£14·95

REF

CW00871124

REFERENCE ONLY

017184

017 184

017184

岭南三通语言工具书系列之一

简明粤英词典
A CONCISE CANTONESE –
ENGLISH DICTIONARY

杨明新

Yang Mingxin

广东高等教育出版社

Guangdong Higher Education Publishing House

1999·广州(Guangzhou)

图书在版编目（CIP）数据

简明粤英词典/杨明新编著 .—广州：广东高等教育出版社，
1999.7
ISBN 7－5361－2350－7

Ⅰ.简… Ⅱ.杨… Ⅲ.①英语－词典 ②词典－粤、英
Ⅳ.H316

中国版本图书馆 CIP 数据核字（98）第 04751 号

广东高等教育出版社出版
社址:广州市林和西横路 邮编:510075 电话:020-83792953
广东省新华书店经销
番禺市石楼官桥彩色印刷厂印刷
850×1168 毫米 32 开本 19.125 印张 600 千字
1999 年 7 月第 1 版 1999 年 7 月第 1 次印刷
印数:0001-2000 册
定价:28.00 元

017184

目　录
CONTENTS

· 2 ·

本书使用说明

本书的编写目的是帮助操英语的人士学习粤语。粤语是汉语的一种方言，它流行于中国南部沿海的开放地带——广东、广西、海南、香港、澳门等省区，以广州音、香港音为标准音。

学习粤语有三个难点：语音、声调和特殊词汇。为攻克这三个难关，本书采取以下三个办法：

一．用中国广东省制定并于 1960 年颁布的《广州话拼音方案》给粤语注音，并在该方案的声母和韵母符号后面用国际音标注明准确的发音。熟悉国际音标的朋友查阅本书是很方便的。如果您不熟悉国际音标，那也不难，有限几十个声母、韵母符号的后面都括注一个汉字，只要您找一位操标准粤语的人发出这个汉字的音，然后您加以分析，问题就解决了。一个汉字，就是一个音节，音节前半部分的辅音就是"声母"，音节后半部分的元音或以元音为主组成的复合音素就是"韵母"。几十个声母、韵母的准确发音熟悉了，一切粤语单字和词语的读音就可以顺利拼出。

二．粤语和中国的普通话一样，有音节中的声调变化，同一个音节，如果声调不同，是代表不同的词，具有不同的意义的。不过，普通话只有四个声调，粤语却有九个声调。本书用 1、2、3、4、5、6、7、8、9 这些阿拉伯数字分别记在各音节注音符号的右上方，表示每个音节应读的声调。这九个声调的音高变化，略如下列五线谱所记：

例字：诗　　史　　试　　时　　市　　事　　色　　锡　　食
注音：xi^1　　xi^2　　xi^3　　xi^4　　xi^5　　xi^6　　xig^7　　xig^8　　xig^9

　　如果您觉得这样描述粤语各声调的特征仍不好理解，那么，简易的办法是：请一位操标准粤语的人把上述"xi(xig)"音节的九个例字的发音读出来，您把它们一一记住了，以后不论遇到什么音节，它的各个声调的音高都与"xi"音节的各调对应相同。如此类推，就可一通百通了。粤语声调最难掌握的是 7、8、9 三个调，这是汉语普通话所没有的，叫做"入声调"，其特点是发音强而有力，时值短，急收煞，略如音乐上的强顿音，又如英语上的以"b"、"d"、"g"、"k"等字母结尾的重读闭音节。

　　三．粤语中大部分的词汇是和汉语普通话相同的。有部分词汇是普通话所不用的，但在粤语口语中却用得非常普遍。对于这部分特殊词汇，本书采取与普通话、与英语找等同关系的办法加以注解。例如：

　　乜野【$med^7 ye^5$ 勿^7 惹】〈pron.〉what ＝【普】什么

　　符号说明：

　　【　】表示它里面是粤语注音

　　【普】汉语普通话

　　〈　〉词类

　　＝　　等于

　　∽　　相似，相近

编者
1999 年 3 月于广州

Notes on the Use of the Dictionary

The aim of this dictionary is to help speakers of English to learn Cantonese —— a dialect spoken in the coastal area of South China, such as Guangdong, Guangxi, Hainan, Hongkong and Macao. The pronunciation in Guangzhou and Hongkong is often regarded as the standard Cantonese.

The most difficult points in learning Cantonese are the pronunciation, tone and special vocabulary. This dictionary adopted three ways to cope with the above-mentioned difficulties accordingly:

⟨ I ⟩ Cantonese characters are noted in accordance with the Cantonese Phonetic Laws issued in 1960 by the Guangdong Province of China and also noted with International Phonetic Symbols as well. It is convenient to those who are familiar with this phonetic system. To those who are not familiar with the International Phonetic Symbols, this dictionary provided a Cantonese character after each of the dozens of consonants and vowels. If you ask a native speaker of Cantonese to pronounce the characters for you, you can solve the problem through comparison and contrast. Each Cantonese character has one syllable, and each syllable consists of the initial consonant and a simple or compound vowel(sometimes with a terminal n or ng). Once you have mastered these consonants and vowels, you can pronounce all the Cantonese characters easily.

⟨ II ⟩ Just like mandarin, a Cantonese also has tone. With different tones, the same syllable may stand for different characters and has different meanings. A mandarin character has four tones only whereas a Cantonese character has nine tones. In this dictionary, an Arabic numeral from 1 through 9 at the upper right corner shows the tone for the syllable. The pitch of each of the nine tones is roughly shown on the staff as follows:

character: 诗　史　试　时　市　事　色　锡　食

phonetics: xi^1　xi^2　xi^3　xi^4　xi^5　xi^6　xig^7　xig^8　xig^9

If you are still not sure of the tones of Cantonese, an even simpler way is to ask a native speaker of Cantonese to pronounce the abovementioned nine characters xi (xig) for you and remember them. All the other syllables have the same nine tones. Once you have mastered these nine tones, you can pronounce any characters correctly with the help of this dictionary. Of all the tones, the most difficult ones are perhaps the 7th, 8th and 9th, which are not found in mandarin. They are named "entering tone", and they are pronounced powerfully, shortly, and with a quick ending, something like the powerful musical pauses, or like the ending "b", "d", "k", "g" in a closed syllable in English.

〈Ⅲ〉The majority of Cantonese vocabularies are the same as the vocabulary of mandarin, however, some of them are not found in mandarin but frequently used in spoken Cantonese. These special words are noted with the equivalent in English and in mandarin as follows:

乜野【med^7 yē^5 勿^7 惹】〈*pron*.〉what＝【普】什么

Captions of the symbols:

【 】 shows the phonetics of Cantonese

【普】 mandarin

〈 〉 parts of speech

＝ equal to

◡◠ resemble;be similar

The Editor

Guangzhou 3/1999

粤语注音符号

The Phonetic Symbols of the Cantonese

一、声母(initial consonant)

声母 initial consonant	国际音标 international phonetic symbols	例字 character	声母 initial consonant	国际音标 international phonetic symbols	例字 character
b	[p]	波 bo¹	h	[h]	何 ho⁴
p	[p']	婆 po⁴	j	[j]	知 ji¹
m	[m]	摸 mo²	q	[ts']	雌 qi¹
f	[f]	科 fo¹	x	[s]	思 xi¹
d	[t]	多 do¹	y	[y]	也 ya⁵
t	[t']	拖 to¹	w	[w]	华 wa⁴
n	[n]	挪 no⁴			
l	[l]	罗 lo⁴			
g	[k]	哥 go¹			
k	[k']	卡 ka¹			
ng	[ŋ]	我 ngo⁵			

二、韵母(simple or compound vowel)

韵母 simple or compound vowel	国际音标 international phonetic symbols	例字 character	韵母 simple or compound vowel	国际音标 international phonetic symbols	例字 character
a	[a]	呀 a¹	ed	[ɐt]	(不)bed⁷
ai	[ai]	挨 ai¹	eg	[ɐk]	(德)deg⁷
ao	[au]	拗 ao²	ēi	[ɛi]	(非)fēi¹
am	[am]	(监)gam¹	ēng	[ɛŋ]	(镜)gēng³
an	[an]	晏 an³	ēg	[ɛk]	(尺)qēg⁸
ang	[aŋ]	罂 ang¹	ê	[œ]	(靴)hê¹
ab	[ap]	鸭 ab⁸	êü	[œjy]	(去)hêü³
ad	[at]	押 ad⁸	ên	[œn]	(春)qên¹
ag	[ak]	(客)hag⁸	ug	[uk]	屋 ug⁷
ē	[ɛ]	(遮)jē¹	i	[i]	衣 yi¹
ei	[ɐi]	矮 ei²	iu	[iu]	妖 yiu¹
eo	[ɐɔ]	欧 eo¹	im	[im]	淹 yim¹
êng	[œŋ]	(香)hêng¹	in	[in]	烟 yin¹
êd	[œt]	(律)lêd⁹	ing	[iŋ]	英 ying¹
êg	[œk]	(约)yêg⁸	ib	[ip]	叶 yib⁹
em	[ɐm]	庵 em¹	id	[it]	热 yid⁹
en	[ɐn]	(恩)yen¹	ig	[ik]	益 yig⁷
eng	[ɐŋ]	莺 eng¹	o	[ɔ]	柯 o¹
eb	[ɐp]	(急)geb⁷	oi	[ɔi]	哀 oi¹

韵母 simple or compound vowel	国际音标 international phonetic symbols	例字 character	韵母 simple or compound vowel	国际音标 international phonetic symbols	例字 character
ou	[ɔu]	奥 ou³	ung	[uŋ]	瓮 wung³
on	[ɔn]	安 on¹	ud	[ut]	活 wud⁹
ong	[ɔŋ]	（康）hong¹	ü	[jy]	于 yü¹
od	[ɔt]	（渴）hod⁸	ün	[jyn]	冤 yün¹
og	[ɔk]	恶 og⁸	üd	[jyt]	月 yüd⁹
u	[u]	乌 wu¹	m	[m]	唔 m⁴
ui	[ui]	煨 wui¹	ng	[ŋ]	五 ng⁵
un	[un]	碗 wun²			

A

丫【a¹ 啊】bifurcation；fork

丫杈【a¹ qa¹ 差】fork(of a free)；crotched；crotch；forked

丫鬟【a¹wan⁴ 环】slave girl；servant girl

呀【a¹ 啊】①〈int.〉ah；oh 呀，落雪啦! = Oh, it's snowing! ②〈auxil.〉佢系边个呀? = Who is he?

阿【a³ 亚】①〈auxil.〉℃the；②play up to

阿飞【a³fēi¹ 非】Teddy boy

阿门【a³mun⁴ 们】amen

阿拉伯【a³lai¹bag⁸ 赖¹ 白¹】Arabian；Arabic；Arab

阿谀【a¹yü⁶ 预】fawn on；flatter

阿弥陀佛【a¹mēi⁴to⁴fed⁸ 眉 驼 罚】① Amitabha ②merciful Buddha

亚【a³ 阿；nga³ 雅³】① inferior；second ②short for Asia

亚军【a³guen¹ 君】second place

亚洲【a³jeo¹ 州】Asia

鸦【a¹ 啊；nga¹ 雅¹】crow

鸦雀无声【a¹jêg⁸nou⁴xing¹ 卓毛升】not even a crow or sparrow can be heard—silence reigns

鸦片【a¹pin³ 骗】opium

哑【a² 丫²；nga² 瓦²】①mute；dumb ②hoarse；husky

哑仔【a²jei² 济²】a dumb person；mute

哑口无言【a²heo²mou⁴yin⁴ 后² 毛然】be left without an argument

啊【a¹ 阿¹；a³ 亚】①〈int.〉Ah 啊，原来系你! = Ah, so it's you! ②〈auxil.〉几咁好嘅呀天气啊! = What a fine day!

鸭【ab⁸"甲"的韵母；ngab⁸】duck

鸭蛋【ab⁸dan² 旦²】duck's egg

鸭绒【ab⁸yung² 拥】duck's down

鸭梨【ab⁸lēi⁴ 离】a kind of pear grown in Hebei Province

押【ad⁸ 压；ngad⁸ 压】①give as security ②detain ③escort ④signature

押当【ad⁸dong³ 档】pawn sth.

押金【ad⁸gem¹ 今】deposit

押送【ad⁸xung³ 宋】escort

押尾【ad⁸mēi⁵ 美】signature

压【ad⁸ 押；ngad⁸ 押】press；push down；hold down；weigh down

压力【ad⁸lig⁹ 历】pressure

压迫【ad⁸big⁷ 逼】oppress；repress

压制【ad⁸jei³ 济】suppress；stifle

压抑【ad⁸yig⁷ 益】constrain；depress

压缩【ad⁸xug⁷ 叔】compress；cut down

挨【ai¹ 埃；ngai¹ 埃；ngai⁴ 捱】① get close to ②in sequence ③suffer

挨近【ai¹gen⁶ 靳】get close to

挨打【ai⁴da² 得亚²】take a beating

挨饿【ai⁴ngo⁶ 卧】suffer from hunger

唉【ai¹ 挨¹；ai⁶ 哎】〈int.〉℃alas 唉，真可惜! = What a pity!

唉声叹气【ai¹xing¹ tan³hēi³ 升炭戏】heave deep sighs; moan and groan

哎 【ai¹ 唉；ēi² 嗳】①〈int.〉∽hey 哎，王先生啊！＝Hey, it's Mr. Wang! ②〈int.〉∽why 哎，真好！＝Why, it's very good!

哎呀【ai¹ya¹ 也¹】〈int.〉∽damn

哎哟【ai¹yo³ 唉唷³】〈int.〉∽"ouch"or "ow"

拗 【ao² 坳²；ngao² 坳²；ao³ 坳³；ngao³ 坳³】①bend so as to break ②hard to pronounce

拗断【ao²tün⁵ 团⁵】break

拗颈【ao³gēng² 镜²】reply defiantly

坳 【ao³ 拗³；ngao³ 拗³】a depression in a mountain range; col

啱 【am¹ 岩；ngam¹ 岩¹】①correct；right＝【普】正确 ②just right＝【普】正好

啱嘅【am¹gē³ 格耶³】correct＝【普】对；正确

啱晒【am¹xai³ 徙³】very good＝【普】正好；好得很

啱先【am¹xin¹ 仙】just now＝【普】刚才

晏 【an³"滩"的韵母】late＝【普】迟

晏起身【an³hēi²xen² 喜新】get up late

罌 【ang¹"硬"的韵母第 1 调；ngang¹ 硬】small-mouthed jar

罌粟【ang¹xug⁷ 叔】opium poppy

B

巴【ba¹ 爸】hope earnestly

巴结【ba¹gid³ 洁】fawn on；curry favour with；make up to

巴掌【ba¹jêng² 蒋】palm；hand

巴士【ba¹xi² 屎】bus＝【普】公共汽车

吧【ba¹ 巴；ba⁶ 罢】①〈onomatopoeia〉∽“crack”②〈auxil.〉我地走吧！＝ Let's go. 佢会来吧？＝ He'll come, won't he?

叭【ba¹】〈onomatopoeia〉

叭闭【ba¹bei³ 蔽】①noise；bustle＝【普】喧闹 ②illustrious；celebrated＝【普】显赫

爸【ba¹；be⁴ 巴⁴】father

爸爸【ba⁴ba¹ 巴⁴ 巴¹】papa；dad；father

笆【ba¹ 巴】basketry

疤【ba¹ 巴】scar

把【ba² 巴²】①hold；grasp ②〈measure word〉一把刀＝a knife

把关【ba²guan¹ 惯¹】guard a pass；check on

把握【ba²ngeg⁷ 厄⁷】grasp；certainty

把屁【ba²pêi³ 譬】useless＝【普】无用；没意思

霸【ba³ 巴³】chief of feudal princes；overlord

霸道【ba³dou⁶ 度⁶】rule by force；over-bearing

霸权【ba³kün⁴ 拳】hegemony

霸王【ba³wong⁴ 黄】overlord；despot

霸占【ba³jim³ 渐³】forcibly occupy；seize

罢【ba⁶ 吧⁶】stop；cease；dismiss

罢免【ba⁶min⁵ 缅】recall

罢休【ba⁶yeo¹ 优】give up；let the matter drop

伯【bag⁸ 百】father's elder brother；earl；count

伯父【bag⁸fu⁶ 付】uncle；old man

伯娘【bag⁸nêng⁴ 良】aunt＝【普】伯母

伯爵【bag⁸jêg⁸ 着⁸】earl；count

白【bag⁹ 百⁹】white；in vain

白色【bag⁹xig⁷ 式】white；White(as a symbol of reaction)

白白【bag⁹bag⁹】in vain；for nothing

白日做梦【bag⁹yed⁹jou⁶mung⁶ 逸造蒙⁶】daydream；vain hope

摆【bai² 拜²】put；place；put on；sway

摆钟【bai²jung¹ 中】pendulum clock

摆档【bai²dong³ 当³】set up a stall＝【普】摆摊子

摆款【bai²hun² 欢³】put on airs；do sth. for show＝【普】摆架子；摆样子

摆阔佬【bai²fud⁸lou² 阔老²】parade one's wealth

摆事实【bai²xi⁶xed⁹ 是失⁹】present the facts

摆乌龙【bai²wu¹lung² 胡¹ 隆²】counter-
　　feit；do mischief；confuse =【普】
　　作假；作怪；搅乱

拜【bai³ 摆³】do obeisance；make a cour-
　　tesy call

拜访【bai³fong² 仿】pay a visit；call on
拜托【bai³tog⁹】request sb. to do sh.
拜佛【bai³fed⁹ 罚】worship Buddha

败【bai⁶ 摆⁶】be defeated；lose；defeat；
　　decay

败坏【bai⁶wai⁶ 怀⁶】ruin；corrupt
败仗【bai⁶jêng³ 胀】lost battle；defeat
败退【bai⁶têû³ 腿³】retreat in defeat
败诉【bai⁶xou³ 数³】lose a lawsuit
败类【bai⁶lêü⁶ 虑】degenerate
败家仔【bai⁶ga¹jei² 加济²】spendthrift

包【bao¹ 胞】wrap；bundle；bag；include

包含【bao¹hem⁴ 陷⁴】contain；embody
包涵【bao¹ham⁴ 函】excuse；forgive
包装【bao¹jong¹ 庄】pack；package
包办【bao¹ban⁶ 板⁶】take care of every-
　　thing concerning a job.
包扎【bao¹jad⁹ 胞砸】wrap；bind up
包围【bao¹wei⁴ 胞维】surround；encircle
包庇【bao¹bei³ 胞比³】shield；harbour
包销【bao¹xiu¹ 胞消】have exclusive sell-
　　ing rights
包租【bao¹jou¹ 胞糟】rent land or a house
　　for subletting

胞【bao¹ 包】afterbirth；born of the same
　　parents　胞兄弟 = full brother

饱【bao² 包²】have eaten one's fill；be
　　full

饱和【bao²wo⁴ 禾】saturation
饱满【bao²mun⁵ 门⁵】full；plump
饱死【bao²xēi² 四²】disagreeable；disgust-
　　ing =【普】讨厌；讨嫌

爆【bao³ 包³】explode；bust；quick-fry

爆发【bao³fad⁹ 法】erupt；burst out
爆炸【bao³ja³ 诈】explode；blow up
爆丈【bao³jêng² 桨】firecracker =【普】爆
　　竹；鞭炮
爆煲【bao³ bou¹ 褒】〈metaphor〉(of a
　　plot, etc.) fall through and stand
　　exposed =【普】败露

龅【bao⁶ 包⁶】龅牙【bao⁶nga⁴ 芽】buck-
　　tooth

班【ban¹ 斑】class；team；shift；duty

班车【ban¹qē¹ 奢】regular bus
班级【ban¹keb⁷ 给】classes and grades in
　　school
班期【bai¹kēi⁴ 其】schedule（for flights,
　　etc.）
班组【ban¹jou² 祖】teams and groups

斑【ban¹ 班】spot；speck；mottled；
　　striped

斑点【ban¹dim² 店²】spot；stain
斑纹【ban¹men⁴ 文】stripe；streak

颁【ban¹ 班】promulgate；issue

颁布【ban¹bou³ 报】promulgate
颁发【ban¹fad⁹ 法】issue

板【ban² 版】board；plank；stiff

板壁【ban²big⁸ 迫⁸】wooden partition
板凳【ban²deng³ 邓³】wooden bench or
　　stool
板滞【ban²jei⁶ 济⁶】stiff；dull

扳【ban² 板；ban³ 板³】pull；turn

扳手【ban²xeo² 搜】spanner；wrench

扳低【ban³dei¹ 底¹】overthrow =【普】打
　　倒；打翻

版【ban² 板】printing plate; edition;
　　page

版本【ban²bun² 叛²】edition

版面【ban²min⁶ 免⁶】space of a whole page

版权【ban²kün⁴ 拳】copyright

版税【ban²xêu³ 碎】royalty

扮【ben⁶ 办】be dressed up as; make
　　faces

扮演【ben⁶yin² 衍】play the part of; act

扮野【ben⁶yē⁵ 惹】put on an act =【普】装
　　模作样

办【ban⁶ 扮】do; handle; manage; set up

办事【ban⁶xi⁶ 士】handle affairs; work

办公【ban⁶gung¹ 工】handle official busi-
　　ness

办报【ban⁶bou³ 布】run a newspaper

泲【ban⁶ 办】泲浆【ban⁶jêng¹ 张】slurry;
　　mud =【普】泥浆

八【bad⁸ 白压⁸】eight

八卦【bad⁸gua³ 挂】①the Eight Diagrams
　　②coquetry of woman =【普】风
　　骚；妖艳 ③womanishly fussy =
　　【普】婆婆妈妈

八仙过海，各显神通【bad⁸xin¹guo³hoi²,
　　gog⁹hin²xen⁴tung¹】like the Eight
　　Immortals crossing the sea, each
　　one showing his or her special
　　prowess

百【bag⁸ 伯】hundred; numerous; all
　　kinds of

百货【bag⁸fo³ 课】general merchandise

百姓【bag⁸xing³ 胜】common people

百依百顺【bag⁸yi¹bag⁸xên⁶ 衣迅⁶】docile

and obedient

跛【bei¹ 闭¹】lame

跛脚【bei¹gêg⁸ 格约⁸】lame in one leg

跛仔【bei¹jei² 济²】lame person

蔽【bei³ 闭】cover; shelter; hide

蔽塞【bei³xeg⁷ 思额⁷】be obstructed; be
　　blocked up

闭【bei³ 蔽】shut; close; stop up; ob-
　　struct

闭塞【bei³xeg⁷ 思额⁷】stop up; close up;
　　unenlightened

闭幕【bei³mog⁹ 莫】the curtain falls; close

闭关自守【bei³guan¹ji⁶xeo²】close the
　　country to international inter-
　　course

弊【bei⁶ 敝】fraud; abuse; disadvantage

弊病【bei⁶bēng⁶ 柄⁶】malady; evil; draw-
　　back

弊端【bei⁶dün¹ 段¹】malpractice; abuse

敝【bei⁶ 弊】①shabby; ragged 敝衣 =
　　ragged clothing ②〈modest.〉my; our
　　敝处 = my place

币【bei⁶ 敝】money; currency
　　币值【bei⁶jig⁹ 直】currency value

毙【bei⁶ 敝】die; get killed; shoot

稗【bei⁶ 敝】barnyard grass

稗仔【bei⁶jei² 知矮²】barnyard grass =
　　【普】稗子

泵【bem¹ 乓】pump 水泵【xêu² 瑞²bem¹】
　　water pump

乒【bem¹ 泵】〈onomatopoeia.〉乒乓

兵【bing¹ 冰 bem¹】ping-pong

宾【ben¹ 缤】guest

宾客【ben¹hag⁸ 赫】guest; visitor

宾馆【ben¹gun² 管】guesthouse

宾至如归【ben¹ji³yū⁴guei¹ 志余龟】guests feel at home (in a hotel, guesthouse, etc.)

缤【ben¹ 宾】in riotous profusion 五彩缤纷【ng⁵qoi²ben¹fen¹】a riot of colour

滨【ben¹ 宾】①bank; brink; shore ②be close to(the sea, a river, etc.)

彬【ben¹ 宾】〈a.〉彬彬有礼【ben¹ben¹yeo⁵lei⁵ 友蠡】refined and courteous; urbane

斌【ben¹ 宾】＝彬

品【ben² 禀】article; product; grade; character; taste sth.

品德【ben²deg⁷ 得】moral character

品质【ben²jed⁷ 知核⁷】character; quality

品性【ben²xing³ 胜】moral character

品种【ben²jung² 肿】breed; variety

品尝【ben²xêng² 常】taste; sample

禀【ben² 禀】report(to one's superior); receive

禀赋【ben²fu³ 富】natural endowment

禀报【ben²bou³ 布】report(to one's superior)

摈【ben³ 殡】①discard; ②carding; ligature

摈弃【ben³hêi³ 气】discard

摈辫【ben³bin¹ 边】ligature pigtails ＝【普】结辫子

鬓【ben³ 摈】temples

鬓发【ben³fad⁸ 法】hair on the temples

殡【ben³ 鬓】lay a coffin in a memorial hall 出殡【qêd⁷ben³】funeral and interment ＝【普】殡葬

殡仪馆【ben³yi⁴gun² 宜管】the undertaker's

笨【ben⁶ 宾⁶】stupid; foolish; clumsy

笨拙【ben⁶jüd⁸ 绝⁸】clumsy; awkward

笨屎虫【ben⁶xi²qung⁴ 史从】cockroach

不【bed⁷ 毕】not; no

不安【bed⁷on¹ 桉】intranquil; unstable; uneasy

不必【bed⁷bid⁷ 别⁷】need not; not have to

不测【bed⁷qog 策⁷】accident; mishap

不曾【bed⁷qeng⁴ 层】never(have done sth.)

不得了【bed⁷deg⁷liu⁵ 德辽⁵】disastrous; extremely

不得人心【bed⁷deg⁷yen⁴xem¹ 德仁深】not enjoy popular support

不得已【bed⁷deg⁷yi⁵ 德耳】act against one's will

不断【bed⁷dün⁶ 段】unceasing

不法【bed⁷fad⁸ 发】lawless; unlawful

不凡【bed⁷fan⁴ 繁】out of the ordinary

不妨【bed⁷fong⁴ 防】there is no harm in

不服【bed⁷fug⁹ 伏】refuse to obey

不符【bed⁷fu⁴ 扶】not agree with

不甘心【bed⁷gem¹xem¹ 金深】not reconciled to

不公【bed⁷gung¹ 工】unjust; unfair

不过【bed⁷guo³ 果³】only; merely; but

不和【bed⁷ wo⁴ 禾】not get along well; discord

不见得【bed⁷gin³deg⁷ 建德】not necessarily

不近人情【bed⁷gen⁶yen⁴qing⁴ 跟⁴ 仁 程】not amenable to reason

不景气【bed⁷ging²hēi³ 境 汽】depression; slump

不堪【bed⁷hem¹ 勘】cannot bear utterly; cannot stand

不卑不亢【bed⁷bei¹bed⁷kong³ 悲抗】neither haughty nor humble

不可告人【bed⁷ho²gou³yen⁴ 河² 高³ 仁】not to be divulged

不可思议【bed⁷ho²xi¹yi⁵ 河² 斯耳】inconceivable

不可一世【bed⁷ho²yed⁷xei³ 河² 日⁷ 细】be insufferably arrogant

不客气【bed⁷hag⁸hēi³ 赫汽】impolite; rude

不愧【bed⁷kuei⁵ 槐⁵】be worthy of

不利【bed⁷lēi⁶ 吏】unfavourable; unsuccessful

不料【bed⁷liu⁶ 尿】unexpectedly

不满【bed⁷mun⁵ 闷⁵】resentful

不免【be⁷min⁵ 勉】unavoidable

不平【bed⁷ping⁴ 萍】injustice; indignant

不切实际【bed⁷qid⁸xed⁹jei³ 彻 失⁸ 济】unrealistic; unpractical

不屈不挠【bed⁷wed⁷bed⁷nao⁴ 乌核⁷ 闹⁴】unyielding; indomitable

不然【bed⁷yin⁴ 言】not so; no; or else

不仁【bed⁷yen⁴ 人】not benevolent; numb

不忍【bed⁷yen² 人²】cannot bear to

不容【bed⁷yung⁴ 熔】not tolerate

不如【bed⁷yü⁴ 鱼】not equal to

不识抬举【bed⁷xig⁷toi⁴gêu² 色台居²】not know how to appreciate favours

不时【bed⁷xi⁴ 是⁴】often; at any time

不适【bed⁷xig⁷ 色】unwell; indisposed

不死心【bed⁷xēi²xem¹ 四² 森】unresigned

不但【bed⁷dan⁶ 旦⁶】not only

不同【bed⁷tung⁴ 铜】not alike; different

不妥【bed⁷tuo⁵ 拖⁵】not proper

不外【bed⁷ngoi⁶ 碍】not beyond the scope of

不惜【bed⁷xig⁷ 色】not stint; not spare

不祥【bed⁷qêng⁴ 肠】ominous

不屑【bed⁷xid⁸ 楔】disdain to do sth.

不懈【bed⁷hai⁶ 械】untiring

不幸【bed⁷heng⁶ 杏】misfortune; unfortunate

不休【bed⁷yeo¹ 优】endlessly; ceaselessly

不朽【bed⁷neo² 纽】immortal

不言而喻【bed⁷yin⁴yi⁴yü⁶ 然移誉】it goes without saying

不宜【bed⁷yi⁴ 而】not suitable

不以为然【bed⁷yi⁵wei⁴yin⁴ 耳围言】object to

不亦乐乎【bed⁷yig⁹log⁸fu⁴ 易落符】extremely

不在乎【bed⁷joi⁶fu⁴ 再⁴ 符】not mind

不在话下【bed⁷joi⁶wa⁶ha⁶ 画⁶ 夏】be a cinch

不约而同【bed⁷yêg⁸yi⁴tung⁴ 跃移铜】take the same action or view without prior consultation

不择手段【bed⁷jag⁹xeo²dün⁶ 泽守锻】by fair means or foul

不只【bed⁷ji² 止】not only; not merely

不中用【bed⁷jung¹yung⁶ 钟容⁶】unfit for anything

不至于【bed⁷ji³jü¹ 置鱼】cannot go so far

不准【bed⁷jên² 津²】not allow; forbid

不自量【bed⁷ji⁶lêng⁶ 治良⁶】not take a proper measure of oneself

毕【bed⁷ 不】finish; conclude; fully

毕竟【bed⁷ging² 境】〈*ad.*〉after all
毕生【bed⁷xeng¹ 牲】all one's life
毕业【bed⁷yib⁹ 叶】graduate; finish school

笔【bed⁷ 不】pen; write

笔画【bed⁷wag⁹ 划】strokes of a Chinese character
笔记【bed⁷ gēi³ 寄】take down（in writing）; notes
笔直【bed⁷jig⁹ 值】perfectly straight

抔【bed⁷ 不】①get things in a spoon =【普】用勺子盛取东西 ②fish for; gain =【普】捞取
抔饭【bed⁷fan⁶ 范】fill a bowl with rice =【普】盛饭

拔【bed⁹ 不⁹】pull out; pull up; choose; pick

拔河【bed⁹ho⁴ 何】tug-of-war
拔海【bed⁹ hoi² 开²】elevation（above sea level）= 海拔
拔尖【bed⁹jim¹ 占¹】tiptop; top-notch
拔苗助长【bed⁹miu⁴jo⁶jêng² 妙⁴ 坐 蒋】spoil things by excessive enthusiasm

跋【bed⁹ 拔】cross mountains; postscript

跋山涉水【bed⁹xan¹xib³xêu² 珊 摄 穗²】scale mountains and ford streams

北【beg⁷ 必黑⁷】north; be defeated

北方【beg⁷fong¹ 芳】north
北京【beg⁷ging¹ 经】Beijing(Peking)
北美洲【beg⁷mēi⁵jeo¹ 尾州】North America
北纬【beg⁷wei⁵ 伟】north latitude

崩【beng¹ 蹦】collapse; be short of

崩溃【beng¹kui² 贿】collapse; crumble
崩口【beng¹heo² 厚²】breach; harelip

蹦【beng¹ 崩】leap; jump

蹦蹦跳【beng¹beng¹tiu³ 条³】bouncing and vivacious

绷【beng¹ 崩】stretch tightly

绷带【beng¹dai³ 戴】bandage

傍【beng⁶ 崩⁶】rely on; depend on =【普】依靠

傍住【beng⁶jŭ⁶ 煮⁶】rely on; count on =【普】依靠着; 依仗
傍爹娘【beng⁶dē¹nêng⁴ 的夜¹ 良】rely on parents =【普】依靠父母

波【bo¹ 坡】wave; disturbance

波动【bo¹dung⁶ 洞】undulate; wave motion
波及【bo¹keb⁹ 级⁹】spread to
波澜【bo¹lan⁴ 兰】great waves; billows
波涛【bo¹tou⁴ 图】great waves; billows
波纹【bo¹men⁴ 文】ripple; corrugation

坡【bo¹ 波】slope; sloping

坡度【bo¹dou⁶ 道】slope; gradient

玻【bo¹ 波】①glass【bo¹lēi¹ 里¹】=【普】玻璃 ②ball =【普】球

玻鞋【bo¹hai⁴ 孩】gym shoes =【普】球鞋
玻胆【bo¹dam² 担²】bladder(of a ball) =【普】球胆
玻台【bo¹toi² 胎²】table of a ball =【普】球桌

播【bo³ 簸】sow; seed; broadcast

播送【bo³xung³ 宋】broadcast; beam
播音【bo³yem¹ 钦】transmit

播种【bo³jung² 总】sowing; seeding

簸【bo³ 播】winnow with a fan; fan

簸箕【bo³gēi¹ 基】a skip for winnow

挏【beo² 白欧²】strike; hit; knock =【普】打棍子

挏冧【beo²lem³ 林³】overthrow =【普】打倒

挏烂【beo²lan⁶ 兰】break; smash =【普】打破

煲【bou¹ 襃】cook in water; boil =【普】熬

煲粥【bou¹jug¹ 竹】cook gruel

煲沉【bou¹qem⁴ 寻】overthrow =【普】打倒

褒【bou¹ 保¹】praise; honour; commend

褒奖【bou¹jêng² 蒋】praise and honour

褒义词【bou¹yi⁶qi⁴ 二辞】commendatory term

保【bou² 宝】protect; keep; guarantee; guarantor

保安【bou²on¹ 桉】ensure public security

保镖【bou²biu¹ 标】bodyguard

保持【bou²qi⁴ 迟】keep; maintain; preserve

保存【bou²qūn⁴ 全】preserve; conserve

保管【bou²gun² 观²】take care of

保护【bou²wu⁶ 户】protect; safeguard

保健【bou²gin⁶ 件】health protection

保留【bou²leo⁴ 流】continue to have

保密【bou²med⁹ 勿】maintain secrecy

保守【bou²xeo² 手】guard; conservative

保卫【bou²wei⁶ 惠】defend; safeguard

保险【bou²him² 欠²】insurance; safe

保修【bou²xeo¹ 收】guarantee to keep sth. in good repair

保佑【bou²yeo⁶ 右】bless and protect

保障【bou²jêng³ 涨】ensure; guarantee

保证【bou²jing³ 正】pledge; guarantee

保重【bou²jung⁶ 仲】take care of oneself

宝【bou² 保】treasure; precious

宝贵【bou²guei³ 桂】valuable; precious

宝物【bou²med⁹ 勿】treasure

宝石【bou²xēg⁹ 锡⁹】precious stones; gem

宝座【bou²jo⁶ 助】throne

补【bou²】mend; patch; fill; nourish

补偿【bou²xêng⁴ 常】compensate; make up

补充【bou²qung¹ 冲】replenish; additional

补救【bou²geo³ 够】remedy

补考【bou²hao² 效²】make-up examination

补课【bou²fo³ 货】make up a missed lesson

补品【bou²ben² 禀】tonic

补缺【bou²küd⁸ 决】fill a vacancy

补贴【bou²tib⁸ 帖】subsidy

补助【bou²jo⁶ 左⁶】subsidy; allowance

布【bou³ 报】cloth; declare; dispose

布料【bou³liu⁶ 廖】cloth

布告【bou³gou³ 高³】notice; bulletin

布局【bou³gug⁹ 焗】overall arrangement

布匹【bou³ped⁷ 拍一⁷】cloth; piece goods

布置【bou³ji³ 至】fix up; arrange; assign

报【bou³ 布】report; reply; requite; newspaper

报纸【bou³ji² 指】newspaper

报告【bou³bou³ 高³】report; talk; speech

报道【bou³dou⁶ 度】report(news); cover

报仇【bou³xeo⁴ 愁】revenge; avenge

报酬【bou³qeo⁴ 筹】reward; pay

报答【bou³dab⁸ 搭】repay；requite

报到【bou³dou³ 度³】report for duty

报复【bou³fug⁹ 伏】make reprisals

报名【bou³mēng² 未镜²】enter one's name

报考【bou³hao³ 孝²】enter oneself for an examination

报应【bou³ying³ 影³】retribution；judgment

步 【bou⁶ 部】step；pace；walk；go on foot

步行【bou⁶hang⁴ 客嚣⁴】go on foot

步伐【bou⁶fed⁹ 佛】step；pace

步骤【bou⁶jao⁶ 找⁶】step；move

步兵【bou⁶bing¹ 冰】foot soldier；infantry

部 【bou⁶ 步】part；section；unit

部队【bou⁶dêü² 对²】army；troops

部分【bou⁶fen⁶ 份】part；section

部件【bou⁶gin² 见²】parts；components

部门【bou⁶mun⁴ 瞒】department；branch

部署【bou⁶qü⁵ 柱】dispose；deploy

部位【bou⁶wei⁶ 胃】position；place

部下【bou⁶ha⁶ 夏】subordinate

怖 【bou³ 布】fear；be afraid of

暴 【bou⁶ 步】sudden and violent；cruel

暴动【bou⁶dung⁶ 洞】insurrection

暴乱【bou⁶lün⁶ 联⁶】riot；rebellion

暴跌【bou⁶did⁸ 得热⁸】slump

暴涨【bou⁶jêng³ 胀】（of floods，prices，etc.）rise suddenly and sharply

暴发【bou⁶fad⁸ 法】break out；get rich quick

暴利【bou⁶lēi⁶ 吏】sudden huge profits

暴风雨【bou⁶fung¹yü⁵ 锋与】rainstorm

暴露【bou⁶lou⁶ 路】expose；reveal

暴行【bou⁶heng⁶ 幸】savage act

暴力【bou⁶lig⁹ 历】violence；force

暴躁【bou⁶qou³ 燥】irascible；irritable

暴政【bou⁶jing³ 正】tyranny

暴君【bou⁶guen¹ 军】tyrant；despot

暴光【bou⁶guong¹ 广¹】exposure

邦 【bong¹ 帮】nation；state；country

邦交【bong¹gao¹ 跤】relations between two countries

帮 【bong¹ 邦】help；assist；gang；band

帮助【bong¹jo⁶ 坐】help；assist

帮忙【bong¹mong⁴ 亡】help；give a hand

帮派【bong¹pai³ 拍埃³】faction

邦手【bong¹xeo² 守】help；assist ＝【普】帮助

帮跤【bong¹gao¹ 交】help to fight ＝【普】帮助打架

榜 【bong² 绑】a list of names posted up

榜样【bong²yêng⁶ 让】example；model

谤 【bong² 榜】slander；defame（see"诽谤"）

绑 【bong² 榜】bind；tie

绑住【bong²jü⁶ 注⁶】truss up；tie up ＝【普】捆绑；捆扎

绑架【bong²ga³ 嫁】kidnap

绑票【bong²piu³ 漂³】kidnap(for ransom)

傍 【bong⁶ 磅】draw near；be close to

傍晚【bong⁶man⁵ 万⁵】＝挨晚【ai¹man⁵】toward evening

磅 【bong⁶ 傍】pound；platform scale

镑【bong⁶ 傍】pound(a currency)

搏【①bog⁷ 博⁷；②bog⁸ 博】① strike; come down with the big stick (upon sb.) ②wrestle; fight

搏湿【bog⁷ xeb⁷ 拾⁷】strike and make to haemorrhage＝【普】打至出血

搏沉【bog⁷qem⁴ 寻】overthrow＝【普】打倒

搏杀【bong⁸xad⁸ 刹】wrestle＝【普】搏斗

搏命【bog⁸ ming⁶ 名⁶(或 mēng⁶)﹞risk one's life; exerting the utmost strength＝【普】拼命

博【bog⁸ 搏⁸】rich; win; gain

博爱【bog⁸oi³ 哀³】universal love

博览【bog⁸lam⁵ 揽⁵】read extensively

博学【bog⁸hog⁹ 鹤】learned

博得【bog⁸deg⁷ 德】win; gain

博士【bog⁸xi⁶ 事】doctor

博彩【bog⁸qoi² 采】try one's luck＝【普】碰运气

膊【bog⁸ 博】arm

膊头【bog⁸teo⁴ 投】shoulder＝【普】肩膀

雹【bog⁹ 薄】hail＝【普】冰雹

薄【bog⁹ 雹】thin; lacking in warmth; cold

薄板【bog⁹ban² 版】sheet metal

薄酬【bog⁹qeo⁴ 绸】the remuneration isn't much

薄命【bog⁹ ming⁶ 名⁶】woman's destiny isn't good

杯【bui¹ 背¹】cup; glass; (prize) cup 一杯茶【yed⁷bui¹qa⁴】a cup of tea

背【bui³ 辈】the back of the body; the back of an object; hide sth. from

背后【bui³heo⁶ 候】behind; behind sb's back

背景【bui³ging² 警】background

背叛【bui³bun⁶ 拌】betray; forsake

背诵【bui³jung⁶ 仲】recite

背心【bui³xem¹ 深】a sleeveless garment

背信弃义【bui³xên³hêi³yi⁶ 讯气二】break faith with sb.; be perfidious

辈【bui³ 背】people of a certain kind; generation

辈分【bui³fen⁶ 份】seniority in the family or clan

焙【bui⁶ 贝⁶】bake over a slow fire

焙干【bui⁶gon¹ 杆¹】dry over a fire

搬【bun¹ 般】take away; move; remove

搬运【bun¹wen⁶ 温⁶】carry; transport

搬家【bun¹ga¹ 加】move(house)

搬弄是非【bun¹lung⁶xi⁶fêi¹ 龙⁶ 事飞】sow discord

般【bun¹ 搬】sort; kind; way

一般【yed⁷bun¹】vague generalization

本【bun² 苯】the root or stem of a plant; this

本地【bun²dêi⁶ 得诶⁶】this locality

本分【bun²fen⁶ 份】one's duty

本钱【bun²qin⁴ 前】capital; principal

本来【bun²loi⁴ 莱】original; originally

本能【bun²neng⁴ 勒莺⁴】instinct

本质【bun²jed⁷ 之屈⁷】essence; nature

本性【bun²xing³ 胜】natural instincts

本义【bun²yi⁶ 二】original meaning

本事【bun²xi⁶ 士】= 本领【bun²ling⁵ 岭】skill

本人【bun²yen⁴ 仁】I（me, myself）；oneself

本身【bun²xen¹ 辛】itself；in itself

本住【bun²jü⁶ 注⁶】in line with =【普】本着

半【bun³ 本³】half；in the middle

半边【bun³bin¹ 鞭】half of sth.

半价【bun³ga³ 嫁】half price

半斤八两【bun³gen¹bad⁸lêng² 根 北压⁸ 俩²】tweedledum and tweedledee

半截【bun³jid⁹ 捷】= 半㮼【bun³küd⁹】= 半秣【bun³lem³】half（a section）=【普】半截子

半路【bun³lou⁶ 露】halfway

半数【bun³xou³ 扫】half the number

半中间【bun³jung¹gan¹ 钟奸】middle；halfway =【普】半中腰

拌【bun⁶ 伴】mix

搅拌【gao²bun⁶】stir；mix

伴【bun⁶】companion；accompany

伴侣【bun⁶lêü⁵ 吕】companion；mate

伴唱【bun⁶qêng³ 昌³】vocal accompaniment

伴奏【bun⁶jeo³ 皱】accompany（with musical instruments）

绊【bun⁶ 伴】stumble；trip

绊脚石【bun⁶gêg⁸xêg⁹ 格约⁸ 硕】stumbling block

叛【bun⁶ 伴】betray；rebel against

叛变【bun⁶bin³ 便³】betray one's country, party, etc.

叛逆【bun⁶yig⁹ 亦】rebel against

叛徒【bun⁶tou⁴ 途】traitor；renegade

畔【bun⁶ 伴】side；bank

河畔【ho⁴bun⁶】river bank

钵【bud⁸ 鉢】earthen bowl 衣钵【yi¹bud⁸】legacy

缽【bud⁸ 钵】a small pottery basin =【普】陶盆子

缽头【bud⁸teo⁴ 投】a small pottery basin

拨【bud⁹ 勃】move with hand；set aside

拨正【bud⁹jing³ 政】set right

拨款【bud⁹fun² 佛碗²】allocate funds

勃【bud⁹ 拨】thriving；vigorous

勃兴【bud⁹hing¹ 兄】rise suddenly

渤【bud⁹ 勃】〈n.〉渤海【bud⁹hoi² 害²】the Bohai Sea

卜【bug⁷ 北屋⁷】divination；fortune-telling

生死未卜【xeng¹xêi²mēi⁶bug⁷】hard to tell whether the person in alive or not

标【biu¹ 彪】mark；sign；put a mark

标明【biu¹ming⁴ 名】mark；indicate

标志【biu¹ji³ 至】sign；mark；indicate

标记【biu¹gêi³ 寄】sign；mark；symbol

标价【biu¹ga³ 嫁】mark a price

标签【biu¹qim¹ 金】label；tag

标点【biu¹dim² 店²】punctuation

标题【biu¹tei⁴ 提】title；heading

标号【biu¹hou⁶ 浩】grade

标准【biu¹jên² 遵²】standard；criterion

标新立异【biu¹xen¹leb⁹yi⁶ 辛粒⁹ 义】start something new in order to be different

镖【biu¹ 标】a dartlike weapon

膘【biu¹ 标】fat(of an animal)

长膘【jêng²biu¹】get fat
【biu¹ 标】violent wind；whirlwind

飙

彪【biu¹ 标】young tiger；very fast

彪形大汉【biu¹ ying⁴ dai⁶ hon³ 仍歹⁶ 看】burly chap

彪起咁快【biu¹hēi¹gem³fai³ 喜禁块】very fast=【普】飞快

表【① biu² 标²；② biu¹ 标】surface；show；a form；model；meter；watch

表达【biu²dad⁹ 得压⁹】express；convey

表格【biu²gag⁸ 革】form；table

表现【biu²yin⁶ 苋】expression；show

表决【biu²küd⁸ 缺】decide by vote

表面【biu²min⁶ 免⁶】surface；face

表明【biu²ming⁴ 名】make known

表亲【biu²qen¹ 趁¹】cousin；cousinship

表情【biu²qing⁴ 程】express one's feelings

表示【biu2xi⁶ 是】show；express

表率【biu²xêd⁷ 恤】example；model

表演【biu² yin² 衍】perform；act；exhibition

表扬【biu²yêng⁴ 羊】praise；commend

表语【biu²yü⁵ 与】predicative

表带【biu¹dai³ 戴】watchband

婊【biu² 表】prostitute

婊子【biu²ji² 止】prostitute；whore

裱【biu² 表】mount(a picture, etc.)

裱画【biu²wa² 话²】mount a picture

边【bin¹ 鞭】① side；margin；border ② what

边际【bin¹jei³ 济】limit；bound

边界【bin¹gai³ 介】boundary；border

边境【bin¹ging³ 景】border；frontier

边沿【bin¹yün⁴ 元】edge；fringe

边个【bin¹go³ 格柯³】who；whom=【普】谁

边处【bin¹qü³ 迟于³；bin¹xü³ 戌】where；what；how=【普】哪里；何处；怎么

边道【bin¹dou⁶ 度】where；what；how=【普】哪里；何处；怎么

边道系【bin¹dou⁶hei⁶ 兮⁶】①where is ②is not；deny；repudiate=【普】不是；哪里是

鞭【bin¹ 边】whip；lash

鞭子【bin¹ji² 止】whip

鞭策【bin¹qag⁷ 测】spur on；urge on

鞭打【bin¹da² 得哑²】whip；lash；flog

鞭炮【bin¹pao³ 泡³】=炮丈【pao³jêng² 蒋】firecrackers

辫【bin¹ 边】plait

辫仔【bin¹jei² 济²】plait；braid=【普】辫子

蝙蝠【bin¹fug⁷ 边幅】〈n.〉bat

扁【bin² 匾】flat

扁虫【bin²qung⁴ 从】flatworm

扁担【bin²bam³ 胆³】=担竿【dam³gon¹

干¹】carrying pole

扁桃体【bin²tou⁴tei² 图睇】tonsil

匾【bin² 扁】

匾额【bin² ngag⁹ 我客⁹】a horizontal inscribed board

贬【bin² 扁】demote; relegate; censure

贬低【bin²dei¹ 底¹】belittle; depreciate

贬值【bin²jig⁹ 直】devalue; depreciate

贬义【bin²yi⁶ 二】derogatory sense

变【bin³ 扁³】change; become; different

变成【bin³xing⁴ 承】change into; become

变动【bin³dung⁶ 洞】change; alteration

变革【bin³gag⁹ 格】transform; change

变更【bin³geng¹ 羹】change; alter

变卦【bin³gua³ 挂】go back on one's word

变化【bin³fa³ 花³】change; vary

变换【bin³wun³ 焕】vary; alternate

变卖【bin³mai⁶ 买⁶】sell off (one's property)

变迁【bin³qin¹ 千】change; vicissitudes

变色【bin³xig⁷ 式】change colour; become angry

变态【bin³tai³ 太】metamorphosis; abnormal

变通【bin³tung¹ 同¹】be flexible; adapt sth to circumstances

变相【bin³xêng³ 商³】in disguised form

变心【bin³xem³ 深】cease to be faithful

变质【bin³jed⁷ 侄⁷】go bad; deteriorate

变种【bin³jung³ 总】mutation; variety

便【bin⁶ 辨】convenient; informal

便当【bin⁶dong³ 档】convenient; handy

便利【bin⁶lêi⁶ 吏】easy; facilitate

便于【bin⁶yü¹ 迂】easy to; convenient for

便饭【bin⁶fan⁶ 范】a simple meal; potluck

便服【bin⁶fug⁹ 伏】everyday clothes

便衣【bin⁶yi¹ 依】civilian clothes; plain clothes

便条【bin⁶tiu⁴ 跳⁴】(informal)note

辨【bin⁶ 便】differentiate; distinguish

辨别【bin⁶bid⁹ 必⁹】differentiate

辨认【bin⁶ying⁶ 应⁶】identify; recognize

辩【bin⁶ 便】argue; dispute

辩驳【bin⁶bog⁸ 博】dispute; refute

辩论【bin⁶lên⁶ 伦⁶】= 拗颈【ao³gêng²】argue

辩护【bin⁶wu⁶ 户】speak in defence; plead

兵【bing¹ 冰】weapons; arms; soldier

兵变【bing¹bin³ 便³】mutiny

兵法【bing¹fad⁸ 发】art of war

兵力【bing¹lig⁹ 历】military strength

兵权【bing¹kün² 拳】military leadership

兵不厌诈【bing¹bed⁷yim³ja³ 毕掩³ 炸】there can never be too much deception in war

兵荒马乱【bing¹fong¹ma⁵lün⁶ 方码联⁶】turmoil and chaos of war

冰【bing¹ 兵】ice; put on the ice; feel cold

冰冻【bing¹dung³ 洞³】freeze

冰冷【bing¹lang⁵ 罗罌⁵】ice-cold

冰凉【bing¹lêng⁴ 良】ice-cold

冰糖【bing¹tong⁴ 塘】crystal sugar

冰箱【bing¹xêng¹ 商】icebox; refrigerator

冰天雪地【bing¹tin¹xüd⁸dêi⁶ 田¹ 说得诶⁶】a world of ice and snow

丙【bing² 秉】the third of the ten Heavenly Stems; third

丙纶【bing²lên¹ 伦】polypropylene fibre

丙种维生素【bing²jung²wei⁴xeng¹xou³ 肿围笙数】vitamin C

炳【bing² 丙】bright; splendid

彪炳【biu¹bing²】shining; splendid

秉【bing² 丙】grasp; hold; control

秉公办理【bing²gung¹ban⁶lēi⁵ 工板⁶ 李】handle a matter impartially

并【①bing³ 丙³；②bing⁶ 丙⁶】combine; and

并发【bing³fad⁸ 法】be complicated by

并肩【bing³gin¹ 坚】shoulder to shoulder

并排【bing³pai⁴ 牌】side by side

并且【bing⁶qē² 扯】〈conj.〉and; besides

并吞【bing³ten¹ 梯因¹】swallow up; annex

并重【bing⁶jung⁶ 仲】lay equal stress on

并驾齐驱【bing⁶ga³qei⁴kêu¹ 嫁妻⁴ 拘】run neck and neck

必【bid⁷ 别⁷】certainly; must; have to

必然【bid⁷yin⁴ 言】inevitable; necessity

必须【bid⁷xêu¹ 需】must; have to

必需【bid⁷xêu¹ 须】essential

必要【bid⁷yiu³ 腰³】necessary

鳖【bid⁸ 别⁸】= 水鱼【xêu²yü² 渔²】=【普】甲鱼 soft-shelled turtle

瘪【bid⁸ 鳖】shrivelled 干瘪【gon¹bid⁸】dry and shrivelled

蹩【①bid⁹ 别；②bei¹ 币¹】sprain(one's ankle or wrist)

蹩足【bid⁹jug⁷ 竹】= 蹩脚【bei¹gêg⁸ 格约⁸】inferior

别【bid⁹ 必⁹】

别号【bid⁹hou⁶ 浩】alias

别人【bid⁹yen⁴ 仁】other people; others

别墅【bid⁹xêu⁵ 穗⁵】villa

别致【bid⁹ji³ 志】= 的式【dig⁷xig⁷】unique

别开生面【bid⁹hoi¹xeng¹min⁶ 海¹ 思萼¹棉⁶】start something new

别有风味【bid⁹yeo⁵fung¹mēi⁵ 油⁵ 丰未】have a distinctive flavour

迫【big⁷ 逼】compel; force; urgent

迫害【big⁷hoi⁶ 亥】persecute

迫切【big⁷gid⁸ 撤】urgent; pressing

迫使【big⁷xei² 洗】force; compel

迫不得已【big⁷bed⁷deg⁷yi⁵ 毕德矣】have no alternative(but to)

逼【big⁷ 迫】force; compel; press for

逼供【big⁷gung¹ 工】extort a confession

逼近【big⁷gen⁶ 靳】press on towards

逼真【big⁷jen¹ 珍】lifelike; true to life

逼上梁山【big⁷xêng⁵lêng⁴xan¹ 尚⁵ 良珊】be driven to revolt

碧【big⁷ 迫】bluish green; blue

碧蓝【big⁷lam⁴ 篮】dark blue

碧绿【big⁷lug⁹ 六】dark green

璧【big⁷ 迫】a round flat piece of jade with a hole in its centre(used for ceremonial purposes in ancient China)

壁【①big⁷ 迫；②bēg⁸ 波尺⁸】wall; cliff

壁报【big⁷dou⁴ 布】wall newspaper

壁灯【big⁷deng¹ 登】wall lamp

壁画【big⁷wa² 话²】mural(painting)

壁垒【big⁷lêū⁵ 吕】rampart；barrier

壁炉【big⁷lou⁴ 劳】fireplace

啤【bē¹ 伯诶¹】beer

生啤【xeng¹bē¹】draught beer

啤酒【bē¹jeo² 走】beer

悲【bēi¹ 碑】sad；sorrowful；compassion

悲哀【bēi¹oi¹ 爱¹】grieved；sorrowful

悲惨【bēi¹qam¹ 杉²】miserable；tragic

悲愤【bēi¹fen⁵ 奋】grief and indignation

悲剧【bēi¹kēg⁶ 屐】tragedy

悲观【bēi¹gun¹ 官】pessimistic

悲伤【bēi¹xêng¹ 商】sad；sorrowful

悲叹【bēi¹tan³ 炭】sigh mournfully

悲痛【bēi¹tung³ 疼】grieved；sorrowful

悲壮【bēi¹jong³ 葬】solemn and stirring

悲欢离合【bēi¹fun¹lêi⁴heb⁹ 宽厘盒】joys and sorrows, partings and re-unions—vicissitudes of life

卑【bēi¹ 悲】low；inferior；modest

卑鄙【bēi¹pēi² 皮²】base；mean

卑贱【bēi¹jin⁶ 箭⁶】lowly；mean and low

卑劣【bēi¹lūd³ 捋】base；mean

卑躬屈膝【bēi¹gung¹wed³qed⁷ 供乌核⁷七】bow and scrape；cringe

碑【bēi¹ 悲】an upright stone tablet

碑文【bēi¹men4 民】an inscription on a tablet

比【bēi² 臂²】match；metaphor；compare

·比喻【bēi²yū⁶ 遇】metaphor；analogy

比如【bēi²yū⁴ 鱼】for example；such as

比较【bēi²gao³ 教】compare；fairly

比例【bēi²lei⁶ 丽】proportion；scale

比赛【bēi²qoi³ 蔡】match；competition

比重【bēi²qung⁵ 从⁵】proportion；specific gravity

俾【bēi² 比】①give；grant =【普】给；②in order to；make；let =【普】使，让

俾我一枝笔【bēi²ngo⁵yed⁷ji¹bed⁷ 鹅⁵ 日⁷之不】give me a pen

俾我地捞到唔少【bēi²ngo⁵dēi⁶lou¹dou³m⁴ xiu³ 鹅⁵ 得诶⁶ 劳¹ 道³m⁴ 小】Let us benefit considerably =【普】让我们得益不少。

畀【bēi² 比】= 俾【bēi² 比】give；let

痹【bēi³ 比³】rheumatism

庇【bēi³ 秘】shelter；protect

庇护【bēi³wu⁶ 户】shelter；shield

秘【bēi³ 庇】secret；keep sth. secret

秘密【bēi³med⁹ 勿】secret；clandestine

秘书【bēi³xū¹ 抒】secretary

秘方【bēi³fong¹ 芳】secret recipe

秘诀【bēi³kūd⁸ 决】secret(of success)

泌【bēi³ 庇】secrete

泌尿器官【bēi³niu⁶hēi³gun¹ 鸟⁶ 气观】urinary organs

臂【bēi³ 庇】arm

手臂【xeo²bēi³】arm =【普】胳臂

髀【bēi² 比】leg =【普】腿

大髀【dai⁶bēi²】thigh =【普】大腿

鸡髀【gei¹bēi²】chicken leg =【普】鸡腿

被【① bēi⁶ 鼻；② pēi⁵ 披⁵】express the passive voice; quit

被迫【bēi⁶big⁷ 逼】be compelled

被动【bēi⁶dung⁶ 洞】passive

被告【bēi⁶gou³ 稿³】defendant

被褥【pēi⁵yug⁹ 育】bedding

被单【pēi⁵dan¹ 丹】(bed)sheet

避【bēi⁶ 备】avoid; evade; prevent

避免【bēi⁶min⁵ 勉】avoid; refrain from

避难【bēi⁶nan⁶ 那晏⁶】take refuge

避孕【bēi⁶yen⁶ 刃】contraception

避重就轻【bēi⁶qung⁵jeo⁶hēng¹ 虫⁵ 袖 何镜¹】avoid the important and dwell on the trivial

鼻【bēi⁶ 备】nose

鼻塞【bēi⁶xeg⁷ 是黑⁷】have a stuffy nose

鼻涕【bēi⁶tei³ 剃】nasal mucus

鼻哥窿【bēi⁶go¹lung¹ 歌 龙¹】nostril ＝【普】鼻孔

备【bēi⁶ 鼻】be equipped with; prepare

备案【bēi⁶ngon³ 按】put on record

备料【bēi⁶liu² 廖²】get the materials ready

备用【bēi⁶yung⁶ 容⁶】reserve; spare

备注【bēi⁶ju³ 著】remarks

惫【bēi⁶ 备】exhausted; fatigued

饼【bēng² 柄²】a round flat cake

饼仔【bēng²jei² 济²】(maize or millet)pancake ＝【普】饼子

饼干【bēng²gon¹ 竿】biscuit; cracker

柄【bēng³ 病³】handle

刀柄【dou¹bēng³】the handle of a knife

窝【bēng³ 柄】hide; conceal ＝【普】藏

窝埋【bēng³mai⁴ 买⁴】conceal; go into hiding ＝【普】藏匿

病【bēng⁶ 柄⁶】ill; sick; disease

病毒【bēng⁶dug⁹ 读】virus

病根【bēng⁶gen¹ 斤】an incompletely cured illness

病虫害【bēng⁶qung⁴hoi⁶ 从亥】plant diseases and insect pests

病历【bēng⁶lig⁹ 力】medical record

病情【bēng⁶qing⁴ 程】state of an illness

病态【bēng⁶tai⁴ 太】morbid state

病痛【bēng⁶tung⁴ 疼】slight illness

病因【bēng⁶yen¹ 姻】cause of disease

病愈【bēng⁶yü⁶ 遇】recover(from an illness)

病危【bēng⁶ngei⁴ 魏⁴】be critically ill

病逝【bēng⁶xei⁶ 誓】die of an illness

病魔【bēng⁶mo¹ 么】serious illness

病入膏肓【bēng⁶yeb⁹gou¹fong¹ 邑⁹ 高方】the disease has attacked the vitals—beyond cure

C

(It is not used in Cantonese.)

D

打【da¹ 得 丫¹; da² 得 丫²】① 〈 *classifier* 〉 dozen 一 打 铅 笔【yed⁷da¹yün⁴bed⁷】a dozen pencils; ②strike; hit; fight; send; ladle

打败【da²bai⁶ 摆⁶】defeat; beat; be defeated

打倒【da²dou² 赌】overthrow

打扮【da²ban⁶ 办⁶】dress up; make up

打断【da²tün⁵ 团⁵】break; interrupt

打哈嗤【da²hed²qi¹ 乞痴】sneeze = 【普】打喷嚏

打击【da²gig⁷ 激】hit; strike

打交【da² gao¹ 胶 】come to blows; fight = 【普】打架

打搅【da²gao² 狡】disturb; trouble

打劫【da²gib⁸ 格叶⁸】rob; plunder; loot

打开【da²hoi¹ 海¹】open; unfold; turn on

打捞【da²lao¹ 罗拗¹】get out of the water

打猎【da²lib⁹ 罗叶⁹】go hunting

打乱【da²lün⁶ 联⁶】throw into confusion

打破沙煲问到笃【da²po³xa¹bou¹men⁶ dou³dug⁷ 婆³ 莎¹ 褒文⁶ 道³ 督】insist on getting to the bottom of the matter = 【普】打破沙锅问到底

打气【da²hēi³ 汽】inflate; pump up; encourage

打散【da²xan³ 汕】break up; scatter

打扫【da²xou³ 数】sweep; clean

打算【da²xün³ 蒜】plan; intend

打碎【da²xêü³ 穗³】break into pieces

打胎【da²toi¹ 台¹】have an(induced) abortion

打通【da²tung¹ 同¹】get through; open up

打头炮【da²teo⁴pao³ 投泡³】fire the first shot

打消【da²xiu¹ 销】give up(an idea, etc.)

打字【da²ji⁶ 治】typewrite; type

打印【da²yen³ 因³】put a seal on; mimeograph

打仗【da²jêng³ 酱】fight; go to war

打针【da²jem¹ 斟】give or have an injection

打中【da²jung³ 种³】hit the mark

打横来【da²wang⁴lei⁴ 划罂⁴ 黎】be impervious to reason = 【普】蛮不讲理

呆【dai¹ 得埃¹; dai² 得埃²; ngoi⁴ 哀⁴】slow-witted; dull; wooden

书呆子【xü¹dai¹ji²】pedant; bookworm

成个呆晒【xēng⁴go³ngoi⁴xai³】dumb as a

wooden chicken =【普】呆若木鸡

老呆【lou⁵dai²】aged；senile =【普】老迈

带【dai³ 戴】belt；girdle；take；bring；bear；lead；look after

带子【dai³ji² 止】belt；girdle

带电【dai³din⁶ 殿】electrified

带动【dai³dung⁶ 洞】drive；spur on

带菌者【dai³kuen²jē² 捆姐】carrier

带领【dai³ling⁵ 岭】lead；guide

带路【dai³lou⁶ 露】show（或 lead）the way

带头【dai³teo⁴ 投】take the lead

戴【dai³ 带】put on；wear；respect

戴眼镜【dai³ngan⁵gēng³ 晏⁵ 颈³】wear glasses

戴孝【dai³hao³ 考³】wear mourning for a parent

大【dai⁶ 歹⁶】big；great；general；size；age

大半【dai⁶bun³ 伴³】more than half

大便【dai⁶bin⁶ 辨】defecate；stool

大臣【dai⁶xen⁴ 神】minister（of a monarchy）

大胆【dai⁶dam² 担²】bold；daring

大道理【dai⁶dou⁴lēi⁵ 度里】major principle

大地【dai⁶dēi⁶ 得诶⁶】earth；mother earth

大多数【dai⁶do¹xou³ 朵¹ 扫】great majority

大方【dai⁶ fong¹ 芳】expert；natural and poised；in good taste

大夫【dai⁶fu¹ 肤】doctor；physician

大肚腩【dai⁶tou⁶nam⁵ 吐⁵ 览】potbellied merchant =【普】大腹贾

大概【dai⁶koi³ 盖】general idea；general

大干【dai⁶gon³ 竿³】work energetically

大纲【dai⁶gong¹ 江】outline

大佬【dai⁶lou² 老²】= 大哥【bai⁶go¹ 歌】eldest brother =【普】老兄

大公无私【dai⁶gung¹mou⁴xi¹ 工毛思】selfless

大功告成【dai⁶gung¹gou³xing⁴ 工高³ 承】be crowned with success

大观【dai⁶gun¹ 官】grand sight

大规模【dai⁶kuei¹mou⁴ 亏毛】large-scale

大镬饭【dai⁶wog⁶fan⁶ 乌恶⁹ 范】mess =【普】大锅饭

大汉【dai⁶hon³ 看】big fellow

大亨【dai⁶heng¹ 铿】big shot；bigwig

大后日【dai⁶heo⁶yed⁹ 候逸】three days from now =【普】大后天

大话【dai⁶wa⁶ 画⁶】big talk；bragging

大家【dai⁶ ga¹ 加】great master；everybody

大街【dai⁶gai¹ 佳】main street

大局【dai⁶gug⁹ 焗】overall situation

大快人心【dai⁶fai³yen⁴xem¹ 块仁深】most gratifying to the people

大老粗【dai⁶lou⁵qou¹ 鲁操】uncouth fellow

大力【dai⁶lig⁶ 历】energetically；vigorously

大量【dai⁶lēng⁶ 亮】a large number；generous

大陆【dai⁶lug⁶ 六】continent；mainland

大麻【dai⁶ma⁴ 马⁴】hemp；marijuana

大马哈【dai⁶ma⁶ha⁶ 麻⁵ 虾】chum salmon

大难【dai⁶nan⁶ 挪晏】catastrophe；disaster

大炮【dai⁶ pao⁶ 泡⁶】big gun；one who speaks boastfully or forcefully

大批【dai⁶pei¹ 皮矮¹】large quantities of

大人【dai⁶yen⁴ 仁】adult；grown-up

大厦【dai⁶ha⁶ 下】large building

大使【dai⁶xi³ 试】ambassador

大事【dai⁶xi⁶ 是】great event

大势【dai⁶xei³ 世】general trend of events

大肆【dai⁶xi³ 试】without restraint

大腿【dai⁶têü² 退²】thigh = 大髀【dai⁶
　　bēi² 比】

大型【dai⁶ying⁴ 形】large-scale

大选【dai⁶xün⁵ 损】general election

大学【dai⁶hog⁹ 鹤】university；college

大众【dai⁶jung³ 中³】the masses；the peo-
　　ple

大意【dai⁶yi³ 义³】general idea；careless

大约【dai⁶yêg⁸ 若⁸】about；probably

大丈夫【dai⁶jêng⁶fu¹ 仗⁶ 肤】true man；
　　real man

大志【dai⁶ji³ 至】high aim；lofty aim

大致【dai⁶ji³ 至】roughly

大自然【dai⁶ji⁶yin⁴ 治言】nature

大份【dai⁶fen⁶ 分⁶】= 大镬【dai⁶wog⁹ 获】
　　= 大单【dai⁶dan¹ 丹】the situation
　　is grave = 【普】事态严重

大槽【dai⁶mung² 梦²】muddled；ignorant；
　　foolish〇【普】大傻瓜

大癫大费【dai⁶din¹dai⁶fei³ 颠废】play to
　　one's heart's content = 【普】纵情
　　玩乐

大把【dai⁶ba² 靶】many；a lot = 【普】很
　　多

大拿拿【dai⁶na⁴na⁴ 那⁴】a lot；many

大枝野【dai⁶ji¹yē⁵ 之惹】proud〇【普】傲
　　慢的样子

大泡和【dai⁶pao¹wo⁴ 炮¹ 禾】someone who
　　is incapable, foolish and unwise

大饐【dai⁶xung³ 宋】one who eats a lot of
　　vegetables = 【普】吃菜多，吃饭
　　少

大嘥【dai⁶xai¹ 晒¹】to waste = 【普】浪费

大食懒【dai⁶xig⁹lan⁵ 色⁹ 兰⁵】one who
　　just eats and does nothing

大耳隆【dai⁶yi⁵lung¹ 尔龙¹】usurer =
　　【普】高利贷者

歹【dai⁶ 大；dai² 大²】bad；evil；vicious

歹徒【dai²tou⁴ 图】scoundrel；evildoer

担【dam¹ 胆¹；dam³ 胆³】carry on a
　　shoulder pole；take on；a unit of
　　weight(= 50 kilograms)

担保【dam¹bou² 宝】assure；guarantee

担当【dam¹dong¹ 党¹】take on；undertake

担任【dam¹yem⁶ 饮⁶】assume the office of

担心【dam¹xem¹ 深】worry；feel anxious

担竿【dam¹gon¹ 干¹】carrying pole =【普】
　　扁担

耽【dam¹ 担¹】delay

耽误【dam¹ng⁶ 悟】delay；hold up

胆【dam² 担²】gallbladder；courage

胆大包天【dam²dai⁶bao¹tin¹ 歹⁶ 胞田¹】
　　audacious in the extreme

胆敢【dam²gem² 感】dare

胆固醇【dam²gu³xên⁴ 故纯】cholesterol

胆量【dam²lêng⁶ 亮】courage；guts

胆识【dam²xig⁷ 色】courage and insight

胆小鬼【dam²xiu²guei² 少² 诡】coward

胆战心惊【dam²jin³xem¹ging¹ 箭深京】
　　tremble with fear

淡【dam⁶ 氮；tam⁵ 谭⁵】thin；tasteless；
　　light；slack

淡薄【dam⁶bog⁹ 泊】thin；flag；dim

淡漠【dam⁶mog⁹ 莫】indifferent；faint

淡水【tam⁵xêü² 穗²】fresh water

淡季【dam⁶guei³ 贵】slack season

淡忘【dam⁶ mong⁴ 亡】fade from one's memory

淡定【dam⁶ding⁶ 订⁶】calm and unhurried ＝【普】从容不迫

啖 【dam⁶ 淡；dam¹ 担】eat；feed；entice

透啖气【tou⁴dam⁶hêi³】draw a breath ＝【普】吸一口气

黄鼠狼啖走一只鸡仔【wong⁴xü²long⁴ dam¹ jeo² yed⁷ jēg⁸gei¹ jei²】a weasel ran off with a chick in its mouth

氮 【dam⁶】nitrogen

氮肥【dam⁶fêi⁴ 飞⁴】nitrogenous fertilizer

丹 【dan¹ 单】red；pellet or powder

丹青【dan¹qing¹ 清】painting

丹桂【dan¹guei³ 贵】orange osmanthus

丹心【dan¹xem¹ 深】a loyal heart

单 【dan¹ 丹】one；single；odd；alone；only

单车【dan¹qē¹ 奢】bicycle

单程【dan¹qing⁴ 情】one way

单纯【dan¹xên⁴ 淳】simple；pure；alone

单词【dan¹qi⁴ 辞】word

单调【dan¹diu⁶ 掉】monotonous；dull

单独【dan¹dug⁶ 毒】alone；by oneself

单价【dan¹ga³ 嫁】unit price

单据【dan¹gêü³ 居³】documents

单身寡佬【dan¹xen¹guo²lou² 辛姑哑²老²】a bachelor ＝【普】单身汉

蛋 【dan² 弹²；dan⁶ 但】egg

蛋白质【dan²bag⁹jed⁷ 伯⁹侄⁷】protein

蛋糕【dan⁶gou¹ 高】cake

蛋挞【dan⁶tad⁷ 塌⁷】egg tart

蛋家【dan⁶ga¹ 加】boat dwellers ＝【普】水上居民

弹 【dan² 蛋；dan⁶ 但；tan⁴ 坛】ball；pellet；bomb；send forth；fluff；pluck

弹药【dan²yêg⁹ 若】ammunition

弹丸【dan⁶yün² 院】pellet；shot

弹弓【dan⁶gung¹ 工】catapult；slingshot

弹力【tan⁴lig⁹ 历】elastic force

弹跳【tan⁴tiu³ 条³】bounce；spring

弹性【tan⁴xing³ 胜】elasticity

弹奏【tan⁴jeo³ 皱】pluck

弹三弹四【tan⁴ xa m¹ tan⁴ xēi³】nitpick；pick holes ＝【普】挑剔毛病

旦 【dan³ 诞】dawn；daybreak；day

旦夕【dan³jig⁹ 直】this morning or evening

诞 【dan³ 旦】birth；birthday；fantastic

诞辰【dan³xen⁴ 神】birthday

诞生【dan³xeng³ 笙】be born；emerge

答 【dab⁸ 搭】answer；respond；reply

答应【dab⁸ying³ 英³】answer；agree

答案【dab⁸ngon³ 按】answer；solution；key

答复【dab⁸fug⁷ 福】answer；reply

答谢【dab⁸ jē⁶ 姐⁶】express appreciation (for sb.'s kindness or hospitality)

搭 【dab⁸ 答】put up；join；add；travel by

搭车【dab⁸qē¹ 奢】travel by car(or taxi)

搭档【dab⁸dong³ 当³】cooperate；partner

搭救【dab⁸geo³ 够】rescue

搭配【dab⁸ pui³ 佩】arrange in pairs or groups

沓 【dab⁹ 答⁹】⟨classifier⟩pile(of paper, etc.)

踏 【dab⁹ 沓】step on；tread；stamp

踏步【dab⁹bou⁶ 部】mark time

踏实【dab⁹xed⁹ 失⁹】steady and sure

挞

【dad⁷ 达⁷；dad⁸ 达⁸；tad⁸ 剔压⁸】flog；whip；strike；fall

挞住个口【dad⁷jü⁶go³heo² 蛙⁶ 哥³ 厚²】gag sb. saying sth. ＝【普】封住嘴巴

挞啲银过去【dad⁸ did⁷ ngen² guo³ hêü⁷ 得热⁷ 额因² 锅³ 许³】give money vehemently ＝【普】甩票子过去（慷慨地给钱）

挞响度【dad⁸hêng²dou⁶ 向² 道】fall ＝【普】跌倒

挞巴掌【dad⁸ba¹jêng² 爸桨】box sb.'s ears ＝【普】"打耳光"或"打嘴巴"

瘩

【dad⁸ 挞⁸】scar

瘩瘌【dad⁸la¹ 刺】scar ＝【普】疤痕

达

【dad⁹ 挞⁹】extend；reach

达成【dad⁹xing⁵ 承】reach(agreement)

达到【dad⁹dou³ 度³】achieve；attain

达观【dad⁹gun¹ 官】take things philosophically

低

【dei¹ 底¹】low；let droop；hang down

低威【dei¹wei¹ 畏¹】without pride；not as good as ；be inferior ～【普】不及；不如；逊色

低级【dei¹keb⁷ 吸】elementary；vulgar

低劣【dei¹lüd⁸ 捋】inferior；low-grade

低微【dei¹mêi⁴ 眉】(of a voice or sound) low；lowly

低温【dei¹wen¹ 瘟】low temperature

低价【dei¹ga³ 嫁】cheap；low

低息【dei¹xig⁷ 色】low interest

低声下气【dei¹xēng¹ha⁶hēi³ 思镜¹ 夏汽】soft-spoken and submissive

底

【dei² 抵】bottom；base；ground；end

底裤【dei²fu³ 富】underwear

底衫【dei²xam¹ 三】bra

底层【dei² qeng⁴ 次肯⁴】ground floor；bottom

底片【dei²pin² 篇²】negative

底色【dei²xig⁷ 式】bottom

底细【dei²xei³ 世】ins and outs

底下【dei²ha⁶ 夏】under；below；next

抵

【dei² 底】support；resist；be equal to

抵达【dei²dad⁹ 达⁹】arrive；reach

抵触【dei²jug⁷ 足】conflict

抵抗【dei²kong³ 亢】resist；stand up to

抵赖【dei²lai⁶ 拉⁶】deny；disavow

抵消【dei²xiu¹ 烧】offset；cancel out

抵押【dei²ad⁸ 压】mortgage

抵死【dei²xēi³ 四²】serve sb. right ＝【普】活该

抵谂【dei²nem² 挪庵²】one who is not too calculative；exercise forbearan e ＝【普】忍让

抵手【dei²xeo² 守】capable；smart ＝【普】能干的

邸

【dei² 底】the residence of a high official

诋

【dei² 底】slander

诋毁【dei²wei² 委】slander；defame

砥

【dei² 底】whetstone

砥砺【dei²lei⁶ 厉】temper；encourage

帝

【dei³ 谛】the Supreme Being；emperor

帝王【dei³wong⁴ 皇】emperor; monarch

帝国【dei³guog² 姑恶²】empire

帝制【dei³jei³ 济】monarchy

谛【dei³ 帝】carefully; meaning; sneer

谛听【dei³ting³ 亭³】listen attentively

谛下佢【dei³ha⁶kêu⁵ 夏拒】speak sarcastically of him = 挖苦一下他(对他稍加嘲讽)

弟【dei⁶ 第】younger brother

弟妹【dei⁶mui⁴ 梅²】younger brother and sister

弟妇【dei⁶fu⁵ 苦⁵】younger brother's wife

第【dei⁶ 弟】the sign of a ordinal number; other

第一【dei⁶yed⁷ 日⁷】first; primary

第三者【dei⁶xam¹jé² 衫姐】a third party (to a dispute, etc.)

第尾【dei⁶méi¹ 味¹】the last one = 【普】末尾的

递【dei⁶ 弟】hand over; pass; give

递交【dei⁶gao¹ 胶】hand over

递时【dei⁶xi⁴ 是⁴】next time = 【普】往后的时间

递日【dei⁶yed⁹ 逸】in the future∽【普】将来

兜【deo¹ 逗¹】a container to keep food for animal; hold

逗【deo¹ 兜; deo⁶ 窦】canvass; go around circles; stay

逗笃【deo¹dug⁷ 督】disclose the whole inside story∽【普】兜底

逗风【deo¹fung¹ 丰】go for a spin

逗圈【deo¹hün¹ 劝¹】go around circles

逗揽【deo¹lam⁵ 览】canvass; solicit

逗售【deo¹xeo⁶ 受】peddle; hawk

逗留【deo⁶leo⁴ 流】stay; stop

逗功【deo¹gung¹ 公】take credit for someone else's achievements = 【普】邀功

豆【deo²; deo⁶ 窦】beans; peas

豆角【deo⁶gog⁸ 阁】long bean

豆豉【deo⁶xi⁶ 是】fermented soya beans

豆腐【deo⁶fu⁶ 父】bean curd

豆浆【deo⁶jêng¹ 张】soya-bean milk

豆沙【deo⁶xa¹ 洒¹】sweetened bean paste

豆芽【deo⁶nga⁴ 牙】bean sprouts

豆咁大粒汗【deo²gem³dai⁶neb⁷hon⁶ 禁歹⁶ 凹焊】a drop of sweat is so big as to seem the bean

豆丁【deo⁶ding¹ 定¹】minute; small

豆泥【deo⁶nei⁴ 尼】inferior quality

斗【deo³ 豆³; deo² 豆²】fight; tussle

斗胆【deo²dam² 淡²】make bold; venture

斗争【deo³jeng¹ 憎】struggle; fight; combat

斗气【deo³héi³ 汽】quarrel or contend with sb. on account of a personal grudge

斗志【deo³ji³ 至】will to fight

斗叻【deo³lég⁷ 沥⁷】battle of wits∽【普】斗智

窦【deo³ 斗³; deo⁶ 豆⁶】hole; sinus; nest

窦口【deo⁶ 窦 heo² 厚²】hole∽【普】洞

窦口【deo³ 窦 heo² 厚²】nest∽【普】窝;巢;居室

痘【deo⁶ 窦⁶】smallpox; smallpox pustule

抖【deo2 斗2】tremble; shake; rouse

抖开【deo2 hoi1 海1】= 扬开【yêng2hoi1 海1】shake; throw up and scatter

抖擞【deo2xeo2 手】enliven; rouse

纠【deo2 斗2; giu2 缴】entangle; correct

纠纷【deo2fen1 分】dispute; issue

纠正【giu2jing3 政】correct; put right

揼【dem1 得庵1】delay; put off

揼时间【dem1xi4gan3 是4 奸3】delay for time =【普】拖延时间

揼揼戚【dem1dem1qig7 赤7】dilatory =【普】拖拖拉拉

抌【dem2 得庵2; dem3 得庵3】throw in; bang down; thump

抌钱落去【dem2qin2log9hêü3 浅洛9 虚3】throw in money =【普】投放钱财

抌心口【dem2xem1heo2 深厚2】to express regret; to blackmail∽【普】"深表后悔"或"敲诈勒索"

抌条绳落去【dem3tiu4xing2log9hêü3 跳4 醒洛9 虚3】make a cord to hang down =【普】使绳子下垂

抌堆【dem3dêü1 对1】aged and often ill =【普】老迈多病

[足冘]【dem6 得庵6】stamp

[足冘]脚【dem6gêg8 格约8】stamp one's foot =【普】顿足

[月敦]【den1 得因1】cheeks 面朱[月敦]【min6 jü1den1 棉6 猪得因1】red cheeks =【普】红红的脸蛋儿

揗【den3 炖3】make drop

揗甩【den3led7 罗不7】exert all one's strength and make drop =【普】使劲令脱落

揗气【den3hêi3 汽】to throw one's temper =【普】发脾气

趸【den2 得因2】wholesale; lay up

趸船【den2xün4 旋】landing stage

趸享度【den2hêng2dou6 响道】lay up here =【普】放在这里

炖【den6 得因6】stew

炖鸡【den6gei1 计1】stewed chicken

墩【den2 趸】pier

桥墩【kiu4den2 乔趸】bridge pier

耷【deb7 特急7】droop; hang down

耷低头【ded7dei1teo4 底1 投】hang down one's head =【普】耷拉着脑袋

[扌耷]【deb9 耷9】beat; lose

[扌耷]烂【deb9lan6 兰6】beat to pieces =【普】捶打至粉碎

[扌耷]左银【deb9jo2ngen2 助2 额因2】lose money =【普】丢了钱

揬【ded7 突7】lay up; sit

揬享度【ded7hêng2dou6 响道】lay up =【普】放置

揬住个位【ded7jü6go3wei2 蛀6 哥3 委】sitting to capture seat =【普】坐占位置

凸【ded9 突】protruding; raised

凸透镜【ded9teo3gêng3 投3 颈3】convex lens

凸版印刷【ded9ban2yen3qad8 板仁3 察】

letterpress

突【ded⁹ 凸】charge; sudden; projecting

突出【ded⁹qêd⁷ 次律⁷】projecting

突击【ded⁹gig⁹ 激】assault; do a crash job

突破【ded⁹ po³ 颇³】break through; surmount

突然【ded⁹yin⁴ 言】suddenly; abruptly

得【deg⁷ 德】get; obtain; gain; all right

得当【deg⁷dong³ 档】apt; appropriate

得力【deg⁷lig⁹ 历】get help from; capable

得到【deg⁷dou³ 度³】get; obtain; gain

得势【deg⁷xei³ 世】be in power

得手【deg⁷ xeo² 守】go smoothly; come off

得闲【deg⁷han⁴ 娴】have leisure

得益【deg⁷yig⁷ 忆】benefit; profit

得意【deg⁷yi³ 义³】① proud of oneself ② interesting = 【普】有趣

得罪【deg⁷jêû⁶ 坠】offend; displease

得把口【deg⁷ba²heo² 巴² 厚²】to describe one who just says and never acts〰【普】光说不干

得把声【deg⁷ ba² xēng¹ 巴² 腥】refer to 〰【普】光会说, 没行动, 无济于事

得个吉【deg⁷go³ged¹ 哥³ 桔】without results〰【普】扑空; 什么也没得到

得米【deg⁷mei⁵ 迷⁵】to achieve one's purpose〰【普】得益; 成功了; 到手了

得人惊【deg⁷yen⁴gēng¹ 仁镜¹】frightening〰【普】使人害怕

得心应手【deg⁷xem¹ying³xeo² 深映³ 守】with facility; serviceable

德【deg⁷ 得】virtue; morals; heart

德行【deg⁷heng⁶ 幸】moral integrity; shameful

德高望重【deg⁷gou¹mong⁶jung⁶ 膏亡⁶ 仲】be of noble character and high prestige

德才兼备【deg⁷qoi¹qim¹bêi⁶ 财格淹¹ 鼻】have both ability and political integrity

特【deg⁹ 得⁹】special; especially

特登【deg⁹deg¹ 灯】purposely = 【普】特地; 故意

特别【deg⁹bid⁹ 必⁹】special; especially

特产【deg⁹qan² 铲²】special local product

特权【deg⁹kün⁴ 拳】privilege

特色【deg⁹xig⁹ 式】characteristic = 特点【deg⁹dim² 店²】

特性【deg⁹xing³ 胜】specific property

特价【deg⁹ga³ 嫁】special offer

特效【deg⁹hao⁶ 校】specially good effect

特殊【deg⁹xü⁴ 薯】special; peculiar

椊【deg⁹ 特】stake; pile = 【普】桩子

心里打个椊【xem¹lêû⁵da²go³deg⁹】be startled suddenly = 【普】突然吃了一惊

多【do¹ 朵¹】many; much; more

多次【do¹qi³ 刺】many times

多数【do¹xou³ 扫】majority; most

多么【do¹mo¹ 魔】= 几咁【gêi²gem³ 纪禁】〈ad.〉how; what

多少【do¹xiu² 小】= 几多【gêi¹do¹ 纪朵¹】①〈num.〉number; somewhat ②〈ad.〉how many; how much

多情【do¹qing⁴ 程】full of tenderness or affection(for a person of the opposite sex)

多事【do¹xi⁶ 士】meddlesome; eventful

多谢【do¹jē⁶ 者⁶】=唔该【m⁴goi¹ 格哀¹】many thanks; thank a lot

多心【do¹xem¹ 深】oversensitive; suspicious

多余【do¹yū⁴ 如】unnecessary; surplus

多嘴【do¹jēu⁴ 咀】speak out of turn

多种多样【do¹ jung² do¹ yēng⁶ 总让】varied; manifold

多才多艺【do¹ qoi⁴ do¹ ngei⁶ 财伪】versatile

多谋善断【do¹meo⁴xin⁶dūn⁴ 某⁴ 擅段】resourceful and decisive

多计【do¹gei² 偈】to describe one who is tricky∽【普】聪明；多计谋

多罗罗【do¹lo⁴lo⁴ 萝萝】many; too much

朵 【do² 躲】〈classifier〉一朵花【yed⁷do²fa¹】a flower

躲 【do² 朵】hide(oneself); dodge

躲避【do²bēi⁶ 备】hide(oneself); avoid

躲藏【do²qong⁴ 床】go into hiding

堕 【do⁶ 惰】fall; sink

堕落【do⁶log⁹ 洛⁹】degenerate; sink low

堕胎【do⁶toi¹ 台¹】induced abortion

惰 【do⁶ 堕】lazy; indolent

惰性【do⁶xing³ 胜】inertia

代 【doi⁶ 袋】take the place of; acting; historical period; generation

代办【doi⁶ban⁶ 板⁶】=代理【doi⁶lēi⁵ 李】do sth. for sb.; act as agent

代表【doi⁶biu² 标²】deputy; represent

代号【doi⁶hou⁶ 好⁶】code name

代价【doi⁶ga³ 嫁】price; cost

代替【doi⁶tei³ 剃】replace; substitute for

代销【doi⁶ xiu¹ 消】sell goods (for the state) on a commission basis

代谢【doi⁶jē⁶ 者⁶】supersession; metabolize

袋 【doi⁶ 代；doi² 代²；doi¹ 代¹】①bag; sack ②child　你个袋【mēi⁵go³doi¹】your child =【普】你的孩子

袋装【doi⁶jong¹ 庄】in bags

黛 【doi⁶ 代】黛绿【doi⁶lug⁶ 六】dark green

玳 【doi⁶ 代】玳瑁【doi⁶mou⁶ 务】hawksbill turtle

当 【dong¹ 党¹；dong³ 档】equal; ought; just at(a time or place); work as

当场【dong¹qēng⁴ 祥】on the spot

当初【dong¹qo¹ 雏】originally

当地【dong¹dēi⁶ 的诶⁶】local

当家【dong¹ ga¹ 加】manage (household) affairs

当今【dong¹gem¹ 金】now; at present

当面【dong¹min³ 免⁶】to sb.'s face

当年【dong¹nin⁴ 捻⁴】in those years

当前【dong¹qin⁴ 钱】before one; present

当时【dong¹xi⁴ 是⁴】then; at that time

当然【dong¹yin⁴ 言】only natural

当权【dong¹kūn⁴ 拳】hold power

当心【dong¹xem¹ 深】take care; look out

当中【dong¹ jung¹ 钟】in the middle; among

当之无愧【dong¹ji¹mou⁴kuei⁵ 支毛亏⁵】be worthy of

当作【dong³jog⁸ 昨】=当做【dong³jou⁶ 造】treat as

当真【dong³jen¹ 珍】take seriously；really true

当铺【dong³pou³ 葡³】pawnshop

当差【dong¹ qia¹ 次埃¹】to become a policeman

当衰【dong¹xêü¹ 绥】unfortunate；unlucky ＝【普】倒霉；碰上厄运

当堂【dong¹tong⁴ 塘】immediately

当佢有来【dong³kêü⁵mou⁵lei⁴ 拒无⁵ 黎】not approve；not serious；needn't worry∽【普】不以为然；不要紧；不用着急

珰 【dong¹ 当】(see"打珰")

铛 【dong¹ 当】(see"铴铛")

挡 【dong² 党】keep off；block

挡箭牌【dong²jin³pai⁴ 战排】shield；excuse

挡土墙【dong²tou⁴qêng⁴ 桃² 祥】retaining wall

党 【dong² 挡】political party；party；clique

党派【dong²pai³ 排³】political parties and groups

党章【dong²jêng¹ 张】party constitution

党纪【dong²gêi² 几】party discipline

党员【dong²yün⁴ 元】party member

党委【dong²wei² 毁】party committee

荡 【dong⁶ 宕】swing；loaf；sway

荡千秋【dong⁶qin¹qeo¹ 迁抽】play on a swing ＝【普】荡秋千

荡平【dong⁶ping⁴ 屏】wipe out

荡涤【dong⁶dig⁹ 敌】cleanse；wash sway

荡漾【dong⁶yêng² 扬²】ripple；undulate

荡失路【dong⁶xed⁷lou⁶ 室露】to lose one's way ＝【普】迷路

档 【dong³ 当】shelves (for files)；files；grade

档口【dong³heo² 厚²】stall

档案【dong³ngon³ 按】files；archives

宕 【dong⁶ 荡】(see"跌宕")

踱 【dog⁹ 得恶⁹】pace；stroll

踱街【dog⁹gai¹ 佳】shopping ＝【普】逛街

踱来踱去【dog⁹lei⁴dog⁹hêü³ 黎虚³】pace to and fro

铎 【dog⁹ 踱】big bell

铎叔【dog⁹xug⁷ 宿】someone who is stingy ＝【普】吝啬鬼；小气鬼

东 【dung¹ 冬】east；master；host

东方【dung¹fong¹ 芳】the east

东南亚【dung¹nam⁴a³ 男阿】Southeast Asia

东道【dung¹dou⁶ 度】host

东家【dung¹ga¹ 加】master；boss

东西【dung¹xei¹ 逝】east and west；thing

东奔西跑【dung¹ben¹xei¹pao² 宾筛泡²】run around here and there；rush about

东拼西凑【dung¹ping³xei¹qeo³ 聘筛臭】scrape together；knock together

东施效颦【dung¹xi¹hao⁶pen⁴ 思校频】blind imitation with ludicrous effect

冬 【dung¹ 东】winter

冬菇【dung¹gu¹ 姑】mushroom

冬天【dung¹tin¹ 田¹】＝ 冬季【dung¹quei³

桂】winter

冬衣【dung¹yi¹ 依】 = 冬装【dung¹jong¹ 庄】winter clothes

董【dung² 懂】direct

董事【dung²xi⁶ 是】director

懂【dung² 董】understand; know

懂得【dung²deg⁷ 德】understand; know

懂事【dung²xi⁶ 是】sensible; intelligent

冻【dung³ 东³】freeze; jelly; feel very cold

冻冰冰【dung³bing¹bing¹ 兵兵】cold; cooling

冻死【dung³xēi² 四²】freeze to death

洞【dung⁶ 栋】hole; thoroughly

洞察【dung⁶qad⁸ 刷】see clearly

洞穴【dung⁶yüd⁸ 月】cave; cavern

洞房【dung⁶fong⁴ 防】bridal chamber

洞箫【dung⁶ xiu¹ 消】a vertical bamboo flute

恫【dung⁶ 洞】fear

恫吓【dung⁶hag⁸ 客】threaten

垌【dung⁶ 洞】〈classifier〉一 垌 田【yed⁷dung⁶tin⁴】a tract of field◯【普】一片田地

栋【dung⁶ 洞】ridgepole; vertical; erect

栋梁【dung⁶ lêng⁴凉】ridgepole and beam —pillar of the state

栋企【dung⁶kēi⁵ 其⁵】erect = 【普】竖立

动【dung⁶ 洞】move; stir; act; change; use

动物【dung⁶med⁹ 勿】animal

动作【dung⁶jog⁸ 昨】movement; act

动态【dung⁶tai³ 太】trends; dynamic state

动手【dung⁶xeo² 守】start work; touch

动武【dung⁶ mou⁵ 母】use force; start a fight

动荡【dung⁶dong⁶ 当⁶】turbulence; unrest

动静【dung⁶jing⁶ 正⁶】the sound of sth. astir; movement

动力【dung⁶lig⁶ 历】motive power; impetus

动机【dung⁶gēi¹ 基】motive; intention

动脉【dung⁶meg⁹ 墨】artery

动人【dung⁶yen⁴ 仁】moving; touching

动情【dung⁶qing⁴ 程】become excited

动听【dung⁶ting³ 亭³】interesting or pleasant to listen to

动工【dung⁶gung¹ 公】begin construction

动用【dung⁶yung⁶ 容⁶】put to use

动员【dung⁶yün⁴ 圆】mobilize

动不动【dung⁶bed⁷dung⁶ 毕洞】easily

咚【dung¹ 东】咚咚【dung¹dung¹ 冬冬】it is onomatopoeia

督【dug⁷ 笃】superintend and direct

督察【dug⁷qad⁸ 刷】superintend

督促【dug⁷qug¹ 速】supervise and urge

笃【dug⁷ 督】①sincere; jab; ②the bottom part = 【普】器皿的底部

笃信【dug⁷xên³ 迅】sincerely believe in

笃穿【dug⁷ qün¹ 川】puncture; expose = 【普】戳穿

毒【dug⁹ 独】poison; cruel; narcotics

毒品【dug⁹ben² 禀】narcotic drugs

毒药【dug⁹yêg⁹ 若】poison

毒性【dug⁹xing³ 胜】toxicity

毒素【dug⁹xou³ 数】toxin; poison

毒饵【dug⁹nēi⁶ 腻】poison bait

毒害【dug⁹hoi⁶ 亥】poison(sb.'s mind)

毒死【dug⁹xēi² 四²】kill with poison

毒化【dug⁹fa³ 花³】poison；spoil

毒辣【dug⁹lad⁹ 捺⁹】sinister；diabolic

毒计【dug⁹gei³ 继】venom；scheme

独【dug⁹ 毒】only；single；alone

独立【dug⁹leb⁹ 粒⁹】stand alone；independence

独自【dug⁹ji⁶ 治】alone；by oneself

独身【dug⁹xen¹ 辛】unmarried；single

独力【dug⁹lig⁹ 历】by one's own efforts

独创【dug⁹qong³ 仓³】original creation

独到【dug⁹dou³ 道³】original

独特【dug⁹deg⁹ 得⁹】unique

独断【dug⁹dün³ 段³】arbitrary

独占【dug⁹jim³ 詹³】monopolize

读【dug⁹ 独】read；attend school

读书【dug⁹xü¹ 舒】read；study

读物【dug⁹med⁹ 勿】reading matter

读音【dug⁹yem¹ 钦】pronunciation

读者【dug⁹jē² 姐²】reader

渎【dug⁹ 读】show disrespect

渎职【dug⁹jig⁷ 织】malfeasance

犊【dug⁹ 读】calf ＝ 牛仔【ngeo⁴jei²】

牍【dug⁹ 读】documents ＝ 文牍【men⁴ dug⁹】

黩【dug⁹ 读】act war wantonly ＝ 黩武【dug⁹mou⁵ 母】

蠹【dug⁹ 读】moth ＝ 蠹虫【dug⁹qung⁴ 从】

啲【di¹ 得衣¹；did⁷ 得热⁷】these；a little

啲人【di⁷yen⁴ 仁】these men(or people) ＝ 【普】这些人

啲多【did⁷do¹ 朵¹】a little ＝【普】一些；一点儿

啲打佬【di¹da²lou² 打老²】a person who plays the trumpet ＝【普】吹唢呐者

丢【diu¹ 刁；diu⁶ 掉⁶】lose

丢失【diu¹xed⁷ 室】lose

丢假【diu¹ga² 加²】lose face ＝【普】丢脸；出丑

丢咗佢【diu⁶ jo² kêü⁵ 阻拒】lose；throw away

丢生【diu¹xang¹ 诗罂¹】careless；negligent

刁【diu¹ 丢；diu² 丢²】tricky

刁难【diu¹nan⁴ 挪晏⁴】create difficulties

刁那妈【diu²na⁵ma¹ 哪吗】〈*vulgar language*〉rape his mother ＝【普】操他娘

刁拆扭拧【diu¹kiu⁴neo²ning⁶ 乔纽宁⁶】to describe someone who is sportful and difficult to get along with∽【普】撒娇

凋【diu¹ 丢】wither

凋谢【diu¹jē 姐⁶】wither and fall

雕【diu¹ 丢】①〈*n*.〉vulture ②〈*v*.〉carve

雕刻【diu¹heg⁷ 克】carve；engrave

雕塑【diu¹sou³ 扫】sculpture

雕虫小技【diu¹qung⁴xiu²gēi⁶ 从少² 伎】insignificant skill(esp. in writing)

貂【diu¹ 丢】marten

貂皮【diu¹pēi⁴ 疲】fur or pelt of marten

吊【diu³ 钓】hang; suspend; condole; revoke

吊车【diu³qē¹ 奢】crane; hoist

吊灯【diu³deng¹ 登】pendent lamp

吊丧【diu³xong³ 桑】pay a condolence call

吊销【diu³xiu¹ 消】revoke; withdraw

吊颈【diu³gēng² 镜²】hang oneself = 【普】上吊

吊味【diu³mēi⁶ 未】to add to the taste

吊瘾【diu³yen⁵ 引】make not to reconciled ∽【普】使不甘心

吊起来卖【diu³hēi²lei⁴mai⁶ 喜黎理⁶】to increase prices of items when they are in high demand∽【普】提高身价

钓【diu³ 吊】angle

钓鱼【diu³yū² 渔²】angle; go fishing

钓饵【diu³nēi⁶ 腻】bait

钓钩【diu³ngeo¹ 勾】fishhook

碉【diu¹ 刁】pillbox = 碉堡【diu¹bou² 保】

调【diu⁶ 掉；tiu³ 跳；tiu⁴ 条】transfer; naughty; adjust

调拨【diu⁶bud⁶ 勃】allot

调动【diu⁶dung⁶ 洞】transfer

调查【diu⁶qa⁴ 茶】investigate

调换【diu⁶wun⁶ 涣】exchange; change

调子【diu⁶ji² 止】tune; tone(of speech)

调皮【tiu³pēi⁴ 疲】naughty

调和【diu⁴wo⁴ 禾】mediate; compromise

调剂【diu⁴jei¹ 挤】adjust

调节【diu⁴jid⁸ 折】regulate

调理【diu⁴lēi⁶ 李】recuperate

调情【diu⁴qing⁴ 程】flirt

调笑【diu⁴xiu³ 少³】make fun; tease

调整【tiu⁴jing² 正²】adjust; regulate

调转头【diu⁶jūn³teo⁴ 钻投】change the direction(or plight) = 【普】调转方向；调换处境

掉【diu⁶ 刁⁶】fall; lose

掉队【diu⁶dēu² 对²】drop out; fall behind

掉以轻心【diu⁶yi⁵hing¹xem¹ 耳兴深】lower one's guard

点【dim² 店²】drop(of liquid); spot; point; put a dot; drip; check one by one; how; why; o'clock

点播【dim²bo³ 波³】dibbling

点菜【dim² qoi³ 蔡】choose dishes from a menu

点火【dim²fo² 伙²】light a fire

点名【dim²mēng² 未镜²】call the roll

点数【dim²xou³ 素】check the number

点头【dim²tou² 投】nod assent

点心【dim²xem¹ 深】pastry

点缀【dim²jêü⁶ 罪】embellish; use sth. merely for show

点样【dim²yêng² 扬²】how = 【普】怎样；怎么样

点解【dim²gai² 介²】why = 【普】为什么；什么原因

点算【dim²xūn² 蒜】What's to be done? = 【普】怎么办

点搞㗎【dim²gao²ga³ 绞嫁】What's all this about? ∽【普】这是怎么弄的？这是怎么回事？

点钟【dim²jung¹ 中】o'clock; hour

玷【dim³ 店】blemish; disgrace

玷污【dim³wu¹ 乌】stain; sully

玷下都唔得【dim³ha⁶dou¹m⁴deg⁷】not allow to touch∽【普】不许动手触摸

店【dim³ 玷】shop; store

店铺【dim³pou³ 甫³】shop; store

店员【dim³yün⁴ 元】shop assistant; clerk

惦【dim³ 店】remember with concern

惦记【dim³gēi³ 寄】keep thinking about

踮【dim³ 店】stand on tiptoe = 踮起脚

踭【dim³hēi²gêng⁸jang¹】=【普】踮足

掂【dim⁶ 店⁶】① perfectly straight = 【普】笔直；②smoothly =【普】顺利

搞掂【jao²dim⁶】be done smoothly =【普】顺利办妥了

唔掂【m⁴dim⁶】not smoothly =【普】不好办

颠【din¹ 癫】crown(fo the head; fall)

颠覆【din¹fug⁷ 福】overturn

颠倒是非【din¹dou²xi⁶fēi¹ 捣事飞】confound right and wrong

颠沛流离【din¹pui³leo⁴léi⁴ 配留漓】lead a vagrant life

巅【din¹ 颠】mountain peak

癫【din 颠】demented; mentally

癫痫【din¹ gan² 简】epilepsy = 发羊吊【fad⁸yêng⁴diu³】

癫狂【din¹kuong⁴ 框⁴】mad; insane

典【din² 碘】standard; ceremony

典当【din²dong³ 档】mortgage

典故【din²gu³ 固】allusion

典型【din²ying² 形】typical case; model

典雅【din²nga⁵ 瓦】elegant

典礼【din²lei⁵ 黎⁵】ceremony

碘【din² 典】iodine

碘酒【din²jeo² 走】tincture of iodine

躺【din² 典】body over and over

躺床躺席【din²qong⁴din²jēg⁹ 厂⁴ 脊⁹】body over and over on the bed — very painful =【普】痛苦极了

垫【din³ 典】fill up; pad

垫平【din³ping⁴ 屏】level up

垫支【din³ji¹ 枝】pay for sb. and expect to be repaid later

奠【din⁶ 电】establish; settle

奠定【din⁶ding⁶ 锭】establish

奠基【din⁶gēi¹ 机】lay a foundation

殿【din⁶ 电】hall; at the rear

殿后【din⁶heo⁶ 候】bring up the rear

殿下【din⁶ha⁶ 夏】〈call .〉Your Highness

佃【din⁶ 电】佃农【din⁶nung⁴ 浓】tenant-peasant

淀【din⁶ 电】form sediment

淀粉【din⁶fen² 分²】starch

淀积【din⁶jig³ 职】illuviation

甸【din⁶ 电】〈n .〉缅甸【min⁵din⁶】Burma

电【din⁶ 甸】electricity; telegram

电子【din⁶ji² 止】electron

电流【din⁶leo⁴ 留】electric current

电压【din⁶ngad⁸ 押】voltage

电阻【din⁶jo² 左】resistance

电功率【din⁶gung¹lêd⁹ 工律】electric power

电力【din⁶lig⁹ 历】= 电功率

电气【din⁶hēi³ 汽】electric

电器【din⁶hēi³ 气】electrical equipment

电灯【din⁶deng¹ 登】electric lamp

电灯胆【din⁶deng¹dam² 登担²】light bulb
=【普】不通气；不予方便

电报【din⁶bou³ 布】telegram; cable

电话【din⁶wa⁶ 画】telephone; phone

电冰箱【din⁶bing¹xēng¹ 兵商】refrigera-
tor; fridge; freezer

电唱机【din⁶qēng³gēi¹ 畅基】electric gramophone

电炉【din⁶lou⁴ 劳】electric stove

电制【din⁶jei³ 济】key; button =【普】电
键；电钮

电机【din⁶gēi¹ 基】electrical machinery

电视【din⁶xi⁶ 示】television(TV)

电台【din⁶toi⁴ 抬】transceiver

电源【din⁶yün⁴ 元】mains; power supply

电路【din⁶lou⁶ 露】electric circuit

电扇【din⁶xin³ 线】electric fan

电线【din⁶xin³ 扇】electric wire

电梯【din⁶tei¹ 锑】lift; elevator

电烫斗【din⁶tong³deo² 趟豆】electric iron
=【普】电熨斗

电烙鸡【din⁶nad⁸gei¹ 捺计¹】electric iron
=【普】电烙铁

丁【ding¹ 叮】man; members of a family;
fourth

丁员【ding¹yün⁴ 元】population

丁等【ding¹deng¹ 邓²】fourth

丁点【ding¹dim² 店²】a tiny bit = 啲咁多
【did⁷gem³do¹】

叮【ding¹ 丁】warn

叮嘱【ding¹jug⁷ 祝】urge again and again

玎【ding¹ 丁】⟨*onomatopoeia* .⟩ding-dong
= 玎珰

顶【ding² 丁²；dēng² 等镜²】the crown
of the head; top; gore; go against

顶点【ding²dim² 店²】apex; acme

顶峰【ding²fung¹ 风】peak

顶用【ding²yung⁶ 庸⁶】be of use(or help)

顶头上司【ding²teo⁴xēng⁶xi¹ 投尚斯】
one's immediate superior

顶住【ding²jü⁶ 著⁶】withstand; stand up to

顶颈【ding²gēng² 镜²】to go against another =【普】顶牛；顶撞；顶嘴

顶证【ding²jing³ 正】to become a witness

顶笼【ding²lung² 龙²】full house; rich; complete =【普】顶多；到顶

顶唔住【ding²m⁴jü⁶ 著⁶】unbearable = 顶
不了

顶心顶肺【ding²xem¹ding²fei⁶ 深费】to be
hurt by others with what others
say∽【普】被顶撞而心里难受

鼎【ding² 顶】tripod

鼎力【ding²lig⁹ 历】your kind effort

鼎盛【ding²xing⁶ 胜⁶】in a period of great
prosperity

鼎立【ding²leb⁹ 粒⁹】tripartite confronta-
tion

订【ding³ 丁³；dēng⁶ 得镜⁶】conclude;
subscribe to; revise

订购【ding³keo³ 扣】order(goods)

订合同【ding³heb⁹tung⁴ 亥急⁹ 铜】enter
into a contract

订货【dēng⁶fo³ 课】order goods

订婚【ding³fen¹ 分】be betrothed

订正【ding³jing³ 政】make corrections

定【ding⁶ 订⁶】calm; stable; decide; fix

定夺【ding⁶düd⁹ 得月⁹】decide

定义【ding⁶yi⁶ 异】definition

定型【ding⁶ying⁴ 形】finalize the design

定性【ding⁶xing³ 胜】determine the nature（of an offence or a case）

定向【ding⁶hêng³ 响³】directional

定局【ding⁶gug⁹ 焗】foregone conclusion

定额【ding⁶ngeg⁹ 我得⁹】quota；norm

定期【ding⁶kēi⁴ 其】fix a date；regular

定理【ding⁶lêi⁵ 里】theorem

定律【ding⁶lêd⁹ 栗】law

定价【ding⁶ga³ 嫁】fix a price

定系【ding⁶ hei⁶ 核矮⁶】of course；or ⌒【普】当然；或者；还是

定当【ding⁶ dong³ 档】sure；certainly ⌒【普】有把握；镇定；从容

定过台油【ding⁶guo³toi⁴yeo⁴ 挞³ 抬尤】to describe that one is calm due to self-confidence =【普】从容不迫

定晒形【ding⁶xai³ying⁴ 徙³ 营】fix one's eyes upon；collect oneself =【普】定睛；定神

碟【dib⁹ 蝶】small plate；small dish

蝶【dib⁹ 碟】butterfly

蝶泳【dib⁹wing⁶ 咏】butterfly stroke

谍【dib⁹ 蝶】espionage；intelligence agent

谍报员【dib⁹bou³yün⁴ 布元】intelligence agent

牒【dib⁹ 蝶】certificate

最后通牒【jêü³heo⁶tung¹dib⁹】ultimatum

叠【dib⁹ 碟】pile up；repeat；fold

叠埋心水【dib⁹mai⁴xem¹xêü² 卖⁴ 深瑞²】to concentrate ⌒【普】一心一意；不想别的

喋【dib⁹ 蝶】chatter away

喋喋不休【dib⁹dib⁹bed⁷yeo¹ 毕优】chatter away

跌【did⁸ 迭⁸】fall；tumble；drop

跌落【did⁸log⁹ 洛⁹】fall；drop

跌倒【did⁸dou² 赌】fall；tumble

跌打损伤【did⁸da²xün¹xêng¹ 得阿² 选湘】injuries from falls，fractures，contusions and strains

跌价【did⁸ga³ 嫁】go down in price

跌跤【did⁸gao¹ 交】fall down

跌左【did⁸jo² 阻】lose =【普】丢失

迭【did⁹ 秩；qid⁸ 切】alternate；change；repeatedly；again and again

迭起【did⁹hēi² 喜】occur repeatedly

唔迭【m²qid⁸】cannot cope；incessantly =【普】不迭

秩【did⁹ 跌⁹】order；decade

秩序【did⁹jêü⁶ 叙】order；sequence

的【dig⁷ 嫡】⟨auxil.⟩

的确【dig⁷kog⁸ 卡恶⁸】indeed；really

的士【dig⁷xi² 史】taxi =【普】出租小汽车

的式【dig⁷xig⁷ 适】delicate；small =【普】标致；小巧

的士高【dig⁷xi⁶gou¹ 是高】disco

的起心肝【dig⁷hēi²xem¹gon¹ 喜深竿¹】to concentrate ⌒【普】下定决心

嫡【dig⁷ 的】of lineal descent

嫡传【dig⁷qün⁴ 存】handed down in a direct line from the master

嫡亲【dig⁷qen¹ 趁】blood relations

滴【dig⁷ 的；dig⁹ 敌】drip；drop

滴虫【dig⁷qung⁴ 从】〈n.〉trichomonad

滴答【dig⁷dag⁷ 得客⁷】〈onomatopoeia.〉

滴水成冰【dig⁷xêü²xing⁴bing¹ 瑞² 承兵】freezing cold

敌【dig⁹ 迪】enemy；foe；oppose；fight；match

敌对【dig⁹xêü³ 队³】hostile；antagonistic

敌情【dig⁹qing⁴ 程】the enemy's situation

敌人【dig⁹yen⁴ 仁】enemy；foe

敌手【dig⁹xeo² 守】match；enemy hands

敌视【dig⁹xi⁶ 示】be hostile to

敌意【dig⁹yi³ 义³】hostility；enmity

涤【dig⁹ 敌】wash；cleanse

涤除【dig⁹qêü⁴ 徐】wash away

涤纶【dig⁹lên⁴ 伦】〈n.〉polyester fibre

迪【dig⁹ 敌】enlighten；guide

嘀【did⁷ 啲】〈onomatopoeia〉嘀咕【did⁷gu¹ 姑】whisper

狄【dig⁹ 敌】a surname

登【deng¹ 灯】ascend；mount；publish；enter

登报【deng¹bou³ 布】publish in the newspaper

登场【deng¹qêng⁴ 祥】come on stage

登高【deng¹gou¹ 糕】ascend a height

登记【deng¹gêi³ 寄】register；check in

登门【deng¹mun⁴ 瞒】call at sb.'s house

登陆【deng¹lug⁹ 六】land；disembark

灯【deng¹ 登】lamp；lantern；burner

灯光【deng¹guong¹ 广⁻¹】lamplight；lighting

灯火【deng¹fo² 伙²】lights

灯泡【deng¹pao² 抛】light bulb ＝ 灯胆【deng¹dam² 担²】

灯红酒绿【deng¹hung⁴jeo²lug⁹ 洪走六】red lanterns and green wine——scene of debauchery

等【deng² 戥】class；grade；wait；await；〈auxil.〉and so on；etc

等待【deng²doi⁶ 代】wait；await ＝ 等候【deng²heo⁶ 后】

等到【deng²dou³ 度³】by the time；when

等等【deng²deng²】and so on；etc

等同【deng²tung⁴ 铜】＝ 等于【deng²yü¹ 迂】equate；be equal；amount to

等号【deng²hou⁶ 好⁶】equal sign

等级【deng²keb⁷ 给】grade；rank

戥【deng² 等】〈n.〉厘戥【lēi⁴deng²】feel sorry for somebody；to balance oneself

瞪【deng¹ 登】open（one's eyes）wide；stare

瞪眼【deng¹ngan⁵ 晏⁵】open（one's eyes）wide

凳【deng³ 登³】stool；bench

邓【deng⁶ 登⁶】a surname

邓小平【deng⁶xiu²ping⁴ 少² 评】Deng Xiao-ping

邓称【deng⁶qing³ 清³】balanced supplement ＝【普】均衡的配搭

都【dou¹ 刀】① 〈ad.〉all；already ② 〈n.〉capital；big city

都啱【dou¹ngam¹ 岩¹】all right = 【普】全对

都系【dou¹hei⁶ 分⁶】also;〈ad.〉had better = 【普】也是；还是

都市【dou¹xi⁵ 是⁵】city; metropolis

刀【dou¹ 都】knife

刀仔【dou¹jei² 济²】small knife = 【普】小刀

刀片【dou¹pin² 偏²】razor blade

刀叉【dou¹qa¹ 差】knife and fork

刀枪【dou¹ qeng¹ 昌】sword and spear; weapons

刀山火海【dou¹xan¹fo²hoi² 珊伙亥²】most severe trials

岛【dou² 倒】island

岛屿【dou²jêu⁶ 序; dou²yu⁵ 与】island and islets

倒【dou² 岛; dou³ 到】fall; fail; change; upside down; pour; move backward

倒闭【dou²bei³ 敝³】close down

倒塌【dou²tab⁸ 塔】collapse; topple down

倒班【dou²ban¹ 斑】change shifts

倒换【dou³wun⁶ 唤】change; rotate

倒车【dou³qe¹ 扯¹】back a car

倒转头【dou³jun³teo⁴ 钻投】①turn round = 【普】掉头 ②on the contrary; instead = 【普】反而；倒是

倒流【dou³leo⁴ 留】flow backwards

倒数【dou³xou⁴ 嫂】count backwards

倒模【dou²mou² 帽】〈v.〉mould

捣【dou²】beat; smash

捣乱【dou²lün⁶ 联⁶】make trouble = 捣蛋【dou²dan² 旦²】

捣毁【dou²wei² 委】smash up; destroy

到【dou³ 倒】arrive; reach; go to; leave for

到处【dou³qü³ 迟于³】everywhere

到达【dou³dad⁹ 得押⁹】arrive; get to

到底【dou³dei² 抵】to the end; at last

到顶【dou³dēng² 得镜²】reach the summit

到期【dou³kēi⁴ 其】become due

到头来【dou³teo⁴loi⁴ 投莱】in the end; finally

到其时【dou²kēi⁴xi⁴ 奇是⁴】when the time comes

道【dou⁶ 导】road; way; say; talk; speak; line

道喜【dou⁶hēi² 起】congratulate sb. on a happy occasion

道德【dou⁶deg⁷ 得】morals; morality

道理【dou⁶lēi⁵ 里】principle; reason

道路【dou⁶lou⁶ 露】road; way; path

道歉【dou⁶hib⁸ 胁】apologize

道义【dou⁶yi⁶ 异】morality and justice

稻【dou⁶ 道】rice; paddy

稻谷【dou⁶gug⁷ 菊】paddy

稻米【dou⁶mei⁵ 迷⁵】rice

稻田【dou⁶tin⁴ 填】(rice) paddy field

酖【dou⁶ 道】kill with poison = 【普】毒杀

酖虫【dou⁶qung⁴ 从】kill in poison bait for the injurious insect

导【dou⁶ 道】lead; guide; conduct; teach

导弹【dou⁶dan² 蛋】guided missile

导电【dou⁶din⁶ 甸】electric conduction

导航【dou⁶hong⁴ 杭】navigation

导师【dou⁶xi¹ 司】tutor; guide of a great cause

导演【dou⁶ yin² 衍】direct（a film, play, etc.）; director

导游【dou⁶yeo⁴ 由】conduct a sightseeing tour

悼　【dou⁶ 道】mourn; grieve

悼念【dou⁶nim⁶ 粘⁶】mourn; grieve over

盗　【dou⁶ 道】steal; rob; thief; robber

盗窃【dou⁶xid⁸ 泄】steal

盗贼【dou⁶qeg⁹ 迟额⁹】robbers; bandits

杜　【dou⁶ 道】birch-1eaf pear; shut out; stop

杜绝【dou⁶jüd⁹ 支月⁹】stop; put an end to

杜撰【dou⁶jan⁶ 栈⁶】fabricate; make up

杜鹃【dou⁶jün¹ 娟】cuckoo; azalea

度　【dou⁶ 道; dog⁹ 铎】linear measure; degree of intensity; degree; limit; time; spend; consideration

度假【dou⁶ga³ 嫁】spend one's holidays

度量【dou⁶lêng⁶ 亮】tolerance; magnanimity

度数【dou⁶xou³ 素】number of degrees

度日如年【dou⁶yed⁹yü⁴nin⁴ 逸鱼捻⁴】one day seems like a year

度度【dog⁹dou² 倒】measurement =【普】量度

度度【dou⁶ dou⁶】everywhere =【普】到处; 每个地方

度侨【dog⁹kiu² 乔²】to plot =【普】想办法; 策划计谋

渡　【dou⁶ 道; dou² 倒】cross（a river, etc.）; ferry

渡河【dou⁶ho⁴ 何】cross a river

渡口【dou⁶heo² 厚²】ferry

花尾渡【fa¹mêi⁵dou² 化¹ 美度²】machine-ship =【普】机器船

镀　【dou⁶ 道】plating

镀金【dou⁶gem¹ 甘】gold-plating; get gilded

妒　【dou³ 到】be jealous of; envy

妒忌【dou³gêi⁶ 己⁶】be jealous of; envy

堵　【dou² 倒】stop up; block up

堵塞【dou²xeg⁷ 是克⁷】stop up; block up

赌　【dou² 倒】gamble; bet

赌博【dou²bog⁸ 搏】gambling

赌钱【dou²qin² 浅】gamble

赌气【dou² hêi³ 戏】feel wronged and act rashly

赌咒【dou²jeo³ 皱】take an oath; swear

睹　【dou² 倒】see

睹物思人【dou²med⁹xi¹yen⁴ 勿司仁】seeing the thing one thinks of the person

嘟　【du¹ 得乌¹】⟨onomatopoeia⟩

舿　【dü¹ 得于¹】⟨onomatopoeia⟩

舿舿【dü⁴dü¹】the sound of child urinate

端　【dǖn¹ 段¹】end; beginning; reason; item

端度【dǖn¹ dog⁹ 铎】look sb. up and down; think over =【普】掂量; 考虑; 端详

端正【dǖn¹jing³ 政】upright; correct

端午节【dǖn¹ng⁵jid⁸ 折】the 5th day of the 5th lunar month

短　【dǖn² 端²】short; lack; fault

短程【dün²qing⁴ 情】short distance

短工【dün²gung¹ 公】casual labourer

短见【dün²gin³ 建】shortsighted view; suicide

短路【dün²lou⁶ 露】short circuit

短命【dün²mēng⁶ 勿镜⁶】die young

短缺【dün²küd³ 决】shortage

短暂【dün²jam⁶ 站】of short duration

短小精悍【dün²xiu¹jing¹hon⁶ 少² 征汗⁴】of short duration

断【dün³ 锻; dün⁶ 段; tün⁵ 团⁵】break; break off; stop; give up; judge

断估【dün³gu² 古】to guess =【普】估计

断定【dün³ding⁶ 订⁶】conclude; decide

断续【tün⁵jug⁹ 逐】off and on

继绝【tün⁵ jüd⁹ 拙⁹】break off; cut off; sever

断送【dün⁶ xung⁷ 宋】forfeit (one's life, etc.)

断然【dün³yin⁴ 言】absolutely

断气【tün⁵hēi³ 戏】die; cut off the gas

段【dün⁶ 锻⁶】section; part; passage

段落【dün⁶log⁹ 洛⁹】paragraph; phase; stage

锻【dün³ 段³】forge

锻炼【dün³lin⁶ 练】take exercise; temper

缎【dün⁶ 段⁶】satin

逇【düd⁷ 夺⁷】逇逇咁去【düd⁷düd⁷gem³ hêu⁶】the vehicle or ship run fast ∽【普】车船快跑状

夺【düd⁹ 得月⁹】take by force; contend for

夺取【düd⁹qêu² 娶】capture; wrest; strive for

夺目【düd⁹mug⁹ 木】dazzle the eyes

哚【dê¹ 的靴¹】a bit; a little

啲哚【did⁷dê¹】a bit; a little =【普】多【did⁷do¹】=【普】一点儿

螫【dê³ 哚³; qig⁷ 斥】sting

螫针【dê³jem¹ 浸】sting; stinger =【普】(黄蜂)刺着

渁【dê⁴ 哚⁴】⟨onomatopoeia⟩

渁渁声【dê⁴dê⁴xēng¹ 思镜¹】the sound of the running water

堆【dêü¹ 队¹】pile up; heap up; pile; heap

堆放【dêü¹fong³ 况】pile up; stack

堆砌【dêü¹qei³ 齐³】pile up(hewn rocks, etc. to build sth.)

堆积【dêü¹jig⁷ 织】pile up; heap up

挃【dêü² 队²】poke; stab; disclose; let out =【普】捅

挃冧佢【dêü²lem⁵kêü⁵ 林³ 拒】poke down to destroy =【普】把某物捅下来(摧毁某物)

对【dêü³ 队³】answer; treat; be trained on; mutual; opposite; suit; check; right

对比【dêü³bēi² 俾】contrast; balance

对唔住【dêü³m⁴jü⁶ 著⁶】I'm sorry; sorry; let sb. down =【普】对不起

对称【dêü³qing³ 清³】symmetry

对待【dêü³doi⁶ 代】treat; handle

对调【dêü³diu⁶ 掉】exchange

对方【dêü³fong¹ 芳】the other side

对付【dêü³fu⁶ 父】deal with; cope with; make do

对话【dêü³wa⁶ 画⁶】dialogue

对头【dêü³teo⁴ 投】correct; on the right

track; enemy

对象【dêū³ jêng⁶ 丈】target; boy or girl f-riend

对应【dêū³ying³ 英³】corresponding

对于【dêū³yū¹ 迂】〈prep.〉∽of; for

对证【dêū³jing³ 正】verify; check

对抗【dêū³kong³ 亢】antagonism; resist

对立【dêū³ leb⁹ 粒⁹】oppose; set sth. a-gainst

对面【dêū³ min³ 免⁶】opposite; right in f-ront

对联【dêū³ lūn⁴ 乱⁴】antithetical couplet (written on scrolls, etc.)

对路【dêū³lou⁶ 露】satisfy the need

兑 【dêū³ 对】exchange; convert

兑换【dêū³wun⁶ 唤】exchange; convert

兑换率【dêū³wun⁶lêd⁹ 律】rate of ex-change

兑现【dêū³ yin⁶ 演⁶】cash(a cheque, etc.); fulfil

碓 【dêū³ 对】a treadle-operated tilt ham-mer for hulling rice

队 【dêū⁶ 对⁶】a row of people; line; team

队伍【dêū⁶ng⁵ 五】troops; ranks

队长【dêū⁶jêng² 蒋】captain; team leader

队员【dêū⁶yūn⁴ 元】team member

敦 【dên¹ 顿¹】honest; sincere

敦促【dên¹qug⁷ 速】urge; press

敦厚【dên¹heo⁵ 后⁵】honest and sincere

敦煌石窟【dên¹wong⁴xēg⁹gued⁹ 王 锡⁹ 掘】〈n.〉The Dunhuang Caves(in China)

吨 【dên¹ 敦】〈classifier〉ton(t.)

吨位【dên¹wei² 委】tonnage

吨公里【dên¹gung¹lēi⁵ 工理】ton kilome-tre

蹲 【dên¹ 敦】squatting down = 踎 低 【meo¹dei¹】

顿 【dên⁶ 囤】pause; suddenly; immedi-ately

顿挫【dên⁶qo³ 错】pause and transition in rhythm or melody

顿时【dên⁶xi⁴ 是⁴】immediately

顿开茅塞【dên⁶hoi¹mao⁴xeg⁷ 海¹ 矛时 克⁷】suddenly see the light

沌 【dên⁶ 顿】(see"混沌")

囤 【dên⁶ 顿】a grain bin; hoard

囤积【dên⁶jig⁷ 织】hoard for speculation

炖 【dên⁶ 顿】stew

炖鸡【dên⁶gei¹ 计¹】stewed chicken

钝 【dên⁶ 顿】blunt; dull; stupid; dull-witted

顿角【dên⁶gog⁸ 阁】obtuse angle

遁 【dên⁶ 顿】escape; flee; fly(see"逃 遁")

蹾 【dêng¹ 得香¹】=【普】啄(see"啄")

蹾住晒【dêng¹jū⁶xai³ 著⁶ 徙⁶】urge again and supervise∽【普】叮咛;督促

啄 【dêg⁸ 琢】peck

啄木鸟【dêg⁸mug⁹niu⁵ 目挪妖⁵】wood-pecker

琢 【dêg⁸ 啄】chisel; carve

琢磨【dêg⁸mo⁴ 摸⁴】carve and polish (jade); polish; refine

斫【dêg⁸ 啄】chop; hack

斫柴【dêg⁸qai⁴ 踩⁴】cut firewood =【普】砍柴

斫烂【dêg⁸lan⁶ 栏⁶】chopped to pieces

爹【dē¹ 嗲¹】father; dad; daddy; pa

爹妈【dē¹ma¹ 吗】father and mother =【普】爹娘

嗲【dē² 爹²】finicky （see"娇嗲"）

嗲嗲噭样【dē²dē²gem²yēng² 敢扬²】delicately pretty∽【普】娇嘀嘀

嗲嗲吊【dē²dē²diu³ 钓】one who is irresponsible =【普】(某人)无责任感;不负责任的样子

嗲嗲渧【dē⁴dē¹dei³ 帝】water that keeps dropping without stopping =【普】口涎流个不断

地【dēi⁶ 得利⁶;dēi² 得利²】①the earth; place; ② the adverbial sign; ③ the sign of the plural of the personal pronoun =【普】们

地板【dēi⁶ban² 版】floor board

地步【dēi⁶bou⁶ 部】condition; extent

地产【dēi⁶qan² 铲】landed estate

地道【dēi⁶dou⁶ 度】genuine; pure; tunnel

地点【dēi⁶dim² 店²】place; site

地方【dēi⁶fong¹ 芳】local; locality; space

地基【dēi⁶jēi¹ 机】ground; foundation

地皮【dēi⁶ pēi⁴ 脾】land for building; ground

地面【dēi⁶min⁶ 免⁶】the earth's surface

地下【dēi⁶ ha⁶ 夏】underground; secret (activity); on the ground

地利【dēi⁶lēi⁶ 例】land productivity

地图【dēi⁶tou⁴ 途】map

地理【dēi⁶lēi⁵ 里】geography

地名【dēi⁶ming⁴ 明】place name

地址【dēi⁶ji² 止】address

地契【dēi⁶kei³ 卡矮³】title deed for land

地球【dēi⁶keo⁴ 求】the earth

地区【dēi⁶kêu¹ 拘】area; prefecture

地形【dēi⁶ying⁴ 仍】topography

地震【dēi⁶jen³ 振】earthquake; seism

地质【dēi⁶jed⁷ 侄⁷】geology

地主【dēi⁶jü² 煮】landlord; host

地租【dēi⁶jou¹ 糟】land rent; ground rent

钉【dēng¹ 盯】to squeeze with one's finger nails; nail; tack; urge

钉仔【dēng¹jei¹ 济²】nail; snag =【普】钉子

钉鞋【dēng¹hai⁴ 谐】spiked shoes

盯【dēng¹ 钉】fix one's eyes on

盯梢【dēng¹xao¹ 捎】shadow sb.; tail sb.

掟【dēng³ 钉³】to throw at a destination; throw; cast; fling =【普】投掷

掟标枪【dēng³biu¹qêng¹ 彪昌】javelin throw =【普】掷标枪

掟煲【dēng³bou¹ 褒】to refer to the breakup of a marriage =【普】吹了(毁掉已有的婚姻或恋爱关系)

蹓【dēg⁸ 得尺⁸】run away; flee; leave

蹓路【dēg⁸lou² 佬】run away; leave =【普】逃跑;速离

蹓更【dēg⁸gang¹ 耕】run away at night =【普】夜逃

蹓甩【dēg⁸led⁷ 罗核⁷】succeed in escaping =【普】逃脱

笛【dēg⁹ 得尺⁹】bamboo flute; whistle

笛子【dēg⁹ji² 止】bamboo flute

E

诶 【ē¹ 欸¹；ē⁴ 欸⁴】〈int.〉show answer, agreement, etc
　诶，我就来! 【ē¹, ngo⁵jeo⁶lei⁴!】Yes, I'll come a minute!

欸 【ē¹ 诶¹；ē⁴ 诶⁴】〇诶
　欸，就噢啦! 【ē⁴, jeo⁶gem²la¹】All right, that's settled.

哎 【ēi¹ 嗳¹；ai¹ 唉¹】〈int.〉show unforeseen, surprised, etc.
　哎，系刘先生! 【ēi¹, hei⁶leo⁴xin¹xang¹】Why, it's Mr. Leo!
　哎呀! 落大雨啦! 【ai¹ya⁴! log⁹dai⁶yü⁵la³】Alas, it's pouring!

嗳 【ēi¹ 哎¹；ai¹ 唉¹】〇哎; show pain
　嗳唷【ēi¹yo¹ 哟¹】= 哎哟【ēi¹yo¹ 唷】〈int.〉show pain

矮 【ei² 矮²】short(of stature);low
　矮仔【ei²jei² 济²】a short person; dwarf = 【普】矮子;矮个儿
　矮仔里头挑高佬【ei²jei²lêu⁶teo⁴tiu¹gou¹lou²】pick a general from among the dwarfs〇【普】矮子里拔将军
　矮唢撰【ei²di¹ded⁷】pudgy〇【普】矮墩墩
　矮仔多计【ei²jei²do¹gei¹ 济² 朵¹ 偈】the dwarf has many schemes = 【普】矮个子多计谋

翳 【ei³ 矮³】nebulous; nebula
　翳气【ei³hēi³ 汽】be unhappy; be vexed

= 【普】烦闷;烦恼

欧 【eo¹ 殴；ngeo¹ 殴】a surname
　欧洲【eo¹jeo¹ 州】Europe
　欧化【eo¹fa³ 花³】Europeanize; westernize

殴 【eo¹;ngeo¹ 欧】beat up; hit
　殴打【eo¹da² 得丫²】beat up; hit

讴 【eo¹ 欧;ngeo¹ 欧】sing; folk songs
　讴歌【eo¹go¹ 哥】sing the praises of

鸥 【eo¹ 欧;ngeo¹ 欧】gull
　海鸥【hoi²eo¹】sea gull

呕 【eo² 欧²;ngeo²】vomit; throw up
　呕吐【eo²tou³ 兔】vomit; throw up
　呕心沥血【eo²xem¹lig⁹hüd⁶ 深力黑月⁸】shed one's heart's blood

沤 【eo³ 欧³;ngeo³ 欧³】soak; steep
　沤肥【eo³fēi⁴ 飞⁴】make compost; wet compost

怄 【eo³ 沤;ngeo³ 沤】annoy; be irritated
　怄气【eo³hēi³ 汽】be difficult and sulky

庵 【em¹ 暗;ngem¹ 暗】hut; nunnery
　草庵【qou²em¹】a thatched hut
　尼姑庵【nēi⁴gu¹em¹】Buddhist nunnery

鹌【em¹ 庵;ngem¹ 庵】(see"鹌鹑")

鹌鹑【em¹qên¹ 春】quail

谙【em¹ 庵】know well

素谙水性【xou³em¹xêǔ²xing³】be a skilful swimmer

揞【em² 庵²】〈v.〉(see"揞住")

揞住【em²jū⁶ 著⁶】apply(medicinal powder to a wound)∽【普】捂着

暗【em³ 庵³;ngem³ 庵³】dark; dim; hidden

暗藏【em³qong⁴ 床】hide; conceal

暗娼【em³qêng¹ 昌】unlicensed prostitute

暗淡【em³dom⁶ 担⁶】dim; faint; dismal

暗害【em³hoi⁶ 亥】kill secretly

暗号【em³hou⁶ 浩】secret signal; countersign

暗示【em³xi⁶ 是】drop a hint; hint

暗礁【em³jiu¹ 招¹】submerged reef

暗算【em³xūn³ 蒜】plot against

暗中【em³jung¹ 钟】in the dark; in secret

暗无天日【em³ mou⁴ tin¹ yed⁹ 毛田¹ 逸】complete darkness; total absence of justice

暗送秋波【em³ xung³ qeo¹ bo¹ 宋抽玻】make eyes at sb. while others are not looking

暗暗沁沁【em³em³xem³xem³ 深³ 深³】not open and not aboveboard∽【普】不光明磊落

黯【em³ 暗】dim; gloomy

黯然失色【em³yin⁴xed⁷xig⁷ 言室式】be overshadowed; dejected

唵【em⁴ 暗⁴;ngem⁴ 暗⁴】wordy

唵唵沉沉【em⁴em⁴qem⁴qem⁴ 寻寻】long-winded; wordy =【普】罗里罗嗦

F

花【fa¹ 化¹】flower；blossom；coloured；dim；fancy；spend

花朵【fa¹do² 躲】flower

花束【fa¹qug⁷ 速】a bunch of flowers

花纹【fa¹men⁴ 文】decorative pattern；figure

花样【fa¹yêng² 扬²】pattern；trick

花款【fa¹fun² 宽²】trick =【普】花样；花式

花斑【fa¹ban¹ 班】piebald

花丛【fa¹qung⁴ 从】flowering shrubs

花絮【fa¹xêü⁵ 穗⁵】titbits(of news)

花卉【fa¹wei⁵ 伟】flowers and plants

花甲【fa¹gab⁸ 格鸭⁸】a cycle of sixty years

花灯【fa¹deng¹ 登】festive lantern

花蜜【fa¹med⁹ 勿】nectar

花露水【fa¹lou⁶xêü² 路瑞²】toilet water

花盆【fa¹pun⁴ 盘】flower vase

花饰【fa¹xig⁷ 色】ornamental design

花费【fa¹fei² 废】spend；expend = 花消【fa¹xiu² 销】

花王【fa¹wong⁴ 皇】a gardener

花樽【fa¹jên¹ 遵】a vase =【普】花瓶

花假【fa¹ga² 贾】pretend to；false；not true =【普】不实在；花架子

花红【fa¹hung⁴ 洪】interest；bonus

花笋【fa¹ xên² 殉²】fashion =【普】流行款式；时髦花样

花士令【fa¹xi⁶ling² 事另²】vaseline

花名【fa¹mêng² 默镜²】nickname =【普】别号；绰号

花洒【fa¹xa² 沙²】shower〇【普】喷水器

花靓仔【fa¹lêng¹jei² 罗镜¹ 济²】young men who are fashion conscious；playboy；playfellow〇【普】不踏实的年轻小伙子

花心萝卜【fa¹xem¹lo⁴bag⁹ 深罗白】to describe men who are not loyal towards love；dandy；coxcomb =【普】花花公子

花哗【fa¹fêd⁷；fa¹fid⁷】frightly coloured；colourful〇【普】花花绿绿

花花世界【fa¹fa¹xei³gai³ 细介】this mortal world

花枝招展【fa¹ji¹jiu¹jin² 支焦剪】(of women)be gorgeously dressed

化【fa³ 花³；fa² 花²】change；turn；convert；open-minded；complete

化学【fa³hog⁹ 鹤】①chemistry ②not long lasting；not trustworthy =【普】不可靠、不耐用的；易坏的

化合【fa³heb⁹ 盒】chemical combination

化名【fa³mêng² 莫镜²】(use an)assumed name

化身【fa³xen¹ 辛】incarnation

化妆【fa³jong¹ 装】put on makeup

化验【fa³yim⁶ 掩⁶】chemical examination

化纤【fa³qim¹ 潜¹】chemical fibre

化为乌有【fa³wei⁴wu¹yeo⁵ 维呜友】melt into thin air

化险为夷【fa³him²wei⁴yi⁴ 欠² 维移】turn danger into safety

化晒【fa³ xai³ 徙³】be disillusioned with the mortal world∽【普】看破红尘

快【fai³ 块³】fast; quick; speed; hurry up; pleased; happy

快速【fai³qug⁷ 促】fast; quick; high-speed

快车【fai³qê¹ 奢】express train or bus

快餐【fai³qan¹ 残¹】quick meal; snack

快信【fai³xên³ 迅】express letter

快趣【fai³qêü³】at once; quickly = 快快趣趣∽【普】赶快

快手【fai³xeo² 守】quick work; deft hand

快活【fai³wud⁹ 乌泼⁹】happy; merry

快乐【fai³log⁹ 落】happy; joyful

快刀斩乱麻【fai³dou¹jam²lün⁶ma⁴ 都眨联⁶嫲】cut a tangled skein of jute with a sharp knife

块【fai³ 快】〈classifier〉piece; lump; chunk

块煤【fai³mui⁴ 媒】lump coal

块喧噉【fai³dad⁸gem² 达⁸ 敢】the looks of a certain person are dull∽【普】其貌不扬；样子呆板

筷【fai³ 快】chopsticks

筷子【fai³ji² 止】chopsticks

翻【fan¹ 反¹】turn over; cross; search; reverse

翻案【fan¹ngon³ 按】reverse a（correct）verdict

翻版【fan¹ban² 板】reprint; reproduction

翻跟斗【fan¹gen¹deo² 斤豆】turn a somersault

翻来复去【fan¹loi⁴fug⁷hêü³ 莱福许³】toss and turn; again and again

翻身【fam¹xen¹ 辛】turn over; free oneself

翻天覆地【fan¹tin¹fug⁷dêi⁶ 田¹ 福得诶⁶】world-shaking

翻译【fan¹yig⁹ 亦】translate; translator

翻印【fan¹yen³ 仁³】reprint; reproduce

翻抄【fan¹qao¹ 吵¹】remanufacture

翻工【fan¹gung¹ 公】go to work = 【普】上班

翻去【fan¹hêü³ 许³】go back =【普】回去

翻学【fan¹ hog⁹ 鹤】= 返学 go to school =【普】上学

翻生【fan¹ xang¹ 是罂¹】to come alive again∽【普】再世；起死回生

翻头婆【fan¹teo⁴po² 投颇】to refer to a woman who marries twice 【普】再嫁的婆娘

番【fan¹ 翻；pun¹ 潘】again; back

番号【fan¹hou⁶ 好⁶】designation（of a military unit）

番茄【fan¹kê² 剧诶²】tomato

番薯【fan¹xü² 暑】sweet potato

番枧【fan¹gan² 简】soap =【普】肥皂

番摊【fan¹tan¹ 滩】a type of gambling

番鬼佬【fan¹guei¹lou² 诡老²】a westerner∽【普】西方强盗；洋鬼子

番鬼【fan¹guei² 诡】be impervious to reason =【普】蛮不讲理

番禺【pun¹ yü⁴ 鱼】the place name of Guangzhou China

反【fan² 返】to joke; turn over; inside out; instead; return; revolt; oppose

反对【fan²dêü³ 队³】oppose; fight; combat

反驳【fan²bog⁸ 博】refute; retort

反击【fan²gig⁷ 激】strike back; beat back

反动【fan²dung⁶ 栋】reaction; reactionary

反常【fan²xêng⁴ 偿】unusual; abnormal

反而【fan²yi⁴ 移】〈conj.〉on the contrary

反感【fan² gem² 敢】be disgusted with

反悔【fan² fui³ 灰³】go back on one's word

反抗【fan² kong³ 慷³】revolt；resist

反叛【fan² bun⁶ 拌】revolt；rebel

反射【fan² xê⁶ 蛇⁶】reflex；reflection

反馈【fan² guei⁶ 跪】feedback

反问【fan² men⁶ 文⁶】ask(a question)in reply

反应【fan² ying³ 英³】reaction；response

反映【fan² ying² 影】reflect；mirror；report

反正【fan² jing³ 政】anyway；anyhow

反复无常【fan² fug⁷ mou⁴ xêng⁴ 福毛偿】changeable

反斗【fan² deo² 豆²】naughty；sporting =【普】调皮捣蛋

反骨【fan² gued⁷ 掘⁷】cruel；ruthless；without mercy∽【普】反叛；恩将仇报

反面【fan² min² 免²】① reverse side ② not on good terms with one =【普】闹翻；反脸

反省【fan² xing² 醒】introspection

返【fan² 反；fan¹ 翻】return

返回【fan² wui⁴ 会⁴】return；come or go back

返销【fan² xiu¹ 消】resold(grain, etc.)

返老还童【fan² lou⁵ wan⁴ tung⁴ 鲁环同】recover one's youthful vigour

返工【fan¹ gung¹ 公】do poorly done work over again

贩【fan³ 泛】buy to resell；dealer

贩卖【fan³ mai⁶ 买⁶】traffic；peddle

贩运【fan³ wen⁶ 混】transport goods for sale

贩毒【fan³ dug⁹ 读】traffic in narcotics

泛【fan³ 败】float；flood；extensive

泛滥【fan³ lam⁶ 缆】be in flood；spread unchecked

泛指【fan³ ji³ 止】make a general reference

泛泛而谈【fan³ fam³ yi⁴ tam⁴ 移谭】talk in generalities

凡【fan⁴ 帆】ordinary；the earth；every；any

凡间【fan⁴ gan¹ 奸】this mortal world

凡人【fan⁴ yen⁴ 仁】① ordinary person ② mortal

凡事【fan⁴ xi⁶ 是】everything

凡是【fan⁴ xi⁶ 事】every；any；all

帆【fan⁴ 凡】sail

帆船【fan⁴ xün⁴ 旋】sailing boat(or ship)

藩【fan⁴】(see"藩篱")

藩篱【fan⁴ lêi⁴ 离】hedge；fence

樊【fan⁴ 凡】(see"樊笼")

樊笼【fan⁴ lung⁴ 龙】bird cage——place or condition of confinement

矾【fan⁴ 凡】vitriol

明矾【ming⁴ fan⁴】alum

烦【fan⁴ 凡】be vexed；be tired；trouble

烦劳【fan⁴ lou⁴ 炉】trouble

烦闷【fan⁴ mun⁶ 门⁶】be unhappy

烦恼【fan⁴ nou⁵ 脑】be vexed；be worried

烦琐【fan⁴ xo² 所】loaded down with trivial details

烦躁【fan⁴ qou⁴ 燥】be fidgety；be agitated

繁【fan⁴ 凡】in great numbers；propagate

繁华【fan⁴wa⁴ 话⁴】flourishing；bustling

繁茂【fan⁴meo⁶ 莫欧⁶】lush；luxuriant

繁盛【fan⁴xing⁶ 剩】thriving；flourishing

繁冗【fan⁴ qung² 宠】prolix；diverse and complicated ＝ 烦冗【fan⁴qung²】

繁衍【fan⁴yin²】multiply

繁育【fan⁴yug⁹ 肉】breed

繁杂【fan⁴jab⁹ 习】many and diverse

繁殖【fan⁴jig⁹ 植】breed；reproduce

繁重【fan⁴qung⁵ 从⁵】heavy；strenuous

繁荣昌盛【fan⁴wing⁴qêng¹xing⁶ 永⁴ 枪 剩】thriving and prosperous

饭【fan⁶ 范】cooked rice or other cereals；meal

饭菜【fan⁶qoi³ 蔡】meal；repast；dishes to go with rice；steamed buns

饭店【fan⁶dim³ 点³】hotel；restaurant

饭厅【fan⁶ têng¹ 听】dining hall；dining room

饭盒【fan⁶heb⁹ 合】lunch-box

饭量【fan⁶lêng⁶ 亮】appetite

饭碗【fan⁶wun² 腕】rice bowl

饭桶【fan⁶ tung² 统】rice bucket；big eater；fathead；good-for-nothing

饭铲头【fan⁶qan²teo⁴ 产投】a cobra

范【fan⁶ 饭】pattern；model；limits

范围【fan⁶wei⁴ 维】scope；limits；range

范例【fan⁶lêi⁶ 丽】model；example

犯【fan⁶ 饭；fan² 反】violate；attack；assail；criminal；commit

犯法【fan⁶fad⁸ 发】violate the law

犯规【fan⁶kuei¹ 亏】break the rules；foul

犯忌【fan⁶gêi⁶ 技】violate a taboo

犯人【fan⁶yen⁴ 仁】prisoner；convict

犯罪【fan⁶jêü⁶ 序】commit a crime

梵【fan⁴ 凡】〈n.〉Buddhist

梵文【fan⁴men⁴ 纹】〈n.〉Sanskrit

梵蒂冈【fan⁴dei³gong¹ 帝江】〈n.〉Vatican

擛【fang³ 符罷³】use a stick to strike

擛佢一棍【fang³kêü⁵yed⁷guen³ 拒壹君³】come down with the big stick upon him

法【fad⁸ 发】law；method；way；mode

法律【fad⁸lêd⁹ 栗】law；statute

法令【fad⁸ling⁶ 另】laws and decrees

法规【fad⁸kuei¹ 亏】laws and regulations

法纪【fad⁸gêi² 己】law and discipline

法人【fad⁸yen⁴ 仁】legal person

法则【fad⁸jeg² 仄】rule；law

法子【fad⁸ji² 止】way；method

法术【fad⁸xêd⁹ 述】magic arts

法宝【fad⁸bou² 保】a magic weapon

法办【fad⁸ban⁶ 板⁶】deal with according to law

法官【fad⁸gun¹ 观】judge；justice

法庭【fad⁸ting⁴ 亭】court；tribunal

法院【fad⁹yün² 元²】court；tribunal

法治【fad⁸ji⁶ 自】rule by law

法制【fad⁸jei³ 济】legal system；legality

法国【fad⁸guog⁸ 帼】France

法西斯【fad⁸xei¹xi¹ 筛司】fascist

砝【fad⁸ 法】（see"砝码"）

砝码【fad⁸ma⁵ 马】weight（used on a balance）

珐【fad⁸ 法】〈n.〉珐琅质【fad⁸long⁴jed⁷ 狼侄⁷】enamel

发【fad⁸ 法】send out; utter; discharge; develop; open-up ; hair

发达【fad⁸ dad⁸ 得押⁹】to become rich; developed

发财【fad⁸ qoi⁴ 才】get rich; make a fortune

发表【fad⁸ biu² 裱】publish; issue

发出【fad⁸ qêd⁷ 迟律⁸】issue; send out; give out

发觉【fad⁸ gog⁸ 角】find; detect

发现【fad⁸ yin⁶ 演⁶】find; discover

发生【fad⁸ xeng¹ 笙】happen; occur; take place

发芽【fad⁸ nga⁴ 牙】germinat; sprout

发育【fad⁸ yug⁶ 肉】growth; development

发展【fad⁸ jin² 剪】develop; grow; recruit

发挥【fad⁸ fei¹ 晖】bring into play; elaborate

发明【fad⁸ ming⁴ 名】invent; expound

发扬光大【fad⁸ yêng⁴ guong¹ dai⁶ 洋 广¹ 带⁶】carry forward

发布【fad⁸ bou³ 报】issue; release

发送【fad⁸ xung³ 宋】transmit by radio; dispatch

发行【fad⁸ heng⁴ 衡】issue; publish; put on sale

发言【fad⁸ yin⁴ 然】speak; take the floor

发炎【fad⁸ yin⁴ 然】inflammation

发烧【fad⁸ xiu¹ 消】have a fever

发火【fad⁸ fo² 伙】catch fire; get angry

发狂【fad⁸ kuong² 确汪⁴】go mad; go crazy

发疯【fad⁸ fung¹ 风】① go mad ② leprosy =【普】麻风病

发癫【fad⁸ din¹ 颠】to become mad∽【普】发狂;发疯

发花癫【fad⁸ fa¹ din¹ 化¹ 颠】mad; insane; oestrus; be in heat∽【普】发情;性欲亢进

发动【fad⁸ dung⁶ 洞】start; call into action

发抖【fad⁸ deo² 豆】= 打冷震【da² lang⁵ jen³ 罗罂⁵ 圳】shiver; shake; tremble

发给【fad⁸ keb⁷ 吸】issue; distribute; grant

发放【fad⁸ fong³ 况】provide; grant

发光【fad⁸ guong¹ 广¹】give out light; shine

发奋【fad⁸ fen⁵ 愤】work energetically

发福【fad⁸ fug⁷ 幅】grow stout; put on weight∽【普】发胖

发毛【fad⁸ mou¹ 无¹】go mouldy and grow mildew∽【普】发霉并长毛

发懵【fad⁸ mung² 梦²】blur; not clear; not sure; stare blankly =【普】发呆

发梦【fad⁸ mung⁶ 懵⁶】dream =【普】作梦

发啷厉【fad⁸ long¹ lei³ 郎¹ 丽³】throw one's temper out of a sudden∽【普】动怒而蛮不讲理

发脾气【fad⁸ pêi⁴ hêi³ 皮戏】lose one's temper

发嗃嘈【fad⁸ meng² jeng² 莫莺² 支莺²】be vexed and lose one's temper =【普】烦恼而发脾气

发嚧风【fad⁸ ngeb⁷ fung¹ 厄急⁷ 丰】to say nonsense =【普】胡说;讲疯话

发瘟【fad⁸ wen¹ 温】one who is out of control of one's action; mad; insane∽【普】发昏;神志不清

发神经【fad⁸ xen⁴ ging¹ 臣京】mad; insane

发吽哣【fad⁸ ngeo⁶ deo⁶ 牛⁶ 豆⁶】feeling stunned; blue; gloomy =【普】发呆

发钱寒【fad⁸ qin² hon⁴ 浅 汗⁴】to describe one who is mad or crazy about money∽【普】钱迷心窍

发烧友【fad⁸xiu¹yeo² 消油²】to refer to one who is crazy about someone or something =【普】入迷地热爱或追求某样东西的人

发型【fad⁸ying⁴ 形】hair style; hairdo

搴
辉【fag⁷ 弗客⁷；fag⁸ 弗客⁸】use stick to strike upward =【普】用棍向上打
【fei¹ 晖】brightness; splendour; shine

辉煌【fei¹wong⁴ 王】brilliant; splendid

辉映【fei¹ying² 影】shine; reflect

晖【fei¹ 辉】sunshine; sunlight

麾【fei¹ 辉】standard of a commander

麾下【fei¹ha⁶ 夏】general; commander

徽【fei¹ 辉】emblem; badge

徽章【fei¹jêng¹ 张】badge; insignia

痱【fei² 费²】〈n.〉热痱【yid⁹fei²】prickly heat =【普】痱子

废【fei³ 费】give up; abandon; waste; useless

废除【fei³qêü⁴ 徐】abolish; abrogate; annul

废弃【fei³hēi³ 气】discard; abandon; cast

废置【fei³ji³ 至】put aside as useless

废物【fei³med⁹ 勿】waste material; trash

废话【fei³wa² 画】superfluous words; nonsense

费【fei³ 废】fee; dues; cost; spend

费事【fei³xi⁶ 是】troublesome; too lazy to do something =【普】太麻烦了，不干

费用【fei³yung⁶ 容⁶】cost; expenses

费力【fei³lig⁹ 历】need or use great effort

费时【fei³xi⁴ 是⁴】take time

费钱【fei³qin² 浅】cost a lot; be costly

费尽心机【fei³jên⁶xem¹gēi¹ 进⁶ 深基】rack one's brains in scheming

肺【fei³ 废】lungs

肺痨【fei³lou⁴ 劳】consumption

肺癌【fei³ngam⁴ 岩】lung cancer

吠【fei⁶ 沸】the dog barks

沸【fei⁶ 吠】boil

沸点【fei⁶dim² 店²】boiling point

沸腾【fei⁶teng⁴ 藤】boiling; boil over

否【feo² 浮²；feo¹ 浮¹】negate; deny; nay; no

否定【feo²ding⁶ 订⁶】negate; negative

否认【feo²ying⁶ 应⁶】deny; repudiate

否决【feo²küd⁹ 缺】vote down; overrule

否则【feo²jeg⁷ 仄】〈conj.〉otherwise; if not；or else

否出去【feo¹qêd⁷hêü³ 迟律⁷ 虚³】negate and remove

浮【feo⁴ 否⁴】float; flighty; hollow

浮沉【feo⁴qem⁴ 寻】now sink, now emerge; drift along

浮荡【feo⁴dong⁶ 当⁶】float in the air

浮动【feo⁴ dung⁶ 洞】float; drift; be unsteady

浮光掠影【feo⁴guong¹lêg⁹ying² 广⁻¹略映】hasty and casual; cursory

浮华【feo⁴wa⁴ 铧】showy; flashy

浮夸【feo⁴ kua¹ 跨】be boastful; exaggerate

浮现【feo⁴ yin⁶ 苋】appear before one's

eyes

浮想【feo⁴xêng¹ 赏】thoughts or recollections flashing across one's mind

浮躁【feo⁴qou³ 煤】impetuous

浮肿【feo⁴jung² 种²】fropsy; edema

浮力【feo⁴lig⁶ 历】buoyancy

浮财【feo⁴qoi⁴ 才】such as cash, grain and clothing

浮雕【feo⁴diu¹ 刁】relief(sculpture)

浮云【feo⁴wen⁴ 匀】floating clouds

浮萍【feo⁴ping⁴ 平】duckweed

浮屠【feo⁴tou⁴ 桃】〈n.〉Buddha; stupa

蜉 【feo⁴ 浮】〈n.〉蜉蝣【feo⁴yeo⁴ 由】mayfly

埠 【feo⁶ 阜⁶】port

埠头地【feo⁶teo⁴dêi² 投 得 希²】port = 【普】通商口岸;商港

分 【fen¹ 芬】divide; part; distribute; distinguish; fraction; one-tenth; point

分开【fen¹hoi¹ 海¹】separate; part

分割【fen¹god⁸ 葛】cut apart; break up

分解【fen¹gai² 介²】resolve; decompose

分类【fen¹lêû⁶ 泪】classify

分离【fen¹lêi⁴ 漓】separate; sever

分裂【fen¹lid⁹ 列】split; divide; fission

分泌【fen¹bêi³ 比³】childbirth

分散【fen¹xan³ 汕】disperse; scatter

分身【fen¹xen¹ 辛】spare time from one's main work to attend to sth. else

分手【fen¹xeo² 守】part company

分辨【fen¹bin⁶ 便】distinguish; resolution

分析【fen¹xig⁷ 识】analyse

分心【fen¹xem¹ 深】divert one's attention

分忧【fen¹yeo¹ 优】share sb'. s cares and burdens

分享【fen¹hêng² 响】share (joy, etc.); partake of

分子【fen¹ji² 止; fen⁶ji² 止】numerator; molecule

分母【fen¹mou⁵ 武; fen⁶mou⁵ 武】denominator

分工【fen¹gung¹ 公】divide the work

分配【fen¹pui³ 沛】distribute; allot

分明【fen¹ming⁴名 】clearly demarcated; plainly

分清【fen¹qing¹ 青】distinguish

分期【fen¹kêi⁴ 其】by stages

分分钟【fen¹fen¹jung¹ 中】at any time; every minute = 【普】随时

分歧【fen¹kêi⁴ 其】difference

分批【fen¹pei¹ 拍矮¹】in batches; in turn

分别【fen¹bid⁹ 必⁹】leave each other; difference; respectively

分寸【fen¹qūn³ 串】sense of propriety

分毫【fen¹hou⁴ 豪】fraction; iota

分秒必争【fen¹miu⁵bid⁷jeng¹ 妙⁵ 别⁷ 憎】seize every minute and second

芬 【fen¹ 分】sweet smell; fragrance

芬芳【fen¹fong¹ 方】sweet-smelling; fragrance

吩 【fen¹ 分】〈n.〉吩咐【fen¹fu³ 富】tell; instruct

纷 【fen¹ 分】confused; many and various

纷纷【fen¹fen¹】one after another; numerous and confused

纷纭【fen¹wen⁴ 云】diverse and confused

纷乱【fen¹lûn⁶ 联⁶】helter-skelter; chaotic

纷争【fen¹jeng¹ 憎】dispute; wrangle

氛 【fen¹ 分】〈n.〉氛围【fen¹wei⁴ 维】atmosphere

酚【fen¹ 分¹】〈n.〉酚醛【fen¹qün⁴ 存】phenolic aldehyde

粉【fen² 分²】powder; white; pink

粉末【fen²mud⁹ 没】powder

粉碎【fen²xêü³ 瑞³】smash; broken to pieces

粉笔【fen²bed⁷ 毕】chalk

粉红【fen²hung⁴ 洪】pink

粉饰【fen²xig⁷ 式】gloss over; whitewash

粉刷【fen²qad⁸ 察】whitewash; plaster

粉身碎骨【fen²xen¹ xêü³gued⁷ 辛瑞³ 掘⁷】have one's body smashed to pieces

粪【fen³ 训】excrement; apply manure

粪便【fen³bin⁶ 辨】excrement and urine

粪坑【fen³hang¹ 黑罌¹】manure basket

瞓【fen³ 粪】又写作"瞓"〈v.〉瞓觉【fen³gao³ 教】sleep =【普】睡觉

训【fen³ 粪】lecture; teach; train; standard

训练【fen³lin⁶ 炼】train; drill

焚【fen⁴ 坟】burn

焚烧【fen⁴xiu¹ 消】burn; set on fire

焚毁【fen⁴wei² 委】destroy by fire; burn down

坟【fen⁴ 焚】grave; tomb

坟墓【fen⁴mou⁶ 雾】grave; tomb

奋【fen⁵ 愤】exert oneself; raise; lift

奋斗【fen⁵deo³ 豆³】struggle; fight

奋发图强【fen⁵fad⁸tou⁴kêng⁴ 弗压⁸ 途卡香⁴】go all out to make the country strong

愤【fen⁵ 奋】=忿【fen⁵ 奋】indignation; anger

愤恨【fen⁵hen⁶ 很⁶】indignantly resent; detest

愤怒【fen⁵nou⁶ 奴⁶】indignation; anger

愤愤不平【fen⁵fen⁵bed⁷ping⁴ 毕萍】be indignant

份【fen⁶ 分⁶】share; portion

份量【fen⁶lêng⁶ 亮】weight

份额【fen⁶ngeg⁶ 我得⁹】share; portion

份内【fen⁶noi⁶ 耐】one's job(or duty)

份外【fen⁶ngoi⁶ 碍】particularly; not one's job

扔【feng³ 弗莺³; fing³ 弗英³; fing⁶ 弗英⁶; wing¹ 乌英¹】

扔甩佢【feng³ led⁷ kêü⁵ 罗不⁷ 拒】leave sb. behind; throw off; swing =【普】甩掉(某人或某物)

扔左佢【wing¹jo²kêü⁵ 佐² 拒】throw away =【普】扔掉(某物)

弗【fed⁷ 拂】not

自愧弗如【ji⁶kuei⁵fed⁷yü⁴ 治葵² 拂鱼】feel ashamed of one's inferiority

拂【fed⁷ 弗】stroke; whisk; flick

拂尘【fed⁷qen⁴ 陈】horsetail whisk

拂袖而去【fed⁷jeo⁶jy⁴hêü³ 就移虚³】leave with a flick of one's sleeve——go off in a huff

氟【fed⁷ 弗】〈n.〉氟里昂【fed⁷lêi⁵ngong⁵ 理憩⁵】freon

窋【fed⁷ 弗】cave; hole; dented =【普】穴; 凹

窋入去【fed⁷yeb⁹hêü³ 挹⁹ 虚³】hollow =【普】凹陷

屎窟【xi² fed⁷ 史 弗】anus；bottom ＝
【普】肛门；屁股

佛【fed⁹ 罚】Buddha；Buddhism

佛教【fed⁹gao³ 较】Buddhism
佛经【fed⁹ging¹ 京】Buddhist Scripture
佛像【fed⁹jêng⁶ 象】figure of Buddha
佛法【fed⁹fad⁹ 发】power of Buddha

罚【fed⁹ 佛】punish；penalize

罚款【fed⁹fun² 欢²】fine；forfeit
罚球【fed⁹keo⁴ 求】penalty shot；penalty
kick

伐【fed⁹ 佛】fell；cut down；strike

伐木【fed⁹mug⁹ 目】felling；lumbering

阀【fed⁹ 佛】valve

阀门【fed⁹mun⁴ 瞒】valve

筏【fed⁹ 佛】raft　橡皮筏【jêng⁶pêi⁴
fed⁹】rubber raft

乏【fed⁹ 佛】lack；tired

乏味【fed⁹mêi⁶ 未】dull；insipid；drab

科【fo¹ 课¹】a branch of academic or vo-
cational study；section；family

科学【fo¹hog⁹ 鹤】science；scientific；k-
nowledge
科技【fo¹gêi⁶ 忌】science and technology
科目【fo¹mug⁹ 木】course；headings in an
account book
科室【fo¹xed⁷ 失】administrative or technical offices
科长【fo¹jêng² 蒋】section chief
科员【fo¹yün⁴ 元】section member
科研【fo¹yin⁴ 言】scientific research

蝌【fo¹ 科】〈n.〉蝌蚪【fo¹deo² 斗²】tad-
pole

火【fo² 伙】fire；urgent；anger；temper

火烛【fo²jug⁷ 祝】＝火灾【fo²joi¹ 哉】、
火警【fo²ging² 景】fire(as a disaster)；conflagration
火光【fo²guong¹ 广¹】flame；blaze
火爆【fo²bao³ 包³】intense；sharp∽【普】
激烈
火滚【fo² guen² 君²】angry；indignant ＝
【普】气愤
火起【fo²hêi² 喜】get angry ＝【普】上火
火气【fo²hêi³ 戏】temper ＝【普】脾气；情
绪
火水【fo²xêu² 瑞²】kerosene ＝【普】煤油
火船【fo²xün⁴ 旋】ferry ＝【普】轮船；机
动船
火花【fo²fa¹ 化¹】spark
火化【fo²fa³ 花³】cremation
火急【fo²geb⁷ 芨】urgent；pressing
火炉【fo²lou⁴ 卢】(heating)stove
火苗【fo²miu⁴ 瞄】a tongue of flame；flame
火钳【fo²kim 拑】fire-tongs；tongs
火热【fo²yid⁹ 孽】burning hot；intimate
火速【fo²qug⁷ 促】at top speed；posthaste
火烧【fo²xiu¹ 消】baked wheaten cake
火山【fo²xan¹ 珊】volcano
火药【fo²yêg⁹ 弱】gunpowder；powder
火腿【fo²têu² 退²】ham
火葬【fo²jong³ 壮】cremation
火上加油【fo²xêng⁶ga¹yeo⁴ 尚家由】pour
oil on the fire

伙【fo² 火】mess；board；company；
group

伙伴【fo²bun⁶ 拌】partner；companion
伙记【fo²gêi³ 寄】workers；employees

伙房【fo² fong⁴ 防】kitchen（in a school, factory）

伙食【fo²xig⁹ 蚀】mess；food

颗【fo² 火；lo² 罗²】〈classifier〉grain；pellet

颗粒归仓【lo²leb⁷guei¹qong¹ 笠龟苍】every grain to the granary

货【fo³ 课】goods；commodity；money

货物【fo³med⁹ 勿】goods；commodity
货色【fo³xig³ 式】goods；stuff；rubbish
货源【fo³yün⁴ 元】source of goods
货车【fo³qē¹ 奢】goods train
货单【fo³dan¹ 丹】manifest；waybill
货价【fo³ga³ 嫁】commodity price
货架【fo³ga² 嫁】goods shelves
货款【fo³fun² 欢²】selling goods；payment for goods
货摊【fo³tan¹ 滩】stall；stand
货主【fo³jü² 煮】owner of cargo
货真价实【fo³jen¹ga³xed⁹ 珍嫁失⁹】genuine goods at a fair price；through and through

课【fo³ 货】subject；class；lesson

课本【fo³bun² 苯】textbook
课堂【fo³tong⁴ 唐】classroom；schoolroom
课文【fo³men⁴ 闻】text
课桌【fo³jêg⁸ 酌】(school)desk
课外【fo³ngoi⁶ 碍】outside class；after school

夥【fo² 火】= 伙【fo²】(see"伙")

方【fong¹ 芳】square；upright；direction；side；place；way；just

方案【fong¹ngon³ 按】scheme；plan
方才【fong¹qoi⁴ 财】just now

方便【fong¹bin⁶ 辨】convenient；go to the lavatory
方法【fong¹fad⁸ 发】method；way；means
方面【fong¹min⁴ 免⁶】respect；aspect；side
方式【fong¹xig⁷ 色】way；fashion
方位【fong¹wei² 委】position；bearing
方向【fong¹hêng³ 香³】direction；orientation
方言【fong¹yin⁴ 然】dialect
方针【fon¹jem¹ 斟】policy
方正【fong¹jing³ 政】upright and foursquare
方兴未艾【fong¹hing¹mēi⁶ngai⁶ 兄味捱⁶】be just unfolding

芳【fong¹ 方】fragrant；good；virtuous

芳草【fong¹qou⁶ 曹²】fragrant grass
芳香【fong¹hêng¹ 乡】fragrant；aromatic

荒【fong¹ 方】waste；desolate；barren；famine

荒诞【fong¹dan³ 旦】fantastic；absurd
荒谬【fong¹meo⁶ 茂】absurd；preposterous
荒唐【fong¹ tong⁴ 堂】absurd；fantastic；loose
荒凉【fong¹lêng⁴ 梁】bleak and desolate；wild
荒芜【fong¹mou⁴ 毛】lie waste
荒地【fong¹dēi³ 得希⁶】wasteland
荒废【fong¹fei⁶ 费】lie waste；neglect
荒疏【fong¹xo¹ 梳】out of practice；rusty
荒淫【fong¹yem⁴ 任⁴】dissolute；licentious
荒年【fong¹nin⁴ 捻⁴】famine(or lean)year

慌【fong¹ 方】flurried；flustered；awfully

慌乱【fong¹ lün⁶ 联⁶】alarmed and bewildered
慌忙【fong¹ mong⁴ 亡】in a great rush；hurriedly

慌张【fong¹ jēng¹ 将】flurried; flustered

谎

谎话【fong¹ wa² 画】= 谎言【fong¹ yin⁴ 然】= 大话【dai⁶ wa⁶ 带⁶ 画⁶】lie; falsehood

谎报【fong¹ bou³ 布】lie about sth.

肓

【fong¹ 方】(see "病入膏肓")

仿

【fong² 访】imitate; copy; resemble

仿佛【fong² fed⁷ 弗】seem; as if; be like

仿效【fong² hao⁶ 校】imitate

仿照【fong² jiu³ 召³】imitate; follow

仿制【fong² jei³ 济】= 仿造【fong² jou⁶ 做】copy

访

【fong² 仿】visit; call on; try to get

访问【fong² men⁶ 文⁶】visit; call on; interview

纺

【fong² 仿】spin; a thin silk cloth

纺织【fong² jig⁷ 职】spinning and weaving

纺纱【fong² xa¹ 沙】spinning

舫

【fong² 仿】boat (see "画舫")

坊

【fong¹ 方; fong² 仿】lane; alley; workshop (see "作坊")

放

【fong³ 况】let go; let off; give out; put; open

放生【fong³ xang¹ 是罂¹】as you like = 【普】任由自便

放胆【fong³ dam² 担²】act boldly and with confidence

放低【fong³ dei¹ 底¹】lay down; put down = 【普】放下

放落【fong³ log⁹ 洛⁹】put; keep; lay up = 【普】放置

放葫芦【fong³ wu⁴ lou² 糊炉】= 卖大包【mai⁶ dai⁶ bao¹ 买⁶ 带⁶ 苞】to tell lie

放大【fong³ dai⁶ 带⁶】enlarge; amplify

放荡【fong³ dong⁶ 当⁶】dissolute; unconventional

放宽【fong³ fun¹ 欢】relax restrictions; relax

放弃【fong³ hēi³ 气】abandon; give up

放任【fong³ yem⁶ 壬⁶】let alone; noninterference

放肆【fong³ xi³ 试】unbridled; wanton

放过【fong³ guo³ 果³】let off; let slip

放心【fong³ xem¹ 深】set one's mind at rest

放手【fong³ xeo² 守】let go; have a free hand

放假【fong³ ga³ 嫁】have a holiday or vacation

放纵【fong³ jung³ 种³】indulge; self-indulgent

放屁【fong³ pēi³ 皮³】fart; talk nonsense

放学【fong³ hog⁹ 鹤】classes are over

放工【fong³ gung¹ 公】(of workers) knock off

放火【fong³ fo² 伙】set fire to

放空炮【fong³ hung¹ pao³ 红¹ 泡³】talk big

况

【fong³】① 〈n.〉condition; situation (see "情况")② 〈conj.〉moreover

况且【fong³ qē¹ 扯】moreover; besides; in addition

恍

【fong² 仿】suddenly; all of a sudden

恍惚【fong² fed⁷ 弗】in a trance; dimly

恍然大悟【fong² yin⁴ dai⁶ ng⁶ 言歹⁶ 误】suddenly see the light

晃【fong² 仿】shake；sway；flash past

晃动【fong²dung⁶ 洞】rock；sway

晃荡【fong²dong⁶ 宕】rock；shake

幌【fong² 仿】〈n.〉幌子【fong²ji² 止】
shop sign；pretence；cover

防【fong⁴ 妨】guard against；defend

防御【fong⁴yü⁶ 预】defence

防止【fong⁴ji² 子】prevent；guard against

防治【fong⁴ji⁶ 自】prevention and cure

防灾【fong⁴ joi¹ 哉】take precautions against natural calamities

防卫【fong⁴wei⁶ 惠】defend

防守【fong⁴xeo² 手】defend；guard

防备【fong⁴bēi⁶ 被】guard against

防火【fong⁴fo² 伙】fire prevention

防盗【fong⁴dou⁶ 道】guard against theft

防患未然【fong⁴wan⁶mēi⁶yin⁴ 宦味言】
take preventive measures

妨【fong⁴ 防】hinder；hamper；impede

妨碍【fong⁴ngoi⁶ 外】hinder；hamper

妨害【fong⁴hoi⁶ 亥】impair；jeopardize

房【fong⁴ 防】house；room

房屋【fong⁴ngug⁷ 喔】house；buildings

房间【fong⁴gan¹ 奸】room

房产【fong⁴qan² 铲】house property

房东【fong⁴ dung¹ 冬】landlady；house-
owner

房客【fong⁴hag⁸ 吓】tenant (of a room)；
lodger

肪【fong¹ 方】(see"脂肪")

霍【fog⁸ 攫】suddenly；a surname

霍乱【fog⁸lün⁶ 联⁶】〈n.〉cholera

霍然【fog⁸yin⁴ 言】suddenly；quickly

攫【fog⁸ 霍】seize；grab

攫取【fog⁸qêü² 娶】seize；grab

豁【fog⁸ 霍；kud⁸ 括】clear；open；ex-
empt

豁口【fog⁸heo² 厚²】opening

豁达【kud⁸dad⁹ 鞑】take things philosophically

豁免【kud⁸min⁵ 缅】exempt；remit

豁然开朗【kud⁸yin⁴hoi¹long⁵ 言亥¹ 琅⁵】
suddenly see the light

夫【fu¹ 孚】husband；man

夫君【fu¹guen¹ 均】husband

夫人【fu¹ yen⁴ 仁】wife；Lady；Madame；
Mrs.

夫妻【fu¹ qei¹ 凄】 = 夫妇【fu¹ fu⁵ 符⁵】
husband and wife

夫子【fu¹ji² 止】pedant

孚【fu¹】〈v.〉深孚众望【xem¹fu¹jung³
mong⁶ 心夫纵亡⁶】enjoy great popularity

肤【fu¹ 夫】skin

肤色【fu¹xig⁷ 式】colour of skin

肤浅【fu¹qin² 钱²】superficial；shallow

麸【fu¹ 夫】〈n.〉麸皮【fu¹pēi⁴ 疲】
(wheat) bran

呋【fu¹ 夫】〈n.〉呋喃【fu¹nam⁴ 男】furan

敷【fu¹ 夫】apply；spread；lay out

敷设【fu¹qid⁸ 切】lay

敷衍【fu¹yin² 演】 = 敷演〈v.〉elaborate；
expound

敷衍了事【fu¹yin²liu⁵xi⁶ 演料⁵ 是】muddle through one's work

孵
【fu¹ 夫】hatch; brood

孵化【fu¹fa³ 花³】hatching; brood
孵卵【fu¹lên² 论²】hatch; brood; incubate

苦
【fu² 虎】bitter; hardship; pain; painstakingly

苦楚【fu²qo² 础】suffering; misery
苦闷【fu²mun⁶ 门⁶】depressed; dejected
苦难【fu²nan⁶ 挪晏⁶】suffering; misery
苦恼【fu²nou⁵ 脑】vexed; worried
苦涩【fu² gib³ 劫】bitter and astringent; pained
苦于【fu² yü¹ 迂】suffer from(a disadvantage)
苦干【fu²gon² 赶³】work hard
苦功【fu²gung¹ 工】hard work
苦口苦面【fu²heo²fu²min⁶ 厚² 免⁶】gloomy =【普】忧郁的样子
苦衷【fu²qung¹ 冲】trouble taken; pains
苦瓜【fu²gua¹ 挂¹】balsam pear
苦口婆心【fu²heo²po⁴xem¹ 厚² 颇⁴ 深】urge sb. time and again with good intentions

虎
【fu² 苦】tiger; brave

虎口【fu²heo² 厚²】tiger's mouth——jaws of death
虎穴【fu²yüd⁹ 月】tiger's den
虎视眈眈【fu²xi⁶dam¹dam¹ 是担担】eye covetously
虎头蛇尾【fu²teo⁴xê⁴mēi⁵ 投佘美】fine start and poor finish

唬
【fu² 苦】bluff

琥
【fu² 苦】〈n.〉琥珀【fu²pag⁸ 拍】amber

甫
【fu² 苦; pou² 普】① just; only; ② 5 km.

抚
【fu² 苦】comfort; nurture; stroke

抚爱【fu²oi³ 哀³】caress; fondle
抚摸【fu²mo² 磨²】= 抚摩【fu²mo¹ 磨¹】stroke
抚弄【fu²lung⁶ 龙⁶】stroke; fondle
抚慰【fu²wei³ 畏】comfort; console
抚养【fu²yêng⁵ 痒】foster; raise
抚育【fu²yug⁶ 玉】foster; nurture; tend
抚恤【fu²xêd⁷ 择】comfort and compensate a bereaved family

府
【fu² 苦】seat of government; office residence

府邸【fu² dei² 底】= 府第【fu² dei⁶ 弟】mansion
府上【fu²xêng⁶ 尚】your home; your family

俯
【fu² 苦】bow (one's head)

俯视【fu²xi⁶ 是】= 俯瞰【fu²hem³ 坎】look down at
俯首【fu²xeo² 手】bow one's head(in submission)

腑
【fu² 苦】(see"脏腑")

富
【fu³ 副】rich; wealthy; abundant; a surname

富贵【fu³guei³ 桂】riches and honour
富有【fu³yeo⁵ 友】rich; rich in; full of
富裕【fu³yü⁵ 预】prosperous
富足【fu³jug⁷ 竹】plentiful; abundant
富翁【fu³yung¹ 雍¹】man of wealth
富余【fu³yü⁴ 鱼】have more than needed

富庶【fu³xü³ 署³】rich and populous

富饶【fu³yiu⁴ 尧】richly endowed; fertile

富强【fu³kêng⁴ 卡香⁴】prosperous and strong

富豪【fu³hou⁴ 毫】rich and powerful people

富丽堂皇【fu³lei⁶tong⁴wong⁴ 厉唐王】sumptuous

赋【fu³ 富】bestow on; tax; compose

赋予【fu³yü⁵ 与】bestow on; give up

赋税【fu³xêü³ 瑞³】taxes

赋诗【fu³xi¹ 思】compose a poem

副【fu³ 富】① deputy; correspond to ② ⟨classifier⟩

副本【fu³bun² 苯】duplicate; copy

副官【fu³gun¹ 观】adjutant

副职【fu³jig⁷ 积】the position of a deputy to the chief of an office, department, etc.

副业【fu³yib⁹ 叶】sideline

副手【fu³xeo² 守】assistant

副刊【fu³hon² 罕】supplement

副食品【fu³xig⁹ben² 蚀禀】non-staple food

库【fu³ 富】warehouse; storehouse

库房【fu³fong⁴ 防】storehouse; storeroom

库藏【fu³qong⁴ 床】have in storage

库存【fu³qün⁴ 泉】stock; reserve

裤【fu³ 富】⟨n.⟩裤子【fu³ji² 止】trousers; pants

裤头带【fu³teo⁴dai² 投歹²】a belt =【普】裤腰带

符【fu⁴ 扶】symbol; tally with

符号【fu⁴hou² 好】symbol; mark

符合【fu⁴heb⁹ 盒】accord with; tally with

符咒【fu⁴jeo³ 皱】Taoist magic figures

符哺【fu⁴fêd⁷】clever device◌【普】巧计

符萨【fu⁴xad⁸ 刹】Bodhisattva =【普】菩萨;神灵

芙【fu⁴ 符】⟨n.⟩lotus

芙蓉【fu⁴yung⁴ 容】cottonrose hibiscus; lotus

扶【fu⁴ 符】support with the hand; help sb. up; help; relieve

扶持【fu⁴qi⁴ 池】help sustain; give aid to

扶助【fu⁴jo⁶ 座】help; assist; support

扶手【fu⁴xeo² 守】handrail; armrest

扶植【fu⁴jig⁹ 殖】foster; prop up

扶疏【fu⁴xo¹ 梳】luxuriant and well-spaced

扶摇直上【fu⁴yiu⁴jig⁹xêng⁵ 尧植尚⁵】rise steeply

妇【fu⁵ 夫⁵】woman; married woman; wife

妇女【fu⁵nêü⁵ 挪去⁵】woman

妇人【fu⁵yen⁴ 仁】married woman

妇产科【fu⁵qan²fo¹ 铲课¹】(department of) gynaecology and obstetrics

妇联【fu⁵lün⁴ 乱⁴】the Women's Federation

腐【fu⁶ 付】rotten; putrid; beancurd

腐蚀【fu⁶xig⁹ 食】corrode; corrupt; etch

腐败【fu⁶bai⁶ 拜⁶】rotten; putrid; corrupt

腐化【fu⁶fa³ 花³】degenerate; corrupt; rot

腐朽【fu⁶neo² 纽】rotten; decadent

腐烂【fu⁶lan⁶ 兰⁶】decomposed; corrupt

腐乳【fu⁶yü⁵ 语】fermented beancurd

付【fu⁶ 附】hand over to; pay

付出【fu⁶qêd⁷ 次律⁷】pay; expend

付款【fu⁶fun² 欢²】pay a sum of money

付息【fu⁶xig⁷ 色】payment of interest
付印【fu⁶yen³ 因³】send to the press
付排【fu⁶pai⁴ 牌】send to the compositor
付诸东流【fu⁶jü¹dung¹leo⁴ 朱冬留】irrevocably lost

赴 【fu⁶ 付】go to；attend
赴约【fu⁶yêg⁸ 若⁸】keep an appointment
赴难【fu⁶nan⁶ 挪晏⁶】go to the aid of one's country
赴汤蹈火【fu⁶tong¹dou⁶fo² 堂¹ 道伙】go through fire and water

仆 【fu⁶ 付；pug⁷ 拍屋⁷；bug⁹ 瀑】fall forward；servant
仆倒【fu⁶ dou²捣；pug⁷ dou²捣】＝跌倒【did⁸dou²】fall；tumble
仆从【bug⁹qung⁴ 虫】footman
仆人【bug⁹yen⁴ 仁】(domestic)servant
仆住【bug⁹jü⁶ 著⁶】follow and keep watch on ＝【普】跟踪监视

附 【fu⁶ 付】add；attach
附带【fu⁶dai³ 戴】in passing；attach；subsidiary
附加【fu⁶ga¹ 家】add；attach；additional
附和【fu⁶wo⁴ 禾】echo；chime in with
附会【fu⁶wui⁶ 汇】draw wrong conclusions by false analogy
附近【fu⁶gen⁶ 靳】nearby；close to
附录【fu⁶lug⁹ 六】appendix
附设【fu⁶qid⁸ 切】have as an attached institution
附属【fu⁶xug⁹ 熟】subsidiary
附庸【fu⁶yung⁴ 容】dependency；vassal
附注【fu⁶jü³ 著】annotations
附着【fu⁶jêg⁹ 之约⁹】adhere to；stick to

驸 【fu⁶ 付】〈n.〉驸马【fu⁶ma⁵ 码】emperor's son-in-law

父 【fu⁶ 付】father；elders
父亲【fu⁶qen¹ 趁¹】father
父母【fu⁶mou⁵ 武】father and mother；parents
父兄【fu⁶hing¹ 兴】father and elder brothers

辅 【fu⁶ 付】assist；complement
辅导【fu⁶dou⁶ 道】give guidance in study；coach
辅助【fu⁶jo⁶ 座】assist；supplementary
辅音【fu⁶yem¹ 钦】consonant

俘 【fu¹ 夫】capture；prisoner of war
俘获【fu¹wog⁶ 镬】capture
俘虏【fu¹lou⁵ 老】capture；captive

呼 【fu¹ 夫】breathe out；shout；call
呼喊【fu¹ham³ 咸³】call out；shout
呼唤【fu¹wun⁶ 换】call；shout to
呼叫【fu¹giu³ 矫³】call out；call；shout
呼吸【fu¹keb⁷ 级】breathe；respire
呼应【fu¹ying³ 英³】echo；work in concert with
呼吁【fu¹yü⁶ 预】appeal；call on
呼呼声【fu⁴fu²xêng¹ 是镜¹】whistle；scream ＝【普】呼啸

乎 【fu⁴ 符】〈auxil.〉＝呢；呀；吗(see "呢"、"呀"、"吗")

咐 【fu³ 富】〈v.〉(see "吩咐")

斧 【fu² 虎】axe；hatchet
斧头【fu²teo⁴ 投】axe；hatchet

斧正【fu² jing³ 政】(please) make corrections

釜【fu² 苦】a kind of cauldron used in ancient China

釜底抽薪【fu²dei²qeo¹xen¹ 邸秋辛】take
away the firewood from under the
cauldron — take a drastic measure
to deal with a situation

负【fu⁶ 腐】shoulder; bear; suffer; owe;
lose; minus

负担【fu⁶dam¹ 胆¹】bear(a burden); load

负荷【fu⁶ho⁴ 何】= 负载【fu⁶joi³ 再】load

负极【fu⁶gig⁹ 激⁹】negative pole

负疚【fu⁶geo³ 救】feel apologetic

负气【fu⁶hēi³ 汽】do sth. in a fit of pique

负伤【fu⁶xêng¹ 商】be wounded

负数【fu⁶xou³ 扫】negative number

负责【fu⁶jag⁸ 泽⁸】be responsible for; conscientious

负债【fu⁶jai³ 寨³】be in debt; incur debt

讣【fu⁶ 父】obituary

讣告【fu⁶gou³ 诰】announce sb.'s death

忽【fed⁷ 拂】neglect; overlook; suddenly

忽然【fed⁷yin⁴ 言】suddenly; all of a sudden

忽视【fed⁷ xi⁶ 是】ignore; overlook; neglect

忽略【fed⁷lêg⁶ 掠】neglect; lose sight

惚【fed⁷ 忽】= 恍【fong²】(see"恍惚")

魁【fui¹ 灰】chief; head; of stalwart build

魁首【fui¹xeo² 手】the brightest and best

魁梧【fui¹ng⁴ 吾】big and tall; stalwart

灰【fui¹ 魁】ash; dust; lime; grey

灰色【fui¹xig⁹ 式】grey; ashy; gloomy

灰暗【fui¹ngem³ 黯】murky grey; gloomy

灰尘【fui¹qen⁴ 陈】dust; dirt

灰烬【fui¹jên⁶ 尽】ashes

灰浆【fui¹jêng¹ 张】mortar

灰心【fui¹xem¹ 深】lose heart; be discouraged

恢【fui¹ 灰】extensive; vast

恢复【fui¹fug⁹ 伏】resume; renew; restore

恢恢【fui¹fui¹】extensive; vast

悔【fui³ 灰³】regret; repent

悔恨【fui³hen³ 很⁶】regret deeply

悔过【fui³guo³ 果³】repent one's error

悔改【fui³goi² 该²】repent and mend one's
ways

悔之莫及【fui³ji¹mog⁹keb⁹ 支漠级⁹】too
late to repent; too late to regret

诙【fui¹ 灰】〈a.〉诙谐【fui¹hai⁴ 鞋】hu-
morous; jocular

晦【fui³ 悔】night; dark; obscure;
gloomy

晦气【fui³hēi³ 汽】unlucky

晦暗【fui³ngem³ 黯】dark and gloomy

晦涩【fui³xab⁸ 时鸭⁸；fui³gib⁸ 格叶⁸】hard
to understand; obscure

诲【fui³ 悔】teach; instruct

诲人不倦【fui³yen⁴bed⁷gün⁶ 仁毕卷⁶】be
tireless in teaching

诲淫诲盗【fui³yem⁴fui³dou⁶ 任⁴度】prop-
agate sex and violence

欢【fun¹ 宽】joyous; merry; jubilant

欢喜【fun¹hēi² 起】joyful; happy; like; be fond of

欢乐【fun¹log⁹ 落】happy; joyous; gay

欢心【fun¹xem¹ 深】favour; liking; love

欢笑【fun¹xiu³ 啸³】laugh heartily

欢迎【fun¹ying⁴ 仍】welcome; greet

欢聚【fun¹jêü⁶ 叙】happy get-together

欢送【fun¹xung³ 宋】see off; send off

欢庆【fun¹hing³ 兴³】celebrate joyously

欢呼【fun¹fu¹ 夫】hail; cheer; acclaim

欢欣鼓舞【fun¹yen¹gu²mou⁵ 因古母】be e-lated

宽【fun¹ 欢】wide; broad; width; relax; extend

宽阔【fun¹fud⁸ 夫活⁸】broad; wide

宽度【fun¹dou⁶ 道】width; breadth

宽敞【fun¹qong² 厂】spacious; roomy

宽大【fun¹dai⁶ 歹⁶】spacious; lenient

宽广【fun¹guong² 光²】broad; extensive

宽厚【fun¹heo⁵ 口⁵】generous

宽容【fun¹yung⁴ 溶】tolerant; lenient

宽恕【fun¹xü³ 署³】forgive

宽慰【fun¹wei³ 畏】comfort; console

宽限【fun¹han⁶ 悭⁶】extend a time limit

宽裕【fun¹yü⁶ 预】well-to-do; ample

宽宏大量【fun¹weng⁴dai⁶lêng⁶ 弘歹⁶ 亮】large-minded; magnanimous

髋【fun¹ 宽】hip

髋骨【fun¹gued⁷ 掘⁷】hipbone

款【fun² 欢²】a sum of money; fund; pattern

款项【fun²hong⁶ 巷】a sum of money; fund

款式【fun²xig⁷ 色】pattern; style; design

款待【fun²doi⁶ 代】treat cordially; entertain

风【fung¹ 丰】wind; winnow; style; scene; news

风波【fung¹bo¹ 坡】disturbance

风暴【fung¹bou⁶ 布⁶】windstorm; storm

风采【fung¹qoi² 彩】elegant demeanour

风潮【fung¹qiu⁴ 瞧】agitation; unrest

风尘【fung¹qen⁴ 陈】travel fatigue

风传【fung¹qün⁴ 存】hearsay; rumour

风度【fung¹dou⁶ 道】demeanour; bearing

风格【fung¹gag⁸ 隔】style

风光【fung¹guong¹ 广⁻¹】scene; view; sight

风化【fung¹fa³ 花³】decency; efflorescence

风纪【fung¹gēi² 己】conduct and discipline

风景【fung¹ging² 竟】scenery; landscape

风浪【fung¹long⁶ 晾】stormy waves

风雷【fung¹lêü⁴ 擂】wind and thunder; tempest

风力【fung¹lig⁹ 历】wind-force

风凉【fung¹lêng⁴ 梁】cool

风流【fung¹leo⁴ 留】distinguished and admirable; dissolute; loose

风貌【fung¹mao⁶ 矛⁶】style and features; view; scene

风靡【fung¹mēi⁴ 眉】fashionable

风气【fung¹ hēi³ 汽】general mood; common

风情【fung¹qing⁴ 程】amorous feelings

风趣【fung¹qêü³ 翠】humour; wit

风骚【fung¹xou¹ 苏】literary excellence; coquettish

风扇【fung¹xin³ 线】electric fan; fan

风尚【fung¹xêng⁶ 上】prevailing custom

风声【fung¹xing¹ 升】rumour

风霜【fung¹xêng¹ 湘】wind and frost

风水【fung¹xêü² 瑞²】geomantic omen

风俗【fung¹jug⁹ 族】custom

风味【fung¹mēi⁶ 未】special flavour

风闻【fung¹men⁴ 文】learn through hearsay

风险【fung¹him² 欠²】risk；hazard

风行【fung¹heng⁴ 衡】be popular

风雅【fung¹ngɑ⁵ 瓦】literary pursuits；elegant

风雨【fung¹yü⁵ 与】wind and rain

风云【fung¹wen⁴ 匀】wind and cloud

风韵【fung¹wen⁵ 酝】graceful bearing；charm

风姿【fung¹ji¹ 支】= 风韵

风筝【fung¹jeng¹ 争】kite

风平浪静【fung¹ping⁴long⁶jing⁶ 屏晾净】calm and tranquil

风起云涌【fung¹hēi²wen⁴yung² 喜匀拥】rolling on with full force

丰【fung¹ 风】abundant；great；fine-looking

丰产【fung¹qɑn² 铲】high yield；bumper crop

丰收【fung¹xeo¹ 修】bumper harvest

丰衣足食【fung¹yi¹jug⁷xig⁹ 依竹蚀】have ample food and clothing

丰年【fung¹nin⁴ 捻⁴】good year

丰富【fung¹fu³ 裤】rich；abundance；enrich

丰满【fung¹mun⁵ 门⁵】plentiful；full and round

丰盛【fung¹xing⁶ 剩】rich；sumptuous

烽【fung¹ 丰】beacon-fire（used to give border alarm in ancient China）

烽火【fung¹fo² 伙】flames of war

烽烟【fung¹yin¹ 胭】beacon；beacon-fire

锋【fung¹ 丰】sharp；keen

锋利【fung¹lēi⁶ 吏】sharp；keen；incisive

锋芒毕露【fung¹mong⁴bed⁷lou⁶ 亡不路】make a showy display of one's abilities

蜂【fung¹ 丰】wasp；bee；in swarms

蜂窠【fung¹deo³ 斗】honeycomb =【普】蜂窝；蜂巢

蜂王【fung¹wong⁴ 黄】queen bee；queen wasp

蜂蜜【fung¹med⁹ 勿】honey

蜂乳【fung¹yü⁵ 雨】= 蜂皇精【fung¹wong⁴jing¹ 王征】royal jelly

蜂拥【fung¹yung² 涌】swarm；flock

峰【fung¹ 丰】peak；summit；hump

峰峦【fung¹lün⁴ 联】ridges and peaks

峰值【fung¹jig⁹ 直】peak value；crest value

封【fung¹ 丰】seal；bank（a fire）；envelope；confer（a title，territory，etc.）upon

封闭【fung¹bei³ 散³】seal；seal off；close

封锁【fung¹xo² 所】blockade；block；seal off

封口【fung¹heo² 厚²】seal；heal

封面【fung¹min² 免²】the title page of a threadbound book；front cover

封建【fung¹gin³ 见】the system of enfeoffment；feudalism

封官许愿【fung¹gun¹hēū²yün⁶ 观栩县】offer official posts and make lavish promises

枫【fung¹ 风】〈n.〉枫树【fung¹xü⁶ 书⁶】Chinese sweet gum

疯【fung¹ 风】mad；insane；spindle

疯子【fung¹ji² 止】lunatic；madman

疯狗【fung¹geo² 久】mad dog；rabid dog

疯疯癫癫【fung¹fung¹din¹din¹ 颠】be flight

疯狂【fung¹kuong⁴ 框⁴】insane；frenzied；

unbridled

俸 【fung² 丰²】pay; salary

俸禄【fung²lug⁹ 录】an official's salary

讽 【fung³ 风³】satirize; mock; chant; intone

讽刺【fung³qi³ 次】satirize; mock

讽喻【fung³yü⁶ 预】parable; allegory

冯 【fung⁴ 逢】a surname

逢 【fung⁴ 冯】meet; come upon

逢迎【fung⁴ying⁴ 营】make up to; fawn on

逢年过节【fung⁴nin⁴guo³jid⁸ 捻⁴ 果³ 折】on New Year's Day or other festivals

缝 【fung⁴ 逢】stitch; sew; seam; crack

缝补【fung⁴bou² 保】sew and mend

缝纫【fung⁴yen⁶ 刃】sewing; tailoring

凤 【fung⁶ 奉】phoenix

凤凰【fung⁶wong⁴ 王】phoenix

凤爪【fung⁶ jao² 找】a chicken's paws = 【普】鸡爪(a dish of Guangzhou)

凤毛麟角【fung⁶mou⁴lên⁴gog⁸ 无伦阁】phoenix feathers and unicorn horns; rarity of rarities

奉 【fung⁶ 凤】give; receive; esteem; wait upon

奉命【fung⁶ming⁶ 名⁶】receive orders

奉承【fung⁶xing⁴ 成】flatter; fawn upon

奉献【fung⁶hin³ 宪】offer as a tribute

奉行【fung⁶ heng⁴ 衡】pursue (a policy, etc.)

奉公守法【fung⁶gung¹xeo²fad⁸ 工手发】be law-abiding

奉养【fung⁶yêng⁵ 仰】support and wait upon

奉送【fung¹xung³ 宋】give away free

奉旨【fung¹ ji² 止】① receive the imperial edict ②in any case; certainly = 【普】无论如何；一定

阔 【fud⁸ 夫活⁸】wide; vast; wealthy; rich; loose

阔步【fud⁸bou² 部】take big strides

阔绰【fud⁸ qêg⁸ 卓】ostentatious; liberal with money

阔气【fud⁸hêi³ 汽】luxurious; lavish

阔落【fud⁸log⁹ 乐】spacious = 【普】地方多；宽松

阔咧啡【fud⁸lêi⁴fê⁴】clothing that is wide and loose = 【普】(衣服)太宽

阔佬【fud⁸lou² 老²】rich man; a person who is generous with money

阔佬懒理【fud⁸lou²lan⁵lêi⁵ 兰² 李】not to bother with others

福 【fug⁷ 幅】good fortune; blessing; happiness

福分【fug⁷fen⁶ 份】= 福气【fug⁷hêi³ 汽】happy lot

福音【fug⁷yem¹ 钦】glad tidings; Gospel

福利【fug⁷ lêi⁶ 俐】material benefits; welfare

福建【fug⁷gin³ 见】〈n.〉Fujian (province)

幅 【fug⁷ 福】width of cloth; size

幅度【fug⁷dou⁶ 道】range; scope; extent

幅员【fug⁷yün⁴ 元】the area of a country's territory

蝠 【fug⁷ 福】〈n.〉bat(see"蝙蝠")

辐 【fug⁷ 福】spoke

辐射【fug⁷xē⁶ 蛇⁶】radiation

服【fug⁹ 伏】clothes; dress; take (medicine); serve; be convinced; obey

服装【fug⁹jong¹ 庄】dress; clothing; costume

服气【fug⁹hēi³ 汽】be convinced

服侍【fug⁹xi⁶ 是】wait upon; attend

服输【fug⁹xū¹ 书】admit defeat

服务【fug⁹mou⁶ 冒】give service to; serve

服役【fug⁹yig⁹ 亦】enlist in the army; do corvèe labour

服用【fug⁹yung⁶ 容⁶】take (medicine)

伏【fug⁹ 服】bend over; subside; hide; volt

伏兵【fug⁹bing 冰】(troops in)ambush

伏击【fug⁹gig⁷ 激】ambush

伏法【fug⁹fad⁸ 发】be executed

伏安【fug⁹on¹ 桉】volt-ampere

伏特【fug⁹deg⁹ 得⁹】volt

伏笔【fug⁹bed⁷ 毕】foreshadowing

茯【fug⁹ 服】〈n.〉poris cocos

袱【fug⁹ 伏】〈n.〉包袱【bao¹fug⁹】① cloth-wrapper; ②load; weight

覆【fug⁷ 福】cover; overturn; upset

覆盖【fug⁷koi³ 概】cover; plant cover

覆灭【fug⁷mid⁹ 蔑】destruction

覆辙【fug⁷qid⁸ 切】the track of an overturned cart

馥【fug⁷ 福】fragrance

馥郁【fug⁷yug⁷ 沃】strong fragrance

腹【fug⁷ 福】belly; abdomen; stomach

腹地【fug⁷dēi⁶ 得气⁶】hinterland

腹稿【fug⁷gou² 告²】mental notes

腹痛【fug⁷tung³ 疼】abdominal pain

腹泻【fug⁷xē³ 舍】diarrhoea

腹背受敌【fug⁷bui³xeo⁶dig⁹ 贝寿滴⁹】be attacked front and rear

嘛【fi¹ 弗依¹;fi⁴ 弗依⁴】〈onomatopoeia〉

嘛嘛声【fi⁴fi⁴xēng¹ 思镜¹】the sound of the wind

甐【fing³ 弗英³;fing⁶ 弗英⁶】make a body to tied cord to revolve and fling out = 【普】使系着绳子的物体旋转后甩出

啡【fē¹ 弗诶¹;fē⁴ 弗诶⁴;fē⁵ 弗诶⁵】〈onomatopoeia〉(see "咖啡" "呢啡")

啡啡声【fē⁴fē⁴xēng¹ 是镜¹】the sound of the gas spray = 【普】气体喷射声

粗【fē³ 弗诶³】the birds used a paw to foot out things

粗晒咕的钱【fē³xai³did⁷qin² 晒得热⁷ 前²】take coins to spend = 【普】把钱花光

飞【fēi¹ 非】fly; flit; swiftly; unexpected

飞虫【fēi¹qung⁴ 从】winged insect

飞花【fēi¹fa¹ 化¹】fly; flyings

飞机【fēi¹gēi¹ 基】aircraft; plane

飞驰【fēi¹qi⁴ 池】speed along

飞船【fēi¹xūn¹ 旋】airship

飞溅【fēi¹jin³ 箭】splash

飞快【fēi¹fai³ 块】very fast

飞发【fēi¹ fad⁸ 法】to have one's hair cut = 【普】理发

飞仔【fēi¹jei² 济²】a gangster = 【普】流氓; 年青歹徒

飞起【fēi¹ hēi² 喜】very; extremely = 【普】很; 凶狠

飞速【fēi¹qug⁷ 促】at full speed

飞行【fēi¹heng⁴ 衡】flight; flying

飞腾【fēi¹teng⁴ 藤】fly swiftly upward

飞舞【fēi¹mou⁵ 武】dance in the air; flutter

飞翔【fēi¹qêng⁴ 祥】circle in the air; hover

飞扬【fēi¹yêng⁴ 杨】fly upward; rise

飞跃【fēi¹yêg⁸ 约】leap

飞涨【fēi¹jêng³ 胀】(of prices, etc.)soar; shoot up

飞黄腾达【fēi¹wong⁴teng⁴dad⁹ 王藤得压⁹】make rapid advances in one's career

非 【fēi¹ 飞】wrong; not; no; not conform to

非难【fēi¹nan⁴ 挪曼⁴】blame; censure; reproach

非议【fēi¹yi⁵ 以】reproach; censure

非正式【fēi¹jing³xig⁷ 政色】unofficial; informal

非洲【fēi¹jeo¹ 州】〈n.〉Africa

非人【fēi¹yen⁴ 仁】inhuman

非分【fēi¹fen⁶ 份】overstepping one's bounds

非凡【fēi¹ fan⁴ 烦 】outstanding; uncommon

非常【fēi¹xêng⁴ 偿】extraordinary; unusual

非但【fēi¹dan⁶ 且⁶】not only

非独【fēi¹dug⁹ 毒】not merely

非法【fēi¹fad⁸ 发】illegal; unlawful

非驴非马【fēi¹lou⁴fēi¹ma⁵ 炉飞码】neither ass nor horse

非……不可【fēi¹……bed⁷ho² 毕何²】must; have to; will inevitably

妃 【fēi¹ 飞】〈n.〉妃子【fēi¹ji² 止】imperial concubine

菲 【fēi¹ 飞】luxuriant; rich with fragrance; poor

菲菲【fēi¹fēi¹】richly fragrant

菲律宾【fēi¹lêd⁹ben¹ 栗彬】the Philippines

菲林【fēi¹lem² 诊】〈n.〉film ＝【普】(照相)胶卷

菲薄【fēi¹bog⁹ 博⁹】humble; poor

霏 【fēi¹ 飞】〈a.〉霏霏【fēi¹fēi¹】falling thick and fast

蜚 【fēi¹ 飞】cockroach

蜚声【fēi¹xing¹ 升】make a name

蜚语【fēi¹yu⁵ 雨】rumours; gossip

绯 【fēi¹ 飞】red

绯红【fēi¹hung⁴ 洪】bright red

扉 【fēi¹ 飞】door leaf

扉页【fēi¹yib⁹ 叶】title page

匪 【fēi² 诽】bandit; brigand; robber

匪徒【fēi²tou⁴ 图】gangster; bandit

匪帮【fēi²bong¹ 邦】bandit gang

匪首【fēi²xeo² 手】bandit chieftain

悱 【fēi² 匪】laden with sorrow ＝ 悱恻【fēi²qeg⁷】

诽 【fēi² 匪】slander

诽谤【fēi²pong³ 旁³】slander; libel

斐 【fēi² 匪】〈a.〉斐然【fēi²yin⁴ 言】striking; brilliant

肥 【fēi⁴ 腓】fat; fertile; fertilizer; loose

肥大【fēi⁴dai⁶ 歹⁶】loose; large; fat; hypertrophy

肥胖【fēi⁴bun⁶ 伴】fat；corpulent

肥美【fēi⁴mēi⁵ 尾】fertile；luxuriant

肥缺【fēi⁴küd⁸ 决】lucrative post

肥料【fēi⁴liu⁶ 廖】fertilizer；manure

肥沃【fēi⁴yug⁷ 郁】fertile；rich

肥壮【fēi⁴jong³ 葬】stout and strong

肥皂【fēi⁴jou⁶ 造】soap

腓【fēi⁴ 肥】calf(of the leg)

腓骨【fēi⁴gued⁷ 掘⁷】fibula

G

家【ga¹ 加】family; home; a specialist in a certain field; school; domestic

家庭【ga¹ting⁴ 廷】family; household

家长【ga¹jêng² 蒋】the head of a family; patriarch

家族【ga¹jug⁹ 俗】clan; family

家眷【ga¹ gün³ 卷³】wife and children; wife

家属【ga¹xug⁹ 熟】family members

家畜【ga¹ qug⁷ 促】domestic animal; livestock

家私【ga¹ xi 诗】= 家产【ga¹ qan² 铲】family property

家具【ga¹ gêû⁶ 巨】= 家俬【ga¹ xi 诗】furniture

家计【ga¹gei³ 继】family livelihood

家教【ga¹gao³ 较】family education

家法【ga¹fad⁸ 发】a rod for punishing children or servants in a feudal household

家丑【ga¹qeo² 绸²】family scandal

家伙【ga¹fo² 火】tool; fellow; guy

家务【ga¹mou⁶ 冒】household duties

家乡【ga¹hêng¹ 香】hometown; native place

家业【ga¹yib⁹ 叶】family property

家公【ga¹gung¹ 工】father-in-law

家婆【ga¹po² 颇】mother-in-law

家姐【ga¹jē¹ 遮】an elder sister = 【普】姐姐

家用【ga¹yung⁶ 容】family allowance

家下【ga¹ha⁶ 夏】= 家阵【ga¹jen⁶ 真⁶】

= 而家【yi⁴ga¹】now; at the moment = 【普】现在

家头细务【ga¹teo⁴xei³mou⁶ 投世冒】housechore; housework = 【普】家庭琐事

家常便饭【ga¹xêng⁴bin⁶fan⁶ 偿卞范】homely food; common occurrence

家喻户晓【ga¹yü⁶wu⁶hiu² 预护器²】widely known

加【ga¹ 家】add; plus; increase; put in

加倍【ga¹pui⁵ 培⁵】double; redouble

加班【ga¹ban¹ 颁】work overtime

加工【ga¹gung¹ 公】process; working

加紧【ga¹gen² 谨】step up; speed up

加剧【ga¹kêg⁹ 屐】aggravate; intensify

加快【ga¹fai³ 块】quicken; speed up

加强【ga¹ kêng⁴卡香⁴】strengthen; enhance

加深【ga¹xem¹ 心】deepen

加入【ga¹yeb⁹ 挹⁹】add; mix; put in; join

加热【ga¹yid⁹ 孽】heating

加油【ga¹yeo² 尤²】oil; refuel; make an extra effort

加以【ga¹yi⁵ 耳】in addition; moreover

加仑【ga¹lên⁴ 伦】gallon

加拿大【ga¹na⁴dai⁶ 哪⁴歹⁶】〈n.〉Canada

袈【ga¹ 加】〈n.〉袈裟【ga¹xa¹ 沙】a patchwork outer vestment worn by a Buddhist monk

痂【ga¹ 加】scab; crust　结痂【gid⁸ga¹】form a scab

笳【ga¹ 加】〈n.〉胡笳【wu⁴ga¹】a reed instrument

嘉【ga¹ 加】good; fine; praise; comment

嘉奖【ga¹jêng² 蒋】comment; cite

嘉宾【ga¹ben¹ 缤】honoured guest; distinguished guest

假【ga² 贾; ga³ 嫁】false; fake; if; suppose; holiday

假扮【ga²ban¹ 办】disguise oneself as

假装【ga²jong¹ 庄】pretend; feign

假冒【ga²mou⁶ 务】pass oneself off as

假话【ga²wa⁶ 画⁶】lie; falsehood

假借【ga² jê³ 蔗】make use of; phonetic loan characters; characters adopted to represent homophones

假定【ga²ding⁶ 锭】suppose; hypothesis

假如【ga²yü⁴ 鱼】= 假若【ga² yêg⁹ 药】if; supposing; in case

假设【ga²qid⁸ 切】suppose; hypothesis

假说【ga²xüd⁸ 雪】hypothesis

假托【ga²tog⁸ 拓】on the pretext of; under sb. else's name; by means of

假想【ga² xêng² 赏】imagination; imaginary

假意【ga²yi³ 义】unction; pretend

假惺惺【ga²xing¹xing¹ 星】hypocritically

假精猫【ga² jêng¹ mao¹ 支镜¹ 矛¹】hypocrite∽【普】伪君子

假公济私【ga²gung¹jei³xi¹ 工制思】use public office for private gain; jobbery

假期【ga³ kēi⁴ 其】vacation; period of leave

假日【ga³ yed³ 逸】holiday; day off

贾【ga² 假²; gu² 古】a surname; merchant

嫁【ga³ 假³】(of a woman)marry; shift; transfer

嫁人【ga³yen⁴ 仁】to get married

嫁娶【ga³qêü² 取】marriage

嫁妆【ga³jong¹ 装】dowry; trousseau

嫁接【ga³jib⁸ 褶】grafting

嫁祸于人【ga³wo⁶yü¹yen⁴ 和⁶ 迁仁】shift the misfortune onto sb. else; put the blame on sb. else

稼【ga³ 嫁】sow(grain); cereals; crops

稼穑【ga³xig⁷ 色】sowing and reaping; farming

价【ga³ 嫁】price; value; valence

价钱【ga³qin⁴ 前】price

价值【ga³jig⁹ 直】value; worth

价格【ga³gag⁸ 隔】price

价目【ga³mug⁹ 木】marked price

驾【ga³ 嫁】harness; draw (a cart, etc.); drive(a vehicle)

驾驶【ga³xei³ 洗】drive(a vehicle)

驾临【ga³lem⁴ 林】your arrival

架【ga³ 嫁】frame; rack; fend off; ward off

架空【ga³hung¹ 红¹】built on stilts; impracticable

架设【ga³qid⁸ 切】erect

架子【ga³ji² 止】frame; framework; airs; unassuming

架势【ga³ xei³ 细】① posture; ② grand; spectacular =【普】显赫; 威风

架罉【ga³qang¹ 撑】tools =【普】工具; 家当

咖【ga³ 嫁】〈n.〉

咖啡【ga³fē¹ 弗诶¹】coffee

咖喱【ga¹lēi¹ 李¹】gamma

佳【gai¹ 阶】good; fine; beautiful

佳话【gai¹wa⁶ 画⁶】a deed praised far and wide

阶【gai¹ 街】steps; stairs; rank

阶层【gai¹qeng⁴ 曾⁴】(social)stratum

阶级【gai¹keb⁷ 给】(social)class

阶段【gai¹dün⁶ 锻】a flight of stairs; ladder

皆【gai¹ 街】all; each and every

皆大欢喜【gai¹dai⁶fun¹hēi² 歹⁶ 宽起】everybody is happy; to the satisfaction of all

皆因【gai¹yen¹ 姻】because of; due to

解【gai² 介²】separate; untie; allay; explain

解开【gai²hoi¹ 海】untie; undo

解剖【gai²feo² 否; gai² peo² 拍欧²】dissect

解除【gai²qêü⁴ 徐】remove; relieve

解放【gai²fong³ 况】liberate; liberation

解答【gai²dab⁸ 搭】answer; explain

解冻【gai²dung³ 栋³】thaw; unfreeze

解毒【gai²dug⁹ 读】detoxify; relieve

解雇【gai²gu³ 故】discharge; dismiss; fire

解救【gai²geo³ 够】save; rescue

解渴【gai²hod⁸ 喝】quench one's thirst

解闷【gai²mun⁶ 门⁶】divert oneself(from boredom)

解囊【gai²nong⁴ 瓢】open one's purse

解散【gai²xan³ 汕】dismiss; dissolve

解释【gai²xig⁷ 析】explain; expound

解脱【gai²tüd⁸ 梯月⁸】free oneself

解约【gai²yêg⁸ 跃】cancel a contract

解送【gai³xung³ 宋】send under guard

介【gai³ 界】be situated between; interpose; take seriously; mind

介词【gai³qi⁴ 迟】preposition

介入【gai³yeb⁹ 挹⁹】intervene; interpose

介绍【gai³xiu⁶ 肇】introduce; recommend; let know

介意【gai³yi³ 义³】take offence; mind

介质【gai³jed⁷ 侄⁷】medium

芥【gai³ 介】mustard

芥菜【gai³qoi³ 蔡】leaf mustard

芥兰【gai³lan³ 烂²】cabbage mustard

芥兰头【gai³lan²teo⁴ 投】brocolli

芥末【gai³mud⁹ 没】mustard

芥蒂【gai³dei³ 帝】ill feeling; grudge

戒【gai³ 介】guard against; exhort; give up

戒备【gai³bēi⁶ 鼻】guard against

戒心【gai³xem¹ 深】vigilance; wariness

戒严【gai³yim⁴ 盐】enforce martial law

戒指【gai³ji² 止】(finger)ring

戒烟【gai³yin¹ 烟】give up smoking

戒骄戒躁【gai³giu¹gai³gou³ 娇 燥】guard against arrogance and rashness

诫【gai³ 介】warn; admonish

告诫【gou³gai³】give warning

疥【gai³】scabies

疥虫【gai³qung⁴ 从】sarcoptic mite

疥疮【gai³qong¹ 仓】scabies

界【gai³ 介】boundary; scope; circles

界线【gai³xin³ 扇】boundary line

届【gai³ 介】fall due

届时【gai³xi⁴ 是⁴】when the time comes

届满【gai³ mun⁵ 门⁵】at the expiration of one's term of office

锴

锴木【gai³mug⁹ 目】saw wood

【gai³ 介】to cut；to saw ＝【普】锯开

交

【gao¹ 郊】hand over；give up；meet；join；cross；associate with；friendship；mate

交叉【gao¹ qa¹ 茶¹】intersect；overlapping；stagger

交出【gao¹ qêd⁷ 次律⁷】surrender；hand over

交错【gao¹qo³ 挫】interlock；staggered

交替【gao¹tei³ 梯³】supersede；in turn

交织【gao¹jig⁷ 积】interweave；mingle

交集【gae¹jab⁸ 习】occur simultaneously

交媾【gao¹keo³ 购】sexual intercourse

交配【gao¹pui³ 沛】mating；copulation

交情【gao¹qing⁴ 程】friendship

交代【gao¹ doi⁶ 待】 hand over；explain；account for

交付【gao¹fu⁶ 父】pay；hand over

交锋【gao¹fung¹ 风】cross swords

交换【gao¹wun⁶ 唤】exchange；swop

交货【gao¹fo³ 课】delivery

交际【gao¹jei³ 济】social intercourse

交接【gao¹jib⁸ 褶】join；associate with；hand over and take over

交界【gao¹gai³ 介】have a common boundary

交纳【gao¹nab⁹ 呐】pay；hand in

交流【gao¹leo⁴ 留】exchange；interflow

交涉【gao²xib⁸ 摄】negotiate

交谈【gao¹tam⁴ 谭】talk with each other；converse

交通【gao¹tung⁴ 同¹】traffic；liaison

交往【gao¹wong⁵ 枉⁵】association；contact

交心【gao¹xem¹ 深】lay one's heart bare

交易【gao¹yig⁹ 亦】business；deal；trade

交谊【gao¹yi⁴ 移】friendship

交响乐【gao¹hêng²ngog⁹ 享岳】symphony

交口称赞【gao¹heo²qing¹jan³ 厚³ 清盏³】unanimously praise

交关【gao¹guan¹ 惯¹】extremely ＝【普】厉害；严重

郊

【gao¹ 交】suburbs；outskirts

郊外【gao¹ngoi⁶ 碍】the countryside around a city

郊区【gao¹kêu¹ 驱】suburban district；outskirts

胶

【gao¹ 交】glue；stick with glue；gluey；rubber

胶乳【gao¹yu⁵ 雨】latex

胶水【gao¹xêu² 瑞²】mucilage；glue

胶合【gao¹heb⁹ 盒】glue together；veneer

胶版【gao¹ban² 板】offset plate

胶印【gao¹ yen³ 人³】offset printing；offset

胶卷【gao² gün¹ 绢²】roll film；film

胶囊【gao¹ nong⁴ 瓤】capsule

胶粘剂【gao¹nim¹jei¹ 捻¹ 济¹】adhesive

胶擦【gao¹ qad⁸ 刷】eraser；rubber ＝【普】胶皮

姣

【gao² 搞】handsome；beautiful-looking

蛟

【gao² 搞】flood dragon, a mythical creature capable of invoking storms and floods

蛟龙【gao²lung⁴ 笼】(see"蛟")

搞

【gao² 姣】do；make；set up；get；work out

搞掂【gao²dim⁶ 店⁶】make a good job of；

do well ＝【普】搞好；办妥

搞错【gao²qo³ 挫】make a mistake ＝【普】弄错

搞鬼【gao²guei² 诡】play tricks

搞搞震【gao²gao²jen³ 振】play tricks ＝【普】搞鬼；挑起事端

搅【gao² 搞】stir；mix；disturb；annoy

搅匀【gao²wen⁴ 云】mix；mess up ＝【普】搞和

搅乱【gao²lün⁶ 联⁶】confuse

搅拌【gao²bun⁶ 伴】stir；agitate

搅屎棍【gao²xi²guen³ 史滚³】the man who sows discord ＝【普】搬弄是非的人

佼【gao² 姣】handsome；beautiful

佼佼【gao²gao²】above average；outstanding

狡【gao² 姣】crafty；foxy；cunning

狡猾【gao²wad⁹ 滑】sly；crafty；cunning

狡辩【gao²bin⁶ 便】quibble；indulge in sophistry

狡赖【gao²lai⁶ 癞⁶】deny（by resorting to sophistry）

皎【gao² 姣】clear and bright

皎洁【gao²gid⁸ 结】（of moonlight）bright and clear

饺【gao² 姣】〈n.〉饺子【gao²ji² 止】dumpling

绞【gao² 姣】twist；wring；wind；reaming

绞车【gao²qē¹ 奢】winch；windlass

绞肉机【gao²yug⁹gēi¹ 玉基】meat mincer

绞刑【gao²ying⁴ 形】death by hanging

绞杀【gao²xad⁸ 萨】strangle

绞痛【gao²tung³ 通³】angina

铰【gao³ 教】〈n.〉铰剪【gao³jin² 展】scissors ＝【普】剪刀

教【gao³ 铰】teach；instruct；religion

教育【gao³yug⁹ 玉】education；teach；educate

教训【gao³fen³ 粪】lesson；chide

教养【gao³yêng⁵ 氧】bring up；breeding

教益【gao³ yig⁷ 亦⁷】benefit gained from sb.'s wisdom

教导【gao³dou⁶ 道】instruct；give guidance；teaching

教诲【gao³fui³ 悔】teaching；instruction

教师【gao³xi¹ 思】teacher

教授【gao³xeo⁶ 受】professor；instruct

教学【gao³hog⁹ 鹤】teaching；teaching and studying

教室【gao³xed⁷ 失】classroom；schoolroom

教会【gao³wui² 汇²】（the Christian）church

教士【gao³ xi⁶ 是 】priest；Christian missionary

教唆【gao³xo¹ 梳】instigate；abet

教条主义【gao³tiu⁴jü²yi⁶ 挑⁴ 煮异】dogmatism

较【gao³ 教】compare；relatively；fairly；quite

较比【gao³bēi² 俾】comparatively；relatively；fairly

较量【gao³lêng⁶ 谅】measure one's strength with；haggle；argue；dispute

窖【gao³ 教】〈n.〉地窖【dēi⁶gao³】cellar

溽【gao³ 教】the intersect of a river；a branch of a river ＝【普】河汉子

监【gam¹ 减¹；gam³ 鉴】supervise；watch；prison

监视【gam¹xi⁶ 示】keep watch on；keep a lookout over

监察【gam¹qad⁸ 刷】supervise；control

监督【gam¹ dug⁷ 笃】supervise；control；supervisor

监护【gam¹wu⁶ 户】guardianship

监制【gam¹ jei³ 济】supervise the manufacture of

监考【gam¹hao² 巧】invigilate．

监狱【gam¹yug⁹ 王】prison；jail ＝ 监仓【gam¹qong¹ 疮】

缄【gam¹ 监】〈a.〉缄默【gam¹meg⁶ 墨】keep silent；缄口【gam¹heo² 厚²】seal

尴【gam¹ 监】〈a.〉尴尬【gam¹gai³ 介】awkward；embarrassed

减【gam² 监²】subtract；reduce；decrease；cut

减少【gam²xiu² 小】reduce；decrease；lessen

减弱【gam²yêg⁹ 药】weaken；abate

减轻【gam²hēng¹ 黑镜¹】lighten；ease；alleviate

减低【gam²dei¹ 底¹】reduction of output

减缓【gam²wun⁴ 换⁴】retard；slow down

减免【gam²min⁵ 勉】mitigate or annul

减产【gam²qan² 铲】reduction of output

减价【gam²ga³ 嫁】reduce the price

减租减息【gam²jou¹gam²xig⁷ 糟熄】reduction of rent for land and of interest on loans

鉴【gam³ 监³】ancient bronze mirror；reflect warning；inspect

鉴别【gam³bid⁹ 必⁹】distinguish；differentiate

鉴定【gam³ding⁶ 锭】appraisal；appraise

鉴赏【gam³xêng² 想】appreciate

鉴戒【gam³ gai³ 介】warning；object lesson

鉴于【gam³yü¹ 迂】in view of；seeing that

撼【gam³ 鉴】actually；strong ＝【普】硬着来；下狠心

撼粗来【gam³qou¹lei⁴ 操黎】force oneself to work hard ＝【普】硬撑着干

撼硬来【gam³ngang²lei⁴ 罌² 黎】act rashly ＝【普】蛮干

撼生壅【gam²xang¹ngung¹是罌¹蕹】bury alive ＝【普】活埋

间【gan¹ 奸；gan³ 奸³】① between；among；room；② space in between；separate；sow discord．

间屋【gan¹ngug⁷ 额谷⁷】a house；a room ＝【普】房子

间断【gan³tün⁵ 团⁵】be disconnected

间隔【gan³gag⁸ 格】interval；intermission

间或【gan³ wag⁹ 惑】occasionally；sometimes ＝ 间中【gan³jung¹ 钟】

间接【gan³jib⁸ 褶】indirect；secondhand

间隙【gan³ kuig⁷ 卡域⁷】interval；gap；space

间歇【gan³hid⁸ 蝎】intermittence

间杂【gan³jab⁹ 习】be mixed

涧【gan³ 谏】〈n.〉溪涧【kei¹gan³】ravine；gully

奸【gan¹ 间】wicked；evil；traitor；self-seeking and wily；illicit sexual relations

奸污【gan¹wu¹ 乌】rape or seduce

奸淫【gan¹yem⁴ 壬】illicit sexual relations；adulter；rape or seduce

奸诈【gan¹ja³ 炸】fraudulent；crafty

奸臣【gan¹xen⁴ 神】treacherous court official

奸商【gan¹ xêng¹ 湘】unscrupulous merchant; profiteer

奸雄【gan¹hung⁴ 红】arch-careerist

奸猾【gan¹wad⁹ 滑】treacherous; crafty

奸笑【gan¹xiu³ 少³】sinister smile

简 【gan² 柬】simple; bamboo slips; letter

简单【gan² dan¹ 丹 】 simple; commonplace; casual

简化【gan²fa³ 花³】simplify

简括【gan²kud⁸ 卡活⁸】compendious

简略【gan²lêg⁹ 掠】simple(in content); brief

简练【gan²lin⁶ 炼】terse; succinct

简洁【gan²gid⁸ 结】succinct; pithy

简明【gan²ming⁴ 名】simple and clear; concise

简朴【gan² pog⁸ 扑 】 simple and unadomed; plain

简要【 gan² yiu³腰³】concise and to the point

简易【gan²yi⁶ 异】simple and easy; simply constructed; unsophisticated

简短【gan²dün² 段²】brief

简陋【gan²leo⁶ 漏】simple and crude

简便【gan²bin⁶ 辨】handy

简写【gan²xē² 舍²】simplify a book for beginners

简称【gan²qing¹ 清】abbreviation; be called sth. for short

简报【gan²bou³ 布】bulletin; brief report

简直【gan²jig⁹ 值】simply; at all

柬 【gan² 简】card; note; letter

柬帖【gan²tib⁸ 贴】note; short letter

柬埔寨【gan²pou²jai⁶ 普债⁶】〈n.〉Kampuchea

枧 【gan² 简】soap =【普】肥皂

枧粉【gan²fen² 分²】detergent =【普】洗衣粉

碱 【gan² 简】alkali; soda

碱金属【gan²gem¹xug⁹ 甘熟】alkali metal

碱性【gan²xing³ 胜】alkaline; basicity

硷 【gan² 简】basic salt

茧 【gan² 简】①〈n.〉蚕茧【qam⁴gan²】silkworm cocoon ②callus

拣 【gan² 简】choose; select; pick out; gather

拣择【gan²jag⁹ 摘】fussy; choosy =【普】挑选

拣饮择食【gan²yem²jag⁹xig⁹ 钦²摘蚀】to be fussy about food =【普】在饮食上挑这选那

艰 【gan¹ 奸】difficult; hard

艰苦【gan¹fu² 虎】arduous; difficult; hard; tough

艰辛【gan¹xen¹ 新】hardships

艰难【gan¹nan¹ 挪晏⁴】difficult; hard

艰巨【gan¹gêü⁶ 具】arduous; formidable

艰深【gan¹ xem¹ 心】 difficult to understand; abstruse

艰危【gan¹ ngei⁴ 巍】difficulties and dangers

艰险【gan¹ him¹ 欠²】 hardships and dangers

谏 【gan³ 间³】expostulate with; admonish

谏诤【gan³jang³ 争³】criticize sb.'s faults frankly

锏【gan² 简】mace

耕【gang¹ 迳¹】plough; till

耕耘【gang¹wen⁴ 云】ploughing and weeding; cultivation

耕种【gang¹jung³ 中³】till; cultivate

耕作【gang¹jog⁸ 昨】tillage; cultivation; farming

耕畜【gang¹qug⁷ 促】farm animal

耕地【gang¹dēi⁶ 得菲⁶】plough; till; cultivated land

更【gang¹ 耕；geng³ 耿³；geng¹ 羹】watch; more; further; change; replace

更夫【gang¹fu¹ 孚】night watchman

更深人静【gang¹xem¹yen⁴jing⁶ 心仁净】deep is the night and all is quiet

更加【geng³ga¹ 家 】more; still more; even more

更进一步【geng³jên³yed⁷bou⁶ 俊壹部】go a step further

更动【gegn¹dung⁶ 洞】change; alter

更改【geng¹goi² 该²】change; alter

更换【geng¹wun⁶ 唤】change; replace

更替【geng¹tei³ 剃】replace

更新【geng¹xen¹ 辛】renew; replace

更生【geng¹xeng¹ 笙】regenerate; revive; renew

更衣【geng¹yi¹ 依】change one's clothes

更正【geng¹jing³ 政】make corrections

挭【gang³ 耕³】(cause to)stumble; trip

挭手挭脚【gang³xeo²gang³gêg⁸ 守格约⁸】be in the way ＝【普】绊手绊脚

跭【gang³ 耕³】wade; ford

跭水过河【gang³xêu²guo⁴ho⁴ 瑞²锅³何】wade(across) a stream ＝【普】蹚水过河

甲【gab⁸ 夹】first; shell; nail; armour

甲级【gab⁸keb⁷ 给】first rate ＝ 甲等【gab⁸deng² 邓²】

甲方【gab⁸fong¹ 芳】first party

甲虫【gab⁸qong⁴ 从】beetle

甲壳【gab⁸hog⁸ 黑恶⁸】crust

甲烷【gab⁸yün² 院】〈n.〉methane

甲骨文【gab⁸gued⁷men⁴ 崛⁷闻】inscription on bones or tortoise shells of the Shang Dynasty

甲状腺【gab⁸jong⁶xin³ 撞线】thyroid gland

夹【gab⁸ 甲】press from both sides; mix; clip; and

夹板【gab⁸ban² 版】splint

夹带【gab⁸dai³ 戴】smuggle; notes smuggled into an examination hall

夹道【gab⁸dou⁶ 度 】a narrow lane; line both sides of the street

夹缝【gab⁸fung⁴ 冯】crack; crevice

夹攻【gab⁸gung¹ 工 】attack from both sides

夹生【gab⁸xang¹ 是嚣¹】half-cooked

夹心【gab⁸xem¹ 深】with filling

夹杂【gab⁸jab⁹ 习】be mixed up with

夹注【gab⁸jü³ 著】interlinear notes

夹衲【gab⁸nab⁹ 纳】lined jacket ＝【普】夹袄

兼夹【gim¹gab⁸】and ＝【普】和；又

革【gag8 格; gab8 甲】leather; hide; change; transform

革除【gag8 qêü4 徐】abolish; get rid of; expel

革命【gab8ming6 名6】revolution

革新【gag8xen1 辛】innovation

革职【gag8 jig7 织】remove from office; cashier

格【gag8 革】check; division; standard; case

格仔【gag8jei2 济2】check = 【普】格子

格式【gag8xig7 色】form; pattern

格局【gag8gug9 焗】pattem; setup

格调【gag8diu6 掉】(literary or artistic) style

格言【gag8yin4 然】maxim; motto

格外【gag8ngoi6 碍】especially; all the more = 宁舍【ling4xē3 玲泻】

格斗【gag8deo3 豆3】grapple; wrestle

格格不入【gag8gag8bed7yeb9 毕邑9】incompatible with

隔【gag8 革】separate; partition; at a distance from

隔断【gag8 tün5 团5】cut off; separate = 隔开【gag8hoi1】

隔篱【gag8lēi4 离】next door = 【普】隔壁

隔离【gag8lēi4 篱】keep apart

隔绝【gag8jüd9 拙9】completely cut off

隔夜【gag8yē6 野6】of the previous night

隔阂【gag8hed9 瞎】estrangement; barrier

隔膜【gag8mog9 莫】unfamiliar with

胳【gag8 革】arm

胳膊【gag8bog8 博】arm

胳肢【gag8 ji1 支】tickle sb. = 㨆【lem1 林1】

胳肋底【gag8lag7dei2 勒客7 抵】armpit = 【普】腋窝; 胳肢窝

骼【gag8 格】(see"骨骼")

嗝【gag8 格】belch; hiccup

膈【gag8 格】diaphragm

膈膜【gag8mog9 莫】diaphragm

浃【gab8 夹】(see"汗流浃背")

挟【gab8 夹; hib8 协】coerce; harbour; pick up

挟持【hib8qi4 迟】hold sb. under duress

挟菜【gab8 qoi3 蔡】pick up food (with chopsticks)

荚【gab8 夹】〈*n.*〉荚果【gab8guo2 过2】, pod; legume

颊【gab8 夹】〈*n.*〉脸颊【lim5gab8】cheek

胛【gab8 甲】〈*n.*〉胛骨【gab8gued7 掘7】shoulder blade

钾【gab8 甲】〈*n.*〉potassium (K)

钾肥【gab8fēi4 非4】potash fertilizer

曱【gad9 戛9】〈*n.*〉曱甴【gad9jad9 戛9 扎9】cockroach; roach = 【普】蟑螂

戛【gad8 甲8】knock gently; tap

戛然而止【gad8yin4ji4ji2 言移指】(of a sound) stop abruptly

几【gēi1 机; gēi2 己】①a small table; nearly; almost ②how many; a few

几案【gēi1ngon3 按】a small table

几乎【gēi1fu4 符】nearly; almost; practically

几多【gēi2do1 朵1】= 几许【gēi2hêü2 去2】how many; how much

几时【gēi² xi⁴ 是⁴】what time；when

几分【gēi² fen¹ 芬】a bit；somewhat；rather

几何【gēi² ho⁴ 河 】① how much；how many ②〈n.〉geometry

· 几内亚【gēi² noi⁶ a³ 耐阿³】〈n.〉Guinea

几大【gēi² dai² 歹²】determined =【普】坚决；无论如何

机【gēi¹ 基】machine；chance；aircraft；crucial point；organic；flexible

机器【gēi¹ hēi³ 气】machine；machinery

机械【gēi¹ hai⁶ 鞋⁶】machinery；mechanical

机件【gēi¹ gin² 见²】parts；works

机组【gēi¹ jou² 祖】unit；set；aircrew

机车【gēi¹ qē¹ 扯¹】locomotive；engine

机床【gēi¹ qong⁴ 藏⁴】machine tool

机房【gēi¹ fong⁴ 防 】generator or motor room

机构【gēi¹ keo³ 购】mechanism；the internal structure of an organization

机关【gēi¹ guan² 惯¹】mechanism；gear；office；organ；body；stratagem；scheme

机会【gēi¹ wui⁶ 汇】chance；opportunity

机密【gēi¹ med² 勿】secret；classified

机警【gēi¹ ging² 景】alert；vigilant

机灵【gēi¹ ling⁴ 玲】clever；smart

机敏【gēi¹ men⁵ 吻】alert and resourceful

机能【gēi¹ neng⁴ 挪莺⁴】function

讥【gēi¹ 机】ridicule；mock；satirize

讥讽【gēi¹ fung³ 风³】ridicule；satirize

讥笑【gēi¹ xiu³ 少³】ridicule；jeer；sneer at

饥【gēi¹ 机】be hungry；starve；famine；crop failure

饥饿【gēi¹ ngo⁶ 我⁶】hunger；starvation

饥荒【gēi¹ fong¹ 方】famine；crop failure；be hard up

饥不择食【gēi¹ bed⁷ jag⁹ xig⁹ 毕摘蚀】a hungry person is not choosy about his food

饥寒交迫【gēi¹ hon⁴ gao¹ big⁷ 韩胶逼】suffer hunger and cold；be poverty-stricken

肌【gēi¹ 机】muscle；flesh

肌肉【gēi¹ yug⁹ 玉】muscle

肌肤【gēi¹ fu¹ 夫】(human) skin

肌体【gēi¹ tei² 睇】human body；organism

基【gēi¹ 机】base；foundation；basic；key；primary

基石【gēi¹ xēg⁹ 硕】foundation stone

基础【gēi¹ qo² 楚】foundation；base；basis

基建【gēi¹ gin³ 见³】capital construction

基金【gēi¹ gem¹ 今】fund

基层【gēi¹ qeng⁴ 次莺⁴】basic level；primary level

基本【gēi¹ bun² 苯²】basic；main；basically

基调【gēi¹ diu⁶ 掉】main key；keynote

基数【gēi¹ xou³ 扫】cardinal number；base

基因【gēi¹ yen¹ 姻】gene

基准【gēi¹ jên² 进²】datum；standard

基于【gēi¹ yü¹ 迂】because of；in view of

基围【gēi¹ we⁴ 为⁴】a dam =【普】堤围

基督【gēi¹ dug⁷ 笃】〈n.〉Christ

箕【gēi¹ 基】〈n.〉簸箕【bo³ gēi¹】dustpan；loop

箕斗【gēi¹ deo² 豆²】skip

觭【gēi¹ 机】corner；horn

觭角【gēi¹ gog⁸ 觉】corner；horn

玑【gēi¹ 机】〈n.〉珠玑【jü¹ gēi¹】pearl；gem

姫【gēi¹ 机】①a complimentary term for women used in ancient China ②a surname

羈【gēi¹ 机】bridle; control; stay

羈絆【gēi¹bun⁶ 伴】trammels; yoke

羈留【gēi¹leo⁴ 流】stay; stop over; detain

羈旅【gēi¹lêü⁵ 吕 】stay long in a strange place

羈押【gēi¹ngad⁸ 压】detain; take into custody

己【gēi² 纪】oneself; one's own; personal

己方【gēi²fong¹ 芳】one's own side

己见【gēi²gin³ 建】one's own views

己任【gēi²yem⁶ 壬⁶】one's own duty

纪【gēi² 己】discipline; record; age; e-poch

纪律【gēi²lêd⁹ 栗】discipline

纪录【gēi²lug⁹ 六】= 记录【gēi³lug⁹ 六】take notes; minutes; notetake; record

纪念【gēi²nim⁶ 粘⁶】commemorate; mark; souvenir

纪实【gēi²xed⁹失⁹】record of actual events

纪要【gēi²yiu³ 腰³】summary

纪年【gēi² nin⁴ 捻⁴】a way of numbering the years; annals

纪元【gēi²yün⁴ 园 】the beginning of an era; epoch; era

杞【gēi² 己】a surname

杞人忧天【gēi²yen⁴yeo¹tin¹ 仁忧田¹】entertain imaginary or groundless fears

记【gēi³ 寄】remember; note; record; mark; sign

记得【gēi³deg⁷ 德】remember

记住【gēi³jü⁶ 著⁶】remember; learn by heart

记性【gēi³xing³ 胜】memory

记忆【gēi³yig⁷ 益】remember; recall; memory

记述【gēi³xêd⁹ 术】record and narrate

记录【gēi³lug⁹ 六】(see"纪录")

记叙【gēi³jêü⁶ 序】narrate

记载【gēi³joi³ 再】record; account

记号【gēi³hou⁶ 好⁶】mark; sign

记帐【gēi³jêng³ 胀】keep accounts; charge to an account

记挂【gēi³gua³ 卦】miss someone = 【普】惦记；想念

记者【gēi³ jē⁶ 姐 】reporter; correspon-dent; newsman

记忆犹新【gēi³yig⁷yeo⁴xen¹ 亿尤辛】remain fresh in one's memory

记认【gēi³ying⁶ 英⁶】a mark = 【普】印记

寄【gēi³ 记】send; post; entrust; deposit; depend on

寄信【gēi³ xên³ 讯 】post a letter; mail a letter

寄存【gēi³ qün⁴ 泉 】deposit; leave with; check

寄卖【gēi³ mai⁶ 买⁶】= 寄销【gēi³ xiu¹ 消】consign for sale on commission

寄托【gēi³tog⁸ 拓】leave with sb.; place (hope, etc.)on

寄予【gēi³yü⁵ 雨】place (hope, etc.) on; show; give

寄语【gēi³yü⁵ 雨】send word

寄宿【gēi³ xug⁷ 缩】lodge; (of students) board

寄生【gēi³xeng¹ 笙】parasitism；parasitic

寄人篱下【gēi³yen⁴lēi⁴ha⁶ 仁离夏】live under another's roof；depend on sb. for a living

既【gēi³ 寄】already；since；as；now that；both…and；as well as

既然【gēi³yin⁴ 言】〈*conj.*〉since；as；now that

既定【gēi³ding⁶ 丁⁶】set；fixed；established

既成事实【gei³xing⁴xi⁶xed⁹ 诚是失⁹】accomplished fact

既往不咎【gēi³wong⁵bed⁷geo³ 枉⁵ 毕够】forgive sb.'s past misdeeds

技【gēi⁶ 妓】skill；ability；trick

技术【gēi⁶ xêd⁹ 述】technology；skill；technique

技能【gēi⁶neng⁴ 挪莺⁴】technical ability

技艺【gēi⁶ngei⁶ 伪】skill；artistry

技巧【gēi⁶hao² 考】skill；technique；craftsmanship

技工【gēi⁶gung¹ 公】skilled worker；technician

技师【gēi⁶xi¹ 司】technician

妓【gēi⁶ 技】prostitute

妓女【gēi⁶ nêû⁵挪去⁵】prostitute ＝ 鸡【gei¹ 计¹】

妓院【gēi⁶ yūn² 婉】brothel＝鸡窦【gei¹ deo³ 斗】

伎【gēi⁶ 妓】〈*n.*〉伎俩【gēi⁶lêng⁵ 两】trick；intrigue；manoeuvre；a professional female dancer or singer in ancient China

忌【gēi⁶ 伎】be jealous of；envy；fear；dread；avoid；shun；abstain from

忌讳【gēi⁶wei⁵ 伟】taboo；avoid as harmful

忌惮【gēi⁶dan⁶ 但】dread；fear；scruple

忌辰【gēi⁶xen⁴ 神】the anniversary of the death of a parent, ancestor, or anyone else held in esteem ＝ 忌日【gēi⁶yed⁹ 逸】

忌口【gēi⁶heo² 厚²】avoid certain food (as when one is ill) ＝ 戒口【gai³ heo²】

觊【gēi³ 寄】covet；cast greedy eyes on

觊觎【gēi³yû⁴ 如】covet；cast greedy eyes on ＝ 瞧住晒【heo¹jû⁶xai³ 候⁶ 著⁶ 晒】

嘅【gē³ 格耶³】"＿'s"；of ＝【普】的

佢嘅书【kêu⁵gē³xü¹】his books

中国嘅地图【jung¹ guog⁸gē³dēi⁶ tou⁴】the map of China

鸡【gei¹ 计¹】①chicken ②prostitute

鸡蛋【gei¹dan² 旦²】(hen's) egg ＝ 鸡春【gei¹qên¹ 蠢¹】

鸡肉【gei¹yug⁹ 玉】chicken (as food)

鸡胸【gei¹hung¹ 空】chicken breast

鸡杂【gei¹jab⁹ 习】chicken giblets

鸡公【gei¹gung¹ 工】a cock ＝【普】公鸡

鸡乸【gei¹na² 挪阿²】a hen ＝【普】母鸡

鸡仔饼【gei¹jei²bēng² 剂² 柄²】a type of biscuit made of sugar and meat which tastes salty and sweet

鸡尾酒【gei¹mēi⁵jeo² 美走】cocktail

鸡佬【gēi¹lou² 老²】the man of homosexuality ＝ 偈佬【gei¹lou²】＝【普】男同性恋者

鸡奸【gei¹gan¹ 间】sodomy；buggery

鸡皮纸【gei¹pēi⁴ji² 疲止】a kind of brown
　　paper
鸡髎唔断【gei¹dêng¹m⁴tūn⁵ 得香¹m⁴ 团⁵】
　　too much to talk = 罗里罗嗦
鸡手鸭脚【gei¹ xeo² ab⁸ gêg⁸守 ab⁸ 格
　　约⁸】a person who is clumsy and
　　who does things slowly = 【普】应
　　急时动作缓慢、笨拙的样子
鸡仔媒人【gei¹ jei² mui⁴ yen² 济² 煤仁²】a
　　person who is busybody = 【普】
　　好拉关系的人; 爱管闲事的人
鸡毛蒜皮【gei¹ mou⁴ xūn³ pēi⁴无 算 疲】
　　chicken feathers and garlic skins;
　　trifles; trivialities
鸡犬不宁【gei¹ hūn² bed⁷ ning⁴劝² 毕狞】
　　even fowls and dogs are not left in
　　peace—general turmoil∽鸡飞狗
　　走【gei¹fēi¹geo²jeo² 菲九酒】
鸡春砍石头【gei¹qên¹hem²xēg⁹teo⁴ 蠢¹
　　嵌² 硕投】like an egg striking a
　　rock — attack sb. far stronger
　　than oneself = 【普】鸡蛋碰石头
鸡蛋里面挑骨头【gei¹dan²lêû⁵min⁶tiu¹gued⁷
　　teo⁴旦¹ 吕⁵ 免⁶ 条¹ 崛⁷投】look for
　　a bone in an egg; find fault

计【gei³ 继; gei² 继²】count; compute;
　　meter; idea; ruse; plan
计策【gei³qag⁸ 册】stratagem; plan
计划【gei³wag⁹ 或⁹】plan; project; map
　　out
计件【gei³gin² 建²】reckon by the piece
计较【yei²gao³ 教 】haggle over; argue;
　　dispute
计量【gei³lêng⁴ 凉】measure; calculate
计谋【gei³meo⁴ 牟】scheme; stratagem
计时【gei³xi⁴ 是⁴】reckon by time

计数【gei³xou³ 扫】count
计算机【gei³xūn³gēi¹ 蒜基】computer; cal-
　　culating
计仔【gei²jei² 济²】(亦作"偈仔")way;
　　stratagem =【普】办法; 计策

继【gei³ 计】continue; succeed; follow;
　　then
继承【gei³xing⁴ 成】inherit; carry on
继续【gei³jug⁹ 逐】continue; go on
继而【gei³yi⁴ 移】then; afterwards
继任【gei³yem⁶ 壬⁶】succeed sb. in a post
继往开来【gei³wong⁵hoi¹loi⁴ 枉⁵ 海¹ 莱】
　　carry forward the cause and forge
　　ahead into the future

髻【gei³ 计】〈n.〉hair worn in a bun or
　　coil

鸠【geo¹ 九¹; keo¹ 沟】① 斑鸠
　　【ban¹geo¹】turtledove ②〈vulgar
　　language〉penis

九【geo² 久】〈num.〉nine; many
九月【geo²yūd⁹ 越】September; the ninth
　　moon
九州【geo²jeo¹ 洲】a poetic name for Chi-
　　na; Kyushu
九泉【geo² qūn⁴ 全 】grave; the nether
　　world
九天【geo² tin¹ 田¹】the Ninth Heaven;
　　the highest of heaven
九霄云外【geo²xiu¹wen⁴ngoi⁶ 消匀碍】
　　beyond the highest heavens
九死一生【geo²xēi²yed⁷xang¹ 四² 壹时
　　罌¹】a narrow escape from death
九牛二虎之力【geo²ngeo⁴yi⁶fu²ji¹lig⁹ 欧⁴
　　义斧支历】tremendous effort

久【geo² 九】for a long time; long

久久【geo² geo²】for a long, long time

久远【geo² yün⁵ 软】far back；ages ago

久而久之【geo² yi⁴ geo² ji¹ 移 支】in the course of time＝【普】时间久了

久病成医【geo²bēng⁶ying⁴yi¹ 柄⁶ 诚衣】prolonged illness makes a doctor of a patient

玖【geo² 九】nine ＝ 九【geo²】

狗【geo² 九】dog；damned；cured

狗虱【geo²xed⁷ 失】dog flea＝【普】狗蚤

狗窦【geo²deo³ 斗】kennel；doghouse＝【普】狗窝

狗屁【geo² pēi³ 臂】horseshit；rubbish；nonsense

狗腿子【geo² tēu⁴ ji² 退⁴止】hired thug；lackey

狗咬狗【geo²ngao⁵geo² 拗⁵】dog-eat-dog

狗头军师【geo²teo⁴guen¹xi¹ 投均司】inept adviser；villainous adviser

狗仗人势【geo² jêng⁶ yen⁴ xei³丈 仁 世】like a dog threatening people on the strength of its master's power

狗胆包天【geo²dam²bao¹tin¹ 担² 胞田¹】monstrous audacity

狗急跳墙【geo² geb⁷ tiu³ qêng⁴格合⁷ 条³祥】a cornered beast will do something desperate

苟【geo² 九】careless；negligent；if

苟安【geo²ngon¹ 氨】seek momentary ease

苟合【geo²heb⁹ 盒】illicit sexual relations

苟且【geo²qē² 扯】drift along；perfunctorily

苟同【geo² tung⁴ 铜】readily subscribe to (sb.'s view)

苟延残喘【geo²yin⁴qan⁴qün⁴ 言灿⁴ 窜】be on one's last legs

枸【geo² 狗】〈n.〉枸杞【geo²gēi² 己】the fruit of Chinese wolfberry

篝【geo¹ 鸠】cage

篝火【geo¹fo² 伙】bonfire；campfire

垢【geo³ 救】dirty；filthy（see"污垢"）

厩【geo³ 救】〈n.〉马厩【ma⁵geo³】stable；cattle-shed

救【geo³ 够】rescue；save；help；relieve

救护【geo³wu⁶ 户】give firstaid；rescue

救急【geo³geb⁷ 格合⁷】help meet an urgent need

救生【geo³xeng¹ 撑】lifesaving

救火【geo²fo² 伙²】fire fighting

救命【geo²mēng⁶ 莫镜⁶】save sb.'s life

救灾【geo²joi¹ 哉】provide disaster relief

救治【geo²ji⁶ 自】treat and cure

救助【geo² jo⁶坐】help sb. in danger or difficulty

救国【geo²guog⁸ 帼】save the nation

救死扶伤【geo²xēi²fu⁴xêng¹ 四² 符湘】heal the wounded and rescue the dying

够【geo³ 救】enough；sufficient；adequate；reach；quite

够本【geo³bun² 苯²】break even

够老鹏【geo³ lou⁵ pang⁵鲁⁵棚⁵】be a friend indeed＝【普】够朋友

够味【geo³mēi⁶ 未】just the right flavour

够胆【geo³dam² 担²】dare＝【普】够勇敢；够胆量

够派【geo²pai¹ 牌¹】fashionable；modern＝【普】时髦的；摩登的

够皮【geo³pēi² 披²】enough; sufficient =【普】足够了

够数【geo³ xou³ 扫】enough; adequate =【普】足够；尚可以

够算【geo³ xūn³ 蒜】enough; satisfied =【普】足够；合算

够运【geo³wen⁶ 混】lucky =【普】好运气；幸好

够钟【geo³jung¹ 中】time's up =【普】到点

咎【geo³ 救】fault; blame; censure; punish

咎由自取【geo³yeo¹ji⁶qêü² 尤治娶】have only oneself to blame

灸【geo³ 救】moxibustion (see "针灸")

究【geo³ 救】study carefully; go into; really

究竟【geo³ging² 警】outcome; actually; after all

究其根源【geo³kēi⁴gen¹yün⁴ 奇斤元】trace sth. to its source

韭【geo² 九】chives

韭菜【geo²qoi³ 蔡】(Chinese) chives

韭黄【geo²wong⁴ 王】hotbed chives

旧【geo⁶ 柩】past; bygone; old; used; worn; former; onetime; old friendship

旧阵时【geo⁶jen⁶xi⁴ 振⁶是⁴】previously; last time 旧底【geo⁶dei² 底】=旧时【geo⁶xi⁴】=旧日【geo⁶yed⁹ 逸】=【普】往日；过去；从前

旧年【geo⁶nin⁴ 捻⁴】last year =【普】去年

旧恶【geo⁶ngog⁸ 额壳⁸】=旧仇【geo⁶

xeo⁴ 愁】=旧怨【geo⁶yün³ 原³】old grievance; old wrong

旧观【geo⁶gun¹ 官】=旧貌【geo⁶ mao⁶ 猫⁶】old look

旧货【geo⁶fo³ 课】secondhand goods; junk

旧交【geo⁶gao¹ 胶】old acquaintance

旧居【geo⁶gêü¹ 举¹】old home

旧历【geo⁶lig⁹ 力】old Chinese calendar

旧式【geo⁶xig⁷ 色】old type

《旧约》【geo⁶yêg⁸ 若⁸】the Old Testament

旧金山【geo⁶gem¹xan¹ 今册】〈n.〉San Francisco

柩【geo⁶ 旧】①a coffin with a corpse in it (see "灵柩")②又作"咀"〈classifier〉a lump =【普】一团

柩(咀)饭嗽【geo⁶fan⁶gem² 范敢】fool; clumsy =【普】笨蛋；笨拙

金【gem¹ 今】gold (Au); golden; metals; money

金器【gem¹hēi³ 气】gold vessel

金币【gem¹bei⁶ 敝】gold coin

金额【gem¹ngag⁹ 岳客⁹】amount of money

金刚石【gem¹gong¹xêg⁹ 硕】diamond

金箍棒【gem¹ku¹pang⁵ 卡乌¹棚⁵】golden cudgel (a weapon used by the Monkey King in the novel Pilgrimage to the West)

金光【gem¹guong¹ 广¹】golden light (or ray)

金黄【gem¹wong⁴ 王】golden yellow

金婚【gem¹fen¹ 分】golden wedding

金库【gem¹fu³ 富】national treasury; exchequer

金钱【gem¹qin⁴ 前】money

金融【gem¹yung⁴ 容】finance；banking

金色【gem¹xig⁷ 式】golden

金鱼黄【gem¹yü⁴wong² 如王²】the bright yellow colour

金属【gem¹xug⁹ 熟】metal

金星【gem¹xing¹ 升】〈n.〉Venus

金鱼【gem¹yü⁴ 如】goldfish

金元【gem¹yün⁴ 园】gold dollar；U. S. dollar

金字塔【gem¹ji⁶tab⁸ 治梯鸭⁸】pyramid

金碧辉煌【gem¹ big⁷ fei¹ wong⁴逼 挥 王】(of a building, etc.) looking splendid in green and gold

金蝉脱壳【gem¹ xim⁴ tüd⁸ hog⁸蝉 铁月⁸ 学⁸】escape by cunning manoeuvring

金山橙【gem¹ xan¹ qang²珊撑²】refer to oranges produced in the United States

金山客【gem¹xan¹hag⁸ 珊吓】refer to the American-born Chinese

今【gem¹ 金】modern；present-day；today；now

今朝【gem¹jiu¹ 焦】this morning；the present

今日【gem¹yed⁹ 逸】today；present；now = 今时【gem¹xi⁴】

今生【gem¹xeng¹ 擤¹】= 今世【gem¹xei³ 细】this life；this age

今天【gem¹ tin¹田¹】today；the present；now

今后【gem¹heo⁶ 候】from now on；in the days to come

今年【gem¹nin⁴ 捻⁴】this year

甘【gem¹ 金】sweet；willingly；pleasant

甘美【gem¹mēi⁵ 尾】sweet and refreshing

甘草【gem¹qou² 操²】licorice root

甘苦【gem¹ fu²虎 】sweetness and bitterness；hardships and difficulties experienced in work

甘露【gem¹lou⁶ 路】sweet dew；manna

甘心【gem¹xem¹ 深】willingly；be reconciled to

甘休【gem¹yeo⁶ 优】be willing to give up

甘油【gem¹yeo⁴ 由】glycerine

甘于【gem¹yü¹ 于】be willing to ; be ready to

甘愿【gem¹yün⁶ 原⁶】willingly；readily

甘蔗【gem¹jē³ 借】sugarcane

甘拜下风【gem¹bai¹ha⁶fung¹ 摆³ 夏锋】candidly admit defeat

柑【gem¹ 金】mandarin orange

柑橘【gem¹gued⁷ 骨】oranges and tangerines；citrus

泔【gem¹ 甘】〈n.〉泔水【gem¹xêü² 瑞²】swill；slops；hogwash = 潲水【xao³xêü² 哨瑞²】

敢【gem² 锦】bold；daring；dare；be certain

敢于【gem²yü¹ 迂】dare to；be bold

敢想【gem²xêng² 赏】dare to think

敢讲【gem²gong² 港】dare to speak = 敢说【gem²xüd⁸ 雪】

敢做【gem² jou⁶造 】dare to act = 敢干【gem²gon³ 杆³】

敢死队【gem²xēi²dêü² 四² 对²】dare-to-die corps

敢怒不敢言【gem²nou⁶bed⁷gem²yin⁴ 奴⁶ 毕然】be forced to keep one's resentment to oneself

噉【gem² 敢】〈*pron.*〉so; such; this way; of that kind; like that; in that way

噉样【gem²yêng² 扬²】so; such; this way; like that =【普】这样；这么样；那样；那么样

橄【gem² 敢】〈*n.*〉橄榄【gem²lam² 览²】Chinese olive; olive

橄榄球【gem²lam²keo⁴ 览² 求】Rugby (football)

锦【gem² 敢】brocade; bright and beautiful

锦缎【gem²dün⁶ 段】brocade

锦锈【gem² xeo³ 瘦 】as beautiful as brocade

锦旗【gem²kēi⁴ 奇】silk banner

锦标【gem²biu¹ 彪】prize; trophy

锦纶【gem²lên⁴ 伦】polyamide fibre

锦上添花【gem²xêng⁶tim¹fa¹ 甜¹ 化¹】add flowers to the brocade—make perfection still more perfect

感【gem² 敢】feel; sense; move; feeling

感觉【gem²gog⁸ 角】sense; sensation; feeling; feel; perceive

感情【gem²qing⁴ 程】emotion; feeling; affection; love

感动【gem²dung⁶ 洞】move; touch

感激【gem²gig⁷ 击】feel grateful; be thankful

感恩【gem²yen¹ 因】feel grateful

感谢【gem²jē⁶ 蔗⁶】thank; be grateful

感想【gem²xêng² 赏】impressions; thoughts

感叹【gem²tan³ 炭】sigh with feeling

感受【gem²xeo⁶ 授】be affected by; experience

感染【gem²yim⁵ 冉⁵】infect; influence

感化【gem²fa³ 花³】help to change by persuasion

感光【gem²guong¹ 广¹】sensitization

感冒【gem²mou⁶ 务】common cold

感慨【gem²koi³ 概】sigh with emotion

咁【gem² 禁】〈*pron.*〉so; such; this way; like that = 咁样【gem²yêng² 扬²】=【普】这样；这么样；那样；那么样

赣【gem³ 禁】another name for Jiangxi Province

禁【gem³ 赣】prohibit; forbid; ban; a taboo; bear; contain oneself

禁锢【gem³gu³ 故】keep in custody; confine

禁忌【gem³ gēi³技 】taboo; avoid; contraindication

禁令【gem³ling⁶ 玲】prohibition; ban

禁区【gem³ kêü¹驱】forbidden zone; preserve

禁止【gem³ji² 子】prohibit; ban; forbid

禁不住【gem³bed⁷jü⁶ 毕著⁶】be unable to bear; can't refrain from

噤【gem³ 禁】keep silent; shiver

噤若寒蝉【gem³yêg⁹hon⁴xim⁴ 药韩婵】as silent as a cicada in cold weather—keep quiet out of fear

揿【gem⁶ 禁⁶】press (with the hand or finger) =【普】摁；(用手)按

揿电制【gem⁶din⁶jei³ 殿济】press (or push)a button =【普】摁电钮

揿住不放【gem⁶jü⁶bed⁷fong³ 著⁶ 毕况】press sth. down and hold it there =【普】压着不放

揿钉【gem⁶dēng¹ 得镜¹】thumb-tack =

【普】图钉；大头钉

庚【geng¹ 羹】the seventh of the ten Heavenly Stems; age 同庚【tung⁴geng¹】of the same age

羹【geng¹ 庚】a thick soup; soup spoon; tablespoon

亘【geng² 耿】extend; stretch

亘古及今【gen²gu²keb⁹gem¹ 鼓给⁹ 金】from time immemorial down to the present day = 从古到今【qung⁴gu²dou³gem¹】

埂【geng² 梗】a low bank of earth between fields

哽【geng² 梗】choke; feel a lump in one's throat

哽咽【geng²yin¹ 烟】choke with sobs

耿【geng² 亘】bright; dedicated; upright

耿直【geng²jig⁹ 值】honest and frank; upright

耿耿【geng²geng²】devoted; be troubled

耿耿于怀【geng² geng² yu¹ wai⁴ 迂坏⁴】take sth. to heart

梗【geng² 亘；guang² 格横²】straighten; obstruct; stem

梗概【geng²koi³ 慨】broad outline; gist = 谱模【pou²mou²】

梗塞【geng² xeg⁷时得⁷】block; clog; infarction

梗阻【geng²jo² 左】block; obstruction

梗系【geng² hei⁶兮⁶】certainly; undoubtedly = 【普】一定；无疑

梗晒【geng²xai³ 徙³】can't move = 【普】不能动弹

梗板【geng² ban² 版】rigid; inflexible = 【普】呆板；没灵活性

菜梗【qoi³guang² 蔡格横²】vegetable stem

更【geng³；gang¹】(see "gang¹")

急【geb⁷ 格合⁷】impatient; worry; irritated; urgent; fast; urgency; be eager to help

急速【geb⁷qug⁷ 促】very fast; rapidly

急促【geb⁷ qug⁷ 速】hurried; rapid; pressing

急于【geb⁷ yü¹ 迂】eager; anxious; impatient

急需【geb⁷xêü¹ 须】be badly in need of; urgent need

急切【geb⁷qid⁸ 设】eager; in a hurry

急迫【geb⁷big² 逼】urgent; pressing

急忙【geb⁷mong⁴ 亡】in a hurry; in haste

急剧【geb⁷ kēg⁹ 屐】torrent; rapids; jet flow

急救【geb⁷geo³ 够】first aid

急诊【geb⁷qen² 陈²】emergency call

急躁【geb⁷qou³ 燥】irritable; impetuous; rash

急不可待【geb⁷bed⁷ho²doi⁶ 毕何² 代】too impatient to wait

急中生智【geb⁷ jung¹ xeng¹ ji³钟 笙 志】show resourcefulness in an emergency

蛤【geb⁸ 急⁸；ha¹ 哈】frog

蛤蚜【geb⁸guai² 拐】a frog = 【普】蛤蟆

蛤乸【geb⁸na² 哪²】an adult frog = 【普】青蛙

拾【geb⁸ 急⁸】gather; collect = 【普】集合；聚集

拾计（偈）【geb⁸gei² 继²】consult; conspire = 【普】合计；合谋

拾手拾脚【geb⁸xeo²geb⁸gêg⁸ 急⁸ 守急⁸

格约⁸】work as one; make concerted efforts = 【普】齐心协力

辩埋晒【geb⁸mai⁴xai³ 买⁴ 徙³】merge; amount = 【普】合起来

毑【geb⁹ 急⁹】shadow sb.; tail sb.

毑紧佢【geb⁹gen²kêû⁵ 谨拒】shadow sb.; tail sb. = 尾随紧盯着某人

鸽【geb⁸ 急⁸】〈n.〉Pigeon; dove

跟【gen¹ 根】heel; follow

跟班【gen¹ban¹斑】join a regular shift or class

跟上【gen¹ xêng⁵尚⁵】keep pace with; catch up with

跟随【gen¹qêû⁴ 徐】follow

跟踪【gen¹jung¹ 中】follow the tracks

跟住【gen¹jǜ⁶ 著⁶】follow in the wake of

跟尾【gen¹mēi⁵美】to follow after = 【普】随后; 后来

跟尾狗【gen¹mēi⁵geo² 美九】to refer to one who does not have his own idea or thinking but agrees to whatever that others say = 【普】自己没主见, 跟着别人说话行事的人

根【gen¹ 跟】root (of a plant); foot; cause; thoroughly; radical

根子【gen¹ji² 止】root; origin

根本【gen¹bun⁴ 搬²】basic; at all; radically

根底【gen¹dei² 抵】foundation; cause

根除【gen¹ qêû⁴徐】thoroughly do away with

根基【gen¹gēi¹ 机】foundation; basis

根据【gen¹gêû³ 句】on the basis of; basis

根苗【gen¹miu⁴ 描】root and shoot

根源【gen¹yün⁴ 元】source; origin

根治【gen¹ji⁶ 自】effect a radical cure

根櫃【gen¹kêng² 强²】root = 【普】(植物的)主根和须根

根深蒂固【gen¹xem¹dei³gu³ 心帝故】deep-rooted

斤【gen¹ 根】a unit of weight (= 1/2 kilogram)

斤两【gen¹lêng² 俩²】weight

斤斤计较【gen¹gen¹gei³gao³ 继教】laggle over every ounce; be calculating

筋【gen¹ 根】muscle; tendon; sinew

筋骨【gen¹gued⁷ 掘⁷】bones and muscles — physique

筋斗【gen¹deo² 豆²】somersault; fall; tumble(over)

筋疲力尽【gen¹pēi⁴lig⁹jên⁶ 皮历进⁶】exhausted

紧【gen² 仅】tight; tighten; urgent; strict

紧逼【gen²big⁷ 迫】press hard; close in on

紧迫【gen²big⁷ 逼】pressing; urgent

紧紧【gen²gen²】closely; firmly

紧要【gen²yiu³ 腰³】critical; crucial

紧密【gen²med⁹ 勿】inseparable; rapid and intense

紧张【gen²jêng¹ 将】nervous; tense

紧缩【gen²xug⁷ 宿】reduce; retrench

紧跟【gen²gen¹ 根】follow closely

紧箍咒【gen²ku¹jeo³ 卡乌¹ 皱】the Incantation of the Golden Hoop, used by the Monk in the novel *Pilgrimage to the West*

谨【gen² 紧】careful; solemnly; sincerely

谨致【gen²ji³ 志】please accept

谨防【gen² fong⁴ 妨】guard against

谨慎【gen² xen⁶ 身⁶】prudent; cautious

谨小慎微【gen² xiu² xen⁶ mēi⁴ 少肾眉】overcautious

谨【gen² 紧】(see"饥馑")

仅【gen² 紧】only; merely

仅仅【gen² gen²】only; merely; barely

巾【gen¹ 斤】a piece of cloth (as used for a towel, etc.)

巾帼【gen¹ guog⁸ 国】ancient woman's headdress; woman

哏【gen¹ 斤; gen³ 艮】amusing; funny; clowning; antic

艮【gen³ 近³; ngen⁶ 银⁶】leathery

狠【gen³ 艮】feel very cold

狠亲【gen³ qen¹ 趁¹】be frostbitten =【普】冻着

茛【gen³ 艮】〈n.〉毛茛【mou⁴ gen³】buttercup

近【gen⁶ 靳】near; close; approaching; close to

近于【gen⁶ yü¹ 于】=近乎【gen⁶ fu⁴ 符】little short of

近郊【gen⁶ gao¹ 交】outskirts of a city; suburbs

近况【gen⁶ fong³ 放】recent developments

近来【gen⁶ loi⁴ 莱】recent; of late; lately

近邻【gen⁶ lên⁴ 伦】near neighbour

近路【gen⁶ lou⁶ 露】shortcut

近旁【gen⁶ pong⁴ 庞】nearby

近期【gen⁶ kēi⁴ 其】in the near future

近亲【gen⁶ qen¹ 趁¹】close relative; near relation

近日【gen⁶ yed⁹ 逸】recently; within the next few days

近视【gen⁶ xi⁶是】myopia; nearsightedness

近似【gen⁶ qi⁵ 此⁵】approximate reading

近水楼台先得月【gen⁶ xêü² leo⁴ toi⁴ xin¹ deg⁷ yüd⁹ 瑞 留抬仙德越】a waterfront pavilion gets the moonlight first—the advantage of being in a favoured position

靳【gen⁶ 近】a surname

吉【ged⁷ 桔】lucky; auspicious; short for Jilin Province

吉利【ged⁷ lēi⁶ 例⁶】lucky; auspicious; propitious

吉祥【ged⁷ qêng⁴ 详】lucky; auspicious; propitious

吉庆【ged⁷ hing³ 兴³】auspicious; propitious; happy

吉兆【ged⁷ xiu⁶ 绍】good omen; propitious sign

吉日【ged⁷ yed⁹ 逸】wedding day

吉凶【ged⁷ hung¹ 空】good or ill luck

吉林【ged⁷ lem⁴ 淋】〈n.〉Jilin(Province)

吉普车【ged⁷ pou² qē¹ 谱奢】jeep

桔【ged⁷ 吉】tangerine

桔汁【ged⁷ jeb⁷ 执】orange juice

桔红【ged⁷ hung⁴ 洪】reddish orange

刮【ged⁷ 吉】stab; prick; jab; poke =【普】刺；戳

刮亲【ged⁷ qen¹ 趁¹】stab and wound =【普】刺伤

刮穿【ged⁷ qün¹ 川】puncture; lay bare =【普】戳穿

尅【ged⁹ 吉⁹】stick up; hold up ＝【普】翘

尅起条尾【ged⁹hēi²tiu⁴mēi⁵ 喜挑⁴ 美】be cocky; get stuck-up ＝【普】翘起尾巴

尅路【ged⁹lou⁶ 露】limp along; walk with a limp ＝【普】一拐一拐地走

尅脚【ged⁹gêg⁸ 格约⁸】lame; inferior ＝【普】跛脚；瘸足

哥【go¹ 歌】elder brother

哥哥【go⁴go¹】elder brother

哥伦比亚【go¹ lên⁴ bēi² nga³沦 髀 哑³】〈n.〉Colombia

哥特式【go¹deg⁹xig⁷ 得⁶ 色】Gothic

歌【go¹ 哥】song; sing

歌唱【go¹qêng³ 畅】sing

歌词【go¹qi⁴ 迟】words of a song

歌谱【go¹pou² 普】music of a song

歌仔【go¹jei² 济²】song ＝【普】歌曲

歌喉【go¹heo⁴ 侯】voice; singing voice

歌手【go¹xeo² 守】singer; vocalist

歌咏【go¹wing⁶ 泳】singing

歌颂【go¹jung⁶ 仲】sing the praises of; extol

歌功颂德【go¹gung¹jung⁶deg⁷ 工 诵 得】eulogize sb.'s virtues and achievements

吤【go² 歌²】that ＝【普】那

吤度【go² dou⁶道】there ＝【普】那里；彼处

吤阵【go² jen⁶ 振⁶】that time; that moment ＝【普】那时；那时候

个【go³ 哥³】①〈classifier〉三个苹果【xam¹go³ping⁴guo²】three apples; ②

individual

个别【go³bid⁹ 必⁹】individual; very few

个把【go³ba² 靶】one or two

个个【go³go³】each and every one; all

个头【go³ teo² 投²】size; height; stature ＝【普】个儿

个样【go³yêng² 扬²】facial feature; looks; shape; manner ＝【普】相貌；样子

个人【go³yen⁴ 仁】individual（person）

个体【go³tei² 睇】individual

个性【go³ xing³胜 】individual character; individuality

个中【go³jung¹ 钟】therein

个噃【go³ bo³播³】to advise; to warn; to confirm ∽【普】的呀；的呵

个啰【go³lo³ 罗³】to show confirmation or satisfaction∽【普】的了；的啦

个喎【go³ wo³窝³】exclamation mark to show dissatisfaction∽【普】的呀；的嘛

翠【go⁶ 个⁶】shield; spoil; dote on（"屙翠"）

叽【gi¹ 格衣¹】〈onomatopoeia〉

叽哩咕噜【gi¹li¹gu¹lu¹ 罗衣¹ 姑罗乌¹】gabble; jabber

该【goi¹ 改¹】ought to; should; deserve; this; that

该当【goi¹dong¹ 珰】deserve; should

该死【goi¹xēi¹ 四²】Oh, no!

该煨【goi¹ wui¹会¹ 】exclamation mark: Oh! No!（to express pity）∽【普】该死；糟糕啦!

赅【goi¹ 该】complete; full 言简意赅【yin⁴gan²yi³goi¹】terse but comprehensive

改【goi² 该²】change; transform; alter; correct

改变【goi²bin³ 边³】change; alter

改革【goi²gag⁸ 格】reform

改换【goi² wun⁶换】change over to; change

改进【goi²jên³ 俊】improve; make better

改良【goi²lêng⁴ 凉】improve; reform

改善【goi²xin⁶ 膳】improve; ameliorate

改造【goi²jou⁶ 做】transform; reform; remould

改正【goi² jing³政】correct; amend; put right

改选【goi²xün² 损】reelect

改过【goi² guo³果³】mend one's ways; correct one's mistakes

改期【goi²kēi⁴ 其】change the date

改装【goi²jong¹ 庄】change one's costume or dress; repackage; refit

改嫁【goi²ga³ 家³】(of a woman)remarry

改头换面【goi² teo⁴ wun⁶ min⁶投 唤 棉⁶】change the appearance

改邪归正【goi²qē⁴guei¹jing³ 斜龟政】give up evil and return to good

盖【goi³ 该³; koi³ 概】lid; cover; canopy; surpass

盖世【goi³xei³ 细】unparalleled; matchless

盖章【koi³jêng¹ 张】affix one's seal; stamp

盖子【goi³ ji²止 】lid; cover; cap; top; shell

盖棺定论【goi³gun¹ding⁶lên⁶ 官 锭伦⁶】final judgment can be passed on a person only when the lid is laid on his coffin

高【gou¹ 膏】tall; high; loud; high-priced; dear

高矮【gou¹ngei² 魏²】height

高低【gou¹dei¹ 底¹】height; sense of propriety; discretion

高度【gou¹ dou⁶道 】altitude; height; highly

高峰【gou¹ fung¹风 】peak; summit; height

高级【gou¹ keb⁷给 】senior; highranking; high-level

高价【gou¹ga³ 嫁】high price

高贵【gou¹guei³ 瑰】noble; highly privileged

高质【gou¹jed⁷ 侄⁷】noble quality

高尚【gou¹xêng⁶ 上】noble

高明【gou¹ming⁴ 名】brilliant; wise

高见【gou¹gin³ 建】your brilliant idea

高手【gou¹xeo² 守】past master; masterhand

高寿【gou¹xeo⁶ 受】longevity; long life; your venerable age

高耸【gou¹xung² 怂】stand tall and erect; tower

高速【gou¹qug⁷ 促】high speed

高压【gou¹ngad⁸ 押】high pressure; high voltage; high-handed

高兴【gou¹hing³ 庆】glad; happy; be willing to

高原【gou¹yün² 元】plateau; highland

高深【gou¹xem¹ 心】advanced; profound

高频【gou¹pen⁴ 贫】high frequency

高炉【gou¹lou⁴ 卢】blast furnace

高烧【gou¹xiu¹ 消】high fever

高涨【gou¹ jêng³胀】rise; upsurge; run high

高亢【gou¹ kong³抗 】loud and sonorous; resounding

高昂【gou¹ngong⁴ 额康⁴】hold high; elated

高傲【gou¹ngou⁶奥⁶】supercilious；arrogant

高产【gou¹qan²铲】high yield；high production

高超【gou¹qiu⁴钊】superb；excellent

高大【gou¹dai⁶歹⁶】tall and big；tall

高等【gou¹deng²戥】higher

高档【gou¹dong³当³】top grade

高举【gou¹gêû¹矩】hold high；hold aloft

高攀【gou¹pan¹盼¹】make friends or claim ties of kinship with someone of a higher social position

高粱【gou¹lêng⁴良　】〈n.〉Chinese sorghum

高利贷【gou¹lêi⁶tai³例态】usury；usurious loan

高窦【gou¹deo³斗】arrogant；proud ＝【普】高傲

高瞻远瞩【gou¹jim¹yün⁵jug⁷詹软足】stand high and see far；show great foresight

高枕无忧【gou¹jem²mou⁴yeo¹针²毛优】shake up the pillow and have a good sleep

高踭鞋【gou¹jang¹hai⁴支罂¹孩】high-heeled shoes ＝【普】高跟鞋

篙【gou¹高】punt-pole

羔【gou¹高】lamb；kid；fawn

糕【gou¹高】cake；pudding

糕点【gou¹dim²店²】cake；pastry

膏【gou¹高】fat；grease；paste；cream

膏药【gou¹gêg⁹若】plaster

睾【gou¹高】〈n.〉睾丸【gou¹yün²院】testis；testicle

镐【gou²稿】〈n.〉镐头【gou²teo⁴投】pick ＝ 锄头【qo⁴teo²】

缟【gou²稿】缟素【gou²xou³扫】white mourning dress

槁【gou²稿】withered

槁木【gou²mug⁹目】dead trees

稿【gou²稿】stalk of grain；draft；manuscript

稿件【gou²jin²见²】manuscript

稿纸【gou²ji²止　】squared or lined paper for making drafts or copying manuscripts

稿费【gou²fei³废】payment for an article or book written；contribution fee

告【gou³诰】tell；accuse；ask for；declare

告诉【gou³xou³数】tell；let know

告知【gou³ji¹支】inform；notify

告示【gou³xi⁶是】official notice；bulletin

告状【gou³jong²撞】go to law against sb.；lodge a complaint against sb. with his superior

告别【gou³bid⁹必⁹】leave；part from；say good-bye to

告辞【gou³qi⁴迟　】take leave（of one's host）

告诫【gou³gai³戒】warn；admonish

告急【gou³geb⁷格合⁷】be in an emergency

告白【gou³bag⁹伯⁹】advertisements＝【普】广告

告假【gou³ga³嫁】to take leave ＝【普】请假

告终【gou³jung¹中】end up

告密【gou³med⁹ 勿】infrom against sb.

诰 【gou³ 告】诰命【gou³ming⁶ 名⁶】imperial mandate

干 【gon¹ 竿；gon³ 擀】① dry；dried food； have to do with ② trunk；cadre；do；work；fight；strike

干鲠鲠【gon¹keng⁵keng⁵ 卡莺⁵】dry = 【普】干巴巴

干枯【gon¹fu¹ 夫】dried-up；withered

干燥【gon¹qou³ 糙】dry；arid；dull

干巴【gon¹ba¹ 爸】dried up；dull and dry

干旱【gon¹hon⁵ 汉⁵】(of weather or soil) arid；dry

干脆【gon¹qêû³ 翠】clear-cut；simply；just

干货【gon¹fo³ 课】fried food and nuts

干涸【gon¹kog³ 确】dry up；run dry

干杯【gon¹bui¹ 背¹】drink a toast

干戈【gon¹ guo¹果¹】weapons of war；arms；war

干净【gon¹ jêng⁶郑 】clean； completely；totally

干亲【gon¹qen¹ 趁】nominal kinship ・

干扰【gon¹yiu⁵ 绕】disturb；interference

干涉【gon¹xib³ 摄】interfere；intervene

干预【gon¹yü⁶ 遇】intervene；interpose

干支【gon¹ji¹ 之】the Heavenly Stems and Earthly Branches

干部【gon³bou⁶ 哺】cadre

干将【gon³ jêng³涨 】 capable person；go-getter

干活【gon³ wud⁹】work = 做野【jou⁶ yê⁵ 造夜⁵】

干劲【gon³ging³ 径】drive；vigour

干掉【gon³diu⁶ 丢】kill；get rid of

干事【gon³xi⁶ 是】a secretary in charge of sth.

干线【gon³xin³ 扇】main line；artery

肝 【gon¹ 竿】liver

肝脏【gon¹jong⁶ 撞】liver

肝炎【gon¹yim⁴ 严】heparin

肝癌【gon¹ngam⁴ 岩】cancer of the liver

肝火【gon¹fo² 伙】irascibility

肝胆相照【gon¹dam²xêng¹jiu³ 担² 双招³】show utter devotion to (a friend, etc.)

肝脑涂地【gon¹nou⁵tou⁴dêi⁶ 恼图得菲⁶】(ready to)die the cruelest death

竿 【gon¹ 肝】pole；rod

酐 【gon¹ 竿】anhydride

杆 【gon¹ 竿】 the shaft or arm of sth.；pole

杆菌【gon¹kuen² 捆】〈n.〉bacillus

擀 【gon² 赶】roll(dough, etc.)

擀面杖【gon²min⁶jêng⁶ 缅⁶ 丈】rolling pin

秆 【gon² 赶】stalk

麻秆【ma⁴gon²】hemp stalk

赶 【gon² 秆】catch up with；overtake；try to catch；drive；drive away

赶路【gon² lou⁶露 】 hurry on with one's journey

赶唔切【gon²m⁴qid⁶ 设】cannot make it to a place or event due to insufficient time = 【普】来不及

赶快【gon²fai³ 块】at once；quickly

赶紧【gon²gen² 谨】lose no time；hasten

赶上【gon² xêng⁶尚⁵】overtake；run-into (a situation)

赶时髦【gon²xi⁴mou¹ 是⁴ 毛¹】follow the fashion

赶走【gon² jeo² 酒】drive away; expel

赶工【gon² gung¹ 攻】to work overtime

赶尽杀绝【gon² jên⁶ xad⁸ jüd⁹ 进⁶ 萨 拙⁹】
　　spare none

江【gong¹ 刚】river; the Changjiang Riv-
　er

江河【gong¹ho⁴ 何】river

江山【gong¹ xan³ 珊】rivers and mountains;
　　land; country

江湖【gong¹ wu⁴ 胡 】 rivers and lakes; all
　　corners of the country; itinerant
　　entertainers, quacks, etc.

刚【gong¹ 江】 firm; strong; just;
　barely; only just

刚才【gon¹qoi⁴ 财】just now; a moment
　　ago ＝ 啱先【ngam¹xin¹】

刚刚【gong¹gong¹】just; only; a moment
　　ago ＝ 啱啱【ngam¹ngam¹】

刚好【gon¹hou² 豪²】just; happen to ＝ 啱
　　好【ngam¹hou²】

刚…就…【gong¹…jeo⁶(袖)…】as soon as
　　… ＝ 正话 … 就 …【jing³wa⁶ …
　　jeo⁶…】

刚健【gon¹gin⁶ 件】vigorous; energetic

刚强【gong¹kêng⁴ 卡香⁴】firm; staunch

刚毅【gong¹ ngei⁶艺 】 resolute and stead-
　　fast

刚劲【gong¹ging³ 敬】bold; vigorous

刚正【gong¹jing³ 政】upright; honourable

刚直【gong¹jig⁹ 值】upright and outspoken

纲【gong¹ 刚】the headrope of a fishing
　net; key link; outline; programme

纲领【gong¹ling⁵ 岭】programme; guiding

纲要【gong¹yiu³ 妖³】outline; essentials

纲举目张【gong¹gêü²mug⁹jêng¹ 矩木章】
　　once the headrope of fishing net is
　　pulled up, all its meshes open

冈【gong¹ 刚】〈n.〉ridge

岗【gong¹ 刚】hillock; mound; ridge;
　welt; sentry

岗仔【gong¹ jei² 济²】mound; hillock ＝
　　【普】小山岗

岗位【gong¹wei² 毁】post; station

岗哨【gong¹ xao³稍³】lookout post; sentry

肛【gong¹ 刚】anus

肛门【gong¹mun⁴ 们】anus ＝ 屎窬
　　【xi²fed⁷ 史弗】

缸【gong¹ 刚】vat; jar; crock

缸仔【gong¹jei² 济²】mug; bowl ＝【普】
　　小瓦缸

缸瓦【gong¹nga⁵ 雅】a compound of sand,
　　clay, etc. for making earthenware

港【gong² 讲】port; harbour

港口【gong²heo² 厚²】port; harbour

港湾【gong²wan¹ 弯】harbour

港纸【gong²ji² 止】the Hong Kong curren-
　　cy

讲【gong² 港】speak; say; tell; explain;
　discuss; stress

讲话【gong²wa⁶ 画⁶】speak; talk; speech;
　　introduction

讲解【gong²gai² 介²】explain

讲价【gong²ga³ 嫁】bargain; haggle over
　　the price

讲和【gong²wo⁴ 禾】make peace; settle a
　　dispute

讲课【gong²fo³ 货】teach; lecture

讲究【gong²geo³ 够】be particular about;
　　exquisite

讲理【gong²lēi⁵ 李】reason with sb.; listen to reason

讲情【gong² qing⁴ 程】intercede；plead for sb.

讲明【gong² ming⁴ 名】explain；make clear

讲求【gong² keo⁴ 球】be particular about

讲述【gong² xêd⁹ 术】tell about；narrate

讲授【gong² xeo⁶ 受】lecture；teach

讲义【gong² yi⁶ 异】teaching materials

讲古【gong² gu³ 鼓】to tell stories =【普】讲故事

讲笑【gong² xiu³ 少³】to joke =【普】开玩笑

讲粗口【gong² qou¹ heo² 操厚²】say words that are nasty

讲大话【gong² dai⁶ wa⁶ 歹⁶ 画⁶】to tell lie；to cheat =【普】说谎

讲数口【gong² xou³ heo² 扫厚²】to bargain =【普】论理，追究责任；算帐

降【gong³ 绛；hong⁴ 杭】fall；drop；lower；surrender；subdue

降低【gong³ dei¹ 帝¹】reduce；cut down；drop；lower

降格【gong³ gag⁸ 隔】lower one's standard or status

降级【gong³ keb⁷ 给】reduce to a lower rank；demote

降临【gong³ lem⁴ 林】befall；come

降落【gong³ log⁹ 洛⁹】descend；land

降温【gong³ wen¹ 瘟】lower the temperature

降压【gng³ ad⁸ 押】step-down

降雨【gong³ yü⁵ 语】rain；precipitation =落雨【log⁹ yü⁵】

降服【hong⁴ fug⁹ 伏】yield；surrender

降伏【hong⁴ fug⁹ 服】subdue；tame

绛【gong³ 降】deep red；crimson

钢【gong³ 降】steel；sharpen；whet；strop

钢铁【gong³ tid⁸ 拖 热⁸】iron and steel；steel

钢材【gong³ qoi⁴ 才】steel products；steels；rolled steel

钢筋【gong³ gen¹ 斤】reinforcing bar

钢板【gong³ ban² 版】steel plate

钢丝【gong³ xi¹ 思】(steel)wire

钢笔【gong³ bed⁷ 毕】pen；fountain pen

钢琴【gong³ kem⁴ 禽】piano

杠【gong³ 钢；gung³ 贡】thick stick；bar

杠棒【gong³ pang⁵ 鹏⁵】stout carrying pole

杠杆【gung³ gon¹ 竿】lever

扛【gong¹ 江】lift with both hands；shoulder

扛枪【gong¹ qêng¹ 昌】shoulder a gun

蚓【gong⁶ 岗⁶】chela；pincers =【普】螯

割【god⁸ 葛】cut

割草【god⁸ qou⁴ 操²】cut grass；mow

割爱【god⁸ ngoi³ 哀³】give up what one treasures

割断【god⁸ tün⁵ 团⁵】sever；cut off

割裂【god⁸ lid⁹ 列】cut apart

割让【god⁸ yêng⁶ 样】cede

葛【god⁸ 割】〈n.〉kudzu vine；a surname

各【gog⁸ 角】each；every；various；different

各个【gog⁸ go³ 哥】each；every；one by one

各人【gog⁸ yen² 仁】each one；everyone

各位【gog⁸ wei² 毁】everybody；every

各自【gog⁸ ji⁶ 治】each；respective

·90· gog. gu

各色【gog⁸xig⁷ 式】of all kinds; assorted

各界【gog⁸gai³ 介】all walks of life

各级【gog⁸keb⁷ 给】all or different levels

角【gog⁸ 各】horn; corner; angle; a fractional unit of money in China

角度【gog⁸dou⁶ 道】angle; point fo view

角尺【gog⁸qēg⁸ 次吃⁸】angle square

角落【gog⁸ log⁹洛⁹】corner; nook = 角落头【gog⁸log⁷teo²】

角钢【gog⁸gong³ 绛】angle steel

角质【gog⁸jed⁷ 侄⁷】cutin

阁【gog⁸ 各】pavilion; cabinet

阁楼【gog⁸leo⁴ 流】attic; loft; garret

阁下【gog⁸ha⁶ 夏】Your Excellency

阁员【gog⁸yūn⁴ 元】member of the cabinet

觉【gog⁸ 各；gao³ 教】sense; feel; wake (up); awake

觉醒【gog⁸xing² 星²】awaken

觉悟【gog⁸ng⁶ 误】consciousness; come to understand

觉察【gog⁸gad⁸ 刷】detect; perceive

觉得【gog⁸deg⁷ 德】feel; think

姑【gu¹ 菇】father's sister; aunt; husband's sister; sister-in-law; husband's mother; nun

姑娘【gu¹nêng⁴ 挪香⁴】girl; daughter

姑姐【gu¹ jē¹遮】father's sister; aunt = 姑妈【gu¹ma¹】= 【普】姑姑；姑母

姑婆【gu¹ po⁴ 颇⁴】grandfather's sisters; grandaunt = 【普】姑奶奶

姑丈【gu¹jêng² 蒋】uncle = 【普】姑夫；姑父

姑且【gu¹ qē²扯 】〈ad.〉tentatively; for the moment

姑息【gu¹xig⁷ 色】appease; indulge; tolerate

菇【gu¹ 姑】〈n.〉mushroom

辜【gu¹ 姑】guilt; crime

辜负【gu¹fu⁶ 父】let down; disappoint

轱【gu¹ 姑】〈n. & a.〉轱辘【gu¹lug⁷ 姑陆⁷】wheel

鸪【gu¹ 姑】(see "鹧鸪")

咕【gu¹ 姑；gu⁴ 姑⁴】〈onomatopoeia〉; 咕喱【gu¹lēi¹ 李¹】a coolie = 【普】搬运工

咕咕声【gu⁴gu²xēng¹ 司镜¹】〈onomatopoeia〉

沽【gu¹ 姑】buy; sell

沽酒【gu¹jeo² 走】buy wine

沽名钓誉【gu¹ming⁴diu³yü⁶ 明吊喻】fish for fame and compliments

孤【gu¹ 姑】(of a child)fatherless; solitary

孤寒【gu¹hon⁴ 韩】stingy; mean = 【普】吝啬

孤寒种【gu¹hon⁴jung² 肿】a person who is stingy = 孤寒铎【gu¹hon⁴dog⁹ 得恶⁹】= 【普】吝啬鬼

孤单【gu¹ dan¹丹】alone; lonely; friendless

孤零零【gu¹ ling¹ ling¹拎 拎】solitary; lone; all alone

孤独【gu¹dug⁹ 毒】lonely; solitary

孤儿【gu¹yi⁴ 移】orphan

孤寂【gu¹jig⁹ 直】lonely

孤立【gu¹leb⁹ 粒⁹】isolated; isolate

孤苦伶仃【gu¹ fu² ling⁴ ding¹ 虎玲丁】orphaned and helpless

孤陋寡闻【gu¹leo⁶guo²men⁴ 漏挂² 文】ignorant and ill-informed

孤注一掷【gu¹ jü³ yed⁷ jag⁹著壹摘】stake everything on a single throw

估 【gu² 姑²】estimate；appraise

估计【gu²gei³ 继】estimate；appraise

估价【gu²ga³ 嫁】appraise；appraised price

估量【gu²lêng⁶ 亮】appraise；estimate

古 【gu² 估】ancient；age-old

古代【gu²doi⁶ 待】ancient time；antiquity

古典【gu²din² 电²】classical allusion；classical

古雅【gu²nga⁵ 瓦】of classic elegance

古人【gu²yen⁴ 仁】the ancients；our forefathers

古老【gu²lou⁵ 鲁】ancient；age-old

古旧【gu²geo⁴ 柩】antiquated；archaic

古朴【gu²pog⁸ 扑】of primitive simplicity

古籍【gu²jig⁹ 直】ancient books

古董【gu²dung² 懂】antique；old fogey

古文【gu²men⁴ 闻】ancient Chinese prose

古语【gu²yü⁵ 雨】archaism；old saying

古往今来【gu²wong⁵gem¹loi⁴ 枉⁵ 金莱】through the ages

古灵精怪【gu²ling⁴jing¹guai³ 宁晶乖³】biarre funny(wearing)；odd-looking⌒【普】古里古怪

古缩【gu²xug⁷ 叔】refer to one who is not sociable；old-fashioned and inflexible ＝【普】古板

鼓 【gu² 古】drum；beat；strike；rouse；bulge

鼓吹【gu²qêü¹ 催】advocate；preach

鼓动【gu²dung⁶ 洞】agitate；instigate

鼓风【gu²fung¹ 丰】blast

鼓励【gu²lei⁶ 丽】encourage；urge

鼓舞【gu²mou⁵ 母】inspire；hearten

鼓噪【gu²qou³ 燥】make an uproar

鼓掌【gu²jêng² 蒋】clap one's hands；applaud

鼓足干劲【gu²jug⁷gon³ging³ 竹杆³ 径】go all out

股 【gu² 古】thigh；section；strand；ply

股本【gu²bun² 苯】capital stock

股份【gu²fen² 粉】share；stock

股东【gu² dung¹ 冬】shareholder；stockholder

股金【gu²gem¹ 今】money paid for shares

股票【gu² piu漂³】share certificate；share；stock

股息【gu²xig⁷ 色】dividend

股肱【gu²gueng¹ 轰】right-hand man

股长【gu²jêng² 蒋】section chief

牯 【gu² 古】bull

臌 【gu² 古】〈n.〉臌胀【gu²jêng³ 帐】tympanites

钴 【gu² 古】〈n.〉cobalt (Co)

瞽 【gu² 古】blind　瞽者【gu²jē² 姐】blind person

蛊 【gu² 古】a legendary venomous insect

蛊惑【gu²wag⁹ 或】poison and bewitch；tricky

蛊惑友【gu²wag⁹yeo² 或油²】people who are tricky⌒【普】鬼计多端的人

蛊惑仔【gu²wag⁹jei² 或济²】a small boy who is tricky⌒【普】鬼计多端的

小子

故【gu³ 固】incident; reason; on purpose; hence; former; old

故事【gu³xi⁶ 是】story; plot

故意【gu³yi³ 衣³】intentionally; wilfully

故伎【gu³gēi⁶ 技】stock trick

故乡【gu³hêng¹ 香】native place

故人【gu³yen⁴ 仁】old friend

故障【gu³jêng³ 涨】hitch; breakdown

故弄玄虚【gu³lung⁶yūn⁴hêü¹ 龙⁶ 元墟】be deliberately mystifying

固【gu³ 故】solid; firmly; solidify; admittedly

固定【gu³ding⁶ 锭】fixed; fix; regular

固守【gu³xeo² 手】defend tenaciously

固态【gu³tai³ 太】solid state

固体【gu³tei⁶ 睇】solid body

固有【gu³yeo⁵ 友】intrinsic; inherent

固执【gu³jeb⁷ 汁】obstinate; persist in

固然【gu³yin⁴言】⟨ad.⟩ no doubt; of course

固步自封【gu³bou⁶ji⁶fung¹ 部治风】be complacent and conservative = 故步自封

雇【gu³ 故】hire; employ

雇工【gu³gung¹ 公】hire labour; hired labourer

雇佣【gu³yung⁴ 容】employ; hire

雇员【gu³ yūn⁴元】employee = 打工仔【da²gung¹jei²】

雇主【gu³jū² 煮】employer = 老细【lou⁵xei³】

顾【gu³ 故】look at; attend to; visit

顾及【gu³keb⁹ 级⁹】attend to

顾忌【gu³gēi⁶ 技】scruple; misgiving

顾住【gu³ jū⁶著⁶】think of someone =【普】请小心；想着；照看着

顾客【gu³hag⁸ 吓】customer; shopper

顾虑【gu³lêü⁶ 泪】misgivings; worry

顾盼【gu³pan³ 攀³】look around

顾问【gu³men⁶ 闻⁶】adviser; consultant

顾此失彼【gu³qi²xed⁷bēi² 齿室比】attend to one thing and lose sight of another

顾名思义【gu³ming⁶xi¹yi⁶ 明司异】seeing the name of a thing one thinks of its function

痼【gu³ 故】chronic; inveterate

痼疾【gu³jed⁹ 侄】chronic illness

锢【gu³ 故】imprison （see"禁锢"）

官【gun¹ 观】government official; officer; organ

官方【gun¹fong¹ 芳】official

官府【gun¹fu² 虎】local authorities; feudal official

官僚【gun¹liu⁴ 辽】bureaucrat

官司【gun¹xi¹ 思】lawsuit

官衔【gun¹ham⁴ 咸】official title

官员【gun¹yūn⁴ 元】official

官职【gun¹jig⁷ 织】official position

官能【gun¹ neng⁴内亨⁴】（organic）function; sense

冠【gun¹ 官；gun³ 贯】hat; corona; crest; precede; first place; the best

冠心病【gun¹xem¹bēng⁶ 深柄⁶】coronary heart disease

冠冕堂皇【gun¹min⁵tong⁵wong⁴ 免唐王】highfalutin

冠军【gun³guen¹ 均】champion; first place

观【gun¹ 官】look at；watch；sight；out-
look；view

观察【gun¹qad⁸ 刷】observe；watch

观看【gun¹hon³ 汉】watch；view

观赏【gun¹xêng² 想】view and admire

观望【gun¹mong⁶ 亡⁶】wait and see；look
on

观音兵【gun¹yem¹bing¹ 钦冰】people who
are willing to do things for women
=【普】乐于听女人调遣的人

观光【gun¹guong¹厂⁻¹】go sightseeing；
visit；tour

观感【gun¹gem² 敢】impressions

观点【gun¹dim² 店²】point of view；view-
point

观念【gun¹nim⁶ 粘⁶】sense；idea；concept

棺【gun¹ 官】coffin

棺材【gun¹qoi⁴ 才】coffin

棺椁【gun¹ guog³国 】inner and outer co-
ffins

倌【gun¹ 官】herdsman；a keeper of domestic animals

管【gun² 灌²】tube；pipe；valve；bother
about；mind；manage；be in charge of

管道【gun²dou⁶ 度】pipeline；piping

管见【gun²gin³ 建】my humble opinion

管弦乐【gun²yin⁴ngog⁹ 言锷】orchestral
music

管理【gun²lēi⁵ 李】manage；run；adminis-
ter

管教【gun² gao³较 】subject sb. to discipline

管束【gun²qug⁷ 促】restrain；check

管辖【gun²hed⁹ 核】have jurisdiction over

管制【gun²jei³ 济】control

管家【gun²ga¹ 加】steward；butler；house-
keeper

管事【gun²xi⁶ 士】run affairs；be in charge

贯【gun³ 灌】pass through；pierce；birth-
place

贯彻【gun³qid⁸ 撤】carry out；implement；
put into effect

贯通【gun³ tung¹ 同¹】be well versed in；
link up

贯穿【gun³ qün¹ 川】 = 贯串【gun³ qün³
寸】run through；permeate

贯注【gun³jü³ 著】concentrate on；be absorbed in

灌【gun³ 贯】irrigate；fill；pour

灌溉【gun³koi³ 概】irrigate

灌浆【gun³ jêng¹张】grouting；form a
vesicle

灌输【gun³xü¹ 书】instil into；inculcate

灌注【gun³jü³ 著】pour into

灌唱片【gun³qêng²pin² 畅 偏²】make a
gramophone record

灌木【gun³mug⁹ 目】bush；shrub

罐【gun³ 灌】jar；pot；tin

罐头【gun³teo² 投²】tin；can

盥【gun³ 灌；fun² 款】wash(the hands or
face)

盥洗【gun³xei² 西²】wash one's hands and
face

鹳【gun³ 灌】stork

公【 gung¹ 工】 public； collective；
common；general；equitable；impar-
tially；public affairs；male

公共【gung¹gung⁶ 贡⁶】public；common；
communal

公德【gung¹ deg⁷得 】morality；social

ethics

公敌【gung¹dig⁹ 迪】public enemy

公仆【gung¹bug⁹ 瀑】public servant

公道【gung¹dou⁶ 度】fair; just; justice

公开【gung¹hoi¹ 海¹】open; overt; make public

公平【gung¹ping⁴ 评】fair; just; impartial

公正【gung¹jing³ 政】just; fair; impartial

公证【gung¹jing³ 正】notarization

公众【gung¹jung³ 种³】the public

公有【gung¹yeo⁵ 友】public-owned; public

公用【gung¹yung⁶佣⁶】for public use; communal

公营【gung¹ying⁴ 盈】publicly-owned

公司【gung¹xi¹ 思】company; corporation

公事【gung¹xi⁶ 士】public affairs; official business

公民【gung¹men⁴ 闻】citizen

公立【gung¹ leb⁹粒⁹】established and maintained by the government; pubilc

公法【gung¹fad⁸ 发】public law

公理【gung¹lēi⁵ 李】generally acknowledged truth; axiom

公里【gung¹lēi⁵ 理】kilometre(km.)

公厘【gung¹lēi⁴ 离】millimetre (mm.)

公斤【gung¹gen¹ 根】kilogram(kg.); kilo

公顷【gung¹king¹ 倾²】hectare (ha.)

公款【gung¹ fun²宽²】public money (or fund)

公家【gung¹ga¹ 加】the state; the public

公元【gung¹ yün⁴员】the Christian era = 公历【gung¹lig⁹ 力】

公务【gung¹mou⁶ 冒】public affairs

公文【gung¹men⁴ 闻】official document

公差【gung¹qai¹ 猜】public errand

公益【gung¹ yig⁷忆 】public good; public welfare

公约【gung¹ yēg⁸跃 】convention; pact; joint pledge

公园【gung¹ yün² 阮】park

公式【gung¹xig⁷ 色】formula

公认【gung¹ying⁶ 英⁶】established

公然【gung¹yin⁴ 言】openly; undisguisedly

公仔【gung¹jei² 济²】doll; cartoon =【普】玩偶娃娃; 漫画; 连环画; 动画

公报【gung¹ bou³布 】bulletin; communique

公布【gung¹ bou³报 】promulgate; announce

公告【gung¹gou³ 诰】announcement; proclamation

公尺【gung¹ qēg⁸赤】metre (m.) = 米【mei¹】

公路【gung¹lou⁶ 露】highway; road

公章【gung¹jēng¹ 张】official seal

公主【gung¹jü² 煮】princess

公子【gung¹ji² 止】son of a feudal prince or high official

公仔书【gung¹jei²xü¹ 济²输】comics =【普】连环画; 小人书

公而忘私【gung¹yi⁴mong⁴xi¹ 移忙思】selfless

工【gung¹ 公】worker; workman; work; skill; be good at

工作【gung¹jog⁸ 昨】work; job

工作者【gung¹jog⁸jē² 姐】worker

工业【gung¹yib⁹ 叶】industry

工具【gung¹gēu⁶ 巨】tool; means

工艺【gung¹ngei⁶ 毅】technology; craft

工人【gung¹yen⁴ 仁】worker; workman

工厂【gung¹ qong²闯 】factory; mill; plant; works

工场【gung¹qēng⁴ 祥】workshop

工程【gung¹qing⁴ 情】engineering; project

工地【gung¹dēi⁶ 得菲⁶】building site

工夫【gung¹ fu¹ 孚】time；work；labour；effort

工效【gung¹hao⁶ 校】work efficiency

工期【gung¹kēi⁴ 其】time limit for a project

工龄【gung¹ling⁴ 玲】length of service

工时【gung¹xi⁴ 是⁴】man-hour

工资【gung¹ji¹ 支】wages；pay

工序【gung¹ jêü⁶ 叙】working procedure；process

工会【gung¹ wui² 汇²】trade union；labour union

工种【gung¹jung² 肿】type of work in production

工整【gung¹jing² 正²】carefully and neatly done

弓【gung¹ 公】bow；bend；arch；anything bow-shaped

弓箭【gung¹jin³ 战】bow and arrow

弓形【gung¹ying⁴ 型】segment of a circle；bow-shaped

弓弦【gung¹yin⁴ 言】bowstring

功【gung¹ 公】service；merit；result；skill；work

功劳【gung¹lou⁴ 卢】contribution；meritorious service

功勋【gung¹fen¹ 分】exploit

功能【gung¹neng⁴ 挪莺⁴】function

功效【gung¹hao⁶ 校】efficacy；effect

功用【gung¹yung⁶ 佣⁶】function；use

功绩【gung¹ jig³织】merits and achievements

功夫【gung¹fu¹ 孚】work；labour；effort

功德【gung¹ deg⁷得】merits and virtues；benefaction

功臣【gung¹xen⁴ 神】a person who has rendered outstanding service

攻【gung¹ 公】attack；accuse；charge；study

攻打【gung¹da¹ 得阿²】attack；assault

攻击【gung¹gig⁷ 激】attack；accuse

攻克【gung¹heg⁷ 黑】capture；take

攻破【gung¹ po³ 婆³】make a breakthrough；breach

攻陷【gung¹ham⁵ 咸⁶】capture；storm

攻心【gung¹xem¹ 深】make a psychological attack

攻读【gung¹dug⁹ 毒】assiduously study

攻其不备【gung¹ kēi⁴ bed⁷ bēi⁶ 奇毕鼻】take sb. by surprise

攻无不克【gung¹mou⁴bed⁷heg⁷ 毛毕黑】all-conquering

供【gung¹ 公】supply；feed；for（the use or convenience of）lay（offerings）；confess；confession

供给【gung¹keb⁷ 级】supply；provide

供销【gung¹xiu¹ 消】supply and marketing

供应【gung¹ying³ 影³】supply

供不应求【gung¹bed⁷ying³keo⁴ 毕影³ 球】supply falls short of demand

供奉【gung¹ fung⁶凤】enshrine and worship；consecrate

供认【gung¹ying⁶ 影⁶】confess

供词【gung¹qi⁴ 迟】confession

供状【gung¹jong⁶ 撞】written confession；deposition

宫【gung¹ 公】palace；temple；womb

宫殿【gung¹din⁶ 电】palace

宫廷【gung¹ting⁴ 亭】palace；court

宫女【gung¹nêü⁵ 那去⁵】a maid in an imperial palace

宫灯【gung¹deng¹ 登】palace lantern

蚣 【gung¹ 公】〈n.〉蜈蚣【ng⁴gung¹】centipede = 百足【bag⁸jug⁷】

躬 【gung¹ 公】personally

躬亲【gung¹qen¹ 趁¹】attend to personally

龚 【ggung¹ 公¹】a surname

恭 【gung¹ 公】respectful; reverent

恭贺【gung¹ho⁶ 何⁶】congratulate
恭候【gung¹heo⁴ 后】await respectfully
恭敬【gung¹ging³ 劲】respectful
恭维【gung¹wei⁴ 围】flatter; compliment
恭喜【gung¹hēi² 起】congratulations

巩 【gung² 拱】consolidate

巩固【gung²gu³ 故】consolidate; solidify; consolidated

拱 【gung² 巩.】cup one hand in the other before the chest; surround; hump up; arch

拱手【gung² xeo²守 】make an obeisance by cupping one hand in the other before one's chest; submissively
拱卫【gung²wei⁶ 惠】surround and protect
拱门【gung²mun⁴ 瞒】arched door
拱桥【gung²kiu⁴ 乔】arch bridge

贡 【gung³ 公³】tribute

贡品【gung³ben² 禀 】articles of tribute; tribute
贡献【gung³hin³ 宪】contribute; dedicate

踬 【gung³ 贡】pass through; cut across = 【普】穿越；穿行

共 【gung⁶ 公⁶】common; general; together; share; altogether; in all; all-told

共同【gung⁶tung⁴ 铜】common; together
共性【gung⁶ xing³胜 】general character; generality
共存【gung⁶qūn⁴ 全】coexist
共和【gung⁶ wo⁴ 禾】republicanism; republic
共鸣【gung⁶ ming⁴ 名】resonance; sympathetic response
共处【gung⁶qū² 此于²】coexist
共事【gung⁶xi⁶ 是】work together; be fellow workers
共通【gung⁶ tung¹统¹】applicable to both or all
共勉【gung⁶ min⁵免 】mutual encouragement
共享【gung⁶ hēng²响 】enjoy together; share
共计【gung⁶gei³ 继】amount to; add up to; total
共产党【gung⁶qan²dong² 铲挡】the Communist Party
共产主义【gung⁶qan²jū²yi⁶ 铲煮异】communism
共埋【gung⁶mai⁴ 买⁴】amount to; together = 【普】共计；合起来

谷 【gug⁷ 菊】valley; gorge; millet

谷物【gug⁷med⁹ 勿】cereal; grain
谷雨【gug⁷yū⁵ 语】Grain Rain (6th solar term)

毂 【gug⁷ 谷】hub

菊 【gug⁷ 谷】chrysanthemum

菊花【gug⁷fa¹ 化¹】chrysanthemum

鞠【gug⁷ 谷】rear；bring up

鞠躬【gug⁷gung¹ 弓】bow

鞠躬尽瘁【gug⁷gung¹jên⁶xêû⁵ 弓进⁶ 穗】bend oneself to a task and exert oneself to the utmost

掬【gug⁷ 谷】hold with both hands；to urge

掬气【gug⁷hêi³ 汽】feel suffocated；choke with resentment =【普】憋气

掬行晒【gug⁷heng⁴xai³ 衡徙³】to urge ∽【普】催促；推进；促进

局【gug⁹】chessboard；game；set；situation；ruse；trap；office；bureau；shop

局部【gug⁹bou⁶ 步】part

局促【gug⁹qug⁷ 速】narrow；feel or show constraint

局面【gug⁹min⁶ 免】aspect；phase

局势【gug⁹xei³ 世】situation

局限【gug⁹han⁶ 黑晏⁶】limit；confine

焗【gug⁹ 局】to force；not airy；stuffy

焗住【gug⁹ jü⁶ 著】be compelled；be forced；can't help；involuntarily =【普】被迫；不由自主

焗炉【gug⁹lou⁴ 卢】an oven

焗闷【gug⁹ mun⁶门⁶】hot and warm；feel oppressed =【普】憋闷

瓜【gua¹ 寡】melon；gourd；die

瓜子【gua¹ji² 止】melon seeds

瓜分【gua¹fen¹ 芬】carve up；partition

瓜葛【gua¹ god⁸割 】connection；implication

瓜熟蒂落【gua¹xug⁹dei³log⁹ 属帝洛⁹】things will be easily settled when conditions are ripe

瓜左【gua¹jo² 助²】= 瓜老衬【gua¹lou⁵ qen³ 鲁趁】die =【普】死了

呱【gua¹ 瓜】⟨onomatopoeia⟩

呱呱叫【gua¹gua¹giu³ 缴³】tiptop；topnotch

寡【gua² 剐】few；scant；tasteless；widowed

寡人【gua²yen⁴ 仁】I，the sovereign

寡妇【gua²fu⁵ 富⁵】widow

寡头【gua²teo⁴ 投】oligarch

寡不敌众【gua²bed⁷dig⁹jung³ 毕迪纵³】be hopelessly outnumbered

剐【gua² 寡】cut to pieces；cut；slit

卦【gua³ 挂】divinatory symbols

褂【gua³ 卦】a Chinese-style unlined garment；gown

挂【gua³ 卦】hang；put up；hitch；be concerned about

挂钩【gua³ngeo¹ 殴】couple；link up with

挂牌【gua³pai¹ 排²】hang out one's shingle

挂名【gua³ mêng⁴默镜²】titular；only in mame

挂号【gua³hou⁴好⁶】register(at a hospital，etc.)

挂帅【gua³ xêû³ 税】be in command；assume command

挂图【gua³ tou⁴途 】wall map；hanging chart

挂档【gua³dong² 党】put into gear

挂齿【gua³qi² 始】mention

挂羊头卖狗肉【gua³yêng⁴teo⁴mai⁶geo² yug⁹ 杨投买⁶ 九玉】hang up a sheep's head and sell dogmeat—

try to palm off sth. inferior to
what it purports to be

挂住【gua³jŭ⁶ 著⁶】= 挂念【gua³nim⁶ 粘⁶】
worry about sb. who is absent;
miss

挂腊鸭【gua³lab⁹ngab⁸ 蜡额甲⁸】to kill
oneself by hanging = 【普】上吊
自杀

乖【guai¹ 怪¹】 well-behaved; good;
clever; alert

乖乖【guai¹guai¹】well-behaved; obedient;
good gracious

乖戾【guai¹lêŭ⁶ 类】perverse(behaviour)

乖谬【guai¹meo⁶ 茂】absurd; abnormal

乖巧【guai¹hao² 考】clever; cute; lovely

拐【guai² 怪²】 turn; limp; crutch;
abduct; swindle

拐杖【guai²jêng⁶ 丈】walking stick

拐弯【guai² wan¹ 湾】 turn a corner; turn
round

拐骗【guai²pin³ 片】abduct; swindle

拐子佬【guai² ji² lou² 止老²】 one who
cheats others for money and
things; abductor = 【普】骗子；
拐子

蜗【guai² 拐】〈n.〉(see"蛤蜗")

怪【guai³ 乖³】strange; wonder; quite;
monster; blame

怪诞【guai³dan³ 旦】weird; strange

怪物【guai³ med⁹ 勿】monster; an eccentric person

怪僻【guai³pig⁷ 辟】eccentric

怪声怪气【guai³xēng¹guai³hēi³ 腥汽】
（speak in a）strange voice or affected manner

怪之得【guai³ji¹deg⁷ 支德】no wonder =

【普】怪不得

关【guan¹ 鳏】stut; close; turn off; lock
up; close down; pass; barrier; concern

关闭【guan¹bei³ 敝³】close; shut

关押【guan¹ngad⁸ 压】lock up; put in
prison

关口【guan¹heo² 厚²】strategic pass; juncture

关卡【guna¹ ka¹ 确亚¹】an outpost of the
tax office

关税【guan¹xêŭ³ 瑞³】customs duty; tariff

关节【guan¹jid⁸ 折】joint; key links; links

关键【guan¹gin⁶ 件】hinge; key; crux

关联【guan¹ lün⁴ 峦】 be related; be connected

关系【guan¹ hei⁶ 兮⁶】 relation; bearing;
concern

关心【guan¹xem¹ 深】 be concerned with;
care for

关怀【guan¹wai⁴ 坏⁴】show loving care for

关注【guan¹jü³ 著】follow with interest

关照【guan¹jiu³ 焦³】 look after; notify by
word of mouth

关于【guan¹ yü¹ 迂】 about; on; with regard to

关斗【guan¹deo² 豆²】a somersault =【普】
筋斗

关刀【guan¹dou¹ 都】a very big knife

关人【guan¹yen⁴ 仁】not to bother oneself
with matters that do not concern
one〇【普】懒得理

鳏【guan¹ 关】wifeless; widowered

鳏夫【guan¹fu¹ 孚】an old wifeless man

惯【guan³ 掼】be used to; indulge

惯性【guan³xing³ 胜】inertia

惯技【guan³gēi⁶ 伎】customary tactic；old trick

惯用【guan³ yung⁶ 佣⁶】consistently use；habitual

惯例【guan³ lei⁶ 丽 】convention；usual practice

掼【guan³ 惯】hurl；fling

掼低【guan³dei¹ 帝¹】fall；tumble ＝【普】跌倒

逛【guang⁶ 格横⁶】stroll；ramble；roam

逛街【guang⁶gai¹ 佳】go window-shopping

刮【guad⁸ 姑押⁸】scrape；plunder；blow

刮刀【guad⁸dou¹ 都】scraping cutter

刮面皮【guad⁸min⁶pēi⁴ 免⁶ 脾】rub the forefinger against one's own check ＝【普】刮脸皮

刮痧【guad⁸ xa¹ 沙 】a popular treatment for sunstroke by scraping the patient's neck, chest or back

刮拢【guad⁸lung² 垄²】corrupted◠【普】搜刮；贪污

刮目相看【guad⁸mug⁹xêng¹hon³ 木商汉】look at sb. with new eyes

掴【guag⁸ 姑客⁸】slap；smack

掴耳光【guag⁸yi⁵guong¹ 尔广¹】box sb.'s ears ＝ 掴巴掌【guag⁸ba¹jêng²】

鬼【guei² 诡】ghost；spirit；stealthy；sinister plot；terrible；clever；very

鬼魂【guei²wen⁴ 云】ghost；spirit

鬼神【guei² xen⁴臣 】ghosts and gods；spirits

鬼怪【guei²guai³ 乖³】ghosts and monsters

鬼魅【guei²mēi⁶ 未】ghosts and goblins

鬼蜮【guei²wig⁹ 域】evil spirit；demon

鬼话【guei²wa⁶ 画⁶】lie

鬼鬼鼠鼠【guei²guei²xü²xü² 署】sneaking；furtive；stealthy ＝【普】鬼鬼祟祟

鬼头鬼脑【guei² teo⁴ guei² nou⁵ 投恼 】thievish；stealthy

鬼迷心窍【guei²mei⁴xem¹kiu³ 米⁴ 深乔³】be possessed

鬼主意【guei² jü² yi³ 煮 义³】evil plan；wicked idea ＝ 鬼点子【guei²dim²ji²】

鬼把戏【guei²ba²hēi³ 巴² 气】sinister plot

鬼混【guei²wen⁶ 运】lead an aimless or irregular existence；fool around

鬼打鬼【guei² da² guei² 得亚²】gangsters who quarrel among themselves

鬼马【guei²ma⁵ 蚂】cunning；not serious；frivolous ＝【普】狡猾的；灵巧的；不严肃的；不正经的

鬼佬【guei²lou² 老²】a westerner ＝【普】洋鬼子

鬼五马六【guei² ng⁵ ma⁵ lug⁹ 伍蚂陆 】messy；frivolous；not serious ＝【普】污秽的；轻佻的；不严肃的

鬼杀咁嘈【guei²xad⁸gem³qou⁴ 萨禁曹】extremely noisy ＝【普】大声吵闹

鬼咁衰【guei² gem³ xêü¹禁绥】very ugly ＝【普】很丑；很糟糕，等等

鬼咁好【guei²gem³hou² 禁号²】very good ＝【普】很好

诡【guei² 鬼】deceitful；tricky；weird

诡辩【guei² bin⁶便 】sophistry；sophism；quibbling

诡计【guei² gei³继 】crafty plot；trick；

ruse

诡谲【guei²küd⁸ 决】strange and change-
ful; treacherous ＝ 诡猾【guei²
wad⁹ 滑】

轨【guei² 鬼】rail; track; course; path

轨道【guei²dou⁶ 度】track; orbit; course;
path

轨迹【guei²jig⁷ 织】locus; orbit

晷【guei² 鬼】a shadow cast by the sun;
time

归【guei¹ 龟】go back to; return; give
back to; converge; turn over to

归来【guei¹ loi⁴莱】return; come back ＝
【普】回来

归期【guei¹kēi⁴ 其】date of return

归程【guei¹qing⁴ 情】return journey

归途【guei¹tou⁴ 图】homeward journey

归并【guei¹bing⁶ 冰⁶】incorporate into

归属【guei¹xug⁹ 熟】belong to

归向【guei¹hêng³ 香³】turn towards

归顺【guei¹xên⁶ 驯⁶】come over and pledge allegiance

归宿【guei¹xug⁷ 叔】a home to return to

归纳【guei¹nab⁹ 呐】induce; sum up

归类【guei¹lêü⁶ 泪】sort out; classify

归结【guei¹ gid⁸洁 】sum up; end (of a
story, etc.)

归咎【guei¹geo³ 究】impute to

归罪【guei¹jêü⁶ 叙】put the blame on; im-
pute to

归于【guei¹yü¹ 迂】belong to; result in

归还【guei¹wan⁴ 环】return; revert

归功于【guei¹gung¹yü¹ 公迂】give the
credit to

归根结底【guei¹gen¹gid⁸dei² 跟洁抵】in
the final analysis

归一【guei¹yed⁷ 壹】neat; tidy ＝【普】完
整的; 不散乱的

龟【guei¹ 归】tortoise; turtle

龟甲【guei¹gab⁸ 格鸭⁸】tortoise-shell

龟缩【guei¹xug² 宿】huddle up like a turtle
drawing in its head and legs

龟头【guei¹teo⁴ 投】glans penis

龟蛋【guei¹dan² 旦²】nasty words used to
scold people∽【普】狗崽子(son of
a bitch)

圭【guei¹ 归】〈n.〉圭臬【guei¹yid⁹ 热】
criterion; standard

闺【guei¹ 归】boudoir

闺房【guei¹fong⁴ 防】boudoir

闺女【guei¹nêü⁵ 挪去⁵】girl; maiden; daughter

硅【guei¹ 归】〈n.〉silicon (Si)

硅钢【guei¹gong³ 绛】silicon steel

硅酸【guei¹xün¹ 孙】silicic acid

硅酸盐【guei¹xün¹yim⁴ 严】silicate

桂【guei³ 贵】cassiabarktree; laurel; bay
tree; sweet-scented osmanthus

桂花【guei³fa¹ 化¹】sweet-scented osmanthus

桂皮【guei³pēi⁴ 脾】cassia bark

桂枝【guei³ji¹ 支】cassia twig

桂圆【guei³yün⁴ 元】longan ＝ 龙眼【lung⁴
ngan⁵】

桂冠【guei³gun¹ 官】laurel

桂林【guei³lem⁴ 淋】〈n.〉Guilin

贵【guei³ 桂】expensive; highly valued;
noble; your

贵重【guei³jung⁶ 仲】valuable; precious

贵族【guei³jug⁹ 俗】noble；aristocrat

贵宾【guei³ben¹ 奔】honoured guest

贵妃【guei³fēi¹ 非】highest-ranking imperial concubine

贵州【guei³jeo¹ 洲】〈n.〉Guizhou（Province）

皈【guei¹ 归】= 归【guei¹】

皈依【guei¹ yi¹ 衣】the ceremony of proclaiming sb. a Buddhist

瑰【guei³ 桂】rare；marvellous

瑰宝【guei³bou² 保】rarity；treasure；gem

瑰丽【guei³lei⁶ 厉】surpassingly beautiful

癸【guei³ 贵】the last of the ten Heavenly Stems

柜【guei⁶ 跪】cupboard；cabinet

柜台【guei⁶toi² 胎²】counter；bar

柜桶【guei⁶tung² 统】drawer = 【普】抽屉

跪【guei⁶ 柜】kneel；go down on one's knees

跪拜【guei⁶ bai³ 摆³】worship on bended knees；kowtow

跪倒【guei⁶ dou² 岛】throw oneself on one's knees；grovel = 跪低【guei⁶dei¹】

馈【guei⁶ 跪】make a present of

馈赠【guei⁶jeng⁶ 增⁶】present（a gift）

匮【guei⁶ 跪】deficient

匮乏【guei⁶fed⁹ 伐】short（of supplies；deficient）

悸【guei³ 贵】（of the heart）throb with terror；palpitate

季【guei³ 贵】season；crop；the last month of a season

季度【guei⁶dou⁶ 道】quarter（of a year）

季风【guei⁶fung¹ 丰】monsoon

季节【guei⁶jid⁸ 折】season

君【guen¹ 军】monarch；gentleman；Mr.

君主【guen¹jü² 煮】monarch；sovereign

君子【guen¹ji² 止】a man of noble character；gentleman

均【guen¹ 君】equal；even；without exception；all

均等【guen¹ deng² 戥】equal；impartial；fair

均衡【guen¹ heng⁴ 恒】balanced；harmonious

均摊【guen¹tan¹ 滩】share equally

均匀【guen¹wen⁴ 云】even；well-distributed

钧【guen¹ 君】an ancient unit of weight

军【guen¹ 君】armed forces；army；troops

军事【guen¹xi⁶ 士】military affairs

军人【guen¹yen⁴ 仁】soldier；armyman

军官【guen¹gun¹ 观】officer

军队【guen¹dêü² 堆²】armed forces；army

军阀【guen¹fed⁹ 佛】warlord

军法【guen¹fad⁸ 发】military law

军纪【guen¹gēi² 己】military discipline

军令【guen¹ling⁶ 另】military orders

军饷【guen¹ hēng² 响】soldier's pay and provisions

军需【guen¹xêü¹ 须】military supplies

军情【guen¹qing⁴ 程】military situation

军心【guen¹xem¹ 深】soldiers' morale

军备【guen¹bēi⁶ 鼻】armament；arms

军火【guen¹fo² 伙】munitions

军费【guen¹fei³ 废】military expenditure

衮【guen² 滚】ceremonial dress for royalty

滚【guen² 衮】roll; get away; beat it; boil; deceive

滚动【guen²dung⁶ 洞】roll; trundle

滚滚【guen²guen²】roll; billow; surge

滚筒【guen²tung² 统】cylinder; roll

滚蛋【guen²dan² 旦²】beat it; scram

滚瓜烂熟【guen²gua¹lan⁶xug⁹ 寡¹ 兰⁶ 属】(recite, etc.) fluently; (know sth.)pat

滚水【guen²xêû² 穗²】boiling hot water = 【普】开水

滚搅【guen²gao² 搞】disturb = 【普】打扰; 添麻烦

滚热辣【guen²yid⁹lad⁹ 孽罗压⁹】boiling hot∽【普】火辣辣; 热得烫手

滚友【guen²yeo² 油²】a liar = 【普】说谎的人

滚红滚绿【guen²hung⁴ guen² lug⁹洪 六】to speak nonsense∽【普】说话荒唐, 胡闹, 用以行骗

棍【guen³ 君³】rod; stick; scoundrel

棍棒【guen³pang⁵ 彭⁵】club; a stick or staff used in gymnastics

郡【guen⁶ 君⁶】prefecture

轰【gueng¹ 姑莺¹】bang; boom; rumble; bombard

轰动【gueng¹dung⁶ 洞】cause a sensation

轰炸【gueng¹ja³ 诈】bomb

轰击【gueng¹gig⁷ 激】shell; bombard

轰轰烈烈【gueng¹gueng¹lid⁹lid⁹ 列】on a grand and spectacular scale; vigorous

肱【gueng¹ 轰】〈n.〉肱骨【gueng¹gued⁷橘】humerus

骨【gued⁷ 橘】bone; skeleton; character

骨骼【gued⁷gag⁸ 格】skeleton

骨架【gued⁷ga³ 嫁】skeleton; framework

骨节【gued⁷jid⁸ 折】joint

骨折【gued⁷jid⁸ 节】fracture

骨肉【gued⁷yug⁹ 玉】flesh and blood; kindred

骨气【gued⁷hêi³ 汽】strength of character

骨干【gued⁷gon³ 竿³】diaphysis; backbone

骨髓【gued⁷xêû⁵ 瑞⁵】marrow

骨子【gued⁷ji² 止】delicate; unique = 【普】精巧; 精致

橘【gued⁷ 骨】tangerine

橘子【gued⁷ji² 止】①tangerine ②delicate = 骨子

倔【gued⁹ 掘】stubborn; gruff

倔强【gued⁹kêng⁵ 卡香⁵】stubborn; unbending

倔毒【gued⁹dug⁹ 独】merciless∽【普】绝情; 倔情

倔笃巷【gued⁹dug⁷hong² 督康²】the lane of not through

倔头倔脑【gued⁹ teo⁴ gued⁹ nou⁵ 投恼】blunt of manner and gruff of speech

倔擂槌【gued⁹lêû⁴qêû⁴ 雷除】blunt; bald = 【普】不尖的; 钝的

掘【gued⁹ 倔】dig

掘进【gued⁹jên³ 俊】driving; tunnelling

掘墓人【gued⁹mou⁶yen⁴ 冒仁】gravedigger

掘土机【gued⁹tou²gêi¹ 图²基】excavator

掘井【gued⁹jēng² 支镜²】dig a well

崛

【gued⁹ 倔】rise abruptly

崛起【gued⁹hēi² 喜】(of a mountain, etc.)rise abruptly; rise(as a political force)

戈

【guo¹ 果¹】dagger-axe (an ancient weapon)

戈壁【guo¹big⁷ 碧】〈 n. 〉gobi; the Gobi Desert

果

【guo² 戈²】fruit; result; resolute; really

果实【guo²xed⁹ 失⁹】fruit; gains; fruits

果仔【guo²jei² 济²】fruit = 【普】果子; 果品

果脯【guo²pou² 普】preserved fruit

果皮【guo²pēi⁴ 牌】the skin of fruit; peel; rind

果汁【guo²jeb⁷ 执】fruit juice

果树【guo²xü⁶ 署⁶】fruit tree

果子狸【guo²ji²lēi⁴ 止厘】masked civet

果真【guo²jen¹ 珍】if indeed; if really; really

果然【guo² yin⁴言 】〈 ad. 〉really; as expected

果断【guo²dün³ 段³】resolute; decisive

果敢【guo²gem² 今²】courageous and resolute

裹

【guo² 果】bind; wrap

裹脚【guo²gêg⁸ 格约⁸】foot-binding

裹蒸粽【guo²jing¹jung³ 精仲³】a kind of dumpling made of pork∽【普】粽子; 糍粑

裹足不前【guo²jug⁷bed⁷qin⁴ 竹毕钱】hesitate to move forward

过

【guo³ 果³】cross; pass; across; past; through; over; spend (time); after; go through; exceed; unduly; go beyond

过来【guo³loi⁴ 莱】come over; come up

过去【guo³ hêü³ 虚³ 】 go over; pass by; formerly

过头【guo³teo⁴ 投】go beyond the limit; overdo

过分【guo³fen⁶ 份】excessive; undue

过失【guo³xed⁷ 室】fault; slip; offence

过错【guo³qo³ 挫】fault; mistake

过得去【guo³deg⁷hêü³ 德虚³】can get through; tolerable; not too bad; feel at ease

过骨【guo³ gued⁷ 倔⁷】get through; crux∽【普】关键的东西; 赖以过关的东西

过气【guo³ hēi³ 戏】to refer to medicine that has been kept too long and cannot be used = 【普】过时无用的

过期【guo³kēi⁴ 其】be overdue

过往【guo³wong⁵ 枉⁵】come and go

过度【guo³dou³ 道】excessive; undue

过渡【guo³dou³ 道】transition; interim

过程【guo³qing⁴ 情】course; process

过后【guo³heo⁶ 候】afterwards; later

过火【guo³fo³ 伙】go too far; overdo

过剩【guo³xing⁶ 胜⁶】excess; surplus

过年【guo³nin⁴ 捻⁴】spend the New Year

过节【guo³jid⁸ 折】celebrate a festival

过滤【guo³lêü⁶ 虑】filter; filtrate

过敏【guo³men⁵ 文⁵】allergy

过细【guo³xei³ 世】meticulous; careful

过硬【guo³ ngang⁶ 额罌⁶】be really up to the mark

过于【guo³yü¹ 迂】〈ad.〉too; unduly; excessively

过瘾【guo³yen⁵ 引】satisfy a craving

过日子【guo³yed⁹ji² 逸止】live; get along

过龙【guo³ lung⁴隆】exceed; in excess =【普】超过;过量;过分

过身【guo³xen¹ 辛】pass away; die =【普】逝世;死了

过不去【guo³bed⁷hêû⁷ 毕虚³】cannot get through; be hard on; embarrass

过意不去【guo³yi³bed⁷hêû³ 蔼毕虚³】feel apologetic; feel sorry

光【guong¹ 胱】light; ray; honour; glory; scenery; smooth; brightness; used up; bare; only

光线【guong¹xin³ 腺】light; ray

光焰【guong¹yim⁶ 艳】radiance; flare

光辉【guong¹fei¹ 晖】radiance; glory; brilliant

光明【guong¹ming⁴ 名】light; bright; promising

光荣【guong¹ wing⁴ 蝾 】honour; glory; credit

光泽【guong¹jag⁴ 摘】lustre; gloss; sheen

光华【guong¹wa⁴ 铧】brilliance; splendour

光滑【guong¹wad⁹ 猾】smooth; glossy

光洁【guong¹gid⁸ 结】bright and clean

光芒【guong¹mong⁴ 亡】rays of light; radiance

光彩【guong¹ qoi² 采】lustre; honourable; glorious

光亮【guong¹lêng⁶ 谅】bright; shiny

光景【guong¹ging² 境】scene; conditions

光复【guong¹fug⁹ 伏】recover

光临【guong¹lem⁴ 林】presence(of a guest, etc.)

光顾【guong¹gu³ 雇】patronize

光阴【guong¹yem¹ 钦】time

光圈【guong¹ hün¹ 喧 】diaphragm; aperture

光谱【guong¹pou² 普】spectrum

光管【guong¹gun² 莞】fluorescent light

光鲜【guong¹ xin¹ 仙】wearing what is neat, tidy and pretty =【普】光洁;新鲜

光脱脱【guong¹tüd⁷tüd⁷ 铁月⁷】empty; naked =【普】光秃秃;全裸露

光棍【gung¹ guen³君³】unmarried man; bachelor

光曈曈【guong¹qang⁴qang⁴ 撑⁴】too bright that the eyes hurt; shining∽【普】光耀夺目;光照太强而刺眼

光天化日【guong¹tin¹fa³yed⁹ 田¹ 花³ 逸】broad daylight

光怪陆离【guong¹guai³lug⁹lêi⁴ 拐³ 六厘】bizarre and motley; grotesque and gaudy

胱【guong¹】〈n.〉(see"膀胱")

桄【guong¹ 光】〈n.〉桄榔【guong¹long⁴狼】gomuti palm

广【guong² 光²】wide; vast; extensive; numerous; expand; spread

广大【guong² dai⁶ 歹⁶】vast; large-scale; numerous

广阔【guong² fud⁸ 夫活⁸ 】vast; wide; broad

广泛【guong² fan³ 范³】extensive; wide-ranging

广度【guong²dou⁶ 道】scope; range

广义【guong²yi⁶ 异】broad sense; generalized

广袤【guong²meo⁶茂】length and breadth of land

广告【guong²gou³ 诰】advertisement

广博【guong²bog⁸ 薄⁸】extensive

广播【guong²bo³ 波³】broadcast

广场【guong²qêng⁴ 祥】square

广东【guong² dung¹ 冬¹ 】〈n.〉Guangdong (Province)

广西【guong²xei¹ 筛】〈n.〉Guangxi

广州【guong²jeo¹ 洲】〈n.〉Guangzhou

广开才路【guong²hoi¹qoi⁴lou⁶ 海¹ 财露】open all avenues for people of talent

广开言路【guong²hoi¹yin⁴lou⁶ 海¹ 然露】encourage the free airing of views

犷【guong² 广】rustic; uncouth; boorish (see"粗犷")

蝈【guog⁸ 国】〈n.〉katydid

帼【guog⁸ 国】〈n.〉(see"巾帼")

国【guog⁸ 蝈】country; state; nation; national; of our country; Chinese

国家【guog⁸ga¹ 加】country; state; nation

国君【guog⁸guen¹ 均】monarch

国王【guog⁸wong⁴ 皇】king

国民【guog⁸men⁴ 文】national

国土【guog⁸tou² 讨】territory; land

国境【guog⁸ging² 景】territory

国情【guog⁸qing⁴ 程】national conditions

国庆【guog⁸hing³ 兴³】National Day

国事【guog⁸xi⁶ 是】national affairs

国法【guog⁸gad⁸ 发】national law

国宝【guog⁸bou² 保】national treasure

国产【guog⁸qan² 铲】made in our country

国会【guog⁸wui² 汇²】parliament

国策【guog⁸qag⁸ 册】national policy

国营【guog⁸ying⁴ 仍】state-operated

国内【guog⁸noi⁶ 耐】internal; domestic

国外【guog⁸ngoi⁶ 碍】external; overseas

国防【guog⁸fong⁴ 妨】national defence

国际【guog⁸jei³ 济】international

国计民生【guog⁸gei³men⁴xeng¹ 继文笙】the national economy and the people's livelihood

郭【guog⁸ 国】the outer wall of a city; a surname

椁【guog⁸ 国】outer coffin(see"棺椁")

瘣【gui⁶ 格会⁶】tired = 【普】疲倦；累了

炯【guing² 迥】bright; shining

炯炯【guing²guing²】(of eyes)bright; shining

迥【guing² 炯】far away; widely different

迥然【guing²yin⁴ 言】far apart; widely different

娇【giu¹ 骄】tender; lovely; fragile; frail; squeamish; finicky; pamper; spoil

娇嗲【giu¹ dê² 爹²】delicately pretty; act like a spoiled child = 【普】娇滴滴；撒娇

娇媚【giu¹ mēi⁴眉】coquettish; sweet and charming

娇嫩【giu¹nün⁶ 暖⁶】tender and lovely; fragile

娇艳【giu¹yim⁶ 验】delicate and charming

娇贵【giu¹guei³ 桂】pampered

娇惯【giu¹guan³ 掼】pamper; coddle; spoil

娇气【giu¹hēi³ 戏】fragile; squeamish

娇生惯养【giu¹xeng¹guan³yêng⁵ 笙掼氧】pampered since childhood

娇小玲珑【giu¹xiu²ling⁴lung⁴ 少² 伶龙】

delicate and exquisite

骄
【giu¹ 娇】proud; arrogant; conceited

骄傲【giu¹ngou⁶ 奥⁶】arrogant; be proud

骄横【giu¹wang⁴ 划嚣⁴】arrogant and imperious; overbearing = 骄蛮【giu¹man⁴ 万⁴】

骄气【giu¹hēi³ 汽】overbearing airs; arrogance

骄纵【giu¹jung³ 中³】arrogant and wilful

骄奢淫逸【giu¹qē¹yem⁴yed⁹ 车任⁴ 日】lordly, luxury-loving, loose-living and idle

缴
【giu² 矫】pay; hand over; hand in; capture

缴获【giu²wog⁹ 镬】capture; seize

缴纳【giu²nab⁹ 呐】pay; hand in = 交纳【gao¹nab⁹】

矫
【giu² 缴】rectify; straighten out; strong

矫正【giu²jing³ 政】correct; put right

矫形【giu²ying⁴ 型】orthopaedic

矫饰【giu²xig⁷ 色】dissemble

矫健【giu²gin⁶ 建⁶】strong and vigorous

矫情【giu²qing⁴ 程】be affectedly unconventional

矫枉过正【giu²wong²guo³jing³ 汪² 果³ 政】exceed the proper limits in righting a wrong; overcorrect

纠
【giu² 矫；deo² 抖】entangle; gather together; correct; rectify

纠正【giu²jing³ 政】correct; put right

纠偏【giu²pin¹ 编】rectify a deviation

纠缠【giu²qin⁴ 前】get entangled; nag; worry

纠葛【deo² god⁸ 割】entanglement; dispute

纠察【deo²qad⁸ 刷】picket

赳
【giu² 矫；deo² 抖】〈a.〉雄赳赳【hung⁴giu²giu²】valiant

叫
【giu³ 矫³】cry; shout; call; greet; hire; name; ask; order

叫喊【giu³ham³ 咸³】shout; yell; howl

叫唤【giu³wun⁶ 换】cry out; call out

叫嚷【giu³yêng⁶ 让】shout; howl

叫做【giu³jou⁶ 造】be called; be known as

叫好【giu³ hou² 蒿²】applaud; shout "Bravo"

叫苦【giu³fu² 虎】complain of hardship or suffering

撬
【giu⁶ 叫⁶】sledge; sled; sleigh

撬墙脚【giu⁶qêng⁴gêg⁸ 祥格约⁸】to refer to the use of mean or illegal methods to achieve what one desires = 【普】挖墙脚——第三者破坏别人的爱情

兼
【gim¹ 检¹】double; concurrently; twice

兼备【gim¹bēi⁶ 鼻】have both...and...

兼并【gim¹bing⁶ 丙⁶】annex(territory, etc.)

兼顾【gim¹ gu³ 雇】give consideration to two or more things

兼任【gim¹ yem⁶阴⁶】hold a concurrent post

兼职【gim¹jig⁷ 织】concurrent post

兼夹【gim¹gab⁸ 甲】couple with = 【普】加上；合在一起

兼听则明，偏信则暗【gim¹ ting³ jeg⁷ ming⁴, pin¹xên³jeg⁷em³ 亭⁶ 侧名，编讯侧庵³】listen to both sides and you will be entlightened; heed only one side and you will be benighted

捡【gim² 检】pick up; collect; gather

捡漏【gim² leo⁶ 流⁶】repair the leaky part of a roof = 执漏【jeb⁷ leo⁶】

捡了芝麻，丢了西瓜【gim² liu⁵ ji¹ ma⁴, diu¹ liu⁵ xei¹ gua¹ 料⁵ 之妈⁴, 凋料⁵ 筛寡¹】pick up the sesame seeds but overlook the watermelons

检【gim² 捡】check up; inspect; examine

检查【gim² qa⁴ 茶】check up; self-criticism

检察【gim² qad⁸ 刷】procuratorial work

检阅【gim² yūd² 月】review; inspect

检举【gim² gêŭ² 矩】report to the authorities

检讨【gim² tou³ 土】self-criticism

检验【gim² yim⁶ 艳】test; examine

检疫【gim² yig⁹ 亦】quarantine

检点【gim² dim² 掂²】examine; check; be cautious

剑【gim³ 兼³】sword; sabre

剑麻【gim³ ma⁴ 妈⁴】sisal hemp

剑拔弩张【gim³ bed⁹ nou⁵ jêng¹ 跋脑章】with swords drawn and bows bent

俭【gim⁶ 检⁶】thrifty; frugal

俭朴【gim⁶ pog⁸ 扑】thrifty and simple; economical

俭用【gim⁶ yung⁶ 佣⁶】spend frugally

坚【gin¹ 肩】hard; solid; fortification; firmly

坚硬【gin¹ ngang⁶ 额罂⁶】hard; solid

坚实【gin¹ xed⁹ 失⁹】solid; substantial

坚强【gin¹ kêng⁴ 卡香⁴】strong; firm; strengthen

坚毅【gin¹ ngei⁶ 艺】firm and persistent

坚定【gin¹ ding⁶ 丁⁶】firm; strengthen

坚固【gin¹ gu³ 故】firm; solid; sturdy

坚决【gin¹ küd⁸ 缺】firm; resolute; determined

坚野【gin¹ yê⁵ 惹】good; true = 【普】好的；真的

坚持不懈【gin¹ qi⁴ bed⁷ hai⁶ 迟毕械】unremitting

坚韧不拔【gin¹ yen⁶ bed⁷ bed⁹ 孕毕跋】firm and indomitable

肩【gin¹ 坚】shoulder; take on; undertake

肩膀【gin¹ bong² 绑】shoulder = 膊头【bog⁸ teo⁴】

肩负【gin¹ fu⁶ 付】take on; undertake

口水肩【heo² xêŭ² gin¹】the necklet of cloth = 布做的项圈（用于小孩围肩，保护衣领清洁）

建【gin³ 见】build; construct; establish; set up; found; propose

建立【gin³ leb⁹ 笠⁹】build; establish; set up; found

建设【gin³ qid⁸ 撤】build; construct

建设性【gin³ qid⁸ xing³ 撤胜】constructive

建树【gin³ xü⁶ 署⁶】make a contribution; contribute

建议【gin³ yi⁵ 耳】propose; suggest; proposal

建造【gin³ jou⁶ 做】build; construct; make

建国【gin³ guog⁶ 帼】found a state; build up a country

建交【gin³ gao¹ 郊】establish diplomatic relations

见【gin³ 建】see; catch sight of; meet with; show evidence of; refer to; meet; view

见面【gin³min⁶ 棉⁶】meet；see

见世面【gin³xei³min⁶ 细棉⁶】see the world

见识【gin³xig⁷ 色】widen one's knowledge；experience

见闻【gin³ men⁴ 文 】what one sees and hears；knowledge

见解【gin³gai² 佳²】opinion；view

见地【gin³dēi⁶ 得菲⁶】insight；judgment

见怪【gin³guai³ 乖³】mind；take offence

见鬼【gin³guei² 轨】fantastic；go to hell

见机【gin³gēi¹ 基】as the opportunity arises

见教【gin³ gao³ 铰】favour me with your advice

见效【gin³hao⁶ 校】become effective

见习【gin³jab⁹ 袭】learn on the job

见外【gin³ ngoi⁶碍】regard sb. as an outsider

见风驶舵【gin³fung¹xei²to⁴ 丰洗驼】trim one's sails

见长【gin³qêng⁴ 祥】be good at

见得【gin³deg⁷ 德】seem；appear

见不得【gin³bed⁷deg⁷ 毕德】not fit to be seen or revealed；not to be exposed to

见笑【gin³xiu³ 少³】laugh at(me or us)

见证【gin³jing³ 正】witness；testimony

见义勇为【gin³yi⁶yung⁵wei⁴ 异拥⁵ 围】ready to take up the cudgels for a just cause

见异思迁【gin³yi⁶xi¹qin¹ 义斯千】change one's mind the moment one sees something new

件 【gin⁶ 健；gin² 见²】letter；paper；correspondence 〈 classifier 〉 一 件 衫 【yed⁷gin⁶xam¹ 】 a shirt；一件工作 【yed⁷gin⁶gung¹jog⁸】a piece of work

健 【gin⁶ 件】healthy；strengthen；be strong in

健康【gin⁶hong¹ 糠】health；physique；healthy

健美【gin⁶mēi⁵ 尾】strong and handsome

健全【gin⁶ qûn⁴存 】sound；perfect；strengthen

健壮【gin⁶jong³ 装³】healthy and strong；robust

健谈【gin⁶tam⁴ 谭】be a good talker

健忘【gin⁶mong⁴ 忙】forgetful

健将【gin⁶jêng¹ 涨】master sportsman

健儿【gin⁶ yi⁴移 】valiant fighter；good athlete

健步【gin⁶ bou⁶部 】walk with vigorous strides

腱 【gin⁶ 件】〈 n. 〉tendon

键 【gin⁶ 件】key；bond

键盘【gin⁶pun⁴ 盆】keyboard；fingerboard

经 【ging¹ 京】warp；channels；longitude；manage；constant；scripture；pass through；as a result of；after；through；stand；bear

经线【ging¹xin³ 扇】warp；meridian(line)

经度【ging¹dou⁶ 道】longitude

经纶【ging¹lên⁴ 伦】comb and arrange silk threads—attend to state affairs；statecraft

经络【ging¹ log⁸洛】main and collateral channels，regarded as a network of passages，through which vital energy circulates and along which the acupuncture points are distributed

经期【ging¹kēi⁴ 其】(menstrual)period

经传【ging¹jūn⁶ 专⁶】classical works; classics

经典【ging¹din² 电²】classics; classical; scriptures

经营【ging¹ying⁴仍】manage; run; engage in

经商【ging¹xêng¹ 双】engage in trade; be in business

经销【ging¹xiu¹消】sell on commission; deal in

经手【ging¹xeo² 守】handle; deal with

经受【ging¹xeo⁶ 授】undergo; experience; withstand

经心【ging¹xem¹深】careful; mindful = 经意【ging¹yi³】

经验【ging¹yim⁶ 艳】experience; go through

经历【ging¹lig⁹ 力】go through; undergo; experience

经理【ging¹lēi⁵ 李】handle; manage; manager; director

经纪【ging¹gēi² 己】manage(a business); manager; broker

经过【ging¹ guo³ 果³】pass; go through; after; through

经费【ging¹fei³ 废】funds; outlay

经济【ging¹ jei³际】economy; economic; economical

经常【ging¹ xêng⁴偿】day-to-day; everyday; daily; frequently; constantly; regularly; often

经由【ging¹yeo⁴ 油】via; by way of

经风雨，见世面【ging¹fung¹yü⁵, gin³xei³min⁶】face the world and brave the storm

经已【ging¹yi⁵ 以】already = 【普】已经

京【ging¹ 经】the capital of a country

京城【ging¹xing⁴ 成】the capital of a country = 京都【ging¹dou¹ 刀】

京畿【ging¹gēi¹ 基】the capital city and its environs

京剧【ging¹kēg⁹ 屐】〈n.〉Beijing opera = 京戏【ging¹hēi³】

惊【ging¹ 京；gēng¹ 镜¹；gēng⁶ 镜⁶】start; surprise; shy; afraid; frightened

惊慌【ging¹fong¹ 方】alarmed; scared

惊恐【ging¹ hung² 孔】alarmed and panicky; terrified

惊险【ging¹ him² 欠²】alarmingly dangerous; breathtaking

惊人【ging¹ yen⁴仁】astonishing; amazing; alarming

惊讶【ging¹nga⁵ 瓦】surprised; amazed

惊奇【ging¹kēi⁴ 其】wonder; be surprised

惊厥【ging¹küd⁸ 决】faint from fear; convulsions

惊扰【ging¹yiu² 要²】alarm; agitate

惊动【ging¹dung⁶ 洞】alarm; alert; disturb

惊叹【ging¹tan³ 炭】wonder at; marvel at

惊叫【ging¹giu³ 娇³】cry in fear; scream

惊呼【ging¹fu¹ 夫】cry out in alarm

惊醒【ging¹xing² 星²】awaken; sleep lightly

惊疑【ging¹ yi⁴移】surprised and bewildered

惊喜【ging¹hēi² 起】pleasantly surprised

惊青【gēng¹qēng¹ 迟镜¹】panic; afraid = 【普】恐慌；畏惧

惊住【gēng⁶jü⁶ 著⁶】worried; anxious; take care = 【普】因为难而不安；倍加小心

惊涛骇浪【ging¹ tou⁴ hai⁵ long⁶ 图蟹狼⁶】 terrifying waves; a situation or life full of perils

惊天动地【ging¹ tin¹ dung⁶ dēi⁶ 田¹ 洞<u>得</u>菲⁶】 shaking heaven and earth; world-shaking

惊心动魄【ging¹ xem¹ dung⁶ pag⁸ 深洞柏】 soul-stirring; profoundly affecting

荆【ging¹ 京】chaste tree; vitex

荆棘【ging¹ gig⁷ 击】thistles and thorns; brambles

荆州【ging¹ jeo¹ 洲】〈n.〉Jingzhou

刭【ging² 景】cut the throat

兢【ging¹ 京】〈a.〉兢兢业业【ging¹ging¹yib⁹yib⁹ 叶叶】cautious and conscientious

儆【ging² 景】warn; admonish

景【ging² 警】view; scenery; situation; scene; admire

景物【ging²med⁹ 勿】scenery
景象【ging²jêng⁶ 像】scene; sight; picture
景色【ging²xig⁷ 式】scenery; view; scene
景况【ging²fong³ 放】situation
景观【ging²gun¹ 官】landscape
景气【ging²hēi³ 汽】prosperity; boom
景仰【ging²yêng⁵ 养】respect and admire

警【ging² 景】alert; warn; alarm; police

警报【ging²bou³ 布】alarm; warning; alert
警察【ging²qad⁸ 刷】police; policeman
警告【ging²gou³ 诰】warn; caution; warning
警戒【ging² gai³ 界】warn; admonish; guard against

警觉【ging²gog⁸ 角】vigilance; alertness
警惕【ging²tig⁷ 剔】be on guard against
警卫【ging²wei⁶ 惠】(security)guard
警钟【ging²jung¹ 中】alarm bell; tocsin

憬【ging² 景】wake up to reality

竟【ging² 景】finish; complete; throughout; whole; in the end; unexpectedly; go so far as to; go to the length of

竟敢【ging²gem² 锦】have the audacity
竟然【ging² yin⁴ 言】unexpectedly; go so far as to

境【ging² 景】border; boundary; place; condition

境地【ging²dēi⁶ <u>得</u>菲⁶】condition; circumstances
境界【ging²gai³ 介】boundary; extent reached; state
境况【ging² fong³ 放】condition; circumstances

竞【ging³ 敬】compete; contest; vie

竞争【ging³jeng¹ 憎】compete
竞赛【ging³qoi³ 菜】contest; competition; race
竞技【ging³gēi⁶ 伎】sports; athletics
竞选【ging³xūn² 损】enter into an election contest; run for

胫【ging³ 径】〈n.〉胫骨【ging³gued⁷ 掘⁷】shin bone

径【ging³ 胫】footpath; way; directly; diameter

径赛【ging³qoi³ 菜】track
径庭【ging³ting⁴ 亭】very unlike
径向【ging³hêng³ 香³】radial
径直【ging³jig⁹ 值】〈ad.〉straight; directly

径自【ging³ji⁶ 治】〈*ad.*〉without leave

劲【ging³ 径；ging⁶ 痉】strong；power-ful；sturdy；strength；vigour；man-ner；interest

劲头【ging³teo⁴ 投】strength；vigour

劲敌【ging³dig⁹ 滴】formidable adversary

劲旅【ging³lêü⁵ 吕】strong contingent

劲抽【ging⁶ qeo¹ 秋】good；very good = 【普】好的；很好的

劲歌【ging⁶go¹ 哥】very pleasant song = 【普】好听的、节奏感很强的歌

敬【ging³ 径】respect；respectfully；offer politely

敬爱【ging³ngoi³ 哀³】respect and love

敬重【ging³jung⁶ 仲】deeply respect；re-vere

敬佩【ging³pui³ 沛】esteem；admire

敬仰【ging³yêng⁵ 养】revere；venerate

敬酒【ging³jeo² 走】propose a toast；toast

敬礼【ging³ lei⁵ 黎⁵】salute；extend one's greetings

敬意【ging³yi³ 薏】respect；tribute

敬而远之【ging³yi⁴yün⁵ji¹ 移软支】stay at a respectful distance from sb.

痉【ging⁶ 劲⁶】convulsion

痉挛【ging⁶lün⁴ 联】convulsion；spasm

矜【ging¹ 京】pity；self-important；re-served

矜持【ging¹qi⁴ 迟】restrained；reserved

矜贵【ging¹guei³ 桂】valuable = 【普】贵重

涩【gib⁸ 劫；xab⁸ 霎】puckery；unsmoo-th；difficult

劫【gib⁸ 涩】rob；plunder；coerce；calamity

劫持【gib⁸qi⁴ 迟】kidnap；hijack

劫夺【gib⁸düd⁹ 得月⁸】seize by force

劫掠【gib⁸lêg⁹ 略⁹】plunder；loot

劫数【gib⁸xou³ 扫】inexorable doom

夹业【gib⁹ 劫⁹】narrow；petty；crowd

窄业【jag⁸gib⁹】narrow；crowd = 【普】窄；挤迫

结【gid⁸ 洁】tie；knit；knot；congeal；settle；node

结合【gid⁸heb⁹ 盒】combine；be united in wedlock

结集【gid⁸jab⁹ 习】concentrate；mass

结成【gid⁸xing⁴ 诚】form

结构【gid⁸keo³ 购】structure；constru-ction；texture

结晶【gid⁸jing¹ 精】crystallize；crystal；crystallization

结交【gid⁸gao¹ 胶】make friends with

结识【gid⁸xig⁷ 色】get to know sb.

结伴【gid⁸bun⁶ 拌】go with

结盟【gid⁸meng⁴ 萌】form an alliance；ally

结恭【gid⁸gung⁷ 公】constipation = 【普】便秘

结仇【gid⁸xeo⁴ 愁】start a feud

结怨【gid⁸yün³ 原³】contract enmity

结婚【gid⁸fen¹ 分】marry；get married

结块【gid⁸fai³ 快】agglomerate；curdle

结冰【gid⁸bing¹ 兵】freeze；ice up

结核【gid⁸hed⁹ 辖】tuberculosis；nodule

结束【gid⁸qug⁷ 促】end；finish；conclude

结果【gid⁸guo² 戈²】result；outcome；kill

结尾【gid⁸mēi⁵ 美】ending；coda

结算【gid⁸xün³ 蒜】settle accounts

结帐【gid⁸jêng³ 涨】settle accounts

结党营私【gid⁸dong²ying⁴xi 挡盈司】form a clique to pursue selfish interests

洁【gid⁸ 结】clean

洁白【gid⁸bag⁹ 伯⁹】spotlessly white; pure white

洁净【gid⁸jing⁶ 静】clean; spotless

噏【gib⁷ 格叶⁷】a suitcase

噏纸【gib⁷ji² 子】artificial bullets used for toy-guns =【普】(玩具枪用的)纸子弹

噏帽【gib⁷mou² 务²】a cap∽【普】工人帽(帽篷上有钮扣的)

噏汁【gib⁷ jeb⁷ 执】ketchup; catchup =【普】番茄酱

挟【gib⁸ 劫；hib⁸ 协】to hold; coerce; harbour

挟制【gib⁸ jei³ 济】force sb. to do one's bidding

挟持【hib⁸ qi⁴迟】seize sb. on both sides by the arms; hold sb. under duress

桀【gid⁹ 杰】the name of the last ruler of the Xia Dynasty(c. 21st — c. 16th century B.C.)

桀骜不驯【gid⁹ngou⁴bed⁷xên⁴ 敖毕纯】stubborn and intractable

杰【gid⁹ 桀】outstanding; prominent; hero

杰出【gid⁹ qêd⁷次律⁷】outstanding; remarkable

杰作【gid⁹jog⁸ 昨】masterpiece

溁【gid⁹ 桀】dense; thick; great

溁嘅【gid⁹gē³ 格诶³】dense; strong; great =【普】浓的；稠的；重大的

击【gig⁷ 激】beat; hit; strike; attack; bump into

击中【gig⁷jung³ 纵³】hit

击破【gig⁷ po³ 颇³】break up; destroy; rout

击败【gig⁷bai⁶ 摆⁶】defeat; beat

击毙【gig⁷bei⁶ 敝】shoot dead

击沉【gig⁷qem⁴ 寻】bombard and sink

击落【gig⁷log⁹ 洛⁹】shoot down

击伤【gig⁷xêng¹ 双】wound(a person)

击退【gig⁷têu³ 腿³】beat back; repel

激【gig⁷ 击】swash; dash; arouse; sharp; fierce

激烈【gig⁷lid⁹ 列】intense; sharp; fierce

激化【gig⁷fa³ 花³】sharpen; intensify

激起【gig⁷hēi² 喜】arouse; stir up; evoke

激发【gig⁷fad⁹ 法】arouse; set off

激荡【gig⁷dong⁶ 当⁶】agitate; surge; rage

激动【gig⁷dung⁶ 洞】excite; stir; agitate

激昂【gig⁷ngong⁴ 额康⁴】excited and indignant

激奋【gig⁷fen⁵ 愤】be roused to action

激进【gig⁷jên³ 俊】radical

激怒【gig⁷nou⁶ 奴⁶】enrage; infuriate

激扬【gig⁷yêng⁴ 杨】encourage; urge

激励【gig⁷lei⁶ 厉】encourage; impel; drive

激光【gig⁷guong¹ 胱】〈n.〉laser

激素【gig⁷xou⁴ 数】〈n.〉hormone

激情【gig⁷qing⁴ 程】intense emotion; enthusiasm

隙【guig⁷ 姑益⁷】crack; chink; gap; loophole; discord

空隙【hung¹guig⁷ 凶】space; gap

仇隙【xeo⁴guig⁷ 愁】feud

戟【gig⁷ 击】halberd

亟【gig⁷ 击】urgently; anxiously; earnestly

极【gig⁹ 击⁹】the utmost point; extreme; pole; extremely; exceedingly; very

极地【gig⁹dēi⁶ 得菲⁶】polar region

极点【gig⁹ dim² 掂²】the limit; the extreme

极之【gig⁹ji¹ 支】extremely; very =【普】很; 极其

极端【gig⁹dün¹ 段¹】extreme; exceeding

极力【gig⁹lig⁹ 历】do one's utmost

极其【gig⁹kēi⁴ 期】most; very; extremely

极度【gig⁹dou⁶ 道】extreme; exceeding

极目【gig⁹ mug⁹ 木】look as far as the eye can see

极盛【gig⁹xing⁶ 剩】heyday; zenith

极限【gig⁹ han⁶ 悭⁶】the limit; the maximum

极权主义【gig⁹kün⁴jü²yi⁶ 拳⁴ 煮异】totalitarianism

极乐世界【gig⁹log⁹xei³gai³ 落细介】pure land; Western Paradise

涓
【gün¹ 娟】a tiny stream

涓涓【gün¹gün¹】trickling sluggishly

鹃
【gün¹ 娟】〈n.〉(see"杜鹃")

娟
【gün¹ 涓】beautiful; graceful

娟秀【gün¹xeo³ 瘦】beautiful; graceful

捐
【gün¹ 娟】relinquish; contribute; tax

捐款【gün¹ fun² 宽²】contribute money; contribution

捐献【gün¹ hin³ 宪】contribute; donate; present

捐弃【gün¹hēi³ 气】relinquish; abandon

捐躯【gün¹kêü¹ 驱】sacrifice one's life

绢
【gün¹ 娟】thin, tough silk

绢花【gün¹fa¹ 化¹】silk flower

卷
【gün² 眷²】roll up; roll; spool; volume

卷入【gün²yeb⁹ 挹⁹】be drawn into

卷筒【gün²tung⁴ 同】reel

卷烟【gün²yin¹ 胭】cigarette; cigar

卷发【gün²fad⁹ 法】curly hair; wavy hair

卷心菜【gün²xem¹qoi³ 深蔡】cabbage

卷扬机【gün²yêng⁴gēi¹ 杨基】hoist; hoister

卷宗【gün²jung¹ 中】folder; file

卷刃【gün² yen⁶孕】(of knife blade) be turned = 岎口【len²heo² 厚²】

卷土重来【gün²tou²qung⁴loi⁴ 讨从莱】stage a comeback

券
【gün³ 眷; hün³ 劝】certificate; ticket

眷
【gün³ 卷³】family dependant; have tender feeling for

眷恋【gün³ lün² 联²】be sentimentally attached to(a person or place)

眷属【gün³xug⁶ 熟】family dependants

蹄
【gün³ 眷; gün¹ 娟】wriggle; squirm

蹄窿蹄罅【gün³lung¹gün³la³ 龙¹啦³】wriggle an exploit an advantage =【普】蠕动而钻缝隙

倦
【gün⁶ 卷⁶】weary; tired

倦怠【gün⁶toi⁵ 台⁵】tired and idle

锯
【gê³ 格靴³; gêü³ 句】saw; cut with a saw

锯条【gê³tiu⁴ 挑⁴】saw blade

锯齿【gê³qi² 耻】sawtooth

锯断【gê³tün⁵ 团⁵】saw to breaking

锯鼻【gê³bēi³ 备】be in love =【普】谈恋爱

居【gêü¹ 句¹】reside; live; house; occupy; claim; lay by

居住【gêü¹jü⁶ 煮⁶】live; reside; dwell

居民【gêü¹men⁴ 文】resident; inhabitant

居留【gêü¹leo⁴ 流】reside

居功【gêü¹gung¹ 公】claim credit for oneself

居心【gêü¹ xem¹ 深】harbour（evil）intentions

居然【gêü¹ yin⁴ 言】〈ad.〉unexpectedly; go so far as to

居高临下【gêü¹gou¹lem⁴ha⁶ 羔林夏】occupy a commanding position

居安思危【gêü¹ngon¹xi¹ngei⁴ 桉司巍】be prepared for danger in times of peace

举【gêü² 矩】lift; hold up; act; start; elect; cite whole

举行【gêü²heng⁴ 衡】hold（a meeting, ceremony, etc.）

举办【gêü²ban⁶ 板⁶】conduct; hold; run

举动【gêü² dung⁶洞】movement; move; act

举手【gêü²xeo² 守】put up one's hand

举荐【gêü²jin³ 箭】recommend（a person）

举例【gêü²lei⁶ 厉】give an example

举目【gêü²mug⁶ 木】raise the eyes; look

举重【gêü²qung⁶ 虫⁵】weight lifting

举世【gêü²xei³ 细】throughout the world

举棋不定【gêü²kêi⁴bed⁷ding⁶ 奇 毕 锭】hesitate about what move to make

举足轻重【gêü²jug⁷hing¹qung⁵ 竹兴¹ 虫⁵】hold the balance

矩【gêü² 举】square; rules; moment

矩形【gêü²ying⁴ 型】rectangle

矩臂【gêü²bêi³ 秘】moment arm

踽【gêü² 举】alone

踽踽独行【gêü²gêü²dug⁹heng⁴ 毒衡】walk alone

龋【gêü² 举】〈n.〉龋齿【gêü²qi² 耻】decayed tooth

据【gêü³ 句】occupy; seize; rely on; according to; evidence

据点【gêü³dim² 掂²】strongpoint; stronghold

据守【gêü³xeo² 手】guard; be entrenched in

据此【gêü³qi² 始】on these grounds; accordingly

据说【gêü³xüd⁸ 雪】it is said; they say; allegedly

据悉【gêü³xig⁷ 识】it is reported

踞【gêü³ 据】crouch; squat; sit

倨【gêü³ 据】haughty; arrogant

遽【gêü⁶ 巨】hurriedly; frightened

遽然【gêü⁶yin⁴ 言】suddenly; abruptly

巨【gêü⁶ 具】huge; tremendous; gigantic

巨大【gêü⁶ dai⁶歹⁶】huge; tremendous; enormous

巨额【gêü⁶ngag⁹ 我客⁹】a huge sum

巨人【gêü⁶yen⁴ 仁】giant; colossus

巨星【gêü⁶xing¹ 升】giant star; giant

巨头【gêü⁶teo⁴ 投】magnate; tycoon

巨著【gêü⁶jü³ 注】monumental work

具【gêü⁶ 巨】utensil; tool; possess; have; provide

具有【gêü⁶ yeo⁵ 友】possess; have; be provided with

具备【gêü⁶bēi⁶ 鼻】= possess
具结【gêü⁶gid⁸ 洁】sign an undertaking
具体【gêü⁶tei² 睇】concrete; specific; particular

惧 【gêü⁶ 巨】fear; dread

惧怕【gêü⁶pa³ 爬³】fear; dread
惧色【gêü⁶xig⁷ 式】a look of fear

炬 【gêü⁶ 巨】torch; fire

飓 【gêü⁶ 巨】〈n.〉飓风【gêü⁶fung¹ 丰】hurricane

句 【gêü³ 据】sentence

句子【gêü³ji² 止】sentence
句型【gêü³ying⁴ 形】sentence pattern
句法【gêü³ fad⁸ 发】 sentence structure; syntax
句读【gêü³deo⁶ 豆】sentences and phrases

姜 【gêng¹ 僵】①ginger ②a surname

姜片虫【gêng¹pin³qung⁴ 骗从】fasciolopsis
姜黄【gêng¹wong⁴ 王】turmeric

羌 【gêng¹ 姜】notopterygium

羌活【gêng¹ wud⁸ 乌阔⁹】notopterygium
羌族【gêng¹jug⁹ 俗】Qiang, an ancient nationality in China

僵 【gêng¹ 姜】stiff; numb; deadlocked

僵硬【gêng¹ngang⁶ 额罂⁶】stiff; rigid
僵化【gêng¹fa³ 花³】become rigid; ossify
僵持【gêng¹qi⁴ 迟】(of both parties)refuse to budge
僵局【gêng¹gug⁹ 焗】deadlock; impasse
僵尸【gêng¹xi¹ 思】corpse

疆 【gêng¹ 姜】boundary; border

疆土【gêng¹tou² 讨】territory
疆域【gêng¹wig⁹ 划益⁹】territory; domain
疆场【gêng¹qêng⁴ 祥】battlefield

缰 【gêng¹ 姜】〈n.〉缰绳【gêng¹xing⁴ 成】reins; halter

犟 【gêng⁶ 姜⁶】obstinate; stubborn; self-willed

脚 【gêg⁸ 格约⁸】foot; base; dregs; leg

脚板【gêg⁸ban² 版】sole(of the foot)= 脚掌【gêg⁸jêng²】
脚踭【gêg⁸jang¹ 支罌¹】heel =【普】脚跟
脚尖【gêg⁸jim¹ 沾】the tip of a toe; tiptoe
脚力【gêg⁸lig⁹ 历】strength of one's legs
脚步【gêg⁸bou⁶ 部】step; pace
脚趾【gêg⁸ji³ 止】toe
脚印【gêg⁸yen³ 忍³】footprint; footmark
脚本【gêg⁸bun² 苯】script; scenario
脚注【gêg⁸jü³ 著】footnote
脚踏车【gêg⁸dab⁹qē¹ 答⁹ 奢】bicycle
脚踏实地【gêg⁸dab⁹xed⁹dēi⁶ 答⁹ 失⁹ 得韮⁶】have one's feet planted on solid ground—earnest and down-to-earth
脚踏两头船【gêg⁸dab⁹lêng⁵teo⁴xün⁴ 答⁹ 俩投旋】straddle two boats—have a foot in either camp

颈 【gēng² 镜²】neck

颈项【gēng²hong⁶ 巷】neck
颈椎【gēng²jêü¹ 追】cervical vertebra
颈链【gēng² lin² 炼²】necklace =【普】项链
颈渴【gēng²hod⁹ 喝】thirsty =【普】口渴

颈巾【gēng² gen¹ 斤】a scarf ＝【普】脖子围巾

猄【gēng¹ 颈¹】〈n.〉黄猄【wong⁴ gēng¹】muntjac

镜【gēng³ 颈³】looking glass; mirror; lens; glass

镜子【gēng³ ji² 止】mirror; looking glass; glasses

镜片【gēng³ pin² 骗²】lens

镜头【gēng³ teo⁴ 投】camera lens; shot; scene

镜框【gēng³ kuang¹ 箍罂¹】picture frame

镜花水月【gēng³ fa¹ xêu² yüd⁹ 化¹ 穗² 越】flowers in a mirror or the moon in the water—an illusion

H

虘【ha^{1} 哈】bully; take advantage of

虘霸【ha^{1}ba^{3} 坝】bully; bully and humiliate; one who loves to bully others =【普】欺负；欺凌

哈【ha^{1} 虾】① breathe out (with the mouth open) ②〈*onomatopoeia*〉show smile or exclaim

哈哈笑【ha^{1} ha^{1} xiu^{3} 少^{3}】laughingly; with a laugh

哈哈镜【ha^{1} ha^{1} gēng^{3} 颈^{3}】distorting mirror

哈密瓜【ha^{1} med^{9} gua^{1} 勿寡^{1}】〈*n*.〉Hami melon

哈萨克【ha^{1} xad^{8} heg^{7} 杀黑】〈*n*.〉the Kazakhs

哈尔滨【ha^{1}yi^{5}ben^{1} 耳宾】〈*n*.〉Harbin

哈巴狗【ha^{1}ba^{1}geo^{2} 爸九】〈*n*.〉Pekinese (a breed of dog); toady; sycophant

哈腰【ha^{1}yiu^{1} 妖】bend one's back; stoop; bow

蛤【ha^{1} 虾; geb^{8} 急^{8}】〈*n*.〉蛤蟆【ha^{1}mou^{1} 毛^{1}】frog; toad; (see"蚧")

虾【ha^{1} 哈】shrimp; prawns

虾公【ha^{9} gung^{1} 功】shrimp; prawns =【普】虾子

虾米【ha^{1}mei^{5} 迷^{5}】small shrimps; shrimp meat =【普】虾仁；虾肉

虾干【ha^{1}gon^{1} 竿】dried shrimps

虾酱【ha^{1}jêng^{3} 涨】shrimp paste

虾饺【ha^{1} gao^{2} 搞】a dumpling with prawns as the ingredient =【普】虾肉饺子

虾笱【ha^{1} geo^{2} 九】a small cage used to catch prawns =【普】捕虾竹篓(虾子能进，不能出)

虾蝾【ha^{1}lad^{8} 捺】a type of small crabs =【普】小螃蟹(生于淡水)

虾兵蟹将【ha^{1}bing^{1}hai^{5}jêng^{3} 冰鞋^{5} 涨】shrimp soldiers and crab generals — ineffective troops

霞【ha^{4} 暇】rosy clouds; morning or evening glow

霞光【ha^{4}guong 胱】rays of morning or evening sunlight

暇【ha^{4} 霞】free time; leisure

遐【ha^{4} 霞】far; distant; lasting; long

遐迩【ha^{4}yi^{5} 耳】far and near

遐想【ha^{4}xêng^{2} 赏】reverie; daydream

瑕【ha^{4} 霞】flaw in a piece of jade; flaw; defect

瑕疵【ha^{4}qi^{1} 痴】flaw; blemish

瑕不掩瑜【ha^{4}bed^{7}yim^{2}yü^{4} 毕淹^{2} 鱼】one flaw cannot obscure the splendour of the jade — the defects cannot obscure the virtues

夏【ha^{6} 下】summer; an ancient name for China

夏季【ha⁶guei³ 桂】summer = 夏天【ha⁶tin¹ 田¹】

夏历【ha⁴ lig⁹力 】the traditional Chinese calendar

夏至【ha⁴ji³ 致】the Summer Solstice(10th solar term)

厦

【ha⁶ 下】a tall building; mansion

厦门【ha⁶mun⁴ 瞒】〈n.〉Xiamen(Amoy)

下

【ha⁶ 夏】below; down; lower; next; latter; descend; alight; fall; go to; exit; leave; apply; use; lay

下巴【ha⁶ba¹爸 】the lower jaw; chin = 下扒【ha⁶pa⁴】

下班【ha⁶ban¹ 斑】come or go off work; knock of

下边【ha⁶bin¹ 鞭】below; under; next = 下面【ha⁶min⁶】

下策【ha⁶qag⁸ 册】a bad plan

下层【ha⁶qeng⁴ 迟莺⁴】lower levels; lower strata

下场【ha⁶qêng⁴ 祥】exit; end; fate

下沉【ha⁶qem⁴ 寻】sink; subside

下垂【ha⁶ xêü⁴水⁴ 】hang down; droop; prolapse

下达【ha⁶dad⁹得压⁹】make known to lower levels

下等【ha⁶deng² 戥】low-grade; inferior

下毒手【ha⁶dug⁹xeo² 独守】strike a vicious blow

下风【ha⁶ fung¹ 丰 】leeward; disadvantageous position

下功夫【ha⁶gung¹fu¹ 工孚】put in time and energy

下怀【ha⁶wai⁴ 坏】one's heart's desire

下跪【ha⁶guei⁶ 馈】kneel down

下级【ha⁶keb⁷给】 lower level; subordi-nate

下降【ha⁶gong³ 钢】descend; go or come down

下贱【ha⁶jin⁶ 煎⁶】low; mean; degrading

下凡【ha⁶fan⁶ 烦】(of gods)descend to the world

下课【ha⁶fo³ 货】get out of class; finish class

下来【ha⁶loi⁴ 莱】come down

下列【ha⁶lid⁹ 裂】listed below; following

下令【ha⁶ling⁶ 另】give orders; order

下落【ha⁶log⁹ 洛⁹】whereabouts; drop; fall

下流【ha⁶ leo⁴ 留 】lower reaches; low-down; mean

下马【ha⁶ ma⁵码 】get down from a horse; discontinue(a project, etc.)

下棋【ha⁶kēi² 其²】play chess = 捉棋【jug⁷kēi²】

下去【ha⁶hêü³ 虚³】go down; descend; go on; continue = 落去【log⁹hêü³】

下手【ha⁶xeo² 守】put one's hand to = 落手【log⁹xeo²】

下属【ha⁶xug⁶ 熟】subordinate

下榻【ha⁶tad⁸ 挞⁸】stay (at a place during a trip)

下台【ha⁶ toi⁴ 抬 】step down from the stage; fall out of power; leave office = 落台【log⁹toi⁴】

下午【ha⁶ng⁵ 五】afternoon

下乡【ha⁶hêng¹ 香】go to the countryside

下游【ha⁶ yeo⁴ 油 】lower reaches (of a river); backward position

下肢【ha⁶ji¹ 支】lower limbs; legs

下意识【ha⁶ji³xig³ 薏色】subconsciousness

下里巴人【ha⁶lēi⁵ba¹yen⁴ 理爸仁】Song of the Rustic Poor(a folk song of

the state of Chu）；popular literature of art

下下【ho⁶ ho²】everytime ＝【普】每时每
刻；经常

下便【ho⁶ bin⁶ 辨】＝下底【ho⁶ dei² 抵】
bottom ＝【普】下边；下面

下晏【ho⁶ngan³ 雁】＝下昼【ho⁶jeo³ 皱】
afternoon ＝【普】下午

下间【ho⁶gan¹ 奸】kitchen ＝【普】厨房；
灶间

下栏【ho⁶lan⁴ 兰】the left-over food；extra
income ＝【普】下脚料；下等的

揩
【hai¹ 鞋¹】to touch；wipe

揩干净【hai¹gon¹jēng⁶ 竿郑】wipe clean

揩油水【hai¹ yeo⁴ xêü² 由瑞²】profit at
other people's expense；favour-
able ＝【普】占便宜

鞋
【hai⁴ 孩】shoes

鞋底【hai⁴dei² 抵】sole(of a shoe)

鞋带【hai⁴dai³ 戴】shoelace；shoestring

鞋垫【hai⁴din³ 电³】shoe-pad；insole

鞋踭【hai⁴jang¹ 支罂¹】heel(of a shoe) ＝
【普】鞋跟

鞋刷【hai⁴qad⁸ 察】shoe brush

鞋油【hai⁴yeo² 有²】shoe polish

嶰
【hai⁴ 鞋】〈a.〉嶰熠熠【hai⁴xab⁹xab⁹】
rough；not smooth ＝【普】粗糙；不光
滑

谐
【hai⁴ 鞋】in harmony；settle；humor-
ous

谐和【hai⁴ wo⁴ 禾】harmonious；concor-
dant

谐谑【hai⁴yêg⁹ 若】banter

谐音【hai⁴yem¹ 钦】homophonic；partials

谐振【hai⁴jen³ 震】resonance

偕
【hai⁴ 鞋；gai¹ 阶】together with；in
the company of

偕老【hai⁴lou¹ 鲁】husband and wife grow
old together

偕同【hai⁴tung⁴ 童】in the company of；a-
long with

孩
【hai⁴ 鞋】child

孩子【hai⁴ji² 止】child；son or daughter；
children ＝细佬哥【xei³lou²go¹】＝
细佬仔【xei³men¹jei²】

孩提【hai⁴tei² 堤】early childhood；infan-
cy

孩子气【hai⁴ji²hēi³ 止戏】childishness

骸
【hai⁴ 鞋】bones of the body；body

骸骨【hai⁴gued⁷ 掘⁷】human bones；skele-
ton

咳
【hai¹ 揩；ked⁷ 卡乞¹】①〈int.〉
Damnit! ②cough

咳嗽【ked⁷xeo³ 秀】cough

蟹
【hai⁵ 鞋⁵】crab

蟹黄【hai⁵wong⁴ 王】the ovary and diges-
tive glands of a crab

懈
【hai⁶ 械】slack；lax

懈怠【hai⁶toi² 台²】slack；sluggish

邂
【hai⁶ 械】meet unexpectedly

邂逅【hai⁶ heo⁶ 后】meet (a relative,
friend, etc.) unexpectedly；run
into sb.

瀣
【hai⁶ 械】〈a.〉沆瀣一气【hong⁴hai⁶
yed⁷hēi³】act in collusion with；like
attracts like

械【hai⁶ 懈】tool; instrument; weapon; fetters

械斗【hai⁶ deo³ 豆³】fight with weapons between groups of people

敲【hao¹ 烤¹】knock; beat; strike; overcharge

敲打【hao¹da² 得阿²】beat; rap; tap

敲诈【hao¹ ja³炸】extort; blackmail; racketeer

敲门砖【hao¹mun⁴jün¹ 瞒专】a stepping-stone to success

敲竹杠【hao¹jug⁷gong³ 足钢】take advantage of sb.'s being in a weak position to overcharge him; fleece

敲骨吸髓【hao¹gued⁷keb⁷xêü⁵ 掘⁷级穗】suck the lifeblood

骇【hai⁵ 蟹】be shocked

烤【hao¹ 敲; hao² 考】bake; roast; scorching

烤炉【hao¹lou⁴ 卢】oven

烤火【hao¹fo² 伙】warm oneself by a fire

烤肉【hao¹yug⁹ 玉】roast meat; roast = 叉烧【qa¹xiu¹】

烤面包【hao¹min⁶bao¹ 免⁶ 胞】toast

吼【hao¹ 敲; heo³ 口³】roar; howl

考【hao² 巧】give or take an examination, test or quiz; check; study; verify

考查【hao²qa⁴ 茶】examine

考察【hao²qad⁸ 刷】inspect; observe and study

考核【hao²hed⁹ 辖】examine; check; assess

考究【hao² geo³够 】observe and study; fastidious; exquisite; fine

考勤【hao²ken⁴ 芹】check on work attendance

考试【hao²xi³ 市³】examination; test

考题【hao²tei⁴ 提】examination question

考卷【hao²gün² 眷】examination paper

考虑【hao²lêü⁶ 泪】think over; consider

考验【hao²yim⁶ 艳】test; trial

考证【hao²jing³ 正】textual criticism

巧【hao² 考】skilful; cunning; opportunely

巧妙【hao²miu⁶ 庙】ingenious; clever

巧计【hao²gei³ 继】clever device

巧合【hao²heb⁹ 盒】coincidence

巧遇【hao²yü⁶ 预】chance encounter

巧手【hao²xeo² 守】a dab hand

巧干【hao²gon³ 竿³】work ingeniously

巧克力【hao²heg⁷lig⁹ 黑历】chocolate

巧夺天工【hao²düd⁹tin¹gung¹ 得月⁹田¹公】wonderful workmanship excelling nature

巧妇难为无米之炊【hao²fu⁵nan⁴wei⁴mou⁴mei⁵ji¹qêü¹ 富⁵挪晏⁴围毛迷⁵支吹】one can't make bricks without straw

拷【hao² 考】flog; beat; torture

拷打【hao²da² 得阿²】flog; beat; torture

拷问【hao² men⁶ 文⁶】torture sb. during interrogation

拷贝【hao²bui³ 背】⟨n.⟩copy

孝【hao³ 考³】filial piety; mourning

孝敬【hao³ging³ 劲】give presents(to one's elders or superiors)

孝顺【hao³xên³ 信⁶】show filial obedience

孝子贤孙【hao³ji²yin⁴xün¹ 止言酸】worthy progeny; true son

婑　【hao⁴ 孝⁴】sexy ∽【普】女性的卖弄
　　风骚
婑 婆【hao⁴po⁴ 破⁴】the woman who
　　shows off coquettish ∽【普】卖弄
　　风情的女人

效　【hao⁶ 考⁶】effect；imitate；render（a
　　service）
效法【hao⁶tad⁸ 发】follow the example of；
　　learn from
效果【hao⁶guo² 过²】effect；sound effects
效劳【hao⁶lou⁴ 炉】work in the service of
效力【hao⁶lig⁹ 历】render a service to；ef-
　　fect
效率【hao⁶lêd⁹ 律】efficiency
效能【hao⁶neng⁴ 挪鸾⁴】efficacy；useful-
　　ness
效益【hao⁶yig⁷ 忆】beneficial result；bene-
　　fit
效应【hao⁶ying³ 英³】effect
效忠【hao⁶jung¹ 中】pledge loyalty to

校　【hao⁶ 效；gao³ 较】school；field offi-
　　cer；check；proofread；compare
校舍【hao⁶ xê³ 泻】schoolhouse；school
　　building
校园【hao⁶yün⁴ 元】campus；school yard
校长【hao⁶ jêng² 蒋】headmaster；presi-
　　dent
校友【hao⁶yeo⁵ 有】alumnus or alumna
校风【hao⁶fung¹ 丰】school spirit
校外【hao⁶ngoi⁶ 碍】outside school；after
　　school
校对【gao³dêu³ 队³】proofread；proofrea-
　　der；check against a standard；
　　calibrate
校勘【gao³hem¹ 堪】collate
校正【gao³jing³ 政】proofread and correct
校样【gao³yêng² 扬²】proof sheet；proof

哮　【hao¹ 敲】heavy breathing；roar；
　　howl
哮喘【hao¹qün² 串²】asthma

喊　【ham³ 咸³】shout；call；cry；weep
喊叫【ham³giu³ 娇³】shout；cry out
喊冤叫屈【ham³yün¹giu³wed⁷ 渊娇³
　　核⁷】cry out about one's grievan-
　　ces
喊包【ham³bao¹ 胞】children who like to
　　cry＝【普】爱哭的小孩
喊苦喊弗【ham³fu²ham³fed⁷ 府拂】end-
　　lessly weep and wail ＝【普】哭哭
　　啼啼

馅　【ham² 咸²；ham⁶ 咸⁶】filling；stuffing
馅饼【ham⁶bēng² 柄²】meat pie

咸　【ham⁴ 函】salted；salty；all
咸水【ham⁴xêü² 瑞²】salt water
咸肉【ham⁴yug⁹ 玉】salt meat；bacon
咸菜【ham⁴qoi³ 蔡】salted vegetables；pi-
　　ckles
咸虾【ham⁴ha¹ 哈】prawn sauce ∽【普】
　　虾酱
咸煎饼【ham⁴jin¹bēng² 战¹柄²】a type of
　　biscuit
咸赧赧【ham⁴nan⁵nan⁵ 难⁵难⁵】salty；bit-
　　ter＝【普】咸味浓烈
咸虫【ham⁴ qung⁴ 从】one who is dirty-
　　minded ＝【普】卑鄙、下流、猥亵
　　的人
咸粒【ham⁴neb⁷ 挪合⁷】eczema on the skin
　　＝【普】皮肤湿疹
咸湿【ham⁴ xeb⁷ 拾⁷】dirty-minded ＝
　　【普】下流猥亵的色情性挑逗

函【ham⁴ 咸】case; envelope; letter

函件【ham⁴ gin² 健²】letters; correspondence

函购【ham⁴ keo³ 构】purchase by mail; mail order

函授【ham⁴ xeo⁶ 受】teach by correspondence

函数【ham⁴ xou³ 扫】function

涵【ham⁴ 咸】contain; culvert

涵洞【ham⁴ dung⁶ 动】culvert

涵养【ham⁴ yêng⁵ 氧】ability to control oneself; conserve

衔【ham⁴ 咸】hold in the mouth; hear; rank

衔接【ham⁴ jib⁸ 支叶⁸】link up; join

衔冤【ham⁴ yūn 渊】nurse a bitter sense of wrong

陷【ham⁶ 咸⁶】pitfall; get stuck or bogged down; sink; frame(up); fall; defect

陷阱【ham⁴ jēng² 井】pitfall; pit; trap

陷害【ham⁴ hoi⁶ 亥】frame(up)

陷落【ham⁴ log⁹ 洛⁹】subside; fall into enemy hands

陷入【ham⁴ yeb⁹ 邑⁹】sink into; be lost in

槛【ham⁵ 函⁵】threshold; banisters

悭【han¹ 闲¹】stingy; to be thrifty; to save up

悭吝【han¹ lên⁶ 论】stingy; miserly

悭俭【han¹ gim⁶兼⁶】to be thrifty = 悭皮【han¹pēi² 脾²】=【普】舍不得花钱而节约、节俭

闲【han⁴ 娴】not busy; idle; not in use; leisure

闲人【han⁴yen⁴ 仁】idler; persons not concerned

闲事【han⁴ xi⁶是 】a matter that does not concern one; unimportant matter

闲散【han⁴ xan² 汕²】free and at leisure; unused

闲居【han⁴gêü¹ 据¹】stay at home idle

闲话【han⁴wo⁶ 华⁶】digression; complaint

闲谈【han⁴tam⁴ 谭】chat; engage in chitchat

闲暇【han⁴ha⁴ 霞】leisure; spare time

闲心【han⁴xem¹ 深】leisurely mood

闲置【han⁴ji³ 至】leave unused; set aside

闲闲地【han⁴han⁴dēi² 得菲²】easy jobs; easy; easily =【普】随随便便的; 一般的

闲情逸致【han⁴qing⁴yed⁹ji³ 程日至】leisurely and carefree mood

娴【han⁴ 闲】refined; adept; skilled

娴静【han⁴jing⁶ 净】gentle and refined

娴熟【han⁴xug⁹ 属】adept; skilled

娴雅【han⁴nga⁵ 瓦】(of a woman) refined; elegant

痫【han⁴ 闲; gan² 简】epilepsy

限【han⁶ 闲⁶】limit; bounds; set a limit

限定【han⁶ ding⁶锭 】prescribe a limit to; limit

限度【han⁶dou⁶ 道】limit; limitation

限额【han⁶ngag⁹ 我客⁹】norm; limit; quota

限量【han⁶lêng⁶ 谅】limit the quantity of

限期【han⁶kēi⁴ 其】within a definite time; time limit; deadline

限于【han⁶yū¹ 迂】be confined to; be limited to

限制【hon⁶ jei³ 济】restrict；limit；confine

坑【hang¹ 夯】hole；pit；tunnel；entrap；cheat

坑道【hang¹ dou⁶ 度】gallery；tunnel

坑害【hang¹ hoi⁶ 亥 】lead into a trap；entrap

坑坑洼洼【hang¹ hang¹ wa¹ wa¹ 娃娃】full of bumps and hollows；bumpy；rough

夯【hang¹ 坑】rammer；ram；tamp

夯土机【hang¹ tou² gēi¹ 讨基】rammer；tamper

行【①hang⁴ 坑⁴；②heng⁴ 衡；③hong⁴ 杭；④heng⁶ 幸】① go；travel ② do；perform；soon；all right；OK.；capable ③line；row；trade；business firm ④behaviour；conduct

品行【ben² heng⁶ 幸】character

行路【hang⁴ lou⁶ 露】to walk =【普】走路

行街【hang⁴ gai¹ 皆】shopping =【普】逛街

行开【hang⁴ hoi¹ 海¹】to be away =【普】走开；滚开

行雷【hang⁴ lēū⁴ 擂】to have thunderstorm =【普】打雷

行运【hang⁴ wen⁶ 温⁶】be lucky =【普】走运

行人路【hang⁴ yen⁴ lou⁶ 仁露】pedestrian crossings

行时【heng⁴ xi⁴ 是⁴】（of a thing）be in vogue

行销【heng⁴ xiu¹ 消】be on sale；sell

行使【heng⁴ xei² 洗】exercise；perform

行事【heng⁴ xi⁶ 士】act；handle；behaviour

行为【heng⁴ wei⁴ 维】action；conduct

行政【heng⁴ jing³ 正】administration

行善【heng⁴ xin⁶ 膳】do good works

行凶【heng⁴ hung¹ 空】commit physical assault or murder；do violence

行刑【heng⁴ ying⁴ 形 】 carry out a death sentence

行李【heng⁴ lēi⁵ 理】luggage；baggage

行动【heng⁴ dung⁶ 洞】 move about；act；take action

行礼【heng⁴ lei⁵ 黎⁵】salute

行将【heng⁴ jêng¹ 张 】 about to；on the verge of

行径【heng⁴ ging³ 劲】act；move

行刺【heng⁴ qi³ 次】assassinate

行不通【heng⁴ bed⁷ tung¹ 毕同¹】won't do；get nowhere ＝ 行唔通【hang⁴ m⁴ tung¹】

行之有效【heng⁴ ji¹ yeo⁵ hao⁶ 支友孝⁶】effective；effectual

行业【hong⁴ yib⁹ 叶】trade；profession

行会【hong⁴ wui² 汇²】guild

行规【hong⁴ kuei¹ 亏】guild regulations

行情【hong⁴ qing⁴ 程】quotations；prices

行长【hong⁴ jêng² 蒋】president（of a bank）

行家【hong⁴ ga¹ 加】expert；connoisseur

行话【hong⁴ wa⁶ 画⁶】jargon；cant

行当【hong⁴ dong³ 档⁶】trade；profession

行列【hong⁴ lid⁹ 裂⁹】ranks

行距【hong⁴ kêū⁵ 拒】row spacing

荚【hab⁸ 呷】the leaf of the taros or vegetables

呷【hab⁸ 荚】to have a sip

呷醋【hab⁸ qou³ 措】to refer to the jealousy between a man-woman relationship ∽【普】妒忌；嫉妒

匣【hab⁹ 峡】a small box（or case）；casket

狎【hab⁹ 峡】be improperly familiar with

峡【hab⁹ 匣】gorge

峡谷【hab⁹gug⁷ 菊】gorge；canyon

狭【hab⁹ 匣】narrow

狭隘【hab⁹ngai³ 艾³】narrow；parochial
狭窄【hab⁹jag⁸ 责】narrow；cramped
狭义【hab⁹yi⁶ 异】narrow sense

侠【hab⁹ 匣】chivalrous

侠客【hab⁹hag⁸ 赫】a person adept in mar-
　　tial arts and given to chivalrous
　　conduct(in olden times)
侠义【hab⁹yi⁶ 异】having a strong sense of
　　justice and ready to help the weak

客【hag⁸ 吓】visitor； traveller；
　　customer；objective
客体【hag⁸tei² 睇】object
客观【hag⁸gun¹ 官】objective
客气【hag⁸hēi³ 汽】polite；courteous；mo-
　　dest
客人【hag⁸yen⁴ 仁】visitor；guest
客套【hag⁸tou³ 吐】polite formula；civili-
　　ties
客车【hag⁸qē¹ 奢】passenger train；bus
客店【hag⁸dim³ 点³】inn＝客栈【hag⁸jan²】
客房【hag⁸fong⁶ 防】guest room
客家【hag⁸ga¹ 加】the Hakkas

吓【hag⁹ 客】frighten；scare；intimidate

吓唬【hag⁹fu² 虎】frighten；scare；intimi-
　　date
吓窒【hag⁸ jed⁸ 侄】 to be so scared that
　　one is stunned＝【普】吓退；吓倒
吓亲【hag⁸qen¹ 趁¹】be frightened＝【普】

　　　受惊
吓破胆【hag⁸po³dam² 婆³ 担²】be scared
　　out fo one's wits

赫【hag⁸ 客】conspicuous；grand；hertz

赫赫【hag⁸hag⁸】illustrious；very impres-
　　sive
赫然【hag⁸ yin⁴ 言】impressively； terribly
　　(angry)
赫兹【hag⁸ji¹ 支】〈n．〉hertz

肹【hei¹ 系¹】〈vulgar language〉
　　woman's pudenda

嚟【hei² 系²】exist；be living；in；at＝
　　【普】在

嚟度【hei²dou⁶ 道】be on the scene；be on
　　the spot；be present＝【普】在场

兮【hei⁴ 奚】〈auxil．〉∽ 啊(see"啊")

奚【hei⁴ 兮】why；how；where；what

奚落【hei⁴log⁹ 洛⁹】scoff at；taunt；gibe

系【hei⁶ 兮⁶】①tie；fasten；system；de-
　　partment；faculty；relate to；feel anx-
　　ious；②be(is，am，are)＝【普】是
系词【hei⁶qi⁴ 迟】copula；copulative verb
系列【hei⁶lid⁹ 裂】series；set
系数【hei⁶xou³ 扫】coefficient
系统【hei⁶tung² 桶】system；systematic
系念【hei⁶nim⁶ 粘⁶】be anxious about
系留【hei⁶leo⁴ 流】moor(a balloon or air-
　　ship)
系啦【hei⁶ la³】＝系嘅【hei⁶ gē³】yes＝
　　【普】是的；对的
系噉【hei⁶gem² 锦】yes；it is this＝【普】
　　是这样

瞭【heo¹ 后¹】like；fix one's eyes on；to
　　woo ∽【普】盯着；想占有；喜欢；

追求

瞅住晒【heo¹jū⁶xɑi³ 著⁶ 徙³】fix one's eyes on; to keep an eye on＝【普】紧盯着

瞅佢【heo¹kêū⁵ 拒】like him＝【普】喜欢他

口【heo² 候²】mouth; opening; entrance

口腔【heo²hong¹ 康】oral cavity

口唇【heo²xên⁴ 纯】lips

口舌【heo²xid⁸ 泄】quarrel; talking round

口气【heo²hēi³ 戏】tone; note

口吻【heo²men⁵ 敏】muzzle; tone; note

口音【heo² yem¹ 钦】oral speech sounds; voice

口味【heo²mēi⁶ 未】a person's taste

口是心非【heo²xi⁶xem¹fēi¹ 士深菲】say yes and mean no

口齿【heo²qi² 始】trustworthiness

口头【heo²teo⁴ 投】oral

口角【heo²gog⁸ 觉】quarrel; bicker

口诀【heo²küd⁸ 决】a pithy formula(often in rhyme)

口才【heo²qoi⁴ 财】eloquence

口述【heo²xêd⁹ 术】oral account

口授【heo²xeo⁶ 受】oral instruction; dictate

口试【heo²xi³ 诗³】oral examination; oral test

口令【heo² ling⁶ 另 】word of command; password

口号【heo²hou⁶ 好⁶】slogan; watchword

口供【heo²gung¹ 公】a statement made by the accused under examination

口袋【heo²doi⁶ 代】pocket

口岸【heo²ngon⁶ 安⁶】port

口语【heo²yü⁵ 雨】spoken language

口蜜腹剑【heo²med⁹fug⁷gim³ 勿福俭³】honey-mouthed and daggerhearted; hypocritical and malignant

口痕【heo²hen⁴ 很⁴】talkative＝【普】多嘴

口多多【heo²do¹do¹ 朵¹】talkative; like to gossip＝【普】多嘴；喜欢抢白

口花花【heo²fɑ¹fɑ¹ 化¹】talkative; like to tease others＝【普】多嘴；爱说没准的话

口水花【heo²xêü²fɑ¹ 瑞² 化¹】saliva

口疏【heo²xo¹ 梳】one who cannot keep a secret＝【普】不能保密；走漏风声

口窒窒【heo²jed⁹jed⁹ 侄】unable to speak fluently＝【普】口吃；说话吞吞吐吐

喉【heo⁴ 侯】larynx; throat

喉咙【heo⁴lung⁴ 龙】throat

喉舌【heo⁴xid⁸ 泄】mouthpiece

喉急【heo⁴geb⁷ 格合⁷】impatient＝【普】没耐性；急于从事

侯【heo⁴ 喉】marquis; a nobleman or a high official

侯爵【heo⁴jêg⁸ 桌】marquis

猴【heo⁴ 侯】monkey; clever boy; smart chap

猴子【heo⁴ji² 止】monkey＝犸㹬【mɑ⁵leo¹ 马留¹】

猴戏【heo⁴hēi³ 气】monkey show＝犸㹬戏【mɑ⁵leo¹hēi³】

厚【heo⁵ 候⁵】thick; deep; kind; large; favour

厚薄【heo⁵bog⁹ 泊】thickness

厚度【heo⁵dou⁶ 道】thickness

厚道【heo⁵dou⁶ 导】honest and kind

厚望【heo⁵mong⁶ 亡⁶】great expectations

厚意【heo⁵yi³ 薏】kind thought；kindness

厚脸皮【heo⁵lim⁵pēi⁴ 殓脾】thick-skinned；brazen；cheeky = 面皮厚【min⁶pēi⁴heo⁵】

厚颜无耻【heo⁵ngan⁴mou⁴qi² 雁⁴ 毛始】impudent

候
【heo⁶ 后】wait；await；inquire after；time

候诊【heo⁶qen² 疹】wait to see the doctor

候审【heo⁶xem² 姊】await trial

候鸟【heo⁶niu⁵ 挪妖⁵】migratory bird；migrant

候选人【heo⁶xūn²yen⁴ 损仁】candidate

候镬【heo⁶wog⁹ 获】chef；cook = 【普】厨师

后
【heo⁶ 候】behind；after；offspring；empress

后面【heo⁶min⁶ 免⁶】at the back；behind；later

后者【heo⁶jē² 姐】the latter

后退【heo⁶tēū³ 推³】draw back；fall back；retreat

后来【heo⁶loi⁴ 莱】afterwards；later

后进【heo⁶ jēn³俊】lagging behind；backward

后方【heo⁶fong⁶ 芳】rear

后顾【heo⁶gu³ 固】turn back；look back

后果【heo⁶ guo² 过²】consequence；aftermath

后患【heo⁶wan⁶ 宦】future trouble

后悔【heo⁶fui³ 晦】regret；repent

后路【heo⁶lou⁶ 露】route of retreat；a way of escape

后门【heo⁶ mun⁴ 瞒】back door；backdoor influence

后备【heo⁶bēi⁶ 避】reserve

后半【heo⁶ bun³ 伴³】 latter half；second half

后继【heo⁶gei³ 计】succeed；carry on

后世【heo⁶xei³ 细】later ages

后台【heo⁶ toi⁴抬】 backstage；backstage supporter

后年【heo⁶nin⁴ 捻⁴】the year after next

后日【heo⁶ yed⁹逸 】the day after tomorrow = 【普】后天

后妈【heo⁶ma¹ 吗】stepmother = 【普】后娘

后裔【heo⁶yêū⁶ 锐】descendant；offspring

后底嬷【heo⁶dei²na² 抵那²】stepmother = 【普】后娘

后边【heo⁶bin¹ 鞭；heo⁶bin⁶ 便】the back；at the back = 【普】后面

后生【heo⁶xang¹ 是罂¹】young = 【普】年青人；年青

后生仔【heo⁶xang¹jei² 济²】young boys = 【普】小伙子

后生女【heo⁶xang¹nêū⁵ 挪去⁵】young girls = 【普】姑娘

逅
【heo⁶ 后】(see "邂逅")

堪
【hem¹ 勘】may；can；bear；endure

堪称佳作【hem¹qing¹gai¹jog⁸ 清皆昨】may be rated as a good piece of writing

勘
【hem¹ 堪】collate；investigate；survey

勘测【hem¹qag⁷ 策⁷】survey

勘探【hem¹tam³ 谈³】exploration；prospecting

勘误【hem¹ng⁶ 悟】correct errors in printing

戡
【hem¹ 堪】suppress

戡乱【hem¹ lün⁶ 联⁶】suppress a rebellion

砍
【hem² 勘²】cut; chop; throw sth. at

砍伐【hem² fed⁹ 佛】fell (trees)

砍头【hem² teo⁴ 投】chop off the head; behead

龕
【hem¹ 堪】niche; shrine

坎
【hem² 砍】bank; ridge; pit; hole

坎坷【hem² ho² 可】bumpy; rough; full of frustrations

磡
【hem³ 砍³】cliff =【普】山崖

嵌
【hem³ 磡; hem⁶ 砍⁶】inlay; embed; set

含
【hem⁴ 坎⁴】keep in the mouth; contain; nurse

含量【hem⁴ lêng⁶ 亮】content

含义【hem⁴ yi⁶ 异】meaning; implication

含混【hem⁴ wen⁶ 运】indistinct; ambiguous

含糊【hem⁴ wu⁴ 胡】ambiguous; careless

含笑【hem⁴ xiu³ 少³】have a smile on one's face

含羞【hem⁴ xeo¹ 修】with a shy look; bashfully

含蓄【hem⁴ qug⁷ 促】contain; implicit; reserved

含冤【hem⁴ yün¹ 渊】suffer a wrong

含怨【hem⁴ yüu³ 渊³】bear a grudge

含情脉脉【hem⁴ qing⁴ meg⁹ meg⁹程 麦】(soft eyes) exuding tenderness and love

含沙射影【hem⁴ xa¹ xê⁶ ying² 莎舍⁶ 映】attack by innuendo; make insinuations

焓
【hem⁴ 含】the fire is vigorous; fierce

焓焓声【hem⁴ hem² xēng¹ 腥】to describe that there are a lot; fierce =【普】火势猛烈；运行快

冚
【hem⁶ 憾; kem² 琴²】tightly closed; all; whole

冚住【kem² jü⁶ 著⁶】cover; closed =【普】盖着；封闭

冚唪呤【hem⁶ bang⁶ lang⁶ 波硬⁶ 冷⁶】all; everything =【普】全部；所有

冚的【hem⁶ did⁷ 得热⁷】all =【普】合把那；全部；通通；统统；所有的

冚家铲【hem⁶ ga¹ qan² 加产】a nasty word used to scold others, it means "go to hell!" ∽【普】满门死尽、灭绝；合家遭殃 (骂人的话)

冚盅【hem⁶ jung¹ 中】a container with cover used to keep sweets, sugar or salt =【普】有盖的小瓦缸或瓷缸

憾
【hem⁶ 含⁶】regret

憾事【hem⁶ xi⁶ 士】a matter for regret

撼
【hem⁶ 憾】shake

撼动【hem⁶ dung⁶ 洞】shake; vibrate

憨
【hem¹ 堪】foolish; straightforward; naive

憨厚【hem¹ heo⁵ 后⁵】straightforward and good-natured

憨直【hem¹ jig⁹ 值】honest and straightforward

憨笑【hem¹ xiu³ 少³】smile fatuously; simper

颔
【hem⁵ 含⁵; ngeb⁹ 额合⁹】chin; nod

颔首【hem⁵ xeo² 守】nod = 岌头【ngeb⁹

teo⁴】＝【普】点头

很【hen² 狠】〈ad.〉very; quite; awfully

很好【hen²hou² 号²】very good

狠【hen² 很】ruthless; firm; resolute

狠毒【hen²dug⁹ 独】vicious; venomous
狠心【hen²xem¹ 深】cruel-hearted; heartless

恳【hen² 很】earnestly; sincerely; request

恳切【hen²qid⁸ 设】earnest; sincere
恳请【hen²qing² 程²】earnestly request
恳求【hen²keo⁴ 球】implore; entreat; beseech

垦【hen² 很】cultivate(land); reclaim

垦荒【hen²fong¹ 方】reclaim wasteland

亨【heng¹ 哼】go smoothly; henry

亨通【heng¹tung¹ 同¹】go smoothly
亨利【heng¹lēi⁶ 俐】〈n.〉henry

哼【heng¹ 亨】groan; snort; hum; croon

哼声【heng¹xēng¹ 腥】hum

铿【heng¹ 亨】〈onomatopoeia〉clang; clatter

铿锵【heng¹qēng¹ 昌】ring; clang

揨【heng¹ 亨】to knock; smash; break

揨烂【heng¹lan⁶ 栏⁶】smash ＝【普】打碎

肯【heng² 啃】agree; consent; be willing to

肯定【heng²ding⁶ 锭】affirm; confirm; definite
肯济【heng² jei³ 际】be willing; wish ＝【普】愿意

啃【heng² 肯】gnaw; nibble

啃骨头【heng²gued⁷teo⁴ 掘⁷ 投】gnaw a bone

衡【heng⁴ 行】the graduated arm of a steelyard; weighing apparatus; weigh; judge

衡器【heng⁴hēi³ 气】weighing apparatus
衡量【heng⁴lêng⁴ 梁】weigh; measure; judge

桁【heng⁴ 衡】purlin

桁架【heng⁴ga³ 嫁】truse

恒【heng⁴ 衡】permanent; lasting; perseverance

恒等【heng⁴deng² 戥】identically equal; identical
恒量【heng⁴lêng⁶ 谅】〈n.〉constant
恒心【heng⁴xem¹ 深】perseverance; constancy of purpose
恒星【heng⁴xing¹ 升】(fixed)star

杏【heng⁶ 幸】apricot

杏红【heng⁶hung⁴ 洪】apricot pink
杏黄【heng⁶wong⁴ 王】apricot yellow
杏仁【heng⁶yen⁴ 人】apricot kernel

幸【heng⁶ 杏】good fortune; favour; rejoice; arrive; fortunately; luckily

幸福【heng⁶fug⁷ 幅】happiness; wellbeing; happy
幸而【heng⁶yi⁴ 移】luckily; fortunately
幸好【heng⁶ hou²号²】fortunately; luckily ＝幸亏【heng⁶kuei¹ 规】
幸免【heng⁶min⁵ 缅】escape by sheer luck
幸运【heng⁶wen⁶ 混】good fortune; fortunate; lucky
幸灾乐祸【heng⁶joi¹log⁹wo⁶ 哉落和⁶】

take pleasure in others' misfortune

悻【heng⁶ 幸】angry; resentful

悻悻【heng⁶heng⁶】angry; resentful

洽【heb⁷ 恰; heb⁹ 合】be in harmony; a-gree; consult; arrange with

洽商【heb⁷ xêng¹ 双 】make arrangements with

洽谈【heb⁷tam⁴ 谭】talk over with

恰【heb⁷ 洽⁷】appropriate; proper; just; exactly

恰当【heb⁷dong³ 档】proper; suitable; fit-ting

恰好【heb⁷hou² 号²】just right =啱好【ngam¹hou²】

恰恰【heb⁷heb⁷】just; exactly =啱啱【ngam¹ngam¹】

恰巧【heb⁷ hao² 考 】by chance; fortuna-tely =咁跷【gem³kiu² 乔²】

恰如其分【heb⁷yü⁴kêi⁴fen⁶ 鱼奇份】apt; just right

瞌【heb⁷ 恰; heb⁹ 合】to close one's eyes

瞌埋眼【heb⁷mai⁴ngan⁵ 买⁴ 雁⁵】to close one's eyes =【普】闭上眼睛

瞌眼瞓【heb⁷ngan⁵fen³ 雁⁵ 训】to yawn; feel sleepy =【普】打盹儿

虓【heb⁷ 恰】bully

虓鸡【heb⁷gei¹ 计¹】bully; treat sb. high-handedly =【普】欺负

焓【heb⁹ 合】burning hot; fiery ∽【普】(热气)腾腾

合【heb⁹ 盒】close; join; whole; suit; proper

合并【heb⁹bing⁶ 丙⁶】merge; amalgamate

合成【heb⁹xing⁴ 绳】compose; compound; synthetize

合力【heb⁹lig⁹ 历】join forces; resultant of forces

合计【heb⁹gei³ 继】amount to; total

合算【heb⁹xün³ 算】paying; reckon up

合作【heb⁹ jog⁸ 昨 】cooperate; work to-gether

合营【heb⁹ying⁴ 仍】jointly owned; jointly operated

合同【heb⁹tung⁴ 铜】contract

合心绪【heb⁹xem¹xêü² 深水】suit; be to one's liking =【普】合意

合法【heb⁹fad⁸ 发】legal; lawful; rightful

合格【heb⁹gag⁸ 隔】qualified; up to stand-ard

合乎【heb⁹fu⁴ 符 】conform with; tally with

合适【heb⁹xig⁷ 色】suitable; right

合理【heb⁹lêi⁵ 李】rational; equitable

合伙【heb⁹fo² 火】form a partnership

合股【heb⁹gu² 古】pool capital; plying

合金【heb⁹gem¹ 甘】alloy

合璧【heb⁹big¹ 碧】match well

合唱【heb⁹qêng³ 畅】chorus

合情合理【heb⁹qing⁴heb⁹lêi⁵ 程李】fair and reasonable

合桃【heb⁹tou⁴ 图】starfruit

盒【heb⁹ 合】box; case

盒子【heb⁹ji² 止】box; case; casket

阖【heb⁹ 合】entire; whole; shut; close

阖家【heb⁹ga¹ 加】the whole family =阖府【heb⁹fu² 虎】

乞【hed⁷ 核⁷】to beg; supplicate

乞儿【hed⁷yi¹ 衣】a beggar＝【普】乞丐

乞食【hed⁷xig⁹ 蚀】to beg for food＝【普】讨饭

乞嚏【hed⁷qi¹ 痴】to sneeze＝【普】喷嚏

乞求【hed⁷keo⁴ 球】beg for；supplicate

乞怜【hed⁷lin⁴ 连】beg for pity(or mercy)

乞灵【hed⁷ ling⁴ 玲 】resort to；seek help from

核【hed⁹ 瞎；wed⁹ 屈⁹】pit；stone；nucleus

核心【hed⁹xem¹ 深】nucleus；core；kernel

核定【hed⁹ding⁶ 锭】check and ratify

核对【hed⁹dêü³ 堆³】check

核实【hed⁹xed⁹ 失⁹】verify；check

核算【hed⁹xün⁴ 算】business accounting

核桃【hed⁹tou⁴ 图】walnut

核能【hed⁹neng⁴ 挪莺⁴】nuclear energy

核武器【hed⁹mou⁵hêi³ 母气】nuclear weap‑on

核战争【hed⁹jin³jeng¹ 贱³ 憎】nuclear war

核糖核酸【hed⁹tong⁴hed⁹xün¹ 唐孙】〈n.〉ribonucleic acid；RNA

瞎【hed⁹ 核】blind；groundlessly；foolishly

瞎子【hed⁹ji² 止】a blind person

瞎扯【hed⁹qê¯ 车²】talk rubbish＝瞎说【hed⁹xüd⁸ 雪】

瞎闹【hed⁹nao⁶ 挠⁶】act senselessly；fool around

瞎指挥【hed⁹ji²fei¹ 旨辉】issue confused orders

劾【hed⁹ 核】expose sb.'s misdeeds or crimes

阂【hed⁹ 核】cut off from；not in communication with

辖【hed⁹ 核】linchpin；have jurisdiction over

辖区【hed⁹kêü¹ 驱】area under one's juris‑diction

黑【heg⁷ 刻】black；dark；secret；wicked

黑色【heg⁷xig⁷ 式】black

黑暗【heg⁷ngem³ 黯】dark

黑白【heg⁷bag⁹ 伯⁹】black and white；right and wrong

黑板【heg⁷ban² 版】blackboard

黑人【heg⁷yen⁴ 仁】Black people；Black；Negro

黑市【heg⁷xi⁵ 是⁵】black market

黑帮【heg⁷bong 邦】reactionary gang

黑心【heg⁷xem¹ 深】black heart；evil mind

黑货【heg⁷fo³ 课】smuggled goods；trash

黑海【heg⁷hoi² 开²】the Black Sea

黑龙江【heg⁷lung⁴gong¹ 隆刚】Heilong‑jiang(Province)

黑幕【heg⁷mog³ 莫】inside story of a plot

黑孖孖【heg⁷ ma¹ ma¹ 吗】black；dark ∽【普】黑漆漆

黑墨墨【heg⁷ meg⁹ meg⁹ 默 】black；dark ∽【普】黑糊糊

黑眯嚙【heg⁷mi¹meng¹ 莫衣¹ 莫莺¹】dark and black；very dark ∽【普】黑咕隆咚

黑古勒特【heg⁷ gu² leg⁹ deg⁹鼓 筋 得⁹】very black ∽【普】黑咕隆咚

黑口黑面【heg⁷heo²heg⁷min⁶ 厚² 免⁶】to have long face to show that one is unhappy＝【普】不满、不愉快的神情

刻【heg⁷ 黑】carve；a quarter (of an hour)；moment；cutting；in the highest degree

刻字【heg⁷ji⁶ 治】carve characters on a

seal, etc.

刻刀【heg⁷dou¹ 都】burin; graver

刻板【heg⁷ban² 版 】cut blocks for printing; mechanical; stiff

刻薄【heg⁷bog⁹ 泊】unkind; harsh; mean

刻毒【heg⁷dug⁹ 独】venomous; spiteful

刻度【heg⁷dou⁶ 道】graduation

刻苦【heg⁷ fu² 虎 】assiduous; simple and frugal

刻意【heg⁷yi³ 薏】painstakingly; sedulously

刻骨铭心【heg⁷gued⁷ming⁵xem¹ 掘⁷ 冥 深】be engraved on one's bones and heart

刻不容缓【heg⁷bed⁷ yung⁴ wun⁴ 毕溶桓】brook no delay; be of great urgency

克【heg⁷ 刻】can; restrain; overcome; digest; a Tibetan unit of volume or dry measure

克复【heg⁷fug⁹ 服】retake; recover

克服【heg⁷fug⁹ 伏】surmount; conquer

克制【heg⁷jei³ 济】restrain; exercise

克扣【heg⁷keo³ 寇】embezzle part of what should be issued

克当量【heg⁷dong¹lêng¹ 档¹ 亮】〈n.〉gram equivalent

克敌制胜【heg⁷dig⁹jei³xing³ 迪济圣】vanquish the enemy

克己奉公【heg⁷ gêi² fung⁶ gung¹ 几 凤 工】wholehearted devotion to public duty

呵【ho¹ 苛;o¹ 柯】breathe out; scold; cherish

呵斥【ho¹qig⁷ 戚】berate; excoriate

呵欠【o¹him³ 何淹³】yawn

呵护【ho¹wu⁶ 户】cherish; take good care of

嗬【ho² 可;ho⁴ 何】show surprised ∽ ah; oh

苛【ho¹ 呵】severe; exacting

苛刻【ho¹heg⁷ 克】harsh

苛求【ho¹keo⁴ 球】make excessive demands

苛捐杂税【ho¹gün¹jab⁹xêü³ 涓习穗³】exorbitant taxes and lexies

可【ho² 嗬】approve; can; may; need; fit; but; yet

可爱【ho²ngoi³ 哀³】lovable; likable; lovely

可悲【ho²bêi¹ 碑】sad; lamentable

可耻【ho²qi² 齿】shameful; disgraceful

可喜【ho²hêi² 起】gratifying; heartening

可笑【ho² xiu³ 少³】laughable; ridiculous; funny

可惜【ho²xig⁷ 识】it's a pity; it's too bad

可观【ho²gun¹ 官】considerable; sizable

可贵【ho² guei³ 桂 】valuable; commendable

可恨【ho²hen⁶ 很⁶】hateful; detestable

可敬【ho²ging³ 径】worthy of respect

可靠【ho²kao³ 卡幼³】reliable; dependable

可怜【ho²lin⁴ 连】pitiful; pity; meagre

可怕【ho²pa³ 爬³】fearful; frightful

可取【ho²qêü² 趣²】desirable

可行【ho²heng⁴ 衡】feasible

可疑【ho²yi⁴ 移】suspicious; questionable

可以【ho²yi⁵ 耳】can; may; passable; not bad

可谓【ho²wei⁶ 卫】it may be said; it may

be called

可是【ho²xi⁶ 士】〈conj.〉but；yet；how-ever

可有可无【ho²yeo⁵ho²mou⁴ 友毛】not essential

可歌可泣【ho²go¹ho²yeb⁷ 哥邑】move one to song and tears

河【ho⁴ 何】river

河流【ho⁴leo⁴ 留】rivers
河道【ho⁴dou⁶ 度】river course
河岸【ho⁴ngon⁶ 安⁶】river bank
河谷【ho⁴gug⁷ 菊】river valley
河运【ho⁴wen⁶ 混】river transport
河山【ho⁴ xan¹ 珊 】rivers and mountains；land

何【ho⁴ 河】〈pron.〉show query ∽ who，when，how，what，where，why，ect.

何必【ho⁴bid⁷ 别⁷】there is not need
何不【ho⁴bed⁷ 毕】why not
何尝【ho⁴xêng⁴ 常】"not that…?" = 何曾【ho⁴qeng⁴】
何等【ho⁴deng² 邓²】what kind；"what …！"
何妨【ho⁴fong⁴ 防】why not；might as well
何况【ho⁴fong³ 放】〈conj.〉much less；let alone
何其【ho⁴kêi⁴ 奇】how；what
何谓【ho⁴wei⁶ 卫】what is meant by
何以【ho⁴yi⁵ 耳】how；why
何在【ho⁴joi⁶ 再⁶】where
何止【ho⁴ji² 子】far more than

荷【ho⁴ 何】lotus；load；burden；grateful

荷花【ho⁴fa¹ 化¹】lotus = 莲花【lin⁴fa¹】

荷包【ho⁴bao¹ 苞】small bag（for carrying money）

荷兰【ho⁴lan¹ 烂¹】〈n.〉the Netherlands（Holland）

荷载【ho⁴joi³ 再】load

贺【ho⁶ 何⁶】congratulate

贺喜【ho⁶ hēi² 起 】congratulate sb. on a happy occasion

贺礼【ho⁶lei⁵ 黎⁵】gift

贺词【ho⁶qi⁴ 迟】speech of congratulation

贺电【ho⁶din¹ 甸】message of congratulation

开【hoi¹ 海¹】open；open up；open out；thaw；set out；run；begin；hold；write out

开始【hoi¹ qi² 耻】begin；start；beginning；outset

开头【hoi¹teo⁴ 投】begin；start

开动【hoi¹dung⁶ 洞】start；set in motion；move

开端【hoi¹dün¹ 段¹】beginning；start

开工【hoi¹ gung¹ 公 】go into operation；start

开车【hoi¹ qē¹ 奢 】 drive or start a car，train，etc.

开办【hoi¹ban⁶ 板⁶】open；set up

开创【hoi¹qong³ 闯³】start；initiate

开导【hoi¹dou⁶ 道】help sb. to see what is right or sensible

开发【hoi¹fad⁸ 法】develop；open up；exploit

开放【hoi¹fong³ 况】come into bloom

开关【hoi¹guan¹ 惯¹】〈n.〉switch

开花【hoi¹fa¹ 化¹】blossom；bloom；flower

开化【hoi¹fa³ 花³】become civilized

开会【hoi¹ wui² 汇²】hold or attend a meeting

开阔【hoi¹ fud⁸ 夫活⁸】open；wide；widen

开朗【hoi¹ long⁵ 郎⁵】open and clear；sanguine

开垦【hoi¹ hen² 很】open up wasteland

开门【hoi¹ mun⁴ 瞒】open the door

开明【hoi¹ ming⁴ 名】enlightened

开幕【hoi¹ mog⁹ 莫】the curtain rises；open

开单【hoi¹ dan¹ 丹】write a receipt＝【普】写发票

开展【hoi¹ jin² 剪】develop；open-minded

开支【hoi¹ ji¹ 支】pay；expenses

开心【hoi¹ xem¹ 深】feel happy；rejoice

开玩笑【hoi¹ wan² xiu³ 环² 少³】crack a joke；joke

开辟【hoi¹ pig⁷ 霹】open up；start

开挖【hoi¹ wad⁸ 乌压⁸】excavate

开拓【hoi¹ tog⁸ 托】open up；developing

开档【hoi¹ dong³ 当³】to start one's business；begin＝【普】开店；开始做生意

开嚟【hoi¹ lei⁴ 黎】to come out form＝【普】出来

开身【hoi¹ xen¹ 新】referring to a ship taking off＝【普】船只开航

开声【hoi¹ xêng¹ 腥】to speak up＝【普】作声

开胃【hoi¹ wei⁶ 卫 】①have a good appetite；②dreams that are not practical ∽【普】异想天开；休想得到

开门见山【hoi¹ mun⁴ gin³ xan¹ 瞒建册】come straight to the point

开明车马【hoi¹ ming⁴ gêū¹ ma⁵ 名居蚂】to state one's intention clearly＝【普】讲明用意；公开战略

海【hoi² 开²】sea or big lake

海洋【hoi² yêng⁴ 杨】seas and oceans；ocean

海皮【hoi² pēi⁴ 脾】beach；seaside；seashore＝【普】海滨；海岸

海滩【hoi² tan¹ 瘫】seabeach；beach

海湾【hoi² wan² 弯】bay；gulf

海峡【hoi² hab⁹ 狭】strait；channel

海水【hoi² xêū² 瑞²】seawater；brine

海味【hoi² mēi² 未²】choice seafood

海鲜【hoi² xin¹ 先】seafood

海港【hoi² gong² 讲】seaport；harbour

海产【hoi² qan² 铲】marine products

海岛【hoi² dou² 倒】island(in the sea)

海鸥【hoi² ngeo¹ 欧】sea gull

海燕【hoi² yin³ 厌】(storm)petrel

海豚【hoi² tūn⁴ 团】dolphin

海内【hoi² noi⁶ 耐】within the four seas

海外【hoi² ngoi⁶ 碍】overseas；abroad

海关【hoi² guan¹ 惯¹】customhouse；customs

海涵【hoi² ham⁴ 咸 】be magnanimous enough to forgive or tolerate

海量【hoi² lêng⁶ 亮 】magnanimity；great capacity for liquor

海市蜃楼【hoi² xi⁵ xen⁵ leo⁴ 是⁵ 身⁵ 流】mirage

海誓山盟【hoi² xei⁶ xan¹ meng⁴ 逝珊萌】(make) a solemn pledge of love

海水不可斗量【hoi² xêū² bed⁷ ho² deo² lêng⁴ 】sea cannot be measured with a bushel—great minds cannot be fathomed

凯【hoi² 海】triumphant strains；triumphant

凯旋【hoi² xün⁴ 船】triumphant return

凯歌【hoi² go¹ 哥】a song of triumph; paean

铠【hoi² 海】〈n.〉铠甲【hoi²gab⁸ 格鸭⁸】(a suit of) armour

害【hoi⁶ 亥】evil；harm；harmful；do harm to kill；suffer from；feel

害虫【hoi⁶qung⁴ 从】injurious insect

害处【hoi⁶qü³ 迂于³】harm

害怕【hoi⁶pa³ 爬³】be afraid；be scared

害羞【hoi²xeo¹ 修】feel ashamed；be bashful；be shy＝怕丑【pa³qeo²】＝【普】害臊

嗐【hoi⁶ 害；hei⁴ 系⁴】〈int.〉show sentimental ∽ oh

亥【hoi⁶ 害】the last of the twelve Earthly Branches

氦【hoi⁶ 亥】〈n.〉helium(He)

蒿【hou¹ 好¹】〈n.〉青蒿【qing¹hou¹】wormwood

好【hou² 号²；hou³ 耗】good；fine；nice；friendly；get well；O.K.；be convenient；very

好人【hou²yen⁴ 仁】good person

好事【hou²xi⁶ 士】good deed；good turn

好心【hou²xem¹ 深】good intention

好睇【hou²tei² 体】good-looking；nice＝【普】好看

好处【hou²qü³ 迂于³】good；benefit；gain

好感【hou²gem² 锦】good opinion；favourable

好听【hou²tēng¹ 厅】pleasant to hear

好意【hou²yi³ 薏】good intention

好使【hou²xei² 洗】be convenient to use

好似【hou²qi⁵ 恃】seem；be like＝【普】好像

好彩【hou²qoi² 采】lucky；luckily＝【普】幸好；好在

好颈【hou²gēng² 镜²】good tempered；kind＝【普】好耐性；好脾气

好劲【hou² ging⁶ 竞】very good ＝【普】很好

好野【hou² yê⁵ 夜⁵】good；cheerio；nice；kind＝【普】好东西；好样的

好比【hou²bēi² 髀】be just like

好闲【hou²han⁴ 娴】never mind＝【普】不要紧；等闲视之

好气【hou² hēi³ 汽】to be talkative；to be patient＝【普】啰嗦；说个不停

好眼界【hou²ngan⁵gai³ 雁介】good eyesight＝【普】好眼力；有眼光；看得准

好心机【hou² xem¹ gēi¹深 基】patient＝【普】好耐性

好声【hou²xēng¹ 腥】careful＝【普】小心；当心

好相与【hou²xêng¹yü⁵ 双雨】easy to get along with＝【普】人际关系好；容易共事合作

好天【hou²tin¹ 田¹】good, clear day＝【普】晴朗；好天气

好话【hou²wa⁶ 华⁶】to answer others"I am fine"when asked＝【普】"我就是这样"(当回答别人问话时骄傲地说)

好人事【hou²yen⁴xi² 仁屎】kindhearted；nice＝【普】慈爱、乐于助人的好品格

好声好气【hou² xēng¹ hou² hēi³腥 汽】to calm down before one negotiates or discusses with others＝【普】说话温和、耐心

好衰唔衰【hou²xêü¹m⁴xêü¹ 水¹】unlucky；

unfortunate =【普】运气不好；真倒霉

好食懒飞【hou³xig⁹lan⁵fēi¹ 蚀烂⁵ 菲】eat but does nothing =【普】好吃懒做

好话唔好听【hou²wa⁶m⁴hou²tēng¹ 华⁶ 厅】frankly speaking =【普】说了别见怪

好地地【hou²dēi⁶dēi⁶ 得菲⁶】in perfectly good condition =【普】好端端；好好儿

好事多磨【hou²xi⁶do¹mo⁴ 是朵¹ 摸⁴】the road to happiness is strewn with setbacks

好景不长【hou²ging²bed⁷qêng⁴ 境毕祥】good times don't last long

耗【hou³ 好³】consume；cost；dawdle；bad news

耗费【hou³fei³ 废】consume；expend

耗损【hou³xūn² 选】consume；waste；lose

耗子【hou³ji² 止】mouse；rat = 老鼠【lou⁵xü²】

豪【hou⁴ 毫】a person of extraordinary powers or endowments；bold and unconstrained；forthright；despotic

豪放【hou⁴ fong³ 况】bold and unconstrained

豪华【hou⁴wa⁴ 铧】luxurious；sumptuous

豪杰【hou⁴ gid⁹ 桀】person of exceptional ability；hero

豪迈【hou⁴ mai⁶ 卖 】bold and generous；heroic

豪强【hou⁴kêng⁴ 卡香⁴】despotic；despot

豪情【hou⁴qing⁴ 程】lofty sentiments

豪爽【hou⁴xong² 丧²】straightforward；forthright

豪言壮语【hou⁴yin⁴jong³yü⁵ 然状³ 雨】brave words

毫【hou⁴ 豪】fine long hair；writing brush；in the least；milli＿；1/10 yuan(money of China)

毫毛【hou⁴mou⁴ 无】soft hair on the body

毫不【hou⁴bed⁷ 毕】not at all

毫厘【hou⁴lēi⁴ 离】the least bit；an iota

毫米【hou⁴mei¹ 莫矮¹】millimeter(mm.)

毫升【hou⁴xing¹ 星】millilitre

壕【hou⁴ 豪】moat；trench

壕沟【hou⁴keo¹ 构¹】trench；ditch

嚎【hou⁴ 豪】howl；wail

嚎啕【hou⁴tou⁴ 陶】cry loudly；wail

嗥【hou⁴ 豪】(of a jackal or wolf)howl

号【hou⁶ 浩】name；mark；sign；number；size；date；order；anything used as a horn

号称【hou⁶qing¹ 清】be known as；claim to be

号角【hou⁶gog⁸ 阁】bugle；bugle call

号令【hou⁶ ling⁶ 拧】verbal command；order

号码【hou⁶ma⁵ 马】number

号召【hou⁶jiu⁶ 赵】call；appeal

浩【hou⁶ 号】great；vast；grand

浩大【hou⁶ dai⁶ 歹⁶ 】very great；huge；vast

浩荡【hou⁶dong⁶ 当⁶】vast and mighty

浩繁【hou⁶fan⁴ 烦】vast and numerous

浩瀚【hou⁶hon⁶ 汗】vast

皓【hou⁶ 号】white；bright

皓首【hou⁶xeo² 手】hoary head

罕【hon² 汉²】rarely; seldom

罕见【hon²gin³ 建】seldom seen; rare

捍【hon² 罕; hon⁶ 汗】defend; guard; protect

捍卫【hon²wei⁶ 为⁶】defend; guard

汉【hon³ 看】the Han Dynasty; the Han nationality; Chinese(language); man

汉人【hon³ yen⁴仁 】the Hans; the Han people

汉语【hon³yū⁵ 雨】Chinese(language)

汉字【hon³ji⁶ 治】Chinese characters

汉族【hon³jug⁹ 俗】the Han nationality

汉子【hon³ji² 止】man; fellow

看【hon³ 汉; hon¹ 汉¹】see; look at; look after; watch; read; think; look upon; visit = 睇【tei²】

看押【hon¹ ngad⁸压 】take into custody; detain

看管【hon¹gun² 官²】look after; attend to

看见【hon³gin³ 建】catch sight of; see

看到【hon³dou³ 度³】= 看见 = 睇到【tei² dou³】catch sight of

看出【hon³ qêd⁷此律⁷】make out; see = 睇出【tei²qêd⁷ 次律⁷】

看病【hon³bēng⁶ 柄⁶】see a patient; see a doctor = 睇病【tei²bēng⁶】

看不惯【hon³ bed⁷ guan³毕 关³】cannot bear the sight of; frown upon = 睇唔惯【tei²m²guan³】

看不起【hon³bed⁷hēi² 毕 喜】look down upon = 睇唔起【m²hēi²】

看成【hon³xing⁴ 承】look upon as; regard as = 睇成【xing⁴】

看穿【hon³qūn¹ 川】see through = 睇穿【qūn¹】

看待【hon³ doi⁶代 】look upon; regard; treat

看得起【hon³deg⁷hēi² 德喜】have a good opinion of = 睇得起【deg⁷hēi²】

看法【hon³fad⁸ 发】a way of looking at a thing; view = 睇法【fad⁸】

看来【hon³loi³ 莱】it seems; it looks as if = 睇嚟【lei⁴】= 睇个样【go³ yêng²】

看齐【hon³qei⁴ 妻⁴】dress; keep up with = 睇齐【qei⁴】

看轻【hon³hing¹ 兴】look down upon = 睇轻【hēng¹】

看上【hon³xêng⁵ 尚²】take a fancy to; settle on = 睇上; 中意【jung¹yi³】; 睇中【jung³】

看透【hon³ teo³头³】see through = 睇透【teo³】

看望【hon³mong⁶ 亡⁶】call on; visit; see

看重【hon³qung⁵ 从⁵】regard as important; value; set store by = 睇重【qung⁵】

看做【hon³jou⁶ 造】look upon as; regard as = 睇作【jog⁸】

看风使舵【hon³fung¹xei¹to⁴ 丰洗驼】trim one's sails

侃【hon² 罕】〈a.〉侃侃而谈【hon²hon²yi⁴tam⁴ 移谭】speak with fervour and assurance ∽ 口水花喷喷【heo²xêū⁵fa¹pen³pen³】

鼾【hon⁴ 寒】〈n.〉鼾声【hon⁴xing¹ 升】sound of snoring

刊【hon² 罕】print; publish; periodical; publication

刊登【hon²deng¹ 灯】publish in a newspaper or magazine; carry = 刊载【hon²joi³ 再】

刊物【hon²med⁹ 勿】publication

寒 【hon⁴ 韩】cold；tremble（with fear）；poor

寒潮【hon⁴qiu⁴ 樵】cold wave

寒风【hon⁴fung¹ 丰】cold wind

寒冷【hon⁴lang⁵ 罗罂⁵】cold；frigid

韩 【hon⁴ 寒】a surname

旱 【hon⁵ 汉⁵】dry spell；drought；dry-land；on land

旱灾【hon⁵joi¹ 哉】drought

旱季【hon⁵guei³ 桂】dry season

旱地【hon⁵dēi⁶ 得菲⁶】dry land

旱情【hon⁵qing⁴ 程】ravages of a drought

旱涝保收【hon⁵lou⁴bou² xeo¹ 劳宝修】ensure stable yields despite drought or excessive rain

翰 【hon⁶ 汗】writing brush；writing

翰林【hon⁶lem⁴ 淋】member of the Imperial Academy

瀚 【hon⁶ 汗】vast

瀚海【hon⁶hoi² 凯】big desert

焊 【hon⁶ 汗】weld；solder

焊工【hon⁶ gung¹ 公 】welding；welder；soldering

焊接【hon⁶jib⁸ 知叶⁸】welding；soldering

悍 【hon⁶ 汗；hon² 旱】brave；bold；fierce

悍然【hon²yin⁴ 言】outrageously；brazenly

汗 【hon⁶ 焊】sweat；perspiration

汗珠【hon⁶jü¹ 朱】beads of sweat

汗衫【hon⁶xam¹ 三】undershirt；T-shirt

汗流浃背【hon⁶ leo⁴ gab⁸ bui³ 留甲贝】streaming with sweat（from fear or physical exertion）

汗马功劳【hon⁶ma⁵gung¹lou⁴ 蚂公涝】distinctions won in battle；one's contributions in work

康 【hong¹ 糠】well-being；health

康健【hong¹ gin⁶ 建⁶ 】healthy；in good health

康乐【hong¹log⁹ 落】peace and happiness

康复【hong¹fug⁹伏 】restored to health；recovered

康庄大道【hong¹jong¹dai⁶dou⁶ 装歹⁶ 度】broad road

匡 【hong¹ 康】rectify；assist

匡正【hong¹jing³ 政】rectify；correct

诓 【hong¹ 匡】deceive；hoax

诓骗【hong¹pin³ 片】deceive；hoax；dupe

框 【hong¹ 匡；kuang¹ 箍罂¹】frame；draw a frame round

框框【kuang¹kuang¹】frame；restriction

筐 【hong¹ 匡；kuang¹ 箍罂¹】basket

筐子【kuang¹ji² 止】small basket ＝ 篓【lēi¹ 哩】

眶 【hong¹；kuang¹ 箍罂¹】the socket of the eye

糠 【hong¹ 康】chaff；bran；husk

糠秕【hong¹bēi² 比】chaff；worthless stuff

粔 【hong² 康²】have not grease；have not profit ＝【普】没油水

炕 【hong³ 康³；kong³ 抗】①bake；roast ②a heatable brick bed

炕干【hong³gon¹ 竿】bake to dry ＝【普】烤干

杭【hong⁴ 航】short for Hangzhou

杭州【hong⁴jeo¹ 洲】Hangzhou

吭【hong⁴ 杭；heng¹ 亨】utter a sound or a word；throat

航【hong⁴ 杭】boat；navigate

航行【hong⁴ heng⁴衡】navigate by water；navigate by air；fly

航海【hong⁴hoi² 凯】navigation

航空【hong⁴hung¹ 胸】aviation

航线【hong⁴ xin³ 扇 】air or shipping line；route

航运【hong⁴wen⁶ 混】shipping

航程【hong⁴ qing⁴情 】voyage；passage；range

航班【hong⁴ban¹ 斑】scheduled flight

巷【hong⁶ 项】lane；alley；tunnel

巷战【hong⁶jin³ 箭】street fighting

巷道【hong⁶dou⁶ 度】tunnel

项【hong⁶ 巷】nape；sum（of money）；term

项链【hong⁶lin² 练²】necklace

项目【hong⁶mug⁹ 木】item

喝【hod⁸ 渴】shout loudly；drink = 饮【yem² 阴】

喝彩【hod⁸qoi² 采】acclaim；cheer

喝令【hod⁸ling¹ 另】shout an order

喝茶【hod⁸qa⁴ 查】drink tea

喝西北风【hod⁸xei¹beg¹fung¹ 筛伯厄⁷丰】drink the northwest wind—have nothing to eat

曷【hod⁸ 喝】= 何【ho⁴】（see"何"）

渴【hod⁸ 喝】thirsty；yearningly

渴望【hod⁸mong⁶ 亡⁶】thirst for；yearn for

褐【hod⁸ 喝】coarse cloth or clothing；brown

褐煤【hod⁸mui⁴ 梅】brown coal；lignite

褐色【hod⁸xig⁷ 式】brown

哭【hug⁷ 酷⁷】cry；weep

哭泣【hug⁷yeb⁷ 邑】cry；weep；sob

哭诉【hug⁷xou³ 数】complain tearfully

哭笑不得【hug⁷xiu³bed⁷deg⁷ 少³ 毕德】not know whether to laugh or to cry

酷【hug⁹ 哭⁹】cruel；oppressive；very；extremely

酷热【hug⁹yid⁹ 孽】extremely hot

酷刑【hug⁹ying⁴ 形】cruel torture

酷爱【hug⁹ngoi³ 哀³】ardently love

酷似【hug⁹qi⁵ 此⁵】be the very image of

空【hung¹ 凶】empty；hollow；void；for nothing

空气【hung¹hēi³ 汽】air；atmosphere

空间【hung¹gan¹ 奸】space

空中【hung¹jung¹ 钟】in the sky；in the air

空旷【hung¹kong³ 抗】open；spacious

空泛【hung¹fan³ 贩】vague and general

空洞【hung¹dung⁶ 动】cavity；empty；hollow

空虚【hung¹hêü¹ 墟】hollow；void

空想【hung¹xêng² 赏】idle dream；fantasy

空谈【hung¹tam² 谭】indulge in empty talk；empty talk = 白讲【bag⁹gong⁹】

空心【hung¹xem¹ 深】hollow

空手【hung¹xeo² 守】empty-handed

空前【hung¹qin⁴ 钱】unprecedented

空军【hung¹guen¹ 君】air force

空运【hung¹wen⁶ 混】air transport；airlift

空喜欢【hung¹hēi²fun¹ 起 宽】rejoice too soon＝白喜欢【bag⁹hēi²fun¹】

空城计【hung¹xing⁴gei³ 成继】empty-city stratagem

空口无凭【hung¹ heo² mou⁴ peng⁴ 厚² 毛 朋】a mere verbal statement is no guarantee

空寥寥【hung¹liu¹liu¹ 了¹ 了¹】＝空窵窐【hung¹lang¹kuang¹】empty＝【普】空空如也

空前绝后【hung¹qin⁴jüd⁹heo⁶ 钱支月⁹ 候】unprecedented and unrepeatable；unique

空中楼阁【hung¹ jung¹ leo⁴ gog⁸ 钟留各】castles in the air

凶【hung¹ 空】inauspicious；fierce；terrible；murder

凶恶【hung¹ngog⁸ 噩】fierce；ferocious；fiendish

凶残【hung¹qan⁴ 灿⁴】fierce and cruel

凶猛【hung¹mang⁵ 孟⁵】violent；ferocious

凶杀【hung¹xad⁸ 煞】homicide；murder

凶手【hung¹xeo² 守】murderer；assassin

凶相【hung¹xêng³ 双³】ferocious features

凶兆【hung¹xiu⁶ 肇】ill omen

凶神恶煞【hung¹xen⁴ngog⁸xad⁸ 辰噩杀】devils；fiends

凶多吉少【hung¹do¹ged⁷xiu² 朵¹ 刮 小】bode ill rather than well

匈【hung¹ 凶】〈n.〉匈奴【hung¹nou⁴ 怒⁴】Xiongnu(Hun), an ancient nationality in China

匈牙利【hung¹nga⁴lēi⁶ 凶芽俐】〈n.〉Hungary

洶【hung¹ 凶】violent

洶洶【hung¹hung¹】the sound of roaring waves violent；tumultuous

洶涌澎湃【hung¹yung²pang⁴pai³ 拥彭派】surging

胸【hung¹ 凶】chest；bosom；mind；heart

胸部【hung¹bou⁶ 步】chest；thorax

胸怀【hung¹wai⁴ 坏⁴】mind；heart

胸襟【hung¹ kem² 禽¹】mind；breadth of mind

胸膛【hung¹tong⁴ 堂】chest

胸脯【hung¹pou² 普】chest

胸有成竹【hung¹yeo⁵xing⁴jug⁷ 友城足】have a well thought out plan, strategem, etc.

孔【hung² 恐】hole；opening；aperture；a surname

孔穴【hung²yüd 月】hole；cavity

孔洞【hung²dung⁶ 动】opening or hole in a utensil, etc.＝窿【lung¹ 龙¹】

孔夫子【hung²fu¹ji³ 孚止】〈n.〉Confucius

孔庙【hung²miu⁶ 妙】Confucian temple

恐【hung² 孔】fear；dread；terrify

恐怖【hung²bou³ 布】terror

恐吓【hung²hag⁸ 客】threaten；intimidate

恐慌【hung²fong¹ 方】panic

恐惧【hung²gêu⁶ 具】fear；dread

恐怕【hung²pa³ 爬³】I'm afraid；perhaps

恐龙【hung²lung⁴ 胧】〈n.〉dinosaur

倥【hung² 孔】〈a.〉倥傯【hung²jung² 总】pressing；destitute

控【hung³ 哄】accuse；control；dominate

控告【hung³gou³ 诰】charge；accuse

控诉【hung³ xou³ 数】accuse; denounce

控制【hung³ jei³ 济】control; command

控【hung³ 哄】look about; peep at ∽【普】探头望；窥视

哄【hung³ 控；hung¹ 空】uproar; fool; bubbub

哄骗【hung³ pin³ 片】cheat; humbug = 咄【tem³ 凶³】

哄动【hung¹ dung⁶ 洞】cause a sensation

哄抬【hung¹ toi⁴ 台】drive up(prices)

哄堂大笑【hung³ tong⁴ dai⁶ xiu³ 唐歹⁶ 少³】the whole room rocking with laughter

讧【hung³ 控】〈n.〉内讧【noi⁶ hung³】internal conflict

红【hung⁴ 洪】red; revolutionary; red cloth; bonus

红色【hung⁴ xig⁷ 式】red; revolutionary

红润【hung⁴ yên⁶ 闰】ruddy; rosy

红脸【hung⁴ lim⁵ 廉⁵】blush; get angry = 面红【min⁶ hung⁴】

红豆【hung⁴ deo⁶ 窦】ormosia; love pea; red beans

红汞【hung⁴ hung³ 控】〈n.〉mercurochrome

红人【hung⁴ yen⁴ 仁】a favourite with sb. in power

红利【hung⁴ lēi⁶ 俐】bonus; extra dividend

红薯【hung⁴ xü⁴ 署⁴】sweet potato = 番薯【fan¹ xü⁴】

红尘【hung⁴ qen⁴ 陈】the world of mortals

红眼【hung⁴ ngan⁵ 雁⁵】pinkeye; see red = 眼红【ngan⁵ hung⁴】

红晕【hung⁴ wen⁶ 运】blush; flush

红运【hung⁴ wen⁶ 晕】good luck

红肿【hung⁴ jung² 总】red and swollen

红装【hung⁴ jong¹ 庄】gay feminine attire

红绿灯【hung⁴ lug⁹ deng¹ 六登】traffic light

红血球【hung⁴ hüd⁸ keo⁴ 黑月⁸ 求】red blood cell

红豆沙【hung⁴ deo⁶ xa¹ 窦 砂】red bean soup

红毛泥【hung⁴ mou⁴ nei⁴ 无尼】cement =【普】水泥

红当荡【hung⁴ dong¹ dong⁶ 噹噹⁶】rosy red; bright red =【普】红彤彤；红通通

红粉花绯【hung⁴ fen² fa¹ fēi¹ 分² 化¹ 飞】brilliant red ∽【普】红艳艳

红光满面【hung⁴ guong¹ mun⁵ min⁶ 胱门⁵ 免⁶】one's face glowing with health; in ruddy health

红十字会【hung⁴ xeb⁹ ji⁶ wui² 拾治汇²】the Red Cross

熊【hung⁴ 红】bear; rebuke; upbraid; scold

熊掌【hung⁴ jêng² 蒋】bear's paw

熊猫【hung⁴ mao¹ 矛¹】panda

熊熊【hung⁴ hung⁴】flaming; ablaze; raging

雄【hung⁴】male; grand; powerful; a person or state having great power and influence

雄壮【hung⁴ jong³ 状³】full of power and grandeur; majestic

雄伟【hung⁴ wei⁵ 韦⁵】grand; imposing

雄浑【hung⁴ wen⁶ 混】vigorous and firm; forceful

雄健【hung⁴ gin⁶ 建⁶】robust; vigorous

雄厚【hung⁴ heo⁵ 候⁵】rich; solid; abundant

雄图【hung⁴ tou⁴ 涛】grandiose plan = 鸿图【hung⁴ tou⁴】

雄辩【hung⁴ bin⁶ 便】convincing argument; eloquence

雄心壮志【hung⁴ xem¹ jong³ ji³深装³至】lofty aspirations and great ideals

雄才大略【hung⁴qoi⁴dai⁶lê̤g⁹ 财歹⁶ 掠】(a man of)great talent and bold vision

烘【hung³ 控】dry or warm by the fire; set off

烘焙【hung³ bui⁶贝⁶】cure (tea or tobacco leaves)

烘干【hung³gon¹ 竿】stoving

烘烤【hung³hao² 考】toast; bake

烘箱【hung³xêng¹ 湘】oven

烘托【hung³tog⁸ 替恶⁸】(in painting)add shading around an object to make it stand out; set off by contrast

洪【hung⁴ 红】big; vast; flood

洪大【hung⁴dai⁶ 歹⁶】loud

洪亮【hung⁴lê̤ng⁶ 量⁶】loud and clear; sonorous

洪水【hung⁴xê̤u² 瑞²】flood; floodwater

洪流【hung⁴leo⁴ 留】mighty torrent; powerful current

虹【hung⁴ 红】rainbow

虹吸管【hung⁴keb⁷gun² 给莞】siphon

鸿【hung⁴ 红】swan goose; letter; great; grand

鸿雁【hung⁴ngan⁶ 眼⁶】swan goose

鸿毛【hung⁴ mou⁴无 】a goose feather — something very light or insignificant

鸿沟【hung⁴keo¹ 购¹】wide gap; chasm

鸿图【hung⁴ tou⁴徒 】great plan; grand prospect＝【普】宏图

鸿鹄之志【hung⁴gug⁷ji¹ji³ 谷支智】high aspirations

訇【hung¹ 空; gueng¹ 轰】loud noise

汞【hung⁶ 红⁶; hung³ 控】〈n.〉mercury (Hg)

薨【hung³ 控; gueng¹ 轰】(of feudal lords or high officials)die; pass away

壳【hog⁸ 学⁸】shell; housing; casing; case

学【hog⁹ 鹤】study; learn; imitate; learning subject of study; school

学习【hog⁹jab⁹ 袭】study; learn; emulate

学问【hog⁹ men⁶ 闻⁶ 】learning; knowledge; scholarship

学说【hog⁹xüd⁹ 雪】theory; doctrine

学术【hog⁹xêd⁹ 述】learning; science

学识【hog⁹xig⁹ 色】learning; knowledge

学生【hog⁹xeng¹ 撑¹】student; pupil

学者【hog⁹jē² 姐】scholar; learned man

学派【hog⁹pai³ 排³】school of thought; school

学校【hog⁹ hao⁶效 】school; educational; institution

学业【hog⁹ yib⁹叶 】one's studies; school work

学院【hog⁹yün² 苑】college; institute

学科【hog⁹fo¹ 课¹】course; subject

学历【hog⁹lig⁹ 力】record of formal schooling

学期【hog⁹kēi⁴ 其】school term; term

学费【hog⁹fei³ 废】tuition fee; tuition

学以致用【hog⁹yi³ji³yung⁶ 耳志容⁶】study for the purpose of application

貉【hog⁹ 学】racoon dog 一丘之貉【yed⁷yeo¹ji¹hog⁹ 休支学】jackals from the same lair; birds of a feather

鹤【hog⁹ 学】crane

鹤嘴锄【hog⁹jêû²qo⁴ 最² 初⁴】pick; pick-axe; mattock

鹤发童颜【hog⁹fad⁸tung⁴ngan⁴ 法同眼⁴】hale and hearty

浇【hiu¹ 嚣】pour liquid on; water; cast

浇灌【hiu¹gun³ 罐】water; irrigate; pour

嚣【hiu¹ 枭】clamour; hubbub; din

嚣张【hiu¹ jêng¹章 】rampant; arrogant; aggressive

枭【hiu¹ 嚣】owlet; fierce and ambitious

枭雄【hiu¹hung⁴ 红】a formidable man

枭首示众【hiu¹xeo²xi⁶jung³ 手视怂】cut off a person's head and hang it up as a warning to all

晓【hiu² 嚣²】dawn; daybreak; know

晓得【hiu²deg⁷ 德】know

晓示【hiu²xi⁶ 视】tell explicitly; notify

翘【hiu³ 黑妖³; kiu³ 乔³】raise; become warped; stick up; hold up

翘首【hiu³ xeo²守 】raise one's head and look

翘尾巴【hiu³mēi⁵ba¹ 美爸】be cocky; get stuck-up

谦【him¹ 欠¹】modest

谦虚【him¹hêû¹ 墟】modest; make modest remarks

谦逊【him¹xên³ 讯】modest; unassuming

谦让【him¹ yêng⁶ 攘】modestly decline

谦恭【him¹gung¹ 公】modest and courteous

险【him² 欠²】narrow pass; defile; dan-ger; sinister; nearly

险阻【him²jo² 左】dangerous and difficult

险峻【him²jên³ 进】dangerously steep; precipitous

险恶【him²ngog⁸ 噩⁸】dangerous; sinister

险境【him²qing² 景】dangerous situation

险些【him²xē¹ 蛇¹】narrowly＝差哋【qa¹ did⁷】

欠【him³ 险³】owe; not enough; raise slightly; yawn

欠债【him³jai³ 斋³】owe a debt; run into debt

欠款【him³fun² 宽²】money that is owing; arrears

欠缺【him³ küd⁸决】be deficient in; defi-ciency

欠妥【him³ to⁵ 陀⁵】not proper＝唔系几妥【m⁴hei⁶gēi²to⁵】

欠佳【him³ gai¹ 皆】not good enough＝唔够好【m⁴geo³hou²】

欠身【him³xen¹ 辛】raise oneself slightly

妗【him⁴ 欠⁴】＝嫌【yim⁴ 艳⁴】(see"嫌")

芡【him³ 欠】〈n.〉Gorgon euryale

芡粉【him³fen² 分²】the seed powder of Gorgon euryale; any starch used in cooking

掀【hin¹ 牵】lift(a cover, ect.)

掀起【hin¹hēi² 喜】lift; surge; set off

掀动【hin¹dumg² 洞】lift; start; set in mo-tion

牵【hin¹ 掀】lead along; pull; involve

牵扯【hin¹qē² 斜²】involve; implicate

牵引【hin¹yen⁵ 瘾】tow; draw

牵线【hin¹xin³ 腺】pull strings; act as go－between

牵涉【hin¹xib⁸摄】involve; drag in

牵制【hin¹jei³济】pin down; tie up; check

牵连【hin¹lin⁴链】involve; tie up with

牵牛花【hin¹ngeo⁴fa¹偶⁴化¹】morning glory

牵肠挂肚【hin¹qêng⁴gua³tou⁵祥卦土⁵】feel deep anxiety about; be very worried about

牵强附会【hin¹kêng⁵fu⁶wui⁶卡香⁵付汇⁶】draw a forced analogy

轩【hin¹牵】high; lofty; a small room or randa with windows

轩昂【hin¹ngong⁴我康⁴】dignified; imposing

轩然大波【hin¹yin⁴dai⁶bo¹言歹⁶坡】a great disturbance

显【hin²遣】apparent; obvious; show; display

显得【hin²deg⁷德】look; seem; appear

显赫【hin²hag⁸客】illustrious; celebrated

显露【hin²lou⁶路】become visible; appear

显然【hin²yin⁴言】obvious; evident

显示【hin²xi⁶是】show; display

显现【hin²yin⁶苋】manifest oneself; appear

显眼【hin²ngan⁵雁】conspicuous; showy

显著【hin²jü³注】notable; marked

显而易见【hin²yi⁴yi⁶gin³移义建】obviously

遣【hin²显】send; dispel; expel

遣送【hin²xung³宋】send back; repatriate

遣返【hin²fan²反】repatriate

遣散【hin²xan³汕】disband; dismiss

谴【hin²显】condemn

谴责【hin²jag⁸窄】condemn; denounce

献【hin³宪】offer; present; dedicate

献计【hin³gei³继】offer advice

献策【hin³qag⁸测⁸】offer advice

献技【hin³gêi⁶忌】show one's skill

献礼【hin³lei⁵黎⁵】present a gift

献媚【hin³mêi¹眉】try to ingratiate

献身【hin³xen¹辛】give one's life for

宪【hin³献】statute; constitution

宪法【hin³fad⁸发】constitution; charter

宪兵【hin³bing¹冰】military police

蚬【hin²显】shell

兴【hing¹兄;hing³庆】prosper; start; promote; get up; permit; interest; excitement

兴起【hing¹hêi¹喜】rise; spring up

兴办【hing¹ban⁶板⁶】initiate; set up

兴奋【hing¹fen⁵愤】be excited; excitation

兴建【hing¹gin³见】build; construct

兴隆【hing¹lung⁴龙】prosperous; thriving

兴盛【hing¹xing³成⁶】prosperous; flourishing

兴旺【hing¹wong⁶王⁶】prosperous; flourishing

兴风作浪【hing¹fung¹jog⁸long⁶丰昨朗⁶】stir up trouble

兴利除弊【hing¹lêi⁶qêü⁴bei⁶俐徐敝】promote what is beneficial and abolish what is harmful

兴趣【hing³qêü³翠】interest = 兴味【hing³mêi⁶未】

兴致【hing³ji³至】interest; mood to enjoy

兴高采烈【hing³gou¹qoi²lid⁹羔彩列】in high spirits

兄【hing¹ 兴¹】elder brother

兄弟【hing¹dei⁶ 递】brothers; fraternal; brotherly

兄长【hing¹jêng² 蒋】a respectful form of address for an elder brother or a man friend

馨【hing¹ 兄】strong and pervasive fragrance

馨香【hing¹hêng¹ 乡】fragrance; smell of burning incense

磬【hing³ 庆】chime stone; inverted bell

罄【hing³ 庆; hing¹ 兄】use up; exhaust

罄尽【hing³jên⁶ 进⁶】with nothing left; all used up

罄竹难书【hing¹jug⁷nan⁴xū¹ 足挪晏⁴ 抒】(of crimes, etc.) too numerous to record

庆【hing³ 磬】celebrate; occasion for celebration

庆典【hing³din² 电²】celebration

庆祝【hing³jug⁷ 足】celebration

庆贺【hing³ ho⁶ 何⁶ 】congratulate; celebrate

庆幸【hing³heng⁶ 杏】rejoice

烘【hing³】buring

烘焰焰【hing³heb⁹heb⁹ 合 合】burnning; burning hot; intimate ∽【普】火热; 热腾腾

歉【hib⁸ 胁】apology; crop failure

歉收【hib⁸xeo¹ 修】crop failure; poor harvest

歉意【hib⁸yi³ 蕙】apology; regret

胁【hib⁸ 协】the upper part of the side of the human body; coerce; force

胁持【hib⁸qi⁴ 迟】= 挟持【hib⁸qi⁴】(see"挟持")

胁迫【hib⁸big⁷ 逼】coerce; force

胁从【hib⁸qung⁴ 虫】be an accomplice under duress

挟【hib⁸ 协; gab⁸ 夹】hold sth. under the arm; coerce; harbour

挟持【hib⁸ qi⁴迟】seize sb. on both sides by the arms; hold sb. under duress

协【hib⁸ 胁】joint; common; assist

协定【hib⁸ding⁶ 锭】agreement; accord

协力【hib⁸lig⁹ 历】unite efforts

协商【hib⁸ xêng¹双 】consult; talk things over

协调【hib⁸ tiu⁴ 条 】coordinate; concert; harmonize

协同【hib⁸ tung⁴铜 】work in coordination with; cooperate with

协议【hib⁸yi⁵ 耳】agree on; agreement

协助【hib⁸jo⁶ 座】assist; help; give assistance

协作【hib⁸jog⁸ 昨】cooperation; coordination

歇【hid⁸ 蝎】have a rest; stop; knock off

歇脚【hid⁸gêg⁸ 格约⁸】stop on the way for a rest

歇凉【hid⁸lêng⁴ 梁】relax in a cool place = 蹛凉【teo²lêng⁴】

歇息【hid⁸xig⁷ 色】have a rest; go to bed = 蹛下【teo²ha⁶】

歇宿【hid⁸xug⁷ 缩】put up for the night = 过夜【guo³yê⁶】

蝎【hid8 歇；kid8 揭】〈*n.*〉scorpion

喧【hün1 圈】noisy

喧哗【hün1wa1 娃】confused noise; hubbub

喧闹【hün1nao6 挠6】noise and excitement; bustle

喧腾【hün1teng4 藤】noise and excitement; hubbub

喧嚣【hün1hiu1 翘1】noisy; clamour; hullabaloo

喧宾夺主【hün1ben1düd9jü2 滨得月9 朱2】a presumptuous guest usurps the host's role

暄【hün1 圈】warmth(of the sun)

圈【hün1 喧；gün6 倦】circle; ring; group; enclose; pen; fold; sty

圈点【hün1dim2 店2】punctuate

圈套【hün1tou3 吐】snare; trap

圈子【hün1ji2 止】circle; ring

圈肥【gün6fêi4 菲4】barnyard manure

犬【hün2 圈2】dog

犬牙交错【hün2nga4gao1qo3 芽郊挫】jigsaw-like

犬马之劳【hün2 ma5 ji1 lou4 蚂支涝】serve like a dog or a horse

劝【hün3 楦】advise; urge; encourage

劝导【hün3dou4 道】try to persuade; advise

劝告【hün3gou3 高3】advise; urge; exhort

劝勉【hün3min5 免】advise and encourage

劝说【hün3xüd8 雪】persuade; advise

劝慰【hün3wei3 畏】console; soothe

劝阻【hün3jo2 左】dissuade sb. from; advise sb. not to

楦【hün3 劝】shoe last; hat block

血【hüd8 黑月8】blood; related by blood

血液【hüd8yig9 亦】blood

血气【hüd8hêi3 汽】sap; courage and uprightness

血管【hüd8gun2 官2】blood vessel

血球【hüd8keo4 求】blood cell

血浆【hüd8jêng1 张】(blood)plasma

血栓【hüd8xan1 山】thrombus

血肉【hüd8yug9 玉】flesh and blood

血腥【hüd8xêng1 是镜1】reeking of blood; bloody

血型【hüd8 ying4形】blood group; blood type

血压【hüd8ngad8 押】blood pressure

血缘【hüd8yün4 元】ties of blood

血债【hüd8jai3 斋3】a debt of blood

血泪【hüd8lêü6 类】tears of blood

血迹【hüd8jig7 织】bloodstain

血战【hüd8jin3 箭】bloody battle

血统【hüd8tung2 桶】blood lineage; extraction

血淋淋【hüd8lem4lem4 林】dripping with blood

血亲【hüd8qen1 趁1】blood relation

血肉相连【hüd8yug9xêng1lin4 玉双链】as close as flesh and blood

靴【hê1 遡1】boots

遡【hê4 靴4】〈*onomatopoeia*〉the sound of the fresh water

遡遡声去【hê4hê2xêng1hêü3 腥虚3】castrate is quick; go very fast ∽【普】去得很快

虚【hêü¹ 墟】void; empty; timid; in vain; false; modest; weak; theory

虚无【hêü¹mou⁴ 毛】nihility; nothingness

虚幻【hêü¹wan⁶ 弯⁶】unreal; illusory

虚假【hêü¹ga² 贾】false; sham

虚伪【hêü¹ngei⁶ 魏】sham; false

虚妄【hêü¹mong⁵ 网】unfounded; invented

虚构【hêü¹keo⁹ 购】fabricate; make up

虚弱【hêü¹yêg⁹ 药】in poor health; weak; feeble

虚设【hêü¹qid⁸ 切】nominal

虚荣【hêü¹wing⁴ 永⁴】vanity

虚心【hêü¹xem¹ 深】open-minded; modest

虚词【hêü¹qi⁴ 迟】function word

虚情假意【hêü¹qing⁴ga²yi³ 程贾薏】false display of affection; hypocritical show of friendship

虚张声势【hêü¹jêng¹xing¹xei³ 章星世】make an empty show of strength; bluff and bluster

墟【hêü¹ 虚】ruins; country fair

圩【hêü¹ 虚】country fair; market

嘘【hêü¹ 虚】breathe out slowly; utter a sigh; scald; sh; hush

嘘寒问暖【hêü¹hon⁴men⁶nün⁵ 韩闻⁶ 嫩⁵】inquire after sb.'s well-being

歔【hêü¹ 虚】sob = 歔欷【hêü¹hêi¹ 希】

栩【hêü² 许】vivid; lively

栩栩如生【hêü²hêü²yü⁴xeng¹ 鱼擤¹】life-like

诩【hêü² 许】brag; boast

自诩为……【ji⁶hêü²wei⁴】style oneself

......

许【hêü² 诩】praise; promise; allow; maybe; a little; place

许多【hêü²do¹ 朵¹】many; much; a lot of

许久【hêü² geo²狗 】for a long time; for ages = 好耐【hou²noi⁶ 奈】

许可【hêü²ho² 何²】permit; allow

许诺【hêü² nog⁸挪恶⁸】make a promise; promise

许配【hêü²pui³ 沛】betroth a girl

许愿【hêü²yün⁶ 元⁶】make a vow; promise sb. a reward

去【hêü³ 虚³】go; leave; remove; be apart from; of last year

去向【hêü³ hêng³ 乡³】the direction in which sb. or sth. has gone

去路【hêü³lou⁶ 露】the way along which one is going; outlet

去处【hêü³qü³ 池于³】place to go; place; site

去世【hêü³xei³ 细】die; pass away

去伪存真【hêü³ngei⁶qün⁴jen¹ 魏全珍】eliminate the false and retain the true

香【hêng¹ 乡】fragrant; savoury; with relish; soundly; popular; perfume or spice; incence

香味【hêng¹mêi¹ 未】sweet smell; scent

香气【hêng¹hêi³ 汽】sweet smell; fragrance; aroma

香水【hêng¹xêü² 瑞²】perfume; scent

香粉【hêng¹fen² 分²】face powder

香精【hêng¹jing¹ 晶】essence

香花【hêng¹fa¹ 化¹】fragrant flower; good writings

香蕉【hêng¹jiu¹ 焦】banana

香皂【hêng¹jou⁶ 造】perfumed soap; toilet

soap

香烟【hêng¹ yin¹ 燕¹】cigarette； incense smoke

香肠【hêng¹ qêng² 祥²】sausage ＝ 腊肠【lab⁹ qêng²】

香料【hêng¹ liu⁶ 廖】perfume；spice

香甜【hêng¹ tim⁴ 添】fragrant and sweet

香烛【hêng¹ jug¹ 竹】joss sticks and candles

香喷喷【hêng¹ pen³ pen³ 贫³】sweet-smelling；savoury

 乡【hêng¹ 香】country； native place； township

乡村【hêng¹ qün¹ 川】village；countryside

乡下【hêng¹ ha² 厦²】village；country ＝ 乡间【hêng¹ gan¹】

乡土【hêng¹ tou² 桃】native soil；local

乡音【hêng¹ yem¹ 阴 】 accent of one's native place

乡亲【hêng¹ qen¹ 趁¹】fellow villager；local people ＝ 乡里【hêng¹ lēi⁵】

乡镇【hêng¹ jen³ 圳】villages and towns

乡巴佬【hêng¹ ba¹ lou² 爸老²】bumpkin ＝ 大乡里【dai⁶ hêng¹ lēi⁵】

享【hêng² 响】enjoy

享受【hêng² xeo⁶ 寿 】 enjoy； enjoyment； treat

享有【hêng² yeo⁵ 友】enjoy

享用【hêng² yung⁶ 容⁶】enjoy the use of； enjoy

享福【hêng² fug⁷ 幅】enjoy a happy life

享乐【hêng² log⁹ 洛⁹】lead a life of pleasure

响【hêng² 享】sound； make a sound； noisy；echo

响亮【hêng² lêng⁶ 谅】loud and clear； resounding

响声【hêng² xing¹ 星】sound；noise

响彻【hêng² qid⁸ 设】resound through

响应【hêng² ying³ 英³】respond；answer

饷【hêng² 响】entertain；pay

飨【hêng² 响】provide dinner for； entertain

向【hêng³ 乡³】direction；face；side with；always

向导【hêng³ dou⁶ 道】guide

向来【hêng³ loi⁴ 莱】always；all along

向着【hêng³ jêg⁹ 桌⁹】turn towards；face； take sb.'s part；side with ＝ 向住【hêng³ jü⁶】

向前【hêng³ qin⁴ 钱】forward；ahead

向上【hêng³ xêng⁶ 尚】upward；up

向下【hêng³ ha⁶ 厦】downward；down

向后【hêng³ heo⁶ 厚⁶】toward the back； backward

向左【hêng³ jo² 助²】toward the left

向右【hêng³ yeo⁶ 佑】toward the right

向往【hêng³ wong⁵ 王⁵ 】 yearn for； look forward to

向上爬【hêng³ xêng⁶ pa⁴ 尚扒】be intent on personal advancement

嘻【hēi¹ 喜¹； hi¹ 黑衣¹】① show exclaim；② ＜onomatopoeia＞ laugh

嘻嘻哈哈【hēi¹ hēi¹ ha¹ ha¹ 希虾】laughing and joking

嬉【hēi¹ 希】play；sport

嬉戏【hēi¹ hēi³ 气】play；sport

嬉皮士【hēi¹ pēi⁴ xi⁶ 脾是】hippy；hippie

嬉皮笑脸【hēi¹ pēi⁴ xiu³ lim⁵ 少廉⁵】grinning cheekily

熹【hēi¹ 希】dawn；brightness

熹微【hēi¹ mēi⁴ 眉】dim；pale

禧【hēi¹ 希】auspiciousness；happiness

曦【hēi¹ 希】sunlight（usu. in early morning）

熙【hēi¹ 希】bright；prosperous；gay

熙熙攘攘【hēi¹hēi¹yêng⁶yêng⁶ 让】bustling with activity

歔【hēi¹ 希】歔歘【hēi¹hêû¹ 虚】sob；sigh

唏【hēi¹ 希】唏嘘【hēi¹hêû¹】=歔歘

晞【hēi¹ 希】dry；daybreak

牺【hēi¹ 希】牺牲【hēi¹xeng¹ 擤¹】sacrifice；sacrifice oneself；give up

稀【hēi¹ 希】rare；sparse；watery；thin

稀薄【hēi¹bog⁹ 泊】thin；rare

稀饭【hēi¹ fan⁶范 】 rice or millet gruel；porridge =粥【jug⁷ 竹】

稀罕【hēi¹hon² 刊】=希罕【hēi¹hon²】（see "希罕"）

稀少【hēi¹xiu² 小】few；rare

稀奇【hēi¹kēi⁴ 其】rare；strange

稀烂【hēi¹lan⁶ 兰⁶】pulpy；broken to bits =溶溶烂烂【yung⁴yung⁴lan⁶lan⁶】

稀释【hēi¹xig¹ 析】dilute

稀疏【hēi¹xo¹ 梳】few and scattered；thin

稀汪汪【hēi¹wang¹wang¹ 横¹】very watery；too thin =【普】很稀（水太多，溶物少）

稀里糊涂【hēi¹lêi⁵wu⁴tou⁴ 理胡桃】muddleheaded

稀有金属【hēi¹ yeo⁵ gem¹ xug⁹友 今 熟】rare metal

希【hēi¹ 稀】hope；rare

希望【hēi¹mong⁶ 亡⁶】hope；wish；expect

希冀【hēi¹kēi³ 暨】hope for；wish for

希腊【hēi¹lab⁹ 蜡】〈n.〉Greece

希罕【hēi¹hon² 旱²】rare；scarce；rare thing；rarity

喜【hēi² 起】happy；delighted；pleased；happy event；pregnancy；be fond of；like

喜悦【hēi²yüd⁹ 月】happy；joyous

喜欢【hēi²fun¹ 宽】like；love；happy；elated

喜爱【hēi² ngoi³ 哀³】like；love；be fond of；be keen on

喜庆【hēi²hing³ 兴³】joyous；happy event

喜鹊【hēi²qêg⁸ 卓】〈n.〉magpie

喜人【hēi²yen⁴ 仁】gratifying；satisfactory

喜事【hēi²xi⁶ 是】happy event；wedding

喜讯【hēi² xên³ 信 】 happy news；good news

喜色【hēi²xig⁷ 式】happy expression；joyful look

喜剧【hēi²kêg⁹ 屐】comedy

喜气洋洋【hēi² hēi³ yêng⁴ yêng⁴汽扬扬 】full of joy

喜闻乐见【hēi²men⁴log⁹gin³ 文落建】love to see and hear

喜笑颜开【hēi² xiu³ ngan⁴ hoi¹少雁⁴ 海¹】light up with pleasure

喜新厌旧【hēi² xen¹ yim³ geo⁶ 辛嫌³ 柩】love the new and loathe the old

起【hēi² 喜】rise；get up；remove；appear；draft；start；case；batch

起来【hēi² loi⁴ 莱；hēi² lei⁴ 黎】stand up；get up；rise

起初【hēi²qo¹ 错¹】originally；at first；in

the beginning

起身【hēi² xen¹ 辛】get up; get out of bed ＝起床【hēi² qong⁴】

起动【hēi² dung⁶ 洞】start

起飞【hēi² fēi¹ 非】(of aircraft) take off

起点【hēi² dim² 掂】starting point

起源【hēi² yün⁴ 元】origin; originate

起伏【hēi² fug⁹ 服】rise and fall; undulate; up and down ＝起落【hēi² log⁹】

起码【hēi² ma⁵ 马】minimum; at least

起讫【hēi² nged⁹ 兀】the beginning and the end

起居【hēi² gêü¹ 据】daily life

起见【hēi² gin³ 建】in order to; for the purpose of

起劲【hēi² ging³ 径】vigorously ＝起势【hēi² xei³ 世】

起草【hēi² qou² 操】draft; make a draft

起哄【hēi² hung³ 控】jeer; boo and hood

起诉【hēi² xou³ 扫 】bring a suit against sb.; sue

起因【hēi² yen¹ 恩】cause; origin

起子【hēi² ji² 止】bottle opener; screwdriver ＝螺丝批【lo⁴ xi¹ pei¹ 罗 思 拍 矮¹】

起誓【hēi² xei⁶ 逝 】swear ＝发誓【fad⁸ xei⁶】

起义【hēi² yi⁶ 异】uprising; revolt

起重机【hēi² qung⁵ gēi¹ 虫² 基】hoist; crane

起早贪黑【hēi² jou² tam¹ heg⁷ 皂² 探¹ 克】work from dawn to dusk

起死回生【hēi² xēi² wui⁴ xeng¹ 四² 汇⁴ 笙】bring the dying back to life

戏【hēi³ 气】play; sport; joke; drama

戏弄【hēi³ lung⁶ 龙⁶】make fun of; play tricks on

戏谑【hēi³ yêg⁹ 若】banter; crack jokes

戏剧【hēi³ kēg⁶ 屐】drama; play; theatre

戏曲【hēi³ kug⁷ 卡屋⁷】traditional opera

戏法【hēi³ fad⁸ 发 】conjuring; juggling; magic

戏院【hēi³ yün² 丸】theatre

气【hēi³ 戏】gas; air; breath; smell; weather; airs; spirit; make angry; get angry; bully

气体【hēi³ tei² 睇】gas

气味【hēi³ mēi⁶ 未】smell; smack

气流【hēi³ leo⁴ 留 】ari current; airflow; breath

气候【hēi³ heo⁶ 后】climate; situation

气氛【hēi³ fen¹ 分】atmosphere

气管【hēi³ gun² 莞】windpipe

气喘【hēi³ qün² 窜】asthma ＝气咳【hēi³ ked⁷】

气化【hēi³ fa³ 花³】gasification

气温【hēi³ wen¹ 瘟】air temperature

气度【hēi³ dou⁶ 道】tolerance ＝气量【hēi³ lêng⁶ 亮】

气力【hēi³ lig⁹ 历】effort; energy

气派【hēi³ pai³ 排³】manner; style

气魄【hēi³ pag⁸ 拍 】boldness of vision; daring

气概【hēi³ koi³ 概】lofty quality; mettle

气节【hēi³ jid⁸ 折】integrity; moral courage

气恼【hēi³ mou⁵ 脑⁵】get angry; take offence

气馁【hēi³ noi⁵ 内⁵】become dejected; lose heart

气象【hēi³ jêng⁶ 丈 】meteorological phenomena; meteorology; atmosphere

气压【hēi³ngad⁸ 押】atmospheric pressure
气焰【hēi³yim⁶ 艳】arrogance; bluster
气质【hēi³jed⁷ 侄⁷】temperament; makings
气势汹汹【hēi³ xei³ hung¹hung¹ 细凶】fierce; overbearing
气味相投【hēi³ mēi⁶ xêng¹ teo⁴未双头】be birds of a feather; be two of a kind
气息奄奄【hēi³ xig⁷ yim¹ yim¹色淹 】at one's last gasp
气势磅礴【hēi³xei³pong⁴bog⁹ 细旁薄】of great momentum

汽 【hēi³ 气】vapour; steam

汽油【hēi³yeo⁴ 由】petrol; gasoline; gas
汽车【hēi³qē¹ 奢】automobile; car
汽船【hēi³xūn⁴ 旋】steamship; steamer
汽笛【hēi³dēg⁹ 获】steam whistle; hooter
汽水【hēi³ xêû²瑞²】 aerated water; soda water

弃 【hēi³ 气】throw away; abandon

弃置【hēi³ji³ 至】discard; throw aside
弃权【hēi³ kūn⁴拳 】 abstain from voting; forfeit
弃旧图新【hēi³geo⁶tou⁴xen¹ 枢途辛】turn over a new leaf

器 【hēi³ 气】implement; organ; capacity

器皿【hēi³ming⁵ 铭】household utensils
器具【hēi³gêû⁶ 巨】utensil; implement
器械【hēi³hai⁶ 鞋⁶】apparatus; appliance
器材【hēi³qoi⁶ 才】equipment; material
器官【hēi³gun¹ 观】organ; apparatus
器重【hēi³jung⁶ 仲】think highly

轻 【hēng¹ 黑镜¹；hing¹ 兄】light; small in number, degree, etc.; not important; gently; belittle

轻轻【hēng⁶hēng¹】lightly; gently
轻便【hēng¹bin⁶ 辨】light; portable
轻快【hing¹fai³ 块】brisk; lively
轻巧【hing¹hao² 考】light and handy
轻柔【hing¹yeo⁴ 油】soft; gentle
轻松【hing¹xung¹ 宋¹】light; relaxed
轻微【hing¹mēi⁴ 眉】light; slight
轻易【hing¹yi⁶ 异】easily; lightly
轻盈【hing¹ying⁴ 仍】slim and graceful; lissom
轻浮【hing¹feo⁴ 否⁴】frivolous; flighty
轻蔑【hing¹mid⁹ 灭】scornful; disdainful
轻视【hing¹xi⁶ 是】despise; look down on
轻佻【hing¹tiu¹ 挑】frivolous; skittish
轻率【hing¹xêd⁷ 恤】rash; hasty
轻敌【hing¹dig⁹ 迪】take the enemy lightly
轻信【hing¹xên³ 讯】be credulous
轻飘飘【hing¹piu¹piu¹ 漂】light; buoyant
轻描淡写【hing¹ miu⁴ dam⁶ xē²苗啖舍²】touch on lightly
轻举妄动【hing¹gêû²mong²dung⁶ 矩网洞】act rashly
轻装上阵【hēng¹jong¹xêng⁵jen⁶ 庄尚⁵ 圳⁶】 go into battle with a light pack
轻而易举【hing¹ yi⁴ yi⁶ gêû²移义矩 】easy to do

吃 【hēg⁸ 黑尺⁸；yag⁸ 衣轭⁸】eat; have one's meals; live on; annihilate; exhaust; absorb; suffer

吃饭【hēg⁸ fan⁸ 范 】 eat; have a meal; make a living
吃苦【hēg⁸fu² 虎】bear hardships
吃亏【hēg⁸kuei¹ 规】suffer losses; at a dis-

advantage

吃惊【hēg⁸gēng¹ 颈¹】be startled

吃力【hēg⁸lig⁹ 历⁹】be a strain

吃透【hēg⁸ teo³偷³】 have a thorough
grasp

吃香【hēg⁸hêng¹ 乡】be very popular

吃不开【hēg⁸ bed⁷ hoi¹ 毕海¹】 be unpop-
ular

吃不消【hēg⁸bed⁷xiu¹ 毕烧】be unable to
stand

吃喝玩乐【hēg⁸hod⁸wan²log⁹ 渴环² 落】
eat, drink and be merry

吃老本【hēg⁸lou⁵bun² 鲁苯】live off one's
past gains

I

(It is not used in the initial consonant.)

J

抓【ja¹ 渣】grab; scratch; arrest; stress; take charge of

抓住【ja¹jü⁶ 注⁶】catch hold of; catch

抓紧【ja¹gen² 谨】firmly grasp; pay close attention to

抓重点【ja¹jung⁶dim² 仲店²】stress the essentials

抓辫子【ja¹bin¹ji² 边止】capitalize on sb.'s vulnerable point

抓颈就命【ja¹gēng²jeo⁶mēng⁶ 镜² 袖莫镜⁶】to be patient with the present situation =【普】认命而吞声忍气

渣【ja¹ 抓】dregs; sediment; residue

渣滓【ja¹joi² 宰】dregs; sediment; residue

楂【ja¹ 抓】〈n.〉山楂【xan¹ja¹】(Chinese) hawthorn; haw

喳【ji¹ji¹ja¹ja¹】〈onomatopoeia〉吱吱喳喳 chirp; twitter

碴【ja¹ 抓; ja⁶ 抓⁶】be cut (by broken glass, china, etc.); block

咱【ja¹ 抓】I; we

咱们【ja¹mun⁴ 门】we = 我们【ngo⁵mun⁴】

= 我地【ngo⁵dēi⁶】

吒【ja¹ 抓】〈n.〉哪吒【na⁴ja¹】name of a god

鲊【ja² 抓²】salted fish; dirty; of inferior quality

鲊斗【ja²deo² 豆²】of low quality = 鲊皮【ja²pēi⁴ 脾²】=【普】不好的；低劣的

腌【ja² 渣²】〈a.〉腍腍腌【na⁵ja²】dirty; filthy =【普】肮脏

腍腍地【ja²ja²dēi² 得菲²】a little bad luck =【普】较差；较糟糕

乍【ja³ 炸】first; suddenly; abruptly

乍到【ja³dou³ 都³】be a newcomer = 初来【qo¹loi⁴】

乍看起来【ja³hon³hēi²loi⁴ 汉喜莱】at first glance

乍暖还寒【ja³ nün⁵ wan⁴ hon⁴ 嫩⁵ 环汗⁴】the temperature changes abruptly

诈【ja³ 乍】cheat; swindle; pretend; feign

诈骗【ja³pin³ 片】defraud; swindle

诈降【ja³hong⁴ 杭】feign surrender

诈死【ja³xēi² 四²】play dead; feign death

诈谛【ja³dei³ 帝】pretend；feign；make believe＝【普】装假

诈假意【ja³ga¹yi¹ 加衣】to pretend＝【普】装假

咋【ja³ 乍】how；why；bite

咋舌【ja³xid⁸ 泄】be left speechless or breathless

咤【ja³ 炸；qag⁷ 测】(see"叱咤风云")

炸【ja³ 诈】explod；blow up；flare up

炸弹【ja³dan² 蛋】bomb

炸药【ja³yêg⁹ 若】explosive；dynamite

榨【ja³ 炸】press；a press for extracting juice, oil, etc.

榨取【ja³qêü² 娶】squeeze；extort

榨油【ja³yeo⁴ 由】extract oil

榨菜【ja³qoi³ 蔡】hot pickled mustard tuber

痄【ja³ 炸】〈n.〉痄腮【ja³xoi¹ 是哀¹】mumps

蚱【ja³ 炸】〈n.〉蚱蜢【ja³mang² 孟²】grasshopper

煠【ja⁴ 炸⁴】〈a.〉煠煠声【ja⁴ja²xêng¹】describe quick；very fast

斋【jai¹ 债¹】abstain from meat, wine, etc.；vegetarian diet；give alms；room or building

斋戒【jai¹ gai³ 介】abstain from meat, wine, etc.；fast

斋期【jai¹kêi⁴ 其】fast days；fast

债【jai³ 斋³】debt

债务【jai³mou⁶ 冒】debt；liabilities

债款【jai³fun² 欢²】loan

债券【jai³gün³ 娟³】bond；debenture

债权【jai³kün⁴ 拳】creditor's rights

债台高筑【jai³toi⁴gou¹jug⁷ 台膏足】be heavily in debt

寨【jai⁶ 债⁶】stockade；stockaded village；camp

嘲【jao¹ 爪¹】ridicule；deride

嘲讽【jao¹fung³ 风³】sneer at；taunt

嘲弄【jao¹lung⁶ 龙⁶】mock；poke fun at

嘲笑【jao¹ xiu³少³】ridicule；deride；jeer at；laugh at

找【jao² 爪】look for；seek；want to see；give change

找寻【jao²qem⁴ 沉】look for；seek＝揾【wen² 温²】

找麻烦【jao² ma⁴ fan⁴ 妈⁴ 凡】look for trouble；cause sb. trouble

找工作【jao²gung¹jog⁸ 公昨】look for a job＝揾野做【wen²yē⁵jou⁶ 夜⁵造】

找钱【jao²qin⁴ 前】give change＝找赎【jao²jug⁹ 续】

爪【jao² 找】claw；talon

爪牙【jao²nga⁴ 芽】talon and fangs—lackeys；underlings

爪哇【jao²wa¹ 娃】〈n.〉Java

笊【jao³ 爪³】〈n.〉笊篱【jao³lēi¹ 离¹】a bamboo, wicker or wire strainer

罩【jao³ 笊】cover；overspread；shade；a bamboo fish trap

罩子【jao²ji² 止】cover；shade；hood；casing

罩灯【jao²deng¹ 登】lampshade

棹【jao⁶ 罩⁶】oar；row(a boat)

棹艇【jao⁶tēng⁵ 厅⁵】row a light boat＝

【普】划小船

棹忌【jao⁶gēi⁶ 机⁶】taboo; dread; far from good =【普】忌讳; 忌惮; 情况不妙

簪

【jam¹ 站¹】hairpin; wear in one's hair

簪子【jam¹ji² 止】hair clasp

簪花【jam¹ fa¹ 化¹】wear flowers in one's hair

斩

【jam² 眨】chop; cut; behead; decapitate

斩头【jam²teo² 投²】behead; decapitate =【普】斩首

斩草除根【jam²qou²qēū⁴gen¹ 操² 徐² 斤】cut the weeds and dig up the roots — destroy root and branch

眨

【jam² 斩; yab⁸ 衣鸭⁸】blink; wink

眨眼【jam²ngan⁵ 雁⁵】wink; very short time

湛

【jam³ 站³】profound; deep; crystal clear

湛蓝【jam³lam⁴ 篮】azure blue; azure

崭

【jam³ 湛; jam² 斩】towering (over); fine; swell

崭新【jam³xen¹ 辛】brand-new = 簇新【qug⁷xen¹】

蘸

【jam³ 湛】dip in(ink, sauce, etc.)

蘸墨水【jam³meg⁹xēū² 麦瑞²】dip in ink

暂

【jam⁶ 站】of short duration; temporary

暂时【jam⁶xi⁴ 思⁴】temporary; transient

暂且【jam⁶qē² 扯】for the time being; for the moment

暂行【jam⁶ heng⁴ 衡 】provisional; temporary

暂停【jam⁶ting⁴ 亭】suspend; time-out

站

【jam⁶ 暂】stand; stop; station

站起来【jam⁶hēi²loi⁴ 喜莱】stand up = 企起来【kēi⁵hēi²lēi⁴】

站住【jam⁶jū⁶ 注⁶】stop; halt; keep one's feet; hold water = 企住【kēi⁵jū⁶】

站稳【jam⁶wen² 揾】come to a stop; stand firm = 企稳【kēi⁵wen²】

站岗【jam⁶gong¹ 冈】stand guard; stand sentry

站台【jam⁶toi⁴ 抬】platform (in a railway station)

錾

【jam⁶ 暂】engrave on gold or silver; carve; chisel

錾刀【jam⁶ dou¹ 都 】(engraver's) burin; graver

錾花【jam⁶fa¹ 化¹】carve flowers or patterns

栈

【jan² 盏】warehouse; inn; shed

栈房【jan²fong⁴ 防】warehouse; inn

栈道【jan²dou⁶度】 a plank road built along the face of a cliff

盏

【jan² 栈】〈classifier〉; small cup

酒盏【jeo²jan²】small wine cup

一盏灯【yed⁷jan²deng⁶】a lamp

攒

【jan² 栈; qūn⁴ 全】collect together; good; ready accumulate

攒聚【jan²jēū⁶ 叙】gather closely together

攒鬼【jan²guei² 诡】save up money; paying; good; reckon up =【普】赚钱; 合算; 有好处

唔攒【m⁴jan²】have not saved up money; no paying =【普】没钱赚; 不合算

攒【jan² 盏】hurry through；urge

走攒【jeo²jam²】leeway；margin =【普】
（回旋）余地

有足够嘅走攒【yeo⁵jug⁷geo³gē³jeo²jan²】
There is plenty of room for manoeuvre =【普】有足够的回旋余
地

赞【jan³ 栈³】support；praise；eulogy

赞成【jan³xing⁴ 承】approve of；favour

赞同【jan³tung⁴ 铜】approve of；agree
with

赞扬【jan³ yêng⁴ 洋 】 speak highly of；
praise

赞赏【jan³xêng² 想】appreciate；admire

赞颂【jan³jung⁶ 仲】extol；eulogize

赞美【jan³mēi⁵ 尾】praise；eulogize

赞叹【jan³ tan³ 炭 】 gasp in admiration；
highly praise

赞歌【jan³go¹ 哥】song of praise；paean

赞助【jan³jo⁶ 座】support；assistance

赚【jan⁶ 栈⁶】make a profit；gain；kid；
profit

赚钱【jan⁶qin² 前²】make money

撰【jan³ 赞】write；compose

撰写【jan³xē² 舍²】write；compose

挣【jang¹ 踭¹；jang⁶ 踭⁶】struggle；
squeeze in

挣扎【jang¹jad⁸ 札】struggle

挣入去【jang⁶yeb⁹hêû³ 邑⁹ 虚³】force
one's way in =【普】挤进去

踭【jang¹ 挣¹】heel

鞋踭【hai⁴jang¹】the heel of a shoe =【普】
鞋后跟

脚踭【gêg⁸jang¹】heel =【普】脚跟

习【jab⁹ 袭】practise；exercise；be used
to；habit

习题【jab⁹tei⁴ 提】exercise

习作【jab⁹jog⁸ 昨】do exercises in composition

习惯【jab⁹ guan³ 关³】 be accustomed to；
habit

习染【jab⁹yim⁵ 冉】contract(a bad habit)；
bad habit

习性【jab⁹xing³ 胜】habits and characteris-
tics

习以为常【jab⁹yi⁵wei⁴xêng⁴ 耳维尝】be
used to sth.

袭【jab⁹ 杂】raid；follow the pattern of

袭击【jab⁹gig³ 激】make a surprise attack
on；raid

袭用【jab⁹yung⁶ 容⁶】take over

杂【jab⁹ 集 】 miscellaneous； mix；
sundry；mingle

杂乱【jab⁹lûn⁶ 联⁶】mixed and disorderly；
in a jumble

杂质【jab⁹jed⁷ 侄⁷】impurity；foreign
matter

杂种【jab⁹jung³ 肿】hybrid；bastard

杂务【jab⁹mou⁶ 冒】odd jobs

杂技【jab⁹gēi⁴ 妓】acrobatics

杂货【jab⁹fo³ 课】sundry goods；groceries

杂志【jab⁹ji³ 至】magazine；records

杂烩【jab⁹ wui⁶ 汇 】 mixed stew； hotch-
potch；mixture

杂牌【jab⁹pai⁴ 排】a less known and inferior brand

杂交【jab⁹gao³ 胶】hybridize；cross

杂糅【jab⁹yeo⁴ 柔】mix；mingle

杂念【jab⁹nim⁶ 粘⁶】distracting thoughts

铡【jab⁹ 习】hand hay cutter；cut up with a hay cutter

铡刀【jab⁹dou¹ 都】hand hay cutter

闸【jab 习】floodgate；dam up water；brake；switch

闸门【jab⁹ mun⁴瞒】sluice gate；gate；throttle valve

闸住【jab⁹ju⁶ 注⁶】stop＝【普】停住

闸仄【jab⁹jeg⁷ 则】to put something in a standing＝【普】歪着；斜着；半转体

集【jab⁹ 习】gather；collect；collection；volume

集中【jab⁹ jung¹ 钟】concentrate；centralize；focus

集合【jab⁹heb⁹ 盒】gather；assemble；call together

集结【jab⁹ gid⁹ 洁】mass；concentrate

集体【jab⁹tei⁶ 睇】collective

集会【jab⁹ wui²汇²】assembly；rally；meeting

集市【jab⁹ 是⁵】country fair；market

集镇【jab⁹jen³ 振】town

集约【jab⁹yêg⁹ 跃】intensive

集资【jab⁹ji¹ 支】raise funds；collect money

集大成【jab⁹dai⁶xing⁴ 歹⁶承】epitomize

集成电路【jab⁹xing⁴din⁶lou⁶承甸露】integrated circuit

集思广益【jab⁹ xi¹ guong² yig⁷司光²忆】pool the wisdom of the masses

集腋成裘【jab⁹ yig⁹ xing⁴ keo⁴亦承球】many a little makes a mickle

栅【jab⁹ 习；xan¹ 山】grid

栅极【xan¹gig⁹ 击⁹】〈n.〉grid；railings；paling

栅栏【jab⁹lan⁴ 兰】railings；paling；boom

扎【jad⁸ 札】prick；run into；get into；tie；bind

扎根【jad⁸gen¹ 斤】take root

扎实【jad⁸xed⁹ 失⁹】sturdy；solid

扎针【jad⁸ jem¹支庵¹】give an acupuncture treatment

扎辫仔【jad⁸ bin¹ jei²边济²】tie up one's plaits＝【普】扎小辫

扎扎跳【jad⁸jad⁸tiu³ 条³】bouncing and vivacious＝【普】蹦蹦跳

札【jad⁸ 扎】thin pieces of wood used for writing on in ancient China；letter

札炮【jad⁸pao³ 泡³】to starve＝【普】捱饿

札记【jad⁸gêi³ 寄】reading notes

匝【jad⁸ 札；jab⁸ 习⁸】circle；dense；full

砸【jad⁸ 札；jab⁸ 习⁸；jag⁹ 宅】pound；tamp；break；smash；fail

砸锅【jad⁸wo¹ 窝】fail；fall through＝掟煲【dêng³bou¹】

砸烂【jad⁸ lan⁶ 兰】break into pieces；smash

咂【jab⁸ 杂⁸；dab⁷ 踏⁷】

咂嘴【jab⁸jêu² 追²】make clicks

咂滋味【dab⁷ji¹mêi⁶ 之未】taste；savour＝【普】品味

责【jag⁸ 窄】duty；demand；question closely；reproach

责任【jag⁸yem⁶ 壬】duty；blame

责备【jag⁸bêi⁶ 鼻】reproach；blame

责成【jag⁸xing⁴ 承】instruct；charge

责怪【jag⁸guai³ 乖³】blame

责令【jag⁸ling⁶ 另】order；instruct

责无旁贷【jag⁸mou⁴pong⁴tai³ 毛蚌⁴太】there is no shirking the responsibility

碛【jag⁸ 责】heavy body press

碛扁【jag⁸bin² 匾】press flat；flatten

碛碎【jag⁸xêü³ 瑞³】crush(to pieces)

宅【jag⁹ 泽】residence；house

宅院【jag⁹yün² 阮】a house with a court-yard；house

窄【jag⁸ 责】narrow；petty；hard up

窄路【jag⁸lou⁶ 露】narrow path

心眼窄【xem¹ngan⁵jag⁸】petty；oversensitive

泽【jag⁹ 宅】pool；damp；luster；favour

泽国【jag⁹guog⁸ 帼】inundated area

啧【jag⁸ 责；jēd⁷ 佢⁷】click of the tongue

啧啧称羡【jag⁸jag⁸qing¹xin⁶ 清善】click the tongue in admiration

择【jag⁹ 摘】select；choose；pick

择交【jag⁹gao¹ 胶】choose friends = 择友【jag⁹yeo⁵ 有】

择善而从【jag⁹xin⁶yi⁴qung⁴ 羡移虫】choose and follow what is good

择食【jag⁹xig⁹ 蚀】to be choosy with food = 【普】挑选好吃的

择使【jag⁹xei² 洗】not easy to use；trou-blesome；difficult = 【普】不好用；不好办；不顺利

掷【jag⁹ 择】throw；cast

掷还【jag⁹wan⁴ 环】please return

掷铁饼【jag⁹tid⁸bēng² 替热⁸ 柄²】discus throw

摘【jag⁹ 择】pick；select；pluck；take off

摘花【jag⁹fa¹ 化¹】pluck flowers

摘除【jag⁹qêü⁴ 徐】excise

摘录【jag⁹lug⁹ 六】take passages；extracts

摘要【jag⁹ yiu³ 妖³】make a summary；summary

挤【jei¹ 剂】to put；to keep；press；jostle；pack

挤拥【jei¹yung² 涌】crowded = 【普】拥挤

挤压【jei¹ngad⁸ 押】extruding = 挬【jid⁷ 节⁷】

挤牙膏【jei¹ nga⁴ gou¹ 芽高】squeeze too-th paste out of a tube = 挬牙膏【jid⁷nga⁴gou¹】

挤眉弄眼【jei¹mēi⁴lung⁶ngan⁵ 微龙⁶ 雁⁵】make eyes；wink

挤享度【jei¹hêng²dou⁶ 响道】lay up here = 【普】放在这里

剂【jei¹ 挤】a pharmaceutical or other chemical preparation

剂量【jei¹lêng⁶ 谅】dosage；dose

剂型【jei¹ying⁴ 形】the form of a drug

齑【jei¹ 剂】fine；powdery

齑粉【jei¹fen² 分²】fine powder；broken bits

仔【jei² 济²；ji² 子】①son；boy；man；②attentive

仔嬷【jei²na² 那²】son and mother = 【普】儿娘

仔女【jei²nêü⁵ 挪去⁵】children = 【普】孩子；儿女

仔细【ji²xei³ 世】careful；attentive；look out

济【jei³ 制；jei² 仔】many；cross a river；help

济济【jei² jei² 仔】(of people) many; numerous

济事【jei³xi⁶ 是】be of help(or use)

制【jei³ 济】①make; restrict; work out; system ②to control; to restrict; willing to

制造【jei³ jou⁶ 做 】make; manufacture; engineer

制作【jei³jog⁸ 昨】make; manufacture

制订【jei³ding³ 定³】work out; formulate

制定【jei³ding⁶ 锭】lay down; draw up

制品【jei³ben² 禀】products; goods

制约【jei³yêg⁸ 若⁸】restrict; condition

制止【jei³ji² 子】check; curb; prevent

制伏【jei³fug⁹ 服】check; subdue

制服【jei³fug⁹ 伏】uniform

制裁【jei³qoi⁴ 才】sanction; punish

制胜【jei³xing³ 圣】get the upper hand of; subdue

制度【jei³dou⁶ 道】system; institution

制得过【jei³ deg⁷ guo³德果³】worthwhile =【普】值得干

制唔制【jei³m⁴jei³】do you like...?; be willing or not; want or not =【普】愿不愿意

滞【jei⁶ 济⁶】stagnant; sluggish; indigestion; not sharp

滞留【jei⁶leo⁴ 流】be detained; be held up

滞销【jei⁶xiu¹ 消】unsalable; unmarketable

滞口【jei⁶heo² 后²】①indigestion and detesting eat ② not smoothly =【普】①消化不良而厌食②不顺利

掣【jei³ 制; qid⁸ 彻】switches; pull; draw

电掣【din⁶jei³】switch =【普】电开关

掣肘【jei³jeo² 走】hold sb. back by the elbow; impede = 托手踭【tog⁸xeo²

jang¹】

周【jeo¹ 邹】circumference; make a circuit; all; thoughtful; week; cycle; a surname

周围【jeo¹wei⁴ 维】around; round

周长【jeo¹qêng⁴ 祥】girth; perimeter

周详【jeo¹qêng⁴ 祥】comprehensive; complete

周到【jeo¹dou³ 度³】attentive and satisfactory

周密【jeo¹med⁹ 勿】careful; through

周全【jeo¹qün⁴ 存】thorough; help sb. attian his aim

周末【jeo¹mud⁹ 没】weekend

周年【jeo¹nin⁴ 捻⁴】anniversary

周期【jeo¹kēi⁴ 其】period; cycle

周旋【jeo¹xün⁴ 船】socialize; deal with

周游【jeo¹yeo⁴ 油】travel round

周折【jeo¹jid⁸ 节】twists and turns; setbacks

周转【jeo¹jün² 专²】turnover; have enough to meet the need

周济【jeo¹jei³ 挤³】help out; relieve

周而复始【jeo¹yi⁴fug⁹qi² 移服齿】go round and begin; move in cycles

周时【jeo¹xi⁴ 是⁴】always =【普】经常

周身屎【jeo¹xen¹xi² 辛史】notorious; to be in trouble =【普】很多罪状、劣迹

周身蚁【jeo¹xen¹ngei⁵ 辛矮⁵】to involve oneself in much trouble =【普】很多难以摆脱的麻烦、困扰

邹【jeo¹ 周】a surname

陬【jeo¹ 周】corner; foot of a hill

走【jeo² 酒】walk；go；run；move；leave；visit；through；to go away

走路【jeo²lou⁶ 露】walk；go on foot = 行路【hang⁴lou⁶】

走动【jeo²dung⁶ 洞】walk about = 行走【hang⁴jeo²】

走向【jeo² hêng³ 香³ 】run；trend；move towards

走卒【jeo² jêd⁷支律⁷】pawn；lackey

走兽【jeo²xeo³ 秀】beast；quadruped

走样【jeo²yêng² 杨²】lose shape

走私【jeo²xi¹ 思】smuggle

走运【jeo²wen⁶ 混】have good luck = 行运【hang⁴wen⁶】

走着瞧【jeo²jêg⁹qiu⁴ 桌⁹ 潮】wait and see = 睇住嚟【tei²jü⁶lei⁴ 注⁴ 黎】

走狗【jeo²geo³ 九】running dog；lackey

走后门【jeo²heo⁶mun⁴ 候们】get in by the back door

走马看花【jeo²ma⁵hon³fa¹ 妈⁵ 汉化¹】look at flowers while riding on horseback

走投无路【jeo²teo⁴mou⁴lou⁶ 头毛露】have no way out

走鸡【jeo² gei¹ 计¹】to lose an opportunity；to run away；wander away =【普】走失

走趱【jeo²jan² 盏】to have room，e.g. for improvement(see"趱")

走人【jeo² yen⁴ 仁】 to leave；sneak away =【普】离去；溜之大吉

走夹唔踎【jeo²gab⁸m⁴teo² 甲头⁴】to run for one's life =【普】慌忙逃跑

酒【jeo² 走】alcoholic drink；wine

酒精【jeo²jing¹ 晶】ethyl alcohol；alcohol

酒饼【jeo²bēng² 柄²】medical wine；distiller's yeast =【普】酒曲

酒店【jeo²dim³ 掂³】a motel；wineshop

酒家【jeo²ga¹ 加】a restaurant；wineshop

酒菜【jeo²qoi³ 蔡】food and drink =【普】酒食

酒席【jeo²jig⁹ 直】feast

酒凹【jeo²neb⁷ 挪合¹】dimple；dimples on the face =【普】酒窝

酒囊饭袋【jeo²nong⁴fan⁶doi⁶ 瓢范代】wine skin and rice bag—a goodfor-nothing

皱【jeo³ 奏】wrinkle；crease

皱纹【jeo³men⁴ 文】wrinkles；lines

皱褶【jeo³jib⁸ 接】fold

皱眉头【jeo³mēi⁴teo⁴ 微投】knit one's brows；frown

绉【jeo³ 奏】crape；crepe

绉纱【jeo²xa¹ 沙】crape

咒【jeo³ 奏】incantation；curse

咒骂【jeo³ma⁶ 妈⁶】curse；swear；abuse；revile

昼【jeo³ 奏】daytime；daylight；day

昼夜【jeo³yē⁶ 野】day and night；round the clock

奏【jeo³ 皱】play(music)；achieve

奏乐【jeo³ngog⁹ 岳】play music；strike up a tune

奏效【jeo³ hao⁶ 吼⁶】 prove effective；be successful

奏章【jeo³jêng¹ 张】memorial to the throne

奏捷【jeo³jid⁹ 截】win a battle

揍【jeo³ 奏】beat; hit; strike

揍他一顿【jeo³ta¹yed⁷dên⁶ 它壹敦⁶】beat
　　him up = 抳佢一餐【qei³kêü⁵yed⁷
　　qɑn¹】

就【jeo⁶ 袖】come near; undertake; ac-
　　complish; suit; concerning; on; at
　　once; as soon as; as much as; only;
　　exactly; even if

就此【jeo⁶qi² 耻】at this point; thus

就地【jeo⁶dēi⁶ 得菲⁶】on the spot

就近【jeo⁶gen⁶ 靳】(do or get sth.) near-
　　by

就范【jeo⁶fɑn⁶ 饭】submit; give in

就是【jeo⁶xi⁶ 士】quite right; even

就任【jeo⁶yem⁶ 壬⁶】take office

就绪【jeo⁶xêü⁵ 瑞】be in order; be ready

就座【jeo⁶jo⁶ 坐】take one's seat

就算【jeo⁶xün³ 蒜】even if; granted that

就要【jeo⁶yiu³ 腰³】be about to; be going
　　to

就业【jeo⁶yib⁹ 叶】obtain employment;
　　get a job

就至【jeo⁶ji³ 志】in the middle of; just =
　　【普】刚才

就嚟【jeo⁶lei⁴ 黎】going to =【普】马上到

就手【jeo⁶xeo² 守】smooth =【普】顺利
　　无阻碍

就事论事【jeo⁶xi⁶lên⁶xi⁶ 是沦⁶ 是】con-
　　sider sth. as it stands

袖【jeo⁶ 就】sleeve; tuck inside the
　　sleeve

袖子【jeo⁶ji² 止】sleeve = 衫袖【xɑm¹jeo⁶】

袖珍【jeo⁶jen¹ 真】pocket-size; pocket

袖手旁观【jeo⁶xeo²pong⁴gun¹ 守膀官】
　　look on with folded arms

宙【jeo⁶ 就】time(conceived as past, pre-
　　sent and future)

纣【jeo⁶ 就】name of the last ruler of the
　　Shang Dynasty, reputedly a tyrant

胄【jeo⁶ 就】helmet; descendants

诌【jeo³ 皱】fabricate(tales, etc.); make
　　up

州【jeo¹ 周】an administrative division;
　　prefecture

洲【jeo¹ 周】continent; islet in a river;
　　sand bar

洲际【jeo¹jei³ 济】intercontinental

舟【jeo¹ 周】boat

舟车【jeo¹qē¹ 奢】vessel and vehicle;
　　journey

箴【jem¹ 针】admonish; exhort

箴言【jem¹yin⁴ 然】admonition; exhorta-
　　tion

砧【jem¹ 针】hammering block; anvil

砧板【jem¹bɑn² 版】chopping block

斟【jem¹ 针】pour(tea or wine)

斟酌【jem¹jêg⁸ 桌】consider; deliberate

斟盘【jem⁶pun⁴ 盆】to hold a talk; to ne-
　　gotiate =【普】洽谈某项生意

针【jem¹ 斟】needle; stitch; injection;
　　acupuncture

针线【jem¹xin³ 扇】needlework

针织【jem¹jig⁷ 积】knitting

针剂【jem¹jei¹ 挤】〈n.〉injection

针砭【jem¹ bin² 贬 】an ancient form of
　　acupuncture; point out sb.'s errors
　　and offer salutary advice

针对【jem¹ dêu³ 堆³】be aimed at; in the light of

针波【jem¹bo¹ 坡】jump ball

针锋相对【jem¹fung¹xêng¹dêu³ 风双堆³】give tit for tat

枕【jem² 针²】pillow; rest the head on; block

枕头【jem²teo⁴ 投】pillow

枕席【jem²jēg⁹ 支尺⁹】a mat used to cover a pillow; bed

枕戈待旦【jem⁹guo¹doi⁶dan³ 果¹ 代诞】be ready for battle

枕长【jem²qêng⁴ 祥】always =【普】一直; 经常

鸩【jem² 枕】〈n.〉鸩毒【jem²dug⁹ 独】poisoned wine

浸【jem³ 枕³; jem⁶ 枕⁶】soak; steep; immerse; a layer

浸泡【jem³pao¹ 抛】soak; immerse

浸染【jem³yim⁵ 冉⁵】be contaminated

浸润【jem³yên⁶ 闰】soak; infiltrate

浸透【jem³teo³ 投³】soak; saturate; steep

浸水【jem⁶ xêu² 绪²】flood; submerge =【普】淹水; 溺水

朕【jem⁶ 浸⁶】I, the sovereign; we(used by a royal person in proclamations instead of I)

真【jen¹ 珍】true; real; truly; really; clearly

真实【jen¹xed⁹ 失⁹】true; real

真相【jen¹ xêng² 双³ 】the real situation; truth

真理【jen¹lêi⁵ 李】truth

真情【jen¹qing² 程】the real situation; true feelings

真谛【jen¹ dei³ 帝 】true essence; true meaning

真空【jen¹hung¹ 匈】〈n.〉vacuum

真挚【jen¹ji³ 志】sincere; cordial

真诚【jen¹xing⁴ 成】sincere; genuine

真假【jen¹ga² 贾】true and false

真知灼见【jen¹ji¹jêg⁸gin³ 支雀建】real knowledge and deep insight

真凭实据【jen¹peng⁴xed⁹gêu³ 朋失⁹ 踞】conclusive evidence; hard evidence

真金不怕火炼【jen¹gem¹bed⁷pa³fo²lin⁶ 今毕耙³ 伙练】true gold fears no fire — a person of integrity can stand severe tests

珍【jen¹ 真】treasure; precious; rare

珍贵【jen¹guei³ 桂】valuable; precious

珍宝【jen¹bou² 补】jewellery; treasure

珍藏【jen¹ qong⁴床 】collect(rare books, etc.)

珍惜【jen¹xig⁷ 色】treasure; value; cherish

珍重【jen¹ jung⁶仲 】 treasure; take good care of yourself

珍馐【jen¹xeo¹ 修】delicacies; dainties

珍珠【jen¹jü¹ 朱】pearl

诊【jen² 缜; qen² 陈²】examine (a patient)

诊病【jen²bēng⁶ 柄⁶】diagnose a disease

诊断【jen²dün³ 段³】diagnose

诊治【jen²ji⁶ 自】make a diagnosis and give treatment = 诊疗【jen²liu⁴ 辽】

诊所【jen²xo² 锁】clinic

诊室【jen²xed⁷ 失】consulting room

畛【jen² 诊】〈n.〉畛域【jen²wig⁹ 划益⁹】boundary

缜【jen² 诊】〈a.〉缜密【jen²med⁹ 勿】careful; deliberate

疹 【jen² 诊；qen² 陈²】rash；measles

振 【jen³ 震】shake；flap；brace up

振荡【jen³dong⁶ 当⁶】vibration；oscillation
振幅【jen³fug⁷ 福】amplitude(of vibration)
振奋【jen³fen⁵ 愤】rouse oneself；inspire
振作【jen³ jog⁸ 昨】bestir oneself；display
　　vigour
振兴【jen³ hing¹ 兄】develop vigorously；
　　promote
振振有辞【jen³jen³yeo⁵qi⁴ 友 词】speak
　　plausibly and at length

震 【jen³ 振】shake；shock；greatly excit-
　　ed；shocked
震颤【jen³jin³ 战】tremble；quiver＝打冷
　　震【da²lang⁵jen³】
震荡【jen³dong⁶ 当⁶】shake；shock
震动【jen³dung⁶ 洞】shake；shock；vibrate
震撼【jen³ham⁶ 陷】shake；shock；vibrate
震惊【jen³ging¹ 京】shoke；amaze；aston-
　　ish
震慑【jen³xib⁸ 摄】awe；frighten
震耳欲聋【jen³yi⁵yug⁹lung⁴ 以玉隆】deaf-
　　ening

赈 【jen³ 振】relieve；aid

赈济【jen³jei³ 际】relieve；aid
赈灾【jen³ joi¹ 哉 】 relieve the people in
　　stricken areas

镇 【jen³ 振】 press down；calm；guard；
　　garrison post；town；ease
镇定【jen³ding⁶ 锭】calm；cool；composed
镇静【jen³jing⁶ 净】calm；cool；composed
镇守【jen³xeo² 手】guard；garrison
镇痛【jen³tung³ 通³】ease pain；analgesia
镇压【jen³ngad⁸ 押】suppress；repress；
　　put down

阵 【 jen⁶　振⁶ 】 battle　array （ or
　　formation）；position；a period of time
阵地【jen⁶dēi⁶ 得菲⁶】position；front
阵容【jen⁶yung⁴ 榕】battle array(or forma-
　　tion)
阵势【jen⁶xei³ 世】battle array；situation
阵线【jen⁶ xin³ 腺 】 front；ranks；align-
　　ment
阵营【jen⁶ying⁴ 仍】a group of people who
　　pursue a common interest；camp
一阵子【yed⁷jen³ji² 壹止】a period of time

轸 【jen² 诊】〈v.〉轸念【jen²nim⁶ 粘⁶】
　　think anxiously about

争 【jeng¹ 铮；jang¹ 踭】contend；vie；
　　strive；argue；dispute；short of；
　　wanting
争霸【jeng¹ba³ 坝】contend for hegemony
　　＝争雄【jeng¹hung⁴ 红】＝争叻
　　【jang¹lēg⁷】
争辩【jeng¹bin⁶ 便】argue；contend ＝ 争
　　鸣【jeng¹ming⁴】
争论【jeng¹ lên⁶ 沦⁶】controversy；dis-
　　pute；contention
争议【jeng¹yi⁵ 耳】dispute；controversy＝
　　争拗【jang¹ao³】
争执【jeng¹jeb⁷ 汁】disagree；dispute
争斗【jeng¹deo² 豆³】fight；struggle
争吵【jeng¹qao² 炒】quarrel；squabble
争夺【jeng¹düd⁹ 得月⁹】fight for；vie with
　　sb. for sth.
争取【jeng¹qêü² 娶】strive for；fight for
争光【jeng¹guong¹ 胱】win honour for
争端【jeng¹ dün¹ 段¹】 controversial issue；
　　dispute
争气【jang¹hēi³ 戏】try to make a good
　　showing

争先恐后【jeng¹ xin¹ hung² heo⁶ 仙孔候 】strive to be the first and fear to lag behind

争权夺利【jang¹ kün⁴ düd⁹lēi⁶ 拳 得月⁹ 俐】scramble for power and profit

增【jeng¹ 争】increase; gain; add

增加【jeng¹ga¹ 家】increase; raise; add

增多【jeng¹ do¹ 朵¹】 grow in number or quantity; increase

增产【jeng¹qan² 铲】increase production

增添【jeng¹tim¹ 甜¹】add; increase

增益【jeng¹yig⁷ 忆】gain

增长【jeng¹jêng² 蒋】increase; rise; grow

增强【jeng¹kêng⁴ 卡香⁴】strengthen; heighten

增进【jeng¹jên⁶ 俊】enhance; promote

增值【jeng¹jig⁹ 直】rise in value; appreciation

增补【jeng¹bou² 保】augment; supplement

增删【jeng¹ xan¹ 山 】 additions and deletions

曾【jeng¹ 增; qeng⁴ 层】relationship between great-grandchildren and great-grandparents; a surname; once

曾孙【jeng¹xün¹ 酸】great-grandson

曾祖【jeng¹ jou² 早 】 (paternal) great-grandfather

曾经【qeng⁴ging¹ 京】once

憎【jeng¹ 增】hate; detest; abhor

憎恨【jeng¹hen⁶ 很⁶】hate; detest

憎恶【jeng¹wu³ 乌³】abhor; loathe; abominate

罾【jeng¹ 增】a square-shaped fishing net with poles as supports

狰【jeng¹ 争】〈a.〉狰狞【jeng¹ning⁴ 宁】ferocious; savage; hideous

峥【jeng¹ 争】〈a.〉峥嵘【jeng¹wing⁴ 荣】lofty and steep; towering; outstanding; extraordinary

睁【jeng¹ 争】open(the eyes)

睁只眼,闭只眼【jeng¹jēg⁸ngan⁵, bei³jēg⁸ ngan⁵ 脊雁⁵】turn a blind eye to sth.; wink at sth.

筝【jeng¹ 争】a 21-or 25-stringed plucked instrument in some ways similar to the zither

铮【jeng¹ 争】〈onomatopoeia〉铮铮【jeng¹jeng¹】clank; clang

怔【jeng² 争²】〈a.〉愣怔【meng²jeng² 盟² 争²】be fidgety; be agitated ∽【普】烦躁;急躁

赠【jeng⁶ 增⁶】give as a present; present as a gift

赠送【jeng⁶xung³ 宋】give as a present

赠品【jeng⁶ben² 裹】gift; giveaway

赠言【jeng⁶yin⁴ 然】words of advice or encouragement given to a friend at parting

执【jeb⁷ 汁】hold; take charge of; persist; observe; catch; to pick up; to pack; to give birth to; to assist in delivering a baby

执行【jeb⁷ heng⁴衡 】 carry out; execute; implement

执掌【jeb⁷jêng² 蒋】wield; be in control of

执法【jeb⁷fad⁸ 发】enforce the law

执拗【jeb⁷ao³ 坳²】stubborn; pigheaded

执意【jeb⁷yi³ 薏】insist on; be bent on

执着【jeb⁷jêg⁹ 支约⁹】inflexible; rigid

执照【jeb⁷jiu³ 召³】license; permit

执政【jeb⁷jing³ 正】be in power; be in office

执迷不悟【jeb⁷mei⁴bed⁷ng⁶ 谜毕误】stick to a wrong course; be perverse

执地【jeb⁷dēi² 得菲²】to collect waste materials =【普】捡破烂

执笠【jeb⁷leb⁷ 立⁷】bankrupt =【普】(店铺)破产倒闭

执漏【jeb⁷leo⁶ 留⁶】to repair a leaking roof =【普】检漏;补漏

执拾【jeb⁷xeb⁹ 十】to pack; to tidy up =【普】收拾;整理

执死鸡【jeb⁷xēi²gei¹ 四² 计¹】to obtain some unexpected benefits =【普】从别人的弃物中捡到有用的东西;幸运得了便宜

执手尾【jeb⁷xeo²mēi⁵ 守美】to clean up; to pack =【普】做扫尾工作

执输【jeb⁷xū¹ 书】to lose; to be at a disadvantage =【普】竞争不过别人;吃了亏

执赢【jeb⁷yēng⁴ 衣镜⁴】to win; to be at an advantage =【普】竞争胜出;得着好处

执人口水尾【jeb⁷yen⁴heo²xêū²mēi⁵ 仁厚² 瑞² 美】to refer to one who has not got his own ideas or thinkings =【普】拾人牙慧

汁【jeb⁷ 执】juice　汁液【jeb⁷yig⁹ 亦】juice

楫【jeb⁷ 室⁷】stopper; cork =【普】塞子

揶【jed⁷ 室⁷】fill in; squeeze in; restrain =【普】硬塞;按捺

揶野入去【jed⁷yē⁵yeb⁹hêū³ 夜⁵ 邑⁹ 虚³】squeeze a few more things in =【普】塞点东西进去

疾【jed⁹ 室】disease; suffering; hate; fast

疾病【jed⁹bēng⁶ 柄⁶】disease; illness

疾苦【jed⁹fu² 虎】suffering; hardships

疾风【jed⁹fung¹ 丰】strong wind; moderate gale

嫉【jed⁹ 疾】be jealous; be envious; hate

嫉妒【jed⁹dou³ 到】be jealous of; envy

嫉恨【jed⁹hen⁶ 很⁶】envy and hate

蒺【jed⁹ 疾】〈n.〉蒺藜【jed⁹lei⁴ 黎】puncture vine

侄【jed⁹ 疾】brother's son; nephew

侄仔【jed⁹jei² 济²】brother's son; nephew =【普】侄子

侄女【jed⁹ nêū² 内去⁵】brother's daughter; niece

侄孙【jed⁹ xūn¹ 酸 】brother's grandson

窒【jed⁹ 疾】stop up; obstructed; afraid; frightened

窒息【jed⁹xig¹ 色】stifle; suffocate

窒脚【jed⁹ gêg⁸ 格约⁸】to stop suddenly for a while when walking =【普】前进中因受阻或受惊而步伐迟疑

仄【jeg⁷ 则】narrow;(see "仄声")

仄声【jeg⁷xing¹ 升】oblique tones, i. e., the falling-rising tone(上声), the falling tone(去声)and the entering tone(入声), as distinct from the level tone(平声)in classical Chinese pronunciation

鲫【jeg⁷ 则】〈n.〉鲫鱼【jeg⁷yū² 渔²】cuttlefish

则【jeg⁷ 仄】standard；rule；imitate；but；〈conj.〉∽ 就

否则【feo²jeg⁷】otherwise；if not；or else

侧【jeg⁷ 则】side；incline；lean

侧面【jeg⁷min⁶ 免⁶】side；aspect

侧边【jeg⁷bin¹ 鞭】next to；beside =【普】旁边

侧门【jeg⁷mun⁴ 们】side door

侧目【jeg⁷mug⁹ 木】sidelong glance

侧身【jeg⁷ xen¹ 辛 】on one's side；sideways

侧重【jeg⁷jung⁶ 仲】lay particular emphasis on

左【jo² 佐²】the left side；the left；east；queer；wrong；different；〈auxil.〉already(此义又写作"咗")=【普】了；了却

左面【jo²min⁶ 免⁶】the left side ＝ 左便【jo²bin⁶】

左手便【jo²xeo²bin⁶ 守辨】left-hand side ＝【普】左手方向

左近【jo²gen⁶ 靳】in the vicinity；around；about；roughly；nearby =【普】大约；差不多；附近

左拗【jo²yao¹ 衣拗¹】left-handed =【普】左手使用能力强于右手的人

左轮【jo²lên² 沦²】revolver

左手【jo²xeo² 守】the left hand

左迁【jo²qin¹ 千】demote

左派【jo² pai³ 排³ 】the Left；the left wing；Leftist

左翼【jo²yig⁹ 亦】left wing；the left wing

左倾【jo²king¹ 顷¹】left-leaning；progressive

左证【jo²jing³ 正】evidence；proof

左右【jo²yeo⁶ 佑】the left and right sides；about；in the vicinity；master；retinue；anyway

左顾右盼【jo² gu³ yeo⁶ pan³ 故 佑 攀³】glance right and left

左右为难【jo²yeo⁶wei⁴nan⁴ 佑维内晏⁴】in a dilemma

阻【jo² 左】hinder；block；obstruct

阻碍【jo²ngoi⁶ 外】hinder；block；impede

阻挡【jo² dong⁶ 当² 】stop；stem；resist；obstruct

阻拦【jo²lan⁴ 兰】stop；obstruct

阻塞【jo²xeg⁷ 是克⁷】block；clog

阻挠【jo²nao⁴ 闹⁴】obstruct；thwart

阻止【jo²ji² 子】prevent；stop；hold back

阻手阻脚【jo²xeo²jo²gêg⁸ 守格约⁸】hinder =【普】阻碍

佐【jo³ 左³】assist；assistant

佐餐【jo³qan¹ 灿¹】be eaten together with rice or bread

佐理【jo³lêi⁵ 李】assist sb. with a task

佐证【jo³jing³ 正】evidence；proof

坐【jo⁶ 助；qo⁵ 错⁵】sit；travel by (a plane, etc.)；have its back towards；put；sink；because

坐低【qo⁵dei¹ 帝¹】sit down =【普】坐下

坐等【jo⁶deng³ 戥】sit back and wait ＝ 坐待【jo⁶doi⁶】

坐标【jo⁶biu¹ 彪】〈n.〉coordinate

坐监【qo⁵gam¹ 鉴¹】be in jail；be imprisoned =【普】坐牢

坐落【jo⁶log⁹ 洛⁹】(of a building) be situated

坐镇【jo⁶ jen³ 振 】assume personal command

坐月【qo⁵ yūd⁹越 】confinement in child-birth

坐视【jo⁶xi⁶ 是】sit by and watch

坐失良机【jo⁶ xed⁷ lêng⁴ gēi¹室凉基】let slip golden opportunity

坐立不安【jo⁶leb⁹bed⁹ngon¹ 笠⁹ 毕桉】be fidgety

坐收渔利【jo⁶ xeo¹ yū⁴ lēi⁶修鱼俐 】reap the spoils of victory without lifting a finger

座【jo⁶ 助;qo⁵ 锄⁵】seat; stand; constel-lation

座谈【jo⁶tam⁴ 谭】have an informal discussion

座谈会【jo⁶tam⁴wui² 谭汇²】forum; symposium

座位【jo⁶wei² 毁】seat; place

座右铭【jo⁶yeo⁶ming⁵ 佑冥】motto; maxim

唑【jo⁶ 坐】〈n.〉噻唑【xeg⁷jo⁶】thiazole

助【jo⁶ 坐】help; assist; aid

助理【jo⁶lēi⁵ 李】assistant

助手【jo⁶xeo² 守】assistant; helper; aide

助长【jo⁶jêng² 掌】encourage; abet; foster

助兴【jo⁶hing³ 庆】liven thing up; add to the fun

助威【jo⁶wei¹ 维¹】boost the morale of

助燃【jo⁶yin⁴ 然】combustion-supporting

助纣为虐【jo⁶jeo⁶wei⁴yêg⁹ 就维药】aid King Zhou in his tyrannical rule; help a tyrant to do evil

灾【joi¹ 栽】calamity; adversity; disaster

灾害【joi¹hoi⁶ 亥】calamity; disaster

灾荒【joi¹ fong¹ 方 】 famine due to crop failures

灾祸【joi¹wo⁶ 窝⁶】disaster; calamity

灾难【joi¹nan⁶ 那晏⁶】suffering; calamity; disaster

灾情【joi¹qing⁴ 程】the condition of a disaster

灾区【joi¹kêu¹ 驱】disaster area

灾民【joi¹ men⁴闻 】 victims of a natural calamity

哉【joi¹ 灾】〈auxil.〉alas; how...; why...; what... = ……呀!;……呢?;……吗? 有何难哉?【yeo⁵ho⁴ nan⁴joi¹】What's so difficult about it?

栽【joi¹ 灾】plant; stick in; impose; tumble

栽培【joi¹pui⁴ 陪】cultivate; grow; foster; patronize

栽种【joi¹jung³ 仲³】plant; grow

栽倒【joi¹dou² 捣】fall down = 跌倒【did⁸ dou²】

宰【joi² 再²】slaughter; govern; government official

宰割【joi² god⁸ 葛 】 invade, oppress and exploit

宰杀【joi² xad⁸ 萨】slaughter; butcher = 剐【tong¹】

宰相【joi² xêng³ 尚³】prime minister (in feudal China)

崽【joi² 宰;jei² 仔】son; young animal; whelp

狗崽子【geo²joi²ji² 九宰止】son of a bitch = 狗种【geo²jung²】

载【joi³ 再】year; put down in writing; record; carry; hold; all over the road; as well as

一年半载【yed⁷ nin⁴ bun³ joi³壹念² 伴³ 宰³】six to twelve months

载重【joi³qung⁵ 从⁵】load；carrying capacity

载货【joi³fo³ 课】carry cargo(or freight)

载波【joi³bo¹ 坡】carrier wave；carrier

载歌载舞【joi³go¹joi³mou⁵ 哥武】festively singing and dancing

再【joi³ 载】〈ad.〉another time；again；moreover

再次【joi³qi³ 刺】once more；once again

再度【joi³dou⁶渡 】once more；a second time

再者【joi³ jē²姐】moreover；furthermore；besides＝再则【joi²jeg⁷】＝再就系【joi³jeo⁶hei⁶】

再三【joi³ xam¹衫 】over and over again；again and again；repeatedly

再见【joi³gin³ 建】good-bye；see you again

再加【joi³ga¹ 家】in addition；besides

再嫁【joi³ga³ 价】(of a woman) remarry

再不【joi³bed⁷ 毕】or else；or；if not＝再不然【yin⁴ 言】

再版【joi³ban² 板】second edition

再造【joi³jou⁶ 做】give sb. a new lease on life

再生【joi³ xeng¹笙 】regeneration；reprocess

再说【joi³xüd⁸ 雪】what's more；besides

再现【joi³yin⁶ 苋】reappear；be reproduced

再接再厉【joi³jib⁸joi³lei⁶ 支叶³ 丽】make persistent efforts；continue to exert oneself

在【joi⁶ 栽⁶】exist；be living；join or belong to an organization；rest with；depend on；in process of；in course of

在行【joi⁶hong⁴ 杭】be expert at sth.

在场【joi⁶qêng⁴ 祥】be on the scene

在乎【joi⁶fu⁴ 符】care about；mind

在即【joi⁶jig⁷ 织】near at hand；shortly；soon

在理【joi⁶ lēi⁵李】reasonable；right ＝ 啱【ngam¹】

在家【joi⁶ga¹ 加】be at home；be in

在世【joi⁶xei³ 细】be living

在望【joi⁶mong⁶ 亡⁶】be visible；be in sight

在先【joi⁶ xin¹仙 】formerly；in the past；before

在野【joi⁶yê⁵ 夜】not be in office

在意【joi⁶yi³ 薏】take notice of；be in custody

在于【joi⁶yü¹ 迂】lie in；be determined by

在职【joi⁶jig⁷ 织】be on the job

在座【joi⁶jo⁶ 坐】be present

在在皆是【joi⁶joi⁶gai¹xi⁶ 佳士】can be seen everywhere

糟【jou¹ 遭】distillers' grains；rotten；in a mess

糟糕【jou¹gou¹ 高】how terrible；too bad

糟糠【jou¹hong¹ 康】distillers' grains, husks, etc.

糟粕【jou¹pag⁸ 魄】waste matter；dross

糟蹋【jou¹tab⁸ 塔】waste；insult；violate

糟掔【jou¹ jed⁷质】 put sb. to great inconvenience；nurse a grievance ＝【普】委屈；糟践

遭【jou¹ 糟】meet with；suffer；round；time

遭到【jou¹dou³ 度³】suffer；meet with

遭受【jou¹xeo⁶ 授】suffer；sustain

遭殃【jou¹yêng¹ 央】suffer disaster；suffer

遭遇【jou¹ yü⁶预】meet with；encounter；(hard)lot

租【jou¹ 遭】rent；charter；rent out；lease；land tax

租借【jou¹jē³ 蔗】rent; hire; lease

租赁【jou¹yem⁶ 任】rent; lease; hire

租金【jou¹gem¹ 甘】rent; rental

租约【jou¹yêg⁸ 若⁸】lease

祖【jou² 早】grandfather; ancestor; founder

祖先【jou²xin¹ 仙】ancestry; forefathers

祖宗【jou²jung¹ 中】forefathers; ancestry

祖辈【jou²bui³ 背】ancestors; forefathers

祖传【jou²qūn⁴ 存】handed down from ancestors

祖父【jou² fu⁶ 付】grandfather＝阿爷【a³ yē⁴】

祖母【jou² mou⁵ 武】grandmother＝阿嬷【a³ma⁴】

祖籍【jou² jig⁹直 】original family home; ancestral home

祖国【jou²guog⁸ 帼】one's country; homeland; motherland; fatherland

组【jou² 祖】organize; form; group; set; series

组合【jou² heb⁹盒 】make up; compose; combination

组织【jou² jig⁷ 积】organize; organization; tissue

组成【jou²xing⁴ 承】form; make up; compose

组阁【jou²gog⁸ 各】form(or set up) a cabinet

组稿【jou²gou² 高²】solicit contributions

早【jou² 祖】morning; long ago; early

早晨【jou²xen⁴ 辰】(early) morning

早安【jou²ngon¹ 桉】good morning

早排【jou²pai⁴ 牌】the previous period＝早个轮【jou²go³lên⁴ 哥³ 伦】＝【普】早些时候

早班【jou²ban¹ 斑】morning shift

早餐【jou²qan¹ 灿¹】breakfast

早期【jou²kēi⁴ 其】early stage; early phase

早日【jou²yed⁹ 逸】at an early date; early; soon

早退【jou²têü³ 推³】leave early

早先【jou²xin¹ 仙】previously; in the past

早已【jou²yi⁵ 以】long ago; for a long time

早早地【jou²jou²dēi² 得希²】as early as possible; well in advance＝【普】早早儿

蚤【jou² 早】flea＝虱【xed⁷ 失】

枣【jou² 早】jujube;（Chinese)date

枣红【jou²hung⁴ 洪】purplish red

枣树【jou²xü⁶ 署⁶】jujube tree

皂【jou² 早；jou⁶ 造】black; soap; runner

皂隶【jou²dei⁶ 弟】runner

皂白【jou²bag⁹ 伯⁹】black and white—right and wrong

皂化剂【jou²fa³jei¹ 花³ 挤】saponifier

造【jou⁶ 做】make; build; invent; train; go to; crop

造成【jou⁶xing⁴ 承】create; cause

造就【jou⁶jeo⁶ 袖】bring up; train; achievements

造福【jou⁶fug⁷ 幅】bring benefit to; benefit

造化【jou⁶fa³ 花³】Nature; good luck

造物【jou⁶med⁹ 勿】Nature

造孽【jou⁶yib⁹ 业】do evil; commit a sin

造反【jou⁶fan² 返】rebel; revolt

造访【jou⁶fong² 仿】pay a visit; call on

造型【jou⁶ying⁴ 形】modelling; model; moulding

造谣【jou⁶yiu⁴ 摇】start a rumour

造诣【jou⁶ngei⁶ 艺】attainments

造作【jou⁶jog⁸ 昨】make；manufacture

灶【jou³ 做³】kitchen range；kitchen

灶头【jou³teo² 投²】a kitchen

灶头君【jou³teo⁴guen¹ 投军】kitchen god ＝【普】灶神

做【jou⁶ 造】make；do；act；cook；become；write；tion；be used as

做工【jou⁶gung¹ 功】work；workmanship

做人【jou⁶yen⁴ 仁】behave；conduct oneself

做事【jou⁶xi⁶ 士】handle affairs；do a deed；work

做官【jou⁶gun¹ 观】be an official

做媒【jou⁶mui¹ 煤】be a matchmaker

做梦【jou⁶mung⁶ 蒙⁶】have a dream；daydream

做戏【jou⁶hēi³ 气】act in a play；playact

做贼心虚【jou⁶qeg⁹xem¹hēü¹ 此克⁹ 深墟】have a guilty conscience

做法【jou⁶fad⁸ 发】method of work；practice

做到【jou⁶dou³ 都³】accomplish；achieve

做低【jou⁶dei¹ 帝¹】to kill ＝【普】打倒

做世界【jou⁶xei³gai³ 细介】to commit crimes ＝【普】投入叛逆战斗；造反

做乜【jou⁶med⁷ 勿⁷】why ＝【普】为什么

做左手脚【jou⁶jo²xeo²gêg⁸ 阻守格约⁸】to set up ＝【普】搞了鬼把戏；假装

庄【jong¹ 装】village；manor；a place of business；serious；a surname

庄家【jong¹ga¹ 加】banker(in a gambling game)

庄园【jong¹yün⁴ 元】manor

庄严【jong¹yim⁴ 盐】solemn；dignified；stately

庄重【jong¹jung⁶ 仲】serious；grave；solemn

桩【jong¹ 庄】stake；pile

打桩【da²jong¹】drive pile

装【jong¹ 庄】dress up；outfit；pretend；load；fit

装扮【jong¹ban⁶ 板⁶】dress up；attire；disguise

装备【jong¹bēi⁶ 鼻】equip；outfit

装饰【jong¹xig⁷ 色】decorate；adorn

装潢【jong¹wong⁴ 王】mount；mounting；decorate

装修【jong¹xeo¹ 收】fit up（a house，etc.）

装门面【jong¹mun⁴min⁶ 们免⁶】put up a front

装假狗【jong¹ga²geo² 贾九】to pretend；make believe；be affected ＝【普】装假；装模作样

装配【jong¹pui³ 沛】assemble；fit together

装束【jong¹qug⁷ 促】dress；attire

装卸【jong¹xē³ 舍】load and unload

装载【jong¹joi³ 再】loading

装订【jong¹ding³ 丁³】binding；bookbinding

装住【jong¹jü⁶ 注⁶】filling ＝【普】盛着

装傻扮彗【jong¹xo⁴ban⁶mung² 梳⁴ 板⁶ 蒙²】feign madness and act like an idiot；play the fool ＝【普】装疯卖傻

妆【jong¹ 装】apply makeup；woman's personal adornments；trousseau

妆奁【jong¹lim⁵ 帘⁵】trousseau

妆饰【jong¹xig⁷ 色】adorn；dress up；deck out

脏【jong¹ 装】stealthily peep at ＝【普】偷偷窥视

壮【jong³ 葬】strong; magnificent; strengthen

壮大【jong³ dai⁶ 歹⁶】grow in strength; expand

壮观【jong³ gun¹ 官】grand sight

壮举【jong³ gêû² 矩】magnificent feat

壮阔【jong³ fud⁸ 夫活⁸】vast; grand

壮丽【jong³ lei⁶ 励】majestic; magnificent

壮烈【jong³ lid⁹ 列】heroic; brave

壮志【jong³ ji³ 至】great aspiration; lofty ideal

壮士【jong³ xi⁶ 是】heroic man; hero; warrior

壮年【jong³ nin⁴ 捻⁴】prime of life

壮胆【jong³ dam² 担²】embolden; boost sb's courage

赃【jong¹ 庄】stolen goods; bribes

赃款【jong¹ fun² 欢²】illicit money

赃物【jong¹ med⁹ 勿】stolen goods; bribes

脏【jong¹ 庄; jong⁶ 撞】dirty; filthy; viscera

脏水【jong¹ xêu² 瑞²】filthy water; slops

脏衣服【jong¹ yi¹ fug⁹ 依伏】dirty linen

脏腑【jong⁶ fu² 府】internal organs including the heart, liver, spleen, lungs, kidneys, stomach, gall, intestines and bladder; viscera

臧【jong¹ 庄】good; right; a surname

葬【jong³ 壮】bury; inter

葬身【jong³ xen¹ 辛】be buried

葬送【jong³ xung³ 宋】ruin; spell an end to

藏【jong⁶ 撞; qong⁴ 床】storing place; depository

藏青【jong⁶ qing¹ 清】dark blue

藏族【jong⁶ jug⁹ 俗】〈n.〉the Zang nationality (Tibetan)

藏匿【qong⁴ nig⁷ 那忆⁷】conceal; hide; go into hiding ＝ 匿埋【nêi¹ mai⁴; nei³ mai⁴】

藏身【qong⁴ xen¹ 辛】hide oneself; go into hiding

藏掖【qong⁴ yig⁹ 亦】try to cover up ＝ 收埋【xeo¹ mai⁴】

藏污纳垢【qong⁴ wu¹ nab⁹ geo³ 乌呐救】shelter evil people and countenance evil practices

状【jong⁶ 撞】form; shape; state; describe; account; plaint; certificate

状况【jong⁶ fong³ 放】condition; state

状貌【jong⁶ mao⁶ 矛⁶】appearance; form

状态【jong⁶ tai³ 太】state; condition

状语【jong⁶ yü⁵ 雨】adverbial modifier

状元【jong⁶ yün⁴ 员】the very best

幢【jong⁶ 撞; tong⁴ 唐】a three-storeyed building; dancing; flickering

撞【jong⁶ 状; jong² 庄²】bump against; run into; meet by chance; bump into

撞击【jong⁶ gig⁷ 激】ram; dash against; strike

撞骗【jong⁶ pin³ 遍】look about for a chance to swindle; swindle

撞见【jong⁶ gin³ 建】meet by chance; to meet; to see ＝【普】遇见; 碰见

撞板【jong⁶ ban² 版】to fail; unfortunately; unlucky ∽【普】倒霉; 遭殃; 碰钉子

撞火【jong⁶ fo² 伙】to feel angry ∽【普】发火; 发怒

撞鬼【jong² guei² 诡 】a phrase used for scolding people; unlucky; unfortunate ∽【普】斥责别人的惯用语,或谓自己运气不好,倒霉

撞彩【jong⁶qoi² 采】try one's luck =【普】碰运气

撞手神【jong⁶xeo²xen⁴ 守臣】try one's luck = 撞彩

作【jog⁸ 昨】do; workshop; make; rise; writings; pretend; regard as; have; be; become

作为【jog⁸ wei⁴维 】deed; regard as; accomplish ; as

作用【jog⁸ yung⁶ 容⁶】act on; effect; acting; motive

作战【jog⁸jin³ 箭】fight; do battle

作证【jog⁸jing³ 正】testify; give evidence

作者【jog⁸jē² 姐】author; writer

作品【jog⁸ben⁶ 禀】works

作文【jog⁸men⁴ 闻】write a composition

作业【jog⁸yib⁹ 叶】school assignment; work

作对【jog⁸ dêü³堆³】set oneself against; oppose

作法【jog⁸fad⁸ 发】way of doing things

作废【jog⁸fei³ 费】become invalid

作风【jog⁸fung¹ 丰】style; style of work

作怪【jog⁸ guai³乖³】 do mischief; make trouble

作弊【jog⁸bei⁶ 敝】practise fraud; cheat

作恶【jog⁸ngog⁸ 噩】do evil

作乐【jog⁸ 乐⁹落 】 make merry; enjoy oneself

作呕【jog⁸ngeo² 欧²】feel sick; to vomit

作状【jog⁸jong⁶ 撞】to pretend to be

作奸犯科【jog⁸gan¹fan⁶fo¹ 间范课¹】violate the law and commit crimes

作威作福【jog⁸wei¹jog⁸fug⁷ 畏¹ 幅】tyrannically abuse one's power

昨【jog⁸ 作】yesterday

昨日【jog⁶yed⁹ 逸】yesterday =【普】昨天

昨晚【jog⁸ man⁵ 万⁵】 yesterday evening; last night

凿【jog⁹ 作⁹】chisel; to steal; authentic

凿山劈岭【jog⁹xan¹pig⁷lēng⁵ 珊辟靓⁵】tunnel through mountains and cut across ridges

凿窿【jog⁹lung¹ 龙¹】bore a hole =【普】开孔

中【jung¹ 宗; jung³ 粽】centre; China; in; middle; mean; in the process of; fit for; hit; be hit by

中间【jung¹gan¹ 奸】among; centre

中等【jung¹deng² 登²】medium; secondary

中部【jung¹bou⁶ 步】central section

中层【jung¹ceng⁴ 迟亨⁴】middle-level

中级【jung¹keb⁷给 】 middle rank; intermediate

中介【jung¹gai³ 界】intermediary; medium

中立【jung¹leb⁹ 笠⁹】neutrality

中和【jung¹wo⁴ 禾】neutralization

中坚【jung¹gin¹ 肩】nucleus; hard core

中继【jung¹gei³ 计】relay

中断【jung¹tün⁵ 团⁵】suspend; break off

中途【jung¹tou⁴ 图】halfway; midway

中枢【jung¹xü¹ 书】centre

中心【jung¹xem¹ 深】centre; heart; core

中央【jung¹yêng¹ 殃】centre; middle; central authorities(of a state, party, etc.)

中午【jung¹ng⁵ 五】midday; noon

中止【jung¹ji² 子】discontinue; suspend

中转【jung¹jun² 专²】change trains

中用【jung¹yung⁶ 容⁶】of use; useful

中国【jung¹guog⁸ 帼】China

中华【jung¹wa⁴ 铧】China

中外【jung¹ngoi⁶ 碍】China and foreign countries

中西【jung¹xei¹ 筛】Chinese and Western

中文【jung¹men⁴ 闻】the Chinese language

中意【jung¹yi³ 薏】like; satisfied =【普】喜欢

中流砥柱【jung¹leo⁴dei²qu⁵ 留底处⁵】firm rock in midstream; mainstay

中毒【jung³dug⁹ 独】poisoning; toxicosis

中风【jung³fung¹ 丰】apoplexy

中奖【jung³ jêng²掌】draw a prizewinning ticket in a lottery

中肯【jung³heng² 亨²】apropos; pertinent

中伤【jung³xêng¹ 商】slander; malign

忠【jung¹ 中】loyal; devoted; honest

忠诚【jung¹xing⁴ 成】loyal; faithful

忠贞【jung¹jing¹ 精】loyal and steadfast

忠于【jung¹yu¹ 迂】true to; loyal to

忠厚【jung¹heo⁵ 候⁵】honest and tolerant

忠实【jung¹xed⁹ 失⁹】true; faithful

忠告【jung¹gou³ 高³】admonish; advice

忠臣【jung¹xen⁴ 神】official loyal to his sovereign

忠心耿耿【jung¹xem¹geng¹geng² 深梗梗】loyal and devoted

盅【jung¹ 中】handleless cup

茶盅【qa⁴jung¹】teacup

钟【jung¹ 中】bell; clock; o'clock; concentrate

钟表【jung¹ biu¹ 标】clocks and watches; timepiece

钟点【jung¹dim² 店²】a time for sth. to be done or to happen; hour = 钟头【jung¹teo⁴】

钟楼【jung¹leo⁴ 留】bell tower; clock tower

钟爱【jung¹ngoi³ 哀³】dote on（a child）; cherish

钟情【jung¹qing⁴ 程】be deeply in love

终【jung¹ 中】end; death; after all; whole

终归【jung¹ guei¹龟】eventually; in the end

终究【jung¹geo³ 够】eventually; in the end

终年【jung¹ nin⁴捻⁴】the year round; the age at which one dies

终身【jung¹xen¹ 辛】lifelong; all one's life

终生【jung¹xeng¹ 笙】all one's life

终于【jung¹yu¹ 迂】at last; in the end; finally

终止【jung¹ji² 子】stop; end; termination

终须【jung¹xêu¹ 需】eventually

舂【jung¹ 中】to give a punch; to fall down

舂米【jung¹mei⁵ 迷⁵】husk rice with mortar and pestle

舂瘟鸡【jung¹wen¹gei¹ 温计¹】to refer to one not walking properly when one is drunk =【普】理智不清醒的无计划的乱奔忙

综【jung¹ 中】put together; sum up

综观【jung¹gun¹ 官】make a comprehensive survey

综合【jung¹heb⁹ 盒】synthesize; synthetical

综述【jung¹xêd⁹ 术】summarize; sum up

宗【jung¹ 中】ancestor；clan；sect；purpose；great master；model

宗族【jung¹jug⁹ 俗】patriarchal clan；clansman

宗派【jung¹pai³ 排³】faction；sect

宗教【jung¹gao³ 较】religion

宗旨【jung¹ji² 子】aim；purpose

棕【jung¹ 中】palm；palm fibre

棕榈【jung¹lêü⁵ 吕】palm

棕毛【jung¹mou⁴ 无】palm fibre

棕色【jung¹xig⁷ 式】brown

踪【jung¹ 中】footprint；track；trace

踪迹【jung¹jig⁷ 织】track；trace

鬃【jung¹ 中】hair on the neck of a pig，horse，etc.

总【jung² 肿】assemble；general；chief；always；anyway；after all

总计【jung²gei³继 】grand total；amount to

总括【jung²kud⁸ 卡活⁸】sum up

总数【jung²xou³ 扫】total；sum total

总体【jung²tei² 睇】overall；total

总揽【jung² lam⁵览 】assume overall responsibility

总监【jung²gam¹ 减¹】inspector general

总理【jung²lêi⁵ 李】premier；prime minister

总统【jung² tung² 捅】president（of a republic）

总结【jung²gid⁸ 洁】sum up；summary

总和【jung²wo⁴ 禾】sum；total；sum total

总汇【jung²wui⁶ 会⁶】come or flow together；confluence；concourse

总共【jung²gung⁶ 供⁶】in all；altogether

总值【jung²jig⁹ 直】total value

总督【jung² dug⁷ 笃 】governor-general；governor

总管【jung²gun² 莞】manager

总得【jung²deg⁷ 德】must；have to

总之【jung²ji¹ 支】in a word；in short；in brief

总算【jung²xün³ 蒜】at long last；finally；considering everything

总 而 言 之【jung²yi⁴yin⁴ji¹ 移 然 支】in short；in a word；in brief

肿【jung² 总】swelling；swollen

肿瘤【jung²leo⁴ 留】tumour

肿胀【jung²jêng³ 涨】swelling

踵【jung² 总】heel＝脚踭【gêg⁸jang¹】

接踵【jib⁸jung²】follow on sb.'s heels

种【jung² 总；jung³ 中³】species；race；seed；guts；kind；grow；plant

种类【jung²lêü⁶ 泪】kind；type

种子【jung²ji² 止】seed

种族【jung²jug⁹ 俗】race

种种【jung²jung²】all sorts of；a variety of

种植【jung³jig⁹ 直】plant；grow

种田【jung³tin⁴ 填】till the land；farm

种瓜得瓜，种豆得豆【jung³gua¹deg⁷gua¹，jung³deo⁶deg⁷deo⁶】as you sow，so will you reap

重【jung⁶ 仲；qung⁵ 从⁵；qung⁴ 从】weight；heavy；deep；lay stress on；discreet；repeat；again；layer

重大【jung⁶dai⁶ 歹⁶】great；weighty；major

重点【jung⁶dim² 店²】focal point；stress

重视【jung⁶xi⁶ 示】attach importance to；value

重心【jung⁶ xem¹ 深 】centre of gravity; heart

重要【jung⁶yiu³ 腰³】important; major

重用【jung⁶ yung⁶容⁶】put sb. in an important position

重担【qung⁵dam³ 胆³】heavy burden

重负【qung⁵ fu⁶ 父 】heavy burden; heavy load

重力【qung⁵lig⁹ 历】〈n.〉gravity

重任【qung⁵yem⁶ 壬⁶】important task

重托【qung⁵tog⁸ 替恶⁸】great trust

重型【qung⁵ying⁴ 形】heavy-duty

重复【qung⁴fug⁷ 福】repeat; duplicate

重迭【qung⁴ did⁹ 秩】one on top of another; overlapping

重合【qung⁴heb⁹ 盒】coincide

重现【qung⁴yin⁶ 苋】reappear

重新【qung⁴xen¹ 辛】again; anew; afresh

重演【qung⁴ yin² 衍】put on an old play; recur

重温【qung⁴wen¹ 瘟】review

重申【qung⁴xen¹ 辛】reaffirm; reiterate

重重【qung⁴qung⁴】layer upon layer

重蹈覆辙【qung⁴tou¹fug⁷qid⁸ 滔福撤】follow the same old disastrous road

重整旗鼓【qung⁴ jing² kēi¹ gu² 精²其古²】rally one's forces(after a defeat)

重系【jung⁶hei⁶ 兮⁶】still=【普】还是

纵【jung¹ 中; jung³ 粽】from north to south; vertical; release; indulge; jump up; even if

纵队【jung¹dêü⁶ 堆⁶】column; file

纵横【jung¹ wang⁴ 乌罂⁴】in length and breadth; with great ease; freely

纵深【jung³xem¹ 心】depth

纵身【jung³xen¹ 辛】jump; leap

纵览【jung³lam⁵ 揽⁵】look far and wide; scan

纵欲【jung³yug⁹ 玉】give way to carnal desires

纵情【jung³qing⁴ 程】to one's heart's content

纵然【jung³yin⁴ 言】even if; even though

纵容【jung³yung⁴ 熔】connive; wink at

纵使【jung³xi² 史】even if; even though

粽【jung³ 纵³】a pyramid-shaped dumpling made of glutinous rice wrapped in bamboo or reed leaves

仲【jung⁶ 中⁶】second; second in order of birth; middle; a surname

仲春【jung⁶ qên¹椿】second month of spring

仲夏【jung⁶ha⁶ 下】second month of summer

仲裁【jung⁶qoi⁴ 才】arbitrate

众【jung³ 种³】many; numerous; crowd

众多【jung³ do¹朵¹】multitudinous; numerous

众数【jung³xou³ 扫】mode

众人【jung³yen⁴ 仁】everybody

众生【jung³xeng¹ 笙】all living creatures

众望【jung³ mong⁶ 亡⁶】people's expectations

众说纷纭【jung³ xüd⁸ fen¹ wen⁴雪分云】opinions vary

众所周知【jung³xo²jeo¹ji¹ 锁邹支】as everyone knows

众怒难犯【jung³ nou⁶ nan⁴ fan⁶ 奴⁶ 挪晏范】you cannot offord to incur public wrath

众志成城【jung³ji³xing⁴xing⁴ 至承】unity is strength

竹【jug⁷ 足】bamboo

竹树【jug⁷xü⁶ 署⁶】bamboo

竹器【jug⁷hēi³ 气】articles made of bamboo

竹笋【jug⁷xên² 荀²】bamboo shoots

竹竿【jug⁷gon¹ 干¹】bamboo pole; bamboo sticks

竹马【jug⁷ma⁵ 码⁵】a bamboo stick used as a toy horse

竹板【jug⁷ban² 版】bamboo clappers

竹篙【jug⁷gou¹ 高】bamboo sticks ∽【普】竹竿

竹篮打水一场空【jug⁷ lam⁴ da² xêu² yed⁷ qêng⁴hung¹】draw water with a bamboo basket——all in vain

烛【jug⁷ 竹】candle; light up

烛光【jug⁷guong¹ 胱】candlepower; candle

足【jug⁷ 竹】foot; leg; sufficient; full; enough

足迹【jug⁷ jig⁷织】footmark; footprint; track

足够【jug⁷geo³ 救】enough; ample; sufficient

足金【jug⁷gem¹ 甘】pure gold; solid gold

足球【jug⁷keo⁴ 求】soccer; football

足见【jug⁷gin³ 建】it serves to show

足以【jug⁷yi⁵ 耳】enough; sufficient

足智多谋【jug⁷ji³do¹meo⁴ 至朵¹ 牟】wise and full of strategems; resourceful

粥【jug⁷ 足】gruel; porridge; congee

祝【jug⁷ 足】express good wishes; wish

祝愿【jug⁷yün⁶ 县⁶】wish

祝贺【jug⁷ho⁶ 何⁶】congratulate

祝福【jug⁷ fug⁷幅】blessing; new year's sacrifice

祝捷【jug⁷jid⁹ 截】celebrate a victory

祝寿【jug⁷xeo⁶ 受】congratulate on his or her birthday

筑【jug⁷ 足】build; construct

筑路【jug⁷lou⁶ 露】construct a road

筑堤【jug⁷tei⁴ 啼】build a dyke

嘱【jug⁷ 足】enjoin; advise; urge

嘱咐【jug⁷fu³ 富】enjoin; tell; exhort

嘱托【jug⁷tog⁸ 替恶⁸】entrust

瞩【jug⁷ 足】gaze; look steadily

瞩目【jug⁷mug⁹ 木】fix one's eyes upon

捉【jug⁷ 足】clutch; hold; catch; capture

捉拿【jug⁷na⁴ 哪⁴】arrest; catch

捉弄【jug⁷long⁶ 龙⁶】tease; make fun of

捉摸【jug⁷mo² 摩²】fathom; ascertain

捉棋【jug⁷kēi² 其²】to play chess =【普】下棋

捉伊人【jug⁷yi¹yen¹ 衣因】hide-and-seek game; be tricky and evasive =【普】捉迷藏

捉襟见肘【jug⁷kem¹gin³jeo² 琴¹ 建走】have too many problems to tackle

捉蛇入屎窟【jug⁷xē⁴yeb⁹xi²fed⁷ 些⁴ 邑⁹ 史弗】to get oneself into trouble =【普】自寻烦恼

镯【jug⁷ 足;jug⁹ 浊】bracelet 玉镯【yug⁹jug⁷】jade bracelet = 玉轭【yug⁹ngag⁸ 厄】

浊【jug⁹ 俗】turbid; deep and thick; chaotic

浊世【jug⁹xei³ 细】the corrupted world

浊音【jug⁹yem¹ 荫】voiced sound

浊亲【jug⁹ qen¹ 趁¹】irritate（respiratory organs）; choke＝【普】(烟或水) 呛着(鼻子或喉头)

俗
【jug⁹ 浊】custom; popular; common; vulgar; secular; lay

俗话【jug⁹ wa⁶ 画⁶】common saying＝俗语【jug⁹ yü⁵】

俗气【jug⁹ hēi³ 汽】vulgar; in poor taste

俗套【jug⁹ tou³ 吐】conventional pattern

俗不可耐【jug⁹ bed⁷ ho² noi⁶ 毕何² 内】unbearably vulgar

族
【jug⁹ 俗】clan; clansman; race; nationality; a class or group of things with common features

族权【jug⁹ kün⁴ 拳】clan authority; clan power

族长【jug⁹ jêng² 掌】clan elder; the head of a clan

逐
【jug⁹ 俗】pursue; drive out; one by one

逐步【jug⁹ bou⁶ 部】step by step

逐一【jug⁹ yed⁷ 壹】one by one＝逐个【jug⁹ go³】

逐渐【jug⁹ jim⁶ 尖⁶】gradually; by degrees

逐鹿【jug⁹ lug⁹ 六】chase the deer—fight for the throne

逐客令【jug⁹ hag⁸ ling⁶ 另】order for guests to leave

续
【jug⁹ 俗】continuous; continue; add

续编【jug⁹ pin¹ 篇】continuation（of a book）; sequel＝续集【jug⁹ jab⁹ 习】

续借【jug⁹ jē³ 蔗】renew（a library book, etc.）

续弦【jug⁹ yin⁴ 言】remarry after the death of one's wife

躅
【jug⁹ 俗】footprint; footmark（see "踯躅"）

轴
【jug⁹ 俗】axle; axis; spool

轴承【jug⁹ xing⁴ 成】bearing

轴线【jug⁹ xin³ 扇】axis; spool thread

轴心【jug⁹ xem¹ 深】axle centre; axis

轴对称【jug⁹ dêu³ qing³ 堆³ 清³】axial symmetry

妯
【jug⁹ 俗】〈n.〉妯娌【jug⁹ lēi⁵ 你】wives of brothers; sisters-in-law

之
【ji¹ 支】①〈pron.〉this; it; ②〈v.〉go; leave; ③〈auxil.〉＝"的"、"嘅"

之前【ji¹ qin⁴ 钱】before; prior to; ago

之后【ji¹ heo⁶ 候】later; after; afterwards

之不过【ji¹ bed⁷ guo³ 毕戈³】just that; but＝【普】但; 可是

支
【ji¹ 之】prop up; put up; raise; support; send away; pay or draw（money）; branch

支承【ji¹ xing⁴ 成】supporting; bearing

支撑【ji¹ qang¹ 橙¹】prop up; sustain; strut

支持【ji¹ qi⁴ 迟】sustain; hold out; support

支柱【ji¹ qü⁵ 储】pillar; prop; mainstay

支配【ji¹ pui³ 沛】arrange; control

支援【ji¹ wun⁴ 垣】support; help

支出【ji¹ qêd⁷ 次律⁷】pay（money）; expenses

支付【ji¹ fu⁶ 父】pay（money）; defray

支取【ji¹ qêü⁵ 娶】draw（money）

支票【ji¹ piu³ 漂³】cheque; check

支使【ji¹ xi² 史】order about; send away

支解【ji¹ gai² 介²】dismemberment

支流【ji¹ leo⁴ 留】tributary; minor aspects

支部【ji¹ bou⁶ 步】branch

支吾【ji¹ ng⁴ 吴】prevaricate; hum and

haw

支离破碎【ji¹lēi⁴po³xêü³ 篱颇³ 瑞³】torn to pieces; fragmented

支整【ji¹jing² 精²】to refer to someone who is over concerned about someone's appearance＝【普】耽于琐事, 延误时间

支质【ji¹ied⁷ 侄¹】redtape＝【普】行动拖拉

吱【ji¹ 支】〈*onomatopoeia .*〉

吱喳【ji¹ja¹ 抓】noisy; talkative

知【ji¹ 之】know; inform; knowledge; administer

知道【ji¹dou³ 到】know; realize

知觉【ji¹gog⁸ 角 】consciousness; ·perception

知悉【ji¹xig⁷ 识】know; learn

知识【ji¹xig⁷ 悉】knowledge; intellectual

知晓【ji¹hiu² 嚣²】know; be aware of; understand

知心【ji¹xem¹ 深】intimate; understanding

知音【ji¹yem¹ 荫】bosom friend

知交【ji¹gao¹ 胶】bosom friend

知情【ji¹qing⁴ 程】be in the know

知趣【ji¹qêü³ 翠】be sensible; be tactful

知行【ji¹heng⁴ 衡】knowing and doing

知识分子【ji¹xig⁷fen⁶ji² 悉份止】intellectual

知己知彼, 百战不殆【ji¹gēi²ji¹bēi², bag⁸ jin³bed⁷toi⁵】know the enemy and know yourself, and you can fight a hundred battles with no danger of defeat

知悭识俭【ji¹han¹xig⁷gim⁶ 黑晏¹ 悉兼⁶】wise and tactful ∽【普】省吃俭用

知书识墨【ji¹xü¹xig⁷meg⁹ 舒悉默】one

who is educated and polite ∽【普】知书识礼

知微麻利【ji¹mēi¹ma⁴lēi⁶ 尾¹ 嫲俐】to refer to one who is calculative＝【普】深谙计算而苛求于人

知生【ji¹xang¹ 是罂¹】if I know such, ...＝【普】早知如此, ...

滋【ji¹ 之】grow; more; moisten; taste; spurt

滋生【ji¹xeng¹ 笙】multiply; cause

滋事【ji¹xi⁶ 士】create trouble

滋蔓【ji¹man⁶ 万】grow and spread

滋补【ji¹bou² 宝】nourishing; nutritious

滋润【ji¹yên⁶ 衣春⁶】moist; moisten

滋味【ji¹mēi⁶ 未】taste; flavour

滋长【ji¹jêng² 掌】grow; develop

滋油佬【ji¹yeo⁴lou² 游老²】the man who is calm(or stable) ∽【普】优哉悠哉的人

滋油淡定【ji¹yeo⁴dam⁶ding⁶ 游啖锭⁶】calm; stable; not panic ∽【普】优游从容;不慌不忙

孳【ji¹ 之】〈*v.*〉孳生【ji¹xeng¹ 擤¹】multiply; propagate

枝【ji¹ 支】branch; twig; 〈*classifier*〉

枝桠【ji¹nga¹ 丫】branch; twig＝【普】枝条

枝叶【ji¹yib⁹ 业】branches and leaves

枝节【ji¹jid⁸ 折】branches and knots—minor matters; complication

芝【ji¹ 之】〈*n.*〉芝麻【ji¹ma⁴ 妈⁴】sesame

芝加哥【ji¹ga¹go¹ 家歌】〈*n.*〉Chicago

肢【ji¹ 支】limb

肢体【ji¹tei² 睇】limbs; limbs and trunk

脂【ji¹ 支】fat; rouge

脂肪【ji¹fong¹ 方】fat

脂油【ji¹yeo⁴ 由】leaf fat

脂膏【ji¹ gou¹ 高】fat; grease; wealth of the people

脂粉【ji¹fen² 分²】rouge and powder; cosmetics

蜘【ji¹ 知】〈n.〉蜘蛛【ji¹jü¹ 朱】spider

卮【ji¹ 支】ancient wine vessel

栀【ji¹ 支】〈n.〉栀子【ji¹ji² 止】Cape jasmine

资【ji¹ 支】money; provide; support; endowment; qualifications

资金【ji¹gem¹ 今】fund

资产【ji¹qan² 铲】property; capital; assets

资本【ji¹bun² 苯】capital; what is capitalized on

资本家【ji¹bun²ga¹ 苯加】capitalist

资本主义【ji¹bun²jü²yi⁶ 苯朱² 异】capitalism

资格【ji¹gag⁸ 隔】qualifications; seniority

资历【ji¹lig⁹力】qualifications and record of service

资料【ji¹liu² 了²】means; data

资源【ji¹ yün⁴元】natural resources; resources

资助【ji¹jo⁶ 左⁶】aid financially; subsidize

孜【ji¹ 支】〈a.〉孜孜不倦【ji¹ji¹bed⁷gün⁶ 毕绢⁶】diligently

咨【ji¹ 支】consult; take counsel

咨文【ji¹men⁴ 民】official communication

咨询【ji¹xên¹ 荀】seek advice from; consult

兹【ji¹ 支】this; now; year

缁【ji¹ 支】〈a.〉black

辎【ji¹ 支】an ancient covered wagon

辎重【ji¹qung⁵ 从⁵】impedimenta; baggage

趑【ji¹ 支】〈a.〉趑趄【ji¹jêü¹ 追】walk with difficulty; hesitate to advance

姿【ji¹ 支】looks; gesture

姿容【ji¹yung⁴ 溶】looks; appearance

姿色【ji¹xig⁷ 式】(of a woman) good looks

姿势【ji¹xei³ 世】posture; gesture

姿态【ji¹tai³ 太】posture; attitude; pose

子【ji² 止】son; person; seed; egg; young; copper; something small and hard; viscount

子弹【ji²dan² 蛋】bullet; cartridge

子弟【ji²dei⁶ 第】sons and younger brothers; children

子宫【ji²gung¹ 工】uterus; womb

子规【ji²kuei⁵ 亏】〈n.〉cuckoo

子女【ji²nêü⁵ 挪去⁵】sons and daughters; children

子孙【ji² xün¹ 酸 】children and grandchildren; descendants

子姜【ji²gêng¹ 姜】young ginger = 【普】嫩姜

子虚【ji²hêü¹ 墟】fictitious; unreal

子夜【ji²yē⁶ 野】midnight

子午线【ji²ng⁵xin³ 五腺】meridian(line)

姊【ji² 止】elder sister; sister

姊妹【ji²mui⁶ 梅⁶】elder sister and younger sister

籽【ji² 子】seed　菜籽【qoi³ji²】vegetable seed

梓【ji² 子】Chinese catalpa; cut blocks for printing

付梓【fu⁶ji²】send to the printers

梓里【ji²lēi⁵ 理】native place; hometown

紫【ji² 子】purple; violet

紫红【ji²hung⁴ 洪】purplish red

紫菜【ji²qoi³ 蔡】laver

紫荆【ji²ging¹ 经】Chinese redbud

紫罗兰【ji²lo⁴lan⁴ 萝栏】〈n.〉violet; common stock

紫外线【ji²ngoi⁴xin³ 碍腺】ultraviolet ray

紫禁城【ji²gem³xing⁴ 咁成】the Forbidden City (in Beijing)

指【ji² 旨】finger; digit; point at; point out; depend on; count on

指甲【ji²gab⁸ 夹】nail

指头【ji²teo⁴ 投】finger; toe

指法【ji²fad⁸ 发】fingering

指标【ji²biu¹ 彪】target; quota; norm

指数【ji²xou³ 扫】index number; index

指导【ji²dou⁶ 度】guide; direct

指教【ji²gao³ 较】give advice or comments

指点【ji² dim² 店²】give directions; show how

指令【ji²ling⁶ 另】instruct; order

指挥【ji² fei¹ 辉】command; direct; conduct

指责【ji²jag⁸ 泽⁸】censure; criticize

指控【ji²hung³ 空³】accuse; charge

指示【ji²xi⁶ 视】indicate; point out; directive

指引【ji²yen⁵ 瘾】point; guide; show

指使【ji²xi² 史】instigate; incite

指派【ji² pai³ 排³】appoint; name; designate

指望【ji²mong⁶ 亡⁶】look to; prospect; hope

指南针【ji²nam⁴jem¹ 男斟】〈n.〉compass

指鹿为马【ji² lug⁹ wei⁴ ma⁵六维蚂】call a stag a horse—deliberately misrepresent

指手划脚【ji²xeo²wag⁹gêg⁸ 守画⁹ 格约⁸】gesticulate; make indiscreet remarks or criticisms

指桑骂槐【ji²xong⁴ma⁶wai⁴ 丧¹ 吗⁶ 怀】point at the mulberry and abuse the locust—point at one but abuse another

旨【ji² 指】purport; aim; tasty

旨意【ji²yi³ 薏】decree; order

祉【ji² 止】happiness; blessedness

止【ji² 指】stop; to; till; only

止步【ji²bou⁶ 哺】halt; stop; go no further

止境【ji²ging² 景】end; limit

止息【ji²xig⁷ 式】cease; stop

止痛【ji²tung³ 通³】relieve pain; stop pain

址【ji²】location; site

纸【ji² 止】paper

纸张【ji²yêng¹ 章】paper

纸烟【ji²yin¹ 燕¹】cigarette

纸币【ji²bei⁶ 弊】paper money; note

纸版【ji²ban² 板】paper mould = 纸型【ji² ying⁴】

纸上谈兵【ji²xêng⁶tam⁴bing¹ 尚潭冰¹】fight only on paper; engage in idle theorizing

纸醉金迷【ji²jêũ³gem¹mei⁴ 最今米⁴】(a life of) luxury and dissipation

纸皮【ji²pēi⁴ 牌】brown rough paper

纸鹞【ji²yiu² 扰】a kite＝【普】风筝

趾
【ji² 止】toe; foot

趾甲【ji²gab⁸ 夹】toenail

趾高气扬【ji²gou¹hēi³yêng⁴ 羔汽洋】strut about and give oneself airs

祇
【ji² 止】only＝只【ji²】

只
【ji² 止；jēg⁸ 隻⁸】single; one only; only; merely

只身【jēg⁸xen¹ 辛】alone; by oneself

只得【ji² deg⁷ 德】have no alternative but to

只顾【ji² gu³ 故】be absorbed in; merely; simply

只好【ji²hou² 蒿²】have to; be forced to

只是【ji² xi⁶士】merely; only; just; simply

只要【ji²yiu³ 腰³】so long as; provided

只有【ji²yeo⁵ 友】only; alone

只不过【ji²bed⁷guo³ 毕戈³】only; just; merely

只要功夫深，铁杵磨成针【ji²yiu³gung¹fu¹ xem¹, tid⁸qũ⁵mo⁴xing⁴jem¹】constant grinding can turn an iron rod into a needle — perseverance spells success

咫
【ji² 只】〈a.〉咫尺【ji²qēg⁸ 次脊⁸】very close

咫尺天涯【ji²qēg⁸tin¹ngai⁴ 次脊⁸ 田¹崖】a short distance away, and yet poles apart—see little of each other though living nearby

黹
【ji² 止】needlework(针黹【jem¹ji²】)

智
【ji³ 至】wisdom; resourcefulness; wit

智慧【ji³wei³ 畏】wisdom; intelligence

智力【ji³lig⁹ 历】intelligence; intellect

智谋【ji³meo⁴ 牟】resourcefulness

智囊【ji³nong⁴ 挪康⁴】brain truster

智取【ji³qêũ² 娶】take by strategy

智勇双全【ji³yung⁵xêng¹qũn⁴ 拥⁵ 商存】both intelligent and courageous

智者千虑，必有一失【ji³jē⁵qin¹lêũ⁶, bid⁷ yeo⁵yed⁷xed⁷】even the wise are not always free from error

至
【ji³ 智】to; until; extremely; most

至诚【ji³xing⁴ 成】complete sincerity; sincere

至宝【ji³bou² 补】most valuable treasure

至迟【ji³qi⁴ 池】at latest

至多【ji³do¹ 朵】at most

至交【ji³gao¹ 胶】best friend

至今【ji³gem¹ 金】up to now; to this day

至亲【ji³qen¹ 趁¹】very close relative; close kin

至少【ji³xiu² 小】at least

至于【ji³yū¹ 迂】as for; as to; go so far as to

至到【ji³dou³ 道】when; until; pertaining to; regarding with＝【普】从……到……（时候）；从……到……（地方）

至高无上【ji³gou¹mou⁴xêng⁶ 羔无尚】most lofty

致
【ji³ 至】send; devote; incur; fine; original in style

致辞【ji³qi⁴ 池】make a speech

致敬【ji³ging³ 劲】salute; pay tribute to

致冷【ji³lang⁵ 罗罂⁵】refrigeration

致力【ji³ lig⁹历 】devote oneself to；work for

致命【ji³ming⁶ 明⁶】causing death；fatal

致使【ji³xei² 洗】cause；result in

致谢【ji³jē⁶ 姐⁶】extend thanks to

致意【ji³yi³ 义³】give one's regards

痣【ji³ 志】nevus；mole＝瘟【meg⁹ 默】

挚【ji³ 至】sincere；earnest

挚友【ji³yeo⁵ 有】intimate friend；bosom friend

置【ji³ 至】place；put；buy

置办【ji³ban⁶ 班⁶】buy；purchase

置换【ji³wun⁶ 唤】displacement

置身【ji³xen¹ 辛】place oneself；stay

置信【ji³xên³ 讯】believe

置疑【ji³yi⁴ 移】doubt

置之不理【ji³ ji¹ bed⁷ lēi⁵支毕李】ignore；brush aside

置之度外【ji³ji¹dou⁶ngoi⁶ 支道碍】give no thought to

志【ji³ 至】will；keep in mind；mark

志气【ji³hēi³ 汽】aspiration；ambition

志趣【ji³qêû³ 翠】aspiration and interest；bent

志向【ji³hêng³ 香³】aspiration；ideal

志愿【ji³yün⁶ 县】aspiration；wish；volunteer

志同道合【ji³tung⁴dou⁶heb⁹ 铜度盒】have a common goal

志在【ji³joi⁶ 再⁶】with the intention of＝【普】目的在于……；看得要紧

枳【ji² 只】〈n.〉trifoliate orange

稚【ji⁶ 治】young；childish

稚气【ji⁶hēi³ 戏】childishness

稚子【ji⁶ji² 止】(innocent)child

彘【ji⁶ 治】pig；swine

治【ji⁶ 自】rule；order；treat；control；punish；study；seat of a local government

治安【ji⁶ngon¹ 桉】public order

治本【ji⁶bun² 苯】effect a permanent cure

治标【ji⁶biu¹ 彪】merely alleviate the symptoms of an illness

治国【ji⁶guog⁸ 帼】administer a country

治理【ji⁶lēi⁵ 李】administer；harness

治疗【ji⁶liu⁴ 辽】treat；cure

治学【ji⁶hog⁹ 鹤】pursue one's studies

治罪【ji⁶jêû⁶ 坠】punish sb. (for a crime)

治病救人【ji⁶bēng⁶geo³yen⁴ 柄⁶ 够仁】cure the sickness to save the patient

痔【ji⁶ 寺】haemorrhoids；piles

痔疮【ji⁶qong¹ 仓】haemorrhoids；piles

寺【ji⁶ 治】temple

寺院【ji⁶yün² 宛】temple；monastery

伺【ji⁶ 治】watch；await；

伺机【ji⁶gēi¹ 基】watch for one's chance

伺候【ji⁶heo⁶ 后】wait upon；serve

俟【ji⁶ 治】wait

饲【ji⁶ 治】raise；rear

饲养【ji⁶yêng⁵ 氧】raise; rear

饲料【ji⁶liu² 辽²】forage; fodder; feed

嗣【ji⁶ 治】succeed; heir

嗣后【ji⁶heo⁶ 候】hereafter; subsequently; later on

祀【ji⁶ 治】offer sacrifices to the gods or the spirits of the dead

巳【ji⁶ 治】the sixth of the twelve Earthly Branches

巳时【ji⁶xi⁴ 是⁴】the period of the day from 9 a. m. to 11 a. m.

字【ji⁶ 治】word; pronunciation; printing type; writings; receipt

字典【ji⁶din² 电²】dictionary

字号【ji⁶hou⁶ 好⁶】the name of a shop

字句【ji⁶ gêu³据 】words and expressions; writing

字据【ji⁶gêu³ 句】written pledge

字母【ji⁶ mou⁵武 】letters of an alphabet; letter

字体【ji⁶ tei²睇 】script; style of calligraphy

字眼【ji⁶ ngan⁵雁⁵】wording; diction

字斟句酌【ji⁶jem¹gêu³jêg⁸ 针据桌】choose one's words with great care; weigh every word

恣【ji¹ 支；ji³ 志；qi³ 次】throw off restraint

恣意【ji¹ yi³薏 】unscrupulous; reckless; wilful

恣睢【ji¹jêü¹ 追】reckless; unbridled

自【ji⁶ 字】self; oneself; certainly; from; since

自己【ji⁶ gêi²几】oneself; closely related; own

自我【ji⁶ ngo⁵鹅⁵】self; oneself ＝ 自身

【ji⁶xen¹ 辛】

自由【ji⁶ yeo⁴油】freedom; free; liberty; unrestrained

自然【ji⁶yin⁴ 言】natural world; naturally; of course; at ease; free from affectation

自如【ji⁶yü⁴ 鱼】freely; smoothly

自若【ji⁶ yêg⁹药 】self-possessed; composed

自行【ji⁶heng⁴ 衡】by oneself; of oneself

自信【ji⁶xên³ 讯】self-confident

自恃【ji⁶qi⁵ 似】count on; capitalize on

自私【ji⁶xi¹ 司】selfish; self-centred

自立【ji⁶leb⁹ 笠⁹】stand on one's own feet

自理【ji⁶lêi⁵ 李】take care of or provide for oneself

自量【ji⁶lêng⁶ 亮】estimate one's own ability or strength

自满【ji⁶mun⁵ 门⁵】complacent; self-satisfied

自慰【ji⁶wei³ 畏】console oneself

自卫【ji⁶ wei⁶为⁶】defend oneself; self-defence

自得【ji⁶ deg⁷德】contented; self-satisfied

自发【ji⁶fad⁸ 法】spontaneous

自封【ji⁶ fung¹丰】proclaim oneself; confine oneself

自负【ji⁶fu⁶ 付】be conceited

自豪【ji⁶hou⁴ 毫】be proud of sth.

自咎【ji⁶geo³ 够】blame oneself

自卑【ji⁶bēi¹ 悲】feel oneself inferior

自爱【ji⁶ngoi³ 哀³】self-respect

自救【ji⁶geo³ 够】save oneself

自荐【ji⁶jin³ 战】recommend oneself

自给【ji⁶keb⁸ 吸】self-sufficient

自决【ji⁶küd⁸ 缺】self-determination

自毁【ji⁶wei² 委】self-destruction

自觉【ji⁶gog⁸ 角】conscious；aware

自动【ji⁶dung⁶ 洞】voluntarily；automatic

自从【ji⁶qung⁴ 虫】since

自称【ji⁶qing¹ 清】call oneself；profess

自来【ji⁶loi⁴ 莱】from the beginning；originally

自新【ji⁶xen¹ 辛】self-confident

自学【ji⁶hog⁹ 鹤】study on one's own

自问【ji⁶men⁶ 文⁶】ask oneself

自愿【ji⁶yün⁶ 县】voluntary；of one's own free will

自治【ji⁶ ji⁶字】 autonomy； self-government

自主【ji⁶jü² 煮】act on one's own；decide for oneself

自尊【ji⁶jün¹ 专】self-respect；self-esteem

自细【ji⁶xei³ 世】since one is young＝【普】从小时候起

自在【ji⁶joi⁶ 再⁶】comfortable；free＝【普】自由；舒适

自梳女【ji⁶xo¹nêü⁵ 疏挪去⁵】a single lady＝【普】不嫁的老姑娘

自作自受【ji⁶jog⁸ji⁶xeo⁶ 昨寿】suffer from one's own actions

自知之明【ji⁶ ji¹ ji¹ ming⁴支支名 】self-knowledge

自始至终【ji⁶ qi² ji³ jung¹ 耻志中 】from start to finish

自相矛盾【ji⁶xêng¹mao⁴tên⁵ 双茅替春⁵】contradict oneself；be self-contradictory

自欺欺人【ji⁶ hēi¹ hēi¹ yen⁴ 希仁】deceive oneself as well as others

自暴自弃【ji⁶bou⁶ji⁶hēi³ 部戏】give oneself up as hopeless

自吹自擂【ji⁶qêü¹ji⁶lêü⁴ 摧雷】blow one's own trumpet

自强不息【ji⁶kêng⁴bed⁷xig⁷ 卡香⁴ 毕色】make unremitting efforts to improve oneself

自力更生【ji⁶lig⁹geng¹xeng¹ 历羹擤¹】self-reliance

招【jiu¹ 焦】beckon； recruit； attract； tease；confess；

招呼【jiu¹fu¹ 夫】call；hail；greet；notify；tell

招手【jiu¹xeo² 守】beckon；wave

招收【jiu¹xeo¹ 修】recruit；take in

招惹【jiu¹yē⁵ 野】provoke；court；tease

招引【jiu¹yen⁵ 瘾】attract；induce

招徕【jiu¹loi⁴ 来】solicit；canvass

招募【jiu¹mou⁶ 务】recruit；enlist

招聘【jiu¹ping³ 拼³】give public notice of a vacancy to be filled

招待【jiu¹doi⁶ 代】receive；entertain

招标【jiu¹biu¹ 彪】invite tenders

招供【jiu¹gung¹ 工】confess

招领【jiu¹lēng⁵ 靓⁵】Found

招数【jiu¹xou³ 扫】trick；device

招牌【jiu¹pai⁴ 排】shop sign；singboard

招兵买马【jiu¹bing¹mai⁵ma⁵ 冰卖⁵ 码】recruit men and buy horses—recruit followers

招致【jiu¹ji³ 至】recruit；incur；lead to

招摇撞骗【jiu¹yiu⁴jong⁶pin³ 尧状片】swindle and bluff

朝【jiu¹ 招； qiu⁴ 潮】morning； day； court；dynasty

朝夕【jiu¹jig⁹ 直】morning and evening；a very short time

朝晖【jiu¹fei¹ 辉】morning sunlight

朝头早【jiu¹teo⁴jou² 投蚤】morning＝【普】早上

朝气蓬勃【jiu¹hēi³fung⁴bud⁹ 戏冯拨】full

of youthful spirit

朝三暮四【jiu¹ xam¹ mou⁶ xēi³ 衫务死³】blow hot and cold

朝思暮想【jiu¹ xi¹ mou⁶ xêng² 司务赏】yearn day and night

朝阳【jiu¹ yêng⁴ 杨】exposed to the sun; sunny

朝拜【qiu⁴bai³ 摆³】pay respects to

朝代【qiu⁴doi⁶ 待】dynasty

朝廷【qiu⁴ting⁴ 亭】royal or imperial court

朝野【qiu⁴yē⁵ 惹】the court and the commonalty

啁　【jiu¹ 招;jeo¹ 周】〈onomatopoeia.〉

啁啁【jiu¹jiu¹】the sound of the bird

啁哳【jiu¹jid⁸ 折】twitter

啾　【jiu¹ 招;jeo¹ 周】= 啁

揪　【jiu¹ 招;jeo¹ 周】hold tight; seize; pull

揪出【jiu¹qêd⁷ 次律⁷】uncover; ferret out

揪心【jiu¹xem¹ 深】anxious; heartrending

焦　【jiu¹ 招】burnt; coke; worried; a surname

焦点【jiu¹ dim² 店²】focal point; focus; central issue

焦炭【jiu¹tan³ 叹】coke

焦急【jiu¹geb⁷ 格合⁷】anxious; worried

焦虑【jiu¹lêu⁶ 滤】feel anxious

焦头烂额【jiu¹teo⁴lan⁶ngag⁹ 投兰⁶ 我客⁹】badly battered

焦积【jiu¹ jig⁷织】clever and seasoned = 【普】精灵;老练

蕉　【jiu¹ 招】〈n.〉香蕉【hêng¹jiu¹】banana

礁　【jiu¹ 招】〈n.〉礁石【jiu¹xēg⁹ 硕】reef; rock

鹪　【jiu¹ 招】〈n.〉鹪鹩【jiu¹liu⁴ 辽】wren

椒　【jiu¹ 招】〈n.〉辣椒【lad⁹jiu¹】chili; red pepper

昭　【jiu¹ 招;qiu¹ 超】clear; obvious

昭雪【jiu¹xüd⁸ 说】exonerate; rehabilitate

昭著【jiu¹jü³ 注】clear; evident; obvious

昭然若揭【jiu¹yin⁴yêg⁹kid⁸ 言药竭】abundantly clear; all too clear

沼　【jiu² 剿】natural pond

沼泽【jiu²jag⁹ 宅】marsh; swamp; bog

沼气【jiu²hēi³ 戏】marsh gas; firedamp

剿　【jiu² 沼】send armed forces to suppress; put down

剿匪【jiu²fēi² 非²】suppress bandits

剿灭【jiu²mid⁹ 蔑】exterminate; wipe out

诏　【jiu³ 照】instruct; imperial edict

诏书【jiu³xü 输】imperial edict

照　【jiu³ 诏】shine; illuminate; reflect; photograph; picture; license; look after; notify; contrast; understand; towards; according to

照明【jiu³ming⁴ 名】illumination; lighting

照耀【jiu³yiu⁶ 要⁶】shine; illuminate

照射【jiu³xē⁶ 些⁶】shine; illuminate; light up

照常【jiu³xêng⁴ 裳】as usual

照旧【jiu³geo⁶ 柩】as before; as of old

照例【jiu³lei³ 丽】as a rule; as usual; usually

照样【jiu³yêng⁶ 让】after a pattern or model; in the same old way; as before

照料【jiu³liu⁶ 廖】take care of; attend to

照顾【jiu³ gu³ 故 】 give consideration to; look after

照应【jiu³ying³ 英³】coordinate; take care of

照办【jiu³ban⁶ 扮】act accordingly; follow

照会【jiu³wui⁶ 汇】present a note to; note

照片【jiu³ pin³偏²】photograph; picture = 相片【xêng³pin²】

照相【jiu³xêng³ 想】take a picture; photo-graph = 映相【ying²xêng³】

照相机【jiu³xêng³gêi⁶ 尚³ 基】camera

照杀【jiu³xad⁸ 煞】to describe that one is confident when promising another to do something = 【普】(当衡量利弊之后作出干脆的决定)"干啦!"

照计【jiu³gei³ 继】by right = 【普】按理说

照板煮碗【jiu³ ban³ ju² wun² 版主腕】to copy; to imitate ∽【普】以其人之道还治其人之身;学着样干

照本宣科【jiu³bun²xun¹fo¹ 苯孙课¹】read item by item from the text

嚼【jiu⁶ 赵】bite slowly in the mouth when eating before one swallows = 【普】慢咬;咀嚼

撨【jiu⁶ 赵】to punch = 【普】拳打

赵【jiu⁶ 召】a surname

召【jiu⁶ 赵】call together; convene; sum-mon

召唤【jiu⁶wun⁶ 换】call; summon

召集【jiu⁶jab⁹ 习】call together; convene

召开【jiu⁶hoi¹ 海¹】convene; convoke

召之即来【jiu³ji¹jig⁷loi⁴ 支织莱】come as soon as called

尖【jim¹ 詹】point; tip; pointed; shrill; sharp; the best of its kind

尖端【jim¹ dün¹ 段¹】pointed end; peak; most advanced

尖利【jim¹lēi⁶ 俐】sharp; keen; shrill

尖锐【jim¹yêü⁶ 蕊⁶】sharp-pointed; pene-trating; shrill; intense

尖酸【jim¹xün¹ 孙】acrid; tart

尖刻【jim¹heg⁷ 黑】acrimonious; biting

尖子【jim¹ ji² 止 】 the best of its kind; a sudden rise in pitch

尖笔甩【jim¹bed⁷led⁷ 毕利核⁷】very sharp = 【普】尖极了

詹【jim¹ 尖】a surname

瞻【jim¹ 尖】look up or forward

瞻仰【jim¹yêng⁵ 养】look at with reverence

瞻前顾后【jim¹qin⁴gu³heo⁶ 钱故候】look ahead and behind—be overcau-tions and indecisive

占【jim¹ 尖;jim³ 尖³】practise divination; occupy; take

占卦【jim¹gua³ 挂】practise divination; di-vine

占据【jim³gêü³ 踞】occupy; hold

占有【jim³yeo⁵ 友】own; have; occupy; hold

占领【jim³ling⁵ 岭】capture; occupy; seize

占便宜【jim³pin⁴yi⁴ 拍烟⁴ 移】gain extra advantage by unfair means; ad-vantageous

沾【jim¹ 尖】moisten; wet; be stained with; touch

沾染【jim¹yim⁵ 冉】be infected with

沾边【jim¹bin¹ 鞭】touch on only lightly; be close to what it should be; be relevant

沾光【jim¹guong¹ 胱】benefit from association with sb. or sth.

沾沾自喜【jim¹jim¹ji⁶hēi² 治起】feel complacent

粘【jim¹ 尖；nim⁴ 念⁴；nim¹ 念¹】sticky; glue；paste

粘米【jim¹mei⁵ 迷⁵】glutinous rice

粘连【jim¹lin⁴ 怜】adhesion

粘贴【nim⁴tib⁸ 帖】paste；stick

粘附【nim¹fu⁶ 付】adhere

粘合【nim¹heb⁹ 盒】bind；bond；adhere = 粳埋【qi¹mai⁴】

粘胶【nim¹gao¹ 交】viscose

粘结【nim¹gid⁸ 洁】cohere

粘膜【nim¹mog⁹ 莫】mucosa

粘土【nim¹tou² 吐²】clay

粘液【nim¹yig⁹ 亦】mucus

粘性【nim¹xing³ 胜】stickiness；viscidity

渐【jim⁶ 尖⁶】gradual；by degrees

渐渐【jim⁶jim²】gradually；by degrees

渐变【jim⁶bin³ 边³】gradual change

渐进【jim⁶jên³ 俊】advance gradually

笺【jin¹ 煎】writing paper；annotation；commentary

笺注【jim¹ jü³ 著】notes and commentary on ancient texts

煎【jin¹ 毡；jin³ 战】fry in shallow oil; decoct

煎熬【jin¹ ngou⁴ 敖⁴】suffering；torture；torment

煎饼【jin¹bēng² 柄²】thin pancake made of millet flour, etc.

煎堆【jin¹ dêü¹ 队¹】a type of fried food made of flour, sesame, sugar and red bean, usually round in shape

∽【普】油煎糍粑（圆型的）

碾【jin² 展】roller；crush；pulverize

碾米机【jin²mei⁵gēi¹ 迷⁵ 基】rice mill

毡【jin² 煎】felt；felt rug；felt blanket

毡帽【jin¹mou² 模²】felt hat

剪【jin² 展】scissors；clip；wipe out

剪刀【jin²dou¹ 都】scissors；shears = 铰剪【gao³jin²】

剪裁【jin²qoi⁴ 才】cut out；tailor；prune

剪辑【jin²qeb⁷ 缉】montage；editing and rearrangement

剪接【jin²jib⁸ 摺】montage；film editing

剪除【jin²qêü⁴ 徐】wipe out；annihilate

展【jin² 剪】open up；put to good use；exhibition

展开【jin²hoi¹ 海¹】spread out；open up；launch

展览【jin²lam⁵lǎm⁵】put on display；exhibit；show

展示【jin²xi⁶ 是】reveal；show

展望【jin² mong⁶ 亡⁶】look into the distance；look ahead

展翅【jin²qi³ 次】spread the wings

辗【jin² 展】〈v.〉辗转【jin²jün² 专²】pass through many hands or places；toss about（in bed）

颤【jin³ 战】tremble；shiver；quiver；vibrate

颤抖【jin³dou² 豆²】shake；tremble = 打冷震（see"打"）

颤音【jin³yem¹ 阴】trill；shake

颤巍巍【jin³ngei⁴ngei⁴ 危】tottering；faltering

箭【jin³ 战】arrow

箭镞【jin³jug⁹ 族】metal arrowhead

箭头【jin³teo⁴ 投】arrowhead; arrow(as a sign)

箭步【jin³bou⁶ 部】a sudden big stride forward

箭靶【jin³ba² 把】target for archery

箭猪【jin³jü¹ 朱】porcupine; pig

战【jin³ 箭】war; warfare; battle; fight; shiver; tremble

战争【jin³jeng¹ 憎】war; warfare

战斗【jin³deo³ 豆³】fight; battle; combat; action

战略【jin³lêg⁹ 掠】strategy

战术【jin³xêd⁹ 述】(military) tactics

战役【jin³yig⁹ 亦】campaign; battle

战乱【jin³lün⁶ 联】chaos caused by war

战祸【jin³wo⁶ 和⁶】disaster of war

战胜【jin³xing³ 性】defeat; vanquish; overcome

战败【jin³bai⁶ 摆⁶】be defeated; defeat

战场【jin³ qêng⁴ 祥 】 battlefield; battleground

战线【jin³xin³ 腺】battle line; front

战士【jin³xi⁶ 是】soldier; champion; fighter

战友【jin³yeo⁵ 有】battle companion

战功【jin³gung¹ 工】battle achievement

战歌【jin³go¹ 哥】battle song

战鼓【jin³gu² 古】war drum; battle drum

战栗【jin³lêd⁹ 律】tremble; shiver

战战兢兢【jin³jin³ging¹ging¹ 京】trembling with fear; with caution; gingerly

战无不胜【jin³mou⁴bed⁷xing³ 毛毕性】invincible

荐【jin³ 箭】recommend; grass; straw mat

荐举【jin³gêü² 矩】propose sb. for an office; recommend

饯【jin³ 箭】give a farewell dinner

饯别【jin³bid⁹ 必⁹】give a farewell dinner

饯行【jin³heng⁴ 衡】give a farewell dinner

践【jin⁶ 贱; qin⁵ 浅】trample; tread; act on

践踏【jin⁶dab⁹ 搭⁹】tread on; trample underfoot

践约【jin⁶yêg⁸ 跃】keep a promise

溅【jin⁶ 贱】splash; spatter

溅落【jin⁶log⁹ 洛⁹】splash down

贱【jin⁶ 溅】low-priced; cheap; lowly; low-down

贱卖【jin⁶mai⁶ 买⁶】sell cheap

贱格【jin³gag⁸ 隔】miserable wretch =【普】贱骨头

精【jing¹ 晶; jēng¹ 郑¹】refined; essence; perfect; fine; smart; skilled; energy; sperm; goblin; bright; cute; selfish

精神【jing¹xen⁴ 臣】vigour; lively; spirit; essence

精彩【jing¹qoi² 采】brilliant; wonderful

精粹【jing¹xêü³ 岁】succinct; pithy; terse

精髓【jing¹xêü⁵ 水⁵】marrow; pith; quintessence

精华【jing¹wa⁴ 铧】cream; essence; quintessence

精干【jing¹gon³ 竿³】crack; keen-witted and capable

精悍【jing¹hon⁶ 汗】capable and vigorous

精简【jing¹gan² 枧】retrench; simplify; cut

精练【jing¹lin⁶ 炼】concise；succinct；terse

精炼【jing¹lin⁶ 练】refine；purify；concise

精锐【jing¹yêu⁶ 蕊⁶】crack；picked

精美【jing¹mēi⁵ 尾】exquisite；elegant

精巧【jing¹hao² 考】exquisite；ingenious

精密【jing¹med⁹ 勿】precise；accurate

精辟【jing¹ pig⁷ 拍益⁷】penetrating；incisive

精确【jing¹kog⁸ 榷】accurate；exact

精深【jing¹xem¹ 心】profound

精心【jing¹xem¹ 深】meticulously；painstakingly

精湛【jing¹ jam³ 暂³】consummate；exquisite

精致【jing¹ji³ 至】fine；exquisite

精通【jing¹ tung¹ 同¹】be proficient in；master

精细【jing¹xei³ 世】meticulous；fine

精制【jing¹jei³ 济】make with extra care；refine

精装【jing¹jong⁶ 妆】clothbound；hardback

精子【jing¹ji² 止】sperm；spermatozoon

精打细算【jing¹da²xei³xün³ 得阿² 世蒜】careful calculation and strict budgeting

精雕细刻【jing¹ diu¹ xei³ heg⁷刁世克 】work at sth. with great care

精明强干【jing¹ming⁴kêng⁴gon³ 名卡香⁴竿³】intelligent and capable

精疲力竭【jing¹pêi⁴lig⁹kid⁸ 皮历揭】exhausted

精益求精【jing¹yig⁷keo⁴jing¹ 忆球】keep improving

精仔【jēng¹jei² 济²】one who grabs any opportunity that one gets ∽【普】机灵、取巧的人

精叻【jēng¹lēg⁷ 沥⁷】smart；capable；bright；spirit；demon；intelligent ∽【普】精灵；聪慧

精出骨【jēng¹qêd⁷gued⁷ 次律⁷ 掘⁷】one who only thinks of oneself；one who is selfish, selfcentred and cunning ∽【普】自私而精于为自己打算

睛【jing¹ 精】eyeball（see"眼睛"）

菁【jing¹ 精】lush；essence

菁华【jing¹wa⁴ 铧】essence；cream；quintessence

旌【jing¹ 精；xing¹ 升】〈n.〉旌旗

【jing¹kēi⁴ 其】banners and flags

征【jing¹ 精】go on a journey；go on an expedition；call up；collect；ask for；proof；sign

征兵【jing¹bing¹ 冰】conscription；draft

征税【jing¹xêu³ 瑞³】levy taxes；taxation

征收【jing¹xeo¹ 修】levy；collect

征讨【jing¹tou² 土】go on a punitive expedition

征战【jing¹jin³ 箭】go on an expedition

征途【jing¹tou⁴ 图】journey

征服【jing¹fug⁹ 伏】conquer；subjugate

征求【jing¹keo⁴ 球】solicit；seek；ask for

征询【jing¹ xên¹ 荀 】seek the opinion of；consult

征集【jing¹jab⁹ 闸】collect；draft

征候【jing¹heo⁶ 后】sign

征象【jing¹jêng⁶ 像】sign；symptom

征引【jing¹yen⁵ 瘾】quote；cite

蒸【jing¹ 精】evaporate；steam

蒸发【jing¹fad⁸ 法】evaporate

蒸馏【jing¹ leo⁶ 漏】distillation

蒸气【jing¹ hēi³ 戏】vapour

蒸汽【jing¹ hēi³ 戏】steam

蒸生瓜【jing¹ xang¹ gua¹ 挂¹】stupid; not alert; not smart ∽【普】不成熟、不稳重、不正经的人

蒸笼【jing¹ lung⁴ 龙】food steamer

蒸饭【jing¹ fan⁶ 范】steam rice

蒸蒸日上【jing¹ jing¹ yed⁹ xêng⁵ 逸尚⁵】flourishing; thriving

晶 【jing¹ 精】brilliant; glittering; quartz; any crystalline substance

晶石【jing¹ xêg⁹ 硕】spar

晶体【jing¹ tei² 睇】crystal

晶体管【jing¹ tei² gun² 睇茺】transistor

晶莹【jing¹ ying⁴ 营】sparkling and crystal-clear

整 【jing² 正²】whole; neat; rectify; repair; fix; do

整数【jing² xou³ 素】integer; round number

整体【jing² tei² 睇】whole; entirety

整个【jing² go³ 哥³】whole; entirety = 成个【xing⁴ go³】

整整【jing² jing²】whole; full

整齐【jing² qei⁴ 妻⁴】in good order; neat; even

整理【jing² lēi⁵ 李】put in order; arrange

整洁【jing² gid⁸ 结】clean and tidy; trim

整饬【jing² qig⁷ 斥】strengthen; neat; tidy

整顿【jing² dên⁶ 吨⁶】rectify; consolidate

整治【jing² ji⁶ 自】renovate; punish; do; work at

整容【jing² yung⁴ 熔】tidy oneself up; face-lifting

整定【jing² ding⁶ 锭】fated to succeed or fail =【普】注定

整古【jing² gu² 鼓】to trick =【普】作难；暗中捣鬼

整色水【jing² xig⁷ xêü² 式瑞²】to pretend =【普】矫揉造作；卖俏

整古作怪【jing² gu² jog⁸ guai³ 鼓昨乖³】to trick =【普】恶作剧；故意捉弄

正 【jing³ 政；jing¹ 精；jēng³ 郑³】straight; main; sharp; right; correct; chief; regular; plus; rectify; just; the first moon

正月【jing¹ yüd⁹ 越】the first month of the lunar year

正常【jing³ xêng⁴ 裳】normal; regular

正当【jing³ dong⁴ 档】proper; appropriate

正当【jing³ dong¹ 珰】just when; just the time for

正大【jing³ dai⁶ 歹⁶】upright; honest

正道【jing³ dou⁶ 度】the right way

正点【jing³ dim² 店²】on time; punctually

正反【jing³ fan² 返】positive and negative

正规【jing³ kuei¹ 亏】regular; standard

正轨【jing³ guei² 鬼】the right path

正好【jing³ hou² 蒿²】just in time; just right; happen to = 啱好【ngam¹ hou²】= 啱晒【ngam¹ xai³】

正经【jing³ ging¹ 京】decent; serious; standard

正门【jing³ mun⁴ 们】front door; main entrance

正面【jing³ min³ 免⁶】front; the right side; positive

正派【jing³ pai³ 排³】upright; honest

正气【jing³ hēi³ 戏】healthy atmosphere

正确【jing³ kog⁸ 榷】correct; right; proper

正视【jing³ ji⁶ 士】face up to; look squarely at

正数【jing³ xou³ 扫】positive number

正统【jing³tung² 桶】legitimism；orthodox

正午【jing³ng⁵ 五】high noon

正业【jing³yib⁹ 叶】regular occupation

正在【jing³ joi⁶ 再 】in process of；in course of

正直【jing³jig⁹ 值】honest；upright

正宗【jing³jung¹ 中】orthodox school

正极【jing³gig⁹ 击⁹】positive electrode

正人君子【jing³yen⁴guen¹ji² 仁 均 止】a man of honour；gentleman

正中下怀【jing³jung³ha⁶wai⁴ 种³ 夏槐】be just what one hopes for＝合晒心水【heb⁹xai³xem¹xêu²】

正话【jing³wa⁶ 画⁶】just now；in the middle of doing or discussing＝【普】刚才；正在

正一【jing³yed⁷ 壹】really；formal＝【普】正式

正野【jêng³ yê⁵惹】certified products（or goods）＝【普】正品；好货

正斗【jêng³ deo²豆²】good；beautiful＝【普】好的；美丽的

贞【jing¹ 精】loyal；chastity or virginity；divination

贞操【jing³ qou¹ 躁】chastity or virginity；divination

贞节【jing¹jid⁸ 折】chastity or virginity，i. e. remaining chaste and faithful to one's husband or betrothed, even after his death, as demanded by the Confucian moral code

贞洁【jing¹gid⁸ 结】chaste and undefiled

侦【jing¹ 精】detect；scout；investigate

侦察【jing¹qad⁸ 刷】reconnoitre；scout

侦缉【jing¹qeb⁷ 辑】track down and arrest

侦探【jing¹ tam³谭³】do detective work；detective

祯【jing¹ 精】auspicious；propitious

帧【jing¹ 精】〈classifier〉一 帧 画【yed⁷jing¹wa²】a picture

帧频【jing¹pen⁴ 贫】picture frequency

静【jing⁶ 精⁶】still；quiet；calm

静止【jing⁶ji² 子】static；motionless

静态【jing⁶tai³ 太】static state

静穆【jing⁶mug⁹ 木】solemn and quiet

静默【jing⁶meg⁹墨 】become silent；observe silence

静脉【jing⁶meg⁹ 默】vein

静电【jing⁶din⁶ 甸】static electricity

静鸡鸡【jing⁶gei¹gei¹ 计¹】secretly；inwardly＝【普】暗地里

静英英【jing⁶ying¹ying¹ 婴】very quiet＝【普】静悄悄

靖【jing⁶ 静】peace；pacify

净【jing⁶ 静；jêng⁶ 郑】clean；completely；only；net

净化【jing⁶fa³ 花³】purify

净水【jing⁶xêu² 瑞²】clean water

净尽【jing⁶jên⁶ 进⁶】completely；utterly

净重【jing⁶qung⁵ 虫⁵】net weight

净系【jing⁶hei⁶ 兮⁶】only；just＝【普】光是；只是

摺【jib⁸ 接】fold

摺叠【jib⁸dib⁹ 蝶】fold

接【jib⁸ 摺】come close to；join；catch；receive；meet；take over

接班【jib⁸ban¹ 斑】take over from；carry on

接触【jib⁸jug⁷ 足】come into contact with；

contact

接待【jib⁸doi⁶ 代】receive; admit

接合【jib⁸heb⁹ 盒】joint

接济【jib⁸jei³ 际】give financial help to

接见【jib⁸gin³ 建】receive sb.

接近【jib⁸gen⁶ 靳】be close to; near

接力【jib⁸lig⁹ 历】relay

接连【jib⁸lin⁴ 莲】on end; in a row

接纳【jib⁸nab⁹ 呐】admit

接洽【jib⁸ heb⁷恰 】arrange with; consult with

接壤【jib⁸ yêng⁶让】border on; be contiguous to

接生【jib⁸xeng¹ 笙】deliver a child

接收【jib⁸ xeo¹修 】 receive; expropriate; admit

接受【jib⁸xeo⁶ 授】accept

接替【jib⁸tei³ 剃】take over; replace

接通【jib⁸tung¹ 同¹】put through

接吻【jib⁸men⁵ 敏】kiss

接续【jib⁸jug⁹ 逐】continue; follow

接应【jib⁸ying³ 英³】coordinate with; reinforce

接住【jib⁸ jü⁶注⁶】catch; follow ＝ 跟住【gen¹ jü⁶】＝【普】接着

接踵【jib⁸ jung² 肿 】 following on sb.'s heels

辄【jib⁸ 接】always; then

疖【jid⁸ 节】〈n〉疖子【jid⁸ji² 止】boil; knob(in wood)

节【jid⁸ 折】joint; section; festival; abridge; save; item; chastity

节操【jid⁸qou¹ 操】high moral principle

节俭【jid⁸gim⁶ 兼⁶】thrifty; frugal

节省【jid⁸xeng² 生²】economize; save

节约【jid⁸yêg⁸ 跃】practise thrift; save

节余【jid⁸yü⁴ 如】surplus

节制【jid⁸jei³ 济】control; temperance

节节【jid⁸jid⁸】successively; steadily

节气【jid⁸hêi³ 戏】solar terms

节日【jid⁸yed⁹ 逸】festival; holiday

节目【jid⁸mug⁹ 木】programme; item

节拍【jid⁸pag⁸ 柏】metre

节奏【jid⁸jeo³ 皱】rhythm

节外生枝【jid⁸ngoi⁶xeng¹ji¹ 碍笙之】side issues or new problems crop up unexpectedly; raise obstacles

节衣缩食【jid⁸yi¹xug⁷xig⁹ 依宿蚀】economize on food and clothing; live frugally

折【jid⁸ 节】break; lose; bend; turn back; be convinced; convert into; discount; fold; folder; roll over

折半【jid⁸ bun³绊³】 reduce（a price）by half

折冲【jid⁸qung¹ 充】repulse or subdue the enemy

折服【jid⁸fug⁹ 伏】subdue; be convinced

折合【jid⁸ heb⁹盒 】convert into; amount to

折回【jid⁸ wui⁴会⁴】turn back ＝ 翻转头【fan¹ jün³teo⁴】

折价【jid⁸ga³ 嫁】convert into money

折旧【jid⁸geo⁶ 柩】depreciation

折扣【jid⁸ keo³购】discount; rebate ＝ 折头【jid⁸teo⁴】

折磨【jid⁸mo⁴ 摸⁴】torment

折射【jid⁸xê⁶ 蛇⁶】refraction

折算【jid⁸xün³ 蒜】convert

折中【jid⁸jung¹ 忠】compromise

折堕【jid⁸ do⁶惰 】conscience; stricken; waste ∽【普】堕落

哲【jid⁸ 折】wise; wise man

哲学【jid⁸hog⁹ 鹤】philosophy
哲理【jid⁸lēi⁵ 李】philosophy
哲人【jid⁸yen⁴ 仁】sage; philosopher

渫【jid⁷ 折⁷】splash on; extruding＝【普】溅；挤压(液体)

蜇【jid⁸ 节】〈n.〉海蜇【hoi²jid⁸】jellyfish

浙【jid⁸ 节】〈n.〉浙江【jid⁸gong¹ 刚】Zhejiang(Province)

截【jid⁹ 节⁹】cut; sever; section; chunk

截断【jid⁹ tün⁵团⁵】 cut off; block; cut short
截止【jid⁹ji² 子】end; close; cut-off
截至【jid⁹ji³ 致】by (a specified time); up to
截击【jid⁹gig⁷ 激】intercept
截面【jid⁹min² 免²】section
截然【jid⁹yin⁴ 言】sharply; completely

捷【jid⁹ 截】victory; prompt

捷报【jid⁹bou³ 布】news of victory
捷径【jid⁹ging³ 劲】shortcut
捷足先登【jid⁹jug⁷xin¹deng¹ 竹仙灯】the swift-footed arrive first

睫【jid⁹ 捷】eyelash; lash

睫毛【jid⁹mou⁴ 无】eyelash; lash

即【jig⁷ 积】approach; assume; at present; be; mean; promptly; even
即系【jig⁷hei⁶ 兮⁶】that is＝【普】即是
即时【jig⁷ xi⁴ 司⁴ 】immediately; forthwith; at once; instantly ＝ 即刻【jig⁷heg⁹ 克】＝【普】立即；马上
即将【jig⁷jêng¹ 章】be about to; be on the

point of
即日【jig⁷yed⁹ 逸】this or that very day; within the next few days
即使【jig⁷ xi² 史 】even; even if ＝ 即便【jig⁷bin⁶】
即位【jig⁷wei⁶ 惠】ascend the throne
即席【jig⁹jig⁹ 直】impromptu; take one's seat
即兴【jig⁷hing³ 庆】impromptu; extemporaneous
即景生情【jig⁷ging²xeng¹qing⁴ 境笙程】the scene brings back memories

迹【jig⁷ 即】a building plan; mark; remains; an outward sign

迹象【jig⁷jêng⁶ 像】sign; indication

积【jig⁷ 即】amass; long-standing; age-old; product

积存【jig⁷qün⁴ 全】store up; lay up
积分【jig⁷fen¹ 熏】integral
积极【jig⁷gig⁹ 击⁹】positive; active
积极性【jig⁷gig⁹xing³ 击⁹ 胜】zeal; initiative
积累【jig⁷lêü⁶ 类】accumulate
积聚【jig⁷jêü⁶ 叙】gather; accumulate
积蓄【jig⁷ qug⁷促 】 put aside; save; savings
积压【jig⁷ngad² 押】overstock
积怨【jig⁷yün³ 渊³】accumulated rancour
积习【jig⁷jab⁹ 袭】old habit; long-standing practice
积劳成疾【jig⁷lou⁴xing⁴jed⁹ 涝承侄】break down from constant overwork
积重难返【jig⁷ qung⁵ nan⁴ fan² 虫⁵挪曼⁴反】bad old practices die hard

瘀【jig⁷ 积】〈n.〉瘀滞【jig⁷jei⁶ 济⁶】indigestion＝【普】积食

漬【jig⁷ 积】a stain, mark or spot on clothing

绩【 jig 积 】 twist hempen thread; achievement; merit

织【jig⁷ 积】weave; knit

织布【jig⁷ bou³ 报 】 weaving cotton cloth; weaving

织造【jig⁷ jou⁶ 做】weaving

织机【jig⁷ gêi¹ 基】loom

织物【jig⁷ med⁹ 勿】fabric

织女【jig⁷ nêu⁵ 挪去⁵ 】 woman weaver; Vega(a Lyrae)

稷【jig⁷ 积】millet; the god of grains worshipped by ancient emperors

寂【jig⁹ 直】quiet; still; lonely; solitary

寂静【jig⁹jing⁶ 净】quiet; still

寂寞【jig⁹mog⁹ 莫】lonely; lonesome

寂寥【jig⁹liu⁴ 聊】solitary; lonesome

直【 jig⁹ 寂 】 straight; straighten; vertical; just; frank; stiff; directly; continuously; simply

直头【jig⁹teo⁴ 投】directly; simply =【普】一直(走); 简直

直程【jig⁹ qing⁴情 】 straight; simply =【普】直线距离; 简直

直笔甩【jig⁹bed⁷led⁷ 毕罗甩⁷ 】very straight =【普】很直

直白【jig⁹bag⁹ 伯⁹】to be frank, true and honest

直达【jig⁹dad⁹ 得押⁹】through; nonstop

直到【jig⁹dou³ 都³】until; up to; till =直至【jig⁹ji³】

直观【jig⁹gun¹ 官】directly perceived through the senses; audio-visual

直角【jig⁹gog⁸ 觉】〈n.〉right angle

直觉【jig⁹gog⁸ 角】intuition

直接【jig⁹jib⁸ 支叶⁸】direct; immediate

直径【jig⁹ging³ 劲】〈n.〉diameter

直属【jig⁹xug⁹ 熟】directly under

直率【jig⁹xêd⁷ 是律⁷】frank; candid

直爽【jig⁹xong² 桑²】frank; candid

直辖【jig⁹hed⁹ 核】directly under the jurisdiction of

直线【jig⁹xin³ 腺】straight line; steep

直译【jig⁹yig⁹ 亦】literal translation

直言不讳【jig⁹ yin⁴ bed⁷ wei⁵ 然毕伟】speak without reservation

直截了当【jig⁹jid⁸liu⁵dong³ 节聊⁵ 荡³】straightforward; blunt; point-blank

席【jig⁹ 直】mat; seat; feast

席位【jig⁹wei⁶ 卫】seat

席卷【jig⁹gün² 娟²】roll up like a mat; engulf

值【jig⁹ 直】value; be worth; happen to; be on duty; value

值得【jig⁹ deg⁷ 德】be worth; merit; deserve

值银【jig⁹ngen² 额恩²】costly; valuable =值钱【jig⁹qin²】

值班【jig⁹ban¹ 斑】be on duty

值勤【jig⁹ken¹ 芹】be on duty; be on point duty

植【jig⁹ 直】plant; grow; set up; establish

植物【jig⁹med⁹ 勿】plant; flora

植树【jig⁹xü⁶ 署⁶】tree planting

植被【jig⁹pêi⁵ 婢】vegetation

殖【jig⁹ 直】breed; multiply

殖民【jig⁹men⁴ 文】establish a colony; colonize

殖民地【jig⁹men⁴dēi⁶ 得希⁶】colony

蹠 【jig⁸ 炙】metatarsus; sole of the foot; tread

蹠骨【jig⁸gued⁷ 掘⁷】metatarsal bones

炙 【jig⁸ 积²; jēg⁸ 脊】broil; roast; roast meat

炙手可热【jig⁸xeo²ho²yid⁹】if you stretch out your hand you feel the heat — the supreme arrogance of a person with great power

籍 【jig⁸ 直】book; registry; native place; membership

籍贯【jig⁹gun³ 灌】the place of one's birth or origin; native place

朱 【jū¹ 珠】vermilion; cinnabar; a surname

朱红【jū¹hung⁴ 洪】vermilion; bright red

朱漆【jū¹qed⁷ 七】red paint; red lacquer

朱砂【jū¹xa¹ 沙】cinnabar

朱门【jū¹mun⁴ 们】vermilion gates — red-lacquered doors of wealthy homes

朱咕力【jū¹gu¹lig⁷ 姑沥】chocolate

诛 【jū¹ 朱】put to death; punish

朱戮【jū¹lug⁹ 六】kill; put to death

侏 【jū¹ 朱】dwarf

侏儒【jū¹yū⁴ 如】dwarf; midget; pygmy

株 【jū¹ 朱】trunk of a tree; plant

株距【jū¹kêū⁵ 拒】spacing in the rows

株连【jū¹lin⁴ 莲】involve in a criminal case; implicate

诸 【jū¹ 朱】all; various =“之于”; a surname

诸多【jū¹do¹ 朵】a good deal; a lot of

诸如【jū¹yū⁴ 鱼】such as

诸位【jū¹wei² 委】you; Ladies and Gentlemen

诸侯【jū¹heo⁴ 喉 】dukes or princes under an emperor

诸葛亮【jū¹god⁸lêng⁶ 割谅】Zhuge Liang, a statesman and strategist in the period of the Three Kingdoms (220—265), who became a symbol of resourcefulness and wisdom in Chinese folklore; mastermind

诸如此类【jū¹yū⁴qi²lêū⁶ 鱼始泪】things like that; such

蛛 【jū¹ 朱】spider

蛛网【jū¹mong⁵ 妄】spider web; cobweb

蛛丝蚂迹【jū¹xi¹ma⁵jig⁷ 司马织】clues; traces

猪 【jū¹ 朱】pig; hog; swine

猪肉【jū¹yug⁹ 玉】pork

猪鬃【jū¹jung¹ 中】(hog) bristles

猪舍【jū¹xē³ 泻】pig house

猪场【jū¹qêng⁴ 祥】pig farm; piggery

猪公【jū¹gung¹ 工】pig(male) =【普】公猪

猪乸【jū¹na² 那²】pig(female) =【普】母猪

猪红【jū¹hung⁴ 洪】the blood of pig =【普】猪血

猪肠粉【jū¹qêng⁴fen² 抢分²】a type of big noodle made of flour

猪手【jū¹xeo² 守】the front legs of pigs =【普】猪前腿

猪杂【jū¹jab⁹ 习】the offals of pigs =【普】猪内脏

猪仔【jū¹jei² 济²】baby pigs; corrupted ministers; people who are cheated

to go overseas to become coolies＝
【普】小猪；旧时代被迫卖去国外
做苦工的人

猪膏【jü¹ gou¹ 高】the oil of pigs＝【普】猪
板油

猪唛【jü¹ meg⁷ 墨⁷】to describe one as stupid as a pig ∽【普】笨蛋；蠢货

猪朋狗友【jü¹ peng⁴ geo² yeo⁵ 凭 九 有】
friends who are not serious ∽
【普】不三不四的朋友；哥们

煮【jü² 主】boil；cook

煮饭【jü² fan⁶ 范】cook rice

煮豆燃其【jü¹ deo⁶ yin⁴ gēi¹ 斗⁶ 言基】burn
beanstalks to cook beans — fratri-
cidal strife

渚【jü² 主】small piece of land surrounded
by water；islet

主【jü² 煮】host；owner；person；God；
Allah；main；manage；indicate；ad-
vocate

主要【jü² yiu³ 腰³】main；chief；principal；
major

主人【jü² yen⁴ 仁】master；host；boss；
owner

主持【jü² qi⁴ 池】take charge of；manage；
preside over；chair；uphold

主次【jü² qi³ 刺】primary and secondary

主从【jü² qung⁴ 虫】principal and subordinate

主导【jü² dou⁶ 道】leading；dominant

主动【jü² dung⁶ 洞】initiative；driving

主妇【jü² fu⁵ 富⁵】housewife；hostess

主干【jü² gon³ 竿³】trunk；mainstay

主顾【jü² gu³ 故】customer；client

主观【jü² gun¹ 官】subjective

主管【jü² gun² 莞】be responsible for；per-

son in charge

主婚【jü² fen¹ 分】preside over a wedding
ceremony

主见【jü² gin³ 建】definite view

主将【jü² jêng³ 涨】chief commander

主角【jü² gog⁸ 阁】leading role；lead

主力【jü² lig⁹ 历】main force

主流【jü² leo⁴ 留】main stream；main trend

主谋【jü² meo⁴ 牟】chief instigator

主权【jü² kün⁴ 拳】sovereign rights；sover-
eignty

主任【jü² yem⁶ 壬⁶】director；head

主编【jü² pin¹ 偏】chief editor；edit

主体【jü² tei² 睇】main body；subject

主席【jü² jig⁹ 直】chairman；president

主演【jü² yin² 衍】act the leading role

主意【jü² yi³ 薏】idea；plan；decision

主义【jü² yi⁶ 异】doctrine；-ism

主语【jü² yü⁵ 雨】subject

主宰【jü² joi² 灾²】dominate；dictate

主张【jü² jêng¹ 章】advocate；hold；main-
tain；view；position；stand

主旨【jü² ji² 止】purport；gist

注【jü³ 著】pour；fix；stakes；annotate；
notes

注册【jü³ qag⁸ 策】register

注定【jü³ ding² 锭】be doomed

注解【jü³ gai² 介²】annotate；note

注释【jü³ xig⁷ 色】explanatory note；anno-
tation

注音【jü³ yem¹ 阴】phonetic notation

注意【jü³ yi³ 薏】pay attention to

注视【jü³ xi⁶ 事】look attentively at；gaze
at

注重【jü³ jung⁶ 仲】lay stress on

注射【jü³ xē⁶ 些⁶】inject

铸【jū³ 注】casting; founding

铸造【jū³jou⁶ 做】casting; founding

铸件【jū³gin² 坚²】cast; casting

铸铁【jū³tid⁸ 替热⁸】iron casting; cast iron

蛀【jū³ 注】moth or any other insect that eats books, clothes, wood, etc.; eat

蛀虫【jū³qung⁴ 从】moth; borer

蛀牙【jū³nga² 芽】decayed tooth

炷【jū³ 注】〈 classifier 〉一 炷 香【yed⁷jū³hêng¹】a burning joss stick

驻【jū³ 注】halt; stay; be stationed

驻守【jū³xeo² 手】garrison; defend

驻扎【jū³jad⁸ 札】be stationed

驻防【jū³fong⁴ 房】garrison

驻地【jū³dēi⁶ 得希⁶】place where troops, etc. are stationed; seat

著【jū³ 注】marked; show; write; book

著作【jū³ jog⁸ 昨】work; book; writings; write

著名【jū³ming⁴ 明】famous; well-known

著称【jū³qing¹ 清】celebrated; famous

箸【jū⁶ 住】chopsticks

住【jū⁶ 箸】live; reside; stay; stop; cease

住房【jū³fong⁴ 防】housing; lodgings

住宅【jū³jag⁹ 泽】residence; dwelling

住处【jū³qū³ 柱³】residence; dwelling (place)

住址【jū³ji² 止】address

专【jūn¹ 砖】focussed on one thing; special; expert

专长【jūn¹qêng⁴ 祥】speciality

专门【jūn¹mun⁴ 们】special; specialized

专一【jūn¹yed⁷ 壹】single-minded; concentrated

专用【jūn¹yung⁶ 拥⁶】for a special purpose

专责【jūn¹jag⁸ 窄】specific responsibility

专职【jūn¹jig⁷ 织】sole duty; full-time

专政【jūn¹jing³ 正】dictatorship

专制【jūn¹jei³ 济】autocracy; autocratic

专断【jūn¹dūn³ 端³】make an arbitrary decision

专横【jūn¹wang⁴ 乌罂⁴】imperious; peremptory

专家【jūn¹ga¹ 加】expert; specialist

专业【jūn¹ yib⁹叶】speciality; discipline; special line

专心【jūn¹xem¹ 深】be absorbed

专利【jūn¹lēi⁶ 例】patent

专卖【jūn¹mai⁶ 买⁶】monopoly

专注【jūn¹jū³ 铸】be absorbed in

专著【jūn¹jū³ 注】monograph; treatise

砖【jūn¹ 专】brick

砖头【jūn¹ teo⁴投 】fragment of a brick; brick

砖坯【jūn¹pui¹ 胚】unfired brick

砖房【jūn¹fong⁴ 防】brick house

砖墙【jūn¹qêng⁴ 祥】brick wall

转【jūn² 专²】turn; change; pass on; transfer

转变【jūn²bin³ 边³】change; transform

转播【jūn²bo³ 波³】relay

转达【jūn²dad⁹ 得押⁹】pass on; convey

转动【jūn²dung⁶ 洞】turn; move; turn round

转告【jūn²gou³ 诰】pass on; communicate

转化【jūn²fa³ 花³】change; transform

转换【jūn²wun⁶ 唤】change; transform

转交【jūn² gao¹ 胶】pass on; transmit

转卖【jūn² mai⁶ 买⁶】resell

转念【jūn² nim⁶ 粘⁶】think better of

转头【jūn² teo⁴ 投】to look back =【普】转过头来；往回走

转下眼【jūn² ha⁶ ngan⁵ 厦雁⁵】to refer that time really flies =【普】眨眼间；瞬间

转让【jūn² yêng⁶ 嚷】make over

转身【jūn² xen¹ 辛】turn round; face about

转手【jūn² xeo² 守】pass on; sell what one has bought

转瞬【jūn² xên³ 信】in a twinkle; in a flash

转述【jūn² xêd⁶ 术】report

转送【jūn² xung³ 宋】pass on; transmit

转弯【jūn² wan¹ 湾】turn a corner; make a turn

转向【jūn² hêng³ 香³】change direction

转眼【jūn² ngan⁵ 雁⁵】in an instant; in a flash

转移【jūn² yi⁴ 而】shift; transfer; metastasis

转运【jūn² wen⁶ 混】transport; have a change of luck

转载【jūn² joi³ 再】reprint

转帐【jūn² jêng³ 涨】transfer accounts

转折【jūn² jid⁸ 浙】a turn in the course of events; transition

转弯抹角【jūn² wan¹ mud⁸ gog⁸ 湾末⁸ 各】full of twists and turns; beat about the bush.

转危为安【jūn² ngei⁴ wei⁴ ngon¹ 巍维氨】pull through

啭【jūn² 转】(of birds) twitter; sing

传【jūn² 转；jūn⁶ 转⁶；qün⁴ 全】commentaries on classics; biography; a novel or story written in historical style; pass; hand down; pass on; spread; transmit; infect

传记【jūn⁶ gêi³ 寄】biography

传略【jūn⁶ lêg⁹ 掠】brief biography

传奇【jūn⁶ kéi⁴ 其 】short stories of the Tang and Song dynasties (618—1279); poetic dramas of the Ming and Qing dynasties (1368—1911); legend; romance

传播【qün⁴ bo³ 波³】disseminate; propagation

传达【qün⁴ dad⁹ 得押⁹】pass on; janitor

传单【qün⁴ dan¹ 丹】leaflet; handbill

传导【qün⁴ dou⁶ 度】conduction

传递【qün⁴ dei⁶ 弟】transmit; deliver

传呼【qün⁴ fu¹ 夫 】notify sb. of a phone call

传令【qün⁴ ling⁶ 另】transmit orders

传染【qün⁴ yim⁵ 冉】infect; be contagious

传神【qün⁴ xen⁴ 臣】vivid; lifelike

传授【qün⁴ xeo⁶ 受】pass on; impart

传输【qün⁴ xü¹ 书】transmission

传说【qün⁴ xüd⁸ 雪 】it is said; they say; legend

传送【qün⁴ xung³ 宋】convey; deliver

传统【qün⁴ tung³ 捅】tradition

传扬【qün⁴ yêng⁴ 杨】spread

传真【qün⁴ jen¹ 珍】portraiture; facsimile

传经送宝【qün⁴ ging¹ xung³ bou² 京宋保】pass on one's valuable experience

钻【jün³ 转³】drill; get into; dig into; auger; jewel; bore

钻窿【jün³ lung¹ 龙¹】drill a hole =【普】钻孔

钻床【jün³ qong⁴ 创⁴】drilling machine

钻机【jūn³gēi¹ 基】(drilling) rig

钻井【jūn³jēng² 支镜²】well drilling

钻石【jūn³ xēg⁹ 硕】diamond; jewel (used in a watch)

钻研【jūn³ yin⁴ 言】study intensively; dig into

钻探【jūn³tam³ 谭³】drilling

钻营【jūn³ying⁴ 仍】secure personal gain

钻空子【jūn³hung¹ji² 孔¹ 止】exploit an advantage

钻牛角尖【jūn³ngeo⁴gog⁹jim¹ 偶⁴ 各沾】split hairs; get into a dead end

纂 【jūn² 转】compile; edit

纂修【jūn²xeo¹ 收】compile; edit

尊 【jūn¹ 专】senior; respect

尊敬【jūn¹ging³ 劲】respect; honour; esteem

尊重【jūn¹jung⁶ 仲】respect; value; esteem

尊贵【jūn¹guei³ 桂】honourable; respectable

尊严【jūn¹yim⁴ 盐】dignity; honour

尊称【jūn¹qing¹ 清】honorific title; address sb. respectfully

鳟 【jūn¹ 尊】〈n.〉鳟鱼【jūn¹yū⁴ 余】trout

嘬 【jūd⁸ 绌】suck; take in; absorb; kiss

嘬奶【jūd⁸nai⁵ 乃】suck the milk

嘬面朱脤【jūd³min⁶jū¹den¹ 缅⁶ 珠得恩¹】kiss＝【普】亲吻

绌 【jūd⁸ 嘬】inadequate; insufficient

拙 【jūd⁸ 绌】clumsy; awkward; dull

拙笨【jūd⁸ben⁶ 奔⁶】clumsy; dull; unskilful

拙劣【jūd⁸lūd⁸ 捋】clumsy; inferior

辍 【jūd⁸ 拙】stop; cease

辍工【jūd⁸gung¹ 公】stop work

啜 【jūd⁸ 辍】sip; sob

啜泣【jūd⁸yeb⁷ 邑】sob

苗 【jūd⁸ 拙】〈a.〉苗壮【jūd⁸jong³ 葬】healthy and strong; sturdy

绝 【jūd⁹ 拙⁹】cut off; sever; exhausted; hopeless; unique; most; absolutely; leaving no leeway

绝对【jūd⁹dêu³ 堆³】absolute; absolutely

绝顶【jūd⁹ding² 鼎】extremely; utterly

绝缘【jūd⁹ yūn⁴元 】insulation; be cut off from

绝迹【jūd⁹jig⁷ 织】disappear; vanish

绝后【jūd⁹heo⁶ 候】without offspring; never to be seen again

绝种【jūd⁹ jung³ 肿 】become extinct; die out

绝望【jūd⁹ mong⁶ 亡⁶】give up all hope; despair

绝食【jūd⁹xig⁹ 蚀】fast; go on a hunger strike

绝症【jūd⁹jing³ 正】incurable disease; fatal illness

绝技【jūd⁹ gēi⁶ 妓】unique skill ＝ 绝招【jūd⁹jiu¹】

绝妙【jūd⁹miu⁶ 庙】extremely clever; perfect

绝路【jūd⁹lou⁶ 露】road to ruin; impasse

绝境【jūd⁹ ging² 景 】hopeless situation; impasse

绝伦【jūd⁹ lên⁴ 沦 】unsurpassed; une-

qualled

绝交【jüd⁹gao¹胶】break off relations

绝密【jüd⁹ med⁹ 勿 】 top-secret; most confidential

绝情【jüd⁹qing⁴ 程】merciless

绝色【jüd⁹xig⁷ 式】exceedingly beautiful

绝处逢生【jüd⁹qü³fung⁴xeng¹ 储³ 冯笙】be unexpectedly rescued from a desperate situation

靰【jê¹ 支靴¹】〈v.〉靰住晒【jê¹jü⁶xai³注⁶ 徙³】twine and question closely =【普】缠绕, 追问

追【jêü¹ 锥】chase after; trace; seek; recall; retroactively

追求【jêü¹keo⁴ 球】seek; woo; pursue; court

追逐【jêü¹jug⁹ 浊】pursue; seek

追赶【jêü¹gon² 干²】run after

追踪【jêü¹ jung³宗 】 follow the trail of; track

追寻【jêü¹qem⁴ 沉】pursue; search

追随【jêü¹qêü⁶ 徐】follow

追忆【jêü¹yig⁷ 益】recollect; recall

追问【jêü¹men⁶ 闻】question closely

追叙【jêü¹jêü⁶ 聚】tell about the past; flashback

追究【jêü¹geo³ 够】look into; investigate

追击【jêü¹gig⁷ 激】pursue and attack; follow up

追捕【jêü¹bou⁶ 步】pursue and capture

追查【jêü¹qa⁴ 茶】investigate; trace

追悼【jêü¹dou⁶ 道】mourn over a person's death

追悔【jêü¹fui³ 灰³】repent; regret

椎【jêü¹ 追】vertebra

椎骨【jêü¹gued⁷ 掘⁷】vertebra

锥【jêü¹ 追; yêü¹ 锐¹】

锥形【jêü¹ying⁴ 型】taper; cone

锥仔【yêü¹jei² 济²】awl =【普】锥子

嘴【jêü² 咀】mouth; anything shaped or functioning like a mouth

嘴唇【jêü²xên⁴ 纯】lip

嘴脸【jêü²lim⁵ 廉⁵】look; features

嘴馋【jêü²qam⁴ 惭】fond of good food

嘴笨【jêü²ben⁶ 奔⁶】inarticulate

嘴乖【jêü² guai⁶怪¹】 clever and pleasant when speaking to elders

嘴尖【jêü²jim¹ 詹】sharp-tongued

嘴甜【jêü²tim⁴ 添⁴】ingratiating in speech

嘴硬【jêü²ngang⁶ 罂⁶】stubborn and reluctant to admit mistakes or defeats

咀【jêü² 嘴】chew

咀嚼【jêü²jêg⁸ 桌】chew; ruminate

沮【jêü² 嘴】stop; turn gloomy

沮丧【jêü²xong³ 桑³】dejected; depressed

诅【jêü² 嘴; jo² 左】〈v.〉诅咒【jêü²jeo³ 皱】curse; swear

最【jêü³ 醉】〈ad.〉most; -est

最初【jêü³qo¹ 雏】initial; first

最低【jêü³dei¹ 底】lowest; minimum

最多【jêü³do¹ 朵¹】at most; maximum

最高【jêü³gou¹ 膏】highest; tallest

最好【jêü³hou² 蒿²】best; first-rate; had better

最后【jêü³heo⁶ 候】final; last

最近【jêü³gen⁶ 靳】recently; lately; soon

最靓【jêü³lêng³ 罗镜³】most beautiful; best =【普】最美; 最佳; 最好

最终【jêü³jung¹ 中】final; ultimate

醉【jêü³ 最】drunk; tipsy; steeped in liquor

醉心【jêü³xem¹ 深】be bent on

醉意【jêü³ yi³薏 】signs or feeling of getting drunk

醉醺醺【jêü³fen¹fen¹ 昏】sottish; drunk; tipsy

醉生梦死【jêü³xing¹mung⁶xêi² 笙蒙⁶ 四²】live as if intoxicated or dreaming

醉翁之意不在酒【jêü³yung¹ yi¹yi³bed⁷joi⁶ jeo² 雍支薏毕再⁶ 走】the drinker's heart is not in the cup — have ulterior motives

罪【jêü⁶ 坠】crime; fault; suffering; put the blame on

罪恶【jêü⁶ngog⁸ 岳⁸】crime; evil

罪过【jêü⁶guo³ 戈³】fault; offence; sin

罪行【jêü⁶heng⁶ 幸】crime; guilt; offence

罪孽【jêü⁶yib⁹ 叶】sin

罪状【jêü⁶jong⁶ 撞】facts about a crime

罪名【jêü⁶ming⁴ 明】charge; accusation

罪犯【jêü⁶fan² 反】criminal; offender

罪证【jêü⁶jing³ 正】evidence of a crime

罪魁【jêü⁶fui¹ 灰】chief criminal

罪大恶极【jêü⁶ dai⁶ ngog⁸ gig⁹歹⁶岳⁸击⁹】be guilty of the most heinous crimes

坠【jêü⁶ 聚】fall; weigh down; weight

坠落【jêü⁶log⁹ 洛⁹】fall; drop

坠毁【jêü⁶wei² 委】fall and break; crash

坠子【jêü⁶ji² 止】weight; ear pendant

聚【jêü⁶ 叙】assemble; gather; get together

聚合【jêü⁶heb⁹ 盒】get together; polymerization

聚集【jêü⁶jab⁹ 习】gather; assemble

聚会【jêü⁶wui⁶ 汇】get together; meet

聚积【jêü⁶jig⁷ 织】accumulate; collect

聚焦【jêü⁶jiu¹ 蕉】focusing

聚居【jêü⁶gêu¹ 据¹】inhabit a region

聚酯【jêü⁶ji¹ 支】polyester

聚餐【jêü⁶qan¹ 灿¹】dine together

聚变【jêü⁶bin³ 边³】fusion

聚精会神【jêü⁶jing¹wui⁶xen⁴ 贞汇臣】concentrate one's attention; be all attention

叙【jêü⁶ 聚】talk; narrate; assess; chat

叙述【jêü⁶xêd⁹ 术】narrate; recount; relate

叙旧【jêü⁶geo⁶ 柩】talk about the old days

叙事【jêü⁶xi⁶ 士】narrate; recount

序【jêü⁶ 叙】order; arrange in order; initial; preface

序列【jêü⁶lid⁹ 裂】alignment; array

序幕【jêü⁶mog⁹ 莫】prologue; prelude

序言【jêü⁶yin⁴ 研】preface; foreword

序曲【jêü⁶kug⁷ 卡屋⁷】overture

缀【jêü⁶ 序；jüd⁸ 苗】sew; compose; embellish

补缀【bou²jêü⁶】mend

点缀【dim²jüd⁸】embellish

赘【jêü⁶ 序】redundant; be burdensome

赘述【jêü⁶xêd⁹ 术】say more than is needed

赘疣【jêü⁶yeo⁴ 尤】wart; anything superfluous or useless

赘婿【jêü⁶xei³ 世】a son-in-law who lives in the home of his wife's parents

惴【jêü³ 最】〈a.〉惴惴不安【jêü³jêü³ bed⁷ngon¹ 毕氨】be anxious and fearful

津【jên¹ 榉】ferry crossing; sweat; moist

津液【jên¹ yig⁹ 亦】body fluid; saliva

津贴【jên¹ tib⁸ 帖】subsidy; allowance

津津有味【jên¹ jên¹ yeo⁵ mēi⁶ 友未】with relish

津津乐道【jên¹ jên¹ log⁹ dou⁶ 落度】take delight in talking about

樽【jên¹ 遵】a kind of wine vessel used in ancient times

遵【jên¹ 津】abide by; obey; observe; follow

遵从【jên¹ qung⁴ 虫】defer to; follow

遵命【jên¹ ming⁶ 名⁶】comply with your wish

遵守【jên¹ xeo² 手】observe; abide by

遵循【jên¹ qên⁴ 巡】follow; abide by

遵照【jên¹ jiu³ 焦³】obey; conform to

准【jên² 津²】allow; in accordance with; standard; accurate; definitely; quasi—

准则【jên² jeg³ 仄】norm; standard

准确【jên² kog⁸ 榷】accurate; exact

准绳【jên² xing⁴ 成】criterion; yardstick

准时【jên² xi⁴ 士⁴】punctual; on time

准许【jên² hêu² 栩】permit; allow

准予【jên² yū⁵ 语】grant; approve

准备【jên² bēi⁶ 鼻】prepare; intend

准将【jên² jêng³ 胀】brigadier; brigadier general

进【jên³ 俊】advance; enter; get into; receive; eat; submit; into; score a goal

进步【jên³ bou⁶ 部】advance; progressive

进程【jên³ qing⁴ 情】course; process

进出【jên³ qêd⁷ 次律⁷】pass in and out; turnover

进度【jên³ dou⁶ 道】rate of progress; planned speed

进而【jên³ yi⁴ 移】proceed to the next step

进攻【jên³ gung¹ 工】attack; assault

进贡【jên³ gung³ 共³】pay tribute

进货【jên³ fo³ 课】stock (a shop) with goods

进化【jên³ fa³ 花³】evolution

进见【jên³ gin³ 建】call on; have an audience with

进军【jên³ guen¹ 君】march; advance

进口【jên³ heo² 后²】enter port; import; entrance; inlet

进来【jên³ loi⁴ 莱】come in; enter

进取【jên³ qêu² 娶】keep forging ahead

进去【jên³ hêu³ 虚³】go in; get in; enter

进入【jên³ yeb⁹ 邑⁹】enter; get into

进食【jên³ xig⁹ 蚀】take food; have one's meal

进退【jên³ têu³ 推³】advance and retreat

进行【jên³ heng⁴ 衡】be in progress; go on; carry on; conduct; march; advance

进修【jên³ xeo¹ 收】engage in advanced studies

进展【jên³ jin³ 剪】make progress; make headway

进一步【jên³ yed⁷ bou⁶ 壹部】go a step further; further

晋【jên³ 进】enter; promote; the Jin Dynasty

晋级【jên³ keb⁷ 给】rise in rank; be promoted

晋升【jên³ xing¹ 星】promote to a higher office

俊【jên³ 进】handsome; a person of outstanding talent

俊杰【jên³ gid⁹ 桀】a person of outstanding talent; hero

俊美【jên³mēi⁵ 尾】pretty

俊俏【jên³qiu³ 峭】pretty and charming

俊秀【jên³xeo³ 瘦】pretty; of delicate beauty

浚【jên³ 进】dredge

浚渠【jên³kêü⁴ 驱⁴】dredge a canal

峻【jên³ 进】(of mountains) high; harsh; severe

峻峭【jên³qiu³ 俏】high and steep

骏【jên³ 进】fine horse; steed

骏马【jên³ma⁵ 蚂】fine horse; steed

竣【jên³ 进】complete; finish

竣工【jên³gung¹ 公】(of a project) be completed

尽【jên⁶ 遵⁶】exhausted; to the utmost; use up; try one's best; all

尽量【jên⁶lêng⁶ 亮】(drink or eat) to the full

尽头【jên⁶teo⁴ 投】end

尽心【jên⁶xem¹ 深】with all one's heart

尽力【jên⁶lig⁹ 历】do all one can; try one's best

尽情【jên⁶qing⁴程】to one's heart's content

尽职【jên⁶jig⁷ 织】fulfil one's duty

尽善尽美【jên⁶xin⁶jên⁶mēi⁵ 膳尾】perfect

尽人皆知【jên⁶yen⁴gai¹ji¹ 仁佳支】be known to all

烬【jên⁶ 尽】cinder

灰烬【fui¹jên⁶】ashes; cinders

将【jêng¹ 章; jêng³ 胀】support; take; bring; take care of; do sth.; check; put sb. on the spot; challenge; with; by; be going to; will; shall; general; commander in chief; lead

将军【jêng¹guen¹ 君】general; check; embarrass

将近【jêng¹gen⁶ 靳】close to; nearly

将就【jêng¹jeo⁶ 袖】make do with; put up with

将来【jêng¹loi⁴ 莱】future

将要【jêng¹yiu³ 妖³】be going to; will; shall

将领【jêng³ling⁵ 岭】general = 将官【jêng³gun¹ 观】

将士【jêng³xi⁶ 事】officers and men

浆【jêng¹ 章】thick liquid; starch

浆液【jêng¹yig⁹ 亦】size

浆洗【jêng¹xei² 驶】wash and starch

张【jêng¹ 章】open; display; magnify; a surname; 〈classifier〉一张纸【yed⁷jêng¹ji²】a piece of paper

张嘴【jêng¹jêü² 咀】open one's mouth

张贴【jêng¹tib⁸ 帖】put up

张扬【jêng¹yêng⁴ 洋】make widely known; publicize

张皇【jêng¹wong⁴ 王】alarmed; magnify

张罗【jêng¹lo⁴ 锣】take care of; raise; attend to

张冠李戴【jêng¹gun¹lēi⁵dai³ 官理带】put Zhang's hat on Li's head — attribute sth. to the wrong person or confuse one thing with another

张牙舞爪【jêng¹nga⁴mou⁵jao² 芽武找】bare fangs and brandish claws — make threatening gestures

章【jêng¹ 张】chapter; order; rules; seal; badge; a surname

章程【jêng¹qing⁴ 情】rules; solution; way

章法【jêng¹ fad⁸ 发 】 art of composition; orderly ways

章节【jêng¹ jid⁸ 折】chapters and sections

彰 【jêng¹ 章】clear; evident; conspicuous

彰明较著【jêng¹ming⁴gao³jü³ 名教注】very obvious

獐 【jêng¹ 章】〈n.〉river deer

璋 【jêng¹ 章】〈n.〉a jade tablet

樟 【jêng¹ 章】camphor tree

樟木【jêng¹mug⁹ 目】camphorwood

樟脑【jêng¹nou⁵ 努】camphor

蟑 【jêng¹ 章】〈n.〉蟑螂【jêng¹long⁴ 郎】cockroach; roach＝甲由【gad⁹jad⁹】

掌 【jêng² 蒋】palm; slap; control; pad; shoe sole or heel; horseshoe

掌心【jêng² xem¹深 】 the centre of the palm

掌声【jêng²xing¹ 星】clapping; applause

掌握【jêng²ngeg⁷ 厄⁷】grasp; master; have in hand

掌管【jêng² gun² 莞 】 be in charge of; administer

掌柜【jêng²guei⁶ 馈】shopkeeper; manager

掌权【jêng² kün⁴拳 】 be in power; wield power

掌上明珠【jêng²xêng⁶ming⁴jü¹ 尚名朱】a pearl in the palm — a beloved daughter

长 【jêng² 掌；qêng⁴ 祥】older; eldest; chief; grow; form; acquire; long; length; lasting; steadily; forte

长辈【jêng²bui 背】older; senior

长大【jêng²dai⁶ 歹⁶】grow up; be brought up

长官【jêng²gun¹ 观】senior officer

长进【jêng²jên³ 俊】progress

长势【jêng²xei³ 世】the way a crop is growing

长相【jêng²xêng³ 商³】looks; features

长度【qêng⁴dou⁶ 道】length

长短【qêng⁴dün⁴ 端²】length; accident; right and wrong

长久【qêng⁴geo² 九】for a long time; permanently

长期【qêng⁴kēi⁴ 其】long-term

长年【qêng⁴nin⁴ 捻⁴】all the year round

长寿【qêng⁴xeo⁶ 受】long life; longevity

长远【qêng⁴ yün⁵ 软 】 long-term; long-range

长征【qêng⁴jing¹ 精】long march

长足【qêng⁴jug⁷ 竹】by leaps and bounds

长工【qêng⁴ gung¹ 公 】 long-term hired hand

长处【qêng⁴qü³ 次于³】good qualities

长途【qêng⁴tou⁴ 图】long-distance

长城【qêng⁴xing⁴ 成】the Great Wall

长江【qêng⁴gong¹ 刚】the Changjiang (Yangtze) River

长篇大论【qêng⁴pin¹dai⁶lên⁶ 偏歹⁶ 伦⁶】a lengthy speech or article

桨 【jêng² 掌】〈n.〉oar

蒋 【jêng² 掌】a surname

奖 【jêng² 掌】encourage; praise; award; prize

奖励【jêng²lei⁶ 丽】encourage and reward; reward

奖赏【jêng²xêng² 想】award; reward

奖金【jêng² gem¹ 今】money award; bonus

奖杯【jêng² bui¹ 背¹】cup(as a prize)

奖品【jêng² ben² 禀】prize; trophy

奖章【jêng² jêng¹ 张】medal; decoration

奖状【jêng² jong⁶ 撞】certificate of merit

酱【jêng³ 帐】a thick sauce made from soya beans, flour, etc.; cooked or pickled in soy sauce; sauce; jam

酱菜【jêng³ qoi³ 蔡】pickles

酱油【jêng³ yeo⁴ 尤】soy sauce; soy = 豉油【xi⁶ yeo⁴】= 抽油【qeo¹ yeo²】

帐【jêng³ 障】curtain; account; account book

帐篷【jêng³ pung⁴ 蓬】tent

帐簿【jêng³ bou² 保】account book

帐单【jêng³ dan¹ 丹】bill; check

帐目【jêng³ mug⁹ 木】accounts

胀【jêng³ 帐】expand; swell

肿胀【jung² jêng³】swollen

胀泵泵【jêng³ bem¹ bem¹ 伯庵¹】too full till bulging out =【普】鼓胀

涨【jêng³ 帐；jêng² 掌】swell after absorbing water, etc.; be swelled by a rush of blood; be more, larger, etc. than expected; rise; go up

涨潮【jêng³ qiu⁴ 瞧】rising tide; flood tide

涨价【jêng³ ga³ 嫁】rise in price

涨落【jêng³ log⁹ 洛⁹】rise and fall; fluctuate

障【jêng³ 帐】hinder; block

障碍【jêng³ ngoi⁶ 外】hinder; obstacle

嶂【jêng³ 帐】a screen-like mountain peak

瘴【jêng³ 帐】miasma

瘴疠【jêng³ lei⁶ 厉　】communicable subtropical diseases, such as pernicious malaria, etc.

瘴气【jêng³ hêi³ 汽】miasma

仗【jêng⁶ 丈；jêng³ 帐】weapons; rely on; war

仗势欺人【jêng⁶ xei³ hêi¹ yen⁴ 世希仁】take advantage of one's or sb. else's power to bully people

仗义疏财【jêng⁶ yi⁶ xo¹ qoi⁴ 异梳才】be generous in aiding needy people

杖【jêng⁶ 丈；jêng³ 蒋】cane; stick; rod or staff used for a specific purpose

丈【jêng⁶ 像】a unit of length(= 3⅓ metres); measure(land); a form of address for certain male relatives by marriage

丈夫【jêng⁶ fu¹ 乎】man; husband

丈量【jêng⁶ lêng⁶ 凉】measure(land)

丈人【jêng⁶ yen⁴ 仁】wife's father = 外父【ngoi⁶ fu²】

丈母娘【jêng⁶ mou⁵ nêng⁴ 武挪香⁴】wife's mother = 外母【ngoi⁶ mou⁵】

象【jêng⁶ 丈】elephant; shape; imitate; be like; look as if; seem; like; such as

象牙【jêng⁶ nga⁴ 芽】elephant's tusk; ivory

象棋【jêng⁶ kêi⁴ 其】(Chinese) chess

象样【jêng⁶ yêng⁶ 让】presentable; decent; sound = 似样【qi⁵ yêng²】

象征【jêng⁶ jing¹ 晶】symbolize; symbol

像【jêng⁶ 丈】likeness(of sb.); portrait; image

像样【jêng⁶ yêng⁶ 让】= 似样【qi⁵ yêng²】presentable; decent

像话【jêng⁶ wa⁶ 华⁶】reasonable; proper; right

橡【jêng⁶ 丈】oak；rubber tree

橡胶【jêng⁶gao¹ 交】rubber

橡皮【jêng⁶pêi⁴ 脾】rubber；eraser

卒【jêd⁷ 支律⁷】soldier；servant；finish；end；finally；at last；die

卒仔【jêd⁷jei² 济²】soldier；private =【普】小兵；小卒

卒之【jêd⁶ ji¹ 支】 finally；ultimately =【普】终于；最终

捽【jêd⁷ 卒】to massage =【普】（用手）推拿

雀【jêg⁸ 酌】sparrow

雀斑【jêg⁸ban¹ 班】freckle

雀跃【jêg⁸yêg⁸ 约】jump for joy

桌【jêg⁸ 雀】table；desk

桌子【jêg⁸ji² 止】table；desk = 台【toi²】

桌面【jêg⁸min⁶ 免⁶】top of a table；table-top = 台面【toi²min⁶】

酌【jêg⁸ 雀】pour out（wine）；drink；a meal with wine；consider；think over

酌量【jêg⁸lêng⁶ 谅】consider；deliberate

酌情【jêg⁸qing⁴ 程】take into consideration the circumstances

灼【jêg⁸ 雀】burn；bright

灼热【jêg⁸yid⁹ 衣泄⁹】scorching hot

灼见【jêg⁸gin³ 建】profound view

着【jêg⁹ 雀⁹；jêg⁸ 雀】wear（clothes）；touch；apply；use；whereabouts；send；a move in chess；trick；touch；burn；being

着数【jêg⁹ xou³扫】beneficial；advantageous =【普】有利；得了好处；占了便宜

着火【jêg⁹fo² 伙】catch fire；be on fire

着急【jêg⁹ geb⁷格恰⁷】worry；feel anxious

着凉【jêg⁹lêng⁴ 量⁴】catch cold

着迷【jêg⁹mei⁴ 谜】be fascinated；be captivated

着魔【jêg⁹mo¹ 么】be bewitched；be possessed

着陆【jêg⁹lug⁹ 六】land；touch down

着落【jêg⁹log⁹ 洛⁹】whereabouts；assured source

着色【jêg⁹xig⁷ 式】put colour on；colour

着实【jêg⁹xed⁹ 失⁹】really；severely

着手【jêg⁹xeo² 守】put one's hand to；set about

着眼【jêg⁹ngan⁵ 雁】see from the angle of

着想【jêg⁹xêng² 赏】consider

着意【jêg⁹yi³ 薏】take pains

着重【jêg⁹jung⁶ 仲】stress；emphasize

着衫【jêg⁸xam¹ 三】wear clothes =【普】穿衣服

嗜【jē¹ 者¹】〈n.〉嗜喱【jē¹lêi² 李²】jelly

嗻【jē¹ 者¹】an exclamation mark used to defend oneself or protest against others

遮【jē¹ 者¹】an umbrella =【普】伞；hide from view；block；keep out

遮骨【jē¹ gued⁷ 姑核⁷】 the frame of an umbrella =【普】伞子的把柄

遮荫【jē¹yem¹ 阴】sunshade =【普】挡阳光

遮蔽【jē¹bei³ 敝³】cover；block；defilade

遮挡【jē¹ dong² 当²】shelter from；keep out

遮掩【jē¹yim² 淹²】cover；overspread；envelop

遮羞【jē¹xeo¹ 修】hush up a scandal

遮盖【jē¹koi³ 概】cover; hide; cover up

姐 【jē² 者；jē¹ 遮】elder sister; a general term for young women

姐姐【jē⁴jē¹】elder sister; sister

姐夫【jē²fu¹ 肤】elder sister's husband; brother-in-law

姐妹【jē² mui² 媒²】sisters; brothers and sisters

蔗 【jē³ 借】sugarcane

蔗糖【jē³tong⁴ 唐】sucrose; cane sugar

蔗渣【jē³ja¹ 抓】bagasse

鹧 【jē³ 借】〈n.〉鹧鸪【jē³gu¹ 姑】partridge; Chinese francolin

锗 【jē² 者】〈n.〉germanium(Ge)

赭 【jē² 者】reddish brown; burnt ochre

赭石【jē²xēg⁹ 硕】ochre

借 【jē³ 蔗】borrow; lend; make use of; use as a pretext

借用【jē³yung⁶ 容⁶】borrow; use sth. for another purpose

借债【jē³ jai³ 斋³】borrow money; raise a loan

借款【jē³fun² 欢²】borrow money; loan

借据【jē³gêu³ 踞】receipt for a loan(IOU)

借贷【jē³tai³ 太】borrow or lend money; debit and credit sides

借口【jē³heo² 候²】use as an excuse

借故【jē³gu³ 固】find an excuse

借鉴【jē³gam³ 监³】use for reference

借以【jē³yi⁵ 耳】so as to; by way of

借问【jē³men⁶ 蚊⁶】may I ask

借一借【jē³yed⁷jē³ 壹】to make way; excuse me =【普】请让路

借帱啲【jē³mē²did⁷】= 借一借 =【普】请让路

借题发挥【jē³tei⁴fad⁸fei¹ 提法辉】make use of the subject under discussion to put over one's own ideas

借刀杀人【jē³ dou¹ xad⁸ yen⁴ 都煞仁】murder with a borrowed knife — make use of another person to get rid of an adversary

借古讽今【jē³gu²fung³gem¹ 鼓风³ 金】use the past to disparage the present

藉 【jē³ 借；jē⁶ 谢；jig⁹ 籍】(see"狼藉")

籍口【jē³heo² 候²】= 借口(see"借口")

籍以【jē³yi⁵ 耳】= 借以(see"借以")

这 【jē⁵ 借⁵】this

这个【jē⁵go³ 哥³】this one = 呢个【ni¹go³】·

这般【jē⁵bun¹ 搬】such; so; like this = 噉样【gem²yêng²】

这边【jē⁵bin¹ 鞭¹】this side; here = 呢边【ni¹bin¹】

这次【jē⁵qi³ 刺】this time; present = 呢次【ni¹qi³】

这时【jē⁵xi⁴ 是⁴】now; at present = 呢阵时【ni¹jen⁶xi⁴】

这里【jē⁵lêu⁵ 罗去⁵】here = 呢度【ni¹dou⁶】 =【普】这儿

这么【jē⁵mo¹ 魔】so; such; this way; like this = 噉样【gem²yêng²】=【普】这样

这些【jē⁵xē¹ 赊】these = 呢啲【ni¹did⁷】

这山望着那山高【jē⁵xam¹mong⁶jēg⁹na⁵ xan¹gou¹】it's always the other mountain that looks higher; never happy where one is

者【jē² 姐】〈*auxil.*〉"＿＿ man"; "the
　　＿＿ one"; "＿＿ er"; etc.

老者【lou⁵jē² 鲁】old man = 老人【lou⁵yen⁴
　　仁】

读者【dug⁹jē² 毒】reader

大者【dai⁶ jē² 歹⁶】the big one = 大嘅
　　【dai⁶gē³】

谢【jē⁶ 树】thank; make an apology; de-
　　cline; wither; a surname

谢谢【jē⁶ jē⁶】thanks; thank you = 多谢
　　【do¹jē⁶】= 唔该【m⁴goi¹】

谢意【jē⁶yi¹ 薏】gratitude; thankfulness =
　　谢忱【jē⁶xem¹ 岑】

谢绝【jē⁶jüd⁹ 支月⁹】refuse; decline

谢幕【jē⁶mog⁹ 莫】answer a curtain call

谢天谢地【jē⁶tin¹jē⁶dēi⁶ 田¹ 得希¹】thank
　　goodness

榭【jē⁶ 谢】a pavilion or house on a ter-
　　race

水榭【xêü²jē⁶ 瑞²】water side pavilion

瑈【jēi¹ 子希¹】sarcoptic mite =【普】疥
　　虫

生瑈【xang¹jēi¹】scabies or mange =【普】
　　长疥疮或疥癣

井【jēng² 郑²】well; sth. in the shape of
　　a well; neat; orderly

井盐【jēng²yim⁴ 严】well salt

井灌【jēng²gun³ 贯】well irrigation

井然【jēng²yin⁴ 言】orderly; shipshape

井井有条【jēng²jēng²yeo⁵tiu⁴ 友挑⁴】in
　　perfect order; shipshape

井底之蛙【jēng²dei²ji¹wa¹ 抵支娃】a frog
　　in a well — a person with a very
　　limited outlook

井水不犯河水【jēng²xêü²bed⁷fan⁶ho⁴xêü²
　　毕范何瑞²】well water does not
　　intrude into river water—I'll mind
　　my own business, you mind yours

郑【jēng⁶ 井⁶】a surname

郑重【jēng⁶ jung⁶ 仲 】serious; solemn;
　　earnest

郑州【jēng⁶jeo¹ 洲】〈*n.*〉Zhengzhou

隻【jēg⁸ 脊】〈*classifier*〉= 只【jēg⁸】(see
　　"只")

脊【jēg⁸ 隻】spine; backbone; ridge

脊梁【jēg⁸ lêng⁴凉 】back (of the human
　　body)

脊梁骨【jēg⁸lêng⁴gued⁷ 姑屈⁷】backbone;
　　spine

脊背【jēg⁸bui³ 贝】back = 背脊【bui³jēg⁸】

脊椎【jēg⁸jêü¹ 追】vertebra

摭【jēg⁸ 脊】pick up; rub with the hands

摭拾【jēg⁸xeb⁹ 十】pick; gather; collect

摭麻【jēg⁸ma⁴ 妈⁴】make cord by twisting
　　hemp fibres between the palms =
　　【普】搓麻绳

瘠【jēg⁸ 脊】lean; barren; poor

瘠土【jēg⁸tou² 讨】poor soil; barren land

K

卡【ka¹ 咳啊¹】block; check

卡片【ka¹pin³ 遍】card

卡车【ka¹qē¹ 奢】lorry; truck

卡钳【ka¹kim⁴ 卡淹⁴】callipers

卡介苗【ka¹gai³miu⁴ 界描】BCG vaccine

卡拉 OK【ka¹lai³ou¹kēi¹】kara OK

卡通片【ka¹tung²pin² 统¹ 偏²】cartoon

卡罅【ka⁶la³ 啦³】a hill＝【普】裂缝；缝隙

夸【kua¹ 垮】exaggerate； overstate； boast; praise

夸大【kua¹ dai⁶ 歹⁶ 】exaggerate； over-state；magnify

夸张【kua¹ jêng¹章 】exaggerate；hyper-bole

夸奖【kua¹jêng² 蒋】praise; commend

夸口【kua¹heo² 厚²】boast; brag; talk big

夸耀【kua¹yiu⁶ 要⁶】brag about; show off; flaunt

夸夸其谈【kua¹kua¹kēi⁴tam⁴ 奇潭】in-dulge in exaggerations

垮【kua¹ 夸】collapse; fall; break down

垮台【kua¹toi⁴ 抬】collapse; fall from power

跨【kua¹ 夸】step; bestride; cut across

跨度【kua¹dou⁶ 道】span

跨越【kua¹yüd⁹ 月】stride across; leap over

跨国公司【kua¹guog⁸gung¹xi¹ 帼工思】transnational corporation

挎【kua¹ 夸】〈n.〉挎包【kua¹bao¹ 胞】satchel

胯【kua¹ 夸】hip

胯骨【kua¹gued⁷ 掘⁷】hipbone; innomi-nate bone

楷【kai² 卡挨²；gai¹ 街】model；pattern

楷模【kai²mou⁴ 毛】model; pattern

楷书【kai²xü¹ 输】(in Chinese calligraphy) regular script

靠【kao³ 铐】lean against; lean on; keep to; near; by; depend on; rely on; trust

靠近【kao³gen⁶ 靳】near; close to; by

靠岸【kao³ngon⁶ 安⁶】pull in to shore

靠边【kao³bin¹ 鞭】keep to the side

靠拢【kao³lung² 垄²】draw close; close up

靠山【kao³xan¹ 珊】backer; patron; back-ing

靠害【kao³hoi³ 亥】specially make disaster ＝【普】专门制造祸害

靠得住【kao³ deg⁷ jü⁶注⁶】 reliable; de-pendable

靠唔住【kao³m⁴jü⁶ 注⁶】unreliable; unde-pendable＝【普】靠不住；不可靠

铐【kao³ 靠】handcuffs; put handcuffs on

槛【kam⁵ 卡岩⁵；ham⁵ 菡】threshold

门槛【mun⁴kam⁵】threshold

畸【kēi¹ 崎；gēi¹ 机】lopsided; irregular; odd lots

畸变【kēi¹bin³ 边³】distortion

畸形【kēi¹ying⁴ 型】deformity; malformation; lopsided; unbalanced

畸士【kēi³xi² 是²】a case＝【普】情况

崎 【kēi¹ 畸】〈a.〉崎岖【kēi¹kêu¹ 驱】rugged

冀 【kēi³ 暨】hope; long for; look forward to

冀望【kēi³mong⁶ 亡⁶】hope for; look forward to

骥 【kēi³ 冀】a thoroughbred horse

暨 【kēi³ 冀】and; up to; till

暨今【kēi³gem¹ 金】up till now

其 【kēi⁴ 奇】his (her, its, their); he (she, it, they); that; such; 〈auxil.〉

其次【kēi⁴qi³ 翅】next; secondly; then

其实【kēi⁴xed⁹ 失⁹】actually; in fact

其他【kēi⁴ta¹ 它】other; else

其余【kēi⁴yü⁴ 如】the others; the rest

其中【kēi⁴jung¹ 钟】among(which, them, etc.); in(which, it, etc.)

奇 【kēi⁴ 其】strange; queer; surprise; wonder

奇怪【kēi⁴guai³乖³】strange; surprising; odd

奇观【kēi⁴gun¹官】marvellous spectacle; wonder

奇景【kēi⁴ging² 境】wonderful view

奇妙【kēi⁴miu⁶庙⁶】marvellous; wonderful

奇特【kēi⁴deg⁹ 得⁹】peculiar; queer; singular

奇闻【kēi⁴men⁴ 文】sth. unheardof

奇异【kēi⁴yi⁶ 义】queer; strange; curious

奇遇【kēi⁴yü⁶ 预】happy encounter; fortuitous meeting; adventure

奇志【kēi⁴ ji³ 至】high aspirations; lofty ideal

奇形怪状【kēi⁴ying⁴guai³jong⁶ 型乖³ 撞】grotesque or fantastic in shape or appearance

奇耻大辱【kēi⁴ qi² dai⁶ yug⁹ 始歹⁶玉 】galling shame and humiliation; deep disgrace

歧 【kēi⁴ 其】fork; branch; divergent

歧路【kēi⁴ lou⁶露 】branch road; forked road

歧途【kēi⁴tou⁴ 图】wrong road

歧视【kēi⁴xi⁶ 示】discriminate against

歧义【kēi⁴yi⁶ 异】different meanings

旗 【kēi⁴ 其】flag; banner; standard

旗帜【kēi⁴ qi³次】banner; flag; standard; colours

旗手【kēi⁴xeo² 守】standard-bearer

旗号【kēi⁴hou⁶ 好⁶】banner; flag

旗袍【kēi⁴pou⁴ 铺⁴】cheongsam

旗鼓相当【kēi⁴gu²xêng¹dong¹ 股双挡¹】be well-matched

旗开得胜【kēi⁴ hoi¹ deg⁷ xing³ 海¹ 德圣】win victory the moment one raises one's standard; win speedy success

棋 【kēi⁴ 其；kēi² 其²】chess or any board game

棋子【kēi⁴ji² 止】piece; chessman

棋盘【kēi⁴ pun⁴盆 】chessboard; checkerboard

棋迷【kēi⁴ mei⁴迷 】chess fan; chess enthusiast

棋逢对手【kēi⁴fung⁴dêu³xeo² 冯队³ 守】

meet one's match in a chess tournament

麒【kēi⁴ 其】〈n.〉麒麟【kēi⁴lên⁴ 邻】(Chinese)unicorn

淇【kēi⁴ 其】(see"冰淇淋")

蜞【kēi⁴ 其】〈n.〉蜞𧋜【kēi⁴na² 挪啊²】leech=【普】蚂蟥

骐【kēi⁴ 其】black horse

琪【kēi⁴ 其】fine jade

祁【kēi 其】a surname

芪【kēi⁴ 其】〈n.〉黄芪【wong⁴kēi⁴】the root of membranous milk vetch

祈【kēi⁴ 其】pray; entreat

祈祷【kēi⁴tou² 讨】pray; say one's prayers

祈求【kēi⁴ keo⁴球 】earnestly hope; pray for

祈望【kēi⁴mong⁶ 亡⁶】hope; wish

祈使句【kēi⁴xei²gêü³ 洗据】imperative sentence

期【kēi⁴ 其】a period of time; phase; stage; scheduled time; make an appointment; expect

期间【kēi⁴gan¹ 奸】time; period

期限【kēi⁴han⁶ 悭⁶】alloted time; time limit

期刊【kēi⁴hon² 罕】periodical

期货【kēi⁴fo³ 课】futures

期满【kēi⁴mun⁵ 门⁵】expire; run out; come to an end

期望【kēi⁴mong⁶ 亡⁶】hope; expectation

期待【kēi⁴doi⁶ 代】expect; await

其【kēi⁴ 其; gei¹ 基】beanstalk

鳍【kēi⁴ 其】〈n.〉鱼鳍【yü⁴kēi⁴】fin

耆【kēi⁴】over sixty years of age; very old

旗【kēi⁴ 其】=旗【kēi⁴】(see"旗")

企【kēi⁵ 其⁵】stand on tiptoe; look forward to

企鹅【kēi⁵ngo⁴ 俄】penguin

企求【kēi⁵keo⁴ 球】desire to gain; seek for

企图【kēi⁵tou⁴ 途】attempt; try; seek

企望【kēi⁵mong⁶ 亡⁶】hope for; look forward to

企业【kēi⁵yib⁹ 叶】enterprise; business

企住【kēi⁵jü⁶ 注⁶】stop; halt; stand firmly on one's feet; stand one's ground; hold water=【普】站住

企堂【kēi⁵tong⁴ 唐】waiters and waitresses

企筵吔【kēi⁵mê²did⁷ 莫耶² 得热⁷】to make way=【普】让路；靠边站

企理【kēi⁵lêi⁵ 李】neat and clean=【普】整齐、清洁

骑【kēi⁴ 奇；kēi⁴ 茄⁴】ride; sit on the back; cavalry

骑马【kēi⁴ma⁵ 玛】ride horse

骑兵【kēi⁴bing¹ 冰】cavalryman

骑缝【kēi⁴fung⁴ 逢】a junction of the edges of two sheets of paper

骑墙【kēi⁴qêng⁴ 祥】sit on the fence

骑士【kēi⁴xi⁶ 是】knight; cavalier

骑术【kēi⁴xêd⁹ 述】horsemanship

骑楼【kēi⁴leo² 纽】corridor=【普】跨进街市的建筑物走廊

骑膊马【kēi⁴bog⁸ma⁵ 博码】when a child rests on the shoulder of the father

=【普】小孩骑在父亲（或其他大人）的肩膀上

溪 【kei¹ 稽】small stream; brook; rivulet

溪涧【kei¹gan³ 间³】mountain stream
溪流【kei¹leo⁴ 留】brook; rivulet

嵠 【kei¹ 溪】a surname

稽 【kei¹ 溪】check; examine; delay; kotow

稽查【kei¹qa⁴ 茶】check; customs officer
稽考【kei¹hao² 烤】ascertain; verify
稽留【kei¹leo⁴ 流】delay; detain
稽首【kei¹xeo² 守】kotow

蹊 【kei¹ 溪; hei¹ 兮】odd; footpath

蹊跷【kei¹kiu² 乔²】odd; queer; fishy
蹊径【kei¹ging³ 劲】path; way

启 【kei² 溪²】open; start; enlighten; inform; letter

启程【kei²qing⁴ 情】set out; start on a journey
启齿【kei²qi² 始】open one's mouth
启动【kei²dung⁶ 洞】start
启发【kei² fad⁸法 】 arouse; inspire; enlighten
启封【kei²fung¹ 丰】unseal; open an envelop
启航【kei²hong⁴ 杭】set sail; weigh anchor
启蒙【kei² mung⁴朦】 impart rudimentary knowledge to beginners; initiate; enlighten
启示【kei² xi⁶士】enlightenment; inspiration
启事【kei²xi⁶ 士】notice; announcement

契 【kei³ 启³; kid⁸ 揭】engrave; contract; deed; agree

契合【kei³heb⁹ 盒】agree with; tally with
契机【kei³gēi¹ 基】moment; turning point; juncture
契约【kei³yêg⁸ 跃】contract; deed
契据【kei³gêu³ 句】deed; contract; receipt
契丹【kid⁸ dan¹ 单】Qidan (Khitan), an ancient nationality in China
契弟【kei³dei⁶ 递】a nasty word of scolding people ∽【普】兔崽子; 没出息的小子
契家佬【kei³ ga¹ lou² 加老²】secret husband =【普】妇人私通的男人
契家婆【kei³ga¹po⁴ 加颇⁴】secret wife = 【普】男人私通的女人
契妈【kei³ ma¹ 吗】adoptive mother = 【普】干妈
契爷【kei³yē¹ 椰】adoptive father =【普】干爹
契仔【kei³jei² 济²】adoptive son =【普】干儿子

亏 【kuei¹ 规】lose; have a deficit; deficient; weak; treat unfairly; fortunately; luckily; wane

亏本【kuei¹bun² 苯】lose money in business = 蚀本【xid⁹bun²】
亏待【kuei¹doi⁶ 代】treat unfairly
亏损【kuei¹ xün² 选】loss; deficit; general debility
亏心【kuei¹ xem¹深 】 have a guilty conscience
亏柴【kuei¹ qai⁴猜⁴】= 亏佬【kuei¹ lou² 老²】a man who is weak ∽【普】体弱多病的人

规 【kuei¹ 亏】compasses; regulation; rule; plan; gauge

规矩【kuei¹gêü² 举】rule; custom; wellbehaved

规定【kuei¹ ding⁶ 锭 】stipulate; fix; set; formulate

规程【kuei¹qing⁴ 情】rules; regulation

规范【kuei¹fan⁶ 犯】standard; norm

规格【kuei¹ gag⁸ 隔 】specifications; standards; norms

规划【kuei¹wag⁹ 或】programme; plan

规律【kuei¹lêd⁹ 栗】law; regular pattern

规则【kuei¹jeg⁷ 仄】rule; regular

规章【kuei¹jêng⁴ 张】rule; regulations

规模【kuei¹mou⁴ 毛】scale; scope; dimensions

规劝【kuei¹hün³ 楦】admonish; advise

窥 【kuei¹ 规】peep; spy

窥测【kuei¹qag⁷ 策⁷】spy out

窥视【kuei¹xi⁶ 示】peep at; spy on

窥伺【kuei¹ji⁶ 自】lie in wait for

窥探【kuei¹tam³ 贪³】spy upon; pry about

盔 【kuei¹ 亏】helmet

盔甲【kuei¹gab⁸ 格鸭⁸】a suit of armour

隗 【kuei⁴ 葵】a surname

葵 【kuei⁴ 隗】certain herbaceous plants with big flowers

葵花【kuei⁴fa¹ 化¹】sunflower

葵扇【kuei⁴xin³ 线】palm-leaf fan

睽 【kuei⁴ 葵】〈a.〉睽睽【kuei⁴kuei⁴】stare; gaze

逵 【kuei⁴ 葵】thoroughfare

馗 【kuei⁴ 葵】= 逵

揆 【kuei⁴ 葵】conjecture; guess; standard

揆度【kuei⁴dog⁹ 铎】estimate; conjecture

傀 【kuei⁵ 愧】〈n.〉傀儡【kuei⁵lêü⁵ 吕】puppet

愧 【kuei⁵ 傀】ashamed; conscience-stricken

愧恨【kuei⁵hen⁶ 很⁶ 】ashamed and remorseful

愧色【kuei⁵xig⁷ 式】a look of shame

抠 【keo¹ 沟】scratch; to mix; carve; delve into

抠埋【keo¹mai⁴ 马埃⁴】to mix =【普】混合; 搀合

抠女【keo¹nêü⁵ 那虚⁵】make friends with girl =【普】结交女孩子

抠字眼【keo¹ji⁶ngan⁵ 自雁⁵】find fault with the choice of words

沟 【keo¹ 扣¹】ditch; groove; rut; gully

沟渠【keo¹kêü⁴ 蘷⁴】irrigation canals and ditches

沟壑【keo¹kog⁸ 确】gully; ravine

沟通【keo¹tung¹ 统¹】link up

媾 【keo³ 扣; geo³ 救】wed; reach agreement; coition

媾和【keo³wo⁴ 禾】make peace

扣 【keo³ 叩】button up; buckle; detain; deduct; discount; knot; smash

扣除【keo³qêü⁴ 徐】deduct

扣留【keo³leo⁴ 流】detain; arrest

扣压【keo³ngad⁸ 押】withhold

扣押【keo³ngad⁸ 压】detain; distain

扣子【keo³ji² 止】knot; button

扣针【keo³jem¹ 斟】a brooch; pin =【普】别针

叩 【keo³ 扣】knock; kotow

叩头【keo³teo⁴ 投】kotow

叩问【keo³men⁶ 闻⁶】make inquiries

购【keo³ 扣】purchase；buy

购买【keo³mai⁵ 卖⁵】purchase；buy

购置【keo³ji³ 至】purchase(durables)

购销【keo³xiu¹ 消】purchase and sale

构【keo³ 扣】construct；form；compose

构成【keo³ xing⁴ 承 】 construct；form；compose

构件【keo³gin² 坚²】member；component (part)

构思【keo³xi¹ 司】conception

构图【keo³tou⁴ 途】composition(of a picture)

构造【keo³jou⁶ 做】structure；tectonic

构筑【keo³jug⁷ 足】construct；build

寇【keo³ 扣】bandit；enemy；invade；a surname

寇仇【keo³xeo⁴ 愁】enemy；foe

蔻【keo³ 扣】(see"豆蔻")

求【keo⁴ 球】beg；request；strive for；seek；try

求人【keo⁴yen⁴ 仁】ask for help

求助【keo⁴jo⁶ 左⁶】seek help

求爱【keo⁴ngoi⁴ 哀³】pay court to；woo

求婚【keo⁴fen¹ 昏】make an offer of marriage；propose

求见【keo⁴jin³ 建】ask to see

求救【keo⁴geo³ 够】call for help(SOS)

求教【keo⁴gao³ 较】ask for advice

求情【keo⁴qing⁴ 程】plead；intercede；ask for a favour

求饶【keo⁴yiu⁴ 尧】beg for mercy；ask for pardon

求学【keo⁴ hog⁹ 鹤 】 go to school；seek knowledge

求援【keo⁴wun⁴ 垣】ask for help

求知【keo⁴ji¹ 支】seek knowledge

求之不得【keo⁴ji¹bed⁷deg⁷ 支毕德】most welcome

求同存异【keo⁴tung⁴qün⁴yi⁶ 铜全义】seek common ground while reserving differences

球【keo⁴ 求】sphere；ball；the globe；the earth

球形【keo⁴ying⁴ 型】spherical；round

球体【keo⁴tei² 睇】spheroid

球场【keo⁴qêng⁴ 祥】court；field

球赛【keo⁴qoi³ 蔡】ball game；match

球队【keo⁴dêü⁴ 对²】(ball game) team

球艺【keo⁴ngei⁶ 毅】ball game skills

球证【keo⁴jing³ 正】a referee =【普】裁判员

球迷【keo⁴mei⁴ 谜】(ball game)fan

裘【keo⁴ 球】fur coat；a surname

舅【keo⁵ 柏】mother's brother；uncle；wife's brother；brother-in-law

舅父【keo⁵fu² 苦】mother's brother；uncle

舅母【keo⁵mou⁵ 武】wife of mother's brother；aunt = 舅妈【keo⁵ma¹ 吗】= 妗母【kem⁵mou⁵】

舅仔【keo⁵jei² 济²】wife's brother =【普】舅子

柏【keo⁵ 舅】〈n.〉乌柏【wu¹keo⁵】Chinese tallow tree

臼【keo⁵ 舅】mortar；any mortarshaped thing；joint

臼齿【keo⁵qi² 始】molar

襟【kem¹ 衾】front of a garment

襟怀【kem¹wai⁴ 槐】bosom；(breadth of) mind

襟兄【kem¹ hing¹ 兴 】 husband of one's wife's elder sister; brother-in-law

襟章【kem¹ jêng¹ 张】a badge =【普】胸章

衾【kem¹ 襟】quilt

肷【kem¹ 衾】lasting long; durable =【普】耐久

肷谂【kem¹ nem² 挪庵²】 to crack one's head ∽【普】费思量

肷着【kem¹ jêg⁸ 雀 】can stand wear and tear; be endurable =【普】耐穿

肷磨【kem¹ mo⁴摩⁴】 wear-resisting; stamina =【普】耐磨

肷用【kem¹yung⁶ 拥⁶】durable =【普】耐用

冚【kem² 食²】to cover

冚住【kem²jŭ⁶ 注⁶】to cover =【普】覆盖; 遮蔽

冚斗【kem²deo² 豆²】=冚档【kem²dong³ 当³】to refer to the closing down of shops due to bankruptcy =【普】(店铺等)停业; 倒闭

琴【kem⁴ 禽】a general name for certain musical instruments

琴弦【kem⁴yin⁴ 言】string(of a musical instrument)

琴键【kem⁴gin⁶ 键】key(on a musical instrument)

琴拨【kem⁴bud⁹ 勃】plectrum

禽【kem⁴ 琴】birds

禽兽【kem⁴xeo³ 秀】birds and beasts

禽兽行为【kem⁴xeo³heng⁴wei⁴ 衡 维】beastial acts

【kem⁴ 禽】capture; catch; crawl; creep; climb

擒上去【kem⁴xêng⁵hêü³ 尚⁵ 虚³】climb up to =【普】爬上去

擒青【kem⁴qēng¹ 次镜¹】to do something without thinking; to be in a hurry =【普】急于求成; 行动匆忙; 慌忙

擒贼先擒王【kem⁴qeg⁹xin¹kem⁴wong⁴ 策⁹ 仙黄】to catch bandits, first catch the ringleader

噙【kem⁴ 禽】hold in the mouth or the eyes

噙着眼泪【kem⁴jêg⁹ngan⁵lêü⁶ 桌⁹ 雁⁵ 类】eyes brimming with tears

蟛【kem⁴ 禽】toad; spider

蟛蟧【kem⁴lou⁴ 劳】spider =【普】蜘蛛

蟛蟧丝网【kem⁴ lou⁴ xi¹ mong¹ 斯虹¹】cobweb =【普】蜘蛛网

蟛蠄【kem⁴kêu² 渠²】toad =【普】蟾蜍; 癞虾蟆

曦【kem⁴ 禽】formerly; go over; last

曦日【kem⁴yed⁹ 逸】yesterday =【普】昨天

曦晚【kem⁴man⁵ 万⁵】last night = 曦晚黑【heg⁷ 克】=【普】昨晚

芹【ken⁴ 勤】〈n.〉芹菜【ken⁴qoi³ 蔡】celery

勤【ken⁴ 芹】diligent; frequently; attendance

勤奋【ken⁴ fen⁵愤】 diligent; assiduous; industrious

勤恳【ken⁴hen² 很 】diligent and conscientious

勤俭【ken⁴ gim⁶ 检⁶ 】 hardworking and thrifty

勤劳【ken⁴lou⁴ 涝】diligent; hardworking

勤务员【ken⁴mou⁶yün⁴ 冒元】odd-jobman; servant

勤工俭学【ken⁴gung¹gim⁶hog⁹ 公检⁶ 鹤】
part-work and part-study system;
work-study programme

坤【kuen¹ 昆】female; feminine (see "乾坤")

昆【kuen¹ 坤】elder brother; offspring

昆虫【kuen¹qung⁴ 从】insect
昆仑【kuen¹ lên⁴伦】the Kunlun Mountains
昆明【kuen¹ming⁴ 名】〈n.〉Kunming
昆仲【kuen¹ jung⁶中⁶】elder and younger brothers; brothers

鲲【kuen¹ 昆】〈n.〉鲲鹏【kuen¹pang⁴ 彭】roc(an enormous legendary bird transformed from a gigantic fish)

捆【kuen² 菌】tie; bind; bundle up; bundle

捆绑【kuen²bong² 榜】truss up; bind; tie up
捆扎【kuen²jad⁸ 札】tie up; bundle up

菌【kuen² 捆】fungus; bacterium; mushroom

菌苗【kuen²miu⁴ 描】vaccine
菌丝【kuen²xi¹ 思】hypha

困【kuen³ 窘】be stranded; surround; tired; sleepy

困难【kuen³ nan⁴ 挪晏⁴】difficulty; difficulties; financial; straitened
困苦【kuen³fu² 虎】(live)in privation
困厄【kuen³ngeg⁷ 握】dire straits; distress
困顿【kuen³ dên⁶ 吨⁶】tired out; in financial straits
困惑【kuen³wag⁹ 或】perplexed; puzzled
困倦【kuen³gün⁶ 卷⁶】sleepy
困扰【kuen³yiu² 妖²】perplex; puzzle
困境【kuen³ ging³景 】difficult position;

straits
困兽犹斗【kuen³xeo³yeo⁴deo³ 秀尤豆³】cornered beasts will still fight

窘【kuen³ 困】in straitened circumstances; hard up; awkward; embarrass

窘境【kuen³ging² 景】predicament; plight
窘迫【kuen³ big⁷碧 】poverty-stricken; hard pressed

群【kuen⁴ 裙】crowd; group; herd; flock

群埋【kuen⁴mai⁴ 卖⁴】to be friend =【普】结伙
群众【kuen⁴jung³ 中³】the masses
群体【kuen⁴tei² 睇】colony
群芳【kuen⁴ fong¹ 方 】beautiful and fragrant flowers
群婚【kuen⁴fen¹ 昏】group marriage
群居【kuen⁴gêü¹ 据¹】living in groups; social
群情【kuen⁴qing⁴ 程】public sentiment
群言堂【kuen⁴yin⁴tong⁴ 然唐】rule by the voice of the many
群策群力【kuen³qag⁸kuen⁴lig⁹ 册历】pool the wisdom and efforts of everyone

裙【kuen⁴ 群】skirt

裙子【kuen⁴ji² 止】skirt
裙带【kuen⁴ dai³ 戴 】connected through one's female relatives

鲠【keng² 卡肯²; geng² 更²】fishbone; get stuck in one's throat

鲠直【geng²jig⁹ 值】honest and frank; upright
鲠颈【keng²gēng² 镜²】to refer to the state when bones are trapped in one's

throat; to do things without suc-cess＝【普】骨头卡住咽喉；（比喻）事情不顺利

肯【keng³ 卡鸶³】good taste; capable; smart＝【普】（酒或烟）气味浓；刺激性强

崧【kueng³ 卡宏³】stumble; trip
崧亲【kueng³qen¹ 趁¹】stumble; trip＝【普】绊着
崧手崧脚【kueng³xeo²kueng³gêg⁸ 守格约⁸】be in the way

级【keb⁷ 给】level; grade; class; step; degree
级别【keb⁷bid⁹ 必⁹】rank; level; grade
级数【keb⁷xou³ 扫】progression; series

岌【keb⁷ 级; ngeb⁹ 额急⁹】lofty; tower-ing; to shake and move
岌岌可危【keb⁷keb⁷ho²ngei⁴ 何² 巍】in imminent danger
岌岌贡【ngeb⁹ngeb⁹gung³ 公³】to keep shaking and moving＝【普】动荡不稳

给【keb⁷ 吸】give; grant; for; let; allow; supply; ample
给以【keb⁷yi⁵ 耳】give; grant
给养【keb³yêng⁵ 氧】provisions; victuals
给予【keb³yü⁵ 语】give; render

吸【keb⁷ 给】inhale; breathe in; absorb; attract
吸引【keb⁷ÿen⁵瘾】attract; draw; fasci-nate
吸收【keb⁷ xeo³ 修】absorb; suck up; re-cruit
吸取【keb⁷qêû² 娶】absorb; draw; assimi-late
吸附【keb⁷fu⁶ 付】absorption

吸毒【keb⁷dug⁹ 读】drug taking
吸烟【keb⁷yin¹ 胭】smoke＝食烟【xig⁹ yin¹】
吸尘器【keb⁷qen⁴hēi³ 陈气】dust catcher
吸血鬼【keb⁷ hüd⁸ guei² 黑月⁸ 诡】blood-sucker

汲【keb⁷ 吸】draw (water)
汲汲【keb⁷keb⁷】anxious; avid
汲取【keb⁷qêû² 娶】draw; derive

及【keb⁹ 级⁹】reach; come up to; in time for
及第【keb⁹dei⁶ 弟】pass an imperial exam-ination
及格【keb⁹gag⁸ 隔】pass a test, examina-tion, etc.; pass
及时【keb⁹ xi⁴ 士⁴ 】timely; in time; promptly
及早【keb⁹ jou² 蚤】at an early stage; be-fore it is too late; as soon as possi-ble
及至【keb⁹ji³ 致】up to; until

咳【ked⁷ 卡核⁷】cough; cut
咳嗽【keb⁷xeo³ 秀】cough

咭【ked⁷ 咳】〈n.〉咭片【ked⁷pin² 遍²】card

梒【keg⁷ 卡黑⁷】〈v.〉梒住【keg⁷jü⁶ 注⁶】block; clog; obstruct＝【普】梗塞；梗阻

慷【kong² 抗²; hong² 康²】vehement
慷慨【kong²koi³ 概】vehement; fervent; generous
慷慨激昂【kong² koi³ gig⁷ ngong⁴ 概 击额康⁴】impassioned; vehement

亢【kong³ 抗】high; haughty; excessive

亢奋【kong³fen⁵ 愤】stimulated; excited

亢进【kong³jên³ 俊】hyperfunction

伉【kong³ 亢】〈n.〉伉俪【kong³lei⁶ 丽】married couple; husband and wife

抗【kong³ 亢】resist; refuse; contend with

抗拒【kong³kêü⁵ 距】resist; defy

抗击【kong³gig⁷ 激】resist; beat back

抗争【kong³jeng¹ 憎】make a stand against; resist

抗议【kong³yi⁵ 耳】protest

抗衡【kong³heng⁴ 行】contend with; match

抗体【kong³tei² 睇】antibody

抗菌素【kong³kuen²xou³ 捆数】antibiotic

抗命【kong³ming⁶ 名⁶】defy orders; disobey

抗震【kong³jen³ 振】anti-seismic

抗洪【kong³hung⁴ 红】fight a flood

抗旱【kong³hon³ 汉⁵】fight a drought

扩【kong³ 抗; kog⁸ 确】expand; enlarge; extend

扩大【kong³dai⁶ 歹】enlarge; expand; extend

扩充【kong³qung¹ 冲】expand; strengthen

扩散【kong³xan³ 汕】spread; diffuse

扩展【kong³jin² 剪】expand; spread; extend

扩张【kong³jêng¹ 章】expand; enlarge; dilate

诳【kuong¹ 卡汪¹; kong⁴ 卡康⁴】lies; falsehood

诳语【kong⁴yü⁵ 雨】lies; falsehood

狂【kuong⁴ 卡汪⁴; kong⁴ 卡康⁴】mad; crazy; violent; wild; arrogant

狂暴【kuong⁴bou⁶ 部】violent; wild

狂妄【kuong⁴mong⁵ 网】wildly arrogant

狂放【kuong⁴fong³ 况】unruly or unrestrained

狂风【kuong⁴fung¹ 丰】whole gale; fierce wind

狂飙【kuong⁴biu¹ 标】hurricane

狂澜【kuong⁴lan⁴ 兰】raging waves

狂热【kuong⁴yid⁹ 衣泄⁹】fanaticism

狂人【kuong⁴yen⁴ 仁】madman; maniac

狂犬【kuong⁴hün² 劝²】bark furiously; howl

狂欢【kuong⁴fun¹ 宽】revelry; carnival

狂喜【kuong⁴hēi² 起】wild with joy

狂笑【kuong⁴xiu³ 少³】laugh wildly

狂言【kuong⁴ yin⁴然】raving; wild language

旷【kong³ 抗】vast; free from worries and petty ideas; neglect; loosefitting

旷野【kong³yē⁵ 惹】wilderness

旷达【kong³ dad⁹ 得压⁹】broad-minded; bighearted

旷工【kong³ gung¹公】stay away from work without leave or good reason

旷课【kong³fo³ 货】cut school

旷日持久【kong³yed⁹qi⁴geo² 逸迟九】protracted; prolonged; long-drawn-out

矿【kong³ 旷】ore deposit; ore; mine

矿藏【kong³qong⁴ 床】mineral resources

矿物【kong³med⁹ 勿】mineral

矿石【kong³xēg⁹ 硕】ore

矿山【kong³xan¹ 删】mine

矿产【kong³qan² 铲】mineral products

矿井【kong³jēng² 支镜²】mine; pit

矿坑【kong³hang¹ 黑罂¹】pit

矿工【kong³gung¹ 公】miner

哐
【kong¹ 旷⁻¹】crash；bang

哐啷【kong¹long¹ 旷⁻¹ 郎¹】〈onomatopoeia .〉crash

慨
【koi³ 概】indignant；deeply touched；generous

慨然【koi³yin⁴ 言】with deep feeling；generously

慨叹【koi³tan³ 炭】sigh with regret

概
【koi³ 忾】general；without exception；deportment

概括【koi³ kud⁸卡活⁸】summarize；generalize；briefly

概要【koi³yiu³ 妖³】essentials；outline

概念【koi³ nim⁶粘⁶】concept；conception；notion

概况【koi³fong³ 放】general situation；survey

概貌【koi³mao⁶ 猫⁶】general picture

概率【koi³lêd⁹ 律】probability

概论【koi³lên⁶ 沦⁶】outline；introduction

溉
【koi³ 概】(see"灌溉")

忾
【koi³ 慨】敌忾【dig⁹koi³】hatred towards the enemy

丐
【koi³ 概】beg；beggar(see"乞丐")

钙
【koi³ 概】〈n .〉calcium(Ca)

钙化【koi³fa³ 花³】calcification

确
【kog⁸ 涸】true；reliable；firmly

确定【kog⁸ding⁶ 锭】define；fix；definite

确实【kog⁸xed⁹ 失⁹】true；reliable；really

确凿【kog⁸jog⁹ 作⁹】conclusive；authentic

确切【kog⁸qid⁸ 撤】definite；exact

确信【kog⁸xên³ 讯】firmly believe；be sure

确认【kog⁸ying⁶ 英⁶】affirm；confirm

确立【kog⁸leb⁹ 罗急⁹】establish

涸
【kog⁸ 确】dry up；humid

涸喉【kog⁸heo⁴ 侯】food that is too dry to swallow＝【普】咽喉干燥；口渴

榷
【kog⁸ 确】discuss　商榷【xêng¹kog⁸】discuss；deliberate over

箍
【ku¹ 卡乌¹】hoop；band；bind round

箍桶匠【ku¹tung²jêng⁶ 统 丈】cooper；hooper

刽
【kui² 绘】cut off；chop off

刽子手【kui²ji²xeo² 止 守】executioner；slaughterer

桧
【kui² 绘】〈n .〉Chinese juniper

绘
【kui² 刽】paint；draw

绘画【kui²wa² 话²】drawing；painting

绘图【kui²tou⁴ 途】charting；drafting

绘声绘色【kui²xing¹ kui²xig⁷ 升式】vivid；lively

荟
【kui³ 绘³；wei³ 畏】luxuriant growth (of plants)

荟萃【kui³xêü⁶ 睡】gather together；assemble

贿
【kui² 绘；fui² 悔²】bribe

贿赂【kui²lou⁶ 路】bribe；bribery

贿选【kui²xün² 损】practise bribery at election；get elected by bribery

括
【kud⁸ 卡活⁸】draw together；contract；include

括号【kud⁸hou⁶ 好⁶】brackets

括弧【kud⁸wu⁴ 胡】parentheses

豁【kud⁸ 括；tog⁸ 霍】clear；open；exempt

曲【kug⁷ 卡屋⁷】bent；wrong；bend(of a river, etc.)；song；music (of a song)；a surname

曲线【kug⁷xin³ 扇】curve

曲折【kug⁷jid⁸ 节】tortuous；winding；complications

曲直【kug⁷jig⁹ 值】right and wrong

曲解【kug⁷gai² 佳²】misinterpret；twist

曲调【kug⁷ diu² 掉 】tune (of a song)；melody

曲子【kug⁷ji² 止】song；tune；melody

曲艺【kug⁷ngei⁶ 毅】folk art forms including ballad singing, story telling, comic dialogues, clapper talks, cross talks, etc.

曲奇【kug⁷kēi⁴ 其】cookies

曲高和寡【kug⁷gou¹wo⁴gua² 膏禾挂²】too highbrow to be popular

麴【kug⁷ 曲】leaven；yeast

麴霉【kug⁷ mui⁴ 梅 】aspergillus ＝ 酒饼【jeo²bēng²】

跷【kiu² 乔】to coincide；fishy；lift up；on tiptoe

跷妙【kui²miu⁶ 庙】funny；strange ＝【普】巧合；奇妙

跷起脚坐响度【kiu²hēi²gêg⁸qo⁵hêng² dou⁶】sit with one's legs crossed

乔【kiu² 乔²】way；means；calculation ＝【普】办法；心计

度乔【dog⁹kiu²】think of a way ＝【普】想办法

绣【kiu⁵ 乔⁵】to coil ＝【普】卷；绕；绕圈

乔【kiu⁴ 桥】tall；disguise；a surname

乔木【kiu⁴mug⁹ 目】arbor；tree

乔迁【kiu⁴ qin¹千 】move to a better place or have a promotion

乔装【kiu⁴jong 妆】disguise

窍【kiu³ 乔³】aperture；a key to sth.

窍门【kiu³mun⁴ 们】key；knack

侨【kiu⁴ 乔 】live abroad；a person living abroad

侨居【kiu⁴gêu¹ 据】live abroad

侨民【kiu⁴men⁴ 文】a national of a particular country residing abroad

侨眷【kiu⁴ gün³卷³】 relatives of nationals living abroad

侨汇【kiu⁴wui⁶ 会】overseas remittance

桥【kiu⁴ 乔】bridge

桥梁【kiu⁴lêng⁴ 凉】bridge

桥拱【kiu⁴gung² 龚²】bridge arch

桥墩【kiu⁴dên² 敦²】bridge pier

桥头堡【kiu⁴teo⁴bou² 投保】bridgehead；bridge tower

荞【kiu⁴ 乔】〈n.〉荞麦【kiu⁴meg⁹ 默】buckwheat

钳【kim⁴ 黔】pincers；pliers；tongs；grip；clamp；restrain

钳工【kim⁴gung¹ 公】benchwork；fitter

钳制【kim⁴ jei³济 】clamp down on；suppress

钳仔【kim⁴ jei²济²】pliers；pincers；forceps ＝【普】钳子

黔【kim⁴ 钳】black；another name for Guizhou Province

黔驴之技【kim⁴lêū⁴ji¹gēi⁶ 雷支妓】tricks not to be feared; cheap tricks

虔【kin⁴ 乾】pious; sincere

虔诚【kin⁴xing¹ 成】pious; devout

乾【kin⁴ 虔】male

乾坤【kin⁴kuen¹ 困¹】heaven and earth; the universe

倾【king¹ 顷¹】incline; collapse; deviation; empty; do all one can

倾斜【king¹qē⁴ 邪】tilt; incline; slope

倾向【king¹hêng³ 香³】tendency; trend; prefer

倾心【king¹xem¹ 深】admire; cordial

倾注【king¹jū² 著】pour into; throw into

倾泻【king¹xē³ 舍】come down in torrents

倾销【king¹xiu¹ 消】dump

倾倒【king¹dou² 捣】tip; pour out; topple over

倾慕【king¹mou⁶ 务】have a strong admiration for; adore

倾诉【king¹xou³ 数】pour out(one's heart, etc.)

倾偈【king¹gei² 鸡²】to chat; have a good chat =【普】聊天; 倾谈

倾轧【king¹jad⁸ 扎】engage in internal strife

倾家荡产【king¹ga¹dong⁶qan² 加当⁶ 铲】lose a family fortune

顷【king² 倾²; king¹ 倾】a unit of area(= 6.6667 hectares); just; just now; a little while

顷刻【king¹heg⁷ 黑】in a moment; instantly

琼【king⁴ 鲸】fine jade

琼阁【king⁴gog⁸ 各】a jewelled palace

琼楼玉宇【king⁴leo⁹yug⁹yū⁵ 留肉语】a richly decorated jade palace

瀄【king⁴ 琼】filter; sediment

瀄干水【king¹gon¹xêū² 竿瑞²】take the water; filter completely =【普】把水滤干

揭【kid⁸ 子】tear off; uncover; lift; expose; raise

揭开【kid⁸hoi¹ 海¹】uncover; reveal

揭露【kid⁸lou⁶ 路】expose; ferret out

揭穿【kid⁸qūn¹ 川】expose; lay bare; show up

揭发【kid⁸fad⁸ 法】expose; unmask

揭示【kid⁸xi⁶ 是】announce; reveal

揭晓【kid⁸hiu² 嚣²】announce; make known

孑【kid⁸ 揭】lonely; all alone

孑孓【kid⁸kūd⁸ 决】wiggler; wriggler

孑然【kid⁸yin⁴ 言】solitary; lonely

竭【kid⁸ 揭】exhaust; use up

竭尽【kid⁸jên⁶ 进⁶】use up; exhaust

竭力【kid⁸lig⁹ 历】do one's utmost

竭诚【kid⁸xing⁴ 成】wholeheartedly

竭泽而渔【kid⁸jag⁹yi⁴yū⁴ 择移鱼】drain the pond to get all the fish

碣【kid⁸ 揭】stone tablet

棘【kig⁷ 卡益⁷; gig⁷ 击】sour jujube; brambles; spine; clumsy; to try; cake

棘住【kig⁷jū⁶ 注⁶】block; check =【普】卡住

棘手【kig⁷xeo² 守】thorny; knotty; difficult

阒【kuig⁷ 箍益⁷】quiet; still; the sound of ram; hit

阒然无声【kuig⁷yin⁴mou⁴xing¹ 言毛升】very quiet

阒沉佢【kuig⁷qem⁴kêü⁵ 寻距】overthrow him

阒火柴【kuig⁷fo²qai⁴ 伙踩⁴】strike a match =【普】划火柴

阒砾㭪嘞【kuig⁷lig⁷kuag⁷lag⁷】the sound of the calculating on an abacus; all things; anything =【普】所有事情；各种各样事情（由打算盘引申出来的意义）

㭪【kuag⁷ 箍客⁷】a round; circle; to surround something with a string ◠【普】一圈；一周；一匝

决【küd⁸ 缺】decide; definitely; certainly; execute a person; burst

决定【küd⁸ding⁶ 锭】decide; resolve; decision

决策【küd⁸ qag⁸ 册】make policy; policy decision

决断【küd⁸dün³ 段³】make a decision; resolve

诀【küd⁸ 决】rhymed formula; knack; part

诀别【küd⁸bid⁹ 必⁹】bid farewell; part

诀窍【küd⁸kiu³ 乔³】secret of success; knack

抉【küd⁸ 决】pick out; single out

抉择【küd⁸jag⁹ 泽】choose

玦【küd⁸ 决】penannular jade ring

厥【küd⁸ 决】faint; fall into a coma; his or her; its; their

蕨【küd⁸ 厥】〈n.〉brake(fern)

蕨类植物【küd⁸lêü⁶jig⁹med⁹ 泪直勿】pteridophyte

獗【küd⁸ 厥】〈a.〉be rampant (see "猖獗")

蹶【küd⁸ 决】fall; suffer a setback 一蹶不振【yed⁷küd⁸bed⁷jen³】collapse after one setback

跑【kê⁴ 卡靴⁴】(limbs)cold ◠【普】手足受冷致不灵便

区【kêü¹ 驱；ngeo¹ 欧】area; district; an administrative division; classify; a surname

区别【kêü¹bid⁹ 必⁹】distinguish; difference

区分【kêü¹ fen¹芬】differentiate; distinguish

区域【kêü¹wig⁹ 乌益⁹】region; area

区区【kêü¹kêü¹】trivial; trifling

岖【kêü¹ 驱】(see"崎岖")

驱【kêü¹ 拘】drive; expel; run quickly

驱除【kêü¹qêü⁴ 徐】drive out; get rid of

驱动【kêü¹dung⁶ 洞】drive

驱使【kêü¹xei² 洗】order about; prompt; urge

驱散【kêü¹xan³ 汕】disperse; dispel

驱逐【kêü¹jug⁹ 浊】drive out; expel

躯【kêü¹ 驱】the human body

躯体【kêü¹tei² 睇】body

躯干【kêü¹gon³ 竿³】trunk; torso

祛【kêü¹ 驱】dispel; remove; drive away

祛除【kêü¹ qêü⁴ 徐 】dispel; get rid of; drive out

祛风【kêü¹ fung¹ 丰】dispel the wind

祛痰【kêü¹ tam⁴ 谭 】make expectoration easy

拘【kêü¹ 驱】arrest; restrain; inflexible

拘捕【kêü¹ bou⁶ 哺】arrest

拘留【kêü¹ leo⁴ 流】detain; intern

拘押【kêü¹ ngad⁸ 压】take into custody

拘束【kêü¹ qug⁷ 促】restrain; restrict

拘礼【kêü¹ lei⁵ 丽⁵】be punctilious

拘谨【kêü¹ gen² 紧】overcautious; reserved

拘泥【kêü¹ nei⁴ 尼】be a strickler for(form, etc.)

俱【kêü¹ 驱】all; complete

俱乐部【kêü¹ log⁹ bou⁶ 落步】club

俱全【kêü¹ qün⁴ 存】complete in all varieties

佢【kêü⁵ 拒】he; she; it =【普】他、她、它

佢地【kêü⁵ dêi⁶ 得希⁶】they =【普】他们; 她们

拒【kêü⁵ 距】resist; repel; refuse; reject

拒绝【kêü⁵ jüd⁹ 嘬⁹】refuse; reject; turn down; decline

拒付【kêü⁵ fu⁶ 父】refuse payment; dishonour

拒捕【kêü⁵ bou⁶ 哺】resist arrest

拒谏饰非【kêü⁵ gan² xig⁷ fêi¹ 简式菲】reject representations and gloss over errors

距【kêü⁵ 拒】distance; be apart from; be at a distance from; spur(of a cock, etc.)

距离【kêü⁵ lêi⁴ 漓】distance; be apart from

驹【kêü¹ 驱】〈n.〉colt; foal

劬【kêü⁴ 渠】fatigued; diligent

劬劳【kêü⁴ lou⁴ 涝】fatigued; overworked

渠【kêü⁴ 劬】canal; ditch; channel

渠灌【kêü⁴ gun³ 罐】canal irrigation

渠道【kêü⁴ dou⁶ 度】irrigation ditch; channel

衢【kêü⁴ 渠】thoroughfare

癯【kêü⁴ 渠】thin; lean

瞿【kêü⁴ 渠】a surname

蕖【kêü⁴ 渠】〈n.〉芙蕖【fu⁴ kêü⁴】=荷花

【ho⁴ fa¹】lotus

蓢【kêng² 强²】root(of a plant)=【普】(植物的)根

强【kêng⁴ 襁⁴; kêng⁵ 襁⁵】stubborn; strong; powerful; by force; better; strive

强大【kêng⁴ dai⁶ 歹⁶】big and powerful; powerful

强暴【kêng⁴ bou⁶ 部】violent; ferocious adversary

强盗【kêng⁴ dou⁶ 道】robber; bandit

强调【kêng⁴ diu⁶ 掉⁶】stress; emphasize

强度【kêng⁴ dou⁶ 道】intensity; strength

强悍【kêng⁴ hon⁶ 汗】intrepid; doughty

强化【kêng⁴ fa³ 花³】strengthen; intensify

强加【kêng⁴ ga¹ 家】impose; force

强奸【kêng⁴ gan¹ 间¹】rape; violate

强劲【kêng⁴ ging³ 径】powerful; forceful

强烈【kêng⁴ lid⁹ 列】strong; intense

强权【kêng⁴kün⁴ 拳】power；might

强盛【kêng⁴ xing⁶剩⁶】（ of a country ）powerful and prosperous

强行【kêng⁴heng⁴ 衡】force

强硬【kêng⁴ngang⁶ 罂⁶】strong；tough

强占【kêng⁴jim³ 詹³】forcibly occupy；seize

强制【kêng⁴jei³ 际】force；compel

强壮【kêng⁴jong³ 葬】strong；sturdy

强中自有强中手【kêng⁴jung¹ji⁶ yeo⁵kêng⁴ jung¹xeo²】 however strong you are， there's always someone stronger

强迫【kêng⁴big⁷ 碧】compel；force＝强逼【kêng⁵big⁷】

强求【kêng⁵keo⁴ 球】insist on；impose

强词夺理【kêng⁴qi⁴düd²lêi⁵ 辞 得月⁹ 李】use lame arguments

强人所难【kêng⁵yen⁴xo²nan⁴ 仁锁挪晏⁴】try to make sb. do sth. which he won't or can't

锂【kêng⁵ 强⁵】〈n.〉锂水【kêng⁵xêü² 瑞²】strong acid

褓【kêng⁵ 锂】〈n.〉褓褓【kêng⁵bou⁴ 保】swaddling clothes

羟【kêng⁵ 锂】〈n.〉羟基【kêng⁵gêi¹ 机】hydroxyl

权【kün⁴ 拳】right；power；advantageous position；weigh；tentatively；expediency

权力【kün⁴lig⁹ 历】power；authority

权术【kün⁴xêd⁹ 述】political trickery

权势【kün⁴xei³ 细】power and influence

权威【kün⁴wei¹ 畏¹】authority；a person of authority

权贵【kün⁴ guei³桂 】influential officials；bigwigs

权利【kün⁴lêi⁶ 俐】right

权益【kün⁴yig⁷ 忆】rights and interests

权衡【kün⁴heng⁴ 恒】weigh；balance

权宜【kün⁴yi⁴ 移】expedient

权且【kün⁴qê² 扯】for the time being

拳【kün⁴ 权】fist；boxing；pugilism

拳头【kün⁴teo⁴ 投】fist

拳术【kün⁴xêd⁹ 述】Chinese boxing

拳击【kün⁴gig⁷ 激】boxing；pugilism

拳打脚踢【kün⁴da²gêg⁸têg⁸ 得啊² 格约⁸ 梯吃⁸】cuff and kick；beat up

颧【kün⁴ 权】cheekbone

颧骨【kün⁴gued⁷ 掘⁷】cheekbone

椰【kē¹ 茄】excrement；faeces；dung；droppings；secretion(of the eye, ear, etc.)

屙椰【o¹kē¹】empty the bowels；shit＝【普】拉屎

椰呢啡【kün⁴ nē¹ fē¹】foolish-looking；muddle-headed ∽【普】傻头傻脑

茄【kē² 卡茄²】eggplant；aubergine

番茄【fan¹kē²】tomato

磋【kē⁴ 茄⁴】strange；odd；queer；curious

磋呢古怪【kē⁴nē⁴gu²guai³ 那耶⁴ 鼓乖³】grotesque or fantastic in shape or appearance ∽【普】奇形怪状；奇里古怪

蹬【kēng³ 卡镜³】ascend；mount；scale

蹬山【kēng³xan¹ 珊】mountain-climbing；mountaineering＝【普】登山

境【kēng⁴ 卡镜⁴】efficacious；effective；right

灵境【lēng⁴kēng⁴】accurate; efficacious ∽
　【普】灵验

起境【hēi²kēng⁴】arrogant because bright
　and capable ∽【普】因聪明能干
　而骄矜

却【kêg⁸ 噱⁸】step back; drive back; de-
　cline; but; yet; however; while; cool
　off

却步【kêg⁸bou⁶ 部】step back; bang back

却之不恭【kêg⁸ji¹bed⁷gung¹ 支毕公】it
　would be impolite to decline

噱【kêg⁹ 却⁹】loud laughter; laugh

噱头【kêg⁹teo⁴ 投】words or act meant to
　amuse or to excite laughter; tricks
　meant to deceive

屐【kêg⁹ 剧】clogs; shoes in general

隻(只)屐噷【jêg⁸kêg⁹gem² 敢】dull be-
　cause tired =【普】因劳累而变得
　呆滞

剧【kēg⁹ 屐】theatrical work; drama;
　play; opera; acute; severe; intense

剧本【kēg⁹bun² 苯²】drama; play; script

剧作家【kēg⁹jog⁸ga¹ 昨加】playwright;
　dramatist

剧中人【kēg⁹jung¹yen⁴ 宗仁】characters in
　a play

剧场【kēg⁹qêng⁴ 祥】theatre

剧院【kēg⁹yūn² 苑】theatre

剧团【kēg⁹ tūn⁴ 梯元⁴】theatrical compa-
　ny; troupe

剧目【kēg⁹mug⁹ 木】a list of plays

剧情【kēg⁹qing⁴ 程】the story of a play

剧终【kēg⁹jung¹ 中】the end; curtain

剧烈【kēg⁹lid⁹ 列】violent; acute; severe

L

啦 【la¹ 罗亚¹；la² 罗亚²；la³ 罗亚³；la⁴ 罗亚⁴】〈*auxil.*〉exclamation mark used to express demand or plead; to show agreement ◡【普】了

佢早来啦！【kêü⁵jou²loi⁴la³ 拒蚤莱】Why, he's been here a long time!

啦啦声【la⁴la²xēng¹ 腥】to act within a short time =【普】很快；很快地

罅 【la³ 啦³】crack; rift; chink

罅隙【la³guig⁷ 姑益⁷】crack; rift; chink

漏罅【leo³ la³ 陋】omission; deficiency =【普】漏水的裂缝

捹 【la² 啦²】to catch; to hurt; to figure out; to stir; exclamation mark used to express doubt ◡【普】抓；抓紧；厉害

捹住【la²jü⁶ 注⁶】to catch hold of; five =【普】（用手）抓住；五（茶楼跑堂者用的暗语）

捹脷【la²lēi¹ 利】to mean that the price is too high that it is unaffordable =【普】价太高，买不起

捹埋【la²mai⁴ 买⁴】generally =【普】一手抓起来；无论什么；什么都在内；包揽

捹西【la² xei¹ 筛】simply; not serious =【普】（办事）粗枝大叶；不细心；不细致

嘞 【la³ 啦³；lag⁸ 罗客⁸】=啦【la³】◡【普】了

喇 【la³ 啦³；la¹ 啦¹】〈*onomatopoeia.*〉；〈*n.*〉

喇叭【la³ba¹ 巴】〈*n.*〉a popular name for Suona, a woodwind instrument; brass-wind instruments in general or any of these instruments; loudspeaker

喇叭花【la³ba¹fa¹ 巴化¹】(white-edged) morning glory

喇嘛【la¹ma⁴ 麻】〈*n.*〉lama

拉 【lai¹ 赖¹】pull; draw; haul; move; play; draw out; help; draw in; press; lift; empty the bowels; slash; slit; chat

拉开【lai¹hoi¹ 海¹】pull open

拉力【lai¹lig⁹ 历】pulling force

拉扯【lai¹qē¹车²】drag; pull; drag in; chat

拉拢【lai¹lung² 龙²】rope in

拉平【lai¹ping⁴ 评】even up

拉手【lai¹xeo² 守】shake hands; handle

拉倒【lai¹dou² 捣】forget about it; drop it

拉链【lai¹lin² 连²】zip fastener; zipper

拉锯【lai¹gê³ 格靴³】work a two-handed saw

拉关系【lai¹guan¹hei⁶ 格弯¹ 兮⁶】cotton up to

拉下水【lai¹ha⁶xêü² 夏端²】drag sb. into the mire

拉大旗作虎皮【lai¹dai⁶kêü⁴jog⁸fu²pēi⁴牙⁶ 奇昨苦脾】drape oneself in the flag to impress people

拉柴【lai¹qai⁴ 猜⁴】die; pass away =【普】死掉

拉线【lai¹xin³ 扇】to foster the relationship between two people =【普】拉关系；牵线搭桥

拉匀【lai¹wen⁴ 云】to balance up =【普】平均

拉头缆【lai¹teo⁴lam⁶ 投滥】to be the first one to start；to lead =【普】牵头；带头

痕
【lai¹ 拉】final；last；end =【普】最后的、末尾的

痕尾【lai¹mēi¹ 美¹】the last one =【普】末尾；末尾的一个

痕仔【lai¹ jei² 济²】the youngest son =【普】最小的儿子

痕女【lai¹nêü² 那去²】the youngest daughter =【普】最小的女儿

癞
【lai³ 赖³】leprosy；favus of the scalp

癞虾蟆【lai³ha¹mou¹ 哈毛¹】〈n.〉toad

癞皮狗【lai³pēi⁴geo² 脾九】mangy dog；loathsome creature

籁
【lai⁶ 赖】an ancient musical pipe；sound；noise

万籁俱寂【man⁶lai⁶kêü¹jig⁹ 慢驱直】silence reigns supreme；all is quiet and still

赖
【lai⁶ 拉⁶；lai³ 癞】rely；hang on in a place；deny one's error or responsibility；blame sb. wrongly；blame；a surname

赖帐【lai⁶ jêng³ 胀 】repudiate a debt；go back on one's word

赖债【lai⁶jai³ 寨³】repudiate a debt

赖猫【lai³mao¹ 矛¹】one who is not serious in attending to anything；rascally；shameless ∽【普】赖皮；不认帐、不认真

醉
【lai⁶ 赖⁶；lüd⁹ 劣⁹】to lose；pour a libation

醉酒【lai⁶jeo² 走】pour a libation

醉低【lai⁶ dei¹帝¹】stay one because forgets =【普】因忘记而留下（没带走）

醉咗【lai⁶jo² 左】to lose =【普】丢失

捞
【lao¹ 罗拗¹；lou¹ 劳¹；lao⁴ 罗拗⁴】drag for；dredge up；fish for；get by improper means；gain；to mix；to earn a living

捞取【lao¹qêü² 娶】fish for；gain

捞一把【lao¹yed⁷ba² 壹巴²】reap some profit；profiteer

捞稻草【lao¹dou⁴qou² 道曹²】(try to) take advantage of sth.

捞家【lou¹ ga¹ 加】 to refer to a gangster who is unemployed and depends on illegal means for a living =【普】善于通过钻营或经营捞取好处的人

捞埋【lou¹mai⁴ 买⁴】mix and stir；blend =【普】拌和

捞匀【lou¹ wen⁴ 云】 mix thoroughly =【普】拌匀

捞鸡【lou¹gei¹ 计¹】to benefit；succeed =【普】成功地捞到了好处

捞起【lou¹hēi² 喜】to become rich =【普】（钻营或经营）取得成效或成功

捞世界【lou¹xei³gai³ 细介】to earn a living ∽【普】闯荡世界；在竞争中奋力图强

榄
【lam² 览²；lam⁵ 览⁵】〈n.〉olive（橄榄【gem²lam²】）

揽
【lam² 览²；lam⁵ 览⁵】to surround；pull sb. into one's arms；fasten with a rope, etc.；canvass；grasp

揽身揽势【lam²xen¹lam²xei³ 辛世】to hug each other ∽【普】(男女相处)动手动脚

揽住【lam²jü⁶ 注⁶】hug; embrace; cuddle =【普】搂抱

蓝【lam⁴ 篮】blue; indigo plant; a surname

蓝靛【lam⁴din⁶ 电】indigo

蓝本【lam⁴bun² 苯】chief source; original version

蓝图【lam⁴tou⁴ 途】blueprint

蓝宝石【lam⁴bou²xêg⁹ 保硕】sapphire

篮【lam⁴ 蓝】basket; goal

篮仔【lam⁴jei² 济²】basket =【普】篮子

篮球【lam⁴keo⁴ 求】basketball

褴【lam⁴ 蓝】〈a.〉褴褛【lam⁴lêü⁵ 吕】lam⁴leo⁵ 柳】ragged; shabby

婪【lam⁴ 蓝】〈a.〉贪婪【tam¹lam⁴ 探¹】avaricious; greedy

览【lam⁵ 揽】〈v.〉look at; see; view; read

一览无余【yed⁷lam⁵mou⁴yü⁴ 壹毛鱼】take in everything at a glance

滥【lam⁶ 缆】overflow; flood; excessive

滥调【lam⁶diu⁶ 掉】hackneyed tune; worn-out theme

滥用【lam⁶ yung⁶ 容⁶】abuse; use indiscriminately

滥竽充数【lam⁶yü¹qung¹xou³ 于冲扫】pass oneself off as one of the players in an ensemble—be there just to make up the number

缆【lam⁶ 滥】hawser; mooring rope; cable

缆索【lam⁶xog⁸ 朔】thick rope; cable

缆车【lam⁶qê¹ 奢】cable car

舰【lam⁶ 滥】warship; naval vessel

舰只【lam⁶ jêg² 脊 】warships; naval vessels

舰艇【lam⁶têng⁵ 厅⁵】naval ships and boats

舰队【lam⁶dêü² 堆²】fleet; naval force

蹒【lan¹ 兰¹】to crawl =【普】匍匐蛇行

蹒尸蹒路【lan¹xi¹ged⁹lou⁶ 司吉⁶ 露】ask someone to get lost ∽【普】滚蛋

蹒出去【lan¹qêd⁷hêü³ 次律⁷ 虚³】get lost =【普】滚开

恻【lan² 兰²】praise oneself; brag =【普】自诩

恻叻【lan²lêg⁷ 沥⁷】praise oneself smart and capable =【普】自诩聪明、有能耐

癞【lan³ 兰³】〈n.〉macula =【普】斑疹

阑【lan⁴ 兰】late; railing; balustrade

阑干【lan⁴gon¹ 竿】crisscross; railing

阑珊【lan⁴xan¹ 山】coming to an end; waning

阑尾炎【lan⁴mēi⁵yim⁴ 美严】appendicitis

岚【lan⁴ 兰】haze; vapour; mist

兰【lan⁴ 岚】orchid

兰花【lan⁴fa¹ 化¹】cymbidium; orchid

兰州【lan⁴jeo¹ 洲】〈n.〉Lanzhou

栏【lan⁴ 兰】fence; railing; pen; shed; column

栏杆【lan⁴gon¹ 竿】railing; banisters

澜【lan⁴ 兰】billows

谰【lan⁴ 兰】calumniate; slander

谰言【lan⁴yin⁴ 然】calumny; slander

斓【lan⁴ 兰】〈a.〉斑斓【ban¹lan⁴】gorgeous

懒【lan⁵ 兰⁵】lazy; indolent; sluggish; languid

懒得【lan⁵ deg⁷德】not feel like (doing sth.)

懒惰【lan⁵do⁶ 堕】lazy

懒佬【lan⁵lou² 老²】sluggard; idler =【普】懒汉

懒散【lan⁵xan² 汕²】sluggish; negligent

懒洋洋【lan⁵yêng⁴yêng⁴ 杨】languid; listless

懒理【lan⁵lêi⁵ 李】not to bother =【普】懒得管

懒蛇【lan⁵ xē⁴射⁴】a lazy bump; lazy ∽【普】懒汉；懒得动

懒佬鞋【lan⁵lou²hai² 老² 孩】slipper =【普】方便鞋(不用系带子的)

拦【lan⁴】bar; block; hold back

拦阻【lan⁴ jo²左】block; hold back; obstruct

拦路【lan⁴lou⁶ 露】block the way

拦截【lan⁴jid⁹ 捷】intercept

拦腰【lan⁴yiu¹ 邀】by the waist; round the middle

拦河坝【lan⁴ho⁴ba³ 何霸】a dam across a river

烂【lan⁶ 兰⁶】sodden; mashed; pappy; rot; fester; worn-out; messy; broken; to break; to spoil; to damage; to tell lie

烂漫【lan⁶man⁶ 慢】bright-coloured; brilliant; unaffected

烂熟【lan⁶xug⁹ 属】thoroughly cooked; know sth. thoroughly

烂醉【lan⁶jêü³ 最】dead drunk

烂摊子【lan⁶tan¹ji² 叹¹ 止】a shamble; an awful mess

烂泥【lan⁶ban⁶ 办】soggy soil =【普】烂泥浆

烂打【lan⁶ da²得阿²】one who likes to fight ∽【普】好斗

烂赌【lan⁶dou² 捣】being addicted to gambling =【普】嗜赌成性

烂瞓【lan⁶fen³ 粪】one who likes to sleep =【普】嗜睡

烂口【lan⁶heo²厚²】nasty words =【普】满口粗言烂语

烂贱【lan⁶ jin⁶ 溅⁶】not worth the money; cheap; low-priced =【普】不值钱

烂命【lan⁶ mēng⁶莫镜⁶】to do something by all means ∽贱命一条；轻生

烂仔【lan⁶jei² 济²】gangsters ∽【普】嗜打好斗、不务正业的小子

烂瘾【lan⁶yen⁵ 引】addicted to ∽【普】着迷

烂蓉蓉【lan⁶yung⁴yung⁴ 容】soggy =【普】稀巴烂

烂泥扶唔上壁【lan⁶nei⁴fu⁴m⁴xêng⁵bēg⁸】to say that one who is incapable, cannot help much =【普】(比喻) 无法帮助其成才的低能儿

毚【lang¹ 罗罂¹】knitting wool =【普】毛线

毚衫【lang¹xam¹ 三】knitting wool-clothes =【普】毛线衣

冷【lang⁵ 罗罂⁵】cold; cooling; frosty; cool; unfrequented; strange; shot from hiding

冷冻【lang⁵dung³ 东³】freezing

冷却【lang⁵kêg⁸ 卡约⁸】cooling

冷静【lang⁵jing⁶ 精⁶】sober; calm

冷落【lang⁵ log⁹ 洛⁹】unfrequented; desolate

冷酷【lang⁵ hug⁹ 黑屋⁹】unfeeling; callous; grim

冷淡【lang⁵ dam⁶ 担⁶】cheerless; indifferent

冷清【lang⁵ qing¹ 称】cold and cheerless; lonely

冷气【lang⁵hēi³ 戏】air conditioning

冷藏【lang⁵ qong⁴床 】refrigeration; cold storage

冷饮【lang⁵yem² 阴²】cold drink

冷门【lang⁵mun² 瞒²】an unexpected winner

冷僻【lang⁵pig⁷ 辟】deserted; rare

冷枪【lang⁵qêng¹ 昌】sniper's shot

冷箭【lang⁵jin³ 战】sniper's shot

冷战【lang⁵jin³ 箭】cold war; shiver

冷遇【lang⁵yǔ⁶ 预】cold reception

冷眼【lang⁵ ngan⁵雁⁵】 cool detachment; cold shoulder

冷笑【lang⁵xiu³ 少³】sneer; laugh grimly

冷板凳【lang⁵ ban² deng³ 版登³】cold bench — an indifferent post or a cold reception

冷不防【lang⁵bed⁷fong⁴ 毕妨】unawares; suddenly

冷嘲热讽【lang⁵jao¹yid⁹fung³ 找¹ 衣泄⁹风³】freezing irony and burning satire

冷巷【lang⁵hong⁶ 康⁶】small paths =【普】小通道；小巷

冷天【lang⁵tin¹ 田¹】winter; cold weather =【普】冬天；寒冷的日子

冷饭【lang⁵fan⁶ 范】the remaining rice; vegetable ∽【普】旧饭；重复提供的东西

冷手执个热煎堆【lang⁵xeo²jeb⁷go³yid⁹ jin¹dêu¹ 守汁哥³ 衣杰⁹ 战¹ 队¹】to be given some unexpected benefit; windfall =【普】白捞；不用付出代价而碰巧得了好处

擸【lab⁸ 腊⁸】to keep; to wrap; to finish buying all; to glance; to step widely ∽【普】攫取；统揽

擸晒【lab⁸xai³ 徙³】all gain =【普】全都取得；统统包揽过来

擸网顶【lab⁸mong⁵dēng² 妄钉²】to be the top; to be the first ∽【普】获取最大的渔利

腊【lab⁹ 蜡】cured (fish, meat, ect., generally done in the twelfth moon)

腊味【lab⁹ mēi² 尾²】 cured meat, fish, etc.

腊肠【lab⁹qêng² 抢】sausage =【普】香肠

腊肉【lab⁹yug⁹ 玉】cured meat; bacon

腊月【lab⁹yüd⁹ 越】the twelfth moon

蜡【lab⁹ 腊】wax; candle; polish

蜡烛【lab⁹jug⁷ 竹】(wax) candle

蜡纸【lab⁹ji² 止】wax paper; stencil paper

蜡笔【lab⁹bed⁷ 毕】wax crayon

辣【lad⁸ 罗压⁸】brand; iron

辣亲【lad⁸qen¹ 趁¹】scald =【普】烫伤

辣鸡【lad⁸gei¹ 计¹】flatiron; iron =【普】烙铁

癞【lad⁸ 辣⁸】〈n.〉癞痢【lad⁸lēi¹ 李¹】favus of the scalp

邋【lad⁹ 辣】〈a.〉邋遢【lad⁹tad⁸ 他压⁸】dirty =【普】肮脏

辣【lad⁹ 罗压⁹】peppery; burn; vicious

辣椒【lad⁹jiu¹ 焦】hot peppery; chilli

辣酱【lad⁹jêng³ 涨】thick chilli sauce

辣手【lad⁹xeo² 守】ruthless method; thorny

辣蓼【lad⁹liu¹ 了¹】〈n.〉knotweed

厉【lei² 厉²】to turn away one's head or body

厉手掉咗【lei²xeo²diu⁶jo² 守丢 左】to throw away things =【普】(接过东西)转手就仍掉(形容不爱惜)

黎【lei⁴ 犁】multitude; host; a surname

黎民【lei⁴ men⁴文】the common people; the multitude

黎明【lei⁴ming⁴ 名】dawn; daybreak

犁【lei⁴ 黎】plough; work with a plough; plough

犁铧【lei⁴wa⁴ 华】ploughshare; share

犁地【lei⁴dēi⁶ 得希⁶】work with a plough

嚟【lei⁴ 黎】come; arrive =【普】来(see "来")

藜【lei⁴ 黎】〈n.〉lamb's-quarters(see "葵藜")

黧【lei⁴ 黎】〈a.〉黧黑【hei⁴heg⁷ 刻】(of complexion)dark

眲【lei⁶ 厉】to look at someone fiercely

眼眲眲【ngan⁵lei⁶lei⁶ 雁⁵】(looking on) helplessly or unfeelingly ∽【普】眼睁睁

骊【lei⁴ 黎】black horse

礼【lei⁵ 蠡】ceremony; rite; courtesy; manners; gift; present

礼貌【lei⁵mao⁶ 猫⁶】courtesy; politeness; manners

礼节【lei⁵jid⁶ 折】courtesy; etiquette; protocol

礼仪【lei⁵yi⁴ 移】etiquette; rite; protocol

礼让【lei⁵yêng⁶ 酿】comity

礼拜【lei⁵bai³ 摆³】religious service; week; day of the week; Sunday

礼堂【lei⁵tong⁴ 唐】assembly hall; auditorium

礼物【lei⁵med⁹勿】gift; present = 礼品【lei⁵ben² 禀²】

礼服【lei⁵fug⁹ 伏】ceremonial robe or dress

礼尚往来【lei⁵xêng⁶wong⁵toi⁴ 上汪⁵ 莱】courtesy demands reciprocity; pay a man back in his own coin

蠡【lei⁵ 礼】dipper; seashell

蠡测【lei⁵qag⁷ 策⁷】measure the sea with an oyeter shell — have a shallow understanding of a person or subject

丽【lei⁶ 厉】beautiful

逦【lei⁵ 礼】〈a.〉迤逦【yi⁵lei⁵】winding; meandering

醴【lei⁵ 礼】〈n.〉sweet wine

厉【lei⁶ 丽】strict; stern; rigorous; severe

厉害【lei⁶ hoi⁶ 亥】terrible; formidable = 犀利【xei¹lēi⁶】

厉行【lei⁶heng⁴ 衡】strictly enforce; rigorously enforce

励【lei⁶ 厉】encourage

励精图治【lei⁶jing¹tou⁴ji⁶ 贞途自】rouse oneself for vigorous efforts to make the country prosperous

砺【lei⁶ 厉】whetstone; whet (see "磨砺")

蛎【lei⁶ 厉】〈n.〉(see"牡蛎")

疠【lei⁶ 厉】pestilence; plague (see "瘰疠")

俪【lei⁶ 丽】pair; husband and wife (see "伉俪")

荔【lei⁶ 例】〈n.〉荔枝【lei⁶ji¹ 支】litchi

例【lei⁶ 厉】example; precedent; case; rule

例如【lei⁶yü⁴ 鱼】for instance; for example (e.g.); such as

例题【lei⁶tei⁴ 提】example

例证【lei⁶jing³ 正】illustrative phrase

例子【lei⁶ji² 止】example; case; instance

例外【lei⁶ngoi⁶ 碍】exception

褛【leo¹ 楼¹; lêü⁵ 吕】①overcoat = 【普】大衣 ②wrap around = 【普】披上; 盖着

搂【leo² 楼²; leo⁵ 柳】hold in one's arms; hug

搂抱【leo²pou⁵ 袍⁵】hug; embrace; cuddle

缕【leo² 搂; lêü⁵ 吕】thread; wisp; strand; detailed

缕缕【leo²leo²】continuously

缕析【lêü⁵xig⁷ 色】make a detailed analysis

篓【leo⁵ 柳; lo¹ 罗¹】basket

字纸篓【ji⁶ji²lo¹】wastepaper basket; wastebasket

喽【leo³ 柳³】invite; request

喽埋一齐【leo³mai⁴yed⁷qei⁴ 买⁴ 壹妻⁴】invite to meet together; call to-

gether = 【普】邀集

嘍口【leo³heo² 厚²】stutter; stammer = 【普】口吃

楼【leo⁴ 留; leo² 搂】a storied building; storey; floor; superstructure

楼房【leo⁴fong⁴防】a building of two or more storeys

楼梯【leo⁴tei¹ 锑】stairs; staircase

楼上【leo⁴xêng⁶ 尚】upstairs

楼下【leo⁴ha⁶ 夏】downstairs

娄【leo⁴ 楼】a surname

娄子【leo⁴ji² 止】trouble; blunder

偻【leo⁴ 娄】〈n.〉佝偻病【kêü¹leo⁴bêng⁶ 驱娄柄⁶】rickets

偻㑩【leo⁴lo⁴ 罗】underling; lackey

髅【leo⁴ 娄】〈n.〉骷髅【fu¹leo⁴ 夫】human skeleton; human skull

镂【leo⁶ 漏】engrave; carve

镂刻【leo⁶heg⁷ 克】engrave; carve

镂空【leo⁶hung¹ 哄¹】hollow out

流【leo⁴ 留】flow; drifting; degenerate; spread; banish; stream of water; current; bad

流体【leo⁴tei² 睇】fluid

流水【leo⁴xêü⁴ 瑞²】running water; turnover

流通【leo⁴tung¹ 同¹】circulate

流动【leo⁴dung⁶ 洞】flow; on the move

流传【leo⁴qün⁴ 存】spread; circulate

流程【leo⁴qing⁴ 情】technological process; circuit

流畅【leo⁴qêng³ 昌³】easy and smooth

流窜【leo⁴qün³ 寸】flee hither and thither

流浪【leo⁴long⁶ 晾】roam about; lead a vagrant life

流利【leo⁴lēi⁶ 俐】fluent; smooth

流露【leo⁴lou⁶ 路】reveal; betray

流氓【leo⁴ mong⁴亡 】hooliganism; indecency

流亡【leo⁴mong⁴ 芒⁴】go into exile

流行【leo⁴heng⁴ 衡】prevalent; popular

流失【leo⁴ xed⁷室 】 run off; be washed away

流毒【leo⁴dug⁹ 独】pernicious influence

流产【leo⁴qan² 铲】abortion; miscarry

流口水【leo⁴heo²xêü² 厚² 瑞²】of low standard; of inferior quality = 【普】垂涎;事情办得糟

流野【leo⁴yē⁵ 夜⁵】〈n.〉product of poor quality; false goods = 【普】劣质品;假货;赝品

流连忘返【leo⁴lin⁴mong⁴fan² 链亡反】enjoy oneself so much as to forget to go home

流离失所【leo⁴ lēi⁴ xed⁷ xo² 漓室锁】become destitute and homeless

流芳百世【leo⁴ fong¹ bag⁸ xei³方伯细 】leave a good name for a hundred generations

刘【leo⁴ 流】a surname

刘海【leo⁴hoi² 凯】bang; fringe

浏【leo⁴ 刘】(of water) clear; (of wind) swift

浏览【leo⁴lam⁵ 缆⁵】glance over; browse

留【leo⁴ 流】remain; stay; ask sb. to stay; reserve; keep; grow; wear; accept; take; leave

留存【leo⁴ qün⁴传 】preserve; keep; remain

留种【leo⁴jung² 肿】reserve seed for planting

留言【leo⁴yin⁴ 然】leave a message

留意【leo⁴yi³ 薏】be careful; look out

留心【leo⁴xem¹ 深】be careful; take care

留情【leo⁴ qing⁴程 】 show mercy or forgiveness

留学【leo⁴hog⁹ 鹤】study abroad

留恋【leo⁴lün² 联²】be reluctant to leave(a place); recall with nostalgia

留念【leo⁴ nim⁶粘⁶】 accept or keep as a souvenir

留级【leo⁴keb⁷ 给】repeat the year's work

留后路【leo⁴heo⁶lou⁶ 候露】leave a way out

留有余地【leo⁴yeo⁵yü⁴dēi⁶ 友如得希⁶】leave some leeway

留得青山在,不怕没柴烧【leo⁴deg⁷qing¹ xan¹joi⁶, bed⁷pa³mud⁹qai⁴xiu¹】as long as the green mountains are there, one need not worry about firewood

留堂【leo⁴ tong⁴唐 】 to be retained in school as a means of punishment = 【普】下课后老师留下学生进行个别教育或令其补习作业

留医【leo⁴yi¹ 衣】to stay in a hospital = 【普】住医院

榴【leo⁴ 留】pomegranate

榴弹【leo⁴dan² 蛋】high explosive shell

榴莲【leo⁴lin² 连】durian

瘤【leo⁴ 留】tumour　毒瘤【dug⁹leo⁴读】malignant tumour

馏【leo⁶ 漏】distillation(蒸馏【jing¹leo⁶】)

溜【leo⁶ 漏;liu¹ 料¹】slide; smooth; slip away

溜冰【leo⁶bing¹ 兵】skating; roller-skating

溜槽【leo⁶qou⁴ 曹⁴】chute

溜光【liu¹guong¹ 胱】very smooth; sleek; glossy

溜之大吉【liu¹ji¹dai⁶ged⁷ 支歹⁶ 格乞⁷】make oneself scarce; sneak away

琉
硫【leo⁴ 流】coloured glaze(琉璃【leo⁴lēi⁴ 离】)

【leo⁴ 流】〈n.〉sulphur(S)

硫磺【leo⁴wong⁴ 王】sulphur

硫酸【leo⁴xūn¹ 孙】sulphuric acid

柳【leo⁵ 流⁵】willow; a surname

柳条【leo⁵tiu⁴ 挑⁴】willow twig; osier

柳絮【leo⁵xêu⁵ 绪⁵】(willow)catkin

漏【leo⁵ 馏】leak; water clock; leak; be missing

漏洞【leo⁶dung⁶ 动】leak; flaw; hole

漏网【leo⁶mong⁵ 妄】slip through the net

漏斗【leo⁶deo² 豆²】funnel

漏电【leo⁶din⁶ 甸】leakage of electricity

漏光【leo⁶guong¹ 胱】light leak

漏风【leo⁶fung¹ 丰】air leak; leak out

陋【leo⁶ 漏】plain; ugly; humble; vulgar; limited

陋俗【leo⁶jug⁹ 族】undesirable customs

陋习【leo⁶jab⁹ 袭】bad habits

绺【leo⁵ 柳】tuft; lock; skein

嘛【lem¹ 林¹】coax a child; make sb. laugh with touching his body ∽【普】哄孩子;触摸身体致笑

冧【lem³ 林³】〈v.〉to collapse

冧档【lem³dong³ 当³】to collapse＝【普】店档倒塌;(势力)瓦解;(谋事)失败

淋【lem⁴ 林】pour; drench; strain; be not hard; be not fierce; kindhearted and weak; soft

淋湿【lem⁴xeb⁶ 拾⁷】drenched

淋浴【lem⁴yug⁹ 玉】shower bath; shower

淋啤啤【lem⁴bē⁴bē⁴ 伯耶⁴】be not hard; very soft＝【普】不坚硬;很柔软

淋善【lem⁴xin⁶擅】be not fierce; kindhearted and weak＝【普】不凶恶;善良柔弱

淋巴【lem⁴ba¹ 爸】lymph

淋菜【lem⁴qoi³ 蔡】water vegetables＝【普】浇菜

淋病【lem⁴bēng⁶ 柄】gonorrhoea

淋漓尽致【lem⁴lēi⁶jên⁶ji³ 离进⁶ 至】incisively and vividly; thoroughly

琳【lem⁴ 林】beautiful jade

琳琅满目【lem⁴long⁴mun⁵mug⁹ 郎螨⁵ 木】a superb collection of beautiful things

霖【lem⁴ 林】continuous heavy rain

啉【lem⁴ 林】〈n.〉喹啉【fui¹lem⁴ 灰】quinoline

林【lem⁴ 淋】forest; woods; grove; circles; forestry

林木【lem⁴mug⁹ 目】forest; woods; forest tree

林海【lem⁴hoi² 开²】immense forest

林区【lem⁴kêu¹ 驱】forest zone

林业【lem⁴yib⁹ 叶】forestry

林立【lem⁴leb⁶ 笠⁶】stand in great numbers

林荫道【lem⁴yem¹dou⁶ 阴度】boulevard; avenue

临【lem⁴ 林】face; arrive; just before; copy

临近【lem⁴gen⁶ 靳】close to; close on

临时【lem⁴xi⁴ 是⁴】at the time when sth. happens; temporary

临到【lem⁴dou³ 都³】just before; befall

临危【lem⁴ ngei⁴ 魏】be dying (from illness); facing death or deadly peril

临别【lem⁴bid⁹ 必⁹】at parting; just before parting

临床【lem⁴qong⁴ 仓⁴】clinical

临摹【lem⁴mou⁴ 毛】copy (a model of calligraphy or painting)

临渴掘井【lem⁴hod⁸gued⁹jēng² 喝骨⁹ 支镜²】not dig a well until one is thirsty — not make timely preparations

临阵磨枪【lem⁴jen⁶mo⁶qêng¹ 振⁶ 摩⁴ 昌】sharpen one's spear only before going into battle — start to prepare only at the last moment

廪【lem⁵ 凛】⟨n.⟩仓廪【qong¹lem⁵ 沧】granary

凛【lem⁵ 廪】cold; strict; severe; afraid

凛冽【lem⁵lid⁹ 裂】piercingly cold

凛凛【lem⁵ lem⁵】cold; stern; awe-inspiring

凛然【lem⁵yin⁴ 言】stern; awe-inspiring

凛瘫【lem⁵ dem² 得庵²】continuously =【普】陆续;不断

埝【lem⁶ 林⁶】to pile up

埝起嚟【lem⁶hēi²lei⁴ 喜黎】to pile up =【普】叠起;堆积

餎【len¹ 罗因¹】⟨v.⟩餎骨【len¹gued⁷ 掘⁷】gnaw a bone =【普】啃骨头

谂【len² 罗因²】⟨v.⟩谂化【len²fa³ 花³】tease =【普】捉弄

拎【len² 罗因²】play with; juggle with; be meticulous in one's work =【普】细致地、慢慢地做某样事情;玩弄玩耍

谞【len³ 罗因³】explained and explained; chatter =【普】说了又说;唠叨

谞谞呻呻【len³len³xen³xen³ 申³】chatter and not decent =【普】唠叨而且不正经

笠【leb⁷ 粒】a large bamboo or straw hat with a conical crown and broad brim; to wear; to coax

笠衫【leb⁷xam³ 三】a sweater =【普】不开纽扣的内衣

笠高帽【leb⁷gou¹mou² 膏冒²】to win one's heart =【普】戴高帽

迾【leb⁹ 立】slow; slowly; stagnant

迾油【leb⁹yeo² 友²】unhurriedly; obstruct =【普】慢腾腾;动作不爽快

立【leb⁹ 笠⁹】stand; set up; erect; found; live; immediate

立正【leb⁹jing³ 政】stand at attention

立定【leb⁹ding⁶ 锭】halt = 企住【kēi⁵ jü⁶ 注⁶】

立场【leb⁹qêng⁴ 祥】position; stand

立方【leb⁹fong¹ 芳】cube; cubic metre

立法【leb⁹fad⁸ 发】legislation

立功【leb⁹gung¹ 工】render meritorious service; win honour

立即【leb⁹jig⁷ 积】immediately; at once

立刻【leb⁹heg⁷ 黑】immediately; right away = 立时【leb⁹xi⁴ 是⁴】

立论【leb⁹lên⁶ 伦⁶】set forth one's views; argument

立体【leb⁹tei² 睇】stereoscopic; solid

立意【leb⁹yi³ 意】be determined；approach

立志【leb⁹ji³ 至】resolve；be determined

立足点【leb⁹ jug⁷ dim² 竹 店²】foothold；
  standpoint

立竿见影【leb⁹gon¹gin³ying² 杆建映】set
  up a pole and see its shadow —
  get instant results

立乱【leb⁹lün² 联²】simply =【普】乱来；随
  意

立立乱【leb⁹leb⁹lün⁶ 联⁶】confusing；wor-
  ried；anxious =【普】乱得很；没头
  绪

粒【leb⁷ 笠】grain；granule；pellet

粒状【leb⁷jong⁶ 撞】granular

粒子【leb⁷ji² 止】〈n.〉particle

粒选【leb⁷xün⁵ 损】grain-by-grain seed selection = 逐粒选择【jug⁹leb⁷xün²
  jag⁹】

甩【led⁷ 罗核⁷】to come off =【普】捽掉；
  摆脱

甩身【led⁷xen¹ 辛】to escape =【普】摆脱
  （困境）

甩须【led⁷ xou¹ 苏】to feel shameful =
  【普】胡须被扯脱；丢脸

勒【leg⁹ 罗黑⁹】rein in；force；carve；tie
  or strap sth. tight

勒令【leg⁹ling⁶ 另】compel；order

勒索【leg⁹xog⁸ 司恶⁸】extort；blackmail

勒紧裤带【leg⁹gen²fu³dai⁶ 谨富戴】tight-
  en the belt

簕【leg⁹ 勒】puncture vine；thorn =【普】
  植物的刺；蒺藜

簕窦【leg⁹deo³ 斗】difficult to come to a
  compromise；difficult to negotiate
  with =【普】不好惹的；难于打交
  道的

啰【lo¹ 罗¹；lo³ 罗³】

啰嗦【lo¹xo¹ 梳】long-winded；wordy；
  overelaborate；troublesome =【普】
  罗嗦

啰啰挛【lo¹lo¹lün¹ 联¹】to refer to a child
  crying when he (or she) does not
  feel well ◇【普】身体有病或心
  中有烦恼时的神态和动作

啰柚【lo¹yeo² 友²】buttock；backside =
  【普】屁股

啰嘛【lo¹bo³ 播】〈auxil.〉exclamation
  mark used to urge or remind ◇
  【普】的呀；的啦（句末表探问语
  气）

捞【lo² 罗²】take；get；fetch；seek；to
  take away

捞翻【lo²fan¹ 番】take back =【普】取回

捞景【lo²ging¹ 境】to look for the correct
  spot for picture-taking；to do
  something on purpose so as to
  make one angry =【普】（摄影时）
  取景；找麻烦；添乱

捞嚟讲【lo²lei⁴gong² 黎港】to say and not
  put what has been said into action
  =【普】找话题来说，没那回事

捞嚟衰【lo²lei⁴xêu¹ 黎需】to find one's
  own trouble；ask for trouble =
  【普】自找麻烦；自讨苦吃

捞命【lo²mēng⁶ 莫镜⁶】terrible；kill；ex-
  tremely；a nuisance =【普】要命

捞便宜【lo²pin⁴yi⁴ 偏⁴ 移】to take advantage =【普】捞好处；占便宜

螺【lo⁴ 罗；lo² 罗²】snail；whorl（in fin-
  gerprint）

螺丝【lo⁴xi¹ 思】screw =【普】螺钉

螺纹【lo⁴men⁴ 闻】whorl（in fingerprint）；

thread

螺旋【lo⁴xün⁴ 船】spiral；screw

螺丝批【lo⁴xi¹pei¹ 思拍矮¹】screw-driver ＝【普】起子

罗【lo⁴ 螺】a net for catching birds；catch birds with a net；collect；display；sieve；a gross；a surname

罗网【lo⁴mong⁵ 妄】net；trap

罗盘【lo⁴pun⁴ 盆】compass

罗列【lo⁴lid⁹ 裂】spread out；enumerate

罗织【lo⁴jig⁷ 积】frame up

咯【lo³ 罗³】〈auxil.〉∽ 啰【lo³】(see "啰")

偻【lo⁴ 罗】〈n.〉(see "偻偻")

锣【lo⁴ 罗】gong

锣鼓【lo⁴gu² 股】gong and drum

萝【lo⁴ 罗】trailing plants

萝卜【lo⁴bug⁹ 仆】boils；radish ＝ 萝白

萝藤【lo⁴teng⁴ 腾】Chinese wistaria

箩【lo⁴ 罗；lo¹ 啰】baskets

箩筐【lo⁴kuang¹ 卡汪¹】a large bamboo or wicker basket

箩仔【lo⁴jei² 济】small baskets ＝【普】小箩筐

箩底橙【lo⁴dei²qang² 邸撑²】the remaining goods, what is left；goods of inferior quality or one who is not educated ＝【普】别人挑剩的东西；智力低下的学生

氯【lo³ 罗³】the smell of things burnt ＝【普】物体烧焦的气味

裸【lo² 啰】bare；naked；exposed

裸露【lo²lou⁶ 路】uncovered；exposed

裸体【lo²tei² 睇】naked；nude

来【loi⁴ 莱；lei⁴ 黎】come；arrive；crop up；coming；future；next；ever since；about

来到【loi⁴dou³ 都³】arrive；come

来临【loi⁴lem⁴ 林】arrive；come；approach

来往【loi⁴wong⁵ 汪⁵】come and go；dealings

来源【loi⁴ yün⁴ 原 】source；origin；stem from

来由【loi⁴yeo² 油】reason；cause

来历【loi⁴lig⁹ 力】origin；source

来势【loi⁴xei³ 世】oncoming force

来回【loi⁴ wui⁴ 会⁴】make a round trip；back and forth；to and fro

来路【loi⁴lou⁶ 露】incoming road；origin

来路货【loi⁴lou²fo³ 佬课】imported goods ＝【普】进口货；舶来品

来客【loi⁴hag⁸ 赫】guest；visitor ＝ 来宾【loi⁴ben¹】

来访【loi⁴fong² 仿】come to visit；come to call

来信【loi⁴xên³ 讯】incoming letter

来电【loi⁴din⁶ 甸】incoming telegram

来年【loi⁴nin⁴ 捻⁴】the coming year；next year

来生【loi⁴xeng¹ 笙】next life ＝ 来世【loi⁴xei³ 细】

来得切【loi⁴ deg⁷ qid⁸ 德彻】in time ＝【普】来得及

来唔切【loi⁴m⁴qid⁸ 彻】won't do；be impermissible ＝【普】来不及

来日方长【loi⁴ yed⁹ fong¹ qêng⁴逸芳祥 】there will be ample time

来龙去脉【loi⁴lung⁴hêü³meg⁹ 隆虚³ 默】origin and development

徕 【loi⁴ 来】〈v.〉招徕（see"招徕"）

莱 【loi⁴ 来】radish

莱菔【loi⁴fug⁹ 服】〈n.〉radish

莱塞【loi⁴xeg⁷ 司克⁷】〈n.〉laser

赉 【loi⁶ 来⁶；lai⁶ 赖】grant；bestow（see "赏赉"）

睐 【loi⁴ 来】look at；glance（see"青睐"）

佬 【lou² 老²】a man ∽【普】汉子

劳 【lou⁴ 唠】work；labour；put sb. to the trouble of；toil；service；reward

劳动【lou⁴dung⁶ 洞】work；labour；physical labour

劳工【lou⁴gung⁴ 功】labourer；worker

劳力【lou⁴lig⁹ 历】labour；labour force

劳资【lou⁴ji¹ 知】labour and capital

劳苦【lou⁴fu² 府】toil；hard work

劳累【lou⁴lêü⁶ 类】tired；overworked

劳碌【lou⁴lug⁷ 辘】work hard；toil

劳气【lou⁴ hēi³ 戏 】to put in efforts ∽ 【普】费口舌；难教育

劳神【lou⁴xen⁴ 臣】bother；trouble

劳役【lou⁴yig⁹ 亦】penal servitude；corvee

劳逸【lou⁴yed⁹ 日】work and rest

劳民伤财【lou⁴men⁴xêng¹qoi⁴ 文湘才】 tire the people and drain the treasury

劳燕分飞【lou⁴yin³fen¹fēi¹ 烟³ 芬 非】 part；separate

唠 【lou⁴ 劳】chatter

唠嘈【lou⁴qou⁴ 曹】to speak loudly =【普】 高声地；大声地

唠叨【lou⁴tou¹ 滔】chatter；be garrulous

痨 【lou⁴ 劳】consumptive disease；tuberculosis

痨病【lou⁴bēng⁶ 柄⁶】tuberculosis

涝 【lou⁴ 劳】waterlogging

涝灾【lou⁴joi¹ 哉】damage or crop failure caused by waterlogging

姥 【lou⁵ 老】grandma

老 【lou⁵ 鲁】old；elderly；big；heavy；pass away；outdated；tough；always；very；the youngest；a surname

老表【lou⁵biu⁴ 标²】cousin ∽【普】表兄弟；表姐妹；乡亲

老卓【lou⁵qêg⁸ 次约⁸】familiar；skillful =【普】精通；熟练

老衬【lou⁵qen³ 趁】foolish；stupid =【普】笨蛋；傻瓜

老抽【lou⁵ qeo¹ 秋 】 concentrated soya sauce =【普】酱油（熟的）

老豆【lou⁵deo⁶ 斗⁶】father =【普】爸爸

老定【lou⁵ding⁶ 锭】calm；stable =【普】镇定；从容

老婵【lou⁵gêü² 举】a prostitute =【普】妓女

老积【lou⁵jig⁷ 织】mature =【普】少年人的成年化；小老头

老辣【lou⁵lad⁹ 捺⁹】cruel；ruthless∽【普】老练；老谋深算

老母【lou⁵mou² 帽²】mother =【普】妈妈

老鹏【lou⁵pang² 棚²】very close friends =【普】很要好的朋友；哥们

老细【lou⁵xei³ 世】boss；manager =【普】老板

老水【lou⁵xêü² 瑞²】one who does things by making use of one's experience ∽【普】办事老练；胸有成竹；不

慌不忙

老野【lou⁵yē⁵ 惹】old man＝【普】老东西；
　　老头

老友【lou⁵yeo⁵ 有】good, close friends ＝
　　老友记【lou⁵yeo⁵gēi³ 寄】＝【普】
　　老朋友；好朋友

老友鬼鬼【lou⁵yeo⁵guei²guei² 诡】friends
　　who have known each other for a
　　very long time and are very close
　　to each other ∽【普】很要好的样
　　子，彼此什么都不计较

老宗【lou⁵jung¹ 中】people with the same
　　surname＝【普】兄弟(同姓的人彼
　　此的称呼)

老鼠【lou⁵xü² 署】mouse; rat

老虎蟹【lou⁵fu²hai⁵ 府鞋】a type of crab;
　　determined; not afraid of anything
　　at all ∽【普】巨型凶恶的螃蟹
　　——很难对付的(也不怕)；铁了
　　心；横下心

老虎乸【lou⁵fu²na² 府那²】female tiger; a
　　fierce woman＝【普】(比喻)悍妇；
　　凶女人

老姑婆【lou⁵gu¹po⁴ 沽颇⁴】an unmarried
　　lady＝【普】老处女；未出嫁的老
　　妇人

老嫖寨【lou⁵ gêü² jai² 举斋²】a house
　　where all the prostitutes stay in＝
　　【普】娼寮；妓女窝

老夭茄【lou⁵ngen¹kē² 银¹卡诶²】to refer
　　to one who is small in size yet hav-
　　ing a mature thinking ∽【普】瘦
　　弱矮小的人(比喻)

老猫烧须【lou⁵mao¹xiu¹xou¹ 矛¹消苏】to
　　refer to the others laughing when
　　one who is experienced or an ex-
　　pert makes mistake ∽【普】老练

的人办事出了差错；丢脸

老虎头上钉虱乸【lou⁵fu²teo⁴xêng⁶dēng¹
　　xed⁷na² 府投尚得镜¹失那²】to
　　refer to one who is very brave ∽
　　【普】太岁头上动土

老龟婆【lou⁵guei¹po² 硅颇】a woman run-
　　ning a brothel; an unmarried lady
　　＝老嫖婆【lou⁵gêü²po⁴】＝【普】老
　　鸨(妓院里管妓女的老妇人)

老人家【lou⁵ yen⁴ ga¹ 仁加】old men or
　　women; the aged; the old; par-
　　ents

老实【lou⁵ xed⁹ 失⁹】honest; frank; well-
　　behaved; naive; simpleminded

老牌【lou⁵pai⁴ 排】old brand

老乡【lou⁵hêng¹ 香】fellow-townsman;
　　fellow-villager

老爷【lou⁵yē⁴ 椰】master; grandpa

老公【lou⁵gung¹ 工】husband＝【普】丈夫

老婆【lou⁵po⁴ 颇⁴】wife＝【普】妻子

老师【lou⁵xi¹ 司】teacher

老手【lou⁵xeo² 守】old-hand; old stager;
　　veteran

老总【lou⁵jung² 肿】an old form of address
　　to a soldier; used with a surname
　　as an affectionate form of addres
　　to a general or high-ranking com-
　　mander of the PLA

老底【lou⁵dei² 低²】sb.'s past

老夫【lou⁵fu¹ 孚】an old fellow like me

老调【lou⁵diu⁶ 掉】hackneyed theme; pla-
　　titude

老本【lou⁵bun² 苯】principal; capital

老成【lou⁵xing⁴ 诚】experienced; steady

老粗【lou⁵qou¹ 操】uneducated person

老伯【lou⁵bag⁸ 白⁸】uncle

老百姓【lou⁵bag⁸xing³ 胜】common people

老大难【lou⁵ dai⁶ nan⁴ 歹⁶ 挪晏⁶】long-standing, big and difficult (problem)

老狐狸【lou⁵ wu⁴ lēi² 胡李²】old fox; crafty scoundrel

老皇历【lou⁵ wong⁴ lig⁹ 王力】last year's calendar; old history

老交情【lou⁵ gao¹ qing⁴ 胶程】long-standing friendship

老毛病【lou⁵ mou⁴ bēng⁶ 无柄⁶】old trouble

老天爷【lou⁵ tin¹ yē²田¹椰】God; Heavens

老顽固【lou⁵ wan⁴ gu³ 环故】old diehard; old fogey

老黄牛【lou⁵ wong⁴ ngeo⁴ 王藕⁴】willing ox; a person who serves the people wholeheartedly

老规矩【lou⁵ kuei¹ gêü² 亏举】old rules and regulations

老资格【lou⁵ ji¹ gag⁷ 知隔】old-timer; veteran

老当益壮【lou⁵ dong¹ yig⁷ jong³ 珰亿葬】old but vigorous

老奸巨猾【lou⁵ gan¹ gêü⁶ wad⁹ 间¹具滑】a past master of machination and manoeuvre

老谋深算【lou⁵ meo⁴ xem¹ xün³ 牟心蒜】circumspect and farseeing

老生常谈【lou⁵ xeng¹ xêng⁴ tam⁴ 笙裳谭】commonplace

老态龙钟【lou⁵ tai⁴ lung⁴ jung¹ 太隆中】senile; doddering

老羞成怒【lou⁵ xeo¹ xing⁴ nou⁶ 修承奴⁶】fly into a rage out of shame

卤【lou⁵ 老】bittern; halogen; stew in soy sauce

卤水【lou⁵ xêü² 瑞²】bittern; brine

卤素【lou⁵ xou³ 数】halogen

卤味【lou⁵ mēi² 未²】pot-stewed fowl, meat, etc. served cold; salted pork

鲁【lou⁵ 老】stupid; rash; rough; rude; a surname

鲁莽【lou⁵ mong⁵ 网】crude and rash; rash

鲁钝【lou⁵ dên⁶ 顿】dull-witted; obtuse; stupid

橹【lou⁵ 鲁】scull; sweep

虏【lou⁵ 老】take prisoner; captive

虏获【lou⁵ wog⁹ 乌恶⁹】capture; men and arms captured

掳【lou⁵ 老】carry off; capture

掳掠【lou⁵ lêg⁹ 略】pillage; loot

卢【lou⁴ 劳】a surname

卢比【lou⁴ bēi² 俾】rupee

卢森堡【lou⁵ xem¹ bou² 心保²】〈n.〉Luxembourg

芦【lou⁴ 劳】reed

芦苇【lou⁴ wei⁵ 伟】reed; bottle gourd

芦笙【lou⁵ xeng¹ 生】a reed-pipe wind instrument, used by the Miao, Yao and Dong nationalities

鸬【lou⁴ 卢】〈n.〉鸬鹚【lou⁴ qi⁴ 慈】cormorant

鲈【lou⁴ 卢】〈n.〉perch

轳【lou⁴ 卢】〈n.〉辘轳【lug⁷ lou⁴】(see "辘轳")

颅【lou⁴ 卢】cranium; skull

颅骨【lou⁴ gued⁷ 掘⁷】skull

路【lou⁶ 露】road; way; distance; means; line; region; route; sort

路数【lou⁶xou³ 扫】plans; way; exact details; a movement in martial arts

路径【lou⁶ging³ 茎】route; way; method

路途【lou⁶tou⁴ 图】road; path; way; journey

路线【lou⁶xin³ 扇】route; line

路上【lou⁶ xêng⁶ 尚】on the road; on the way

路面【lou⁶min⁶ 免⁶】road surface

路口【lou⁶heo² 候²】crossing

路标【lou⁶biu¹ 彪】road sign; route sign

路灯【lou⁶deng¹ 登】road lamp

路轨【lou⁶guei² 鬼】rail; track

路过【lou⁶guo³ 戈³】pass by or through(a place)

路障【lou⁶jêng³ 涨】roadblock

路遥知马力【lou⁶yiu⁴ji¹ma⁵lig⁹ 摇支玛历】distance tests a horse's stamina

露【lou⁶ 路】dew; syrup; show; reveal

露水【lou⁶xêu² 瑞²】dew

露珠【lou⁶jü¹ 朱】dewdrop

露天【lou⁶tin¹ 田¹】in the open(air); outdoors

露宿【lou⁶xug⁷ 缩】sleep in the open

露骨【lou⁶gued⁷ 掘⁷】thinly veiled; undisguised

露头角【lou⁶teo⁴gog⁸ 投各】budding

赂【lou⁶ 路】〈v.〉贿赂【fui²lou⁶ 灰²】bribe; bribery

鹭【lou⁶ 路】〈n.〉egret; heron

璐【lou⁶ 路】〈n.〉jade

萠【long¹ 啷】〈n.〉萠其【long¹gêi¹ 箕】brake(fern)=【普】蕨(生于山野, 茎硬似骨)

啷【long¹ 萠】〈onomatopoeia〉

啷啷响【long¹long¹hêng² 享】the sound of bell

潝【long² 郎²】to wash

潝口【long²heo² 厚²】to gargle=【普】漱口

【long³ 朗³】fill up=【普】垫起

郎【long⁴ 狼】an ancient official title; my son; my darling

儿郎【yi⁴long⁴ 而】my son

郎君【long⁴guen¹ 军】my darling

狼【long⁴ 郎】wolf

狼忙【long⁴ mong⁴ 亡 】in a hurry; in a rush=【普】匆忙

狼胎【long⁴toi¹ 台¹】fierce; heartless=【普】凶狠

狼狗【long⁴geo² 九】wolfhound

狼藉【long⁴jig⁹ 直】in disorder

狼狈【long⁴bui³ 背】in a difficult position

狼狈为奸【long⁴ bui³ wei⁴ gan¹ 背维间¹】act in collusion with each other

狼吞虎咽【long⁴ten¹fu²yin³ 替因¹ 府燕】rapacious as a wolf and savage as a cur; cruel and unscrupulous; ungrateful

廊【long⁴ 郎】porch; corridor; veranda

画廊【wa²long⁴ 话²】picture gallery

榔【long⁴ 郎】〈n.〉槟榔【ben¹long⁴ 宾】a species of apple which is slightly sour and astringent

螂【long⁴ 郎】〈n.〉螳螂【tong⁴long⁴】(see "螳螂")

锒【long⁴ 郎】iron chains; clang

锒铛入狱【long⁴dong¹yeb⁹yug⁹ 当邑⁹ 玉】be chained and thrown into prison

琅【long⁴ 郎；long⁵ 朗】〈onomatopoeia〉

琅琅读书声【long⁵long⁵dug⁹xü¹xing¹ 独输升】the sound of reading aloud

朗【long⁵ 郎⁵】light; bright; loud and clear

朗读【long⁵dug⁹ 独】read aloud

朗诵【long⁵ jung⁶ 仲】read aloud with expression; recite

塱【long⁵ 朗】a vast field ∽【普】大片的田野

浪【long⁶ 晾】wave; billow; unrestrained

浪潮【long⁶qiu⁴ 樵】tide; wave

浪花【long⁶fa¹ 化¹】spray; spindrift

浪头【long⁶teo⁴ 投】wave; trend

浪荡【long⁶dong⁶ 当⁶】loiter about; dissolute

浪费【long⁶fei³ 废】waste; squander

浪漫【long⁶man⁶ 万】romantic

浪子回头【long⁶ji²wui⁴teo⁴ 止会⁴ 投】return of the prodigal son

晾【long⁶ 浪】dry in the air; dry in the sun

晾干【long⁶gon¹ 竿】dry by airing

晾衫【long⁶xam¹ 三】sun clothes =【普】晾衣服

撨【log⁷ 落⁷】pull out =【普】拨掉(牙齿、钉子之类)

撨牙【log⁷nga⁴ 芽】pull out a tooth =【普】拔牙

嗠【log⁷ 洛⁷】〈onomatopoeia〉

嗠嗠声【log⁷log⁷xēng¹ 是镜¹】metaphor language is fluent =【普】语言流利(比喻)

骆【log⁸ 洛】camel; a surname

骆驼【log⁸to⁴ 拖⁴】camel

洛【log⁸ 骆】〈n.〉洛阳【log⁸yêng⁴ 杨】Luoyang

荦【log⁸ 骆】prominent; outstanding

荦荦大方【log⁸log⁸dai⁶fong¹ 歹⁶ 芳】salient points

络【log⁸ 骆】sth. resembling a net; branches of channels; twine; wind

络脉【log⁸meg⁹ 默】collaterals which connect channels

络腮胡子【log⁸xoi¹wu⁴ji²是哀¹ 糊止】whiskers

络绎不绝【log⁸yig⁹bed⁷jüd⁹ 亦毕嗄⁹】in an endless stream

珞【log⁸ 洛】〈n.〉赛璐珞【qoi³lou⁶log⁸ 路洛】celluloid

落【log⁹ 乐】fall; drop; lower; leave behind; down; lag behind; fall onto; receive

落地【log⁹dēi⁶ 得希⁶】fall to the ground

落车【log⁹qē 奢】to get down from a car =【普】下车

落定【log⁹ dēng⁶得镜⁶】to pay deposit =【普】给定金

落力【log⁹lig⁹ 历】serious; hardworking =【普】下力气

落堂【log⁹tong⁴ 唐】recess time at schools =【普】下课；放学

落面【log⁹ min² 免²】to feel ashamed = 【普】丢脸

落形【log⁹ying⁴ 仍】to refer to one being too thin that one can hardly be recognized by others = 【普】(身体)消瘦得不像样

落成【log⁹xing⁴ 承】completion(of a building, etc.)

落得【log⁹deg⁷ 德】get；end in

落第【log⁹ dei⁶弟 】fail in an imperial examination

落后【log⁹heo⁶ 候】fall behind；backward

落空【log⁹hung¹ 红¹】come to nothing；fall

落难【log⁹ nan⁶ 挪晏⁶】meet with misfortune

落实【log⁹xed⁹ 失⁹】practicable；carry out

落魄【log⁹pag⁸ 拍】be in dire straits；casual

落网【log⁹mong⁵ 妄】fall into the net—be caught；be captured

落选【log⁹xün³ 损】fail to be elected

落井下石【log⁹jēng²ha⁶xēg⁹ 支镜⁹ 夏硕】hit a person when he's down

落荒而逃【log⁹fong¹yi⁴teo⁴ 方移图】take to the wilds—be defeated and flee the battlefield；take to flight

落手落脚【log⁹xeo²log⁹gêg⁸ 守格约⁸】to do things on one's own ∽【普】动手动脚——真参与

落雨丝湿【log⁹yü⁵xi¹xeb⁷ 语句拾⁷】to refer to the roads becoming slippery due to rain ∽【普】因雨而路滑

乐【log⁹ 落；ngog⁹ 岳】happy；cheerful；joyful；enjoy；laugh；music；a surname

乐呵呵【log⁹ ho¹ ho¹贺¹】buoyant；happy and gay

乐滋滋【log⁹ji¹ji¹ 支】contented；pleased

乐陶陶【log⁹tou⁴tou⁴ 图】cheerful；joyful

乐观【log⁹gun¹ 官】optimistic；hopeful

乐趣【log⁹qêü³ 翠】delight；pleasure；joy

乐意【log⁹yi³ 薏】be willing to；pleased

乐于【log⁹yü¹ 迂】be happy to

乐得【log⁹deg⁷ 德】be only too glad to

乐园【log⁹yün⁴ 元】paradise

乐不可支【log⁹bed⁷ho²ji¹ 毕何² 之】overjoyed

乐极生悲【log⁹ gig⁹ xeng¹ bēi¹击⁹ 笙卑】extreme joy begets sorrow

乐队【ngog⁹dêü² 堆²】orchestra；band

乐曲【ngog⁹kug⁹ 卡屋⁷】musical composition；music

乐器【ngog⁹hēi³ 气】musical instrument

乐谱【ngog⁹pou² 普】music score；music

烙【log⁸ 洛】brand；iron；bake in a pan

烙饼【log⁸bēng² 柄²】a kind of pancake

烙印【log⁸yen³ 因³】brand

爧【lung¹ 龙¹】burn till burnt

烧爧【xiu¹lung¹ 消¹】burn till burnt = 【普】烧焦；烧糊了

傮【lung³ 龙³】bow (one's head) = 【普】俯

傮低【lung³dei¹ 帝¹】bow (one's head or body) = 【普】弯腰俯身

隆【lung⁴ 龙】grand；intense；prosperous；swell

隆重【lung⁴jung⁶ 仲】grand；solemn

隆冬【lung⁴dung¹ 东】midwinter

隆情厚谊【lung⁴qing⁴heo⁵yi⁴ 程候⁵ 移】profound sentiments of friendship

窿【lung¹ 龙¹】〈n.〉窟窿【gued⁹ lung¹ 掘】hole; debt

窿窿罅罅【lung¹ lung¹ la³ la³ 罗啊³】places that are isolated and small ∽【普】小孔和缝隙（形容很细微的地方）

龙【lung⁴ 隆】dragon; imperial; a huge extinct reptile; a surname

龙王【lung⁴ wong⁴ 黄】the Dragon King (the God of Rain in Chinese mythology)

龙头【lung⁴ teo⁴ 投】tap; faucet; handle-bar

龙虾【lung⁴ ha¹ 哈】lobster

龙舟【lung⁴ jeo¹ 周】dragon boat = 龙船【lung⁴ xün⁴】

龙眼【lung⁴ ngan⁵ 雁⁵】longan =【普】桂圆

龙虱【lung⁴ xed⁷ 室】predacious diving beetle

龙卷风【lung⁴ gün² fung¹ 绢² 丰】tornado

龙飞凤舞【lung⁴ fēi¹ fung⁶ mou⁵ 非风⁶ 母】like dragon flying and phoenixes dancing—lively and vigorous flourshes in calligraphy

龙腾虎跃【lung⁴ teng⁴ fu² yêg⁸ 藤府约】dragon rising and tigers lea-ping—a scene of bustling and enthusiasm

龙争虎斗【lung⁴ jeng¹ fu² deo³ 憎府豆³】a fierce struggle between two evenly – matched opponents

龙精虎猛【lung⁴ jing¹ fu² mang⁵ 贞府锰】lively; energetic

笼【lung⁴ 龙; lung⁵ 龙⁵】cage; coop; basket; (food) steamer envelop; cover; a large box or chest; trunk

笼鸟【lung⁴ niu⁵ 挪妖⁵】cage bird

鸡笼【gei¹ lung⁴ 计¹】chicken coop

笼络【lung⁵ log⁸ 洛】draw over

笼统【lung⁵ tung² 桶】general; sweeping

笼罩【lung⁵ jao³ 爪³】envelop; shroud

垄【lung⁵ 拢】ridge (in a field); raised path between fields

垄沟【lung⁵ keo¹ 卡欧¹】field ditch; furrow

垄断【lung⁵ dün⁶ 段】monopolize

拢【lung² 龙²】approach; reach; sum up; hold together

靠拢【kao³ lung⁵ 卡拗³】draw close; close up

陇【lung⁵ 垄】another name for Gansu Province

聋【lung⁴ 龙】deaf; hard of hearing

聋哑【lung⁴ nga² 雅²】deaf and dumb; deaf—mutes

咙【lung⁴ 龙】〈n.〉喉咙 (see "喉咙")

栊【lung² 拢】cage; case

趟栊【tong³ lung² 烫】a lig wooden case used to keep clothes

胧【lung⁴ 龙】〈a.〉朦胧【mung⁴ lung⁴】(see "朦胧")

珑【lung⁴ 龙】〈a.〉玲珑【ling⁴ lung⁴】(see "玲珑")

茏【lung⁴ 龙】verdant

茏葱【lung⁴ qung¹ 冲】verdant; luxuriantly green

弄【lung⁶ 龙⁶】play with; play; do; get; lane; alley

弄错【lung⁶ qo³ 挫】make a mistake; misunderstand

弄坏【lung⁶ wai⁶ 歪⁶】ruin; put out of order

弄僵【lung⁶gêng¹ 羌】bring to a deadlock; deadlock

弄清【lung⁶qing¹ 青】make clear; clarify

弄通【lung⁶tung¹ 同¹】get a good grasp of

弄假成真【lung⁶ ga² xing⁴ jen¹ 贾承珍 】 what was make-believe has become reality

弄巧反拙【lung⁶hao²fan²jüd⁸ 考返嘅】try to be clever only to end up with a blunder; outsmart oneself

碌【lug⁷ 辘】commonplace; mediocre; busy; roll

碌碌【lug⁷lug⁷】mediocre; busy with miscellaneous work

碌柚【lug⁷yeo² 由²】pomelo＝【普】柚子

辘【lug⁷ 碌】windlass; winch; roll

辘轳【lug⁷lou⁴ 卢】windlass; winch

辘辘【lug⁷lug⁷】〈onomatopoeia〉rumble

辘落嚟【lug⁷log⁹lei⁴ 乐黎】rolling down＝【普】滚下来

陆【lug⁹ 六】land; six; a surname

陆地【lug⁹dēi⁶ 得希⁶】dry land; land

陆路【lug⁹lou⁶ 露】land route

陆军【lug⁹ guen¹君 】 ground force; land force; army

陆续【lug⁹jug⁹ 逐】one after another

陆运【lug⁹wen⁶ 混】land transportation

六【lug⁹ 陆】six

六月【lug⁹yūd⁹ 越】June; the Sixth moon

六面体【lug⁹min⁶tei² 免² 睇】hexahedron

六腑【lug⁹fu² 府】the six hollow organs

六亲不认【lug⁹qen¹bed⁷ying⁶ 趁¹ 毕英⁶】 refuse to have anything to do with all one's relatives and friends

六神无主【lug⁹xen⁴mou⁴jū² 臣毛煮】all six vital organs failing to func-tion—in a state of utter stupefaction

录【lug⁹ 六】record; copy; write down; employ; tape-record; register

录取【lug⁹qêū² 娶】enroll; recruit

录用【lug⁹yung⁶ 容⁶】employ

录音【lug⁹yem¹ 阴】sound recording

录像机【lug⁹jêng⁶gēi¹ 象基】videocorder

禄【lug⁹ 六】official's salary in feudal China

绿【lug⁹ 六】green

绿叶【lug⁹yib⁹ 业】green leaves

绿洲【lug⁹jeo¹ 州】oasis

绿化【lug⁹fa³ 花³】afforest

绿茶【lug⁹qa⁴ 查】green tea

绿豆【lug⁹deo⁶ 窦】mung bean; green gram

绿灯【lug⁹deng¹ 登】green light

绿林好汉【lug⁹lem⁴hou²hon³ 淋蒿² 看】 heroes of the greenwood; forest outlaws; brigands

戮【lug⁹ 六】kill; to step on; unite; join

戮力同心【lug⁹lig⁹tung⁴xem¹ 历铜深】u-nite in a concerted effort

鹿【lug⁹ 六】deer

鹿茸【lug⁹yung⁴ 容】pilose antler（of a young stag）

鹿死谁手【lug⁹xēi²xêū⁴xeo² 四² 垂守】at whose hand will deer die—who wins the prize

麓【lug⁷ 碌】the foot of a hill or mountain

椂【lug⁷ 碌】⟨*classifier*⟩ the unit of rod, club, cudgel, stick, etc.

一椂木【yed⁷lug⁷mug⁹ 碌目】a wood—cannot move =【普】一根木头（似的），不推不动

煪【lug⁹ 六】to boil with hot water

煪亲【lug⁹qen¹ 趁¹】to boil ⌒【普】（被热的东西）烫着

睩【lug⁷ 碌】to open one's eyes really big（眼睩睩【ngan⁵lug⁷lug⁷】）

撩【liu¹ 了¹；liu² 了²；liu⁴ 聊】tease; tantalize; provoke; stir up; hold up; sprinkle(water)

撩落嚟【liu²log⁹lei⁴ 洛⁹ 黎】tease down ⌒【普】撩拨（高处物体）使之落下

撩拨【liu² bud² 勃】tease; banter; incite; provoke

撩㑞【liu²nou¹ 挪欧¹】tease to make sb. angry =【普】挑逗使某人恼怒

鹩【liu¹ 了¹；liu⁴ 辽】⟨*n.*⟩鹩哥【liu¹go¹ 歌】hill myna

缭【liu⁴ 辽；liu² 了²】entangled; sew with slanting stitches

缭绕【liu⁴yiu⁵ 妖⁵】curl up; wind around

缭乱【liu⁴lün⁶ 联】confused; in a turmoil

蓼【liu¹ 了¹】knotweed(see"辣蓼")

潦【liu⁴ 辽；lou⁵ 老】sloppy; hasty; careless

潦草【liu⁴qou² 曹²】(of handwriting)hasty and careless; sloppy; slovenly

潦倒【liu⁴dou² 捣】be frustrated

燎【liu⁴ 辽】singe; burn

燎原【liu⁴yün⁴ 元】set the prairie ablaze

燎天【liu⁴tin¹ 田¹】inappropriate request ⌒

【普】妄求

獠【liu⁴ 辽】long, sharp, protruding teeth(獠牙【liu⁴nga⁴ 芽】)

嘹【liu⁴ 辽】⟨*a.*⟩嘹亮【liu⁴lêng⁶ 量⁶】loud and clear

寮【liu⁴ 辽】small house; hut

寮棚【liu⁴pang⁴ 鹏】shed; hut

僚【liu⁴ 辽】official; an associate in office

僚属【liu⁴xug⁹ 熟】officials under someone in authority; staff

寥【liu⁴ 辽】few; silent

寥廓【liu⁴kuog⁸ 郭】boundless; vast

寥落【liu⁴log⁹ 洛⁹】few and between; sparse

寥寥无几【liu⁴liu⁴mou⁴gēi² 毛己】very few

聊【liu⁴ 辽】merely; just; a little; chat

聊且【liu⁴qē² 扯】tentatively; for the moment

聊天【liu⁴ tin¹ 田¹】chat = 倾闲偈【king¹ han⁴gei²】

聊以自慰【liu⁴yi⁵ji⁶wei³ 耳治畏】just to console oneself

辽【liu⁴ 僚】distant; faraway

辽阔【liu⁴fud⁸ 夫活⁸】vast; extensive

辽远【liu⁴yün⁵ 软】distant; faraway

辽宁【liu⁴ning⁴ 拧⁴】Liaoning Province

了【liu⁵ 撩⁵；liu⁴ 辽】know clearly; understand; end; finish; settle; dispose of; entirely; ⟨*auxil.*⟩show v. + ed

了事【liu⁵ xi⁶士】dispose of a matter; get sth. over

了却【liu⁵kêg⁸ 卡约⁸】settle；solve

了结【liu⁵gid⁸ 洁】finish；wind up

了得【liu⁵deg⁷ 德】how outrageous = 得了【deg⁷liu⁵】

了解【liu⁵gai² 介²】understand；find out

了望【liu⁴mong⁶ 亡·⁶】watch from a height or a distance

了不得【liu⁵bed⁷deg⁷ 毕德】terrific；terrible

了不起【liu⁵bed⁷hêi² 毕喜】amazing；terrific

料【liu² 撩²；liu⁶ 廖】expect；anticipate；material；stuff；(grain)feed；makings

料车【liu²qê¹ 奢】skip；skip car

料到【liu⁶dou³ 都³】foresee；expect

料想【liu⁶ xêng² 赏 】expect；think；presume

料理【liu⁶lêi⁵ 李】arrange；manage

料峭【liu⁶qiu³ 俏】chilly

料事如神【liu⁶xi⁶yü⁴xen⁴ 士鱼臣】predict like a prophet

疗【liu⁴ 辽】treat；cure

疗法【liu⁴fad⁸ 发】therapy；treatment

疗程【liu⁴qing⁴ 情】course of treatment

疗效【liu⁴hao⁶ 考⁶】curative effect

疗养【liu⁴yêng⁵ 氧】recuperate；convalesce

廖【liu⁶ 料⁶】a surname

摺【liu¹ 了¹】put down；throw down；shoot down

摺担子【liu¹dam³ji² 胆³ 止】throw down one's job.

镣【liu⁴ 辽】fetters

镣铐【liu⁴kao³ 靠】fetters and handcuffs

敛【lim⁶ 帘⁶；lim⁵ 帘⁵】hold back；collect

敛财【lim⁶qoi⁴才 】accumulate wealth by unfair means

敛迹【lim⁵jig⁷ 即】lie low

敛容【lim⁵yung⁴ 溶】assume a serious expression

脸【lim⁵ 廉⁵】face；countenance；front

脸色【lim⁵xig⁷ 式】complexion；facial expression

脸皮【lim⁵pêi⁴ 脾】face；cheek

脸谱【lim⁵pou² 普】types of facial makeup in operas

脸红脖子粗【lim⁵hung⁴bud⁸ji²qou¹ 洪勃止操】flush with agitation

殓【lim⁵ 脸】put a body into a coffin；encoffin

奁【lim⁴ 帘；lim⁵ 脸】a toilet case used by women in ancient China

帘【lim⁴ 廉】flag as shop sign；curtain

窗帘【qêng¹lim⁴ 昌】window curtain

帘布【lim⁴bou³ 报】cord fabric(in tyres)

廉【lim⁴ 帘】honest and clean；inexpensive

廉耻【lim⁴qi³ 始】sense of honour

廉洁【lim⁴gid⁸ 结】honest

廉价【lim⁴ga³ 嫁】low-priced；cheap

镰【lim⁴ 廉】sickle(镰刀【lim⁴dou¹ 都】)

镰鱼【lim⁴yü² 淤】moorish idol

鲢【lin⁴ 连】silver carp(鲢鱼【lin⁴yü² 淤】)

连【lin⁴ 鲢】link；join；in succession；repeatedly；including；company；even；a surname

连带【lin⁴dai³ 戴】related

连贯【lin⁴gun³ 罐】link up；coherent；consistent

连接【lin⁴jib⁸ 支叶⁸】join；link

连续【lin⁴jug⁹ 逐】continuous；successive

连同【lin⁴ tung⁴铜 】 together with；along with

连绵【lin⁴min⁴ 棉】continuous；unbroken

连连【lin⁴lin⁴】repeatedly；again and again

连忙【lin⁴mong⁴ 亡】promptly；at once

连环【lin⁴wan⁴ 寰】chain of rings

连日【lin⁴yed⁹ 逸】day after day

连气【lin⁴ hēi³ 戏 】 continuously；nonstop ∽【普】接连

连埋【lin⁴mai⁴ 买⁴】to keep；to tidy up；to remove；to shift ∽【普】连同

连年【lin⁴nin⁴ 捻⁴】for years running

连任【lin⁴ yem⁶ 壬⁶】 renew one's term of office

连夜【lin⁴yē⁶ 野⁶】the same night

连队【lin⁴dêü² 堆²】company

连缀【lin⁴ jüd⁸绝⁸】 join together；put together

连珠炮【lin⁴jü¹pao³ 朱泡³】continuous firing

连篇累牍【lin⁴ pin¹ lêü⁶ jug⁹ 编类续】lengthy and tedious

连锁反应【lin⁴xo²fan²ying³ 所返英³】chain reaction

连累【lin⁴lêü⁶ 类】implicate；involve

莲【lin⁴ 连】lotus

莲花【lin⁴fa¹ 化¹】lotus flower

莲子【lin⁴ji² 止】lotus seed

涟【lin⁴ 连】〈n.〉涟漪【lin⁴yi² 椅】ripples

撵【lin⁵ 辇】drive out；oust；catch up

辇【lin⁵ 撵】a man-drawn carriage used in ancient times；imperial carriage

怜【lin⁴ 连】sympathize with；love tenderly

怜爱【lin⁴ngoi³ 外³】love tenderly

怜悯【lin⁴men⁵ 敏】pity；take pity on

怜惜【lin⁴xig⁷ 色】take pity on；have pity for

练【lin⁶ 炼】white silk；boil and scour raw silk；practise；train；experienced

练功【lin⁶gung¹ 工】practise one's skill

练习【lin⁶jab⁹ 袭】practise；exercise

练球【lin⁶keo⁴ 求】practise a ball game

炼【lin⁶ 练】smelt；refine；temper with fire

炼钢【lin⁶gong³ 岗³】steelmaking；steel-smelting

炼铁【lin⁶tid⁸ 替热⁸】iron-smelting

炼奶【lin⁶ nai⁵乃 】condensed milk＝【普】炼乳

炼制【lin⁶jei³ 济】refine

揵【lin² 炼²】pinch；mould；fabricate

揵埋【lin²mai⁴ 买⁴】mediate；carry on with sb.

链【lin⁶ 练；lin² 练²】chain；cable length

链条【lin⁶tiu⁴ 挑⁴】chain；roller chain

链轨【lin²guei² 鬼】caterpillar track

链球菌【lin⁶keo⁴kuen² 求捆】streptococcus

链霉素【lin⁴mui⁴xou³ 梅数】streptomycin

楝【lin⁶ 练；lin¹ 练】〈n.〉苦楝树【fu²lin¹xü⁶书¹】chinaberry

拎【ling¹ 令¹】carry；to take；to hold；use as ∽【普】提；提取；拿

拎住【ling¹ jū⁶ 注⁶】was carrying =【普】提着

拎走【ling¹ jeo² 酒】take it away =【普】拿去

羚【ling³ 令³】the surface of a body is glossy and has lustre

羚蜡蜡【ling³ lab⁸ lab⁸ 罗鸭⁸】very glossy and lustrous =【普】很光滑，充满光泽

玲【ling⁴ 灵】exquisitely carved

玲珑浮突【lin⁴ lung⁴ feo⁴ ded⁹ 灵龙否⁴ 得核⁹】to describe things that are delicate, clear, elegant and beautiful ∽【普】玲珑剔透

伶【ling⁴ 玲】actor or actress

伶仃【ling⁴ ding¹ 丁 】left alone without help; lonely

伶俐【ling⁴ lēi⁶ 利】clever; bright

铃【ling⁴ 玲；ling¹ 拎】bell; anything in the shape of a bell

铃铃【ling¹ ling¹】small bell =【普】铃铛

铃鼓【ling⁴ gu² 古】tambourine

瓴【ling⁴ 玲】water jar

囹【ling⁴ 玲】〈n.〉囹圄【ling⁴ yū⁵ 语】jail; prison

羚【ling⁴ 玲】〈n.〉羚羊【ling⁴ yêng⁴ 洋】antelope

聆【ling⁴ 玲】〈v.〉聆听【ling⁴ ting³ 亭³】listen; hear

翎【ling⁴ 玲】〈n.〉翎毛【ling⁴ mou⁴ 无】plume

苓【ling⁴ 玲】〈n.〉茯苓【fug⁹ ling⁴ 伏】fuling(poris cocos)

凌【ling⁴ 玲】insult; rise high

凌辱【ling⁴ yug⁹ 玉】insult; humiliate

凌厉【ling⁴ lei⁶ 丽】swift and fierce

凌驾【ling⁴ ga³ 价】override

凌云【ling⁴ wen⁴ 魂】reach the clouds

凌晨【ling⁴ xen⁴ 辰】in the small hours

菱【ling⁴ 玲】ling; water chestnut

菱角【ling⁴ gog⁸ 各】ling; water chestnut

菱形【ling⁴ ying⁴ 型】rhombus

陵【ling⁴ 玲】hill; mausoleum

陵墓【ling⁴ mou⁶ 务】mausoleum; tomb

陵园【ling⁴ yün⁴ 元】cemetery

绫【ling⁴ 玲】damask silk

绫罗绸缎【ling⁴ lo⁴ qeo⁴ dün⁶ 锣筹段】silk and satins

棱【ling⁴ 玲】arris; ridge

棱角【ling⁴ gog⁸ 各 】edges and corners; edge

棱镜【ling⁴ gēng³ 格颈³】prism

愣【ling⁴ 玲】distracted; rash

愣神【ling⁴ xen⁴ 臣】stare blankly

鲮【ling⁴ 玲；lēng⁴ 罗镜⁴】〈n.〉鲮鱼【ling⁴ yū² 淤²】dace

灵【ling⁴；lēng⁴ 罗镜⁴】quick; clever; effective spirit; fairy; bier

灵魂【ling⁴ wen⁴ 云】soul; spirit

灵活【ling⁴ wud⁹ 乌阔⁹】nimble; agile; elastic

灵敏【ling⁴ men⁵ 蚊⁵】sensitive; keen

灵巧【ling⁴ hao² 考】dexterous; nimble

灵机【ling⁴ gēi¹ 基】sudden inspiration

灵感【ling⁴gen² 锦】inspiration

灵验【ling⁴yim⁶ 艳⁶】effective; right

灵枢【ling⁴geo⁶ 旧】bier

灵芝【ling⁴ji¹ 之】glossy ganoderma

灵丹妙药【ling⁴dan¹miu⁶yêg⁹ 单庙若】miraculous cure; panacea

棂　【ling⁴ 玲】(window) lattice; lattice-work

零　【ling⁴ 玲】zero sign (0); nought; odd; zero; part; wither and fall; nill

零丁【ling⁴ding¹ 定¹】not whole number =【普】不完整；余下零数

零舍【ling⁴xê³ 泻】special = 宁舍【ling⁴xê³】=【普】特别；分外；格外

龄　【ling⁴ 玲】age; years; duration

领　【ling⁵ 岭⁵；lêng⁵ 罗镜⁵】neck; collar; outline; lead; receive; understand

领导【ling⁵dou⁶ 道】lead; leader; leadership

领教【ling⁵gao³ 较】much obliged; ask advice

领会【ling⁵wui⁶ 汇】understand; grasp

领悟【ling⁵ng⁶ 误】comprehend; grasp

领先【ling⁵xin¹ 仙】lead

领头【ling⁵teo⁴ 投】take the lead

领土【ling⁵tou² 吐²】territory

领袖【ling⁵jeo⁶ 就】leader

领事【ling⁵xi⁶ 是】consul

领域【ling⁵wig⁹ 乌益⁹】territory; field

领带【lêng⁵dai² 歹】necktie; tie

领取【lêng⁵qêü² 娶】draw; receive

领情【lêng⁵qing⁴ 程】feel grateful to sb.

领咗野【lêng⁵jo⁵yê⁵ 助² 惹】fall into an ambush =【普】中了计

岭　【ling⁵ 令²；lêng⁵ 罗镜⁵】mountain; mountain range; ridge

岭南【ling⁵nam⁴ 男】south of the Five Ridges (the area covering Guangdong, Guangxi and Hainan)

令　【ling⁶ 另】command; order; make; season; good; your; an ancient official title; drinking game

令尊【ling⁶jün¹ 专】your father

令行禁止【ling⁶heng⁴gem³ji² 衡咁³ 子】strict enforcement of orders and prohibitions

另　【ling⁶ 令】other; another; separate

另外【ling⁶ngoi⁶ 碍】in addition; moreover

另眼相看【ling⁶ ngan⁵ xêng¹ hon¹ 雁⁵ 双 汉¹】regard sb. with special respect; see sb. in a new light

另起炉灶【ling⁶hêi²lou⁴jou³ 喜卢做³】set up a separate cover—make a fresh start

猎　【lib⁹ 罗叶⁹】hunt

猎获【lib⁹wog⁹ 镬】capture or kill in hunting; bag

猎取【lib⁹qêü² 娶】hunt; seek; hunt for

猎奇【lib⁹kēi⁴ 其】hunt for novelty

猎手【lib⁹xeo² 守】hunter

猎枪【lib⁹qêng¹ 昌】hunting rifle; shotgun

猎狗【lib⁹geo² 九】hunting dog; hound

猎场【lib⁹qêng⁴ 祥】hunting ground

列　【lid⁹ 烈】arrange; list; row; kind; various

列车【lid⁹qē¹ 奢】train

列举【lid⁹gêü² 矩²】enumerate; list

列席【lid⁹jig⁹ 直】attend (a meeting) as a nonvoting delegate

列传【lid⁹jün² 转】biographies

洌【lid⁹ 列】(see "凛洌")

趔【lid⁹ 列】〈a.〉趔趄【lid⁹qid⁸ 切】stagger; reel

烈【lid⁹ 列】strong; violent; staunch; upright; sacrificing oneself for a just cause

烈性【lid⁹xing³ 胜】spirited; strong

烈风【lid⁹fung¹ 丰】strong gale

烈火【lid⁹fo² 伙】raging fire; raging flames

烈日【lid⁹yed⁹ 逸】burning sun

烈士【lid⁹xi⁶ 是】martyr; a person of high endeavour

烈火见真金【lid⁹fo²gin³jen¹gem¹ 伙建珍甘】pure gold proves its worth in a blazing fire — people of worth show their mettle during trials and tribulations

裂【lid⁹ 列】split; crack; rend

裂开【lid⁹hoi¹ 海¹】split open; rend

裂口【lid⁹ heo² 厚²】breach; gap; split; vent

裂缝【lid⁹fung⁴ 冯】rift; crevice; crack

裂痕【lid⁹hen⁴ 很⁴】rift; crack; fissure

裂变【lid⁹bin³ 鞭³】fission

沥【lig⁴ 力; lig⁷ 力⁷; lēg⁴ 罗尺⁹】drip; trickle; drop

沥水【lig⁷ xêû² 瑞²】waterlogging caused by excessive rainfall

沥青【lig⁷qing¹ 清】pitch; asphalt = 蜡青【lab⁹gēng¹】

砾【lig⁷ 力⁷】gravel; shingle

砾石【lig¹xēg⁹ 硕】gravel

雳【lig⁷ 砾】〈n.〉霹雳【pig⁷lig⁷ 辟】thunderbolt

力【lig⁹ 历】power; strength; force; physical strength; do all one can

力量【lig⁹ lêng⁶亮 】physical strength; power; force

力气【lig⁹hēi³ 戏】physical strength; effort

力度【lig⁹dou⁶ 道】dynamics

力争【lig⁹jeng¹ 憎】work hard for; argue strongly

力图【lig⁹tou⁴ 途】try hard to; strive to

力求【lig⁹keo⁴ 球】do one's best to; strive to

力戒【lig⁹gai³ 介】strictly avoid; guard against

力不从心【lig⁹bed⁷qung⁴xem¹ 毕虫深】ability falling short of one's wishes

力所能及【lig⁹ xo² neng⁴ keb⁹锁 挪莺⁴级⁹】in one's power

力挽狂澜【lig⁹wan⁵kuong⁴lan⁴ 环⁵ 卡汪⁴兰】make vigorous efforts to turn the tide

历【lig⁹ 历】go through; undergo; experience; all previous; one by one; calendar

历史【lig⁹xi² 屎】history; past records

历程【lig⁹qing⁴ 情】course

历来【lig⁹loi⁴ 莱】always; constantly

历次【lig⁹qi³ 刺³】all previous

历时【lig⁹xi⁴ 思⁴】last (a period of time)

历代【lig⁹doi⁶ 袋】past dynasties

历法【lig⁹fad⁸ 发】calendar

历数【lig⁹xou² 嫂】count one by one; enumerate

历历在目【lig⁹lig⁹joi⁶mug⁹ 再⁶ 木】come clearly into view; leap up vividly before the eyes

栃【lig¹ 砺】manger

挛【lün¹ 联¹；lün⁴ 联】crooked；contraction

挛拱【lün¹ gung¹ 公 】curl；coil；twist；
hump up ＝【普】蜷曲；拱起

挛毛【lün¹ mou¹ 冒¹】curly hair；one with
curly hair ＝【普】头发蜷曲；蜷
发的人

挛埋晒【lün¹mai⁴xai³ 买⁴ 徙³】contracture
＝【普】挛缩

恋【lün² 联²】love；long for；feel attached
to

恋爱【lün²ngoi³ 哀³】love

恋恋不舍【lün²lün²bed⁷xē² 毕写】be reluctant to part with；hate to see
sb. go

鸾【lün⁴ 联】a mythical bird like the
phoenix

鸾凤【lün⁴fung⁶ 奉】husband and wife

銮【lün⁴ 联】a small tinkling bell

脔【lün⁴ 联】a small slice of meat

栾【lün⁴ 联】goldenrain tree；a surname

峦【lün⁴ 联】low but steep and pointed
hill；mountains in a range

孪【lün⁴ 联】twin

孪生【lün⁴xeng¹ 笙】twin

联【lün⁴ 孪】ally oneself with；unite；
join；antithetical couplet

联合【lün⁴ heb⁹盒 】unite；ally；alliance；
union；joint

联盟【lün⁴meng⁴ 萌】alliance；coalition；u-

nion

联系【lün⁴ hei⁶分⁶】contact；touch；integrate；relate；link

联络【lün⁴log⁸ 洛】get in touch with

联想【lün⁴xêng² 赏】associate；connect in
the mind

联翩【lün⁴pin¹ 篇】together

联运【lün⁴wen⁶ 混】through transport

联欢【lün⁴fun¹ 欢】have a get-together

联邦【lün⁴bong¹ 帮】federation；union

联合国【lün⁴heb⁹guog⁸ 盒帼】the United
Nations(U. N.)

乱【lün⁶ 联⁶】in disorder；in a mess；
chaos；riot；confuse；mix up；
jumble；confused；random；promiscuity

乱笼【lün⁶lung⁴ 隆】confusing；muddle
things up ∽【普】乱了套

乱咁春【lün⁶ gem³ jung¹禁中 】to wander
around ∽【普】到处碰；瞎跑

乱立立【lün⁶leb⁹leb⁹ 笠⁹】confusing；in a
mess ∽【普】乱哄哄

乱纷纷【lün⁶fen¹fen¹ 分】disorderly；confused

乱糟糟【lün⁶jou¹jou¹ 租】chaotic；confused

乱子【lün⁶ji² 止】disturbance；trouble

乱讲【lün⁶gong² 港】speak carelessly

乱离【lün⁶lêi⁴ 厘】be separated by war

乱世【lün⁶xei³ 细】troubled times

乱弹琴【lün⁶tan⁴kem⁴ 坛禽】act or talk
like a fool

乱七八糟【lün⁶qed⁷bad⁸jou¹ 柒捌租】at
sixes and sevens；in a mess

乱伦【lün⁶lên⁴ 沦】commit incest

滑【lüd⁷ 劣⁷】slippery；smooth

滑滑滑【wad⁹lüd⁷lüd⁷ 挖⁹】slick；smooth；

slippery ∽【普】滑溜溜

捋【lüd⁸ 劣；lüd⁹ 劣⁹】smooth out with the fingers; stroke; rub one's palm along

捋起衫袖【lüd⁸hēi²xam¹jeo⁶ 喜三就】push up one's sleeve =【普】捋起袖子

捋胡须【lün⁹wu⁴xou¹ 糊苏】stroke one's beard =【普】捋胡子

劣【lüd⁸ 捋⁸】bad; inferior; of low quality

劣等【lüd⁸deng² 登²】low-grade; poor

劣质【lüd⁸jed⁷ 侄⁷】of poor quality; inferior

劣种【lüd⁸jung² 肿】inferior strain

劣势【lüd⁸xei³ 世】inferior strength

劣迹【lüd⁸jig⁷ 织】misdeed; evil doing

呕【lê¹ 罗靴¹；dêd⁷ 得律⁷】vomit; throw up; tut-tut

呕骨【lê¹gued⁷ 掘⁷】vomit the bone =【普】吐骨头

呕呕怪事【dêd⁷dêd⁷guai³xi⁶ 乖³ 士¹】monstrous absurdity

嗻【lê² 罗靴²；yü⁴ 如】insist on; impose; speak haltingly

嗻银【lê² ngen² 额因²】(children) impose the coins ∽【普】讨零花钱

嗫嗻【jib⁸yü⁴ 接】speak haltingly

擂【lêü¹ 累¹；lo⁴ 罗】pile up; repeat; fold; press

擂埋去【lêü¹ mai⁴hêü³ 买⁴ 虚³】force one's way in; squeeze in =【普】挤进去

擂砖【lêü¹jün¹ 专】pile up the brick =【普】叠砖头

擂【lêü⁴ 雷】hit; beat; pestle; pound; arena

擂台【lêü⁴toi⁴ 抬】ring (for martial con-

tests); arena

雷【lêü⁴ 擂】thunder; mine; a surname

雷电【lêü⁴din⁶ 甸】thunder and lightning

雷公【lêü⁴gung¹ 工】Thunder God

雷公劈【lêü⁴gung¹pēg⁸ 工辟尺⁸】be struck by lightning =【普】雷击

雷鸣【lêü⁴ming⁴ 明】thunderous; thundery

雷达【lêü⁴dad⁶ 得压⁹】radar

雷管【lêü⁴gun² 莞】detonator

雷厉风行【lêü⁴ lei⁶ fung¹ heng⁴ 励丰衡】vigorously and speedily; resolutely

雷霆万钧【lêü⁴ting⁴man⁶guen¹ 庭慢君】as powerful as a thunderbolt

雷打不动【lêü⁴da²bed⁷dung⁶ 得阿² 毕洞】unshakable; final; inviolate

镭【lêü⁴】radium (Ra)

镭射【lêü⁴xē⁶ 舍⁶】radium

蕾【lêü⁴ 雷；lêü⁵ 偏】flower bud; bud

儡【lêü⁵ 屡】〈n.〉傀儡【fai³lêü⁵ 块】puppet

磊【lêü⁵ 吕】〈a.〉磊落【lêü⁵log⁹ 洛⁹】open and upright

吕【lêü⁵ 吕】a surname

吕宋【lêü⁵xung³ 送】〈n.〉Luzon

侣【lêü⁵ 吕】companion; partner (see "伴侣")

铝【lêü⁵ 吕】〈n.〉aluminium (Al)

铝箔【lêü⁵bog⁹ 薄】aluminium foil

闾【lêü⁵ 吕】the gate of an alley; alleys and lanes

闾里【lêü⁵ lêi⁵李】native village; home town

屡【lêü⁵ 吕】repeatedly；time and again

屡次【lêü⁵qi³ 刺】time and again；repeatedly

屡见不鲜【lêü⁵gin³bed⁷xin¹ 建毕仙】common occurrence

屡教不改【lêü⁵gao³bed⁷goi² 较毕该²】refuse to mend one's ways despite repeated admonition

梠【lêü⁵ 吕】〈n.〉棕榈【jung¹lêü⁵】（see "棕榈"）

旅【lêü⁵ 吕】travel；brigade；troops；force

旅行【lêü⁵heng⁴ 衡】travel；journey；tour

旅伴【lêü⁵bun⁶ 拌】travelling companion

旅程【lêü⁵qing⁴ 情】route；itinerary

旅途【lêü⁵tou⁴ 图】journey；trip

旅店【lêü⁵dim³ 点³】inn

旅馆【lêü⁵gun² 管】hotel ＝ 旅社【lêü⁵xê⁵ 舍⁵】

旅费【lêü⁵fei³ 废】travelling expenses

旅游【lêü⁵yeo⁴ 油】tour；tourism

褛【lêü⁵ 吕；leo⁵ 柳】（see "褴褛"）

履【lêü⁵ 吕；lêi⁵ 李】shoe；tread on；footstep；fulfil

履历【lêü⁵lig⁹ 力】personal details；antecedents

履行【lêi⁵heng⁴ 衡】perform；fulfil；carry out

垒【lêü⁵ 吕】build by piling up bricks，stones，earth，etc.

垒球【lêü⁵keo⁴ 求】〈n.〉softball

唳【lêü⁵ 吕】cry（of a crane）

膂【lêü⁵ 吕】backbone

膂力【lêü⁵lig⁹ 历】muscular strength；brawn

累【lêü⁵ 吕；lêü⁶ 类；lêü⁴ 雷】pile up；repeated；involve；tired；tire；work hard；toil

累累【lêü⁵lêü⁵；lêü⁴lêü⁴】gaunt；clusters of；again and again；countless

累赘【lêü⁶jêü⁶罪】burdensome；wordy；burden

累积【lêü⁶jig³ 织】accumulate

累计【lêü⁶gei³ 继】add up；grand total

累卵【lêü⁴lên² 论²】a stack of eggs — liable to collapse any moment；precarious

劳累【leo⁴lêü⁶ 卢】（see "劳累"）

戾【lêü⁶ 类】crime；sin；perverse；unreasonable

泪【lêü⁶ 类】tear；teardrop

泪水【lêü⁶xêü² 瑞】tear；teardrop ＝ 泪珠【lêü⁶jü¹ 朱】

泪花【lêü⁶fa¹ 化¹】tears in one's eyes

泪痕【lêü⁶hen⁴ 很⁴】tear stains

泪眼【lêü⁶ngan⁵ 雁⁵】tearful eyes

类【lêü⁶ 泪】kind；type；class；resemble

类别【lêü⁶bid⁹ 必⁹】classification；category

类比【lêü⁶bêi² 俾】analogy

类型【lêü⁶ying⁴ 形】type

类似【lêü⁶qi⁵ 特】similar；analogous

类推【lêü⁶têü¹ 退¹】analogize；reason by analogy

虑【lêü⁶ 泪】consider；ponder；concern；anxiety；worry

滤【lêü⁶ 泪】strain；filter

滤纸【lêü⁶ji² 止】filter paper

滤色镜【lêû⁶ xig⁷ gēng³ 式颈³】(colour) filter

滤波器【lêû⁶bo¹hēi³ 坡戏】wave filter

驴【lêû⁴ 雷】donkey; ass

卵【lên² 论²】ovum; egg; spawn

卵子【lên²ji² 止】ovum; egg

卵巢【lên²qao⁴ 抄²】ovary

卵石【lên² xêg⁹ 硕】cobble; pebble; shingle

卵生【lên²xing¹ 笙】oviparity

卵翼【lên² yig⁹亦】cover with wings as in brooding; shield

躏【lên⁶ 吝】〈v.〉蹂躏【yeo⁴lên⁶ 柔】trample on; ravage

蔺【lên⁶ 吝】a surname

吝【lên⁶ 蔺】stingy; mean; closefisted

吝惜【lên⁶xig⁷ 色】grudge; stint

吝啬【lên⁶xig⁷ 色】stingy; niggardly = 孤寒【gu¹hon⁴】

磷【lên⁴ 邻】phosphors (P)

磷肥【lên⁴fēi⁴ 非⁴】phosphata fertilizer

粼【lên⁴ 邻】〈a.〉粼粼【lên⁴lên⁴】(of water, stone, etc.) clear; crystalline

嶙【lên⁴ 邻】〈a.〉嶙峋【lên⁴xen¹ 荀】(of mountain rocks, cliffs, etc.) jagged; (of person) bony

遴【lên⁴ 邻】〈v.〉遴选【lên⁴xün² 损】select sb. for a post; select

鳞【lên⁴ 邻】scale (of fish, etc.); like the scales of a fish

鳞甲【lên⁴gab⁸ 夹】scale and shell

鳞爪【lên⁴ jao⁵ 找】scales and nails; small bits

鳞次栉比【lên⁴qi³jid⁸bēi² 刺节俾】(of houses, etc.) row upon row of

邻【lên⁴ 磷】neighbour; neighbouring; near

邻近【lên⁴gen⁶ 靳】near; close to

邻居【lên⁴gêu¹ 巨¹】neighbour = 邻舍【lên⁴ xê³ 泻】

邻里【lên⁴ lêi⁵理 】neighbourhood; neighbours

仑【lên⁴ 邻】logical sequence; coherence

伦【lên⁴ 仑】human relations, esp. as conceived by feudal ethics; logic; peer

伦常【lên⁴xêng⁴ 裳】feudal order of importance or seniority in human relationships

伦比【lên⁴bēi² 俾】rival; equal

伦次【lên⁴qi³ 刺】coherence

伦理【lên⁴lêi⁵ 李】ethics; moral principles

沦【lên⁴ 仑】sink; fall

沦落【lên⁴log⁹ 洛⁹】fall low

沦陷【lên⁴ham⁶ 憾】(of territory, etc.) be occupied by the enemy

沦亡【lên⁴mong⁶ 忙】(of a country) be annexed

纶【lên⁴ 仑】black silk ribbon; fishing line; synthetic fibre

囵【lên⁴ 仑】(see "囫囵")

轮【lên⁴ 仑】wheel; disc; ring; steamboat; take turns; round

轮子【lên⁴ji² 止】wheel

轮胎【lên⁴toi¹ 台¹】tyre = 轮呔【lên⁴tai¹ 太¹】

轮换【lên⁴wun⁶ 唤】rotate; take turns

轮流【lên⁴leo⁴ 留】take turns

轮船【lên⁴xūn⁴ 旋】steamer; steamship

轮机【lên⁴gēi¹ 基】turbine; engine

轮廓【lên⁴kuog⁸ 郭】outline; contour

论【lên⁶ 仑⁶; lên³ 仑³】discuss; talk about; view; dissertation; theory; mention; determine; by; essay

论点【lên⁶dim² 店²】argument; thesis

论调【lên⁶diu⁶ 掉】view; argument

论据【lên⁶gêü³ 踞】argument; grounds of argument

论证【lên⁶jing³ 正】demonstration; proof

论理【lên⁶lēi⁵ 李】normally; logic

论述【lên⁶xê d⁹ 术】discuss; expound

论战【lên⁶jin³ 箭】polemic; debate

论著【lên⁶jü³ 注】treatise; work; book

论断【lên⁶dün⁶ 段】inference; thesis

论处【lên⁶qü² 柱²】punish

论功行赏【lên⁶gung¹heng⁴xêng² 工衡想】dispense rewards or honours according to merit

论咗又论【lên³ jo² yeo⁶ lên³左右】explained and explained = 【普】说了又说

论尽【lên⁶ jên⁶ 进⁶】clumsy; inconvenient = 【普】(老人、病人或小孩)行动不便的样子;麻烦;糟了

良【lêng⁴ 粮】good; fine; good people; very

良好【lêng⁴hou² 蒿²】good; well

良心【lêng⁴xem¹ 深】conscience

良知【lêng⁴ji¹ 支】intuitive knowledge

良策【lêng⁴qag⁸ 册】good plan

良方【lêng⁴ fong¹ 芳】good recipe; sound strategy

良材【lêng⁴qoi⁴ 才】good timber;able person

良种【lêng⁴ jung² 肿 】improved variety; fine breed

良机【lêng⁴gēi¹ 基】good opportunity

良久【lêng⁴geo² 九】a long time

良药苦口【lêng⁴yêg⁹fu²heo² 若府厚²】good medicine tastes bitter

两【lêng⁵ 俩; lêng² 良²】two; both (sides); either(side); a few; a unit of weight (= 50 grams)

两边【lêng⁵bin¹ 鞭】both sides; both parties

两面【lêng⁵min⁶ 免⁶】two sides; dual

两头【lêng⁵teo⁴ 投】both ends; both parties

两可【lêng⁵ho² 何²】both will do

两难【lêng⁵nan⁴ 挪晏⁴】face a difficult choice

两讫【lêng⁵nged⁹ 兀】the goods are delivered and the bill is cleared

两性【lêng⁵ xing³胜 】both sexes; amphiprotic

两样【lêng⁵yêng⁶ 让】different

两用【lêng⁵yung⁶ 容⁶】dual purpose

两栖【lêng⁵qei¹ 妻】amphibious

两极【lêng⁵gig⁹ 击⁹】the two poles of the earth; the two poles (of a magnet or an electric battery)

两面派【lêng⁵ min⁶ pai³免⁶排³】doubledealer

两回事【lêng⁵wui⁴xi⁶ 会⁴ 士】two entirely different things

两败俱伤【lêng⁵bai⁶kêü¹xêng¹ 摆⁶ 拘双】both sides suffer

两全其美【lêng⁵ qün⁴ kēi⁴ mēi⁵泉奇尾 】satisfy both sides

两相情愿【lêng⁵xêng¹qing⁴yün⁶ 商程县⁶】both parties are willing

俩【lêng⁵ 两】two; trick（see "伎俩"）

魉【lêng⁵ 两】（see "魍魉"）

粮【lêng⁴ 良】grain; food; provision

粮食【lêng⁴xig⁹ 蚀】grain; cereals; food

粮饷【lêng⁴hêng² 响】provisions and funds for troops

粮店【lêng⁴dim³ 点³】grain shop

粮仓【lêng⁴qong¹ 苍】granary; barn

粱【lêng⁴ 梁】a fine strain of millet; fine grain

梁【lêng⁴ 良】roof beam; bridge; ridge; a surname

梁上君子【lêng⁴ xêng⁶ guen¹ ji² 尚军止】gentleman on the beam — burglar; thief

量【lêng⁴ 良；lêng⁶ 亮】measure; capacity; amount; estimate

量度【lêng⁴dog⁹ 铎】measurement

量子【lêng⁶ji² 止】quantun

量变【lêng⁶bin³ 边³】quantitative change

量力而行【lêng⁶lig⁹yi⁴heng⁴ 历移衡】do what one is capable of

辆【lêng⁶ 亮】〈classifier〉一辆汽车【yed⁷lêng⁶hêi³qê¹ 壹戏奢】a bus (or car)

凉【lêng⁴ 良】make or become cool; cool; cold; discouraged

凉快【lêng⁴fai³ 块】nice and cool; cool off

凉爽【lêng⁴xong³ 桑²】nice and cool

凉菜【lêng⁴qoi³ 蔡】cold dish

凉水【lêng⁴xêu² 瑞²】cold water

凉亭【lêng⁴ting² 停】wayside pavilion; kiosk

谅【lêng⁶ 亮】forgive; understand; I think

谅解【lêng⁶gai² 介²】understand

谅必如此【lêng⁶bid⁷yü⁴qi² 别¹ 鱼次²】I think it must be so

亮【lêng⁶ 谅】bright; light; enlightened; show

亮光【lêng⁶guong¹ 胱】light

亮度【lêng⁶dou⁶ 道】brightness; brilliance

亮相【lêng⁶xêng³ 双³】strike a pose on the stage; state one's views

亮晶晶【lêng⁶ jing¹ jing¹ 精】glittering; sparkling

亮堂堂【lêng⁶tong⁴tong⁴ 唐】brightly lit; well lit

律【lêd⁹ 栗】law; statute; rule; restrain

律师【lêd⁹xi¹ 思】lawyer; barrister; attorney

律诗【lêd⁹xi¹ 思】a poem of eight lines, each containing five or seven characters, with a strict tonal pattern and rhyme scheme

率【lêd⁹ 律；xêd⁷ 恤】rate; ratio; proportion; lead; command; rash; frank; generally

效率【hao⁶lêd⁹ 考⁶】efficiency

率尔【xêd⁷yi⁵ 耳】rashly; hastily

率领【xêd⁷ling⁵ 岭】lead; head; command

率先【xêd⁷xin¹ 仙】take the lead in doing sth.

率直【xêd⁷jig⁹ 值】forthright and sincere; blunt

栗【lêd⁹ 律】chestnut; tremble; a surname

栗子【lêd⁹ji² 止】chestnut ＝ 风栗【fung¹ lêd⁹ 丰】

栗色【lêd⁹ xig⁷ 式 】chestnut colour；maroon

傈【lêd⁹ 律】〈n.〉傈僳族【lêd⁹xug⁷jug⁹ 叔俗】the Lisu nationality

略【lêg⁹ 掠】brief；sketchy；slightly；summary；omit；strategy；capture

略略【lêg⁹lêg⁹】slightly；briefly

略微【lêg⁹mêi⁴ 眉】slightly；a little

略见一斑【lêg⁹gin³yed⁷ban¹ 建壹班】catch a glimpse of

略知一二【lêg⁹ji¹yed⁷yi⁶ 支壹义】have a smattering of

掠【lêg⁹ 略】plunder；pillage；sack；sweep past

掠夺【lêg⁹dūd⁹ 得月⁹】plunder；rob；pillage

掠取【lêg⁹gêū² 娶】seize；grab；plunder

掠过水面【lêg⁹guo³xêū²min⁶ 果³ 瑞³ 免⁶】skimmed over the water

哩【lê¹ 罗诶¹；lê³ 罗诶³；lēi¹ 罗希¹；li¹ 罗衣¹】①〈auxil.〉∽ "呢" "啦"，show the state-tone，its used to sentence end ②〈onomatopoeia〉scattered

天仲早哩！【tin¹jung⁶jou²lê³】It's still early！＝【普】天还早哩！

哩哩啦啦【li¹li¹la¹la¹】scattered；sporadic

厘【lēi⁴ 离】a unit of length (= ⅓ millimetre)；a unit of weigh (= 0.05 grams)；a unit of area (= 0.666 square metres)；one thousandth of a yuan；a unit of monthly interest rate (= 0.1%)；a fraction

厘定【lēi⁴ding⁶ 锭】collate and stipulate

厘米【lēi¹mei¹ 迷¹】centimetre

喱【lēi¹ 李¹】〈n.〉咖喱【ga³lēi¹ 加³】(see "咖喱")

离【lēi⁴ 漓】leave；part from；off；away；without

离开【lēi⁴hoi¹ 海¹】leave；depart from

离别【lēi⁴bid⁹ 必⁹】part；leave

离散【lēi⁴xan³ 汕】dispersed；scattered about

离心【lēi⁴xem¹ 深】dissension；centrifugal

离间【lēi⁴gan³ 涧】sow discord

离职【lēi⁴jig⁷ 织】leave office

离境【lēi⁴ging² 景】leave a country or place

离婚【lēi⁴fen¹ 昏】divorce

离子【lēi⁴ji² 止】〈n.〉ion

离合器【lēi⁴heb⁹hēi³ 盒戏】〈n.〉clutch

离奇【lēi⁴kēi⁴ 其】odd；fantastic

离乡别井【lēi⁴hêng¹bid⁹jēng² 香必⁹ 支镜²】leave one's native place

离心离德【lēi⁴xem¹lēi⁴deg⁷ 深得】disunity

漓【lēi⁴ 离】(see "淋漓")

璃【lēi⁴ 离；lēi¹ 喱】(see "玻璃"、"琉璃")

骊【lēi⁴ 离】black horse

狸【lēi⁴ 离；lēi² 李²】racoon dog

狸猫【lēi⁴mao¹ 矛⁻¹】leopard cat

梨【lēi⁴ 离；lēi 利²】pear

罹【lēi⁴ 离】suffer from；meet with

罹难【lēi⁴nan⁶ 挪晏⁶】die in a disaster or an accident；be murdered

篱【lēi⁴ 离；lēi¹ 离¹】hedge；fence

篱笆【lēi⁴ba¹ 巴】bamboo or twig fence

笊篱【jɑo³lēi¹ 罩】a utensil that salvages things in the soup ∽【普】小捞网（用在汤或油里打捞东西）

蜊 【lēi⁶ 利】(see"蛤蜊")

痢 【lēi⁶ 利；lēi¹ 喱】dysentery；(see"瘌痢")

痢疾【lēi⁶jed⁹ 佚】dysentery

犛 【lēi⁴ 离】yak

里 【lēi⁵ 李；lêû⁵ 吕】in；inside；lining；inner；neighbourhood；home-town；a Chinese unit of length（= 1/2 kilometre)

里程【lēi⁵qing⁴ 情】mileage；course

里程碑【lēi⁵qing⁴bēi 情卑】milestone

里边【lêû⁵ bin¹ 鞭 】inside；in；within = 里便【lêû⁵bin⁶】

里面【lêû⁵min⁶ 免⁶】inside；interior

里头【lêû⁵teo⁴ 投】inside；interior

里里外外【lêû⁵ lêû⁵ ngoi⁶ ngoi⁶ 碍 】inside and outside

里应外合【lêû⁵ying³ngoi⁶heb⁹ 英³ 碍盒】act from inside in coordination with forces attacking from outside

俚 【lēi⁵ 李】vulgar

俚俗【lēi⁵jug⁹ 族】vulgar；unrefined

俚语【lēi⁵yū⁵ 雨】slang

娌 【lēi⁵ 李】〈n.〉妯娌【jug⁹lēi⁵ 俗】wives of brothers

理 【lēi⁵ 李】texture；reason；manage；put in order；pay attention to

理论【lēi⁵lên⁶ 吝】theory

理性【lēi⁵xing³ 胜】reason

理智【lēi⁵ji³ 至】reason；intellect

理想【lēi⁵xêng² 赏】ideal

理事【lēi⁵xi⁶ 士】member of a council；director

理财【lēi⁵qoi⁴ 才】manage money matters

理发【lēi⁵fad⁸ 法】haircut；hairdressing

理睬【lēi⁵qoi² 采】pay attention to

理会【lēi⁵wui⁶ 汇】understand；take notice of

理解【lēi⁵gɑi² 介²】understand；comprehend

理亏【lēi⁵kuei¹ 规】be in the wrong

理疗【lēi⁵liu⁴ 辽】physiotherapy

理屈词穷【lēi⁵wed⁷qi⁴kung⁴ 乌核⁷ 辞穷】fall silent on finding oneself bested in argument

理所当然【lēi⁵ xo² dong¹ yin⁴锁珰言】of course；naturally

理直气壮【lēi⁵jig⁹hēi³jong³ 值戏葬】with justice on one's side, one is bold and assured

锂 【lēi⁵ 理】lithium（Li）

鲤 【lēi⁵ 理】carp（鲤鱼【lēi⁵yū² 语²】）

李 【lēi⁵ 理】plum；a surname

李代桃僵【lēi⁵doi⁶tou⁴gêng¹ 袋图羌】substitute one thing for another；sacrifice oneself for another person

利 【lēi⁶ 俐】sharp；advantage；favourable；profit；do good to；benefit

利益【lēi⁶yig⁷ 亿】interest；benefit

利害【lēi⁶hoi⁶ 亥】gains and losses；terrible

利润【lēi⁶yên⁹ 闰】profit

利率【lēi⁶lêd⁹ 律】interest rate

利落【lēi⁶ log⁹洛⁹】agile；nimble；neat；settled

利息【lēi⁶ xig⁷ 色】interest

利器【lēi⁶ hēi³ 戏 】 sharp weapon; good tool

利弊【lēi⁶bei⁶ 币】pros and cons

利用【lēi⁶ yung⁶ 容⁶】 use; make use of; take advantage of; exploit

利令智昏【lēi⁶ ling⁶ ji³ fen¹ 另至分】be blinded by lust for gain

利欲熏心【lēi⁶yug⁹fen¹xem¹ 玉分深】be blinded by greed

利市【lēi⁶ xi⁶ 吏示】money given during the Chinese New Year =【普】押岁钱

俐 【lēi⁶ 利】(see "伶俐")

脷 【lēi⁶ 利】tongue =【普】舌头

猪脷【jü¹lēi⁶ 朱】the tongue of a pig

吏 【lēi⁶ 利】official; mandarin (see "官吏")

莉 【lēi⁶ 利】(see "茉莉")

莅 【lēi⁶ 利】arrive; be present

莅临【lēi⁶lem⁴ 林】arrive; be present

猁 【lēi⁶ 利】〈n.〉猞猁【xē³lēi⁶ 舍】lynx

靓 【lēng³ 罗镜³；jing⁶ 静】① beautiful; pretty; good; handsome =【普】美丽；②dress up

靓仔【lēng³ jei² 济²】beautiful young man =【普】漂亮的小伙子

靓女【lēng³ nêü² 挪去²】beaufiul girl =【普】漂亮的姑娘

靓野【lēng³yē⁵ 夜⁵】good thing =【普】好东西

篗 【lēng¹ 靓¹】fish-basket =【普】鱼篗（口小，腹大）

入篗【yeb⁹lēng¹ 挹⁹】be taken in =【普】上当；入圈套

篗仔【lēng¹ jei² 济²】a young man who is hasty and of no use ∽【普】小子（贬义）

叻 【lēg⁷ 罗吃⁷】smart and capable =【普】聪明的；有能耐的

叻仔【lēg⁷jei² 济²】a smart boy; one who is smart; smart; bright = 【普】好小子；聪明能干的小伙；好样的

叻女【lēg⁷ nêü² 挪去²】a smart girl; one who is smart; smart; bright =【普】聪慧的姑娘；巧姑娘

坜 【lēg⁹ 叻⁹】ridge (in a field) =【普】（种作物的）地垄

M

唔【m²“吾”的韵尾】no；not =【普】不；并不；并非（表示否定）

唔抵【m⁴dei² 底】not worthwhile；not deserved =【普】不值得；不合算

唔定【m⁴ding⁶ 锭】maybe；perhaps =【普】未定；(说)不定

唔化【m⁴fa³ 花³】stubborn；narrow-minded =【普】执迷不误；没看透事物的本质

唔够【m⁴geo³ 救】not enough；insufficient =【普】不够

唔系【m⁴hei⁶ 兮⁶】no；otherwise =【普】不是

唔该【m⁴goi¹ 改¹】thank you；to thank =【普】谢谢

唔好【m⁴ hou⁴ 蒿²】not good；do not =【普】不好；不要

唔拘【m⁴kêü¹ 驱】never mind =【普】不要紧；没关紧；随便

唔捞【m⁴ lou¹ 老¹】cannot work；not worth it =【普】不成功；(事情)办坏了

唔啱【m⁴ngam¹ 岩¹】not correct；wrong；not suitable；otherwise =【普】不对；不正确；错了

唔似【m²qi⁵ 恃】do not look like；cannot compare with =【普】不像；不一样

唔恨【m²hen⁶ 狠⁶】not to cherish =【普】不想要

唔切【m⁴qid⁸ 撤】cannot make it =【普】太急于；忙不及

唔使【m⁴xei² 洗】not necessary；no need =【普】用不着；不需要

唔识【m⁴xig⁷ 色】do not know；cannot do =【普】不懂得；不认识；不晓得

唔制【m⁴jei³ 济】not willing =【普】不愿意；不干

唔单只【m⁴ dan¹ ji² 丹止】not only … but also =【普】不光；不单

唔得闲【m²deg⁷han⁴ 娴】busy；not free =【普】忙着；没空

唔抵得【m²dei²deg⁷ 底德】unbearable =【普】不服气；不甘心

唔等使【m²deng²xei² 灯²洗】useless；not beneficial =【普】不中用；不合用；没用的

唔化算【m⁴fa³xün³ 花³蒜】not worth it =【普】不合算

唔忿气【m⁴ fen⁶ hēi³ 份戏】not convincing =【普】不服气

唔够气【m⁴geo³hēi³ 救戏】lack of oxygen =【普】力气不足

唔够喉【m⁴ geo³ heo⁴ 救侯】not satisfied =【普】吃了嫌不足，还想吃

唔觉眼【m⁴ gog⁸ ngan⁵ 各雁⁵】not observant =【普】没留神；没看到

唔觉意【m⁴gog⁸yi³ 各薏】not careful =【普】没留意；没注意

唔怪之【m⁴guai³ji¹ 乖³支】not wonder =【普】怪不得

唔关事【m⁴guan¹xi⁶ 惯¹士】not related to =【普】没牵扯

唔系路【m⁴ hei⁶ lou⁶ 兮⁶露】to sense that

something is wrong = 【普】不是办法;不对劲

唔开胃【m⁴ hoi¹ wei⁶ 海¹ 卫】no appetite; to show disgust about someone or something = 【普】没兴趣;不想要

唔知丑【m⁴ ji¹ qeo² 支次欧²】not to mind = 【普】不要脸;不害羞

唔精神【m⁴ jing¹ xen⁴ 贞臣】sick; not feeling well = 【普】(生病)不舒服

唔啈耕【m⁴ na¹ gang¹ 拿¹ 格罂¹】not related to = 【普】(两事)毫无关系

唔啱㤿【m⁴ ngam¹ kiu² 岩¹ 乔²】cannot get along with = 【普】(两人)不合心计,想法、兴趣不同;兴味不相投

唔似样【m⁴ qi⁵ yêng⁵ 恃杨⁵】to refer that one has done too much or has gone too far = 【普】不像样

唔生性【m⁴ xang¹ xing³ 是罂²胜】ignorant; naive; not knowing what is right or wrong; useless = 【普】(孩子)不懂事;不听话;不正经,不持重

唔使慌【m⁴ xei²fong¹ 洗方】no need to be afraid; no need to worry = 【普】不用害怕;别慌张

唔使计【m⁴ xei²gei³ 洗继】do not mention it = 【普】别计较;不用算

唔使恨【m⁴ xei²hen⁶ 洗很⁶】no need to hope = 【普】别指望

唔熟性【m⁴ xug⁹xing³ 淑胜】not being understanding = 【普】不懂世故;不懂投其所好办事

唔通气【m⁴ tung¹hēi³ 同¹ 戏】not considerate; not understanding = 【普】不懂避忌、避让,有碍别人成事

唔话得【m⁴ wa⁶deg⁷ 画⁶ 德】no complaints for one who has done a good job = 【普】很不错;没说的

唔争在【m⁴jang¹joi⁶ 支罂¹ 再⁶】not to calculate ∽【普】给吧,别为这小意思争了

唔中用【m⁴jung¹yung⁶ 钟容⁶】not applicable; useless = 【普】不中用;不顶用

唔抵得谂【m⁴ dei² deg⁷ nem² 底德挪庵²】not calculative = 【普】不会忍让,怕吃亏

唔够佢嚟【m⁴geo³kêu⁵lei⁴ 救拒黎】cannot fight with one who is too strong = 【普】斗不过他;智能不及他高强

唔经唔觉【m⁴ ging¹ m⁴ gog³ 京角】without one realizing it ∽【普】屈指细算,(时间已过去很长一段)

唔好手脚【m⁴hou²xeo²gêg⁸ 蒿²,守格约⁸】one who tends to steal = 【普】手脚不干净(指某人曾有偷窃之类的坏行为)

唔合何尺【m⁴ heb⁹ ho⁴ qê¹ 盒河车】not matching = 【普】(两人)想的、做的不一致;不合拍;不协调

唔使指倚【m⁴ xei² ji² yi⁵ 洗止以】to say that one should not dream and do nothing and hope that one will achieve what one wants ∽【普】别指望(得到某人的帮助)

唔识驾步【m⁴ xig⁷ga⁷bou⁶ 色价部】do not know what to do = 【普】不内行;不懂办事的方法与门路

唔制得过【m⁴ jei³ deg⁷ guo³ 济德果³】not worth it; not deserve = 【普】不合算;不干为好

唔衰拗嚟衰【m⁴xêu¹lo²lei⁴xêu¹ 需罗² 黎

需】to find one's own trouble =
【普】自讨苦吃;自找麻烦

孖【ma¹ 妈】two objects sticking
together; to join; to be together; one
pair (twin) = 【普】双;成双成对的

孖仔【ma¹jei² 济】twin brothers = 【普】
孪生兄弟

孖女【ma¹nêû² 挪去²】twin sisters =【普】
孪生姐妹

孖铺【ma¹pou¹ 普¹】two people sleeping
on one bed = 【普】二人同床睡

妈【ma¹ 孖】mother; ma; mum; mum-
my

妈妈【ma⁴ma¹】mother; ma; mum; mum-
my

吗【ma¹ 妈】〈auxil.〉show query mood
in the sentence end; what

吗啡【ma¹fê¹ 夫诶¹】morphine

麻【ma⁴ 妈⁴】a general term for hemp;
sesame; rough; pocked; tingle;
anaesthesia; a surname

麻绳【ma⁴xing⁴成 】rope made of hemp,
flax, jute, etc.

麻线【ma⁴xin³ 扇】flaxen thread

麻布【ma⁴bou⁶ 报】gunny (cloth); linen

麻袋【ma⁴doi⁶ 代】gunny-bag

麻痹【ma⁴bêi³ 秘】paralysis; benumb;
lower one's guard

麻醉【ma⁴jêû³ 最】anaesthesia; poison

麻风【ma⁴fung¹ 丰】leprosy

麻将【ma⁴jêng³ 涨】mahjong

麻药【ma⁴yêg⁹ 若】anaesthetic

麻油【ma⁴yeo⁴ 由】sesame oil

麻疹【ma⁴qen² 诊】measle

麻烦【ma⁴fan⁴ 凡】troublesome; put sb.
to trouble

麻甩【ma⁴led⁷ 罗核⁷】sparrow = 【普】麻

雀

麻甩佬【ma⁴led⁷lou² 罗核⁷ 老²】one who
is immoral = 【普】不正派的、猥
亵的男人

麻麻地【ma⁴ma²dêi² 吗² 得希²】general;
common = 【普】普普通通

麻雀虽小, 五脏俱全【ma⁴jêg⁸xêû¹xiu²,
ng⁵jong⁶kêû¹qün⁴ 酌 须 少², 伍 撞
驱存】the sparrow may be small
but it has all the vital organs —
small but complete

麻木不仁【ma⁴mug⁹bed⁷yen⁴ 目毕人】ap-
athetic; unfeeling

嘛【ma⁴ 麻;ma³ 麻³】〈auxil.〉show obvious mood in the sentence end

嫲【ma⁴ 麻;ma¹ 妈】wet nurse; grandmother = 【普】奶奶

蟆【ma⁴ 麻;mou¹ 毛¹】frog; toad

马【ma⁵ 蚂】horse; a surname

马匹【ma⁵ped⁷ 拍乙⁷】horses

马力【ma⁵lig⁹ 历】horsepower (h.p.)

马达【ma⁵dad⁹ 得压⁹】motor

马车【ma⁵qê¹ 奢】(horse-drawn) carriage;
cart

马路【ma⁵lou⁶ 露】road; street; avenue

马夫【ma⁵fu¹ 孚】groom

马蜂【ma⁵fung¹ 丰】hornet; wasp

马虎【ma¹fu¹ 妈夫】careless; casual

马上【ma⁵xêng⁶ 尚】at once; immediately

马桶【ma⁵tung² 统】nightstool; commode
= 屎塔【xi²tab⁸ 史塔】

马戏【ma⁵hêi³ 气】circus

马术【ma⁵xêd⁹ 述】horsemanship

马仔【ma⁵jei² 济²】bodyguards; followers

=【普】部下;听差的;跑腿的

马骝【ma⁵leo¹ 褛¹】monkey =【普】猴子

马骝精【ma⁵leo¹jing¹ 贞】to refer to a child who is playful and sporting 【普】调皮的、好玩耍的小孩

马蹄【①ma⁵ tei⁴ 提;②ma⁵ tei² 睇】① horse's hoof;② water chestnuts =【普】荸荠

马蹄粉【ma⁵tei⁴fen² 提分²】water chestnut powder

马拉松【ma⁵ lai¹ xung¹ 罗埃¹ 宋¹】marathon

马赛克【ma⁵qoi³heg⁷ 蔡黑】masaic

马蜂窝【ma⁵fung¹wo¹ 风蜗】hornet's nest = 黄蜂窦【wong⁴fung⁴deo³ 王风斗】

马铃薯【ma⁵ling⁵xü⁴ 伶书⁴】potato = 薯仔【xü⁴jei²】

马后炮【ma⁵ heo⁶ pao¹候泡³】belated effort

马列主义【ma⁵ lid⁹ jü² yi⁶ 烈煮异】Marxism-Leninism

马不停蹄【ma⁵ bed⁷ thing⁴ tei⁴ 毕亭提】nonstop

马到功成【ma⁵dou³gung¹xing¹ 都³工承】win instant success

蚂【ma⁵ 马】

蚂蚁【ma⁵ngei⁵ 危⁵】ant

蚂蟥【ma⁵wong⁴ 王】leech

蚂螂狂【ma⁵long⁴kuóng⁴ 郎卡汪⁴】cockroach =【普】螳螂

玛【ma⁵ 马】

玛瑙【ma⁵nou⁵ 脑】agate

骂【ma⁶ 马⁶】abuse; curse; swear; condemn; scold

骂街【ma⁶gai¹ 佳】shout abuses in the street

码【ma⁵ 马】a sign or thing indicating number; pile up; stack; yard (yd.)

码头【ma⁵teo⁴ 投】wharf; dock; port city

码子【ma⁵ji² 止】numeral; counter; chip

埋【mai⁴ 买⁴】cover up; bury; blame; complain; near; next to; to close

埋藏【mai⁴qong⁴ 床】bury; lie hidden in the earth

埋葬【mai⁴jong³ 壮】bury

埋伏【mai⁴fug⁹ 服】ambush; hide; lie low

埋没【mai⁴mud⁹】bury; cover up; neglect

埋怨【mai⁴yün³ 院³】blame; complain

埋便【mai⁴ bin⁶ 边⁶】to pay for bills =【普】里边

埋去【mai⁴heü³ 虚³】to go near =【普】走近去

埋嚟【mai⁴lei¹ 黎】to come =【普】走近来

埋位【mai⁴wei² 毁】to be on each's seat in a party where meals are served =【普】入席;就座

埋手【mai⁴xeo² 守】to tackle =【普】动手

埋数【mai⁴ xou³扫】to pay for bills =【普】结数

埋单【mai⁴ dan¹ 丹】to pay for bills =【普】结帐

埋尾【mai⁴ mēi⁵美】to be over; to finish =【普】扫尾(工作)

埋头埋脑【mai⁴teo⁴mai⁴nou⁵ 投瑙】to refer to one being engrossed in one's work =【普】全神贯注(某项工作)

买【mai⁵ 埋⁵】buy; purchase

买卖【mai⁵ mai⁶埋⁶】buying and selling;

business; deal; transaction

买主【mai⁵jŭ²煮】buyer; customer

买价【mai⁵ga³嫁】buying price

买帐【mai⁵ jêng³涨】acknowledge the superiority or seniority of; show respect for

买空卖空【mai⁵hung¹mai⁶hung¹红¹埋⁶】speculate (in stocks, etc.)

卖【mai⁶埋⁶】sell; exert to the utmost; betray; show off

卖主【mai⁶jŭ²煮】seller

卖力【mai⁶lig⁹历】exert all one's strength

卖命【mai⁶mēng⁶莫镜⁶】work oneself to the bone for sb.; die (unworthily) for

卖唱【mai⁶qêng⁴畅】sing for a living

卖艺【mai⁶ngei⁶毅 】make a living as a performer

卖淫【mai⁶yem⁴壬】prostitution

卖座【mai⁶jo⁶坐】(of a theatre, etc.) draw large audiences

卖国【mai⁶guog⁸帼】betray one's country

卖价【mai⁶ga⁴嫁】selling price

卖弄【mai⁶nung⁶挪翁⁶】show off; parade

卖俏【mai⁶qiu³峭】play the coquette; coquette

卖关子【mai⁶guan¹ji²惯¹止】keep people guessing

卖身投靠【mai⁶xen¹teo⁴kao³新头卡拗³】barter away one's honour for sb.'s pstronage

卖面光【mai⁶min⁶guong¹免⁶胱】to please one's heart; not being sincere ∽【普】装门面

卖猪仔【mai⁶jū¹jei²朱济²】people who are cheated to work overseas ∽【普】贩卖劳工

卖大包【mai⁶dai⁶bao¹歹⁶苞 】to sell cheaply or to offer free gifts for purchases of customers ∽【普】扯大炮;放葫芦

迈【mai⁶卖】step; stride; old; aged

迈步【mai⁶bou⁶部】take a step; make a step

迈进【mai⁶jên³俊】stride forward; forge ahead

猫【mao¹矛¹】cat

猫仔【mao¹jei²济²】kitten =【普】小猫

猫公【mao¹gung¹工】tomcat =【普】雄猫

猫乸【mao¹na²拿²】damcat =【普】母猫

猫姨【mao¹yi¹衣】cat =【普】猫儿

猫头鹰【mao¹teo⁴ying¹投英】owl

猫哭老鼠【mao¹hug⁷lou⁵xū²酷⁷鲁署】the cat weeping over the dead mouse — shed crocodile tears

猫刮咁嘈【mao¹guad⁸gem³qou⁴姑压⁸禁曹】too loud that it is just like the cat making sexual intercourse ∽【普】吵闹得令人讨厌

锚【mao⁴矛】anchor

锚地【mao⁴dēi¹得希⁶】anchorage

矛【mao⁴锚】lance; pike; spear

矛盾【mao⁴tên⁵替春⁵】contradictory; contradiction

矛头【mao⁴teo⁴投】spearhead

茅【mao⁴矛】cogongrass; a surname

茅寮【mao⁴liu²撩】small huts =【普】小茅房

茅棚【mao⁴pang⁴彭】thatched shed

茅厕【mao⁴qi³ 次】latrine

茅屋【mao⁴ngug⁷ 额哭⁷】thatched cottage

茅草【mao⁴qou² 操²】cogongrass

茅塞顿开【mao⁴xeg⁷dên⁶hoi¹ 是黑⁷ 敦⁶ 海¹】suddenly see the light

悉【mao⁴ 矛】flurried; flustered; arbitrarily

发晒悉【fad⁸xai³mao⁴ 法徙³】flurried; flustered ⌒【普】慌张；慌乱

悉赖【mao⁴lai³ 拉³】sb. does not acknowledge a debt arbitrarily; make a scene; raise hell =【普】耍赖

蟊【mao⁴ 矛】an insect destructive of the roots of seedlings

蟊贼【mao⁴qeg⁹ 次黑⁹】a person harmful to the country and people; pest

卯【mao⁵ 牡】the fourth of the twelve Earthly Branches; mortise

卯时【mao⁵xi⁴ 是⁴】the period of the day from 5 a.m. to 7 a.m.

铆【mao⁵ 卯】riveting

铆接【mao⁵jib² 支叶⁸】riveting; rivet joint

铆钉【mao⁵dēng¹ 得镜¹】rivet

貌【mao⁶ 矛⁶】looks; appearance

貌似【mao⁶qi⁵ 恃】seemingly; in appearance

貌合神离【mao⁶heb⁹xen⁴lēi⁴ 盒臣离】(of two persons or parties) seemingly in harmony but actually at variance

牡【mao⁵ 卯】male

牡丹【mao⁵dan¹ 单】tree peony; peony

牡蛎【mao⁵lei⁶ 丽】oyster

扮【man¹ 万¹】pull; turn ⌒【普】扳

扮低【man¹dei¹ 底¹】pull down =【普】扳倒

扮车边【man¹qē¹bin¹ 奢鞭】to get a free lift; to get beside one who is smart or popular ⌒【普】沾（某人）的光；托赖（某人）关照

蛮【man⁴ 万⁴】rough; fierce; reckless; unreasoning; quite; pretty

蛮干【man⁴gon³ 杆³】act rashly; act recklessly

蛮横【man⁴wang⁴ 乌嚣⁴】rude and unreasonable; arbitrary; peremptory

蛮不讲理【man⁴bed⁷gong²lēi⁵ 毕港李】be impervious to reason

晚【man⁵ 万⁵】evening; night; late; younger; junior

晚上【man⁵ xêng⁶尚 】(in the) evening; (at) night

晚安【man⁵ngon¹ 胺】good night

晚辈【man⁵bui³ 背】the younger generation

晚餐【man⁵ qan¹产¹】supper; dinner = 晚饭【man⁵fan⁶】

晚点【man⁵ dim² 掂²】(of a train, ship, etc.) late

晚间【man⁵ gan¹奸 】= 晚上（see "晚上"）

晚会【man⁵ wui² 汇²】soiree; social evening; evening party

晚年【man⁵ nin⁴ 捻⁴】 old age; one's later years

晚期【man⁵kēi⁴ 其】later period

晚霞【man⁵ ha⁴ 遐 】 sunset glow; sunset clouds

晚节【man⁵jid⁸ 折】integrity in one's later years

晚黑【man⁵ heg⁷ 克 】= 晚头黑【man⁵ teo⁴heg⁷ 投克】a night =【普】晚上

万【man⁶ 慢】ten thousand; myriad; absolutely

万般【man⁶ bun¹ 搬】all the different kinds; utterly; extremely

万端【man⁶dün¹ 段¹】multifarious

万分【man⁶fen¹ 芬】very much; extremely

万难【①man⁶nan⁴ 挪晏⁴；②man⁶nan⁶ 挪晏⁶】① extremely difficult；② all difficulties

万能【man⁶ neng⁴挪莺⁴】all-powerful; universal

万千【man⁶qin¹ 迁¹】multifarious; myriad

万全【man⁶qün⁴ 存】perfectly sound; sure-fire

万万【man⁶ man⁶】absolutely; wholly; hundred million

万一【man⁶yed⁷ 壹】just in case; contingency; one ten thousandth

万物【man⁶med⁹ 勿】all things on earth

万象【man⁶ jêng⁶像】every phenomenon on earth

万状【man⁶jong⁶ 撞】extremely

万幸【man⁶heng⁶ 杏】very lucky; by sheer luck

万有引力【man⁶yeo⁵yen⁵lig⁹ 友瘾历】(universal) gravitation

万事通【man⁶xi⁶tung¹ 是同¹】know-all

万应灵丹【man⁶ ying³ ling⁴ dan¹英³ 伶单】cure-all; panacea

万众一心【man⁶jung⁶yed⁷xem¹ 中⁴ 壹深】millions of people all of one mind

万无一失【man⁶mou⁴yed⁷xed⁷ 毛壹室】no risk at all

万事亨通【man⁶ xi⁶ heng¹ tung¹是铿同¹】everything goes well

万事大吉【man⁶xi⁶dai⁶ged⁷ 是歹⁶ 格核⁷】everything is just fine; all's well

万紫千红【man⁶ji²qin¹hung⁴ 止纤洪】a riot of colour

万变不离其宗【man⁶bin³bed⁷lēi⁴kēi⁴jung¹ 边³ 毕滴奇中】change ten thousand times without departing from the original aim or stand

万事俱备，只欠东风【man⁶xi⁶kêü¹bēi⁶, ji²him³dung¹fung¹ 士驱鼻，止谦³ 冬丰】everything is ready, and all that we need is an east wind — all is ready except what is crucial

曼【man⁶ 万】graceful; prolonged

曼延【man⁶yin⁴ 言】draw out; stretch

曼陀林【man⁶to⁴lem⁴ 驼淋】mandolin

蔓【man⁶ 万】trailing plant (蔓生植物【man⁶xeng¹jig⁹med⁹】)

蔓菁【man⁶jing¹ 精】turnip

蔓延【man⁶yin⁴ 言】spread; extend

慢【man⁶, 曼】slow; postpone; defer; rude

慢走【man⁶ jeo² 酒 】don't go yet; stay; wait a minute; good-bye; take care

慢车【man⁶qē¹ 奢】slow train

慢性【man⁶xing³ 胜】chronic; slow

慢慢【man⁶man² 万²】slowly; gradually

慢吞吞【man⁶ten¹ten¹ 替因¹】unhurriedly =【普】慢腾腾

慢条斯理【man⁶tiu⁴xi¹lēi⁵ 挑⁴ 司李】leisurely

漫【man⁶ 万】overflow; brim over; flood; free

漫步【man⁶bou⁶ 部】stroll；roam

漫长【man⁶qêng⁴ 祥】very long；endless

漫漫【man⁶man⁶】very long；boundless

漫谈【man⁶ tam⁴谭】（have an）informal discussion

漫说【man⁶xüd⁸ 雪】let alone；to say nothing of

漫天【man⁶ tin¹ 田¹】all over the sky；boundless

漫游【man⁶yeo⁴ 油】go on a pleasure trip；roam

漫无边际【man⁶ mou⁴ bin¹ jei³毛鞭制】boundless；rambling；discursive

漫不经心【man⁶bed⁷ging¹xem¹ 毕京深】careless

谩【man⁶ 曼】disrespectful；rude；deceive

谩骂【man⁶ma⁶ 马⁶】hurl invectives；rail

鳗【man⁶ 曼】eel（鳗鲡【man⁶lei⁶ 丽】）

馒【man⁶ 曼】steamed bun（馒头【man⁶teo⁴ 投】）

幔【man⁶ 曼】curtain；screen

幔帐【man⁶jêng³ 涨】curtain；screen

掹【mang¹ 孟¹；meng¹ 莫莺¹；meng³ 莫莺³】pull；drag

掹掹紧【mang¹mang¹gen² 谨】one who is not ample pays expenses ＝【普】经济开支不宽裕

掹出去【meng¹ qêd⁷ hêü³次律⁷虚³】pull out ＝【普】拉出去

掹过嚟【meng¹guo³lei⁴ 果³ 黎】rope in ＝【普】拉拢来

掹秧【meng³yêng¹ 央】pull up seedlings ＝【普】拔秧

蜢【mang² 孟²；mang⁵ 猛】grasshopper

蚱蜢【ja³mang² 炸】grasshopper

锰【mang⁵ 猛；mang¹ 孟¹】manganese（Mn）

锰钢【mang⁵gong³ 岗³】manganese steel

锰铁【mang⁵tid⁸ 替热⁸】ferromanganese

猛【mang⁵ 孟⁵】fierce；violent；suddenly；abruptly

猛烈【mang⁵lid⁹ 列】fierce；vigorous；violent

猛力【mang⁵lig⁹ 历】vigorously；with sudden force

猛进【mang⁵jên³ 俊】push ahead vigorously

猛禽【mang⁵kem⁴ 擒】bird of prey

猛不防【mang⁵ bed⁷ fong⁴毕妨】by surprise；unawares

猛咁【mang⁵gem³ 禁】very；hardworking；vigorously；desperately ＝【普】起劲地；拼命地

猛料【mang⁵liu² 廖²】brilliant data ＝【普】精彩材料

孟【mang⁶ 猛⁶】the first month（of a season）；eldest（brother）；a surname

孟子【mang⁶ji² 止】〈n.〉Mencius

孟浪【mang⁶long⁶ 朗】rash；impetuous

孟加拉【mang⁶ ga¹ lai¹家 赖¹】＜n.＞Bengal

盲【mang⁴ 孟⁴】blind

盲眼【mang⁴ngan⁵ 雁】blind

盲肠【mang⁴qêng⁴ 抢】caecum

盲公【mang⁴gung¹ 工】a blind man ＝【普】瞎子（男性的）

盲婆【mang⁴po² 颇】a blind lady ＝【普】盲人（女性的）

盲摸摸【mang⁴ mo² mo² 摩²】 to follow blindly; the situation is not clear ＝【普】盲目地

盲从【mang⁴qung⁴ 虫】follow blindly

盲动【mang⁴dung⁶洞 】 act blindly; act rashly

抹

【mad⁸ 莫压⁸; mud⁸莫活⁸】to wipe

抹台布【mad⁸toi²bou³ 抬² 报】table towel

掰

【mag⁸ 莫客⁸】to tear; to rip

掰烂【mag⁸lan⁶ 兰⁶】 tear up; tear to shreds ＝【普】(把布、纸等)撕毁

米

【mei⁵ 迷⁵; mei¹ 迷¹】rice; shelled or husked seed; metre; a surname

米波【mei¹bo¹ 坡】〈n.〉metre wave

米粒【mei⁵neb⁷ 挪恰⁷】grain of rice

米饭【mei⁵fan⁶ 范】(cooked) rice

米粉【mei⁵ fen² 分²】 ground rice; rice flour; rice-flour noodles

米酒【mei⁵jeo² 走】rice wine

咪

【mei¹ 迷¹; mei⁵ 米】read and dig into; no; not

咪书【mei¹xū¹ 输】read and dig into; study hard

咪先【mei⁵xin¹ 仙】＝ 未自先【mēi⁵ji⁶xin¹ 味⁵ 治仙】do not move at before; not beforehand ＝【普】先别动

迷

【mei⁴ 谜⁴】be confused; be lost; be fascinated by; confuse; perplex; fascinate

迷惑【mei⁴wag⁶ 或】puzzle; confuse; perplex

迷路【mei⁴ lou⁶露 】 lose one's way; get lost

迷茫【mei⁴mong⁴ 亡】vast and hazy; confused

迷失【mei⁴xed⁷ 室】lose

迷惘【mei⁴mong⁵ 网】be perplexed; be at a loss

迷离【mei⁴lēi⁴ 漓】blurred

迷恋【mei⁴lūn² 联²】madly cling to

迷糊【mei⁴ wu⁴ 胡 】 misted; blurred; dazed; confused

迷信【mei⁴xên³ 讯】superstition; have blind faith in

迷宫【mei⁴gung¹ 公】labyrinth; maze

迷魂阵【mei⁴wen⁴jen⁶ 云镇⁶】maze; trap

迷魂汤【mei⁴wen⁴tong¹ 云堂¹】magic potion

迷途知返【mei⁴tou¹ji¹fan² 图之反】recover one's bearings and return to the fold

谜

【 mei⁴ 迷 】 riddle; conundrum; enigma; puzzle

谜语【mei⁴yū⁵ 雨】riddle; conundrum

谜底【mei⁴ dei²抵 】 answer to a riddle; truth

踎

【meo¹ 茂¹】to squat down ＝【普】蹲下

踎墩【meo¹den¹ 得因¹】unemployed ＝【普】失业

踎享曙【meo¹hêng²xū³ 响 署³】squatting down here ＝【普】蹲在这里

某

【meo⁵ 亩】certain; some

某某【meo⁵meo⁵】so-and-so

某日【meo⁵yed⁹ 逸】on a certain date

某人【meo⁵yen⁴ 仁】a certain person; as for me

谋

【meo⁴ 牟】stratagem; plan; work for; seek; plot; consult

谋求【meo⁴keo⁴ 球】seek; strive for

谋划【meo⁴wag⁹ 或】plan; scheme

谋略【meo⁴lêg⁹ 掠】strategy

谋生【meo⁴ xeng¹ 笙 】 seek a livelihood;
　　make a living

谋事【meo⁴xi⁶ 士】plan matters; look for a
　　job

谋士【meo⁴xi⁶ 事】adviser; counsellor

谋害【meo⁴hoi⁶ 亥】plot to murder

谋反【meo⁴fan² 返】plot a rebellion

谋财害命【meo⁴qoi⁴hoi⁶ming⁶ 才亥名⁶】
　　murder sb. for his money

牟 【meo⁴ 谋】try to gain; seek; obtain; a
　　surname

牟取【meo⁴qêü² 娶】try to gain; seek; ob-
　　tain = 谋取【meo⁴qêü²】

眸 【meo⁴ 牟】pupil (of the eye); eye

缪 【meo⁶ 茂; meo⁴ 谋; miu⁶ 妙】a sur-
　　name

绸缪【qeo⁴ meo⁴ 稠 】 sentimentally atta-
　　ched

纰缪【pēi¹meo⁶ 披】error; mistake

茂 【meo⁶ 贸】luxuriant; profuse; exu-
　　berant; rich and splendid

茂密【meo⁶med⁶ 勿】dense; thick

茂盛【meo⁶ xing¹升⁶】 luxuriant; exuber-
　　ant

懋 【meo⁶ 茂】diligent; luxuriant; profuse

贸 【meo⁶ 茂】trade

贸然【meo⁶yin⁴ 言】rashly; hastily

贸易【meo⁶yig⁹ 亦】trade

袤 【meo⁶ 茂】length and breadth of land
　　(see "广袤")

袤狸【meo⁶lêi² 离²】fool; blockhead ∽
　　【普】傻瓜

饛 【mem¹ 莫庵】〈n.〉饛饛【mem¹mem¹】
　　soggy rice = 【普】糊饭(供婴儿吃
　　的)

蚊 【men¹ 文¹】mosquito

蚊仔【men¹jei² 济²】mosquito = 【普】蚊
　　子

蚊帐【men¹jêng³ 涨】mosquito net

蚊香【men¹hêng¹ 乡 】 mosquito-repellent
　　incense

蚊睏【men¹fen³ 训】too late = 【普】太晚
　　了

蚊蟻【men¹ji¹ 支】small insects = 【普】野
　　外小黑蚊

炆 【men¹ 蚊】to simmer; cook in water
　　∽【普】熬(文火长时间地煎熬)

炆淋【men¹lem⁴ 林】boil to become soft ∽
　　【普】熬至软化

扻 【men² 敏²】wipe; extruding and make
　　into or clean

扻墙窿【men²qêng⁴lung¹ 祥龙¹】extruding
　　the mud into the small hole that is
　　on wall ∽【普】填补墙上的窟窿

扻屎【men²xi² 史】clean the buttocks =
　　【普】擦屁股

抿 【men³ 蚊³】be close to end = 【普】接
　　近尽头;差不多没了

时间抿【xi⁴gan¹men³ 是⁴ 奸】the time is
　　close to end = 【普】没多少时间
　　了

抿抿莫【men³men³mog⁸ 剥⁸】be close to
　　need and insufficient ∽【普】勉强
　　够用;马马虎虎

文 【men⁴ 民】character; writing; lan-
　　guage; formal ritual; culture;
　　civilian; gentle; cover up; a cash; a
　　surname

文字【men⁴ji⁶ 治】characters; writing

文章【men⁴ jêng¹ 张 】 essay; literary works; hidden meaning

文明【men⁴ming⁴ 名】civilization; culture; civilized

文化【men⁴fa³ 花³】civilization; culture; education

文武【men⁴mou⁵ 母】civil and military

文学【men⁴hog⁹ 鹤】literature

文艺【men⁴ngei⁵ 毅】literature and art

文件【men⁴gin² 坚²】documents; papers

文献【men⁴hin³ 宪】documents; literature

文物【men⁴med⁹ 勿】cultural relic

文采【men⁴ qoi² 彩 】 rich and bright colours; literary grace

文告【men⁴ gou³ 诰 】 proclamation; message

文豪【men⁴ hou⁴毫 】 literary giant; great writer

文笔【men⁴bed⁷ 毕】style of writing

文身【men⁴xen¹ 辛】tattoo

文雅【men⁴nga⁵ 瓦】elegant; refined

文具【men⁴ gêû⁶巨 】 writing materials; stationery

文质彬彬【men⁴jed⁷ben¹ben¹ 侄¹ 宾宾】gentle; suave

文过饰非【men⁴ guo³ xig⁷ fêi¹ 果³ 式菲】conceal faults and gloss over wrongs

文化衫【men⁴fa³xêd⁷ 摔 】 short-sleeved round collar shirt

民【men⁴ 文】the people; a member of a nationality; a person of a certain occupation; folk; civilian

民众【men⁴jung³ 纵³】the common people; the populace

民权【men⁴kün⁴ 拳】civil rights; civil liberties

民族【men⁴jug⁹ 俗】nation; nationality

民生【men⁴ xeng¹笙 】 the people's livelihood

民俗【men⁴jug⁹ 族】folk custom; folkways

民情【men⁴qing⁴ 程】condition of the people

民意【men⁴yi³ 薏】the will of the people

民心【men⁴xem¹ 深】popular feelings

民用【men⁴yung⁶ 容⁶】civil

民政【men⁴jing³ 正】civil administration

民主【men⁴jü² 煮】democracy; democratic

民间【men⁴gan¹ 奸】popular; nongovernmental

民运【men⁴ wen⁶混 】 civil transport; the movement for democracy

民航【men⁴hong⁴ 杭】civil aviation

民警【men⁴ging² 景】people's policeman

民工【men⁴ gung¹公 】 a labourer working on a public project

民办【men⁴ban⁶ 班⁶】run by the local people

民歌【men⁴go¹ 哥】folk song

民愤【men⁴fen⁵ 奋】popular indignation

民不聊生【men⁴ bed⁷ liu⁴ xeng¹毕辽笙 】 the people have no means of livelihood

民怨沸腾【men⁴yün³fei⁶teng⁴ 渊³ 费⁶ 藤】the people are boiling with resentment

氓【men⁴ 民;meng⁴ 萌; mong⁴ 亡】the common people; rogue（see "流氓"）

闻【men⁴ 文;men² 文²】hear; news; famous; reputation; smell; a surname

闻讯【men⁴xên³ 信】hear the news

闻名【men⁴ ming⁴ 明 】 well-known; famous; be familiar with sb.'s name

闻风而动【men⁴ fung¹ yi⁴ dung⁶ 丰移洞】immediately respond to a call

闻过则喜【men⁴ guo³ jeg⁷ hēi² 果³ 仄起】feel happy when told of one's errors

闻所未闻【men⁴ xo² mēi⁶ men⁴ 锁味】unheard of

纹【men⁴ 文】lines; veins; grain

纹理【men⁴lēi⁵ 李】veins; grain

纹路【men⁴lou⁶ 露】lines; grain; method

纹丝不动【men⁴xi¹bed¹dung⁶ 司毕洞】absolutely still

吻【men⁵ 敏】lips; kiss; an animal's mouth

吻合【men⁵heb⁹ 盒】be identical; coincide; tally

刎【men⁵ 敏】cut one's own throat (自刎【ji⁶men⁵】)

闽【men⁵ 敏】another name for Fujian Province

悯【men⁵ 敏】commiserate; pity; sorrow

泯【men⁵ 敏】vanish; die out

泯灭【men⁵mid⁹ 蔑】die out; vanish

泯没【men⁵mud⁹ 末】vanish; become lost

闵【men⁵ 敏】a surname

抿【men⁵ 敏】smooth (hair, etc.) with a wet brush; close lightly; furl; sip

抿着嘴笑【men⁵jêg⁹jêu²xiu³ 雀⁹ 追² 少³】smile with closed lips

敏【men⁵ 闽】quick; nimble; agile

敏感【men⁵gem² 敢】sensitive; susceptible

敏捷【men⁵jid⁹ 截】quick; nimble; agile

敏锐【men⁵yêü⁶ 衣去⁶】sharp; acute

紊【men⁶ 问】disorderly; confused

紊乱【men⁶lün⁶ 联】disorder; chaos; confusion

瘤【meng¹ 莫莺¹】< n. >瘤鸡【meng¹gei¹ 计¹】the scars on eyelid; one who has got scars on the eyelid = 【普】眉眼附近的疮疤或伤疤

㦒【meng² 盟²】< a. >㦒悖【meng²jeng² 争²】hot-tempered; frustrated ∽【普】暴躁的；烦躁的；易激怒的

萌【meng⁴ 盟】sprout; shoot forth; bud; germinate

萌发【meng⁴ fad⁸ 法】sprout; germinate; shoot

萌芽【meng⁴ nga⁴ 牙】sprout; germinate; rudiment

盟【meng⁴ 萌】alliance; league; sworn (brothers)

盟誓【meng⁴xei⁶ 逝】take an oath; make a pledge

盟约【meng⁴yêg⁸ 跃】oath of alliance

盟友【meng⁴yeo⁵ 有】ally

盟邦【meng⁴bong¹ 帮】allied country; ally

盟主【meng⁴ jü² 煮】the leader of an alliance

盟笼【meng⁴lung² 拢】seal = 【普】密封、密闭状态

乜【med⁷ 勿⁷】what; whatever; why = 【普】什么;何;哪;怎

乜野【med⁷yê⁵ 夜⁵】what = 【普】什么；啥东西

乜东东【med⁷dung⁷dung¹ 冬】what is it = 【普】什么东西

乜鬼【med⁷guei² 诡】what is it = 【普】什么鬼名堂

乜谁【med7xêü2 水】who =【普】谁；何人

乜乜物物【med7med7med9med9 勿】this, that and the others ∽【普】什么什么，这个那个

乜都有【med7dou1yeo5 刀友】have all =【普】什么都有

乜都假【med7dou1ga2 刀贾】to show that one is determined to achieve what one wants; not being able to help ∽【普】说啥我也不信

袜【med9 勿】socks; stockings; hose =【普】袜子

勿【med9 密】no; not; do not

勿歇【med9hid8 蝎8】continuously; non-stop =【普】不断；不停

密【med9 勿】close; intimate; fine; secret

密闭【med9bei3 蔽】airtight; hermetic

密布【med9bou3 报】densely covered

密封【med9fung1 风】seal up; seal airtight

密集【med9jab9 习】concentrated

密码【med9ma5 马】cipher; cipher code

密斟【med9 jem1针 】to negotiate; to discuss; hold private counsel =【普】密谈；密商

密谋【med9meo4 牟】conspire; plot

密约【med9yêg8 跃】secret agreement

密友【med9yeo5 有】close friend

密实【med9 xed9 失9 】tightly-closed; quiet; closely knit

密揎揎【med9jed7jed7 质】thick (refer to the growing of hair); dense =【普】密匝匝

密密麻麻【med9 med9 ma4 ma4妈4】close and numerous

密切【med9qid8 设】close; intimate; carefully

密底算盘【med9dei2xün3pun4 抵算盆】one who plans carefully before doing anything ∽【普】老谋深算(做每样事情之前都考虑、计划得很周到密实)

蜜【med9 勿】honey; honeyed; sweet

蜜蜂【med9fung1 风】honeybee; bee

蜜饯【med9jin3 箭】candied fruit

蜜蜡【med9lab9 腊】bee wax

蜜糖【med9tong4 唐】honey

蜜枣【med9jou2 早】candied date or jujube

蜜月【med9yüd9 越】honeymoon

谧【med9 密】quiet; still; tranquil (see "静谧")

宓【med9 密】tranquil; quiet; a surname

物【med9 勿】thing; matter; other people; content

物质【med9jed7 窒7】matter; substance

物体【med9 tei2睇】body; substance; object

物品【med9ben2 禀】article; goods

物件【med9gin2 坚2】thing; article

物价【med9ga3 嫁】(commodity) prices

物产【med9qan2 铲】products; produce

物理【med9 lēi5李 】innate laws of thing; physics

物资【med9ji1 支】goods and materials

物证【med9jing3 正】material evidence

物色【med9 xig7式 】look for; seek out; choose

物以类聚【med9yi5lêü6jêü6 耳泪叙】things of one kind come together

物尽其用【med9jên6kēi4yung6 进6 奇容6】make the best use of everything

物极必反【med⁹gig⁹bid⁷fan² 击⁹ 别⁷ 返】things will develop in the opposite direction when they become extreme

唛【meg⁷ 麦⁷】mark；trademark；mug = 【普】牌子；样式；款式；商标

唛头【meg⁷teo² 投²】the look = 【普】样子；模样

㧯【meg⁷ 唛】tail sb. and press hard

㧯实【meg⁷xed⁹ 失⁹】tail sb. and press hard = 【普】(打球时)盯着而且紧逼(对方球员)

墨【meg⁹ 默】ink；ink stick；learning；black；graft；a surname

墨水【meg⁹xêü² 瑞²】ink；book learning

墨汁【meg⁹jeb⁷ 执】prepared Chinese ink

墨迹【meg⁹jig⁷ 积】ink marks；sb.'s writing or painting

墨守成规【meg⁹xeo⁹xing⁴kuei¹ 手承亏】stick to conventions

默【meg⁹ 麦】silent；tacit；write from memory

默哀【meg⁹ngoi¹ 爱¹】stand in silent tribute

默读【meg⁹dug⁹ 独】read silently

默默无闻【meg⁹meg⁹mou⁴men⁴ 毛文】unknown to the public

麦【meg⁹ 默】wheat；a surname

脉【meg⁹ 麦】arteries and veins；vein

脉搏【meg⁹bog⁸ 博】pulse

脉冲【meg⁹qung¹ 充】pulse

脉络【meg⁹ log⁹ 洛 】vein (of a leaf, etc.)；thread of thought

脉脉【meg⁹meg⁹】affectionately；lovingly

瘼【meg⁹ 麦】freckles = 【普】痣

么【mo¹ 摩；ma¹ 吗】〈auxil .〉① usually suffix of a word (see "什么"、"多么"、"怎么")；② = 吗

摩【mo¹ 魔；mo⁴ 磨】rub；scrape；touch；mull over；study

摩擦【mo¹qad⁸ 刷】rub；friction；clash

摩登【mo¹deng¹ 灯】modern；fashionable

摩托【mo¹tog⁸ 替恶⁸】motor

摩打【mo¹ da² 得阿²】motor = 【普】马达、电动机

摩肩接踵【mo⁴ gin¹ jib⁸ jung²坚支叶⁸ 肿】jostle each other in a crowd

摩拳擦掌【mo⁴kün⁴qad⁸jêng² 权刷蒋】rub one's fists and wipe one's palms — be eager for a fight

魔【mo¹ 摩¹】evil spirit；demon；magic

魔鬼【mo¹guei² 诡】devil；demon；monster

魔力【mo¹lig⁹ 历】magic power；magic

魔术【mo¹xed⁹ 述】magic；conjuring

魔掌【mo¹jêng² 蒋】devil's clutches

魔爪【mo¹jao² 找】devil's talons；claws

摸【mo² 么²】feel；feel for；feel out；stroke

摸索【mo²xog⁸ 朔】grope；feel about

摸底【mo²dei² 抵】know the real situation；sound sb. out

馍【mo¹ 么；mo⁴ 磨】steamed bun；steamed bread

磨【mo⁴ 么⁴；mo⁶ 么⁶】

磨砺【mo⁴ lei⁶厉 】 go through the mill；steel oneself；harden oneself

磨光【mo⁴guong¹ 胱】polish

磨练【mo⁴lin⁶ 炼】temper oneself

磨难【mo⁴ nan⁶ 挪晏⁶】 tribulation; hardship

磨损【mo⁴xūn² 选】wear and tear

磨灭【mo⁴mid⁹ 蔑】wear away; efface

磨蹭【mo⁴xeng³ 摛】move slowly; dawdle

磨牙【mo⁴ nga⁴牙】grind one's teeth; indulge in idle talk = 打牙铰【da² nga⁴gao³】

磨洋工【mo⁶yêng⁴gung¹ 羊公】loaf on the job

磨嘴皮【mo⁶jêü²pēi⁴ 追² 脾】jabber; do a lot of talking

蘑【mo⁴ 么⁴】mushroom

蘑菇【mo⁴gu¹ 姑】mushroom; worry; dawdle

髦【mou¹ 毛；mo⁴ 毛】fashionable; stylish (时髦【xi⁴mo¹】)

帽【mou² 毛²; mou⁶ 冒】headgear; hat; cap

帽子【mou²ji² 止】headgear; hat; cap; label; tag

帽徽【mou⁶fei¹ 辉】insignia on a cap

毛【mou⁴ 无】 hair; feather; wool; mildew; semifinished; gross; little; panick; a fractional unit of money in China; a surname

毛皮【mou⁴pēi⁴ 脾】fur; pelt

毛线【mou⁴xin³ 扇】knitting wool

毛纺【mou⁴fong² 访】wool spinning

毛巾【mou⁴gen¹ 斤】towel = 手巾【xeo² gen¹】

毛毯【mou⁴tan² 坦】woollen blanket

毛毡【mou⁴jin¹ 笺】felt

毛孔【mou⁴hung² 恐】pore

毛虫【mou⁴qung⁴ 从】caterpillar

毛笔【mou⁴bed⁷ 毕】writing brush

毛病【mou⁴bēng⁶ 柄⁶】trouble; defect

毛重【mou⁴qung⁵ 充⁵】gross weight

毛利【mou⁴lēi⁶ 俐】gross profit

毛衣【mou⁴yi¹ 依】woollen sweater; sweater

毛细管【mou⁴xei³gun² 世莞】capillary

毛毛雨【mou⁴mou⁴yü⁵ 语】drizzle

毛茸茸【mou⁴ xeng⁴ xeng⁴ 笙⁴】 hairy; downy ∽【普】毛茸茸

毛遂自荐【mou⁴xêü⁶ji⁶jin³ 瑞治箭】volunteer one's services

牦【mou⁴ 毛】yak（牦牛【mou⁴ngeo⁴ 藕⁴】)

耄【mou⁶ 冒】octogenarian; advanced in years

巫【mou⁴ 毛】shaman; witch; a surname

诬【mou⁴ 毛】accuse falsely

诬告【mou⁴gou³ 诰】lodge a false accusation against

诬蔑【mou⁴mid⁹ 灭】slander; vilify

诬陷【mou⁴ham⁶ 咸⁶】frame a case against

无【mou⁴ 毛】nothing; nil; not have; not; regardless of; without

无比【mou⁴bēi² 俾】incomparable; matchless

无偿【mou⁴xêng⁴ 常】free; gratis

无耻【mou⁴qi² 始】shameless; brazen

无从【mou⁴qung⁴ 虫】have no way

无端【mou⁴dün¹ 段¹】for no reason

无法【mou⁴fad⁸ 发】unable; incapable

无妨【mou⁴fong² 防】there's no harm

无非【mou⁴fēi¹ 飞】nothing but; simply; only

无辜【mou⁴ gu¹ 姑】innocent；an innocent person

无故【mou⁴gu³ 固】without cause or reason

无怪【mou⁴guai³ 乖³】no wonder

无关【mou⁴ guan³ 惯¹】have nothing to do with

无稽【mou⁴kei¹ 溪】unfounded；fantastic

无愧【mou⁴kuei⁵ 亏⁵】feel no qualms

无赖【mou⁴lai⁶ 拉⁶】rascally；rascal

无理【mou⁴ lēi⁵里】unreasonable；unjustifiable

无聊【mou⁴liu⁴ 辽】bored；senseless；silly

无奈【mou⁴noi⁶ 内】cannot help but；but

无能【mou⁴neng⁴ 挪莺⁴】incompetent；incapable

无情【mou⁴qing⁴ 程】merciless；ruthless

无穷【mou⁴kung⁴ 穷】infinite；endless

无任【mou⁴ yem⁶ 壬⁶】extremely；immensely

无上【mou⁴xêng⁶ 尚】supreme；highest

无视【mou⁴xi⁶ 示】ignore；disregard

无双【mou⁴ xêng¹相】unparalleled；unrivalled

无私【mou⁴xi¹ 司】selfless；unselfish

无谓【mou⁴wei⁶ 卫】no need；senseless

无畏【mou⁴wei³ 喂】fearless；dauntless

无限【mou⁴ han⁶ 悭⁶】infinite；limitless；boundless

无效【mou⁴hao⁶ 孝⁶】of no avail；invalid

无心【mou⁴ xem¹深】not be in the mood for；unwittingly

无须【mou⁴xêū¹ 需】need not

无恙【mou⁴yêng⁶ 让】in good health；well；safe

无疑【mou⁴yi⁴ 移】undoubtedly

无异【mou⁴yi⁶ 义】not different from；the same as

无益【mou⁴yig⁷ 忆】useless；no good

无意【mou⁴yi³ 薏】have no intention；unwittingly

无用【mou⁴yung⁶ 容】useless；of no use

无知【mou⁴ji¹ 支】ignorant

无拘束【mou⁴kêū¹qug⁷ 驱促】unrestrained

无所谓【mou⁴ xo² wei⁶锁卫 】cannot be designated as；not matter

无线电【mou⁴xin³din⁶ 扇甸】radio

无形中【mou⁴ying⁴jung¹ 型钟】imperceptibly

无意识【mou⁴yi³xig⁷ 薏式】unconscious

无端白事【mou⁴dün¹bag⁹xi⁶ 段¹伯⁹士】 without any reason ∽【普】无缘无故

无事生非【mou⁴ xi⁶ xeng¹ fēi¹士笙飞 】 make trouble out of nothing

无所事事【mou⁴ xo² xi⁶ xi⁶锁士 】have nothing to do

无所适从【mou⁴ xo² xig⁷ qung⁴锁式虫】 not know what course to take

无微不至【mou⁴ mēi⁴ bed⁷ ji³眉毕致】 meticulously

无以复加【mou⁴yi⁵fug⁹ga¹耳伏家】the extreme

无与伦比【mou⁴yü⁵lên⁴bēi²语沦俾】incomparable

无可非议【mou⁴ ho² fēi¹ yi⁵贺² 飞耳】 blameless

无可救药【mou⁴ho²geo³yêg⁹贺²够若】 incurable

无动于衷【mou⁴dung⁶yü¹qung¹洞迂冲】 unmoved

无恶不作【mou⁴ngog⁸bed⁷jog⁸噩毕昨】 stop at nothing in doing evil；stop at no evil

无法无天【mou⁴fad⁸mou⁴tin¹发田¹】defy

laws human and divine

无中生有【mou⁴jung¹xeng¹yeo⁵ 钟笙友】
purely fictitious

无的放矢【mou⁴dig⁷fong³qi² 滴⁷ 况始】
shoot at random

模【mou⁴ 毛；mou² 毛²】

模具【mou⁴geu⁶ 巨】mould；matrix

模样【mou⁴ yêng⁶让 】appearance；look；
approximately

模范【mou⁴fan⁶饭】an exemplary person
or thing；model；fine example

模仿【mou⁴fong² 访】imitate；copy

模拟【mou⁴yi⁴ 移】imitate；simulate

模糊【mou⁴ wu⁴胡 】blurred；dim；blur；
obscure

模型【mou⁴ying⁴ 形】model；mould

模特儿【mou⁴deg⁹yi⁴ 得⁹ 而】model

模棱两可【mou⁴ling⁴lêng⁵ho² 陵俩贺²】e-
quivoval

摹【mou⁴ 毛】copy；trace

摹本【mou⁴bun² 苯】facsimile；copy

摹写【mou⁴xê² 舍²】copy；depict

摹刻【mou⁴ heg⁷黑 】carve a reproduction
of an inscription or painting

母【mou⁵ 武⁵】mother；one's female el-
ders；female (animal)；nut；origin

母亲【mou⁵qen¹ 趁¹】mother

母爱【mou⁵ngoi³ 哀³】mother love；mater-
nal love

母本【mou⁵bun² 苯】female parent

母性【mou⁵xing³ 胜】maternal instinct

母系【mou⁵hei⁶ 兮⁶】maternal side；matri-
archal

母校【mou⁵hao⁶ 效】one's old school；Al-
ma Mater

拇【mou⁵ 母】〈n.〉拇指【mou⁵ji² 止】
thumb；big toe

姆【mou⁵ 母】〈n.〉保姆【bou²mou⁵ 宝】
(children's) nurse

冇【mou⁵ 母】do not have；do not win ＝
【普】没有；无

冇乜【mou⁵ med⁷勿⁷】 nothing much to
say；not really ∽【普】没什么；没
要说的了

冇料【mou⁵liu² 撩】not knowledgeable ＝
【普】没知识；没本领；没什么东
西

冇谱【mou⁵pou² 普】abnormal；to reach a
degree at which it is unbearable ∽
【普】乱来；没章法；没准绳；没个
大概

冇符【mou⁵ fu⁴乎 】 fail to tackle with a
problem after using all possible
means ∽【普】没办法；无法对付

冇解【mou⁵ gai²介² 】rude；no manners；
funny；strange ∽【普】没道理；
无法解释

冇瘾【mou⁵ yen⁵引 】boring；meaningless
∽【普】没意思；没兴趣

冇话【mou⁵wa⁶ 画⁶】have no say；never
∽【普】没说

冇益【mou⁵yig⁷ 忆】not beneficial ∽【普】
没好处

冇野到【mou⁵yê⁵dou³ 惹都³】have no benefit ∽【普】没得好处；没东西送
到

冇得弹【mou⁵deg⁷tan⁴ 德坛】excellent；
very good ∽【普】无法挑剔的；
好得很

冇踏霎【mou⁵dab⁹xab⁹ 搭⁹ 是鸭⁹】not
giving full concentration when doing things；not serious ∽【普】做

事情松松垮垮,拖拖拉拉,没条理,没计划

冇几何【mou⁵ gēi² ho⁴ 纪何 】sometimes; hardly ◯【普】次数不多;不很经常

冇记性【mou⁵ gēi² xing³ 寄胜 】absent-minded ◯【普】健忘;记忆力差

冇口齿【mou⁵ heo² qi² 厚² 齿】not trustworthy ◯【普】说话不算数;不讲信用

冇眼睇【mou⁵ ngan⁵ tei² 雁⁵ 替²】not to bother any more ◯【普】不愿看到;看了难堪

冇声气【mou⁵ xēng¹ hēi³ 腥戏 】no more hope; no more news ◯【普】没消息;没希望

冇心机【mou⁵ xem¹ gēi¹ 深基¹】impatient; not concentrating ◯【普】提不起兴趣;不想干

冇相干【mou⁵ xēng¹ gon¹ 双竿】never mind ◯【普】没关系;不要紧

冇走鸡【mou⁵ jeo² gei¹ 酒计¹】be bound to get ◯【普】必定得到;不会错失

冇走栈【mou⁵ jeo² jan² 酒盏】confident; sure of winning ◯【普】只能这样办;没有回旋的余地

冇腰骨【mou⁵ yiu¹ gued⁷ 妖掘¹】unreliable ◯【普】缺乏德性,不念亲情、友情,把事做绝了;没骨气

冇头乌蝇【mou⁵ teo⁴ wu¹ ying¹ 投污英】to refer to one who does things without proper planning ◯【普】形容某人缺乏理智,办事忙乱,没计划,乱碰乱闯

冇晒表情【mou⁵ xai³ biu² qing⁴ 徙³ 标² 程²】to describe one's feeling when one is troubled by some unfortunate happenings ◯【普】情绪低落;发呆;无精打采

冇厘神气【mou⁵ lēi⁴ xen⁴ hēi³ 离臣戏】in a bad mood; not feeling good ◯【普】无精打采

募【mou⁶ 务】raise; collect; enlist; recruit

募集【mou⁶ jab⁹ 习】raise; collect

募捐【mou⁶ gūn¹ 娟】solicit contributions

墓【mou⁶ 务】grave; tomb; mausoleum

墓地【mou⁶ dēi⁶ 得希⁶】graveyard; cemetery

墓穴【mou⁶ yüd⁹ 月】coffin pit

墓碑【mou⁶ bēi¹ 悲 】tombstone; gravestone

慕【mou⁶ 务】admire; yearn for

爱慕【ngoi³ mou⁶ 哀³】love; adore

慕名【mou⁶ ming⁴ 明】out of admiration for a famous person

暮【mou⁶ 务】dusk; evening; towards the end

暮霭【mou⁶ ngoi² 哀²】evening mist

暮色【mou⁶ xig⁷ 式】dusk; twilight

暮气【mou⁶ hēi³ 戏】lethargy; apathy

暮年【mou⁶ nin⁴ 捻⁴】old age

冒【mou⁶ 务】emit; risk; boldly; falsely

冒充【mou⁶ qung¹ 冲】pretend to be (sb. or sth.)

冒犯【mou⁶ fan⁶ 范】offend; affront

冒火【mou⁶ fo² 伙】burn with anger; flare up

冒尖【mou⁶ jim¹ 詹】a little over

冒进【mou⁶ jên³ 俊】premature advance

冒失【mou⁶ xed⁷ 室】rash; abrupt

冒险【mou⁶him² 欠²】take a risk

冒牌【mou⁶pai⁴ 排】imitation; fake

冒天下之大不韪【mou⁶tin¹ha⁶ji¹dai⁶bed⁷ wei⁵ 田¹ 夏支歹⁶ 毕伟】defy world opinion

瑁【mou⁶ 务】〈n.〉玳瑁【doi⁶mou⁶ 代】hawksbill turtle

戊【mou⁶ 务】the fifth of the ten Heavenly Stems

务【mou⁶ 冒】affair; business; be engaged in; must; be sure to

务必【mou⁶bid⁷ 别⁷】must; be sure to = 务须【mou⁶ xêu¹ 需】

务使【mou⁶xei² 洗】make sure; ensure

务实【mou⁴ xed⁹失⁹】deal with concrete matters relating to work

武【mou⁵ 冇】military; connected with boxing skill, swordplay, etc.; valiant; dispute

武力【mou⁵lig⁹ 历】force; military force

武器【mou⁵hêi³ 戏】weapon; arms

武士【mou⁵xi⁶ 是】palace guards in ancient times; warrior; knight

武术【mou⁵ xêd⁹ 述】martial arts such as shadowboxing, swordplay, etc., formerly cultivated for self-defence, now a form of physical culture

武装【mou⁵jong¹ 妆】arms; armed forces; arms

鹉【mou⁵ 武】〈n.〉鹦鹉【ying¹mou² 英】parrot

侮【mou⁵ 武】insult; bully

侮辱【mou⁵yug⁹ 玉】insult; humiliate

舞【mou⁵ 武】dance; move about as in a dance; flourish; dance with sth. in one's hands

舞蹈【mou⁵dou⁶ 道】dance

舞会【mou⁵wui² 汇²】dance; ball

舞伴【mou⁵bun⁶ 拌】dancing partner

舞台【mou⁵toi⁴ 抬】stage; arena

舞弄【mou⁵lung² 龙⁶】wave; wield

舞弊【mou⁵bei⁶ 币】malpractices

妩【mou⁴ 无】〈a.〉妩媚【mou⁴mêi⁴ 眉】lovely; charming

芜【mou⁴ 无】〈a.〉芜杂【mou⁴jab⁹ 习】mixed and disorderly; miscellaneous

杧【mong¹ 芒¹】〈n.〉杧果【mong1guo² 裹】mango

捆【mong¹ 杧】use paper, skin, silk, etc., to cover on =【普】用纸、皮革、丝绸等蒙紧在某物上

芒【mong¹ 亡; mong¹ 杧】awn; beard; arista

芒种【mong⁴jung³ 钟³】Grain in Ear (9th solar term)

芒刺在背【mong¹qi³joi⁶bui³ 次再⁶ 辈】feel prickles down one's back — feel nervous and uneasy

硭【mong⁴ 亡】〈n.〉硭硝【mong⁴xiu¹ 矛】mirabilite

茫【mong⁴ 亡】boundless and indistinct; ignorant

茫茫【mong⁴ mong⁴】boundless and indistinct; vast

茫然【mong⁴yin⁴ 言】ignorant; at a loss

忙【mong⁴ 亡】busy; fully; hurry; hasten

忙碌【mong⁴ lug⁷ 陆⁷】be busy; bustle about

忙乱【mong⁴lün⁶ 联⁶】be in a rush and a muddle

莽【mong⁵ 网】rank grass；rash

莽苍【mong⁵qong¹ 仓】(of scenery) blurred；misty

莽汉【mong⁵hon³ 看】a boorish fellow；a boor

莽撞【mong⁵jong⁶ 壮⁶】crude and impetuous；rash

蟒【mong⁵ 莽】〈 n.〉蟒蛇【mong⁵xē⁴ 些⁴】boa；python

亡【mong⁴ 忙】flee；run away；die；lose；deceased；conquer

亡命【mong⁴ming⁶ 名⁶】flee；desperate

亡灵【mong⁴ling⁴ 玲】ghost；spectre

亡国【mong⁴guog⁸ 帼】subjugate a nation

亡羊补牢【mong⁴yêng⁴bou²lou⁴ 杨保劳】mend the fold after a sheep is lost

虻【mong¹ 亡¹】〈 n.〉牛虻【ngeo⁴mong¹ 欧⁴】gadfly

忘【mong⁴ 亡】forget；overlook；neglect

忘记【mong⁴gēi³ 寄】forget；overlook

忘却【mong⁴kêg⁸ 卡约⁸】forget

忘我【mong⁴ ngo⁵鹅⁵】oblivious of oneself；selfless

忘本【mong⁴ bun² 苯】forget one's class origin

忘形【mong⁴ ying⁴型 】be beside oneself（with glee, etc.）

忘恩负义【mong⁴ yen¹ fu⁶ yi⁶因付异】devoid of gratitude；ungrateful

忘乎所以【mong⁴fu⁴xo²yi⁵ 符锁耳】forget oneself

妄【mong⁵ 网 】absurd；preposterous；presumptuous

妄想【mong⁵xêng² 赏】vain hope；wishful thinking

妄图【mong⁵ tou⁴途 】try in vain；vainly attempt

妄动【mong⁵dung⁶ 洞】rash action

妄自尊大【mong⁵ji⁶jūn¹dai⁶ 治专歹⁶】be overweening

网【mong⁵ 妄】net；network；catch with a net；cover or enclose as with a net

网兜【mong⁵deo¹ 逗¹】string bag

网罗【mong⁵lo⁴锣 】trap；enlist the services of

网络【mong⁵log⁸ 诺】network

网球【mong⁵keo⁴ 求】tennis；tennis ball

罔【mong⁵ 妄】deceive；no；not

惘【mong⁵ 妄】feel frustrated；feel disappointed

惘然【mong⁵ yin⁴言 】frustrated；disappointed

魍【mong⁵ 妄】〈 n.〉魍魉【mong⁵lêng⁵两】demons and monsters

望【mong⁶ 亡⁶】look over；call on；hope；reputation；full moon；the 15th day of a lunar month

望族【mong⁶jug⁹ 俗】distinguished family

望远镜【mong⁶yün⁵gēng³ 软颈³】telescope

望尘莫及【mong⁶qen⁴mog⁹keb⁹ 陈膜级⁹】so far behind that one can only see the dust of the rider ahead；too far behind to catch up

望穿秋水【mong⁶ qün¹ qeo¹ xêu²川抽瑞²】anxiously gaze till one's eyes are strained

望而生畏【mong⁶ yi⁴ xeng¹ wei³移笙喂】forbidding

望洋兴叹【mong⁶yêng⁴hing¹tan³ 羊兄炭】lament one's littleness before the vast ocean — bemoan one's inadequacy in the face of a great task

望梅止渴【mong⁶mui⁴ji²hod⁸ 煤子喝】feed on fancies

望天打卦【mong⁶ tin¹ da² gua³ 田¹ 得阿² 挂】to say that one should not be lazy but should work hard to earn a living ∽【普】盼老天爷开恩

剥【mog⁷ 莫⁷】shell; peel; skin

剥花生【mog⁷fa¹xeng¹ 化¹ 笙】shell peanuts

剥落【mog⁷log⁹ 洛⁹】peel off =剥甩【mog⁷ led⁷】

剥夺【mog⁷düd⁹ 得月⁹】deprive; strip

剥削【mog⁷xêg⁸ 是约⁸】exploit

莫【mog⁹ 漠】no one; nothing; none; no; not; don't; a surname

莫不【mog⁹ bed⁷毕】there's no one who doesn't or isn't

莫非【mog⁹fêi¹ 飞】can it be that

莫大【mog⁹dai⁶ 歹⁶】greatest; utmost

莫如【mog⁹yü⁴ 鱼】would be better

莫过于【mog⁹guo³yü¹ 果³ 迂】nothing is more … than

莫须有【mog⁹xêü¹yeo⁵ 需友】unwarranted

莫名其妙【mog⁹ming⁴kêi⁴miu⁶ 明奇庙】be baffled; inexplicable; odd

寞【mog⁹ 莫】lonely; deserted（see "寂寞"）

漠【mog⁹ 莫】desert; indifferent

漠视【mog⁹xi⁶ 示】treat with indifference; ignore

漠然【mog⁹yin⁴ 言】indifferently; apathetically

漠不关心【mog⁹bed⁷guan¹xem¹ 毕惯深】indifferent

幕【mog⁹ 莫】curtain; screen; act

幕布【mog⁹bou³ 报】curtain; screen

幕后【mog⁹ heo⁶候 】behind the screen; backstage

膜【mog⁹ 莫】membrane; film; thin coating

膜片【mog⁹pin³ 遍】diaphragm

膜拜【mog⁹ bai³ 摆³】prostrate oneself; worship

妹【mui² 梅²; mui¹ 梅¹; mui⁶ 梅⁶】younger sister

妹妹【mui⁴mui²】younger sister

妹夫【mui⁶fu¹ 孚】younger sister's husband

妹钉【mui¹dêng¹ 得镜¹】small young girls =【普】小姑娘

妹仔【mui¹jei² 济²】servants =【普】丫头

梅【mui⁴ 媒】plum; a surname

梅仔【mui⁴jei² 济²】plum =【普】梅子

梅花【mui⁴fa¹ 化¹】plum blossom; wintersweed

梅雨【mui⁴ yü⁵语 】 plum rains = 黄梅雨【wong⁴mui⁴yü⁵ 王】

梅毒【mui⁴dug⁹ 独】syphilis

莓【mui⁴ 梅】<n.> 草莓【qou² mui⁴ 操²】strawberry

酶【mui⁴ 梅】<n.> enzyme; ferment

霉【mui⁴ 梅】mould; mildew; damaged

霉菌【mui⁴kueu⁴ 捆】mould

霉烂【mui⁴lan⁶ 兰⁶】mildew and rot

霉菜【mui⁴qoi³ 蔡】a type of dried preserved vegetable

媒【mui⁴ 梅】matchmaker；go-between；
　　intermediary
媒婆【mui⁴po⁴ 颇⁴】woman matchmaker
媒人【mui⁴yen¹ 仁】matchmaker；go-be-
　　tween
媒介【mui⁴ gai³ 戒 】 intermediary；medi-
　　um；vehicle
媒质【mui⁴jed⁷ 侄⁷】medium

煤【mui⁴ 梅】coal

煤矿【mui⁴kong³ 抗³】coal mine；colliery
煤炭【mui⁴tan³ 叹】coal
煤油【mui⁴yeo⁴ 由】kerosene；paraffin ＝
　　火水【fo²xêü²】
煤渣【mui⁴ja¹ 抓】coal cinder
煤气【mui⁴hēi³ 汽】coal gas；gas

玫【mui⁵ 梅】＜n.＞ 玫瑰【mui⁴ guei³
　　桂】rugosa rose；rose

枚【mui⁴ 梅；mui² 妹；mui⁵ 每】＜classi-
　　fier＞ 一枚古币【yed⁷mui⁴gu²bei⁶】an
　　ancient coin
枚举【mui⁵gêü² 矩】enumerate one by one

昧【mui⁶ 妹⁶】be ignorant of；hide；con-
　　ceal

寐【mui⁶ 昧】sleep

每【mui⁵ 梅⁵】every；each；per；often

每当【mui⁵ dong¹ 珰 】 whenever；every
　　time
每每【mui⁵mui⁵】often
每况愈下【mui⁵fong⁵yüd⁹ha⁶ 放 月 夏】
　　steadily deteriorate

瞒【mun⁴ 门】hide the truth from

瞒骗【mun⁴pin³ 片】deceive
瞒上欺下【mun⁴xêng⁶hēi¹ha⁶ 尚希夏】de-
ceive those above and bully those
below
瞒天过海【mun⁴tin¹guo³hoi² 田¹ 果³ 开²】
　　cross the sea by a trick — practise
　　deception

门【mun⁴ 们】 entrance； door； gate；
　　valve；knack；family；class；phylum；
　　a surname；＜classifier＞　一门大炮
　　【yed⁷mun⁴dai⁶pao³】a cannon
门口【mun⁴heo² 厚²】entrance；doorway
门面【mun⁴ min⁶ 免⁶】 shop front；appear-
　　ance；facade
门牌【mun⁴pai⁴ 排】(house) number
　　plate；house number
门路【mun⁴ lou⁶ 露 】 knack；way；social
　　connections
门市【mun⁴xi⁵ 史⁵】retail sales
门卫【mun⁴wei⁶ 惠】entrance guard
门诊【mun⁴qen² 陈²】outpatient service
门徒【mun⁴tou⁴ 图】disciple；follower
门径【mun⁴ging³ 经³】access；key；way
门楣【mun⁴mēi⁴ 眉】lintel (of a door)
门扇【mun⁴xin³ 线】door leaf
门槛【mun⁴ham⁵ 咸⁵】threshold
门框【mun⁴kuang¹ 卡横¹】doorframe
门闩【mun⁴xan¹ 珊】(door) bolt；(door)
　　bar
门户【mun⁴wu⁶ 护】door；gateway；faction
门第【mun⁴dei⁶ 弟】family status
门外汉【mun⁴ngoi⁶hon³ 碍看】layman；the
　　uninitiated
门庭若市【mun⁴ting⁴yêg⁹xi⁵ 廷药史⁵】the
　　courtyard is as crowded as a mar-
　　ketplace — a much visited house

们【mun⁴ 门】show the plural form of the
　　personal pronoun 他们【ta¹mun⁴ 它】
　　they

钔【mun⁴ 门 】 < n. > mendelevium（Md）

扪【mun⁴ 门】touch; stroke

扪心自问【mun⁴xem¹ji⁶men⁶ 深治文⁶】examine one's conscience

满【mun⁵ 螨】full; filled; fill; expire; completely; satisfied; complacent; a surname

满足【mun⁵jug⁷ 竹】satisfied; content; satisfy

满意【mun⁵yi³ 薏】satisfied; pleased

满载【mun⁵joi³ 再】loaded to capacity; fully loaded

满额【mun⁵ngag⁹ 我客⁹】fulfil the（enrolment, etc.）quota

满月【mun⁵ yüd⁹越 】full moon; a baby's completion of its first month of life

满师【mun⁵xi¹ 思】serve out one's apprenticeship

满杯【mun⁵ wai⁴槐】be imbued with; all with young

满不在乎【mun⁵bed⁷joi⁶fu⁴ 毕再⁶ 符】not worry at all

满城风雨【mun⁵ xing⁴ fung¹ yü⁵成丰语】（become）the talk of the town

满目疮痍【mun⁵ mug⁹ qong¹ yi⁴木仓夷 】everywhere a scene of devastation meets the eye

螨【mun⁵ 满】< n. > mite

懑【mun⁶ 闷】< a. > 烦懑 【fan⁴mun⁶凡】be unhappy

闷【mun⁶ 懑】stuffy; cover tightly; muffled; shut oneself or sb. indoors; bored; sealed

闷气【mun⁶ hēi³戏 】 stuffy; close; the sulks

闷热【mun⁶yid⁹ 衣泄⁹】hot and suffocating; sultry

闷雷【mun⁶lêu⁴ 擂】muffled thunder

闷葫芦【mun⁶wu⁴lou⁴ 胡卢】enigma; puzzle; riddle

闷闷不乐【mun⁶mun⁶bed⁷log⁹ 毕落】depressed; in low spirits

懵【mung² 蒙²】blur; ambiguous; muddled; ignorant

懵懂【mung²dung² 董】muddled; ignorant

懵闭闭【mung²bei³bei³ 蔽】blur; not sure ＝ 懵盛盛【mung²xing⁶xing⁶ 成⁶】 ＝【普】(理智)不清醒;糊里糊涂

檬【mung¹ 蒙¹】< n. > 柠檬【ning⁴ mung¹ 宁】lemon

蒙【mung⁴ 朦】cheat; deceive; make a wild guess; unconscious; cover; receive; ignorant

蒙古【mung⁴gu² 鼓】Mongolia

蒙骗【mung⁴ pin³遍 】deceive; cheat; delude

蒙蔽【mung⁴bei³ 闭】hoodwink; deceive

蒙混【mung⁴ wen⁶运 】deceive or mislead people

蒙昧【mung⁴mui⁶ 妹⁶】barbaric; ignorant

蒙受【mung⁴xeo⁶ 授】suffer; sustain

蒙难【mung⁴nan⁶ 挪晏⁶】be confronted by danger

蒙太奇【mung⁴tai³kēi⁴ 泰其】< n. > montage

蒙在鼓里【mung⁴joi⁶gu²lêu⁵ 再⁶ 古吕】be kept inside a drum — be kept in the dark

蒙头转向【mung⁴ teo⁴ jün² hêng³ 投专² 香³ 】lose one's bearings

濛【mung⁴ 蒙】< a . > 濛濛【mung⁴ mung⁴】drizzly; misty = 蒙蒙【mung⁴ mung⁴】

朦【mung⁴ 蒙; mung¹ 檬】< a . > 朦胧【mung⁴ lung⁴ 龙】dim moonlight; obscure; dim

朦朦光【mung¹ mung¹ guong¹ 胱】dawn; first glimmer of dawn; daybreak = 【普】蒙蒙亮

矇【mung⁴ 蒙; mung¹ 檬】drowsy

矇眬【mung⁴ lung⁴ 龙】half asleep; somnolent

眼矇矇【ngan⁵ mung¹ mung¹ 雁⁵】eyes heavy with sleep

矇茶茶【mung⁴ qa⁴ qa⁴ 查】blur; one who is not sure; one not knowing the real situation ∽ 【普】懵懂; 糊里糊涂

梦【mung⁶ 蒙⁶】dream

梦幻【mung⁶ wan⁶ 弯⁶】illusion; dream

梦境【mung⁶ ging² 竟】dreamland; dreamworld = 梦乡【mung⁶ hêng¹ 香】

梦想【mung⁶ xêng² 赏】dream of; fond dream

梦见【mung⁶ gin³ 建】see in a dream

梦呓【mung⁶ ngei⁶ 艺】somniloquy; rigmarole; daydream = 梦话【mung⁶ wa⁶ 画⁶】

梦幻泡影【mung⁶ wan⁶ pao¹ ying² 弯⁶ 抛 映】pipe dream; bubble; illusion

梦寐以求【mung⁶ mui⁶ yi⁵ keo⁴ 昧 耳 球】crave sth. so that one even dreams about it

木【mug⁹ 目】tree; made of wood; wooden; coffin; numb

木材【mug⁹ qoi⁴ 才】wood; timber; lumber = 木料【mug⁹ liu² 撩】

木板【mug⁹ ban² 版】plank; board

木头【mug⁹ teo⁴ 投】wood; log; timber

木器【mug⁹ hêi³ 气】wooden furniture

木工【mug⁹ gung¹ 功】woodwork; woodworker

木匠【mug⁹ jêng⁶ 丈】carpenter

木刻【mug⁹ heg⁷ 克】woodcut; wood engraving

木屋【mug⁹ ngug⁷ 额哭⁷】log cabin

木屐【mug⁹ kēg⁹ 剧】clogs

木瓜【mug⁹ gua¹ 寡¹】< n . > Chinese flowering quince; papaya

木耳【mug⁹ yi⁵ 以】an edible fungus

木筏【mug⁹ fed⁹ 伐】raft

木炭【mug⁹ tan³ 叹】charcoal

木薯【mug⁹ xü⁴ 书⁴】cassava

木棉【mug⁹ min⁴ 绵】silk cotton; kapok

木独【mug⁹ dug⁹ 毒】stunned; not enough sleep∽ 【普】睡眠不足时不清醒、发木的样子;不合群,孤独

木偶【mug⁹ ngeo⁵ 藕】wooden image; puppet

木星【mug⁹ xing¹ 升】< n . > Jupiter

木兰【mug⁹ lan⁴ 栏】lily magnolia

木乃伊【mug⁹ nai⁵ yi¹ 奶 衣】mummy

木然【mug⁹ yin⁴ 言】stupefied

木已成舟【mug⁹ yi⁵ xing⁴ jeo¹ 耳承周】the wood is already made into a boat — what is done cannot be undone

目【mug⁹ 木】eye; look; regard; order; catalogue

目标【mug⁹ biu¹ 彪】objective; goal; aim

目的【mug⁹ dig⁹ 得益⁷】purpose; aim

目光【mug⁹ guong¹ 胱】sight; gaze; look

目睹【mug⁹ dou² 赌 】see with one's own eyes; witness

目击【mug⁹gig⁷ 激】= 目睹【mug⁹dou²】

目录【mug⁹lug⁹ 六】catalogue; contents

目前【mug⁹qin⁴ 钱】at present

目送【mug⁹xung³ 宋】watch sb. go; gaze after

目眩【mug⁹yün⁴ 原】dizzy; dazzled

目中无人【mug⁹jung¹mou⁴yen⁴ 钟毛仁】be overweening

目无法纪【mug⁹ mou⁴ fad⁸ gēi² 毛发儿】disregard law and discipline

目空一切【mug⁹hung¹yed⁷qei³ 凶壹砌】be supercilious

目不转睛【mug⁹ bed⁷ jün² jing¹ 毕专¹ 精】look with fixed eyes

目瞪口呆【mug⁹ deng¹ heo² ngoi⁴ 登厚² 碍⁴】gaping; stupefied

沐【mug⁹ 木】wash one's hair

沐浴【mug⁹yug⁹ 玉】have a bath; bathe; immerse

苜【mug⁹ 目】< n. > 苜蓿【mug⁹xug⁷ 宿】lucerne; alfalfa

钼【mug⁹ 目】< n. > molybdenum (Mo)

牧【mug⁹ 木】herd; tend

牧民【mug⁹ men⁴ 文 】herdsman = 牧人【mug⁹yen⁴ 仁】

牧场【mug⁹ qêng⁴祥 】grazing land; pastureland

牧童【mug⁹tung⁴ 同】shepherd boy

牧师【mug⁹xi¹ 司】pastor; minister

牧歌【mug⁹go¹ 哥】pastoral song; madrigal

牧羊人【mug⁹yêng⁴yen⁴ 洋仁】shepherd

睦【mug⁹ 目】peaceful; harmonious

睦邻【mug⁹lên⁴ 伦】good-neighbourliness

穆【mug⁹ 目】solemn; reverent; a surname

穆罕默德【mug⁹hon²meg⁹deg⁷ 汗² 墨得】Mohammed

穆斯林【mug⁹xi¹lem⁴ 司临】Moslem; Muslim

咪【mi¹ 莫衣¹; mēi¹ 微¹】

咪咪【mi¹mi¹】① < onomatopoeia > mew; miaow (the sound of cat calling) ② < a. > smilingly

喵【miu¹ 苗¹】< onomatopoeia > miaow (the sound of cat calling)

苗【miu⁴ 描】young plant; seedling; the young of some animals; vaccine; sth. resembling a young plant; a surname

苗子【miu⁴ji² 止】young plant; young successor

苗裔【miu⁴yêü⁶ 锐】progeny; offspring

苗头【miu⁴teo⁴ 投】symptom of a trend

苗条【miu⁴tiu⁴ 挑⁴】(of a woman) slender; slim

苗圃【miu⁴pou² 普】nursery stock

瞄【miu⁴ 苗】take aim

瞄准【miu⁴jên² 遵²】take aim; aim; train on

描【miu⁴ 苗】trace; copy; touch up; retouch

描画【miu⁴wag⁹ 或】draw; paint; depict

描绘【miu⁴kui² 剑】depict; describe; portray

描述【miu⁴xêd⁹ 术】describe

描图【miu⁴tou⁴ 途】tracing

描写【miu⁴xē² 舍²】describe

秒【miu⁵ 渺】second (= 1/60 of a minute)

秒表【miu⁵biu¹ 标】stopwatch；chronograph

秒针【miu⁵jem¹ 斟】second hand（of a clock or watch）

渺【miu⁵ 秒】（of an expanse of water）vast；vague；tiny

渺茫【miu⁵mong⁴ 亡】distant and indistinct；vague；uncertain

渺小【miu⁵xiu² 少²】tiny；negligible；insignificant

杳【miu⁵ 秒；yiu² 绕²】distant and out of sight

杳无音信【miu⁵mou⁴yem¹xên³ 毛阴讯】have never been heard of since

淼【miu⁵ 秒】（of an expanse of water）vast

淼茫【miu⁵mong⁴ 亡】（of an expanse of water）stretch as far as the eye can see

缈【miu⁵ 秒】<a.>缥渺【piu¹miu⁵ 飘】dimly discernible

邈【miu⁵ 秒；mog⁹ 莫】far away；remote

藐【miu⁵ 秒】small；petty；slight；despise

藐视【miu⁵xi⁶ 示】despise；look down upon

藐小【miu⁵xiu² 少²】tiny；negligible；paltry

妙【miu⁶ 庙】wonderful；excellent；fine；ingenious

妙计【miu⁶gei³ 继】excellent plan；brilliant scheme

妙语【miu⁶yǔ⁵ 雨】witty remark；witticism

妙用【miu⁶yung⁶ 容⁶】magical effect

妙趣横生【miu⁶qêü³wang⁴xeng¹ 翠鸟罂⁴笙】full of wit and humour；very witty

妙手回春【miu⁶xeo²wui⁴qên¹ 守会⁴椿】（of a doctor）effect a miraculous cure and bring the dying back to life

庙【miu⁶ 妙；miu² 秒²】temple；temple fair

庙宇【miu⁶yǔ⁵ 雨】temple

庙会【miu⁶wui⁶ 汇²】temple fair；fair

棉【min⁴ 绵】a general term for cotton and kapok；cotton；cotton-padded；quilted

棉花【min⁴fa¹ 化¹】cotton

棉田【min⁴tin⁴ 天⁴】cotton field

棉纱【min⁴xa¹ 沙】cotton yarn

棉布【min⁴bou³ 报】cotton cloth；cotton

棉纺【min⁴fong² 访】cotton spinning

棉衣【min⁴yi¹ 依】cotton-padded clothes = 棉袄【nab⁹ 纳】

棉裤【min⁴fu³ 富】cotton-padded trousers

棉袄【min⁴ou³ 澳】cotton-padded jacket = 棉褛【leo¹ 楼¹】

棉被【min⁴ pēi⁴ 婢 】 a quilt with cotton wadding

棉絮【min⁴xêü⁵ 绪】cotton fibre；a cotton wadding

绵【min⁴ 棉】silk floss；continuous；soft

绵薄【min⁴ bog⁹ 泊 】（my）meagre strength；humble effort

绵亘【min⁴geng² 耿】（of mountains, etc.）stretch in an unbroken chain

绵绵【min⁴min⁴】continuous；unbroken

绵延【min⁴yin⁴ 言】be continuous

绵羊【min⁴ yêng⁴ 洋】sheep

眠【min⁴ 棉】sleep; dormancy

免【min⁵ 勉】excuse sb. from sth.; exempt; dismiss; avoid; avert; not allowed

免除【min⁵ qêū⁴ 徐 】prevent; avoid; remit; excuse; exempt; relieve

免得【min⁵ deg⁷ 德 】so as not; so as to avoid

免费【min⁵fei³ 废】free of charge; free; gratis

免票【min⁵piu³ 漂³】free pass; free ticket; free of charge

免税【min⁵ xêū³绪³】exempt from taxation; tax-free

免疫【min⁵ yig⁹亦 】 immunity (from disease)

免职【min⁵jig⁷ 织】remove sb. from office

免罪【min⁵ jêū⁶序 】 exempt from punishment

免不了【min⁵bed⁷liu⁵ 毕辽⁵】be unavoidable

免验放行【min⁵yim⁶fong³heng⁴ 艳况衡】pass without examination (P. W. E.)

勉【min⁵ 免】exert oneself; strive; encourage; urge; exhort; strive to do what is beyond one's power

勉励【min⁵lei⁶ 厉】encourage; urge

勉强【min⁵ kêng⁶卡香⁵】 manage with an effort; reluctantly; force sb. to do sth.; inadequate; barely enough

娩【miu⁵ 免】childbirth; delivery (see "分娩")

冕【miu⁵ 免】crown (see "冠冕")

缅【miu⁵ 免 】remote; far back

缅甸【min⁵din⁶ 电】<n.>Burma

缅怀【min⁵ wai⁴槐 】 cherish the memory of; recall

腼【min⁵ 免】<a.>腼腆【min⁵tin² 天²】shy; bashful = 怕丑【pa³qeo² 秋²】

湎【min⁵ 免】<v.>沉湎【qem⁴min⁵ 侵⁴】wallow

面【min⁶ 免⁶; min² 免²】face; surface; top; personally; cover; outside; an entire area; side extent; range; wheat flour; flour; powder; noodles; soft and floury

面容【min⁶yung⁴ 溶】facial features; face

面色【min⁶xig⁷ 式】complexion; facial expression

面貌【min⁶mao⁶ 卯⁶】face; look; aspect

面目【min⁶ mug⁹ 木】face; features; look; aspect

面颊【min⁶ gab⁸夹 】cheek; face = 面珠墩【min⁶jū¹den¹】

面庞【min⁶pong⁴ 旁】contours of the face; face

面孔【min⁶hung² 恐】face

面子【min⁶ji² 止】outer part; face; reputation

面衫【min² xam¹三】jacket = 【普】上衣; 外套

面巾【min⁶ gen¹斤 】towel = 手巾【xeo² gen¹】=【普】脸巾

面对【min⁶dêū³ 队³】face; confront

面临【min⁶lem⁴ 林】be faced with

面前【min⁶qin⁴ 钱】in the face of; before

面谈【min⁶ tam⁴谭】speak to sb. face to face

面向【min⁶ hêng³ 香³】turn one's face to;

face

面额【min⁶ngag⁹ 我赫⁹】denomination；
　face value ＝ 面值【min⁶jig⁹ 直】
面善【min⁶ xin⁶ 美】look familiar ＝ 面熟
　【min⁶xug⁹ 属】
面纱【min⁶xa¹ 沙】veil
面具【min⁶gêu⁶ 巨】mask
面积【min⁶jig⁷ 织】area
面粉【min⁶fen² 分²】wheat flour；flour
面条【min⁶tiu⁴ 挑⁴】noodles
面包【min⁶bao¹ 苞】bread
面黄肌瘦【min⁶ wong⁴ gêi¹ xeo³ 王机秀】
　sallow and emaciated
面红耳赤【min⁶ hung⁴ yi⁵ qêg⁸ 洪以尺】be
　red in the face；be flushed
面面俱到【min⁶ min⁶ kêu¹ dou³ 驱度³】at-
　tend to each and every aspect of a
　matter
面红面绿【min⁶ hung⁴ min⁶ lug⁹ 洪 六 】to
　blush when one feels shy ∽【普】
　面红耳赤（一个人害怕、害羞或
　发怒时的面色）
面青青【min⁶qêng¹ qêng¹ 次镜¹】look pale
　∽【普】脸色苍白（害怕或病态）
面皮厚【min⁶ pêi⁴ heo⁵ 候⁵】one who is
　thick-skinned，i.e. one who does
　not get shy easily ＝【普】脸皮厚
　（不知羞耻）

明【ming⁴ 鸣；ming² 铭²】bright；light；
　clear；open；overt；sharp-eyed；hon-
　est；sight；know；brilliant；the Ming
　Dynasty（1368－1644）
明暗【ming⁴ngem³ 庵³】light and shade
明灯【ming⁴deng¹ 登】bright lamp；beacon
明亮【ming⁴lêng⁶ 谅】light；bright；shin-
　ing；become clear

明朗【ming⁴ long⁵ 浪⁵】 bright and clear；
　clear；forthright
明净【ming⁴jing⁶ 静】bright and clean
明快【ming⁴fai³ 块】lucid and lively；for-
　thright
明丽【ming⁴lei⁶ 厉】bright and beautiful
明媚【ming⁴mêi⁴ 眉】bright and beautiful
明晰【ming⁴xig⁷ 析】distinct；clear
明显【ming⁴ hin² 献²】clear；obvious；evi-
　dent
明确【ming⁴ kog⁸ 榷 】clear-cut；explicit；
　make clear
明知【ming⁴ji¹ 之】know perfectly well
明了【ming⁴ liu⁴辽 】 understand；clear；
　plain
明白【ming⁴bag⁹ 伯⁹】clear；frank；sensi-
　ble；know
明智【ming⁴ji³ 至】sensible；sagacious；
　wise
明明【ming⁴ming⁴】obviously；plainly
明珠【ming⁴jü¹ 朱】bright pearl；jewel
明星【ming⁴xing¹ 升】star
明证【ming⁴jing³ 正】clear proof
明令【ming⁴ling⁶ 另】explicit order
明码【ming⁴ma⁵ 马】plain code
明年【ming⁴nin⁴ 捻⁴】next year
明天【ming⁴ tin¹ 田¹】tomorrow；the near
　future ＝ 明日【ming⁴yed⁹ 逸】
明火【ming⁴fo² 伙】to cook using hot fire
明虾【ming⁴ha¹ 哈】prawn
明辨是非【ming⁴bin⁶xi⁶fêi¹ 辩士飞】make
　a clear distinction between right
　and wrong
明知故问【ming⁴ ji¹ gu³ men⁶ 支固闻⁶】ask
　while knowing the answer
明知故犯【ming⁴ji¹gu³fan⁶ 支固范】know-
　ingly violate

明哲保身【ming⁴ jid⁸ bou² xen¹ 折宝辛】be worldly wise and play safe

明争暗斗【ming⁴ jeng¹ ngem³ deo³ 憎庵豆³】both open strife and veiled struggle

明目张胆【ming⁴mug⁹jêng¹dam² 木章担²】brazenly

明枪易躲，暗箭难防【ming⁴qêng¹ yi⁶do²，ngem³jin³nan¹fong⁴ 昌义朵，庵战那晏⁴ 妨】it is easy to dodge a spear in the open, but hard to guard against an arrow shot from hiding

名【ming⁴ 明；mēng² 莫镜²】name; given name; fame; renown; famous; noted; express; <classifier> unit of a man

名字【ming⁴ji⁶ 自】name; (given)name

名称【ming⁴qing¹ 清】name (of a thing or organization)

名誉【ming⁴yũ⁶ 预】fame; honorary

名义【ming⁴yi² 异】name; nominal; in name

名声【ming⁴xing¹ 升】reputation; renown

名气【ming⁴hēi³ 戏】reputation; fame

名目【ming⁴mug⁹ 木】names of things; items

名堂【ming⁴tong⁴ 唐】variety; item; result; reason

名片【ming⁴pin² 偏²】visiting card; calling card

名单【ming⁴dan¹ 丹】name list

名次【ming⁴qi⁴ 刺】position in a name list

名词【ming⁴qi⁴ 辞】noun; term

名家【ming⁴ga¹ 加】famous expert; master

名著【ming⁴jũ³ 注】famous book; famous work

名产【ming⁴qan² 铲】famous product

名贵【ming⁴ guei³桂 】 famous and precious; rare

名言【ming⁴yin⁴ 然】well-known saying

名利【ming⁴lēi⁶ 例】fame and gain

名不副实【ming⁴bed⁷fu³xed⁹ 毕富失⁹】the name falls short of the reality

名副其实【ming⁴fu³kēi⁴xed⁹ 富奇失⁹】the name matches the reality ＝ 名符其实

名正言顺【ming⁴ jing³ yin⁴ xên⁶ 政然信⁶】come within one's jurisdiction

名存实亡【ming⁴ qūn⁴ xed⁹ mong⁴ 全失⁹ 芒】cease to exist except in name

名列前茅【ming⁴lid⁹qin⁴mao⁴ 烈钱矛】be among the best of the successful candidates

鸣【ming⁴ 名】the cry of birds, animals or insects; ring; express; voice

鸣锣开道【ming⁴lo⁴hoi¹dou⁶ 罗海¹ 度】prepare the public for a coming event

鸣冤叫屈【ming⁴yūn¹giu³wed⁷ 渊娇³ 乌核⁷】complain and call for redress

酩【ming⁴ 名】<a.> 酩酊大醉【ming⁴ding¹dai⁶jêū³ 丁歹⁶ 最】be dead drunk

咯【ming¹ 名】small ＝【普】小的

狗咯【geo²ming¹ 九】a small dog ＝【普】小狗

茗【ming⁴ 名；ming⁵ 名⁵】tender tea leaves; tea

铭【ming⁵ 皿】inscription; engrave

铭记【ming⁵gēi³ 寄】engrave on one's mind

铭刻【ming⁵heg⁷ 克】inscription；engrave on one's mind；always

皿 【ming⁵ 铭】household utensils（器皿【hēi³ming⁵】）

冥 【ming⁴ 名；ming⁵ 铭】dark；deep；dull；underworld

冥王星【ming⁴wong⁴xing¹ 黄升】＜n.＞ Pluto

冥顽【ming⁵wan⁴ 环】thickheaded；stupid

冥思苦想【ming⁵ xi¹ fu² xêng² 司府赏】think long and hard

瞑 【ming⁵ 铭；ming⁴ 名】close eyes

瞑目【ming⁵mug⁹ 木】close one's eyes in death — die content

暝 【ming⁵ 铭；ming⁴ 名】（of the sun）set；（of the sky）grow dark；dark

溟 【ming⁵ 铭；ming⁴ 名】sea

东溟【dung¹ming⁵ 冬】the east sea

命 【ming⁶ 铭；mēng⁶ 莫镜⁶】life；lot；fate；order；command；assign

命脉【ming⁶meg⁹ 默】lifeblood；lifeline

命运【ming⁶wen⁶ 混】destiny；fate；lot

命根子【mēng⁶gen¹ji² 斤 止】one's very life；lifeblood

命名【ming⁶ming⁴ 明】name（sb. or sth.）

命题【ming⁶tei⁴ 提】assign a topic

命中【ming⁶jung³ 种³】hit the target

搣 【mid⁷ 灭⁷】pinch and twist ＝【普】捏着加拧

搣甩【mid⁷led⁷ 罗核⁷】pinch and twist to make drop ∽【普】（用手指）捏着加拧使脱落

瘪 【mid⁸ 灭⁸】not plump；shrivelled ∽【普】瘪；不饱满

瘪谷【mid⁸gug⁷ 菊】shrivelled millet ＝【普】瘪谷子

灭 【mid⁹ 篾】go out；extinguish；put out；drown；destroy；submerge

灭亡【mid⁹mong⁴ 忙】be destroyed；die out

灭顶【mid⁹ding² 鼎】be drowned

灭口【mid⁹heo² 厚²】do away with a witness or accomplice

灭迹【mid⁹ jig⁹ 织】destroy the evidence（of one's evildoing）

灭火【mid⁹fo² 伙】put out a fire；cut out an engine

灭绝人性【mid⁹jüd⁹yen⁴xing³ 拙⁹ 仁胜】inhuman；savage

蔑 【mid⁹ 灭】slight；nothing；smear（see "诬蔑"）

蔑视【mid⁹xi⁶ 示】despise；scorn

篾 【mid⁹ 灭】thin bamboo strip；the rind of reed or sorghum

篾片【mid⁹ pin³ 遍】thin bamboo strip；hanger-on

篾青【mid⁹qēng¹ 次镜¹】the outer cuticle of a bamboo stem

篾席【mid⁹jēg⁹ 脊⁹】a mat made of thin bamboo strips

搣 【mig⁷ 幂⁷】break off ＝【普】掰

搣开【mig⁷hoi¹ 海¹】use hands to break off ＝【普】用两手使原来粘合的物体分开

幂 【mig⁹ 觅】power；cloth cover

幂级数【mig⁹keb⁷xou³ 给扫】power series

觅 【mig⁹ 幂】look for；hunt for；seek

觅食【mig⁹xig⁹ 蚀】look for food ＝ 搵食【wen²xig⁹】

咩【mē¹ 孭】① < *onomatopoeia* > show a sound of baa (or bleat) ② < *auxil.* > show query mood ∽【普】吗

孮【mē² 咩²】askew; crooked; slanting ∽【普】歪

孮孮斜斜【mē²mē²qē²qē² 扯】crooked; askew; aslant =【普】歪斜

孮嘴【mē²jêû²迫²】askew mouth =【普】歪嘴巴

孭【mē¹ 咩】bear; carry on the back =【普】背负

孭仔【mē¹jei² 济²】carry a baby on one's back = 背孩子

孭镬【mē¹wog⁹ 获】be make a scapegoat ∽【普】背黑锅

搣【mēi² 未²】seek; look for =【普】寻找；寻觅

搣翻【mēi²fan¹ 番】seek back =【普】找回来

搣唔翻【mēi²m⁴fan¹ 番】can not seek back =【普】找不回来

眉【mēi⁴ 媚】eyebrow; brow; the top margin of a page

眉毛【mēi⁴mou⁴ 无】eyebrow; brow

眉睫【mēi⁴ jid⁹捷】the eyebrow and eyelashes

眉目【mēi⁴ mug⁹木 】features; looks; logic; prospect of a solution

眉头【mēi⁴teo⁴ 投】brows

眉梢【mēi⁴xao¹ 筲】the tip of the brow

眉批【mēi⁴pei¹ 拍矮¹】notes and commentary at the top of a page

眉豆【mēi⁴deo² 斗²】a type of bean

眉飞色舞【mēi⁴fêi¹xig⁷mou⁵ 非式武】with dancing eyebrows and radiant face — enraptured; exultant

眉精眼企【mēi⁴jēng¹ngan⁵kēi⁵ 雁⁵ 奇⁵】a cunning look =【普】样子很帅或很秀气

眉开眼笑【mēi⁴hoi¹ngan⁵xiu³ 海¹ 雁⁵ 少³】be all smiles; beam with joy

眉来眼去【mēi⁴loi⁴ngan⁵hêû³ 莱雁⁵ 虚³】make eyes at each other; flirt with each other

媚【mēi⁴眉】fawn on; charming

媚敌【mēi⁴dig⁹ 迪】curry favour with the enemy

媚人景色【mēi⁴yen⁴ging²xig⁷ 仁境式】enchanting scenery

楣【mēi⁴眉】lintel(over a door)

鹛【mēi⁴眉】< n. > babbler

糜【mēi⁴眉】gruel; rotten; wasteful; a surname

糜烂【mēi⁴lan⁶ 兰⁶】rotten to the core; erosion

靡【mēi⁴眉】waste; blown away by the wind; no; not

靡费【mēi⁴fei³ 废】waste; spent extravagantly

靡靡之音【mēi⁴mēi⁴ji¹yem¹ 支阴】decadent music

麋【mēi⁴眉】elk

麋鹿【mēi⁴lug⁹ 六】mi-lu; David's deer

蘼【mēi⁴眉】< n. > 荼蘼【tou⁴mēi⁴ 涂】roseleaf raspberry

猕【mēi⁴眉】< n. > 猕猴【mēi⁴heo⁴ 侯】macaque

娓【mēi⁵美】< a. > 娓娓【mēi⁵mēi⁵】(talk)tirelessly

眯【mēi¹ 美¹】narrow (one's eyes); take a nap

笑眯眯【xiu³mēi¹mēi¹ 少³】narrow one's eyes into a smile =【普】眯着眼睛笑

眯住眼睇【mēi¹jü⁶ngan⁵tei² 注⁶ 雁⁵ 体】squint at =【普】眯着眼瞧

微【mēi⁴ 眉】minute; tiny; profound; decline; one millionth part; micro

微小【mēi⁴xiu² 肖²】small; little

微弱【mēi⁴yêg⁹ 若】faint; feeble; weak

微粒【mēi⁴neb⁷ 挪合⁷】particle; corpuscle

微薄【mēi⁴bog⁹ 博⁹】meagre; scanty

微量【mēi⁴lêng⁶ 亮】trace; micro-

微微【mēi⁴mēi⁴】slight; faint; pico-

微型【mēi⁴ying⁴ 形】miniature; mini-

微观【mēi⁴gun¹ 官】microcosmic

微贱【mēi⁴jin⁶ 战⁶】humble; lowly

微茫【mēi⁴mong¹ 亡】blurred; hazy

微风【mēi⁴fung¹ 丰】gentle breeze

微笑【mēi⁴xiu³ 少³】smile

微波【mēi⁴bo¹ 坡】microwave

微米【mēi⁴mei¹ 迷¹】micron (μ)

微妙【mēi⁴miu⁶ 庙】delicate; subtle

微不足道【mēi⁴bed⁷jug⁷dou⁶ 毕竹度】not worth mentioning; insignificant

微乎其微【mēi⁴fu⁴kēi⁴mēi⁴ 符奇眉】very little

薇【mēi⁴ 微】(see "蔷薇")

尾【mēi⁵ 美; mēi¹ 眯】tail; end; remnant

尾后【mēi⁵heo⁶ 候】=尾迩【mēi¹nai¹ 拉】=迩尾【nai¹mēi¹】final; last; later =【普】最后; 后来

尾二【mēi¹yi² 椅】second last =【普】倒数第二

尾巴【mēi⁵ba¹ 叭】tail; tail-like part; a person shadowing sb.

尾声【mēi⁵xing¹ 升】coda; epilogue; end

尾数【mēi⁵xou³ 扫】odd amount in addition to the round number

尾随【mēi⁵qêü⁴ 徐】tail behind; tag along after =跟住尾【gen¹jü⁶mēi⁵ 根注⁶】

尾追【mēi⁵jêü¹ 椎】in hot pursuit =追住尾【jêü¹jü⁶mēi⁵ 椎注⁶】

美【mēi⁵ 尾⁵】beautiful; pretty; good; short for America

美丽【mēi⁵lei⁶ 厉】beautiful =靓【lēng³ 罗镜³】

美好【mēi⁵hou² 蒿】fine; happy; glorious

美差【mēi⁵qai¹ 猜】cushy job

美称【mēi⁵qing¹ 清】good name

美德【mēi⁵ deg⁷ 得】virtue; moral excellence

美感【mēi⁵gem² 敢】aesthetic feeling

美观【mēi⁵ gun¹ 官】pleasing to the eye; beautiful

美化【mēi⁵fa³ 花³】beautify; prettify

美景【mēi⁵ging² 境】beautiful scenery

美满【mēi⁵mun⁵ 螨】happy; perfectly satisfactory

美梦【mēi⁵mung⁶ 蒙⁶】fond dream

美妙【mēi⁵miu⁶ 庙】beautiful; splendid

美人【mēi⁵yen⁴ 仁】beautiful woman; beauty

美容【mēi⁵yung⁴ 熔】improve looks; cosmetology

美术【mēi⁵ xêd⁹ 述】the fine arts; art; painting

美味【mēi⁵ mēi⁶ 未】delicious food; delicious

美言【mēi⁵yin⁴ 然】put in a good word for sb.

美元【mēi⁵ yün⁴原 】American dollar; U. S. dollar

美国【mēi⁵guog⁸ 帼】the United States of America（U.S.A.）

美洲【mēi⁵jeo¹ 州】America

美滋滋【mēi⁵ji¹ji¹ 支】very pleased with oneself

美不胜收【mēi⁵bed⁷xing³xeo¹ 毕性修】so many beautiful things that one simply can't take them all in

美中不足【mēi⁵ jung¹ bed⁷ jug⁷钟毕竹】a blemish in an otherwise perfect thing

镁【mēi⁵ 美】magnesium（Mg）

镁光【mēi⁵guong¹ 胱】magnesium light

魅【mēi⁶ 未】evil spirit; demon

魅力【mēi⁶lig⁹ 历】glamour; charm

味【mēi⁶ 未】taste; smell; interest; distinguish the flavour of; <classifier> ingredient (of a Chinese medicine prescription)

味道【mēi⁶dou⁶ 度】taste; flavour

味精【mēi⁶ jing¹ 贞 】 monosodium glutamate

味觉【mēi⁶gog⁸ 角】sense of taste

味同嚼蜡【mēi⁶tung⁴jêg⁸lab⁹ 铜爵垃】it is like chewing wax — insipid

未【mēi⁶ 味】have not; did not; not; the eight of the twelve Earthly Branches

未必【mēi⁶bid⁷ 别⁷】may not; not necessarily

未曾【mēi⁶qeng⁴ 层】have not; did not = 未尝【mēi⁶xêng⁴】

未定【mēi⁶ding⁶ 锭】uncertain; undecided

未决【mēi⁶küd⁸ 缺】unsettled; outstanding

未婚【mēi⁶fen¹ 分】unmarried; single

未可【mēi⁶ho² 何²】cannot

未来【mēi⁶ loi⁴莱 】coming; approaching; next; future

未了【mēi⁶ liu⁵ 辽⁵】unfinished; outstanding

未免【mēi⁶min⁵ 缅】rather; a bit too; truly

未能【mēi⁶neng⁴ 挪莺⁴】fail to; cannot

未遂【mēi⁶ xêu⁶ 穗⁶】 not accomplished; abortive

未完【mēi⁶yün⁴ 元】unfinished

未详【mēi⁶qêng⁴ 祥】unknown

未央【mēi⁶yêng¹ 秧】not ended

未知数【mēi⁶ji¹ xou³扫 】unknown number; unknown

未卜先知【mēi⁶bug⁷xin¹ji¹ 伯屋⁷ 仙支】foresee; have foresight

未敢苟同【mēi⁶gem²geo²tung⁴ 感九铜】beg to differ; cannot agree

未雨绸缪【mēi⁶yü⁵qeo⁴meo⁴ 语筹谋】repair the house before it rains; take precautions

末【mud⁹ 没】tip; end; nonessentials; last stage; powder; dust

末尾【mud⁹mēi⁵ 美】end

末后【mud⁹heo⁵ 候】finally

末了【mud⁹liu⁵ 辽⁵】last; finaly

末路【mud⁹lou⁶ 露】dead end; impasse

末期【mud⁹kêi⁴ 其】last phase; last stage

末日【mud⁹yed⁹ 逸】doomsday; doom; end

末世【mud⁹xei³ 细】last phase (of an age)

末代【mud⁹doi⁶ 袋】the last reign of a dynasty

末叶【mud⁹yib⁹ 业】last years

沫【mud⁹ 末】foam; froth (see "泡沫")

茉【mud⁹ 末】< n . > 茉莉【mud⁹lēi⁴ 离】jasmine

殁【mud⁹ 末】die

没【mud⁹ 末】sink; overflow; hide; confiscate; till the end; not have

没落【mud⁹log⁹ 洛⁹】decline; wane

没收【mud⁹ xeo¹ 修】confiscate; expropriate

没趣【mud⁹ qêü³翠 】 feel put out; feel snubbed

没有【mud⁹ yeo⁵ 友】not have; there is not; not so . . . as; less than

没什么【mud⁹xem⁶mo¹ 甚魔】it's nothing = 冇乜野【mou⁵med⁷yē⁵】

没错【mud⁹ qo³挫】I'm quite sure; can't go wrong = 冇错【mou⁵qo³ 武挫】

没关系【mud⁹guan¹hei⁶ 惯¹ 兮⁶】it doesn't matter; it's nothing = 冇关系【mou⁵guan¹hei⁶】

没法子【mud⁹fad⁹ji² 发止】can do nothing about it; can't help it = 冇法子【mou⁵fad⁹ji²】

没命【mud⁹mēng⁶ 莫镜⁶】lose one's life; die; recklessly = 冇命【mou⁵mēng⁶】

没奈何【mud⁹moi⁶ho⁴ 耐河】have no way out

没齿不忘【mud⁹qi²bed⁷mong⁴ 耻毕亡】will never forget to the end of one's days

揩【mēng² 莫镜²; mēng⁴ 莫镜⁴】have not; did not = 未曾【mēi⁶qeng⁴ 味层】

N

瘌【na¹ 那¹】scar =【普】疤痕

喧瘌【dad⁶na¹ 达⁸】a scar =【普】一个疤痕

嘠【na¹ 那¹】and; with; contact; relation =【普】和;同;联系;关系

嘠绠【na¹ gang¹ 耕】contact; relation =【普】联系;关系

嘠埋【na¹mai⁴ 买⁴】and; with =【普】和;与;同;同……一起

姆【na² 那²】female =【普】母性的

猪姆【jü¹na² 朱】sow =【普】母猪

冇姆教【mou⁵na²gao³ 武 较】have not mother's teaching =【普】没娘教育

拿【na⁴ 那⁴; na² 那²】hold; take; seize; capture; be able to do = 将【jêng¹】

拿住【na² jü⁶注⁶】①catch; grip =【普】抓住;②five =【普】五(茶楼暗语)

拿获【na⁴ wog⁹ 镬】apprehend = 捉住【jug¹jü⁶】

拿手【na⁴xeo² 守】adept; expert; good at
拿主意【na⁴jü²yi³ 煮蒽】make a decision
拿不出手【na⁴bed⁷qêd⁷xeo² 毕次律⁷守】not be presentable = 扐唔出手【lig⁷m⁴qêd⁷xeo²】
拿埋都风湿【na²mai⁴dou¹fung³xeb⁷ 买⁴刀丰拾⁷】all maintain; all will maintain ∽【普】(以为)全是一样

剢【na² 那²】strong stimulus to make body shrink =【普】(酸、碱、盐等)强刺激使物体收缩

剢脷【na²lêi⁶ 利】strong stimulus on tongue; terrible; formidable =【普】舌头受到强刺激;厉害

那【na⁵ 哪】that; then; in that case

那个【na⁵go³ 哥³】that = 吓个【go²go³】
那里【na⁵lêü⁵ 吕】that place; there = 吓度【go²dou⁶】
那么【na⁵mo¹ 魔】like that; about; or so; then = 噉样【gem²yêng² 扬²】
那时【na⁵ xi⁴ 史⁴】at that time; then; in those days = 吓时【go²xi⁴】= 吓阵时【go²jen⁶xi⁴】
那些【na⁵xē¹ 赊】those = 吓啲【go²did⁷】
那样【na⁵ yêng⁶ 让】of that kind; like that; such; so = 吓样【go²yêng⁶】;噉样【gem²yêng² 扬²】
那么点儿【na⁵mo¹dim²yi⁴ 魔店² 移】so little; so few = 个啲咁多【go³did⁷gem³do¹】

哪【na⁵ 那】which; what

哪个【na⁵go³】which; who = 边个【bin¹go³】
哪里【na⁵lêü⁵ 吕】where; wherever = 边度【bin¹dou⁶】
哪怕【na⁵pa³ 爬³】even; even if; even though = 即使【jig⁷xi² 史】;就算系【jeo⁶xün³hei⁶】

哪些【na⁵ xē¹ 赊】which；who；what =
　　边啲【bin¹did⁷】

哪样【na⁵yêng⁶ 让】what kind of = 边样
　　【bin¹yêng⁶ 让】

哪时【na⁵ xi⁴ 是⁴】when；whenever；any
　　time ＝ 边时【bin¹xi⁴】；乜时候
　　【med⁷xi⁴heo⁶】；几时【gēi²xi⁴】

孻【nai¹ 乃¹】tail；end；the smallest ＝
　　【普】最后的；最小的

孻仔【nai¹ jei² 济】the smallest son ＝
　　【普】最小的儿子

孻尾【nai¹mēi¹ 美¹】final；last；later ＝
　　【普】最后；后来

朚【nai² 乃²】know very well；be familiar
　　with ＝【普】熟悉；知晓

唔朚架步【m⁴nai²ga³bou⁶ 乃²价步】not
　　know the way ＝【普】不懂方法；
　　不熟门路

乃【nai⁵ 奶⁵】be；so；therefore；only
　　then；you；your

乃是【nai⁵xi⁶ 士】be

乃至【nai⁵ji³ 致】and even

奶【nai⁵ 乃；nai¹ 孻】breasts；milk；
　　suckle

奶头【nai⁵ teo⁴ 投】nipple；teat；nipple（of
　　a feeding bottle）

奶水【nai⁵xêu² 绪】milk ＝ 奶汁【nai⁵
　　jeb⁷ 执】

奶粉【nai⁵ fen² 分²】milk powder；dried
　　milk

奶酪【nai⁵log⁸ 洛】cheese

奶油【nai⁵yeo⁴ 由】cream

奶茶【nai⁵qa⁴ 查】tea with milk

奶品【nai⁵ben² 禀】milk products

奶奶【nai⁴ nai⁵】grandmother；a respect-
　　ful form of address for an old
　　woman

师奶【xi¹ nai⁵ 司】teacher's wife ＝【普】
　　师娘

少奶【xiu³nai⁵ 笑】young married woman
　　＝【普】少妇；少奶奶

氖【nai⁵ 乃】＜ n. ＞ neon（Ne）

氖灯【nai⁵deng¹ 登】neon lamp；neon
　　light

氖管【nai⁵gun² 莞】neon tube

迺【nai⁵ 乃】＝ 乃【nai⁵】

鼐【nai⁵ 乃】a big tripod

疷【nai⁴ 乃⁴】paralysis of the foot ＝
　　【普】足瘫

软疷疷【yün⁵nai⁴nai⁴ 远】tired out and can
　　not move ＝【普】累坏了，不能动
　　弹

闹【nao⁶ 挠⁶】noisy；make a noise；give
　　vent；suffer from；do；make

闹市【nao⁶xi⁵ 士⁵】busy street；busy
　　shopping centre

闹钟【nao⁶jung¹ 中】alarm clock

闹交【nao⁶ gao¹胶】 to argue；to quarrel
　　＝【普】吵架

闹事【nao⁶xi⁶ 士】make trouble

闹翻【nao⁶fan¹ 蕃¹】fall out with sb.

闹剧【nao⁶kēg⁸ 屐】farce

闹哄哄【nao⁶ hung³ hung³ 控】clamorous；
　　noisy

闹嚷嚷【nao⁶yêng⁶yêng⁶ 让】noisy

闹翻天【nao⁶fan¹tin¹ 蕃¹ 田¹】raise hell

闹别扭【nao⁶bid⁹neo² 必⁹ 纽】be difficult
　　with sb.

闹情绪【nao⁶qing⁴xêu⁵ 程絮】be disgrun-
　　tled

闹意见【nao⁶yi³gin³ 蕙建】be on bad

terms because of a difference of
opinion

闹意气【nao⁶yi³hēi³ 蕙戏】sulk

闹笑话【nao⁶xiu³wa² 少³ 画²】make a fool
of oneself

闹着玩【nao⁶jêg⁹wan² 雀⁹ 环²】joke

挠【nao⁴ 闹⁴】scratch; hinder; yield

不屈不挠【bed¹wed⁷bed⁷nao⁴ 毕乌核⁷】
indomitable

铙【nao⁴ 挠】< n. > 铙钹【nao⁴bed⁹
拔】big cymbals

猱【nao⁴ 挠】< n. > 猱犬【nao⁴hūn²
劝²】dhole; red dog

蹿【nam³ 南³】steps【普】跨；跨步
大步蹿过【dai⁶bou⁶nam³guo³ 部南
戈³】steps with a big step =【普】
大步跨过

蹿一日去一趟【nam³yed⁷yed⁹hêu³yed⁷
tong³ 壹逸虚³ 壹烫】every alternate day go once =【普】每隔一
天去一次

捅【nam⁵ 腩】to hit with a long stick

捅佢一棍【nam⁵kêū⁵yed⁷guen³ 拒壹君³】
hit him with a long stick =【普】
打他一棍子

腩【nam⁵ 南²】to refer to the flesh on the
abdomen of cows =【普】腹部脂肪
多的皮肉

大肚腩【dai³tou⁴nam⁵ 歹⁶ 吐⁵】a big tripe
(or belly) =【普】大肚皮；大肚
子

鱼腩【yū⁴nam⁵ 余】fish belly; fish maw =
【普】鱼肚；鱼腹

南【nam⁴ 男】south; a surname

南无【nam⁴mo⁴ 磨】to pray ∽【普】祭神
祈祷

南无佬【nam⁴mo⁴lou² 磨老²】a witch ∽
【普】巫师；神棍；祭礼的主持者

南洋【nam⁴yêng² 样²】the south-east is-
lands; south-east Asia =【普】东
南亚

南乳【nam⁴yū⁵ 语】a type of sauce made of
yam =【普】一种用芋头粉发酵
腌制的腐乳

南方【nam⁴fong¹ 芳】south

南部【nam⁴bou⁶ 步】southern part

南风【nam⁴fung¹ 丰】south wind

南瓜【nam⁴gua¹ 挂¹】pumpkin; cushaw

南国【nam⁴guog⁸ 帼】the southern part of
the country; the south

南海【nam⁴ hoi² 凯】the Nanhai Sea; the
South China Sea

南极【nam⁴gig⁹ 击⁹】the South Pole

南京【nam⁴ging¹ 经】< n. > Nanjing

南纬【nam⁴wei⁵ 伟】south latitude

南美洲【nam⁴mēi⁵jeo¹ 尾州】South America

南柯一梦【nam⁴ ngo¹yed⁷mung⁶ 屙壹蒙⁶】
Nanke dream; illusory joy; fond
dream

南腔北调【nam⁴ hong¹ beg⁷ diu⁶康伯得⁷
掉】(speak with) a mixed accent

南征北战【nam⁴jing¹beg⁷jin³ 贞伯得⁷ 箭】
fight north and south on many
fronts

男【nam⁴ 南】man; male; son; boy;
baron

男仔【nam⁴ jei²济²】guys; boys =【普】小
伙子；男孩子

男人【nam⁴ yen² 忍 】man; menfolk; husband

男性【nam⁴xing³ 胜】the male sex；man

男生【nam⁴xeng¹ 笙】man student；
　　schoolboy

男装【nam⁴jong¹ 庄】men's clothing

男声【nam⁴xing¹ 升】male voice

男爵【nam⁴jêg⁸ 桌】baron

男朋友【nam⁴peng⁴yeo⁵ 凭有】boyfriend

男厕所【nam⁴ qi³ xo²次锁】men's lava-
　　tory；Gentlemen；Men；Gents

男盗女娼【nam⁴dou⁶nêū⁵qêng¹ 道那虚⁵
　　昌】 behave like thieves and
　　whores；be out-and-out scoundrels

喃【nam⁴ 南】< onomatopoeia > 喃喃
　　【nam⁴nam⁴】mutter；murmur

楠【nam⁴ 南】< n. > 楠木【nam⁴mug⁹
　　目】nanmu

蝻【nam⁴ 南】< n. > 蝻蛇【nam⁴xē⁴
　　射⁴】a python

难【nan⁴ 那晏⁴；nan⁶ 那晏⁶】difficult；
　　hard；put sb. into a difficult position；
　　hardly possible；calamity；disaster；
　　take to task；blame

难处【nan⁴qū³ 次于³】difficulty；trouble

难关【nan⁴guan¹ 惯¹】difficulty；crisis

难点【nan⁴ dim² 店²】difficult point；diffi-
　　culty

难题【nan⁴tei⁴ 提】difficult problem；poser

难度【nan⁴dou⁶ 道】degree of difficulty

难道【nan⁴ dou⁶ 度】 < ad. > show a
　　mood of rhetorical question = 唔
　　通【m⁴tung¹】

难倒【nan⁴dou⁴ 捣】daunt；baffle；beat

难得【nan⁴ deg⁷ 德 】 hard to come by；
　　rare；seldom；rarely

难怪【nan⁴guai³ 乖³】no wonder；pardon-
　　able

难过【nan⁴ guo³ 戈³】 have a hard time；
　　feel sorry

难堪【nan⁴ hem¹ 勘】 intolerable；embar-
　　rassed

难睇【nan⁴tei² 体】ugly；shameful ＝【普】
　　难看

难受【nan⁴ xeo⁶ 授】feel unwell；feel ill；
　　feel unhappy；feel bad

难讲【nan⁴gong² 港】it's hard to say

难听【nan⁴ tēng¹ 厅 】unpleasant to hear；
　　offensive；coarse

难做【nan⁴jou⁶ 造】embarrass；press；be a
　　tough job to ∽【普】难为

难忘【nan⁴mong⁴ 亡】unforgetable；mem-
　　orable

难以【nan⁴yi⁵ 耳】difficult to

难产【nan⁴qan² 铲】difficult labour；be
　　slow in coming

难顶【nan⁴ding² 鼎】unbearable ＝【普】难
　　以抵挡；难于对付

难闻【nan⁴ men⁴文 】 smell unpleasant；
　　smell bad

难民【nan⁶men⁴ 文】refugee

难兄难弟【nan⁶hing¹nan⁶dei⁶ 兴第】fellow
　　sufferers

难为情【nan⁴wei⁴qing⁴ 维程】ashamed；
　　shy；embarrassing

难能可贵【nan⁴ neng⁴ ho² guei³那莺⁴ 河²
　　桂】estimable；commendable

难言之隐【nan⁴yin¹ji¹yen² 然支忍】a
　　painful topic

难舍难分【nam⁴xē²nan⁴fen¹ 写芬】loath to
　　part from each other

赧【nan⁵ 难⁵】blushing

赧然【nan⁵yin⁴ 言】blushing

赧颜【nan⁵ ngan⁴雁⁴】 blush；be shamefaced

齉【nang³ 那罌³】< a. > describe the woman to play the coquette

齉齆【nang³xang³ 是罌³】the woman is playing the coquette =【普】骚女人卖弄风情

呐【nab⁹ 纳】< v. > 呐喊【nab⁹ham³ 咸³】shout loudly; cry out

纳【nab⁹ 呐】receive; accept; enjoy; pay; sew close stitches

纳入【nab⁹ yeb⁹ 邑⁹】bring (or channel) into

纳税【nab⁹xêü³ 碎】pay taxes

纳凉【nab⁹lêng⁴ 良】enjoy the cool

纳闷【nab⁹mun⁶ 门⁶】feel puzzled; wonder

纳新【nab⁹ xen¹ 辛】take in the fresh — take in new party members

纳降【nab⁹ hong⁴杭】accept the enemy's surrender

纳罕【nab⁹hon² 汗²】be surprised; marvel

纳粹【nab⁹xêü⁵ 税⁵】Nazi

衲【nab⁹ 纳】patch up; patchwork vestment worn by a Buddhist monk

钠【nab⁹ 纳】< n. > sodium (Na)

钠玻璃【nab⁹bo¹lēi¹ 坡 离¹】soda-lime glass

捺【nad⁹ 挪压⁹】press down; restrain; right-falling stroke (in Chinese characters)

泥【nei⁴ 那矮⁴】mud; mire; mashed vegetable or fruit; stubborn, bigoted; obstinate; soil

泥泞【nei⁴ban⁶ 办】soggy =【普】烂泥巴

泥尘【nei⁴qen⁴ 陈】dirt =【普】泥垢；灰尘

泥土【nei⁴tou² 桃²】earth; soil; clay

泥沙【nei⁴xa¹ 纱】silt

泥浆【nei⁴jêng¹ 张】slurry; mud

泥泞【nei⁴ning⁴ 宁】muddy; miry

泥潭【nei⁴tam⁴ 谈】mire; quagmire

泥沼【nei⁴jiu² 剿】mire; swamp; slough

泥坑【nei⁴hang¹ 黑罌¹】mud pit; morass

泥塑【nei⁴xog⁸ 索】clay sculpture

泥鳅【nei⁴qeo¹ 秋】loach

泥古【nei⁴ gu² 鼓】have bigoted belief in the ancients

泥水佬【nei⁴xêü²lou² 绪² 老²】bricklayer; tiler; plasterer =【普】泥水匠

泥菩萨过河【nei⁴pou⁴xad⁸guo⁸ho⁴ 莆煞戈³ 何】like a clay idol fording a river — hardly able to save oneself

尼【nēi⁴ 妮】Buddhist nun

尼姑【nēi⁴gu¹ 菇】Buddhist nun

尼姑庵【nēi⁴gu¹ngem¹ 鹤】Buddhist nunnery

尼龙【nēi⁴lung⁴ 胧】nylon

尼古丁【nēi⁴gu²ding¹ 鼓叮】nicotine

尼泊尔【nēi⁴bog⁹yi⁵ 薄耳】Nepal

妮【nēi⁴ 尼】girl; lass

怩【nēi⁴ 尼】(see "忸怩")

旎【nēi⁵ 你】< a. > 旖旎【yi²nēi⁵ 倚你】charming and gentle

弥【nēi⁴ 尼；mēi⁴ 眉】full; cover; fill; more

弥补【nēi⁴ bou⁴保】make up; remedy; make good

弥漫【nēi⁴man⁶ 万】fill the air

弥留【nēi⁴leo⁴ 流】be dying

睨【nēi¹ 尼¹；ngei⁶ 伪】strabismus

射睨【xē⁶nēi¹ 舍⁶】strabismus; look sideways

腻【nēi⁶ 饵; nēi³ 饵³; nēi¹ 饵¹】greasy; oily; be bored; be fed up; loathe; hate; dirt; meticulous

腻味【nēi³mēi⁶】get fed up

好多腻【hou²do¹nēi¹ 蒿¹ 朵¹】many dirt = 好多老泥【lou⁵nei⁴】= 【普】很多尘腻（或积垢）

你【nēi⁵ 尼⁵】you; one; anyone = 您【nēi⁵】

你好【nēi⁵hou² 蒿²】how do you do; how are you; hello = 【普】你好；您好

你地【nēi⁵dēi⁶ 得希⁶】you（second person plural）= 【普】你们

你死我活【nēi⁵xēi²ngo⁵wud⁹ 四² 鹅⁵ 乌阔⁹】life-and-death; mortal

你追我赶【nēi⁵jêü¹ngo⁵gon² 椎鹅⁵ 竿²】try to overtake each other in friendly emulation

你哋人【nēi⁵did⁷yen⁴ 得热⁷ 仁】all of you = 【普】你们这些人

饵【nēi⁶ 腻】cakes; pastry; bait; entice

饵以重利【nēi⁵yi⁵qung⁵lēi⁶ 尔从⁵ 例】use great wealth as a bait

孬【neo¹ 】bad; cowardly

孬种【neo¹jung² 肿】coward

忸【neo² 扭】<a.> 忸怩【neo²nēi⁴ 尼】blushing; bashful

扭【neo² 忸】turn round; twist; sprain; roll; swing; seize

扭打【neo²da² 得阿²】wrestle; grapple

扭捏【neo²nib⁹ 聂】be affectedly bashful

扭伤【neo²xêng¹ 湘】sprain; wrench

扭转【neo²jün² 专²】turn round; reverse

扭拧【neo² ning⁶宁⁶】shy; blushing; behave coyly = 【普】扭捏；忸怩作态

扭计【neo² gei² 偈】sporting; naughty = 【普】(小孩)以俾嗔的办法邀宠；(大人)故意刁难，斗智谋

扭计师爷【neo²gei²xi¹yê⁴ 偈思椰】one who has a lot of funny ideas ∽ 扭计祖宗【neo²gei²jou²jung¹ 早中】∽ 【普】诡计多端的人；刁难、斗智的军师

扭纹【neo²men⁴ 文】refer to children being sporting ∽ 【普】孩子不听话，撒野

扭纹柴【neo²men⁴qai⁴ 文猜⁴】wood with flowery pattern; children who like to cry = 【普】纹理不直的木头；不听话的、撒野的孩子

纽【neo² 扭】handle; knob; button; bond

纽带【neo²dai³ 戴】link; tie; bond

纽扣【neo²keo³ 购】button

纽约【neo²yêg⁸ 跃】<n.> New York

钮【neo² 扭】<n.> 电钮【din⁶neo² 甸】push button

狃【neo² 扭】be bound by

狃于习俗【neo²yü¹jab⁹jug⁹ 迂袭族】be bound by custom

妞【neo² 纽】girl

耨【neo⁶ 扭⁶】weeding hoe; weeding; fed up

耨喉【neo⁶heo⁴ 侯】fed up ∽ 【普】吃腻了

朽【neo² 扭】rotten; decayed; senile

朽木【neo²mug⁹ 目】rotten wood or

tree; a hopeless case

嬲【neo¹ 孬】又写作"㜝" hate; angry; fury＝【普】恨;发怒

嬲死佢【neo¹xēi²kêu⁵ 四² 拒】hate sb. to the marrow of one's bones ∽【普】恨死他;恨之入骨

发嬲【fad⁸neo¹ 法】get angry; fury＝【普】恼怒;发怒

谂【nem² 挪庵²】to think; to consider

谂头【nem² teo⁴ 投】idea; thinking; to think＝【普】想法;考虑

谂计【nem²gei² 偈】think of a way; do everything possible＝【普】想办法;想方设法

谂真啲【nem²jen¹did² 珍 得热⁷】to really think about something＝【普】想清楚点儿;考虑成熟些

谂缩数【nem²xug⁷xou³ 叔扫】to think for the good of oneself only ∽【普】为自己占便宜想简便的方法

瞒【nem⁶ 谂⁶】soundly＝【普】酣畅

瞓得好瞒【fen³deg⁷hou²nem⁶ 训德蒿²】to sleep soundly＝酣睡

褮【neng³ 能³】tie; fasten; involve; tie up with

褮住【neng³jū⁶ 注⁶】be tieing; fasten＝【普】系着

㩥褮【la¹neng³ 啦¹】involve; tie up with＝【普】牵连

能【neng⁴ 那亨⁴】ability; capability; skill; energy; able; capable; can; be able to

能干【neng⁴gon³ 竿³】able; capable; competent

能够【neng⁴ geo³究 】can; be able to; be capable of

能力【neng⁴lig⁹ 历】ability; capability

能量【neng⁴lêng⁶ 亮】energy; capabilities

能耐【neng⁴noi⁶ 内】ability; capability; skill

能人【neng⁴yen⁴ 仁】able person

能手【neng⁴xeo² 守】dab; expert

能源【neng⁴yün⁴ 原】energy resources

能说会道【neng⁴xüd⁸wui⁵dou⁶ 雪汇⁵ 度】have the gift of the gab

能者为师【neng⁴ jē² wei⁴ xi¹ 姐维司】let those who know teach

粒【neb⁷ 那急⁷】grain; granule; pellet; ＜classifier＞

粒状【neb⁷jong⁶ 撞】granular

粒子【neb⁷ji² 止】＜n.＞ particle

粒声都唔出【neb⁷xēng¹dou¹m⁴qêd⁷】to keep quiet＝【普】啥话也不说

凹【neb⁷ 粒】concave; hollow; sunken

凹陷【neb⁷ham⁶ 咸⁶】hollow; sunken; depressed

凹版【neb⁷ban² 板】intaglio; gravure

凹透镜【neb⁷teo³gēng³ 偷³ 颈³】concave lens

泅【neb⁹ 粒⁹】rusty; sticky ∽【普】停滞;缺少活动性

泅糯【neb⁹no⁶ 懦】slowly ∽【普】慢腾腾

泅黐黐【neb⁹qi¹qi¹ 痴】sticky ∽【普】黏黏糊糊;很不干脆

泅油【neb⁹ yeo² 由²】not smooth (machines); slow; not alert＝【普】(行动)不快捷;不干脆利索

挪【no⁴ 懦⁴】move; shift＝逪【ten³ 吞³】

挪动【no⁴dung⁶ 洞】move; shift

挪用【no⁴yung⁶ 容⁶】divert (funds); misappropriate

挪威【no⁴wei¹ 畏¹】< n. > Norway

挼 【no⁴ 挪】rub; knead = 揉搓

将信挼成一团【jêng¹xên³no⁴xing⁴ yed⁷tün⁴ 张讯承壹替冤⁴】crumple a letter into a ball

糯 【no⁶ 懦】glutinous (cereal)

糯米【no⁶mei⁵ 迷⁵】polished glutinous rice

糯米屎窬【no⁶mei⁵xi²fed⁷ 迷⁵ 吏弗】guest is sitting long time and does not want to go out ∽【普】客人长时间地坐着不想走

懦 【no⁶ 糯】cowardly; weak

懦弱【no⁶yêg⁹ 若】cowardly; weak

懦夫【no⁶fu¹ 孚】coward; craven; weaking

娜 【no⁴ 挪; na⁴ 拿】< a. > 婀娜【ngo¹no⁴】(of a woman's bearing) graceful

喏 【no⁶ 糯; yê⁵ 野】< int. > used to bring to sb. 's attention; ∽ look

耐 【noi⁶ 奈】be able to bear or endure; long time

好耐【hou² noi⁶蒿²】for a long time =【普】很久

耐烦【noi⁶fan² 凡】patient

耐火【noi⁶fo² 伙】fire-resistant; refractory

耐久【noi⁶geo² 九】lasting long; durable

耐力【noi⁶lig⁹ 历】endurance; staying power

耐磨【noi⁶ mo⁴ 摩⁴】(of metals) wear-resisting; wearproof

耐热【noi⁶ yid⁹ 衣泄⁹】heat-resisting; heatproof

耐酸【noi⁶ xün¹ 孙 】acidproof; acid-resisting

耐用【noi⁶yung⁶ 容⁶】durable

耐中【noi⁶jung¹ 钟】sometimes = 耐唔中【noi⁶m⁴jung¹】=【普】有时候；有些时候

耐心【noi⁶xem¹ 深】patient

耐性【noi⁶xing³ 胜】patience; endurance

耐不耐【noi⁶bed⁷noi⁶ 毕】occasionally =【普】间中；间或

耐人寻味【noi⁶yen⁴qen⁴mēi⁶ 仁沉未】afford food for thought

奈 【noi⁶ 耐】< ad. > 奈何【noi⁶ho⁴ 河】how; to no avail; do sth. to a person

萘 【noi⁶ 奈】< n. > naphthalene

内 【noi⁶ 耐】inner; within; inside; one's wife or her relatives

内部【noi⁶bou⁶步】inside; internal; interior

内地【noi⁶dēi⁶ 得希⁶】inland; hinterland

内服【noi⁶fug⁹ 伏】to be taken orally

内阁【noi⁶gog⁸ 角】cabinet

内涵【noi⁶ham⁶ 咸】intension; connotation

内行【noi⁶hong⁴ 航】expert; adept

内河【noi⁶ho⁴ 何】inland river

内讧【noi⁶hung³ 控】internal conflict

内奸【noi⁶gan¹ 间¹】hidden traitor

内疚【noi⁶geo³ 够】compunction

内科【noi⁶fo¹ 课¹】(department of) internal medicine

内涝【noi⁶lou⁶ 劳】waterlogging

内乱【noi⁶ lün⁶联⁶】 civil strife; internal disorder

内幕【noi⁶mog⁹ 莫】inside story

内亲【noi⁶qen¹ 趁¹】a relative on one's wife's side; in-law

内情【noi⁶qing⁴ 程】inside information

内人【noi⁶yen⁴ 仁】my wife = 内子【noi⁶ji² 止】

内容【noi⁶yung⁴ 熔】content; substance

内伤【noi⁶xêng¹ 双】internal injury

内外【noi⁶ngoi⁶ 碍 】 inside and outside; around

内务【noi⁶mou⁶ 冒】internal affairs

内线【noi⁶xin³ 扇】planted agent; interior lines; inside（telephone）

内向【noi⁶hêng³ 香³】introversion

内销【noi⁶xiu¹ 消】sold inside the country

内心【noi⁶xem¹ 深】heart; innermost being

内省【noi⁶xing² 醒】introspection

内衣【noi⁶yi¹ 依】underwear; underclothes

内因【noi⁶yen¹ 茵】internal cause

内应【noi⁶ ying³英³】a planted agent; a plant

内在【noi⁶joi⁶ 载⁶】inherent; internal

内脏【noi⁶ jong⁶撞 】internal organs; viscera

内战【noi⁶jin³ 箭】civil war

内政【noi⁶jing³ 正】internal affairs

内助【noi⁶jo⁶ 左⁶】wife

内燃机【noi⁶yin⁴gêi¹ 言基】internal-combustion engine

内分泌【noi⁶fen¹bēi³ 芬痹】endocrine

内忧外患【noi⁶yeo¹ngoi⁶wan⁶ 优碍环⁶】domestic trouble and foreign invasion

奴 【nou⁴ 驽】bondservant; slave; enslave

奴役【nou⁴yig⁹ 亦】enslave; keep in bondage

奴仆【nou⁴bug⁹ 伯屋⁹】servant; lackey

奴隶【nou⁴dei⁶ 弟】slave

奴化【nou⁴fa³ 花³】enslave

奴性【nou⁴xing³ 胜】servility; slavishness

奴颜婢膝【nou⁴ngan⁴pēi⁵xed⁷ 雁⁴ 披⁵ 失】subservient; servile

孥 【nou⁴ 奴】children; wife and children

驽 【nou⁴ 奴 】 inferior horse;（of a person）dull

驽马【nou⁴ma⁵ 码】inferior horse; jade

驽钝【nou⁴dên⁶ 顿】dull; stupid

弩 【nou⁵ 脑】crossbow

弩弓【nou⁵gung¹ 工】crossbow

脑 【nou⁵ 恼】brain

脑子【nou⁵ ji² 止 】 brain; brains; mind; head

脑筋【nou⁵ gen¹斤 】 brain; mind; head; ideas

脑汁【nou⁵jeb⁷ 执】brains

脑袋【nou⁵doi² 代²】head

脑海【nou⁵hoi² 凯】brain; miad

脑浆【nou⁵jêng¹ 张】brain = 脑髓【nou⁵xêu⁵】

脑电图【nou⁵din⁶tou⁴ 甸途】electroencephalogram

脑震荡【nou⁵ jen³ dong⁶ 振当⁶】cerebral concussion

脑溢血【nou⁵yed⁹hüd⁸ 日黑月⁸】cerebral haemorrhage

脑满肠肥【nou⁵mun⁵qêng⁴fēi⁴ 螨祥飞⁴】heavy-jowled and pothellied — the idle rich

恼 【nou⁵ 脑】angry; irritated; unhappy; worried; annoyed

恼恨【nou⁵hen⁶ 很⁶】resent; hate

恼火【nou⁵fo² 伙】annoyed; irritated;

vexed

恼怒【nou⁵nou⁶ 奴⁶】angry; indignant; furious

恼人【nou⁵yen⁴ 仁】irritating; annoying

恼羞成怒【nou⁵xeo¹xing⁴nou⁶ 收承奴⁶】
fly into a rage from shame

瑙【nou⁵ 恼】< n. > 玛瑙【ma⁵nou⁵】
（see"玛瑙"）

怒【nou⁶ 努⁶】anger; rage; fury

怒火【nou⁶fo² 伙】flames of fury; fury

怒气【nou⁶hēi³ 戏】anger; rage; fury

怒斥【nou⁶qig⁷ 戚】angrily rebuke

怒号【nou⁶hou⁶ 好⁶】howl; roar

怒吼【nou⁶hao¹ 蔽】roar; howl

怒视【nou⁶xi¹ 士】glare at; glower at

怒容【nou⁶ yung⁴ 溶】an angry look ＝ 怒
色【nou⁶xig⁷】

怒潮【nou⁶qiu⁴ 瞧】angry tide; bore

怒涛【nou⁶tou⁴ 图】furious billows

怒冲冲【nou⁶qung¹qung¹ 充】in a rage; furiously ＝ 嬲爆爆【neo¹bao³bao³】

怒发冲冠【nou⁶fad⁸qung¹gun¹ 法充官】
bristle with anger; be in a towering rage

怒不可遏【nou⁶bed⁷ho²ngod⁸ 毕贺² 额
割⁸】be beside oneself with anger; boil with rage

努【nou⁵ 恼】put forth (strength); exert (effort); protrude; bulge

努力【nou⁵ lig⁹历】make great efforts; try hard; exert oneself

努嘴【nou⁵ jêü²追²】pout one's lips as a signal

囊【nong⁴ 那康】bag; pocket; anything shaped like a bag

囊括【nong⁴kud⁸ 卡活⁸】include; embrace

囊虫【nong⁴qung⁴ 从】cysticercus

囊肿【nong⁴jung² 种²】cyst

囊中物【nong⁴ jung¹ med⁹钟勿 】sth.
which is in the bag — sth. certain of attainment

囊空如洗【nong⁴hung¹yü⁴xei² 凶鱼逝²】
with empty pockets; penniless; broke

曩【nong⁵ 囊】former; past

曩时【nong⁵xi⁴ 是⁴】in olden days; of yore

瓤【nong⁴ 囊】pulp; flesh; pith; the interior part of certain things

西瓜瓤【xei¹gua¹nong⁴ 筛格娃¹】the pulp of a watermelon

诺【nog⁹ 那恶⁹】promise; yes

诺言【nog⁹yin⁴ 然】promise

锘【nog⁹ 诺】< n. > nobelium (No)

鸟【niu⁵ 那妖⁵】bird

鸟类【niu⁵lêü⁶ 泪】birds

鸟笼【niu⁵lung⁴ 隆】birdcage

鸟枪【niu⁵qēng¹ 昌】fowling piece; air gun

鸟兽【niu⁵xeo³ 秀】birds and beasts

鸟瞰【niu⁵hem³ 勘】get a bird's-eye view;
general survey of a subject

袅【niu⁵ 鸟】slender and delicate

袅袅【niu⁵niu⁵】curl upwards; wave in the wind; linger

袅娜【niu⁵ no⁴挪 】slender and graceful;
willowy

茑【niu⁵ 鸟】< n. > 茑萝【niu⁵lo⁴ 罗】
cypress vine

尿【niu⁶ 鸟⁶】urine; urinate; make water; pass water

尿道【niu⁶dou³ 度】urethra

尿布【niu⁶bou³ 报】diaper; napkin; nappy

尿床【niu⁶qong⁴ 苍⁴】wet the bed; bed-wetting

尿频【niu⁶pen⁴ 贫】frequent micturition

尿素【niu⁶xou³ 扫】urea; carbamide

尿酸【niu⁶xün¹ 孙】uric acid

尿毒症【niu⁶dug⁹jing³ 独正】oliguria

尿失禁【niu⁶xed⁷gem³ 室咁】urinary incontinence

脲【niu⁶ 尿】urea; carbamide

脲醛塑料【niu⁵qün⁴xog⁹liu² 全索了²】urea-formaldehyde plastics

黏【nim¹ 念¹; jim¹ 占¹】= 粘（see "粘"）

拈【nim¹ 念¹】pick up (with the thumb and one or two fingers)

拈轻怕重【nim¹hing¹pa³qung⁵ 兴扒³ 充⁵】prefer the light to the heavy — pick easy jobs and shirk hard ones

念【nim⁶ 那艳⁶】think of; miss; thought; idea; read aloud; study; attend school

念叨【nim⁶tou¹ 滔】talk about again and again in recollection or anticipation; talk over; discuss

念经【nim¹ging¹ 京】recite or chant scriptures

念头【nim⁶teo⁴ 投】thought; idea; intention

念旧【nim⁶geo⁶ 柩】keep old friendships in mind; for old time's sake

腍【nin¹ 捻¹】breast; mamma; milk = 【普】乳房；乳汁

捻【nin² 年²; nen² 挪恩²】twist with the fingers; sth. made by twisting

捻死【nin²xéi² 四²】twist to die; firmly grasp ∽【普】(把人或动物)捏死；抓紧；不放松

捻针【nen²jem² 斟】twirling or rotating of the acupuncture needle

年【nin⁴ 捻⁴】year; annual; yearly; age; New Year; a period in one's life; a period in history; harvest; a surname

年月【nin⁴yüd⁹ 越】days; years

年份【nin⁴fen⁶ 分⁶】a particular year; age; time

年度【nin⁴dou⁶ 道】year

年头【nin⁴ teo⁴ 投 】year; years; ays; harvest

年岁【nin⁴xêü³ 碎】age; years

年龄【nin⁴ling⁴ 玲】age

年纪【nin⁴géi² 己】age

年级【nin⁴keb⁷ 给】grade; year

年华【nin⁴wa⁴ 铧】time; years

年代【nin⁴doi⁶ 袋】age; years; time; a decade of a century

年轮【nin⁴lên⁴ 伦】annual ring

年利【nin⁴lêi⁶ 俐】annual interest = 年息【nin⁴xig⁷】

年成【nin⁴ xing⁴ 承】the year's harvest = 年景【nin⁴ging²】

年初【nin⁴ qo¹ 楚¹】the beginning of the year

年底【nin⁴ dei² 抵】the end of the year; year-end = 年终【nin⁴jung¹】年尾【nin⁴méi⁵】

年青【nin⁴qing¹ 清】young = 年轻【nin⁴hing¹】

年迈【nin⁴mai⁶ 卖】old; aged

年富力强【nin⁴fu³lig⁹kêng⁴ 赋历卡香⁴】in

the prime of life; in one's prime

年深日久【nin⁴ xem¹ yed⁹ geo² 心逸九】
with the passage of time; as the
years go by

拧【ning² 宁²; ning⁶ 宁⁶】twist; wring;
pinch; tweak; screw

拧头【ning⁶teo⁴ 投】to shake one's head =
【普】摇头（不同意）

拧干衣服【ning²gon¹yi¹fug⁹ 竿依伏】wr-
ing out wet clothes = 【普】把衣
服拧干

拧开樽盖【ning⁶hoi¹jên¹goi³ 海¹ 遵该³】
twist the cap off a bottle = 【普】
拧开瓶盖

宁【ning⁴ 拧⁴】rather; would rather; better; could there be; a surname; peaceful; tranquil; another name for Nanjing

宁静【ning⁴ jing⁶ 净 】peaceful; tranquil;
quiet

宁可【ning⁴ho² 贺²】would rather; better
= 宁愿【ning⁴yün⁶ 县】= 宁肯
【ning⁴heng² 亨²】

宁缺勿滥【ning⁴küd⁸med⁹lam⁶ 决物缆】
rather go without than have something shoddy — put quality before
quantity

宁死不屈【ning⁴xēi²bed⁷wed⁷ 四² 毕乌
核⁷】rather die than submit

柠【ning⁴ 宁】< n. > 柠檬【ning⁴mung¹
蒙¹】(see"柠檬")

咛【ning⁴ 宁】< v. > 叮咛【ding¹ning⁴
丁】warn

泞【ning⁴ 宁】(see "泥泞")

狞【ning⁴ 宁】ferocious; hideous

狞笑【ning⁴xiu³ 少³】grin hideously

佞【ning⁶ 拧⁶】given to flattery

佞人【ning⁶yen⁴ 仁】sycophant;
toady

镍【nib⁷ 聂; nib⁹ 聂】nickel

镍币【nib⁷bei⁶ 敝】nickel coin; nickel

聂【nib⁹ 捏】a surname

镊【nib⁹ 聂】tweezers（镊子【nib⁹ji² 止】）

颞【nib⁹ 聂】< n. > 颞颥【nib⁹yü⁴ 儒】
temple

蹑【nib⁹ 聂】lighten （one's step）;
follow; tread

蹑手蹑脚【nib⁹xeo²nib⁹gêg⁹ 守格约⁹】
walk gingerly

涅【nib⁹ 捏】alunite; dye sth. black

涅白【nib⁹bag⁹ 百⁹】opaque white

涅槃【nib⁹pun⁴ 盘】nirvana

捏【nib⁹ 涅】hold between the fingers;
pinch

捏合【nib⁹heb⁹ 盒】mediate; carry on with
sb.

捏造【nib⁹jou⁶ 做】fabricate; concoct;
fake

捏一把汗【nib⁹yed⁷ba²hon⁶ 壹巴² 翰】be
breathless with anxiety or tension

搦【nig⁷ 匿】hold; take; grasp = 【普】
拿;持

搦来【nig⁷loi⁴ 莱】bring it here = 【普】拿
来

搦去【nig⁷hêü³ 虚】take it away = 【普】
拿走

搦唔出手【nig⁷m⁴qêd⁷xeo³ 次律⁷ 守】not
be presentable = 【普】拿不出手

溺【nig⁹ 匿⁹；niu⁶ 尿】drown；be addicted to

溺死【nig⁹xêi² 四²】be drowned

溺爱【nig⁹ngoi³ 哀³】spoil（a child）；dote on（a child）

昵【nig⁷ 搦】close；intimate

亲昵【qen¹nig⁷ 趁¹】very intimate

匿【nig⁷ 搦】hide；conceal

匿迹【nig⁷jig⁷ 织】go into hiding

匿名【nig⁷ming⁴ 明】anonymous

女【nêü⁵ 挪去⁵】woman；female；daughter；girl

女子【nêü⁵ji² 止】woman；female

女仔【nêü⁵jei² 济】girl；virgin =【普】女孩

女儿【nêü⁵yi⁴ 移】daughter；girl

女士【nêü⁵xi⁶ 是】lady；madam

女郎【nêü⁵long⁴ 狼】young woman；maiden；girl

女流【nêü⁵leo⁴ 留】the weaker sex

女性【nêü⁵xing³ 胜】the female sex；woman

女色【nêü⁵xig⁷ 式】woman's charms

女神【nêü⁵xen⁴ 臣】goddess

女婿【nêü⁵xei³ 世】son-in-law

女红【nêü⁵hung⁴ 洪】needlework

女工【nêü⁵gung¹ 功】woman worker

女生【nêü⁵xeng¹ 笙】girl student；schoolgirl

女王【nêü⁵wong⁴ 黄】queen

女朋友【nêü⁵peng⁴yeo⁵ 凭有】girl friend

女主人【nêü⁵jü²yen⁴ 煮仁】hostess

女厕所【nêü⁵qi³xo² 次锁】woman's lavatory；ladies' room；Ladies；Women

馁【nêü⁵ 女；noi⁵ 内⁵】hungry；famished；disheartened；dispirited；（of fish）putrid

气馁【hêi³nêü⁵ 戏】lose heart

暖【nüu⁵ 嫩⁵】warm；genial；warm up

暖和【nün⁵wo⁴ 禾】warm；nice and warm；warm up

暖流【nün⁵leo⁴ 留】warm current

暖气【nün⁵hêi³ 戏】central heating

暖烘烘【nün⁵ hung³ hung³ 控】nice and warm

暖水壶【nün⁵ xêü² wu⁴ 绪²胡 】thermos flask；thermos bottle =【普】暖水瓶

嫩【nün⁶ 暖⁶】tender；delicate；inexperienced；unskilled

嫩叶【nün⁶yib³ 业】tender leaves

嫩绿【nün⁶lug⁹ 六】light green

嫩蚊仔【nün⁶men¹jei² 炆 济²】boy and girl；boy；child =【普】小孩

娘【nêng⁴ 挪香⁴；nêng¹ 挪香¹】ma；mum；mother；a form of address for an elderly married woman；a young woman

娘亲【nêng⁴qen¹ 趁¹】mother

娘娘【nêng⁴ nêng⁴】empress or imperial concubine of the first rank；goddess

娘家【nêng⁴ga¹ 加】a married woman's parents' home

娘胎【nêng⁴toi¹ 台¹】mother's womb

娘子【nêng⁴ ji² 止 】a form of address for one's wife；a polite form of address for a young woman

呢【nē¹ 挪耶¹；nei⁴ 泥；nēi¹ 尼¹；ni¹ 挪衣¹】①＜auxil.＞show query mood

in the sentence end; show stress or stop; ② < *pron* . > this; ③ < *n* . > wool; woollen cloth

呢绒【nēi⁴yung² 拥】woollen goods; wool fabric

呢个系乜野?【nēi¹go³hei⁶med⁷yē⁵】what is this? =【普】这个是什么?

呢啲【ni¹did⁷ 得热⁷】these =【普】这些

呢度【nēi¹dou⁶ 道】here =【普】这里

呢排【nēi¹pai⁴ 牌】recently; lately ∽【普】这些日子

呢笼野【nēi¹lung⁵yē⁵ 陇惹】this type of thing ∽【普】这些东西;这一套;这些鬼名堂

吴【ng⁴ 吾】the Kingdom of Wu(222 - 280), one of the Three Kingdoms; a surname

梧【ng⁴ 吴】< *n* . > 梧桐【ng⁴tung⁴ 同】Chinese parasol (tree)

蜈【ng⁴ 吴】< *n* . > 蜈蚣【ng⁴gung¹ 公】centipede

吾【ng⁴ 吴】I or we

吾国【ng⁴guog⁸ 帼⁸】my or our country

吾人【ng⁴yen⁴ 仁⁴】we

吾辈【ng⁴bui³ 背】we

五【ng⁵ 伍】five

五倍【ng⁵pui⁵ 陪⁵】fivefold

五彩【ng⁵ qoi² 采】the five colours (blue, yellow, red, white and black); multicoloured

五谷【ng⁵ gug⁷ 菊】the five cereals (rice, two kinds of milled, wheat and beans); food crops

五更【ng⁵gang¹ 耕】the five watches of the night; the fifth watch of the night

五官【ng⁵ gun¹ 观 】the five sense organs (ears, eyes, lips, nose and tongue); facial features

五金【ng⁵gem¹ 今】the five metals (gold, silver, copper, iron and tin); metals; hardware

五经【ng⁵ging¹ 京】the Five Classics, namely, The Book of Songs, the Book of History, the Book of Change, the Book of Rites and Spring and Autumu Annals

五岭【ng⁵ling⁵ 领】the Five Ridges

五内【ng⁵moi⁶ 耐】viscera

五味【ng⁵ mēi⁶ 未 】the five flavous (sweet, sour, bitter, pungent and salty); all sorts of flavours

五行【ng⁵ heng⁴ 衡 】the five elements (metal, wood, water, fire and earth)

五月【ng⁵yüd⁹ 越】May; the fifth moon

五岳【ng⁵ngog⁹ 颚】the Five Mountains

五脏【ng⁵jong⁶ 撞】the five internal organs (heart, liver, spleen, lungs and kidneys)

五线谱【ng⁵xin³pou² 扇普】staff; stave

五光十色【ng⁵ guong¹ xeb⁹ xig⁷ 胱拾式】multicoloured; of great variety

五颜六色【ng⁵ngan⁴lug⁹xig⁷ 雁⁴ 绿式】of various colours; multicoloured

五湖四海【ng⁵ wu⁴ xēi³ hoi² 胡跟凯】all corners of the land

五花八门【ng⁵ fa¹ bad⁸ mun⁴ 化¹ 捌瞞】multifarious

五体投地【ng⁵tei²teo⁴dēi⁶ 睇头得希⁶】prostrate oneself before sb. in admiration

午【ng⁵ 五】noon；midday；the seventh of the twelve Earthly Branches

午前【ng⁵qin⁴ 钱】forenoon；before noon；morning

午后【ng⁵heo⁶ 候】afternoon

午饭【ng⁵fan⁶ 范】midday meal；lunch

午睡【ng⁵xêu⁶ 绪⁶】afternoon nap；take a nap after lunch

午休【ng⁵ yeo¹优】noon break；midday rest

午夜【ng⁵yê⁶ 野⁶】midnight

伍【ng⁵ 五】five (used for the numeral 五 on cheques, banknotes, etc, to avoid mistakes or alterations)；army；company；a surname

忤【ng⁵ 午】disobedient；uncongenial

忤逆【ng⁵yig⁹ 亦】disobedient

误【ng⁶ 悟】mistake；error；miss；harm；by mistake

误差【ng⁶qa¹ 叉】error

误会【ng⁶ wui⁶汇 】mistake；misunderstanding

误解【ng⁶ gai²戒²】misread；misunderstanding

误事【ng⁶ xi⁶是 】cause delay in work；bungle matters

悟【ng⁶ 误】realize；awaken

悟性【ng⁶xing³ 姓】comprehension

晤【ng⁶ 悟】meet；interview；see

晤面【ng⁶min⁶ 免⁶】meet；see

寤【ng⁶ 悟】awake

寤寐【ng⁶mêi⁶ 味】awake and a sleep

嗯【ng² 吾²；ng⁴ 吾】＜int.＞ show a sound of question or promise

嗯，你讲乜野？【ng²，nêi⁵gong²med⁷yê²】what？what did you say？＝【普】嗯，你说什么？

嗯，好啦！【ng⁴，hou²la¹】O.K.，it's settled！＝【普】嗯，就这么办！

桠【nga¹ 额丫¹】fork (of a tree)

桠杈【nga¹ qa¹ 叉】fork (of a tree)；crotch；crotched；forked

伢【nga¹ 桠；nga¹ 牙】child；kid

伢伢仔【nga⁴nga¹jei² 济²】child；kid；baby ＝【普】婴儿；小孩

砑【nga² 牙²；nga⁴ 牙】not bright-coloured；have not lustre；press and smooth；calender

砑光【nga²guong¹ 胱】calender

砑色【nga²xig⁷ 式】not bright-coloured；have not lustre ＝【普】不鲜艳；没有光泽

氩【nga³ 亚】＜n.＞ argon（Ar）

牙【nga⁴ 芽⁴】tooth；tooth-like thing；ivory

牙齿【nga⁴qi² 耻】tooth

牙关【nga⁴guan¹ 惯¹】mandibular joint

牙垢【nga⁴geo³ 救】tartar；dental calculus ＝ 牙屎【nga⁴xi² 史】

牙痛【nga⁴tung³ 通³】toothache

牙医【nga⁴yi¹ 衣】dentist

牙龈【nga⁴ngen⁴ 银】gum

牙膏【nga⁴gou¹ 高】toothpaste

牙刷【nga⁴qad⁸ 察】toothbrush

牙签【nga⁴qim¹ 潜¹】toothpick

牙雕【nga⁴diu¹ 刁】ivory carving

牙铰【nga⁴ gao³教 】chin =【普】颏；下巴

牙罅【nga⁴ la³啦³】the space between the teeth =【普】牙缝

牙烟【nga⁴ yin¹燕¹】dangerous; terrible; horrible; ugly; simply; of low quality =【普】危险得很；好险

牙擦【nga⁴ qad⁸刷 】boastful; one who says a lot to defend oneself = 牙擦擦　牙斩斩【nga⁴jam²jam²斩²】=【普】骄傲；自负

牙尖嘴利【nga⁴jim¹jêü²lêi⁶ 詹追² 俐】one who can speak very well =【普】说话嘴快，而且说得刻薄，不饶人

牙齿当金使【nga⁴qi²dong³gem¹xei² 始档 今洗】to make a promise and to honour the promise ∽【普】说得出，做得到；讲信誉

芽　【nga⁴ 牙】bud; sprout; shoot

芽豆【nga⁴deo⁶ 窦】sprouted broad bean

芽菜【nga⁴qoi³ 蔡】bean sprouts =【普】豆芽儿

蚜　【nga⁴ 牙】< n . > 蚜虫【nga⁴qung⁴从】aphid; aphis

迓　【nga⁶ 讶】welcome; meet

讶　【nga⁶ 迓；nga⁵ 瓦】be surprised; be astonished

雅　【nga⁵ 瓦】standard; proper; refined; elegant; acquaintance; friendship

雅观【nga⁵ gun¹官 】refined (in manner, etc.); in good taste

雅致【nga⁵ji³ 至】refined; tasteful

雅兴【nga⁵hing³ 庆】aesthetic mood

雅意【nga⁵ yi³蕙 】your kindness; your kind offer

雅量【nga⁵lêng⁶亮 】magnanimity; great capacity for liquor

雅俗共赏【nga⁵jug⁹gung⁶xêng² 族贡⁶ 想】(of a work of art or literature) appeal to both the more and the less cultured

衙　【nga⁴ 牙】< n . > 衙门【nga⁴mun⁴瞒】government office in feudal China

瓦　【nga⁵ 雅】tile; made of baked clay; watt

瓦屋【nga⁵ ngug⁷ 额哭⁷】tile-roofed house =【普】瓦房

瓦工【nga⁵ gung¹功 】bricklayer; tiler =【普】瓦匠

瓦砾【nga⁵lig⁷ 力¹】rubble; debris

瓦特【nga⁵deg⁹ 得⁹】watt

瓦时【nga⁵xi⁴ 史⁴】watt-hour

瓦解【nga⁵gai² 介²】disintegrate; collapse

瓦罉【nga⁵qang¹ 撑】clay pot = 瓦煲【nga⁵ bou¹ 褒】=【普】瓦锅

瓦背【nga⁵bui³ 辈】roof = 瓦背顶【nga⁵ bui³dēng²】=【普】房子的瓦面

瓦坑【nga⁵hang¹ 黑罂²】rooftop =【普】瓦面的泻水槽

掗　【nga⁶ 讶】to open wide one's legs

掗碴【nga⁶ja⁶ 榨⁶】to take up much place; bulky; one who is nasty =【普】霸占；霸道

搯　【ngao¹ 拗¹】use the hand or claw to scratch where it itches

搯痒【ngao¹ yêng⁵氧 】scratch where it itches =【普】搔痒

嘐　【ngao¹ 坳¹；ngao³ 坳³】the tiger's (or demon's) howl; argue or quarrel

嘐呜婆【ngao¹wu¹po⁴ 乌颇⁴】type of gi-

ant in tales used to scare children
〇【普】女魔鬼;女妖怪(大人捏
造用以唬小孩的)

唔颈【ngao³gēng² 镜²】to go against; to
be very stubborn; argue; quarrel
〇【普】争辩;争吵;顶牛

肴

【ngao⁴ 淆】meat and fish dishes

肴馔【ngao⁴jan⁶ 栈⁶】sumptuous courses at
a meal

淆

【ngao⁴ 肴】confuse; mix

淆乱【ngao⁴lün⁶ 联⁶】confuse; befuddle

咬

【ngao⁵ 肴⁵】bite; snap at; grip; bark;
pronounce; be nitpicking

咬住【ngao⁵jü⁶ 注⁶】bite into; grip

咬牙切齿【ngao⁵ nga⁴ qid⁸ qi²芽 彻 始】
gnash one's teeth

咬文嚼字【ngao⁵men⁴jê̂g⁸ji⁸ 闻 桌 自】pay
excessive attention to wording

咬唔入【ngao⁵m⁴yeb⁹ 邑⁹】cannot be bit-
ten; cannot take one's advantage
〇【普】抓不住把柄;攻不下;奈
何不了

啱

【ngam¹ 岩】correct; right; proper =
【普】正确

岩

【ngam⁴ 癌】rock; cliff; crag

岩石【ngam⁴xē̄g⁹ 硕】rock

岩浆【ngam⁴jêng¹ 张】magma

岩层【ngam⁴qeng⁴ 次莺⁴】rock stratum

岩洞【ngam⁴dung⁶ 动】grotto

癌

【ngam⁴ 岩】cancer; carcinoma

癌症【ngam⁴jing³ 正】cancer

罱

【ngam³ 岩³】make the body to press
close into

罱讲【ngam³ban⁶ 办】(the ox) lie down
into mire = 【普】(牛)躺倒在泥
浆里

埃

【ngai¹ 艾¹; ngoi¹ 哀】dust

埃及【ngai¹keb⁹ 级⁹】< n. > Egypt

欸

【ngai² 埃²; ē¹ 诶¹】< int. > 〇 hey

欸乃【ngai²nai⁵ 奶】< onomatopoeia >
the creak of an oar

艾

【ngai⁶ 隘】Chinese mugwort; end;
stop; a surname

艾绒【ngai⁶yung⁴ 容】moxa

艾灸【ngai⁶geo³ 够】moxibustion

隘

【ngai⁶ 艾】narrow; pass

隘口【ngai⁶heo² 厚²】(mountain)pass

喺

【ngai³ 艾³】shout; scold

喺交【ngai³gao¹ 胶】quarrel = 【普】对
骂;互相指责;争吵

捱

【ngai⁴ 崖】= 挨【ngai⁴】suffer; drag
out; delay; bear

捱饿【ngai⁴ngo⁶ 卧】suffer from hunger

捱世界【ngai⁴xei³gai³ 细介】survive in the
society 〇【普】辛苦劳碌过日子

捱更抵夜【ngai⁴gang⁴dei²yē⁶ 耕底野⁶】
sleep late so as to try to complete a
project; wake up early and sleep
late 〇【普】彻夜不眠地辛苦劳
作

崖

【ngai⁴ 涯】precipice; cliff

崖壁【ngai⁴big⁸ 碧⁸】precipice

涯

【ngai⁴ 崖】margin; limit

涯际【ngai⁴jei³ 济】margin; border

颜【ngan⁴ 雁⁴】face；countenance；prestige；colour；a surname

颜面【ngan⁴min⁶ 免⁶】face；prestige

颜料【ngan⁴liu⁶ 辽⁶】pigment；colour

颜色【ngan⁴xig⁷ 式】colour；countenance；pigment

礶【ngan⁴ 雁⁴】grind；roller

礶碎【ngan⁴xêü³ 绪³】pulverize = 【普】碾碎

礶成粉【ngan⁴xing⁴fen² 承分²】grind into fine powder = 【普】研成粉末

眼【ngan⁵ 雁⁵】eye；look；glance；small hole

眼睛【ngan⁵jing¹ 精】eye

眼珠【ngan⁵jü¹ 朱】eyeball = 眼球【ngan⁵keo⁴】= 眼核【ngan⁵wed⁹】

眼眶【ngan⁵hong¹ 康】eye socket；rim of the eye

眼泪【ngan⁵lêü⁶ 类】tears = 眼水【ngan⁵xêü²】

眼帘【ngan⁵lim⁴ 廉】eye

眼光【ngan⁵guong¹ 胱】eye；sight；foresight

眼力【ngan⁵lig⁹ 历】eyesight；vision；judgment

眼界【ngan⁵gai³ 介】field of vision；outlook

眼色【ngan⁵xig⁷ 式】hint given with the eyes；wink

眼神【ngan⁵xen⁴ 臣】expression in one's eyes；eyesight

眼生【ngan⁵xeng¹ 笙】look unfamiliar

眼熟【ngan⁵xug⁹ 孰】look familiar

眼看【ngan⁵hon³ 汉】soon；in a moment；watch helplessly = 眼睇【ngan⁵tei² 体】

眼前【ngan⁵qin⁴ 钱】before one's eyes；at the moment；now

眼馋【ngan⁵qan² 产】covet；be envious

眼福【ngan⁵fug⁷ 幅】the good fortune of seeing sth. rare or beautiful

眼红【ngan⁵hung⁴ 洪】covet；be envious；furious

眼里【ngan⁵lêü⁵ 吕】in one's eyes

眼瞓【ngan⁵fen³ 训】sleepy = 【普】眼累了；要睡

眼枷【ngan⁵ga¹ 加】spectacles = 【普】眼镜

眼眉【ngan⁵mēi⁴ 媚】eyebrow = 眼眉毛【ngan⁵mēi⁴mou⁴】

眼浅【ngan⁵qin² 钱²】get upset easily = 【普】眼光短；看不开

眼屎【ngan⁵xi² 史】mucus in the eyes；gum (in the eyes) = 【普】眼垢

眼甘甘【ngan⁵gem¹gem¹ 今】not to stop looking at something that one really wants to obtain ∽【普】看得入了迷；贪恋地看的样子

眼光光【ngan⁵guong¹ guong¹ 胱】open one's eyes；anxiously；helplessly ∽【普】眼巴巴

眼凸凸【ngan⁵ded⁹ded⁹ 突】frustrated and shocked due to failure；unfeelingly ∽【普】眼睁睁(感到突然时失望的眼神)

眼定定【ngan⁵ding⁶ding⁶ 锭】stare = 【普】凝神注视

眼辘辘【ngan⁵lug⁷lug⁷ 碌】open one's eyes big；show that one is angry ∽【普】提起精神，密切关注情况变化的样子

眼眨眨【ngan⁵jam²jam² 斩】wink one's eyes to show that one is pitiful

【普】悲怜的样子;眼泪快要夺眶
而出时的神色

眼眲眲【ngan⁵lei⁶lei⁶ 厉】keep staring at
something ∽【普】使眼色

眼湿湿【ngan⁵xeb⁷xeb⁷ 拾⁷】with tears in
one's eyes ∽【普】泪水盈眶

眼朦朦【ngan⁵ mung¹ mung¹ 樣¹】describe
one's look who just up from sleep;
half-close one's eyes ∽【普】睡眼
朦胧

眼掘掘【ngan⁵gued⁹gued⁹ 骨⁹】angry eyes
=【普】发怒时的眼色

眼揾毛【ngan⁵ yeb⁷ mou¹ 无¹】eyelash =
【普】睫毛

眼明手快【ngan⁵ming⁴xeo²fai³ 名守块】
quick of eye and deft of hand

眼高手低【ngan⁵gou¹xeo²dei¹ 糕守底¹】
have grandiose aims but puny abilities

眼花缭乱【ngan⁵fa¹liu⁴lün⁶ 化¹ 辽联⁶】be
dazzled

雁【ngan⁶ 眼⁶】< n. > wild goose

俺【ngan² 雁²; an²】I; we (northern di-
alect)

硬【ngang⁶ 额罷⁶; ngang² 额罷²】hard;
stiff; tough; strong; firm; manage to
do sth. with difficulty; abie (person)

硬币【ngang⁶bei⁶ 敝】coin; specie

硬度【ngang⁶dou⁶ 道】hardness

硬汉【ngang⁶hon³ 看】a man of iron

硬化【ngang⁶fa³ 花³】harden; sclerosis

硬件【ngang⁶gin² 建²】hardware

硬朗【ngang⁶long⁵ 浪⁵】hale and hearty

硬性【ngang⁶xing³ 胜】rigid; stiff; inflexible

硬拼【ngang⁶ping³ 聘】fight recklessly

硬水【ngang⁶xêü² 绪²】hard water

硬说【ngang⁶xüd⁸ 雪】stubbornly insist;
assert

硬系【ngang²hei⁶ 兮⁶】must; actually;
simply; always =【普】硬是;总
是;必然

硬颈【ngang⁶gēng² 镜²】stubborn =【普】
硬性子;不听劝告

硬打硬【ngang⁶da²ngang⁶ 得阿²】true ∽
【普】真家伙;实实在在

硬晒舦【ngang⁶xai³tai⁵ 徙³ 太⁵】put something in a mess and it cannot be
solved ∽【普】启动不了;无法干
(某事)

硬碰硬【ngang⁶pung³ngang⁶ 捧³】confront
the tough with toughness

硬骨头【ngang⁶gued⁷teo⁴ 掘⁷ 投】hard bone
— a dauntless, unyielding person

硬功夫【ngang⁶gung¹fu¹ 工孚】great profi-
ciency

硬邦邦【ngang⁶ bong¹ bong¹ 帮 】very
hard; very stiff

硬着头皮【ngang⁶jêg⁹teo⁴pēi⁴ 桌⁹ 投脾】
toughen one's scalp — brace oneself

轭【ngag⁸ 额⁸】< n. > yoke

钜【ngag⁸ 轭】bracelet =【普】手镯

玉钜【yug⁸ngag⁸ 肉】jade bracelet =
【普】玉镯

额【ngag⁹ 轭⁹】forehead; a horizontal
tablet; a specified number or amount

额骨【ngag⁹gued⁷ 掘⁷】frontal bone

额角【ngag⁹gog⁸ 各】frontal eminence

额定【ngag⁹ding⁶ 锭】specified; rated

额外【ngag⁹ngoi⁶ 碍 】extra; additional;

added

啮【ngad⁹ 额压⁹；ngid⁹ 额热⁹】gnaw; bite

啮齿动物【ngid⁹qi²dung⁶med⁹ 此洞勿】rodent

有得啮【mou⁵deg⁷ngad⁹ 武德】have no food = 【普】没食物

庶【ngad 压】the smell of the urine (尿庶【niu⁶ngad⁸】)

噯【ngei¹ 矮¹】plead = 【普】哀求

噯求【ngei⁴keo⁴ 球】plead; beg = 【普】哀求；缠着苦求

矮【ngei² 伪²】short (of stature); low

矮胖【ngei² bun⁶ 伴】short and stout; dumpy

矮小【ngei² xiu² 少²】short and small

矮仔【ngei²jei² 济²】a short person; dwarf = 【普】矮子；矮个儿

矮瓜【ngei²gua¹ 挂¹】brinjal = 【普】茄瓜

矮咕咕【ngei²ded⁷ded⁷ 凸⁷】very short; pudge; short and plump = 矮凳凳【ngei²den²den² 得因²】= 【普】矮墩墩

翳【ngei³ 矮³；ei³】slight corneal opacity; nebula; dark; dim; in a bad mood; not feeling good;make someone angry

翳焗【ngei³ gug⁹ 局】warm = 【普】（天气）闷热

翳气【ngei³hēi³ 戏】be in a bad mood after being scolded = 【普】（办事遇到梗阻时）心情不舒爽；烦恼

缢【ngei³ 翳；ei³】bang

自缢【ji⁶ngei³ 治】bang oneself

危【ngei⁴ 伪⁴】danger; peril; endanger; dying; proper

危危乎【ngei⁴ngei⁴fu⁴ 符】dangerous

危险【ngei⁴him² 谦²】dangerous; perilous

危殆【ngei⁴toi⁵ 怠】in great danger; in jeopardy

危害【ngei⁴ hoi⁶ 亥】harm; endanger; jeopardize

危机【ngei⁴gēi¹ 基】crisis

危急【ngei⁴geb⁷ 格合⁷】critical; in imminent danger

危难【ngei⁴nan⁶ 挪晏⁶】danger and disaster

危亡【ngei⁴mong⁴ 忙】in peril; at stake

危言耸听【ngei⁴yin⁴xung²ting³ 然崇² 挺³】say frightening things just to raise an alarm

危在旦夕【ngei⁴joi⁶dan³jig⁹ 再⁶ 诞直】on the verge of death or destruction

巍【ngei⁴ 危】towering; lofty

巍峨【ngei⁴ngo⁴ 鹅】towering; lofty

巍然【ngei⁴yin⁴ 言】towering; lofty; majestic

巍巍【ngei⁴ngei⁴】towering; lofty

蚁【ngei⁵ 伪⁵】ant

蚁窦【ngei⁵deo³ 斗】ant nest = 【普】蚁巢

蚁丘【ngei⁵yeo¹ 休】ant hill

魏【ngei⁶ 艺】the Kingdom of Wei (220－265); a surname

伪【ngei⁶ 艺】false; fake; bogus; puppet

伪装【ngei⁶jong¹妆】pretend; disguise; camouflage

伪造【ngei⁶jou⁶ 做】forge; falsify; fabricate

伪善【ngei⁶xin⁶ 膳】hypocritical

伪钞【ngei⁶qao¹ 抄】counterfeit money = 【普】伪币

伪君子【ngei⁶guen¹ji² 军止】hypocrite

蚬【ngei⁴ 巍】lofty; towering

霓【ngei⁴ 危】secondary rainbow

霓红灯【ngei⁴hung⁴deng¹ 登】neon lamp; neon light

倪【ngei⁴ 危】clue; inkling; a surname

艺【ngei⁶ 伪】skill; art

艺术【ngei⁶xêd⁹ 述】art; skill; craft; conforming to good taste

艺人【ngei⁶yen⁴ 仁】actor or artist; artisan

毅【ngei⁶ 艺】firm; resolute

毅力【ngei⁶lig⁹ 历】willpower; will; stamina

毅然【ngei⁶yin⁴ 言】resolutely; firmly

呓【ngei⁶ 艺】talk in one's sleep

呓语【ngei⁶yü⁵ 雨】talk in one's sleep = 讲梦话【gong²mong⁶wa²】

诣【ngei⁶ 艺】call on (sb. one respects); visit; (academic or technical) attainments

欧【ngeo¹ 殴¹；eo¹】short for Europe; a surname

欧洲【ngeo¹jeo¹ 州】Europe

欧化【ngeo¹fa³ 花³】Europeanize; westernize

欧姆【ngeo¹mou⁵ 母】ohm

欧阳【ngeo¹yêng⁴ 扬】a surname

殴【ngeo¹ 欧；eo¹】beat up; hit

殴打【ngeo¹da² 得阿²】beat up; hit

瓯【ngeo¹ 欧；eo¹】bowl; cup; small bowls

鸥【ngeo¹ 欧；eo¹】gull

海欧【hoi²ngeo¹】sea gull

讴【ngeo¹ 欧；eo¹】sing; folk songs; ballads

讴歌【ngeo¹go¹ 哥】sing the praises of; eulogize

区【ngeo¹ 欧；kêü¹ 驱】a surname; area; district; region; an administrative division; distinguish; classify

区别【kêü¹bid⁹ 必⁹】distinguish; differentiate; difference

区分【kêü¹fen¹ 芬】differentiate; distinguish

区划【kêü¹wag⁹ 或】division into districts

区域【kêü¹wig⁹ 乌益⁹】region; area; district

区区【kêü¹kêü¹】trivial; trifling

勾【ngeo¹ 欧】cancel; cross out; strike out; tick off; delineate; draw; point; thicken; induce; evoke; collade with

勾搭【ngeo¹dab⁸ 答】gang up with; seduce

勾画【ngeo¹wag⁹ 划】draw the outline of; delineate

勾勒【ngeo¹ leg⁹ 罗克⁹】draw the outline of; outline

勾通【ngeo¹tung¹ 同¹】collude with

勾销【ngeo¹xiu¹ 消】liquidate; write off

勾引【ngeo¹yen⁵ 瘾】tempt; entice; seduce

勾心斗角【ngeo¹xem¹deo³gog⁸ 深豆³ 各】intrigue against each other = 钩

心斗角

勾股定理【ngeo¹ gu² ding⁶ lēi⁵ 古锭李】the Pythagorean theorem

钩【ngeo¹ 欧】hook; hook stroke; tick; crochet; sew with large stitches

钩针【ngeo¹ jem¹ 浸¹】crochet hook

钩虫【ngeo¹ qung⁴ 从】hookworm

钓鱼钩【diu⁴ yü⁴ ngeo¹ 吊渔】fishhook

呕【ngeo² 欧²】vomit; throw up

呕吐【ngeo² tou³ 套】vomit; throw up; be sick

呕血【ngeo² hüd⁸ 黑月⁸】haematemesis

呕心沥血【ngeo² xem¹ lig⁹ hüd⁸ 深力黑月⁸】shed one's heart's blood; take in-·finite pains

炰【ngeo³ 欧³】use the small fire to boil for a long time =【普】熬

沤【ngeo³ 欧³】soak; steep; macerate; soak in water; spoiled; use a long time to cook

沤肥【ngeo³ fēi⁴ 非⁴】make compost; wet compost

怄【ngeo³ 沤】irritate; annoy; be irritated

怄气【ngeo³ hēi 戏】be difficult and sulky

牛【ngeo⁴ 欧⁴】ox; a surname

牛鬼蛇神【ngeo⁴ guei² xē⁴ xen⁴ 诡射⁴ 臣】monsters and demons — forces of evil

牛牯【ngeo⁴ gu⁴ 古】bull =【普】公牛

牛牸【ngeo⁴ na² 那²】cow =【普】母牛

牛肉【ngeo⁴ yug⁹ 玉】beef

牛奶【ngeo⁴ nai⁵ 乃】milk

牛马【ngeo⁴ ma⁵ 码】oxen and horses — beasts of burden

牛痘【ngeo⁴ deo⁶ 斗⁶】cowpox; smallpox pustule

牛腩【ngeo⁴ nam⁵ 南⁵】sirloin; tenderloin

牛毛【ngeo⁴ mou⁴ 无】ox hair

牛皮【ngeo⁴ pēi⁴ 脾】cattlehide

牛虻【ngeo⁴ mong¹ 网¹】gadfly

牛栏【ngeo⁴ lan⁴ 兰】cattle pen

牛劲【ngeo⁴ ging³ 径】great strength; obstinacy

牛河【ngeo⁴ ho² 可】rice noodle cooked with beef =【普】牛肉炒粉条

牛精【ngeo⁴ jing⁴ 睛】inconsiderate; stubbornness; unreasonable =【普】牛脾气

牛扒【ngeo⁴ pa² 耙】steak

牛油【ngeo⁴ yeo⁴ 由】butter

牛仔【ngeo⁴ jei² 济²】baby cows; cangsters

牛王【ngeo⁴ wong⁴ 黄】barbarian ∽【普】蛮不讲理;横行霸道

牛犊【ngeo⁴ dug⁹ 读】calf

牛王头【ngeo⁴ wong⁴ teo⁴ 黄投】one who is unreasonable ∽【普】蛮不讲理、横行霸道的人;恶棍

牛颈【ngeo⁴ gēng² 镜²】obstinate; stubborn; self-willed =【普】犟脾气

牛噍牡丹【ngeo⁴ jiu⁶ mao⁵ dan¹ 赵貌⁵ 单】fail to differentiate between good and bad ∽【普】品不出味

牛仔裤【ngeo⁴ jei² fu³ 济² 富】close-fitting pants; jeans

牛头不对马嘴【ngeo⁴ teo⁴ bed⁷ dêu³ ma⁵ jêu² 投毕队³ 蚂追²】incongruous; irrelevant

牛角尖【ngeo⁴ gog⁹ jim¹ 各沾】the tip of a horn — an insignificant or insoluble problem

偶【ngeo⁵ 藕】image; idol; mate; spouse; by chance; by accident

偶尔【ngeo⁵yi⁵ 耳】once in a while; occasionally

偶然【ngeo⁵ yin⁴言 】accidental; fortuitous; chance

偶合【ngeo⁵heb⁹ 盒】coincidence

偶数【ngeo⁵xou³ 扫】even number

偶像【ngeo⁵jêng⁶ 匠】image; idol

耦【ngeo⁵ 偶】in pairs; mate; spouse

耦合【ngeo⁵heb⁹ 盒】coupling

藕【ngeo⁵ 偶】lotus root

藕粉【ngeo⁵fen² 分²】lotus root starch

藕断丝连【ngeo⁵tün⁵xi¹lin⁴ 团⁵ 思连】the lotus root snaps but its fibres stay joined — apparently severed, actually still connected

吽【ngeo⁶ 牛⁶】< a. > 吽呾【ngeo⁶deo⁶ 豆】not energetic; not lively = 【普】痴呆

庵【ngem¹ 鹌; em¹】hut; nunnery

鹌【ngem¹ 庵; em¹】< n. > 鹌鹑【ngem¹ qên¹春】quail

揞【ngem² 庵²】use hand to cover a body; seal; cover; muffle; apply (medicinal powder to a wound)

揞住个鼻【ngem²jü⁶go³bêi⁶ 注⁶ 哥³ 备】cover one's nose with one's hand = 【普】捂鼻子

揞住耳仔【ngem²jü⁶yi⁵jei² 注⁶ 尔济²】stap one's ears = 【普】捂着耳朵

暗【ngem³ 庵³; em³】(see "em³")

黯【ngem³ 暗; em³】dim; gloomy

黯淡【ngem³dam⁶ 担⁶】dim; faint; dismal; gloomy

黯然【ngem³yin⁴ 言】dim; faint; dejected; low-spirited; downcast

谙【ngem¹ 庵; em¹】know well

谙练【ngem¹lin⁶ 炼】conversant; skilled; proficient

搎【ngem⁴ 庵⁴】draw out; pull out; fish out

搎手枪【ngem⁴ xeo² qêng¹守 昌 】draw a pistol = 【普】掏手枪

搎荷包【ngem⁴ho⁴bao¹ 何苞】pay out of one's own pocket; foot a bill; pick sb.'s pocket = 【普】掏腰包

噷【ngem⁴ 庵⁴; em⁴】with bated breath to speak

噷沉【ngem⁴qem⁴ 寻】with bated breath to speak; long-winded; wordy; be talkative = 【普】低音说话;罗嗦

奀【ngen¹ 银¹】thin and small = 【普】瘦小

奀孱【ngen¹ji¹ 支】thin and small = 【普】瘦小

奀裊裊【ngen¹niu¹niu¹ 鸟¹】tall and thin

银【ngen⁴ 奀⁴; ngen² 奀²】silver (Ag); relating to currency or money; silver-coloured

银纸【ngen⁴ ji² 止 】 money; bank-note paper; note = 【普】钞票;银钱

银包【ngen⁴bao¹ 苞】wallet; purse

银行【ngen⁴hong² 杭】bank

银根【ngen⁴gen¹ 跟】money market; money

银币【ngen⁴bei⁶ 敝】silver coin

银两【ngen⁴lêng² 良²】silver（used as currency）

银元【ngen⁴yün⁴ 圆】silver dollar

银器【ngen⁴hêi³ 气】silverware

银牌【ngen⁴pai² 排²】silver medal = 银质奖【ngen⁴jed⁷jêng² 侄⁷ 蒋】

银白【ngen⁴bag⁹ 伯⁹】silver white

银灰【ngen⁴fui¹ 恢】silver grey

银幕【ngen⁴ mog⁹ 莫 】（motion-picture）screen

银河【ngen⁴ho⁴ 何】the Milky Way

银婚【ngen⁴fen¹ 分】silver wedding

银鸡【ngen⁴ gei¹ 计¹】whistle = 【普】哨子

龈 【ngen⁴ 银】gum（see "牙龈"）

垠 【ngen⁴ 银】boundary; limit

狺 【ngen⁴ 银】< onomatopoeia > yap; yelp

狺狺狂吠【ngen⁴ngen⁴kuong⁴fei⁶ 诳⁴ 废⁶】bark frenziedly

踉 【ngen³ 银³】（person or animal）squatting on plank（or tree）rock; make something move

踉踉脚【ngen³ ngen³ gêg⁸格约⁸】sit cross-legged and make to rock — the model of a happy life ∽【普】晃动跷起的二郎腿——享乐的样子

踉踉跳【ngen³ngen³tiu³ 条³】the model of worry; run around on sinister errands ∽【普】上窜下跳（着急的样子）

韧 【ngen⁶ 银⁶；yen⁶ 孕】pliable but strong; tenacious; tough

韧带【yen⁶dai³ 戴】ligament

韧性【ngen⁶xing³ 姓】toughness; tenacity

韧皮【ngen⁶pêi⁴ 脾】naughty =【普】顽皮

莺 【ngeng¹ 额亨¹；eng¹】varbler; oriole

莺歌燕舞【ngeng¹go¹yin³mou⁵ 哥彦武】orioles sing and swallows dart — the joy of spring

礑 【ngeng² 莺²】the body be gored from under =【普】物体下面被东西顶着

礑心礑肺【ngeng²xem¹ngeng²fei³ 深费】the heart and lungs be gored — be bullied; feel unwell ∽【普】受气；难受

嘡 【ngeng⁴ 莺⁴】< onomatopoeia > get angry with bated breath

嘡嘡声【ngeng⁴ngeng²xêng¹ 是镜¹】get angry with bated breath ∽【普】表示不满的唠唠叨叨

罨 【ngeb⁷ 额急⁷；yim² 掩】apply medicine; not ventilated; instead of wrapping it in papers; put some seeds in a container so that they can grow

罨烂【ngeb⁷lan⁶ 兰⁶】wet and not ventilated, make body mildew and rot =【普】潮湿和不通风致使物体霉烂

罨汁【ngeb⁷jeb⁷ 执】not ventilated, wet, narrow and untidy =【普】（地方）狭窄、潮湿，不通风，不干净

噏 【ngeb⁷ 额洽⁷】speak; say; tell

乱噏【lün⁶ngeb⁷ 联⁶】speak indiscreetly = 发噏疯【fad⁸ngeb⁷fung¹ 法风】=【普】乱说

噏一套，做一套【ngeb⁷yed⁷tou³，jou⁶yed⁷tou³】say one thing and do another =【普】讲的是一套，做的是另一

套

擙【ngeb⁷】apply (powder, ointment, etc.)

擙药【ngeb⁷yêg⁹ 若】apply the medicinal powder =【普】敷药

岌【ngeb⁹ 额洽⁹；keb⁷ 级】shake and move

岌岌贡【ngeb⁹ngeb⁹gung³ 拱³】keep shaking and moving；rock；sway = 岌岌喐【yug⁷ 郁】=【普】晃动、不稳的样子；岌岌可危

抁【nged⁷ 额乞⁷】use the hands to extrude

抁住【ngeb⁷jū⁶ 注⁶】use the hands to extrude =【普】用手按着挤压

抁入去【ngeb⁷yeb⁹hêû³ 挹⁹ 虚³】extruding into =【普】挤压进去

抁只死猫食【ngeb⁷jēg⁸xēi²mao¹xig⁹ 脊四² 矛¹ 蚀】force sb. to admit crime (or wrong) =【普】强迫认罪(或错)

兀【nged⁹ 迄】rising to a height；towering；bald

兀立【nged⁹leb⁹ 笠⁹】stand upright

兀自【nged⁹ji⁶ 治】still

迄【nged⁹ 兀】up to；till；so far；all along

迄今【nged⁹gem¹ 金】up to now；to this day

讫【nged⁹ 兀】settleed；completed；end

收讫【xeo¹nged⁹ 修】received in full

起讫【hēi²nged⁹ 喜】the beginning and the end

屹【nged⁹ 兀】towering like a mountain peak

屹立【nged⁹leb⁹ 笠⁹】stand erect

屹然【nged⁹yin⁶ 言】towering；majestic

握【ngeg⁷ 厄；eg⁷】hold；grasp

握拳【ngeg⁷kûn⁴ 权】make a fist；clench one's fist

握手【ngeg⁷xeo² 守】shake hands；clasp hands

幄【ngeg⁷ 握；eg⁷】tent

齷【ngeg⁷ 握；eg⁷】< a. > 齷齪

齪【ngeg⁷qug⁸ 促】dirty；filthy

厄【ngeg⁹ 握⁹；eg⁹】strategic point；adversity；be stranded

厄水【ngeg⁹xêû² 绪²】against the current =【普】逆水

厄运【ngeg⁹ wen⁶ 混】adversity；misfortune

扼【ngeg⁷ 握；eg⁷】clucth；grip；guard；control

扼杀【ngeg⁷xad⁸ 煞】strangle；smother

扼守【ngeg⁷xeo² 手】hold；guard

扼要【ngeg⁷yiu² 腰³】to the point

呃【ngeg⁷ 握；eg⁷】①hiccup ②deceive

打呃【da²ngeg⁷ 得阿²】hiccup =【普】呃逆

呃呃骗骗【ngeg⁷ngeg⁷pin³pin³ 片】deceive；cheat；dupe = 呃呃谝谝【ngeg⁷ngeg⁷tem³tem³ 拖庵³】=【普】欺骗

屙【ngo¹ 疴；o¹】discharge (excrement or urine)

屙屎【ngo¹xi² 史】empty the bowels；shit =【普】拉屎；大便

屙底【ngo¹dei² 抵】the bottom of utensil is pierced

屙尿【ngo¹niu⁶ 鸟⁶】pass urine =【普】拉

尿;小便

疴【ngo¹ 屙;o¹】illness
沉疴【qem⁴ngo¹ 侵⁴】severe and lingering illness

婀【ngo¹ 屙;o¹ 呵】<a.> 婀娜【ngo¹ no⁴挪⁴】(of woman's bearing) graceful

俄【ngo⁴ 鹅】very soon; presently; suddenly
俄顷【ngo⁴king¹ 倾】in a moment; presently
俄罗斯【ngo⁴lo⁴xi¹ 萝司】Russian

鹅【ngo⁴ 俄;ngo² 俄²】goose
鹅毛【ngo⁴mou⁴ 无】goose feather
鹅绒【ngo⁴yung² 拥】goose down
鹅卵石【ngo⁴ lên² xēg⁹ 论² 硕】cobblestone; cobble

峨【ngo⁴ 鹅】high (see "巍峨")

娥【ngo⁴ 鹅】pretty young woman
娥眉【ngo⁴ mēi⁴ 媚】delicate eyebrows; beautiful woman

蛾【ngo⁴ 鹅】moth (飞蛾【fēi¹ngo⁴ 非】)
蛾眉【ngo⁴mēi⁴ 媚】delicate eyebrows

讹【ngo⁴ 鹅】erroneous; mistaken; extort; blackmail; bluff
讹传【ngo⁴qün⁴ 存】false rumour
讹误【ngo⁴ng⁶ 悟】error (in a text)
讹诈【ngo⁴ja³ 炸】blackmail

我【ngo⁵ 鹅⁵】I; we; self; my; our
我地【ngo⁵dēi⁶ 得希⁶】we =【普】我们
我方【ngo⁵fong¹ 芳】our side

我嘅【ngo⁵gē³ 格耶³】my =【普】我的
我行我素【ngo⁵heng⁴ngo⁵xou³ 衡扫】persist in one's old ways (no matter what others say)

卧【ngo⁶ 饿】lie; (of animals or birds) crouch; sit; for sleeping in; poach (eggs)
卧倒【ngo⁶dou² 捣】drop to the ground = 瞓低【fen³dei¹ 训底¹】
卧床【ngo⁶qong⁴ 苍⁴】lie in bed
卧病【ngo⁶bēng⁶ 柄⁶】be confined to bed
卧室【ngo⁶xed⁷ 失】bedroom
卧榻【ngo⁶tad⁸ 替压⁸】bed
卧铺【ngo⁶ pou⁴ 普】sleeping berth; sleeper
卧薪尝胆【ngo⁶xen¹xêng⁴dam² 辛常担²】sleep on brushwood and taste gall — undergo self-imposed hardships so as to strengthen one's resolve to wipe out a national humiliation

饿【ngo⁶ 卧】hungry; starve
饿饭【ngo⁶fan⁶ 范】go hungry; go without food
饿殍【ngo⁶piu⁵ 漂⁵】bodies of the starved

哀【ngoi¹ 爱¹;oi¹】grief; sorrow; mourning; pity
哀愁【ngoi¹xeo⁴ 仇】sad; sorrowful
哀怨【ngoi¹yün³ 渊³】sad; plaintive
哀痛【ngoi¹tung³ 通³】grief; deep sorrow
哀伤【ngoi¹ xêng¹ 湘】grieved; sad; distressed
哀思【ngoi¹xi¹ 司】sad memories; grief
哀叹【ngoi¹ tan³ 炭】lament; bewail; bemoan

哀告【ngoi¹gou³ 诰】beg piteously; supplicate

哀求【ngoi¹keo⁴ 球】entreat; implore

哀悼【ngoi¹ dou⁶ 道 】grieve over sb.'s death

哀歌【ngoi¹go¹ 哥】a mournful song; dirge

哀鸿遍野【ngoi¹ hung⁴ pin³ yē⁵红片夜⁵】 disaster victims everywhere

哀兵必胜【ngoi¹bing¹bid⁷xing³ 冰别⁷性】 an army burning with righteous indignation is bound to win

蔼【ngoi² 霭】friendly; amiable

蔼然可亲【ngoi² yin⁴ ho² qen¹言河² 趁¹】 kindly; amiable; affable

霭【ngoi² 蔼】mist; haze

爱【ngoi³ 暧；oi³】love; affection; like; cherish; be apt to

爱护【ngoi³wu⁶ 户】cherish; treasure

爱惜【ngoi³xig⁷ 色】cherish; treasure; use sparingly＝爱锡【ngoi³xēg⁸ 石⁸】

爱抚【ngoi³fu² 府】show tender care for

爱好【ngoi³hou³ 蒿³】love; like; interest; hobby

爱慕【ngoi³mou⁶ 务】adore; admire

爱怜【ngoi³lin⁴ 连】show tender affection for

爱恋【ngoi³lūn² 孪²】be in love with

爱情【ngoi³ qing⁴程】love (between man and woman)

爱戴【ngoi³dai³ 带】love and esteem

爱国【ngoi³guog⁸ 帼】love one's country

爱人【ngoi³ yen⁴ 仁 】husband or wife; sweetheart

爱憎【ngoi³jeng¹ 增】love and hate

爱面子【ngoi³min⁶ji² 免⁶ 止】be concerned about face-saving

爱不释手【ngoi³ bed⁷ xig⁷ xeo²毕式守】 fondle admiringly

爱屋及乌【ngoi³ngug⁷keb⁹wu¹ 额哭⁷级⁹ 污】love me, love my dog

爱理不理【ngoi³ lēi⁵bed⁷ lēi⁵李毕】look cold and indifferent

爱莫能助【ngoi³ mog⁹ neng⁴ jo⁶漠那亨 座】willing to help but unable to do so

呆【ngoi⁴ 外⁴；dai¹ 歹¹】＜a.＞呆板 【ngoi⁴ban² 版】stiff; rigid; inflexible

暧【ngoi³ 爱】＜a.＞暧昧【ngoi³mui⁶ 妹⁶】ambiguous; shady; dubious

碍【ngoi⁶ 外；oi⁶】hinder; obstruct; be in the way of

碍事【ngoi⁶xi⁶ 士】be in the way; matter

碍眼【ngoi⁶ ngan⁵ 雁⁵】be unpleasant to look

碍手碍脚【ngoi⁶xeo²ngoi⁶gêg⁸ 守格约⁸】 be in the way＝阻埞【jo²dēng⁶】

碍于情面【ngoi⁶yū¹qing⁴min⁶ 迂程免⁶】for fear of hurting sb.'s feelings

外【ngoi⁶ 碍；oi⁶】outer; outward; outside; other; not closely related; besides; unofficial

外边【ngoi⁶bin¹ 鞭】outside; out; exterior

外表【ngoi⁶biu² 标²】outward appearance; exterior

外部【ngoi⁶ bou⁶ 步 】outside; external; exterior; surface

外地【ngoi⁶dēi⁶ 得希⁶】parts of the country other than where one is

外观【ngoi⁶gun¹ 官】outward appearance; exterior

外国【ngoi⁶guog⁸ 帼】foreign country

外行【ngoi⁶ hong⁴ 杭 】layman; nonprofessional; lay

外汇【ngoi⁶ wui⁶ 会⁶】foreign exchange

外籍【ngoi⁶ jig⁹ 直】foreign nationality

外加【ngoi⁶ ga¹ 家】more; additional; extra

外间【ngoi⁶ gan¹ 奸 】outer room; outside circles

外交【ngoi⁶ gao¹ 胶 】diplomacy; foreign affairs

外界【ngoi⁶ gai³ 介 】the outside world; outside

外科【ngoi⁶ fo¹ 课¹】surgical department

外壳【ngoi⁶hog⁸ 学⁸】outer covering; shell; case

外来【ngoi⁶loi⁴ 莱】outside; external; foreign

外力【ngoi⁶lig⁹ 历】outside force; external force

外贸【ngoi⁶meo⁶ 茂】foreign trade

外貌【ngoi⁶mao⁶ 矛⁶】appearance; exterior; looks

外面【ngoi⁶min⁶ 免⁶】outside; out = 外头【ngoi⁶teo⁴】

外人【ngoi⁶ yen⁴ 仁】stranger; foreigner; alien

外伤【ngoi⁶xêng¹ 湘】an injury or wound; trauma

外套【ngoi⁶tou³ 吐】overcoat; loose coat

外文【ngoi⁶ men⁴闻 】 foreign language = 外语【ngoi⁶yü⁵】

外围【ngoi⁶wei⁴ 维】periphery

外向【ngoi⁶hêng³ 乡³】extroversion

外销【ngoi⁶xiu¹ 消】for sale abroad or in another part of the country

外形【ngoi⁶ying⁴ 仍】appearance; external form

外衣【ngoi⁶yi¹ 依】coat; jacket; semblance

外因【ngoi⁶yen¹ 恩】external cause

外援【ngoi⁶ wun⁴垣 】 foreign aid; outside help

外债【ngoi⁶jai³ 斋³】external debt; foreign debt

外在【ngoi⁶joi¹ 再⁶】external; extrinsic

外资【ngoi⁶ji¹ 支】foreign capital

外公【ngoi⁶ gung¹工 】(materal) grandfather

外婆【ngoi⁶ po⁴ 颇⁴】(maternal) grandmother

外父【ngoi⁶fu² 府】wife's father = 【普】岳父

外甥【ngoi⁶xeng¹ 笙】sister's son; nephew

外甥女【ngoi⁶xeng¹nêü⁵ 笙那去⁵】sister's daughter; niece

外孙【ngoi⁶xün¹ 酸】daughter's son; grandson

外孙女【ngoi⁶xün¹nêü⁵ 酸那去⁵】daughter's daughter; granddaughter

外强中干【ngoi⁶kêng⁴jung⁴gon¹ 卡香⁴ 宗竿】outwardly strong but inwardly weak

揂【ngou¹ 奥¹】use a hand to implicate or to pluck = 【普】用手攀扯或采摘

揂唔到【ngou¹m⁴dou³ 度³】too high so implicate to = 【普】太高, 攀扯不到

奥【ngou³ 澳; ou³】profound; abstruse; oersted

奥妙【ngou³ miu⁶ 庙⁶】profound; subtle; secret

奥秘【ngou³bēi³ 泌】profound mystery

奥地利【ngou³dēi³lēi⁶ 得希⁶ 俐】< n. > Austria

奥运会【ngou³wen⁶wui² 混汇²】the Olympic Games

澳【ngou³ 奥】an inlet of the sea; bay; short for Aomen

澳门【ngou³mun² 打²】< n. > Aomen (Macao)

澳大利亚【ngou³dai⁶lēi⁶nga³ 歹⁶ 俐哑³】Australia

懊【ngou³ 奥】regretful; remorseful; annoyed

懊悔【ngou³fui³ 灰³】feel remorse; repent; regret

懊恼【ngou³nou⁵ 脑】annoyed; vexed; upset

懊丧【ngou³xong³ 桑³】dejected; despondent

敖【ngou⁴ 熬】a surname

熬【ngou⁴ 敖】cook in water; boil; stew; decoct; endure; hold out

熬煎【ngou⁴jin¹ 笺】suffering; torture

熬夜【ngou⁴ yē⁶ 野⁶】stay up late or all night

鳌【ngou⁴ 敖】a huge legendary turtle

螯【ngou⁴ 敖】chela; pincers = 弧【gong⁶ 杠⁶】

聱【ngou⁴ 敖】(see "佶屈聱牙")

骜【ngou⁴ 敖】(see "桀骜不驯")

鏖【ngou⁴ 敖】engage in fierce battle

鏖战【ngou⁴jin³ 箭】fight hard; engage in fierce battle

袄【ngou³ 奥;ou³】a short Chinese-style coat or jacket

媪【ngou² 奥²;ou²】old woman = 伯爷婆【bag⁸yē¹po²】

傲【ngou⁶ 奥⁶】proud; haughty; brave; defy

傲然【ngou⁶yin⁴ 言】loftily; proudly; unyieldingly

傲视【ngou⁶xi⁶ 是】turn up one's nose at; show disdain for

傲慢【ngou⁶man⁶ 万】arrogant; haughty

傲气【ngou⁶ hēi³ 戏】air of arrogance; haughtiness

傲骨【ngou⁶ gued⁷ 格屈⁷】lofty and unyielding character

翱【ngou⁴ 敖】take wing

翱翔【ngou⁴qêng 祥⁴】hove; soar

搋【ngou⁴ 敖】use hands to shake the body = 【普】摇撼

搋唔郁【ngou⁴m⁴yug⁷ 郁】can not make to shake = 【普】动摇不了

安【ngon¹ 桉;on¹】peaceful; quiet; calm; safe; find a place for; install; give; harbour; where; how; ampere

安全【ngon¹qün⁴ 存】safe; secure

安乐【ngon¹log⁹ 落】peace and happiness

安静【ngon¹jing⁶ 净】quiet; peaceful

安宁【ngon¹ning⁴ 柠】peaceful; calm

安定【ngon¹ding⁶ 锭】stable; quiet; settled; maintain

安康【ngon¹hong¹ 糠】good health

安适【ngon¹xig⁷ 式】quiet and comfortable

安息【ngon¹xig⁷ 式】rest; go to sleep; rest in peace

安闲【ngon¹han⁴ 娴】peaceful and carefree

安详【ngon¹qêng⁴ 祥】serene; composed

安逸【ngon¹ yed⁹ 日】easy and comfortable; easy

安排【ngon¹ pai⁴ 牌】arrange；plan；fix up

安置【ngon¹ ji³ 至 】find a place for；arrange for

安装【ngon¹ jong¹ 妆】install；erect；fix

安放【ngon¹ fong³ 况】lay；place

安危【ngon¹ ngei⁴ 巍】safety and danger

安设【ngon¹ qid⁸ 彻】install；set up

安插【ngon¹ qab⁸ 次鸭⁸】place in a certain position

安身【ngon¹ xen¹ 辛】make one's home

安顿【ngon¹ dên⁶ 敦⁶】find a place for；arrange for

安抚【ngon¹ fu² 府】placate；appease

安慰【ngon¹ wei³ 畏】comfort；console

安然【ngon¹ yin⁴ 言】safely；peacefully

安家【ngon¹ ga¹ 加】settle down；set up a home

安眠【ngon¹ min⁴ 棉】sleep peaceful

安心【ngon¹ xem¹ 深 】feel at ease；keep one's mind on sth.

安生【ngon¹ xeng¹ 笙】peaceful；still

安稳【ngon¹ wen² 温²】smooth and steady

安葬【ngon¹ jong³ 壮】bury（the dead）

安分守己【ngon¹ fen⁶ xeo² gēi¹ 份手几】abide by the law and behave oneself

安居乐业【ngon¹ gêü¹ log⁹ yib⁹ 举¹ 落叶】live and work in peace and contentment

安如泰山【ngon¹ yū⁴ tai³ xan¹ 鱼太珊】as solid as a rock

桉【ngon¹ 安；on¹】< n. > 桉树

桉【ngon¹ xū⁶ 署⁶】eucalyptus

氨【ngon¹ 安；on¹】ammonia

氨基【ngon¹ gēi¹ 机】amino；amino-group

氨水【ngon¹ xêü² 绪²】ammonia water

胺【ngon¹ 安；on¹】amine

胺盐【ngon¹ yim⁴ 严】amine salt

鞍【ngon¹ 安；on¹】< n. >（马鞍【ma⁵ ngon¹】saddle）

鞍马【ngon¹ ma⁵ 码】pommelled horse；side horse

按【ngon³ 安³；on³】press；push down；shelve；restrain；keep one's hand on；according to；check；refer to

按捺【ngon³ nad⁹ 那压⁹】restrain；control

按摩【ngon³ mo¹ 么】massage

按钮【ngon³ neo² 纽】push button

按期【ngon³ kēi⁴ 其】on schedule；on time

按时【ngon³ xi⁴ 是⁴】on time；on schedule

按理【ngon³ lēi⁵ 李】according to reason；normally

按照【ngon³ jiu³ 焦³】according to；in the light of

按语【ngon³ yū⁵ 雨】note；comment

按兵不动【ngon³ bing¹ bed⁷ dung⁶ 冰毕洞】not throw the troops into battle；bide one's time

按部就班【ngon³ bou⁶ jeo⁶ ban¹ 步袖斑】follow the prescribed order

按劳分配【ngon³ lou⁴ fen¹ pui³ 卢芬佩】distribution according to work

案【ngon³ 按；on³】table；desk；case；record；proposal

案件【ngon³ gin² 坚²】law case；case

案情【ngon³ qing⁴ 程】details of a case；case

案卷【ngon³ gün² 绢²】records；files；archives

案头【ngon³ teo⁴ 投】on one's desk

岸【ngon⁶ 安⁶；on⁶】bank；shore；coast；lofty

上岸【xêng⁵ngon⁶ 尚⁵】go ashore

岸然【ngon⁶yin⁴ 言】in a solemn manner

盎【ngong³ 昂³；ong³】an ancient vessel with a big belly and a small mouth

盎然【ngong³yin⁴ 言】abundant；full；overflowing

盎司【ngong³xi¹ 斯】ounce

肮【ngong¹ 昂¹；ong¹】< a . > 肮脏【ngong¹ jong¹ 装】dirty；filthy = 邋遢【lad⁹ tad⁸辣替押⁸】

戇【ngong⁶ 昂⁶；jong³ 壮】dull；blunt and tactless

戇车【ngong⁶gêû¹ 居】foolish；stupid；dull；dull-looking = 戇车车【ngong⁶gêû¹ gêû¹居居】= 【普】傻里傻气；呆头呆脑

戇车佬【ngong⁶gêû¹lou² 居老²】idiot；simpleton；fool；blockhead = 【普】呆子；傻瓜

戇直【jong³jig⁹ 值】blunt and tactless

昂【ngong⁴ 盎⁴；ong⁴】hold（one's head）high；high；soaring

昂昂【ngong⁴ngong⁴】high-spirited；brave-looking

昂扬【ngong⁴yêng⁴ 洋】high-spirited

昂然【ngong⁴yin⁴ 言】upright and unafraid

昂贵【ngong⁴guei³ 桂】expensive；costly

昂首阔步【ngong⁴xeo²fud⁸bou⁶ 手夫活⁸ 部】stride forward with one's chin up

遏【ngod⁸ 额渴⁸；ad⁸ 压】check；hold back

遏止【ngod⁸ji² 子；ad⁸ji² 子】check；hold back

遏制【ngod⁸jei³ 济；ad⁸jei³ 济】keep within limits；contain

唔【ngog⁷ 岳⁷】< onomatope . > 唔唔脆【ngog⁷ngog⁷qêû³ 翠】the sound from when mull over food of the dry and hard = 【普】咀嚼干和硬的食物时发出的声音

恶【①ngog⁸ 岳⁸；og⁸；②wu³ 乌³】①evil；vice；fierce；bad；② loathe；dislike；hate

恶霸【ngog⁸ba³ 坝】local tyrant

恶爷【ngog⁸ yê¹ 耶¹】fierce，nasty，evil person；villain = 【普】恶人

恶报【ngog⁸bou³ 布】retribution for evildoing

恶果【ngog⁸guo² 戈²】evil consequence

恶魔【ngog⁸mo¹ 摩】demon；devil

恶棍【ngog⁸guen³ 君³】ruffian；bully

恶毒【ngog⁸dug¹ 独】vicious；malicious

恶习【ngog⁸jab³ 袭】bad habit

恶性【ngog⁸xing³ 姓】malignant；vicious

恶化【ngog⁸fa³ 花³】worsen；deteriorate

恶意【ngog⁸yi³ 薏】evil intentions；malice

恶浊【ngog⁸jug⁹ 续】foul；filthy

恶作【ngog⁸jug⁸ 昨】difficult to handle = 【普】难搞；难做

恶死【ngog⁸xēi² 四²】fierce；not easy to get along with；one who likes to play trick = 【普】（某人）诸多刁难，不易与之打交道；刁钻古怪的脾气

恶围【ngog⁸fen³ 训】unable to get to sleep soundly = 【普】难于进入酣睡状态

恶狠狠【ngog⁸hen²hen² 很】fierce；ferocious

恶作剧【ngog⁸ jug⁸ kēg⁹ 昨屐】practical joke；prank

恶贯满盈【ngog⁸gun³mun⁵ying⁴ 灌门⁵ 营】

face retribution for a life of crime

憎恶【jeng¹wu³ 增乌³】abhor; loather; abominate

噩【ngog⁸ 岳⁸】shocking; upsetting

噩耗【ngog⁸ hou³ 好³】sad news of the death of one's beloved

噩梦【ngog⁸ mung⁶ 蒙⁶】frightening dream; nightmare

萼【ngog⁹ 岳】calyx（花萼【fa¹ngog⁹】）

鳄【ngog⁹ 岳】crocodile; alligator（鳄鱼【ngog⁹yü⁴】）

颚【ngog⁹ 岳】jaw; palate

颚骨【ngog⁹gued⁷ 掘⁷】jawbone

上颚【xêng⁶ngog⁹ 尚】upper jaw

下颚【ha⁶ngog⁹ 夏】lower jaw

愕【ngog⁹ 岳】stunned; astounded

愕然【ngog⁹yin⁴ 言】stunned; astounded

鄂【ngog⁹ 岳】another name for Hubei Province; a surname

岳【ngog⁹ 萼】high mountain; wife's parents; a surname

岳父【ngog⁹fu⁶ 付】wife's father; father-in-law

岳母【ngog⁹mou⁵ 武】wife's mother; mother-in-law

颐【ngog⁹ 岳】to raise one's head

颐高头【ngog⁹gou¹teo⁴ 膏投】to raise one's head =【普】抬起头

壅【ngung¹ 瓮¹; yung¹ 雍】① heap soil or fertilizer over and around the roots（of plants and trees）; use soil to cover ② stop up

壅泥【ngung¹ nei⁴ 那矮⁴】use mud to cover; hilling

壅肥【ngung¹ fêi⁴ 非⁴】heap fertilizer around the roots

壅塞【yung¹ xeg⁷ 是克⁷】clogged up; jammed

搿【ngung² 瓮²】push; pull open =【普】推; 操

搿开【ngung²hoi¹ 海¹】pull open =【普】推开

搿冧【ngung²lem³ 林³】push over; repudiate =【普】推倒

瓮【ngung³ 蕹; wung³ 乌空³】urn; earthen jar

瓮中之鳖【ngung³jung¹ji¹bid⁹ 宗支别】a turtle in a jar — bottled up; trapped

瓮中捉鳖【wung³jung¹jug⁷bid⁹ 宗足别】catch a turtle in a jar — go after an easy prey

蕹【ngung³ 翁; ung³】water spinach

蕹菜【ngung³ qoi³ 蔡】water spinach =【普】通菜; 通心菜

屋【ngug⁷ 额哭⁷; ug⁷】house; room

屋仔【ngug⁷jei² 济】small room =【普】小屋

屋顶【ngug⁷dēng² 得镜²】roof; housetop

屋脊【ngug⁷jēg⁸ 隻】ridge（of a roof）

屋檐【ngug⁷xim⁴ 婵】eaves

屋宇【ngug⁷yü⁴ 语】house

诶【ngē⁴; ē⁴; ē¹; ē²】< int. > show the sound of agree, surprised, etc.

唔唔诶诶【m⁴m⁴ngē⁴ngē⁴】speak in a low voice; hum and haw ∽【普】低声说话; 支吾其词

呃【ngē¹ 额夜¹】make a sound; speak = 【普】做声；说话

有得呃【mou⁵ deg⁷ ngē¹ 武德】be in the wrong and have nothing to say = 【普】理亏而无话可说

O

呵 【o¹ 柯；ho¹ 苛】① ＜int.＞ show the pleasantly surprised；② breathe out（with the mouth open）；scold

呵,原来系你！【o¹, yün⁴loi⁴hei⁶nēi⁵ 元 菜兮⁶ 那希⁵】Ah, so it's you! ＝【普】原来是你!

呵欠【o¹him³ 谦³】yawn

呵呵大笑【ho¹ho¹dai⁶xiu³ 歹⁶ 少³】laugh loudly

呵护【ho¹ wu⁶ 户】caress and protect ＝【普】抚爱和保护

呵罖【o¹go⁶ 个⁶】shield and spoil ＝【普】卵翼并溺爱

柯 【o¹ 呵；ngo¹ 屙】stalk or branch；helve；a surname

珂 【o¹ 呵】a jade-like stone；an ornament on a bridle

坷 【o¹ 柯；ho² 可】（see "坎坷"）

诃 【o¹ 柯；ho¹ 苛】scold

诃子【o¹ji² 止】〈n.〉myrobalan

哦 【o² 柯²；o⁴ 柯⁴】＜int.＞ show the doubt or comprehend

哦! 会有噉嘅事?【o², wui⁵yeo⁵gem² gē³xi⁶】what! How can that be? ＝【普】哦! 会有这样的事?

哦,我知啦。【o⁴, ngo⁵ji¹la³】Oh, I see. ＝【普】哦,我懂了。

P

趴【pa¹ 怕¹】lie on one's stomach; bend over

趴享地面【pa¹hêng² dēi⁶min⁶ 响 得希⁶ 免⁶】lie on the ground =【普】趴在地上

趴台【pa¹toi² 胎²】bending over the desk; drawing =【普】趴在桌子上;伏桌子

筢【pa² 趴¹; pa⁴ 耙】bamboo rake

爬【pa⁴ 耙】crawl; creep; climb; clamber

爬行【pa⁴heng⁴ 衡】crawl; creep

爬虫【pa⁴qung⁴ 从】reptile

爬头【pa⁴teo⁴ 投】be ahead of others

杷【pa⁴ 爬】(see "枇杷")

扒【pa⁴ 爬; pa² 爬²】gather up; rake up; stew; braise; row (a boat)

扒钱【pa⁴ qin⁴浅】pick others pocket =【普】捞钱

扒手【pa⁴xeo² 守】pickpocket

牛扒【ngeo⁴pa² 藕⁴】stewed beef

扌扌【pa⁴ 爬】rob; take things without permission

扌扌手【pa⁴xeo² 守】pickpocket =【普】扒手

耙【pa⁴ 爬】rake; harrow

犁耙【lei⁴pa⁴ 黎】plough and rake

耙平唛地【pa⁴ ping⁴ dad⁸ dēi⁶ 萍 达⁸

得希⁶】rake the soil level =【普】把地耙平

耙灰公【pa⁴fui¹gung¹ 恢工】cuckold =【普】王八

琶【pa⁴ 爬】(see "琵琶")

琶音【pa⁴yem¹ 暗】< n. > arpeggio

怕【pa³ 扒³】fear; dread; be afraid of; perhaps

怕丑【pa³qeo³ 秋²】shy; coy; bashful =【普】怕羞;害羞

怕事【pa³xi⁶ 士】be afraid of getting into trouble

怕死【pa³xēi² 四²】fear death

派【pai³ 排³;pai¹ 排¹】group; school; faction; clique; style; send; dispatch; appoint

派款【pai³fun² 宽²】impose levies of money

派遣【pai³hin² 显】send; dispatch

派驻【pai³jū³ 注】accredit

派系【pai³hei⁶ 兮⁶】factions

派生【pai³xeng¹ 笙】derive

派别【pai³bid⁹ 必⁹】group; school; faction

派头【pai¹teo⁴ 投】style; manner

排【pai⁴ 牌】arrange; put in order; row; line; platoon; rehearse; raft; exclude; push

排字【pai⁴ ji⁶ 治】composing; typesetting = 排版【ban²】

排印【pai⁴yen³ 恩³】typesetting and printing

排场【pai⁴ qêng⁴ 祥】ostentation and extravagance

排斥【pai⁴qig⁷ 戚】repel; exclude

排除【pai⁴qêu⁴ 徐】get rid of; remove

排队【pai⁴dêu² 对²】form a line; line up

排骨【pai⁴gued⁷ 掘⁷】spareribs

排灌【pai⁴gun³ 贯】irrigation and drainage

排挤【pai⁴jei² 剂】push aside; push out

排练【pai⁴lin⁶ 炼】rehearse

排列【pai⁴lid⁹ 烈】arrange; range; permutation

排遣【pai⁴hin² 显】divert oneself from loneliness and boredom

排球【pai⁴keo⁴ 求】volleyball

排水【pai⁴xêu² 瑞²】drain off water

排气【pai⁴hēi³ 戏】exhaust

排泄【pai⁴xid⁶ 屑】drain; excrete

排他性【pai⁴ta¹xing³ 它姓】exclusiveness

排山倒海【pai⁴xan³dou²hoi² 珊捣凯】topple the mountains and overturn the seas

排难解纷【pai⁴ nan⁶ gai² fen¹ 那晏⁶ 介² 分】mediate a dispute

牌【pai⁴ 排; pai² 排²】plate; tablet; brand; cards, dominoes, etc.

例牌【lei⁶pai² 丽】an old rule; as a rule = 【普】照例; 例规

牌子【pai⁴ji² 止】plate; sign; brand

牌号【pai⁴hou⁶ 好⁶】the name of a shop; shop sign; trademark

牌照【pai⁴ jiu³ 赵³】license plate; license tag

牌坊【pai⁴fong¹ 方】memorial archway

湃【pai³ 派; bai³ 拜】(see "澎湃")

抛【pao¹ 泡】throw; fling; leave behind

抛掷【pao¹jag⁹ 择】throw; cast

抛弃【pao¹hēi³ 戏】abandon; forsake; cast aside

抛售【pao¹ xeo⁶受】sell (goods, shares, etc.) in big quantities, usu. in anticipation of or in order to bring about a fall in price

抛锚【pao¹mao⁴ 矛】drop anchor; (of vehicles) break down

抛物线【pao¹med⁹xin³ 勿扇】parabola

抛头露面【pao¹teo⁴lou⁶min⁶ 投路缅⁶】show one's face in public

泡【pao¹ 抛; pao³ 炮; pou⁵ 抱; peo³ 剖³】bubble; sth. shaped like a bubble; steep; sth. puffy and soft; spongy

泡沫【pao¹mud⁹ 末】foam; froth

泡影【pao¹ying³ 映】bubble

泡茶【pao³qa⁴ 查】make tea

起泡【hēi²pou⁵ 喜】send up foam (or bubble) = 【普】冒泡

泡木【peo³mug⁹ 目】the wood is not solid = 【普】不坚实的、疏松的木头

泡桐【pao³tung⁴ 同】< n. > paulownia

泡瓢冬瓜【peo³nong⁴dung¹gua¹ 囊东挂¹】metaphor: sb.' physique is very weak and often falls ill = 【普】(比喻)体弱多病的人

泡打粉【pao¹da²fen² 得阿² 分²】powder

跑【pao² 泡²】run; run away; walk; run about doing sth. away; off

跑步【pao² bou⁶部】run; march at the double

跑道【pao³dou⁶ 度】runway; track

跑马【pao³ma⁵ 码】have a ride on a horse; horse race

跑腿【pao³ têu² 退²】run errands; do legwork

跑龙套【pao³lung⁴tou³ 笼吐】play a bit

role

炮【pao³ 豹】big gun; cannon; artillery piece; quick-fry

炮弹【pao³dan² 蛋】(artillery) shell

炮兵【pao³bing¹ 冰】artillery; artillerymen

炮轰【pao³gueng¹ 姑莺¹】bombard; shell

炮火【pao³fo² 伙】artillery fire; gunfire

炮台【pao³toi¹ 胎²】fort; battery

炮羊肉【pao³yêng⁴yug⁹ 杨玉】quick-fry mutton

炮战【pao³jin³ 箭】artillery action

炮声【pao³xing¹ 升】report (of a gun)

炮灰【pao³fui¹ 恢】cannon fodder

炮仗【pao³jêng² 掌】firecracker; firework

炮制【pao³jei³ 济】deal with; concoct; cook up

庖【pao⁴ 刨】kitchen; cook

庖代【pao⁴doi⁶ 袋】act in sb.'s place = 代庖

庖丁【pao⁴ding¹ 叮】cook = 厨师【qêü⁴xi¹】

咆【pao⁴ 刨】<v.> 咆哮【pao⁴hao¹ 蔽】roar; thunder

豹【pao³ 炮】leopard; panther

刨【pao⁴ 庖】plane sth. down; plane; planer; slice

刨板【pao⁴pan² 版】plane a board

刨刀【pao⁴dou¹ 都】plane tool

刨工【pao⁴gung¹ 功】planing; planer

刨床【pao⁴qong⁴ 苍⁴】planer; planing machine

刨花【pao⁴fa¹ 化¹】wood shaving

刨书【pao⁴xü¹ 输】engross oneself in books ∽【普】攻读

疱【pao³ 炮】blister; bleb

疱疹【pao³qen² 陈²】bleb; herpes

攀【pan¹ 盼¹】climb; clamber; seek connections in high places; involve; implicate

攀登【pan¹ deng¹ 灯】climb; clamber; scale

攀缘【pan¹yün⁴ 沿】climb; clamber

攀谈【pan¹tam⁴ 谭】engage in small talk

攀折【pan¹jid⁶ 节】pull down and break off

攀亲道故【pan¹ qen¹ dou⁶ gu³趁¹ 度固】claim ties of blood or friendship

攀龙附凤【pan¹lung⁴fu⁶fung⁶ 隆付奉】play up to people of power and influence

襻【pan³ 盼;ban³ 办³】a loop for fastening a button; sth. shaped like a button loop or used for a similar purpose; fasten with a rope, string, etc.; tie

用绳襻住【yung⁶xing²ban³jü⁶】fasten with a rope =【普】用绳子横勒上

盼【pan³ 攀³】hope for; long for; expect; look

盼望【pan³mong⁶ 芒⁶】hope for; long for; look forward to

㧒【pang¹ 彭¹】rush; chase someone out; drive out =【普】撵；驱逐；驱赶

㧒走【pang¹ jeo² 酒】drive out; chase someone out =【普】驱逐；撵跑

镑【pang¹ 彭¹】pan =【普】平底锅;金属盘子

锑镑【tei¹pang¹ 梯】aluminium pan

棚【pang⁴ 彭】canopy or awning of reed mats, etc.; shed; shack

凉棚【lêng⁴pang⁴ 梁】awning

草棚【qou²pang⁴ 曹²】straw mat shed

彭【pang⁴ 棚】a surname

澎【pang⁴ 棚】splash; spatter

澎湃【pang⁴pai³ 派】surge

膨【pang⁴ 彭】expand; swell

膨胀【pang⁴jêng³ 涨】expand; swell; dilate; inflate

膨大【pang⁴dai⁶ 歹⁶】expand; inflate

蟛【pang⁴ 彭】< n. > amphibious crab (蟛蜞【pang⁴kêi² 企²】)

鹏【pang⁴ 彭】roc

鹏程万里【pang⁴qing⁴man⁶lêi⁵ 情曼李】(make) a roc's flight of 10,000 kilometre — have a bright future

烹【pang¹ 彭¹】boil; cook

烹饪【pang¹yem⁶ 任】cooking; culinary

烹调【pang¹tiu⁴ 条】cook (dishes)

棒【pang⁵ 彭⁵】stick; club; cudgel

棒槌【pang⁵qêü⁴ 徐】wooden club

棒球【pang⁵keo⁴ 求】baseball

拍【pag⁸ 粕】clap; pat; beat; bat; shoot; send (a telegram, etc.); flatter

拍手【pag⁸xeo² 守】clap one's hands; applaud

拍板【pag⁸ban² 版】clappers; beat time with clappers; rap the gavel

拍打【pag⁸da² 得亚²】pat; slap

拍卖【pag⁸mai⁶ 买⁶】auction; sale

拍摄【pag⁸xib⁸ 司叶⁸】take (a picture); shoot; photograph = 拍照【pag⁸jiu³焦³】

拍子【pag⁸ji² 止】bat; racket; beat; time

拍拖【pag⁸ to¹ 陀¹】the lovers hand in hand to go sight-seeing = 【普】情侣结伴而游

拍马屁【pag⁸ma⁵ pêi³ 码披³】lick sb.'s boots; flatter; soft-soap = 托大脚【tog⁸dai⁶gêg⁸】

拍档【pag⁸ dong³ 当³】work together; partner = 【普】合作;合作者

拍硬档【pag⁸ngang⁶dong³ 罂⁶ 当³】work in close-knit; cooperation with others = 【普】加强合作;通力合作

拍得住【pag⁸ deg⁷ jü⁶ 德注⁶】match = 【普】匹配;比得上

拍心口【pag⁸xem¹heo² 深厚²】guarantee others that one is going to finish the job or project = 【普】捶胸发誓;表决心

拍乌蝇【pag⁸wu¹ying¹ 污英】describe that business is not good = 【普】生意冷淡,没人光顾(店员打苍蝇)

拍案叫绝【pag⁸ngon³giu³jüd⁸ 按娇³ 拙⁹】thump the table and shout "bravo!"

帕【pag⁸ 拍】< n. > 手帕【xeo²pag⁸ 守】handkerchief = 手巾仔【xeo²gen¹jei²守斤济²】

粕【pag⁸ 拍;pog⁸ 扑】dregs of rice (see "糟粕")

珀【pag⁸ 拍】amber (琥珀【fu²pag⁸ 虎】)

魄【pag⁸ 拍】soul; vigour; spirit

魄力【pag⁸lig⁹ 历】daring and resolution; boldness

柏【pag⁸ 拍】cypress

柏树【pag⁸xū⁶ 署⁶】cypress

柏油【pag³yeo⁴ 由】pitch; tar; asphalt

啪【pag⁷ 拍⁷】< *onomatepoeia* > show the shot, etc.

棵【po¹ 婆¹】< *classifier*. > the unit of the plant

一棵树【yed⁷po¹xū⁶】a tree

颇【po² 巨】inclined to one side; oblique; partial; quite; rather

颇佳【po²gai 街】quite good

巨【po² 颇】impossible = 不可【bed⁷ ho²】

巨测【po²qag⁷ 策⁷】unfathomable

破【po³ 婆³】broken; damaged; torn; break; split; destroy; defeat; lay bare; paltry

破坏【po³wai⁶ 怀⁶】destroy; do great damage to; change completely or violently; violate; decompose

破裂【po³lid⁹ 列】burst; split

破碎【po³xêü³ 绪³】tattered; broken; crush

破损【po³xūn² 选】damaged; worn; torn

破烂【po³lan⁶ 兰⁶】tattered; ragged; junk

破产【po³qan² 铲】go bankrupt; fall through

破除【po³ qêü⁴徐】do away with; eradicate

破费【po³fei³ 废】spend money

破格【po³gag⁸ 隔】break a rule

破例【po³lei⁶ 丽】break a rule

破案【po³ngon³ 按】solve a case

破财【po³ qoi⁴才 】suffer unexpected personal finacial losses

破相【po³xêng³ 商³】be marred by a scar

破灭【po³mid⁹ 莫热⁹】be shattered

破天荒【po³tin¹fong¹ 田¹ 方】be unprece-

dented

破釜沉舟【po³fu²qem⁴jeo¹ 府侵⁴ 周】burn one's boats

破旧立新【po³geo⁶leb⁹xen¹ 枢笠⁹ 辛】destroy the old and establish the new

破涕为笑【po³tei⁶wei¹xiu³ 剃维少³】smile through tears

婆【po⁴ 破⁴; po² 颇】old woman; husband's mother; mother-in-law; a woman in a certain occupation

婆家【po⁴ga¹ 加】husband's family

婆娘【po⁴nêng⁴ 那香⁴】young married woman; wife

婆婆【po⁴po⁴】husband's mother; grandmother

婆娑【po⁴xo¹ 梳】whirling; dancing

婆婆妈妈【po⁴po⁴ma¹ma¹ 吗】womanishly fussy; sentimental

铺【pou¹ 普¹; pou³ 普³】spread; extend; pave; lay

铺陈【pou¹qen⁴ 尘】narrate in detail

铺张【pou¹jêng¹ 章】extravagant

铺开【pou¹hoi¹ 海¹】spread out; sprawl

铺盖【pou¹koi³ 概】bedding; bedclothes

铺设【pou¹qid⁸ 彻】lay; build

铺垫【pou¹din³ 电³】bedding; foreshadowing

铺头【pou³teo² 投²】shops; stalls = 【普】店铺

甫【pou² 普; pou³ 铺³; fu² 苦】10 Chinese-mile; just; only; one's courtesy name

脯【pou² 普; fu² 苦】dried meat; preserved fruit; chest; breast

普【pou² 谱】general; universal

普通【pou² tung¹同¹】ordinary; common;

average

普及【pou² keb⁹级⁹】popularize; disseminate; universal; popular

普选【pou²xün² 损】general election

普照【pou²jiu³ 焦³】illuminate all things

普查【pou²qa⁴ 茶】general investigation

普天同庆【pou²tin¹tung⁴hing³ 田¹ 铜兴³】
the whole world or nation joins in
the jubilation

谱【pou² 普】table; chart; register

谱表【pou²biu² 标²】stave; staff

谱号【pou²hou⁶ 好⁶】clef

谱系【pou²hei⁶ 兮⁶】pedigree

谱写【pou²xē² 舍²】compose (music)

圃【pou² 普】garden

苗圃【miu⁴pou²】seed plot

溥【pou² 普】broad; common

匍【pou⁴ 蒲】<v.>匍匐【pou⁴fug⁹ 伏】
crawl; creep; lie prostrate

菩【pou⁴ 匍】pipal; Bodhisattva

菩萨【pou⁴xad⁸ 杀】Bodhisattva; Buddha

菩提树【pou⁴tei⁴xü⁶ 题署⁶】pipal; bo tree

菩提子【pou⁴tei⁴ji² 止】grapes

葡【pou⁴ 匍】grape

葡萄【pou⁴tou⁴ 陶】grape

葡萄牙【pou⁴tou⁴nga⁴ 陶芽】Portugal

浦【pou⁴ 匍; pou² 普】riverside; river
mouth; float; a surname

浦头【pou⁴teo⁴ 投】floats on water; (sb.)
has emerged = 【普】浮上来; 浮
在水上

蒲【pou⁴ 匍】cattail; a surname

蒲草【pou⁴ qou² 操²】the stem or leaf of
cattail

蒲团【pou⁴tün⁴ 替远⁴】cattail hassock

蒲席【pou⁴jēg⁹ 脊⁹】cattail mat

蒲扇【pou⁴xin³ 线】cattail leaf fan

蒲柳【pou⁴leo⁵ 纽⁵】big catkin willow

蒲公英【pou⁴gung¹ ying¹ 工婴】dandelion

抱【pou⁵ 普⁵】hold or carry in the arms;
embrace; bug; hang together; cherish; harbour

抱负【pou⁵fu⁶ 付】aspiration; ambition

抱歉【pou⁵hib³ 胁】be sorry; regret

抱怨【pou⁵yün³ 渊³】complain; grumble

抱恨【pou⁵ hen⁶ 很⁶】have a gnawing regret

抱病【pou⁵ bēng⁶ 柄⁶】be ill; be in bad
health

抱不平【pou⁵bed⁷ping⁴ 毕萍】be outraged
by an injustice

抱残守缺【pou⁵qan⁴xeo²küd⁸ 灿⁴ 手决】
cherish the outmoded and preserve
the outworn — be conservative

旁【pong⁴ 滂】side; other; else

旁边【pong⁴bin¹ 鞭】side

旁门【pong⁴mun⁴ 瞒】side door

旁人【pong⁴yen⁴ 仁】other people = 第啲
人【dei⁶did⁷yen⁴】

旁听【pong⁴ tēng¹ 厅】be a visitor at a
meeting, in a school class, etc.

旁观【pong⁴ gun¹ 官】look on; be an on-
looker

旁证【pong⁴ jing³ 正】circumstantial evidence

旁敲侧击【pong⁴hao¹jeg⁷gig⁷ 烤¹ 仄激】attack by innuendo; make oblique references

旁若无人【pong⁴yêg⁹mou⁴yen⁴ 药毛仁】act as if there was no one else present — self-assured or supercilious

膀【pong⁴ 旁】< n . > 膀胱【pong⁴guong¹光】(urinary) bladder

螃【pong⁴ 旁】< n . > 螃蟹【pong⁴hai⁵械⁵】crab

彷【pong⁴ 旁】< a . > 彷徨【pong⁴wong⁴王】walk back and forth, not knowing which way to go; hesitate

滂【pong⁴ 旁】< a . > 滂沱【pong⁴to⁴陀】torrential

庞【pong⁴ 旁】huge; innumerable and disordered; face; a surname

庞大【pong⁴ dai⁶ 歹⁶】buge; enormous; colossal

庞杂【pong⁴jab⁹ 习】numerous and jumbled

蚌【pong⁵ 旁⁵】freshwater mussel; clam

朕【pog⁷扑⁷】①air bladder (of fish); ②courage; guts; pluck = 【普】鱼鳔; 胆量

够朕【geo³pog⁷ 究】bold; daring = 【普】大胆

朴【① pog⁸ 扑; ② piu⁴ 瓢】① simple; plain; ② a surname

朴实【pog⁸xed⁹ 失⁹】simple; plain

朴素【pog⁸xou³ 扫】simple; plain

扑【pog⁸ 朴】throw oneself on; pounce on; rush at; flap; bend over

扑打【pog⁸da² 得阿²】swat; beat; pat

扑救【pog⁸geo³ 够】put out a fire to save life and property

扑面【pog⁸min⁶ 缅⁶】blow on one's face

扑鼻【pog⁸bēi⁶ 备】assail the nostrils

扑空【pog⁸hung¹ 孔¹】fail to get or achieve what one wants

扑灭【pog⁸mid⁹ 蔑】stamp out; put out; exterminate

扑克【pog⁸heg⁷ 黑】poker = 迓【pē】

噗【pog⁸ 扑】< onomatope . > puff

噗嗤【pog⁸qi¹ 疵】< onomatope . > titter; snigger

璞【pog⁸ 扑】uncut jade (璞玉【pog⁸yug⁹肉】)

批【pei¹ 皮矮¹】slap; criticize; refute; write instructions or comments on; wholesale; batch; lot; group

批驳【pei¹bog⁸ 博】refute; criticize; rebut

批评【pei¹ping⁴ 平】criticize; criticism

批判【pei¹pun³ 潘³】criticize; critique

批示【pei¹ xi⁶ 是】written instructions or comments on a report, etc. submitted by a subordinate

批注【pei¹ jü³ 著】annotate and comment on; marginalia

批改【pei¹goi² 该²】correct

批准【pei¹jên² 遵²】ratify; approve; sanction

批发【pei¹ fad⁸ 法】wholesale; be authorized for dispatch

批量【pei¹lêng⁶ 亮】batch; lot

刉【pei¹ 批】pare with a knife = 【普】用刀削

刉苹果【pei¹ping⁴guo² 萍戈²】pare an apple = 【普】削苹果

刉 铅笔【pei¹yün⁴bed⁷ 元毕】sharpen a pencil = 【普】削铅笔

孵【peo³ 拍殴³】not solid；the volume is big and weight is light；unreliable；cannot be trusted；weak；not strong ∽【普】不坚实；不结实；体积大而重量轻

孵腩【peo³nam⁵ 南⁵】the flesh at the abdomen of pigs＝【普】猪腹中的肥肉块

喷【pen³ 贫³】spurt；spout；spray；sprinkle

喷射【pen³xē⁶ 蛇⁶】spray；spurt；jet

喷薄【pen³bog⁹ 泊】gush；spurt

喷雾【pen³mou⁶ 务】spraying

喷泉【pen³qün⁴ 全】fountain

喷漆【pen³ qed⁷ 七 】spray paint；spray lacquer

喷灌【pen³gun³ 贯】sprinkling irrigation

喷饭【pen³ fan⁶ 范 】laugh so hard as to spew one's food

喷嚏【pen³tei³ 涕】sneeze＝打哈嚏【da² ha¹qi¹】

喷枪【pen³qêng¹ 昌】spray gun

喷嘴【pen³ jêü² 咀 】spray nozzle；spray head

贫【pen⁴ 频】poor；needy；impoverished；inadequate；garrulous

贫穷【pen⁴kung⁴ 穹】poor；needy；impoverished

贫乏【pen⁴fed⁹ 佛】poor；short；lacking

贫寒【pen⁴ hon⁴ 韩 】poor；poverty-stricken

贫瘠【pen⁴jêg⁸ 脊】barren；infertile；poor

贫贱【pen⁴jin⁶ 溅⁶】poor and lowly

贫苦【pen⁴fu² 府】poor；poverty-stricken

贫困【pen⁴kuen³ 昆³】poor；impoverished

贫民【pen⁴men⁴ 文】poor people；pauper

贫弱【pen⁴ yêg⁹ 若 】(of a county) poor and weak

贫血【pen⁴hüd⁸ 黑月⁸】anaemia

贫病交迫【pen⁴bēng⁶gao¹big⁷ 柄⁶ 胶碧】sick as well as poor

频【pen⁴ 贫】frequently；repeatedly；frequency

频率【pen⁴lêd⁹ 律】frequency

频繁【pen⁴fan⁴ 凡】frequently；often

频频【pen⁴pen⁴】again and again；repeatedly

频仍【pen⁴ying⁴ 形】frequent

频带【pen⁴dai³ 戴】frequency band

频道【pen⁴dou⁶ 度】frequency channel

频扑【pen⁴ pog⁸ 朴】rush to a few places；be in a hurry all the time＝频频扑扑＝【普】奔波劳碌

频轮【pen⁴lên⁴ 伦】rush；be in a hurry＝【普】仓促；急速

蘋【pen⁴ 频】< n. > clover fern

颦【pen⁴ 频】knit the brows

凭【peng⁴ 朋】lean on；rely on；proof；go by；base on

凭据【peng⁴gêü³ 踞】evidence；proof

凭单【peng⁴dan¹ 丹】voucher

凭借【peng⁴jē³ 姐³】rely on；depend on

凭空【peng⁴hung¹ 凶】out of the void；groundless

凭证【peng⁴ jing³ 正 】proof；evidence；voucher

凭眺【peng⁴tiu³ 跳】gaze from a high place into the distance

凭吊【peng⁴diu³ 掉】visit and ponder on the past

朋【peng⁴ 凭；pang² 棚²】friend

朋友【peng⁴yeo⁵ 有】friend; boy friend or girl friend

朋党【peng⁴dong² 挡】clique; cabbal

朋比为奸【peng⁴bēi⁴wei⁴gan¹ 髀维间¹】act in collusion with; conspire; collude

硼 【peng⁴ 朋】< n. > boron (B)

硼砂【peng⁴xa¹ 沙】boron; sodium borate

硼酸【peng⁴xūn¹ 孙】boric acid

匹 【ped⁷ 拍乞⁷】be equal to; be a match for; < onomatopoeia > the unit of a horse or cloth (a bolt)

匹配【ped⁷pui³ 沛】mate; marry; matching

匹夫【ped⁷fu¹ 肤】ordinary man; an ignorant person

匹敌【ped⁷ dig⁹ 迪】be equal to; be well matched

坯 【pui¹ 培¹; pēi¹ 丕】base; blank; unburnt brick; adobe

坯子【pui¹ji² 止】semifinished product; base

坯件【pui¹gin² 建²】blank

配 【pui³ 佩】join in marriage; mate; compound; opportion; find sth. to fit or replace sth. else; match; deserve

配合【pui³heb⁹ 盒】coordinate; cooperate; concert

配对【pui³ dêu³队³】pair; (of animals) mat

配偶【pui³ngeo³ 耦】spouse

配套【pui³tou³ 吐】form a complete set

配搭【pui³dab⁸ 答】supplement; match

配备【pui³bēi⁶ 鼻】allocate; provide; dispose; deploy; outfit; equipment

配方【pui³fong¹ 芳】fill a prescription

配药【pui³yêg⁹ 若】make up a prescription

配制【pui³jei³ 济】compound; make up

配置【pui³ji³ 至】dispose; deploy

配给【pui³keb⁸ 级】ration

配件【pui³gin³ 见²】fittings; replacement

配料【pui³liu² 撩】burden

配角【pui³gog⁸ 各】costar; supporting role

配音【pui³yem¹ 阴】dub (a film, etc.)

配乐【pui³ ngog⁹岳 】dub in background music

配种【pui³jung² 肿】breeding

佩 【pui³ 配】wear; admire

佩带【pui³dai³ 戴】wear

佩服【pui³fug⁹ 伏】admire

沛 【pui³ 配】copious; abundant

霈 【pui³ 沛】heavy rain

旆 【pui³ 沛】flag

培 【pui⁴ 赔】bank up with earth; earth up; cultivate; foster; train

培土【pui³tou² 肚²】hill up; earth up

培训【pui³fen³ 分³】cultivate; train

培养【pui³yêng⁵ 氧】foster; train; culture

培育【pui³yug⁹ 玉】cultivate; foster; breed

培植【pui³jig⁹ 直】cultivate; foster; train

赔 【pui⁴ 培】compensate; pay for; stand a loss

赔本【pui⁴bun² 苯 】sustain losses in business

赔偿【pui⁴xêng⁴ 常】compensate; pay for

赔款【pui⁴fun² 欢²】pay an indemnity; reparations

赔礼【pui⁴lei⁵ 厉⁵】offer an apology; apologize

赔笑【pui⁴ xiu³ 少³】smile obsequiously or apologetically

赔罪【pui⁴jêü⁶ 叙】apologize

陪【pui⁴ 培】accompany; keep sb. company

陪伴【pui⁴ bun⁶ 绊】accompany; keep sb. company

陪同【pui⁴tung⁴ 铜】accompany

陪衬【pui⁴qen³ 趁】set off; foil; setoff

陪客【pui⁴ hag⁸ 赫】a guest invited to a dinner party to help entertain the guest of honour

陪审【pui⁴ xem² 婶 】act as an assessor; serve on a jury

裴【pui⁴ 陪】a surname

蓓【pui⁴ 陪】< n. > 蓓蕾【pui⁴lêü⁴ 雷】bud

倍【pui⁵ 陪⁵】times; ____ fold; double; twice as much

倍数【pui⁵xou³ 扫】multiple

倍增【pui⁵jeng¹ 憎】redouble

潘【pun¹ 判¹】a surname

拼【pun² 潘²; ping¹ 聘¹】be ready to risk one's life; go all out in work

拼命【pun² mēng⁶莫镜⁶】risk one's life; defy death; exerting the utmost strength; desperately

拼死【pun² xēi²四²】risk one's life; defy death

拼𢱸【pun²pē⁵ 拍耶⁵】make a scene; wash one's hands of the business ∽【普】撒赖；撒手不管

判【pun³ 潘³】distinguish; obviously; judge; decide; sentence; condemn

判别【pun³ bid⁹ 必⁹】differentiate; distin-

guish

判定【pun³ding⁶ 锭】judge; decide

判断【pun³ dūn³ 段³】judge; decide; judgment

判处【pun³qü² 次于²】sentence; condemn

判决【pun³ küd⁸ 缺】court decision; judgment

判罪【pun³jêü⁶ 坠】declare guilty; convict

盘【pun⁴ 盆】tray; plate; dish; market quotation; transfer; game; set; a surname

盘仔【pun⁴jei² 济²】tray; plate; dish

盘旋【pun⁴xün⁴ 船】spiral; wheel; linger; stay

盘踞【pun⁴gêü³ 据】illegally or forcibly; be entrenched

盘算【pun⁴xün³ 蒜】calculate; figure; plan

盘问【pun⁴ men⁶ 文⁶】cross-examine; interrogate

盘点【pun⁴ dim² 店²】check; make an inventory of

盘桓【pun⁴wun⁴ 垣】stay; linger

盘查【pun⁴ qa⁴ 茶】interrogate and examine

盘缠【pun⁴qin⁴ 前】money for the journey

盘剥【pun⁴ mog⁷ 莫⁷】practise usury; exploit

盘根错节【pun⁴gen¹qo³jid⁸ 斤挫折】complicated and difficult to deal with; deep-rooted

盆【pun⁴ 盘】basin; tub; pot

盆地【pun⁴dēi⁶ 得希⁶】basin

盆花【pun⁴fa¹ 化¹】potted flower

盆景【pun⁴ging² 竟】potted landscape

盆腔【pun⁴hong¹ 康】pelvic cavity

磐【pun⁴ 盘】< n. > 磐石【pun⁴xēg⁹ 硕】huge rock

槃【pun⁴ 盘】< v. > 涅槃(see "涅槃")

蟠【pun⁴ 潘⁴】coil; curl

蟠桃【pun⁴tou⁴ 图】flat peach; peach of immortality in Chinese mythology

捧【pung² 蓬²】hold or carry in both hands; boost; exalt; extol; flatter

捧场【pung²qêng⁴ 祥】boost; flatter

捧腹【pung²fug² 福】split one's sides with laughter

碰【pung³ 蓬³; pung¹ 蓬¹】touch; bump; meet; run into

碰撞【pung³jong⁶壮⁶】collide; run into; impact

碰杯【pung³bui¹ 背¹】clink glasses

碰壁【pung³big⁸ 碧⁸】run up against a stone wall; be rebuffed

碰尘【pung¹qen⁴ 陈】dirt = 【普】蒙尘

碰见【pung³ gin³ 建】meet unexpectedly; run into

碰彩【pung³ qoi² 采】try one's luck = 【普】碰运气

碰巧【pung³hao² 考】by chance; by coincidence = 碰啱【pung³ngam¹ 岩¹】

碰头【pung³teo⁴ 投】meet and discuss

碰钉子【pung³ dēng¹ ji² 得镜¹ 止】meet with a rebuff

碰运气【pung³wen⁶hēi³ 混戏】try one's luck

蓬【pung⁴ 篷; fung⁴ 逢】bitter fleabane; fluffy; dishevelled

蓬勃【pung⁴bud⁹ 拨】vigorous; flourishing

蓬莱【fung⁴ loi⁴来】a fabled abode of immortals

蓬松【pung⁴xung¹ 送¹】fluffy; puffy

蓬头垢面【pung⁴teo⁴geo³min⁶ 投够缅⁶】unkempt

篷【pung⁴ 蓬】covering or awning on a car, boat, etc.; sail (of a boat)

篷布【pung⁴bou³ 报】tarpaulin

篷车【pung⁴qē¹ 奢】boxcar; covered truck

泼【pud⁸ 拍活⁸】sprinkle; splash; spill; shrewish

泼辣【pud⁸lad⁹ 罗压⁹】rude and unreasonable; shrewish; pungent; forceful

泼妇【pud⁸fu⁵ 苦⁵】shrew; vixen

泼冷水【pud⁸lang⁵xêü² 罗罂⁵ 瑞²】pour cold water on; dampen the enthusiasm

搫【pud⁸ 泼】fan

搫扇【pud⁸xin³ 线】fan oneself; use a fan = 【普】摇扇子；扇扇子

躄【pug⁷ 拍屋⁷】rest on the table; fall = 【普】(向前)跌倒

躄街【pug⁷ gai¹ 佳】a nasty word, e. g. "go to hell" ∽ 【普】"死去吧!"(骂人的话)

躄转【pud⁸jün³ 钻】turn something over = 【普】反转物体，使凹面朝下

飘【piu¹ 缥¹】wave to and fro; float; flutter

飘带【piu¹dai³ 戴】streamer; ribbon

飘荡【piu¹dong⁶ 当⁶】drift; wave; flutter

飘忽【piu¹fed⁷ 弗】move swiftly; fleet; mobile

飘零【piu¹ling¹ 凌】faded and fallen; wandering; adrift

飘洒【piu¹xa² 耍】float; drift

飘扬【piu¹yêng⁴ 杨】wave; flutter; fly

飘摇【piu¹yiu⁴ 遥】sway; shake; totter

飘逸【piu¹ yed⁹ 日】possessing natural grace; elegant

飘飘然【piu¹piu¹yin⁴ 言】smug; self-satisfied

漂【piu¹ 飘; piu³ 票】float; drift; bleach; rinse

漂浮【piu¹feo⁴ 否⁴】float; superficial; showy

漂流【piu¹leo⁴ 留】drift about; be driven by the current

漂白【piu³bag⁹ 伯⁹】bleach

漂泊【piu¹bog⁹ 薄】lead a wandering life; drift

漂亮【piu³lêng⁶ 量⁶】handsome; beautiful; good-looking; brilliant

缥【piu¹ 飘】< a. > 缥缈【piu¹miu⁵ 秒】dimly discernible; misty

殍【piu⁵ 漂⁵】(see "饿殍")

螵【piu¹ 飘】< n. > 螵蛸【piu¹xiu¹ 消】the egg capsule of a mantis

骠【piu¹ 飘; biu¹ 标】(of horses) fast; brave

票【piu³ 漂³】ticket; ballot; hostage; amateur performance

票子【piu³ji² 止】bank note; paper money; bill

票价【piu³ga³ 嫁】the price of a ticket; admission fee

票据【piu³ gêu³ 踞】bill; note; voucher; receipt

票额【piu³ngag⁹ 我客⁹】denomination; face value

剽【piu⁴ 嫖】rob; nimble; swift

剽窃【piu⁴xid⁸ 泄】plagiarize; lift

剽悍【piu⁴hon⁶ 汗】agile and brave

瞟【piu⁵ 漂⁵】look sidelong at; glance sideways at

嫖【piu⁴ 剽】visit prostitutes; go whoring

瓢【piu⁴ 剽】gourd ladle; wooden dipper

瓢泼大雨【piu⁴pud⁸dai⁶yü⁵ 拍活⁸ 歹⁶ 语】heavy rain

编【pin¹ 篇】weave; plait; organize; edit; write fabricate; part of a book

编次【pin¹qi³ 刺】order of arrangement

编辑【pin¹qeb⁷ 缉】edit; compile; editor; compiler

编写【pin¹xê² 舍²】compile; write; compose

编著【pin¹jü³ 注】compile; write

编纂【pin¹jün² 转】compile

编审【pin¹xem¹ 婶】read and edit; copy editor

编导【pin¹dou⁶ 道】write and direct; playwright - director

编剧【pin¹kêg⁹ 屐】write a play; playwright

编织【pin¹jig⁷ 积】weave; knit; plait

编制【pin¹ jei³ 济】weave; work out; establishment

编排【pin¹pai⁴ 牌】arrange; lay out

编目【pin¹mug⁹ 木】catalogue; list

编码【pin¹ ma⁵ 马】coding; serial number = 编号【hou⁶】

偏【pin¹ 编】inclined to one side; slanting; partial; prejudiced; leaning

偏爱【pin¹ ngoi³ 衰³】have partiality for sth.

偏心【pin¹ xem¹深】partiality; bias; eccentric

偏差【pin¹qa¹ 叉】deviation; error

偏废【pin¹fei³ 费】do one thing and neglect another

偏激【pin¹gig⁷ 击】extreme

偏见【pin¹gin³ 建】prejudice; bias

偏离【pin¹lêi⁴ 漓】deviate; diverge

偏僻【pin¹pig⁷ 辟】remote; out-of-the-way

偏远【pin¹yün⁵ 软】remote; faraway

偏偏【pin¹pin¹】< ad. > show "intentionally" or "opposite" or "only"

偏颇【pin¹po² 婆²】biased; partial

偏巧【pin¹hao² 考】it so happened that = 有咁啱得咁跷【yeo⁵gem³ngam¹ deg⁷gem³kiu²】

偏袒【pin¹ tan² 坦】be partial to and side with = 偏护【wu⁶ 户】= 争住晒【jang¹jü⁶xai³】

偏向【pin¹hêng³ 香³】deviation; be partial to

偏重【pin¹jung⁶ 仲】lay particular stress on

偏转【pin¹jün² 专²】deflection

偏听偏信【pin¹ting³pin¹xên³ 亭³讯】heed and trust only one side

篇【pin¹ 编】a piece of writing; sheet; < classifier. > the unit of paper, etc.

篇幅【pin¹fug⁷ 福】length; space

篇目【pin¹mug⁹ 木】table of contents; contents

篇章【pin¹jêng¹ 张】sections and chapters; writings

翩【pin¹ 篇】lightly

翩翩【pin¹pin¹】lightly; elegant

翩跹【pin¹qin¹ 迁】lightly; trippingly

片【pin³ 骗】a flat; thin piece; slice; flake; part of a place; cut into slices; incomplete; partial; < classifier. > the unit showing the flat-body

片段【pin³ dün⁶ 缎 】 part; passage; fragment

片剂【pin³jei¹ 挤】tablet

片刻【pin³ heg⁷ 黑 】a short while; a moment = 片时【xi⁴】

片面【pin³min⁶ 缅⁶】unilateral; one-sided

片言【pin³yin⁴ 然】a few words

片甲不存【pin³gab⁸bed⁷qün⁴ 夹毕全】the army is completely wiped out

骗【pin³ 片】deceive; fool; hoodwink; cheat

骗人【pin³yen⁴ 仁】deceive people

骗取【pin³qêü² 娶】gain sth. by cheating; defraud

骗局【pin³gug⁹ 焗】fraud; hoax; swindle

骗术【pin³xêd⁹ 述】deceitful trick; ruse

骗子【pin³ji² 止】swindler; impostor; cheat

拼【ping¹ 聘¹; ping³ 聘】put together; piece together

拼凑【ping³qeo³ 臭】piece together; rig up

拼盘【ping³pun² 盆²】assorted cold dishes

拼版【ping³ban² 板】makeup

拼写【ping³xé² 舍²】spell; transliterate

拼音【ping¹yem¹ 阴】combine sounds into syllables; spell; phoneticize

姘【ping³ 聘; ping¹ 拼¹】have illicit relations with

姘居【ping³gêü¹ 据¹】live illicitly as husband and wife; cohabit

姘头【ping³teo⁴ 投】paramour

聘【ping³ 姘³】engage; betroth

聘请【ping³qing² 逞】engage; invite

聘任【ping³yem⁶ 壬⁶】engage; appoint to a position

聘书【ping³xü¹ 输】letter of appointment;

脾脏【pēi⁴jong⁶ 撞】spleen

脾胃【pēi⁴wei⁶ 卫】taste

脾气【pēi⁴hēi³ 戏】temperament；bad temper

罴【pēi⁴ 皮】< n. > brown bear

貔【pēi⁴ 皮】a mythical bearlike wild animal

貔貅【pēi⁴yeo¹ 休】a mythical wild animal；brave troops

鼙【pēi⁴ 皮】a drum used in the army in ancient China

蚍【pēi⁴ 皮】< n. > 蚍蜉【pēi⁴feo⁴ 浮】ant

蚍蜉撼大树【pēi⁴feo⁴ham⁶dai⁶xū⁶ 陷歺⁶署⁶】an ant trying to topple a giant tree—ridiculously overrating one's own strength

疲【pēi⁴ 皮】tired；weary；exhausted

疲惫【pēi⁴bēi⁶ 备】tired out；exhausted

疲乏【pēi⁴fed⁹ 佛】weary；tired

疲倦【pēi⁴gün⁶ 卷⁶】tired；weary

疲劳【pēi⁴lou⁴ 卢】tired；fatigue；weary

疲软【pēi⁴yün⁵ 远】fatigued and weak；weaken

疲塌【pēi⁴tab⁸ 塔】slack；negligent

疲于奔命【pēi⁴yü¹ben¹ming⁶ 迂宾铭⁶】be weighed down with work

楞【pēng¹ 拍镜¹】the back of a chair for one to lean against =【普】椅子后面让人靠背的板或木条

捱楞椅【ngai¹pēng¹yi² 挨²倚】chair =【普】靠背椅

楞骨【pēng¹gued⁷ 掘⁷】rib =【普】肋骨

刷【pēng² 平镜²】fell；cut；sweep away =【普】砍；横扫

刷沉【pēng²qem⁴ 侵⁴】cut down；sweep away；defeat the opponents ∽【普】砍倒；横扫；击沉

Q

叉【qa¹ 权；qa³ 岔】fork；work with a fork；cross；block up；jam

叉子【qa¹ji² 止】fork

餐叉【qan¹qa¹ 灿¹】(table) fork

叉鱼【qa¹yü² 于²】spear fish

叉腰【qa¹yiu¹ 邀】akimbo

叉住【qa¹jü⁶ 注⁶】block up；jam

叉烧【qa¹xiu¹ 消】roast meat =【普】烤肉

杈【qa¹ 叉；qa³ 岔】wooden fork；kay-fork；pitchfork；branch (of a tree)

树杈【xü⁶qa¹ 署⁶】a branch of a tree

衩【qa¹ 叉；qa³ 岔】vent in the side of a garment

裤衩【fu³qa¹ 富】underpants = 三角裤【xam¹gog⁹fu³】

蹅【qa¹ 叉】trudge（in mud, snow, etc.）= 踩【qai²】

差【qa¹ 叉；qai¹ 猜；qi¹ 疵】difference；mistake；dispatch；errand；job；differ from；wrong；wanting；poor；uneven

差别【qa¹bid⁹ 必⁹】difference；disparity

差错【qa¹ qo³挫 】mistake；slip；error；mishap

差额【qa¹ngag⁹ 轭⁹】difference；balance

差距【qa¹ kêü⁵拒】gap；disparity；difference

差异【qa¹yi⁶ 义】difference；divergence

差强人意【qa¹kêng⁵yen⁴yi³ 卡香⁵ 仁薏】just passable

差之毫厘，谬以千里【qa¹ji¹hou⁴lêi⁴, meo⁶yi⁵qin¹lêi⁵ 】an error the breadth of a single hair can lead you a thousand li astray

差皮【qa¹pēi⁴ 脾】not smart；poor =【普】差劲

差迟【qa¹qi⁴ 池】mistake =【普】差错；过失

差唔多【qa¹m⁴do¹ 朵¹】almost；nearly =【普】差不多；还可以

差啲【qa¹ did⁷跌⁷】not quite up to the mark；not good enough；almost；nearly =【普】差点儿

差馆【qai¹gun² 管】police station ∽【普】警察局

差遣【qai¹hin² 显】send sb. on an errand；assign

差人【qai¹yen⁴ 仁】police =【普】警察

差使【qai¹ xi² 史 】send；assign；official post

差事【qai¹xi⁶ 是】errand；send

差役【qai¹yig⁹ 亦】corvee

参差【qem¹qi¹ 侵】irregular；uneven

镲【qa² 查²；qa⁴ 查】cymbals =【普】钹（乐器）

镲镲【qa⁴qa²】cymbals

铃铃镲镲都掉埋【ling¹ling¹qa¹qa²dou¹diu⁶ mai⁴】The family belongings were all lost—have not all hope =【普】全部家当丢光——全无希望

岔【qa³ 叉³】branch off；fork；trun off；accident；trouble

岔开【qa³hoi¹ 海¹】branch off；diverge to；stagger

岔口【qa³heo² 厚²】fork（in a road）

岔路【qa³lou⁶ 露】branch road; byroad

岔子【qa³ji² 止】accident; trouble

诧

【qa³ 岔】be surprised

诧异【qa³yi⁶ 义】be surprised; be astonished

姹

【qa³ 岔】beautiful

姹紫嫣红【qa³ji²yin¹hung⁴ 止烟洪】brilliant purples and reds — beautiful flowers

汊

【qa³ 岔】branch of a river = 湆【gao³教】

槎

【qa⁴ 查】raft; stubble; crop

浮槎【feo⁴qa⁴ 否⁴】raft = 木筏【mug⁹fed⁹ 伐】

茬

【qa⁴ 查】stubble; crop; batch

麦茬【meg⁹qa⁴ 默】wheat stubble

查

【qa⁴ 茶】check; examine; look into; look up

查点【qa⁴dim² 店²】check the number or amount of

查对【qa⁴dêu³队³】check; verify

查访【qa⁴fong² 仿】go around and make inquiries

查封【qa⁴fung¹ 风】seal up; close down

查禁【qa⁴gem³ 咁】ban; prohibit

查看【qa⁴hon³ 汉】look over; examine

查明【qa⁴ming⁴ 名】find out; ascertain

查票【qa⁴piu³ 漂】examine tickets

查清【qa⁴qing¹ 青】check up on

查收【qa⁴xeo¹ 修】please find

查问【qa⁴men⁶ 敏⁶】question; interrogate

查询【qa⁴xên¹ 荀】inquire about

查验【qa⁴yim⁶ 艳】check; examine

查阅【qa⁴yüd⁹ 月】consult; look up

查证【qa⁴jing³ 正】investigate and verify; check

茶

【qa⁴ 查】tea; certain kinds of drink or liquid food

茶叶【qa⁴yib⁹ 业】tea; tea-leaves

茶水【qa⁴xêu² 瑞²】tea or boiled water

茶杯【qa⁴bui¹ 背¹】teacup

茶壶【qa⁴wu² 湖²】teapot

茶色【qa⁴xig⁷ 式】dark brown

茶味【qa⁴mēi⁶ 未】tea flavour

茶馆【qa⁴gun² 管】teahouse

茶点【qa⁴dim² 店²】tea and pastries

茶会【qa⁴wui² 汇²】tea party

茶座【qa⁴jo⁶ 坐】teahouse; seats in a teahouse or teagarden

茶花【qa⁴fa¹ 化¹】camellia

茶油【qa⁴yeo² 由】tea oil

茶亭【qa⁴ting² 廷²】tea-booth; tea-kiosk

茶果【qa⁴guo² 戈²】dessert

茶居【qa⁴gêu¹据¹】restaurant（for tea, drink and meals）; teahouse = 【普】茶馆

茶楼【qa⁴leo² 榴²】the teahouse of upstairs

搽

【qa⁴ 茶】put（powder, ointment, etc.）on the skin; apply ∽【普】涂

搽药【qa⁴yê⁹ 若】apply ointment, lotion, etc.

搽雪花膏【qa⁴xüd⁸fa¹gou¹ 说化¹糕】put on vanishing cream

扠

【qa⁵ 叉⁵】erase with a pen or pencil; play with = 【普】乱画; 玩弄

扠祸【qa⁵wo⁵ 和⁵】ruin; put out of order; make trouble = 【普】捣乱; 弄坏

猜【qai¹ 钗】guess; speculate; suspect

猜测【qai¹qag⁷ 侧】guess; conjecture

猜度【qai¹dog⁹ 铎】surmise; conjecture

猜忌【qai¹gēi⁶ 基⁶】be suspicious and jealous of

猜谜【qai¹mei⁴ 迷】guess a riddle; guess

猜拳【qai¹kün⁴ 权】afinger-guessing game; mora = 猜程沉【qai¹qing⁴qem⁴ 情侵⁴】

猜想【qai¹xêng² 赏】suppose; guess; suspect

钗【qai¹ 猜】hairpin（formerly worn by women for adornment)

搋【qai¹ 猜】rub; knead

搋面【qai¹min⁶ 缅⁶】knead dough

踩【qai² 猜²】step on; trample; ride

踩线【qai²xin³ 扇】step on the line; footfault

踩单车【qai²dan¹qē¹ 丹奢】ride a bicycle =【普】骑自行车

柴【qai⁴ 豺】firewood; faggot; a surname

柴草【qai⁴qou² 曹²】firewood; faggot
柴火【qai⁴fo² 伙】firewood; faggot
柴油【qai⁴yeo⁴ 由】diesel oil
柴米油盐【qai⁴mei⁵yeo⁴yim⁴ 迷⁵ 由严】fuel, rice, oil and salt — chief daily necessities

豺【qai⁴ 柴】jackal

豺狼【qai⁴long⁴ 郎】jackals and wolves — cruel and evil people

侪【qai⁴ 柴】fellows; associates

踹【qai² 踩；qai⁴ 柴；yai² 衣埃²】kick; tread

踹台【qai⁴toi⁴ 抬】make catcalls; hoot; boo =【普】喝倒彩

踹哇哇【qai⁴wa¹wa¹ 娃】simply go to do; not serious; trifling matter ∽【普】简单从事；儿戏；不严肃认真

抄【qao¹ 钞】copy; plagiarize; search and confiscate; fold（one's arms); grab

抄写【qao¹xē² 舍²】copy; transcribe
抄录【qao¹lug⁹ 六】make a copy of; copy
抄袭【qao¹ jab⁹习】plagiarize; lift; borrow indiscriminately from other people's experience
抄家【qao¹ga¹ 加】search sb.'s house and confiscate his property
抄后路【qao¹heo⁶lou⁶ 候露】outflank the enemy and attack him in the rear

钞【qao¹ 抄】bank note; paper money; collected writings

钞票【qao¹piu³ 漂³】paper money; bill = 银纸【ngen⁴ji²】

吵【qao² 炒】make a noise; quarrel; wrangle; make a row; kick up a racket

吵架【qao² ga³嫁 】quarrel; wrangle; bicker = 嗌交【ai³gao¹ 胶】
吵闹【qao² nao⁶那拗⁶】wrangle; din; hubbub
吵嚷【qao² yêng⁶让 】make a racket; clamour

炒【qao² 吵】stir-fry; fry

炒菜【qao² qoi²蔡】stir-fry; a fried dish; a dish cooked to order

炒货【qao²fo³ 课】roasted seeds and nuts

炒冷饭【qao²lang⁵fan⁶ 罗罳⁵ 范】heat leftover rice — say or do the same old thing; rehash

炒鱿鱼【qao²yeo⁴yü² 尤余²】refer to one being sacked from one's job; discharge; dismiss = 【普】解雇

炒虾嚓蟹【qao²ha¹qad⁸hai⁵ 哈察械⁵】use coarse or vulgar language; people who always say rude things or dirty words = 【普】粗言烂语;说话粗俗

㩧【qao³ 抄³】seek; look for; search for; hunt for; scout around = 【普】寻找;搜索

㩧出来【qao³qêd⁷loi⁴ 次律⁷ 莱】search for sth. to come out = 【普】(把某人或物)搜寻出来

巢【qao⁴ 抄⁴】nest

巢穴【qao⁴yüd⁹ 月】lair; den; nest; hideout

皺【qao⁴ 巢】have the wrinkles or fold = 【普】起皱纹

皺皮【qao⁴pēi⁴ 疲】the surface having the wrinkles or fold; (refer to the skin) not elastic anymore; wrinkled = 【普】(物体)表面起皱纹或皱褶

参【qam¹ 惨¹; qem¹ 侵; xem¹ 心】join; enter; refer; call to pay one's respects to; impeach an official before the emperor; uneven; ginseng

参加【qam¹ga¹ 家】join; attend; take part in

参与【qam¹yü⁵ 语】participate in; have a hand in

参半【qam¹bun³伴³】half; half-and-half

参观【qam¹gun¹ 官】visit; look around

参考【qam¹hao² 巧】consult; refer to; reference

参谋【qam¹meo⁴ 牟】staff officer; give advice

参事【qam¹xi⁶ 是】counsellor; adviser

参数【qam¹xou³ 素】parameter

参天【qam¹tin¹ 田¹】reaching to the sky; towering

参赞【qam¹jan³ 撰】counsellor

参照【qam¹jiu³ 焦³】cousult; refer to

参议院【qam¹yi⁵yün² 耳丸】senate

参议员【qam¹yi⁵yün⁴ 耳元】senator

人参【yen⁴xem¹ 仁心】ginseng

参差【qem¹qi¹ 侵妣】(see "差")

搀【qam¹ 参】help by the arm; mix

搀扶【qam¹fu⁴ 符】support sb. with one's hand

搀杂【qam¹jab⁹ 习】mix; mingle

惨【qam² 篸】miserable; pitiful; tragic; cruel; savage; disastrously

惨状【qam²jong⁶ 撞】miserable condition

惨痛【qam²tung³ 通³】deeply grieved; painful; bitter

惨重【qam²jung⁶ 仲】heavy; grievous

惨案【qam²ngon³ 按】massacre; murder case

惨败【qam²bai⁶ 拜⁶】crushing defeat

惨死【qam²xēi² 四²】die a tragic death

惨剧【qam²kēg⁹ 屐】tragedy; calamity

惨遭不幸【qam²jou¹bed⁷heng⁶ 糟毕杏】die a tragic death

惨不忍睹【qam²bed⁷yen²dou² 毕隐倒】too horrible to look at

惨无人道【qam² mou⁴ yen⁴ dou⁶ 毛 仁 度】
    inhuman

惨绝人寰【qam² jüd⁹ yen⁴ wan⁴ 嘬⁹ 仁环】
    extremely tragic

惨淡经营【qam² dam⁶ ging¹ ying⁴ 担⁶ 京
    仍】keep（an enterprise, etc.）go-
    ing by painstaking effort

簸【qam² 惨】a dustpan; winnowing fan
    ～【普】竹筐

杉【qam³ 参³】China fir

杉【qam⁴ mug⁹ 目】China fir

忏【qam⁴ 杉】< v. > 忏悔【qam⁴ fui³
    灰³】repent; confess

蚕【qam⁴ 参⁴】silkworm

蚕虫【qam⁴ qung² 宠】silkworm
蚕蛹【qam⁴ yung² 拥】silkworm chrysalis
蚕茧【qam⁴ gan² 简】silkworm cocoon
蚕丝【qam⁴ xi¹ 思】natural silk; silk
蚕蛾【qam⁴ ngo² 鹅】silk moth
蚕豆【qam⁴ deo² 斗²】broad bean
蚕食【qam⁴ xig⁹ 蚀】nibble

惭【qam⁴ 蚕】feel ashamed

惭愧【qam⁴ kuei⁵ 葵⁵】be ashamed

馋【qam⁴ 蚕】greedy; gluttonous ＝ 为
    食【wei⁶ xig⁹】

馋涎欲滴【qam⁴ yin⁴ yug⁹ dig⁹ 言 玉 敌】
    mouth drooling with greed

巉【qam⁴ 蚕】dangerously steep; precipi-
    tous

岩岩巉巉【ngam⁴ ngam⁴ qam⁴ qam⁴ 喵⁴】
    full of bumps and holes; uneven
    ＝【普】凹凸不平

谗【qam⁴ 蚕】slander

谗言【qam⁴ yin⁴ 然】calumny

劖【qam⁵ 蚕⁵】① a big chisel, its blade
    being long；② be assassinated

劖刀【qam⁵ dou¹ 都】a big chisel, its blade
    being long ＝【普】长刃的大凿子

劖亲【qam⁶ qen¹ 趁】be assassinated

餐【qan¹ 产¹】eat; food; meal; regular
    meal

餐具【qan¹ gêü⁶ 巨】tableware; dinner ser-
    vice

餐巾【qan¹ gen¹ 斤】table napkin

餐厅【qan¹ têng¹ 剔镜¹】dining room; res-
    taurant

餐车【qan¹ qê¹ 奢】restaurant car; dining
    car

产【qan² 铲】give birth to; produce;
    yield; product; property; estate

产生【qan² xeng¹ 笙】produce; engender;
    emerge; come into being

产妇【qan² fu⁵ 付⁵】lying-in woman

产房【qan² fong⁴ 防】delivery room

产科【qan⁴ fo¹ 课¹】obstetrics

产假【qan² ga³ 价】maternity leave

产卵【qan² lên² 伦²】lay eggs

产品【qan² ben² 禀】product; produce

产物【qan² med⁹ 勿】outcome; result; pro-
    duct

产量【qan² lêng⁶ 亮】output; yield

产销【qan² xiu¹ 消】production and mar-
    keting

产值【qan² jig⁹ 直】value of output; output
    value

产业【qan² yib⁹ 叶】estate; property; in-
    dustrial

产权【qan² kün⁴ 拳】property right

产地【qan² dêi⁶ 得希⁶】place of production

铲【qan² 产】shovel；lift or move with a shovel

铲车【qan²qē¹ 奢】forklift（truck）

铲除【qan²qêü⁴ 徐】root out；uproot

粲【qan³ 灿】bright；beaming；smile

粲然【qan³yin⁴ 言】bright；smiling broadly

璨【qan³ 灿】(see "璀璨")

灿【qan³ 粲】＜a.＞灿烂【qan³lan⁶ 兰⁶】magnificent；splendid；resplendent；bright

残【qan⁴ 灿⁴】incomplete；remnant；injure

残暴【qan⁴bou⁶ 部】cruel and ferocious；ruthless

残害【qan⁴hoi⁶ 亥】cruelly injure or kill

残酷【qan⁴hug⁹ 哭³】cruel；brutal

残忍【qan⁴yen² 隐】cruel；ruthless

残杀【qan⁴xad⁸ 煞】murder；massacre

残余【qan⁴yü⁴ 鱼】remnants；remains

残存【qan⁴qün⁴ 全】remnant；remain ＝残留【leo⁴】

残废【qan⁴fei³ 费】maimed；crippled；cripple

残疾【qan⁴jed⁹ 侄】deformity

残局【qan⁴gug⁹ 焗】the final phase of a game of chess

残破【qan⁴po³ 婆³】broken；dilapidated

残缺【qan⁴küd⁸ 决】incomplete；fragmentary

残生【qan⁴xeng¹ 笙】one's remaining years

残年【qan⁴nin⁴ 捻⁴】the last days of the year；the evening of life

残阳【qan⁴yêng⁴ 杨】the setting sun

残骸【qan⁴hai⁴ 鞋】remains；wreckage

残兵败将【qan⁴bing¹bai⁶jêng³ 冰拜⁶ 涨】remnants of a routed army

残渣余孽【qan⁴ja¹yü⁴yib⁹ 抓鱼叶】evil elements from the old society

撑【qang¹ 橙¹；qang³ 橙³】prop up；push or move with a pole；maintain；keep up；open；brace；stay

撑持【qang¹qi⁴池】prop up；shore up；sustain

撑腰【qang¹yiu¹邀】support；back up

撑臂【qang³bēi³痹】brace

撑门面【qang¹mun⁴min²瞒缅²】keep up appearance

撑竿跳高【qang¹gon¹tiu³gou¹ 杆挑³盖】pole vault

鐣【qang¹ 撑¹】a flat wok for cooking ＝【普】烹调小锅

瓦鐣【nga⁵qang¹ 雅】clay pot ＝【普】砂锅

橙【qang² 撑²】orange；orange colour

橙子【qang²ji² 止】orange

橙黄色【qang²wong⁴xig⁷ 王式】orange colour

瞠【qang⁴ 撑⁴】＜v.＞瞠眼【qang⁴ngan⁵ 雁⁵】open one's eyes really big；dizzy；dazzled ＝【普】强光刺眼

枨【qang⁴ 橙⁴】use body to move sb.

枨鸡【qang⁴gei¹ 计¹】a nasty woman ＝枨鸡婆【po⁴】＝【普】泼辣、淫猥的妇人

插【qab⁸ 次鸭⁸】stick in；insert；interpose

插入【qab⁸yeb⁹ 邑⁹】squeeze in；edge in；take part in

插手【qab⁸xeo² 守】take part in；lend a

hand; have a hand in

插足【qab⁸jug⁷ 竹】put one's foot in; participate

插嘴【qab⁸jêü² 咀】interrupt; chip in

插苏【qab⁸xou¹ 搔】plug; bolt = 【普】插头；插销

插座【qab⁸jo⁶ 助】socket; outlet

插话【qab⁸ wa⁶ 画⁶】interpose; chip in; digression

插曲【qab⁸kug⁷ 卡屋⁷】interlude; episode

插图【qab⁸tou⁴ 途】illustration; plate

插秧【qab⁸yêng¹ 央】transplant rice seedlings

插翼难飞【qab⁸yig⁸nan⁴fēi¹ 亦那晏⁴ 非】unable to escape even if given wings

锸【qab⁸ 插】spade

嚓【qad⁸ 察】① < onomatopoeia > the sound of the car stop, etc. ② eat

嚓饭【qad⁸fan⁶ 范】eat; have a meal = 【普】吃饭

唰【qad⁸ 察】< onomatopoeia > the sound of rain, etc.

察【qad⁸ 刷】examine; look into; scrutinize

察看【qad⁸hon³ 汉】watch; look carefully at

察觉【qad⁸gog⁸ 各】be conscious of; perceive

察颜观色【qad⁸ngan⁴gun¹xig⁷ 雁⁴ 官式】watch a person's every mood

擦【qad⁸ 察】rub; wipe; spread on; brush; scrape (into shreds)

擦拭【qad⁸xig⁷ 式】clean; cleanse

擦边球【qad⁸bin¹keo⁴ 鞭求】edge ball; touch ball

擦亮眼睛【qad⁸lêng⁶ngan⁵jing¹ 量⁶ 雁⁵ 精】remove the scales from one's eyes

刷【qad⁸ 察】brush; scrub; daub; paste up; remove

刷洗【qad⁸xei² 驶】scrub

刷新【qad⁸ xen¹ 辛 】renovate; refurbish; break

刷牙【qad⁸nga³ 芽】brush one's teeth

刷鞋【qad⁸hai⁴ 孩】brush shoes

刷子【qad⁸ji² 止】brush; scrub

测【qag⁷ 策⁷; qeg⁷ 次克】survey; fathom; conjecture

测定【qag⁷ding⁶ 锭】determine

测绘【qag⁷ kui² 剑】survey and drawing; mapping

测量【qag⁷ lêng⁴梁 】survey; measure; gauge

测验【qag⁷yim⁶ 艳】test

策【qag⁷ 测; qag⁸ 册】plan; scheme; strategy; whip; a type of essay in ancient China

策动【qag⁸dung⁶ 洞】instigate; engineer

策划【qag⁸wag⁹ 或】plan; plot; scheme

策应【qag⁸ ying³ 英³】support by coordinated action

策略【qag⁸lêg⁹ 掠】tactics; tactful

策源地【qag⁸yün⁴dēi⁶ 元得希⁶】source; place of origin

策励【qag⁷lei⁶ 厉】encourage; spur on

册【qag⁸ 策⁸】volume; book; copy

册子【qag⁸ji² 止】book; volume

拆【qag⁸ 册】tear open; take apart; pull down; dismantle

拆除【qag⁸ qêü⁴徐】demolish; dismantle; remove

拆毁【qag⁸wei² 委】demolish；pull down

拆伙【qag⁸ fo²火】dissolve a partnership

折开【qag⁸hoi¹ 海¹】take apart；open

拆散【qag⁸xan³ 汕】break（a set）；break up

拆卸【qag⁸xē⁴ 舍】dismantle；dismount

拆台【qag⁸ toi⁴抬】cut the ground from under sb.'s feet；pull away a prop

坼【qag⁸ 册】split open；crack

爆坼【bao³qag⁸ 包³】split open；rend ＝【普】裂开

贼【qag⁹ 册⁹】thief；traitor；enemy；crooked；wicked；evil；furtive

贼心【qag⁸xem¹ 深】wicked heart；evil designs

贼赃【qag⁹jong¹ 装】stolen goods；booty

贼头贼脑【qag⁹teo⁴qag⁹nou⁵ 投恼】behaving stealthily like a thief；stealthy

贼喊捉贼【qag⁹ham³jug⁷qag⁹ 咸³ 竹】a thief crying "stop thief"

贼佬【qag⁹lou² 老²】robber；thief ＝ 贼仔【jei² 济²】

妻【qei¹ 萋】wife

妻子【qei¹ji² 止】wife；wife and children

妻孥【qei¹nou⁴ 奴】wife and children

妻离子散【qei¹lēi⁴ji²xan³ 漓止汕】breaking up or scattering of one's family

凄【qei¹ 萋】chilly；cold；bleak and desolate；sad；wretched

凄凉【qei¹lêng⁴ 梁】dreary；desolate

凄惨【qei¹ qam² 参²】wretched；miserable；tragic

凄厉【qei¹lei⁶ 励】sad and shrill

凄切【qei¹qid⁸ 设】plaintive；mournful

凄然【qei¹yin⁴ 言】sad；mournful

凄风苦雨【qei¹fung¹fu²yū⁵ 丰府语】wailing wind and weeping rain — wretched circumstances

萋【qei¹ 妻】＜a.＞萋萋【qei¹qei¹】luxuriant

栖【qei¹ 妻】（of birds）perch；dwell；stay

栖身【qei¹xen¹ 辛】stay；sojourn

栖息【qei¹xig⁷ 式】(of birds) perch；rest

砌【qei³ 齐³】build by laying bricks or stones；step

砌砖【qei³jūn¹ 专】lay bricks

砌墙【qei³qêng⁴ 祥】build a wall

咽【qei³ 砌】eat；take

咽一餐【qei³yed⁷qan¹ 壹灿¹】have a eat

掔【qei³ 砌】＜v.＞boxing ＝【普】拳击

掔一拳【qei³yed⁷kün⁴ 壹权】give a punch

齐【qei⁴ 妻⁴】neat；even；on a level with；together；all ready；alike；a surname

齐整【qei⁴jing¹ 正²】neat；uniform

齐全【qei⁴qūn⁴ 存】complete；all in readiness

齐备【qei⁴bēi⁶ 鼻】all ready

齐名【qei⁴ming⁴ 明】enjoy equal popularity

齐心【qei⁴xem¹ 深】be of one mind

齐声【qei⁴xing¹ 升】in chorus；in unison

齐奏【qei⁴jeo³ 咒】unison；playing in unison

齐头并进【qei⁴teo⁴bing⁶jên³ 投丙⁶ 俊】advance side by side

荠【qei⁵ 齐；jei³ 济】(see "荸荠")

秋【qeo¹ 抽】autumn; harvest time; year

秋季【qeo¹guei³ 桂】autumn = 秋天【qeo¹ tin¹田¹】

秋色【qeo¹xig⁷ 式】autumn scenery

秋千【qeo¹qin¹ 浅¹】swing

秋水【qeo¹ xêü² 瑞²】autumn waters – limpid eyes

秋波【qeo¹bo¹ 坡】bright eyes of a beautiful woman

秋毫无犯【qeo¹hou⁴mou⁴fan⁶ 豪毛范】not encroach on the interests of the people to the slightest degree

秋后算帐【qeo¹ heo⁶ xün³ jêng³ 候蒜胀】wait until after a political movement is over to settle accounts with the leadership or the masses

抽【qeo¹ 秋】take out (from in between); take (a part from a whole); put forth; obtain by drawing, etc.; lash; whip

抽查【qeo¹qa⁴ 茶】selective examination; spot check

抽搐【qeo¹qug⁷ 畜】twitch; tic

抽打【qeo¹da² 得阿²】lash; whip; thrash

抽调【qeo¹diu⁶ 掉】transfer

抽风【qeo¹fung¹ 丰】convulsions

抽水【qeo¹xêü² 瑞²】draw water

抽税【qeo¹xêü⁵ 瑞³】levy a tax

抽穗【qeo¹xêü⁵ 瑞⁵】heading; earing

抽屉【qeo¹tei³ 替】drawer = 柜筒【guei⁶ tung²】

抽象【qeo¹jêng⁶ 像】abstract

抽烟【qeo¹yin¹ 燕¹】smoke

抽样【qeo¹yêng² 扬²】sample; sampling

抽筋【qeo¹ gen¹ 斤】pull out a tendon; cramp

抽油【qeo¹yeo² 友²】soya sauce = 【普】酱油

抽空【qeo¹hung¹ 凶】manage to find time

抽泣【qeo¹yeb⁷ 邑】sob

抽签【qeo¹qim¹ 金】draw lots

抽球【qeo¹keo⁴ 求】drive

抽纱【qeo¹xa¹ 沙】drawnwork .

抽薪止沸【qeo¹xen¹ji²fei⁶ 辛子吠】take drastic measures to stop sth.

丑【qeo² 秋²】ugly; unsightly; disgraceful; shameful; clown in Beijing Opera, etc.; the second of the twelve Earthly Branches

丑恶【qeo²ngog⁸ 噩】ugly; repulsive; hideous

丑化【qeo²fa³ 花³】smear; uglify; defame; vilify

丑剧【qeo²kêg⁹ 展】farce

丑角【qeo²gog⁸ 各】clown; buffoon

丑陋【qeo²leo⁶ 漏】ugly

丑时【qeo² xi⁴是⁴】the period of the day from 1 a.m. to 3 a.m.

丑事【qeo²xi⁶ 士】scandal

丑态【qeo²tai³ 太】ugly performance; buffoonery

丑闻【qeo²men⁴ 文】scandal

丑八怪【qeo²bad⁸guai³ 捌乖³】a very ugly person

瞅【qeo² 丑;qeo¹ 秋】look at

瞅见【qeo²gin³ 建】see

臭【qeo³ 嗅】smelly; foul; stinking; disgusting; odour; smell

臭味相投【qeo³mêi⁶xêng¹teo⁴ 未双头】share the same rotten tastes habits, etc.; be two of a kind

臭虫【qeo³qung⁴ 从】bedbug = 木虱【mug⁹】

xed⁷ 目失】

臭哼哼【qeo³heng¹heng¹ 亨】stinking;
foul-smelling =【普】臭烘烘

臭气【qeo³hēi³ 戏】bad smell；stink

臭骂【qeo³ma⁶ 吗⁶】curse roundly

臭烹烹【qeo³pang¹pang¹ 棚¹】= 臭哼哼
【heng¹ 亨】

臭名远扬【qeo³ ming⁴ yūn⁵ yêng⁴明软洋】
notorious

臭名昭著【qeo³ming⁴qiu¹jū³ 明超注】of ill
repute；notorious

臭青【qeo³ qēng¹ 次镜¹】the taste of raw
vegetable =【普】没煮熟的青菜
给人的味觉

臭丸【qeo³yūn² 院】mothballs =【普】樟
脑丸

臭屁蝲【qeo³pēi³lad⁸ 披³捺】a type of insect which is dark grey in colour
and which can discharge smelly
liquid =【普】一种被捕时能放出
刺激性臭味的小飞虫

嗅 【qeo³ 臭】smell；scent；sniff

嗅觉【qeo³gog⁸ 各】(sense of) smell；
scent

溴 【qeo³ 臭】<n.> bromine (Br)

溴水【qeo³xêū² 瑞²】bromine water

凑 【qeo³ 臭】gather together；pool；hap-
pen by chance；move close to；press
near

凑合【qeo³ heb⁹盒】gather together；col-
lect；improvise；make do；pass-
able

凑集【qeo³jab⁹ 习】gather together

凑数【qeo³xou³ 素】serve as a stopgap

凑巧【qeo³hao² 考】luckily；fortunately

凑跷【qeo³ kiu² 荞²】coincidence =【普】
巧合；一致

辏 【qeo³ 凑】<n.> 辐辏【fug⁷qeo³】con-
verge

绸 【qeo⁴ 筹】silk fabric；silk

绸缎【qeo⁴dūn⁶ 段】silks and satins

绸缪【qeo⁴meo⁶ 茂】① sentimentally attached ②（see "未雨绸缪"）

稠 【qeo⁴ 绸】thick；dense

稠密【qeo⁴med⁹ 蜜】dense

酬 【qeo⁴ 绸】propose a toast；toast；re-
ward；friendly exchange；fulfil

酬答【qeo⁴dab⁶ 搭】thank sb. with a gift

酬金【qeo⁴gem¹ 今】monetary reward；
remuneration

酬劳【qeo⁴lou⁴ 卢】recompense；reward

酬谢【qeo⁴jē⁶ 樹】thank sb. with a gift

俦 【qeo⁴ 绸】companion

畴 【qeo⁴ 绸】farmland；kind；division

踌 【qeo⁴ 绸】hesitate；smug

踌躇【qeo⁴qêū⁴ 徐】hesitate；shilly-shally

踌躇满志【qeo⁴qêū⁴mun⁵ji³ 徐门⁵ 至】en-
ormously proud of one's success；
smug；complacent

筹 【qeo⁴ 绸】chip；counter；prepare；
plan

筹码【qeo⁴ma⁵ 马】chip；counter

筹备【qeo⁴bēi⁶ 鼻】prepare；arrange

筹划【qeo⁴wag⁹ 或】plan and prepare

筹办【qeo⁴ban⁶ 板⁶】make preparations

筹建【qeo⁴gin³ 见】prepare to construct or
establish sth.

侵【qem¹ 寝¹】invade; intrude into; approaching

侵犯【qem¹fan⁶ 范】encroach on; violate

侵略【qem¹lêg⁹ 掠】aggression; invasion

侵入【qem¹yeb⁹ 邑⁹】invade; intrude into

侵扰【qem¹yiu² 要²】invade and harass

侵蚀【qem¹xig⁹ 食】corrode; erode

侵吞【qem¹ten³ 替因¹】embezzle; annex

侵占【qem¹ jim³ 詹³】 invade and occupy; seize

寝【qem² 侵²】sleep; coffin chamber; stop; end

寝食【qem²xig⁹ 蚀】sleeping and eating

寝室【qem²xed³ 失】bedroom; dormitory

覃【qem⁴ 寻; tam⁴ 谭】a surname

沉【qem⁴ 寻】sink; keep down; lower; deep; heavy; profound

沉浸【qem⁴jem³ 针³】immerse; steep

沉淀【qem⁴din⁶ 电】sediment; precipitate

沉积【qem⁴jig⁷ 织】deposit

沉寂【qem⁴jig⁹ 直】quiet; still; no news

沉静【qem⁴jing⁶ 净】quiet; calm; serene

沉默【qem⁴ meg⁹ 麦】reticent; taciturn; silent

沉闷【qem⁴mun⁶ 门⁶】oppressive; depressing; depressed

沉思【qem⁴xi¹ 司】ponder; meditate

沉痛【qem⁴tung³ 通³】deep feelings of grief or remorse; deeply felt; bitter

沉吟【qem⁴ yem⁴ 淫 】 mutter to oneself, unable to make up one's mind

沉郁【qem⁴yug⁷ 沃】depressed; gloomy

沉冤【qem⁴yün¹ 渊】gross injustice

沉疴【qem⁴ ngo¹ 屙】severe and lingering illness

沉沦【qem³lên⁴ 伦】sink into

沉迷【qem⁴mei⁴ 谜】indulge; wallow

沉没【qem⁴mud⁹ 抹⁹】sink

沉溺【qem⁴nig⁹ 那益⁹】indulge; wallow

沉睡【qem⁴xêü⁶ 穗⁶】be sunk in sleep

沉香【qem⁴ hêng¹ 乡】 ＜n.＞ a galloch eaglewood

沉重【qem⁴jung⁶ 仲】heavy; serious

沉渣【qem⁴ja¹ 抓】sediment; dregs

沉着【qem⁴jêg⁹ 桌⁹】cool-headed; composed; calm

沉醉【qem⁴jêü³ 最】get drunk

沉沉【qem⁴qem⁴】heavy; deep

沉甸甸【qem⁴din⁶din⁶ 电】heavy

谶【qem³ 侵³】augury

嗪【qem³ 侵³】add; say and say

嗪气【qem³hêi³ 戏】long-winded; explained and eplained ＝【普】啰嗦;说了又说

亲【qen¹ 陈¹】parent; blood relation; relative; marriage; match; bride; close; dear; in person; kiss

亲爱【qen¹ngoi³ 哀³】dear; beloved

亲近【qen¹gen⁶ 靳】be close to

亲口【qen¹heo² 厚²】(say sth.) personally

亲密【qen¹med⁹ 勿】close; intimate

亲昵【qen¹nig⁷ 挪益⁷】very intimate

亲戚【qen¹qig⁷ 次益⁷】relative

亲切【qen¹qid⁸ 设】cordial; kind

亲热【qen¹ yid⁹衣泄⁹】affectionate; intimate

亲人【qen¹ yen⁴ 仁 】one's family members; dear ones; those dear to one

亲善【qen¹xin⁶ 膳】goodwill

亲身【qen¹xen¹ 辛】personal；firsthand

亲自【qen¹ ji⁶治】personally；in person；
oneself

亲手【qen¹xeo²守】withone's own hands；
personally

亲生【qen¹ xeng¹笙】one's own（children，
parents）

亲事【qen¹xi⁶ 士】marriage

亲属【qen¹xug⁹熟】kinsfolk；relatives

亲信【qen¹xên³ 讯】trusted follower

亲眼【qen¹ngan⁶ 雁⁵】with one's own eyes；
personally

亲友【qen¹yeo⁵ 有】relatives and friends

亲嘴【qen¹jêû² 咀】kiss

亲者痛，仇者快【qen¹jē²tung³，xeo⁴jē²
fai³】sadden one's own people and
gladden the enemy

诊【qen² 疹；jen² 真²】examine（a
patient）（see "jen²"）

疹【qen² 陈²；jen² 真²】rash

疹子【qen²ji² 止】measles＝痲疹【ham⁴
lan³ 兰³】；痲粒【ham⁴neb⁷ 那合⁷】

趁【qen³ 衬】take advantage of；while；
go to market

趁墟【qen³hêü¹ 虚】go to market＝【普】
赶集

趁便【qen³bin⁶ 辨】when it is convenient

趁机【qen³ gēi¹基 】take advantage of the
occasion

趁势【qen³xei³ 世】take advantage of a favourable situation

趁早【qen³jou² 祖】as early as possible

趁热打铁【qen³yid⁹da²tid⁸ 衣泄⁹ 得亚²
替热⁸】strike while the iron is hot

趁火打劫【qen³fo²da²gib⁸ 伙 得亚² 格

业⁸】loot a burning house

槟【qen³ 趁】coffin

衬【qen³ 趁】line；lining；liner；set off

衬托【qen³tog⁸ 梯恶⁸】set off；serve as a
foil to

衬衫【qen³xam¹ 三】shirt

衬衣【qen³yi¹ 依】underclothes；shirt

陈【qen⁴ 尘】lay out；put on display；
state；old；a surname

陈列【qen⁴lid⁹ 裂】display；set out

陈设【qen⁴qid⁸ 彻】display；set out；fur-
nishings

陈旧【qen⁴geo⁶ 柩】outmoded；obsolete

陈迹【qen⁴jig⁷ 织】a thing of the past

陈腐【qen⁴fu⁶ 付】old and decayed；stale

陈皮【qen⁴pēi⁴ 脾】dried tangerine or orange peel

陈述【qen⁴xê²⁹ 术】state

陈陈相因【qen⁴qen⁴xêng¹yen¹ 双欣】fol-
low a set routine

陈词滥调【qen⁴qi⁴lam⁶diu²迟缆掉】hack-
neyed and stereotyped expressions

尘【qen⁴ 陈】dust；dirt；this world

尘埃【qen⁴ai¹ 挨¹】dust

尘土【qen⁴tou² 桃²】dust

尘垢【qen⁴geo³ 救】dust and dirt；dirt

尘世【qen⁴ xei³细 】this world＝ 尘寰
【wan⁴ 环】

层【qeng⁴ 次莺⁴】layer；tier；stratum；a
component part in a sequence

层次【qeng⁴ qi³ 刺】administrative levels；
arrangement of ideas

层云【qeng⁴wen⁴ 匀】stratum

层层【qeng⁴qeng⁴】layer upon layer

层峦迭嶂【qeng⁴lün⁴did⁹jêng³ 联秩障】peaks rising one higher than another

层出不穷【qeng⁴qêd⁷bed⁷kung⁴ 次律⁷ 毕穷】emerge in an endless stream

辑【qeb⁷ 缉】collect; compile; edit; part; volume; division

辑录【qeb⁷lug⁹ 六】compile

缉【qeb⁷ 辑】seize; arrest

缉捕【qeb⁷bou⁶ 暴】seize; arrest

缉拿【qeb⁷na⁴那亚⁴】seize; arrest; apprehend

缉私【qeb⁷xi¹ 司】suppress smuggling

葺【qeb⁷ 辑】cover a roof with straw; thatch; repair; mend

七【qed⁷ 柒】seven

七月【qed⁷ yüd⁹越 】July; the seventh mooth

七情【qed⁷qing⁴ 程】the seven human e-motions, namely, joy, anger, sorrow, fear, love, hate and desire

七夕【qed⁷jig⁹ 直】the seventh evening of the seventh moon

七零八落【qed⁷ling⁴bad⁸log⁹ 凌捌洛⁹】in disorder

七七八八【qed⁷qed⁷bad⁸bed⁸ 捌】refer to a piece of work that is almost finished ＝【普】差不多；接近完成

七拼八凑【qed⁷ping³bad⁸qeo³ 聘³ 捌臭】piece together; knock together

七嘴八舌【qed⁷ jêü² bad⁸ xid⁸ 司热⁸】all talking at once

七老八十【qed⁷ lou⁵ bad⁸ xeb⁹鲁捌拾】old; elderly; aged ＝【普】年迈；年纪大

七窍生烟【qed⁷kiu³xeng¹yin¹ 乔³ 笙燕¹】fume with anger; foam with rage

七国咁乱【qed⁷ guog⁶ gem³ lün² 幗禁联⁶】describe a situation that is very confused and messy ＝【普】大混乱；乱成一团

柒【qed⁷ 七】seven (used for the numeral 七 on cheques, etc., to avoid mistakes or alterations)

漆【qed⁷ 七】lacquer; paint; coat with lacquer

漆树【qed⁷xü⁶ 署⁶】lacquer tree

漆器【qed⁷hêi³ 戏】lacquerware; lacquer-work

漆工【qed⁷gung¹ 公】lacquering; lacquerer

漆包线【qed⁷bao¹xin³ 苞腺】enamel - insulated wire

漆黑一团【qed⁷heg⁷yed⁷tün⁴ 克壹梯元⁴】pitch-dark; be in the dark

朏【qed⁹ 七⁹】penis (vulgar language)

恻【qeg⁷ 次克⁷】sorrowful; sad

恻隐【qeg⁷yen² 忍】compassion; pity

恻隐之心【qeg⁷yen²ji¹xem¹ 忍支深】sense of pity

初【qo¹ 搓】at the beginning of; first; for the first time; elementary; original; a surname

初步【qo¹bou⁶部 】initial; preliminary; tentative

初创【qo¹qong³ 苍³】newly established

初次【qo¹qi³ 刺】the first time

初级【qo¹keb⁷ 给】elementary; primary

初交【qo¹gao¹ 郊】new acquaintance

初恋【qo¹lün² 联²】first love

初期【qo¹kēi⁴ 其】initial stage; early days

初试【qo¹xi³史³】 first try; preliminary examination

初学【qo¹hog⁹ 鹤】begin to learn

初小【qo¹xiu² 少²】lower primary school

初中【qo¹jung¹ 宗】junior middle school

初等【qo¹deng² 登²】 elementary mathematics

初犯【qo¹fan⁶ 范】first offender; first offence

初选【qo¹xün² 损】primary election

初衷【qo¹qung¹ 冲】original intention

初生之犊【qo¹xeng¹ji¹dug⁹ 笙支读】new-born calf

初出茅庐【qo¹qêd⁷mao⁴lou⁴ 次律矛卢】young and inexperienced

初露锋芒【qo¹lou⁶ fung¹ mong⁴路风亡】display one's talent for the first time

雏【qo¹ 初】young（bird）; nestling; fledgling

雏鸟【qo¹niu⁵ 那妖⁵】nestling; fledgling

雏形【qo¹ ying⁴型】embryonic form; embryo

刍【qo¹ 初】hay; fodder; cut grass

刍议【qo¹yi⁵ 耳】my humble opinion

反刍【fan²qo¹ 返】ruminate; chew the cud

搓【qo¹ 初】rub with the hands

搓板【qo¹ban² 版】washboard

搓麻绳【qo²ma⁴xing⁴ 妈⁴ 成】make cord by twisting hemp fibres between the palms

搓手取暖【qo¹xeo²qêü²nün⁵ 守娶那元⁵】rub one's hands together to warm them

磋【qo¹ 初】consult

磋商【qo¹xêng¹ 双】consult; exchange views

蹉【qo¹ 初】< v. > 蹉跎【qo¹to⁴ 陀】waste time

楚【qo² 础】clear; neat; pang; suffering; a surname (see "清楚"; "苦楚")

楚楚【qo²qo²】clear; tidy; neat

础【qo² 楚】plinth (see "基础")

错【qo³ 挫】interlocked and jagged; intricate; grind; rub; alternate; wrong; mistaken; fault; bad; poor

错误【qo³ng⁶ 悟】wrong; mistaken; mistake; error; blunder

错过【qo³guo³ 戈³】miss; let slip

错处【qo³qü³ 次于³】fault; demerit

错乱【qo¹lün⁶ 联⁶】in disorder; deranged

错觉【qo³ gog⁸角】 illusion; wrong impression

错爱【qo³ngoi³ 哀³】undeserved kindness

错怪【qo³guai³ 乖³】blame sb. wrongly

错案【qo³ngon³ 按】misjudged case

错字【qo³ji⁶ 治】wrongly written character; misprint

错开【qo³hoi¹ 海¹】stagger

错杂【qo³jab⁹ 习】mixed; heterogeneous; jumbled

错落【qo³log⁹ 洛⁹】strew at random

错综复杂【qo³jung⁶fug⁷jab⁹ 宗幅习】intricate; complex

挫【qo³ 错】defeat; frustrate; subdue; lower

挫折【qo³jid⁸ 节】setback; reverse

挫伤【qo³xêng¹ 双】contusion；dampen

挫败【qo³bai⁶ 拜⁶】frustrate；foil；defeat

锉

【qo³ 错】file；make smooth with a file

锉刀【qo³dou¹ 都】file

锉光【qo³guogn¹ 桄¹】file sth. smooth

痤

【qo⁴ 锄】< n. >痤疮【qo⁴qong¹ 苍】acne = 青春痘【qing¹qên¹deo²】

锄

【qo⁴ 痤】hoe；work with a hoe；uproot；eliminate；wipe out

锄头【qo⁴teo² 投²】hoe

锄草【qo⁴qou² 操²】hoe up weeds

锄奸【qo⁴gan¹ 间¹】eliminate traitors

啋

【qoi¹ 采¹】exclamation mark ∽【普】呸！别说 。(制止别人说不中听的话)

采

【qoi² 彩】pick；pluck；mine；extract；adopt；select；complexion；spirit

采撷【qoi²kid⁸ 揭】pick；pluck；gather

采摘【qoi²jag⁹ 择】pluck；pick

采择【qoi²jag⁹ 摘】select and adopt

采取【qoi²qêü² 娶】adopt；take

采纳【qoi²nab⁹ 呐】accept；adopt

采用【qoi²yung⁶ 拥⁶】adopt；use；employ

采伐【qoi²fed⁹ 乏】fell；cut

采集【qoi²jab⁹ 习】gather；collect

采种【qoi²jung² 肿】seed collecting

采掘【qoi²gued⁹ 骨⁹】excavate

采药【qoi²yêg⁹ 若】gather medicinal herbs

采制【qoi²jei³ 济】collect and process

采购【qoi²keo³ 构】purchase

彩

【qoi² 采】colour；coloured silk；variety；prize；blood from a wound

彩色【qoi²xig⁷ 式】multicolour；colour

彩虹【qoi²hung⁴ 红】rainbow

彩霞【qoi²ha⁴ 暇】rosy clouds

彩绸【qoi²qeo⁴ 稠】coloured silk

彩带【qoi⁴dai³ 戴】coloured ribbon

彩旗【qoi²kêi⁴ 其】coloured flag；bunting

彩绘【qoi² kui² 剑】coloured drawing or pattern

彩塑【qoi²xog⁸ 索】coloured modelling

彩印【qoi²yen³ 因³】colour printing

彩陶【qoi²tou⁴ 图】ancient painted pottery

彩排【qoi²pai³ 牌】dress rehearsal

彩票【qoi²piu³ 漂³】lottery ticket

睬

【qoi² 采】pay attention to；take notice of

睬佢都傻【qoi³kêü⁵dou¹xo⁴ 拒刀梳⁴】not to both with someone =【普】管他是多余的

菜

【qoi³ 蔡】vegetable；greens；food；dish

菜肴【qoi³ngao⁴ 淆】cooked food

菜蔬【qoi³xo¹ 梳】vegetables；greens；dishes at a meal

菜单【qoi³dan¹ 丹】menu；bill of fare

菜刀【qoi³dou¹ 都】kitchen knife

菜花【qoi³fa¹ 化¹】cauliflower；rape flower

菜心【qoi³xem¹ 深】heart（of a cabbage，etc.）；Chinese vegetable

菜豆【qoi³deo⁶ 斗⁶】kidney bean

菜干【qoi³ gon¹ 竿 】a type of dried vegetable =【普】干白菜

菜瓜【qoi³gua¹ 寡¹】snake melon

菜油【qoi³yeo⁴ 由】rapeseed oil；rape oil

菜摊【qoi³tan¹ 滩】vegetable stall

菜市【qoi³xi⁵ 是⁵】food market

蔡

【qoi³ 菜】a surname

才

【qoi⁴ 财】ability；talent；gift；capable person；people of a certain type；< ad. > show "just now"，"then"， "after that", etc.

才子【qoi⁴ji² 止】gifted scholar

才干【qoi⁴gon³ 杆³】ability; competence

才华【qoi⁴wa⁴ 娃⁴】literary talent

才能【qoi⁴neng⁴ 那莺⁴】ability; talent

才气【qoi⁴hēi³ 戏】literary talent

才识【qoi⁴xig⁷ 色】ability and insight

才思【qoi⁴xi¹ 司】imaginative power; cre-
　　ativeness

才智【qoi⁴ji³ 至】ability and wisdom

才疏学浅【qoi⁴xo¹hog⁹qin² 梳鹤千²】have
　　little talent and less learning

财【qoi⁴ 才】wealth; money

财宝【qoi⁴bou² 保】money and valuables

财产【qoi⁴qan² 铲】property

财富【qoi⁴fu³ 副】wealth; riches

财力【qoi⁴lig⁹ 历】financial resources

财经【qoi⁴ging¹ 京】finance and economics

财团【qoi⁴tūn⁴ 梯元⁴】financial group

财神【qoi⁴xen⁴ 臣】the God of Wealth

财务【qoi⁴mou⁶ 冒】financial affairs

财物【qoi⁴med⁹ 勿】property; belongings

财源【qoi⁴yūn⁴ 元】financial resources

财政【qoi⁴jing³ 正】(public) finance

财主佬【qoi⁴jū²lou² 煮鲁²】rich man;
　　moneybags ＝【普】财主

裁【qoi⁴ 才】cut (paper, cloth, etc.) in-
　　to parts; reduce; cut down; judge;
　　check; mental planning

裁缝【qoi⁴fung⁴ 逢】tailor; dressmaker

裁剪【qoi⁴jin² 展】cut out

裁定【qoi⁴ding⁶ 锭】ruling

裁决【qoi⁴kūd⁹ 缺】ruling; adjudication

裁判【qoi⁴qun³ 潘³】judgment; referee

裁减【qoi⁴gam² 监²】reduce; cut down

裁员【qoi⁴yūn⁴ 元】reduce the staff

操【qou¹ 粗】grasp; hold; act; do;
　　speak; drill; exercise; conduct

操持【qou¹qi⁴ 池】manage; handle

操劳【qou¹lou⁴ 卢】work hard; take care

操练【qou¹lin⁶ 炼】drill; practice

操守【qou¹xeo² 手】personal integrity

操心【qou¹xem¹ 深】worry about; trouble
　　about; rack one's brains

操行【qou¹heng⁶ 杏】behaviour or conduct
　　of a student

操纵【qou¹jung³ 种³】operate; control;
　　rig; manipulate

操作【qou¹jog⁸ 昨】operate; manipulate

粗【qou¹ 操】wide; thick; coarse; crude;
　　gruff; careless; rude; roughly;
　　slightly

粗暴【qou¹bou⁶ 部】rude; rough; crude

粗糙【qou¹qou³ 燥】coarse; rough; crude

粗大【qou¹dai⁶ 歹⁶】thick; bulky; loud

粗放【qou¹fong³ 况】extensive

粗犷【qou¹guong² 广】rough; rude;
　　rugged

粗话【qou¹wa⁶ 画⁶】vulgar language

粗鲁【qou¹lou⁵ 老】rough; rude; boorish

粗略【qou¹lêg⁹ 掠】rough; sketchy

粗浅【qou¹qin² 钱²】superficial; simple

粗人【qou¹yen⁴ 仁】rough fellow; boor

粗疏【qou¹xo¹ 梳】careless; inattentive

粗口【qou¹ heo² 厚²】say words that are
　　nasty, unpleasant and rude ＝
　　【普】说话粗俗；粗言烂语

粗俗【qou¹jug⁹ 族】vulgar; coarse

粗细【qou¹xei³ 世】(degree of) thickness

粗心【qou¹xem¹ 深】careless; thoughtless

粗野【qou¹yē⁵ 惹】rough; boorish

粗重【qou¹ qung⁵ 冲⁵】loud and jarring;

big and heavy；thick and heavy；
strenuous

粗壮【qou¹jong³ 装³】sturdy；thick and
strong

粗枝大叶【qou¹ji¹dai⁶yib⁹ 支歹⁶ 业】slop-
py；slapdash

粗制滥造【qou¹jei³lam⁶jou⁶ 济缆做】man-
ufacture in a rough and slipshod
way

草【qou² 操²】grass；straw；careless；
draft

草丛【qou² qung⁴ 虫 】a thick growth of
grass

草地【qou²dēi⁶ 得希⁶】grassland；lawn

草披【qou²pēi¹ 皮¹】lawn =【普】草坪

草原【qou²yūn⁴ 元】grasslands；prairie

草棚【qou²pang⁴ 鹏】thatched shack

草鞋【qou²hai⁴ 孩】straw sandals

草席【qou²jēg⁹ 支吃⁹】straw mat

草帽【qou²mou² 模²】straw hat

草纸【qou²ji² 止】rough straw paper；arti-
ficial paper

草药【qou²yêg⁹ 若】medicinal herbs

草鱼【qou²yü⁴ 余】grass carp

草蜢【qou²mang⁵ 孟²】grasshopper

草菇【qou²gu¹ 姑】straw mushroom

草莓【qou²mui⁴ 梅】strawberry

草芥【qou²gai³ 介】trifle；mere nothing

草寇【qou²keo³ 扣】robbers in the green-
wood；bandits

草莽【qou² mong⁵ 网 】a rank growth of
grass；wilderness

草创【qou²qong³ 苍³】start

草案【qou²ngon³ 按】draft

草包【qou²bao¹ 苞】straw bag；idiot；
blockhead

草草【qou²qou²】carelessly；hastily

草稿【qou²gou² 高²】rough draft；draft

草拟【qou²yi⁴ 移】draw up；draft

草签【qou²qim¹ 潜¹】initial

草书【qou²xü¹ 输】cursive hand

草率【qou²xêd⁷ 恤】careless；rash

草图【qou²tou⁴ 途】sketch（map）；draft

草菅人命【qou²gan¹yen⁴mēng⁶ 奸仁莫
镜⁶】treat human life as if it were
not worth a straw

草木皆兵【qou²mug⁹gai¹bing¹ 目佳冰】
every bush and tree looks like an
enemy — a state of extreme ner-
vousness

糙【qou³ 曹³】rough；coarse

糙米【qou³mei⁵ 迷⁵】brown rice；unpol-
ished rice

燥【qou³ 糙】dry

燥热【qou³yid⁹ 衣泄⁹】hot and dry

躁【qou³ 燥】rash；impetuous；restless
（see "急躁"，"暴躁"）

噪【qou³ 燥】（of birds，insects，etc.）
chirp；a confusion of voices

噪音【qou³yem¹ 阴】noise

厝【qou³ 措】lay；place；place a coffin in
a temporary shelter，pending burial

措【qou³ 燥】arrange；handle；make
plans

措辞【qou³qi⁴ 池】wording；diction

措施【qou³xi¹ 司】measure；step

措手不及【qou³xeo²bed⁷keb⁹ 守毕级⁹】be
caught unprepared

醋【qou³ 措】vinegar；jealousy（as in love
affair）

呷醋【hab⁸qou³ 黑鸭⁸】feel jealous =【普】吃醋

醋意【qou³yi³ 薏】(feeling of) jealous

醋精【qou³jing¹ 贞】vinegar concentrate

醋酸【qou³xün¹ 孙】acetic acid

槽【qou⁴ 曹】trough; groove; slot

马槽【ma⁵qou⁴ 码】manger

水槽【xêü²qou⁴ 瑞²】water trough

槽钢【qou⁴gong³ 刚³】channel (iron)

曹【qou⁴ 槽】people of the same kind; a surname

尔曹【yi⁵qou⁴ 耳】all of you; you = 你们【nêi⁵mun⁴】

嘈【qou⁴ 曹】noise; din

嘈杂【qou⁴jab⁹ 习】noisy

嘈生晒【qou⁴xang¹xai³ 是嚣徙³】noisy; making too much noises; clamour ∽【普】吵嚷

嘈喧巴闭【qou⁴hün¹ba¹bei³ 劝¹ 爸蔽】noisy; wrangle; bustle; racket; clamour ∽【普】吵闹；喧闹；喧嚣

揩【qou⁵ 曹⁵】save money; save bit by bit; gather; build up; accumulate

揩埋【qou⁵mai⁴ 买⁴】save bit by bit; gather; build up; accumulate =【普】积攒；积聚；积蓄

揩钱【qou⁵qin² 浅】save money =【普】积攒钱财

仓【qong¹ 苍】storehouse; warehouse

仓储【qong¹qü⁵忙】keep grain, goods, etc. in a storehouse

仓库【qong¹fu¹ 富】warehouse; storehouse

仓租【qong¹ jou¹ 糟】warehouse storage charges

仓促【qong¹qug¹ 速】hurriedly; hastily

仓皇【qong¹wong⁴ 王】in a flurry; in panic

苍【qong¹ 仓】dark green; blue; grey; ashy

苍白【qong¹bag⁹ 伯⁹】pale; pallid; wan

苍苍【qong¹qong¹】grey; vast and hazy

苍翠【qong¹qêü³ 脆】dark green; verdant

苍黄【qong¹wong⁴ 王】greenish yellow; in panic

苍劲【qong¹ging³ 径】old and strong; bold

苍老【qong¹lou⁵ 鲁】old; aged; vigorous; forceful

苍凉【qong¹lêng⁴ 梁】desolate; bleak

苍茫【qong¹ mong⁴ 亡】vast; boundless; in-distinct

苍穹【qong¹kung⁴ 穷】the firmament

苍天【qong¹tin¹ 田】the blue sky; Heaven

苍蝇【qong¹ ying⁴ 营】fly = 乌蝇【wu¹ying¹英】

沧【qong¹ 仓】(of the sea) dark blue

沧海【qong¹hoi² 凯】the blue sea; the sea

沧海一粟【qong¹hoi²yed⁷xug⁷ 凯壹宿】a drop in the ocean

沧桑【qong¹ xong¹ 丧¹】seas change into mulberry fields and mulberry fields into seas — time brings great changes to the world = 沧海桑田【qong¹hoi²xong¹tin⁴ 凯丧¹天⁴】

舱【qong¹ 仓】cabin; module

舱室【qong¹xed⁷ 失】cabin

客舱【hag⁸qong¹ 赫】(passenger) cabin

疮【qong¹ 仓】sore; skin ulcer; wound

疮口【qong¹ heo² 候²】the open part of a sore

疮疤【qong¹ba¹ 巴】scar

疮痍满目【qong¹yi⁴mun⁵mug⁹ 而螨木】everywhere a scene of devastation meets the eyes

闯【qong² 厂】rush; dash; charge; temper oneself

闯劲【qong²ging³ 径】the spirit of a pathbreaker; pioneering spirit

闯将【qong²jêng³ 酱】daring general; pathbreaker

闯祸【qong²wo⁶ 涡⁶】get into trouble

闯江湖【qong²gong¹wu⁶ 岗胡】make a living wandering from place to place

厂【qong² 闯】factory; mill; plant; works; yard; depot

厂房【qong² fong⁴防 】factory building; workshop

厂矿【qong²kong³ 邝】factories and mines

厂商【qong²xêng¹ 双】firm

厂长【qong²jêng² 蒋】factory director

厂址【qong²ji² 止】the site of a factory

敞【qong² 厂】spacious; open; uncovered

敞开【qong²hoi¹ 海¹】open wide

宽敞【fun¹qong² 欢】spacious; roomy

敞亮【qong²lêng⁶ 量⁶】light and spacious; clear

敞篷车【qong²pung⁴qê¹ 捧⁴奢】open car

创【qong³ 仓³】wound; start (doing sth.); achieve (sth. for the first time)

创伤【qong³xêng¹ 双】wound; trauma

创办【qong³ban⁶ 班⁶】establish; set up

创建【qong³gin³ 见】found; establish

创举【qong³gêu² 矩】pioneering work

创立【qong³leb⁹ 笠⁹】found; originate

创始【qong³qi² 耻】originate; initiate

创新【qong³xen¹ 辛】bring forth new ideas

创业【qong³yib⁹ 叶】start an undertaking

创造【qong² jou⁶ 做】create; produce; bring about

创制【qong³jei³ 济】formulate; institute

创作【qong³jog⁹ 昨】create; produce; write; creative work; creation

怆【qong³ 创】sorrowful

怆然泪下【qong³yin⁴lêi⁶ha⁶ 言类夏】burst into sorrowful tears

藏【qong⁴ 床; jong⁶ 撞】(see "jong⁶")

床【qong⁴ 仓⁴】bed; sth. shaped like a bed

床铺【qong⁴pou¹ 普¹】bed

床架【qong⁴ga³ 价】bedstead

床单【qong⁴dan¹ 丹】sheet

床垫【qong⁴din³ 电³】mattress

床头柜【qong⁴ teo⁴ guei⁶ 投骥】bedside cupboard

戳【qog⁸ 次恶⁸; qê⁸ 卓】jab; poke; stab; sprain; blunt; stamp; seal

戳穿【qog⁸ qün¹ 川】puncture; lay bare; expose

戳记【qog⁸gêi³ 寄】stamp; seal

揯【qog⁸ 戳】pull with force =【普】(突然)用力猛拉

揯甩【qog⁸led⁷ 罗乞⁷】pull to drop =【普】拉脱

冲【qung¹ 充】pour boiling water on; thoroughfare; develop; punching

冲动【qung¹dung⁶ 洞】impulse; get excited

冲锋【qung¹fung¹ 风】charge；assault

冲击【qung¹gig⁷ 激】lash；pound；charge

冲破【qung¹po³ 颇³】break through；
breach

冲散【qung¹xan³ 汕】break up；scatter

冲杀【qung¹xad⁸ 煞】charge；rush ahead

冲刺【qung¹qi³ 次】spurt；sprint

冲突【qung¹ded⁹ 凸】conflict；clash

冲撞【qung¹jong⁶ 状】collide；bump；give
offence；ram；offend

冲洗【qung¹xei² 驶】rinse；wash；develop

冲淡【qung¹tam⁵ 谭⁵】dilute；water down；
weaken

冲积【qung¹jig⁷ 织】alluvia

冲垮【qung¹kua¹ 夸】burst；shatter

冲力【qung¹lig⁹ 历】impulsive force；mo-
mentum

冲晒【qung¹xai³ 徙³】develop and print

冲刷【qung¹qad⁸ 察】erode；scour；wash
out

冲帐【qung¹jêng³ 涨】strike a balance；re-
verse an entry

冲床【qung¹qong⁴ 藏⁴】punch（press）；
punching machine

冲压【qung¹ngad⁸ 押】stampling；punch-
ing

冲昏头脑【qung¹fen¹teo⁴nou⁵ 恼】turn sb.'s
head

冲凉【qung¹lêng⁴ 梁】bath；take a shower
=【普】洗澡

冲锋陷阵【qung¹fung¹ham⁶jen⁶ 风咸⁶振⁶】
charge and shatter enemy posi-
tions；charge forward

充【qung¹ 冲】sufficient；full；fill；serve
as；pose as

充斥【qung¹qig⁷ 戚】flood；congest

充当【qung¹dong¹ 珰】serve as；act as

充电【qung¹din⁶ 甸】charge（a battery）

充分【qung¹fen⁶ 份】full；ample

充公【qung¹gung¹ 工】confiscate

充饥【qung¹gēi¹ 机】allay one's hunger

充军【qung¹guen¹ 君】banish

充满【qung¹mun⁵ 螨 】full of；brimming
with

充沛【qung¹pui³ 配】plentiful；abundant

充塞【qung¹xeg⁷ 是克⁷】fill（up）；cram

充实【qung¹xed⁹ 失⁹】substantial；rich；
substantiate；enrich

充数【qung¹xou³ 素】make up the number

充溢【qung¹yed⁹ 日】full to the brim；ex-
uberant

充裕【qung¹yü⁶ 遇】abundant；ample

充足【qung¹jug⁷竹 】adequate；sufficient；
ample

充其量【qung¹kēi⁴lêng⁶ 亮】at most；at
best

充耳不闻【qung¹yi⁵bed⁷men⁴尔毕文】
turn a deaf ear to

充大头鬼【qung¹dai⁶teo⁴guei²歹⁶投诡】
pretend；pretend to be（sb. or
sth. else）=【普】装假；冒充

憧【qung¹ 充】long for

憧憬【qung¹ging² 景】long for；look forward to

忡【qung¹ 充】<a.> 忡忡【qung¹qung¹】
laden with anxiety；careworn

匆【qung¹ 充】hastily；hurriedly

匆匆【qung¹qung¹】hurriedly

匆促【qung¹qug⁷ 速】hastily；in a hurry =
匆忙【qung¹mong⁴ 亡】

葱【qung¹ 匆】onion；scallion；green

葱白【qung¹bag⁹ 伯⁹】scallion stalk

葱花【qung¹fa¹ 化¹】chopped green onion

葱头【qung¹teo⁴ 投】onion

葱翠【qung¹qêu³ 脆】fresh green

葱绿【qung¹lug⁹ 六】pale yellowish green; light green

葱茏【qung¹lung⁴ 龙】verdant; luxuriantly green

囱【qung¹ 充】< n. > 烟囱【yin¹qung¹】(see "yin¹")

铳【qung¹ 充】blunderbuss

聪【qung¹ 充】faculty of hearing; acute hearing

聪明【qung¹ming⁴名】intelligent; bright; clever

聪慧【qung¹wei³ 尉】bright; intelligent

聪颖【qung¹wing⁶ 泳】intelligent; bright; clever

骢【qung¹ 充】a horse of green and white

宠【qung² 冢】dote on; bestow favour on

宠爱【qung²ngoi³ 哀³】make a pet of sb.; dote on

宠信【qung² xên³ 讯 】be specially fond of and trust unduly (a subordinate)

宠儿【qung²yi⁴ 而】pet; favourite

宠坏【qung²wai⁶ 怀⁶】spoil

冢【qung² 宠】tomb; grave

扰【qung³ 冢³】poke; stab; disclose =【普】捅

扰跌【qung³did⁸ 得热⁸】poke down =【普】捅(某物)使掉下

从【qung⁴ 虫; xung¹ 崇¹】< prep. > from; through; < ad. > ever; fol-low; join; follower; secondary; calm

从…到…【qung⁴…dou³…】from . . . to . . .

从此【qung⁴ qi²始 】from this time on; from now on; henceforth; there-upon

从而【qung⁴ yi⁴移 】< conj. > thus; thereby

从犯【qung⁴ fan²返】accessary criminal; accessary

从简【qung⁴gan² 柬】conform to the prin-ciple of simplicity

从军【qung⁴guen¹ 君】join the army; enlist

从来【qung⁴ loi⁴莱】always; at all times; all along

从略【qung⁴lêg⁹ 掠】be omitted

从前【qung⁴ qin⁴ 钱 】before; formerly; in the past

从事【qung⁴xi⁶ 示】go in for; deal with

从属【qung⁴xug⁹ 熟】subordinate

从速【qung⁴qug⁷ 促】as soon as possible

从头【qung⁴ teo⁴ 投】from the beginning; anew; once again

从小【qung⁴xiu² 少²】from childhood; as a child

从中【qung⁴jung¹ 宗】out of; from among

从容【xung⁴ yung⁴ 熔 】calm; unhurried; plentiful

从长计议【qung⁴qêng⁴gei³yi⁵ 祥继耳】give the matter further thought and discuss it later

丛【qung⁴ 虫】crowd together; clump; grove; crowd; a surname

丛林【qung⁴lem⁴ 淋】jungle; forest

丛生【qung⁴ xeng¹ 笙 】(of plants) grow thickly; break out

丛书【qung⁴xü¹ 输】a series of books; collection

虫【qung⁴ 丛】insect；worm

虫虫【qung⁴qung²】insect；worm ＝【普】
虫儿；虫子

虫灾【qung⁴joi¹ 哉】plague of insects

虫情【qung⁴qing⁴ 程】insect pest situation

虫害【qung⁴hoi⁶ 亥】insect pest

束【qug⁷ 速】bind；tie；bunch；bundle；
control；restrain；a surname

束缚【qug⁷bog⁸ 驳】tie；bind up；tetter

束手【qug⁷xeo² 守】have one's hands tied；
be helpless

束手无策【qug⁷xeo²mou⁴qag⁸ 守毛册】be
at a loss what to do；feel quite
helpless

束之高阁【qug⁷ji¹gou¹gog⁸ 支糕各】lay a-
side and neglect；shelve

速【qug⁷ 束】fast；rapid；quick；speedy；
speed；velocity；invite

速度【qug⁷dou⁶ 道】speed；velocity；rate；
pace；tempo

速成【qug⁷xing⁴ 承 】 speeded-up educational program

速冻【qug⁷dung³ 东³】quick-froozen

速决【qug⁷küd⁸ 缺】quick decision

速记【qug⁷gēi³ 寄】shorthand；stenog-
raphy

速效【qug⁷hao⁶ 考⁶】quick results

促【qug⁷ 束】（of time）short；hurried；
urgent；urge；promote；close to；near

促成【qug⁷xing⁴ 承】help to bring about；
facilitate

促进【qug⁷jên³俊】promote；advance；ac-
celerate

促使【qug⁷xei² 洗】impel；urge；spur

促膝谈心【qug⁷xed⁷tam⁴xem¹ 失谭深】sit

side by side and talk intimately

簇【qug⁷ 束】form a cluster；pile up；
cluster；bunch

簇拥【qug⁷yung² 涌】cluster round

簇新【qug⁷xen¹ 辛】brand new

簌【qug⁷ 束】< onomatopoeia > rustle；
（tears）streaming

蹙【qug⁷ 束】pressed；knit one's brows
（蹙额【qug⁷ngag⁹】）

蹴【qug⁷ 束】kick；tread

一蹴即就【yed⁷qug⁷jig⁷jeo⁶ 促积袖】
reach the goal in one step

蓄【qug⁷ 畜】store up；save up；grow；
entertain（ideas）；harbour

蓄积【qug⁷jig⁷ 织】store up；save up

蓄水【qug⁷xêü² 瑞²】retain water

蓄意【qug⁷ yi³ 蒽】premeditated；delib-
erate

蓄谋【qug⁷meo⁴ 牟】premeditate

蓄电池【qug⁷din⁶qi⁴ 甸迟】strorage bat-
tery；accumulator

搐【qug⁷ 畜】（see "抽搐"【qeo¹qug⁷】）

畜【qug⁷ 束】raise（domestic animals）；
domestic animal；livestock

畜生【qug⁷xang¹ 是罂¹】domestic animal；
beast

畜类【qug⁷lêü⁶ 泪】domestic animals

畜力【qug⁷lig⁹ 历】animal power

畜牧【qug⁷mug⁹ 木】raise livestock or
poultry

畜养【qug⁷yêng⁵ 氧】raise（domestic ani-
mals）

畜产【qug⁷qan² 铲】livestock products

蚩【qi¹ 嗤】ignorant；stupid

蚩

嗤【qi¹ 蚩】sneer

嗤笑【qi¹ xiu³ 少³】laugh at; sneer at

嗤之以鼻【qi¹ ji¹ yi⁵ bēi⁶ 支尔备】give a snort of contempt; despise

哧【qi¹ 蚩】＜ *onomatopoeia*〉哧哧发笑【qi¹ qi¹ fad⁸ xiu³ 法少³】titter

雌【qi¹ 蚩】female（雌性【qi¹ xing³ 姓】）

雌雄【qi¹ hong⁴ 红】male and female; victory and defeat

痴【qi¹ 蚩】silly; idiotic; crazy about; insane; mad

痴呆【qi¹ ngoi⁴ 外⁴】dull-witted; stupid; dementia

痴迷【qi¹ mei⁴ 谜】infatuated; obsessed; crazy

痴情【qi¹ qing⁴ 程】unreasoning passion; infatuation

痴心【qi¹ xem¹ 深】infatuation

痴心妄想【qi¹ xem¹ mong⁵ xêng² 深网赏】wishful thinking; fond dream

疵【qi¹ 痴】flaw; defect; blemish

疵点【qi¹ dim² 店²】flaw; fault; defect

疵毛【qi¹ mou⁴ 无】defective wool

魑【qi¹ 痴；lêi⁴ 离】＜ *n.* ＞ 魑魅魍魉【qi¹ mēi⁴ mong⁵ lêng⁵ 未网俩】evil spirits; demons and monsters

媸【qi¹ 蚩】ugly; unsightly; hideous

眵【qi¹ 蚩】＜ *n.* ＞ 眼眵【ngan⁵ qi¹ 雁⁵】gun（in the eyes）＝ 眼屎【ngan⁵ xi²】

鸱【qi¹ 蚩】＜ *n.* ＞ 鸱鸺【qi¹ yeo¹ 休】owl ＝ 猫头鹰【mao¹ teo⁴ ying¹】

黐【qi¹ 蚩】stick; take advantage of women; disturb; sticky ＝【普】黏

黐埋【qi¹ mai⁴ 买⁴】bind; bond ＝【普】黏着

黐缠【qi¹ qin⁴ 前】twine; bind; loath to part from each other ＝【普】（情人）难舍难分

黐牙【qi¹ nga⁴ 芽】food is trapped in between the teeth ＝【普】食物黏着牙齿

黐线【qi¹ xin³ 腺】something wrong; insane; mad ＝【普】疯了；神经错乱

此【qi² 始】this

此处【qi² qū³ 次于³】this place; here

此等【qi² deng³ 戥】this kind

此辈【qi² bui³ 背】people of this type; such people

此后【qi² heo⁶ 候】after this; hereafter

此间【qi² gan¹ 奸】around here; here

此刻【qi² heg⁷ 克】this moment; now; at persent

此时【qi² xi⁴ 是⁴】this moment; right now

此外【qi² ngoi⁴ 碍】besides; moreover

此路不通【qi² lou⁶ bed⁷ tung¹ 露毕同¹】dead end; blind alley

此起彼伏【qi² hēi² bēi² fug⁹ 喜比服】as one falls, another rises

此一时，彼一时【qi² yed⁷ xi⁴, bēi² yed⁷ xi⁴ 壹是⁴, 比壹是⁴】This is one situation and that was another — time has changed.

此地无银三百两【qi² dēi⁶ mou⁴ ngen⁴ xam¹ bag⁸ lêng²】No 300 taels of silver buried here

始【qi² 此】beginning; start; ＜ *ad.* ＞ only then

始祖【qi²jou² 早】first ancestor；earliest ancestor

始末【qi² mud⁹ 没】beginning and end — the whole story

始终【qi²jung¹ 中】from beginning to end；all along

始终如一【qi²jung¹yü⁴yed⁷ 中鱼壹】constant；consistent；persistent

矢　【qi² 始】arrow；vow；swear

矢量【qi²lêng⁶ 亮】＜ n . ＞ vector

矢口否认【qi²heo²feo²ying⁶ 厚² 浮² 英⁶】flatly deny

矢志不移【qi²ji³bed⁷yi⁴ 至毕而】vow to adhere to one's chosen course

豕　【qi² 始】pig

齿　【qi² 始】tooth；a tooth – like part of anything；age；mention

齿龈【qi²ngen⁴ 银】gums

齿轮【qi²lên⁴ 伦】gear wheel；gear

侈　【qi² 始】wasteful；exaggerate

侈谈【qi²tam⁴ 谭】talk glibly about；prate about

耻　【qi² 始】shame；disgrace；humiliation

耻辱【qi²yug⁹ 玉】shame；disgrace

耻笑【qi² xiu³ 少³】hold sb. to ridicule；sneer at；mock

褫　【qi² 始】strip；deprive

褫职【qi²jig⁷ 积】deprive sb. of his post

褫夺【qi²düd⁹ 得月⁹】strip；deprive

次　【qi³ 刺】order；sequence；second；next；second-rate；inferior；hypo；stopover；＜ classifier . ＞ the unit of the movement

次数【qi³xou³ 素】number of times；frequency

次序【qi³jêü⁶ 叙】order；sequence

次第【qi³dei⁶ 弟】order；one after another

次等【qi³dêng² 邓²】second-class；inferior

次货【qi³fo³ 课】inferior goods

次品【qi³ben² 禀】substandard products

次要【qi³ yiu³ 腰³】less important；secondary

次之【qi³ji³ 支】take second place

刺　【qi³ 次】thorn；splinter；stab；prick；assassinate；irritate；criticize；visiting card

刺刀【qi³dou¹ 都】bayonet

刺杀【qi³xad⁸ 煞】assassinate；bayonet charge

刺激【qi³gig⁷ 击】stimulate；provoke；upset

刺眼【qi³ ngan⁵ 雁】dazzling；offending to the eye

刺耳【qi³ yi⁵尔】grating on the ear；jarring；harsh

刺骨【qi³gued⁷ 掘⁷】piercing to the bones；biting

刺探【qi³tam³ 贪³】pry；spy

刺客【qi³hag⁸ 赫】assassin

刺绣【qi³xeo³ 秀】embroider；embroidery

刺猬【qi³wei⁶ 胃】hedgehog

赐　【qi³ 次】grant；favour；gift

赐予【qi³yü⁵ 与】grant；bestow

赐教【qi³gao³ 较】condescend to teach；grant instruction

厕　【qi³ 次】lavatory；toilet；washroom；W. C.

厕所【qi³xo² 锁】lavatory；toilet；W. C.

雉【qi⁴ 迟】pheasant

雉鸡【qi⁴gei¹ 计¹】untamed chicken

池【qi⁴ 迟】pool; pond; an enclosed space with raised sides; stalls; moat; a surname

池塘【qi⁴tong⁴ 堂】pond; pool

池沼【qi⁴jiu³ 剿】pond; pool

池盐【qi⁴yim⁴ 严】lake salt

弛【qi⁴ 池】relax; slacken

弛缓【qi⁴wun⁴ 垣】relax; calm down

驰【qi⁴ 池】speed; gallop; spread; turn eagerly

驰骋【qi⁴qing² 逞】gallop

驰驱【qi⁴kêü¹ 拘】gallop; do one's utmost in sb.'s service

驰名【qi⁴ming⁴ 明 】known far and wide; famous

迟【qi⁴ 池】slow; tardy; late; a surname

迟慢【qi⁴man⁶ 万】slow; tardy

迟缓【qi⁴wun⁴ 垣】slow; tardy; sluggish

迟钝【qi⁴dên⁶ 顿】slow (in thought or action); obtuse

迟到【qi⁴dou³ 都³】be late; come late

迟迟【qi⁴qi⁴】slow; tardy

持【qi⁴ 池】hold; grasp; support; manage; run; oppose

持枪【qi⁴qêng¹ 昌】hold a gun; port arms

持家【qi⁴ga¹ 加】run one's home; keep house

持论【qi⁴ lên⁶ 伦⁶】present an argument; put a case

持有【qi⁴yeo⁵ 友】hold

持重【qi⁴jung⁶ 仲】prudent; cautious; discreet

匙【qi⁴ 池；xi⁴ 时】spoon; key

匙羹【qi⁴geng¹ 更¹】a spoon

锁匙【xo²xi⁴ 琐】a key ＝【普】钥匙

踟【qi⁴ 池】＜a.＞踟蹰【qi⁴qü⁴ 处⁴】hesitate; waver

瓷【qi⁴ 池】porcelain; china

瓷土【qi⁴tou² 肚²】porcelain clay; china clay

瓷器【qi⁴hêi³ 戏】porcelain; chinaware

瓷碗【qi⁴wun² 腕】china bowl

瓷砖【qi⁴jün¹ 专】ceramic tile; glazed tile

瓷雕【qi⁴diu¹ 刁】porcelain carving

瓷漆【qi⁴qed⁷ 七】enamel paint; enamel

磁【qi⁴ 池】magnetism; porcelain; china

磁场【qi⁴qêng⁴ 祥】magnetic field

磁针【qi⁴jem¹ 斟】magnetic needle

磁性【qi⁴xing³ 姓】magnetism; magnetic

磁铁【qi⁴tid⁸ 替热⁸】magnet

磁体【qi⁴tei² 睇】magnetic body; magnet

磁石【qi⁴xêg⁹ 硕】magnetic; magnet

磁力【qi⁴lig⁹ 历】magnetic force

磁极【qi⁴gig⁹ 击⁹】magnetic pole

磁化【qi⁴fa³ 花³】magnetization

磁带【qi⁴dai³ 戴】magnetic tape

磁盘存储器【qi⁴pun⁴qün⁴qü⁵hêi³ 盆全贮戏】magnetic disc store

糍【qi⁴ 池；qêi² 次希²】＜n.＞糍粑【qi⁴ba¹ 巴】cooked glutinous rice pounded into paste; glutinous rice cake

鹚【qi⁴ 池】＜n.＞鸬鹚【lou⁴qi⁴ 卢池】(see "鸬"【lou⁴】)

慈【qi⁴ 池】kind; loving; mother

慈祥【qi⁴qêng⁴ 场】kindly

慈爱【qi⁴ngoi³ 哀³】love；affection；kindness

慈善【qi⁴xin⁶ 膳】charitable；benevolent

慈悲【qi⁴bēi¹ 碑】mercy；benevolence；pity

慈母【qi⁴mou⁵ 武】loving mother

慈菇【qi⁴gu¹ 沽】water chestnut＝【普】荸荠

祠【qi⁴ 池】ancestral temple

祠堂【qi⁴tong⁴ 塘】ancestral hall；memorial temple

茨【qi⁴ 池】thatch（a roof）；puncture vine

辞【qi⁴ 池】diction；phraseology；take leave；decline；dismiss；shirk；a form of classical poetry

辞别【qi⁴bid⁹ 必⁹】bid farewell；say good-bye

辞行【qi⁴ heng⁴ 衡】say good-bye before setting out on a journey

辞让【qi⁴yêng⁶ 样】politely decline

辞退【qi⁴têu³ 推³】dismiss；discharge

辞职【qi⁴jig⁷ 积】resign

辞谢【qi⁴jē⁶ 榭】decline with thanks

辞令【qi⁴ling⁶ 另】language appropriate to occasion

辞呈【qi⁴qing² 请】（written）resignation

辞章【qi⁴jêng¹ 张】poetry and prose；rhetoric

辞典【qi⁴din² 电²】dictionary

辞藻【qi⁴jou² 早】flowery language；rhetoric

词【qi⁴ 池】word；term；speech；statement

词汇【qi⁴wui⁶ 会⁶】vocabulary；words and phrases

词句【qi⁴gêu³ 据】words and phrases

词类【qi⁴lêu⁶ 泪】parts of speech

词序【qi⁴jêu⁶ 叙】word order

词义【qi⁴yi⁶ 异】the meaning of a word

词语【qi⁴ yü⁵ 雨】words and expressions；terms

词典【qi⁴din² 电²】dictionary

脐【qi⁴ 池】navel；umbilicus（肚脐【tou⁵qi⁴】）

脐带【qi⁴dai³ 戴】umbilical cord

翅【qi³ 次】wing；shark's fin

翅膀【qi³pong⁴ 旁】wing

笞【qi¹ 雌】beat with a stick，cane，etc.

鞭笞【bin¹qi¹ 边】flog；whip

炽【qi³ 次】flaming；ablaze

炽热【qi³yid⁹ 衣泄⁹】red-hot；blazing；passionate

啻【qi³ 翅】only＝只【ji² 止】

恃【qi⁵ 似】rely on；depend on

恃势欺人【qi⁵ xei³ hēi¹ yen⁴世希仁】take advantage of one's or sb. else's power to bully people＝【普】仗势欺人

恃强凌弱【qi⁵kêng⁴ling⁴yêg⁹ 卡香⁴ 陵若】use one's strength to bully the weak

柿【qi⁵ 似】persimmon

柿仔【qi⁵jei² 济²】persimmon＝【普】柿子

柿饼【qi⁵bēng² 柄²】dried persimmon

似【qi⁵ 恃】simiar；like；seem；appear

似乎【qi⁵fu⁴ 符】it seems；as if；seemingly

似是而非【qi⁵xi⁵yi⁴fēi¹ 士移飞】apparently right but actually wrong；specious

似模似样【qi⁵mou⁴qi⁵yêng⁶ 毛让】resemble；look alike＝【普】很像样子

似足【qi⁵jug⁷ 竹】resemble＝【普】全像

似样【qi⁵yêng² 扬²】look alike＝【普】像样

超【qiu¹ 钊】exceed；surpass；overtake；ultra－；super－；extra－；transcend

超过【qiu¹guo³ 戈³】outstrip；surpass；exceed

超出【qiu¹qêd⁷ 次律⁷】overstep；exceed

超越【qiu¹yüd⁹ 月】surmount；overstep；surpass

超脱【qiu¹tüd⁸ 替月⁸】unconventional；original；be detached；stand aloof

超然【qiu¹yin¹ 言】aloof；detached

超前【qiu¹qin⁴ 钱】lead

超群【qiu¹ kuen⁴ 裙】head and shoulders；above all others；preeminent

超级【qiu¹keb⁵ 给】super

超等【qiu¹deng² 邓²】of superior grade；extra fine

超导【qiu¹dou⁶ 道】superconduction

超度【qiu¹dou⁶ 道】release souls from purgatory

超支【qiu¹ji¹ 之】overspend

超载【qiu¹joi³ 再】overload

超重【qiu¹qung⁵ 从⁵】overload；overweight

超产【qiu¹qan² 铲 】overfulfil a production target

超车【qiu¹ qē¹ 奢 】overtake other cars on the road

超速【qiu¹qug⁷ 促】exceed the speed limit；hypervelocity

超人【qiu¹yen⁴ 仁】be out of the common run；superman

超负荷【qiu¹ fu⁶ ho⁴ 付河】excess load；overload

超声波【qiu¹ xing¹ bo¹ 升坡】ultrasonic（wave）

超短波【qiu¹dün²bo¹ 段² 坡】ultrashort wave

刨【qiu¹ 超】encourage；spur；exhort

锹【qiu¹ 超】spade

悄【qiu² 超²】quiet；silent；sad；worried；grieved

悄然【qiu²yin⁴ 言】sorrowfully；sadly；quietly；softly

悄声【qiu²xing¹ 升】quietly；in a low voice＝细细声【xei³xei³xēng¹】

悄悄【qiu²qiu²】quietly；on the quiet＝静静鸡【jing⁶jing²gei¹】＝静鸡鸡【jing⁶gei¹gei¹】

愀【qiu² 悄】＜a.＞愀然【qiu²yin⁴ 言】sorrowful-looking；stern；grave-looking

鞘【qiu³ 俏；sao¹ 梢】sheath；scabbard；shiplash

俏【qiu³ 峭】pretty；smart；handsome；sell well

俏丽【qiu³lei⁶ 厉】handsome；pretty

俏皮【qiu³ pēi⁴ 脾】good-looking；smart；witty

俏皮话【qiu³pēi⁴wa² 脾画²】witty remark；witticism；sarcastic remark

诮【qiu³ 俏】censure；blame（see "讥诮"）

峭【qiu³ 俏】high and steep; precipitous; severe

峭拔【qiu³bed⁹ 跋】high and steep; vigorous

峭壁【qiu³big⁸ 璧】cliff; precipice

谯【qiu⁴ 樵】< n. > 谯楼【qiu⁴leo⁴ 流】watchtower; drum tower

憔【qiu⁴ 樵】< a. > 憔悴【qiu⁴xêu⁶ 睡】wan and sallow; thin and pallid; (of plants) withered

樵【qiu⁴ 潮】gather firewood; firewood

樵夫【qiu⁴fu¹ 肤】woodcutter

瞧【qiu⁴ 潮】look; see

瞧见【qiu⁴gin³ 建】see; catch sight of = 睇见【tei²gin³】

瞧不起【qiu⁴ bed⁷ hēi² 毕喜 】look down upon = 睇唔起【tei²m⁴hēi²】

瞧不上眼【qiu⁴ bed⁷ xêng⁵ ngan⁵ 毕 尚⁵ 雁⁵】consider beneath one's notice = 睇唔上眼【tei²m⁴xêng⁵ngan⁵】

瞧得起【qiu⁴deg⁷hēi² 德喜】think much of sb. = 睇得起【tei²deg⁷hēi²】

潮【qiu⁴ 瞧】tide; (social) upsurge; damp

潮流【qiu⁴leo⁴ 留】tide; tidal; trend

潮水【qiu⁴xêu² 瑞²】tidewater; tidal water

潮汐【qiu⁴jig⁹ 夕】morning and evening tide

潮湿【qiu⁴xeb⁷ 拾⁷】moist; damp

晁【qiu⁴ 潮】a surname

签【qim¹ 次淹¹】sign; make brief comments on a document; bamboo slips used for divination or drawing lots; label; a slender pointed piece of bamboo or wood; tack

抽签【qeo¹qim¹ 秋】draw lots

牙签【nga⁴qim¹ 芽】tooth pick

签名【qim⁴mēng² 莫镜²】sign one's name; autograph

签字【qim⁴ji⁶ 治】sign; affix one's signature

签署【qim⁴xü² 暑】sign

签订【qim⁴ding³ 丁³】conclude and sign

签发【qim⁴fad⁷ 法】sign and issue

签收【qim⁴xeo¹ 修】sign after receiving sth.

签证【qim⁴jing³ 政】visa; vise

谄【qim² 签²】flatter; fawn on

谄媚【qim²mēi⁴ 眉】flatter; fawn on; toady

谄笑【qim²xiu³ 少³】ingratiating smile

谄上欺下【qim²xêng⁶hēi¹ha⁶ 尚 希 夏】fawn on those above and bully those below

纤【qim¹ 签;hin¹ 牵】fine; minute; tow line

纤维【qim¹wei⁴ 围】fibre; staple

纤夫【hin¹fu¹ 肤】boat tracker

暹【qim³ 堑】< n. > 暹罗【qim³lo² 箩²】Thailand

堑【qim³ 暹】moat; chasm

堑壕【qim³hou⁴ 豪】trench; entrenchment

潜【qim⁴ 签⁴】latent; hidden; stealthily; secretly

潜藏【qim⁴qong⁴ 床】hide; go into hiding

潜伏【qim⁴fug⁹ 服】hide; conceal; lie low

潜力【qim⁴lig⁹ 历】latent capacity; potential

潜入【qim⁴yeb⁹ 邑⁹】slip into; sneak into;

dive

潜水【qim⁴xêū² 瑞²】go under water；dive

潜逃【qim⁴tou⁴ 桃】abscond

潜艇【qim⁴tēng⁵ 厅⁵】submarine

潜心【qim⁴xem¹ 深】with greal concentration

潜在【qim⁴joi⁶ 再⁶】latent；potential

潜意识【qim⁴yi³xig⁷ 薏式】the subconscious

潜移默化【qim⁴yi⁴meg⁹fa³ 而墨花³】imperceptibly influence

撏【qim⁴ 潜】pull out；pull up ＝【普】（用两只手指）拔出

撏毛【qim⁴mou⁴ 无】pull up the hair ∽【普】拔毛

千【qin¹ 仟】thousand；a great amount of

千克【qin¹heg⁷ 黑】kilogram（kg.）

千米【qin¹mei¹ 米¹】kilometer（km.）

千瓦【qin¹nga⁵ 雅】kilowatt（kw）

千伏【qin¹fug⁹ 服】kilovolt（kv.）

千周【qin¹jeo¹ 邹】kilocycle（kc）

千斤【qin¹gen¹ 根】very heavy；weighty

千里【qin¹lēi⁵ 李】a long distance

千秋【qin¹qeo¹ 抽】a thousand years；centuries

千万【qin¹man⁶ 慢】ten million；millions upon millions

千祈【qin¹kēi⁴ 奇】must ＝【普】必须；一定要

千斤顶【qin¹gen¹ding² 根鼎】hoisting jack；jack

千里马【qin¹lēi⁵ma⁵ 李码】a winged steed

千变万化【qin¹bin³man⁶fa³ 边³慢花³】ever changing

千差万别【qin¹qa¹man⁶bid⁹ 叉慢必⁹】differ in thousands of ways

千锤百炼【qin¹qêū⁴bag⁸lin⁶ 除伯练】thoroughly tempered；be highly finished

千方百计【qin¹fong¹bag⁸gei³ 芳伯继】in a thousand and one ways

千钧一发【qin¹ guen¹ yed⁷ fad⁸君壹法】a hundredweight hanging by a hair — in imminent peril

千头万绪【qin¹ teo⁴ man⁶ xêū⁵投慢穗⁵】a multitude of things

千辛万苦【qin¹ xen¹ man⁶ fu²新慢府】untold hardships

迁【qin¹ 千】move；change

迁移【qin¹yi 而】move；remove

迁就【qin¹ jeo⁶ 袖】accommodate oneself to；yield to

仟【qin¹ 千】thousand（used for the numeral 千 on cheques，etc.，to avoid mistakes or alterations）

阡【qin¹ 千】＜n.＞阡陌【qin¹meg⁹ 默】crisscross footpaths between fields

扦【qin¹ 千】a short slender pointed piece of metal，bamboo，etc.

扦队【qin¹dêū² 对²】sb. stick into formation ＝【普】（某人）插进正在等候的队列

扦插【qin¹qab⁸ 锸】cuttage

钎【qin¹ 千】drill rod；drill steel；borer

浅【qin² 钱²】shallow；simple；easy；superficial；not intimate；（of colour）light；not long in time

浅海【qin²hoi² 开²】shallow sea

浅滩【qin²tan¹ 摊】shoal；shallows

浅薄【qin²bog⁹ 泊】shallow；meagre

浅近【qin²gen⁶ 靳】simple；plain

浅陋【qin²leo⁶ 漏】meagre; mean

浅显【qin²hin² 蚬】plain

浅色【qin²xig⁷ 式】light colour

浅见【qin²gin³ 建】superficial view

浅尝辄止【qin²xêng⁴jib⁸ji² 常 接子】be satisfied with a smattering of a subject

钱【qin⁴ 前; qin² 浅】copper coin; cash; money; fund; sum; a unit of weight (= 5 grams); a surname

钱罂【qin⁴ang¹】a saving box = 【普】钱罐子; 钱盒子

钱币【qin⁴bei⁶ 敝】coin

钱包【qin⁴bao¹ 苞】wallet; purse

钱财【qin⁴qoi⁴ 才】wealth; money

前【qin⁴ 缠】front; forward; ago; before; preceding; former; formerly; first

前边【qin⁴bin¹ 鞭】in front; ahead; above

前方【qin⁴gong¹ 芳】ahead; the front

前后【qin⁴heo⁶ 候】around (a certain time); about; from beginning to end; altogether; in front and behind

前进【qin⁴jên³ 俊】advance; go forward

前景【qin⁴ging² 境】foreground; prospect; vista

前列【qin⁴ lid⁹ 裂】front row; forefront; van

前例【qin⁴lei⁶ 丽】precedent

前门【qin⁴mun⁴ 们】front door

前面【qin⁴min⁶ 缅⁶】in front; ahead; above

前排【qin⁴pai² 碑²】earlier; at the previous time = 【普】前些日子

前年【qin⁴nin⁴ 捻⁴】the year before last

前期【qin⁴kêi⁴ 其】earlier stage; early days

前人【qin⁴yen⁴ 仁】forefathers; predecessors

前日【qin⁴yed⁹ 逸】the day before yesterday = 【普】前天

前导【qin⁴dou⁴ 道】precede; guide

前哨【qin⁴xao³ 捎³】outpost; advance guard

前身【qin⁴xen¹ 辛】predecessor

前世【qin⁴xei³ 势】previous existence = 【普】前生

前台【qin⁴toi⁴ 抬】proscenium; (on) the stage

前提【qin⁴tei⁴ 题】premise; prerequisite

前途【qin⁴tou⁴ 图】future; prospect = 前程【qin⁴qing⁴】

前往【qin⁴ wong⁵ 枉⁵】go to; leave for; proceed to

前夕【qin⁴jig⁹ 直】eve = 前夜【qin⁴yē⁶】

前线【qin⁴xin³ 扇】front; frontline

前兆【qin⁴xiu⁶ 绍】omen; forewarning

前者【qin⁴jē² 姐】former

前奏【qin⁴jeo³ 咒】prelude

前车之鉴【qin⁴qē¹ji¹gam³ 奢支监³】warning taken from the overturned cart ahead

前赴后继【qin⁴ fu⁶ heo⁶ gei³ 付候计】advance wave upon wave

前功尽弃【qin⁴gung¹jên⁶hēi³ 工俊⁶ 气】all that has been achieved is spoiled

前仆后继【qin⁴ fu⁶ heo⁶ gei³ 付候计】no sooner has one fallen than another steps into the breach

前所未有【qin⁴xo²mēi⁶yeo⁵ 锁味友】hitherto unknown

前因后果【qin⁴ yen¹ heo⁶ guo² 恩候戈²】cause and effect

缠【qin⁴ 前; jin⁶ 贱】twine; wind; tangle; tie up

缠绕【qin⁴yiu⁵ 扰】twine; bind; wind; worry

缠绵悱侧【qin⁴min⁴fêi²qeg⁷ 棉匪次克⁷】(of writing) exceedingly sentimental

缠脚【jin⁶gêg⁸ 格约⁸】foot-binding

践【qin⁵ 浅; jin⁶ 贱】trample; tread; act on

践踏【qin⁵dab⁹ 答⁹】tread on; trample underfoot

践约【qin⁵yêg⁸ 跃】keep a promise

青【qing¹ 清; qêng¹ 次镜¹】blue or green; black; green grass; young crops

青草【qing¹qou² 操²】green grass

青菜【qêng¹qoi³ 蔡】green vegetables; greens

青春【qing¹qên¹ 椿】youth; youthfulness

青葱【qing¹qung¹ 匆】verdant; fresh green

青翠【qing¹qêü³ 脆】verdant; fresh and green

青豆【qêng¹deo² 斗²】green soya bean

青海【qing¹hoi² 凯】< n. > Qinghai(Province)

青筋【qêng¹gen¹ 斤】blue veins

青睐【qing¹loi⁶ 来⁶】favour; good graces

青绿【qêng¹lug⁹ 六】dark green

青梅【qing¹mui⁴ 莓】green plum

青苗【qing¹miu⁴ 描】young crops; green shoots of grains

青年【qing¹nin⁴ 捻⁴】youth; young people

青山【qing¹xan¹ 珊】green hill

青史【qing¹xi² 屎】annals of history

青丝【qing¹xi¹ 司】black hair

青松【qing¹qung⁴ 虫】pine

青苔【qing¹toi⁴ 抬】moss

青天【qing¹tin¹ 田¹】blue sky; a just judge

青蛙【qing¹wa¹ 娃】frog

青鱼【qing¹yü⁴ 渔】black carp

青云【qing¹wen⁴ 耘】high official position

青黄不接【qing¹ wong⁴ bed⁷ jib⁸王毕支叶⁸】When the new crop is still in the blade and the old one is all consumed — temporary shortage.

青出于蓝【qing¹qêd⁹yü¹lam⁴ 次律⁷迁篮】Indigo blue is extracted from the indigo plant — the pupil surpasses the master.

清【qing¹ 青】unmixed; clear; distinct; clarified; quiet; completely; settle; count; the Qing Dynasty (1644 – 1911)

清楚【qing¹qo² 础】clear; distinct; be clear about

清澈【qing¹qid⁸ 设】limpid; clear

清洁【qing¹gid⁸ 结】clean

清白【qing¹ bag⁹ 伯⁹】pure; clean; stainless

清凉【qing¹lêng⁴ 梁】cool and refreshing

清爽【qing¹xong² 桑²】fresh and cool

清淡【qing¹ dam⁶ 担⁶】light; weak; dull; slack

清晰【qing¹xig⁷ 析】distinct; clear

清新【qing¹xen¹ 辛】pure and fresh; fresh

清幽【qing¹yeo¹ 优】quiet and beautiful

清静【qing¹jing⁶ 净】quiet

清风【qing¹fung¹ 丰】cool breeze

清茶【qing¹ qa⁴查】green tea; tea served without refreshments

清香【qing¹ hêng¹ 乡】delicate fragrance; faint scent

清汤【qing¹tong¹ 剉】clear soup; light soup

清贫【qing¹ pen⁴ 频】be poor

清廉【qing¹ lim⁴ 帘】honest and upright

清高【qing¹ gou¹ 膏】aloof from politics and material pursuits

清官【qing¹ gun¹ 观】honest and upright official

清理【qing¹ lēi⁵ 李】put in order; check up; clear

清查【qing¹ qa⁴ 茶】check; uncover; comb .out

清点【qing¹ dim² 店²】check; make an inventory

清算【qing¹ xūn³ 蒜】clear (accounts); settle accounts

清帐【qing¹ jêng³ 涨】square an account

清单【qing¹ dan¹ 丹】detailed list; detailed account

清除【qing¹ qêu⁴ 徐】clear away; eliminate

清洗【qing¹ xei² 驶】rinse; wash; clean; purge

清醒【qing¹ xing² 星²】clear-headed; sober; regain consciousness

清早【qing¹ jou² 枣】early morning = 清晨【xen⁴】

清脆【qing¹ qêu³ 翠】clear and melodious

清秀【qing¹ xeo³ 瘦】delicate and pretty

清明【qing¹ ming⁴ 名】Pure Brightness (5th solar term); clear and bright

清一色【qing¹ yed⁷ xig⁷ 壹式】flush; uniform

清景【qing¹ ging² 境】elegant; beautiful = 【普】清幽；清秀

清补凉【qing¹ bou² lêng⁴ 保梁】a type of Chinese dessert with different types of herbs

清规戒律【qing¹ kuei¹ gai³ lêd⁹ 亏介栗⁹】regulations, taboos and commandments for Buddhists or Taoists; restrictions and fetters

蜻【qing¹ 清】dragonfly (蜻蜓【qing¹ ting⁴ 亭】)

蜻蜓点水【qing¹ ting⁴ dim² xêu² 亭店² 瑞²】like a dragonfly skimming the surface of the water — touch on sth. without going into it deeply

氰【qing¹ 清】cyanogen; dicyanogen

氰化物【qing¹ fa³ med⁹ 花³ 勿】cyanide

称【qing¹ 清；qing³ 秤】call; name; say; state; commend; weigh; fit; match

称号【qing¹ hou⁶ 好⁶】title; name

称呼【qing¹ fu¹ 夫】call; address; form of address

称谓【qing¹ wei⁶ 卫】appellation; title

称快【qing¹ fai³ 块】express one's gratification

称颂【qing¹ jung⁶ 仲】praise; extol; eulogize

称赞【qing¹ jan³ 撰】praise; acclaim; commend

称心【qing³ xem¹ 深】find sth. satisfactory; be gratified

称职【qing³ jig⁷ 积】be competent

秤【qing³ 称³】balance; steelyard; hold

秤杆【qing³ gon¹ 竿】the arm of a steelyard

秤钩【qing³ ngeo¹ 欧】steelyard hook

秤砣【qing³ to⁴ 陀】the sliding weight of a steelyard

逞【qing² 请】show off; flaunt; indulge

逞能【qing² neng⁴ 那亨⁴】show off one's skill or ability; parade one's ability

逞强【qing² kêng⁴ 卡香⁴】flaunt one's superiority

逞凶【qing²hung¹ 空】act violently

拯【qing² 请】save; rescue; deliver

拯救【qing²geo³ 够】save; rescue; deliver

骋【qing² 请; ping³ 聘】gallop; give free rein to (see "驰骋"【qi⁴qing²】)

请【qing² 逞; qēng² 次镜²】request; ask; invite; please

请求【qing²keo⁴ 球】ask; request

请问【qing²men⁶ 蚊⁶】excuse me; please; It may be asked; One may ask

请示【qing²xi⁶ 是】ask for instructions

请教【qing²gao³ 较】ask for advice; consult

请安【qing²ngon¹ 胺】pay respects to sb.

请便【qing²bin⁶ 辨】please yourself

请假【qing²ga³ 价】ask for leave

请客【qing²hag⁸ 赫】stand treat

请帖【qing²tib⁸ 贴】invitation card = 请柬【qing²gan²】

请命【qing²ming⁶ 名⁶】plead on sb.'s behalf

请愿【qing² yün⁶县⁶】present a petition; petition

请战【qing²jin³ 箭】ask for a battle assignment

请罪【qing²jêü⁶ 聚】apologize

情【qing⁴ 程】feeling; affection; sentiment; love; passion; favour; situation; stances; condition

情感【qing⁴gem² 敢】emotion; feeling

情怀【qing⁴wai⁴ 槐】feelings

情意【qing⁴yi³ 薏】tender regards; goodwill

情义【qing⁴yi⁶ 异】ties of friendship, comradeship, etc.

情谊【qing⁴yi⁴ 宜】friendly feelings

情欲【qing⁴yug⁹ 玉】sexual passion; lust

情况【qing⁴fong³ 放】situation; condition; military situation ·

情景【qing⁴ging³ 境】scene; sight

情境【qing⁴ging² 景】circumstances; situation

情形【qing⁴ying⁴ 型】circumstances; situation

情绪【qing⁴ xêü⁵ 穗⁵】morale; feeling; mood

情态【qing⁴tai³ 太】spirit; mood

情愿【qing⁴yün⁶ 县⁶】be willing to; would rather

情理【qing⁴lêi⁵ 李】reason; sense

情趣【qing⁴qêü⁴ 翠】temperament and interest; interest; appeal

情面【qing⁴min⁶ 缅⁶】feelings; sensibilities

情报【qing⁴bou³ 布】intelligence; information

情操【qing⁴qou¹ 躁¹】sentiment

情调【qing⁴diu⁶ 掉】sentiment; emotional appeal

情敌【qing⁴dig⁹ 迪】rival in love

情分【qing⁴fen⁶ 份】mutual affection

情人【qing⁴yen⁴ 仁】sweetheart

情侣【qing⁴lêü⁵ 旅】sweethearts; lovers

情夫【qing⁴fu¹ 肤】lover

情妇【qing⁴fu³ 府⁵】mistress

情节【qing⁴jid⁸ 折】plot; circumstances

情由【qing⁴yeo⁴ 油】the hows and whys

情有可原【qing⁴yeo⁵ho²yün⁴ 友贺² 源】excusable

情投意合【qing⁴teo⁴yi³heb⁹ 头薏盒】find each other congenial; hit it off perfectly

情不自禁【qing⁴bed⁷ji⁶gem³ 毕治咁】can-

not refrain from; cannot help (doing sth.)

程【qing⁴ 情】rule; regulation; order;
journey; distance; a surname

程数【qing⁴ xou³ 扫】possibility; percentage ∽【普】可能性;百分比

程度【qing⁴dou⁶ 道】level; degree; extent

程式【qing⁴ xig⁷色 】form; pattern; formula

程序【qing⁴ jêü⁶ 叙 】 order; procedure;
programme

惩【qing⁴ 情】punish; penalize

惩办【qing⁴ban⁶ 版⁶】punish

惩处【qing⁴qü² 次于²】penalize; punish

惩罚【qing⁴fed⁹ 佛】punish; penalize

惩治【qing⁴ji⁶ 自】punish; mete out pun-
ishmet to

惩戒【qing⁴gai³ 介】punish sb. to teach
him a lesson

惩一儆百【qing⁴yed⁷ging²bag⁸ 壹警伯】
punish one to warn a hundred

罌【qing⁴ 呈】earthen jar =【普】坛子

一罌醋【yed⁷qing⁴qou³ 壹燥】a jar of
vinegar

澄【qing⁴ 情;king⁴ 琼】clear; transparent

澄清【qing⁴ qing¹ 青】clear; transparent;
clear up; clarity

澄清【king⁴qing¹ 青】(of a liquid) settle;
become clear

晴【qing⁴ 情】fine; clear

晴空【qing⁴hung¹ 凶】clear sky; cloudless
sky

晴朗【qing⁴long⁵ 琅⁵】fine; sunny

晴天【qing⁴tin¹ 田¹】fine day; sunny day

晴天霹雳【qing⁴tin¹pig⁷lig⁷ 田¹ 辟砾】a
bolt from the blue

呈【qing⁴ 情】assume; submit; present;
petition

呈现【qing⁴ yin⁶燕⁶】 present; appear; e-
merge

呈报【qing⁴bou³ 布】submit a report; report a matter

呈递【qing⁴dei⁶ 弟】present; submit

妾【qib⁸ 次叶⁸】concubine

妾侍【qib⁸xi⁵ 氏】concubine =【普】小老
婆

切【qid⁸ 设;qei³ 砌】cut; slice; tangent;
correspond to; eager; be sure to

切除【qid⁸qêü⁴ 徐】excision; resection

切断【qid⁸tün⁵ 团⁵】cut off

切开【qid⁸hoi¹ 海¹】incision

切片【qid⁸pin⁵ 骗】cut into slices; section

切削【qid⁸xêg⁸ 是约⁸】cutting

切齿【qid⁸qi² 始】gnash one's teeth

切合【qid⁸heb⁹ 盒】suit; fit in with

切记【qid⁸gêi³ 寄】must always remember

切近【qid⁸gen⁶ 靳】close to

切忌【qid⁸gêi³ 技】must guard against

切脉【qid⁸meg⁹ 麦】feel the pulse

切切【qid⁸qid⁸】be sure to

切菜【qid⁸qoi³ 蔡】dry sliced carrots

切身【qid⁸xen¹ 辛】of immediate concern
to oneself personal

切醋【qid⁸qou³ 措】a type of vinegar red in
colour

切实【qid⁸ xed⁹失⁹】 feasible; practical;
earnestly

切题【qid⁸tei⁴ 提】keep to the point

切中【qid⁸jung³ 种³】hit (the mark)

一切【qid⁸ qei³ 壹砌 】all; every; everything

设【qid⁸ 撤】set up; found; work out; given; if

设备【qid⁸ bēi⁶ 鼻】equipment; installation; facilities

设法【qid⁸fad⁸ 发】think of a way; try

设计【qid⁸gei³ 继】design; plan

设立【qid⁸leb⁹ 笠⁹】establish; set up; found

设若【qid⁸yêg⁹ 药】if; suppose; provided

设施【qid⁸xi¹ 司】installation; facilities

设想【qid⁸ xêng² 赏】imagine; envisage; tentative plan; tentative

设宴【qid⁸yin³ 燕】give a banquet; fete

设置【qid⁸ji² 至】set up; put up

撤【qid⁸ 设】remove; take away; withdraw; evacuate

撤除【qid⁸qêū⁴ 徐】remove; dismantle

撤换【qid⁸wun⁶ 焕】dismiss and replace; recall; replace

撤回【qid⁸wui⁴ 汇⁴】recall; revoke

撤离【qid⁸lêi⁴ 漓】withdraw from; leave

撤退【qid⁸têū³ 推³】withdraw; pull out

撤销【qid⁸xiu¹ 消】cancel; rescind

撤职【qid⁸jig⁷ 积】dismiss sb. from his post

撤走【qid⁸jeo² 酒】withdraw

彻【qid⁸ 设】thorough; penetrating

彻底【qid⁸dei² 抵】thorough; thoroughgoing

彻头彻尾【qid⁸ teo⁴ qid⁸ mēi⁵投美 】out and out; through and through; downright

彻夜【qid⁸yê⁶ 野⁶】all night; all through the night

彻骨【qid⁸gued⁷ 掘⁷】to the bone

澈【qid⁸ 设】(of water) clear; limpid (see "清沏")

掣【qid⁸ 设;jei³ 制】pull; tug; draw (see "风驰电掣"【fung¹qi⁴din⁶qid⁸】)

斥【qig⁷ 叱】upbraid; scold; repel; exclude; oust; open up; expand; scout

斥力【qig⁷lig⁹ 历】< n. > repulsion

斥骂【qig⁷ma⁶ 马⁶】reproach; upbraid; scold

斥退【qig⁷ têū³ 推³ 】dismiss sb. from his post; shout at sb. to go away

斥责【qig⁷jag⁸ 窄】reprimand; rebuke

叱【qig⁷ 斥】loudly rebuke; shout at

叱喝【qig⁷hod⁸ 渴】shout at; bawl at

叱责【qig⁷jag⁸ 窄】scold; upbraid; rebuke

叱咤风云【qig⁷ja³fung¹wen⁴ 炸丰匀】commanding the wind and the clouds; all-powerful

撖【qig⁷ 斥】carry (with a hand) =【普】(用手)提

撖起【qig⁷hēi¹ 喜】carry up (with a hand) =【普】(用手)提起

饬【qig⁷ 斥; xig⁷ 式】put in order; readjust; orderly; order (see "整饬"【jing²qig⁷】)

敕【qig⁷ 斥】imperial order; edict

戚【qig⁷ 斥】relative; sorrow; woe; a surname (see "亲戚"【qen¹qig⁷】, "休戚相关"【yeo¹qig⁷xêng¹guan¹】)

处【qū³ 柱³;qū² 贮;xū³ 恕】place; point; part; office; get along (with sb.); be situated in; manage; punish; live

处所【qü³xo² 锁】place；location

处处【qü³qü³】everywhere；in all respects

处罚【qü²fed⁹ 佛】punish；penalize

处分【qü³ fen¹ 芬】take disciplinary action against；punish

处方【qü³ fong¹ 芳】write out a prescription；prescribe；prescription

处境【qü³ging³ 景】plight

处理【qü²lêi⁵ 李】handle；deal with；treat by a special process；sell at reduced prices

处女【qü³nêû⁵ 那去⁵】virgin；maiden

处世【qü³xei³ 细】conduct oneself in society

处暑【qü³xü² 署】the Limit of Heat (14th solar term)

处死【qü² xêi²四²】put to death；execute = 处决【küd⁸】

处刑【qü²ying⁴ 型】condemn；sentence

处治【qü²ji⁶ 自】punish

处置【qü²ji³ 至】handle；deal with；punish

边处【bin¹xü³ 鞭恕】where = 【普】哪里

厨【qü⁴ 橱；qêü⁴ 除】kitchen

厨房【qü⁴gong¹ 防】kitchen

厨师【qü⁴xi¹ 司】cook

橱【qü⁴ 厨；qêü⁴ 除】cabinet；closet

橱窗【qü⁴qêng¹ 昌】show window；showcase；glass-fronted billboard

蹰【qü⁴ 厨；qêü⁴ 除】(see "踌躇"【qeo⁴qü⁴】)

躇【qü⁴ 厨；qêü⁴ 除】(see "踟躇"【qi⁴qü⁴】)

楮【qü² 处²】＜n.＞楮实【qü²xed⁹ 失⁹】paper mulberry fruit

褚【qü² 贮²】a surname

储【qü⁵ 柱】store up；a surname

储备【qü⁵bēi⁶ 避】store for future use；lay in；resere

储藏【qü⁵gong⁴ 床】save and preserve；store；deposits

储存【qü⁵qün⁴ 全】lay in；lay up；store

储蓄【qü⁵qug⁷ 促】save；deposit

储量【qü⁵lêng⁶ 亮】reserves

诸君【qü⁵guen¹ 军】crown prince

贮【qü⁵ 储】store；save；lay aside

贮备【qü⁵bēi⁶ 避】store up；lay aside

贮藏【qü⁵qong⁴ 床】store up；lay in

贮存【qü⁵qün⁴ 全】store；keep in storage

柱【qü⁵ 储】post；upright；pillar；sth. shaped like a column；cylinder

柱子【qü⁵ji² 止】post；pillar

柱石【qü⁵xêg⁹ 硕】pillar；mainstay

柱身【qü⁵xen¹ 辛】shaft

柱头【qü⁵teo⁴ 投】column cap；column head

柱砖【qü⁵den² 得因²】a concrete column；column base = 【普】柱座

杼【qü⁵ 柱】reed；shuttle

拄【qü⁵ 柱；jü² 主】lean on (a stick, etc.)

拄拐杖【qü⁵guai²jêng² 乖² 丈²】lean on a stick

拄咪【jü²mei⁵ 米】go to law against sb.；inform against sb. = 【普】告状；告密

伫【qü⁵ 贮】stand for a long while

伫立【qū⁵leb⁹ 笠⁹】stand still for a long while

苎【qū⁵ 贮】< n. > 苎麻【qū⁵ma⁴ 妈⁴】ramie

川【qūn¹ 穿】river; plain; short for Sichuan Province

川贝【qūn¹bui³ 背】tendril-leaved frifillary bulb

川芎【qūn¹gung¹ 弓】the rhizome of Ligus- ticum wallichii

川流不息【qūn¹leo⁴bed⁷xig³ 留毕色】nev- er-ending

穿【qūn¹ 川】pierce through; penetrate; pass through; cross; wear; put on

穿窿【qūn¹lung¹ 隆¹】bore a hole; perfora- tion; perforate = 【普】穿孔

穿插【qūn¹qab⁸ 锸】alternate; subplot; weave in

穿戴【qūn¹dai³ 带】apparel; dress = 穿着 【qūn¹jêg⁸ 爵】

穿梭【qūn¹xo¹ 梳】shuttle back and forth

穿越【qūn¹yūd⁹月 】pass through; cut across = 穿过【guo³】

穿凿【qūn¹ jog⁹ 作⁹】read too much into sth.

穿煲【qūn¹ bou¹ 褒】reveal a secret = 【普】(秘密)泄露或败露

穿针引线【qūn¹jem¹yen⁵xin³ 浸¹ 癮扇】act as a go-between

喘【qūn² 串²】breathe heavily; pant; asthma

喘气【qūn² hēi³ 戏】breathe (deeply); pant; gasp

喘息【qūn²xig⁷ 色】pant; breather; respire

揣【qūn² 喘; qêū² 取】hide or carry in one's clothes; estimate; surmise; conjecture

揣测【qūn²qag⁷ 策⁷】guess; conjecture

揣度【qūn²dog⁹ 铎】estimate; appraise

揣摩【qūn²mo² 摸】try to fathom

窜【qūn³ 寸】flee; scurry; change; alter

窜扰【qūn³yiu² 妖²】harass

窜逃【qūn³tou⁴ 途】flee in disorder; scurry off

窜改【qūn³goi² 该²】alter; tamper with

蹿【qūn¹ 村】leap up

搋【qūn³ 寸】throw; fling; do in a hurry; fly into a rage

搋掇【qūn³jūd³ 拙】urge; egg on

钏【qūn³ 寸】bracelet

村【qūn¹ 川】village; hamlet; rustic; boorish

村庄【qūn¹jong¹ 装】village; hamlet = 村 落【log⁸ 洛】= 邨【qūn¹】

村镇【qūn¹jen³ 振】villages and small towns

串【qūn³ 寸】string together; conspire; gang up; get things mixed up; run about; rove; act; < classifier. > string

串通【qūn³tung¹ 同¹】gang up; collude

串联【qūn³lün⁴ 李】establish ties; series connection

串珠【qūn³jū¹ 朱】a string of beads

串门【qūn³mun⁴ 们】call at sb.'s home; drop in

串讲【qūn³gong² 港】construe

串供【qūn³ gung¹ 攻】act in collusion to make each other's confessions tally

串仔【qūn³jei² 济²】gangsters (boys) ∽ 【普】(乱搞两性关系的)坏小子

串女【qün³nêü² 那去²】gangsters（girls）∽【普】(乱搞两性关系的)坏女子

寸【qün³ 串】a unit of length（= 1/3 decimetre）; very little; very short; small

寸步【qün³ bou⁶ 部】a tiny step; a single step

寸心【qün³xem¹ 深】feelings

寸金难买寸光阴【qün³gem¹nan⁴mai⁵qün³ guong¹yem¹】Money can't buy time. Time is more precious than gold.

忖【qün² 喘】turn over in one's mind; ponder

忖度【qün²dog⁹ 铎】speculate; conjecture; surmise

忖量【qün² lêng⁴ 梁】think over; conjecture; guess

全【qün⁴ 存】complete; whole; entire; full; entirely; completely; keep intact; a surname

全体【qün⁴tei² 睇】all; entire; whole

全部【qün⁴bou⁶ 步】whole; complete; total; all

全局【qün⁴gug⁹ 焗】overall situation

全面【qün⁴min² 缅²】overall; all-round

全盘【qün⁴pun⁴ 盆】overall; wholesale

全数【qün⁴xou³ 扫】total number; whole amount

全都【qün⁴dou¹ 刀】all; without exception

全然【qün⁴yin⁴ 言】completely; entirely

全球【qün⁴keo⁴ 求】the whole world

全国【qün⁴ guog⁸ 帼】the whole nation; nationwide; countrywide

全民【qün⁴men⁴ 文】the whole people; all the people

全身【qün⁴xen¹ 辛】the whole body

全貌【qün⁴mao⁶ 矛⁶】complete picture; full view

全景【qün⁴ging² 境】pull view; whole scene

全力【qün⁴lig⁹ 历】with all one's strength; all-out

全权【qün⁴kün⁴ 拳】full powers; plenary powers

全能【qün⁴neng⁴ 那莺⁴】all-round

全才【qün⁴qoi⁴ 财】a versatile person; all-rounder

全速【qün⁴qug⁷ 促】full speed

全程【qün⁴qing⁴ 程】whole journey; whole course

全套【qün⁴tou³ 兔】complete set

全等【qün⁴deng² 戥】congruent

全天候【qün⁴tin¹heo⁶ 田¹ 后】all-weather

全年【qün⁴nin⁴ 捻⁴】annual; yearly

全盛【qün⁴ xing⁶ 升⁶】flourishing; in full bloom

全神贯注【qün⁴ xen⁴ gun³ jü³臣灌著】be absorbed in; be preoccupied with

全心全意【qün⁴xem¹qün⁴yi³ 深薏】wholeheartedly

诠【qün⁴ 全】< v. > 诠释【qün⁴xig⁷ 色】annotation; explanatory notes

痊【qün⁴ 全】recover from an illness

痊愈【qün⁴yü⁶ 预】full recover from an illness

醛【qün⁴ 全】aldehyde

醛酯【qün⁴ji² 旨】aldehydo-ester

泉【qün⁴ 全】spring; an ancient term for coin

泉水【qūn⁴xêü² 瑞】spring water; spring

泉源【qūn⁴ yūn⁴ 原】wellspring; spring-
head; source

存【qūn⁴ 全】exist; live; store; keep;
collect; deposit; leave with; retain;
be in stock; cherish

存在【qūn⁴joi⁶ 再⁶】exist; be

存储【qūn⁴qū⁵ 柱】memory; storage

存亡【qūn⁴mong⁴忘】live or die; survive
or perish

存货【qūn⁴fo³ 课】goods in stock; existing
stock

存款【qūn⁴fun² 宽²】deposit; bank savings

存放【qūn⁴fong³ 况】leave with

存单【qūn⁴dan¹ 丹】deposit receipt

存根【qūn⁴gen⁸ 斤】counterfoil; stub

存折【qūn⁴ jid⁸ 节】deposit book; bank-
book

存底【qūn⁴dei² 抵】keep a file copy

存身【qūn⁴xen¹ 辛】take shelter; make
one's home

存心【qūn⁴xem¹ 深】cherish certain intentions

存疑【qūn⁴yi¹ 而】leave a question open

椽【qūn⁴ 全】rafter

椽条【qūn⁴tiu⁴ 挑⁴】rafter

筌【qūn⁴ 全】a bamboo fish trap

撮【qūd⁸ 次月⁸】gather; bring together;
scoop up; <*classifier.*> pinch; tuft

撮合【qūd⁸heb⁹ 盒】make a match; act as
go-between

撮要【qūd⁸yiu³ 腰³】make an abstract; abstract

一小撮【yed⁷xiu²qūd⁸ 壹少²】a handful

一撮毛【yed⁷qūd⁸mou⁴ 壹无】a tuft of hair

＝一执毛【yed⁷jeb⁷mou¹】

趌【qūd⁸ 撮】wheelly flight

趌来趌去【qūd⁸loi⁴qūd⁸hêü³ 莱虚³】wheelly
flight ＝【普】盘旋飞行

吹【qêü¹ 催】blow; puff; play; boast;
brag; break off

吹风【qêü¹ fung¹ 丰】catch a chill; dry
with a blower; let sb. in on sth.
in advance

吹拂【qêü¹fed⁷ 弗】sway; stir

吹嘘【qêü¹hêü¹ 虚】lavish praise on oneslf
or other

吹奏【qêü¹ jeo³ 绉】play (wind instruments)

吹牛【qêü¹ ngeo⁴ 偶⁴】boast; brag; talk
big

吹捧【qêü¹pung² 碰²】flatter; lavish praise
on

吹吹拍拍【qêü¹qêü¹pag⁸pag⁸ 柏】boasting
and toadying

吹毛求疵【qêü¹mou⁴keo⁴qi¹ 无球痴】find
fault; pick holes; nitpick

炊【qêü¹ 吹】cook a meal

炊事【qêü¹xi⁶ 士】cooking; kitchen work

炊具【qêü¹gêü⁶ 巨】cooking utensils

炊烟【qêü¹yin¹ 咽】smoke from kitchen
chimneys

崔【qêü¹ 吹】a surname

崔巍【qêü¹ngei⁴ 危】lofty; towering

崔嵬【qêü¹ngei⁴ 危】rocky mound; high

催【qêü¹ 推】urge; hurry; press; hasten;
speed up

催促【qêü¹qug⁷ 速】urge; hasten; press

催逼【qêü¹big¹ 迫】press

催化【qêü¹fa³ 花】catalysis

催眠【qêü¹min⁴ 棉】lull（to sleep）；hypnotism

催泪弹【qêü¹lêü⁶dan² 类蛋】tear bomb

摧【qêü¹ 催】break；destroy

摧残【qêü¹qan⁴ 灿⁴】wreck；destroy；devastate

摧毁【qêü¹wei² 委】destroy；smash；wreck

摧枯拉朽【qêü¹fu¹lai¹neo² 夫罗埃¹ 纽】（as easy as）crushing dry weeds and smashing rotten wood

璀【qêü¹ 崔】＜a.＞璀璨【qêü¹qan³ 灿】bright；resplendent

取【qêü² 娶】take；get；fetch；aim at；seek；adopt；assume；choose

取得【qêü²deg⁷ 德】gain；acquire；obtain

取材【qêü²qoi⁴ 才】draw materials

取代【qêü²doi³ 袋】replace；supersede；supplant

取道【qêü²dou⁶ 度】by way of；via

取缔【qêü²dei³ 帝】outlaw；ban；suppress

取经【qêü²ging¹ 京】go on a pilgrimage for Buddhist scriptures；learn from sb. else's experience

取决【qêü²küd⁸ 缺】be decided by；depend on

取乐【qêü²log⁹ 落】seek pleasure；amuse oneself

取悦【qêü²yüd⁹ 月】try to please

取暖【qêü²nün⁵ 那远⁵】warm oneself（by a fire，etc.）

取法【qêü²fad³ 发】take as one's model

取巧【qêü²hao² 考】resort to trickery to serve oneself

取胜【qêü²xing³ 性】win victory；score a success

取舍【qêü²xê³ 泻】accept or reject

取消【qêü²xiu¹ 销】cancel；call off；abolish

取笑【qêü²xiu³ 少】ridicule；make fun of

取长补短【qêü²qêng⁴bou²dün² 祥保段²】learn from others' strong points to offset one's weaknesses

娶【qêü² 取】marry（a woman）；take as wife

娶亲【qêü²qen¹ 趁¹】（of a man）get married

趋【qêü¹ 催】hasten；hurry along；tend towards

趋势【qêü¹xei³ 世】trend；tendency

趋向【qêü¹hêng³ 香³】tend to；incline to；trend

趋时【qêü¹xi⁴ 是⁴】follow the fashion

趋附【qêü¹fu⁶ 付】ingratiate oneself with

趋炎附势【qêü¹yim⁴fu⁶xei³ 严付世】curry favour with the powerful

趋之若鹜【qêü¹ji¹yêg⁹mou⁶ 支药务】go after sth. like a flock of ducks

趣【qêü³ 翠】interest；interesting；bent；purport

趣事【qêü³xi⁶ 是】an interesting episode

趣味【qêü³mêi⁶ 未】interest；delight

脆【qêü³ 翠】fragile；crisp；clear；brittle；neat

脆性【qêü³xing³ 姓】brittleness

脆弱【qêü³yêg⁹ 若】fragile；frail；weak

翠【qêü³ 趣】emerald green；green；kingfisher；jade

翠绿【qêü³lug⁹ 六】emerald green；jade green

翠竹【qêü³jug⁷ 足】green bamboos

翠微【qêü³mêi⁴眉】a shady retreat on a green hill

淬【qêū³ 脆；xêū⁶ 睡】temper by dipping in water, oil, etc.; quench

淬火【qêū³fo² 伙】quench

毳【qêū³ 趣】fine hair on animals; down

除【qêū⁴ 徐】get rid of; eliminate; remove; except; besides; divide; doorsteps

除草【qêū⁴qou² 曹²】weeding

除根【qêū⁴gen¹ 斤】dig up the roots; root out

除咗【qêū⁴jo² 佐²】except; besides =【普】除了

除外【qêū⁴ngoi⁶ 碍】except; not counting

除夕【qêū⁴jig⁹ 直】New Year's Eve

除非【qêū⁴fēi¹ 飞】< conj. > only if; only when; unless

除法【qêū⁴fad⁸ 发】< n. > division

除数【qêū⁴xou³ 扫】< n. > divisor

除旧布新【qêū⁴geo⁶bou³xen¹ 柩报辛】get rid of the old to make way for the new

徐【qêū⁴ 除】slowly; gently; a surname

徐步【qêū⁴bou⁶ 部】walk slowly; stroll

徐徐【qêū⁴qêū⁴】slowly; gently

隋【qêū⁴ 随】the Sui Dynasty（581 – 618); a surname

随【qêū⁴ 除】follow; comple with; let; along with; look like

随住【qêū⁴jü⁶ 注⁶】along with; in pace with =【普】随着

随便【qêū⁴bin² 圆】casual; random; do as one pleases; careless; wanton; anyhow; any

随从【qêū⁴ qung⁴ 虫】attend; retinue; suite

随处【qêū⁴ qü³ 厨³】everywhere; anywhere = 随地【dēi⁶】

随和【qêū⁴wo⁴ 禾】amiable; obliging

随后【qêū⁴heo⁶ 候】soon afterwards = 跟住【gen¹jü⁶】

随即【qêū⁴jig⁷ 积】immediately; presently = 跟手【gen¹xo²】

随口【qêū⁴heo² 厚²】speak thoughtlessly or casually

随身【qêū⁴xen¹ 辛】(carry) on one's person

随时【qêū⁴xi⁴ 是⁴】at any time; whenever necessary

随手【qêū⁴xeo² 守】conveniently

随俗【qêū⁴ jug⁹ 族】comply with convention

随同【qêū⁴tung⁴ 铜】be in company with

随意【qêū⁴yi³ 薏】at will; as one pleases

随风倒【qêū⁴fung¹dou² 丰捣】bend with the wind — be easily swayed

随声附和【qêū⁴xing¹fu⁶wo⁴ 升付禾】echo what others say; chime in with others

随机应变【qêū⁴gēi¹ying³bin³ 基英³边³】adapt oneself to changing conditions

随遇而安【qêū⁴yü⁶yi⁴ngon¹ 预移胺】feel at home wherever one is

随心所欲【qêū⁴xem¹xo²yug⁹ 深锁玉】follow one's inclinations

嗖【qêū⁴ 徐】smell; odour; flavour =【普】气味

一嘬嗖【yed⁷bung⁶qêū⁴ 壹伯瓮⁶】a puff of smell =【普】一股气味

捶【qêū⁴ 徐】beat; thump; pound

捶打【qêū⁴da² 得阿²】beat; thump

捶胸顿足【qêü⁴hung¹dên⁶jug⁷ 空敦⁶ 竹】beat one's breast and stamp one's feet

锤【qêü⁴ 徐】hammer; mace; hammer into shape; weight

铁锤【tid⁸qêü⁴ 替热⁸】iron hammer

锤仔【qêü⁴jei² 济²】hammer＝【普】锤子

锤炼【qêü⁴ lin⁶ 练】hammer into shape; temper

槌【qêü⁴ 徐】mallet; beetle

鼓槌【gu²qêü⁴ 古】drumstick

春【qên¹ 椿】spring; love; lust; life; a surname

春天【qên¹tin¹ 田¹】spring; springtime＝春季【guei³】

春风【qên¹fung¹ 丰】spring breeze

春播【qên¹bo³ 波³】spring sowing

春耕【qên¹gang¹ 格罂¹】spring ploughing

春光【qên¹guong¹ 胱】spring scenery＝春色【xig⁷】

春节【qên¹jid⁸ 折】the Spring Festival

春雷【qên¹lêü⁴ 擂】spring thunder

春联【qên¹lün⁴ 李】Spring Festival couplets

春梦【qên¹mung⁶ 蒙⁶】spring dream; transient joy

春秋【qên¹ qeo¹ 抽】spring and autumn; year; the Spring and Autumn Period (770－476B.C.); annals; history

春笋【qên¹ xên² 荀²】bamboo shoots in spring

春意【qên¹ yi³ 薏】spring in the air; the beginning of spring; thoughts of love

春游【qên¹yeo⁴ 由】spring outing

椿【qên¹ 春】Chinese toon; tree of heaven

椿象【qên¹jêng⁶ 丈】< n. > stinkbug; shieldbug

蠢【qên² 春²】stupid; foolish; dull; clumsy; wriggle

蠢笨【qên²ben⁶ 宾⁶】clumsy; awkward; stupid

蠢材【qên²qoi² 才】idiot; fool

蠢货【qên²fo³ 课】blockhead; dunce; idiot

蠢人【qên²yen⁴ 仁】fool; blockhead

蠢猪【qên¹jü¹ 朱】idiot; stupid swine; ass

蠢蠢欲动【qên²qên²yug⁹dung⁶ 玉洞】ready to start wriggling — ready to make trouble

鹑【qên¹ 春；xên⁴ 纯】quail (see "鹌鹑"【ngem¹qên¹】)

巡【qên⁴ 循】patrol; make one's rounds; round of drinks

巡逻【qên⁴lo⁴ 罗】go on patrol; patrol

巡回【qên⁴wui⁴ 会⁴】go the rounds; tour

巡查【qên⁴qa⁴ 茶】go on a tour of inspection

巡捕【qên⁴bou⁶ 哺】police or policeman

巡警【qên⁴ging² 景】policeman

巡视【qên⁴xi⁶ 是】make an inspection tour; tour

巡礼【qên⁴lei⁵ 丽⁵】visit a sacred land; tour

巡航【qên⁴hong⁴ 杭】cruise

循【qên⁴ 巡】follow; abide by

循序【qên⁴jêü⁶ 叙】in proper order or sequence

循环【qên⁴wan⁴ 还】circulate; cycle

循规蹈矩【qên⁴kuei¹dou⁶gêü² 亏道举】

follow rules, orders, etc. docilely; toe the line

循循善诱【qên⁴ qên⁴ xin⁶ yeo⁵ 美友 】 be good at giving systematic guidance

秦【qên⁴ 巡】the Qin Dynasty (221 – 207 B. C.); a surname; another name for Shanxi Province

秦腔【qên⁴hong¹ 康】Shanxi opera, popular in the northwestern provinces

旬【qên⁴ 巡】a period of ten days; a period of ten years in a person's age

旬刊【qên⁴hon² 罕】a publication appearing once every ten days

昌【qêng¹ 窗】prosperous; flourishing

昌明【qêng¹ming⁴ 名】flourishing; thriving

昌盛【qêng¹xing⁶ 剩】prosperous

菖【qêng¹ 昌】< n. > 菖蒲【qêng¹pou⁴ 普⁴】calamus

鲳【qêng¹ 昌】< n. > 鲳鱼【qêng¹yü⁴ 如】silvery pomfret

猖【qêng¹ 昌】savage; be rampant

猖獗【qêng¹küd⁸ 蕨】 be rampant; run wild

猖狂【qêng¹kuong⁴ 卡汪⁴】savage; furious

娼【qêng¹ 昌】prostitute

娼妇【qêng¹fu⁵ 府⁵】bitch; whore

娼妓【qêng¹gêi⁶技 】 prostitute; streetwalker

伥【qêng¹ 昌；qang¹ 撑】(see " 为虎作伥")

窗【qêng¹ 昌】window

窗口【qêng¹heo² 厚²】window; wicket

窗户【qêng¹wu⁶ 护】window; casement

窗框【qêng¹kuang¹ 卡横¹】window frame

窗帘【qêng¹lim⁴ 廉】(window) curtain

窗纱【qêng¹xa¹ 沙】window screening

窗棂【qêng¹ling⁴ 灵】window lattice

窗玻璃【qêng¹bo¹lêi¹ 波喱】windowpane

窗明几净【qêng¹ming⁴gêi¹jing⁶ 名机静】 bright and clean

枪【qêng¹ 昌】rifle; gun; firearm; spear

枪支【qêng¹ji¹ 枝】firearms = 枪械【hai⁶】

枪炮【qêng¹pao³ 泡³】firearms; arms; guns

枪声【qêng¹xing! 升】report of a gun; shot

枪手【qêng¹xeo² 守】marksman; gunner

枪弹【qêng¹dan² 蛋】cartridge; bullet

枪法【qêng¹fad⁸ 发】marksmanship

枪毙【qêng¹bei¹ 敝】execute by shooting = 枪决【qêng¹küd⁸】

枪杀【qêng¹xad⁸ 煞】shoot dead

枪伤【qêng¹xêng¹ 湘】bullet wound

枪林弹语【qêng¹lem⁴dan⁶yü⁵ 淋蛋语】a hail of bullets

锵【qêng¹ 昌】clang; gong (see "铿锵")

呛【qêng¹ 昌；qêng³ 唱】choke; irritate

抢【qêng² 枪²】rob; loot; snatch; grab; vie for; scrape

抢夺【qêng²düd⁹ 得月⁹】snatch; wrest; seize

抢野【qêng²yê⁵ 夜⁵】rob; loot; plunder = 抢劫【qêng²gib⁸ 格叶ꟼ】

抢掠【qêng²lêg⁹ 略】loot; sack; plunder

抢救【qêng²geo³ 够】rescue; save

抢险【qêng² him² 欠²】rush to deal with an emergency

抢购【qêng² keo³ 构】rush to purchase

抢修【qêng² xeo¹ 收】rush to repair

抢先【qêng² xin¹ 仙】anticipate

抢占【qêng² jim³ 詹】race to control; seize

抢白【qêng² bag⁹ 伯⁹】reprove or satirize sb. to his face

抢时间【qêng² xi⁴ gan¹ 是⁴ 奸】race against time

唱【qêng³ 畅】sing; call; cry

唱歌【qêng³ go¹ 哥】sing (a song)

唱和【qêng³ wo⁴ 禾】one singing a song and the others joining in the chorus

唱腔【qêng³ hong¹ 康】music for voices in a Chinese opera

唱戏【qêng³ hêi³ 气】act in an opera

唱片【qêng³ pin³ 偏²】gramophone record; disc

唱机【qêng³ gêi¹ 基】gramophone; phonograph

唱票【qêng³ piu³ 漂³】call out the name of those voted for while counting ballot-slips

唱反调【qêng³ fan² diu⁶ 返掉】sing a different tune

唱对台戏【qêng³ dêu³ toi⁴ hêi³ 堆³ 抬气】put on a rival show; enter into rivalry

畅【qêng³ 唱】smooth; unimpeded; free

畅通【qêng³ tung¹ 同¹】unimpeded; unblocked

畅快【qêng³ fai³ 块】free from inhibitions; carefree

畅谈【qêng³ tam⁴ 谭】talk freely and to one's heart's content; speak glowingly of

畅销【qêng³ xiu¹ 消】be in great demand; sell well

畅游【qêng³ yeo⁴ 油】have a good swim; enjoy a sightseeing tour

畅所欲言【qêng³ xo² yug⁹ yin⁴ 锁玉然】speak one's mind freely; speak out freely

怅【qêng³ 唱】disappointed; sorry

怅然【qêng³ yin⁴ 言】disappointed; upset

怅惘【qêng³ mong⁵ 妄】distracted; listless

倡【qêng¹ 昌; qêng³ 唱】initiate; advocate

倡导【qêng¹ dou⁶ 道】initiate; propose

倡议【qêng¹ yi⁵ 耳】propose

场【qêng⁴ 祥】a place where people gather; farm; stage; field; a level open space; < classifier. > the unit of rain, ill, film, match, etc.

场地【qêng⁴ dêi⁶ 得希⁶】space; place; site

场所【qêng⁴ xo² 锁】place; arena

场合【qêng⁴ heb⁹ 盒】occasion; situation

场面【qêng⁴ min² 缅²】scene; spectacle; occasion; appearance; front

场次【qêng⁴ qi³ 刺】the number of showings of a film, play, etc.

肠【qêng⁴ 场; qêng² 抢】intestines

肠胃【qêng⁴ wei⁶ 惠】intestines and stomach; stomach; belly

肠炎【qêng⁴ yim⁴ 严】enteritis

肠梗阻【qêng⁴ geng² jo² 耿左】intestinal obstruction

祥【qêng⁴ 详】auspicious; propitious; lucky

祥瑞【qêng⁴xêü⁶ 睡】auspicious sign; propitious omen

详【qêng⁴ 祥】detailed; minute; details; know clearly

详细【qêng⁴xei³ 世】detailed; minute

详尽【qêng⁴ jên⁶进⁶】detailed; exhaustive; thorough

详实【qêng⁴xed⁹ 失⁹】full and accurate

详情【qêng⁴ qing⁴程 】detailed information; details

详明【qêng⁴ming⁴ 名】full and clear

翔【qêng⁴ 详】circle in the air

翔实【qêng⁴xed⁹ 失⁹】full and accurate

出【qêd⁷ 次律⁷】go or come out; exceed; issue; put up; produce; turn out; arise; happen; rise well; put forth; vent; expend; a dramatic piece

出现【qêd⁷yin⁶ 燕⁶】appear; arise; emerge

出生【qêd⁷xing¹ 笙】be born

出世【qêd⁷xei³ 细】come into the world; be born

出身【qêd⁷xen¹ 辛】class origin; family background; one's previous experience or occupation

出土【qêd⁷ tou²肚²】be unearthed; come up out to the ground

出脱【qêd⁷tüd⁸ 替月⁸】manage to sell; acquit

出去【qêd⁷hêü³ 虚】go out; get out

出来【qêd⁷loi⁴ 莱】come out; emerge

出没【qêd⁷mud⁵ 末】appear and disappear; haund

出入【qêd⁷yeb⁹ 邑⁹】cone in and go out; discrepancy; divergence

出口【qêd⁷heo² 厚²】speak; utter; exit

出路【qêd⁷lou⁶ 露】way out; outlet

出境【qêd⁷ging² 景】leave the country

出界【qêd⁷gai³ 介】out-of-bounds; outside

出发【qêd⁷fad⁸ 法】set out; start off; start from

出产【qêd⁷qan² 铲】produce; manufacture

出品【qêd⁷ben² 禀】produce; manufacture

出版【qêd⁷ ban²板 】come off the press; publish; come out

出动【qêd⁷dung⁶ 洞】set out; start off; send out

出厂【qêd⁷qong² 敞】(of products)leave the factory

出差【qêd⁷qai¹ 猜】be away on official business

出错【qêd⁷qo³ 挫】make mistakes

出丑【qêd⁷qeo² 秋²】make a fool of oneself

出工【qêd⁷gung¹ 功】go to work

出恭【qêd⁷gung¹ 公】go to the lavatory = 〔普〕上厕所

出轨【qêd⁷guei² 鬼】be derailed; overstep the bounds

出汗【qêd⁷hon² 焊】perspire; sweat

出击【qêd⁷gig² 激】hit out; make a sally

出家【qêd⁷ga¹ 加】become a monk or nun

出嫁【qêd⁷ga³ 价】(of a woman) get married; marry

出力【qêd⁷ lig⁹历 】put forth one's strength

出笼【qêd⁷ lung⁴ 龙 】come out of the steamer; appear; come forth

出马【qêd⁷ma⁵码】go into action; take the field

出卖【qêd⁷mai⁶ 买⁶】sell; sell out; betray

出面【qêd⁷min² 缅²】appear personally

出名【qêd7 ming4 明】famous; lend one's name

出气【qêd7hēi3 戏】vent one's spleen

出纳【qêd7nab9 呐】receive and pay out money or bills

出奇【qêd7 kei4其】unusually; extraordinarily

出色【qêd7 xig7 式】outstanding; remarkable

出使【qêd7 xi3 试】serve as an envoy abroad

出示【qêd7xi6 视】show; produce

出售【qêd7xeo6 受】offer for sale; sell

出息【qêd7xig7 式】promise; prospects

出席【qêd7jig8 直】attend; be present

出租【qêd7jou1 糟】hire;let

出众【qêd7jung3 种3】be outstanding

出于【qêd7yü1 迂】start from; stem from

出计仔【qêd7gei2jei2 继2 济2】offer advice =[普]出点子

出猫仔【qêd7 mao1 jei2 矛1 济2】practise fraud; cheat; indulge in corrupt practices =[普]作弊;耍鬼把戏

出洋相【qêd7yêng4xêng3 杨商3】make an exhibition of oneself

出尔反尔【qêd7yi5fan2yi5 耳返】go back on one's word

出类拔萃【qêd7 lêü6 bed9 xêü5 泪跋穗5】stand out from one's fellows

出谋献策【qêd7 meo4 hin3 gag8 牟宪册】give counsel

出奇制胜【qêd7kēi4jei3xing3 其济姓】defeat one's opponent by a surprise move

出人意外【qêd7 yen4 yi3 ngoi6仁薏碍】exceeding all expectations

出生入死【qêd7xing1yeb9xēi2 笙邑9 四2】go through fire and water

卓

【qêg8 绰】tall and erect; outstanding; eminent; a surname

卓越【qêg8yüd9 月】outstanding; brilliant

卓绝【qêg8jüd9 拙9】unsurpassed; extreme

卓著【qêg8 jü3注 】distinguished; outstanding

卓见【qêg8gin3 建】excellent opinion

卓有成效【qêg8yeo5xing4hao6 友承孝6】fruitful

焯

【qêg8 卓】scald(as a way of cooking) =[普]把(青菜等)放进开水里烫一烫,使之消毒

焯一焯【qêg8yed7gêg9】scald∽[普]烫一烫

绰

【qêg8 卓】ample;spacious

绰号【qêg8 hou6好6】 nickname = 花名【fa1mēng2】

绰约【qêg8yêg8 若8】(of a woman) graceful

绰绰有余【qêg8qêg8yeo5yü4 友如】more than sufficient; enough and to spare

芍

【qêg8 卓】<*n*.>芍药〔qêg8yêg9 若〕Chinese berbaceous peony

啅

【qêg8 卓】eloquence

啅头【qêg8teo4 投】eloquence; sweet taste ∽[普]口才;甜头

落足啅头【log9jug7qêg8teo4 洛9 竹投】full exert eloquence; use all one's resources∽[普]充分使用口才;使出全副本领

赤

【qēg8 尺】red; loyal; sincere; bare

赤色【qēg8xig7 式】red

赤诚【qēg⁸xìng⁴ 成】absolute; sincerity

赤子【qēg⁸ji² 止】a newborn baby

赤字【qēg⁸ji⁶ 自】deficit

赤露【qēg⁸lou⁶ 路】bare

赤裸裸【qēg⁸lo²lo² 螺²】without a stitch of clothing; stark-naked; naked; out-and-out

赤脚【qēg⁸qēg⁸ 格约⁸】barefoot

赤贫【qēg⁸pen⁴ 频】utterly destitute

赤道【qēg⁸ dou⁶ 度】the equator; the celestial equator

赤膊上阵【qēg⁸bog⁸xêng⁵jen⁶ 博尚⁵. 珍⁶】go into battle stripped to the waist; throw away all disguise

赤胆忠心【qēg⁸ dam² jumg¹ xem¹担² 中深】utter devotion; loyalty

痎 【qēg⁸ 赤】frozen stiff and feel unwell =[普]冻僵而感到难受

手痎脚痎【xeo²qēg⁸gêg⁸qēg⁸ 守格约⁸】the hands and the foots frozen stiff to feel unwell=【普】手脚冻僵而感到难受

肉痎【yug⁹qēg⁸ 玉】heartbreak; unhappy; grudge∽【普】心疼;可惜;舍不得

尺 【qēg⁸ 赤】a unit of length(= 1/3 metre); rule; ruler; an instrument in the shape of a rule

尺子【qēg⁸ji² 止】rule; ruler

尺寸【qēg⁸qūn³ 串】measurement; size

尺码【qēg⁸ma⁵ 马】size; measures

尺度【qēg⁸ dou⁶ 道】yardstick; measure; scale

尺蠖【qēg⁸wog⁹ 获】looper; inchworm

车 【qē¹ 奢; gêû¹ 居】①vehicle; wheeled machine or instrument; machine; lathe; turn; lift water by water-wheel; a surname; ② chariot, one of the pieces in Chinese chess

车仔【qē¹jei² 济²】small vehicle =【普】车子

车辘【qē¹lug⁷ 鹿⁷】wheel(of a vehicle) =【普】车轮

车呔【qē¹tai¹ 太¹】tyre=【普】车胎;轮胎

车厢【qē¹xêng¹ 湘】railway carriage; railroad car

车辆【qē¹lêng² 两²】vehicle; car

车次【qē¹ qi³ 刺】train number; motorcoach number

车票【qē¹piu³ 漂³】automobile ticket

车费【qē¹fei³ 废】fare

车技【qē¹gêi⁶ 伎】trick-cycling

车速【qē¹qug⁷ 促】speed of a vehicle

车祸【qē¹wo⁶ 和⁶】traffic accident

丢卒保车【diu¹jêd⁷bou²gêû¹】give up a pawn to save a chariot — sacrifice minor things to save major ones

车站【qē¹jam⁶ 暂】station; depot; stop

车床【qē¹qong⁴ 藏⁴】lathe

车刀【qē¹dou¹ 都】lathe tool

车工【qē¹gung¹ 功】lathe work; lathe operator

车水马龙【qē¹xêû²ma⁵lung⁴ 瑞² 码隆】incessant stream of horses and carriages — heavy traffic

哷 【qē¹ 车】< int . > show negation; ∽ no

扯 【qē² 车²; qē⁵ 车⁵】pull; tear; buy; chat; gossip; both hands forward to grope

扯盲摸【qē⁵mang⁴mo¹ 猛⁴ 摩】grope one's way on a dark night; both hands forward to grope in dark =【普】摸黑儿

扯谈【qē²tam⁴ 谭】talk nonsense; nonsense

扯谎【qē²fong¹ 荒】tell a lie；lie

扯皮【qē²pēi⁴ 脾】dispute over trifles；wrangle

扯猫尾【qē²mao¹mēi⁵ 矛¹ 美】hold sb. back（from action）；be a drag on sb.；be a hindrance to sb. ∽【普】扯后腿

跩【qē² 扯】get away；leave；beat it ＝【普】离开；走开；滚蛋

奢【qē¹ 车】luxurious；extravagant；excessive；inordinate

奢侈【qē¹qi² 齿】luxurious；extravagant

奢华【qē¹wa⁴ 铧】luxurious；sumptuous

奢望【qē¹mong⁶ 亡⁶】extravagant hopes；wild wishes

斜【qē⁴ 邪；qē³ 邪³】oblique；slanting；inclined；tilted

斜坡【qē³bo¹ 波】slope

斜路【qē³lou⁶ 露】wrong path

斜角【qē³gog⁸ 各】oblique angle；bevel angle

斜边【qē⁴bin¹ 鞭】hypotenuse；bevel edge

斜线【qē⁴xin³ 扇】oblique line

斜纹【qē⁴men⁴ 文】twill（weave）

斜面【qē⁴min² 缅²】inclined plane

斜率【qē⁴lēd⁹ 律】slope

斜视【qē⁴ xi⁶示 】strabismus；look sideways

斜阳【qē⁴yêng⁴ 杨】setting sun

邪【qē⁴ 斜⁴】evil；heretical；irregular；unhealthy environmental influences that cause disease

邪道【qē⁴dou⁶ 度】evil ways；vice ＝ 邪路【lou⁶】

邪恶【qē⁴ngog⁸ 噩】evil；wicked；vicious

邪心【qē⁴xem¹ 深】evil thought；wicked idea ＝ 邪念【lim⁶】

邪气【qē⁴hēi³ 戏】perverse trend；evil influence

邪说【qē⁴xüd⁸ 雪】heresy；heretical ideas；fallacy

邪门歪道【qē⁴mun⁴wai¹dou⁶ 满⁴ 怀¹ 度】crooked ways；dishonest practices

R

(It is not used in Cantonese.)

S

(It is not used in Cantonese.)

T

他【ta¹ 她】he; him = 佢【kêu⁵】

他们【ta¹ mun⁴ 门】they; them = 佢地【kêu⁵dēi⁶ 得希⁶】

他们㗎【ta¹mun⁴dig⁷ 门滴⁷】their = 佢地嘅【kêu⁵dēi⁶gē³】

他的【ta¹dig⁷ 滴⁷】his = 佢嘅【kêu⁵gē³】

他人【ta¹ yen⁴仁】another person; other people; others

他日【ta¹yed⁹ 逸】some other time; some day = 递日【dēi⁶yed⁹】

他乡【ta¹hêng¹ 香】an alien land

他杀【ta¹xad⁸ 煞】homicide

他妈的【ta¹ma¹dig⁷ 吗滴⁷】damn it; blast it = 佢老母【kêu⁵lou⁵mou²】

她【ta¹ 他】she; her

她的【ta¹dig⁷ 滴⁷】her; hers = 佢嘅【kêu⁵gē³】

她们【ta¹mun⁴ 门】they;them = 佢地【kêu⁵dēi⁶】

她们的【ta¹mun⁴dig⁷ 门滴⁷】their = 佢地嘅【kêu⁵dēi⁶gē³】

它【ta¹ 他】it = 佢【kêu⁵】

它的【ta¹dig⁷ 滴⁷】its = 佢嘅【kêu⁵ gē³】

它们【ta¹ mun⁴门】them; they = 佢地【kêu⁵ dēi⁶】

它们的【ta¹mun⁴dig⁷ 门滴⁷】their = 佢地嘅【kêu⁵dēi⁶gē³】

它逍【ta¹tiu⁴ 条】leisurely and carefree; be well; firm; calm; comfortable = 【普】舒服；优游自在

呔【tai¹ 太¹】tyre = 【普】轮胎

补呔【bou²tai¹ 保】mend the tyre = 【普】修补轮胎

太【tai³ 汰】highest; greatest; remotest; more or most senier; excessively; too; over; extremely; very

太空【tai³hung¹ 凶】the firmament; outer space

太阳【tai³ yêng⁴ 杨】the sun; sunshine;

sunlight

太平【tai³ping⁴ 苹】peace and tranquility

太公【tai³gung¹ 工】great-grandfather

太婆【tai³po² 颇】great-grandmother

太太【tai³tai²】Mrs; madame; lady

太后【tai³heo⁶ 候】mother of an emperor; queen mother

太监【tai³gam³ 鉴】(court)eunuch

太上皇【tai³xêng⁶wong⁴ 尚王】a title assumed by an emperor's father who abdicated in favour of his son; overlord; supersovereign

太子爷【tai³ji²yê² 止夜²】crown prince; refer to a young boss

太平洋【tai³ping⁴yêng⁴ 苹杨】the Pacific (Ocean)

汰 【tai¹ 呔】a.tie

领汰【lêng⁵tai⁵ 罗镜⁵】necktie; tie =【普】领带

钛 【tai³ 太】〈n.〉titanium

酞 【tai³】〈n.〉phthalein

泰 【tai³ 太】safe; peaceful; extreme; most

泰国【tai³guog⁸ 帼⁸】Thailand

泰然【tai³yin⁴ 言】calm; composed; self-possessed

泰山【tai³xan¹ 珊】Mount Taishan; Taishan Mountain

舦 【tai⁵ 太⁵】the steering on a ship =【普】舵

逴舦【tên³tai⁵ 吞论³】hang back; not do =【普】退却；不干

汰 【tai³ 太】discard; eliminate (see "淘汰")

贪 【tam¹ 探¹】corrupt; venal; have an insatiable desire for; covet

贪心【tam¹xem¹ 深】greed; avarice; greedy

贪婪【tam¹lan⁴ 蓝】avaricious; greedy

贪恋【tam¹lün² 乱²】hate to leave; cling to

贪图【tam¹tou⁴ 途】seek; hanker after; covet

贪污【tam¹wu¹ 乌】corruption; graft

贪便宜【tam¹pin⁴yi⁴ 片⁴ 移】anxious to get things on the cheap

贪得意【tam¹deg⁷yi³ 德薏】seek interesting =【普】贪好玩；图取乐

贪生怕死【tam¹xeng¹pa³xêi² 笙扒³ 四²】cravenly cling to life instead of braving death

贪赃枉法【tam¹jong¹wong²fad⁸ 装汪² 发】take bribes and bend the law

探 【tam³ 贪³】try to find out; explore; sound; scout; spy; visit; pay a call on

探测【tam³qag⁷ 次轭⁷】survey; sound; probe

探访【tam³ fong² 坊】seek by inquiry or search; pay a visit to; visit

探矿【tam³kong³ 抗】go prospecting; prospect

探亲【tam³qen¹ 趁¹】go home to visit one's family or go to visit one's relatives

探索【tam³xog⁸ 溯】explore; probe

探讨【tam³tou² 桃²】inquire into; probe into

探听【tam³ting³ 亭³】try to find out; make inquiries

探望【tam³mong⁶ 亡⁶】look about; visit

探险【tam³him² 欠²】explore; make explorations

探询【tam³xên¹ 荀】inquire after =探问【men⁶】

探囊取物【tam³nong⁴qêû²med⁹ 那康⁴ 婜 勿】like taking something out of one's pocket—as easy as winking; as easy as falling off a log

探家【tam³ga¹ 加】visit one's parents at home

探热针【tam³yid⁹jem¹ 衣泄⁹ 浸¹】a thermometer =【普】体温计

燂【tam⁴ 谭】roast =【普】(用火)烧烤; 焙烘

燂隌咗【tam⁴lung¹jo² 隆¹ 佐²】burnt = 【普】烧焦了

覃【tam⁴ 谭; qem⁴ 寻】deep; a surname

谭【tam⁴ 潭】a surname

潭【tam⁴ 谭】deep pool; pond

一潭死水【yed⁷tam⁴xêi²xêû² 壹四² 瑞²】a pond of stagnant water

谈【tam⁴ 谭】talk; chat; discuss; what is said or talked about; a surname

谈话【tam⁴wa⁶ 画⁶】conversation; talk; chat; statement

谈论【tam⁴lên⁶ 沦⁶】discuss; talk about

谈到【tam⁴dou³ 度³】speak of; talk about

谈判【tam⁴pun³ 潘³】negotiations; talks

谈心【tam⁴xem¹ 深】heart-to-heart talk

谈笑风生【tam⁴xiu³fung¹xeng¹ 少³ 丰笙】talk cheerfully and humorously

谈何容易【tam⁴ho⁴yung⁴yi⁶ 河熔异】easier said than done; by no means easy

痰【tam⁴ 谈】phlegm; sputum

痰盂【tam⁴yü² 余²】spittoon; cuspidor

滩【tan¹ 摊】beach; sands; shoal;

滩多水急【tan¹do¹xêû²geb⁷ 朵¹ 瑞² 格合⁷】with many shoals and rapids

摊【tan¹ 滩】spread out; take a share in; vendor's stand; booth; stall; fry batter in a thin layer; < classifier. > a pool of

摊档【tan¹dong³ 当³】vendor's stand; booth; stall; setup =【普】摊子

摊贩【tan¹fan² 反】street pedlar

摊牌【tan¹pai² 排²】lay one's cards on the table; show one's hand; have a showdown

摊冻【tan¹dung³ 东³】lay up the hot thing to change cold slowly =【普】放着 热物使之慢慢变凉

摊直【tan¹jig⁹ 值】die =【普】死了

瘫【tan¹ 滩; tan² 滩²】paralysis

瘫痪【tan¹wun⁶ 换】paralysis; palsy; be paralysed; break down

瘫软【tan¹yün⁵ 远】(of arms, legs, etc.) weak and limp

炭【tan³ 叹】charcoal

炭火【tan³fo² 伙】charcoal fire

炭笔【tan³bed⁷ 毕】charcoal pencil

炭画【tan³wa² 话²】charcoal drawing; charcoal

碳【tan³ 炭】〈n.〉carbon(C)

碳精【tan³jing¹ 贞】< n. >carbon(C)

碳化【tan³fa³ 花³】carbonization

碳酸【tan³xün³ 孙】carbonic acid

碳水化合物【tan³xêü²fa³heb⁹med⁹ 瑞² 花³ 盒勿】carbohydrate

錟【tan³炭】enjoy；rest＝【普】享受；休息

錟世界【tan³xei³gai³ 势介】enjoy＝【普】享受；享乐

坦【tan² 祖】level；smooth；calm；open

坦途【tan²tou⁴ 逃】level road；highway

坦白【tan² bag⁹ 伯⁹】honest；frank；confess；own up

坦荡【tan²dong⁶ 当⁶】broad and level；magnanimous

坦然【tan²yin⁴ 言】calm；unperturbed

坦率【tan²xêd⁷ 是律⁷】candid；frank

祖【tan² 坦】leave(the upper part of the body)uncovered；shield；shelter

祖护【tan²wu⁶ 户】give unprincipled protection to；be partial to；shield

祖胸露臂【tan²hung¹lou⁶bêi³ 凶路秘】exposing one's neck and shoulders

毯【tan² 坦】blanket；rug；carpet(地毯【dêi⁶tan²】)

忐【tan² 坦】〈a.〉忐忑【tan²tig⁷ 惕】perturbed；mentally disturbed；uneasy

叹【tan³炭】sigh；exclaim in admiration；acclaim

叹词【tan³ qi⁴ 辞】interjection；exclamation

叹气【tan³hêi³ 戏】sigh；heave a sigh＝叹息【xig⁷】

叹服【tan³fug⁹ 伏】gasp in admiration

叹为观止【tan³wei⁴gun¹ji² 维官子】acclaim(a work of art, etc.)as the acme of perfection

檀【tan⁴ 坦】wingceltis；a surname

檀香【tan⁴hêng¹ 乡】whit sandalwood

檀香山【tan⁴hêng¹xan¹ 乡珊】< n.> Honolulu

昙【tan⁴ 坛】covered with clouds

昙花【tan⁴fa¹ 化¹】broad-leaved epiphyllum

昙花一现【tan³fa¹ yed⁷yin⁶ 化¹ 壹燕⁶】flower briefly as the broad-leaved epiphyllum；last briefly

坛【tan⁴ 昙；tam⁴ 谭】altar；a raised plot of land for planting flowers, etc.；forum；platform；earthen jar；jug；circles

坛子【tan⁴ji² 止】earthen jar

坛坛罐罐【tam⁴tam⁴gun³gun³ 贯】pots and pans—personal possessions

塔【tab⁸ 塌】Buddhist pagoda；pagoda；tower；column

塔吊【tab⁸diu² 丢³】tower crane

塌【tab⁸ 塔】collapse；fall down；cave in；sink；droop；calm down

塌陷【tab⁸ham⁶ 咸】cave in；subside；sink

塌方【tab⁸fong¹ 芳】cave in；collapse；landship

塌台【tab⁸ toi⁴ 抬】collapse；fall from power

蹋【tab⁸ 塔；tad⁸ 遢】(see"糟蹋")

挞【tad⁸ 拖压⁸】flog；whip(see"鞭挞")

鳎【tad⁸ 挞；tab⁸ 塔】sole

鳎沙鱼【tab⁸xa¹yü² 纱如²】sole

遢【tad⁸ 挞】〈a.〉邋遢【lad⁹tad⁸ 辣】dirty；filthy＝【普】肮脏

遢订【tad⁸dêng⁶ 得镜⁶】default the sub-

scription（rate）=【普】拖欠订货
款

榻【tad⁸ 挞；tab⁸ 塔】a long, narrow and low bed；couch（see"下榻"）

嗒【tad⁸ 挞；tab⁸ 塔】< onomatopoeia >

嗒然【tab⁸yin⁴ 言】dejected；depressed

梯【tei¹ 锑】ladder；steps；stairs；shaped like a staircase；terraced

梯子【tei¹ji² 止】ladder；stepladder

梯级【tei¹ked⁷ 给】stair；step

梯队【tei¹dêû⁶ 对⁶】echelon

梯田【tei¹tin⁴ 天⁴】terraced fields；terrace

梯形【tei¹ ying⁴ 型】ladder-shaped；trapezoid

锑【tei¹ 梯】〈n.〉antimony；stibium（Sb）

体【tei² 睇】body；part of the body；substance；style；form；personally do or experience sth.；system；aspect（of a verb）

体积【tei²jig⁷ 织】volume；bulk

体质【tei²jed⁷ 侄⁷】physique；constitution

体重【tei²qung⁵ 冲⁵】（body）weight

体格【tei²gag⁸ 隔】physique；build

体魄【tei²pag⁸ 拍】physique

体力【tei²lig⁹ 历】physical strength；physical power

体态【tei²tai³ 太】posture；carriage

体形【tei²ying⁴ 型】bodily form；build

体育【tei²yug⁹ 玉】physical culture；sports

体温【tei²wen¹ 瘟】（body）temperature

体操【tei²qou¹ 粗】gymnastics

体会【tei²wui⁶ 汇】know from experience；realize

体验【tei²yim⁶ 艳】learn through practice

体现【tei²yin⁶ 燕⁶】embody；incarnate；reflect

体恤【tei²xêd⁷ 率】show solicitude for

体察【tei²qad⁸ 刷】experience and observe

体贴【tei²tib⁸ 帖】give every care to

体谅【tei²lêng⁶ 量⁶】make allowances

体念【tei²nim⁶ 粘⁶】give sympathetic consideration to

体面【tei² min⁶ 缅⁶】dignity；face；honourable

体系【tei²hei⁶ 兮⁶】system；setup

体制【tei²jei³ 济】system of organization；system

体裁【tei²qoi⁴ 材】types or forms of literature

体无完肤【tei²mou⁴yûn⁴fu¹ 毛元夫】be a mass of bruises；be thoroughly refuted

睇【tei² 体】watch；see；read=【普】看；观；读

睇白【tei²bag⁹ 伯】most probably=【普】估计；料定

睇病【tei² bēng⁶柄⁶】see a doctor=【普】看病；就诊

睇医生【tei²yi¹xeng¹ 衣笙】visit a doctor=【普】看大夫；就诊

睇化【tei²fa³ 花】not to hold a serious attitude towards every incident that happens in this world ∽【普】看透（事物的本质）；看破红尘

睇法【tei² fad⁸发 】 opinion；thinking=【普】看法

睇死【tei²xēi² 四²】sure=【普】确信；肯定无疑

睇衰【tei²xêu¹ 须】look down on=【普】瞧不起；看扁

睇小【tei²xiu² 少²】look down on=【普】瞧不起；小视

睇数【tei² xou³ 素】pay for bills =【普】结帐（茶馆、酒楼用语）

睇㖩凑【tei² lei⁶ qeo³ 黎臭】depend on circumstances =【普】看情况而定

睇住嚟【tei² jü⁶ lei⁴ 注⁶ 黎】wait and see =【普】等着瞧吧

替【tei³ 涕】take the place of；replace；for；on behalf of；decline

替代【tei³ doi⁶ 袋】substitute for；replace

替换【tei³ wun⁶ 焕】replace；substitute for；displace

替身【tei³ xen¹ 辛】substitute；replacement；scapegoat

替死鬼【tei³ xēi² guei² 四² 诡 】scapegoat；fall guy

替罪羊【tei³ jêü⁶ yêng⁴ 聚洋】scapegoat

嚔【tei³ 涕】sneeze（see"喷嚔"）

涕【tei³ 替】tears；mucus of the nose；snivel

剃【tei³ 替】shave

剃刀【tei³ dou¹ 都】razor

剃头【tei³ teo⁴ 投 】have one's head shaved；have a haircut

剃度【tei³ dou⁶ 道】tonsure

剃须【tei³ xou¹ 苏】have a shave；clean one's beard

剃刀门楣【tei³ dou¹ mun⁴ mēi⁴ 都 们 微 】money-changers =【普】狠心的敛财者，出入都括

屉【tei³ 替】steamer tray；drawer

抽屉【qeo¹ tei³ 秋】drawer = 柜桶【guei⁶ tung²】

啼【tei⁴ 提】cry；weep aloud；crow；caw

啼哭【tei⁴ hug⁷ 酷⁷】cry；wail

啼笑皆非【tei⁴ xiu³ gai¹ fēi¹ 少³ 佳飞】not know whether to laugh or cry

蹄【tei⁴ 提】hoof

马蹄【ma⁵ tei⁴ 码】horse's hoofs

醍【tei⁴ 提】〈n.〉醍醐【tei⁴ wu⁴ 胡】finest cream

题【tei⁴ 提】topic；subject；title；problem；inscribe

题目【tei⁴ mug⁹ 木】title；subject；topic；exercise problems；examination questions

题字【tei⁴ ji⁶ 治】inscribe；inscription

题词【tei⁴ qi⁴ 辞】appreciation or commemoration；inscription；foreword

题名【tei⁴ ming⁴ 明】inscribe one's name；autograph

题解【tei⁴ gai² 介²】key to exercises or problems；explanatory notes on the title or background of a book

题材【tei⁴ qoi⁴ 才】subject matter；theme

堤【tei⁴ 提】dyke；embankment

堤岸【tei⁴ ngon⁶ 安⁶】embankment

堤坝【tei⁴ ba³ 霸】dykes and dams

堤防【tei⁴ fong⁴ 妨】dyke；embankment

提【tei⁴ 堤】carry；lift；raise；put forward；draw out；mention；refer to；dipper；rising stroke

提防【tei⁴ fong⁴ 妨】take precautions against；beware of

提案【tei⁴ ngon³ 按】motion；proposal

提拔【tei⁴ bed⁹ 跋】promote

提包【tei⁴ bao¹ 苞】handbag；bag；valise

提倡【tei⁴ qêng¹ 昌】advocate；promote

提成【tei⁴ xing⁴ 诚】deduct a percentage

提出【tei⁴ qêd⁷次律⁷】put forward; advance; pose

提纯【tei⁴xên⁴ 醇】purify; refine

提起【tei⁴hēi⁴ 喜】raise; brace up; speak of

提高【tei⁴ gou¹糕】raise; heighten; enhance; increase

提取【tei⁴ qêû²娶】draw; pick up; extract; abstract

提前【tei⁴ qin⁴钱】move up; in advance; ahead of time

提升【tei⁴xing¹ 星¹】promote; hoist; elevate

提示【tei⁴xi⁶ 视】point out; prompt

提问【tei⁴men⁶ 文⁶】put questions to; quiz

提携【tei⁴kuei⁴ 葵】lead by the hand; guide and support = 带挟【dai³ hib⁸】

提醒【tei⁴xēng² 是镜²】remind; warn

提要【tei⁴yiu³ 腰³】summary; abstract; epitome

提议【tei⁴yi⁵ 耳】propose; move; proposal; motion

提早【tei⁴jou² 枣】shift to an earlier time

提炼【tei⁴lin⁶ 练】extract and purify; refine

提纲【tei⁴gong¹ 岗】outline

提供【tei⁴gung¹ 公】provide; supply; offer

提货【tei⁴fo³ 课】pick up goods

提款【tei⁴fun² 宽²】draw money

提交【tei⁴gao² 胶】submit to; refer to

提心吊胆【tei⁴xem¹diu³dam² 深掉³ 担²】have one's heart in one's mouth; be on tenterhooks

娣【tei⁵ 替⁵】younger sister

偷【teo¹ 头¹】steal; pilfer; find(time)

偷窃【teo¹xid⁸ 泄】steal; pilfer

偷盗【teo¹dou⁶ 道】steal; pilfer

偷懒【teo¹lan⁵ 兰⁵】loaf on the job; be lazy

偷偷【teo¹teo¹】stealthily; secretly; covertly

偷空【teo¹hung¹ 凶】take time off; snatch a moment

偷税【teo¹xêû³ 衰³】evade taxes

偷情【teo¹qing⁴ 程】carry on a clandestine love affair

偷袭【teo¹jab⁹ 习】sneak attack; sneak raid

偷工减料【teo¹gung¹gam²liu² 功监² 了²】scamp work and stint material; jerry-build

偷偷摸摸【teo¹teo¹mo¹mo¹ 摩】furtively; covertly

偷梁换柱【teo¹lêng⁴wun⁶qū⁵ 凉焕拄】perpetrate a fraud

偷鸡唔到蚀抓米【teo¹gei¹m⁴dou²xid⁹ja¹ mei⁵】try to steal a chicken only to end up losing the rice; go for wool and come back shorn =【普】偷鸡不着蚀把米

嗒【teo² 透】have a rest =【普】歇息

嗒下先【teo²ha⁶xin¹ 夏仙】have a short rest =【普】歇一会儿

透【teo³ 偷³; teo² 偷²】penetrate; pass through; seep through; fully; thoroughly; tell secretly; appear; show

透彻【teo³qid⁸ 撤】penetrating; through

透顶【teo³dēng² 钉²】thoroughly; downright

透气【teo³ hēi³ 戏 】ventilate; breathe freely

透火【teo³fo² 伙】start a fire =【普】生火；点炉子

透风【teo³ fung¹ 丰】let in air; ventilate; leak

透光【teo³guong¹ 桄¹】bright; transparent

透明【teo³ming⁴ 名】transparent

透视【teo³xi⁶ 示】perspective; fluoroscopy

透镜【teo³gēng³ 颈³】lens

透露【teo³ lou⁶路 】divulge; leak; disclose; reveal

透辟【teo³pig⁷ 僻】penetrating; incisive

透气【teo²hēi³ 戏】breathe; respire =【普】呼吸

透大气【teo²dai⁶hēi³ 歹⁶ 戏】take a deep breath =【普】喘气；深呼吸

头【teo⁴ 投; teo² 透】head; hair or hair style; top; end; beginning or end; remnant; chief; side; first; last; before; < *classifier*. > the unit of cattle, etc.

头脑【teo⁴nou⁵ 恼】brains; mind; clue

头颅【teo⁴lou⁴ 卢】head = 头壳【hog⁸】

头发【teo⁴fad⁸ 法】hair

头顶【teo⁴ dēng² 得镜²】the top of the head

头等【teo⁴deng² 戥】first-class; first-rate

头子【teo⁴ji² 止】chieftain; chief; boss

头目【teo⁴mug⁹ 木】head of a gang; chieftain

头头【teo⁴teo²】head; chief; leader; initially

头绪【teo⁴xêū² 穗²】main threads = 头路【lou⁶】

头晕【teo⁴wen⁴ 云】dizzy; giddy = 头昏【fen¹】

头痛【teo⁴tung³ 通³】(have a) headache = 头瘭【qēg⁸】

头衔【teo⁴ham⁴ 咸】title

头先【teo⁴xin¹ 仙】just now =【普】刚才

头车【teo⁴qē¹ 奢】the first bus or train to travel according to the schedule =【普】第一班车；早班车

头大【teo⁴dai⁶ 歹⁶】= 头婷【teo⁴peo³ 拍欧³】troublesome; difficult to solve; knotty =【普】伤脑筋

头莙【teo⁴log⁷ 洛⁷】chief; first in command =【普】头号人物；第一把手

头皮【teo⁴pēi⁴ 脾】dandruff

头耷耷【teo⁴deb⁷deb⁷ 得合⁷】keep one's head down; the expression when one is low, blue =【普】垂头丧气

头颐颐【teo⁴ ngog⁹ ngog⁹ 岳 】look around everywhere =【普】仰起头，发呆的样子

头重脚轻【teo⁴qung⁵gêg⁸hēng¹ 虫⁵ 格约⁸ 黑镜¹】top-heavy

头头是道【teo⁴ teo⁴ xi⁶ dou⁶ 示度】clear and logical

头痛医头，脚痛医脚【teo⁴tung³yi¹teo⁴, gêg⁹tung³yi¹gêg⁹】treat symptoms but not the disease

投【teo⁴ 头】throw; fling; hurl; put in; drop; cast; send; go to; fit in with

投掷【teo⁴jag⁹ 泽】throw; hurl

投奔【teo⁴ben¹ 宾】go to for shelter

投入【teo⁴yeb⁹ 邑⁹】throw into; put into

投身【teo⁴xen¹ 辛】throw oneself into

投标【teo⁴biu¹ 彪】submit a tender; enter a bid

投产【teo⁴qan² 铲】put into production

投递【teo⁴dei⁶ 第】deliver

投合【teo⁴heb⁹ 盒】agree; get along; cater to

投机【teo⁴gēi¹ 基】congenial; speculate; seize a chance to seek private gain

投票【teo⁴piu³ 漂】vote; cast a vote

投靠【teo⁴kɑo³ 卡坳³】go and seek refuge with sb.

投亲【teo⁴qen¹ 趁¹】go and live with relatives

投资【teo⁴ji¹ 支】invest; money invested

投放【teo⁴fong³ 况】throw in; put in

投降【teo⁴hong⁴ 项⁴】surrender; capitulate

投胎【teo⁴toi¹ 台¹】reincarnation

投影【teo⁴ying² 映】projection

投桃报李【teo⁴tou⁴bou⁴lēi⁵ 陶布理】return present for present; exchange gifts

投鼠忌器【teo⁴xü²gēi⁶hēi⁵ 署技气】hesitate to pelt a rat for fear of smashing the dishes beside it

诵【tem³ 凼³】fool; humbug; coax; humour =【普】哄

诵细蚊仔【tem⁴xei³men¹jei² 世炆济²】coax a child; handle children =【普】哄小孩

凼【tem⁵ 梯暗⁵】small puddle

水凼【xêü²tem⁵ 瑞²】a small puddle

吞【ten¹ 饨】swallow; gulp down; take possession of; annex

吞并【ten⁴bing⁶ 丙⁶】annex; gobble up

吞没【ten¹mud⁹ 末】embezzle; swallow up; engulf

吞声【ten¹xēng¹ 腥】gulp down one's sobs

吞噬【ten¹xei⁶ 逝】swallow; gobble up; engulf

吞吐【ten¹tou³ 套】swallow and spit – take in and send out in large quantities

吞枪【ten¹qēng¹ 昌 】kill oneself with a pistol

吞吞吐吐【ten¹ten¹tou³tou³ 套】hesitate in speech; hem and haw

饨【ten¹ 吞】dumpling soup(see"云吞")

褪【ten³ 吞³; têü³ 退】step back; withdraw; shift; move; slip out of sth.; take off; shed; fade

褪出【ten³qêd⁷ 次律⁷】slip out

迍【ten³ 褪; ten⁴ 褪⁴】move; remove; shift =【普】移动; 挪动

迍过去【ten³guo³hêü³ 戈³ 虚³】move over to =【普】移过去; 挪过去

迍来迍去【ten⁴loi⁴ten⁴hêü³ 莱虚³】go out and come in; go out and come; be busy ∽【普】出出进进; 忙来忙去

胗【ten⁴ 吞⁴】shiver due to shock and terror; shake =【普】振动; 震动

胗胗震【ten⁴ten²jen³ 振】keep shivering =【普】发抖; 心慌意乱

肥胗胗【fēi⁴ten⁴ten⁴ 非⁴】overfat ∽【普】过度肥胖

腾【teng⁴ 誊】gallop; jump; prance; rise; soar; clear out; vacate; toss about

腾空【teng⁴hung¹ 凶】soar; rise high into the air; rise to the sky

腾越【teng⁴yüd⁹ 月】jump over

腾云驾雾【teng⁴wen⁴gɑ³mou⁶ 匀架务】speed across the sky; feel giddy

藤【teng⁴ 腾】cane; rattan; vine

藤萝【teng⁴lo⁴ 罗】Chinese wistaria

藤条【teng⁴tiu² 跳²】rattan

藤笈【teng⁴gib⁷ 格业⁷】a box made of rattan＝【普】藤箱子；藤箧；

滕【teng⁴ 腾】a surname

誊【teng⁴ 腾】transcribe；copy out

誊写【teng⁴xē² 舍²】transcribe；copy out

誊清【teng⁴qing¹ 青】make a fair copy of

韬【teb⁷ 梯急⁷】usie the sheath to slip on sth.＝【普】用套子套上

韬韬客【teb⁷ teb⁷ hem⁶ 坎⁶】using the sheath to slip on sth. is very suitable＝【普】用套子套上某物很合适

拖【to¹ 妥¹】pull；drag；haul；delay；drag on

拖拉【to¹lai¹ 赖¹】dilatory；slow；sluggish

拖欠【to¹him³ 谦³】be in arrears；default

拖累【to¹lêu⁶ 虑】encumber；implicate

拖沓【to¹dab⁹ 踏】dilatory；sluggish

拖鞋【to¹hai⁴ 孩】slippers

拖车【to¹qē¹ 奢】trailer

拖船【to¹xün⁴ 旋】tugboat；tug

拖后腿【to¹heo⁶têü² 候退²】hinder sb.；hold sb. back

拖拉机【to¹lai¹gēi¹ 赖¹ 基】tracter

拖泥带水【to¹ nei⁴ dai³ xêü² 尼戴瑞²】messy；sloppy

唾【to³ 拖³；tê³ 梯靴³】saliva；spittle；spit

唾液【to³yig⁹ 亦】saliva＝口水【heo²xêü²】

唾沫【to³mud⁹ 没】saliva；spittle

唾骂【to³ma⁶ 马⁶】spit on and curse；revile

唾弃【to³hēi³ 戏】cast aside；spurn

佗【to⁴ 驼】shoulder a burden；conceive＝【普】负荷；拖累

佗衰【to⁴xêü¹ 需】involve others in one's problems；get sb. into trouble＝【普】连累；被牵连而受罪

砣【to⁴ 驼】the sliding weight of a steelyard；stone roller

砣表【to⁴biu¹ 标】a small round clock worn inside one's clothing＝【普】怀表

砣仔【to⁴jei² 济²】be pregnant＝【普】怀孕

驮【to⁴ 驼；do⁶ 惰】carry on the back

驮畜【to⁴qug⁷ 促】pack animal

驼【to⁴ 驮】camel；hunchbacked

驼峰【to⁴ fung¹ 风 】hump（of a camel）；hump

驼背【to⁴ bui³辈 】hunchback；hunchbacked

驼子【to⁴ji² 止】hunchback；hunchbacked＝阿驼【a³to²】

阿驼行路——中中地【a³to²hang⁴lou⁶, jung¹jung¹dēi²】the state of being middling ∽【普】不上不下，中游状态

舵【to⁴ 驼】rudder；helm

舵手【to⁴xeo² 守】steersman；helmsman

陀【to⁴ 驼】〈n.〉陀螺【to⁴lo⁴ 罗】top

沱【to⁴ 驼】a small bay in a river

鸵【to⁴ 驼】〈n.〉鸵鸟【to⁴niu⁵ 那妖⁵】ostrich

跎【to⁴ 驼】(see"蹉跎"【qo¹to⁴】)

鼍【to⁴ 驼】〈n.〉鼍龙【to⁴lung⁴ 隆】Chinese alligator = 猪婆龙【jü¹po⁴lung⁴】

妥【to⁵ 驼⁵】appropriate; proper; ready; settled

妥当【to⁵dong³ 档】appropriate; proper

妥善【to⁵xin⁶ 膳】appropriate; proper

妥帖【to⁵ tib⁸ 贴】appropriate; fitting; proper

妥协【to⁵hib⁸ 惬】come to terms; compromise

胎【toi¹ 台¹】foetus; embryo; birth; padding; roughcast; tyre

胎儿【toi¹yi⁴ 而】foetus; embryo

胎盘【toi¹pun⁴ 盆】placenta

胎生【toi¹xeng¹ 笙】viviparity

台【toi⁴ 抬; toi² 抬²】platform; stage; terrace; stand; support; table; desk; broadcasting station; a special telephone service; < pron. > you; < classifier. > the unit of a play, etc.

台布【toi⁴bou³ 报】tablecloth

台词【toi⁴qi⁴ 辞】actor's lines

台风【toi⁴fung¹ 丰】typhoon

台阶【toi⁴gai¹ 皆】a flight of steps; chance to extricate oneself from an awkward position; bench

台面【toi⁴min² 缅】table; mesa

台球【toi⁴keo⁴ 求】billiards; billiard ball; table tennis

台湾【toi⁴wan¹ 弯】Taiwan(Province)

苔【toi⁴ 台】live mosses(see"青苔")

苔藓植物【toi⁴xin²jig⁹med⁹ 洗直勿】bryophyte

抬【toi⁴ 台】lift; raise; carry; rise

抬头【toi⁴teo⁴ 投】raise one's head; gain ground; rise; look up; hoist; go up; ascend

抬举【toi⁴gêü² 矩】praise or promote sb. to show favour; favour sb.

殆【toi⁵ 怠; doi⁶ 代】danger; nearly; almost

怠【toi⁵ 台⁵】idle; remiss; slack

怠工【toi⁵gung¹ 功】slow down; go slow

怠慢【toi⁵man⁶ 万】cold-shoulder; slight

韬【tou¹ 滔】sheath or bow case; hide; the art of war

韬略【tou¹lêg⁹ 掠】military strategy

韬光养晦【tou¹guong¹yêng⁵fui³ 胱庠悔】hide one's capacities and bide one's time

滔【tou¹ 韬】inundate; flood

滔滔【tou¹tou¹】torrential; surging; keeping up a constant flow of words

滔天【tou¹tin¹ 田¹】dash to the skies; heinous

叨【tou¹ 滔; dou¹ 刀】be favoured with

叨光【tou¹guong¹ 胱】much obliged to you

饕【tou¹ 滔】〈n.〉饕餮【tou¹tid⁸ 铁】a mythical ferocious animal; a fierce and cruel person; voracious eater; glutton

绦【tou¹ 滔】silk ribbon; silk braid

绦虫【tou¹qung⁴ 从】tapeworm; cestode

土【tou² 肚²】soil; earth; land; ground; local; homemade; unrefined; opium

土地【tou²dêi⁶ 得希⁶】land; soil; territory

土壤【tou²yêng⁶ 让】soil

土木【tou²mug⁹ 目】building; construction

土豆【tou²deo⁶ 窦】potato

土产【tou²qan² 铲】local product

土法【tou²fad⁸ 发】local method

土方【tou²fong¹ 芳】cubic metre of earth；
　　earthwork

土气【tou²hēi³ 戏】rustic；uncouth

土著【tou² ju³ 注】original inhabitants；a-
　　boriginals

土语【tou²yü⁵ 雨】local dialect＝土话
　　【wa⁶】

土匪【tou²fēi² 非²】bandit；brigand

土豪【tou²hou⁴ 毫】local tyrant

土佬【tou²lou² 老²】one who is local；clod-
　　hopper＝【普】土包子

土星【tou²xing¹ 升】〈n.〉Saturn

土鲮鱼【tou² lēng⁴ yü² 靓⁴ 于²】a type of
　　fish

土霉素【tou²mui⁴xou³ 梅数】terramycin

土耳其【tou²yi²kēi⁴ 尔奇】〈n.〉Turkey

土皇帝【tou²wong⁴dei³ 王谛】local despot

土洋结合【tou² yêng⁴ gid⁸ heb⁹ 杨洁盒】
　　combine indigenous and foreign
　　methods

土崩瓦解【tou²beng¹nga⁵gai² 蹦雅介²】
　　disintegrate

钍【tou² 土】〈n.〉thorium（Th）

吐【tou³ 套】spit；say；tell；vomit；dis-
　　gorge

吐痰【tou³tam⁴ 谭】spit；expectorate

吐血【tou³hüd⁸ 黑月⁸】spitting blood；hae-
　　matemesis

吐露【tou³lou⁶ 路】reveal；tell

吐气【tou³ hēi³ 戏　】feel elated and exul-
　　tant；aspirated

吐弃【tou³hēi³ 戏】spurn；cast aside；re-
　　ject

吐故纳新【tou³gu³nab⁹xen¹ 固呐辛】get
　　rid of the stale and take in the
　　fresh

兔【tou³ 吐】hare；rabbit

兔仔【tou³jei² 济²】hare；rabbit＝【普】兔
　　子

兔崽子【tou³joi²ji² 宰止】brat；bastard

兔死狐悲【tou³xēi²wu⁴bēi¹ 四² 胡卑】like
　　grieves for like

兔子不食窝边草【tou³ji²bed⁷xig⁹wo¹bin¹
　　qou² 止毕蚀锅鞭曹²】a villain
　　doesn't harm his nextdoor neigh-
　　bours

菟【tou³ 兔】〈n.〉菟丝子【tou³xi¹ji² 司
　　止】the seed of Chinese dodder

屠【tou⁴ 涛】butcher；massacre；slaugh-
　　ter；a surname

屠宰【tou⁴joi² 哉²】butcher；slaughter

屠杀【tou⁴xad⁸ 煞】massacre；butcher

屠夫【tou⁴fu¹ 肤】butcher；a ruthless ruler

屠刀【tou⁴dou¹ 都】butcher's knife

徒【tou⁴ 屠】on foot；empty；bare；only；
　　in vain；pupil；follower；person；fel-
　　low；sentence

徒弟【tou⁴dei² 抵】apprentice；disciple

徒步【tou⁴bou⁶ 部】on foot

徒手【tou⁴xeo² 守】bare-handed；unarmed

徒然【tou⁴yin⁴ 言】in vain；for nothing

徒刑【tou⁴ying⁴ 型】imprisonment；sen-
　　tence

徒劳无功【tou⁴lou⁴mou⁴gung¹ 卢毛工】
　　make a futile effort；work to no
　　avail

徒子徒孙【tou⁴ji²tou⁴xün¹ 止酸】disciples
　　and followers；adherents

途
【tou⁴ 图】way; road; route

途径【tou⁴ging³ 劲】way; channel

途经【tou⁴ging¹ 京】by way of

途中【tou⁴jung¹ 钟】on the way

途程【tou⁴ging⁴ 情】road; way; course

涂
【tou⁴ 图】spread on; apply; smear; blot out; cross out; a surname

涂改【tou⁴goi² 该²】alter

涂料【tou⁴liu² 撩】coating; paint

涂抹【tou⁴mud⁸ 末⁸】daub; paint; scribble

涂炭【tou⁴tan³ 叹】utter misery; great affliction

涂脂抹粉【tou⁴ji¹mud⁸fen² 支末⁸ 分²】apply powder and paint; prettify; whitewash

荼
【tou⁴ 图】a bitter edible plant; the white flower of reeds, etc.

荼毒【tou⁴dug⁹ 独】torment

荼蘼【tou⁴mēi⁴ 眉】< n. > roseleaf raspberry

图
【tou⁴ 徒】picture; drawing; chart; map; plan; seek; pursue; intention; intent

图画【tou⁴wa² 话²】drawing; picture

图片【tou⁴pin² 偏²】picture; photograph

图样【tou⁴ yēng² 扬²】pattern; design; draft

图形【tou⁴ying⁴ 型】graph; figure

图像【tou⁴jêng⁶ 象】picture; image

图表【tou⁴biu² 标²】chart; diagram; graph

图案【tou⁴ngon³ 按】pattern; design

图景【tou⁴ging² 境】view; prospect

图谋【tou⁴ meo⁴ 牟】plot; scheme; conspire

图书【tou⁴xū⁶ 输】books

图腾【tou⁴teng⁴ 藤】totem

图章【tou⁴jêng¹ 张】seal; stamp

淘
【tou⁴ 涛】wash in a pan or basket; tax; naughty; clean out; dredge

淘米【tou⁴mei⁵ 迷⁵】wash rice

淘金【tou⁴gem¹ 今】panning

淘气【tou⁴hēi³ 戏】naughty; mischievous

淘汰【tou⁴tai³ 太】eliminate through selection or competition; die out; fall into disuse

陶
【tou⁴ 淘】pottery; make pottery; mould; happy; a surname

陶器【tou⁴hēi³ 戏】pottery; earthenware

陶瓷【tou⁴ qi⁴ 迟】pottery and porcelain; ceramics

陶然【tou⁴yin⁴ 言】happy and carefree

陶冶【tou⁴yē⁵ 野】make pottery and smelt metal; exert a favourable influence; mould

陶醉【tou⁴jêü³ 最】be intoxicated; revel in

萄
【tou⁴ 图】grapes(see"葡萄")

啕
【tou⁴ 图】cry loudly(号啕【hou⁶tou⁴】)

掏
【tou⁴ 陶】draw out; pull out; fish out; dig; hollow out; steal from sb's pocket

掏腰包【tou⁴yiu¹bao¹ 邀苞】foot a bill; pick sb.'s pocket = 摱荷包【ngem⁴ho⁴bao¹】

涛
【tou⁴ 图】great waves; billows(see"波涛")

桃
【tou⁴ 图】peach; a peach-shaped thing

桃树【tou⁴xü⁶ 书⁶】peach(tree)

桃花【tou⁴fa¹ 化¹】peach blossom

桃红【tou⁴hung⁴ 洪】pink

桃仔【tou⁴jei² 济²】peach =【普】桃子

桃李【tou⁴lēi⁵ 理】peaches and plums——one's pupils or disciples

讨【tou² 土】send armed forces to suppress; denounce; condemn; demand; ask for; marry; invite; discuss; study

讨伐【tou² fed⁹ 乏】send armed forces to suppress

讨饭【tou² fan⁶ 范】beg for food = 乞饭【hed⁷ fan⁶】

讨好【tou²hou² 蒿²】fawn on; toady to; be rewarded with a fruitful result

讨还【tou²wan⁴ 环】get sth. back

讨价【tou² ga³ 嫁】ask a price = 问价钱【men⁶ ga³qin⁴】

讨教【tou²gao³ 较】ask for advice

讨论【tou²lên⁶ 沦⁶】discuss; talk over

讨饶【tou² yiu⁴ 尧】beg for mercy = 求饶【keo⁴yiu⁴】

讨嫌【tou²yim⁴ 严】annoying; disagreeable

讨厌【tou²yim³ 染³】disagreeable; disgusting; hard to handle; troublesome

讨价还价【tou² ga³ wan⁴ ga³嫁环】bargain; haggle

逃【tou⁴ 桃】run away; escape; flee; evade; dodge; shirk

逃走【tou⁴jeo² 酒】run away; flee

逃跑【tou⁴pao² 泡²】run away; flee; take flight

逃甩【tou⁴led⁷ 罗核⁷】succeed in escaping =【普】逃脱

逃避【tou⁴bēi⁶ 鼻】escape; evade; shirk

逃难【tou⁴nan⁶ 那晏⁶】flee from a calamity

逃荒【tou⁴fong¹ 方】flee from famine

逃命【tou⁴mēng⁶ 莫镜⁶】run for one's life

逃兵【tou⁴ bing¹冰 】army deserter; deserter

逃窜【tou⁴qün³ 寸】run away; flee in disorder

逃亡【tou⁴mong⁴ 忙】flee from home

逃税【tou⁴xêü³ 瑞³】evade a tax

逃之夭夭【tou⁴ji¹yiu¹yiu¹ 支妖】decamp; make one's getaway

套【tou³ 吐】sheath; case; covers; sleeve; cover with; slip over; that which covers; batting; traces; hitch up; knot; loop; tie; copy; formula; coax a secret out of sb. ; <classifier> the unit of the books, etc.

套子【tou³ji² 止】sheath; case; cover

套筒【tou³tung² 桶】sleeve; muff

套间【tou³ gan¹ 奸 】inner room; apartment; flat

套包【tou³bao¹ 苞】collar for a horse

套购【tou³keo³ 扣】illegally buy up

套色【tou³xig⁷ 式】chromatography

套印【tou³yen³ 因³】chromatography

套话【tou³wa⁶ 华⁶】polite formula = 套语【yü⁵ 雨】

套问【tou³ men⁶ 文⁶】tactfully sound sb. out

套用【tou³yung⁶ 容⁶】apply mechanically

肚【tou⁵ 土⁵】tripe; belly; abdomen; stomach

肚子【tou⁵ji² 止】belly; abdomen

肚皮【tou⁵pēi⁴ 脾】belly

肚脐【tou⁵qi⁴ 迟】navel; belly button

肚腩【tou⁵ nam⁵ 那南⁵】one's stomach; belly ∽【普】肚皮

肚屙【tou⁵ngo¹ 柯】diarrhoea =【普】拉肚子

汤【tong¹ 凼】hot water; boiling water; hot springs; soup; broth; decoction; a surname

清汤【qing¹ tong¹ 青】clear soup

汤匙【tong¹qi⁴ 迟】tablespoon；soupspoon

汤勺【tong¹ xêg⁸ 削】soup ladle ＝ 汤壳【hog⁸】

汤碗【tong¹wun² 宛】soup bowl

汤面【tong¹min⁶ 缅⁶】noodles in soup

汤药【tong¹yêg⁹ 若】a decoction of medicinal ingredients

汤丸【tong¹ yün² 院 】red flour balls eaten during Chinese New Year ＝【普】汤圆

剸【tong¹ 汤】slaughter；cut open ＝【普】宰杀

剸猪【tong¹ju¹ 朱】cut a pig

剸 死 牛【tong¹xêi²ngeo⁴ 四² 偶⁴】rob someone at the road ＝【普】路上强抢；掠夺

羰【tong¹ 汤】carbonyl（group）

羰基【tong¹gêi¹ 机】carbonyl（group）

躺【tong² 汤²】lie；recline

躺倒【tong²dou² 捣】lie down ＝ 睏低【fen³ dei¹】

躺椅【tong²yi² 绮】deck chair；sling chair

趟【tong³ 烫】〈classifier.〉the unit of walking about

烫【tong³ 趟】scald；burn；warm；very hot；iron；press；perm

烫发【tong³fad⁸法】give or have a permanent wave；perm

烫衫【tong³xam¹三】iron clothes ＝【普】烫衣服

烫金【tong³gem¹今】gilding；bronzing

烫伤【tong³xêng¹双】scald ＝ 㷫亲【lad⁸qen¹】

耥【tong³ 烫；tong² 躺】weed and loosen the soil

耥耙【tong³pa⁴ 爬】paddy-field harrow

淌【tong² 躺；tong⁵ 躺⁵】drip；shed；trickle

淌眼泪【tong²ngan⁵lêü⁶ 雁⁵ 类】shed tears

倘【tong² 躺】if；supposing；in case

倘若【tong²yêg⁹ 药】if；supposing；in case ＝ 倘或【wag⁹】＝ 倘使【xei²】

倘有不测【tong²yeo⁵bed⁷qag⁷ 友毕策⁷】in case of accidents

蹚【tong³ 趟；tong² 倘】wade；ford

蹚水过河【tong³xêü²guo³ho⁴ 瑞² 戈³ 何】wade（across）a stream

唐【tong⁴ 糖】the Tang Dynasty（618～907）；a surname

唐突【tong⁴ded⁹ 凸】brusque；rude；offensive

唐人【tong⁴yen⁴ 仁】Chinese

唐诗【tong⁴xi¹ 司】Tang poetry

唐人街【tong⁴yen⁴gai¹ 仁皆】Chinese town

唐山【tong⁴xan¹ 珊】motherland；China

糖【tong⁴ 唐】sugar；sugared；sweets

糖类【tong⁴lêü⁶ 泪】carbohydrate

糖水【tong⁴xêü² 瑞²】syrup；a type of dessert

糖果【tong⁴guo² 戈²】sweets；candy

糖精【tong⁴jing¹ 贞】saccharin；gluside

糖醋【tong⁴qou³ 措】sweet and sour

糖尿病【tong⁴niu⁶bêng⁶ 鸟⁶ 柄⁶】diabetes

糖衣炮弹【tong⁴yi¹pao¹dan² 依泡蛋】sugarcoated bullet

塘【tong⁴ 唐】dyke; pool; pond

鱼塘【yü⁴tong⁴ 余】fish pond
塘泥【tong⁴nei⁴ 尼】pond sludge; pond silt
塘虱【tong⁴xed⁷ 失】a type of fish =【普】
　　塘角鱼

搪【tong⁵ 淌⁵】ward off; keep out;
　　evade; daub
搪瓷【tong⁵qi⁴ 迟】enamel
搪塞【tong⁵xeg⁷ 时克⁷】stall sb. off

棠【tong⁴ 堂】〈n.〉birchleaf pear

棠梨【tong⁴lêi⁴ 离】birchleaf pear
棠棣【tong⁴dei⁶ 弟】Chinese bush cherry;
　　a kind of white poplar

堂【tong⁴ 棠】the main room of a house;
　　a hall for a specific purpose; court of
　　law; of the same clan; < classifier. >
　　the unit of a classes, etc.
堂屋【tong⁴ngug⁷ 额哭⁷】central room
堂兄弟【tong⁴hing¹dei⁶ 兴第】cousins
堂堂【tong⁴tong⁴】dignified; imposing
堂皇【tong⁴wong⁴ 王】grand; stately
堂堂正正【tong⁴tong⁴jing³jing³ 政】impre-
　　ssive or dignified in personal ap-
　　pearance; open and aboveboard

膛【tong⁴ 堂】thorax; chest; chamber

胸膛【hung¹tong⁴ 凶】chest

镗【tong⁴ 堂; tong¹ 汤】boring

镗床【tong⁴qong¹ 仓⁴】boring machine

螳【tong⁴ 堂】mantis

螳螂【tong⁴long⁴ 郎】mantis
螳蜋【tong⁴mêi¹ 尾¹】flying dragons; a
　　boat =【普】蜻蜓

螳臂挡车【tong⁴bêi³dong²qē¹ 秘当² 奢】a
　　mantis trying to stop a chariot
　　——overrate oneself and try to
　　hold back an overwhelmingly su-
　　perior force

托【tog⁸ 柝】hold in the palm; sth. serv-
　　ing as a support; set off; ask; plead;
　　owe to
托付【tog⁸fu⁶ 附】entrust; commit sth. to
　　sb.'s care
托管【tog⁸gun² 莞】trusteeship
托福【tog⁸fug⁷ 幅】thanks to you
托故【tog⁸ gu³ 固】give a pretext; make
　　an excuse
托词【tog⁸qi⁴ 辞】find a pretext; pretext
托人情【tog⁸ yen⁴ qing⁴仁程 】gain one's
　　end through pull
托儿所【tog⁸yi⁴xo² 而锁】nursery; creche
托拉斯【tog⁸lai¹xi¹ 赖¹ 司】trust
托大脚【tog⁸ dai¹ gêg⁶ 歹⁶ 格约⁸】please
　　one intentionally so as to benefit
　　from that being pleased ∽【普】阿
　　谀逢迎
托手踭【tog⁸ xeo² jang¹守支罂¹】prevent
　　one from doing something; decline
　　to help people =【普】阻碍别人达
　　到目的或谢绝帮助别人

柝【tog⁸ 托】watchman's clapper

拓【tog⁸ 托; tab⁸ 塌】open up; develop;
　　rubbing
拓荒【tog⁸fong¹ 方】open up virgin soil
拓片【tog⁸pin² 偏²】rubbing

通【tung¹ 桶¹】open; through; open up
　　or clear out by poking or jabbing; lead
　　to; go to; connect; tell; know; ex-
　　pert; logical; all; whole; common;

< *classifier.* > the unit of the speak or movement

通达【tung¹dad⁹ 得压⁹】understand; passage

通畅【tung¹qêng³ 唱】unobstructed; clear; easy and smooth

通街【tung¹gai¹ 皆】common; everywhere ＝【普】到处

通顺【tung¹xên⁶ 信⁶】clear and coherent; smooth

通行【tung¹heng⁴ 衡】pass through; current

通过【tung¹guo³ 戈³】pass through; get past; pass; carry; by; through; ask the consent or approval of

通水【tung¹xêü² 瑞²】convey messages ＝【普】透露内情

通道【tung¹dou⁶ 度】passageway; passage ＝通路【lou⁶】

通衢【tung¹kêü⁴ 渠】thoroughfare ＝通途【tou⁴】

通商【tung¹ xêng¹ 双 】(of nations) have trade relations

通邮【tung¹ yeo⁴ 由】asessible by postal communication

通信【tung¹xên³ 讯】communicate by letter

通讯【tung¹xên³ 信】communication; newsreport

通航【tung¹hong⁴ 杭】be open to navigation or air traffic

通车【tung¹ qē¹奢 】be open to traffic; have transport service

通话【tung¹wa⁶ 华⁶】converse; communicate by telephone

通货【tung¹ fo³课 】currency; current money

通力【tung¹lig⁹ 历】concerted effort

通气【tung¹hēi³ 戏】ventilate; be in touch with each other

通风【tung¹fung¹ 丰】ventilate; divulge information

通婚【tung¹fen¹ 分】intermarry

通奸【tung¹gan¹ 间¹】commit adultery

通缉【tung¹qeb⁷ 辑】order the arrest of a criminal at large

通告【tung¹gou³ 诰】announce; public notice

通知【tung¹ji¹ 支】notify; inform; notice

通晓【tung¹ hiu² 翘²】 thoroughly understand

通常【tung¹xêng⁴ 偿】general; usual; normal

通通【tung¹tung¹】all; entirely; completely

通俗【tung¹jug⁹ 族】popular; common

通行证【tung¹heng⁴jing³ 衡正】pass; permit

通融【tung¹yung⁴ 容】make an exception in sb.'s favour; accommodate sb. with a short-term loan

通菜【tung¹qoi³ 蔡】a type of vegetable

通情达理【tung¹qing⁴dad⁹lēi⁵ 程 得压⁹ 李】showing good sense; reasonable

统【tung² 捅】interconnected system; gather into one; unite; all; togther; any tube-shaped part of an article of clothing, etc.

统一【tung² yed⁷ 壹 】unify; unite; integrate; unified; unitary

统制【tung²jei³ 济】control

统治【tung²ji⁶ 自】rule; dominate

统帅【tung² xêü³ 税】commander; command

统率【tung²xêd⁷ 恤】command

统统【tung²tung²】all; completely; entirely

统计【tung² gei³ 继】statistics; add up; count

统筹【tung²qeo⁴ 绸】plan as a whole

统称【tung²qing¹ 清】be called by a joint name; a general designation

捅【tung² 统】poke; stab; disclose; give away

捅刺刀【tung²qi³dou¹ 次都】stab with a bayonet

捅马蜂窝【tung²ma⁵fung¹wo¹ 码风锅】stir up a hornets' nest; bring a hornets' nest about one's ears

桶【tung² 捅】tub; pail; bucket; keg; barrel

水桶【xêü² tung² 瑞²】water bucket

筒【tung² 桶; tung⁴ 同】a section of thick bamboo; a thick tube-shaped object

笔筒【bed⁷tung⁴ 毕】brush pot

痛【tung³ 疼】ache; pain; sadness; sorrow; extremely; deeply

痛苦【tung³fu² 府】pain; suffering; agony

痛楚【tung³qo²挫²】pain; anguish; suffering

痛心【tung³ xem¹ 深】pained; distressed; grieved

痛惜【tung³xig⁷ 式】deeply regret; deplore

痛切【tung³qid⁸ 设】with intense sorrow

痛恨【tung³hen⁶ 狠⁶】hate bitterly; utterly detest

痛哭【tung³hug⁷ 酷】cry bitterly; wail

痛斥【tung³qig⁷ 戚】bitterly attack

痛处【tung³qü³ 储³】sore spot; tender spot

痛痒【tung³ yêng⁵ 仰】sufferings; importance

痛心疾首【tung³xem¹jed⁹xeo² 深佳守】with bitter hatred

痛改前非【tung³goi²qin⁴fēi¹ 该² 钱飞】sincerely mend one's ways

疼【tung³ 痛】love; kiss; ache; pain; sore; love dearly

头疼【teo⁴tung³ 投】have a headache

疼锡【tung³xēg⁸ 石⁸】love dearly =【普】疼爱

同【tung⁴ 铜】same; alike; similar; be the same as; together; in common; < conj. > ∽ and; < prep. > ∽ with

同性【tung⁴xing³ 姓】of the same sex; of the same nature or character

同样【tung⁴yêng⁶ 让】same; equal; similar

同一【tung⁴yed⁷ 壹】same; identical

同埋【tung⁴mai⁴ 买⁴】together; and; with =【普】和……一起

同时【tung⁴ xi⁴ 是⁴】at the same time; moreover

同步【tung⁴bou⁶ 部】synchronism

同路【tung⁴lou⁶ 露】go the same way

同行【tung⁴heng⁴ 衡】travel together

同行【tung⁴hong⁴ 杭】of the same trade or occupation; the same trade or business

同屋【tung⁴ngug⁷ 额哭⁷】stay in the same house with others

同事【tung⁴xi⁶ 示】work in the same place; work together

同仁【tung⁴ yen⁴ 人】colleagues = 同人【yen⁴】

同伙【tung⁴fo² 火】collude; partner

同心【tung⁴xem¹ 深】concentric; with one heart

同情【tung⁴qing⁴ 程】sympathize with; show sympathy for

同谋【tung⁴meo⁴ 牟】conspire；accomplice

同盟【tung⁴meng⁴ 萌】alliance；league

同伴【tung⁴bun⁶ 拌】companion

同学【tung⁴ hog⁹ 鹤】be in the same school；schoolmate；fellow student＝同窗【qeng¹】

同乡【tung⁴ hêng¹ 香】a fellow villager，townsman or provincial

同胞【tung⁴bao¹ 包】born of the same parents；fellow countryman；compatriot

同感【tung⁴gem² 敢】the same feeling

同志【tung⁴ji³ 至】comrade

同宗【tung⁴jung¹ 中】of the same clan

同意【tung⁴ yi³ 薏】agree；consent；approve

同化【tung⁴ fo³花³】assimilate；assimilation

同上【tung⁴xêng⁶ 尚】ditto

同室操戈【tung⁴xed⁷qou¹guo¹ 失操¹果¹】internal strife

同床异梦【tung⁴qong⁴yi⁶mung⁶ 苍⁴义蒙⁶】be strange bedfellows

同流合污【tung⁴ leo⁴ heb⁹ wu¹ 留盒乌】wallow in the mire with sb.

同病相怜【tung⁴bêng⁶xêng¹lin⁴ 柄⁶双连】Fellow sufferers commiserate with each other.

同仇敌忾【tung⁴ xeo⁴ dig⁹ koi³ 愁迪概】share a bitter hatred of the enemy

同甘共苦【tung⁴gem¹gung⁶fu² 今贡⁶府】share weal and woe

同心同德【tung⁴xem¹tung⁴deg⁷ 深得】be of one heart and one mind

同心协力【tung⁴ xem¹ hib⁸ lig⁹深胁历】work together with one heart

同舟共济【tung⁴jeo¹gung⁶jei³ 周贡⁶制】cross a river in the same boat

铜【tung⁴ 同】copper(Cu)

铜器【tung⁴hêi³ 戏】copper ware

铜丝【tung⁴xi¹ 司】copper wire

铜像【tung⁴jêng⁶ 匠】bronze statue

铜钱【tung⁴qin⁴ 前】copper cash

铜版【tung⁴ban² 板】copperplate

铜臭【tung⁴qeo³ 嗅】the stink of money

铜管乐器【tung⁴gun²ngog⁹hêi³ 莞岳戏】brass wind

蒿【tung⁴ 同】〈n.〉茼蒿【tung⁴hou¹ 好¹】crowndaisy chrysanthemum

桐【tung⁴ 同】a general term for paulownia，phoenix tree and tung tree

桐油【tung⁴yeo⁴ 由】tung oil

彤【tung⁴ 同】red

彤云【tung⁴ wen⁴ 匀】red clouds；dark clouds

佟【tung⁴ 同】a surname

童【tung⁴ 同】child；virgin；bare；bald

童子【tung⁴ji² 止】boy；lad

童贞【tung⁴jing¹ 精】virginity；chastity

童心【tung⁴xem¹ 深】childlike innocence；childishness；playfulness

童年【tung⁴nin⁴ 捻⁴】childhood

童话【tung⁴wa² 画²】children's stories

童工【tung⁴gung¹ 功】child labour

童声【tung⁴xing¹ 升】child's voice

童谣【tung⁴yiu⁴ 摇】children's folk rhymes

瞳【tung⁴ 童】pupil(of the eye)

瞳孔【tung⁴hung² 恐】pupil

瞳人【tung⁴yen⁴ 仁】pupil(of the'eye)＝

瞳仁【yen⁴】

酮【tung⁴ 同】〈n.〉ketone

秃【tug⁷ 替屋⁷】bald；bare；blunt；incomplete

秃顶【tug⁷dēng² 钉²】bald＝光头【guong¹teo⁴】

秃子【tug⁷ji² 止】baldhead＝光头佬【guong¹teo⁴lou²】

秃发病【tug⁴fad⁸bēng⁶ 法柄⁶】alopecia

挑【tiu¹ 佻】select；choose；pick；shoulder；raise；poke；stir up；instigate

挑剔【tiu¹tig⁷ 惕】nitpick；be fastidious

挑选【tiu¹xūn 损】choose；select；pick out

挑拣【tiu¹gan² 柬】pick；pick and choose

挑唆【tiu¹xo¹ 梳】incite；abet

挑动【tiu¹dung⁶ 洞】provoke；stir up

挑衅【tiu¹yen⁶ 孕】provoke

挑战【tiu¹jin³箭】throw down the gauntlet；challenge to a contest

挑逗【tiu¹deo¹ 兜】provoke；tease；tantalize

挑肥拣瘦【tiu¹fēi⁴gan²xeo³ 飞⁴ 柬秀】pick the fat or choose the lean — choose whichever is to one's personal advantage

挑拨离间【tiu¹bud⁹lēi⁴gan³ 勃漓柬³】sow dissension；foment discord

佻【tiu¹ 挑】〈a.〉轻佻【hing¹tiu¹ 兴】frivolous；giddy

祧【tiu¹ 挑】be or become heir to

跳【tiu³ 挑³】jump；leap；spring；beat；skip

跳动【tiu³ dung⁶ 洞】move up and down；beat

跳高【tiu³gou¹ 糕】high jump

跳过【tiu³guo³ 戈³】leap over

跳开【tiu³hoi³ 海¹】jump off

跳板【tiu³ ban² 版】gangplank；springboard

跳跃【tiu³yêg⁸ 约】jump；leap；bound

跳远【tiu³yün⁵ 软】long jump；broad jump

跳水【tiu³xêu² 瑞】dive

跳舞【tiu³mou⁵ 武】dance

跳蚤【tiu³ jou²早】flea＝狗虱【geo²xed⁷九室】

跳梁小丑【tiu³lêng⁴xiu²qeo² 凉少² 绸²】a buffoon who performs antics

眺【tiu³ 跳】look into the distance from a high place

眺望【tiu³mong⁵ 亡⁶】look into the distance from a high place

粜【tiu³ 跳】sell grain（粜米【tiu³mei⁵】）

窕【tiu⁵ 条⁵】〈a.〉窈窕【yiu²tiu⁵ 绕】gentle and graceful

笤【tiu⁴ 条】〈n.〉笤帚【tiu⁴jeo² 走】whisk broom

髫【tiu⁴ 条】a child's hanging hair

迢【tiu⁴ 条】far；remote

迢迢【tiu⁴tiu⁴】far away；remote

条【tiu⁴ 迢；tiu² 迢²】twig；strip；slip；item；order；< *classifier.* > the unit of a fish，a ship，etc.

条子【tiu⁴ ji² 止】strip；a brief informal note

条文【tiu⁴men⁴ 闻】article；clause

条约【tiu⁴yêg⁸ 跃】treaty；pact

条款【tiu⁴ fun² 欢²】clause；article；provision

条例【tiu⁴lei⁶ 丽】regulations；rules

条件【tiu⁴gin² 健²】condition；term；factor；requirement；prerequisite

条理【tiu⁴lēi⁵ 李】orderliness；method

条气唔顺【tiu⁴hēi³m⁴xên⁶ 戏讯⁶】feeling angry for not being convinced about something＝【普】气不顺；不服气

条分缕析【tiu⁴fen¹lêu⁵xig⁷ 芬吕式】make a careful and detailed analysis

条条框框【tiu⁴tiu⁴kuang¹kuang¹ 卡横¹】rules and regulations；conventions

添【tim¹ 甜】add；increase；have a baby

添置【tim¹ji³ 至】add to one's possessions；acquire

添丁【tim¹ding¹ 叮】have a baby born into the family

添补【tim¹bou¹ 保】replenish；get more

添枝加叶【tim¹ji¹ga¹yib⁹ 支家业】embellish a story

舔【tim² 忝】lick；lap

舔嘴唇【tim²jêu²xên⁴ 咀纯】moisten one's lips with the tongue

忝【tim² 舔】be unworthy of the honour

恬【tim⁴ 甜】quiet；tranquil；calm；not care at all

恬淡【tim⁴dam⁶ 担⁶】indifferent to fame or gain

恬静【tim⁴jing⁶ 净】quiet；peaceful

恬不知耻【tim⁴bed⁷ji¹qi² 毕之始】not feel ashamed；be shameless

甜【tim⁴ 恬】sweet；honeyed；sound

甜蜜【tim⁴med⁹ 勿】sweet；happy

甜美【tim⁴mēi⁵ 尾】sweet；luscious；pleasant

甜味【tim⁴mēi⁶ 未】sweet taste

甜头【tim⁴teo⁴ 投】sweet taste；good

甜水【tim⁴ xêu² 瑞²】fresh water；sugar water；happiness

甜品【tim⁴ ben² 禀】sweetmeats；sweet food ＝甜食【xig⁹】

甜耶耶【tim⁴ yē⁴ yē⁴ 椰】sweet；lovely feeling＝【普】太甜；很甜

甜滋滋【tim⁴ji¹ji¹ 支】pleasantly sweet

甜言蜜语【tim⁴yin⁴med⁹yü⁵ 然勿雨】sweet words and honeyed phrases

天【tin¹ 田¹】sky；heaven；overhead；day；season；weather；nature；God；Heaven

天空【tin¹hung¹ 凶】sky；heaven

天体【tin¹tei² 睇】celestial body

天边【tin¹bin¹ 鞭】horizon；remotest places

天下【tin¹ha⁶ 夏】land under heaven—the world；rule；domination

天棚【tin¹pang² 鹏²】the corridor＝【普】天台；楼顶

天地【tin¹ dēi⁶ 得希⁶】heaven and earth；world；field of activity

天堂【tin¹tong⁴ 塘】paradise；heaven

天公【tin¹ gung¹ 工】the ruler of heaven；God

天国【tin¹guog⁸ 帼】the Kingdom of Heaven

天宫【tin¹gung¹ 公】heavenly palace

天河【tin¹ ho⁴ 何】the Milky Way；the Galaxy

天使【tin¹xi³ 试】angel

天才【tin¹qoi⁴ 材】genius；talent；gift

天赋【tin¹ fu³ 富】inborn；innate；natural gift；talent＝天资【tin¹ji¹】

天分【tin¹fen⁶ 份】natural gift；talent

天干【tin¹gon¹ 竿】the ten Heavenly Stems

天机【tin¹gēi¹ 基】nature's mystery; God's design

天命【tin¹ming⁶ 名⁶】God's will; destiny; fate

天理【tin¹lēi⁵ 李】heavenly principles; justice

天良【tin¹lêng⁴ 梁】conscience

天伦【tin¹lên⁴沦 】the natural bonds and ethical relationships between members of a family

天光【tin¹guong¹ 桄¹】daybreak; dawn = 【普】天亮；天明

天色【tin¹ xig⁷式 】 colour of the sky; weather

天气【tin¹hēi³ 戏】weather

天时【tin¹xi⁴ 是⁴】weather; climate; timeliness

天然【tin¹yin⁴ 言】natural

天真【tin¹jen¹ 珍】innocent; artless

天职【tin¹jig⁷ 积】bounden duty; vocation

天性【tin¹ xing³姓 】 natural instincts; nature

天子【tin¹ji² 止】the Son of Heaven—the emperor

天险【tin¹him² 欠²】natural barrier

天敌【tin¹dig⁹ 迪】natural enemy

天窗【tin¹qêng¹ 昌】skylight

天井【tin¹jēng² 支镜²】small yard; courtyard

天线【tin¹xin³ 扇】aerial; antenna

天桥【tin¹kiu⁴ 乔】overline bridge

天文【tin¹men⁴ 闻】astronomy

天仙【tin¹xin¹ 先】goddess; a beauty

天时冷【tin¹xi⁴lang⁵ 是罗罍⁵】winter = 【普】冬天；天气冷

天鹅【tin¹ngo⁴ 峨】swan

天时热【tin¹xi⁴yid⁹ 是⁴ 衣泄⁹】summer = 【普】夏天；天气热

天花乱坠【tin¹fa¹lūn⁶jêū⁶ 化¹ 联⁶ 聚】as if it were raining flowers—give an extravagantly colourful description

天昏地暗【tin¹ fen¹ dēi⁶ ngem³分 得希⁶ 庵³】a murky sky over a dark earth; dark all round

天经地义【tin¹ging¹dēi⁶yi⁶ 京 得希⁶ 异】unalterable principle—right and proper

天罗地网【tin¹lo⁴dēi⁶mong⁵ 萝得希⁶ 妄】nets above and snares below

天诛地灭【tin¹ jū¹ dēi⁶ mid⁹ 朱得希⁶ 篾】stand condemned by God

天灾人祸【tin¹joi¹yen⁴wo⁶ 哉仁和⁶】natural and man-made calamities

天有不测风云【tin¹ yeo⁵ bed⁷ qag⁷ fung¹ wen⁴友毕策⁷ 丰匀】A storm may arise from a clear sky.

天无绝人之路【tin¹mou⁴jūd⁹yen⁴ji¹lou⁶ 毛 支月⁹ 仁支露】Heaven never seals off all the exits—there is always a way out.

田【tin⁴ 天⁴】field; farmland; cropland; a surname

田地【tin⁴ dēi⁶得希⁶】field; farmland; plight

田埂【tin⁴ geng²梗】a low bank of earth between fields; ridge = 田 基【gēi¹】

田间【tin⁴gan¹ 奸】field; farm

田野【tin⁴yē⁵ 惹】field; open country

田园【tin⁴yūn⁴ 元】field and gardens; countryside

田鸡【tin⁴gei¹ 计¹】frog =【普】青蛙

田螺【tin⁴lo² 罗²】river snail; snails

填【tin⁴ 田】fill; stuff; write; fill in

填空【tin⁴hung¹ 凶】fill a vacancy

填充【tin⁴ qung¹ 冲】fill up; stuff; fill in the blanks(in a test paper)

填补【tin⁴ bou² 保】fill (a vacancy, gap, etc.)

填平【tin⁴ping⁴ 萍】fill and level up

填写【tin⁴xē² 舍²】fill in; write

殄【tin⁵ 天⁵】extirpate; exterminate

腆【tin² 田²】rich; protrude; thrust out

腆胸【tin²hung¹ 凶】stick out one's chest

靦【tin² 田²】ashamed; brazen

靦颜【tin²ngan⁴ 雁⁴】ashamefaced

靦着脸【tin²jēg¹lim⁵ 桌⁹ 廉⁵】brazen it out

听【ting¹ 亭¹; ting³ 亭³; tēng¹ 厅¹】listen; hear; heed; obey; manage; allow

听见【tēng¹ gin³ 建】hear = 听闻【tēng¹ men⁴】

听说【tēng¹xūd⁸ 雪】be told; hear of; listen to a talk = 听讲【gong²】

听话【tēng¹ wa⁶华⁶】heed what an elder or superior says; be obedient

听从【tēng¹qung⁴ 虫】obey; heed

听信【tēng¹xên³ 讯】wait for information

听取【tēng¹qêū² 娶】listen to

听任【ting³yem⁶ 阴⁶】allow; let

听候【ting³heo² 后】wait for

听差【ting³qai¹ 钗】manservant; office attendant

听课【tēng¹fo³ 货】visit a class

听诊【ting¹qen² 陈²】auscultation

听众【ting¹jung³ 种³】audienece; listeners

听起来【tēng¹hēi²loi⁴ 喜莱】sound; ring

听其自然【ting³kēi¹yi⁶yin⁴ 奇治言】let things take their own course

听天由命【ting³tin¹yeo⁴ming⁶ 田¹ 油名⁶】submit to the will of Heaven; trust to luck

烃【ting¹ 汀】〈n.〉hydrocarbon

汀【ting¹ 亭¹】low, level land along a river; spit of land

廷【ting⁴ 亭】the court of a feudal ruler; the seat of a monarchic government

挺【ting⁵亭⁵】straight; erect; stiff; stick out; endure; stand; hold out; < classifier. > the unit of a machine gun

挺拔【ting⁵bed⁹ 跋】tall and straight; forceful

挺进【ting⁵jên³ 俊】press onward

挺立【ting⁵leb⁹ 笠⁹】stand upright

挺身而出【ting⁵xen¹yi⁴qêd⁷ 辛移次律⁷】come out boldly

铤【ting⁵ 挺】(run)quickly

铤而走险【ting⁵yi⁴jeo²him² 移酒欠²】risk danger in desperation; make a reckless move

庭【ting⁴ 亭】front courtyard; law court

庭园【ting⁴yūn⁴ 元】flower garden; grounds

庭院【ting⁴yūn² 苑】courtyard

亭【ting⁴ 停】pavilion; kiosk; wellbalanced; even

亭子【ting⁴ji² 止】pavilion; kiosk

亭亭玉立【ting⁴ting⁴yug⁹leb⁹ 肉笠⁹】(of a

woman)slim and graceful; tall and erect

停【ting⁴ 亭】stop; cease; halt; stop over; stay; be parked

停止【ting⁴ ji² 子】stop; cease; halt; suspend

停留【ting⁴leo⁴ 流】stop; stop for a time

停滞【ting⁴jei⁶ 济⁶】stagnate; bog down

停息【ting⁴xig⁷ 色】stop; cease

停歇【ting⁴ hib⁸ 协】stop doing business; stop

停顿【ting⁴dên⁶ 吨⁶】stop; halt; pause

停放【ting⁴fong³ 况】park; place

停靠【ting⁴kao³ 卡拗³】stop; berth

停泊【ting⁴bog⁹ 薄】anchor; berth

停车【ting⁴ qē¹ 奢】stop; pull up; park; stall

停产【ting⁴qan² 铲】stop production

停工【ting⁴gung¹ 功】stop work

停业【ting⁴ yib⁹ 叶】stop doing business; close down

停火【ting⁴fo² 伙】cease fire; armistice = 停战【jin³】

停学【ting⁴hog⁹ 鹤】stop going to school

停航【ting⁴hong³ 杭】suspend air or shipping service

婷【ting⁴ 亭】graceful

蜓【ting⁴ 亭】(see "蜻蜓")

霆【ting⁴ 亭】thunderbolt(see "雷霆")

帖【tib⁸ 贴】submissive; well-settled; invitation; note; a book containing models of handwriting or painting for learners to copy

服帖【fug⁹tib⁸ 伏】docile and obedient

请帖【qing²tib⁸ 逞】invitation

字帖【ji⁶tib⁸ 治】calligraphy models

贴【tib⁸ 帖】paste; stick; keep close to; subsidies; < classifier . > the unit of a medicated plaster, etc.

贴近【tib⁸gen⁶ 靳】press close to

贴切【tib⁸qid⁸ 设】(of words)apt; suitable

贴身【tib⁸xen¹ 辛】next ot the skin

贴心【tib⁸xem¹ 深】intimate; close

贴补【tib⁸ bou² 保】subsidize; help financially

贴错门神【tib⁸qo³mun⁴xen⁴ 挫们臣】refer to two persons not on good terms = 【普】比喻两人关系不和, 整天吵嘴

贴花【tib⁸fa¹ 化¹】applique

贴金【tib⁸gem¹ 今】cover with gold leaf; gild; touch up; prettify

铁【tid⁸ 餐】iron(Fe); arms; weapon; hard or strong as iron; resolve

铁器【tid⁸hēi³ 戏】ironware

铁线【tid⁸xin³ 扇】iron wire = 【普】铁丝

铁皮【tid⁸pēi⁴ 脾】iron sheet

铁枝【tid⁸ji¹ 支】sheet = 【普】铁条; 钢筋

铁桶【tid⁸tung² 统】metal drum

铁锤【tid⁸qêü⁴ 槌】iron hammer

铁钉【tid⁸dēng¹ 得镜¹】iron nail

铁砧【tid⁸jem⁹ 针】anvil

铁闸【tid⁸jab⁹ 习】a gate

铁笔【tid⁸ bed⁷ 毕】a cutting tool used in carving seals, etc.; stencil pen

铁饼【tid⁸bēng² 柄²】discus; discus throw

铁箍【tid⁸ku¹ 卡乌¹】iron hoop

铁管【tid⁸gun² 莞²】iron pipe; iron tube

铁链【tid⁸lin² 连²】iron chain; shackles

铁路【tid⁸ lou⁶ 露】railway；railroad ＝ 铁道【dou⁶】

铁轨【tid⁸guei² 鬼】rail

铁索【tid⁸xog⁸ 塑】cable；iron chain

铁窗【tid⁸qêng¹ 昌】a window with iron grating；prison

铁锈【tid⁸xeo³ 秀】rust

铁腕【tid⁸wun² 碗】iron hand

铁蹄【tid⁸tei⁴ 啼】iron heel—cruel oppression of the people

铁证【tid⁸jing³ 正】ironclad proof

铁汉【tid⁸ hon³ 看】man of iron；a strong determined person

铁饭碗【tid⁸ fan⁶ wun² 范腕】iron rice bowl—a secure job

铁嘴鸡【tid⁸jêu²gei¹ 咀 计¹】one who is good at talking ＝【普】善于辩驳，耍嘴皮的人

铁石心肠【tid⁸xêg⁹xem¹qêng⁴ 硕深祥】be ironhearted；be hardhearted

铁面无私【tid⁸min⁶mou⁴xi¹ 缅⁶ 毛司】impartial and incorruptible

饕【tid⁸ 铁】greedy for food(see"饕餮")
惕

惕【tig⁷ 剔】cautious；watchful

警惕【ging²tig⁷ 景】be on the alert；watch out

剔【tig⁷ 惕】pick；pick out and throw away；reject

剔除【tig⁷qêu⁴ 徐】reject；get rid of

团【tün⁴ 屯】round；circular；roll sth. into a ball；roll；group；society；regiment；the League；< classifier . > the unit of a flour，etc.

团结【tün⁴gid⁸ 洁】unite；rally

团聚【tün⁴jêu⁶ 叙】reunite

团粒【tün⁴neb⁷ 那合⁷】granule

团体【tün⁴ tei² 睇】organization；group；team

团团【tün⁴tün⁴】round and round；all round

团员【tün⁴ yün⁴ 元】member；League Member

团长【tün⁴ jêng² 蒋】regimental commander；head of a delegation，troupe，etc.

抟【tün⁴ 团】roll sth. into a ball；roll

屯【tün⁴ 团】collect；store up；station；quarter；village

屯兵【tün⁴bing¹ 冰】station troops

屯粮【tün⁴lêng⁴ 梁】store up grain

豚【tün⁴ 团】suckling pig；pig

鲀【tün⁴团】globefish；balloonfish；puffer

臀【tün⁴ 团】buttocks

臀部【tün⁴bou⁶ 步】buttocks

脱【tüd⁸ 梯月⁸】shed；come off；take off；escape from；get out of；miss out；slight；if；< classifier . > the unit of the people of a cretain kind

一脱人【yed¹tüd⁸yen⁴ 壹仁】the people of a cretain kind ＝【普】一辈人

脱离【tüd⁸ lêi⁴漓】separate oneself from；break away from

脱落【tüd⁸ log⁹ 洛⁹】drop；fall off；come off

脱节【tüd⁸ jid⁸折】come apart；be out of line with

脱毛【tüd⁸mou⁴ 无】moult；shed

脱发【tüd⁸fad⁸ 法】trichomadesis

脱臼【tüd⁸keo⁵ 舅】dislocation＝脱位【wei⁶】

脱身【tüd⁸xen¹ 辛】get away；get free

脱手【tüd⁸xeo² 守】slip out of the hand；sell

脱水【tüd⁸ xêu² 瑞²】deprivation of body fluids；dehydration

脱脂【tüd⁸ji¹ 支】de-fat；degrease

脱险【tüd⁸him² 欠²】escape danger

脱俗【tüd⁸jug⁹ 族】free from vulgarity；refined

脱销【tüd⁸xiu¹ 消】out of stock；sold out

脱粒【tüd⁸neb⁷ 那合⁷】threshing；shelling

脱漏【tüd⁸leo⁶ 馏】be left out；be missing

脱轨【tüd⁸guei² 鬼】derail

脱缰之马【tüd¹ gêng¹ ji¹ ma⁵ 羌支码】a run-away horse—uncontroll-able；running wild

脱胎换骨【tüd⁸toi¹wun⁶gued⁷ 台¹ 唤掘⁷】be reborn

脱颖而出【tüd⁸wing⁶yi⁴qêd⁷ 泳移次律⁷】talent showing itself

推【tēū¹ 退¹】push；shove；grind；pare；promote；advance；infer；push away；put off；elect；choose；hold in esteem

推动【tēū¹dung⁶ 洞】push forward；promote

推移【tēū¹yi⁴ 而】(of time) elapse；pass；develop

推倒【tēū¹dou² 捣】push over；overturn；repudiate

推翻【tēū¹fan¹ 蕃】overthrow；topple；repudiate

推广【tēū¹guong² 光²】popularize；spread；extend

推进【tēū¹jên³ 俊】push on；advance；push；drive

推行【tēū¹heng⁴ 衡】carry out；pursue；practise

推荐【tēū¹jin³ 战】recommend

推举【tēū¹gêu² 矩】elect；choose；press＝推选【xün²】

推卸【tēū¹xě³ 舍】shirk

推辞【tēū¹qi⁴ 迟】decline

推崇【tēū¹xung⁴ 宋⁴】hold in esteem

推测【tēū¹qag⁷策⁷】infer；conjecture；guess

推论【tēū¹lên⁶ 沦⁶】inference；deduction

推理【tēū¹lêi⁵ 李】inference；reasoning

推算【tēū¹xün³ 蒜】calculate；reckon

推断【tēū¹dün³ 段】deduce；infer

推让【tēū¹yêng⁶ 酿】decline

推却【tēū¹kêg⁸ 卡约⁸】refuse；decline

推托【tēū¹tog⁸ 替恶⁸】offer as an excuse；plead

推波助澜【tēū¹bo¹jo⁶lan⁴ 坡左⁶ 兰】add fuel to the flames

推陈出新【tēū¹qen⁴qêd⁷xen¹ 亲⁴ 次律⁷辛】weed through the old to bring forth the new

推推撞撞【tēū¹tēū¹jong⁶jong⁶ 状】push and shove＝【普】推推搡搡

推心置腹【tēū¹xem¹ji³fug⁷ 深至福】repose full confidence in sb.；confide in sb.

推己及人【tēū¹gēi²keb⁹yen⁴ 几给⁹ 仁】put oneself in the place of another；be considerate

腿【tēū² 退²】leg；a leglike support；ham

大腿【dai⁶tēū² 歹²】thigh

小腿【xiu²tēū² 少²】shank

腿子【tēū²ji² 止】hired thug；lackey；henchman

腿肚子【têū²tou⁵ji² 桃⁵ 止】calf (of the leg) = 脚锄肚【gêg⁸long¹tou⁵】

退【têū³ 推³】move back; retreat; withdraw; remove; quit; decline; ebb; fade; return; cancel; break off

退回【têū³wui⁴ 会⁴】return; send back; go back

退出【têū³ qêd⁷次律⁷】withdraw from; quit

退还【têū³wan⁴ 环】return

退却【têū³ kêg⁸ 卡约⁸】retreat; hang back; flinch

退避【têū³bêi⁶ 备】keep out of the way

退让【têū³yêng⁶ 酿】yield; give in

退步【têū³ bou⁶ 部 】lag behind; retrogress; leeway

退缩【têū³ xug⁷宿 】shrink back; flinch; cower

退潮【têū³qiu⁴ 瞧】ebb tide; ebb

退化【têū³fa³ 花³】degeneration; degenerate

退路【têū³lou⁶ 露】route of retreat; leeway

退票【têū³piu³ 漂³】return a ticket

退色【têū³xig⁷ 式】fade

退烧【têū³ xiu¹消 】bring down a fever; come down = 退热【yid⁹】

退学【têū³hog⁹ 鹤】leave school

退伍【têū³ng⁵ 五】leave the army

退职【têū³jig⁷ 积】quit working

蜕【têū³ 退】slough off; exuviae; exuviate

蜕皮【têū³pêi⁴ 牌】cast off a skin; exuviate

蜕化【têū³fa³ 花³】slough off; exuviate; degenerate

蜕变【têū³bin³ 边³】change qualitatively; transform; decay

颓【têū⁴ 退⁴】ruined; declining; dejected

颓废【têū⁴fei³ 费】dispirited; decadent

颓唐【têū⁴tong⁴ 塘】dejected; dispirited

颓丧【têū⁴xong³ 桑³】dejected; dispirited

盾【tên⁵ 梯论⁵】shield

盾牌【tên⁵pai⁴ 排】shield; pretext; excuse

啐【tê³ 梯靴³; qêū³ 翠】spit; expectorate

啐佢一督口水【tê³kêū⁵yed⁷dug⁷heo²xêū² 拒壹笃厚² 瑞²】spit at him = 【普】啐他一口

厅【tēng¹ 艇¹】hall; office; a government department at the provincial level

饭厅【fan⁶tēng¹ 范】dining hall = 餐厅【qan¹tēng¹】

会议厅【wui⁶yi⁵tēng¹ 汇耳】conference hall

踢【tēg⁸ 梯吃⁸】kick; play(football)

踢波【tēg⁸bo¹ 玻】play football = 【普】踢足球

踢脚【tēg⁸ gêg⁸ 格约⁸ 】get into deep trouble = 【普】事情遇到麻烦、故障,令人苦恼

U

(It is not used in Cantonese.)

V

(It is not used in Cantonese.)

W

洼【wa¹ 蛙】hollow; low-lying; depression

洼地【wa¹dēi⁶ 得希⁶】depression; low-lying land

哇【wa¹ 注】〈*onomatopoeia*〉∽ hullabaloo; uproar; din

蛙【wa¹ 注】frog

蛙人【wa¹yen⁴ 仁】frogman

蛙泳【wa¹wing⁶ 咏】breaststroke

娃【wa¹ 注】baby; child; newborn animal

娃娃【wa¹wa¹】baby; child

娃娃鱼【wa¹wa¹yü² 余²】giant salamander

哗【wa¹ 注; wa² 注²; wa⁴ 华】noise; clamour

哗变【wa¹bin³ 边³】mutiny

哗哗声【wa⁴wa⁴xēng¹ 腥】in an uproar = 【普】哗然

哗众取宠【wa¹jung³qêü²qung² 纵娶虫²】try to please the public with claptrap

挓【wa²注²; wē² 乌耶²】scratch =【普】用爪子抓东西；捞取

挓痕【wa²hen⁴ 很⁴】scratch due to itchiness =【普】抓痒

挓银【wē² ngen² 哭²】accumulate wealth by unfair means ∽【普】捞钱；敛财

华【wa⁴ 铧; wa⁶ 话】magnificent; prosperous; cream; flashy; grey; China; corona; a surname

华丽【wa⁴ lei⁶ 厉】magnificent; resplendent

华贵【wa⁴guei³ 桂】luxurious; sumptuous

华夏【wa⁴ha⁶ 下】an ancient name for China

华灯【wa⁴ deng¹ 登】colourfully decorated lantern

华盖【wa⁴koi³ 概】canopy; aureole

华侨【wa⁴kiu⁴ 桥】overseas Chinese

华裔【wa⁴yêu⁶ 锐】foreign citizen of Chinese origin

华尔街【wa⁴yi⁵gai¹ 耳佳】〈n.〉Wall Street

华而不实【wa⁴yi⁴bed⁷xed⁹ 移毕失⁹】flashy and without substance; superficially clever

铧【wa⁴ 华】ploughshare

桦【wa⁴ 华】〈n.〉birch

画【wa² 乌亚²；wag⁹ 或；wa⁶ 话⁶】draw; paint; drawing; picture; stroke (of a Chinese character)

画画【wag⁹wa²】draw a picture

画片【wa²pin⁴ 遍²】a miniature reproduction of a painting

画幅【wa²fug⁷ 福】picture; size of a picture

画册【wa²qag⁸ 策】picture album

画刊【wa²hon² 罕】pictorial

画像【wa²jêng⁶ 匠】portray; portrait

画面【wa²min² 缅²】tableau; frame

画师【wa²xi¹ 司】painter

画家【wa²ga¹ 加】painter; artist

画卷【wa²gün² 捐²】picture scroll

画廊【wa²long⁴ 郎】painted corridor; gallery

画展【wa²jin² 剪】art exhibition

画皮【wa²pēi⁴ 脾】disguise or mask of an evildoer

画眉【wa²mēi⁴ 媚】a kind of thrush

画法【wag⁹fad⁸ 发】technique of painting or drawing

画笔【wa²bed⁷ 毕】painting brush; brush

画稿【wa²gou² 缟】rough sketch (for a painting)

画龙点睛【wag⁹lung⁴dim²jing¹ 胧店² 贞】add the finishing touch; add a word or two to clinch the point

画蛇添足【wag⁹xē⁴tim¹jug⁷ 写⁴ 甜¹ 竹】draw a snake and add feet to it — ruin the effect by adding sth. superfluous

话【wa⁶ 华⁶；wa² 华²】word; talk; tell; speak about

话音【wa⁶yem¹ 阴】one's voice in speech; tone

话筒【wa⁶tung² 统】microphone

话题【wa⁶tei⁴ 提】subject of a talk

话剧【wa⁶kēg⁹ 屐】modern drama; stage play

话别【wa⁶bid⁹ 必⁹】say good-bye

话柄【wa⁶bēng³ 病³】subject for ridicule; handle

话里有话【wa⁶lêu⁵yeo⁵wa² 吕友】The words mean more than they say.

话落【wa⁶log⁹ 洛⁹】leave a message =【普】事前的吩咐

话实【wa⁶xed⁹ 失⁹】confirm; persuade; convince =【普】表态；说定

话事【wa⁶xi⁶ 士】be in charge =【普】掌权；说了算

话斋【wa⁶jai¹ 支埃¹】just like what one says =【普】正像(某人)说的

话唔定【wa⁶m⁴ding⁶ 锭】= 话唔埋【wa⁶m⁴mai⁴ 卖⁴】perhaps; difficult to predict =【普】也许；说不定

话你知【wa⁶nēi⁵ji¹ 那希⁵ 支】tell you =【普】告诉你

歪【wai¹ 坏¹】askew；crooked；devious；underhand

歪斜【wai¹qē⁴ 邪】crooked；askew；aslant

歪曲【wai¹ kug⁷ 卡屋⁷】distort；misrepresent；twist

歪风【wai¹fung¹ 丰】evil wind；unhealthy trend

歪门邪道【wai¹mun⁴qē⁴dou⁶ 们斜度】(see "邪门歪道")

怀【wai⁴ 淮】bosom；mind；keep in mind；think of；conceiye(a child)

怀抱【wai⁴pou⁵ 普⁵】bosom；cherish

怀恋【wai⁴lün² 联²】think fondly of；look back nostalgically

怀念【wai⁴ nim⁶ 粘⁶】cherish the memory of；think of

怀古【wai⁴gu² 鼓】meditate on the past

怀旧【wai⁴ geo⁶ 柩】remember past times or old acquaintances

怀疑【wai⁴yi⁴ 而】doubt；suspect

怀胎【wai⁴toi¹ 台¹】be pregnant

怀孕【wai⁴yen⁶ 刃】be pregnant

淮【wai⁴ 怀】〈n.〉淮河【wai⁴ho⁴ 何】the Huaihe River

槐【wai⁴ 怀】〈n.〉槐树【wai⁴xü⁶ 署⁶】Chinese scholartree

坏【wai⁶ 怀⁶】bad；go bad；spoil；badly；evil idea

坏人【wai⁶yen⁴ 仁】bad person；evil doer

坏事【wai⁶xi⁶ 士】bad thing；ruin sth.

坏处【wai⁶qü³ 次于³】harm；disadvantage

坏蛋【wai⁶dan² 单²】bad egg；bastadrel

坏到加零一【wai⁶ dou³ ga¹ ling⁴ yed⁷度³ 家凌壹】the worst ＝【普】坏极了；坏透了

弯【wan¹ 湾】curved；crooked；bend；turn

弯曲【wan¹ kug⁷ 卡屋⁷】winding；meandering；zigzag

弯路【wan¹ lou⁶露】crooked road；roundabout way

弯子【wan¹ji² 止】bend；turn；curve

湾【wan¹ 弯】a bend in a stream；gulf；bay；moor

玩【wan² 弯²；wan⁴ 还；wun⁶ 换】play；have fun；employ；trifle with；enjoy；object for appreciation

玩笑【wan²xiu³ 少³】joke；jest

玩弄【wan²lung⁶ 龙⁶】dally with；play with

玩具【wan²gêu⁶ 巨】toy；play thing

玩完【wan²yün⁴ 原】die；pass away ＝【普】死；去世

玩火自焚【wan²fo²ji⁶fen⁴ 伙治汾】He who plays with fire will get burnd.

玩忽职守【wun⁶fed⁷jig⁷xeo² 弗积手】neglect of duty

玩偶【wun⁶ngeo⁵ 藕】doll；toy figurine

玩赏【wun⁶xêng² 想】enjoy；take pleasure in

玩味【wun⁶mêi⁶ 未】ponder；ruminate

玩耍【wun⁶xa² 洒²】play；have fun

玩物丧志【wun⁶med⁹xong³ji³ 勿桑³ 至】Riding a hobby saps one's will to make progress.

顽【wan⁴ 环】stupid；stubborn；naughty；dense

顽固【wan⁴ gu³ 故 】obstinate；stubborn；die-hard

顽皮【wan⁴pêi⁴ 脾】naughty；mischievous

顽童【wan⁴ tung⁴ 同 】naughty child；urchin

顽症【wan⁴jing³ 正】chronic and stubborn

disease

顽强【wan⁴ kêng⁴ 卡香⁴】indomitable; staunch

顽抗【wan⁴kong³ 炕】stubbornly resist

环【wan⁴ 顽】ring; hoop; link; surround; hem in

环抱【wan⁴ pou⁵ 普⁵】surround; encircle; hem in

环顾【wan⁴gu³ 固】look round = 环视【xi⁶ 示】

环城【wan⁴xing⁴ 成】around the city

环节【wan⁴jid⁸ 折】link; segment

环球【wan⁴keo⁴ 求】round the world; the earth

环绕【wan⁴yiu⁵ 扰⁵】surround; encircle

环形【wan⁴ying⁴ 型】annular; ringlike

寰【wan⁴ 环】extensive region

寰球【wan⁴keo⁴ 求】the earth; the whole world = 环球【wan⁴keo⁴】= 寰宇【yü⁵ 雨】

鬟【wan⁴ 环】bun(of hair)

绾【wan² 玩²】coil up

挽【wan⁵ 弯⁵】draw; pull; roll up

挽回【wan⁵wui⁴ 会⁴】retrieve; redeem

挽救【wan⁵geo³ 够】save; remedy

挽留【wan⁵leo⁴ 流】urge sb. to stay

輓【wan⁵ 挽】pull; draw; lament sb.'s death

輓歌【wan⁵go¹ 哥】dirge; elegy

輓联【wan⁵lün⁴ 李】elegiac couplet

还【wan⁴ 环】go (or come) back; give back; repay; give or do sth. in return; 〈ad.〉still; yet; also; too;

as well; even

还好【wan⁴ hou²蒿²】not bad; passable; fortunately = 仲算好【jung⁶xün³ hou³】

还是【wan⁴ xi⁶士】〈ad.〉still; nevertheless; had better = 仲系【jung⁶hei⁶】

还原【wan⁴yün⁴ 元】restore; reduction

还愿【wan⁴ yün⁶ 县】redeem a vow to a god; fulfil one's promise

还清【wan⁴qing¹ 称】pay off

还击【wan⁴gig⁷ 激】figth back; riposte

还手【wan⁴xeo² 守】strike back

还价【wan⁴ga³ 嫁】counter-offer; counter-bid

还礼【wan⁴lei⁵ 黎⁵】return a salute; present a gift in return

还债【wan⁴jai³ 寨³】pay one's debt; repay a debt

还嘴【wan⁴jêü² 咀】answer back; retort

还乡【wan⁴ hêng¹香】 return to one's native place

幻【wan⁶ 患】unreal; imaginary; magical

幻灯【wan⁶ deng¹ 登】slide show; slide projector

幻景【wan⁶ging⁶ 境】illusion; mirage

幻境【wan⁶ging⁶ 景】dreamland; fairyland

幻觉【wan⁶gog⁸ 各】hallucination

幻灭【wan⁶mid⁹ 篾】vanish into thin air

幻术【wan⁶xêd⁹ 述】magic; conjuring

幻想【wan⁶xêng⁶ 赏】illusion; fancy; fantasy

幻象【wan⁶jêng⁶ 像】mirage; phantom

幻影【wan⁶ying⁶ 映】unreal image

宦【wan⁶ 患】official; eunuch; a surname

宦官【wan⁶gun¹ 观】eunuch

宦海【wan⁶ hoi² 凯 】officialdom；official circles

患 【wan⁶ 宦 】trouble；peril；anxiety；worry；contract

患病【wan⁶bēng⁶ 柄】fall ill；be ill

患处【wan⁶qū³ 次于³】affected part

患者【wan⁶jē² 姐】sufferer；patient

患难【wan⁶nan⁶ 那晏⁶】adversity；trouble

患得患失【wan⁶deg⁷wan⁶xed⁷ 德室⁷】worry about personal gains and losses

豢 【wan⁶ 患 】〈v.〉豢养【wan⁶yêng⁵ 氧】feed；groom；keep

鲩 【wan⁵ 挽 】〈n.〉鲩鱼【wan⁶yū² 淤】grass carp

潢 【wang¹ 横¹】watery；be defeated；be defeated and dispersed

稀潢潢【hēi¹wang¹wang¹ 希】very watery ＝【普】很稀

潢晒【wang¹ xai³ 徙³】＝潢潢公司【wang¹wang¹gung¹xi¹ 工 斯】be defeated＝【普】完了；全盘皆输

横 【wang⁴ 乌罂⁴；wang² 乌罂²】horizontal；across；traverse；turbulently；violently；perverse；unexpected

横向【wang⁴hêng³ 香³】crosswise

横跨【wang⁴ kua¹ 夸】stretch over or a-cross

横亘【wang⁴geng³ 耿】lie across；span

横切【wang⁴qid⁸ 设】crosscut

横生【wang⁴xeng¹ 笙】grow wild；happen unexpectedly；be full of

横扫【wang⁴xou³ 素】sweep away

横巷【wang⁴hong² 康²】crosscut

横梁【wang⁴ lêng⁴ 凉】crossbeam；cross member

横眉【wang⁴mēi⁴ 微】frown；scowl

横肉【wang⁴yug⁹ 王】look ugly and ferocious

横掂【wang⁴dim⁶ 店⁶】in any case；anyway＝【普】横竖；反正

横水渡【wang⁴xêu²dou² 瑞² 倒】a boat for crossing rivers＝【普】渡江轮船

横祸【wang⁴wo⁶ 禾⁶】unexpected calamity

横财【wang⁴qoi⁴ 才】ill-gotten wealth

横断面【wang⁴tūn⁵min² 团⁵ 缅²】cross section

横膈膜【wang⁴gag⁸mog⁹ 格莫】diaphragm

横冲直撞【wang⁴qung¹jig¹jong⁶ 充值壮⁶】push one's way by shoving or bumping；barge about

横七竖八【wang⁴qed⁷xū⁶bad⁸ 柒树捌】in disorder

横行霸道【wang⁴heng⁴ba³dou⁶ 衡坝度】ride roughshod

横征暴敛【wang⁴jing¹bou⁶lim⁵ 贞保⁶ 廉⁵】levy exorbitant taxes

挖 【wad⁸ 滑⁸】dig；excavate

挖掘【wad⁸gued⁹ 骨⁹】excavate；unearth

挖根【wad⁸ gen¹ 跟】dig sth. up by the roots；uproot

挖苦【wad⁸ fu² 府 】speak sarcastically or ironically

挖墙脚【wad⁸qêng⁴gêg⁸ 祥格约⁸】undermine the foundation

挖空心思【wad⁸ hung¹ xem¹ xi¹ 凶深司】rack one's brains

挖肉补疮【wad⁸yug⁹bou²qong¹ 玉保仓】cut out a piece of one's flesh to cure a boil —— resort to a remedy worse than the ailment

滑【wad⁹ 猾】slippery; smooth; slip; slide; cunning

滑捋捋【wad⁹lüd⁷lüd⁷ 劣⁷ 劣⁷】slippery; slick; smooth =【普】滑溜

滑潺潺【wad⁹ xan⁴ xan⁴】oily; velvety; creamy =【普】滑腻

滑牙【wad⁹nga² 哑】refer to the loosening of screws in machines =【普】齿轮打滑

滑牛【wad⁹ngeo² 偶²】fried beef =【普】牛肉酱

滑动【wad⁹dung⁶ 洞】slide

滑行【wad⁹heng⁴ 衡】slide; coast

滑翔【wad⁹qêng⁴ 祥】glide

滑坡【wad⁹bo¹ 波】landslide; landslip

滑梯【wad⁹tei¹ 锑】(children's)slide

滑冰【wad⁸ bing¹ 兵】ice-skating; skating

滑雪【wad⁹xüd⁸ 说】skiing

滑头【wad⁹ teo² 投²】slippery fellow; slippery; slick

滑稽【wad⁹ kei¹ 溪】funny; amusing; comic talk

猾【wad⁹ 滑】cunning; crafty; sly

或【wag⁹ 惑】〈ad.〉perhaps; maybe; 〈conj.〉or; either ... or ...; someone; some people

或许【wag⁹ hêü² 诩】〈ad.〉perhaps; maybe

或者【wag⁹ jē² 姐】〈ād.〉perhaps; maybe; 〈conj.〉or; either... or...

惑【wag⁹ 或】be puzzled; be bewildered; delude

划【wag⁹ 或; wa¹ 哇; fa³ 化】delimit; transfer; plan; draw; mark; stroke; paddle; row; pay; scratch

划分【wag⁹fen¹ 芬】divide; differentiate

划清【wag⁹qing¹ 青】draw a clear line of demarcation

划定【wag⁹ding⁶ 锭】delimit; designate

划归【wag⁹guei¹ 龟】put under; incorporate into

划界【wag⁹gai³ 介】delimit a boundary

划一【wag⁹ yed⁷ 壹】standardized; uniform

划时代【wag⁹xi⁴doi⁶ 士⁴ 袋】epoch-making

划船【wa¹xün¹ 旋】paddle(or row)a boat

划算【fa³xün³ 蒜】calculate; weigh; be to one's profit; pay

威【wei¹ 萎¹】impressive strength; might; by force

威水【wei¹ xêü² 瑞²】striking; bright; smart; feeling good ∽【普】好看; 好样的

威吔【wei¹ya² 也²】wire =【普】钢丝绳

威风【wei¹fung¹ 丰】power and prestige; imposing

威力【wei¹lig⁹ 历】power; might

威势【wei¹xei³ 世】power and influence

威吓【wei¹hag⁸ 客】intimidate; threaten; bully

威武【wei¹mou⁵ 母】might; power; powerful; mighty

威胁【wei¹hib⁸ 协】threaten; menace; imperil

威慑【wei¹xib⁸ 摄】terrorize with military force

威逼【wei¹big⁷ 迫】threaten by force; coerce

威严【wei¹ yim⁴ 盐】dignified; stately; dignity

威信【wei¹xên³ 讯】prestige; popular trust

威仪【wei¹yi⁴ 移】impressive and dignified manner

威士忌【wei¹xi⁶gēi⁶ 事几⁶】whisky

威风凛凛【wei¹fung¹lem⁵lem⁵ 丰林⁵】majestic-looking；awe-inspiring

威风扫地【wei¹fung¹xou³dēi⁶ 丰素得希⁶】with every shred of one's prestige swept away—completely discredited

委【wei² 萎】entrust；appoint；throw away；roundabout；shift；end；listless；actually；committee member；committee

委靡【wei²mēi⁴ 微】listless；dispirited

委派【wei²pai² 排³】appoint；delegate

委屈【wei²wed⁷ 乌核⁷】feel wronged；put sb. to great inconvenience

委任【wei²yem⁶ 阴⁶】appoint

委实【wei²xed⁹ 失⁹】really；indeed

委托【wei²tog⁸ 梯恶⁸】entrust；trust

委婉【wei²yūn² 院】mild and roundabout；tactful

委员【wei²yūn⁴ 元】committee member

萎【wei² 委】wither；wilt；fade；decline

萎靡【wei²mēi⁴ 微】listless；dispirited

萎缩【wei² xug⁷ 宿】wither；shrivel；shrink；sag；atrophy

萎谢【wei²jē⁶ 榭】wither；fade

痿【wei² 委】〈n.〉痿症【wei²jing³ 正】flaccid paralysis

毁【wei² 委】destroy；ruin；burn up；defame；refashion

毁谤【wei²bong² 榜】slander；malign；calumniate

毁坏【wei²wai⁶ 怀⁶】destroy；damage

毁灭【wei²mid⁹ 篾】destroy；exterminate

毁弃【wei²hēi³ 戏】scrap；annul

毁约【wei²yêg⁸ 跃】break one's promise；scrap a contract or treaty

诿【wei² 委】shift（推诿【têū¹wei²】

畏【wei³ 尉】fear；respect

畏惧【wei³gêu⁶ 巨】fear；dread

畏怯【wei³hib⁸ 协】cowardly；timid

畏难【wei³nan⁴ 那晏⁴】be afraid of difficulty

畏缩【wei³xug⁷ 宿】recoil；shrink；flinch

畏途【wei³tou⁴ 涂】a dangerous road

畏罪【wei³jêu⁶ 聚】dread punishment for one's crime

喂【wei³ 畏】〈int.〉∽ hello；hey；〈v.〉feed

喂奶【wei³nai⁵ 乃】breast-feed；suckle；nurse

喂养【wei³yêng⁵ 氧】feed；raise；keep

尉【wei³ 畏】a junior officer；a surname

尉官【wei³gun¹ 观】a military officer above the rank of warrant officer and below that of major

蔚【wei³ 尉】luxuriant；grand；colourful

蔚蓝【wei³lam⁴ 篮】azure；sky blue

蔚然成风【wei³yin⁴xing⁴fung¹ 言承丰】become common practice

蔚为大观【wei³ wei⁴ dai⁶ gun¹ 维歹⁶ 官】present a splendid sight

慰【wei³ 尉】console；comfort；be relieved

慰劳【wei³lou⁴ 涝】bring gifts to, or send one's best wishes to, in recognition of services rendered

慰问【wei³men⁶ 蚊⁶】express sympathy and solicitude for; salute

慧【wei³ 尉; wei⁶ 胃】intelligent; bright

慧眼【wei⁶ngan⁵ 雁⁵】mental discernment; insight

秽【wei³ 尉】dirty; ugly; abominable

污秽【wu¹wei³ 乌】filthy

秽行【wei³heng⁴ 衡】abominable behaviour

遗【wei⁴ 维; wei⁶ 惠】offer as a gift; lose; something lost; omit; leave behind; bequeath

遗产【wei⁴qan² 铲】legacy; heritage

遗传【wei⁴qun⁴ 存】heredity; inheritance

遗憾【wei⁴hem⁶ 含⁶】regret; pity

遗恨【wei⁴hen⁶ 很⁶】eternal regret

遗留【wei⁴leo² 流】leave over; hand down

遗漏【wei⁴leo⁶ 馏】omit; leave out

遗弃【wei⁴hēi³ 戏】abandon; forsake; cast off

遗失【wei⁴xed⁷ 室】lose

遗忘【wei⁴mong⁴ 忙】forget

遗体【wei⁴tei² 睇】remains(of the dead)

遗物【wei⁴med⁹ 勿】things left behind by the deceased

遗像【wei⁴jêng⁶ 象】a portrait of the deceased

遗愿【wei⁴yun⁶ 县】last wish

遗嘱【wei⁴jug⁷ 足】testament; will

遗著【wei⁴jū³ 注】posthumous work

遗址【wei⁴ji² 止】ruins; relics

遗迹【wei⁴jig⁷ 积】vestige; traces

遗志【wei⁴ji³ 至】unfulfilled wish; behest

唯【wei⁴ 维】only; alone; yea

唯一【wei⁴yed⁷ 壹】only; sole

唯恐【wei⁴hung² 孔】for fear that; lest

唯独【wei⁴dug⁹ 毒】only; alone

唯有【wei⁴yeo⁵ 友】only; alone

唯利是图【wei⁴ lēi⁶ xi⁶ tou⁴ 莉士途】be bent solely on profit

唯命是听【wei⁴ming⁶xi⁶ting³ 名⁶ 事亭³】always do as one is told

唯我独尊【wei⁴ ngo⁵ dug⁹ jūn¹ 鹅⁵ 毒专】overweening

唯物主义【wei⁴med⁹jū²yi⁶ 勿煮异】materialism

唯心主义【wei⁴xem¹jū²yi⁶ 深煮异】idealism

唯物辩证法【wei⁴med⁹bin⁶jing⁶fad⁸ 勿便正发】materialist dialectics

唯唯诺诺【wei⁴wei⁴nog⁶nog⁶ 那恶⁸】be a yes-man

惟【wei⁴ 唯】only; alone; but; thinking

惟妙惟肖【wei⁴miu⁶wei⁴qiu³ 庙俏】remarkably true to life = 维妙维肖【wei⁴miu⁶wei⁴qiu³】

维【wei⁴ 唯】tie up; maintain; thinking; dimension

维持【wei⁴qi⁴ 迟】keep; maintain

维护【wei⁴wu⁴ 户】safeguard; defend

维系【wei⁴hei⁶ 兮⁶】hold together; maintain

维修【wei⁴xeo¹ 收】keep in repair; service

维新【wei⁴xen¹ 辛】reform; modernization

维尼纶【wei⁴nēi⁴lên⁴ 你⁴ 伦】vinylon

维生素【wei⁴xeng¹xou³ 笙数】vitamin

帷【wei⁴ 维】curtain

帷幕【wei⁴mog⁹ 莫】heavy curtain = 帷幔【man⁶】

帷幄【wei⁴ngeg⁷ 握】army tent

韦 【wei⁴ 维；wei⁵ 伟】a surname; leather

苇 【wei⁵ 伟】reed(see"芦苇")

闱 【wei⁴ 维】a side gate of an imperial palace; imperial examination hall

桅 【wei⁴ 维】mast(桅杆【wei⁴gon¹ 竿】

围 【wei⁴ 维】enclose; surround; all round; around

围墙【wei⁴ qêng⁴场 】enclosure; enclosing wall

围绕【wei⁴ yiu⁵要⁵】round; around; centre on

围困【wei⁴ kuen³昆³】besiege; hem in; pin down

围攻【wei⁴ gung¹工 】besiege; jointly attack sb.

围剿【wei⁴jiu² 召²】encircle and suppress

围巾【wei⁴gen¹ 斤】muffler; scarf

围裙【wei⁴kuen² 菌】apron

围棋【wei⁴·kēi⁴奇 】a game played with black and white pieces on a board of 361 crosses

违 【wei⁴ 维】disobey; violate; be separated

违背【wei⁴bui³ 辈】violate; go against

违法【wei⁴fad⁸ 法】break the law; be illegal

违反【wei⁴fan² 返】violate; run counter to

违犯【wei⁴fan⁶ 范】violate; infringe

违禁【wei⁴gem³ 咁】violate a ban

违抗【wei⁴kong³ 亢】disobey; defy

违例【wei⁴lei⁶ 丽】breach of rules

违心【wei⁴xem¹ 深】against one's will

违约【wei⁴yêg⁸ 若⁸】break a contract; break one's promise

违章【wei⁴jêng¹ 张】break rules and regulations

为 【wei⁴ 维；wei⁶ 惠】do; act; act as; become; be; mean; 〈prep.〉 show the target, cause, purpose, etc.

为难【wei⁴ nan⁴那晏⁴】feel embarrassed; make things difficult for

为皮【wei⁴ pēi² 鄙】cost; capital; high capital cost =【普】估定成本；估定代价

为期【wei⁴kēi⁴ 其】by a definite date

为人【wei⁴yen² 仁】behave; conduct oneself

为首【wei⁴xeo² 守】headed by

为数【wei⁴xou³ 素】amount to; number

为止【wei⁴ji² 纸】up to; till

为得过【wei⁴deg⁷guo³ 德戈³】worthwhile =【普】还合算

为重【wei⁴ jung⁶仲 】attach most importance to

为主【wei⁴jŭ² 煮】give first place to; give priority to

为咗【wei⁶jo² 阻】for; for the sake of =【普】为了

为此【wei⁶ qi² 次²】to this end; for this reason

为何【wei⁶ho⁴ 河】why; for what reason

为食【wei⁶ xig⁹蚀 】glut; a glutton =【普】嘴馋

为乜野【wei⁶ med⁷ yē⁵勿⁷夜⁵】why =【普】为什么

为虎作伥【wei⁶fu²jog⁸qêng¹ 苦昨昌】help a villain do evil

为民请命【wei⁶men⁴qing²ming⁶ 文逞名⁶】plead for the people

伟【wei⁵ 纬】big；great

伟大【wei⁵dai⁶ 歹⁶】great；mighty

伟人【wei⁵yen⁴ 仁】a great man

伟绩【wei²jig⁷ 积】great feats；great exploits

伟业【wei²yib⁹ 叶】great cause；exploit

纬【wei⁵ 纬】weft；woof；latitude

纬度【wei⁵dou⁶ 度】latitude

纬线【wei⁵xin³ 扇】paralleled；weft

韪【wei⁵ 伟】fault；slip；offence（不韪【bed⁷wei²】）

偎【wei³ 畏；wui¹ 煨】snuggle up to；lean close to

偎依【wei³ yi¹ 衣】snuggle up to；lean close to

逶【wei¹ 威】〈a.〉逶迤【wei¹yi⁴ 移】winding；meandering

卫【wei⁶ 惠】defend；guard；protect；a surname

卫兵【wei⁶ bing¹ 冰】guard；bodyguard ＝ 卫士【xi⁶ 事】

卫护【wei⁶wu⁶ 户】protect；guard

卫戍【wei⁶xü³ 书³】garrison

卫生【wei⁶xeng¹ 笙】hygiene；health；sanitation

卫星【wei⁶xing¹ 升】satellite；moon；artificial satellite

位【wei⁶ 卫；wei² 委】place；location；position；throne；figure；〈class-ifier.〉the unit of a man

座位【jo⁶wei² 助】seat

位次【wei⁶qi³ 厕】precedence；seating arrangement

位于【wei⁶ yü¹ 迂 】be located；be situated；lie

位置【wei⁶ji³ 至】seat；place；position

猬【wei⁶ 胃】〈n.〉hedgehog

渭【wei⁶ 胃】short for the Weihe River

猥【wei² 委】numerous；base；obscene；indecent

猥鄙【wei²pēi² 皮²】base；mean；despicable

猥琐【wei²xo² 所】of wretched appearance

猥亵【wei²xid⁸ 泄】obscene；salacious；act indecently towards（a woman）

卉【wei² 委】（various kinds of）grass

讳【wei⁵ 传】avoid as taboo；taboo；the name regarded as taboo, of a deceased emperor or head of a family

讳言【wei⁵yin⁴ 然】dare not or would not speak up

讳疾忌医【wei⁵jed⁹gēi⁶ji¹ 侄技衣】hide one's sickness for fear of treatment—conceal one's fault for fear of criticism

惠【wei⁶ 卫】favour；kindness；benefit；a surname

惠存【wei⁶qün⁴ 泉】please keep；so-and-so

惠顾【wei⁶gu³ 故】your patronage

蕙【wei⁶ 卫】〈n.〉蕙兰【wei⁶lan⁴ 栏】a species of orchid

蟪【wei⁶ 卫】〈n.〉蟪蛄【wei⁶gu¹ 姑】a kind of cicada

温【wen¹ 瘟】warm；lukewarm；warm up；review；revise；a surname

温暖【wen¹nün⁵ 嫩⁵】warm

温度【wen¹dou⁶ 道】temperature

温饱【wen¹bao² 包²】dress warmly and eat one's fill

温床【wen¹ qong⁴ 苍⁴】hotbed；breeding ground

温室【wen¹xed³ 失】hothouse；greenhouse

温带【wen¹dai³ 戴】temperate zone

温存【wen¹ qün⁴ 全 】attentive；gentle；kind

温泉【wen¹qün⁴ 全】hot spring

温和【wen¹wo⁴ 禾】temperate；mild；gentle；warm；lukewarm

温厚【wen¹ heo⁵ 口⁵】gentle and kind；good-natured

温情【wen¹ qing⁴ 程】tender feeling；too softhearted

温柔【wen¹yeo⁴ 油】gentle and soft

温顺【wen¹xên⁶ 讯⁶】docile；meek

温驯【wen¹ xên⁴纯 】(of animals) docile；meek；tame

温习【wen¹jab⁹ 袭】review；revise

温故知新【wen¹gu³ji¹xen¹ 固支辛】gain new insights through restudying old material；reviewing the past helps one to understand the present

温文尔雅【wen¹men⁴yi⁵nga⁵ 闻耳瓦】gentle and cultivated

瘟【wen¹ 温】acute communicable diseases

瘟病【wen¹bēng⁶ 柄⁶】seasonal febrile diseases

瘟神【wen¹xen⁴ 臣】god of plague

瘟疫【wen¹yig⁹ 亦】pestilence

瘟瘟沌沌【wen¹wen¹den⁶den⁶ 炖】blur；ambiguous ∽【普】糊糊涂涂；头脑不清醒

揾【wen² 稳】look for；search；seek

揾钱【wen²qin² 浅】= 揾食【wen²xig⁹ 蚀】work so as to earn a living =【普】设法赚钱；谋生

揾笨【wen²ben⁶ 宾⁶】= 揾老衬【weɲ²lou⁵ qen³ 鲁趁】cheat；take advantage；take advantage of others ∽【普】欺负低能儿；占笨蛋的便宜

揾野做【wen²yē⁵jou⁶ 惹造】look for a job =【普】找工作；找活干

韫【wen³ 温³】keep animals in the cages；confinement；shut in a pen；pen in =【普】收藏；禁闭；把(牲口)圈起来；把(人)关起来

韫住【wen³jü⁶ 注⁶】shut in a pen；pen in =【普】把……圈起来

韫实【wen³xed⁹ 失】be placed in confinement =【普】关紧；禁闭

匀【wen⁴ 云】even；even up；divide evenly；spare

匀巡【wen⁴ qên⁴ 旬 】distributed evenly；even and orderly；well-distributed =【普】均匀；匀整

匀称【wen⁴ qing³ 秤】well-proportioned；symmetrical

匀净【wen⁴jing⁶ 静】uniform；even

匀速运动【wen⁴qug⁷wen⁶dung⁶ 促混洞】uniform motion

云【wen⁴ 匀】say；cloud；a surname

云彩【wen⁴qoi² 采】cloud

云雾【wen⁴mou⁶ 务】cloud and mist；mist

云吞【wen⁴ten¹ 梯因¹】dumpling soup =【普】馄饨

云团【wen⁴tün⁴ 梯元⁴】cloud atlas

云霞【wen⁴ha⁴ 哈】rosy clouds

云烟【wen⁴yin¹ 燕¹】cloud and mist

云雨【wen⁴ yü⁵ 与】sexual intercourse; make love

云云【wen⁴wen⁴】show the omit of saying

云端【wen⁴dün¹ 段¹】high in the clouds

云汉【wen⁴hon³ 看】the Milky Way

云集【wen⁴ jab⁹ 习】come together in crowds; gather

云母【wen⁴mou⁵ 武】mica

云南【wen⁴nam⁴ 男】〈n.〉Yunnan (Province)

云雀【wen⁴jêg⁸ 桌】〈n.〉skylark

云杉【wen⁴qam³ 参³】dragon spruce

云梯【wen⁴tei¹ 锑】scaling ladder

云霄【wen⁴xiu¹ 消】the skies

云游【wen⁴yeo⁴ 油】roam; wander

云消雾散【wen⁴xiu¹mou⁶xan³ 烧冒汕】The clouds melt and the mists disperse — vanish into thin air.

芸【wen⁴ 云】〈n.〉芸香【wen⁴hêng¹ 乡】rue

芸芸众生【wen⁴wen⁴jung³xeng¹ 种³ 笙】all living things; all mortal beings

纭【wen⁴ 云】〈a.〉纭纭【wen⁴wen⁴】numerous and disorderly; diverse and confused

耘【wen⁴ 云】weed

耘田【wen⁴tin⁴ 天⁴】weed the fields

晕【wen⁴ 云; wen⁶ 运】dizzy; giddy; swoon; faint; halo

晕厥【wen⁴küd⁸ 缺】syncope; faint

晕低【wen⁴ dei¹ 底¹】fall in a faint; pass out =【普】晕倒

晕车【wen⁴qê¹ 奢】carsickness

晕船【wen⁴xün⁴ 旋】seasickness

晕酡酡【wen⁴to⁴to⁴ 驼】dizzy; giddy =【普】晕晕忽忽

晕头转向【wen⁴teo⁴jün²hêng³ 投专² 乡³】confused and disoriented

晕浪【wen⁴long⁶ 晾】sea-sick

稳【wen² 揾】steady; firm; sure; certain

稳步【wen² bou⁶ 部】with steady steps; steadily

稳当【wen² dong³ 档】reliable; secure; safe

稳定【wen²ding⁶ 锭】stable; steady; stabilize

稳固【wen²gu³ 故】firm; stable

稳健【wen²gin⁶ 腱】firm; steady

稳妥【wen²to⁵ 拖⁵】safe; reliable

稳重【wen²jung⁶ 仲】steady; staid; sedate

稳操胜券【wen²qou¹xing³hün³ 躁圣劝】have full assurance of success

稳阵【wen²jen⁶ 珍⁶】calm; stable; firm =【普】稳定; 没危险

允【wen⁵ 陨】permit; allow; consent; fair; just

允许【wen⁵hêü² 栩】permit; allow

允诺【wen⁵ nog⁸ 那恶⁸】promise; consent; undertake

愠【wen³ 韫】angry; irritated

愠怒【wen³nou⁶ 奴⁶】be inwardly angry

韵【wen⁵ 陨】musical sound; rhyme; charm

韵脚【wen⁵gêg⁸ 格约⁸】the rhyming word that ends a line of verse; rhyme

韵律【wen⁵ lêd⁹ 栗】metre; rules of rhyming

韵母【wen⁵mou⁵ 武】simple or compound vowel

韵事【wen⁵xi⁶ 士】literary or artistic pursuits, often with pretence to good taste and refinement; romantic affair

韵味【wen⁵mēi⁶ 未】lingering charm

韵文【wen⁵ men⁴ 闻】literary composition in rhyme; verse

陨【wen⁵ 韵】fall from the sky or outer space

陨石【wen⁵xēg⁹ 硕】aerolite; stony meteorite

陨落【wen⁵log⁹ 洛⁹】fall from the sky or outer space

殒【wen⁵ 陨】perish; die

殒灭【wen⁵mid⁹ 篾】meet one's death; perish

蕴【wen⁵ 允】accumulate; hold in store; contain

蕴藏【wen⁵ qong⁴ 床】hold in store; contain

蕴涵【wen⁵ham⁴ 函】contain; implication

蕴藉【wen⁵jē³ 借】temperate and refined

酝【wen⁵ 允】〈v.〉酝酿【wen⁵yēng⁶ 让】brew; ferment; delicates

熨【wen⁶ 运; wed⁷ 屈】iron; press

熨斗【wen⁶deo² 豆²】flat iron; iron = 烫斗【tong³deo²】

熨衣服【wen⁶yi¹fug⁹ 依伏】iron clothes = 烫衣服【tong³yi¹fug⁹】

郓【wen⁶ 运】a surname

浑【wen⁶ 运】muddy; turbid; foolish; simple and natural; whole; all over

浑身【wen⁶xen¹ 辛】from head to foot; all over

浑厚【wen⁶ heo⁵ 口⁵】simple and honest; simple and vigorous

浑然一体【wen⁶yin⁴yed⁷tei² 言壹睇】one integrated mass; an integral whole

浑浑噩噩【wen⁶ wen⁶ ngog⁶ ngog⁶ 噩】ignorant; simple-minded; muddle-headed

诨【wen⁶ 运】joke; jest

诨名【wen⁶ming⁴ 明】nickname = 花名【fa¹mēng²】

混【wen⁶ 运】mix; confuse; pass for; muddle along; get along with sb.; thoughtlessly

混沌【wen⁶ dên⁶顿】chaos; innocent as a child

混合【wen⁶heb⁹ 盒】mix; blend; mingle

混迹【wen⁶ jig⁷ 积 】unworthily occupy a place among

混进【wen⁶jên³ 俊】infiltrate; sneak into

混乱【wen⁶lün⁶ 联⁶】confusion; chaos

混同【wen⁶tung⁴ 铜】confuse; mix up

混淆【wen⁶ngao⁴ 肴】obscure; blur; confuse; mix up

混杂【wen⁶jab⁹ 习】mix; mingle

混战【wen⁶jin³ 箭】tangled warfare

混浊【wen⁶jug⁹ 续】muddy; turbid

混帐【wen⁶jêng³ 涨】scoundrel; bastard

混吉【wen⁶ged⁷ 格核⁷】do things without results =【普】做事情没得到预料的结果; 白辛苦; 徒劳无益

混蛋【wen⁶dan² 单²】blackguard; wretch; scoundrel; skunk

混凝土【wen⁶ying⁴tou² 营肚²】concrete

混为一谈【wen⁶wei⁴yed⁷tam⁴ 维壹谭】lump together

混水摸鱼【wen⁶xêü²mo²yü⁴ 瑞²摩²余】fish in troubled waters

混世魔王【wen⁶xei³mo¹wong⁴ 细摩黄】

fiend in human shape; devil incarnate

魂【wen⁴ 云】soul; mood; the lofty spirit of a nation

魂魄【wen⁴pag⁸ 柏】soul＝魂灵【ling⁴】

魂不附体【wen⁴bed⁷fu⁶tei² 毕付睇】as if the soul had left the body

运【wen⁶ 混】motion; carry; use; fortune; luck

运动【wen⁶ dung⁶ 洞】motion; sports; movement

运输【wen⁶ xū¹ 书】transport; carriage; conveyance

运送【wen⁶ xung³ 宋】transport; ship; convey

运行【wen⁶heng⁴ 衡】move; be in motion

运转【wen⁶ jūn² 专²】revolve; turn round; work

运费【wen⁶fei³ 废】transportation expenses; freight; carriage

运算【wen⁶xūn³ 蒜】operation

运用【wen⁶ yung⁶容⁶】utilize; wield; apply

运气【wen⁶hēi³ 戏】fortune; luck

运动会【wen⁶ dung⁶ wui² 洞汇²】sports meet; games

运筹帷幄【wen⁶qeo⁴wei⁴ngeg¹ 绸维握】devise strategies within a command tent

弘【weng⁴ 宏】great; grand; enlarge; expand

弘大【weng⁴dai⁶ 歹⁶】grand

泓【weng⁴ 弘】(of water) deep; ⟨classifier.⟩ the unit of a clear spring

宏【weng⁴ 弘】great; grand; magnificent

宏伟【weng⁴wei⁵ 讳】magnificent; grand

宏大【weng⁴dai⁶ 歹⁶】grand; great

宏观【weng⁴gun¹ 官】macroscopic

宏论【weng⁴lên⁶ 沦⁶】informed opinion

宏图【weng⁴ tou⁴途】great plan; grand prospect

宏愿【weng⁴ yün⁶ 县】great aspirations

宏旨【weng⁴ji² 止】main theme

屈【wed⁷ 乌核⁷】bend; bow; crook; subdue; wrong; injustice; in the wrong; a surname

屈服【wed⁷ fug⁹ 伏】surrender; yield; knuckle under

屈辱【wed⁷yug⁹ 玉】humiliation; mortification

屈从【wed⁷qung² 虫】submit to; yield to

屈曲【wed⁷kug⁷ 卡屋⁷】bend to winding＝【普】使弯曲

屈膝【wed⁷ xed⁷ 失】go down on one's knees

屈节【wed⁷jid⁸ 折】forfeit one's honour

屈才【wed⁷qoi⁴ 财】submit to; yield to

屈驾【wed⁷ ga³ 价 】condescend to make the journey

屈尊【wed⁷jūn¹ 专】condescend

屈指可数【wed⁷ ji² ho² xou² 止河² 嫂】very few

屈打成招【wed⁷da²xing⁴jiu¹ 得阿² 承焦】confess to false charges under torture

屈㞘【wed⁷ jed⁷质 】crowded; small; bored＝【普】(地方)窄小; 拥挤; 令人烦恼

煀【wed⁷ 屈】grill; smoke＝【普】烤; 烟熏

煀蚊【wed⁷men¹ 文¹】smoke the mosquito＝【普】烟熏蚊子

䯲【wed⁹ 屈】⟨a.⟩䯲突【wed⁹ded⁹ 凸】ugly; terrible; rude＝【普】丑陋; 肮

脏；难看

涡【wo¹ 蜗】whirlpool；eddy

涡流【wo¹leo⁴ 留】whirling fluid；eddy
涡轮【wo¹lên⁴ 轮】turbine

蜗【wo¹ 涡】snail

蜗牛【wo¹ngeo⁴ 藕⁴】snail
蜗居【wo¹gêü¹ 据¹】humble abode
蜗轮【wo¹lên⁴ 伦】worm gear

窝【wo¹ 蜗】nest；lair；den；pit；harbour hold in；check；bend；litter；brood

窝藏【wo¹qong⁴ 床】harbour；shelter
窝棚【wo¹pang⁴ 彭】shack；shed；shanty
窝工【wo¹gung¹功】hold up in the work through poor organization
窝囊【wo¹nong⁴ 那康⁴】feel vexed；good-for-nothing

倭【wo¹ 蜗】an old name for Japan

倭寇【wo¹keo³ 扣】Japanese pirates

挝【wo¹ 蜗；ja¹ 抓】〈n.〉老挝【lou⁵wo¹ 鲁】Laos

肞【wo⁵ 蜗】the egg being spoiled＝【普】（鸟）蛋变质、变坏

扠肞【qa⁵wo⁵ 叉⁵】mess up a matter＝【普】把事情弄坏、弄糟

呙【wo³ 窝³】（of the mouth）awry；〈auxil.〉exclamation mark；express protest；convey others，messages；show surprise，shock；show defence

禾【wo⁴ 和】standing grain（esp，rice）；paddy

禾苗【wo⁴ miu⁴ 描】seedlings of cereal crops
禾虫【wo⁴ qung² 宠】an insect living in streams

禾秆【wo¹gon² 赶】straw＝【普】稻草
禾花雀【wo¹fa¹jêg⁸ 化¹ 桌】a kind of bird
禾秆冚珍珠【wo¹gon²kem²jen¹jü¹ 赶襟² 真朱】refer to rich people who pretend to be poor＝【普】富人装穷

和【wo⁴ 禾；wo¹ 涡】gentle；mild；kind；harmonious；peace；tie；together with；sum；join in the singing；mix；and；a surname

和味【wo¹mēi¹ 尾¹】delicious；tasty＝【普】好味道；美味
和暖【wo⁴nün⁵ 那渊⁵】luke-warm＝【普】暖和
和蔼【wo⁴ngoi² 霭】kindly；affable；amiable
和好【wo⁴hou² 蒿²】become reconciled
和解【wo⁴gai² 介²】become reconciled
和局【wo⁴ gug⁹ 焗】drawn game；draw；tie
和睦【wo⁴ mug⁹ 目 】harmony；concord；amity
和平【wo⁴ping⁴ 萍】peace；mild
和气【wo⁴ hēi³ 戏】gentle；kind；polite；amiable
和善【wo⁴xin⁶ 膳】kind and gentle；genial
和谈【wo⁴tam² 谭】peace talks
和约【wo⁴yêg⁸ 若⁸】peace treaty
和声【wo⁴xing¹ 升】harmony
和弦【wo⁴yin⁴ 言】chord
和谐【wo⁴hai⁴ 鞋】harmonious
和尚【wo⁴xêng² 想】Buddhist monk
和事老【wo⁴xi⁶lou⁵ 士鲁】peacemaker
和风细雨【wo⁴fung¹ xei³yü⁵ 丰世语】like a gentle breeze and a mild rain—in a gentle and mild way

和盘托出【wo⁴pun⁴tog⁸qêd⁷ 盆拓次律⁷】reveal everything

和颜悦色【wo⁴ ngan⁴ yüd⁹ xig⁷雁⁴ 月式】with a kind and pleasant countenance

和衷共济【wo⁴qung¹ gung⁶jei³ 冲贡⁶ 制】work together with one heart

和稀泥【wo⁴hēi¹nei⁴ 希尼】try to smooth things over

祸【wo⁶ 和⁶】misfortune; disaster; calamity; ruin

祸害【wo⁶hoi⁶亥】disaster;curse;scourge; damage; destroy

祸患【wo⁶wan⁶ 弯⁶】disaster; calamity

祸首【wo⁶xeo² 手】chief culprit

祸心【wo⁶xem¹ 深】evil intention

祸胎【wo⁶toi¹ 台¹】the root of the trouble

祸根【wo⁶ gen¹ 斤】the root of trouble; bane

祸国殃民【wo⁴guog⁸yêng¹men⁴ 帼央文】bring calamity to the country and the people

祸不单行【wo⁶ bed⁷ dan¹ heng⁴毕丹衡】Misfortunes never come singly.

祸起萧墙【wo⁶ hēi² xiu¹ qêng¹喜消场】Trouble arises within the family.

汪【wong¹ 枉¹】①(of liquid) collect; accumulate; ②〈classifier.〉 ∽ a puddle(of rainwater); ③〈onomatope.〉 ∽ bark; bow-wow; ④a surname

汪汪【wong¹ wong¹】tears welling up; tearful

汪洋【wong¹ yêng⁴羊 】(of a body of water)vast; boundless

枉【wong² 汪²】crooked; twist; pervert; wrong; in vain; of no avail

枉法【wong²fad⁸ 发】pervert the law

枉费【wong²fei³ 废】waste; try in vain

枉然【wong²yin⁴ 言】futile; in vain

王【wong⁴ 黄】king; monarch; grand; great; a surname

王朝【wong⁴ qiu⁴樵】imperial court; dynasty

王国【wong⁴ guog⁸帼】kingdom; realm; domain

王公【wong⁴gung¹ 工】princes and dukes; the nobility

王侯【wong⁴heo⁴ 喉】princes and marquis; the nobility

王后【wong⁴heo⁶ 候】queen consort;queen

王子【wong⁴ji² 止】king's son; prince

王孙【wong⁴xün¹ 酸】prince's descendants

王宫【wong⁴gung¹ 工】(imperial)palace

王储【wong⁴qü⁵ 柱】crown prince

王法【wong⁴fad⁸ 发】the law of the land; the law

王道【wong⁴dou⁶ 度】kingly way; benevolent government

王牌【wong⁴pai² 排²】trump card

王八【wong⁴ bad⁸ 捌】tortoise; cuckold = 忘八【mong⁴】

皇【wong⁴ 王】emperor; sovereign

皇帝【wong⁴dei³ 低³】emperor

皇后【wong⁴heo⁶ 候】empress

皇冠【wong⁴gun¹ 官】imperial crown

皇宫【wong⁴gung¹ 工】(imperial) palace

皇家【wong⁴ ga¹ 加】imperial family = 皇室【xed⁷】

皇族【wong⁴ jug⁹ 俗】people of imperial lineage

皇上【wong⁴ xêng⁶ 尚】the emperor; Your Majesty

皇权【wong⁴kün⁴ 拳】imperial power

黄【wong⁴ 王】 yellow; sallow; fall through; a surname

黄色【wong⁴ xig⁷式 】 yellow; decadent; obscene

黄豆【wong⁴deo⁶ 窦】soya bean; soybean

黄瓜【wong⁴gua¹ 寡¹】cucumber

黄蜂【wong⁴fung¹ 风】wasp

黄犬【wong⁴hün² 劝²】earthworms =【普】蚯蚓

黄麻【wong⁴ma⁴ 妈⁴】(roundpod) jute

黄蚑【wong⁴kēi² 其²】ants =【普】蚂蟥

黄牛【wong⁴ngeo⁴ 偶⁵】ox; cattle

黄鳝【wong⁴xin⁵ 善】ricefield eel

黄花筒【wong⁴fa¹tung² 化¹ 统】a type of fish

黄连【wong⁴ lin⁴ 莲】the rhizome of Chinese goldthread

黄芽白【wong⁴nga⁴bag⁹ 牙伯⁹】big Chinese lettuce =【普】大白菜

黄猄【wong⁴gēng¹ 镜¹】muntjac

黄土【wong⁴ tou²肚 】loess; yellow soil = 黄泥【nei⁴】

黄熟【wong⁴ xug⁹ 属】pale =【普】(脸色) 苍白、淡黄

黄莺【wong⁴ngeng¹ 额亨¹】oriole

黄铜【wong⁴tung¹ 同】brass

黄金【wong⁴gem¹ 今】gold

黄泉【wong⁴qün⁴ 存】netherworld

黄昏【wong⁴fen¹ 分】dusk

黄丝蚁【wong⁴ xi¹ ngei⁵ 司伪⁵】yellow small ants =【普】小黄蚁

黄鼠狼【wong⁴ xü² long⁴ 署郎 】 yellow weasel

黄灿灿【wong⁴ qan³ qan³ 璨】bright yellow; golden

黄粱美梦【wong⁴lêng⁴mēi⁵mung⁶ 凉尾莫 瓮⁶】Golden Millet Dream; pipe dream

黄绿医生【wong⁴lug⁹yi¹xeng¹ 六衣笙】doctors who are not really smart or good =【普】医技、医德很糟的庸医

凰【wong⁴ 王】(see“凤凰”【fung⁶wong⁴】)

隍【wong⁴ 王】dry moat outside a city wall

惶【wong⁴ 王】fear; anxiety; trepidation

惶惶不可终日【wong⁴wong⁴bed⁷ho²jung¹ yed⁹ 毕贺² 中逸】be in a constant state of anxiety

惶惑【wong⁴wag⁹ 或】perplexed and alarmed

惶恐【wong⁴hung² 孔】terrified

徨【wong⁴ 王】bright; brilliant (see “辉煌”)

潢【wong⁴ 王】(see“装潢”【jong¹wong⁴】)

蝗【wong⁴ 王】〈n.〉蝗虫【wong⁴qung⁴ 从】locust

篁【wong⁴ 王】bamboo grove; bamboo

磺【wong⁴ 王】sulphur

磺胺【wong⁴ ngon¹ 安】 sulphanilamide (SN)

蟥【wong⁴ 王】(see“蚂蟥”【ma⁵wong⁴】)

簧【wong⁴ 王;wong² 枉】reed; spring

往【wong⁵ 王⁵】go; in the direction of; toward; to

往返【wong⁵ fan² 反 】go there and back; journey to and fro

往复【wong⁵ fug⁷ 幅 】move back and forth; reciprocate

往来【wong⁵ loi⁴ 莱】come and go; contact

往常【wong⁵ xêng⁴ 尝 】habitually in the past

往昔【wong⁵ xig⁷ 色 】in the past; in former times

往往【wong⁵ wong⁵】〈ad.〉often; frequently

往年【wong⁵ nin⁴ 捻⁴】(in) former years

往日【wong⁵ yed⁹ 逸】(in) former days

往事【wong⁵ xi⁶ 士】past events; the past

往时【wong⁵ xi⁴ 是⁴】previously; last time

往前看【wong⁵ qin⁴ hon³ 钱汉 】look forward

旺【wong⁶ 王⁶】prosperous; flourishing; vigorous; merry; joyous; good business; season

旺盛【wong⁶ xing⁶ 乘⁶】vigorous; exuberant

旺季【wong⁶ guei³ 桂】peak period; busy season

获【wog⁹ 蠖】capture; catch; obtain; win; reap

获得【wog⁹ deg⁷ 德】gain; obtain; win; acquire

获胜【wog⁹ xing³ 圣】win victory; be victorious

获悉【wog⁹ xig⁷ 色】learn(of an event)

蠖【wog⁹ 获】looper; inchworm (尺蠖【qēg⁴ wog⁹】)

镬【wog⁹ 获】cauldron; big pot = 【普】锅；大锅

镬铲【wog⁹ qan² 产】a cooking utensil used to fry food

乌【wu¹ 污】crow; black; dark; a surname

乌黑【wu¹ heg⁷ 克 】pitch-black; jet-black

乌龟【wu¹ guei¹ 归】tortoise; cuckold

乌鸦【wu¹ nga¹ 丫】crow

乌云【wu¹ wen⁴ 耘 】black clouds; dark clouds

乌贼【wu¹ qag⁹ 册⁹】cuttlefish; inkfish = 墨鱼【meg⁹ yü⁴】

乌鱼【wu¹ yü⁴ 余】snakehead; snakeheaded fish = 生鱼【xang¹ yü²】

乌桕【wu¹ keo⁵ 舅】Chinese tallow tree

乌蝇【wu¹ ying¹ 英】a fly = 【普】苍蝇

乌榄【wu¹ lam² 揽²】olive

乌鸡【wu¹ gei¹ 计¹】rust; black mark

乌龙【wu¹ lung² 笼²】irresponsible; unwise; deceive; confused = 【普】糊涂的；乱来的；不负责任的

乌龙王【wu¹ lung² wong⁴ 笼² 黄】one who is blurred ∽【普】糊涂虫；瞎搞糊弄的头领

乌哝哝【wu¹ lüd⁷ lüd⁷ 抒⁷】black and shining = 【普】乌亮；乌黑发亮

乌纱帽【wu¹ xa¹ mou² 沙冒²】black gauze cap; official post

乌托邦【wu¹ tog⁹ bong¹ 梯恶⁸ 帮】Utopia

乌合之众【wu¹ heb⁹ ji¹ jung³ 盒支纵³】a disorderly band; rabble; mob

乌烟瘴气【wu¹ yin¹ jêng³ hēi³ 咽障戏】foul atmosphere

乌灯黑火【wu¹ deng¹ heg⁷ fo² 登克伙 】completely dark = 【普】没有一点亮光；很黑

乌喱单刀【wu¹ lēi¹ dan¹ dou¹ 李¹ 丹都】Blur; in a mess ∽【普】乱七八糟；乌七八糟

邬【wu¹ 乌】a surname

钨【wu¹ 乌】tungsten; wolfram(W)

钨钢【wu¹gong³ 岗³】wolfram steel; tungsten steel

钨砂【wu¹xa¹ 沙】tungsten ore

钨丝【wu¹xi¹ 司】tungsten filament

呜【wu¹ 乌】〈onomatope.〉∽toot; hoot; zoom

呜咽【wu¹yin¹ 烟】sob; whimper

呜呼哀哉【wu¹fu¹ngoi¹joi¹ 夫爱¹灾】alas; dead and gone; all is lost

俛【wu³ 乌³】bow (one's head) =【普】俯

俛低【wu³dei¹ 底¹】bend down =【普】俯身向下

壶【wu⁴ 胡; wu² 浒】kettle; pot; bottle; flask

茶壶【qa⁴wu² 查】teapot

浒【wu² 壶²】waterside

胡【wu⁴ 糊】introduced from the northern and western nationalities or abroad;〈ad.〉recklessly; wantonly;〈pron.〉why; moustache, beard or whiskers; a surname

胡哩马汉【wu⁴li¹ma⁵qa⁵ 罗衣¹ 码叉⁵】in a mess ∽【普】(写得)乌七八糟

胡椒【wu⁴jiu¹ 焦】pepper

胡琴【wu⁴kem² 禽】a general term for certain two-stringed bowed instruments, such as"erhu", etc.

胡须【wu⁴ xou¹ 苏】beard, moustache or whiskers

胡乱【wu⁴lün⁶ 联】carelessly; casually

胡闹【wu⁴nao⁶ 那拗⁶】run wild; be mischievous

胡来【wu⁴ loi⁴莱 】mess things up; run wild = 乱嚟【lün²lei⁴】

胡说【wu⁴ xüd⁸雪】 talk nonsense; nonsense = 乱讲【lün²gong²】

胡杨【wu⁴ yêng⁴ 洋 】 diversiform-leaved poplar

胡胡混混【wu⁴ wu⁴ wen⁶ wen⁶ 运】ordinary; common ∽【普】混日子

胡思乱想【wu⁴ xi¹ lün⁶ xêng² 司联⁶ 赏】 imagine things; go off into wild flights of fancy

胡作非为【wu⁴jog⁸fêi¹wei² 昨飞维】commit all kinds of outrages

胡须簕特【wu⁴xou¹leg⁹deg⁹ 苏勒得⁹】the look of one who has got beard ∽【普】满脸胡须茬子

糊【wu⁴ 胡; wu² 浒】paste; stick with paste; (of food) burnt; plaster

糊料【wu⁴liu² 撩】thickener

糊涂【wu⁴ tou⁴ 途】muddled; confused; bewildered

糊墙纸【wu⁴qêng⁴ji² 场止】wall paper

葫【wu⁴ 胡】〈n.〉葫芦【wu⁴lou² 卢²】bottle gourd; calabash; things; sayings that are false

葫芦王【wu⁴lou⁴wong⁴ 卢² 黄】One who likes to tell lies. ∽【普】吹牛大王

湖【wu⁴ 胡】lake

湖泊【wu⁴bog⁹ 薄】lake

湖滨【wu⁴ben¹ 宾】lakeside

湖南【wu⁴ nam⁴ 男】〈n.〉Hunan (Province)

湖北【wu⁴ beg⁷ 伯克⁷】〈n.〉Hubei (Province)

猢【wu⁴ 胡】〈n.〉猢狲【wu⁴xün¹ 孙】macaque

煳【wu⁴ 胡】(of food) burnt = 燶【lung¹】)

瑚【wu⁴ 胡】(see"珊瑚"【xan¹wu⁴】)

蝴【wu⁴ 胡】〈n.〉蝴蝶【wu⁴dib⁹ 碟】butterfly

醐【wu⁴ 胡】(see"醍醐"【tei⁴wu⁴】)

弧【wu⁴ 胡】arc

弧度【wu⁴dou⁶ 道】radian

弧形【wu⁴ying⁴ 型】arc；curve

弧光【wu⁴guong¹ 胱】arc light；arc

狐【wu⁴ 胡】fox

狐狸【wu⁴lēi² 李²】fox

狐臭【wu⁴ qeo³ 嗅】body odour；bromhidrosis

狐裘【wu⁴keo⁴ 求】fox-fur robe

狐疑【wu⁴yi⁴ 移】doubt；suspicion

狐狸精【wu⁴lēi⁴jing¹ 离贞】fox spirit — seductive woman

狐群狗党【wu⁴kuen⁴geo²dong² 裙九挡】a pack of rogues；a gang of scoundrels

污【wu¹ 乌】dirt；filth；dirty；filthy；defile

污秽【wu¹wei³ 畏】filthy；foul

污垢【wu¹geo³ 够】dirt；filth

污点【wu¹dim² 店²】stain；spot；blemish

污迹【wu¹jig⁷ 积】stain；smear；smudge

污泥【wu¹nei⁴ 尼】mud；mire；sludge

污水【wu¹ xêü²瑞²】foul water；sewage；slops

污浊【wu¹jug⁹ 续】dirty；muddy；foul

污染【wu¹yim⁵ 冉】pollute；contaminate

污辱【wu¹ yug⁹ 玉】humiliate；insult；defile；sully

污糟【wu¹jou¹ 遭】dirty = 【普】肮脏

污糟邋遢【wu¹ jou¹ lad⁹ tad⁸遭辣梯压⁸】dirty；nasty = 【普】很肮脏

污七八糟【wu¹qed⁷bad⁸joi¹ 柒捌遭】in a horrible mess；obscene；dirty；filthy

户【wu⁶ 护】door；household；family；account

户口【wu⁶ heo² 厚²】number of household and total population；registered permanent residence

户籍【wu⁶ jig⁹直 】census register；registered permanent residence

户主【wu⁶jü² 煮】head of a household

户枢不蠹【wu¹xü¹bed⁷dug⁹ 书毕毒】a door-hinge is never worm-eaten

互【wu⁶ 户】mutual；each other

互相【wu⁶ xêng¹商 】〈ad.〉mutual；each other

互助【wu⁶jo⁶ 座】help each other

互利【wu⁶lēi⁶ 俐】mutually beneficial

互惠【wu⁶wei⁶ 卫】mutually beneficial

互换【wu⁶wun⁶ 唤】exchange

互访【wu⁶fong² 坊²】exchange visits

互感【wu⁶gem² 敢】mutual inductance

互通有无【wu⁶tung¹yeo⁵mou⁴ 统¹ 友毛】each supplies what the other needs

沪【wu⁶ 户】another name for Shanghai

护【wu⁶ 户】protect；guard；be partial to

护卫【wu⁶ wei⁶ 惠】protect；guard；bodyguard

护理【wu⁶lēi⁵ 李】nurse; tend and protect

护送【wu⁶xung³ 宋】escort; convoy

护养【wu⁶yēng⁵ 氧】cultivate; nurse; maintain

护士【wu⁶xi⁶ 事】(hospital) nurse

护航【wu⁶hong⁴ 杭】escort; convoy

护短【wu⁶ dün² 端²】shield a shortcoming or fault

护照【wu⁶jiu³ 赵³】passport

扈【wu⁶ 户】retinue; a surname

扈从【wu⁶qung⁴ 虫】retinue; retainer

怙【wu⁶ 户】rely on

怙恶不悛【wu⁶ngog⁸bed⁷xün¹ 噩毕宣】be steeped in evil and refuse to repent

祜【wu² 浒】blessing; bliss

瓠【wu⁶ 户】a kind of edible gourd

芋【wu⁶ 户】taro

芋头【wu⁶teo⁴ 投】taro; sweet potato

煨【wui¹ 会¹】cook over a slow fire; stew; simmer; roast(sweet potatoes, etc.)in fresh cinders

煨牛肉【wui⁶ngeo⁴yug⁹ 偶⁴ 玉】stewed beef

会【wui² 煨²; wui⁶ 汇; wui⁶ 汇⁵】get together; meet; see; meeting; party; association; a temple fair; chief city; opportunity; understand; can; be able to; be good at; be likely to; a moment

会见【wui⁶gin³ 建】meet with

会面【wui⁶min⁶ 缅⁶】meet

会晤【wui⁶ng⁶ 误】meet

会谈【wui⁶tam⁴ 谭】talks

会同【wui⁶tung⁴ 铜】jointly with other organizations concerned

会错意【wui⁶qo³yi³ 挫薏】misunderstand =【普】误会对方的意思

会心【wui⁶ xem¹ 深 】 understanding; knowing

会意【wui⁶yi³ 薏】understanding; knowing

会议【wui⁶yi⁵ 尔】meeting; conference

会合【wui⁶heb⁹ 盒】join; meet; converge

会师【wui⁶ xi¹司 】 join forces; effect a junction

会战【wui⁶jin³ 箭】meet for a decisive battle; join in a battle

会诊【wui⁶qen² 陈²】constitution of an association

会堂【wui⁶tong⁴ 塘】assembly hall; hall

会场【wui⁶qêng⁴ 祥】meeting-place; conference hall

会得【wui⁵deg⁷ 德】know =【普】晓得; 懂得

会员【wui²yün⁴ 元】member

会客【wui⁶hag⁸ 吓】receive a visitor

荟【wui⁶ 会; kui³ 溃³】luxuriant growth

荟萃【wui⁶xêü⁶ 睡】gather together; assemble

烩【wui⁶ 汇】braise; cook with meat, vegetables and water

汇【wui⁶ 烩】converge; gather together; things collected; assemblage; collection; remit

汇报【wui⁶bou³ 布】report; give an account of

汇编【wui⁶pin¹ 篇】compilation; collection

汇兑【wui⁶dêü³ 对】remittance

汇款【wui⁶ fun² 欢²】remit money; remittance

汇率【wui⁶lêd⁹律】exchange rate

汇票【wui⁶piu³漂³】draft; money order

汇费【wui⁶fei³废】remittance fee

汇合【wui⁶heb⁹盒】converge; join

汇集【wui⁶jɑb⁹习 】collect; compile; come together

汇总【wui⁶jung²肿】gather; collect; pool

回【wui⁴ 茴】circle; wind; return; go back; turn round; answer; reply; 〈classifier.〉∽ chapter; the unit of a motion; 〈n.〉the Hui nationality

回来【wui⁴loi⁴莱 】return; come back; back

回去【wui⁴hêû³虚³】return; go back; be back; back

回旋【wui⁴xūn⁴船】circle round; manoeuvre

回归【wui⁴guei¹龟】regression

回避【wui⁴bēi⁶备】evade; dodge

回报【wui⁴bou³布 】report back on what has been done; repay; requite

回南【wui⁴nɑm⁴男】the winter is turning to summer＝【普】天气转暖，吹南风，空气潮湿

回潮【wui⁴qiu⁴樵】resurgence; reversion

回春【wui⁴qên¹椿】return of spring; bring back to life

回答【wui⁴dɑb⁸搭 】answer; reply; response

回荡【wui⁴dong⁶当⁶】resound; reverberate

回复【wui⁴fug⁷幅】reply (to a letter)

回合【wui⁴heb⁹盒】round; bout

回话【wui⁴wɑ⁶华⁶】reply; answer

回击【wui⁴gig⁷激】fight back; return fire

回扣【wui⁴keo³寇】sales commission

回礼【wui⁴lei⁵厉⁵】return a salute; send a present in return

回廊【wui⁴long⁴郎】winding corridor

回路【wui⁴lou⁶露】return circuit; return; loop

回升【wui⁴xing¹星】rise again; pick up

回首【wui⁴xeo²手】turn one's head; turn round; look back

回收【wui⁴xeo¹修】retrieve; recover; reclaim

回头【wui⁴teo⁴投】turn one's head; repent

回味【wui⁴mēi⁶未】aftertaste; call sth. to mind and ponder over it

回乡【wui⁴hêng¹香】return to one's home village

回响【wui⁴hêng²向²】reverberate; echo; resound

回想【wui⁴xêng²赏】think back; recollect; recall

回信【wui⁴xên³讯】write in reply; write back; a letter in reply; reply

回音【wui⁴yem¹阴】echo; reply; turn

回忆【wui⁴yig⁷亿】call to mind; recollect; recall

回执【wui⁴jeb⁷汁】a short note acknowledging receipt of sth.; receipt

回族【wui⁴jug⁹俗】the Hui nationality

回顾【wui⁴gu³故】look back; review

回归线【wui⁴guei¹xin³龟扇】tropic

回马枪【wui⁴mɑ²qêng¹码昌】back thrust

回心转意【wui⁴ xem¹ jūn² yi³ 深专² 意】change one's views; come around

回头是岸【wui⁴teo⁴xi⁶ngon⁶投示安⁶】repent and be saved

茴【wui¹回】〈n.〉茴香【wui⁴hêng¹乡】fennel; aniseed

蛔【wui⁴ 回】〈n.〉蛔虫【wui⁴qung⁴ 从】roundworm; ascarid

碗【wun² 腕】bowl

惋【wun² 碗】sigh

惋惜【wun²xig⁷ 色】feel sorry for sb. or about sth.; sympathize with

腕【wun² 碗】wrist

手腕【xeo²wun² 守】wrist

缓【wun⁶ 换; wun⁴ 桓】slow; unhu-ried; delay; postpone; not tense; recuperate; revive

缓冲【wun⁶ qung¹ 充】buffer; cushion

缓和【wun⁶ wo⁴ 禾】relax; ease up; mitigate

缓急【wun⁴geb⁷ 格合⁷】pressing or otherwise; emergency

缓慢【wun⁴man⁶ 万】slow

缓坡【wun⁶bo¹ 波】gentle slope

缓期【wun⁶ kēi⁴其 】postpone a deadline; suspend

缓刑【wun⁶ying⁴ 型】temporary suspension of the execution of a sentence; reprieve

缓征【wun⁶ jing¹精】postpone the imposition of a tax or levy

缓兵之计【wun⁴bing¹ji¹gei³ 冰支继】stalling tactics

桓【wun⁴ 缓⁴】a surname

垣【wun⁴ 桓】wall

援【wun⁴ 缓⁴; yün⁴ 元】pull by hand; hold; quote; cite; help; aid; rescue

援救【wun⁴ geo³ 够 】rescue; save; deliver from danger

援例【wun⁴lei⁶ 厉】cite a precedent

援引【wun⁴ yen⁵ 瘾】quote; cite; recommend or appoint one's friends or favourites

援助【wun⁴jo⁶ 座】help; support; aid

浣【wun² 碗; wun⁵ 碗⁵】wash; any of the three ten-day divisions of a month

浣衣【wun⁵yi¹ 依】wash clothes

爰【wun⁴ 桓; yün⁴ 元】whence; from what place; hence; thereupon

换【wun⁶ 唤】exchange; barter; trade; change

换班【wun⁶ban¹ 斑】change shifts; relieve a person on duty; changing of the guard

换车【wun⁶qē¹ 奢】change trains or buses

换人【wun⁶ yen⁴ 仁】substitution（of players)

换岗【wun⁶gong¹ 江】relieve a sentry

换工【wun⁶gung¹ 公】exchange labour

换货【wun⁶fo³ 课】exchange goods; barter

换钱【wun⁶qin¹ 前】change money; sell

换季【wun⁶guei³ 贵】change garments according to the season

换气【wun⁶hēi³ 戏】take a breath（in swimming)

换取【wun⁶ qêu²娶 】 exchange sth. for; get in return

换算【wun⁶xün³ 蒜】conversion

换汤不换药【wun⁶tong¹bed⁷wun⁶yêg⁹ 堂¹毕若】the same medicine differently prepared

涣【wun⁶ 换】melt; vanish

涣然【wun⁶yin⁴ 言】melt away; vanish

涣散【wun⁶xɑn³ 汕】lax；slack

唤

【wun⁶ 换】call out

唤起【wun⁶hēi² 喜】arouse；call；recall

唤醒【wun⁶xing² 星²】wake up；awaken

焕

【wun⁶ 换】shining；glowing

焕发【wun⁶fɑd⁸ 法】shine；glow；irradiate

焕然一新【wun⁶ yin⁴ yed⁷ xen¹ 言壹辛】
　　take on an entirely new look；look
　　brand-new

瘓

【wun⁶ 换】(see"瘫痪"【tɑn¹wun⁶】)

活

【wud⁹ 乌括⁹】live；alive；living；save；
　　vivid；lively；movable；moving；sim-
　　ply；exactly；work

活泼【wud⁹ pud⁸拍活⁸】lively；vivid；re-
　　active

活跃【wud⁹yêg⁸ 约】brisk；active；enliven

活动【wud⁹dung⁶ 洞】move about

活化【wud⁹fɑ³ 花³】activation

活性【wud⁹xing³ 姓】active；activated

活该【wud⁹goi¹ 改¹】serve sb. right ＝ 抵
　　死【dei²xēi²】

活像【wud⁹jêng⁶ 象】look exactly like ＝ 似
　　晒【qi⁵xɑi³】

活活【wud⁹wud⁹】while still alive

活力【wud⁹lig⁹ 历】vigour；vitality；ener-
　　gy

活路【wud⁹ lou⁶露 】way out；workable
　　method

活络【wud⁹log⁹ 洛】loose；noncommittal

活命【wud⁹mēng⁶ 莫镜⁶】earn a bare liv-
　　ing；save sb.'s life

活期【wud⁹kēi⁴ 其】current

活塞【wud⁹xeg⁷ 是克⁷】piston

活现【wud⁹yin⁶ 燕⁶】appear vividly；come
alive

活生生【wud⁹xeng¹xeng¹ 笙】real；living；
　　while still alive

活见鬼【wud⁹ gin³ guei² 建轨 】It's sheer
　　fantasy. ＝ 撞鬼【jung²guei²】

活受罪【wud⁹xeo⁶jêū⁶ 授坠】have a hell of
　　a life

活灵活现【wud⁹ling⁴wud⁹yin⁶ 凌燕⁶】
　　vivid；vitality

躯

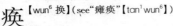

【wi¹ 乌衣¹】〈onomatopoeia〉

躯哗鬼震【wi¹wɑ¹guei²jen³ 娃诡振】
　　wrangle； hubbub； clamour ∽
　　【普】吵吵闹闹；吵吵嚷嚷

永

【wing⁵ 荣⁵】perpetually；forever；al-
ways

永恒【wing⁵heng⁴ 衡】eternal；perpetual；
　　forever

永远【wing⁵yün⁵ 软】always；forever；ever

永久【wing⁵geo² 九】permanent；perpetu-
　　al；forever

永别【wing⁵bid⁹ 必⁹】part forever ＝ 永诀
　　【küd⁸】

永生【wing⁵xeng¹ 笙】eternal life；immor-
　　tal

永世【wing⁵xei³ 细】forever

永志不忘【wing⁵ ji³ bed⁷ mong⁴ 至毕亡】
　　will always bear in mind

永垂不朽【wing⁵xêū⁴bed⁷neo² 谁毕纽】be
　　immortal

泳

【wing⁶ 咏】swim

咏

【wing⁶ 泳】chant；intone；express or
narrate in poetic form

咏赞【wing⁶jɑn³ 支晏³】sing the praises
　　of；praise

咏叹【wing⁶tɑn³ 炭】intone；chant；sing

荣【wing⁴ 永⁴】grow luxuriantly; flourish; honour; glory; a surname

荣辱【wing⁴yug⁹ 玉】honour or disgrace

荣誉【wing⁴yü⁶ 喻】honour; credit; glory

荣耀【wing⁴yiu⁶ 要⁶】honour; glory

荣幸【wing⁴heng⁶ 杏】be honoured

荣获【wing⁴wog⁹ 蠖】have the honour to get

荣归【wing⁴guei¹ 龟】return in glory

荣华富贵【wing⁴wa⁴fu³guei³ 铧裤桂】glory, splendour, wealth and rank

嵘【wing⁴ 荣】(see "峥嵘"【jeng¹wing⁴】)

域【wig⁹ 蜮】land within certain boundaries; territory; region

阈【wig⁹ 域】threshold; doorsill

蜮【wig⁹ 域】〈n.〉鬼蜮【guei²wig⁹ 诡】demon

X

卅【xa¹ 沙】thirty

沙【xa¹ 纱】sand; granalated; husky; a surname

沙子【xa¹ji² 止】sand; grit; small grains; pellets

沙丘【xa¹yeo¹ 休】(sand) dune

沙滩【xa¹tan¹ 摊】sandy beach

沙洲【xa¹ jeo¹ 州】shoal; sandbar; sandbank

沙漠【xa¹mog⁹ 莫】desert

沙场【xa¹ qêng⁴ 祥】battlefield; battleground

沙发【xa¹fa² 化²】sofa; settee

沙拉【xa¹lai¹ 罗埃¹】salad

沙梨【xa¹lêi² 李²】sand pear

沙参【xa¹xem¹ 心】the root of straight ladybell

沙哑【xa¹nga² 雅²】hoarse; husky

沙眼【xa¹ngan⁵ 雁⁵】trachoma

沙锥【xa¹jêü¹ 追】snipe = 沙虫【xa¹qung² 宠】

沙丁鱼【xa¹ding¹yü² 余²】sardine

沙俄【xa¹ngo⁴ 鹅⁴】tsarist Russia

沙特阿拉伯【xa¹deg⁹a¹lai¹bag⁸】Saudi Arabia

沙虱【xa¹xed⁷ 失】sand hopper = 【普】沙蚤

沙河粉【xa¹ho²fen²何²分²】a type of noodle

沙田柚【xa¹tin⁴yeo²友²】a type of pomelo

沙尘【xa¹qen⁴ 陈】= 沙尘白霍【xa¹qen⁴bag⁹fog⁸ 陈伯⁹夫恶⁸】describe one who is proud, arrogant, boastful and frivolous = 【普】卖脸光；通过装扮显示气派

砂【xa¹ 沙】sand; grit

砂砾【xa¹lig⁷ 力⁷】gravel; grit

砂煲兄弟【xa¹bou¹hing¹dei⁶ 褒兴第】good friends that share happiness and burden ∽【普】分享快乐与患难的朋友；哥们

砂轮【xa¹lên⁴轮】emery wheel; grinding wheel

砂布【xa¹bou³ 报】emery cloth

砂纸【xa¹ji² 止】sand paper

砂土【xa¹tou² 肚】sandy soil; sand

砂岩【xa¹ngam⁴ 癌】sandstone

砂糖【xa¹tong⁴ 唐】granulated sugar

砂煲罂罉【xa¹bou¹ngang¹qang¹ 硬¹撑】tins and bottles = 【普】煮吃工具；家当

纱【xa¹ 沙】yarn; gauze; sheer

纱布【xa¹bou³ 报】gauze

纱窗【xa¹qêng¹ 昌】screen window

纱罩【xa¹jao³ 爪³】gauze or screen covering; mantle(of a lamp)

纱灯【xa¹deng¹ 登】gauze lantern

纱锭【xa¹ding⁶ 定】spindle

纱线【xa¹xin³ 扇】yarn

纱笼【xa¹lung⁴ 龙】sarong

裟【xa¹ 沙】〈n.〉袈裟【ga¹xa¹】(see"袈裟")

鲨【xa¹ 沙】〈n.〉鲨鱼【xa¹yū⁴ 余】shark

鲨胆【xa¹dam² 担²】bold；daring =【普】大胆

痧【xa¹ 沙】acute diseases such as cholera and sunstroke

洒【xa² 沙²】sprinkle；spray；spill；shed

洒泪【xa²lêü⁶ 类】shed tears

洒扫【xa² xou³ 素】sprinkle water and sweep the floor；sweep

洒脱【xa² tüd⁸ 梯月⁸】free and easy

揰【xa² 洒；xa⁴ 沙⁴】shake one's hand

揰手兼拧头【xa¹xeo²gim¹ning⁶teo² 守检¹宁⁶ 投²】shake one's hand and shake one's head to denote disagreement =【普】摇手、摇头，表示不合适、不同意

揰揰滚【xa⁴xa⁴guen² 均²】careless；fail to plan；without planning = 揰哩弄抗【xa⁴li¹lung⁶qung³ 罗衣¹ 龙充³】=【普】做事不按方法步骤，乱来

耍【xa² 洒；xa³ 沙³】play；play with；flourish；play(tricks)

去耍【hêü³xa³ 虚³】go to play

耍弄【xa²lung⁶ 龙⁶】make fun of；deceive

耍笔杆【xa²bed⁷gon¹ 毕竿】wield a pen

耍花招【xa²fa¹jiu¹ 化¹ 焦】play tricks

耍滑头【xa² wad⁹ teo² 挖⁹ 投²】act in a slick way

耍流氓【xa²leo⁴mong⁴ 留亡】behave like a hoodlum

耍脾气【xa²pēi⁴hēi³ 皮戏】get into a huff

耍威风【xa² wei¹ fung¹ 委¹ 丰】make a show of authority

耍无赖【xa²mou⁴ lai² 毛拉²】act shamelessly

耍嘴皮【xa² jêü⁴ pēi⁴ 咀脾 】talk glibly；mere empty talk ∽ 卖口乖【mai⁶heo²guai¹】

嚡【xai¹ 徙】waste；squander；it's a pity

嚡遢【xai¹tad⁸ 梯压⁸】waste =【普】浪费；糟蹋

嚡晒【xai¹ xai³ 徙³】waste；it's a pity =【普】浪费；可惜

嚡时间【xai¹xi⁴gan¹ 是⁴ 奸】waste the time =【普】浪费时间

嚡气【xai¹ hēi³ 戏 】waste one's energy；not practical =【普】说了没用

嘲【xai¹ 徙¹】ridicule；deride =【普】揶揄

嘲下佢【xai¹ha⁶kêü⁵ 夏拒】ridicule him =【普】揶揄他

晒【xai³ 徙】(of the sun) shine upon；dry in the sun；bask；come to an end；be over

冇晒【mou⁵xai³ 武】come to an end =【普】完了

晒粮食【xai³lêng⁴xig⁹ 良蚀】dry grain in the sun

晒坪【xai³ping⁴ 平】sunning ground

晒图【xai³ tou⁴ 途 】make a blueprint；blueprint

晒棚【xai³ pang² 彭²】an area inside the house which is not covered by roof =【普】天台；阳台

徙【xai² 晒²】move(from one place to another)

徙居【xai²gêu¹ 据¹】move house

玺 【xai² 徙】imperial or royal seal(see"玉玺")

梢 【xao¹ 捎】tip; the thin end of a twig, etc.

梢头【xao¹teo⁴ 投】the tip of a branch; top log

筲 【xao¹ 梢】〈n.〉筲箕【xao¹gēi¹ 机】pail(usu. made of bamboo strips or wood); bucket

捎 【xao¹ 梢】take along sth. to or for sb.; bring to sb.

捎带【xao¹dai³ 戴】incidentally; in passing

艄 【xao¹ 梢】stern; rudder; helm

艄公【xao²gung¹ 工】helmsman; boatman

稍 【xao² 梢²】〈ad.〉a little; a bit; slightly; a trifle

稍为【xao²wei⁴ 维】a little; a bit; slightly a trifle=【普】稍微;稍许

稍息【xao²xig⁷ 式】stand at ease

稍纵即逝【xao²jung³jig⁷xei⁶ 种³ 积誓】transient; fleeting

哨 【xao³ 潲】sentry post; post; chirp; whistle; the front tooth revealing out

哨牙【xao³nga⁴ 芽】the front tooth revealing out=【普】门牙外露

哨兵【xao³bing¹ 冰】sentry; guard

哨所【xao³xo² 锁】sentry post; post

哨子【xao³ji² 止】whistle

潲 【xao³ 哨】hogwash; swill; slops

猪潲【jü¹xao³ 朱】hogwash; swill =【普】猪食

潲水【xao³xêu² 瑞²】swill; slops=【普】泔水

鞘 【xao¹ 梢;qiu³ 俏】whiplash; scabbard

三 【xam¹ 衫】three; more than two; several; many

三方【xam¹fong¹ 芳】tripartite

三角【xam¹ gog⁸ 各】triangle; trigonometry

三昧【xam¹ mui² 妹】samadhi; secret; knack

三国【xam¹guog⁸ 帼】the Three Kingdoms (220~265)

三月【xam¹ yüd⁹越 】March; the third month of the lunar year; the third moon

三相【xam¹xêng³ 商³】three-phase

三部曲【xam¹bou⁶kug⁷ 步卡屋⁷】trilogy

三段论【xam¹dün⁶lên⁶ 端⁶ 沦⁶】syllogism

三伏天【xam¹fug⁹tin¹ 服田】dog days

三合板【xam¹ heb⁹ ban² 盒版】three-ply board; plywood

三棱镜【xam¹ling⁴gêng³ 凌颈³】(triangular) prism

三轮车【xam¹lên⁴qē¹ 纶奢】tricycle; pedicab

三只手【xam¹jēg⁸xeo² 脊守】pickpocket; a thief

三幅被【xam¹fug⁷pēi⁵ 福皮⁵】not creative =【普】不新鲜的话题;老调重弹

三脚凳【xam¹ gêg⁸ deng⁸ 格约⁸邓³】 one who cannot be relied upon; a trap set up to trap others ∽【普】不可靠、不能信赖的人;陷阱;圈套

三文治【xam¹men⁴ji⁶ 民自】sandwich

三行仔【xam¹ hong² jei² 巷² 济²】carpenters, painters and bricklayer = 【普】木匠、泥水匠、油漆匠等建筑工匠

三岔路口【xam¹qa³lou⁶heo²　叉³露厚²】a fork in the road; a junction of three roads

三长两短【xam¹qêng⁴lêng⁵dün²　场俩端²】unexpected misfortune; sth. unfortunate, esp. death

三番五次【xam¹fan¹ng⁵qi³　翻伍刺】again and again; time and again; repeatedly

三令五申【xam¹ling⁶ng⁵xen¹　另伍辛】repeated injunctions

三教九流【xam¹ gao³ geo² leo⁴　较久留】people in various trades; people of all sorts

三生有幸【xam¹xeng¹yeo⁵heng⁶　笙友杏】consider oneself most fortunate

三思而行【xam¹xi⁴yi⁴heng⁴　司移衡】think thrice before you act; look before you leap

三头六臂【xam¹ teo⁴ lug⁹ bêi³　投陆泌】(with) three heads and six arms — superhuman

三心两意【xam¹xem¹lêng⁵yi³　深俩薏】be of two minds; shilly-shally; half-hearted

三民主义【xam¹ men⁴ jü² yi⁶　文煮异】the Three People's Principles(Nationalism, Democracy and the People's Livelihood), put forward by Dr. Sun Yat-sen

三九两丁七【xam¹geo²lêng⁵ding¹qed⁷　久俩叮柒】describe that there are very few people walking on the street ∽【普】没几个人

三句不离本行【xam¹gêu³bed⁷lêi⁴bun²hong⁴　据毕漓苯航】can hardly open one's mouth without talking shop;

talk shop all the time

三十六计, 走为上计【xam¹xeb⁹lug⁹gei³, jeo²wei²xêng⁶gei³】Of the thirty-six stratagems, the best is running away—the best thing to do now is to quit.

三个臭皮匠, 合成一个诸葛亮【xam¹go³ qeo³pêi⁴jêng⁶, heb⁹xing⁴yed⁷go³ jü²god⁸lêng⁶】Three cobblers with their wits combined equal Zhuge Liang the master mind—the wisdom of the masses exceeds that of the wisest individual.

叁【xam¹　三】three(used for the numeral "三" on cheques, etc. to avoid mistakes or alterations)

衫【xam¹　三】a blouse; clothing(general) =【普】上衣; 衣服

衫刷【xam¹ qad⁸　察　】a brush used for washing clothes=【普】洗衣刷子

衫架【xam¹go³　价】clothes hangers=【普】衣架

衫裙【xam¹kuen⁴　群】a dress=【普】女服; 盛装

衫钮【xam¹neo²　纽】buttons=【普】衣服扣子

衫袖【xam¹jeo⁶　就】sleeves=【普】衣袖

芟【xam¹　衫】〈v.〉芟除【xam¹qêü⁴　徐】mow; cut down; delete

山【xan¹　珊】hill; mountain; anything resembling a mountain; a surname

山头【xan¹teo⁴　投】hilltop; mountain stronghold

山岳【xan¹ngog⁹　尊】lofty mountains

山崖【xan¹ngai⁴　涯】cliff

山冈【xan¹gong¹　岗】low hill ;hillock

山岭【xan¹ling⁵　领】mountain ridge

山峦【xan¹lün⁴ 联】chain of mountains

山脉【xan¹meg⁹ 默】mountain range

山坳【xan¹ngao³ 拗³】col

山顶【xan¹dēng² 钉²】hilltop; the summit of a mountain

山崩【xan¹beng¹ 蹦】landslide; landslip

山茶【xan¹qa⁴ 查】camellia

山川【xan¹qün¹ 穿】mountains and rivers —land

山村【xan¹qün¹ 穿】mountain village

山东【xan¹dung¹ 冬】〈n.〉Shandong(Province)

山西【xan¹ xei¹ 筛】〈n.〉Shanxi(Province)

山歌【xan¹go¹ 哥】folk song

山沟【xan¹keo¹ 扣¹】gully; ravine;(mountain) valley

山谷【xan¹gug⁷ 菊】mountain valley

山河【xan¹ho⁴ 何】mountains and rivers— the land of a country

山洪【xan¹hung⁴ 红】mountain torrents

山货【xan¹fo³ 课】mountain products

山溪【xan¹kei¹ 稽】mountain stream = 山涧【gan³】

山脚【xan¹gêg⁸ 格约⁸】the foot of a hill = 山麓【lug⁷】

山林【xan¹lem⁴ 淋】mountain forest

山坡【xan¹bo¹ 波】mountain slope

山墙【xan¹qêng⁴ 场】gable

山区【xan¹kêü¹ 驱】mountain area

山泉【xan¹qün⁴ 存】mountain spring

山水【xan¹xêü² 瑞²】water from a mountain; mountains and rivers; landscape

山乡【xan¹hêng¹ 香】mountain area

山寨【xan¹jai⁶ 斋⁶】mountain fastness

山庄【xan¹jong¹ 装】mountain villa

山羊【xan¹yêng⁴ 洋】goat; buck

山楂【xan¹ ja¹抓 】(Chinese) hawthorn; haw

山鸡【xan¹gei¹ 继¹】wild chicken; pheasant

山猪【xan¹jü¹ 朱】boar=【普】野猪

山窿【xan¹ lung⁴隆¹】 a cave; cavern =【普】山洞

山窿山罅【xan¹ lung¹ xan¹ la³ 隆¹ 罗亚³】isolated mountain areas =【普】深山里的洞谷;偏远山区

山明水秀【xan¹ming⁴xêü²xeo³ 名瑞² 瘦】green hills and clear waters—picturesque scenery

山珍海味【xan¹jen¹hoi²mēi² 真凯未²】delicacies from land and sea

山盟海誓【xan¹ meng⁴ hoi² xei² 萌凯逝】(make) a solemn pledge of love

山雨欲来风满楼【xan¹yü⁵yug⁹loi⁴fung¹ mun⁵leo⁴ 语玉莱丰蠓流】The wind sweeping through the tower heralds a rising storm in the mountains.

舢【xan¹ 山】〈n.〉舢板【xan¹ban² 版】sampan

册【xan¹ 山】delete; leave out

删除【xan¹qêü⁴ 徐】delete; strike out

删改【xan¹ goi² 该²】 delete and change; revise

删节【xan¹jid⁸ 折】abridge; abbreviate

删繁就简【xan¹fan⁴jeo⁶gan² 烦袖柬】simplify sth. by cutting out the superfluous

珊【xan¹ 山】〈n.〉珊瑚【xan¹wu⁴ 胡】coral

栅【xan¹ 册;qag³ 册;jab⁹ 闸】

栅极【xan¹gig⁹ 激⁹】grid
木栅【mug⁹jab⁹ 目】paling;palisade

姗【xan¹ 册】〈a.〉姗姗来迟【xan¹xan¹ loi⁴qi⁴ 莱池】be slow in coming;be late

跚【xan¹ 山】(see"蹒跚"【mun⁴xan¹】)

潸【xan¹ 山】in tears;tearfully

潸然泪下【xan¹yin⁴leü⁶ha⁶ 言类下】tears tricking down one's cheeks

闩【xan⁴ 山】bolt;latch;fasten with a bolt or latch

闩住门【xan¹jü⁶mun⁴ 注⁶ 们】bolt the door ＝【普】把门闩好

拴【xan¹ 山;qün⁴ 全】tie;fasten

栓【xan¹ 山】bolt;plug;stopper;cork

栓塞【xan¹xeg⁷ 是克⁷】embolism

散【xan² 山²;xan³ 汕】come loose;fall a-part;scattered;medicinal powder;break up;disperse;distribute;give out;dispel

散纸【xan²ji² 止】small change ＝【普】零钱;零钞
散收收【xan²xeo¹xeo¹ 修】not organized;loose ＝【普】散乱;不整齐
散手【xan²xeo² 守】skill;technic;exper-tise ＝【普】武术小套路;小本领
散仔【xan²jei² 济²】one who does nothing ∽【普】游手好闲的小子
散档【xan³dong³ 当³】be over ＝【普】散伙
散光【xan²guong¹ 桃¹】astigmatism
散货【xan²fo³ 课】bulk cargo

散剂【xan²jei¹ 挤】powder;pulvis
散居【xan²geü¹ 据¹】live scattered
散漫【xan²man⁶ 万】undisciplined;unor-ganized
散文【xan²men⁴ 民】prose
散装【xan²jong¹ 妆】bulk;in bulk
散播【xan³bo³ 波³】disseminate;spread
散布【xan³bou³ 报】spread;scatter;dif-fuse
散步【xan³bou⁶ 部】take a walk;go for a walk
散场【xan³qêng⁴ 祥】empty after the show
散发【xan³fad⁸ 法】send out;give out
散会【xan³ wui² 汇²】(of a meeting) be over
散失【xan³ xed⁷室 】scatter and dis-appear;be lost
散心【xan³xem¹ 深】relieve boredom
散兵游勇【xan³bing¹yeo⁴yong⁵ 冰由拥⁵】stragglers and disbanded soldiers

疝【xan³ 汕】hernia(疝气【xan³hêi³ 戏】)

伞【xan³ 汕】umbrella;sth. shaped like an umbrella

伞兵【xan³bing¹ 冰】paratrooper;parach-uter

汕【xan³ 散³】〈n.〉汕头【xan³teo⁴ 投】Shantou(City)

孱【xan⁴ 山⁴;qan³ 灿】frail;weak

孱弱【xan⁴yêg⁹ 若】frail;delicate

潺【xan⁴ 孱】〈onomatope.〉

潺潺【xan⁴xan⁴】murmur;babble;purl
潺湲【xan⁴yün⁴ 圆】flow slowly

生【xang¹ 是罂¹;xeng¹ 笙】give birth to;
bear; grow; existence; life; livelihood; living; get; have; unripe; light
(a fire); raw; unrefined; unfamiliar;
stiff; very; student; pupil

生抽【xang¹qeo¹ 秋】soya sauce =【普】用
大豆制成的酱油

生菜【xang¹ qoi³ 蔡】a type of vegetable;
romaine lettuce; cos lettuce

生粉【xang¹fen² 分²】starch flour =
【普】米粉

生胶【xang¹gao¹ 交】a type of rubber used
for shoes bases =【普】像胶初制
品(未经硫化的)

生鬼【xang¹ guei² 诡】lively; humorous;
vivid and vigorous =【普】生动;生
动活泼

生猛【xang¹mang⁵ 孟⁵】energetic; be alive;
brave; brimmig with energy =
【普】生命力很强;生龙活虎

生果【xang¹guo² 戈²】fruits =【普】水果

生癍【xang¹ji¹ 支】infected with skin diseases; pests that live on trees =
【普】动物身上的皮肤病,湿疹之
类

生疳【xang¹jig⁷ 积】indigestion =【普】疳
积(中医所称儿童的肠胃病)

生油【xang¹yeo⁴ 由】peanut oil =【普】未
经炼制的花生油

生盐【xang¹yim⁴ 严】salt =【普】未经炼制
的食盐

生性【xang¹ xing³ 姓】know what is right
and wrong and what to do =【普】
(小孩)懂事理;听话

生病【xeng¹bēng⁶ 柄⁶】fall ill

生产【xeng¹qan²铲】produce; give birth
to a child

生日【xang¹yed⁹ 逸】birthday = 生辰
【xeng¹xen⁴】

生存【xeng¹qūn⁴ 全】subsist;exist; live

生根【xeng¹gen¹ 跟】take root; strike root

生活【xeng¹wud⁹ 乌括⁹】life; live; livelihood

生机【xeng¹gēi¹ 基】lease of life; life; vitality

生计【xeng¹gei³ 继】means of livelihood;
livelihood

生成【xeng¹xing⁴ 诚】be born with =【普】
生就

生冷【xang¹lang⁵ 罗罂⁵】raw or cold food

生理【xeng¹xēi⁵ 李】physiology

生路【xeng¹lou⁶ 露】means of livelihood;
way out

生命【xeng¹ming⁶ 名⁶】life

生怕【xeng¹pa³ 爬³】for fear that; lest

生僻【xeng¹pig⁷ 辟】uncommon; rare

生平【xeng¹ping⁴ 萍】all one's life

生气【xeng¹ hēi³ 戏】①life; vitality; ②
take offence; get angry = 发娄
【fad⁸leo¹】

生前【xeng¹qin⁴ 钱】before one's death

生色【xeng¹xig⁷ 式】add colour to

生事【xeng¹ xi⁶ 士】make trouble = 惹事
【yē⁵xi⁶】

生手【xeng¹xeo² 守】sb. new to a job

生疏【xeng¹ xo¹ 梳】not familiar; rusty;
not as close as before

生态【xeng¹tai³ 太】ecology

生铁【xeng¹tid⁸ 梯热⁸】pig iron

生物【xeng¹med⁹ 勿】living things; organ-
isms

生息【xeng¹ xig⁷色】bear interest; live;
grow

生效【xeng¹hao⁶ 烤⁶】go into effect；become effective

生锈【xeng¹xeo³ 秀】get rusty

生涯【xeng¹ngai⁴ 崖】career；profession

生疑【xeng¹yi⁴ 移】be suspicious

生意【xeng¹yi³ 蕫】business；trade

生硬【xeng¹ngang⁶ 罂⁶】stiff；rigid；harsh

生育【xeng¹yug⁹ 玉】give birth to；bear

生长【xeng¹jêng⁶ 掌】grow；grow up

生殖【xeng¹jig⁹ 直】reproduction

生字【xeng¹ji⁶ 自】new word

生命线【xeng¹ming⁶xin³ 名⁶ 扇】lifeline；lifeblood

生力军【xeng¹ lig⁹ guen¹ 历君】fresh troops；new force

生勾勾【xang¹ ngeo¹ ngeo¹ 欧】alive；lively；not ripe；raw；have great vitality＝【普】生命力强；生蹦活跳

生安白造【xang¹ngon¹bag⁹jou⁶ 胺伯⁹ 做】not to tell the true story；coin；fabricate＝【普】生造；捏造

生搬硬套【xang¹ bun¹ ngang⁶ tou³ 般罂⁶ 吐】copy mechanically in disregard of specific conditions

生老病死【xeng¹ lou⁵ bêng⁶ xêi² 鲁柄⁶ 四²】birth，age，illness and death

生离死别【xeng¹ lêi⁴xêi²bid⁹ 漓四² 必⁹】part never to meet again；part for ever

生灵涂炭【xeng¹ling⁴tou⁴tan³ 棱图叹】The people are plunged into an abyss of misery.

生人唔生胆【xang¹yen⁴m⁴xang¹dam² 仁担²】timid；easily frightened ∽ 【普】长身体不长勇气；胆小怕事

省【xang² 是罂²】；xing² 醒；xeng² 笙²】economize；save；omit；province

省份【xang²fen⁶ 分⁶】province

省城【xang²xing⁴ 成】provincial capital ＝省会【wui⁶】

省力【xang² lig⁹ 历】save effort ＝悭力【han¹lig⁹】

省钱【xang² qin⁴ 前】save money ＝悭钱【han¹qin⁴】

省事【xang²xi⁶ 士】save trouble ＝悭工夫【han¹gung¹fu¹】

省悟【xing²ng⁶ 误】wake up to reality

省亲【xeng²qen¹ 趁¹】pay a visit to one's parents or elders ＝探亲【tam³qen¹】

揩【xang² 是罂²】clean by brushing with soap；reprimand；be hit by balls；polish；burnishing；criticize ＝【普】磨光；批评

揩到蜡蜡烫【xang²dou³lab⁸lab⁸ling³ 度³ 拉⁸ 灵³】take a body to burnishing；severe criticism ＝【普】把物体磨得闪闪发亮；严厉的批评

揩牛王【xang²ngeo⁴wong⁴ 偶⁴ 黄】take away the belongings of one before，without one's permission ＝【普】在未经允许时把属于别人的东西取走

嗓【xang³ 省³】（see"襲嗓"【nang³xang³】）

霎【xab⁸ 是鸭⁸】a very short time；moment；instant；snap a photograph；wink one's eyes

霎时间【xab⁸xi⁴gan¹ 是⁴ 奸】in a twinkling；in a split second；in a jiffy

霎气【xab⁸hêi³ 戏】disobedient（child-ren）＝【普】孩子不听话，令监护者气恼

圾【xab⁸ 雯】〈n.〉垃圾【lab⁹xab⁸ 蜡】rubbish；garbage

歃【xab⁸ 雯】suck

歃血【xab⁸hüd⁸ 黑月⁸】smear the blood of a sacrifice on the mouth—an ancient form of swearing an oath

煔【xab⁹ 雯】cook with water =【普】用水煮

煔熟狗头【xab⁹xug⁹geo²teo⁴ 属九投】laugh foolishly；giggle；smirk =【普】(比喻)傻笑的样子(露出门牙)

飒【xab⁸ 圾】〈a.〉飒爽【xab⁸xong² 丧²】valiant

煞【xad⁸ 杀】evil spirit；goblin；very；stop；halt；weaken；take off；exceedingly；tighten

煞白【xad⁸bag⁹ 伯⁹】ghastly pale；pallid

煞尾【xad⁸ mēi⁵美】finish off；wind up；final stage；end；ending

煞有介事【xad⁸yeo⁵gai³xi⁶ 友戒士】make a great show of being in earnest

煞费苦心【xad⁸fei³fu²xem¹ 废府心】cudgel one's brains

杀【xad⁸ 煞】kill；slaughter；fight；weaken；abate；take off；in the extreme

杀食【xad⁸xig⁹ 蚀】have skill；competent =【普】有本领；胜任

杀摊【xad⁸ tan¹ 滩】complete；finish =【普】结束；收场；收摊

杀起【xad⁸hēi¹ 喜】determined to accomplish a project =【普】统揽；包起

杀头【xad⁸teo⁴ 投】behead；decapitate

杀敌【xad⁸dig⁹ 迪】fight the enemy

杀菌【xad⁸kuen² 捆】disinfect；sterilize

杀害【xad⁸hoi⁶ 亥】murder；kill

杀戮【xad⁸lug⁹ 六】massacre；slaughter

杀伤【xad⁸xêng¹ 双】kill and wound

杀气【xad⁸hēi³ 戏】murderous look；vent one's ill feeling

杀虫剂【xad⁸qung⁴jei¹ 从挤】insecticide；pesticide

杀风景【xad⁸fung¹ging² 丰境】spoil the fun

杀身之祸【xad⁸xen¹ji¹wo⁶ 辛支窝⁶】a fatal disaster

杀身成仁【xad⁸xen¹xing⁴yen⁴ 辛承人】die to achieve virtue—die for a just cause

杀人如麻【xad⁸yen⁴yü⁴ma⁴ 仁余妈⁴】kill people like flies

杀一儆百【xad⁸ yed⁷ ging² bag⁸ 壹警伯】execute one as a warning to a hundred

杀鸡吓猴【xad⁸ gei¹ hag⁸ heo⁴继¹ 客侯】kill the chicken to frighten the monkey—punish someone as a warning to others

杀人不眨眼【xad⁸yen⁴bed⁷jam²ngan⁵ 仁毕斩雁⁵】kill without batting an eyelid

杀人不见血【xad⁸yen⁴bed⁷gin³hüd⁸ 仁毕建黑月⁸】kill without spilling blood；kill by subtle means

刹【xad⁸ 杀】put on the brakes；stop；check；Buddhist temple

刹那【xad⁸na⁵ 哪】instant；split second

刹车【xad⁸qē¹ 奢】stop a vehicle by applying the brakes；turn off a machine；brake

萨【xad⁸ 杀】a surname

萨克风【xad⁸heg⁷fung¹ 黑丰】saxophone

萨其马【xad⁸kēi⁴ma⁵ 奇码】a kind of candied fritter

萨尔瓦多【xad⁸ yi¹ nga⁵ do¹ 耳雅朵¹】El Salvador

萨拉热窝【xad⁸lai¹yid⁹wo¹ 罗埃¹ 衣泄⁹ 祸¹】Sarajevo

撒【xad⁸ 杀】cast；let go；let out；let oneself go；scatter；spread；spill；drop

撒谎【xad⁸fong¹ 荒】tell a lie；lie = 讲大话【gong²dai⁶wa⁶】

撒娇【xad⁸giu¹ 骄】act like a spoiled child

撒赖【xad⁸ lai⁶拉⁶】make a scene；raise hell

撒尿【xad⁸niu⁶ 鸟⁶】piss；pee = 屙尿【ngo¹ niu⁶】

撒泼【xad⁸ pud⁸ 拍活⁸】be unreasonable and make a scene

撒野【xad⁸yē⁵ 惹】act wildly；behave atrociously

撒播【xad⁸bo³ 鄱】broadcast sowing

撒粉【xad⁸fen² 分²】dusting

撒手锏【xad⁸xeo²gan³ 守柬】an unexpected thrust with the mace—one's trump card

撒哈拉沙漠【xad⁸ha¹lai¹xa¹mog⁹】the Sahara

瓠【xag⁸ 是轭⁸】half of sth.；one side of sth.

一瓠【yed⁷xad⁸ 壹】half of sth.；one side of sth. = 【普】物体(瓜、果之类)的半边或半个

西【xei¹ 筛】west；Occidental；Western

西方【xei¹fong¹ 芳】the west；the West；the Occidental

西风【xei¹fung¹ 丰】west wind

西南【xei¹nam⁴ 男】southwest；southwest China

西北【xei¹beg⁷ 伯得⁷】northwest；northwest China

西安【xei¹ngon¹ 氨】Xi'an

西欧【xei¹ngeo¹ 殴¹】western Europe

西洋【xei¹yêng⁴ 羊】the West；the Western world

西餐【xei¹qan¹ 残¹】Western-style food

西服【xei¹fug⁹ 伏】Western-style clothes = 西装【jong¹】

西瓜【xei¹gua¹ 寡¹】watermelon

西晒【xei¹ xai³ 徙³】(of a room) with a western exposure

西式【xei¹xig⁷ 色】Western style

西天【xei¹tin¹ 田¹】Western Paradise

西医【xei¹yi¹ 衣】Western medicine；a doctor trained in Western medicine

西药【xei¹yêg⁹ 若】Western medicine

西乐【xei¹ngog⁹ 岳】Western music

西藏【xei¹jong⁶ 撞】Xizang(Tibet)

西红柿【xei¹hung⁴qi⁵ 洪似】tomato = 番茄【fan¹kē²】

西班牙【xei¹ban¹nga⁴ 斑芽】Spain

西洋景【xei¹yêng⁴ging² 羊境】peep show；hank-panky

西洋菜【xei¹ yêng⁴ qoi³羊蔡 】a type of vegetable

西装友【xei¹jong¹yeo² 妆有²】refer to one who wears business suits and trousers ◯【普】穿西装的人；时髦打扮者

西伯利亚【xei¹bag⁸lēi⁶nga³ 白⁸ 俐瓦³】Siberia

茜【xei¹ 西；xin⁶ 善】madder；alizarin dyes

硒【xei¹ 西】selenium(Se)

犀【xei¹ 西】rhinoceros

犀牛【xei¹ngeo⁴ 偶⁴】rhinoceros

犀利【xei¹lēi⁶ 例】sharp; incisive; terrific; good; smart

筛【xei¹ 西】sieve; sifter; screen; sift; riddle

筛糠【xei¹hong¹ 康】shiver

筛选【xei¹xün² 损】screening; sieving

使【xei² 洗；xi² 史；xi³ 试】send; use; employ; apply; make; cause; envoy; messenger; if

使用【xei²yung⁶ 庸⁶】expenses; allowances; make use of; use; employ

使唤【xei²wun⁶ 换 】order about; use; handle

使到【xei²dou³ 道³】can be used; usable; workable; make; cause; render＝【普】使得

使得【xei²deg⁷ 德】capable; smart; effective＝【普】有能耐；干得好

使出【xei²qêd⁷ 次律⁷】use; exert

使劲【xei²ging³ 径】exert all one's strength＝出力【qêd⁷lig⁹】

使性【xei²xing³ 姓】get angry; lose one's temper; throw one's temper＝使颈【gēng²】

使眼色【xei²ngan⁵xig⁷ 雁⁵ 式】tip sb. the wink; wink

使妈【xei²ma¹ 吗】servants＝【普】女佣人；家庭女工

使牛【xei²ngeo⁴ 偶⁴】use cows to plough＝【普】驱牛耕地；掌牛

使乜【xei²med⁷ 勿⁷】not nood＝【普】不用；用不着

使乜讲【xei²med⁷gong² 勿⁷ 港】sure; of course; do not have to say; a fact that cannot be argued any more＝【普】不用说；当然啦

使命【xi²ming⁶ 名⁶】mission

使者【xi³ jê² 姐】emissary; envoy; messenger

使馆【xi³gun² 管】diplomatic mission; embassy

洗【xei² 西²】wash; bathe; baptize; redress; right; kill and loot; sack; develop(a film); shuffle(cards, etc.)

洗涤【xei²dig⁹ 迪】wash; cleanse

洗刷【xei²qad⁸ 察】wash and brush; scrub; wash off

洗身【xei² xen¹ 辛】have a bath; bath＝【普】洗操

洗衫【xei²xam¹ 三】wash clothes＝【普】洗衣服

洗白白【xei²bag⁹bag⁹ 伯⁹】bathe (for child)＝【普】给孩子洗澡

洗尘【xei²qen⁴ 陈】give a dinner of welcome (to a visitor from afar)

洗礼【xei²lei² 厉⁵】baptism; severe test

洗手【xei² xeo² 守】wash one's hands of sth.; stop doing evil and reform oneself

洗头【xei²teo⁴ 投】wash one's hair; shampoo

洗印【xei²yen³ 因³】developing and printing; processing

洗劫【xei²gib⁸ 格业⁸】loot; sack

洗雪【xei²xüd⁸ 说】wipe out; redress

洗耳恭听【xei²yi⁵gung¹ting³ 尔公亭³】listen with respectful attention

洗心革面【xei²xem¹gag⁸min⁶ 深格缅⁶】turn over a new leaf; thoroughly

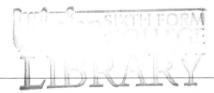

reform oneself

荽【xei¹ 西；xêû¹ 需】〈n.〉芫荽【yūn⁴xei¹ 元】coriander

细【xei³ 世】thin；slender；fine；thin and soft；exquisite；careful；minute；trifling

细胞【xei³bao¹ 包】cell

细菌【xei³kuen² 捆】germ；bacterium

细节【xei³jid⁸ 折】details；particulars

细故【xei³gu³ 固】trivial matter；trifle

细工【xei³gung¹ 功】fine workmanship

细微【xei³mēi⁴ 眉】slight；fine；subtle

细小【xei³xiu² 少²】very small；tiny；fine

细碎【xei³xêû³ 瑞³】in small，broken bits

细目【xei³mug⁹ 木】detailed catalogue；detail

细则【xei³jeg⁷ 仄】detailed rules and regulations

细密【xei³ med⁹ 勿】fine and closely woven；close；meticulous；detailed

细嫩【xei³nūn⁶ 暖⁶】delicate；tender

细腻【xei³ nēi⁶ 那希⁶】fine and smooth；minute

细软【xei³yūn⁵ 远】jewelry；expensive clothing and other valuables

细弱【xei³yêg⁹ 若】thin and delicate

细纱【xei³xa¹ 沙】spun yarn

细雨【xei³yū⁵ 语】drizzle；fine rain

细帐【xei³jêng³ 胀】itemized account

细致【xei³ji³ 至】careful；meticulous；painstaking

细作【xei³jog⁸ 昨】spy；secret agent

细胆【xei³dam² 担²】timid =【普】胆小怕事

细个【xei³go³ 哥³】young =【普】年纪小

细佬【xei³lou² 老²】young brother =【普】老弟；小兄弟

细时【xei³xi⁴ 是⁴】during one's childhood =【普】小时候；孩提时

细馂【xei³xung³ 送】eat very little =【普】不用很多菜就能吃饱饭

细佬哥【xei³lou²go¹ 老² 歌】= 细路哥【xei³lou⁶go¹ 露歌】children；young boy =【普】小孩子

细蚊仔【xei³men¹jei² 文¹ 济²】children；young kids =【普】小孩子；小娃娃

细路女【xei³ lou⁶ nêû² 露那去²】young girl；girl =【普】小女孩；女孩

细声细气【xei³xēng¹xei³hēi³ 是镜¹ 戏】in a soft voice；soft-spoken

细水长流【xei³ xêû² qêng⁴ leo²瑞² 场留】economize to avoid running short；go about sth. little by little without a letup

细枝末节【xei³ji¹mud⁹jid⁸ 支没折】minor details

世【xei³ 细】lifetime；life；generation；age；era；world；epoch

世界【xei³gai³ 介】world

世代【xei³doi⁶ 袋】for generations；generation

世道【xei³ dou⁶ 度】the manners and morals of the time

世故【xei³gu³ 固】the ways of the world；worldly-wise

世纪【xei³gēi³ 几】century

世家【xei³ga¹ 加】aristocratic family

世交【xei³gao¹ 胶】old family friends；friendship spanning two or more generations

世面【xei³min⁶ 缅⁶】society；world

世上【xei³ xêng⁶ 尚 】in the world；on earth

世人【xei³yen⁴ 仁】common people

世事【xei³xi⁶ 士】affairs of human life

世俗【xei³jug⁹ 浊】common customs; secular; worldly

世态【xei³tai³ 太】the ways of the world

世袭【xei³jab⁹ 习】hereditary

世侄【xei³jed⁹ 室】a more polite address for young people, however, it sometimes carries the meaning of insult ∽【普】孩子;老弟(长辈对晚辈男子的亲切或客气的称呼)

世界仔【xei³gai³jei² 介济²】one who lives for benefits and who forgets easily those who have done him ∽【普】善于钻营、图谋私利的人

势【xei³ 世】power; force; momentum; tendencey; the outward appearance of a natural object; situation; sign; male genitals

势力【xei³lig⁹ 历】force; power; influence

势头【xei³ teo⁴ 投】impetus; momentum; tendency

势利【xei³lēi⁶ 俐】snobbish

势必【xei³ bid⁷ 别⁷】certainly will; be bound to

势利眼【xei³lēi⁶ngan⁵ 俐雁⁵】snobbish attitude; snob

势如破竹【xei³yū⁴po³jug⁷ 余颇³ 足】like splitting a bamboo; like a hot knife cutting through butter; with irresistible force

势不可挡【xei³bed⁷ho²dong² 毕何² 当²】irresistible

势不两立【xei³ bed⁷ lêng⁵ leb⁹ 毕俩笠⁹】mutually exclusive; irreconcilable

势均力敌【xei³ guen³ lig⁹ dig⁹ 君历迪】match each other in strength

势凶夹狼【xei³hung¹gab⁸long⁴ 空甲郎】be aggressive; ambitious; show that one has done too much ∽【普】心狠手辣

噬【xei⁴ 世⁴;xei⁶ 誓】bitten by dogs

噬咗一啖【xei⁴jo²yed⁷dam⁶ 佐² 壹淡】take a bite =【普】咬了一口

驶【xei² 洗】sail; drive; speed

驶入【xei²yeb⁹ 邑⁹】sail into

誓【xei⁶ 逝】swear; vow; pledge; oath

誓死【xei⁶xēi² 四²】pledge one's life; dare to die

誓言【xei⁶ yin⁴ 然】oath; pledge = 誓词【xei⁶qi⁴】

誓愿【xei⁶yūn⁶ 县】swear

誓师【xei⁶xi¹ 司】a rally to pledge resolution before going to war; take a mass pledge

誓不两立【xei³bed⁷lêng⁵leb⁹ 毕俩笠⁹】swear not to coexist with one's enemy; be irreconcilable

誓不罢休【xei³bed⁷ba⁶yeo¹ 毕吧⁶ 丘】swear not to stop; swear not to rest

逝【xei⁶ 誓】pass; die; pass away

消逝【xiu¹xei⁶ 销】vanish; pass;fade away

逝世【xei⁶xei³ 细】pass away; die

收【xeo¹ 修】receive; accept; put away; take in; collect; money received; income; harvest; gather in; close; stop; restrain; control

收档【xeo¹dong³ 当³】close one's shop; finish; complete; keep =【普】收摊;关店;完事

收科【xeo¹ fo¹ 课¹】clean up a mess ＝【普】收场的戏路；了事的方案

收山【xeo¹ xan¹ 删】discontinue one's career; retire from one's career ∽【普】结束某事；退隐, 不再出而谋事

收尾【xeo¹ mēi⁵ 美】lastly; finally; wind up; ending(of an article, etc.)

收兵【xeo¹ bing¹ 冰】withdraw troops; call off a battle

收藏【xeo¹ qong⁴ 床】collect; store up

收场【xeo¹ qêng⁴ 祥】wind up; end up; stop; end

收成【xeo⁹ xing⁴ 承】harvest; crop

收到【xeo¹ dou³ 道³】receive; get; achieve

收发【xeo¹ fad⁸ 法】receive and dispatch; dispatcher

收费【xeo¹ fei³ 废】collect fees; charge

收复【xeo¹ fug⁹ 伏】recover; recapture

收割【xeo¹ god⁹ 格渴⁹】reap; harvest; gather in

收工【xeo¹ gung¹ 功】stop work for the day; pack up

收购【xeo¹ keo³ 寇】purchase; buy

收回【xeo¹ wui⁴ 苗】take back; call in; regain

收获【xeo¹ wog⁹ 镬】gather in the crops; harvest; results; gains

收集【xeo¹ jab⁹ 习】collect; gather

收缴【xeo¹ giu² 矫】take over; capture

收紧【xeo¹ gen² 仅】tighten up

收据【xeo¹ gêü³ 踞】receipt ＝收条【tiu⁴】

收口【xeo¹ heo² 厚²】(of a wound)close up; stop saying

收敛【xeo¹ lim⁵ 帘⁵】weaken; restrain oneself; convergence; astringent

收殓【xeo¹ lim⁵ 帘⁵】lay a body in a coffin

收留【xeo¹ leo⁴ 流】take sb. in; have sb. in one's care

收录【xeo¹ lug⁹ 六】employ; include; take down; record

收罗【xeo¹ lo⁴ 锣】collect; gather; enlist

收买【xeo¹ mai⁵ 卖⁵】purchase; buy in; buy over

收盘【xeo¹ pun⁴ 盆】closing quotation

收起【xeo¹ hēi² 喜】pack up; stop

收容【xeo¹ yung⁴ 熔】take in; accept; house

收讫【xeo¹ nged⁹ 兀】payment received; received in full

收入【xeo¹ yeb⁹ 邑⁹】income; revenue; receipts; take in; include

收拾【xeo¹ xeb⁹ 十】put in order; tidy; pack; repair; mend; settle with; punish

收缩【xeo¹ xug⁷ 宿】contract; draw back; systole

收听【xeo¹ tēng¹ 厅】listen in to

收效【xeo¹ hao⁶ 烤⁶】yield results; bear fruit

收益【xeo¹ yig⁷ 亿】income; profit; gains

收心【xeo¹ xem¹ 深】get into the frame of mind for work; have a change of heart

收押【xeo¹ ngad⁸ 压】take into custody; detain

收养【xeo¹ yêng⁵ 氧】take in and bring up

收支【xeo¹ ji¹ 之】income and expenses

收音机【xeo¹ yem¹ gēi¹ 阴基】radio(set); wireless(set)

修【xeo¹ 收】embellish; repair; mend; write; study; build; trim; long

修补【xeo¹ bou² 保】mend; repair; patch up

修长【xeo¹qêng⁴ 祥】tall and thin；slender

修辞【xeo¹qi⁴ 词】rhetoric

修道【xeo¹dou⁶ 度】cultivate oneself according to a religious doctrine

修订【xeo¹ding³ 丁³】revise

修复【xeo¹fug⁹ 伏】repair；restore

修改【xeo¹ goi² 该²】revise；modify；amend

修好【xeo¹ hou² 蒿²】foster cordial relations between states；do good words

修建【xeo¹ gin³ 见】build；construct ＝ 修筑【jug⁷】

修理【xeo¹ lēi⁵ 李】repair；mend；overhaul；fix

修缮【xeo¹ xin⁶ 善】repair；renovate ＝ 修葺【qeb⁷】

修饰【xeo¹xig⁷ 式】decorate；make up and dress up；polish；qualify；modify

修养【xeo¹yêng⁵ 氧】mastery；self-cultivation

修业【xeo¹yib⁹ 叶】study at school

修整【xeo¹jing² 正²】repair and maintain；prune

修正【xeo¹jing³ 政】revise；amend；mutilate

脩【xeo¹ 修】a private tutor's remuneration

羞【xeo¹ 修】shy；bashful；shame；disgrace；feel ashamed

羞家【xeo¹ga¹ 加】bring about shame；feel embarrassed or ashamed ∽【普】丢人

羞涩【xeo¹gib⁸ 格叶⁸】shy；bashful；embarrassed

羞愧【xeo¹kuei² 亏⁶】ashamed；abashed ＝ 羞惭【qam⁴】

羞耻【xeo¹qi² 始】sense of shame；shame

羞怯【xeo¹hib⁸ 协】shy；timid；sheepish

羞辱【xeo¹yug⁹ 玉】shame；humiliate；put sb. to shame

馐【xeo¹ 羞】delicacy；dainty

手【xeo² 守】hand；hold；handy；personally；a person doing or good at a certain job

手掌【xeo²jêng² 蒋】palm＝手板堂【xeo²ban²tong⁴】

手指【xeo²ji² 止】finger

手背【xeo²bui³ 辈】the back of the hand

手心【xeo²xem¹ 深】the palm of the hand；control

手臂【xeo²bēi³ 泌】arm

手段【xeo²dün⁶端⁶】means；medium；trick；artifice

手法【xeo²fad⁸ 发】skill；technique；trick

手工【xeo²gung¹ 功】handwork；by hand；manual

手势【xeo² xei³ 世】gesture；sign；signal；luck

手术【xeo² xêd⁹ 述】surgical operation；operation

手腕【xeo²wun² 碗】artifice；finesse；stratagem

手续【xeo²jug⁹ 逐】procedures；formalities

手艺【xeo²ngei⁶ 伪】workmanship；handicraft；trade

手淫【xeo²yem⁴ 壬】masturbation

手巧【xeo²hao² 考】deft；dexterous

手快【xeo²fai³ 快】deft of hand

手软【xeo²yün⁵ 远】be soft-hearted

手枪【xeo²qêng¹ 昌】pistol

手钳【xeo²kim⁴ 卡淹⁴】hand vice；pliers

手头【xeo² teo⁴投 】on hand；at hand；

one's financial condition at the
moment

手下【xeo²ha⁶ 夏】under；at hand；at the
hands of sb.；one's financial condition at the moment

手抽【xeo²qeo¹ 秋】handbags made of rat-
tans＝【普】手提篮子或袋子(用
于盛蔬菜等物)

手甲【xeo²gab⁸ 夹】finger nails＝【普】指
甲

手巾【xeo²gen¹ 斤】towel

手巾仔【xeo²gen¹jei² 斤济²】handkerchief
＝【普】手帕

手瓜【xeo²gua¹ 寡¹】＝手臂瓜【xeo²bēi³
gua¹】the upper arms＝【普】上臂

手瓜硬【xeo²gua¹ngang⁶ 寡¹ 罂⁶】having
a solid or strong foundation＝【普】
(比喻)实力强

手袜【xeo²med⁹ 勿】hand gloves ＝【普】
纺织品手套

手尾【xeo² mēi⁵ 美 】 the remaining job
which is yet to be completed＝
【普】未完成的一点工作；未办完
的一点事情

手信【xeo²xên³ 讯】gifts for friends or relatives when paying them visits＝
【普】拜访时随手带备的礼物

手睁【xeo²jang¹ 支罂¹】elbow＝【普】肘子

手作【xeo²jog⁸ 昨】skill；expertise＝【普】
手工工艺；手工工作

手作仔【xeo² jog⁸ jei² 昨济²】one who is
good at handicraft＝【普】手工业
工匠

手指公【xeo²ji²gung¹ 止工】thumb＝【普】
大姆指

手指尾【xeo²ji²mēi¹ 止美¹】the last finger
＝【普】小指

手指模【xeo² ji² mou⁴ 止毛】finger mould
＝【普】指模；指印

手指罅【xeo²ji²la³ 止罗亚³】the space between fingers＝【普】指间缝隙

手腈脚震【xeo² ten⁴ gêg⁸ jen³ 吞⁴ 格约⁸
振】nervous and shivering due to
lack of skill or confidence＝【普】
(慌乱以致)手脚发抖

手急眼快【xeo²geb⁷ngan⁵fai³ 格合⁷ 雁⁵
块】quick of eye and deft of hand
＝【普】手疾眼快

手不释卷【xeo²bed⁷xig⁷gün² 毕式捐²】al-
ways have a book in one's hand；
be very studious

手忙脚乱【xeo² mong⁴ gêg⁸ lün⁶ 亡格约⁸
联⁶】running around in circles；in
a muddle

手无寸铁【xeo² mou⁴ qün³ tid⁸ 毛川³ 替
热⁸】unarmed；bare-handed；de-
fenceless

手舞足蹈【xeo² mou⁵ jug⁷ dou⁶ 武竹道】
dance for joy

手下留情【xeo² ha⁶ leo⁴ qing⁴ 夏流程】
show mercy；be lenient

守【xeo² 手】guard；defend；keep
watch；observe；close to

守卫【xeo²wei⁶ 惠】guard；defend

守护【xeo²wu⁶ 户】guard；defend

守候【xeo² heo⁵ 后】wait for；expect；
keep watch

守法【xeo²fad⁸ 发】abide by the law

守业【xeo² yib⁹叶 】 safeguard one's heritage

守寡【xeo²gua² 瓜²】remain a widow

守旧【xeo²geo⁶ 柩】adhere to past practices

守门【xeo² mun⁴ 瞒】be on duty at the door or gate

守夜【xeo² yē⁶ 野⁶】keep watch at night

守则【xeo² jeg⁷ 仄】rules; regulations

守势【xeo² xei³ 世】defensive

守株待兔【xeo² jū¹ doi⁶ tou³ 朱代吐】trust to chance and windfalls

首【xeo² 手】head; first; leader; chief; 〈classifier.〉the unit of a poem

首先【xeo² xin¹ 仙】first; first of all; above all

首长【xeo² jêng² 掌】leading cadre

首要【xeo² yiu² 腰³】first; chief

首创【xeo² qong³ 苍³】initiate; originate

首次【xeo² qi³ 刺】for the first time; first

首都【xeo² dou¹ 刀】capital

首恶【xeo² ngog⁸ 噩】chief criminal

首领【xeo² ling⁵ 岭】chieftain; leader; head

首肯【xeo² heng² 亨²】nod approval; approve

首饰【xeo² xig⁷ 式】ornaments; jewelry

首尾【xeo² mēi⁵ 美】the head and the tail; from beginning to end

首屈一指【xeo² wed⁷ yed⁷ ji¹ 乌核⁷ 壹止】come first on the list

首当其冲【xeo² dong¹ kēi⁴ qung¹ 珰奇充】bear the brunt

狩【xeo³ 瘦】hunting(esp. in winter)

狩猎【xeo³ lib⁹ 罗叶⁹】hunting

叟【xeo² 手】old man

艘【xeo² 手】〈classifier.〉the unit of a ship

擞【xeo³ 秀; xeo² 手】(see "抖擞"【deo² xeo²】)

嗖【xeo¹ 收】〈onomatopoeia〉∽ whiz

飕【xeo¹ 收】〈onomatopoeia〉the sound of the wind

馊【xeo¹ 收; xug⁷ 叔】sour; spoiled

馊主意【xeo¹ jū² yi³ 煮薏】rotten idea; lousy idea

饭菜馊咗【fan⁶ qoi³ xug⁷ jo² 范蔡阻】The food has spoiled. =【普】饭菜馊了

薮【xeo² 手】a shallow lake overgrown with wild plants; den

嗽【xeo³ 秀】cough (see "咳嗽"【ked⁷ xeo³】)

搜【xeo² 手】search

搜查【xeo² qa⁴ 茶】search; ransack; rummage

搜索【xeo² xog⁸ 朔】search for; hunt for

搜集【xeo² jab⁹ 习】collect; gather; recruit = 搜罗【lo⁴】

搜刮【xeo² guad⁸ 格挖⁸】extort; plunder; expropriate

搜索枯肠【xeo² xog⁸ fu¹ qêng⁴ 朔夫场】rack one's brains(for fresh ideas or apt expressions)

瘦【xeo³ 秀】thin; lean; tight; not fertile

瘦弱【xeo³ yêg⁹ 若】thin and weak; emaciated

瘦小【xeo³ xiu² 少²】thin and small

瘦削【xeo³ xêg⁸ 是约⁸】very thin; gaunt

瘦蜢蜢【xeo³ mang² mang² 孟²】= 瘦骨如柴【xeo³ gued⁷ yü⁴ qai⁴ 掘⁷ 余猜⁴】very thin =【普】很瘦(形状如蚱蜢,如干柴)

兽【xeo³ 秀】beast; animal; beastly

兽类【xeo³lêü⁶ 泪】beasts; animals

兽性【xeo³ xing³姓 】brutish nature; barbarity

兽欲【xeo³yug⁹ 玉】animal desire

兽医【xeo³yi¹ 衣】veterinary surgeon; vet

秀【xeo³ 锈】put forth flowers or ears; elegant; beautiful; excellent

秀才【xeo³qoi⁴ 财】scholar; skilful writer

秀丽【xeo³ lei⁶厉】beautiful; handsome; pretty

秀美【xeo³mēi⁵ 尾】graceful; elegant

秀气【xeo³ hēi³戏】elegant; fine; refined; delicate and well-made

锈【xeo³ 秀】rust; become rusty

锈蚀【xeo³xig⁹ 食】=生锈【xang¹xeo³】become rusty

绣【xeo³ 秀】embroider; embroidery

绣花【xeo³fa¹ 化¹】embroider; do embroidery

绣球【xeo³keo⁴ 求】a ball made of strips of silk

仇【xeo⁴ 愁】enemy; foe; hatred; enmity; a surname

仇敌【xeo⁴dig⁹ 迪】foe; enemy

仇人【xeo⁴yen⁴ 仁】personal enemy

仇恨【xeo⁴hen⁶ 很⁶】hatred; enmity; hostility

仇杀【xeo⁴xad⁸ 刹】kill in revenge

仇视【xeo⁴xi⁶ 示】regard as an enemy

仇隙【xeo⁴ guig¹ 姑益¹】 bitter quarrel; feud =仇口【xeo⁴heo²】

愁【xeo⁴ 仇】worry; be anxious

愁闷【xeo⁴mun⁶ 门⁶】feel gloomy; be depressed

愁容【xeo⁴yung⁴ 熔】worried look

愁绪【xeo⁴xêü⁵ 穗⁵】gloomy mood

愁苦【xeo⁴fu² 府】anxiety; distress

愁眉【xeo⁴mēi⁴ 微】knitted brows

愁眉苦脸【xeo⁴mēi⁴fu²lim⁵ 微府敛】have a worried look; pull a long face

愁肠百结【xeo²qêng⁴bag⁸gid⁸ 祥伯洁】weighed down with anxiety

受【xeo⁶ 授】receive; accept; suffer; stand; endure; bear

受害【xeo⁶hoi⁶ 亥】suffer injury; fall victim

受益【xeo⁶yig⁷ 亿】profit by; benefit from

受挫【xeo⁶qo³ 错】be foiled; be baffled

受罚【xeo⁶fed⁹ 佛】be punished

受贿【xeo⁶fui² 悔²】accept bribes

受奖【xeo⁶jêng² 掌】be rewarded

受惊【xeo⁶ gēng¹ 镜¹】 be frightened; be startled

受尽【xeo⁶jên⁶ 进⁶】suffer enough from

受精【xeo⁶jing¹ 贞】be fertilized

受苦【xeo⁶fu² 府】suffer; have a rough time

受累【xeo⁶ lêü⁶类 】 get involved on account of sb. else; be put to much trouble

受难【xeo⁶nan⁶ 那晏⁶】suffer calamities or disasters

受骗【xeo⁶pin³ 片】be deceived

受气【xeo⁶ hēi³ 戏】be bullied; suffer wrong

受权【xeo⁶kün⁴ 拳】be authorized

受辱【xeo⁶ yug⁹玉 】 be insulted; be disgraced

受伤【xeo⁶ xêng¹ 双 】 be injured; be wounded

受托【xeo⁶tog⁹ 梯恶⁹】be entrusted

受用【xeo⁶ yung⁶容⁶】benefit from; enjoy; profit by

受灾【xeo⁶joi¹ 哉】be hit by a natural adversity

受罪【xeo⁶jêü⁶ 聚】have a hard time

受宠若惊【xeo⁶qung² yêg⁹gēng¹ 充² 药镜¹】feel extremely flattered

授【xeo⁶ 受】award; vest; confer; give; teach; instruct

授予【xeo⁶yü⁵ 与】confer; award

授课【xeo⁶ fo³货 】give lessons; give instruction

授权【xeo⁶kün⁴ 拳】empower; authorize

授计【xeo⁶gei³ 继】confide a stratagem to sb.

授意【xeo⁶ yi³惹】incite sb. to do sth.; inspire

授受【xeo⁶ xeo⁶】grant and receive; give and accept

绶【xeo⁶ 受】〈n.〉绶带【xeo⁶dai³ 戴】ribbon

售【xeo⁶ 受】sell; make work; carry out

售货【xeo⁶fo³ 课】sell goods

售货员【xeo⁶ fo³ yün⁴课元 】 shop assistant; salesclerk

售价【xeo⁶ga³ 嫁】selling price; price

售票处【xeo⁶piu³qü³ 漂³ 次于³】ticket office; wicket

售票员【xeo⁶piu³yün⁴ 漂³ 元】ticket seller

寿【xeo³ 受】longevity; life; age; birthday; for burial; a surname; foolish and stupid

寿命【xeo³ming⁶ 名⁶】life-span; life

寿辰【xeo³xen⁴ 神】birthday

寿星【xeo³xing¹ 升】the god of longevity; a elderly person whose birthday is being celebrated

寿终正寝【xeo³jung¹jing³qem² 中政侵²】die in bed of old age; die a natural death

寿头寿脑【xeo³ teo⁴ xeo³ nou² 投恼】the manner of foolish and stupid =【普】愚钝、糊涂的样子

寿仔【xeo³jei² 济²】a fool =【普】笨人; 傻子

寿星公【xeo³xing¹gung¹ 升工】one who is long-lived

心【xem¹ 深】the heart; heart; mind; feeling; centre; core

心脏【xem¹jung² 撞】the heart

心思【xem¹xi¹ 司】thought; idea; thinking; mood

心绪【xem¹xêü⁵ 穗⁵】state of mind

心意【xem¹yi³ 惹】regard; feelings; intention

心愿【xem¹ yün⁶远⁶】cherished desire; wish

心血【xem¹xüd⁸ 黑月⁸】painstaking care

心术【xem¹xêd⁹ 述】intention; design

心事【xem¹xi⁶ 士】sth. weighing on one's mind; worry

心情【xem¹qing⁴ 程】frame of mind; mood

心机【xem¹gēi¹ 基】effort thinking; scheming; mood

心计【xem¹gei³ 继】calculation; planning

心理【xem¹lēi⁵ 李】psychology; mentality

心爱【xem¹ngoi³ 哀³】love; treasure

心肠【xem¹ qêng⁴祥 】heart; state of mind; mood

心得【xem¹deg⁷ 德】what one has learned from work, study, etc.

心肝【xem¹ gon¹ 竿】conscience；darling；dear

心慌【xem¹ fong¹ 方】be flustered；palpitate

心急【xem¹ geb⁷ 格合⁷】impatient

心里【xem¹ lêü⁵ 吕】in the heart；at heart

心灵【xem¹ ling⁴ 棱】clever heart；soul

心软【xem¹ yün⁵ 远】be softhearted

心酸【xem¹ xün¹ 孙】be grieved；feel sad

心疼【xem¹ tung³ 痛】love dearly；feel sorry

心细【xem¹ xei³ 世】careful；scrupulous

心胸【xem¹ hung¹ 空】breadth of mind

心照【xem¹ jiu³ 赵³】understand without being told

心服【xem¹ fug⁹ 伏 】be genuinely convinced

心口【xem¹ heo² 厚²】heart＝【普】心脏；胸脯

心水【xem¹ xêü² 瑞²】suit one's taste；mind＝【普】心思；心绪

心淡【xem¹ tam⁵ 探⁵】disappointed；lose interest in sb. or sth.＝【普】失望了；欲念不强；不多想

心肝芋【xem¹ gon¹ ding³ 定³】the loved ones＝【普】心爱的人

心抱【xem¹ pou⁵ 铺⁵】an address for the son's wife by the mother＝【普】儿媳妇

心多多【xem¹ do¹ do¹ 朵¹】hesitated；not decisive＝【普】想法很多，拿不定主意

心思思【xem¹xi¹xi¹ 司】think of＝【普】老是想着

心喐喐【xem¹yug⁷yug⁷ 郁】do something but have not put it into action ∽【普】跃跃欲试

心大心细【xem¹dai⁶xem¹xei³ 歹⁶世】hesitated＝【普】想这想那，拿不定主意

心慈手软【xem¹qi⁴xeo²yün⁵ 迟守远】softhearted

心腹之患【xem¹fug⁷ji¹wan⁶ 福支幻】serious hidden trouble or danger

心甘情愿【xem¹gem¹qing⁴yün⁶ 今程怨⁶】be most willing to；be perfectly happy to

心花怒放【xem¹fa¹nou⁶fong³ 化¹奴⁶况】burst with joy；be wild with joy；be elated

心灰意懒【xem¹ fui¹ yi³ lan⁵ 恢薏兰⁵】be disheartened

心惊胆战【xem¹ging¹dam²jin³ 京担²箭】tremble with fear

心里话【xem¹lêü⁵wa⁶ 吕华⁶】one's innermost thoughts and feelings

心连心【xem¹lin⁴xem¹ 莲】heart linked to heart

心满意足【xem¹ mun⁵ yi³ jug⁷ 螨薏竹】be perfectly content

心平气和【xem¹ ping⁴ hēi³ wo⁴ 萍弃禾】even-tempered and good-humoured；calm

心如刀割【xem¹yü⁴dou¹god⁸ 余都葛】feel as if a knife were piercing one's heart

心心相印【xem¹ xem¹ yêng¹ yen³ 双因³】have mutual affinity

心血来潮【xem¹hüd⁸loi⁴qiu⁴ 黑月⁸莱樵】be prompted by a sudden impulse

心猿意马【xem¹yün⁴yi³ma⁵ 元薏码】restless and whimsical

心悦诚服【xem¹yüd⁹xing⁴fug⁹ 月承伏】feel a heartfelt admiration

心直口快【xem¹jig⁹heo²fai³ 值厚² 块】
　　frank and outspoken

心中有数【xem¹jung¹yeo⁵xou³ 钟友素】
　　have a pretty good idea of

心有余而力不足【xem¹yeo⁵yü⁴yi⁴lig⁹bed⁷
　　jug⁷ 友鱼移历毕竹】The spirit is
　　willing, but the flesh is weak.

芯【xem¹ 心】rush pith; core

深【xem¹ 森】deep; difficult; profound;
　　penetrating; close; dark; late; very

深奥【xem¹ngou³ 澳】abstruse; profound

深长【xem¹qêng⁴ 祥】profound

深沉【xem¹qem⁴侵⁴】dark; deep; con-
　　cealing one's real feelings

深处【xem¹qü³ 次于³】depths; recesses

深度【xem¹dou⁶ 道】depth; profundity

深厚【xem¹heo⁵后⁵】deep; solid; deep-
　　seated

深化【xem¹fa³ 花³】deepen

深究【xem¹geo³ 够】go into seriously

深刻【xem¹heg⁷ 克】deep; profound

深浅【xem¹qin² 千²】depth; proper limits;
　　shade

深切【xem¹qid⁸设 】heartfelt; deep; pro-
　　found

深入【xem¹ yeb⁹ 邑⁹】go deep into; deep-
　　going

深深【xem¹xem¹】profoundly; deeply

深山【xem¹xan¹ 珊】remote mountains

深水【xem¹xêü² 瑞²】deepwater

深思【xem¹xi¹ 司】think deeply about

深邃【xem¹xêü⁶ 睡】deep; profound

深夜【xem¹yê⁶ 野⁶】late at night

深渊【xem¹yün¹ 冤】abyss

深远【xem¹yün⁵ 软】profound and lasting

深造【xem¹jou⁶ 做】pursue advanced stud-
　　ies

深重【xem¹jung⁶ 仲】very grave; extreme-
　　ly serious

深谋远虑【xem¹ meo⁴ yün⁵ lêü⁶ 牟软累】
　　think deeply and plan carefully

深入浅出【xem¹yeb⁹qin²qêd⁷ 邑⁹ 前² 次
　　律⁷】explain the profound in sim-
　　ple terms

深思熟虑【xem¹xi¹xug⁹lêü⁶ 司属类】care-
　　ful consideration

深恶痛绝【xem¹ wu³ tung³ jüd⁹乌³ 同³ 支
　　月⁹】hate bitterly; abhor; detest

森【xem¹ 深】full of trees; multitu-
　　dinous; dark; gloomy

森林【xem¹lem⁴ 淋】forest

森严【xem¹yim⁴ 盐】stern; strict; forbid-
　　ding

森然【xem¹ yin⁴ 言】dense; thick; awe-in-
　　spiring

森森【xem¹xem¹】dense; thick

沈【xem² 审】a surname

沈阳【xem²yêng⁴ 杨】〈n.〉Shenyang

审【xem² 沈】careful; examine; go over;
　　interrogate; try; know; indeed; real-
　　ly

审查【xem²qa⁴ 茶】examine; investigate

审核【xem²hed⁹ 辖】examine and verify

审计【xem²gei³ 继】audit

审理【xem²lêi⁵ 李】try; tear

审美【xem² mêi⁵尾 】 appreciation of the
　　beautiful

审判【xem²pun³ 潘³】bring to trial; try

审批【xem² pei¹ 皮矮¹】 examine and ap-
　　prove

审慎【xem²xên⁶ 信⁶】cautious；careful

审讯【xem²xên³ 信】interrogate；try

审议【xem²yi⁵ 尔】consideration；deliberation

审阅【xem²yüd⁹ 月】check and approve

【xem² 审】wife of father's younger brother；aunt；a form of address to a woman about one's mother's age；auntie

　婶母【xem²mou⁵ 武】wife of father's younger brother；aunt

渗【xem³ 沁】ooze；seep

　渗漏【xem³leo⁶ 留⁶】seepage；leakage

　渗入【xem³yeb⁹ 邑⁹】permeate；seep into；infiltrate

　渗透【xem³teo³ 偷³】osmosis；permeate；seep；infiltrate

沁【xem³ 渗】ooze；seep；exude

　沁人心脾【xem³yen⁴xem¹pêi⁴ 仁深皮】gladdening the heart and refreshing the mind；refreshing

葚【xem⁴ 岑】〈n.〉桑葚【xong¹xem⁴】mulberry

岑【xem⁴ 葚】high hill；a surname

涔【xem⁴ 岑】rainwater in puddles

　涔涔【xem⁴xem⁴】dripping；streaming

甚【xem⁶ 岑⁶】very；extremely；more than

　甚至【xem⁶ji³ 志】even；（go）so far as to；so much so that；even if = 甚至无【xem⁶ji³mou⁴】= 甚而至于【xem⁶yi⁴ji³yü¹】

　甚嚣尘上【xem⁶hiu¹gen⁴xêng⁶ 晓¹陈尚】

cause a temporary clamour

什【xem⁶ 甚；xeb⁹ 拾；jab⁹ 习】what；assorted；varied；ten

　什么【xem⁶mo¹摸¹】what = 乜野【med⁷yê⁵】

　什物【xeb⁹med⁹ 勿】articles for daily use；sundries

　什锦【jab⁹gem² 敢】assorted；mixed

申【xen¹ 伸】state；express；explain；a surname；the ninth of the twelve Earthly Branches；another name for Shanghai

　申报【xen¹bou³ 布】report to a higher body；declare sth.

　申辩【xen¹bin⁶ 便】defend oneself

　申明【xen¹ming⁴ 名】declare；state；avow

　申请【xen¹qing² 逞】apply for.

　申诉【xen¹xou⁵ 素】appeal

　申述【xen¹xêd⁹ 术】state；explain in detail

　申冤【xen¹ yün¹ 渊】redress an injustice；appeal for redress of a wrong = 伸冤【xen¹yün¹】

伸【xen¹ 申】stretch；extend

　伸手【xen¹ xeo²守】stretch out one's hand；ask for help，etc.

　伸缩【xen¹ xug⁷宿】stretch out and draw back；expand and contract；flexible；elastic

　伸展【xen¹jin² 剪】spread；extend；stretch

　伸张【xen¹jêng¹ 章】uphold；promote

　伸腰【xen¹yiu¹ 夭】straighten one's back

　伸懒腰【xen¹lan⁵yiu¹ 兰⁵夭】stretch oneself

身【xen¹ 申】body；life；oneself；one's moral character and conduct；the main part of a structure；〈classifier.〉suit

身家【xen¹ ga¹ 加 】 wealth；one's be-
longings＝【普】一个人的家产

身体【xen¹tei² 睇】body；health

身子【xen¹ji² 子】body；pregnancy；health

身躯【xen¹kêu¹ 驱】body；stature

身边【xen¹bin¹ 鞭】at one's side；with one

身爀【xen¹hing³ 庆】fever＝【普】身体发
热；发烧

身材【xen¹qoi⁴ 才】stature；figure

身分【xen¹fen² 粉】status；capacity；dig-
nity

身高【xen¹gou⁴ 糕】height(of a person)

身后【xen¹heo⁶ 候】after one's death

身价【xen¹ ga³ 嫁】social status；the selling price of a slave

身教【xen¹gao³ 较】teach others by one's
own example

身纪【xen¹gêi¹ 几】pregnancy＝【普】身孕

身上【xen¹ xêng⁶尚 】 on one's body；on
one

身世【xen¹ xei³ 细】one's life experience；
one's lot

身手【xen¹xeo² 守】skill；talent

身心【xen¹xem¹ 深】body and mind

身受【xen¹xeo⁶ 授】experience

身败名裂【xen¹ bai⁶ ming⁴ lid⁹ 摆⁶ 明列】
lose all standing and reputation

身不由己【xen¹bed⁷yeo⁴gêi² 毕油几】in-
voluntarily；in spite of oneself

身强力壮【xen¹ kêng⁴ lig⁹ jong³卡香⁴ 历
撞³】(of a person) strong；tough

身体力行【xen¹ tei² lig⁹ heng⁴睇历衡 】
earnestly practise what one advo-
cates

身先士卒【xen¹xin¹xi⁶jêd⁷ 仙事支律⁷】
lead one's men in a charge

呻【xen¹ 申】〈v.〉呻吟【xen¹yêm⁴ 淫】
groan；moan

绅【xen¹ 申】〈n.〉绅士【xen¹xi⁶ 事】gen-
tleman；gentry

砷【xen¹ 申】〈n.〉arsenic(As)

辛【xen¹ 申】hot；pungent；hard；suffer-
ing；the eighth of the ten Heavenly
Stems；a surname

辛苦【xen¹ fu² 府】hard；toilsome；work
hard

辛辣【xen¹lad⁹ 那压⁹】pungent；hot；bit-
ter

辛劳【xen¹lou⁴ 痨】pains；toil

辛勤【xen¹ ken⁴ 芹 】 industrious；hard-
working

辛酸【xen¹xün¹ 孙】sad；bitter；miserable

锌【xen¹ 辛】zinc(Zn)

锌白【xen¹bag⁹ 伯⁹】zinc white

锌粉【xen¹fen² 分²】zinc powder

锌版【xen¹ban² 板】zinc plate；zincograph

莘【xen¹ 辛】〈a.〉莘莘【xen¹xen¹】nu-
merous

新【xen¹ 辛】new；fresh；newly；recent-
ly married

新鲜【xen¹xin¹ 仙】fresh；new；novel

新兴【xen¹ hing¹ 兄】new and developing；
rising

新式【xen¹xig⁷ 色】new type；latest type

新型【xen¹ ying⁴形 】 new type；new pattern

新颖【xen¹ wing⁶咏 】 new and original；
novel

新奇【xen¹kêi⁴ 其】strange；novel；new

新生【xen¹xeng¹ 笙】newborn；newly
born；new life；rebirth

新人【xen¹ yen⁴ 仁】people of a new type;
new personality

新手【xen¹ xeo² 守 】new hand; raw recruit

新闻【xen¹ men⁴ 文】news

新装【xen¹ jong¹ 妆】new clothes

新年【xen¹ nin⁴ 捻⁴】New Year

新婚【xen¹ fen¹ 分】newly-married

新郎【xen¹ long⁴ 廊】bridegroom = 新郎哥
【go¹】

新娘【xen¹ nêng⁴ 罗香⁴】bride = 新心抱
【xem¹ pou⁵】

新居【xen¹ gêū¹ 据¹】new home; new residence

新近【xen¹ gen⁶ 靳】 recently; lately; in
recent times

新潮【xen¹ qiu⁴ 樵】modern; fashionable

新疆【xen¹ gêng¹ 羌】〈n.〉Xinjiang

新篇章【xen¹ pin¹ jêng¹ 编张】new page

新大陆【xen¹ dai⁶ lug⁹ 歹⁶ 六】 the New
World——the Americas

新闻纸【xen¹ men⁴ ji² 文止】newspapers

新陈代谢【xen¹ qen⁴ doi⁶ jê⁶ 尘袋榭】meta-
bolism; the new superseding the
old

新仇旧恨【xen¹ xeo⁴ geo⁶ hen⁶ 愁枢狠⁶】
old scores and new

新鲜滚热辣【xen¹ xin¹ guen² yid⁹ lad⁹ 仙君²
衣 泄⁹ 罗 压⁹】 something new;
something that just takes place ◇
【普】(刚煮好的食物的) 新鲜烫
热情况; 事情刚发生的情况

新西兰【xen¹ xei¹ lan⁴ 茜栏】New Zealand

新加坡【xen¹ ga³ bo¹ 嫁波】Singapore

薪【xen¹ 辛】 firewood; faggot; fuel;
salary

薪水【xen¹ xêū² 瑞²】salary; pay; wages

薪金【xen¹ gem¹ 今】salary; pay

臣【xen⁴ 神】official under a feudal ruler;
subject

臣服【xen⁴ fug⁹ 伏】submit oneself to the
rule of

臣民【xen⁴ men⁴ 文 】 subjects of a feudal
ruler

臣子【xen⁴ ji² 止】official in feudal times

辰【xen⁴ 神】celestial bodies; any of the
traditional twelve two-hour periods of
the day; time; day

辰时【xen⁴ xi⁴ 是⁴】the period of the day
from 7 a.m. to 9 a.m.

晨【xen⁴ 神】morning

晨光【xen¹ guong¹ 胱】the light of the early morning sun

晨曦【xen⁴ hēi¹ 希】first rays of the morning sun

晨星【xen⁴ xing¹ 升】stars at dawn; morning star

神【xen⁴ 臣】god; deity; supernatural;
magical; spirit; mind; expression;
look; clever

神采【xen⁴ qoi² 彩】expression; look

神甫【xen⁴ fu⁶ 父】Catholic father; priest
= 神父【fu⁶】

神怪【xen⁴ guai³ 乖】gods and spirits

神化【xen⁴ fa³ 花】deify

神话【xen⁴ wa³ 华²】mythology; myth;
fairy tale

神魂【xen⁴ wen⁴ 云】state of mind; mind

神经【xen⁴ ging¹ 京】 nerve; something
wrong; insane

神灵【xen⁴ ling⁴ 玲】gods; deities; divini-
ties

神秘【xen⁴bēi³ 泌】mysterious; mystical

神妙【xen⁴miu⁶ 庙】wonderful; marvellous

神明【xen⁴ming⁴ 名】gods; deities

神奇【xen⁴kēi⁴ 其】magical; mystical

神气【xen⁴hēi³ 戏】expression; spirited

神情【xen⁴qing⁴ 程】expression; look

神色【xen⁴xig⁷ 式】expression; look

神圣【xen⁴xing³ 胜】sacred; holy

神思【xen⁴xi¹ 斯】state of mind; mental state

神似【xen⁴qi⁵ 次⁵】be alike in spirit

神速【xen⁴qug⁷ 促】marvellously quick

神态【xen⁴tai³ 太 】expression; manner; mien

神通【xen⁴tung¹ 同¹】remarkable ability

神童【xen⁴tung⁴ 同】child prodigy

神往【xen⁴wong⁵ 旺⁵】be carried away

神威【xen⁴wei¹ 畏¹】martial prowess

神仙【xen⁴xin¹ 先】supernatural being

神韵【xen⁴wen⁵ 阻】romantic charm

神志【xen⁴ji³ 至】senses; mind

神州【xen⁴jeo¹ 洲】the Divine Land (a poetic name for China)

神心【xen⁴ xem¹ 深】determined; consistent =【普】对菩萨虔诚之心;虔诚

神神经经【xen⁴xen⁴ging¹ging¹ 京】say that one does not behave the way one should; neuropathy; mental disorder ∽【普】神经病的样子

神高神大【xen⁴gou¹xen⁴dai⁶ 糕歹⁶】refer to one who is tall and strong and big size ∽【普】个子高大,魁梧

神出鬼没【xen⁴qêd⁷guei²mud⁹ 次律⁷ 诡末】come and go like a shadow

神机妙算【xen⁴ gēi¹ miu⁶ xün³ 基庙蒜】wonderful foresight (in military operations, etc.)

神经过敏【xen⁴ging¹guo³men⁵ 京戈³闽】neuroticism; neurotic

神气活现【xen⁴ hēi³ wud⁹ yin⁶ 戏乌阔⁹ 燕⁶】very cocky

蜃

【xen⁵ 身⁵】clam

蜃景【xen⁵ging² 境】mirage

瘛

【xen⁵ 蜃;xen⁴ 神】refer to food that contains high carbohydrate such as yam, potato, etc.; describe that one is stubborn and not creative

瘛仔【xen⁵jei² 济²】a fool ∽【普】神经不很正常的人;愚笨者

瘛瘛化化【xen⁴xen⁴fa³fa³ 花³】one who does not behave normally =【普】神经不很正常;行为反常

瘛咗【xen⁴jo² 左】(machine, etc.) become bad =【普】(机器等)坏了

诇

【xen³ 申】scold =【普】唠唠叨叨

慎

【xen⁶ 身⁶】careful; cautious

慎重【xen⁶jung⁶ 仲】cautious; careful; prudent

肾

【xen⁶ 慎;xen⁵ 慎⁵】kidney

肾脏【xen⁶jung⁶ 撞】kidney

肾炎【xen⁶yim⁴ 严】nephritis

肾结石【xen⁶gid⁸xēg⁹ 硕】kidney stone

笙

【xeng¹ 生】a reed pipe wind instrument

笙歌【xeng¹go¹ 哥】playing and singing

甥

【xeng¹ 笙;xang¹ 是罂¹】sister's son; nephew (see"外甥"【ngoi⁶xeng¹】)

牲

【xeng¹ 笙;xang¹ 是罂¹】domestic animal; animal sacrifice

牲畜【xeng¹qug⁷ 促】livestock；domestic animals

牲口【xang¹heo² 厚²】draught animals

擤【xeng³ 笙³】blow（one's nose）

擤鼻涕【xeng³bēi⁶tei³ 备替】blow one's nose

湿【xeb⁷ 十⁷】wet；damp；humid

湿度【xeb⁷dou⁶ 道】humidity

湿气【xeb⁷hēi³ 戏】moisture；eczema

湿润【xeb⁷yēn⁶ 闰】moist

湿透【xeb⁷teo³ 投³】wet through

湿疹【xeb⁷qen³ 陈²】eczema

湿热【xeb⁷ yid⁹ 衣泄⁹】damp and hot；sth. is not smooth

湿滞【xeb⁷jei⁶ 济⁶】sth. is not smooth =【普】（事情）不顺利；难办

湿立立【xeb⁷leb⁹leb⁹ 笠⁹】wet；damp；dripping wet =【普】湿漉漉；湿淋淋

十【xeb⁹ 拾】ten；topmost

十分【xeb⁹fen¹ 芬】very；fully

十足【xeb⁹ jug¹ 竹】100 per cent；sheer；downright

十月【xeb⁹ yüd² 越】October；the tenth moon

十一月【xeb⁹yed⁷yüd⁹ 壹越】November；the eleventh moon

十二月【xeb⁹ yi⁶ yüd⁹ 异越】December；the twelfth moon

十二指肠【xeb⁹ yi⁶ ji² qêng⁴ 拾异子祥】duodenum

十字路口【xeb⁹ ji⁶ lou⁶ heo² 自露厚²】crossroads

十恶不赦【xeb⁹ngog⁸bed⁷xē³ 岳⁸ 毕舍】guilty of unpardonable evil

十拿九稳【xeb⁹na⁴geo²wen² 那⁴ 久温²】90 percent sure；in the bag

十全十美【xeb⁹ qün⁴ xeb⁹ mēi⁵ 存尾】be perfect in every way

十万火急【xeb⁹man⁶fo²geb⁷ 慢伙格合⁷】posthaste

拾【xeb⁹ 十】pick up（from the ground）；collect；ten

拾取【xeb⁹qêü² 娶】pick-up；collect

拾遗【xeb⁹wei⁴ 维】appropriate lost property；make good omissions

拾金不昧【xeb⁹gem⁶bed⁷mui⁶ 今毕妹】not pocket the money one picks up

失【xed⁷ 室】lose；miss；let slip；fail to achieve one's end；mishap；defect；deviate from the normal；break

失咗【xed⁷jo² 左】lose；miss =【普】丢失

失去【xed⁷hêü³ 虚】lose = 失落【xed⁷log⁹ 洛⁹】

失败【xed⁷ bai⁶ 摆⁶】be defeated；lose（a war, etc.）

失策【xed⁷qag⁸ 册】unwise；inexpedient

失常【xed⁷xêng⁴ 裳】not mormal；odd

失宠【xed⁷qung² 充²】fall into disfavour

失传【xed⁷qün⁴ 全】be lost

失火【xed⁷fo² 伙】catch fire；be on fire

失魂【xed⁷wen⁴ 云】panic；be scared to death；lose one's presence of mind；lose one's head ∽【普】惊惶失措

失控【xed⁷hung³ 哄】out of control；runaway

失礼【xed⁷ lei⁵厉⁵】breach of etiquette；not in well manner or rude

失利【xed⁷lēi⁶ 莉⁶】suffer a setback

失恋【xed⁷ lün²联²】be disappointed in a

love affair

失灵【xed⁷ling⁴ 玲】be out of order

失眠【xed⁷min⁴ 棉】(suffer from)insomnia

失明【xed⁷ming⁴ 名】lose one's sight; go blind

失散【xed⁷xɑn³ 汕】be scattered

失色【xed⁷xig⁷ 式】turn pale; be eclipsed

失实【xed⁷xed⁹ 室⁹】inconsistent with the facts

失势【xed⁷ xei³ 世】lose power and influence

失事【xed⁷xi⁶ 士】(have an)accident

失手【xed⁷xeo² 守】accidentally drop

失守【xed⁷xeo² 手】fall

失算【xed⁷xūn³ 蒜】miscalculate; misjudge

失态【xed⁷tai³ 太】forget oneself

失调【xed⁷ tiu⁴条 】imbalance; lack of proper care

失望【xed⁷ mong⁶亡⁶】lose hope; disappointed

失物【xed⁷med⁹ 勿】lost article

失误【xed⁷ng⁶ 悟】fault; muff

失陷【xed⁷hɑm⁶ 咸⁶】(of cities, etc.)fall

失效【xed⁷hɑo⁶ 校】lose efficacy

失信【xed⁷xên³ 讯】break one's promise

失修【xed⁷xeo¹ 收】be in bad repair

失学【xed⁷hog⁹ 鹤】be unable to go to school

失言【xed⁷yin⁴ 然】make an indiscreet remark

失业【xed⁷yib⁹ 叶】lose one's job

失意【xed⁷yi³ 薏】be frustrated

失约【xed⁷ yêg⁸ 跃】fail to keep an appointment

失真【xed⁷jen¹ 珍】lack fidelity

失职【xed⁷jig⁷ 织】neglect one's duty

失重【xed⁷qung⁵ 虫⁵】weightlessness

失主【xed⁷jū² 煮】owner of lost property

失踪【xed⁷jung¹ 中】be missing

失足【xed⁷ jug⁷竹 】lose one's footing; slip; take a wrong step in life

失魂鱼【xed⁷wen⁴yū² 云余²】refer to the expression on one's face when one is scared to death ∽【普】惊惶失措的样子;跑来跑去,忙来忙去,忙不出什么名堂

失惊无神【xed⁷gēng¹mou⁴xen⁴ 颈¹ 毛臣】refer to one's look after being frightened by someone or something; driven to distraction ∽【普】失魂落魄

失道寡助【xed⁷dou⁶guɑ²jo⁶ 度瓜² 左⁶】An unjust cause finds scant support.

虱 【xed⁷ 失】〈n.〉虱子【xed⁷ji² 止】louse

虱乸【xed⁷nɑ² 那²】fleas

室 【xed⁷ 失】room

室内【xed⁷noi⁶ 耐】indoor; interior

室外【xed⁷ngoi⁶ 碍】outdoor; outside

实 【xed⁹ 失⁹】solid; true; real; reality; fact; fruit; seed

实际【xed⁹jei³ 济】reality; practice; practical; real; realistic

实地【xed⁹dēi⁶ 得希⁶】on the spot

实干【xed⁹gon⁶ 竿⁶】get right on the job; do solid work

实话【xed⁹wɑ⁶ 华⁶】truth

实惠【xed⁹wei⁶ 卫】material benefit; solid

实价【xed⁹gɑ³ 嫁】actual price

实践【xed⁹qin⁵ 千⁵】practice; put into practice

实力【xed⁹ lig⁹ 历 】strength; actual strength

实例【xed⁹lei⁶ 厉】living example; example

实情【xed⁹qing⁴ 程】the true state of affairs

实权【xed⁹kün⁴ 拳】real power

实施【xed⁹xi¹ 司】put into effect

实数【xed⁹ xou³素 】 the actual amount; real number

实体【xed⁹tei² 睇】substance; entity

实物【xed⁹ med⁹勿 】 material object; in kind

实习【xed⁹jab⁹ 杂】practice; fieldwork

实现【xed⁹yin⁶ 苋】realize; achieve

实验【xed⁹yim⁶ 艳】experiment; test

实业【xed⁹yib⁹ 叶】industry and commerce; industry

实用【xed⁹yung⁶ 容⁶】practical; functional

实在【xed⁹ joi⁶再⁶】 true; real; in fact; (of work)well-done

实则【xed⁹jeg⁷ 仄】actually; in fact

实质【xed⁹jed⁷ 侄⁷】substance; essence

实净【xed⁹ jēng⁶郑】strong; firm（body）=【普】（木制家具等的）坚实

实食有黐牙【xed⁹xig⁹mou⁵qi¹nga⁴ 蚀武 痴芽】confident of winning or achieving at a purpose ∽【普】稳操胜券

实事求是【xed⁹xi⁴keo⁴xi⁶ 士球示】seek truth from facts; be practical and realistic

塞【xeg⁷ 是得⁷; qoi³ 蔡】fill in; stuff; stopper; a place of strategic importance

个塞【go³xeg⁷ 哥³】stopper; cork; plug =【普】塞子

塞住【xeg⁷jü⁶ 朱⁶】be clogged up

塞责【xeg⁷jag⁸ 泽⁸】not do one's job conscientiously

塞外【qoi³ ngoi⁶碍 】 beyond the Great Wall

塞翁失马，安知非福【qoi³yung¹xed⁹ma⁵, ngon¹ji¹fēi¹fug⁷】A loss may turn out to be a gain.

疏【xo¹ 梳】dredge; thin; sparse;（of family or social relations）distant; not familiar with; neglect; scanty; disperse

疏打【xo¹da² 得亚²】soda

疏导【xo¹dou⁶ 道】dredge

疏忽【xo¹fed⁷ 弗】carelessness; oversight

疏浚【xo¹jên³ 进】dredge

疏懒【xo¹lan⁵ 兰⁵】careless and lazy; indolent

疏漏【xo¹leo⁶ 陋】careless omission; slip

疏密【xo¹med⁹ 勿】density; spacing

疏散【xo¹xan³ 汕】sparse; evacuate

疏堂【xo¹tong⁴ 唐】cousins ∽【普】非直系亲属——宗亲

疏松【xo¹xung¹ 松】loose; loosen

疏通【xo¹ tung¹痛¹】dredge; mediate between two parties

疏嘞嘩【xo¹lag⁸kuag⁸ 罗轭⁸卡或⁸】loose; thin; not densed =【普】很疏

疏远【xo¹yün⁵ 软】drift apart; become estranged

蔬【xo¹ 梳】vegetables

蔬菜【xo¹qoi³ 蔡】vegetables; greens

梳【xo¹ 疏】comb; comb one's hair, etc.

梳仔【xo¹jei² 济²】comb =【普】梳子

梳理【xo¹lēi⁵ 李】carding
梳洗【xo¹xei² 驶】wash and dress
梳妆【xo¹jung¹ 装】dress and make up

锁【xo² 琐】lock; lock up; lockstitch

锁链【xo²lin² 连²】chain; shackles
锁紧【xo²gen² 谨】locking
锁匙【xo²xi⁴ 时】key; strategic gateway＝【普】锁钥
锁骨【xo²gued⁷ 掘⁷】clavicle; collarbone

唢【xo² 锁】〈n.〉唢呐【xo²nab⁹ 腊】suona horn, a woodwind instrument

琐【xo² 锁】trivial; petty

琐事【xo²xi⁶ 士】trifles; trivial matters
琐碎【xo²xêü³ 瑞³】trifling; trivial
琐屑【xo²xid⁸ 泄】trifling; trivial

所【xo² 锁】place;〈classifier.〉a house;"被……所……"or"为……所……"constitute passive form;〈conj.〉"所以" join result
所以【xo²yi⁵ 耳】〈conj.〉so; therefore; as a result
所得【xo² deg⁷ 德】income; earnings; gains
所属【xo²xug⁹ 熟】what is subordinate to one or under one's command; what one belongs to or is affiliated with
所谓【xo² wei⁶ 惠】what is called; so-called
所有【xo²yeo⁵ 友】own; possess; possessions; all
所在【xo²joi⁶ 再⁶】place; location
所致【xo²ji³ 至】be caused by; be the result of
所向披靡【xo²hêng³pēi¹mēi⁴ 香³ 屁¹ 眉】sweep away all obstacles

所向无敌【xo²hêng³mou⁴dig⁹ 香³ 毛迪】be invincible

娑【xo¹ 梳】(see "婆娑"【po⁴xo¹】)

唆【xo¹ 梳】instigate; abet

唆使【xo¹xei² 洗】instigate; abet

嗦【xo¹ 梳】(see "啰嗦" or " 罗嗦"【lo¹xo¹】)

梭【xo¹ 梳】shuttle

飞梭【fēi¹xo¹ 非】shuttle＝【普】梭子
梭标【xo¹biu¹ 彪】spear

羧【xo¹ 梳】carboxyl

羧基【xo¹ gēi¹机 】carboxyl; carboxyl group
羧酸【xo¹xün¹ 孙】carboxylic acid

蓑【xo¹ 梳】〈n.〉蓑衣【xo¹yi¹ 依】straw or palm-bark rain cape

桫【xo¹ 梳】

桫椤【xo¹lo⁴ 罗】〈n.〉spinulose tree fern
桫麻柚【xo¹ma⁴yeo² 妈⁴ 由²】shaddock; pomelo＝【普】柚子

腮【xoi¹ 鳃】cheek

鼓起泡腮【gu²hēi²pao¹xoi¹ 古喜炮¹ 鳃】let cheek to pluck up—the manner of anger＝【普】怒气或生气的样子

鳃【xoi¹ 腮】〈n.〉鱼鳃【yü⁴xoi¹ 余】gill; branchia

苏【xou¹ 酥】revive; come to; short for Jiangsu Province; Soviet; a surname

苏醒【xou¹ xing²星²】revive; come to; come round

苏州【xou¹jeo¹ 洲】〈n.〉Suzhou

苏维埃【xou¹wei⁴ngai¹ 围捱¹】Soviet

苏丹【xou¹dan¹ 单】〈n.〉the Sudan; sultan

酥 【xou¹ 苏】revive; come to

酥 【xou¹ 苏】crisp; short; shortbread; limp; soft

酥油【xou¹yeo⁴ 由】butter

酥脆【xou¹qêū³ 翠】crisp

酥软【xou¹yūn⁵ 远】limp; weak; soft

骚 【xou¹ 苏】disturb; upset; short for "Li Sao"(《离骚》); literary writings; coquettish

骚动【xou¹ dung⁶洞】disturbance; be in a tumult

骚乱【xou¹lūn⁶ 联⁶】disturbance; riot

骚扰【xou¹yiu⁵ 绕⁵】harass; motest

骚客【xou¹hag⁸ 赫⁸】poet

搔 【xou¹ 苏】scratch; pay attention to

搔痒【xou¹yêng⁵ 养】scratch where it itches = 挈痒【ngao¹yêng⁵】

搔首【xou¹xeo² 守】scratch one's head = 挈头【ngao¹teo⁴】

唔搔佢【m⁴xou¹kêū⁵ 拒】pay no attention to him =【普】不理睬他

缫 【xou¹ 苏】reel silk from cocoons; reel

缫丝【xou¹xi¹ 司】silk reeling; filature

臊 【xou¹ 苏；xou³ 扫】shy; bashful; the smell of urine; foul smell; give birth to; the unpleasant smell of beef and mutton

臊虾【xou¹ha¹ 哈】a baby =【普】婴儿

臊虾仔【xou¹ha¹jei² 哈济²】a baby boy =【普】男婴

臊虾女【xou¹ha¹nêū⁵ 那虚⁵】a baby girl =【普】女婴

嫂 【xou² 素²】elder brother's wife; sister

阿嫂【a³xou² 丫³】elder brother's wife; sister-in-law =【普】嫂嫂；嫂子

数 【xou³ 素；xou² 嫂】count; be reckoned as exceptionally; number; figure; several; a few; fate; destiny

数数【xou²xou³】count; reckon

数落【xou²log⁹ 洛⁹】scold sb. by enumerating his wrongdoings; rebuke; enumerate

数一数二【xou²yed⁷xou²yi⁶ 壹义】count as one of the very best

数额【xou³ngag⁹ 轭⁹】number; amount

数据【xou³gêū³ 踞】data

数量【xou³lêng⁶ 亮】quantity; amount

数码【xou³ma⁵ 马】numeral; number; amount

数学【xou³hog⁹ 鹤】mathematics

数值【xou³jig⁹ 直】numerical value

数字【xou³ji⁶ 治】numeral; figure; digit; quantity; amount

漱 【xou³ 数；xeo³ 秀】gargle; rinse

漱口【xou³heo² 厚】rinse the mouth; gargle = 滦口【long²heo²】

扫 【xou³ 数】sweep; clear away; pass quickly along or over; put all together; broom

扫帚【xou³jeo² 走】broom = 扫把【xou³ba²】

扫除【xou³ qêū⁴ 徐 】cleaning; cleanup; clear away; remove

扫荡【xou³dong⁶ 当⁶】mop up

扫地【xou³ dēi⁶ 得希⁶】sweep the floor;

reach rock bottom

扫描【xou³miu⁴ 苗】scanning

扫墓【xou³mou⁶ 务】sweep a grave—pay respects to a dead person at his tomb＝拜山【bai³xan¹】

扫平【xou³ping⁴ 萍】put down; crush

扫射【xou³xē⁶ 舍⁶】strafe

扫尾【xou³mēi⁵ 美】wind up; round off

扫兴【xou³hing³ 庆】feel disappointed

诉【xou³ 素】tell; relate; inform; complain; accuse; appeal to; resort to

诉苦【xou³fu² 府】vent one's grievances

诉说【xou³xūd⁸ 雪】tell; relate; recount

诉讼【xou³jung⁶ 颂】lawsuit; litigation

诉状【xou³jong⁶ 撞】plaint; indictment

素【xou³ 扫】white; plain; quiet; native; element; usually; always

素材【xou³qoi⁴ 才】source material; material

素菜【xou³qoi³ 蔡】vegetable dish

素食【xou³xig⁹ 蚀】vegetarian diet

素淡【xou³dam⁶ 担⁶】quiet(colour)

素来【xou³loi⁴ 莱】always; usually

素描【xou³miu⁴ 苗】sketch; literary sketch

素馨【xou³hing⁵ 兴】jasmine

素雅【xou³nga⁵ 瓦】simple but elegant

素养【xou³yêng⁵ 痒】attainment

素质【xou³jed⁷ 侄⁷】quality; diathesis

愫【xou³ 素】sincere feeling; sincerity

溯【xou³ 素】go against the stream; recall

溯源【xou³yūn⁴ 原】trace to the source

塑【xou³ 素；xog⁸ 索】model; mould

塑像【xou³jêng⁶ 丈】statue

塑造【xou³jou⁶ 做】model; mould; portray

塑料【xou³liu² 了²】plastics＝塑胶【xog⁸ gao¹】

桑【xong¹ 嗓】white mulberry; mulberry; a surname

桑树【xong¹xū⁶ 署⁶】white mulberry; mulberry

桑葚【xong¹xem⁴ 岑】mulberry

桑蚕【xong¹qam⁴ 惭】silkworm

桑梓【xong¹ji² 子】one's native place

桑榆暮景【xong¹yū⁴mou⁶ging² 如务境】the evening of one's life

嗓【xong¹ 桑】throat; larynx; voice

嗓子【xong¹ji² 止】throat; larynx; voice

嗓门【xong¹mun⁴ 门】voice

嗓音【xong¹yem¹ 阴】voice

丧【xong¹ 桑；xong³ 桑³】lose; funeral; mourning

丧事【xong¹xi⁶ 士】funeral arrangements

丧葬【xong¹jong³ 壮】burial; funeral

丧礼【xong¹lei⁵ 厉⁵】obsequies; funeral

丧乱【xong³lün⁶ 联⁶】disturbance; turmoil

丧钟【xong³jung¹ 中】funeral bell; knell

丧失【xong³xed⁷ 室】lose; forfeit

丧命【xong³ming⁶ 名⁶】meet one's death; get killed

丧胆【xong³dam² 担²】be terror-stricken

丧偶【xong³ngeo⁵藕 】bereft of one's spouse, esp. one's wife

丧气【xong³hēi³戏 】feel disheartened; lose heart; be unlucky; be out of luck

丧心病狂【xong³xem¹bēng⁶kuong⁴ 深柄⁶ 卡汪⁴】frenzied

丧尽天良【xong³jên⁶tin¹lêng⁴ 进⁶ 田¹ 量⁴】utterly devoid of conscience; heartless

丧魂落魄【xong³wen⁴log⁹pag⁸ 云洛⁹ 柏】be driven to distraction

丧家之犬【xong³ga¹ji¹hün² 加支劝²】stray cur

丧权辱国【xong³kün⁴yug⁹guog⁸ 拳玉帼】humiliate the nation and forfeit its sovereignty

颡【xong² 爽】forehead

搡【xong² 爽】push violently

爽【xong² 搡】bright; clear; frank; feel well; deviate; crunchy; soft and fining; comfortable

爽口【xong²heo² 厚²】tasty and refreshing

爽快【xong² fai³ 块 】refreshed; frank; readily

爽朗【xong²long⁵郎⁵】bright and clear; hearty

爽利【xong²lêi⁶ 俐】brisk and neat; excited; feeling good

爽直【xong²jig⁹ 值】frank; candid

爽手【xong²xeo² 守】the good feeling that one gets when touching something smooth and soft; do things really fast ∽【普】办事行动快，干脆利落

爽脆【xong² qêü³ 翠】crunchy; do th-ings fast and be responsible

搂【xog⁷ 索⁷】hit one's head =【普】敲打（某人的头部）

索【xog⁸ 朔】large rope; search; demand; ask; exact; all alone; dull; a string; make a knot; chain; a surname

索道【xog⁸dou⁶ 度】cableway; ropeway

索取【xog⁸qêü²娶】ask for; demand; exact

索性【xog⁸xing³ 姓】〈ad.〉∽clear-cut; simply

索引【xog⁸yen⁵ 隐⁵】index

索然【xog⁸yin⁴ 言】dull; dry; insipid

索水【xog⁸xêü² 瑞】absorb water =【普】（用干物）把水吸去

索油【xog⁸ yeo⁴由】①absorb oil; ②take advantage of women ∽【普】缠绕女性，企图占便宜

朔【xog⁸ 索】new moon; the first day of the lunar month; north

朔望【xog⁹ mong⁶亡⁻⁶】the first and the fifteenth day of the lunar month; syzygy

朔风【xog⁹fung¹ 丰】north wind

嗍【xog⁸ 索】sip =【普】吮吸

嗍气【xog⁹hêi³ 戏】keep breathing after a strenuous journey; difficult; tiring ∽【普】气喘呼呼；疲劳

松【xung¹ 松；qung⁴ 虫】pine; loose; slack; loosen; slacken; not hard up; soft; dried meat floss; a surname

松弛【xung¹qi⁴ 池】limp; slack; lax

松绑【xung¹bong² 梆】untie a person

松动【xung¹dung⁶ 洞】become less crowded; not hard up; become flexible

松紧【xung¹ gen² 谨】degree of tightness; elasticity

松劲【xung¹ging³ 敬】relax one's efforts

松气【xung¹hêi³ 戏】relax one's efforts

松软【xung¹yün⁵ 远】soft; spongy; loose

松散【xung¹ xan² 山²】loose; inattentive; relax

松化【xung¹ fa³ 花³】crunchy; tasty ∽【普】（食物）松软，一进口就溶化

松姈【xung¹ peo³ 剖³】soft and fender =

【普】物质结构松软，体积大而重量少

松手【xung¹ xeo² 守】lossen one's grip; let go

松土【xung¹ tou² 肚²】loosen the soil

松懈【xung¹ hai⁶ 械】relax; slacken

松骨【xung¹ gued⁷ 掘⁷】massage; give someone a punch＝【普】捶骨

松人【xung¹ yen⁴ 仁】free oneself; sneak away ∽【普】溜之大吉

松糕【xung¹ gou¹ 高】cake; pastry＝【普】米粉糕儿

松树【qung⁴ xü⁶ 署⁶】pine tree; pine

松明【qung⁴ ming⁴ 名】pine torches

松鼠【qung⁴ xü² 署】squirrel

松香【qung⁴ hêng¹ 乡】rosin; colophony

松脂【qung⁴ ji¹ 支】rosin; pine rosin

松节油【qung¹ jid⁸ yeo⁴ 折由】turpentine (oil)

松松垮垮【xung¹ xung¹ kua¹ kua¹ 夸】be slack and perfunctory

嵩【xung¹ 淞】(of mountains) high; lofty

淞【xung¹ 嵩】〈n.〉吴淞【ng⁴ xung¹】Wusong (in Shanghai)

忪【xung¹ 嵩】(see "惺忪"【xing¹ xung¹】)

怂【xung² 耸】〈v.〉怂恿【xung² yung² 拥】instigate; incite; egg sb. on; abet

悚【xung² 耸】〈a.〉悚然【xung² yin⁴ 言】terrified; horrified

耸【xung² 怂】towering; lofty; alarm; shock

耸动【xung² dung⁶ 洞】shrug; create a sensation

耸立【xung² leb⁹ 笠⁹】tower aloft

耸肩【xung² gin¹ 坚】shrug one's shoulders

耸人听闻【xung² yen⁴ ting³ men⁴ 仁亭³ 文】deliberately exaggerate so as to create a sensation

耸入云霄【xung² yeb⁹ wen⁴ xiu¹ 邑⁹ 纭消】tower to the skies

悚【xung² 悚】＝悚 (see "悚"【xung²】)

宋【xung³ 送】the Song Dynasty (960～1279); a surname

送【xung³ 宋】deliver; carry; give; see sb. off or out; accompany; escort

送信【xung³ xên³ 讯】deliver a letter; send word

送别【xung³ bid⁹ 必⁹】see sb. off; wish sb. bon voyage; give a send-off party＝送行【heng⁴】

送殡【xung³ ben³ 宾³】attend a funeral＝送葬【jong³】

送终【xung³ jung¹ 中】attend upon a dying parent or other senior member of one's family; bury a parent

送货【xung³ fo³ 课】deliver goods

送给【xung³ keb⁷ 级】give as a present; give

送交【xung³ gao¹ 胶】deliver; hand over

送客【xung³ hag⁸ 赫】see a visitor out

送礼【xung³ lei⁵ 厉⁵】give sb. a present

送命【xung³ mêng⁶ 莫镜⁶】lose one's life; get killed

送死【xung³ xêi² 四²】court death

送人情【xung³ yen⁴ qing⁴ 仁程】do favours at no great cost to oneself; make a gift of sth.

送旧迎新【xung³ geo⁶ ying⁴ xen¹ 柩仍辛】see off the old and welcome the new

餸【xung³ 送】dishes to be served with rice＝【普】菜肴

大餸【dai⁶xung³ 歹⁶】one who eats a lot of vegetables＝【普】（用餐时）菜肴吃得多

崇【xung⁴ 送⁴】high; lofty; sublime; esteem; worship; a surname

崇高【xung⁴gou¹ 糕】lofty; sublime; high

崇尚【xung⁴xêng⁴ 上】uphold; advocate

崇拜【xung⁴bai³ 摆³】worship; adore

崇敬【xung⁴ging³ 劲】esteem; respect; revere

叔【xug⁷ 宿】father's younger brother; uncle; a form of address for a man about one's father's age

叔伯【xug⁷bag⁸ 百】relationship between cousins of the same grandfather or great-grandfather

叔父【xug⁷fu⁶付】father's younger brother; uncle

叔母【xug⁷mou⁵ 武】wife of father's younger brother;aunt＝姊娘【xem²nêng⁴ 那香⁴】

叔叔【xug⁷ xug⁷】father's younger brother; uncle＝阿叔【a³xug⁷】

叔公【xug⁷gung¹ 工】grandfather's younger brother; granduncle＝【普】叔祖

叔婆【xug⁷po⁴ 颇⁴】wife of grandfather's younger brother; grandaunt＝【普】叔祖母

菽【xug⁷ 叔】beans

宿【xug⁷ 叔】lodge for the night; stay overnight; long-standing; old; veteran; a surname

宿舍【xug⁷xê³ 泻】hotel; living quarters

宿营【xug⁷ying⁴ 仍】take up quarters

宿怨【xug⁷yün² 元³】old grudge; old scores

宿愿【xug⁷yün⁶ 县】long-cherished wish

夙【xug⁷ 叔】early in the morning; long-standing

夙愿【xug⁷yün⁶ 县】long-cherished wish

夙兴夜寐【xug⁷hing¹yê⁶mui⁶ 兄野⁶ 昧】rise early and retire late—hard at work night and day

粟【xug⁷ 叔】millet; a surname

粟米【xug⁷mei⁵ 迷⁵】corns＝【普】玉米

倏【xug⁷ 叔】swiftly

倏忽【xug⁷fed⁷ 弗】swiftly; in the twinkling of the eye＝倏然【xug⁷yin⁴ 言】

肃【xug⁷ 叔】respectful; solemn

肃静【xug⁷jing⁶ 净】solemn silence

肃立【xug⁷leb⁹ 笠⁹】stand as a mark of respect

肃穆【xug⁷mug⁹ 目】solemn and respectful

肃清【xug⁷qing¹ 称】eliminate; clean up

肃然起敬【xug⁷yin⁴hēi²ging³ 言喜径】be filled with deep veneration

缩【xug⁷ 叔】contract; shrink; draw back; recoil

缩短【xug⁷dün² 瑞²】shorten; curtail; cut down

缩减【xug⁷gam² 监²】reduce; cut

缩小【xug⁷xiu² 少²】reduce; lessen; shrink

缩写【xug⁷xē² 舍²】abbreviation; abridge

缩影【xug⁷ying² 映】epitome; miniature

缩水【xug⁷xêu² 瑞】(of cloth through wetting)shrink

缩骨【xug⁷ gued⁷ 掘⁷】one who is selfish and cunning 〇【普】巧计谋私

缩沙【xug⁷ xa¹ 砂】withdraw at the last minute 〇【普】见势不妙而退走

缩数【xug⁷ xou³ 素】be calculative 〇【普】谋私的精巧打算

缩头龟【xug⁷ teo⁴ guei¹ 投归】one who is timid 〇【普】怕死鬼

缩开啲【xug⁷hoi¹did⁷ 海¹ 得热⁷】give way to others =【普】请(别人)让开点位置

缩骨遮【xug⁷gued⁷jē¹ 掘⁷ 姐¹】umbrellas =【普】把柄能伸缩的伞子

缩埋一咕【xug⁷mai⁴yed⁷geo² 买⁴ 壹旧】coil one's body 〇【普】缩成一团

缩埋一二角【xug⁷mai⁴yed⁷yi⁶gog⁸ 买⁴ 壹义各】hide oneself in a corner due to extreme horror 〇【普】退至阴暗角落

淑 【xug⁹ 熟】kind and gentle; fair

淑女【xug⁹nêü⁵ 那虚⁵】a fair maiden

蜀 【xug⁹ 熟】another name for Sichuan Province

赎 【xug⁹ 熟; jug⁷ 逐】redeem; ransom; atone for(a crime)

赎买【xug⁹mai⁵ 卖⁵】redeem; buy out

赎身【xug⁹ xen¹ 辛】buy back one's freedom

赎罪【xug⁹jêü⁶ 聚】atone for one's crime

赎金【xug⁹ gem¹今】ransom money; ransom

赎钱【jug⁹ qin² 浅】give back the spare money =【普】退回余钱

属 【xug⁹ 熟; jug⁷ 足】category; genus; under; belong to; family members; be; be born in the year of; join; com-

bine; fix(one's mind)on

属于【xug⁹yü¹ 迂】belong to; be part of

属性【xug⁹xing³ 姓】attribute; property

属地【xug⁹dēi⁶ 得希⁶】possession

属国【xug⁹guog⁸ 帼】vassal state

属意【jug⁷yi³ 薏】fix one's mind on sb. (as one's choice, favourite, etc.)

孰 【xug⁹ 熟】who; which; what

孰是孰非【xug⁹xi⁶xug⁹fēi¹ 士菲】Which is right and which is wrong.

塾 【xug⁹ 熟】private school

熟 【xug⁹ 属】ripe; cooked; done; processed; familiar; skilled; practised; deeply

熟谙【xug⁹ em¹庵】be familiar with; be good at

熟记【xug⁹gēi³ 寄】learn by heart; memorize

熟客【xug⁹ hag⁸赫】frequent visitor; clients

熟练【xug⁹lin⁶ 炼】skilled; practised

熟料【xug⁹liu² 了²】grog; clinker

熟路【xug⁹lou⁶ 露】familiar route; beaten track

熟人【xug⁹yen⁴ 仁】acquaintance; friend

熟食【xug⁹xig⁹ 蚀】prepared food; cooked food

熟识【xug⁹xig⁷ 式】know well

熟悉【xug⁹xig⁷ 式】know sth. or sb. well

熟睡【xug⁹xêü⁶ 瑞】sleep soundly

熟习【xug⁹jab⁹ 杂】be skilful at

熟知【xug⁹ji¹ 支】know very well

熟行【xug⁹ hong⁴ 杭】expert; good at =【普】懂行规,知行情

熟落【xug⁹ log⁹ 洛⁹】efficient；fest；good ＝【普】熟门熟路；不生疏

熟性【xug⁹ xing³ 姓】considerate；understanding◯【普】懂世故，会做人

熟盐【xug⁹yim⁴ 严】cooking salt

熟烟【xug⁹yin¹ 言】tobacco used to make cigarette

熟能生巧【xug⁹neng⁴xeng¹hao² 那莺⁴ 笙 考】Skill comes from practice.

熟视无睹【xug⁹xi⁶mou²dou² 示毛倒】pay no attention to a familiar sight；ignore

诗 【xi¹ 思】poetry；verse；poem

诗歌【xi¹go¹ 哥】poems and songs；poetry

诗集【xi¹jab⁹ 习】collection of poems；poetry anthology

诗经【xi¹ging¹ 京】The Book of Songs

诗句【xi¹gêü³ 据】verse；line

诗篇【xi¹pin¹ 编】poem；inspiring story

诗人【xi¹yen⁴ 仁】poet

诗意【xi¹yi³ 薏】poetie quality or flavour

师 【xi¹ 诗】teacher；master；model；a person skilled in a certain profession；of one's master or teacher；division；army；troops；a surname

师奶【xi¹nai¹ 乃¹】the wife of teacher or master ＝【普】师娘

师长【xi¹ jêng² 掌】teacher；division commander

师表【xi¹ biu² 标²】a person of exemplary virtue

师范【xi¹ fan⁶ 饭】teacher-training；normal school

师傅【xi¹ fu⁶ 附】master worker ＝ 师父 【xi¹fu⁶ 附】

师兄【xi¹ hing¹ 兴】senior fellow appren-

tice；the son of one's master

师姑【xi¹gu¹ 估¹】a monk ＝【普】尼姑

师爷【xi¹yê⁴ 椰】private adviser

师团【xi¹tün⁴ 梯元⁴】division

狮 【xi¹ 诗】lion

狮子【xi¹ji² 止】lion

施 【xi¹ 诗】execute；carry out；bestow；hand out；exert；impose；use；a surname

施放【xi¹fong³ 况】discharge；fire

施加【xi¹ga¹ 家】exert；bring to bear on

施舍【xi¹xê² 写】give alms；give in charity

施行【xi¹ heng⁴ 衡】put in force；execute；perform

施用【xi¹yung⁶ 容⁶】use；employ

施与【xi¹yü⁵ 语】grant；bestow

施展【xi¹jin² 剪】put to good use

施工【xi¹gung¹ 功】construction

施肥【xi¹fêi⁴ 非⁴】spread manure

施政【xi¹jing³ 正】administration

司 【xi¹ 思】take charge of；attend to；manage；department；a surname

司法【xi¹fad⁸ 发】administration of justice；judicature

司机【xi¹gêi¹ 基】driver

司炉【xi¹lou⁴ 卢】stoker；fireman

司仪【xi¹yi⁴ 而】master of ceremonies

司令【xi¹ ling⁶ 另】commander；commanding officer

司空【xi¹hung¹ 凶】a surname

司马【xi¹ma⁵ 码】a surname

司徒【xi¹tou⁴ 图】a surname

司空见惯【xi¹hung¹gin³guan³ 凶建关³】a common sight；a common occurrence

丝【xi¹ 诗】silk; a threadlike thing; trace; a unit of weight (= 0.0005 grams)

丝绸【xi¹qeo⁴ 筹】silk cloth; silk

丝带【xi¹dai³ 戴】silk ribbon; silk sash

丝瓜【xi¹gua³ 寡¹】towel gourd

丝毫【xi¹hou⁴ 豪】a bit; a particle; an iota

丝绵【xi¹min⁴ 棉】silk floss; velour

丝绒【xi¹yung⁴ 容】velvet; velour

丝网【xi¹nong⁵冈】silk fabrics and woodwind instruments; music

丝织品【xi¹jig⁷ben² 积裹】silk fabrics; silk knit goods

丝丝入扣【xi¹xi¹yeb⁹keo³ 邑⁹ 寇】(done) with meticulous care and flawless artistry

私【xi¹ 司】personal; private; selfish; secret; illicit

私人【xi¹yen⁴ 仁】private; one's own man

私自【xi¹ji⁶ 治】privately; secretly

私下【xi¹ha⁶ 夏】in private; in secret

私奔【xi¹ben¹ 宾】elopement

私产【xi¹qan² 铲】private property

私仇【xi¹xeo⁴ 愁】personal morals

私邸【xi¹dei¹ 底】private residence

私房【xi¹fong⁴ 防】private savings; confidential

私愤【xi¹fen⁵ 奋】personal spite

私货【xi¹fo³ 课】smuggled goods; contraband goods

私立【xi¹leb⁹ 笠⁹】privately run; private

私利【xi¹lēi⁶ 俐】private interests; personal gain

私家【xi¹ga¹ 加】private＝【普】私人的

私囊【xi¹nong⁴ 那昂⁴】private purse

私情【xi¹qing⁴ 程】personal relationships

私事【xi¹xi⁶ 士】private affairs

私通【xi¹tung¹ 同¹】illicit intercourse; adultery

私心【xi¹ xem¹深】selfish motives; selfishness

私营【xi¹ ying⁴仍 】privately owned; private

私有【xi¹ ying⁴ 友 】privately owned; private

私语【xi¹yǔ 与】whisper; confidence

私欲【xi¹yug⁹ 玉】selfish desire

私章【xi¹gêng¹ 张】personal seal; signet

思【xi¹ 司】think; consider; think of; thought

思想【xi¹ xêng² 赏 】thought; thinking; idea; ideology

思绪【xi¹xêū⁵ 水⁵】train of thought; thinking; feeling

思维【xi¹wei⁴ 围】thought; thinking

思思缩缩【xi¹xi¹xug⁷xug⁷ 宿】feel restricted, not free; suspicious∽【普】想干又不敢干,行动不果断

思潮【xi¹qiu⁴ 樵】trend of thought; thoughts

思忖【xi¹qūn² 喘】ponder; consider

思考【xi¹ hao² 巧 】think deeply; ponder over

思量【xi¹lêng⁴ 凉】consider; turn sth. over in one's mind

思疑【xi¹yi⁴ 移】suspect∽【普】怀疑;疑虑

思路【xi¹ lou⁶ 露】train of thought; thinking

思虑【xi¹ lêū⁶ 类】consider carefully; contemplate

思慕【xi¹ mou⁶ 务 】think of sb. with respect; admire

思念【xi¹nim⁶ 粘⁶】think of; miss

斯【xi¹ 司】this; then; thus; a surname

斯文【xi¹men⁴ 闻】refined; gentle

斯里兰卡【xi¹lēi⁵lan⁴ka¹ 李栏其亚¹】Sri Lanka

锶【xi¹ 司】〈n.〉strontium (Sr)

咝【xi¹ 司】〈onomatope.〉whistle

蛳【xi¹ 司】(see "螺蛳" 【lou⁴xi¹】)

厮【xi¹ 司】male servant; fellow; guy; together

厮打【xi¹da² 得亚²】come to blows; tussle

厮杀【xi¹xad⁸ 煞】fight at close quarters

撕【xi¹ 司】tear; rip

撕毁【xi¹wei² 委】tear up; tear to shreds

嘶【xi¹ 司】neigh; hoarse

嘶哑【xi¹nga² 瓦²】hoarse

尸【xi¹ 司】corpse; dead body; remains

尸体【xi¹tei² 睇】corpse; dead body; remains

尸骨【xi¹gued⁷ 掘⁷】skeleton = 尸骸【xi¹hai⁴】

尸横遍野【xi¹ wang⁴ pin³ yē⁵乌嚣⁴ 片惹】field littered with corpses

屎【xi² 史】excrement; faeces; dung; secretion; poor; of inferior quality

笨屎虫【ben⁶xi²qung⁴ 奔⁶ 从】dung beetle = 【普】屎壳郎

屎窟【xi²fed⁷ 弗】buttock = 【普】屁股; 肛门

屎坑【xi² hang¹黑嚣¹】toilet = 【普】茅坑; 茅厕; 厕所

屎斗【xi²deo² 豆】of poor performance; of inferior quality ∽ 【普】笨拙; 愚笨; 不聪明

屎计【xi² gei²偈】plans or ideas that are not really good or smart ∽ 【普】下策; 不高明的计划、打算

史【xi² 屎】history; a surname

史册【xi²qag⁸ 策】history; annals

史书【xi²xü¹ 输】history; historical records = 史籍【jig⁹】

史诗【xi²xi¹】epic

史实【xi²xed⁹ 失⁹】historical facts

史料【xi²liu⁶ 了⁶】historical data; historical materials

史前【xi²qin⁴ 钱】prehistoric

史迹【xi²jig⁷ 积】historical site or relics

史学【xi²hog⁹ 鹤】the science of history

史无前例【xi²mou⁴qin⁴lei⁶ 毛钱厉】without precedent in history; unprecedented

弑【xi³ 试】murder(one's sovereign of father)

试【xi³ 谥】try; test; examination

试验【xi³yim⁶ 艳】trial; experiment; test

试行【xi³heng⁴ 衡】try out

试纸【xi³ji² 止】test paper

试剂【xi³jei¹ 挤】reagent

试管【xi³gun¹ 莞】test tube

试题【xi³tei⁴ 提】examination questions

试卷【xi³ gün²绢²】examination paper; test paper

试点【xi³dim² 店²】make experiments; experimental unit

试车【xi³qē¹ 奢】test run; trial run

试飞【xi³fēi¹ 非】test flight; trial flight

试航【xi³hong⁴ 杭】trial trip; shake down

试探【xi³ tam³ 贪³】sound out; feel out; probe

试图【xi³tou⁴ 徒】attempt; try

试问【xi³men⁶ 闻⁶】We should like to ask. May we ask?

试想【xi³xêng² 赏】just think

试销【xi³xiu¹ 消】place goods on trial sale; trial sale

试用【xi³yung⁶ 容⁶】try out; on probation

试制【xi³jei³ 济】trial-produce

试过【xi³guo³ 戈³】having done something before = 【普】已经尝试了

谥【xi³ 试】〈n.〉谥号【xi³hou⁶ 毫⁶】the honorific title given to a dead person

时【xi⁴ 是衣⁴】time; times; days; fixed time; hour; season; current; present; chance; now and then; now... now...; tense; a surname

时常【xi⁴xêng⁴ 尝】often; frequently

时辰【xi⁴xen⁴ 晨】one of the 12 two-hour periods into which the day was traditionally divided, each being given the name of one of the 12 Earthly Branches

时代【xi⁴doi⁶ 袋】times; age; era; a period in one's life

时而【xi⁴ yi⁴ 移】sometimes; now ... now ...

时分【xi⁴fen⁶ 份】time

时光【xi⁴guong¹ 胱】time; times; days

时候【xi⁴heo⁶ 后】time; moment

时价【xi⁴ga³ 嫁】current price

时间【xi⁴gan³ 奸³】time

时节【xi⁴jid⁶ 折】season; time

时局【xi⁴gug⁹ 焗】the current political situation

时刻【xi⁴ heg⁷ 克 】time; hour; moment; always

时髦【xi⁴ mou¹ 毛¹】fashionable; stylish; in vogue

时期【xi⁴kêi¹ 其】period

时尚【xi⁴xêng⁶ 上】fashion; fad

时时【xi⁴ xi⁴】often; constantly; always; usually

时势【xi⁴xei³ 细】the current situation

时事【xi⁴xi⁶ 士】current events

时速【xi⁴qug⁷ 促】speed per hour

时态【xi⁴tai³ 太】tense

时务【xi⁴mou⁶ 冒】current affairs

时新【xi⁴xen¹ 辛】stylish; trendy

时兴【xi⁴hing¹ 兄】fashionable; in vogue; popular

时宜【xi⁴yi⁴ 而】what is appropriate to the occasion

时年【xi⁴nin⁴ 捻⁴】the whole year = 【普】年景

时运【xi⁴wen⁶ 混】luck; fortune

时钟【xi⁴jung¹ 中】clock

时装【xi⁴jong¹ 妆】fashionable dress

时菜【xi⁴qoi³ 蔡】delicacies of the season

时下【xi⁴ha⁶ 夏】at present

时不时【xi⁴bed⁷xi⁴ 毕】occassionally; on and off

时至今日【xi⁴ji³gem¹yed⁹ 志金逸】at this late hour

时哩沙啦【xi⁴li¹xa⁴la⁴ 罗衣¹ 砂⁴ 罗亚⁴】refer to the rapid progress of a project or event due to considerable man-power∽【普】形容动作快捷，但不过细

市【xi⁵ 时⁵】market; city; pertaining to the Chinese system of weights and measures

市廛【xi⁵ qin⁴ 前 】 stores in a market or street；market

市场【xi⁵qêng⁴ 祥】marketplace；market

市秤【xi⁵ qing³ 称³】Chinese scale of weights

市尺【xi⁵ qêg⁸ 赤】a unit of length（= 50 kilograms）

市集【xi⁵jab⁹ 习】fair；small town

市价【xi⁵ga³ 嫁】market price

市斤【xi⁵gen¹ 根】a unit of weight（= ½ kilogram）

市井【xi⁵jêng² 支镜²】marketplace；town

市侩【xi⁵kui² 绘】sordid merchant

市面【xi⁵min⁶ 缅⁶】market conditions；business

市民【xi⁵ men⁴文 】 residents of a city；townspeople

市区【xi⁵ kêu¹ 驱】city proper；urban district

市容【xi⁵yung⁴ 熔】the appearance of a city

市镇【xi⁵jen³ 振】small town；towns

氏 【xi⁶ 士】family name；surname

氏族【xi⁶jug⁹ 俗】clan

示 【xi⁶ 士】show；notify；instruct

示范【xi⁶fan⁶ 饭】set an example；demonstrate

示例【xi⁶lei⁶ 厉】give typical examples

示弱【xi⁶yêg⁹ 药】take sth. lying down

示威【xi⁶wei¹ 卫¹】demonstrate；put on a show of force

示意【xi⁶ji³ 薏】signal；hint；motion

示众【xi⁶ jung³ 纵 】 publicly expose；put before the public

士 【xi⁶ 示】bachelor（in ancient China）；a social stratum in ancient China, between senior officials and the common people；scholar；noncommissioned officer；a person trained in a certain field；（commendable）person；bodyguard, one of the pieces in Chinese chess

士兵【xi⁶bing¹ 冰】rank-and-file soldiers；privates

士卒【xi⁶jêd⁷ 支律⁷】soldiers；privates

士气【xi⁶hêi³ 戏】morale

士担【xi⁶dam¹ 胆¹】stamp =【普】邮票

士多【xi⁶do¹ 朵】store =【普】店铺；商店

士呖【xi⁶lig⁷ 历】slick =【普】清漆

士巴拿【xi⁶ba¹na² 吧¹ 嗱】spanner =【普】扳手

士挞胆【xi⁶tad⁷dam² 替压⁷ 担²】starter =【普】启辉器

事 【xi⁶ 士】 matter； affair； thing； trouble；accident；job；work；responsibility；wait upon；serve；be engaged in

事物【xi⁶med⁹ 勿】thing；object

事情【xi⁶qing⁴ 程】affair；matter；thing

事件【xi⁶gin² 坚²】incident；event

事变【xi⁶bin³ 边³】incident；emergency；exigency

事端【xi⁶dün¹ 段¹】disturbance；incident

事故【xi⁶gu³ 固】accident；mishap

事后【xi⁶ heo⁶ 候】after the event；afterwards

事迹【xi⁶jig⁷ 迹】deed；achievement

事理【xi⁶lêi⁶ 李】reason；logic

事例【xi⁶lei⁶ 厉】example；instance

事前【xi⁶ qin⁴钱 】 before the event；beforehand

事实【xi⁶xed⁹ 失⁹】fact

事事【xi⁶xi⁶】everything

事态【xi⁶tai³ 太】state of affairs；situation

事务【xi⁶mou⁶ 冒】work；general affairs

事先【xi⁶xin¹ 仙】in advance；beforehand；prior

事项【xi⁶hong⁶ 巷】item；matter

事业【xi⁶yib⁹ 叶】cause；enterprise

事宜【xi⁶ yi⁴移 】matters concerned；arrangements

事由【xi⁶yeo⁴ 游】particulars of a matter；main content

事干【xi⁶ gon³ 竿³】matter；event＝【普】事情

事头【xi⁶teo⁴ 投²】boss；owner＝【普】老板

事头婆【xi⁶ teo⁴ po⁴ 投颇⁴】lady-boss；lady-owner＝【普】老板娘

事实上【xi⁶xed⁹xêng⁴ 失⁹ 尚】in fact；in reality

事半功倍【xi⁶bun³gung¹pui⁵ 伴³ 工陪⁵】get twice the result with half the effort

事倍功半【xi⁶pui⁵gung¹bun³ 陪⁵ 工伴³】get half the result with twice the effort

事不宜迟【xi⁶ bed⁷ yi⁴ qi⁴毕移池】One must lose no time in doing it.

事出有因【xi⁶qêd⁷yeo⁵yen¹ 次律⁷ 友恩】There is good reason for it.

事与愿遗【xi⁶yû⁵yûn⁶wei⁴ 语县维】Things go contrary to one's wishes.

事在人为【xi⁶joi⁶yen⁴wei⁴ 再⁶ 仁维】It all depends on human effort

事急马行田【xi⁶geb⁷ma⁵hang⁴tin⁴ 格合⁷ 码坑⁴ 天⁴】refer to the use of illegal means ∽【普】（比喻）危急关头，不按常规办事

仕【xi⁶ 士】be an official；fill an office；bodyguard, one of the pieces in Chinese chess

仕途【xi⁶tou⁴ 图】official career

仕女【xi⁶nêû⁵ 那虚⁵】traditional Chinese painting of beautiful women

视【xi⁶ 示】look at；regard；inspect；watch

视察【xi⁶qad⁸ 刷】inspect

视角【xi⁶ gog⁸各 】angle of view；visual angle

视觉【xi⁶gog⁸ 各】visual sense；vision

视力【xi⁶lig⁹ 历】vision；sight

视听【xi⁶ ting³亭 】seeing and hearing；what is seen and heard

视线【xi⁶ xin³扇 】line of vision；line of sight

视野【xi⁶yê⁵ 惹】field of vision

视而不见【xi⁶ yi⁴ bed⁷ gin³移毕建】look but see not

视若无睹【xi⁶ yêg⁸ mou⁴ dou² 药毛岛】take no notice of what one sees

视死如归【xi⁶xêi²yû⁴guei¹ 四² 余龟】look upon death as going home

侍【xi⁶ 是】wait upon；attend upon；serve

侍从【xi⁶qung⁴ 虫】attendants；retinue

侍奉【xi⁶gung⁶ 凤】wait upon；attend upon

侍卫【xi⁶wei⁶ 惠】imperial bodyguard

侍者【xi⁶jê² 姐】attendant；servant；waiter

伺【xi⁶ 是；ji⁶ 自】watch；await

伺候【xi⁶heo⁶ 后】wait upon；serve

伺机【xi⁶gêi¹ 基】watch for one's chance

驷【xi³ 试】〈n.〉驷马【xi³mα⁵ 码】a team of four horses

肆【xi³ 试；xēi³ 四】wanton；unbridled；shop；four

肆虐【xi³yêg⁹ 若】wreak havoc

肆意【xi³yi³ 薏】wantonly；wilfully

肆无忌惮【xi³mou⁴gēi⁶dαn⁶ 毛技但】unbridled；brazen；unscrupulous

是【xi⁶ 示】correct；right；yes；this；praise；justify

是的【xi⁶dig⁷ 滴⁷】yes；right；that's it ＝系嘅【hei⁶gē³】＝啱嘅【ngαm¹gē³】

是非【xi⁶fēi¹ 飞】right and wrong；quarrel；dispute

是否【xi⁶ feo² 浮²】whether or not；whether；if

是必【xi⁶bid⁷ 别⁷】may be；possible；must ∽【普】势必；一定

是但【xi⁶dαn⁶ 蛋⁶】simply ＝【普】随便；哪个都行

豉【xi⁶ 是】fermented soya beans，salted or otherwise

豉油【xi⁶yeo⁴ 由】soya sauce ＝【普】酱油

豉汁【xi⁶jeb⁷ 执】black bean sauce ＝【普】以豆豉、酱油为主体熬成的调味液

莳【xi⁶ 是；xi⁴ 时】transplant

莳秧【xi⁶yêng¹ 央】transplant rice seedlings ＝插秧【qαb⁸yêng¹】

消【xiu¹ 销】disappear；vanish；eliminate；dispel；remove；while away（the time）；need

消沉【xiu¹ qem⁴侵⁴】downhearted；low-spirited；dejected；depressed

消除【xiu¹ qêû⁴徐 】eliminate；dispel；remove

消毒【xiu¹dug⁹ 独】disinfect；sterilize

消防【xiu¹fong⁴ 房】fire control；fire fighting

消费【xiu¹fei³ 废】consume

消耗【xiu¹hou³ 好³】consume；use up；deplete

消化【xiu¹fa³ 花³】digest

消极【xiu¹gig⁹ 激⁹】megative；passive

消灭【xiu¹mid⁹ 蔑】perish；die out；eliminate

消磨【xiu¹ mo⁴摩⁴】wear down；while away

消遣【xiu¹hin² 显】divert oneself；pastime

消散【xiu¹xαn³ 汕】scatter and disappear；dissipate

消失【xiu¹xed⁷ 室】disappear；vanish；dissolve

消逝【xiu¹ xei⁶ 誓】die away；vanish；elapse

消瘦【xiu¹xeo³ 秀】become thin

消亡【xiu¹mong⁴ 忘】wither away；die out

消息【xiu¹xig⁷ 色 】news；information；tidings

消炎【xiu¹yim⁴ 严】diminish inflammation

消夜【xiu¹yē⁶ 野⁶】midnight snack；have a midnight snack；supper ＝【普】夜餐

消肿【xiu¹ jung² 种² 】subsidence of a swelling；detumescence

烧【xiu¹ 消】burn；cook；bake；heat；stew after frying or fry after stewing；roast；run a fever；fever

烧饼【xiu¹bēng² 柄²】sesame seed cake

烧火【xiu¹fo² 伙】make a fire；light a fire

烧酒【xiu¹jeo² 走】spirit usu. distilled from sorghum or maize；white spirit

烧卖【xiu¹ mαi²埋²】a steamed dumpling

with the dough gathered at the top

烧伤【xiu¹xêng¹双】burn

烧香【xiu¹hêng¹乡】burn joss sticks(before an idol)

烧灼【xiu¹jêg³雀】burn; scorch; singe

烧鸡【xiu¹gei¹继¹】roast chicken

烧肉【xiu¹yug⁹玉】roasted pork =【普】烤猪肉

烧乳猪【xiu¹yü⁵jü¹语朱】roasted small pig =【普】烤小猪

宵 【xiu¹消】night

宵禁【xiu¹gem³咁】curfew

逍 【xiu¹消】〈a.〉逍遥【xiu¹yiu⁴尧】free and unfettered

逍遥法外【xiu¹yiu⁴fad⁸ngoi⁶尧发碍】go scot-free

萧 【xiu¹消】desolate; dreary; a surname

萧墙【xiu¹qêng⁴场】screen wall facing the gate of a Chinese house

萧瑟【xiu¹xêd⁷恤】rustie in air; bleak

萧疏【xiu¹xo¹梳】desolate; thinly scattered

萧索【xiu¹xog⁹是恶⁸】bleak and chilly; desolate

萧条【xiu¹tiu⁴跳⁴】desolate; bleak; depression

潇 【xiu¹消】(of water)deep and clear

潇洒【xiu¹xa²耍²】natural and unrestrained

潇潇【xiu¹xiu¹】whistling and pattering; drizzly

潇湘【xiu¹xêng¹双】slim; pretty

箫 【xiu¹消】a vertical bamboo flute

霄 【xiu¹消】clouds; sky; heaven

霄汉【xiu¹hon³看】the sky; the firmament

硝 【xiu¹消】nitre; saltpetre; tawing

硝石【xiu¹xêg⁹硕】nitre; saltpetre

硝酸【xiu¹xün¹孙】nitric acid

硝化【xiu¹fa³花³】nitrify

硝烟【xiu¹yin¹燕¹】smoke of gunpowder

销 【xiu¹消】melt(metal); cancel; annul; sell; market; expend; spend; pin

销毁【xiu¹wei²委】destroy by melting or burning

销魂【xiu¹wen⁴云】feel transported

销路【xiu¹lou⁶露】sale; market

销售【xiu¹xeo⁶受】sell; be on sale

销量【xiu¹lêng⁶亮】sales volume

销赃【xiu¹jong¹妆】disposal of stolen goods

小 【xiu²少²】small; little; petty; minor; for a while; for a short time; young

小半【xiu²bun³搬³】less than half; lesser part

小便【xiu²bin⁶辨】urinate; pass water; urine

小菜【xiu²qoi³蔡】pickles; common dishes

小肠【xiu²qêng⁴场】small intestine

小车【xiu²qē¹奢】wheelbarrow; sedan (car)

小食【xiu²xig⁹蚀】snack; cold dish =【普】小吃

小刀【xiu²dou¹都】small sword; pocket knife = 刀仔【dou¹jei²济²】

小调【xiu²diu⁶掉】ditty; minor

小队【xiu²dêu⁶对⁶】team; squad

小儿【xiu²yi⁴移】children; my son

小贩【xiu²fan²反】pedlar; vendor; hawker

小费【xiu² fei³ 废】tip; gratuity

小鬼【xiu² guei² 轨 】imp; goblin; little devil

小孩【xiu² hai⁴ 鞋】child = 细佬哥【xei³ lou² go¹】

小伙子【xiu² fo² ji² 火止】lad; young fellow = 后生哥【heo⁶ xang¹ go¹】

小结【xiu² gid⁸ 洁 】brief summary; summarize briefly

小姐【xiu² jē² 借²】Miss; young lady

小看【xiu² hon³ 汉】look down upon; belittle = 睇小【tei² xiu²】

小康【xiu² hong¹ 匡】comparatively well-off

小麦【xiu² meg⁹ 默】wheat

小米【xiu² mei⁵ 迷⁵】millet

小品【xiu² ben² 禀】essay; sketch

小气【xiu² hēi³ 器 】stingy; mean; petty; get angry and unhappy very fast

小人【xiu² yen⁴ 仁】a person of low position; a base person; villain

小时【xiu² xi 是⁴】hour

小事【xiu² xi⁶ 士】trifle; petty thing

小数【xiu² xou³ 素】decimal

小说【xiu² xūd⁸ 雪】novel; fiction

小偷【xiu² teo¹ 投¹】petty thief; pilferer

小心【xiu² xem¹ 深】take care; be careful

小型【xiu² ying⁴ 形】small-sized; miniature

小学【xiu² hog⁹ 鹤】primary school; elementary school

小子【xiu² ji² 止】boy; bloke; fellow; chap = 靓仔【lēng¹ jei²】

小组【xiu² jou² 祖】group

小册子【xiu² qag⁸ ji² 策止】booklet; pamphlet

小聪明【xiu² qung¹ ming⁴ 充名】cleverness in trivial matters; petty trick

小轿车【xiu² kiu⁴ qē¹ 乔奢 】sedan (car); limousine

小老婆【xin² lou⁵ po⁴ 鲁颇⁴】concubine

小两口【xiu² lêng⁵ heo² 俩厚²】young couple

小卖部【xiu² mai⁶ bou⁶ 买⁶ 步】a small shop; buffet

小朋友【xiu² peng⁴ yeo⁵ 凭有】children; little boys or girls

小便宜【xiu² pin⁴ yi⁴ 片⁴ 移】small gain

小人物【xiu² yen⁴ med⁹ 仁勿】a nobody; cipher

小商品【xiu² xêng¹ ben² 双禀】small commodities

小时候【xiu² xi⁴ heo⁶ 是⁴ 后】in one's childhood

小市民【xiu² xi⁵ men⁴ 示⁵ 文】urban petty bourgeois

小算盘【xiu² xün³ pun⁴ 蒜盆】selfish calculations

小提琴【xiu² tei⁴ kem⁴ 堤禽】violin

小学生【xiu² hog⁹ xeng¹ 鹤笙】pupil; schoolchild

小夜曲【xiu² yē⁶ kug⁷ 野⁶ 卡屋⁷】serenade

小意思【xiu² yi³ xi¹ 薏司】mere trifle

小儿科【xiu² yi⁴ fo¹ 移货¹】paediatrics; a trivial matter; naive

小心眼【xiu² xem¹ ngan⁵ 深雁⁵】narrow-minded; petty = 心胸窄【xem¹ hung¹ jag⁸】

小本经营【xiu² bun² ging¹ ying⁴ 苯京仍】business with a small capital; do business in a small way

小道消息【xiu² dou⁶ xiu¹ xig⁷ 度烧式】hearsay; grapevine

小恩小惠【xiu² yen¹ xiu² wei⁶ 因卫】petty favours

小巧玲珑【xiu² hao² ling⁴ lung⁴ 考铃龙】small and exquisite

小手小脚【xiu² xeo² xiu² gêg⁸ 守格约⁸】stingy; timid

小题大作【xiu² tei⁴ dai⁶ jog⁸ 题歹⁶ 昨】make a mountain out of a molehill

小心翼翼【xiu² xem¹ yig⁹ yig⁹ 深亦亦】with great care; cautiously

小巫见大巫【xiu² mou⁴ gin³ dai⁶ mou⁴ 毛建歹⁶】like a small sorcerer in the presence of a great one—feel dwarfed

少 【xiu³ 笑; xiu² 小】young; young master; few; little; less; be short; lack; lose; be missing; a little while; a moment; stop; quit

少壮【xiu³ jong³ 葬】young and vigorous

少妇【xiu³ fu⁵ 付⁵】young married woman

少奶【xiu³ nai¹ 那埃¹】young mistress of the house =【普】少奶奶

少女【xiu³ nêû⁵ 那虚⁵】young girl

少爷【xiu³ yê⁴ 椰 】young master of the house

少将【xiu³ jêng³ 酱】major general; rear admiral

少量【xiu² lêng⁶ 亮】a small amount; a little; a few

少刻【xiu² heg⁷ 克】after a little while; a moment later; presently = 一阵间【yed⁷ jen⁶ gan¹】=【普】少顷

少数【xiu² xou² 素】small number; few; minority

少许【xiu² hêû² 栩】a little; a few = 啲哚【did⁷ dê¹】

啸 【xiu³ 笑】whistle; howl; roar

笑 【xiu³ 啸】smile; laugh; ridicule; laugh at

笑柄【xiu³ bêng³ 病³】laughingstock; butt

笑话【xiu³ wa² 华²】joke; jest; laugh at; ridicule

笑脸【xiu³ lim⁵ 廉⁵】smiling face

笑剧【xiu³ kêg⁹ 展】farce

笑料【xiu³ liu² 了²】laughingstock; joke

笑纳【xiu³ nab⁹ 呐】kindly accept

笑容【xiu³ yung⁴ 熔】smiling expression; smile

笑谈【xiu³ tam⁴ 谭】laughingstock

笑窝【xiu³ wo¹ 涡】dimple

笑颜【xiu³ ngan⁴ 雁⁴】smiling face

笑靥【xiu³ yib⁸ 叶⁸】dimple; smiling face

笑哈哈【xiu³ ha¹ ha¹ 虾】laughingly; with a laugh

笑眯眯【xiu³ mêi¹ mêi¹ 尾¹】smilingly

笑嘻嘻【xiu³ hēi¹ hēi¹ 希】grinning; smiling broadly

笑里藏刀【xiu³ lêu⁵ qong⁴ dou¹ 吕床都】hide a dagger in a smile — with murderous intent behind one's smiles

笑吟吟【xiu³ yem⁴ yem⁴ 淫】smiling

笑逐颜开【xiu³ jug⁹ ngan⁴ hoi¹ 浊雁⁴ 海¹】beam with smiles; be wreathed in smiles

笑口噬噬【xiu³ heo² xei⁴ xei⁴ 厚² 逝⁴】smiling at all times

韶 【xiu⁴ 少⁴】splendid; beautiful

韶光【xiu⁴ guong¹ 胱 】beautiful springtime; glorious young

绍 【xiu⁶ 肇】carry on; continue

绍菜【xiu⁶ qoi³ 蔡】Chinese lettuce

绍兴酒【xiu⁶hing¹jeo² 兄走】Shaoxing rice wine

邵【xiu⁶ 绍】a surname

肇【xiu⁶ 绍】start; commence; cause (trouble, etc.)

肇端【xiu⁶dün¹ 段¹】beginning

肇祸【xiu⁶wo⁶ 和⁶】cause trouble

肇事【xiu⁶xi⁶ 示】cause trouble

兆【xiu⁶ 绍】sign; omen; protend; foretell; million; a million millions; billion

兆头【xiu⁶teo⁴ 投】sign; omen; portent

闪【xim² 陕】dodge; get out of the way; twist; sprain; lightning; flash; shine; leave behind

闪避【xim²bēi⁶ 备】dodge; sidestep

闪躲【xim²do² 朵】dodge; evade

闪开【xim² hoi¹ 海¹】get out of the way; dodge

闪电【xim²din⁶ 甸】lightning

闪光【xim²guong¹ 胱】flash of light; gleam

闪闪【xim²xim²】sparkle; glisten

闪烁【xim² xêg⁸ 削 】twinkle; glimmer; evasive; scintillation

闪现【xim²yin⁶ 燕⁶】flash before one

闪耀【xim²yiu⁶ 尧⁶】glitter; shine

陕【xim² 闪】short for Shanxi Province

陕西【xim²xei¹ 筛】Shanxi(Province)

婵【xim⁶ 蝉】lovely

婵娟【xim⁴gün¹ 捐】lovely(used in ancien-writings to describe women); the moon

蝉【xim⁴ 蝉】cicada

蝉联【xim⁴lün⁴ 李】continue to hold a post or title

禅【xim⁴ 蝉; xin⁶ 善】deep meditation; dhyana; Buddhist

禅师【xim⁴xi¹ 司】honorific title for a Buddhist monk

禅宗【xim⁴jung¹ 中】the Chan sect; Dhyana; Zen

禅让【xin⁶ yêng⁶ 样】abdicate and hand over the crown to another person

蟾【xim⁴ 蝉】〈n.〉蟾蜍【xim⁴qü⁴ 厨】toad; the fabled toad in the moon; the moon

蟾宫【xim⁴gung¹ 公】the moon

赡【xim⁶ 蝉⁶】〈v.〉赡养【xim⁶yêng⁵ 氧】support; provide for

檐【xim⁴ 蝉】eaves; ledge; brim

檐沟【xim⁴keo¹ 购¹】eaves gutter＝瓦坑【nga⁵hang¹】

仙【xin¹ 先】celestial being; immortal

仙人【xin¹ yen⁴ 仁】celestial being; immortal

仙女【xin¹nêü⁵ 那虚⁵】female celestial

仙姑【xin¹ gu¹ 菇 】female immortal; sorceress

仙鹤【xin¹hog⁹ 学】red-crowned crane

仙境【xin¹ging² 景】fairyland; wonderland

仙丹【xin¹dan¹ 单】elixir of life

仙逝【xin¹xei⁶ 誓】pass away

仙人掌【xin¹yen⁴jêng² 仁蒋】＜n.＞cactus

仙山琼阁【xin¹xan¹king⁴gog⁸ 珊倾⁴角】a jewelled palace in elfland's hills

仙屄【xin¹xi² 史】cents＝【普】金属分币; 零钱

先【xin¹ 仙】earlier; before; first; elder generation; deceased; late; earlier on; then

先时【xin¹xi⁴ 是⁴】last time = 【普】从前; 以前

先头【xin¹teo⁴ 投】just now = 头先【teo⁴ xin¹】=【普】刚才

先生【xin¹ xang¹ 是罂¹】teacher; an address for men; Mr. (mister); gentleman; sir

先排【xin¹pai² 牌²】some time ago = 【普】前一段时间

先辈【xin¹ bui³背 】elder generation; ancestor

先导【xin¹dou⁶ 度】guide; forerunner

先锋【xin¹fung¹ 风】vanguard; van

先后【xin¹heo⁶ 候】early or late; priority; order; successively

先进【xin¹jên³ 俊】advanced

先例【xin¹lei⁶ 厉】precedent

先烈【xin¹lid⁹ 列】martyr

先令【xin¹ling⁶ 另】shilling; schilling

先前【xin¹qin⁴ 钱】before; previously

先遣【xin¹xin² 显】sent in advance

先驱【xin¹kêü¹ 拘】pioneer; forerunner

先人【xin¹ yen⁴仁 】ancestor; my late father

先世【xin¹xei³ 细】forefathers; ancestors

先天【xin¹tin¹ 田¹】congenital; innate

先行【xin¹heng⁴ 衡】go ahead of the rest; beforehand

先兆【xin¹xiu⁶ 肇】omen; portent; sign

先知先觉【xin¹ji¹xin¹gog⁸ 之角】a person of foresight; having foresight

先见之明【xin¹gin³ji¹ming⁴ 建支名】prophetic vision

先发制人【xin¹fad⁸jei³yen⁴ 法济仁】gain the initiative by striking first

先礼后兵【xin¹ lei⁵ heo⁶ bing¹厉⁵ 候冰】take strong measures only after courteous ones fail

先入为主【xin¹ yeb⁹ wei⁴ jü² 邑⁹ 维煮】First impressions are strongest. be prejudiced

先声夺人【xin¹ xing¹ düd⁹ yen⁴升得月⁹仁】forestall one's opponent by a show of strength

先斩后奏【xin¹jam⁶heo⁶jeo³ 湛² 候周³】act first and report afterwards

先下手为强【xin¹ha⁶xeo²wei⁴kêng⁴ 夏守维卡香⁴】He who strikes first gains the advantage.

鲜【xin¹ 仙; xin² 冼】little; rare; fresh; bright; tasty; delicacy; aquatic foods

鲜甜【xin¹tim⁴ 添⁴】tasty; delicious = 【普】新鲜甜美

鲜见【xin²gin³ 建】rarely seen

鲜花【xin¹fa¹ 化¹】fresh flowers; flowers

鲜货【xin¹fo³ 课】fresh fruit; fresh aquatic foods; fresh medicinal herbs

鲜美【xin¹mēi⁵ 尾】delicious; tasty

鲜明【xin¹ ming⁴名 】(of colour) bright; distinct clear-cut

鲜嫩【xin¹nün⁶ 那渊⁶】fresh and tender

鲜血【xin¹hüd⁸ 黑月⁸】blood

鲜艳【xin¹yim⁶ 验】bright-coloured

酰【xin¹ 先】〈n.〉acyl

冼【xin² 藓】a surname

藓【xin² 冼】〈n.〉moss

癣【xin² 冼】tinea; ringworm

铣【xin² 冼】mill

铣床【xin² qong⁴ 苍⁴】milling machine; miller

铣刀【xin²dou¹ 都】milling cutter

跣【xin² 冼】barefooted(跣足【xin²jug⁷】)

线【xin³ 腺】thread; string; wire; sth. shaped like a line, thread, etc.; made of cotton thread; line; route; boundary; brink; clue; a ray; a gleam

线步【xin³bou⁶部】stitches on clothing = 【普】车缝时的线路痕迹;车缝时的走线功夫

线材【xin³qoi⁴ 才】wire rod

线段【xin³dün⁶ 端⁶】line segment

线路【xin³lou⁶ 露】circuit; line; route

线描【xin³miu⁴ 苗】line drawing

线圈【xin³hün¹ 喧】coil

线索【xin³xog⁸ 司恶⁸】clue; thread

线条【xin³tiu⁴ 跳⁴】line; lines

线头【xin³teo⁴ 投】the end of a thread; an odd piece of thread

线性【xin³xing³ 姓】linear

腺【xin³ 扇】gland

扇【xin³ 线】fan; leaf; 〈classifier.〉a door(or window);incite; fan up; stir up

扇子【xin³ji² 止】fan

扇形【xin³ying⁴ 型】fan-shaped; sector

扇动【xin³ dung⁶洞 】fan; flap; instigate; stir up

扇风点火【xin³fung¹dim²fo² 丰店² 伙】fan the flames; inflame and agitate people

煽【xin³ 扇】incite; instigate; fan up; stir up

蹁【xin³ 扇】slip and fall down =【普】打滑;滑脱

蹁脚【xin³gê⁸ 格约⁸】The foot is sliped. =【普】脚踩不稳,滑脱

劏【xin³ 扇】〈n.〉劏鸡【xin³gei¹ 继¹】capon =【普】阉鸡

鳝【xin⁵ 扇⁵】eel; finless eel

善【xin⁶ 膳】good; satisfactory; perfect; kind; friendly; be good at; properly; be apt to

善良【xin⁶lêng⁴ 凉】good and honest;kind-hearted

善心【xin⁶xem¹ 深】mercy; benevolence

善意【xin⁶ yi³ 薏】goodwill; good intentions

善举【xin⁶ gêü² 矩】philanthropic act or project

善于【xin⁶yü¹ 迂】be good at ; be adept in

善后【xin⁶ heo⁶ 候】deal with problems arising from an accident, etc.

善终【xin⁶jung¹ 中】die a natural death

善罢甘休【xin⁶ba⁶gem¹yeo¹ 吧⁶ 金优】leave the matter at that; let it go at that

善始善终【xin⁶qi²xin⁶jung¹ 齿 中】start well and end well

善有善极,恶有恶报【xin⁶yeo⁵xin⁶bou³, ngog⁸yeo⁵ngog⁸bou³ 友布岳⁸】Good will be rewarded with good, and evil with evil.

膳【xin⁶ 善】meals; board

膳食【xin⁶xig⁹ 蚀】meals; food

膳费【xin⁶fei³ 废】board expenses

缮【xin⁶ 善】repair; mend; copy; write out

房屋修缮【fong⁴ngug⁷xeo¹xin⁶ 防额哭⁷收】house repairing

缮写【xin⁶xē² 舍²】write out; copy

擅【xin⁶ 善】arrogate to oneself; be good at

擅自【xin⁶ji⁶治 】do sth. without authorization

擅长【xin⁶qêng⁴ 祥】be good at; be expert in

擅离职守【xin⁶lēi⁴jig⁷xeo² 漓积手】be absent from one's post without leave

嬗【xin⁶ 善】evolution

嬗变【xin⁶bin³ 边³】evolution; transmutation

升【xing¹ 星】rise; hoist; go up; promote; litre; a unit of dry measure for grain（＝1 litre）

升级【xing¹ keb⁷ 给】go up（one grade, etc.）; escalate

升格【xing¹gag⁸ 隔】promote; upgrade

升腾【xing¹teng⁴ 藤】lea pup; rise

升华【xing¹ wa⁴铧】sublimation; distillation

升平【xing¹ping² 屏】peace

升旗【xing¹kēi⁴ 奇】hoist a flag

升学【xing¹ hog⁹ 鹤】go to a school of a higher grade

升值【xing¹jig⁹ 直】revalue; appreciate

升降机【xing¹gong³gēi¹ 钢基】elevator; lift

声【xing¹ 升；xēng¹ 是镜¹】sound; voice; make a sound; initial consonant; tone; reputation;〈classifier.〉the unit of sound

声音【xing¹yem¹ 阴】sound; voice

声波【xing¹ bo¹坡 】sound wave; acoustic wave

声浪【xing¹long⁶ 朗⁶】voice; clamour

声称【xing¹ qing¹ 清】profess; claim; assert

声带【xing¹dai³ 戴】vocal cords; sound track

声调【xing¹diu⁶ 掉】tone; note

声名【xing¹ ming⁴ 明】reputation = 名声【ming⁴ xing¹】

声明【xing¹xing⁴ 名】state; declare; statement

声母【xing¹mou⁵ 武】initial consonant

声气【xēng¹ hēi³戏】information; voice; tone; hope; news

声频【xing¹pen⁴ 贫】acoustic frequency

声讨【xing¹tou² 土】denounce; condemn

声喉【xing¹heo⁴ 侯】the part of the throat that produces voice =【普】嗓子；嗓音

声望【xing¹mong⁶ 亡】popularity; prestige

声威【xing¹wei¹ 委¹】renown; prestige

声息【xing¹ xig⁷色】sound; noise; information

声响【xing¹hêng² 享】sound; noise

声言【xing¹ yin⁴然 】profess; claim; declare

声誉【xing¹yü 预】reputation; fame; prestige

声援【xing¹ yün⁴元】express support for; support

声乐【xing¹ngog⁹ 岳】vocal music

声张【xing¹jêng¹ 章】make public; disclose

声东击西【xing¹dung¹gig⁷xei¹ 冬激筛】make a feint to the east and attack in the west

声泪俱下【xing¹ lêü⁶ kêü¹ ha⁶ 类拘夏】shedding tears while speaking

声色俱厉【xing¹ xig⁷ kêü¹ lei⁶ 式拘励】stern in voice and countenance

声嘶力竭【xing¹xi¹lig⁹kid⁸ 司历揭】shout oneself hoarse

星【xing¹ 升】star; heavenly body; bit; particle; small marks on the arm of a steelyard indicating "jin" and its fractions

星星【xing¹xing¹】tiny spot; star

星辰【xing¹xen⁴ 臣】stars

星斗【xing¹deo² 豆】stars

星河【xing¹ho⁴ 何】the Milky Way

星火【xing¹fo² 伙】spark; shooting star

星期【xing¹kêi⁴ 其】week; Sunday

星球【xing¹keo⁴ 求】celestial body

星散【xing¹xan³ 汕】scattered far and wide

星体【xing¹tei² 睇】celestial body

星宿【xing¹xug⁷ 缩】constellation

星夜【xing¹yē⁶ 野⁶】on a starlit night; by night

星云【xing¹wen⁴ 耘】nebula

星座【xing¹jo⁶ 坐】constellation

星君【xing¹ guen¹ 军】a naughty boy =【普】顽皮的小孩;淘气鬼

星罗棋布【xing¹lo⁴kêi⁴bou³ 锣其棋报】scattered all over like stars in the sky or men on a chessboard

星星点点【xing¹ xing¹ dim² dim² 店²】tiny spots

星转斗移【xing¹jün²deo²yi⁴ 专² 豆² 而】change in the positions of the stars—change of the seasons; passage of time

惺【xing¹ 星】clearheaded

惺忪【xing¹xung¹ 嵩】(of eyes)not yet fully open on waking up

惺惺【xing¹ xing¹】clearheaded; awake; wise

惺惺作态【xing¹xing¹jog⁸tai³ 昨太】be affected; simulate

猩【xing¹ 星】orangutan

猩猩【xing¹xing¹】orangutan

猩红【xing¹hung⁴ 洪】scarlet; bloodred

猩红热【xing¹hung⁴yid⁹ 洪 衣泄⁹】scarlet fever

腥【xing¹ 星;xēng¹ 是镜¹】raw meat or fish; having the smell of fish, seafood, etc.

腥味【xēng¹ mēi⁶ 未】smelling of fish; fishy

腥臭【xing¹qeo³ 凑】stinking smell of rotten fish

腥气【xēng¹ hēi³戏 】the smell of fish, seafood, etc.; stinking; fishy

腥鳁鳁【xēng¹wen¹wen¹ 温】the unpleasant smell from fish∽【普】很腥;腥气袭人

醒【xing² 星²;xēng² 是镜²】regain consciousness; sober up; come to; wake up; be clear in mind; be striking

醒目【xing²mug⁹ 木】catch the eye; be striking; smart; intelligent

醒目仔【xing²mug⁹jei² 木济²】one who is smart and wise =【普】聪明的小子

醒定【xing²ding⁶ 锭】pay attention =【普】警惕性高而又沉着镇定;充分注意;留心

醒水【xing² xêü² 瑞²】alert; alarmed =【普】机警;警惕;警戒

醒胃【xing² wei⁶ 卫】appetizing＝【普】刺激食欲

醒酒【xing² jeo² 走】dispel the effects of alcohol

醒悟【xing² ng⁶ 误】come to realize the truth, one's error, etc.; wake up to reality

性【xing³ 姓】nature; character; property; quality; sex; gender

性别【xing³ bid⁹ 必⁹】sexual; distinction; sex

性病【xing³ bēng⁶ 柄⁶】venereal disease; V.D.

性欲【xing³yug⁹ 玉】sexual desire

性器【xing³ hēi³戏】sexual organs; genitals

性交【xing³gao¹ 胶】sexual intercourse

性命【xing³ming⁶ 名⁶】life

性格【xing³gag⁸ 隔】nature; disposition

性急【xing³ geb⁷格合⁷】impatient; short-tempered

性能【xing³ neng⁴那莺⁴】function; property

性情【xing³qing⁴ 程】disposition; temper

性质【xing³jed⁷ 侄⁷】quality; nature

性状【xing³ jong⁶ 撞 】shape and properties; properties

性子【xing³ ji² 止】temper; strength; potency

姓【xing³ 性】surname; family name

姓名【xing³ming⁴ 明】surname and personal name; full name

姓氏【xing³xi⁶ 示】surname

胜【xing³ 姓】victory; success; surpass; superb; be equal to; bear

胜败【xing³ bai⁶摆⁶】victory or defeat; success or failure＝胜负【xing³fu⁶】

胜利【xing³lēi⁶ 俐】victory; triumph; successfully

胜券【xing³hün³ 劝】confidence in victory

胜任【xing³ yem⁶壬⁶】competent; qualified; equal

胜似【xing³qi⁵ 恃】be better than; surpass

胜诉【xing³xou³ 素】win a lawsuit

胜算【xing³xün³ 蒜】a stratagem which ensures success

胜仗【xing³ jêng³ 涨】victorious battle; victory

圣【xing³ 胜】sage; saint; holy; sacred; emperor

圣诞【xing³dan³. 旦】the birthday of Jesus Christ

圣地【xing³ dēi⁶得希⁶】the Holy Land; sacred place; shrine

圣洁【xing³ gid⁸ 结】holy and pure

圣经【xing³ ging¹京 】the Holy Bible; the Bible

圣母【xing³ mou⁵武】a female deity; the (Blessed) Virgin Mary; Madonna

圣人【xing³yen⁴ 仁】sage; wise man

圣贤【xing³ yin⁴言 】sages and men of virtue

圣旨【xing³ji² 止】imperial edict

蛏【xing³】razor clam(蛏子【xing³ji² 止】)

丞【xing⁴ 成】assist; assistant officer

丞相【xing⁴xêng³ 商³】prime minister

成【xing⁴ 诚；xêng³ 是镜⁴】accomplish; succeed; become; achievement; result; fully grown; established; in considerable numbers or amounts; all right; O.K.; able; one tenth; a surname

成败【xing⁴bai⁶ 摆⁶】success or failure

成本【xing⁴bun² 苯】cost

成材【xing⁴qoi⁴ 才】grow to full size; become a useful person

成都【xing⁴dou¹ 刀】Chengdu

成堆【xēng⁴dêü⁴ 队¹】form a pile; be in heaps

成分【xing⁴ fen⁶ 份】composition; component part; one's profession or economic status

成风【xing⁴ fung¹ 丰】become a common practice

成个【xēng⁴ go³ 哥³】be well formed; grow to a good size; be in the proper form; whole =【普】成个儿;整个

成功【xing⁴gung¹ 工】succeed; success

成果【xing⁴ guo² 戈²】achievement; fruit; gain

成婚【xing⁴ fen¹ 分】get married = 成家【xēng⁴ga¹】= 成亲【xing⁴qen¹】

成活【xing⁴wud⁹ 乌阔⁹】survive

成绩【xing⁴ jig⁷ 积】result; achievement; success

成见【xing⁴ gin³ 建】preconceived idea; prejudice

成交【xing⁴ gao¹ 胶】strike a bargain; clinch a deal

成就【xing⁴jeo⁶ 袖】achievement; success

成立【xing⁴ leb⁹ 笠⁹】found; set up; be tenable

成命【xing⁴ming⁶ 名⁶】order already issued

成年【xing⁴nin⁴ 捻⁴】grow up; adult; year after year

成批【xēng⁴pei¹ 拍矮¹】group by group; in batches

成品【xing⁴ben² 禀】end product

成全【xing⁴qün⁴ 存】help

成群【xing⁴kuen⁴ 裙】in groups

成人【xing⁴yen⁴ 仁】grow up; adult; grown-up

成仁【xing⁴ yen⁴ 人】die for a righteous cause

成色【xing⁴ xig⁷ 式】the percentage of gold; quality

成事【xing⁴ xi⁶ 士】accomplish sth.; succeed

成熟【xing⁴xug⁹ 孰】ripe; mature

成套【xing⁴tou⁴ 兔】form a complete set; whole set

成为【xing⁴wei⁴ 维】become; turn into

成效【xing⁴hao⁶ 考⁶】effect; result

成性【xing⁴xing³ 姓】by nature

成衣【xing⁴ yi¹ 依】tailoring; ready-made clothes

成因【xing⁴ yen¹ 恩】cause of formation; contributing factor

成语【xing⁴yü⁵ 雨】set phrase; idiom

成员【xing⁴yün⁴ 元】member

成灾【xing⁴joi¹ 哉】cause disaster

成长【xing⁴ jêng² 掌】grow up; grow to maturity

成盘【xing⁴pun⁴ 盆】closing a sales =【普】整盘

成世【xēng⁴xei³ 细】the whole life =【普】整个一生

成日【xēng⁴ yed⁹ 逸】the whole day =【普】整天

成问题【xing⁴men⁶tei⁴ 蚊⁶ 堤】be a problem; be open to question

成气候【xing⁴hēi³heo⁶ 戏后】make good

成龙配套【xing⁴lung⁴pui³tou³ 隆佩吐】fill in the gaps to complete a chain

成人之美【xing⁴ yen⁴ ji¹ mēi⁵ 仁支尾】help sb. to fulfil his wish

成竹在胸【xing⁴ jug⁷ joi⁶ hung¹ 足再⁶ 空】（see"胸有成竹"【hung¹ yeo⁵ xing⁴ jug⁷】）

诚【xing⁴ 成】sincere; honest; really

诚心【xing⁴ xem¹ 深】sincere desire; intentionally

诚恳【xing⁴ hen² 很】sincere

诚然【xing⁴ yin⁴ 言】true; indeed; be sure

诚实【xing⁴ xed⁹ 失⁹】honest

诚意【xing⁴ yi³ 薏】good faith; sincerity

诚挚【xing⁴ ji³ 至】sincere; cordial

承【xing⁴ 成】bear; hold; undertake; be indebted; continue; carry on

承办【xing⁴ ban⁶ 板⁶】undertake

承包【xing⁴ bao¹ 苞】contract

承担【xing⁴ dam¹ 胆¹】bear; undertake

承当【xing⁴ dong¹ 铛】take; bear

承继【xing⁴ gei³ 计】be adopted as heir to one's uncle; adopt one's brother's son

承接【xing⁴ jib⁸ 支叶⁸】continue; carry on; hold out a vessel to have liquid poured into it

承蒙【xing⁴ mung⁴ 朦】be indebted; be granted a favour

承诺【xing⁴ nog⁸ 那恶⁸】promise to undertake

承平【xing⁴ ping⁴ 萍】peaceful

承认【xing⁴ ying⁶ 英⁶】admit; acknowledge; recognize

承受【xing⁴ xeo⁶ 寿】bear; support; inherit

承载【xing⁴ joi³ 再】bear the weight of

承重【xing⁴ qung⁵ 虫⁵】bearing; load-bearing

城【xing⁴ 成】city wall; wall; city; town

城墙【xing⁴ qêng⁴ 场 】city wall = 城垣【xing⁴ wun⁴】

城市【xing⁴ xi⁵ 是⁵】town; city

城镇【xing⁴ jen³ 振】cities and towns

城里【xing⁴ lêû⁵ 吕 】inside the city; in town

城区【xing⁴ kêû¹ 拘】the city proper

城郊【xing⁴ gao¹ 交】outskirts of a town

城门【xing⁴ mun⁴ 扪】city gate

城楼【xing⁴ leo⁴ 留 】a tower over a city gate; gate tower

城池【xing⁴ qi⁴ 迟】city wall and moat; city

城堡【xing⁴ bou² 保】castle

城邦【xing⁴ bong¹ 帮】city-state

城门失火，殃及池鱼【xing⁴ mun⁴ xed⁷ fo², yêng¹ keb⁹ qi⁴ yü⁴ 们室伙，央级⁹ 迟余】When the city gate catches fire, the fish in the moat suffer.

绳【xing⁴ 成；xing² 醒】rope; cord; string; restrict

绳仔【xing⁴ jei² 济² 】small cord; small string = 普 小绳子

绳索【xing⁴ xog⁸ 是恶⁸】rope; cord

绳墨【xing⁴ meg⁹ 默】carpenter's line marker; rules and regulations

乘【xing⁴ 成；xing⁶ 盛】ride; take advantage of; multiply; a war chariot drawn by four horses

乘搭【xing⁴ dab⁸ 答】ride in(a bus, etc.)

乘便【xing⁴ bin⁴ 辨】when it is convenient

乘法【xing⁴ fad⁸ 发】multiplication

乘数【xing⁴ xou³ 素】multiplier

乘方【xing⁴ fong¹ 芳】involution; power

乘积【xing⁴jig⁷ 织】product

乘机【xing⁴gēi¹ 基】seize the opportunity

乘客【xing⁴hag⁸ 赫】passenger

乘凉【xing⁴lêng⁴ 量⁴】enjoy the cool

乘胜【xing⁴xing³ 姓】exploit a victory

乘兴【xing⁴hing³ 庆】while one is in high spirits

乘虚【xing⁴ hêü¹ 墟 】take advantage of a weak point in an opponent's defence

乘风破浪【xing⁴fung¹po³long⁶ 丰颇³ 朗⁶】ride the wind and cleave the waves

剩

【xing⁶ 盛】surplus; remnant

剩低【xing⁶dei¹ 底¹】be left(over); remain = 剩落【xing⁶log⁹ 洛⁹】=【普】剩下

剩余【xing⁶yü⁴ 鱼】surplus; remainder

盛

【xing⁶ 剩】flourishing; prosperous; vigorous; energetic; magnificent; grand; abundant; popular; common; greatly; deeply; a surname; fill; ladle; hold; contain

盛产【xing⁶qan² 铲】abound in; teem with

盛大【xing⁶dai⁶ 歹⁶】grand; magnificent

盛典【xing⁶din² 电²】grand ceremony

盛况【xing⁶fong⁶ 放】grand occasion

盛情【xing⁶qing⁴ 程】great kindness

盛世【xing⁶xei³ 细】flourishing age; heyday

盛事【xing⁶ xi⁶ 士】grand occasion; great event

盛衰【xing⁶ xêü¹ 须】prosperity and decline; rise and fall; ups and downs

盛夏【xing⁶ha⁶ 下】the height of summer; midsummer

盛行【xing⁶ heng⁴ 衡】be current; be in vogue

盛意【xing⁶ yi³ 薏】great kindness; generosity

盛誉【xing⁶yü⁶ 预】great fame

盛赞【xing⁶jan³ 撰】highly praise

盛装【xing⁶gong¹ 妆】splendid attire; rich dress

盛器【xing⁶hēi³ 戏】vessel; receptacle

盛饭【xing⁶fan⁶ 范】fill a bowl with rice = 装饭【jong¹fan⁶】

盛极一时【xing⁶gig⁹yed⁷xi⁴ 击⁹ 壹 士⁴】be in fashion for a time

盛气凌人【xing⁶ hēi³ ling⁴ yen⁴ 戏陵仁】domineering; arrogant; overbearing

塍

【xing⁴ 成】a path between fields

摄

【xib⁸ 涉】absorb; assimilate; shoot; conserve; act for

摄石【xib⁸xēg⁶ 硕】magnet =【普】磁石

摄取【xib⁸qêü² 娶】absorb; take in; shoot

摄影【xib⁸ ying² 映】take a photograph; shoot a film

摄制【xib⁸jei³ 济】produce

摄政【xib⁸jing³ 正】act as regent

摄像机【xib⁸ jêng⁶ gēi¹象基】pickup camera

摄影机【xib⁸ying²gēi¹ 映基】camera

摄氏温度计【xib⁸xi⁶wen¹dou⁶gei³ 士瘟道继】Celsius thermometer

慑

【xib⁸ 涉】fear; be awed

慑服【xib⁸fug⁹ 伏】submit because of fear; succumb; cow sb. into submission

涉

【xib⁸ 摄】wake; ford; go through; involve

涉及【xib⁸keb⁹ 级⁹】involve; relate to

涉猎【xib⁸lib⁹ 罗叶⁹】do desultory reading

涉嫌【xib⁸yim⁴ 严】be suspected

涉足【xib⁸jug⁷ 竹】set foot in

楔【xid⁸ 泄】wedge

楔子【xid⁸ji² 止】dedge; peg; prologue or interlude in Yuan Dynasty drama; prologue in some modern novels

揳【xid⁸ 楔;xib⁸ 涉】drive (a wedge; nail, etc.)

屑【xid⁸ 泄】bits; scraps; crumbs; trifling

纸屑【ji²xid⁸ 止】scraps of paper

不屑【bed⁷xid⁸ 毕】disdain to do sth.

薛【xid⁸ 泄】a surname

亵【xid⁸ 泄】treat with irreverence; obscene; indecent

亵渎【xid⁸dug⁹ 读】blaspheme; profane; pollute

泄【xid⁸ 屑】let out; discharge; release; let out; leak; give vent to; vent

泄漏【xid⁸leo⁶ 馏】leak; let out; divulge

泄露【xid⁸lou⁶ 路】let out; reveal

泄密【xid⁸med⁹ 勿】divulge a secret

泄气【xid⁸hēi³ 戏】lose heart; feel discouraged; disappointing; frustrating

泄水【xid⁸xêu² 瑞²】sluicing

舌【xid⁸ 泄】tongue(of a human being or animal); sth. shaped like a tongue

舌头【xid⁸teo⁴ 投】tongue＝脷【lēi⁶ 利】

舌苔【xid⁸toi⁴ 台】coating on the tongue; fur

舌战【xid⁸ jin³ 箭 】 have a verbal battle with; argue heatedly

式【xig⁷ 拭】type; style; pattern; form; ceremony; ritual; formula; mood; mode

式样【xig⁷yêng² 扬²】style; type; model

式子【xig⁷ji² 止】posture; formula

拭【xig⁷ 式】wipe away; wipe

拭目以待【xig⁷mug⁹yi⁵doi⁶ 木尔代】wait and see

饰【xig⁷ 式】decorations; ornaments; play the role of; impersonate

饰物【xig⁷med⁹ 勿】jewelry; ornaments; decorations

适【xig⁷ 式】fit; suitable; proper; right; comfortable; well; go; follow; pursue

适才【xig⁷qoi⁴ 财】just now＝【普】刚才

适当【xig⁷xong³ 档】suitable; proper

适度【xig⁷dou⁶ 道】appropriate measure

适合【xig⁷heb⁹ 盒】suit; fit

适龄【xing⁷ling⁴ 玲】of the right age

适时【xig⁷xi⁴ 是⁴】at the right moment; in good time; timely

适宜【xig⁷yi⁴ 而】suitable; fit; appropriate

适应【xig⁷ying³ 映³】suit; adapt; fit

适意【xig⁷ yi³ 薏 】agreeable; enjoyable; comfortable

适用【xig⁷yung⁶ 庸⁶】suit; be applicable

适值【xig⁷jig⁹ 直】just when

适中【xig⁷jung¹ 钟】moderate; well situated

适者生存【xig⁷jē²xeng¹qūn⁴ 姐笙全】survival of the fittest

适可而止【xig⁷ ho² yi⁴ ji² 贺² 移子】stop before going too far; not overdo it

适得其反【xig⁷deg⁷kēi⁴fan² 德奇返】run counter to one's desire

释【xig⁷ 析】explain; elucidate; clear up; dispel; let go; release; set free;

Sakyamuni; Buddhism

释放【xig⁷fong³ 况】release; set free

释然【xig⁷ yin⁴言】 feel relieved; feel at ease

释迦牟尼【xig⁷ga¹meo⁴nēi⁴ 家谋你⁴】 Sakyamuni, the founder of Buddhism

析【xig⁷ 色】divide; separate; analyse; dissect

析义【xig⁷yi⁶ 异】analyse the meaning(of a word)

析疑【xig⁷yi⁴ 移】resolve a doubt

析出【xig⁷qêd⁷ 次律⁷】separate out

昔【xig⁷ 惜】former times; the past

昔年【xig⁷nin⁴ 捻⁴】in former years

昔日【xig⁷yed⁹ 溢】in former days

惜【xig⁷ 式】cherish; value highly; spare; grudge; have pity on sb.; feel sorry for sb.

惜别【xig⁷bid⁹ 必⁹】hate to see sb. go

惜力【xig⁷lig⁹ 历】be sparing of one's energy

息【xig⁷熄】breath; news; cease; stop; rest; grow; interest; one's children

息怒【xig⁷nou⁶ 奴⁶】cease to be angry

息肉【xig⁷yug⁹ 玉】polyp; polypus

息事宁人【xig⁷ xi⁶ ning⁴ yen⁴ 士拧⁴ 仁⁴】 patch up a quarrel and reconcile the parties concerned; make concessions to avoid trouble

息息相关【xig⁷xig⁷xêng¹guan¹ 双惯¹】be closely linked; be closely bound up

熄【xig⁷ 息】extinguish; put out

熄灯【xig⁷deng¹ 登】put out the light

熄灭【xig⁷mid⁹ 篾】go out; die out

媳【xig⁷ 息】daughter-in-law

媳妇【xig⁷fu⁵ 府⁵】son's wife; daughter-in-law; the wife of a relative of the younger generation

淅【xig⁷ 析】wash rice

淅沥【xig⁷lig⁷ 历⁷】〈onomatope.〉the sound of rain

晰【xig⁷ 析】clear; distinct

清晰【qing¹xig⁷ 称】distinct

皙【xig⁷ 析】fair-skinned; light-complexioned

蜥【xig⁷ 析】〈n.〉蜥蜴【xig⁷yig⁹ 易】lizard

螅【xig⁷ 息】〈n.〉水螅【xêü²xig⁷ 瑞²】hydra

悉【xig⁷ 息】all; entirely; know; learn; be informed of

悉数【xig⁷xou³ 素】all; enumerate in full detail

悉心【xig⁷xem¹ 深】devote all one's attention; take the utmost care

蟋【xig⁷ 悉】〈n.〉蟋蟀【xig⁷xêd⁷ 摔】cricket

色【xig⁷ 式】colour; look; countenance; kind; scene; scenery; quality; woman's looks; dice

色狼【xig⁷long⁴ 郎】one who is sex-minded ∽【普】色情狂

色彩【xig⁷ qoi² 采】colour; hue; tint; shade

色水【xig⁷xêü² 瑞²】colour; complexion =【普】颜色;面色

色调【xig⁷diu⁴ 掉】tone; hue

色盲【xig⁷mang⁴ 孟⁴】achromatopsia

色情【xig⁷qing⁴ 程】pornographic；sexy

色素【xig⁷xou³ 扫】pigment

色泽【xig⁷jag⁹ 掷】colour and lustre

色纸【xig⁷ji² 止】coloured paper

色仔【xig⁷jei² 济²】dice＝【普】色子

色厉内荏【xig⁷lei⁶noi⁶yem⁶ 丽耐任】fierce of mien but faint of heart

啬【xig⁷ 色】stingy；miserly

穑【xig⁷ 色】(see"稼穑"【ga³xig⁷】)

铯【xig⁷ 色】cesium(C₈)

识【xig⁷ 色】know；knowledge；remember；mark；sign

识记【xig⁷gēi¹ 寄】remember

识别【xig⁷bid⁹ 必⁹】distinguish；discern；spot

识货【xig⁷fo³ 课】know all about the goods

识破【xig⁷po³ 颇³】see through；penetrate

识趣【xig⁷qêu³ 翠】know how to behave in a delicate situation

识字【xig⁷ji⁶ 治】learn to read；become literate

识穿【xig⁷qūn¹ 川】reveal ∽【普】看透

食【xig⁹ 蚀】eat；meal；food；feed；edible；eclipse；bring food to

食物【xig⁹ med⁹勿 】food；eatables；edibles

食品【xig⁹ben² 禀】foodstuff；food

食道【xig⁹dou² 度】esophagus

食量【xig⁹ lêng⁶ 亮】capacity for eating；appetite

食粮【xig⁹lêng⁴ 凉】grain；food

食积【xig⁹jig⁹ 织】dyspepsia；indigestion

食客【xig⁷hag⁸ 赫】a person sponging on an aristocrat

食宿【xig⁹xug⁷ 缩】board and lodging

食堂【xig⁹ tong⁴唐 】dining room；mess hall

食糖【xig⁹tong⁴ 唐】sugar

食盐【xig⁹yim⁴ 严】table salt；salt

食言【xig⁹yin⁴ 然】go back on one's word

食谱【xig⁹pou² 普】recipes；cookbook

食油【xig⁹yeo⁴ 由】edible oil；cooking oil

食用【xig⁹yung⁶ 庸⁶】edible

食欲【xig⁹yug⁹ 玉】appetite

食指【xig⁹ji² 止】index finger；forefinger

食塞米【xig⁹xeg⁷mei⁵ 是黑¹ 迷⁵】one who is not sure of many things＝食屈米【xig⁹wed⁷mei⁵】∽【普】饭桶(比喻某人只会吃饭，办什么事都不可靠、没有把握)

食古不化【xig⁹gu²bed⁷fa³ 鼓毕花³】swallow ancient learning without digesting it；be pedantic

食碗面反碗底【xig⁹wun²min²fan²wun²dei² 腕免² 返抵】not to appreciate or remember the kindness that one has done∽【普】受人恩惠不感恩图报，反而做出对不起恩人的事

蚀【xig⁹ 食；xid⁹ 舌⁹】lose；erode；eclipse

蚀刻【xig⁹heg⁷ 克】etching

蚀本【xid⁹ bun² 苯 】lose one's capital；make a lose in business

蚀底【xid⁹dei² 抵】be disadvantaged；lose out＝【普】吃亏

书【xū¹ 抒】write；style of calligraphy；script；book；letter；document

书本【xū¹bun² 苯】book

书包【xū¹bao¹ 苞】satchel；schoolbag

书页【xū¹yib⁹ 叶】page

书桌【xū¹ jêg⁸ 着⁸】desk；writing desk＝

书台【xū¹ toi²】

书房【xū¹ fong⁴ 防】study

书库【xū¹ fu³ 富】stack room

书店【xū¹ dim³ 点³】bookshop；bookstore

书架【xū¹ ga³ 驾】bookshelf

书籍【xū¹ jig⁹ 直】books；works；literature

书刊【xū¹ hon² 罕】books and periodicals

书摊【xū¹ tan¹ 滩】bookstall；bookstand

书名【xū¹ ming⁴ 明】the title of a book；title

书目【xū¹ mug⁹ 木】booklist；title catalogue

书法【xū¹ fad⁸ 发】penmanship；calligraphy

书记【xū¹ gēi³ 寄】secretary clerk

书面【xū¹ min² 缅²】written；in written form

书皮【xū¹ pēi⁴ 脾】book cover；jacket；cover

书生【xū¹ xeng¹ 笙】intellectual；scholar

书写【xū¹ xē² 舍²】write

书信【xū¹ xên³ 讯】letter；written message ＝书札【xū¹ jad⁸】＝书简【xū¹ gan²】

书友【xū¹ yeo⁵ 有】ex-classmates

书生气【xū¹ xeng¹ hēi³ 笙戏】bookishness

枢【xū¹ 书】pivot；hub；centre

枢纽【xū¹ neo² 扭】pivot；hub；axis

抒【xū¹ 书】express；convey；give expression to

抒发【xū¹ fad⁸ 法】express；voice；give expression to

抒情【xū¹ qing⁴ 程】express one's emotion

舒【xū¹ 抒】stretch；unfold；easy；a surname

舒服【xū¹ fug⁹ 伏】comfortable；be well

舒畅【xū¹ qêng³ 唱】happy；entirely free from worry

舒适【xū¹ xig⁷ 式】comfortable；cosy；snug

舒展【xū¹ jin² 剪】unfold；extend；limber up

舒张【xū¹ jêng¹ 章】diastole

输【xū¹ 书】transport；convey；contribute money；donate；lose；be beaten

输出【xū¹ qêd⁷ 次律⁷】export；output

输入【xū¹ yeb⁹ 邑⁹】import；input

输送【xū¹ xung³ 宋】carry；transport；convey

输血【xū¹ hüd⁸ 黑月⁸】blood transfusion；bolster up

输液【xū¹ yig⁹ 亦】infusion

输氧【xū¹ yêng⁵ 养】oxygen therapy

输电【xū¹ din⁶ 甸】transmit electricity

输理【xū¹ lēi⁵ 李】be in the wrong

输赌【xū¹ dou² 倒】bet ＝【普】打赌

输蚀【xū¹ xid⁹ 舌⁹】poorer；weaker；be disadvantaged ＝【普】比不上别人；吃亏

黍【xū² 暑】broomcorn millet

暑【xū² 署】heat；hot weather

暑天【xū² tin¹ 田¹】hot summer days；dog days

暑热【xū² yid⁹ 衣泄⁹】hot summer weather

暑期【xū² kēi¹ 其】summer vacation time

暑假【xū² ga³ 嫁】summer vacation

署【xū² 暑】a government office；office；make arrangements for；handle by proxy；sign

署名【xū² ning⁴ 明】sign；put one's signature to

鼠【xū² 暑】mouse; rat

鼠辈【xū²bui³ 背】mean creatures; scoundrels

鼠窜【xū²qūn³ 寸】scamper off like a rat

鼠疫【xū²yig⁹ 亦】the plague

鼠目寸光【xū²mug⁹qūn³guong¹ 木川³ 胱】a mouse can see only an inch; be short-sighted

曙【xū⁵ 暑⁵;qū⁵ 柱】daybreak; dawn

曙光【xū⁵guong¹ 胱】first light of morning; dawn

曙色【xū⁵xig⁷ 式】light of early dawn

薯【xū⁴ 殊】potato; yam; stupid

薯莨【xū⁴lêng⁴ 良】〈n.〉dye yam

薯头【xū⁴teo⁴ 投】stupid; a stupid fellow ∽【普】愚笨的;反应迟钝的;笨蛋;傻瓜

殊【xū⁴ 薯】different; outstanding; special; very much; really

殊勋【xū⁴fen¹ 分】outstanding merit

殊死【xū⁴ xēi² 四²】desperate; life-and-death

殊不知【xū⁴bed⁷ji¹ 毕支】little imagine; hardly realize

殊途同归【xū⁴tou⁴tung⁴guei¹ 图铜龟】reach the same goal by different routes

戍【xū³ 暑³】defend; garrison

戍边【xū³bin¹ 鞭】garrison the frontiers

恕【xū³ 戍】forgive; pardon; excuse; excuse me; beg your pardon; forbearance

恕罪【xū³jêū⁶ 叙】pardon an offence; forgive a sin

庶【xū³ 戍】multitudinous; of or by the concubine; so that; so as to

庶几【xū³gēi² 纪】so that; so as to

庶民【xū³men⁴ 文】the common people; the multitude

庶务【xū³mou⁶ 冒】general affair; a person in charge of business matters

竖【xū⁶ 树】vertical; upright; set upright; erect; stand; vertical stroke

竖立【xū⁶leb⁹ 笠⁹】erect; set upright; stand

竖起【xū⁶hēi² 喜】hold up; erect

竖琴【xū⁶kem⁴ 禽】〈n.〉harp

竖子【xū⁶ ji² 止】boy; lad; mean fellow; fellow

树【xū⁶ 竖】tree; plant; cultivate; set up; uphold

树木【xū⁶mug⁹ 目】trees

树林【xū⁶lem⁴ 临】woods; grove

树苗【xū⁶miu⁴ 描】sapling

树皮【xū⁶pēi⁴ 脾】bark

树梢【xū⁶xao¹ 稍¹】the tip of a tree; treetop

树阴【xū⁶yem¹ 音】shade (of a tree)

树枝【xū⁶ji¹ 支】branch; twig

树脂【xū⁶ji¹ 支】resin

树干【xū⁶gon³ 竿³】tree trunk; trunk

树立【xū⁶leb⁹ 笠⁹】set up; establish

树敌【xū⁶dig⁹ 迪】make an enemy of sb.; antagonize

树碑立传【xū⁶bēi¹leb⁹jūn² 悲笠⁹ 转】build up sb.'s public image

树大招风【xū⁶ dai⁶ jiu¹ fung¹ 歹⁶ 焦¹ 丰】A tall tree catches the wind—a person in a high position is liable to be attacked.

树倒猢狲散【xü⁶dou²wu⁴xün¹xan³ 捣胡孙汕】When the tree falls the monkeys scatter—when an influential person falls from power, his hangers-on disperse.

树高万丈，叶落归根【xü⁶gou¹man⁶jêng⁶, yib⁹log⁹guei¹gen¹ 羔慢杖，业洛⁹龟斤】A person residing away from home eventually returns to his native soil.

树欲静而风不止【xü⁶yug⁹jing⁶ yi⁴fung¹ bed⁷ji² 玉净移丰毕子】The tree may prefer calm, but the wind will not subside—the enemies always want to make trouble.

撌【xü² 鼠】⟨n.⟩steal; pilfer

撌野【xü²yē⁵ 惹】steal article =【普】偷东西

孙【xün¹ 狲】grandson; generations below that of the grandchild; second growth of plants; a surname

孙子【xün¹ji² 止】grandson = 个孙【go³ xün¹】= 孙仔【jei²】

孙女【xün¹nêü⁵ 那去⁵】granddaughter

孙媳妇【xün¹ xig⁷ fu⁵ 息付⁵】grandson's wife

狲【xün¹ 孙】(see"猢狲"【wu⁴xün¹】)

酸【xün¹ 孙】acid; sour; tart; sick at heart; grieved; pedantic; tingle; ache

酸味【xün¹mēi⁶ 未】tart flavour; acidity

酸性【xün¹xing³ 姓】acidity

酸痛【xün¹tung³ 同】ache

酸软【xün¹yün⁵ 远】aching and limp

酸梅【xün¹ mui⁴ 霉】smoked plum; dark plum

酸菜【xün¹ qoi³ 蔡】pickled Chinese cabbage

酸牛奶【xün¹ ngeo⁴ nai⁵ 偶⁴ 乃】yoghurt; sour milk

酸溜溜【xün¹ liu¹ liu¹ 辽¹】sour; tingle; ache; sad; mournful

酸微微【xün¹mēi¹mēi¹ 尾¹】sour =【普】(味觉上的)酸溜溜

酸枝【xün¹ji¹ 支】a type of red wood usually used to make furniture

酸甜苦辣【xün¹tim⁴fu²lad⁹ 添⁴ 府罗压⁹】sour, sweet, bitter, hot—joys and sorrows of life

酸㷛烂臭【xün¹ xug⁷ lan⁶ qeo³ 粟兰⁶ 溴】unpleasant smell∽【普】发霉发臭的各种气味集大成

宣【xün¹ 孙】declare; proclaim; announce; lead off; a surname

宣布【xün¹bou³ 报】declare; proclaim; announce

宣称【xün¹qing¹ 清】assert; declare; profess

宣传【xün¹ qün¹全】conduct propaganda; propagate; disseminate; give publicity to

宣告【xün¹gou¹ 高³】declare; proclaim

宣判【xün¹pun³ 潘³】pronounce judgment

宣誓【xün¹xei⁶ 逝】take an oath; make a vow

宣泄【xün¹xid⁸ 屑】lead off; drain; unbosom oneself

宣言【xün¹yin⁴ 盐】declaration; manifesto

宣扬【xün¹yêng¹ 洋】publicize; propagate; advocate

宣战【xün¹jin³ 箭】declare war

宣纸【xün¹ji² 止】Xuan paper, a high quality paper made in Xuancheng

渲【xūn¹ 宣】wash(a piece of drawing paper)with watercolours

渲染【xūn¹ yin⁵ 演⁵】apply colours to a drawing; play up; exaggerate; pile it on

飧【xūn¹ 宣】〈n.〉supper; dinner

选【xūn² 损】select; choose; pick; elect; selections; anthology

选拔【xūn²bed⁹ 跋】select; choose

选材【xūn¹qoi⁴ 才】select material

选购【xūn² keo³ 构】pick out and buy; choose

选集【xūn²jab⁹ 习】selected works; selections

选举【xūn²gêū² 矩】elect

选民【xūn² men⁴ 文】voter; elector; electorate

选票【xūn²piu⁵ 飘³】vote; ballot

选取【xūn²qêū² 娶】select; choose

选手【xūn²xeo² 守】an athlete selected for a sports meet; contestant; player

选修【xūn² xeo¹收】take as an elective course

选样【xūn²yêng² 扬²】sampling; sample

选择【xūn²jag⁹ 泽】select; choose; opt

选种【xūn²jung² 总】seed selection

损【xūn² 选】decrease; lose; harm; damage; sarcastic; caustic; cutting; hurt(skin)

损害【xūn²hoi⁶ 亥】harm; damage; injure

损耗【xūn²hou³ 好³】loss; wear and tear; wastage

损坏【xūn²wai⁶ 怀⁶】damage; injure

损失【xūn²xed⁷ 室】lose; loss; damage

损人利己【xūn²yen⁴lēi⁶gēi² 仁俐几】harm others to benefit oneself

损手烂脚【xūn²xeo²lan⁶gêg⁸ 守兰⁶ 格约⁸】hurt（limbs）=【普】手脚受损伤,发炎而至霉烂

算【xūn³ 蒜】calculate; reckon; compute; include; count; plan; think; suppose; consider; carry weight; at long last; finally; let it be; let it pass

算术【xūn³xêd⁸ 述】arithmetic

算法【xūn³fad⁸ 发】algorithm

算命【xūn³mēng⁶ 莫镜⁶】fortune-telling

算盘【xūn³pun⁴ 盆】abacus

算数【xūn³xou³扫】count; hold; stand; never mind

算系【xūn³hei⁶ 兮⁶】at last =【普】算是

算帐【xūn²jêng³涨】do accounts; balance the books; get even with sb.

算死草【xūn³xēi²qou² 四² 操²】one who is mean, stingy and calculative =【普】(形容某人)自私、吝啬而又精于计算

蒜【xūn³ 算】garlic

蒜苗【xūn³miu⁴ 描】garlic bolt

蒜头【xūn³teo⁴ 投】the head of garlic

蒜茸【xūn³yung⁴ 容】mashed garlic =【普】蒜泥

旋【xūn⁴ 船】whirl; lathe; pare; at the time; revolve; circle; spin; return; come back; part of the scalp where the hair is whorled; soon

旋转【xūn⁴ jūn² 专²】revolve; gyrate; rotate; spin

旋绕【xūn⁴yiu⁵ 尧⁵】curl up; wind around

旋钮【xūn⁴neo² 扭】knob

旋涡【xūn⁴wo¹ 窝】whirlpool; vortex; eddy

旋律【xūn⁴lêd⁹ 栗】melody

旋风【xūn⁴fung¹ 丰】whirlwind

旋即【xūn⁴jig⁹ 积】at the time; at the last moment

旋转乾坤【xūn⁴jūn²kin⁴kuen¹ 专² 卡烟⁴ 昆】be earthshaking

船【xūn⁴ 旋】boat; ship

船只(隻)【xūn⁴jēg⁸ 脊】shipping; vessels

船舶【xūn⁴ pag⁸ 拍】shipping; boats and ships

船队【xūn⁴dêü² 对²】fleet; flotilla

船坞【xūn⁴wu¹ 乌】dock; shipyard

船闸【xūn⁴jab⁹ 习】(ship)lock

船舱【xūn⁴qong¹ 仓】ship's hold; cabin

船篷【xūn⁴pung⁴ 碰⁴】sail

船票【xūn⁴piu³ 飘³】steamer ticket

船期【xūn⁴kēi⁴ 其】sailing date

船家【xūn⁴gai¹ 加】boatman

船夫【xūn⁴fu¹ 敷】boatman

船工【xūn⁴gung¹ 功】boatman; junkman

船长【xūn⁴jêng² 蒋】captain; skipper

船头慌鬼，船尾慌贼【xūn⁴ teo⁴ fong¹guei²，xūn⁴mēi⁵fong¹qag⁹ 投方诡，美方 册⁹】fear this and fear that; timid and overcautious =【普】(比喻)怕这怕那；胆小怕事

吮【xūn⁵ 船⁵】suck

吮吸【xūn⁵keb⁷ 级】suck

说【xüd⁸ 雪；xêü³ 税】speak; talk; say; explain; theory; teachings; doctrine; scold; try to persuade

说话【xüd⁸ xa⁶ 华⁶】advice; speak; talk; say; chat; gossip

说道【xüd⁸dou⁶ 度】say

说明【xüd⁸ ming⁴ 名 】explain; illustrate; show; explanation; directions; caption

说白【xüd⁸ bag⁹伯⁹】spoken parts in an opera

说唱【xüd⁸ qêng³ 畅 】a genre of popular entertainment consisting mainly of talking and singing, e. g. comic dialogue, etc.

说穿【xüd⁸qūn¹ 川】tell what sth. really is; reveal = 讲穿【gong²qün¹】

说定【xüd⁸ding⁶ 锭】settle; agree on = 讲定【gong²ding⁶】

说法【xüd⁸fad⁸ 发】wording; statement = 讲法【gong²fad⁸】

说服【xêü³ fug⁹ 伏】persuade; convince; prevail on

说好【xüd⁸hou² 蒿²】come to an agreement = 讲好【gong²hou²】

说谎【xüd⁸fong¹ 方】tell a lie; lie = 讲大话【gong²dai⁶wa⁶】

说理【xüd⁸ lēi⁵李 】argue; reason things out = 讲理【gong²lēi⁵】

说情【xüd⁸ qing⁴ 程】plead for mercy for sb. ; intercede for sb. = 讲情【gong²qing⁴】

说书【xüd⁸xü¹ 抒】storytelling

说死【xüd⁸xēi² 四²】fix definitely = 讲死【gong²xēi²】

说妥【xüd⁸to⁵ 陀⁵】come to an agreement = 讲妥【gong²to⁵】

说笑【xüd⁸ xiu³ 少】chatting and laughing = 讲笑【gong²xiu³】

说不定【xüd⁸ bed⁷ ding⁶毕锭】perhaps; maybe = 话唔定【wa⁶m⁴ding⁶ 锭】

说不上【xüd⁸bed⁷xêng⁵ 毕尚⁵】cannot say = 讲唔出【gong²m²qêd⁷】

说到做到【xüd⁸dou³jou⁶dou³ 度³ 造度³】

do what one says = 讲到做到
【gong²dou³jou⁶jou³】

说得过去【xŭd⁸deg⁷guo³hêü³ 德戈³ 虚³】
justifiable; passable = 讲得过去
【gong²deg⁷guo³hêü³】

雪【xŭd⁸ 司月⁸】snow; wipe out; avenge

雪花【xŭd⁸fa¹ 化¹】snowflake = 雪片【xŭd⁸
pin³】

雪白【xŭd⁸ bag⁹ 伯⁹】snow-white; snowy
white

雪亮【xŭd⁸ lêng⁶ 量⁶】bright as snow;
shiny

雪茄【xŭd⁸kē² 卡舍²】cigar

雪堆【xŭd⁸dêü¹ 队¹】snow drift

雪崩【xŭd⁸beng¹ 绷】snowslide

雪糕【xŭd⁸gou¹ 高】ice cream

雪条【xŭd⁸tiu² 跳²】ice-lolly; ice cream roll
= 【普】冰棒

雪批【xŭd⁸pei¹ 拍矮¹】ice cream pie

雪屐【xŭd⁸kēg⁹ 剧】a roller skate = 【普】
溜冰鞋

雪梨【xŭd⁸lēi⁴ 离】a type of fruit

雪橇【xŭd⁸hiu³ 嚣】sled; sledge

雪柜【xŭd⁸guei⁶ 聩】a refrigerator

雪藏【xŭd⁸qong⁴ 床】freeze

雪冤【xŭd⁸ yün¹ 渊】 clear sb. of a false
charge; redress a wrong

雪恨【xŭd⁸ hen⁶ 很⁶】 wreak vengeance;
avenge

雪花膏【xŭd⁸fa¹gou¹ 化¹ 高】vanishing
cream

雪上加霜【xŭd⁸xêng⁶ga¹xêng¹ 尚家湘】
snow plus frost—one disaster after
another

雪中送炭【xŭd⁸gung¹xung³tan³ 宗宋叹】
send charcoal in snowy weather—
provide timely help

靸【xê¹ 是靴¹】〈 onomatopoeia 〉 the
sound of the running water, etc.

逇【xê⁴ 是靴⁴】slide; coast = 【普】滑动;
滑行

逇滑梯【xê⁴wad⁹tei¹ 挖⁹ 替¹】sit the slide
= 【普】坐滑梯

擎【xê⁴ 是靴⁴】steal

掔野【xê⁴yē⁵ 惹】steal; pilfer = 【普】盗
窃;偷东西

需【xêü¹ 须】need; want; require; nec-
essaries

需求【xêü¹keo⁴ 球】requirement; demand

需要【xêü¹yiu³ 腰³】need; want; require;
demand; needs

须【xêü¹ 需; xou¹ 苏】must; have to;
await; beard; mustache; palpus; tas-
sel

须要【xêü¹yiu³ 腰³】must; have to

须知【xêü¹ ji¹ 之 】 one should know that;
notice

须臾【xêü¹yü⁶ 预】moment; instant

须发【xou¹fad⁸ 法】beard and hair

须根【xou¹gen¹ 斤】〈 n . 〉fibrous root

须眉【xou¹ mēi⁴微 】 beard and eyebrows—a man

胥【xêü¹ 虽】petty official; all; a surname

胥吏【xêü¹lēi⁶ 利】petty official

绥【xêü¹ 虽】peaceful; pacify

绥靖【xêü¹jing⁶ 静】pacify; appease

虽【xêü¹ 衰】〈conj.〉though; although;
even if

虽然【xêū¹yin⁴ 言】though；although

虽说【xêū¹xüd⁸ 雪】though；although

虽则【xêū¹jeg⁷ 仄】though；although

衰【xêū¹ 虽】decline；wane；unlucky；unfortunate

衰败【xêū¹bai⁶ 摆⁶】decline；wane；be at a low ebb

衰减【xêū¹gam² 监²】attenuation

衰退【xêū¹têū³ 推³】fail；decline

衰竭【xêū¹ kid⁹ 揭】exhaustion；prostration

衰老【xêū¹ lou⁵ 鲁】old and feeble；decrepit

衰弱【xêū¹yêg⁹ 若】weak；feeble

衰微【xêū¹mēi⁴ 眉】decline；wane

衰亡【xêū¹ mong⁴ 忙】become feeble and die；wither away；decline and fall

衰人【xêū¹ yen⁴ 仁】a word for scolding people∽【普】坏种；糟糕的、没出息的人

衰仔【xêū¹ jei² 济²】words used to scold children or young people∽【普】坏孩子；没出息的小子

衰女【xêū¹nêū² 那去²】=衰女包【xêū¹nêū²bao¹ 那去² 苞】a word for scolding daughter or girl∽【普】不听话的娃，没出息的娃

衰公【xêū¹ gung¹ 工】a word for scolding husband or man∽【普】没出息的汉

衰婆【xêū¹ po² 颇】a word for scolding wife or women∽【普】令人讨厌的婆娘

衰神【xêū¹xen⁴ 臣】=衰鬼豆【xêū¹guei² deo⁶ 诡窦】a word used to scold people；a nasty phrase used to scold people∽【普】(俾嗔骂人)坏家伙；没出息的

水【xêū² 瑞²】water；river；a liquid；a surname

水分【xêū² fen⁶ 份】moisture content；exaggeration

水流【xêū²leo⁴ 留 】rivers；streams；current；flow

水性【xêū²xing³ 姓】ability in swimming

水路【xêū²lou⁶ 露】waterway；water route

水力【xêū² lig⁹ 历】waterpower；hydraulic power

水利【xêū²lēi⁶ 例】water conservancy；irrigation works

水电【xêū²din⁶ 甸】water and electricity

水客【xêū² hag⁸ 赫】one who depends on commission as a living by delivering foreign currencies for others

水脚【xêū² gêg⁸ 格约⁸】transportation fees；fare =【普】盘缠；路费；旅费

水喉【xêū² heo⁴ 侯】pipes；waterpipe =【普】水管

水壳【xêū² hog⁸学⁸】a container to keep water；water ladle =【普】水瓢

水圳【xêū²jen³ 振】drains；ditch=【普】水沟

水坑【xêū² hang¹ 黑罂¹】puddle；pool；water hole

水抱【xêū²pou⁵ 铺⁵】blisters；a float used by children when swimming =【普】救生圈；救生衣

水尾【xêū²mēi⁵ 美】the remaining goods∽【普】后到的、人家要了而剩下的货(没多少好东西)

水汪【xêū²xong¹ 王¹】of a slim hope；handle affairs how is not do one's best (or not proper)∽【普】办事不得

力,没有落实措施办妥,令人失望

水蟣【xêū²ji¹ 支】minute organics that live under the sea

水坝【xêū²ba³ 霸】dam

水泵【xêū²bem¹ 伯庵¹】water pump

水笔【xêū²bed⁷ 毕】(fountain)pen

水表【xêū²biu¹ 标】water meter

水兵【xêū²bing¹ 冰】seaman; sailor

水草【xêū²qou² 曹²】water and grass; waterweeds

水彩【xêū²qoi² 采】watercolour

水产【xêū²qan² 铲】aquatic product

水池【xêū²qi⁴ 迟】pond; pool; cistern

水稻【xêū²dou⁶ 道】paddy(rice); rice

水果【xêū²guo² 戈²】fruit

水壶【xêū²wu⁴ 胡⁴】kettle; canteen; watering can

水晶【xêū²jing¹ 精】crystal; rock crystal

水井【xêū²jēng² 支镜²】well

水灾【xêū²joi¹ 哉】flood; inundation

水泥【xêū²nei⁴ 那矮⁴】cement

水牛【xêū²ngeo⁴ 偶⁴】(water)buffalo

水泡【xêū²pao¹ 抛】blister; bubble

水平【xêū²ping⁴ 萍】horizontal; standard; level

水渠【xêū²kêū⁴ 驱⁴】ditch; canal

水球【xêū²keo⁴ 求】water polo

水势【xêū²xei³ 细】the flow of water

水压【xêū²ngad⁸ 押】water pressure

水手【xêū²xeo² 守】seaman; sailor

水塔【xêū²tab⁸ 替鸭⁸】water tower

水潭【xêū²tam⁴ 谈】puddle; pool

水塘【xêū²tong⁴ 唐】pool; pond

水田【xêū²tin⁴ 天⁴】paddy field

水桶【xêū²tung² 统】pail; bucket

水箱【xêū²xêūg¹ 湘】water tank

水乡【xêū²hêng¹ 香】a region of rivers and lakes

水文【xêū²men⁴ 民】hydrology

水银【xêū²ngen⁴ 天⁴】mercury

水域【xêū²wig⁹ 乌益⁹】waters; water area

水源【xêū²yûn⁴ 元】headwater; water-head

水运【xêū²wen⁶ 混】water transport

水闸【xêū²jab⁹ 习】water gate; sluice

水藻【xêū²jou² 早】algae

水质【xêū²jed⁷ 侄⁷】water quality

水蛭【xêū²jed⁹ 侄】leech

水榭【xêū²jé⁶ 谢】waterside pavilion

水肿【xêū²jung² 总】oedema; dropsy

水准【xêū²jên² 进²】level; standard

水族【xêū²jug⁹ 俗】aquatic animals

水豆【xêū² deo² 斗²】the level of knowledge or technology that is inferior ＝【普】知识或技术水平低下

水龙头【xêū²lung⁴teo⁴ 隆投】(water)tap; faucet

水蒸气【xêū²jing¹hēi³ 精气】steam; water vapour

水到渠成【xêū²dou³kêū⁴xing⁴ 度³ 薹诚】When conditions are ripe, success will come.

水滴石穿【xêū² dig⁹ xēg⁹ qūn¹ 迪硕川】Dripping water wears through rock—constant effort brings success.

水落石出【xêū² log⁹ xēg⁹ qêd⁷ 洛⁹ 硕次律⁷】When the water subsides the rocks emerge—the whole thing comes to light.

水乳交融【xêū²yū⁵gao¹yung⁴ 语胶容】as well blended as milk and water—

in complete harmony

水深火热【xêü² xem¹ fo² yid⁹ 心伙衣泄⁹】extreme misery

水泄不通【xêü² xid⁸ bed⁷ tung¹ 屑毕痛¹】Not even a drop of water could trickle through.

水涨船高【xêü² jêng³ xün³ gou¹ 帐旋糕】When the river rises the boat goes up—particular things improve with the improvement of the general situation.

水中捞月【xêü² jung¹ lao¹ jüd⁹ 钟挠¹ 越】fish for the moon in the water—make impractical or vain efforts

嗉【xêü³ 碎；xou³ 素】the stomach of birds；crop=【普】鸟类的胃

鸡嗉【gei¹xêü³ 岁】the stomach of a chicken =【普】鸡胃

鸡嗉咁多【gei¹xêü³gem³do¹ 岁禁朵¹】a little；a few=【普】很少；一点儿

岁【xêü³ 碎】year；year(of age)；year(for crops)

岁数【xêü³xou³ 扫】age；years

岁月【xêü³yüd⁹ 越】years

岁暮【xêü³mou⁶ 务】the close of the year

碎【xêü³ 岁】break to pieces；smash；broken；garrulous

碎纸【xêü³ji² 止】small change=【普】零钞；零钱

碎步【xêü³bou⁶ 部】quick short steps

碎石【xêü³xēg⁹ 硕】crushed stones；broken stones

碎湿湿【xêü³xeb⁷xeb⁷ 拾⁷】= 湿湿碎【xeb⁷xeb⁷xêü³】torn to small pieces=【普】不足珍惜的一点儿

谁【xêü⁴】who；someone；anyone=边个【bin¹go³】

谁不知【xêü⁴bed⁷ji¹ 毕支】I see!；Who don't know?

垂【xêü⁴ 谁】hang down；droop；let fall；bequeath to posterity；nearing；approaching；condescend

垂直【xêü⁴jig⁹ 值】perpendicular；vertical

垂涎【xêü⁴yin⁴ 言】drool；slaver；covet = 流口水【leo⁴heo²xêü²】

垂危【xêü⁴ngei⁴ 巍】critically ill

垂死【xêü⁴xēi² 四²】moribund；dying

垂青【xêü⁴qing¹ 清】show appreciation for sb.；look upon sb. with favour

垂钓【xêü⁴ diu³ 吊】fish with a hook and line

垂柳【xêü⁴leo⁵ 罗欧⁵】weeping willow

垂头丧气【xêü⁴teo⁴xong³hēi³ 投桑³ 戏】crestfallen

陲【xêü⁴ 垂】frontiers；borders

祟【xêü⁶ 瑞】evil spirit；ghost

作祟【jog⁸xêü⁶ 昨】act like an evil spirit

髓【xêü⁵ 绪】marrow；pith(see"脊髓")

绪【xêü⁵ 髓】thread；order in sequence or arrangement；mental or emotional state；task；cause

绪论【xêü⁵lên⁶ 吝】introduction

绪言【xêü⁵yin⁴ 然】introduction

絮【xêü⁵ 绪】(cotton)wadding；sth. resembling cotton；wad with cotton；garrulous

絮叨【xêü⁵ dou¹ 刀】long-winded；garrulous

絮棉【xêü⁵min⁴ 绵】cotton for wadding

穗【xêü⁶ 瑞】the ear of grain；spike；tassel；fringe；another name for Guangzhou

遂【xêû⁶ 穗】satisfy; fulfil; then; thereupon; succeed

遂心【xêû⁶ xem¹ 深 】after one's own heart; to one's liking

遂意【xêû⁶yi³ 薏】to one's liking

隧【xêû⁶ 遂】〈n.〉隧道【xêû⁶dou⁶ 度】tunnel

邃【xêû⁶ 遂】remote; deep; profound

燧【xêû⁶ 睡】flint; beacon fire

燧石【xêû⁶xēg⁹ 硕】flint

睡【xêû⁶ 遂】sleep

睡觉【xêû⁶ gog⁷ 各 】sleep = 瞓瞓【fen³ gao³】

睡眠【xêû⁶min⁴ 棉】sleep

睡梦【xêû⁶mung⁶ 蒙⁶】sleep; slumber

睡醒【xêû⁶ xēng² 腥²】wake up = 瞓醒【fen³ xēng²】

睡意【xêû⁶yi³ 薏】sleepiness; drowsiness

睡衣【xêû⁶yi¹ 依】night clothes; pajamas

税【xêû³ 碎】tax; duty

税收【xêû³xeo¹ 修】tax revenue

税率【xêû³lêd⁹ 律】tax rate; rate of taxation

税制【xêû³jei³ 济】tax system; taxation

税款【xêû³fun² 欢²】tax payment; taxation

荀【xên¹ 殉】a surname

殉【xên¹ 询】be buried alive with the dead; sacrifice one's life for

殉难【xên¹ nan⁶ 那晏⁶】die (for a just cause)

殉国【xên¹guog⁸ 帼】die for one's country

殉职【xên¹jig⁷ 积】die at one's post

询【xên¹ 荀】ask; inquire

询问【xên¹men⁶ 闽⁶】ask about; inquire

徇【xên¹ 荀；xên⁶ 顺】give in to; submit to; comply with; sacrifice one's life for

徇情【xên¹qing⁴ 程】act wrongly out of personal considerations; practise favouritism

徇私枉法【xên¹xi¹wong²fad⁸ 思汪² 发】bend the law for the benefit of relatives or friends

笋【xên² 信²】bamboo shoot

笋尖【xên²jim² 詹】tender tips of bamboo shoots

笋干【xên²gon¹ 竿】dried bamboo shoots

笋野【xên²yē⁵ 惹】something that is beneficial〇【普】有利、有益的事情；好东西

信【xên³ 讯】true; confidence; trust; faith; believe; profess faith in; believe in; at will; at randon; letter; mail message; word; fuse

信件【xên³gin² 建²】letters = 信札【xên³ jad⁸】

信纸【xên³ji³ 止】letter paper = 信笺【xên³ jin¹ 毡】

信封【xên³fung¹ 风】envelope

信息【xên³ xig⁷ 识 】information; news; message

信仰【xên³yêng² 氧】faith; belief; conviction

信念【xên³nim⁶ 粘⁶】faith; belief; conviction

信贷【xên³tai³ 太】credit

信步【xên³bou⁶ 部】take a leisurely walk; stroll

信奉【xên³fung⁶ 凤】believe in

信服【xên³fug⁹ 伏】completely accept

信号【xên³hou⁶ 豪⁶】signal

信赖【xên³lai⁶ 拉⁶】trust; count on

信任【xên³ yem⁶ 壬⁶】trust; have confidence in

信实【xên³xed⁹ 失⁹】trustworthy; honest

信守【xên³xeo² 手】abide by; stand by

信徒【xên³tou⁴ 图】believer; disciple; follower

信托【xên³tog⁸ 替恶⁸】trust; entrust

信物【xên³med⁹ 勿】token; keepsake

信心【xên³xem¹ 深】confidence; faith

信用【xên³yung⁶ 容⁶】trustworthiness; credit

信誉【xên³yü⁶ 预】prestige; credit; reputation

信口雌黄【xên³heo²qi¹wong⁴ 厚² 痴王】make irresponsible remarks

信口开河【xên³heo²hoi¹ho⁴ 厚² 海¹ 何】talk irresponsibly; talk nonsense

信誓旦旦【xên³xei⁶dan³dan³ 逝诞诞】vow solemnly

讯 【xên³ 信】interrogate; question; message; dispatch

讯问【xên³ men⁶ 文⁶】interrogate; question; ask about

汛 【xên³ 信】flood; high water

汛期【xên³kêi⁴ 其】flood season

迅 【xên³ 信】fast; swift

迅疾【xên³jed⁹ 侄】swift; rapid

迅捷【xên³jid⁹ 截】fast; agile; quick

迅速【xên³qug⁷ 促】rapid; swift; speedy; prompt

迅猛【xên³mang⁵ 孟⁵】swift and violent

迅雷不及掩耳【xên³lêü⁴bed⁷keb⁹yim²yi⁵ 擂毕级⁹ 淹² 尔】as sudden as lightning

逊 【xên³ 信】abdicate; modest; inferior

逊色【xên³xig⁷ 式】be inferior

逊位【xên³wei⁶ 卫】abdicate

纯 【xên⁴ 淳】pure; unmixed; simple; skilful; practised; well versed

纯粹【xên⁴xêü⁵ 绪】pure; unadulterated

纯度【xên⁴dou⁴ 道】purity; pureness

纯碱【xên⁴gan² 间²】soda ash

纯洁【xên⁴gid⁸ 结】pure; clean and honest

纯净【xên⁴jing⁶ 静】pure; clean

纯朴【xên⁴pog⁸ 扑】honest; simple

纯熟【xên⁴xug⁹ 属】skilful; practised

纯真【xên⁴jen¹ 珍】pure; sincere

纯正【xên⁴jing³ 政】pure; unadulterated

纯种【xên⁴jung² 总】purebred

驯 【xên⁴ 纯】tame and docile; tame; domesticate

驯服【xên⁴ fug⁹ 伏】docile; tame; tractable

驯化【xên⁴fa³ 花³】domestication; taming

驯良【xên⁴lêng⁴ 凉】tractable; docile

驯养【xên⁴yêng⁵ 氧】raise and train; domesticate

唇 【xên⁴ 纯】lip

唇膏【xên⁴gou¹ 糕】lipstick

唇舌【xên⁴xid⁸ 泄】words; argument

唇枪舌剑【xên⁴qêng¹xid⁸gim³ 昌泄兼³】cross verbal swords

唇亡齿寒【xên⁴mong⁴qi²hon⁴ 忘始韩】If

the lips are gone, the teeth will be cold. share a common lot

莼【xên⁴ 纯】 water shield （莼菜【xên⁴qoi³】)

淳【xên⁴ 纯】pure; honest

淳厚【xên⁴heo⁵ 后⁵】pure and honest

淳朴【xên⁴pog⁸ 扑】honest; simple

淳于【xên⁴yü¹ 迂】a surname

醇【xên⁴ 纯】mellow wine; good wine; pure; unmixed; alcohol

醇厚【xên⁴heo⁵ 后⁵】mellow; rich; pure and honest

醇化【xên⁴fa³ 花³】refine; purify; alcoholization

顺【xên⁶ 信⁶】in the same direction as; with; along; arrange; put in order; obey; yield to; suitable; take the opportunity to; in sequence

顺便【xên⁶bin⁶ 辨】conveniently; in passing

顺畅【xên⁶qêng³ 唱】smooth; unhindered

顺次【xên⁶qi³ 刺】in order; in succession

顺从【xên⁶qung⁴ 虫】be obedient; submit to

顺当【xên⁶dong³ 档】smoothly; without a bitch

顺耳【xên⁶yi⁵ 尔】pleasing to the ear

顺风【xên⁶fung 封】have a tail wind

顺口【xên⁶ heo² 厚²】read smoothly; say offhandedly

顺利【xên⁶lêi⁶ 俐】smoothly; successfully

顺路【xên⁶ lou⁶ 露】on the way; direct route

顺势【xên⁶ xei³ 细】take advantage of an opportunity

顺手【xên⁶ xeo² 守】smoothly; conve-

niently; do sth. as a natural sequence; handy

顺水【xên⁶xêü² 瑞】downstream

顺心【xên⁶xem¹ 深】satisfactory

顺序【xên⁶ jêü⁶ 叙】sequence; order; in proper order; in turn

顺延【xên⁶yin⁴ 言】postpone

顺眼【xên⁶ngan⁵ 雁⁵】pleasing to the eye

顺应【xên⁶ ying³ 映³】comply with; conform to

顺风转舵【xên⁶ fung¹ jün² to⁴ 丰专² 陀】trim one's sails; take one's cue from changing condition

顺理成章【xên⁶lêi⁵xing⁴jêng¹ 李承张】To write well, you must follow a logical train of thought. To do some work well, you must follow a rational line.

顺水推舟【xên⁶xêü²têü¹jeo¹ 瑞² 退¹ 周】push the boat along with the current—make use of an opportunity to gain one's end

顺藤摸瓜【xên⁶teng⁴mo¹gua¹ 腾摩寡¹】follow the vine to get the melon—track down sb. or sth. by following clues

顺我者昌，逆我者亡【xên⁶ngo⁵jê²qêng¹, yig³ngo²jê²mog⁴ 鹅⁵ 姐枪，亦鹅⁵ 姐忘】Those who submit will prosper, and those who resist shall perish.

舜【xên³ 信】Shun, the name of a legendary monarch in ancient China

瞬【xên³ 信】wink; twinkling

瞬时【xên³xi⁴ 是⁴】instantaneous

瞬息【xên³xig⁷ 式】twinkling

伤【xêng¹ 双】wound; injury; injure; hurt; be distressed; get sick of sth.; be harmful to; hinder

伤害【xêng¹hoi⁶ 亥】injure; harm; hurt

伤痕【xêng¹hen⁴ 很⁴】scar; bruise

伤疤【xêng¹ba 巴】scar

伤口【xêng¹heo² 厚】wound; cut

伤员【xêng¹ yün⁴ 元】wounded personnel; the wounded

伤亡【xêng¹mong⁴ 忘】injuries and deaths

伤心【xêng¹xem 深】sad; grieved

伤感【xêng¹gem² 敢】sick at heart; sentimental

伤寒【xêng¹hon⁴ 韩】typhoid fever; febrile disease

伤风【xêng¹ fung¹ 丰】catch cold; have a cold

伤脑筋【xêng¹ nou⁵ gen¹ 瑙斤】knotty; troublesome

伤风败俗【xêng¹fung¹bai⁶jug⁹ 丰摆⁶族】offend public decency

殇【xêng¹ 双】die young

觞【xêng¹ 双】wine cup; drinking vessel

商【xêng¹ 双】discuss; consult; trade; commerce; merchant; trader; the Shang Dynasty(C. 16th～11th century B.C.); a surname

商量【xêng¹lêng⁴ 凉】consult; discuss

商谈【xêng¹ tam⁴谭】exchange views; confer

商讨【xêng¹ tou² 桃】discuss; deliberate over

商榷【xêng¹kog⁸ 确】discus; deliberate

商议【xêng¹yi⁵ 耳】confer; discuss

商约【xêng¹yêg⁸ 若⁸】commercial treaty

商人【xêng¹ yen⁴ 仁】businessman; merchant; trader

商贾【xêng¹gu² 古】merchants

商务【xêng¹mou⁶ 冒】commercial affairs

商业【xêng¹yib⁹ 叶】commerce; trade; business

商行【xêng¹hong² 项²】trading company

商店【xêng¹dim³ 点³】shop; store

商标【xêng¹biu¹ 彪】trade mark

商贩【xêng¹fan² 反】small retailer; pedlar

商场【xêng¹qêng⁴ 祥】market; bazaar

商埠【xêng¹feo⁶ 浮⁶】commercial port

商港【xêng¹gong² 讲】commercial port

商定【xêng¹ding⁶ 锭】agree

双【xêng¹ 商】two; twin; both; dual; pair; even; double; twofold

双方【xêng¹fong¹ 芳】both sides; the two parties

双边【xêng¹bin¹ 鞭】bilateral

双层【xêng¹qeng⁴ 次莺⁴】double-deck

双重【xêng¹qung⁴ 虫】double; dual; twofold

双关【xêng¹ guan¹ 惯¹】having a double meaning

双轨【xêng¹guei² 鬼】double track

双交【xêng¹gao¹ 胶】double cross

双料【xêng¹liu² 辽²】extra quality

双全【xêng¹qün⁴ 存】complete in both respects

双生【xêng¹xeng¹ 笙】twin

双日【xêng¹yed⁹ 逸】even-numbered day

双手【xêng¹xeo² 守】both hands

双数【xêng¹xou³ 素】even numbers

双双【xêng¹xêng¹】in pairs

双喜【xêng¹hēi² 起】double happiness

双胞胎【xêng¹bao¹toi¹ 包台¹】twins

双眼皮【xêng¹ ngan⁵ pêi⁴ 雁⁵ 脾】double eyelid

双爵墙【xêng¹yü⁴qêng⁴ 如场】walls made of double layers of bricks =【普】双砖墙

双簧管【xêng¹wong⁴gun² 王莞】oboe

双人舞【xêng¹ yen⁴ mou⁵ 仁武】dance for two people

双氧水【xêng¹ yêng⁵ xêü² 仰瑞²】hydrogen peroxide solution

双管齐下【xêng¹gun²qei⁴ha⁶ 莞妻⁴ 夏】paint a picture with two brushes at the same time—work along both lines

霜【xêng¹ 双】frost; frostlike powder; white; hoar

霜冻【xêng¹dung³ 东³】frost

霜期【xêng¹kêi⁴ 其】frost season

霜叶【xêng¹ yib⁹业】 red leaves; autumn maple leaves

孀【xêng¹ 双】widow

孀妇【xêng¹fu⁵】widow

孀居【xêng¹gêü¹ 句¹】live in widowhood

相【xêng¹ 双;xêng³ 尚³】each other; one another; mutually; see for oneself; a surname; looks; appearance; bearing; look at and appraise; assist; prime minister; photograph; phase; elephant, one of the pieces in Chinese chess

相比【xêng¹bêi² 悲²】compare

相差【xêng¹qa¹ 叉】differ

相称【xêng¹qing³ 秤】match; suit

相持【xêng¹ qi⁴迟 】be locked in a stalemate

相处【xêng¹qü² 次于²】get along(with one another)

相传【xêng¹ qün⁴ 存】according to legend; hand down or pass on from one to another

相当【xêng¹dong¹ 铛】match; balance; fit; quite

相等【xêng¹deng² 邓²】be equal

相抵【xêng¹dei² 底】offset; balance

相对【xêng¹ dêü³ 堆³】opposite; relative; relatively

相反【xêng¹fan² 返】opposite; contrary

相逢【xêng¹fung⁴ 冯】meet; come across

相符【xêng¹fu⁴ 乎】conform to; tally with

相干【xêng¹gon¹ 竿】have to do with; coherent

相隔【xêng¹gag⁸ 格】be separated by; be apart

相关【xêng¹guan¹ 惯¹】be interrelated

相好【xêng¹ hou² 蒿²】 be on intimate terms; intimate friend; lover or mistress

相片【xêng³pin² 遍²】photograph; photo

相互【xêng¹ wu⁶ 护 】mutual; reciprocal; each other

相继【xêng¹gei³ 计】in succession; one after another

相交【xêng¹gao¹ 胶】intersect

相间【xêng¹gan³ 奸³】alternate with

相貌【xêng³ mao⁶矛⁶】facial features; looks

相近【xêng¹gen⁶ 靳】close; near; be similar to

相距【xêng¹kêü⁵ 拒】apart; away from

相连【xêng¹lin⁴ 莲】be linked together; be joined

相识【xêng¹ xig⁷悉 】 be acquainted with each other; acquaintance

相思【xêng¹ xi¹ 司】yearning between lovers; lovesickness

相声【xêng³ xing¹ 升 】comic dialogue; cross talk

相似【xêng¹qi⁵ 次⁵】resemble; be similar

相通【xêng¹ tung¹同¹】communicate with each other

相同【xêng¹tung⁴ 铜】identical; the same; alike

相投【xêng¹teo⁴ 头】be congenial

相像【xêng¹jêng⁶ 象】resemble; be similar

相信【xêng¹ xên³ 讯】believe in; be convinced of

相依【xêng¹yi¹ 衣】depend on each other

相应【xêng¹ying³ 映³】corresponding; relevant

相约【xêng¹ yêg⁸ 若⁸ 】agree (on meeting place, etc.)

相机【xêng³ gêi¹基】watch for an opportunity; camera

相知【xêng¹ji¹ 支】be well acquainted with each other; bosom friend

相宜【xêng¹yi⁴ 而】cheap; suitable; fitting

相与【xêng¹ yü⁵ 语 】negotiate; get along ＝【普】打交道;相处

相安无事【xêng¹ngon¹mou⁴xi⁶ 胺毛士】 live in peace with each other

相得益彰【xêng¹ deg⁷yig⁷jêng¹ 德忆章】 complement each other

相辅相成【xêng¹ fu⁶ xêng¹ xing⁴父诚】 supplement each other

相提并论【xêng¹tei⁴bing⁶lên⁶ 堤丙⁶ 吝】 place on a pair

相形见绌【xêng¹ ying⁴ gin³ jüd⁸ 型建苗】 prove definitely inferior; be outshone

湘【xêng¹ 双 】short for the Xiangjiang River; another name for Hunan Province

厢【xêng¹ 湘】wing; wing-room; railway carriage; box; the vicinity outside of a city gate; side

厢房【xêng¹fong² 仿】wing; wing-room

箱【xêng¹ 湘】chest; box; case; trunk; anything in the shape of a box

箱仔【xêng¹ jei² 济²】chest; box; case; trunk＝【普】箱子

箱笼【xêng¹lung⁵ 垄】boxes and baskets; luggage; baggage

襄【xêng¹ 湘】assist; help

襄助【xêng¹jo⁶ 座】assist

镶【xêng¹ 湘】inlay; set; mount; rim; edge

镶嵌【xêng¹hem³ 勘³】inlay; set; mount

镶牙【xêng¹nga⁴ 芽】put in a false tooth

想【xêng² 赏 】think; suppose; reckon; consider; want to; would like to; feel like; miss; remember with longing

想话【xêng² wo⁶ 华⁶】just want to say＝【普】正想;正想说

想野【xêng²yê⁵ 惹】think over a problem ＝【普】想问题

想必【xêng² bid⁷ 别⁷】presumably; must probably

想到【xêng² dou³ 都³ 】think of; call to mind

想法【xêng²fad⁸ 发】think of a way; try; idea; opinion

想见【xêng²gin³ 建】infer; gather

想来【xêng² loi⁴莱 】It may be assumed that. presumably

想念【xêng²nim⁶ 粘⁶】remember with

longing; long to see again; miss

想起【xêng² hêi² 喜】remember; recall; think of

想通【xêng²tung¹ 同】straighten out one's thinking; come round

想望【xêng²mong⁶ 亡⁶】desire; long for

想象【xêng²jêng⁶ 像】imagine; fancy; visualize; imagination

想唔到【xêng² m⁴ dou³ 道³】unexpected =【普】想不到

想唔开【xêng²m⁴hoi¹ 海¹】take things too hard; take a matter to heart =【普】想不开

想得开【xêng²deg⁷hoi¹ 德海¹】not take to heart

想当然【xêng² dong¹ yin⁴ 铛言】assume sth. as a matter of course

想方设法【xêng²fong¹qid⁸fad⁸ 芳切发】do everything possible; try every means

想入非非【xêng² yeb⁹ fêi¹ fêi¹ 邑⁹ 飞】indulge in fantasy; allow one's fancy to **run wild**

赏【xêng² 想】grant a reward; award; reward; admire; enjoy; appreciate

赏赐【xêng²qi³ 次】grant a reward; award

赏罚【xêng² fed⁹ 佛】rewards and punishments

赏光【xêng² guong¹胱 】request the pleasure of your company

赏识【xêng² xig⁷ 式】recognize the worth of; appreciate

赏心悦目【xêng²xem¹yüd⁹mug⁹ 深越木】find the scenery pleasing both the eye and the mind

尝【xêng⁴ 偿】taste; try the flavour of; ever; once

尝试【xêng⁴xi³ 示³】attempt; try

尝新【xêng⁴xen¹ 申】have a taste of what is just in season

偿【xêng⁴ 尝】repay; compensate for

偿还【xêng⁴wan¹ 环】repay; pay back

偿债【xêng⁴jai³ 寨³】pay a debt

偿命【xêng⁴mêng⁶ 莫镜⁶】pay with one's life

偿心愿【xêng⁴ xem¹ yün⁶ 深县】have fulfilled one's long-cherished wish

徜【xêng⁴ 尝】〈v.〉徜徉【xêng⁴yêng⁴ 洋】wander about unhurriedly

常【xêng⁴ 尝】ordinary; common; normal; constant; frequently; often; usually; a surname

常常【xêng⁴ xêng⁴】frequently; often; usually; generally

常规【xêng⁴ kuei¹ 亏】convention; rule; routine

常轨【xêng⁴guei² 鬼】normal practice

常见【xêng⁴gin³ 建】common

常例【xêng⁴lei⁶ 厉】common practice

常年【xêng⁴nin⁴ 捻⁴】throughout the **year**; perennial; year in year out; average year

常青【xêng⁴qing¹ 清】evergreen

常情【xêng⁴qing⁴ 程】person; sense

常人【xêng⁴yen⁴ 仁】ordinary person

常任【xêng⁴yem⁶ 壬⁶】permanent; standing

常设【xêng⁴qid⁸ 切】standing; permanent

常驻【xêng⁴jü³ 注】resident; permanent

常识【xêng⁴ xig⁷ 式】general knowledge; common sense

常数【xêng⁴xou³ 扫】constant

常态【xêng⁴tai³ 太】normality; normal behaviour

常温【xêng⁴ wen¹ 瘟】normal atmosphere temperature; homoiothermy

常务【xêng⁴mou⁶ 冒】day-to-day business; routine

常言【xêng⁴yin⁴ 然】saying

常用【xêng⁴yung⁶ 庸】in common use

常备不懈【xêng⁴bēi⁶bed⁷hai⁶ 鼻毕械】always be on the alert

裳【xêng⁴ 常】skirt(worn in ancient China)(see"衣裳"【yi¹xêng⁴】)

嫦【xêng⁴ 常】〈n..〉嫦娥【xêng⁴ngo⁴ 俄】the goddess of the moon

上【xêng⁶ 尚;xêng⁵ 尚⁵】upper; up; upward; higher; first (part); preceding; the emperor; go up; mount; go to; leave for; submit; send in; present; go ahead; enter; fill; supply; set; fix; apply; paint; be put on record; wind; be engaged at a fixed time; up to; <prep.>on...;at...

上班【xêng⁵ban¹ 斑】go to work; start work

上边【xêng⁶bin¹ 鞭】above; over; on top of; above-mentioned; aforesaid; the higher-ups; aspect; respect =上面【xêng⁶min⁶】

上堂【xêng⁵tong⁴ 唐】have a lesson in a class; attend class; go to class; give lesson =【普】上课

上便【xêng⁶bin⁶ 辨】the top; over; above; aspect; on top of =【普】上面

上高【xêng⁶gou¹ 膏】the top part; higher level =【普】上头;上级;上面

上下【①xêng⁶ha⁶ 尚夏;②xêng⁶ ha² 尚夏²】① high and low; up and down; ② almost; going to; down;

roughly; estimated to =【普】大约;左右;差不多

上昼【xêng⁶jeo³ 奏】in the morning; forenoon =【普】上午

上宾【xêng⁶ben¹ 奔】guest of honour

上策【xêng⁶ qag⁸ 册】the best plan; the best way out

上层【xêng⁶qeng⁴ 次莺⁴】upper strata; uper levels

上场【xêng⁵ qêng⁴ 祥】enter; enter the court

上床【xêng⁵qong⁴ 苍⁴】go to bed

上苍【xêng⁶qong¹ 仓】Heaven; God =上天【tin¹】

上当【xêng⁵ dong³ 档】be taken in; be fooled

上等【xêng⁶ deng² 邓²】first-class; first-rate

上帝【xêng⁶dei³ 蒂】God

上吊【xêng⁵diu³ 掉³】hang oneself

上风【xêng⁶ fung¹ 丰】windward; advantage

上钩【xêng⁵ngeo¹ 欧】rise to the bait; get hooked

上官【xêng⁶gun¹ 观】a surname

上海【xêng⁶hoi² 凯】Shanghai

上缴【xêng⁶ giu² 矫】turn over(revenues, etc.)to the higher authorities

上街【xêng⁵gai¹ 佳】go into the street

上进【xêng⁶jên³ 俊】go forward

上空【xêng⁶hung¹ 凶】in the sky

上来【xêng⁵loi⁴ 莱】come up

上门【xêng⁵mun¹ 们】visit; bolt the door

上去【xêng⁵hêü³ 虚】go up

上任【xêng⁵yem⁶ 壬⁶】assume office

上色【xêng⁵ xig⁷ 式】colour (a picture, map, etc.)

上升【xêng⁶ xing¹ 声】rise; go up; ascend

上市【xêng⁵ xi⁵ 示⁵】go on the market

上手【xêng⁵ xeo² 守】left-hand; start

上书【xêng⁵ xü¹ 输】submit a written-statement to a higher authority

上述【xêng⁶ xêd⁹ 术】above-mentioned

上司【xêng⁶ xi¹ 思】superior; boss

上诉【xêng⁶ xou³扫 】appeal (to a higher court)

上算【xêng⁶ xün³ 蒜】paying; worthwhile

上台【xêng⁵ toi⁴ 抬】appear on the stage; assume power

上限【xêng⁶ han⁶ 悭⁶】upper limit

上学【xêng⁵ hog⁹ 鹤】go to school

上旬【xêng⁶ qên⁴ 巡】the first ten-day period of a month

上演【xêng⁶ yin² 衍】put on the stage; perform

上瘾【xêng⁵ yen⁵引 】 be addicted (to sth.); get into the habit(of doing sth.)

上游【xêng⁶ yeo⁴ 由】upper reaches; advanced position

上涨【xêng⁶ jêng³ 帐】rise; go up

上阵【xêng⁵ jen⁶ 振⁶】go into battle

上轨道【xêng⁵ guei² dou⁶ 鬼度】get on the right track

上议院【xêng⁶ yi⁵ yün² 尔丸】upper house

上窜下跳【xêng⁶ qün³ ha⁶ tiu³ 寸夏条³】run around on sinister errands

上方宝剑【xêng⁶ fong¹ bou² gim³ 芳保俭³】the imperial sword

上行下效【xêng⁶ heng⁴ ha⁶ hao⁶ 衡夏孝⁶】Those in subordinate positions will follow the example set by their superiors.

尚【xêng⁶ 上⁶】〈ad.〉still; yet; 〈v.〉esteem; value; 〈n.〉a surname

尚且【xêng⁶ qê² 扯】〈conj.〉even

尚书【xêng⁶ xü¹ 输】a high official in ancient China

蟀【xêd⁷ 摔】(see"蟋蟀"【xig⁷ xêd⁷】)

摔【xêd⁷ 蟀】fall; tumble; lose one's balance; hurtle down; plunge; break; cast; throw; fling

摔打【xêd⁷ da² 得亚²】beat; knock; rough it

摔交【xêd⁷ gao¹ 胶】tumble; trip up; wrestling

摔跟头【xêd⁷ gen¹ teo⁴ 斤投】tumble; trip and fall; trip up; turn somersault ＝翻筋斗【fan¹ gen¹ deo²】

恤【xêd⁷ 摔】pity; sympathize; give relief; compensate; bottle cover; lock

恤金【xêd⁷ gem¹ 今】pension for a disabled person or the family of the deceased

恤衫【xêd⁷ xam¹ 三】shirt＝【普】衬衣

术【xêd⁹ 述】 art; skill; technique; method; tactic

术语【xêd⁹ yü⁵ 雨】technical terms; terminology

述【xêd⁹ 术】state; relate; narrate

述说【xêd⁹ xüd⁸雪 】state; recount; narrate

述评【xêd⁹ping⁴ 平】review; commentary

述职【xêd⁹jig⁷ 积】report on one's work; report

削【xêg⁸ 是约⁸】pare (or peel) with a knife; cut; chop; whittle

削铅笔【xêg⁸ yün⁴ bed⁷ 元毕】sharpen a

pencil

削球【xêg⁸keo⁴ 求】cut；chop

削减【xêg⁸gam² 监²】cut(down)；reduce；slash

削弱【xêg⁸yêg⁹ 若】weaken；cripple

削足适履【xêg⁸jug⁷xig⁷lēi⁵ 竹式李】cut the feet to fit the shoes

桨【xêg⁸ 削】refer to the flesh on the body which is loose and not firm；soggy＝【普】拌和粉或泥时，水分太多，不粘稠

桨揸揸【xêg⁸dad⁹dad⁹ 达】body flesh which is loose＝【普】稀烂，不粘稠

勺【xêg⁸ 削；jêg⁸ 桌】spoon；ladle；an old unit of capacity(＝1 centilitre)

勺子【xêg⁸ji² 止】ladle；scoop＝壳仔【hog⁸jei²】

些【xē¹ 赊】slightly；a little；a bit；a few

些少【xē¹xiu² 小】a bit；a little；a few＝【普】一点儿

些微【xē¹mēi⁴ 眉】slightly；a little；a bit

赊【xē¹ 些】buy or sell on credit

赊住先【xē¹jü⁶xin¹ 注⁶ 仙】buy or sell on credit；give or get credit＝【普】赊欠；赊帐

赊购【xē¹keo³ 扣】buy on credit

赊销【xē¹xiu¹ 消】sell on credit

写【xē² 舍²】write；compose；describe；depict；paint；draw；enjoyable

写稿【xē²gou² 缟】write for a magazine，etc.

写生【xē²xeng¹ 笙】paint from life

写实【xē²xed⁹ 失⁹】write or paint realistically

写意【xē²yi³ 薏】freehand brushwork in traditional Chinese painting；comfortable；enjoyable

写作【xē²jog⁸ 昨】writing

写照【xē²jiu³ 焦³】portrayal；portraiture

写真【xē²jen³ 珍】portray a person；portrait；describe sth. as it is

写字台【xē²ji⁶toi⁴ 治抬】writing desk

泻【xē³ 舍³】flow swiftly；rush down；pour out；have loose bowels；have diarrhoea

泻肚【xē³tou⁵ 土⁵】have loose bowels；have diarrhoea＝屙肚【ngo¹tou⁵】

泻药【xē³yêg⁹ 若】laxative；cathartic；purgative

卸【xē³ 泻】unload；discharge；lay down；remove；strip；get rid of；shirk

卸车【xē³qē¹ 奢】unload from a vehicle；unload

卸货【xē³fo³ 课】unload cargo；unload

卸任【xē³yem⁶ 壬⁶】be relieved of one's office

卸装【xē³jong¹ 妆】remove stage makeup and costume

舍【xē³ 泻；xē² 写】house；shed；hut；give up；give alms

舍下【xē³ha⁶ 夏】my humble abode；my house

舍亲【xē²qen¹ 趁¹】my relative

舍弃【xē²hēi³ 戏】give up；abandon

舍身【xē²xen¹ 辛】give one's life；sacrifice oneself

舍得【xē²deg³ 德】be willing to part with；not grudge

舍不得【xē²bed⁷deg⁹ 毕德】hate to part with or use；grudge＝唔舍得

【m⁴xē²deg⁷】

舍本逐末【xē²bun²jog⁹mud⁹ 苯续没】attend to trifles to the neglect of essentials

舍己为人【xē²gēi²wei⁶yen⁴ 几卫仁】sacrifice one's own interests for the sake of others

舍生取义【xē²xeng¹qēû²yi⁶ 笙娶二】lay down one's life for a just cause

佘【xē⁴ 蛇】a surname

畲【xē⁴ 蛇】〈n.〉畲族【xē⁴jug⁹ 俗】the She nationality, distributed over Fujian, Zhejiang, Jiangxi and Guangdong

猞【xē³ 卸】〈n.〉猞猁【xē³lēi⁶ 利】lynx

蛇【xē⁴ 余；yi⁴ 而】snake; serpent; winding; lazy

蛇蝎【xē⁴kid⁸ 揭】snakes and scorpions —— vicious people

蛇蜕【xē⁴tēû³ 退】snake slough

蛇形【xē⁴ying⁴ 仍】snakelike; S-shaped

蛇行【xē⁴heng⁴ 衡】move with the body on the ground; crawl

委蛇【wei²yi⁴ 而】winding; meandering

蛇王【xē⁴wong⁴ 皇】lazy; lazybones =【普】懒惰；懒汉

蛇仔【xē⁴ jei⁹ 济²】unlicensed cars that take passengers by the roadside; assistants to drivers〇【普】帮助主子拉客或逐客的人

蛇头鼠眼【xē⁴teo⁴xū²ngan⁵ 投署雁⁵】one who causes suspicion by behaving suspiciously〇【普】笨拙贪婪的样子；面目可憎

死【xēi² 四²】die; to the death; to death; extremely; implacable; deadly; fixed; rigid; impassable; closed

死亡【xēi²mong⁴ 忘】death; doom

死难【xēi² nan⁶ 那晏⁶】die in an accident or a political incident

死人【xēi² yen⁴ 仁 】a dead person; the dead

死者【xēi²jē² 姐】the dead; the deceased

死罪【xēi²jēû⁶ 叙】capital offence

死囚【xēi²qeo⁴ 筹】a convict sentenced to death

死刑【xēi²ying⁴ 型】death penalty; death sentence

死尸【xēi²xi¹ 司】corpse; dead body

死党【xēi² dong² 挡 】very close friends; sworn followers

死火【xēi²fo² 伙】jam(cars); break down; barriers to stop an event from being successful =【普】机器不能启动；办事因故中止，无法再继续办下去

死鬼【xēi² guei² 轨 】an address for one who is dead; a word used to scold people; devil

死揸【xēi² lēû⁴雷】work very hard〇【普】埋头苦干

死佬【xēi² lou² 老²】bad guys〇【普】坏小子；坏汉

死敌【xēi²dig⁹ 迪】deadly enemy

死地【xēi² dēi⁶ 得希⁶】a fatal position; deathtrap

死活【xēi²wūd⁹ 乌括⁹】life or death; fate; anyway

死角【xēi²gog⁸ 各】dead angle; dead space

死结【xēi²gid⁸ 洁】fast knot

死力【xēi²lig⁹ 历】all one's strength

死路【xēi²lou⁶ 露】blind alley; the road to ruin = 崛头路【gued⁹teo⁴lou⁶】

死命【xēi² mēng⁶ 莫镜⁶】doom；death；desperately

死守【xēi² xeo² 手】defend to death；rigidly adhere to

死水【xēi² xêu² 瑞】stagnant water

死心【xēi² xem¹ 深】drop the idea forever；have no more illusions about the matter

死讯【xēi² xên³ 信】news of sb.'s death

死硬【xēi² ngang⁶ 罂⁶ 】stiff；inflexible；very obstinate；die-hard；have no hope

死板【xēi²ban² 版】rigid；inflexible；stiff

死咕咕【xēi² gu⁴ gu⁴ 古⁴】rigid；not creative；not lively；dead∽【普】一副呆滞模样；毫无生气；毫无动静

死妹钉【xēi²mui¹dēng¹ 梅¹ 得镜¹】=死女包【xēi²nêu²bao¹ 那去² 苞】a phrase to scold people（girl）=【普】死丫头

死死下【xēi²xēi²ha² 夏²】not lively=【普】（工作到）累极了

死死自气【xēi²xēi²ji⁶hēi³ 治戏】not on one's own free will；be in a bed mood∽【普】不乐意地、闹着脾气地（去做某事）

死牛一边颈【xēi²ngeo⁴yed⁷bin⁶gēng²偶⁴壹便镜²】one who is stubborn and who insists on his own thinking and opinion∽【普】固执己见

死鸡撑饭盖【xēi²gei²qang³fan⁶goi³ 计¹橙³ 范该³ 】=死鸡撑硬脚【xēi²gei²qang³ngang⁶gêg⁸ 计¹ 橙³罂⁶ 格约⁸】argue or protest though one is on the wrong side∽【普】不认输,强词掩饰失败

死不瞑目【xēi²bed⁷ming⁵mug⁹ 毕冥木】not close one's eyes when one dies—die with a grievance or everlasting regret

死而后已【xēi²yi⁴heo⁶ yi⁵ 移候尔】until one's dying day；to the end of one's days

死灰复燃【xēi² fui⁵ fug⁹yin⁴ 恢伏言】dying embers glowing again — resurgence；revival

死记硬背【xēi²gēi³ngang⁶bui⁶ 寄罂⁶ 辈⁶】mechanical memorizing

死里逃生【xēi² lêu⁵ tou⁴xeng¹ 吕图笙】escape by the skin of one's teeth；have a narrow escape

死皮赖脸【xēi² pēi⁴ lai⁶ lim⁵ 脾拉⁶ 廉⁵】thick-skinned and hard to shake off

死气沉沉【xēi²hēi³qem⁴qem⁴ 戏侵⁴】lifeless；spiritless

死过翻生【xēi²guo³fan¹xang¹ 戈³ 蕃 是罂¹】half dead；hovering between life and death=【普】死去活来

死心塌地【xēi²xem¹tab⁸dēi⁶ 深塌得希⁶】be dead set；be hell-bent

死有余辜【xēi² yeo⁵ yü⁴gu¹ 友鱼姑】Even death would be too good for him.

死于非命【xēi²yü¹fēi¹ming⁶ 迂飞名⁶】die an unnatural death

四【xēi³ 死³】four

四正【xēi³jēng³ 郑²】neat and tidy=【普】（样子）端正（或端装）

四边【xēi³bin¹ 鞭】(on)four sides

四处【xēi³ qü³ 次于³】all around；everywhere

四川【xēi³qūn¹ 穿】Sichuan(Province)

四方【xēi³ fong¹芳 】the four directions; square

四海【xēi³ hoi² 凯】the four seas; the whole world

四季【xēi³guei³ 桂】the four seasons＝四时【xi⁴】

四面【xēi³min⁶ 缅⁶】(on)four sides；(on) all sides

四起【xēi³hēi² 喜】rise from all directions

四散【xēi³xan³ 汕】scatter in all directions

四围【xēi³ wei⁴维 】all around ＝四周【jeo¹】

四野【xēi³yē⁵ 惹】the surrounding country

四月【xēi³yūd⁹ 越】April; the fourth moon

四肢【xēi³ji¹ 支】the four limbs; arms and legs

四分五裂【xēi³fen¹ng⁵lid⁹ 芬吴⁵ 列】fall apart; disintegrate

四面八方【xēi³min⁶bad⁸fong¹ 缅⁶ 捌芳】all directions; all around; far and near

四面楚歌【xēi³min⁶qo²go¹ 缅⁶ 础哥】be besieged on all sides

四平八稳【xēi³ping⁴bad⁸wen² 苹捌温²】very steady; lacking in initiative and overcautious

四舍五入【xēi³ xē² ng⁵ yed⁹写吴⁵ 邑⁹】rounding (off)；to the nearest whole number

四通八达【xēi³tung¹bad⁸dad⁹ 同¹ 捌挞⁹】extend in all directions

四块半【xēi³fai³bun³ 快拌³】a coffin ＝【普】棺材

四方木【xēi³fong¹mug⁹ 芳目】one who is passive and rigid＝【普】(比喻)没有主动性、积极性的人

四眼佬【xēi³ ngan⁵ lou² 雁⁵ 老²】a man who wears spectacles ＝【普】(戏称)戴眼镜的男人

四体不勤，五谷不分【xēi³tei²bed⁷ken⁴, ng⁵gug⁷bed⁷fen¹ 睇毕芹，吴⁵ 菊毕芬】can neither use one's four limbs nor tell the live grains apart

锃【xēng³ 是镜³】rust; rusty ＝【普】锈；铁锈

生锃【xang¹xēng³ 是罂¹】get rusty＝【普】生锈

锡【xēg⁸ 石⁸；xig⁸ 食⁸】tin(Sn)

锡矿【xēg⁸kong³ 抗】tin ore

锡纸【xēg⁸ji² 止】silver paper; tinfoil

锡箔【xēg⁸bog⁹ 薄】tinfoil paper

锡【xēg⁸ 锡】love dearly; cherish; kiss (又写作"锡")

锡住晒【xēg⁸jū⁶xai³ 注⁶ 徙³】love dearly; cherish＝【普】疼爱；爱惜

锡啖【xēg⁸dam⁶ 淡】kiss＝【普】亲吻；亲嘴

锡力【xēg⁸ lig⁹历】not do one's best ＝【普】惜力；不愿出大力气

Y

吔【ya¹ 衣亚¹；ya² 衣亚²；ya³ 衣亚³；ya⁴
衣亚⁴】〈int.〉ah；oh；hey；ouch；∽
【普】呀

吔吔乌【ya⁴ya⁴wu¹ 呜】what bad luck；
too bad＝【普】糟糕得很

扡【ya⁶ 也⁶】〈a.〉扡 文 扡 武
【ya⁶men⁴ya⁶mou⁵ 民 母】show off
one's strength or power；parade one's
superiority and strive to outshine oth-
ers∽【普】逞威风；逞强好胜

也【ya⁵ 扡⁵】〈ad.〉also；too；as well；
either；〈int.〉∽呀【a³ 阿】

也罢【ya⁵ba⁶ 吧】let it be；let it pass；all
right

也好【ya⁵hou² 蒿²】may as well；whether
...or...

也门【ya⁵mun⁴ 们】Yemen

也许【ya⁵hêü² 诩】〈ad.〉perhaps；pro-
bably；maybe

廿【ya⁶ 也⁶】twenty

幺【yao¹ 衣幼¹；yiu¹ 腰】one（used for
the numeral"一"orally）

躏【yang³ 衣罂³】use the foot to support
or pedal＝【普】用脚撑开或蹬踏

躏开【yang³hoi¹ 海】use the foot to support out＝【普】用脚（把东西）撑
开

裇【yag⁸ 衣轭⁸】eat＝【普】吃（see"吃"
【hēg⁸】）

搋【yei⁵ 衣矮⁵】（the child）be naughty＝
【普】（孩子）顽皮；不听话

曳【yei⁶ 拽】drag；haul；tug；tow

曳绳钓【yei⁶xing⁴diu³ 成吊】trolling

拽【yei⁶ 曳】fling；throw；harl；pull；
drag；haul

拽住不放【yei⁶jü⁶bed⁷fong³ 注⁶ 毕况】
catch hold of sb. or sth. and let go

丘【yeo¹ 邱】mound；hillock；grave；a
surname

丘陵【yeo¹ling⁴ 棱】hills

丘疹【yeo¹qen² 陈²】papule

邱【yeo¹ 丘】a surname

蚯【yeo¹ 丘】〈n.〉蚯 蚓【yeo¹yen⁵ 瘾】
earthworm＝黄犬【wong⁴hün²】

优【yeo¹ 丘】excellent；actor or actress

优待【yeo¹doi⁶ 代】give preferential treatment

优等【yeo¹ deng² 邓²】high-class；excel-
lent

优点【yeo¹dim² 店²】merit；strong point；
virtue

优厚【yeo¹heo⁵ 后⁵】munificent；liberal

优惠【yeo¹ wei⁶ 卫】preferential；favour-
able

优良【yeo¹lêng⁴ 凉】fine；good

优伶【yeo¹ling⁴ 玲】actor or actress

优胜【yeo¹xing³ 圣】winning；superior

优势【yeo¹ xei³ 细】superiority；prepon-
derance

优先【yeo¹xin¹ 仙】have priority

优秀【yeo¹xeo³ 瘦】outstanding；excellent

优异【yeo¹yi⁶ 二】excellent；outstanding

优游【yeo¹yeo⁴ 由】leisurely and carefree

优越【yeo¹ yüd⁹ 月 】superior； advanta-geous

优质【yeo¹ ji¹侄¹】 high quality； high grade

优柔寡断【yeo¹yeo⁴gua²dün³ 由挂² 段³】irresolute and hesitant；indecisive

优哉游哉【yeo¹joi¹jeo⁴joi¹ 由灾】living a life of ease and leisure； leisurely and carefree

忧【yeo¹ 优】worry； be worried；sorrow；anxiety

忧愁【yeo¹xeo⁴ 仇】sad；worried

忧愤【yeo¹fen⁵ 奋】worried and indignant

忧患【yeo¹wan⁶ 幻】suffering；misery

忧虑【yeo¹lêü⁶ 累】worried；anxious

忧伤【yeo¹xêng¹ 双】distressed

忧心【yeo¹xem¹ 深】worry；anxiety

忧郁【yeo¹yug⁷ 沃】melancholy；dejected

幽【yeo¹ 优】deep and remote；dim；se-cret；hidden；quiet；imprison；of the nether world

幽暗【yeo¹ngem³ 庵³】dim；gloomy

幽谷【yeo¹ gug⁷ 菊】a deep and secluded valley

幽会【yeo¹ wui⁶ 汇】a secret meeting of lovers

幽魂【yeo¹wen⁴ 云】ghost

幽禁【yeo¹ gem³ 咁】put under house ar-rest

幽静【yeo¹jing⁶ 净】quiet and secluded

幽灵【yeo¹ling⁴ 玲】ghost；spectre

幽默【yeo¹meg⁹ 麦】humorous

幽深【yeo¹xem¹ 心】deep and serene

幽思【yeo¹ xi¹ 司】ponder； thoughts on things remote

幽微【yeo¹mēi⁴ 眉】faint；weak

幽香【yeo¹hêng¹ 乡】a delicate fragrance

幽雅【yeo¹nga⁵ 瓦】quiet and tasteful

幽咽【yeo¹yin¹ 烟】whimpering；murmur-ing

幽怨【yeo¹yün³ 渊³】hidden bitterness

柚【yeo² 优²】shaddock；pomelo；teak

梳麻柚【xo¹ma⁴yeo² 疏妈⁴】= 碌柚【lug⁷yeo² 六⁷】shaddock；pomelo ＝【普】柚子

柚木【yeo²mug⁹ 目】teak

铀【yeo² 柚】〈n.〉uranium(U)

釉【yeo² 柚】glaze

釉陶【yeo²tou⁴ 图】glazed pottery

釉面砖【yeo²min⁶jün⁴ 缅⁶ 专】glazed tile

呦【yeo¹ 休】〈int.〉∽hey；〈onomatope.〉the sound of deer

休【yeo¹ 优】stop；cease；cast off one's wife and send her home；don't

休息【yeo¹xig⁷ 式】have a rest；rest

休假【yeo¹ga³ 价】have a holiday or vaca-tion；be on leave or furlough

休克【yeo¹heg⁷ 刻】shock

休眠【yeo¹min¹ 绵】dormancy

休戚【yeo¹ qig⁷ 斥】weal and woe；joys and·sorrows

休憩【yeo¹hēi³ 戏】have a rest；rest

休闲【yeo¹han⁴ 娴】lie fallow

休想【yeo¹ xêng² 赏】don't imagine that it's possible

休养【yeo¹ yêng⁵ 痒】recuperate；conva-lesce

休战【yeo¹jin³ 箭】truce；cease-fire

休整【yeo¹ jing² 精²】rest and reorganization

休止【yeo¹ji² 纸】stop；cease

休养生息【yeo¹yêng⁵xeng¹xig⁷ 痒笙式】rest and build up strength

咻
【yeo¹ 休】make a din

貅
【yeo¹ 休】(see"貔貅"【pêi⁴yeo¹】)

幼
【yeo³ 蚴】young；under age；children

幼虫【yeo³qung⁴ 从】larva

幼儿【yeo³yi⁴ 移】child；infant

幼苗【yeo³miu⁴ 描】seedling

幼年【yeo³nin⁴ 捻⁴】childhood；infancy

幼小【yeo³xiu² 少²】immature

幼细【yeo³xei³ 世】fine, delicate＝【普】细小；纤细

幼芽【yeo³nga⁴ 牙】young shoot；bud

幼稚【yeo³ji⁶ 自】young；childish；puerile

蚴
【yeo³ 幼】the larva of a tapeworm or the cercaria of a schistosome

悠
【yeo⁴ 攸】long-drawn-out；leisurely；swing

悠长【yeo⁴qêng⁴祥 】long；long-drawn-out

悠荡【yeo⁴dong⁶ 当⁶】swing；sway

悠久【yeo⁴geo² 九】long；long-standing；age-old

悠然【yeo⁴yin⁴ 言】carefree and leisurely；long

悠闲【yeo⁴han⁴ 娴】leisurely and carefree

悠扬【yeo⁴yêng⁴ 杨】rising and falling

悠悠【yeo⁴yeo⁴】long；remote；leisurely

悠远【yeo⁴ yün⁵ 软】a long time ago；far off

悠悠荡荡【yeo⁴ yeo⁴ dong⁶ dong⁶ 当⁶】floating about

攸
【yeo⁴ 尤】a matter

性命攸关【xing³ming⁶yeo⁴guan¹ 圣名⁶惯¹】a matter of life and death

尤
【yeo⁴ 犹】outstanding；particularly；fault；blame；a surname

尤其【yeo⁴kêi⁴ 奇】especially；particularly

犹
【yeo⁴ 尤】just as；like；still

犹如【yeo⁴yü⁴ 余】just as；like；as if

犹疑【yeo⁴yi⁴ 而】hesitate

犹豫【yeo⁴yü⁴ 余】hesitate；be irresolute

犹大【yeo⁴dai⁶ 歹⁶】Judas

犹太人【yeo⁴tai³yen⁴ 态仁】Jew；Jewess

鱿
【yeo⁴ 尤】〈n.〉鱿鱼【yeo⁴yü⁴ 余】squid

疣
【yeo⁴ 尤】wart

由
【yeo⁴ 尤；yeo² 柚】cause；reason；because of；due to；by；through；follow；obey；from

由佢【yeo²kêü⁵ 拒】＝由得佢【yeo²deg⁷kêü⁵ 德拒】let＝【普】不理；任由

由此【yeo⁴qi² 次²】from this；there from；thus

由来【yeo⁴loi⁴ 莱】origin

由于【yeo⁴yü¹ 迂】owing to；thanks to；due to

由衷【yeo⁴qung¹ 冲】sincere；heartfelt

油
【yeo⁴ 尤；yeo² 柚】oil；fat；grease；apply tung oil or paint；oily；glib

油角【geo⁴ gog⁸ 各 】a type of fried dumpling with flour stin and peanuts, sesame, sugar and coconuts as the ingredients

油气【yeo⁴hêi³ 戏】fried food＝【普】油炸

类食品

油脂【yeo⁴ji¹ 支】oil；fat；grease

油蟙【yeo⁴ji¹ 支】a type of skin disease in which case the skin is itchy

油泵【yeo⁴bem¹ 伯庵¹】oil pump

油布【yeo⁴bou³ 报】oilcloth；oilskin

油彩【yeo⁴qoi² 采】greasepaint；paint

油灯【yeo⁴deng¹ 登】oil lamp

油茶【yeo⁴qa⁴ 查】tea-oil tree

油菜【yeo⁴qoi³ 蔡】rape

油管【yeo⁴gun¹ 莞】oil pipe；oil tube

油光【yeo⁴guong¹ 胱】glossy；shiny

油滑【yeo⁴wad⁹ 挖⁹】slippery；foxy

油画【yeo⁴wa² 话】oil painting

油灰【yeo⁴fui¹ 恢】putty

油迹【yeo⁴jig⁷ 织】oil stains；grease spots

油库【yeo⁴fu³ 富】oil depot

油门【yeo⁴mun¹ 们】throttle；accelerator

油墨【yeo⁴meg⁹ 麦】printing ink

油腻【yeo⁴nêi³ 尼³】greasy；oily

油漆【yeo⁴ qed⁷ 七】paint；cover with paint

油然【yeo⁴yin⁴ 言】spontaneously；densely

油水【yeo⁴xêu² 瑞²】grease；profit

油田【yeo⁴tin⁴ 天⁴】oil field

油桶【yeo⁴tung⁴ 统】oil drum

油污【yeo⁴wu¹ 乌】greasy dirt

油箱【yeo⁴xêng¹ 湘】fuel tank

油烟【yeo⁴yin¹ 燕¹】lampblack

油印【yeo⁴yen³ 人³】mimeograph

油渣【yeo⁴ja¹ 抓】dregs of fat；oil residue

油麦菜【yeo⁴meg⁹qoi³ 墨蔡】a type of green vegetable which is not bitter in taste

油香饼【yeo⁴hêng¹bêng² 乡柄²】a type of fried biscuit＝【普】油炸面饼

油炸鬼（桧）【yeo⁴ja³ guei² 诈轨】fried stick food made of flour，sugar and salt＝【普】油条

油罧罧【yeo⁴nem⁶nem⁶ 那庵⁶】oily〰【普】油腻

油头粉面【yeo⁴teo⁴fen²min⁶ 投分² 缅⁶】sleek-haired and creamy-faced—coquettish or dandified in appearance

油腔滑调【yeo⁴ hong¹ wad⁹ diu⁶ 康⁹ 挖⁹ 掉】glib；unctuous

油嘴滑舌【yeo⁴jêu²wad⁹xid⁶ 咀挖⁹ 泄】glib-tongued

邮 【yeo⁴ 由】post；mail；postal

邮寄【yeo⁴gēi³ 记】post；send by post

邮包【yeo⁴bao¹ 苞】postal parcel；parcel

邮件【yeo⁴gin² 建²】postal matter；post；mail

邮箱【yeo⁴xêng¹ 湘】postbox；mailbox

邮局【yeo⁴gug⁹ 菊⁹】post office

邮票【yeo⁴piu⁸ 漂³】postage stamp；stamp

邮戳【yeo⁴qog⁸ 次恶⁸】postmark

邮递【yeo⁴ dei⁶ 弟】send by post；postal delivery

邮差【yeo⁴ qai¹ 猜】postman＝【普】邮递员

邮购【yeo⁴keo³ 构】mail-order

邮汇【yeo⁴wui⁶ 会】remit by post

邮费【yeo⁴fei³ 废】postage＝邮资【yeo⁴ji¹ 支】

邮政【yeo⁴jing³ 正】postal service

邮政编码【yeo⁴jing³pin¹ma⁵ 正偏马】postcode

游 【yeo⁴ 由】swim；rove around；wander；travel；tour；roving；associate with；part of a river；a surname

游逛【yeo⁴guang⁶ 姑罍⁶】go sight-seeing

游玩【yeo⁴wan² 挽²】amuse oneself；play；stroll about

游览【yeo⁴lam⁵ 揽⁵】go sight-seeing；tour；visit

游荡【yeo⁴dong⁶ 当⁶】loaf about；wander

游历【yeo⁴ lig⁹ 力】 travel for pleasure；tour

游记【yeo⁴gēi³ 寄】travel notes；travels

游戏【yeo⁴hēi³ 气】recreation；game；play

游人【yeo⁴yen⁴ 仁】visitor；sightseer；tourist ＝ 游客【yeo⁴hag⁸】

游离【yeo⁴lēi⁴ 漓】dissociate；free

游民【yeo⁴men⁴ 文】vagrant；vagabond

游移【yeo⁴yi⁴ 而】waver；vacillate；wobble

游水【yeo⁴ xēü² 瑞²】swim ＝ 游泳【yeo⁴ wing⁶】

游说【yeo⁴ xēü³ 税】 go about selling an idea；go canvassing

游行【yeo⁴heng⁴ 衡】parade；march

游弋【yeo⁴yig⁹ 亦】cruise

游艇【yeo⁴ tēng⁵ 厅⁵】 yacht；pleasure-boat

游艺【yeo⁴ngei⁶ 毅】entertainment

游击【yeo⁴gig⁷ 激】guerrilla warfare

游牧【yeo⁴mug⁹ 木】rove around as a nomad

游子【yeo⁴ji² 止】man travelling or residing in a place far away from home；decoy

游兴【yeo⁴ hing³庆】interest in going on an excursion or sight-seeing

游河【yeo⁴ho² 可】tour on river ＝【普】在河上游览

游车河【yeo⁴qē¹ho² 奢可】travel in a car ＝【普】乘车到处游览

游手好闲【yeo⁴ xeo² hou³ han⁴ 守蒿³ 娴】idle about；loaf

酋【yeo⁴ 由；qeo⁴ 绸】chief of a tribe；chieftain

酋长【yeo⁴jêng² 掌】chief of a tribe；emir

酋长国【yeo⁴jêng²guog² 掌帼】sheikhdom；emirate

柔【yeo⁴ 油】soft；supple；flexible；soften；gentle；yielding；mild

柔道【yeo⁴dou⁶ 度】judo

柔和【yeo⁴wo⁴ 禾】soft；gentle；mild

柔媚【yeo⁴mēi⁴ 眉】gentle and lovely

柔情【yeo⁴qing⁴ 程】tender feelings；tenderness

柔软【yeo⁴yün⁶ 远】soft；lithe

柔弱【yeo⁴yêg⁹ 药】weak；delicate

柔顺【yeo⁴xên⁶ 信⁶】gentle and agreeable；meek

揉【yeo⁴ 油】rub；knead

揉搓【yeo⁴qo¹ 初】rub；knead

糅【yeo⁴ 油】mix；mingle

糅合【yeo⁴heb⁹ 盒】mix；form a mixture

蹂【yeo⁴ 油】trample on

蹂躏【yeo⁴lên⁶ 论】trample on；ravage；make havoc of；devastate

遒【yeo⁴ 由】powerful；forceful

遒劲【yeo⁴ging³ 径】powerful；vigorous

黝【yeo² 釉】black；dark

黝黑【yeo²heg⁷ 克】dark；swartby

有【yeo⁵ 友】have；possess；there is；exist；some；again

有宝【yeo⁵bou² 保】the attitude of one not

to cherish certain things〜【普】宝贵；有法宝

有突【yeo⁵ded⁹ 凸】excessive；odd＝【普】多出；有余

有得【yeo⁵deg⁷ 德】available〜【普】可以得到；能够获得

有限【yeo⁵han⁶ 悭⁶】limited＝【普】不很多

有行【yeo⁵hong⁴ 航】say that there is a hope that the expectations will come true〜【普】有获利的希望；有利可图

有之【yeo⁵ji¹ 支】maybe；perhaps；possible＝【普】有可能；或许会

有排【yeo⁵pai⁴ 牌】still a long time to go〜【普】还要待很久；时间远未到

有心【yeo⁵xem¹深】a word used to express thank and appreciation to one who shows concern and care＝【普】多谢关心

有瘾【yeo⁵yen⁵ 引】interesting；show one's interest＝【普】有趣；有兴趣

有碍【yeo⁵ngoi⁶ 外】be a hindrance to；obstruct

有待【yeo⁵doi⁶ 代】remain；await

有啲【yeo⁵did⁷ 得热⁷】some；somewhat；rather＝【普】有的；有些

有底【yeo⁵dei² 抵】know how things stand and feel confident of handling them

有方【yeo⁵fong¹ 芳】with the proper method；in the right way

有功【yeo⁵gung¹ 工】have rendered great service

有关【yeo⁵guan¹ 惯¹】have a bearing on；relate to；concern

有鬼【yeo⁵guei² 轨】There's something fishy.

有害【yeo⁵hoi⁶ 亥】harmful；pernicious

有机【yeo⁵gēi¹ 基】organic

有赖【yeo⁵lai⁶ 拉⁶】depend on；rest on

有力【yeo⁵lig⁹ 历】strong；powerful；forceful

有利【yeo⁵lēi⁶俐】advantageous；beneficial

有名【yeo⁵ ming⁴ 明】well-known；famous

有钱【yeo⁵qin⁴ 前】rich；wealthy

有时【yeo⁵xi⁴ 是⁴】sometimes；at times

有事【yeo⁵ xi⁶士】when problems crop；busy

有数【yeo⁵ xou³ 扫】know exactly how things stand

有所【yeo⁵ xo² 锁】to some extent；somewhat

有望【yeo⁵mong⁶ 亡⁶】hopeful

有为【yeo⁵wei⁴ 维】promising

有效【yeo⁵ hao⁶ 考⁶】efficacious；effective；valid

有益【yeo⁵yig⁷ 亿】profitable；beneficial

有助于【yeo⁵jo⁶yü¹ 左⁶ 迂】be conducive to

有计划【yeo⁵gei³wag⁹ 继或】according to plan

有的是【yeo⁵ dig⁷ xi⁶嫡示】have plenty of；there's no lack of＝大把【dai⁶ba²】

有分数【yeo⁵ fen¹ xou³芬素】know what to do＝【普】有把握；心中有数

有路数【heo⁵lou⁶xou³ 露素】have one's own way of doing something〜【普】有办法

有声气【yeo⁵ xēng¹ hēi³ 腥戏】express that there is still a hope〜【普】有

好消息;有希望

有着数【yeo⁵jêg⁹xou³ 桌⁹扫】beneficial﹀【普】有利;有便宜可占;合算

有几何【yeo⁵gēi²ho²纪可】rarely﹀【普】难得;少有

有冇搞错【yeo⁵mou⁵gao²qo³ 武绞挫】It means:"are you sure?"﹀【普】有否弄错

有型有款【yeo⁵ying⁴ yeo⁵ fun²形欢²】act and look like﹀【普】很像样子;很中看

有头威有尾阵【beo⁵teo⁴wei¹mou⁵mēi⁵ jen⁶ 投畏¹武美珍】be very hard-working and determined in the very beginning but fail to insist on till the last minute﹀【普】(做事)虎头蛇尾;有始无终

有备无患【yeo⁵bēi⁶mou⁴wan⁶ 鼻无宦】Preparedness averts peril.

有的放矢【yeo⁵dig⁷ fong³ qi²嫡况始】shoot the arrow at the target —— have a definite object in view

有机可乘【yeo⁵gēi¹ho²xing⁴ 基何²成】There's loophole that can be used.

有利可图【yeo⁵lēi⁶ ho² tou⁴例何²途】have good prospects of gain

有口难言【yeo⁵heo² nan⁴ yin⁴ 厚³那晏然】cannot bring oneself to mention sth.

有名无实【yeo⁵ming⁴mou⁴xed⁹ 明毛失⁹】in name but not in reality

有目共睹【yeo⁵mug⁹gung⁶dou² 木供⁶倒】be there for all to see

有声有色【yeo⁵xing¹yeo⁵xig⁷ 升式】full of sound and colour——vivid and dramatic

有生以来【yeo⁵xeng¹ yi⁵loi⁴ 笙尔莱】ever since one's birth

有史以来【yeo⁵ xi² yi⁵ loi⁴ 屎尔莱】throughout history

有恃无恐【yeo⁵qi⁵mou⁵hung² 似毛孔】secure in the knowledge that one has strong backing

有条不紊【yeo⁵tiu⁴bed⁷men⁶ 挑⁴毕问】in an orderly way; methodically

有勇无谋【yeo⁵yung⁵mou⁴meo⁴ 拥⁵毛牟】have valour but lack strategy; be foolhardy

有朝一日【yeo⁵ jiu¹ yed⁷ yed⁹焦壹逸】some day; one day

有眼不识泰山【yeo⁵ngan⁵bed⁷xig⁷tai³ xan¹ 雁⁵毕色太珊】entertain an angel unawares

有志者事竟成【yeo⁵ji³zê²xi⁶ging²xing⁴ 至姐士境承】Where there's a will there's a way.

有福同享,有祸同当【yeo⁵fug⁷tung⁴ hêng², yeo⁵wo⁶tung⁴dong¹ 幅铜响,禾⁶铜铛】share joys and sorrows; share weal and woe

友【yeo⁵ 有;yeo² 柚】friend; friendly

友仔【yeo²jei² 济】guy﹀【普】小子;家伙

友爱【yeo⁵KG＊6Ⅱngoi³ 哀³】friendly affection; fraternal love

友邦【yeo⁵ bong¹ 帮】friendly nation(or country)

友好【yeo⁵hou⁴ 蒿²】close friend; friend; friendly

友情【yeo⁵ qing⁴程】friendly sentiments; friendship

友人【yeo⁵yen⁴ 仁】friend

友善【yeo⁵xin⁶ 膳】friendly; amiable

友谊【yeo⁵yi⁴ 移】friendship

齴【yeo⁵ 有】the teeth of the twelve Earthly Branches

诱【yeo⁵ 有】guide；lead；induce；lure；seduce；entice

诱导【yeo⁵dou⁶ 道】guide；lead；induce

诱饵【yeo⁵nēi⁶ 腻】bait

诱发【yeo⁵fad⁸ 法】bring out；induce

诱惑【yeo⁵ wag⁹ 或】entice；tempt；attract

诱骗【yeo⁵ pin³ 片】inveigle；cajole；trap；trick

诱降【yeo⁵hong⁴ 航】lure into surrender

又【yeo⁶ 右】again；and；

又及【yeo⁶keb⁹ 级⁹】postscript(ps)

又惊又喜【yeo⁶ging¹yeo⁶hēi² 京起】be pleasantly surprised

又平又靓【yeo⁶pēng⁴yeo⁶lēng³ 拍镜⁴ 罗镜³】cheap but good

牖【yeo⁵ 友】window

莠【yeo⁵ 友】green bristlegrass；bad people

右【yeo⁶ 又】the right side；the right；west；the right side as the side of precedence；the Right

右边【yeo⁶ bin¹ 鞭 】the right side；the right

右面【yeo⁶min⁶ 缅⁶】the right side

右手【yeo⁶xeo² 守】the right hand

右首【yeo⁶ xeo²守】the right-hand side ＝ 右手便【yeo⁶xeo²bin⁶】

右派【yeo⁶pai³ 排³】the Right；Rightist

右倾【yeo⁶king¹ 顷¹】Right deviation

右翼【yeo⁶yig⁹ 亦】right wing；the Right

佑【yeo⁶ 右】help；protect；bless

宥【yeo⁶ 右】excuse；forgive

囿【yeo⁶ 右】animal-farm；enclosure；park；limited；hampered

阴【yem¹ 音】the feminine or negative principle in nature；the moon；overcast；shade north of a hill or south of a river；back；in intaglio；hidden；secret；of the nether world；negative；private parts；a surname

阴功【yem¹gung¹ 工】express sympathy∽【普】残忍；凄惨；没积阴德

阴湿【yem¹xeb⁷ 拾】cunning；sinister ＝【普】阴险

阴阴笑【yem¹yem¹xiu³ 少³】one privately smiles to oneself∽【普】暗笑；暗自欢喜

阴声细气【yem¹xēng¹xei³hēi³ 腥世戏】soft-spoken＝【普】(女性)温柔地小声说话

阴暗【yem¹ngem³ 庵³】dark；gloomy

阴沉【yem¹qem⁴ 侵⁴】cloudy；overcast

阴德【yem¹ deg⁷ 得】a good deed to the doer's credit in the next world

阴道【yem¹dou⁶ 度】vagina

阴茎【yem¹ging³ 径】penis

阴电【yem¹din⁶ 甸】negative electricity

阴风【yem¹fung¹ 丰】ill wind

阴极【yem¹gig⁹ 击⁹】negative pole

阴魂【yem¹wen⁴ 云】soul；spirit

阴间【yem¹gan¹ 奸】the nether world

阴历【yem¹lig⁹ 力】lunar calendar

阴凉【yem¹ lēng⁴ 梁】shady and cool；shady

阴霾【yem¹mei⁴ 迷】haze

阴谋【yem¹meo⁴ 牟】plot；scheme

阴森【yem¹xem¹ 心】gloomy；gruesome

阴私【yem¹xi¹ 司】shameful secret

阴天【yem¹ tin¹ 田¹】overcast sky; cloudy day

阴文【yem¹ men⁴ 民】characters cut in intaglio

阴险【yem¹him² 欠²】sinister; insidious

阴性【yem¹ xing³ 姓】negative; feminine gender

阴阳【yem¹ yêng⁴ 杨】the two opposing principles in nature, the former feminine and negative, the latter masculine and positive

阴影【yem¹ying² 映】shadow

阴雨【yem¹yǔ⁵ 语】overcast and rainy

阴郁【yem¹yug⁷ 沃】gloomy; dismal

阴云【yem¹wen⁴ 魂】dark clouds

阴差阳错【yem¹qa¹yêng⁴qo³ 叉杨挫】a strange combination of circumstances

音【yem¹ 阴】sound; news; tidings; tone

音响【yem¹hêng² 享】sound; acoustics

音信【yem¹xên³ 讯】mail; message; news

音乐【yem¹ngog⁹ 岳】music

音质【yem¹jed⁷ 侄⁷】tone quality; acoustic fidelity

音容【yem¹ yung⁴ 熔】the likeness of the deceased

音素【yem¹xou³ 扫】phoneme

音节【yem¹jid⁸ 折】syllable

音调【yem¹diu⁶ 掉】tone

音符【yem¹fu⁴ 芙】note

音量【yem¹lêng⁶ 亮】volume

音律【yem¹lêd⁹ 栗】temperament

音频【yem¹pen⁴ 贫】audio frequency

暗【yem¹ 音】silent; mute

饮【yem² 音²】drink; keep in the heart; nurse; give water to drink

饮食【yem²xig⁹ 蚀】food and drink; diet

饮料【yem²liu⁶ 了⁶】drink; beverage

饮恨【yem²hen² 很⁶】nurse a grievance

饮泣【yem²yeb⁷ 邑】weep in silence

饮马【yem²ma⁵ 码】water a horse

饮茶【yem²qa⁴ 查】drink tea; drink water; eat dim sum in restaurants

饮胜【yem² xing³ 圣】propose a toast ∽【普】干杯; 喝完

荫【yem³ 任³; yem¹ 音】penetrate; water the paddy field; shade; shady; confer privileges on sb.'s descendants in consideration of his distinguished service

荫庇【yem³bēi³ 臂】protection by one's elders or ancestors

荫凉【yem¹lêng⁴ 梁】shady and cool

荫蔽【yem³ bei³ 闭】be shaded or hidden by foliage; cover; conceal

鬠【yem⁴ 壬】fringes in front of the forehead

褛鬠妹【leo¹yem⁴mui² 流¹ 壬 梅²】girl; young girl =【普】姑娘; 少女

壬【yem⁴ 淫】the ninth of the ten Heavenly Stems

淫【yem⁴ 壬】excessive; loose; wanton; lewd; licentious; obscene

淫荡【yem⁴ dong⁶ 当⁶】loose in morals; lascivious

淫秽【yem⁴wei³ 畏】obscene; salacious

淫乱【yem⁴ lün⁶ 联⁶】(sexually) promiscuous; licentious

淫威【yem⁴wei¹ 伟¹】abuse of power

吟【yem⁴ 淫】chant; recite; song; the cry of certain animals

吟诵【yem⁴jung⁶ 颂】chant; recite

吟咏【yem⁴ wing⁶ 泳】recite with a cadence; chant

湴【yem⁵ 吟⁵】dip in (ink, sauce, etc) =【普】蘸

湴墨水【yem⁵meg⁹xêü² 麦瑞²】dip in ink

任【yem⁶ 壬⁶】appoint; assume a post; take up a job; office; let; allow; not matter; a surname

任务【yem⁶mou⁶ 冒】assignment; mission; task; job

任用【yem⁶yung⁶ 庸⁶】appoint

任职【yem⁶jig⁷ 织】hold a post; be in office

任命【yem⁶ming⁵ 名⁶】appoint

任免【yem⁶min⁵ 缅】appoint and remove

任何【yem⁶ho⁴ 河】any; whichever; whatever

任凭【yem⁶ peng⁴朋】at one's convenience; no matter

任性【yem⁶ xing³ 姓】wilful; self-willed wayward

任意【yem⁶yi³ 薏】wantonly; wilfully

任由【yem⁶ yeo⁴ 油】as you like; as you see fit =【普】任便

任……唔嬲【yem⁶…m⁴neo¹ 那欧¹】It is up to you! ∽【普】随便……也不生气

任重道远【yem⁶ jung⁶ dou⁶ yün⁵ 仲度软】The burden is heavy and the road is long—shoulder heavy responsibilities.

任人唯亲【yem⁶yen⁴wei⁴qen¹ 仁维趁¹】appoint people by favouritism

任人唯贤【yem⁶yen⁴wei⁴yin⁴ 仁维言】appoint people on their merits

饪【yem⁶ 任; yem⁵ 任⁵】(see "烹饪"【pang¹yem⁶】)

妊【yem⁴ 吟】be pregnant

妊娠【yem⁴xen¹ 身】gestation; pregnancy

荏【yem⁵ 任⁵; yem⁶ 任】weak; weakkneed; common perilla

荏苒【yem⁵yin⁵ 染】(of time)elapse quickly or imperceptibly; slip by

因【yen¹ 恩】follow; carry on; on the basis of; cause; reason; because of; as a result of

因此【yen¹qi² 次²】therefore; for this reason

因而【yen¹yi⁴ 移】thus; as a result

因果【yen¹guo² 裹】cause and effect; karma

因素【yen¹xou³ 扫】factor; element

因为【yen¹ wei⁶ 卫】because; for; on account of

因循【yen¹ qên⁴ 巡】follow; continue in the same old rut; procrastinate

因由【yen¹yeo⁴ 油】reason; cause; origin

因缘【yen¹ yün⁴ 元】principal and subsidiary causes; cause; predestined relationship

因何【yen¹ho⁴ 河】why =【普】为何;为什么

因住【yen¹jü⁶ 注⁶】beware; be careful; estimate =【普】小心;提防;别乱来

因材施教【yen¹qoi⁴xi¹gao³ 才司较】teach students in accordance with their aptitude

因陋就简【yen¹ lou⁶ jeo⁶ gan² 漏袖束】make do with whatever is available

因势利导【yen¹ xei³ lêi⁶ dou⁶世俐道】adroitly guide action according to circumstances

恩【yen¹ 因】kindness; favour; grace

恩爱【yen¹ngoi³ 哀³】conjugal love

恩赐【yen¹qi³ 次】bestow; favour; charity

恩德【yen¹ deg⁷ 得 】favour; kindness; grace

恩惠【yen¹wei⁶ 卫】favour; kindness; bounty

恩情【yen¹qing⁴ 程】loving-kindness

恩人【yen¹ yen⁴ 仁】benefactor

恩怨【yen¹yün³ 愿³】feeling of gratitude or resentment; resentment; grievance

恩将仇报【yen¹jêng¹xeo⁴bou³ 章愁布】 requite kindness with enmity

茵【yen¹ 因】nattress

茵陈【yen¹qen⁴ 趁⁴】capillary artemisia

姻【yen¹ 因】marriage; relation by marriage

姻亲【yen¹qen¹ 趁¹】relation by marriage

姻缘【yen¹yün⁴ 元】the happy fate which brings lovers together

甄【yen¹ 因】discriminate; distinguish; examine; a surname

甄别【yen¹bid⁹ 必⁹】examine and distinguish; screen; reexamine a case

铟【yen¹ 因】indium（In）

殷【yen¹ 因】abundant; rich; eager; ardent; hospitable; blackish red; the Yin Dynasty, the later period of the Shang Dynasty; a surname

殷红【yen¹ hung⁴洪 】blackish red; dark red

殷切【yen¹qid⁸ 设】ardent; eager

殷勤【yen¹ ken⁴ 芹】eagerly attentive; solicitous

殷实【yen¹ xed⁹ 失⁹】well-off; substantial

殷鉴不远【yen¹gam³bed⁷yün⁵ 监³ 毕软】 One need not look far a lesson.

隐【yen² 忍】hidden from view; concealed; latent dormant; lurking

隐蔽【yen²bei³ 闭】conceal; take cover

隐藏【yen²qong⁴ 床】hide; conceal

隐患【yen²wan⁶ 幻】hidden trouble; hidden danger

隐忧【yen²yeo¹ 优】secret worry

隐讳【yen² wei⁵ 伟 】avoid mentioning; cover up

隐晦【yen²fui³ 悔】obscure; veiled

隐居【yen²gêü¹ 举¹】live in seclusion; be a hermit

隐瞒【yen² mun⁴ 门】conceal; hide; hold back

隐情【yen² qing⁴ 程】facts one wishes to hide

隐私【yen²xi¹ 司】one's secrets

隐退【yen²têü³ 推³】go and live in seclusion

隐性【yen²xing⁵ 姓】recessiveness

隐语【yen²yün⁵ 雨】enigmatic language

隐喻【yen²yü⁶ 誉】metaphor

隐约【yen²yêg⁸ 跃】indistinct; faint

隐衷【yen² qung¹ 冲 】feelings or troubles one wishes to keep to oneself

忍【yen² 隐】bear; endure; tolerate; put up with; be hardhearted enough to

忍心【yen²xem¹ 深】have the heart to

忍耐【yen² noi⁶奈 】exercise patience; exercise restraint

忍让【yen²yêng⁶ 样】exercise forbearance

忍受【yen²xeo⁶ 授】bear; endure; stand

忍痛【yen²tung³ 通³】very reluctantly

忍唔住【yen²m⁴jü⁶ 注⁶】unable to bear ＝

【普】忍不住

忍无可忍【yen² mou⁴ ho² yen² 毛苟²】be driven beyond (the limits of) forbearance

忍气吞声【yen² hēi³ ten¹ xēng¹ 汽替因¹ 腥】swallow an insult; submit to humiliation

忍辱负重【yen² yug⁹ fu⁶ jung⁶ 玉父仲】endure humiliation in order to carry out an important mission

胭【yen² 闰²】liver; liver in animals' bodies =【普】肝

胭肠【yen² qêng² 抢】sausages made of pork liver and pork =【普】以动物肝脏为主要原料制成的香肠

韧【yen⁶ 孕; ngen⁶ 银⁶】pliable but strong; tenacious; tough

韧带【yen⁶ dai³ 戴】ligament

韧性【yen⁶ xing³ 姓】toughness; tenacity

韧皮【ngen⁶ pēi⁴ 牌】naughty =【普】(小孩)顽皮

纫【yen⁶ 刃】sew; stitch; thread (a needle)

刃【yen⁶ 纫】the edge of a knife, sword, etc; blade; sword; knife; kill with a sword or knife (see "刀刃"【dou¹ yen⁶】)

仞【yen⁶ 刃】an ancient measure of length equal to seven or eight chi (尺)

孕【yen⁶ 刃】pregnant

孕育【yen⁶ yug⁹ 玉】be pregnant with; breed

孕妇【yen⁶ fu⁵ 苦⁵】pregnant woman

闰【yen⁶ 润】intercalary

闰年【yen⁶ nin⁴ 捻⁴】leap year

闰月【yen⁶ yüd⁹ 越】intercalary month in the lunar calendar; leap month

润【yen⁶ 闰】moist; smooth; sleek; moisten; embellish; profit; benefit

润滑【yen⁶ wad⁹ 挖⁹】lubricate

润色【yen⁶ xig⁷ 式】polish; touch up = 润饰【yen⁶ xig⁷ 式】

润泽【yen⁶ jag⁹ 择】moist; smooth; moisten

印【yen³ 刃³】seal; stamp; chop; mark; print; engrave; tally; a surname

印刷【yen³ qad⁸ 察】printing

印花【yen³ fa¹ 化¹】printing

印染【yen³ yim⁵ 冉⁵】printing and dyeing

印章【yen³ jêng¹ 张】seal; signet; stamp

印鉴【yen³ gam³ 监³】a specimen seal impression for checking when making payments

印象【yen³ jêng⁶ 丈】impression

印证【yen³ jing³ 正】confirm; verify

印数【yen³ xou³ 扫】printing; impression

印度【yen³ dou⁶ 道】India

印度洋【yen³ dou⁶ yêng⁴ 道羊】the Indian Ocean

印把子【yen³ ba² ji² 巴² 止】official seal

印度尼西亚【yen³ dou⁶ nēi⁴ xei¹ a³ 道你⁴ 筛阿】Indonesia

寅【yen⁴ 人】the third of the twelve Earthly Branches

寅时【yen⁴ xi⁴ 是⁴】the period of the day from 3 a.m. to 5 a.m.

引【yen⁵ 蚓】draw; stretch; lead; guide; leave; lure; attract; cause; make; quote; cite; a unit of length (= 33⅓ metres)

引导【yen⁵ dou⁶ 道】guide; lead

引渡【yen⁵ dou⁶ 道】extradite

引发【yen⁵fad⁸ 法】initiation

引起【yen⁵hēi² 喜】give rise to; lead to

引出【yen⁵ qêd⁷次律⁷】draw forth; lead to

引入【yen⁵yeb⁹ 邑⁹】lead into; draw into

引进【yen⁵jên³ 俊】recommend; introduce from elsewhere

引申【yen⁵xen¹ 辛】extend

引用【yen⁵yung⁶ 庸⁶】quote; cite; recommend

引文【yen⁵men⁴ 民】quoted pasage; quotation

引线【yen⁵ xin³扇】 lead（wire）; go-between; catalyst

引号【yen⁵hou⁶ 好⁶】quotation marks

引荐【yen⁵jin³ 箭】recommend

引咎【yen⁵geo³ 够】take the blame

引力【yen⁵lig⁹ 历】gravitation; attraction

引擎【yen⁵king⁴ 琼】engine

引诱【yen⁵yeo⁵ 友】lure; seduce

引人注目【yen⁵yen⁴jū³mug⁹ 仁蛀木】noticeable

引人入胜【yen⁵yen⁴yeb⁹xing³ 仁邑⁹ 性】fascinating; enchanting; bewitching

引狼入室【yen⁵long⁴yeb⁹xed⁷ 郎邑⁹ 失】invite a wolf into the house——open the door to a dangerous foe

引以为戒【yen⁵yi⁵wei⁴gai³ 尔维介】learn a lesson; take warning

蚓【yen⁵ 引】(see "蚯蚓"【yeo¹yen⁵】)

瘾【yen⁵ 引】addiction; strong interest

瘾头【yen⁵teo⁴ 投】addiction; strong interest

胤【yen⁶ 刃】offspring; posterity

人【yen⁴ 仁】human being; man; person; people; adult; grown-up; a person engaged in a particular activity; other people; personality; how one feels everybody; each; manpower

人民【yen⁴men⁴ 文】the people

人员【yen⁴yūn⁴ 元】personnel; staff

人命【yen⁴mēng⁶ 莫镜⁶】human life

人体【yen⁴tei² 睇】human body

人手【yen⁴xeo² 守】manpower; hand

人身【yen⁴xen¹ 辛】livng body of a human being; person

人口【yen⁴ heo² 厚²】population; number of people

人群【yen⁴kuen⁴ 裙】crowd; throng

人类【yen⁴lêü⁶ 泪】mankind; humanity

人力【yen⁴ lig⁹ 历】 manpower; labour ower

人工【yen⁴ gung¹ 功】 man-made; manual work; manpower; man-day

人心【yen⁴xem¹ 深】popular feeling; public feeling

人性【yen⁴ xing³ 姓】human nature; humanity; normal human feelings; reason

人格【yen⁴ gag⁸ 隔】personality; human dignity

人品【yen⁴ben² 禀】moral standing; looks

人情【yen⁴ qing⁴ 程】human feeling; human relationship; favour; gift; present

人权【yen⁴ kün⁴拳】human rights; rights of man

人事【yen⁴ xi⁶ 示】human affairs; personnel matters; ways of the world; consciousness of the outside world; what is humanly possible

人士【yen⁴xi⁶ 是】personage; public figure

人生【yen⁴xeng¹ 笙】life

人世【yen⁴xei³ 细】the world; man's world =人间 gan¹】

人伦【yen⁴lên⁴ 纶】human relations

人们【yen⁴ mun⁴ 门 】people; men; the public

人人【yen⁴yen⁴】everybody; everyone

人家【yen⁴ ga¹ 加】household; family; other people

人物【yen⁴med⁹ 勿】figure; personage; character

人道【yen⁴ dou⁶ 度】humanity; human; humane

人称【yen⁴qing¹ 清】person

人才【yen⁴qoi⁴ 材】a person of ability; talent; a talented person; handsome appearance

人为【yen⁴wei⁴ 维】artificial; man-made

人造【yen⁴jou⁶ 做】man-made; imitation

人参【yen⁴xem¹ 心】ginseng

人质【yen⁴ji² 至】hostage

人迹【yen⁴jig⁷ 织】human footmarks

人和【yen⁴wo⁴ 禾】support of the people

人烟【yen⁴yin¹ 燕¹】signs of human habitation

人地【yen⁴dēi⁶ 得希⁶】others =【普】别人;人家

人客【yen⁴hag⁸ 赫】guests =【普】客人

人渣【yen⁴ja¹ 抓】people who are useless to the society =【普】败类

人头涌涌【yen⁴ teo⁴ yung² yung² 投拥】crowded; too many people =【普】

人多拥挤

人细鬼大【yen⁴ xei³ guei² dai⁶世诡歹⁶】one who is young at age but mature in thinking =【普】年纪少而懂事多、计谋多

人定胜天【yen⁴ding⁶xing³tin¹ 锭性田¹】Man can conquer nature.

人面兽心【yen⁴min⁶xeo³xem¹ 缅⁶ 秀深】have the face of a man but the heart of a beast——a beast in human shape

人云亦云【yen⁴wen⁴yig⁹wen⁴ 魂逆】echo the views of others; parrot

人情世故【yen⁴ qing⁴ xei³ gu³ 程细固】worldly wisdom

人之常情【yen⁴ji¹xêng⁴qing⁴ 支裳程】the way of the world

人同此心, 心同此理【yen⁴tung⁴qi²xem¹, xem¹ tung⁴qi²lêi⁵ 铜次² 深李】Everybody feels the same about this.

人不为己, 天诛地灭【yen⁴bed⁷wei⁶gēi², tin¹jü¹dēi⁶mid⁹ 毕卫儿, 田¹ 朱得希⁶ 蔑】everyone for himself and the devil take the hindmost

仁【yen⁴ 人】benevolence; kindheartedness; humanity; sensitive; kernel

仁爱【yen⁴ngoi³ 哀³】kindheartedness

仁慈【yen⁴ qi⁴ 迟】benevolent; merciful; kind

仁兄【yen⁴hing¹ 兴】my dear friend

仁政【yen⁴jing³ 正】policy of benevolence

仁义道德【yen⁴yi⁶dou⁶deg⁷ 异度得】humanity; justice and virtue

仁至义尽【yen⁴ji³yi⁶jên⁶ 志异进⁶】do everything called for by humanity and duty

泣【yeb⁷ 揖】weep; sob; tears

泣不成声【yeb⁷bed⁷xing⁴xing¹ 毕承升】choke with sobs

挹【yeb⁷ 泣】scoop up; ladle out; pull

揖【yeb⁷ 泣】(make a) bow with hands clasped

邑【yeb⁷ 泣】city; county

悒【yeb⁷ 泣; yab⁸】sad; worried

悒悒不乐【yeb⁷yeb⁷bed⁷log⁹ 毕落】feel depressed; mope

发悒【fad⁸yab⁸ 法】feel gloom and get angry＝【普】愁闷而发脾气

翕【yeb⁷ 泣】amiable and compliant; furl; fold; shut

翕张【yeb⁷jêng¹ 章】close and open

翕手【yeb⁷ xeo² 守】wave at ∽【普】挥手; 以手示意邀对方过来或送别

入【yeb⁹ 泣⁹】enter; join; be admitted into; income; conform to; keep

入门【yeb⁹ mun⁴ 们】cross the threshold; elementary course; ABC

入口【yeb⁹heo² 厚²】enter the mouth; entrance

入场【yeb⁹qêng⁴ 祥】entrance; admission

入耳【yeb⁹yi⁵ 尔】pleasant to the ear

入港【yeb⁹gong² 讲】enter a port; in full agreement

入伙【yeb⁹ fo² 火】join a gang; join a mess; shift to a new house

入股【yeb⁹gu² 古】buy a share; become a shareholder

入境【yeb⁹ging² 景】enter a country

入库【yeb⁹fu³ 富】be put in storage

入梦【yeb⁹ mung⁶ 蒙⁶】fall asleep; appear in one's dream

入睡【yeb⁹ xêü⁶ 穗⁶】go to sleep; fall asleep

入迷【yeb⁹mei⁴ 米⁴】be infatuated

入魔【yeb⁹mo¹ 摩】be infatuated

入神【yeb⁹xen⁴ 臣】be entranced; superb

入侵【yeb⁹qem¹ 沉¹】invade; intrude

入声【yeb⁹ xing¹ 升】entering tone, one of the four tones in classical Chinese pronunciation, still retained in certain dialects

入手【yeb⁹xeo² 守】start with; begin with

入微【yeb⁹mēi⁴ 眉】in every possible way

入选【yeb⁹xün² 损】be selected; be chosen

入学【yeb⁹ hog⁹ 鹤】start school; enter a school

入帐【yeb⁹ jêng³ 涨】enter an item in an account

入赘【yeb⁹ jêü⁶ 罪】marry into and live with one's bride's family

入数【yeb⁹xou³ 扫】take into account ∽【普】进帐; 算进去

入围【yeb⁹wei⁴ 维】qualify; be employed ＝【普】进入了……范围; 入选

入息【yeb⁹xig⁷ 式】salary＝【普】薪金; 月收入

入味【yeb⁹mēi⁶ 未】tasty; interesting

入便【yeb⁹bin⁶ 辨】inside＝【普】里边

入院【yeb⁹yün² 阮】be admitted to hospital

入狱【yeb⁹yug⁹ 玉】be put in prison

入境问俗【yeb⁹ging²men⁶jug⁹ 景闻⁶族】on entering a country, inquire about its customs

一【yed⁷ 壹】one; single; alone; only one; same; whole; all; each; per; every time; also; wholehearted;

once; as soon as; extremely

一哥【yed⁷ go¹ 歌】number one; the authority; one who will not admit that one fails∽【普】第一把手；头头；首领；群体中权力最大、地位最高的人

一系【yed⁷hei⁶ 兮⁶】or =【普】或者；要不然

一自【yed⁷yi⁶ 治】at the same time =【普】（在同一时间）一边（干）……一边（干）……

一于【yed⁷yü¹ 迂】insist on ∽【普】一定（照这样办）

一阵【yed⁷ jen⁶珍⁶】a while; after some time; hold on for a while = 一阵间【yed⁷jen⁶gan¹ 珍⁶ 奸】=【普】一会儿；一阵子

一般【yed⁷ bun¹ 搬】same as; general; common

一半【yed⁷ bun³ 搬³ 】one half; half; in part

一边【yed⁷bin¹ 鞭】one side; at the same time

一次【yed⁷qi³ 刺】once

一旦【yed⁷dan³ 诞】in a single day; once

一齐【yed⁷qei⁴ 妻⁴】together; at the same place; in company; in all =【普】一道；一起；一块儿；一同

一等【yed⁷ deng² 邓² 】first-class; first-rate; top-grade = 一流【yed⁷leo⁴ 留】

一定【yed⁷ ding⁶ 锭】fixed; definite; certainly; surely; given; certain

一概【yed⁷koi³ 慨】one and all; totally

一共【yed⁷gung⁶ 贡⁶】altogether; in all

一贯【yed⁷gun³ 灌】consistent; all along

一晃【yed⁷fong² 仿】slash;（of time）pass in a flash

一经【yed⁷ ging¹ 京】〈ad.〉as soon as; once

一举【yed⁷gêü² 矩】with one action

一口【yed⁷heo² 厚²】a bite; readily

一连【yed⁷lin⁴ 莲】〈ad.〉in a row; running

一路【yed⁷ lou⁶ 露】all the way; of the same kind; go the same way; single file

一律【yed⁷lêü⁹ 栗】same; alike; uniform; all

一面【yed⁷min⁶ 缅⁶】one side; one aspect; at the same time

一气【yed⁷hêi³ 戏】at one go; a spell; a fit

一切【yed⁷qei³ 砌】all; every

一生【yed⁷xeng¹ 笙】all one's life

一时【yed⁷xi⁴ 是⁴】a period of time; for a short while; now..., now...

一手【yed⁷ xeo² 守】skill; move; all by oneself; all alone

一瞬【yed⁷xên³ 信】an instant; a flash

一味【yed⁷mêi² 未²】〈ad.〉blindly

一下【yed⁷ ha⁶ 夏】one time; once; in a short while; all at once

一向【yed⁷ hêng³ 乡³】earlier on; lately; all along

一些【yed⁷xê¹ 赊】a number of; some; certain; a few; a little

一心【yed⁷xem¹ 深】wholeheartedly; heart and soul; of one mind; at one

一样【ged7yêng⁶ 让】the same; equally; alike

一一【yed⁷yed⁷】one by one; one after another

一月【yed⁷yüd⁹ 越】January

一再【yed⁷joi³ 载】time and again; repeatedly

一早【yed⁷jou² 蚤】early in the morning

一直【yed⁷jig⁹ 值】straight; always; all along; all the way

一致【yed⁷ ji³ 至】showing no difference; identical; unanimous; consistent

一头…一头…【yed⁷teo⁴…yed⁷teo⁴…投】at the same time... and... =【普】(在同一时间)一边…一边…

一日【yed⁷yed⁹ 逸】one day; according to the reasoning =【普】一天;全都

一堆垒【yed⁷dêü¹lêü¹ 对¹ 吕¹】one pile◯【普】全都放在一起;垒成一堆

一脚踢【yed⁷gêg⁸têg⁹ 格 约⁸ 替吃⁸】do everthing on one's very own; all; everything =【普】全部包揽;一揽子解决

一咀饭【yed⁷geo⁶fan⁶ 旧范】= 一辘木【yed⁷lug⁹mug⁹ 六⁷ 目】stupid; not alert; not smart =【普】饭桶;呆子(比喻某人愚笨,没有主动性、灵活性)

一个对【yed⁷go³dêü³ 哥³ 堆³】the entire night =【普】从一天的某时刻到第二天的同一时刻;一昼夜(24小时)

一个骨【yed⁷go³gued⁷ 哥³ 掘³】one quarter =【普】一刻钟

一个字【yed⁷go³ji⁶ 哥³ 治】five minutes =【普】五分钟

一枝公【yed⁷ji¹gung¹ 支工】single(refer to a man) =【普】独自一人;自个儿

一窿蛇【yed⁷ lung¹ xê⁴隆¹ 余】one group of gangsters◯【普】蛇鼠一窝;一班坏家伙

一粒色【yed⁷ neb⁷ xig⁷笠式】describe one who is small in size◯【普】小个子

一身蚁【yed⁷ xen¹ ngei⁵ 辛矮⁵】get involved in deep trouble =【普】(惹来)一大堆麻烦

一镬粥【yed⁷ wog⁹ pou⁵ 获抱】describe that a matter is in a mess and is difficult to solve =【普】一团糟;一塌糊涂

一镬熟【yed⁷ wog⁹ xug⁹ 获孰】Everyone bears the consequences when an unfortunate event happens. ◯【普】一揽子解决。

一时时【yed⁷xi⁴xi⁴ 是⁴】sometimes◯【普】一时一变样

一只(隻)屐【yed⁷jêg⁸kêg⁹ 脊剧】describe the expression on one's face when one is low, blue or moody =【普】(比喻)累得难受

一栋都冇晒【yed⁷dung⁶dou¹mou⁵xai³ 洞刀武徙³】cannot do anything =【普】全盘输光;啥办法也没了

一眼关七【yed⁷ngan⁵guan¹qed⁷ 雁⁵ 惯¹柒】take care of a few things at the same time◯【普】眼观六路;全面关注情况

一手一脚【yed⁷xeo²yed⁷gêg⁸ 守格 约⁸】finish a project or a piece of work all by oneself◯【普】全过程由一人亲自操办

一日到黑【yed⁷ yed⁹ dou¹heg⁷ 逸度³ 克】the whole day; according to the reasoning =【普】一天到晚;从早到晚;整天;老是

一败涂地【yed⁷bai⁶tou⁴dêi⁶ 摆⁶ 图得希⁶】suffer a crushing defeat

一个鼻哥窿出气【yed⁷ go³ bêi⁶ go¹ lung¹

qêd⁷hēi³ 哥³ 备哥隆¹ 次律⁷ 戏】
breathe through the same nos-trils
— sing the same tune

一朝天子一朝臣【yed⁷qiu⁴tin¹ji²yed⁷qiu⁴
xen⁴ 瞧田¹ 止神】Every new
sovereign brings his own cour-tiers
— a new chief brings in new
aides.

一帆风顺【yed⁷ fan⁴ fung¹ xên⁶凡丰信⁶】
plain sailing

一鼓作气【yed⁷gǔ⁴jog⁸hēi³ 古昨戏】press
on to the finish without letup

一见钟情【yed⁷gin³jung¹qing⁴建中程】fall
in love at first sight

一箭双雕【yed⁷ jin³ xêng¹ diu¹ 战商刁】
shoot two hawks with one arrow;
kill two birds with one stone = 一
举两得【yed⁷gêǔ¹lêng⁵deg¹ 矩俩
德】

一鸣惊人【yed⁷ming⁴ ging¹ yen⁴ 名京仁】
set the world on fire

一丘之貉【yed⁷yeo¹ji¹hog⁹优支学】birds
of a feather

一人得道，鸡犬升天【yed⁷yen⁴deg¹dou⁶,
gei¹hūn²xing¹tin¹ 仁德度，继¹ 劝²
声田¹】When a man attains the
Tao(enlightenment and immortality), even his pets ascend to heav-
en——when a man gets to the
top, all his friends and relations get
there with him.

一失足成千古恨【yed⁷xed⁷jug⁷xing⁴qin¹
gǔ¹hen⁶ 室竹承迁鼓很⁶】A single
slip may cause lasting sorrow.

一视同仁【yed⁷xi⁶tung⁴yen⁴ 示铜人】treat
equally without discrimination

一往情深【yed⁷wong⁵ qing⁴xem¹ 汪⁵ 程

心】be head over heels in love

一物治一物【yed⁷med⁹ji⁶yed⁷med⁹ 勿自】
There is always one thing to conquer another.

一息尚存【yed⁷xig⁹ xêng⁶ qūn¹ 色上泉】so
long as one still has a breath left

一心一德【yed⁷xem¹yed⁷deg¹ 深得】be of
one heart and one mind

一言以蔽之【yed⁷yin⁴yi⁵bei³yi¹ 然尔闭
支】sum up in a word

一叶知秋【yed⁷yib⁹ ji¹ qeo¹ 业支抽】The
falling of one leaf heralds the autumn.

一叶障目，不见泰山【yed⁷yib⁹jêng³mug⁹,
bed⁷gin³tai³xan¹ 业涨木, 毕建太
珊】A leaf before the eye shuts out
Mount Taishan—have one's view
of the important overshadowed by
the trivial.

一枕黄梁【yed⁷jem²wong⁴lêng⁴ 针² 王
梁】Golden Millet Dream — a
brief dream of grandeur

一着不慎，全盘皆输【yed⁷jêg⁹bed⁷xen⁶,
qūn⁴pun⁴gai¹xū¹ 雀⁹ 毕辛⁶, 存盆
街书】One careless move and the
whole game is lost.

壹 【yed⁷ 一】one (used as the numeral
on cheques, banknotes, etc. to
avoid mistakes or alterations)

日 【yed⁹ 逸】sun; daytime; day; daily;
every day; time

日头【yed⁹teo² 投²】sunlight; day time =
【普】白天

日日【yed⁹yed⁹】every day =【普】天天

日间【yed⁹gan¹ 奸】in the daytime

日本【yed⁹bun² 苯】Japan

日常【yed⁹xêng⁴ 裳】day-to-day; everyday

日光【yed⁹guong¹ 胱】sunlight; sunbeam

日后【yed⁹heo⁶ 候】in the future; in days to come

日见【yed⁹gin³ 建】=日渐【yed⁹jim⁶ 尖⁶】with each passing day; day by day

日历【yed⁹lig⁹ 力】calendar

日食【yed⁹xig⁹ 蚀】solar eclipse

日内【yed⁹noi⁶ 耐】in a few days

日前【yed⁹qin⁴ 钱】a few days ago

日期【yed⁹kēi⁴ 其】date

日夜【yed⁹yē⁶ 野⁶】day and night; round the clock

日子【yed⁹ji² 止】day; date; time; life

日趋【yed⁹qêü¹ 吹】with each passing day; day by day

日益【yed⁹ yig⁷忆】increasingly; day by day

日薄西山【yed⁹bog⁹xei¹xan¹ 博⁹ 筛珊】The sun is setting beyond the western hills — declining rapidly.

日暮途穷【yed⁹mou⁶tou⁴kung⁴ 务图穹】The day is waning and the road is ending—approaching the end of one's days.

日新月异【yed⁹ xen¹ yüd⁹ yi⁶辛越异】change with each passing day

日以继夜【yed⁹yi⁵gei³yē⁶ 尔计野⁶】night and day; round the clock

日积月累【yed⁹jig⁷yüd⁹lêü⁶ 织越类】accumulate over a long period

逸 【yed⁹ 日】ease; leisure; escape; flee; be lost; excel

逸乐【yed⁹log⁹ 落】comfort and pleasure

逸事【yed⁹xi⁶ 士】anecdote

逸闻【yed⁹men⁴ 民】anecdote

溢 【yed⁹ 日】overflow; spill; excessive

溢出【yed⁹qêd⁷ 次律⁷】spill over; overflow

溢美【yed⁹ mēi⁵ 尾】undeserved praise; compliment

佚 【yed⁸ 日】be lost; excel

轶 【yed⁹ 日】be lost; excel

轶事【yed⁹xi⁶ 士】anecdote

唷 【yo¹ 哟】〈int.〉╭oh;〈auxil.〉╭ho

哟 【yo¹ 唷】〈int.〉╭oh;〈auxil.〉╭ho

雍 【yung¹ 痈】harmony; a surname

雍容【yung¹yung⁴ 熔】natural, graceful and poised

壅 【yung¹ 雍;ngung¹ 瓮¹】stop up; heap soil or fertilizer over and around the roots

壅塞【yung¹ xeg⁷ 是克⁷】clogged up; jammed

壅泥【ngung¹nei⁴ 黎】hilling =【普】壅土

痈 【yung¹ 雍】carbuncle

痈疽【yung¹jêü¹ 追】ulcer

邕 【yung¹ 雍】another name for Nanning

翁 【yung¹ 雍】old man; father; father-in-law; a surname

翁姑【yung⁹gu¹ 孤】a woman's parents-in-law

嗡 【yung¹ 翁】〈onomatope.〉drone; buzz; bum

鶲【yung¹ 翁】〈n.〉flycatcher

拥【yung² 甬】hold in one's arms; embrace; hug; gather around; crowd; support; have; possess

拥抱【yung²pou⁵ 铺⁵】embrace; hug

拥戴【yung²dai³ 带】support(sb. as leader)

拥护【yung²wu⁶ 户】support; uphold

拥挤【yung²jei¹ 剂】crowd; push and squeeze

拥墩【yung²den² 得因²】the man who supports sb. =【普】某人的狂热拥护者

拥塞【yung²xeg⁷ 是克⁷】jam; congest

拥有【yung²yeo⁵ 友】possess; have; own

甬【yung² 拥】another name for Ningbo

甬道【yung²dou⁶ 度】paved path leading to a main hall or a tomb; corridor

涌【yung² 甬】gush; well; pour; surge; rise; emerge

涌现【yung²yin⁶ 燕⁶】emerge in large numbers; spring up

踊【yung² 甬】leap up; jump up

踊跃【yung²yêg⁸ 约】leap; jump; eagerly; enthusiastically

恿【yung² 甬】(see"怂恿"【xung²yung²】)

蛹【yung² 甬】pupa(see"蚕蛹"【qam⁴ yung²】)

俑【yung² 甬】wooden or earthen human figure buried with the dead in ancient times; tomb figure; figurine

慵【yung⁴ 容】weary; lethargic; languid

庸【yung⁴ 容 】commonplace; inferior; need; how could

庸人【yung⁴yen⁴ 仁】mediocre person

庸才【yung⁴qoi⁴ 财】mediocre person; mediocrity

庸碌【yung⁴lug⁷ 六⁷】mediocre and unambitious

庸俗【yung⁴jug⁹ 族】vulgar; philistine

庸人自扰【yung⁴yen⁴ji⁶yiu² 仁治妖²】worry about troubles of one's own imagining

臃【yung² 甬²】〈a.〉臃肿【yung²jung² 总】too fat to move; overstaffed

佣【yung⁴ 容;yung² 甬】hire(a labourer); servant; commission

佣工【yung⁴gung¹ 功】hired labourer; servant

佣金【yung²gem¹ 今】commission; brokerage

戎【yung⁴ 容】army; military affairs; an ancient name for the peoples in the west; a surname

戎马【yung⁴ma⁵ 码】army horse

茸【yung⁴ 容】(of grass, etc.) fine, soft; downy; young pilose antler; thick (hair)

茸茸【yung⁴yung⁴】(of grass, hair, etc.) fine, soft and thick; downy

绒【yung⁴ 容;yung² 甬】fine hair; down; cloth with a soft nap or pile on one or either side; fine floss for embroidery

绒毛【yung⁴mou⁴ 无】fine hair; down; nap; pile

绒花【yung⁴fa¹ 化¹】velvet flowers, birds, etc.

绒布【yung² bou³ 报】flannelette; cotton flannel

绒线【yung² xin³ 腺】floss for embroidery; knitting wool

绒绣【yung² xeo³ 秀】woollen embroidery

绒衫【yung² xam³ 三】sweat shirt

绒裤【yung² fu³ 富】sweat pants

蓉

【yung⁴ 容】(see "芙蓉" 【fu⁴ yung⁴】)

容

【yung⁴ 蓉】hold; contain; tolerate; permit; facial expression; looks; appearance; a surname

容纳【yung⁴ nab⁹ 呐】hold; accommodate

容器【yung⁴ hēi³ 戏】container; vessel

容积【yung⁴ jig⁷ 织】volume

容量【yung⁴ lêng⁶ 亮】capacity

容人【yung⁴ yen⁴ 仁】tolerant towards others

容忍【yung⁴ yen² 隐】tolerate; condone

容许【yung⁴ hêu² 诩】tolorate; permit; possibly

容易【yung⁴ yi⁶ 义】easy; easily; likely; apt

容颜【yung⁴ ngan⁴ 雁⁴】appearance; looks

容貌【yung⁴ mao⁶ 矛⁶】appearance; looks

容乜易【yung⁴ med⁷ yi⁶ 勿⁷ 义】not difficult; very easy = 【普】不难；很容易

容光焕发【yung⁴ guong¹ wun⁶ fad⁸ 胱换法】one's face glowing with health

溶

【yung⁴ 容】dissolve; spoiled

溶化【yung⁴ fa³ 花³】dissolve; melt

溶剂【yung⁴ jei¹ 挤】solvent

溶溶烂烂【yung⁴ yung⁴ lan⁶ lan⁶ 兰⁶】spoiled; torn into pieces; completely mashed; pulpy = 【普】稀巴烂

溶解【yung⁴ gai² 介²】dissolve

溶液【yung⁴ yig⁹ 亦】solution

溶质【yung⁴ jed⁷ 侄⁷】solute

熔

【yung⁴ 容】melt; fuse; smelt

熔点【yung⁴ dim² 店²】melting point

熔化【yung⁴ fa³ 花³】melt

熔剂【yung⁴ jei¹ 挤】flux

熔解【yung⁵ gai² 介²】fuse; fusion

熔炼【yung⁴ lin⁶ 练】smelt

熔炉【yung⁴ lou⁴ 芦】smelting furnace; crucible

熔岩【yung⁴ ngam⁴ 癌】lava

熔铸【yung⁴ jü³ 注】founding; casting

融

【yung⁴ 容】melt; thaw; blend; fuse

融合【yung⁴ heb⁹ 盒】mix together

融化【yung⁴ fa³ 花】melt; thaw

融洽【yung⁴ heb⁷ 恰】harmonious; on friendly terms

融融【yung⁴ yung⁴ 容】happy and harmonious; warm

融会贯通【yung⁴ wui⁶ gun³ tung¹ 汇灌同¹】achieve mastery through a comprehensive study of the subject

勇

【yung⁵ 甬⁵】brave; valiant; courageous

勇敢【yung⁵ gem² 锦】brave; courageous

勇猛【yung⁵ mang⁵ 孟⁵】bold and powerful

勇气【yung⁵ hēi³ 戏】courage; nerve

勇士【yung⁵ xi⁶ 事】a brave and strong man; warrior

勇武【yung⁵ mou⁵ 母】valiant

勇于【yung⁵ yü¹ 迂】be brave in; be bold in

勇往直前【yung⁵ wong⁵ jig⁹ qin⁴ 汪⁵ 值钱】march forward courageously; advance bravely

用

【yung⁶ 庸⁶】use; employ; apply; expenses; outlay; usefulness; need;

eat; drink; hence; therefore

用处【yung⁶qū³ 次于³】use; good

用场【yung⁶qêng⁴ 祥】use

用法【yung⁶fad⁸ 发】use; usage

用功【yung⁶ gung¹ 工 】hardworking; diligent

用户【yung⁶wu⁶ 护】consumer; user

用具【yung⁶gêû⁶ 巨】utensil; apparatus; appliance

用力【yung⁶ lig⁹ 历 】 exert oneself; put forth one's strength

用品【yung⁶ben² 禀】articles for use

用人【yung⁶yen⁴ 仁】choose a person for a job; need hands; servant

用事【yung⁶xi⁶ 士】act; be in power

用武【yung⁶mou⁵ 母】use force

用途【yung⁶tou⁴ 图】use

用心【yung⁶xem¹ 深】diligently; motive

用意【yung⁶yi³ 薏】intention; purpose

用语【yung⁶yû⁵ 雨】choice of words; term

郁【yug⁷ 沃；wed⁷ 屈】strongly fragrant; lush; gloomy; a surname

郁郁【yug⁷yug⁷】lush; luxuriant; gloomy; strongly fragrant; elegant

郁结【yug⁷gid⁸ 洁】=郁积【yug⁷jig⁷ 织】pent-up

郁闷【wed⁷mun⁶ 门⁶】gloomy; depressed

郁金香【wed⁷gem¹hêng¹ 今乡】tulip

喐【yug⁷ 沃】move; touch=【普】动

喐动【yug⁷dung⁶ 洞】move around; be active=【普】移动;动弹

喐喐贡【yug⁷yug⁷gung³ 供³】always moving around; active=【普】不隐,动来动去

喐不得其正【yug⁷bed⁷deg⁷kêi⁴jing³ 毕德奇政】cannot move at all=【普】全都不能动;动弹不得

沃【yug⁷ 郁】fertile; rich; irrigate

沃土【yug⁷tou² 讨】fertile soil; rich soil

沃野千里【yug⁷yê⁵qin¹lêi⁵ 惹仟李】a vast expanse of fertile land

煜【yug⁷ 沃】illuminate; shine

昱【yug⁷ 沃】sunlight; shine

旭【yug⁷ 沃】brilliance of the rising sun

旭日【yug⁷yed⁹ 逸】the rising sun

玉【yug⁹ 肉】jade;（of a person, esp. a woman）pure; handsome; beautiful; your

玉石【yug⁹xêg⁹ 硕】jade

玉器【yug⁹hêi³ 气】jade article

玉玺【yug⁹xai² 徙²】imperial jade seal

玉米【yug⁹ mei⁵ 迷⁵】maize; corn; ear of maize

玉兰【yug⁹lan⁴ 栏】〈n.〉yulan magnolia

玉帛【yug⁹ bag⁹ 白】jade objects and silk fabrics, used as state gifts in ancient China

玉雕【yug⁹diu¹ 刁】jade carving

玉兔【yug⁹tou³ 吐】the Jade Hare — the moon

玉宇【yug⁹yû⁵ 语】residence of the immortals; the universe

玉成【yug⁹xing⁴ 诚】kindly help sculpture the success of sth.

玉皇大帝【yug⁹wong⁴dai⁶dei³ 王歹⁶ 蒂】the Jade Emperor（the Supreme Deity of Taoism）

玉洁冰清【yug⁹gid⁸bing¹qing¹ 结兵青】as pure as jade and as clean as ice; pure and noble

玉石俱焚【yug⁹xēg⁹kêü¹fen⁴ 硕驱汾】jade and stone burned together — destruction of good and bad alike

狱【yug⁹ 玉】prison; jail; lawsuit; case

狱吏【yug⁹lēi⁶ 利】warder; prison officer; jailer

狱卒【yug⁹jêd⁷ 支律⁷】prison guard; turn-key

浴【yug⁹ 玉】bath; bathe

浴场【yug⁹qêng⁴ 祥】outdoor bathing place

浴池【yug⁹qi⁴ 迟】common bathing pool; public baths

浴盆【yug⁹pun⁴ 盆】bathtub

浴巾【yug⁹gen¹ 斤】bath towel

浴血【yug⁹ hüd⁸ 黑月⁸】bathed in blood; bloody

欲【yug⁹ 玉】desire; longing; wish; want; about to; just going

欲望【yug⁹mong⁶ 亡⁶】desire; wish; lust

欲盖弥彰【yug⁹ goi³ nēi⁴ jêng¹ 该¹ 尼章】The more one tries to hide, the more one is exposed.

欲壑难填【yug⁹kog⁸nan⁴tin⁴ 确那晏⁴ 田】Greed is like a valley that can never be filled. Avarice knows no bounds.

欲擒故纵【yug⁹kem⁴gu³jung³ 禽固种³】leave sb. at large the better to apprehend him

欲速则不达【yug⁹qug⁷jeg⁷bed⁷dad⁹ 促仄毕得压⁹】More haste, less speed. Haste makes waste.

肉【yug⁹ 玉】meat; flesh; pulp; flesh(of fruit)

肉食【yug⁹xig⁹ 蚀】carnivorous; meat

肉店【yug⁹dim³ 惦】butcher's (shop)

肉丁【yug⁹ding¹ 叮】diced meat

肉片【yug⁹pin³ 骗】sliced meat

肉丝【yug⁹xi¹ 司】shredded meat

肉饼【yug⁹bēng² 柄²】meat pie

肉汤【yug⁹tong¹ 堂¹】broth

内体【yug⁹tei² 睇】the human body; flesh

肉丸【yug⁹yün² 阮】meatball

肉刑【yug⁹ying⁴ 形】corporal punishment

肉欲【yug⁹yug⁹】carnal desire

肉桂【yug⁹guei³ 贵】Chinese cassia tree

肉瘤【yug⁹leo⁴ 留】sarcoma

肉麻【yug⁹ma⁴ 马⁴】nauseating; sickening

肉搏【yug⁹bog⁸ 博】figh hand-to-hand

肉中刺【yug⁹ jung¹ qi³ 钟次】a thorn in one's flesh

肉痹【yug⁹ qēg⁸ 赤】= 肉痛【yug⁹tung³ 同³】heartbreak; unhappy =【普】心痛; 舍不得

肉紧【yug⁹gen² 谨】nervous; frustrated =【普】神经紧张; 把某事看得很要紧

肉酸【yug⁹ xün¹ 孙】ugly; terrible =【普】肮脏; 难看; 不堪入目

衣【yi¹ 依】clothing; clothes; coating; covering; afterbirth

衣车【yi¹ qē¹奢】a sewing-machine =【普】缝纫机

衣着【yi¹ jêg⁸ 桌】clothing; headgear and footwear

衣服【yi¹fug⁹ 伏】clothing; clothes

衣料【yi¹liu² 了²】material for clothing

衣物【yi¹med⁹ 勿】clothing and other articles of daily use

衣架【yi¹ga² 假】coat hanger; clothes tree

衣冠【yi¹gun¹ 官】hat and clothes; dress

衣柜【yi¹guei⁶ 聰】wardrobe

衣裳【yi¹xêng⁴ 常】clothing; clothes

衣襟【yi¹ kem¹ 衾 】the one or two pieces making up the front of a Chinese jacket

衣钵【yi¹ bud⁸ 波活⁸】a Buddhist monk's mantle and alms bowl which he hands down to his favourite disciple; legacy

衣食住行【yi¹ xig⁹ jû⁶ heng⁴ 蚀注⁶ 衡】food, clothing, shelter and transportation—basic necessities of life

衣冠禽兽【yi¹gun¹kem⁴xeo³ 官琴秀】a beast in human attire; brute

伊【yi¹ 衣】he or she; a surname

伊始【yi¹qi² 齿】beginning

伊面【yi¹min⁶ 缅】a type of noodle

伊捞七【yi¹lou¹qed⁷ 劳¹ 柒】generally speaking=【普】一般来说；通常情况下

伊甸园【yi¹din⁶yün⁴ 电元】the Garden of Eden; paradise

伊朗【yi¹long⁵ 郎⁵】Iran

伊拉克【yi¹lai¹heg⁷ 赖¹ 刻】Iraq

伊斯兰教【yi¹xi¹lan⁴gao³ 司栏较】Islam; Islamism

医【yi¹ 衣】doctor(of medicine); medical science; medicine; cure; treat

医疗【yi¹liu⁴ 辽】medical treatment

医生【yi¹xeng¹ 笙】doctor; medical man = 医师【xi¹】

医术【yi¹ xêd⁹述 】 medical skill; art of healing

医务【yi¹mou⁶ 冒】medical matters

医学【yi¹hog⁹ 鹤】medical science; medicine

医药【yi¹yêg⁹ 若】medicine

医院【yi¹yün² 阮】hospital

医治【yi¹yi⁶ 自】cure; treat; heal

医嘱【yi¹jug⁷ 竹】doctor's advice

依【yi¹ 衣】depend on; comply with; yield to; according to; in the light of

依时依候【yi¹xi⁴yi¹heo⁶ 是⁴ 后】be on time; punctual =【普】按时；准时

依次【yi¹qi³ 刺】in proper order; successively

依从【yi¹qung⁴ 虫】comply with; yield to

依附【yi¹fu⁶ 父】depend on; attach oneself to

依旧【yi¹geo⁶ 九⁶】as before; still

依据【yi¹gêü³ 踞】according to; basis

依照【yi¹ jiu³ 赵³ 】 according to; in the light of

依靠【yi¹kao³ 卡考³】rely on; depend on; support; backing

依赖【yi¹ lai⁶ 拉⁶】rely on; be dependent on

依恋【yi¹lün² 联²】be reluctant to leave

依然【yi¹yin⁴ 言】still; as before

依稀【yi¹hêi¹ 希】vaguely; dimly

依依【yi¹yi¹】reluctant to part

依仗【yi¹jêng⁶ 丈】count on; rely on

咿【yi¹ 衣】⟨onomatopoeia⟩; ⟨auxil.⟩

咿呀【yi¹a¹ 亚¹】⟨onomatopoeia⟩ squeak; creak; prattle; babble

咿挹【yi¹yeb⁷ 邑】refer to a boy-girl relationship that is not serious∽【普】男女间的猥亵举动

咿唪【yi¹ yug⁷郁】move around and make

noises；make a move∽【普】动作；动静

龂 【yi¹ 衣】smile；bare；show＝【普】龇
龂牙哗哨【yi¹nga⁴bang⁶xao³ 芽伯罂⁶梢³】smile；show one's teeth；look fierce；grimace in pain∽【普】龇牙咧嘴；令人生厌的傻笑

噫 【yi¹ 衣】〈int.〉alas

咦 【yi² 椅】〈int.〉well；why；an exclamation mark to express shock

椅 【yi² 咦】chair
椅仔【yi²jei² 济²】a small chair＝【普】小椅子

倚 【yi² 椅】lean on or against；rest on；count on；biased；partial
倚靠【yi²kao³ 卡考³】lean on or against；rest on
倚赖【yi²lai⁶ 拉⁶】rely on；be dependent on
倚仗【yi²jêng⁶ 丈】rely on；count on
倚重【yi² jung⁶仲 】rely heavily on sb.'s service
倚老卖老【yi²lou⁵mai⁶lou⁵ 鲁买⁶】take advantage of one's seniority or old age；flaunt one's seniority

绮 【yi² 椅】damask；beautiful；gorgeous
绮丽【yi²lei⁶ 厉】beautiful；gorgeous

旖 【yi²】〈a.〉旖旎【yi²nêi⁵ 你】charming and gentle

漪 【yi¹ 衣】ripples

猗 【yi¹ 衣】(see"涟猗"【lin⁴yi¹】)

意 【yi³ 薏】meaning；idea；wish；desire；intention；anticipate；expect；hint；trace
意见【yi³ gin³ 建 】idea；view；opinion；suggestion；objection；complaint
意思【yi³xi¹ 司】meaning；idea；opinion；wish；a token of affection，appreciation，gratitude，etc.；suggestion；hint；interest；fun
意会【yi³wui⁶ 汇】sense
意境【yi³ging² 景】artistic conception
意料【yi³liu⁶ 了⁶】anticipate；expect
意气【yi³hêi³ 戏】will and spirit；temperament；personal feelings
意趣【yi³qêu³ 翠】interest and charm
意识【yi³ xig⁷ 式】consciousness；be conscious of；realize；awake to
意图【yi³tou⁴ 徒】intention；intent
意外【yi³ngoi⁶ 碍】unexpected；accident
意味【yi³mêi⁶ 未】meaning；interest
意想【yi³xêng² 赏】imagine；expect
意向【yi³hêng³ 乡³】intention；purpose
意义【yi³yi⁶ 异】meaning；sense
意愿【yi³yün⁶ 县】wish；desire；aspiration
意志【yi³ji³ 至】will
意旨【yi³ji³ 止】intention；wish；will
意中人【yi³jung¹yen⁴ 钟仁】the person one is in love with
意味着【yi³mêi⁶jêg⁹ 桌⁹】signify；mean；imply
意大利【yi³dai⁶lêi⁶ 歹⁶ 俐】Italy
意头【yi³teo⁴ 投】symptom∽【普】征候；征兆
意在言外【yi³joi⁶yin⁴ngoi⁶ 再⁶ 然碍】the meaning is implied

薏 【yi³ 意】Job's tears

薏苡【yi³yi⁵ 尔】Job's tears

薏米【yi³mei⁵ 迷⁵】the seed of Job's tears

姨【yi⁴ 而；yi¹ 衣】one's mother's sister; aunt; one's wife's sister; sister-in-law

姨妈【yi⁴ ma¹ 吗】the sisters of one's mother; aunt；（married）maternal aunt

姨丈【yi⁴jêng² 掌】uncle; the husband of one's maternal aunt =【普】姨夫；姨父

姨仔【yi¹jei² 济²】the sisters of one's wife =【普】小姨子

姨表【yi⁴biu² 标²】maternal cousin

姨太太【yi⁴tai³tai² 泰³ 泰²】concubine

胰【yi⁴ 而】pancreas

胰岛【yi⁴dou² 倒】pancreas islet

胰腺【yi⁴xin³ 线】pancreas

胰岛素【yi⁴dou²xou³ 扫】insulin

夷【yi⁴ 而】smooth; safe; raze; exterminate; wipe out; a name for ancient tribes in the east; foreign country; foreigner

痍【yi⁴ 而】wound; trauma

仪【yi⁴ 而】appearance; bearing; ceremony; rite; present; apparatus

仪表【yi⁴ biu² 标】appearance; bearing; meter

仪器【yi⁴hêi³ 戏】instrument; apparatus

仪容【yi⁴yung⁴ 熔】looks; appearance

仪态【yi⁴tai³ 太】bearing; deportment

仪仗【yi⁴jêng⁶ 丈】flags, weapons, etc. carried by a guard of honour

仪式【yi⁴xig⁷ 色】ceremony; rite; function

宜【yi⁴ 而】 suitable; appropriate; should; ought to

宜人【yi⁴yen⁴ 仁】pleasant; delightful

宜得【yi⁴deg⁷ 德】want; can't wait to see ∽【普】想要；急不及待

谊【yi⁴ 而】friendship

怡【yi⁴ 而】happy; joyful; cheerful

怡然【yi⁴yin⁴ 言】happy; contented

贻【yi⁴ 而】make a gift of sth.; present; bequeath; leave behind

贻害【yi⁴hoi⁶ 亥】leave a legacy of trouble

贻误【yi⁴ng⁶ 悟】affect adversely; bungle

贻笑大方【yi⁴xiu³dai⁶fong¹ 少³ 歹⁶ 芳】make a laughingstock of oneself before experts

移【yi⁴ 而】 move; remove; shift; change; alter

移动【yi⁴dung⁶ 洞】move; shift

移交【yi⁴ gao¹ 胶】turn over; transfer; hand over one's job to a successor

移居【yi⁴gêü¹ 据¹】move one's residence; migrate

移民【yi⁴men⁴ 文】migrate; emigrate; immigrate; emigrant; immigrant

移植【yi⁴jig⁹ 直】transplant; grafting

移风易俗【yi⁴fung¹yig⁹jug⁹ 丰亦族】change prevailing habits and customs

移花接木【yi⁴fa¹jib⁸mug⁹ 化¹ 支业⁸ 目】graft one twig on another; stealthily substitute one thing for another

移山倒海【yi⁴xan¹dou²hoi² 珊岛凯】remove mountains and drain seas — transform nature

疑【yi⁴ 而】doubt; disbelieve; suspect; doubtful; uncertain

疑问【yi⁴ men⁶ 文⁶】query; question;

doubt

疑点【yi⁴dim² 店²】doubtful point

疑窦【yi⁴deo⁶ 豆】cause of suspicion

疑团【yi⁴tün⁴ 替元⁴】doubts and suspicions

疑心【yi⁴xem¹ 深】suspicion

疑惑【yi⁴wag⁹ 或】feel uncertain

疑惧【yi⁴gêü⁶ 具】apprehensions; misgivings

疑虑【yi⁴ lêü⁶ 类】apprehensions; misgivings

疑难【yi⁴nan⁴ 那晏⁴】difficult; knotty

疑案【yi⁴ngon³ 按】doubtful case; mystery

疑义【yi⁴yi⁶ 异】doubt; doubtful point

疑神疑鬼【yi⁴xen⁴yi⁴guei² 臣诡】be terribly suspicious

彝【yi⁴ 而】wine vessel

彝族【yi⁴jug⁹ 俗】the Yi nationality, distributed over Yunnan, Sichuan and Guizhou

颐【yi⁴ 而】cheek; keep fit

颐养【yi⁴yêng⁵ 氧】keep fit; take care of oneself

颐和园【yi⁴wo⁴yün⁴ 禾元】the Summer Palace(in Beijing)

儿【yi⁴ 而 】child; youngster; youth; son; male

儿子【yi⁴ji² 止】son

儿女【yi⁴nêü⁵ 那虚⁵】sons and daughters; children; young man and woman (in love)

儿孙【yi⁴ xün¹ 酸】children and grandchildren

儿童【yi⁴ tung⁴ 同】children

儿戏【yi⁴ hêi³ 气】 trifing matter; unreliable; not firm; not solid

儿歌【yi⁴go¹ 哥】children's song

儿科【yi⁴fo¹ 蝌】paediatrics

而【yi⁴ 儿】〈conj.〉and; but; to; if

而家【yi⁴ga¹ 加】now; at the present time ＝【普】而今; 现在

而后【yi⁴heo⁶ 候】after that; then

而且【yi⁴qê² 扯】and

而已【yi⁴yi⁵ 耳】〈auxil.〉that is all; nothing more

以【yi⁵ 耳】use; take; according to; because of; in order to; so as to; at (a certain time); on (a fixed date); and; as well as

以便【yi⁵bin⁶ 辨】so that; in order to; so as to

以后【yi⁵heo⁶ 候】after; afterwards; later

以及【yi⁵keb⁹ 级⁹】as well as; along with; and

以来【yi⁵loi⁴ 莱】since

以近【yi⁵gen⁶ 靳】up to

以远【yi⁵yün⁵ 软】beyond

以免【yi⁵min⁵ 缅】in order to avoid; lest

以内【yi⁵noi⁶ 耐】within; less than

以外【yi⁵ ngoi⁶ 碍 】beyond; outside; except

以前【yi⁵qin⁴ 钱】before; formerly; previously

以求【yi⁵ keo⁴ 球】in order to; in an attempt to

以上【yi⁵ xêng⁶ 尚】more than; over; the above

以下【yi⁵ ha⁶ 夏 】below; under; the following

以太【yi⁵tai³ 泰】ether

以往【yi⁵wong⁵ 枉⁵】before; formerly; in

the past

以为【yi⁵wei⁴ 围】think; believe; consider

以至【yi⁵ ji³志】down to; up to; so... that...

以致【yi⁵ji³ 至】so that; consequently; as a result

以资【yi⁵ji¹ 支】as a means of

以德报怨【yi⁵ deg⁹bou³yün³ 得布元³】return good for evil

以点带面【yi⁵dim²dai³min² 店² 戴缅²】fan out from point to area

以毒攻毒【yi⁵ dug⁹gung¹gug⁹ 独工³】combat poison with poison

以讹传讹【yi⁵ ngo⁴qün⁴ngo⁴ 鹅存】incorrectly relay an erroneous message

以怨报德【yi⁵ yün³bou³deg⁷ 元³ 布得】return evil for good

以攻为守【yi⁵gung¹wei⁴xeo² 工维手】use attack as a means of defence

以退为进【yi⁵ têü³wei⁴jên³ 推³ 维俊】retreat in order to advance

以己度人【yi⁵gēi²dog⁹yen⁴ 几铎仁】judge others by oneself

以假乱真【yi⁵ ga²lün⁶jen¹ 贾联⁶ 珍】mix the spurious with the genuine

以礼相待【yi⁵ lei⁵ xêng¹ doi⁶黎¹ 双代】treat sb. with due respect

以理服人【yi⁵ lēi⁵fug⁹yen⁴ 李伏仁】convince people by reasoning

以邻为壑【yi⁵lên⁴wei⁴kog⁸ 伦维确】shift one's troubles onto others

以身作则【yi⁵xeo¹jog⁸jeg⁷ 辛咋仄】set an example

以逸待劳【yi⁵ yed⁹doi⁶lou⁴ 日代卢】wait at one's ease for an exhausted enemy or opponent

以…为…【yi⁵... wei⁴...维】take...

as...; regard...as...

矣【yi⁵ 已】〈auxil.〉∽"了""啊""呀"

迤【yi⁵ 以】go towards

迤逦【yi⁵lei⁵ 礼】winding; tortuous; meandering

已【yi⁵ 以】stop; cease; end; already; thereafter; afterwards; too

已故【yi⁵gu³ 固】deceased; late

已经【yi⁵jing¹ 京】already

已然【yi⁵yin⁴ 言】be already so

已往【yi⁵ wong⁵ 枉⁵】before; previously; in the past

耳【yi⁵ 以】ear; on both sides; side; only; just

耳朵【yi⁵do² 躲】ear＝耳仔【yi⁵jei² 济²】

耳背【yi⁵bui⁶ 杯⁶】hard of hearing

耳垂【yi⁵xêü⁴ 睡⁴】earlobe

耳屎【yi⁵xi² 史】earwax＝耳垢【yi⁵geo³】

耳环【yi⁵wan² 玩²】earrings＝【普】耳坠子

耳窿【yi⁵lung¹ 隆¹】earhole＝【普】耳孔

耳轮【yi⁵lên⁴ 伦】helix

耳机【yi⁵gēi¹ 基】earphone

耳鸣【yi⁵ming⁴ 名】tinnitus

耳目【yi⁵mug⁹ 木】what one sees and hears; knowledge; one who spies for sb. else

耳塞【yi⁵xeg⁷ 是克⁷】earplug

耳生【yi⁵ xang¹ 是罂¹】unfamiliar to the ear

耳熟【yi⁵xug⁹ 孰】familiar to the ear

耳挖【yi⁵wad⁸ 滑⁸】earpick＝【普】耳挖子

耳语【yi⁵ yü⁵ 雨】whisper in sb.'s ear; whisper

耳聪目明【yi⁵ qung¹ mug⁹ ming⁴冲木名】have good ears and eyes; have a thorough grasp of the situation

耳目一新【yi⁵mug⁹yed⁷xen¹ 木壹辛】find everything fresh and new

耳濡目染【yi⁵ yū⁴ mug⁹ yim⁵ 余木艳⁵】be imperceptibly influenced by what one constantly sees and hears

耳闻目睹【yi⁵ men⁴ mug⁹ dou² 文木倒】what one sees and hears

尔【yi⁵ 耳】you; like that; so; that

尔曹【yi⁵qou⁴ 槽】you people; you and your kind

尔虞我诈【yi⁵yū⁴ngo⁵ja³ 余鹅⁵ 炸】each trying to cheat or outwit the other

尔后【yi⁵heo⁶ 候】thereafter

迩【yi⁵ 尔】near(see"遐迩"【ha⁴yi⁵】)

洱【yi⁵ 耳; nēi² 腻²】(see " 普洱 "【pou²nēi²】)

二【yi⁶ 义】two; second; different

二月【yi⁶ yūd⁹越 】February; the second moon

二心【yi⁶xem¹ 深】disloyalty; halfheartedness

二等【yi⁶deng² 邓²】second-class; second-rate

二流子【yi⁶ leo⁴ ji² 留止 】 loafer; idler; bum

二级风【yi⁶keb⁷fung¹ 给丰】force 2 wind

二重性【yi⁶qung⁴xing³ 虫姓】dual character; duality

二元论【yi⁶yūn⁴lūn⁶ 原沦⁶】dualism

二世祖【yi⁶ xei³ jou²细早】The man by all means spends money. =【普】败家子

二十八宿【yi⁶xeb⁹bad⁸xug⁷ 拾捌叔】the lunar mansions

二手货【yi⁶ xeo² fo³ 守课】secondhand goods

二仔底【yi⁶jei²dei² 济² 抵】refer to one who is not capable⌒【普】底子薄; 没本事

贰【yi⁶ 二】two (used for the numeral "二" on cheques, banknotes, etc. to avoid mistakes or alterations)

肄【yi⁶ 义】study

肄业【yi⁶yib⁹ 叶】study in school or at college

义【yi⁶ 二】justice; righteousness; righteous; human ties; relationship; meaning; adopted; false

义气【yi⁶ hēi³戏 】 code of brotherhood; personal loyalty

义士【yi⁶xi⁵ 示】a high-minded or chivalrous person; righteous man

义举【yi⁶gēu² 矩】a magnanimous act undertaken for the public good

义务【yi⁶mou⁶ 冒】duty; obligation; volunteer

义演【yi⁶yin² 衍】benefit performance

义不容辞【yi⁶ bed⁷ yung⁴ qi⁴半溶池】be duty-bound; have an unshirkable duty

义愤填膺【yi⁶ fen⁵ tin⁴ ying¹ 奋田英】be filled with (righteous) indignation

义无反顾【yi⁶mou⁴fan²gu³ 毛返固】Honour permits no turning back.

义正词严【yi⁶jing³qi⁴yim⁴ 政池盐】speak sternly out of a sense of justice

议【yi⁵ 尔】opinion; view; discuss; talk over

议论【yi⁵lên⁶ 沦⁶】comment; talk; discuss

议事【yi⁵xi⁶ 士】discuss official business

议题【yi⁵tei⁴ 提】subject under discussion

议案【yi⁵ngon³ 按】proposal; motion

议程【yi⁵qing⁴ 情】agenda

议定【yi⁵ding⁶ 锭】pass a resolution

议员【yi⁵ yǔn⁴ 元】member of a legislative assembly

议会【yi⁵wui² 汇】parliament

议席【yi⁵ jig⁹ 直】seat in a legislative assembly

议价【yi⁵ga³ 嫁】negotiate a price; negotiated price

异【yi⁶ 义】different; strange; unusual; surprised; other; another; separate

异彩【yi⁶qoi² 采】extraordinary splendour

异常【yi⁶xêng⁴ 裳】unusual; extremely

异端【yi⁶dün¹ 短】heterodoxy; heresy

异国【yi⁶guog⁸ 帼】foreign country

异化【yi⁶fa³ 花³】alienation

异己【yi⁶gêi² 几】dissident; alien

异同【yi⁶ tung⁴铜 】similarities and differences

异物【yi⁶med⁹ 勿】foreign matter; ghost

异乡【yi⁶hêng¹ 香】foreign land

异心【yi⁶xem¹ 深】infidelity; disloyalty

异性【yi⁶ xing³ 姓】the opposite sex; different in nature

异相【yi⁶ xêng³ 商³】terrible; ugly =【普】样子难看;丑陋

异样【yi⁶yêng⁶ 让】difference; unusual

异议【yi⁶yi⁵ 尔】objection; dissent

异乎寻常【yi⁶fu⁴qem⁴xêng⁴ 符沉尝】unusual

异口同声【yi⁶ heo² tung⁴ xing¹ 厚² 铜升】with one voice in unison

异曲同工【yi⁶kug⁷tung⁴gung¹ 卡屋铜功】different in approach but equally satisfactory

异想天开【yi⁶xêng¹tin¹hoi¹ 赏田¹ 海¹】indulge in the wildest fantasy

懿【yi⁶ 义】exemplary

懿行【yi⁶heng⁴ 衡】exemplary conduct

腰【yiu¹ 邀】①waist; small of the back; pocket; middle; ②kidney =【普】肾

腰骨【yiu¹ gued⁷掘⁷】back; backing; the waist; one who has got pride =【普】腰板儿;腰杆子;自尊心

腰包【yiu¹ bao¹ 苞】purse; pocket = 荷包【ho⁴bao¹】

腰带【yiu¹dai³ 戴】waistband; belt; girdle = 裤头带【fu³teo⁴dai²】

腰身【yiu¹xen¹ 辛】waistline; girth

腰痛【yiu¹tung³ 通³】lumbago

腰斩【yiu¹jam² 湛²】cutting sb. in two at the waist; cut sth. in half

腰椎【yiu¹jêü¹ 追】lumbar vertebra

腰果【yiu¹guo² 戈²】cashew

吆【yiu¹ 腰】<v.> 吆喝【yiu¹hod⁸ 渴】cry out; call; cry one's wares; loudly urge on

夭【yiu¹ 腰; yiu² 扰】die young; tender; young

夭折【yiu²jid⁸ 节】die young; come to a premature end

夭亡【yiu²mong⁴ 忙】die young

妖【yiu¹ 腰; yiu² 扰】goblin; demon; evil and fraudulent; bewitching

妖怪【yiu²guai³ 拐³】monster; bogy; goblin; demon

妖精【yiu²jing¹ 贞 】evil spirit; alluring woman

妖孽【yiu²yid⁹ 热】person or event associated with evil or misfortune; evil doer

妖娆【yiu¹yiu⁴ 尧】enchanting; fascinating

妖艳【yiu²yim⁶ 验】pretty and coquettish = 妖冶【yiu²yē⁵ 野】

妖魔鬼怪【yiu¹mo¹guei²guai³ 么诡乖³】demons and ghosts

邀【yiu¹ 腰】invite; request; solicit; seek

邀功【yiu¹gung¹ 工】take credit for someone else's achievements

邀集【yiu¹jab⁹ 习】invite to meet together

邀请【yiu¹ging² 逞²】invite

扰【yiu² 夭²; yiu⁵ 绕】harass; trouble; trespass on sb.'s hospitality

扰乱【yiu⁵lün⁶联⁶】harass; disturb; confusion

扰攘【yiu²yêng⁶ 让】hustle and bustle; tumult

要【yiu³ 夭³; yiu¹ 腰】important; want; ask for; wish; ask sb. to do sth.; want to; wish to; must; should; shall; will; need; take; if; suppose; ask; demand; force

要求【yiu¹keo⁴ 球】ask; demand; require; claim

要挟【yiu¹hib⁸ 协】coerce; threaten

要紧【yiu³ gen² 谨】important; essential; be critical; matter

要点【yiu³dim² 店²】main points; key strongpoint

要旨【yiu³ji² 止】main idea; gist

要领【yiu³ling³ 岭】main points; gist; essentials

要害【yiu³ hoi⁶ 亥】vital part; strategic point

要素【yiu³xou³ 数】essential factor

要不【yiu³bed⁷ 毕】otherwise; or else; or

要么【yiu³mo¹ 摩】or; either...or...

要不是【yiu³bed⁷xi⁶ 毕示】if it were not for

要好【yiu³hou² 蒿²】be on good terms; eager to improve oneself

要价【yiu³ga³ 嫁】ask a price; charge

要命【yiu³ mēng⁶ 莫镜⁶】kill; extremely; awfully

要塞【yiu³qoi³ 菜】fort; fortress

要职【yiu³jig⁷ 织】important post

要道【yiu³dou⁶ 度】thoroughfare

要是【yiu³xi⁶ 示】if; suppose; in case

娆【yiu⁴ 尧】(see "妖娆"【yiu¹yiu⁴】)

尧【yiu⁴ 摇】〈n.〉尧舜【yiu⁴xên³ 信】Yao and Shun, legendary monarchs in ancient China—ancient sages

饶【yiu⁴ 尧】rich; plentiful; let sb. off; forgive; give sth. extra; although; a surname

饶命【yiu⁴mēng⁶ 莫镜⁶】spare sb.'s life

饶恕【yiu⁴xü³ 树³】forgive; pardon

饶舌【yiu⁴xid⁸ 泄】too talkative; shoot off one's mouth

鹞【yiu⁴ 遥】harrier; sparrow hawk

姚【yiu⁴ 遥】a surname

窑【yiu⁴ 遥】kiln; pit; cave dwelling

窑洞【yiu⁴dung⁶ 动】cave dwelling

谣【yiu⁴ 遥】ballad; rumour

谣言【yiu⁴yin⁴ 然】rumour; groundless

遥【yiu⁴ 摇】distant; remote

遥远【yiu⁴ yūn⁵ 软】distant; remote; far-away

遥遥【yiu⁴yiu⁴】far away; a long way off

遥望【yiu⁴ mong⁶ 亡⁶】look into the distance

遥测【yiu⁴qag⁷ 策⁷】telemetering

遥控【yiu⁴ hung³ 哄】remote control; telecontrol

遥相呼应【yiu⁴xêng¹fu¹xing³ 双孚映³】echo each other at a distance

摇 【yiu⁴ 尧】shake; wave; rock; turn

摇摆【yiu⁴bai² 败²】sway; swing; rock

摇荡【yiu⁴dong⁶ 当⁶】rock; sway

摇动【yiu⁴ dung⁶ 洞 】sway; rock; wave; shake

摇晃【yiu⁴fong² 仿²】rock; sway; shake

摇撼【yiu⁴ ham⁶ 陷 】give a violent shake to; rock

摇手【yiu⁴xeo² 守】shake the hand

摇头【yiu⁴teo⁴ 投】shake one's head

摇曳【yiu⁴yei⁶ 拽】flicker; sway

摇尾乞怜【yiu⁴mēi⁵hed⁷lin⁴ 美核⁷ 连】wag the tail ingratiatingly—fawn

摇摇欲坠【yiu⁴ yiu⁴ yug⁹ jêū⁶ 玉叙】tottering

摇唇鼓舌【yiu⁴xên⁴gu²xid⁸ 纯古泄】wag one's tongue; engage in loose talk

摇身一变【yiu⁴ xen¹ yed⁷ bin³辛壹边³】suddenly change one's identity

徭 【yiu⁴ 摇】< n. >徭役【yiu⁴yig⁹ 亦】coree

瑶 【yiu⁴ 摇】precious jade

瑶族【yiu⁴jug⁹ 俗】the Yao nationality

鳐 【yiu⁴ 瑶】〈n.〉ray; skate

窈 【yiu² 夭²】<a.>窈窕【yiu²tiu⁴ 条】= 苗条【miu⁴tiu⁴】(of a woman) gentle and graceful

舀 【yiu⁵ 绕】ladle out; spoon up; scoop up

舀汤【yiu⁵tong¹ 当】ladle out soup

绕 【yiu⁵ 舀】wind; coil; move round; bypass; go round; confuse; baffle

绕道【yiu⁵dou⁶ 度】make a detour = 运路【wen⁶lou⁶】

绕圈子【yiu⁵hün¹ji² 喧止】circle; go round and round; go for a stroll

绕弯子【yiu⁵wan¹ji² 湾止】go the long way round

耀 【yiu⁶ 天⁶】shine; illuminate; dazzle; boast of; laud

耀眼【yiu⁶ngan⁵ 雁⁵】dazzling

耀武扬威【yiu⁶mou⁵yêng⁴wei¹ 母杨畏¹】make a show of one's strength; swagger around

阉 【yim¹ 奄】castrate or spay

阉鸡【yim¹gei¹ 计¹】capon

阉猪【yim¹jū¹ 朱】hog

阉割【yim¹god⁸ 葛】castrate or spay; deprive a theory

奄 【yim¹ 阉】cover; overspread; suddenly

奄奄【yim¹yim¹】feeble breathing

淹 【yim¹ 奄】flood; submerge; be tingling from sweat

淹没【yim¹mud⁹ 末】submerge; flood; inundate

淹死【yim¹xēi² 四²】drown

腌 【yim¹ 奄; yib⁸ 叶⁸】preserve in salt; preserve; attack; salt; pickle; cure

腌咸菜【yib⁸ham⁴qoi³ 陷⁴ 蔡】pickled vegetables; choosy

腌鱼【yib⁶yü² 余²】salted fish

腌臜【yim¹ jam¹ 簪】filthy; dirty

腌尖【yim¹ jim¹ 詹】choosy; fussy =【普】苛求；诸多挑剔

腌尖声闷【yim¹jim¹xēng¹mun⁶ 詹腥门⁶】hated or unwelcomed by others when one is too fussy ∽【普】苛刻待人；诸多挑剔

掩【yim² 淹²】cover; hide; shut; close; attack by surpise

掩蔽【yim²bei³ 敝³】screen; shelter; cover

掩护【yim²wu⁶ 户】screen; shield; cover

掩盖【yim²goi³ 该³】cover; conceal

掩埋【yim²mai⁴ 买⁴】bury; close; shut

掩饰【yim²xig7 式】cover up; gloss over; conceal

掩映【yim²ying² 影】set off (one another)

掩人耳目【yim²yen⁴yi⁵mug⁹ 仁尔木】deceive the public; hoodwink people

掩耳盗铃【yim²yi⁵dou⁶ling⁴ 尔道零】plug one's ears while stealing a bell; deceive oneself

揜【yim² 掩】have a scar = 痂【ga¹】∽【普】伤疤

厌【yim³ 染³】be disgusted with; detest; be fed up with; be bored with; be tired of; be satisfied

厌烦【yim³fan⁴ 凡】be sick of; be fed up with

厌倦【yim³gün⁴ 卷⁶】be weary of; be tired of

厌弃【yim³hei³ 气】detest and reject

魇【yim² 掩】have a nightmare

餍【yim³ 厌】have enough (food); be satiated; satisfy

偃【yim² 掩；yin² 演】fall on one's back; lay down; desist; cease

偃旗息鼓【yim²kēi⁴xig7gu² 其式古】lower the banners and muffle the drums—cease all activities

严【yim⁴ 盐】tight; strict; severe; stern; father; a surname

严办【yim⁴ban⁶ 班⁶】deal with severely

严惩【yim⁴qing⁴ 程】punish severely

严词【yim⁴qi⁴ 辞】in strong terms

严冬【yim⁴dung¹ 东】severe winter

严寒【yim⁴hon⁴ 韩】severe cold

严防【yim⁴fong⁴ 房】be strictly on guard against

严格【yim⁴gag⁸ 隔】strict; rigorous; rigid

严谨【yim⁴gen² 紧】rigorous; strict; compact

严禁【yim⁴gem³ 咁】strictly forbid

严紧【yim⁴gen² 谨】tight; close

严峻【yim⁴ jên³ 进】stern; severe; rigorous; grim

严酷【yim⁴hug⁹ 哭⁹】harsh; bitter; grim; cruel

严厉【yim⁴lei⁶ 励】stern; severe

严密【yim⁴med⁹ 勿】tight; close

严明【yim⁴ming⁴ 名】strict and impartial

严肃【yim⁴xug7 宿】serious; solemn

严刑【yim⁴ying⁴ 形】cruel torture

严整【yim⁴jing⁴ 精²】in neat formation

严正【yim⁴jing³ 政】solemn and just

严重【yim⁴jung⁶ 仲】serious; grave

严阵以待【yim⁴jen⁶yi⁵doi⁶ 镇⁶ 尔代】be ready in full battle array

盐【yim⁴ 严】salt

盐水【yim⁴xêü² 瑞】salt solution; brine

盐罂【yim⁴ ngang¹ 硬¹】saltcellar; saltshaker＝【普】盐瓶

盐酸【yim⁴xūn¹ 孙】hydrochloric acid

盐田【yim⁴tin¹ 填】salt pan; salina

盐业【yim⁴yib⁹ 叶】salt industry

炎【yim⁴ 严】scorching; burning hot; inflammation

炎热【yim⁴yid⁹ 衣泄⁹】scorching; blazing; burning hot

炎症【yim⁴jing³ 正】inflammation

阎【yim⁴ 严】the gate of a lane; a surname

阎罗【yim⁴lo⁴ 罗】＜n.＞Yama

阎王【yim⁴wong⁴ 黄】Yama; King of Hell; an extremely cruel and violent person

染【yim⁵】dye; catch; acquire; soil; contaminate

染病【yim⁵bēng⁶ 柄⁶】catch an illness

染缸【yim²gong¹ 岗】dye vat; dyejigger

染料【yim²liu⁶ 了⁶】dyestuff; dye

染液【yim²yig⁹ 亦】dye liquor

染色【yim²xig⁷ 式】dyeing; colouring

染指【yim²ji² 止】encroach on

染色体【yim²xig⁷tei² 式睇】chromosome

髯【yim⁴ 炎】whiskers; beard

冉【yim⁵ 染】slowly; a surname

冉冉【yim⁵yim⁵】slowly; gradually

苒【yim⁵ 染】(see"荏苒"【yem⁶yim⁵】)

焰【yim⁶ 艳】flame; blaze

焰火【yim⁶fo² 伙】fireworks

艳【yim⁶ 焰】gorgeous; colourful; gaudy; amorous; admire; envy·

艳丽【yim⁶ lei⁶ 厉】bright-coloured and beautiful

艳阳天【yim⁶yêng⁴tin¹ 杨 田¹】bright spring day

验【yim⁶ 艳】examine; check; test; prove effective

验收【yim⁶xeo¹ 修】check and accept

验证【yim⁶jing³ 正】test and verify

验血【yim⁶hüd⁸ 黑月⁸】blood test

验算【yim⁶xün³ 蒜】checking computations

烟【yin¹ 咽¹】smoke; mist; (of eyes) be irritated by smok; tobacco or cigarette; opium

烟叶【yin¹yeb⁹ 业】tobacco leaf

烟草【yin¹qou² 操²】tobacco

烟丝【yin¹xi¹ 司】cut tobacco

烟仔【yin¹jei² 济²】cigarette＝【普】烟卷儿

烟友【yin¹yeo⁵ 有】one who smokes

烟屎【yin¹ xi² 史】smoke wastes; an addicted smoker＝【普】烟斗中的油垢

烟斗【yin¹deo² 豆²】(tobacco) pipe

烟杠【yin¹gong³ 钢】one who is addicted to smoking＝【普】吸烟的瘾君子;沉溺于吸烟者

烟铲【yin¹ gan² 产】a cigarette-addict; heavy smoker ∽【普】烟鬼;大量吸烟的人

烟头【yin¹teo² 投²】cigarette end ＝【普】烟蒂

烟囱【yin¹gung¹ 充】chimney; funnel

烟灰【yin¹fui¹ 恢】tobacco or cigarette ash

烟火【yin¹ fo² 伙】smoke and fire; fire works

烟波【yin¹bo¹ 坡】mist-covered waters

烟幕【yin¹mog⁹ 莫】smoke screen

烟雾【yin¹mou⁶ 务】smoke; mist; smog

烟霞【yin¹ ha⁴ 遐】mist and clouds in the twilight

烟雨【yin¹yü⁵ 语】misty rain

烟瘾【yin¹yen⁵ 引】a craving for tobacco

烟尘【yin¹qen⁴ 陈】dirt ∽【普】尘埃

烟消云散【yin¹xiu¹wen⁴xan³ 烧匀汕】vanish

蔫【yin¹ 焉】< a . > 蔫韧【yin¹ngen⁶ 额恩⁶】difficult to bite; very close boy-girl relationships =【普】韧性强;难舍难分

胭【yin¹ 烟】< n . > 胭脂【yin¹ji¹ 支】rouge

咽【yin¹ 烟;yin³ 燕;yid⁸ 噎】pharynx; swallow

咽气【yin¹hēi³ 戏】breathe one's last; die

咽喉【yin¹ heo⁴ 侯】pharynx and larynx; throat; key link

咽炎【yin¹yim⁴ 严】pharyngitis

焉【yin¹ 烟;yin⁴ 言】here; herein; how; why

嫣【yin¹ 烟】handsome; beautiful

嫣红【yin¹hung⁴ 洪】bright red

嫣然【yin¹yin⁴ 言】beautiful; sweet

演【yin² 衍】develop; evolve; deduce; e-laborate; drill; practise; perform; play; act

演唱【yin²qêng³ 畅】sing

演奏【yin² jeo³ 皱】play a musical instrument

演戏【yin²hēi³ 气】put on a play; playact

演员【yin² yün³ 元】actor or actress; performer

演变【yin²bin³ 边³】develop; evolve

演出【yin²gêd⁷ 次律⁷】perform; show

演讲【yin²gong² 港】give a lecture; lecture

演说【yin²xüd⁸ 雪】deliver a speech; speech

演习【yin²jab⁹ 袭】manoeuvre; exercise

演义【yin²yi⁶ 异】historical novel

演绎【yin²yig⁹ 亦】deduction

衍【yin² 演】spread out; develop; redundant

衍变【yin²bin³ 边³】develop; evolve

衍射【yin²xē 麝】diffraction

衍生物【yin²xeng¹med⁹ 笙勿】derivative

燕【yin³ 宴;yin¹ 烟】northern Hebei Province; swallow; feast; a surname

燕子【yin³ji² 止】swallow

燕窝【yin³wo¹ 涡】edible bird's nest

燕麦【yin³meg⁹ 默】oats

燕尾服【yin³mēi⁵fug⁹ 美伏】swallowtail; tails

宴【yin³ 燕】entertain at a banquet; fete; feast; ease and comfort

宴会【yin³wui⁶ 汇】banquet; feast; dinner party

宴请【yin³qing² 逞】entertain; fete

宴席【yin³jig⁹ 直】banquet; feast

堰【yin² 演】weir

言【yin² 然 】speech; word; say; talk; speak; character; a surname

言论【yin⁴ lên⁶沦⁶】opinion on public affairs; speech

言谈【yin⁴ tam⁴ 谭】the way one speaks or what he says

言语【yin⁴ yü⁵ 雨】spoken language; speech; speak; talk; answer

言辞【yin⁴qi⁴ 词】one's words; what one says

言传身教【yin⁴ qün⁴ xen¹ gao³ 存辛较】teach by personal example as well as verbal instruction

言简意赅【yin⁴gan²yi³goi¹ 東薏该】concise and comprehensive; compendious

言过其实【yin⁴guo³kēi⁴xed⁹ 戈³ 奇失⁹】exaggerate; overstate

言不由衷【yin⁴bed⁷yeo⁴qung¹ 毕尤冲】speak insincerely

言而无信【yin⁴ yi⁴ mou⁴ xên³移毛讯】fail to keep faith; go back on one's word

言外之意【yin⁴ngoi⁶ji¹yi³ 碍支薏】implication

言之有据【yin⁴ji¹yeo⁵gêû³ 支有踞】speak on good grounds

言之成理【yin⁴ji¹xing⁴lēi⁵ 支承李】sound reasonable

言者无罪，闻者足戒【yin⁴jē²mou⁴jêû⁶, men⁴jē²jug⁷gai³ 姐毛坠，民竹介】blame not the speaker but be warned by his words

言必信，行必果【yin⁴bid⁷xên³, heng⁴bid⁷guo² 别⁷讯，衡别⁷ 戈²】Promises must be kept and action must be resolute.

然【yin⁴ 言】right; correct; so; like that; but; nevertheless; however; obviously

然而【yin⁴yi⁴ 移】yet; but; however

然后【yin⁴heo⁶ 候】then; after that; afterwards = 然之后【yin⁴ji¹heo⁶】

然则【yin⁴jeg⁷ 仄】in that case; then

燃【yin⁴ 言】burn; ignite; light

燃烧【yin⁴xiu¹ 消】burn; kindle; combustion

燃料【yin⁴liu² 了²】fuel

燃眉之急【yin⁴mēi⁴ji¹geb⁷ 微支格合⁷】as pressing as a fire singeing one's eyebrows—a pressing need

延【yin⁴ 言】prolong; extend; protract; postpone; delay; engage; send for

延长【yin⁴qêng⁴ 祥】lengthen; prolong

延迟【yin⁴qi⁴ 池】delay; postpone; defer

延缓【yin⁴ wun⁴ 垣】delay; postpone; put off

延期【yin⁴ kēi⁴ 其】postpone; delay; put off

延伸【yin⁴xen¹ 辛】extend; elongate

延误【yin⁴ng⁶ 悟】incur loss through delay

延续【yin⁴jug⁹ 浊】continue; go on; last

延年益寿【yin⁴nin⁴yig⁷xeo⁶ 捻⁴ 忆受】prolong life

涎【yin⁴ 言】saliva

蜒【yin⁴ 言】(see"蜿蜒"【yün²yin⁴】)

筵【yin⁴ 言】< n. > 筵席【yin⁴jig⁹ 直】seats arranged at a banquet; feast; banquet

妍【yin⁴ 言】beautiful

研【yin⁴ 言】grind; pestle; study

研究【yin⁴geo³ 够】study; research; consider; discuss; deliberate

贤【yin⁴ 言】virtuous; worthy; able; a worthy person

贤人【yin⁴ yen⁴ 仁】a person of virtue; worthy

贤良【yin⁴lêng⁴ 凉】(of a man) able and virtuous

贤惠【yin⁴wei⁶ 卫】(of a woman) virtuous

贤达【yin⁴dad⁹ 得压⁹】prominent personage

弦【yin⁴ 言】bowstring; string; the string of a musical instrument; chord; hypotenuse

弦乐器【yin⁴ngog⁹hēi³ 岳气】stringed instrument

弦外之音【yin⁴ngoi⁶ji¹yem¹ 碍支阴】overtones

嫌【yim⁴ 盐】suspicion; ill will; resentment; enmity; dislike; mind

嫌弃【yim⁴hēi³ 戏】dislike and avoid

嫌恶【yim⁴wu³ 乌³】detest; loathe

嫌疑【yim⁴yi⁴ 而】suspicion

苋【yin⁶ 现】amaranth

苋菜【yin⁶qoi³ 蔡】three-coloured amaranth

现【yin⁶ 苋】present; current; existing; in time of need; on hand; cash; show; appear

现在【yin⁶joi⁶ 再⁶】now; at present; today

现状【yin⁶jong⁶ 撞】present situation

现有【yin⁶yeo⁵ 友】now available; existing

现行【yin⁶heng⁴ 衡】in force; in operation; active

现形【yin⁶ ying⁴ 刑】reveal one's true features

现象【yin⁶ jêng⁶ 像 】appearance; phenomenon

现实【yin⁶xed⁹ 失⁹】reality; actuality; real; actual

现时【yin⁶xi⁴ 是⁴】now; at present

现今【yin⁶gem¹ 金】nowadays; these days

现金【yin⁶ gem¹ 今】ready money; cash; cash reserve in a bank = 现银【yin⁶ngen²】

现款【yin⁶fun² 欢²】ready money; cash = 现钱【qin²】

现货【yin⁶ fo³ 课 】merchandise on hand; spots

现代【yin⁶doi⁶ 袋】modern time; modern

现存【yin⁶qūn⁴ 全】extant; in stock

现成【yin⁶xing⁴ 诚】ready-made

现场【yin⁶qêng⁴ 祥】scene; site; spot

现代化【yin⁶doi⁶fa³ 待花³】modernize

现身说法【yin⁶xen¹xüd⁸fad⁸ 辛雪发】advise sb. or explain sth. by using one's own experience as an example

砚【yin⁶ 现】inkstone; inkslab

彦【yin⁶ 现】a man of virtue and ability

谚【yin⁶ 现】proverb; saying; adage; saw

谚语【yin⁶yü⁵ 雨】proverb; saying; adage; saw

唁【yin⁶ 现】extend condolences

唁电【yin⁶din⁶ 甸】telegram of condolence

英【ying¹ 婴】flower; hero; outstanding person; a surname

英豪【ying¹ hou⁴ 毫 】heroes; outstanding figures

英雄【ying¹hung⁴ 红】hero

英勇【ying¹yung⁵ 甬⁵】heroic; valiant; brave; gallant

英明【ying¹ming⁴ 名】wise; brilliant

英姿【ying¹ji¹ 支】heroic bearing

英灵【ying¹ling⁴ 玲】spirit of a martyr

英俊【ying¹ jên³ 进】eminently talented; brilliant; smart

英才【ying¹ goi⁴财】person of outstanding ability

英国【ying¹guog⁸ 帼】Britain; England

英语【ying¹ yü⁵ 雨】English（language）

英镑【ying¹bong⁶ 磅】pound sterling

英尺【ying¹qēg⁸ 赤】foot

英寸【ying¹qūn³ 串】inch

英里【ying¹lēi⁵ 李】mile

婴【ying¹ 英】< n. >婴儿【ying¹yi⁴ 而】baby；infant

缨【ying¹ 英】tassel；sth. shaped like a tassel；ribbon

樱【ying¹ 英】cherry；oriental cherry

樱花【ying¹fa¹ 化¹】oriental cherry

樱桃【ying¹tou⁴ 图】cherry

膺【ying¹ 英】breast；bear；receive

鹰【ying¹ 英】hawk；eagle

鹰犬【ying¹hūn² 劝²】falcons and hounds—lackeys

映【ying² 影】reflect；mirror；shine

映照【ying²jiu³ 焦³】shine upon；cast light upon

映射【ying²xē⁶ 舍⁶】shine upon；cast light upon

映象【ying²jêng⁶ 丈】image

映衬【ying²qen³ 趁】set off

影【ying² 映】shadow；reflection；image；trace；photograph；picture；film；movie；reflex

影子【ying²ji² 止】shadow；reflection；trace；sign

影片【ying²pin² 骗²】film；movie

影院【ying²yūn² 阮】cinema；movie theatre

影印【ying² yen³ 因³】photomechanical printing

影响【ying²hêng² 享】influence；effect；aff-ect

影相【ying² xêng³ 商³】take a photo-graph =【普】照相

影相机【ying²xêng³gēi¹ 商³ 基】a camera =【普】照相机

应【ying¹ 英；ying³英³】answer；respond；agree；accept；should；ought；echo；comply with；grant；suit；deal with；a surname

应份【ying¹fen⁶ 分⁶】ought to；should =【普】应该

应承【ying¹ xing⁴成】promise =【普】答应

应当【ying¹dong¹ 铛】should；ought to

应得【ying¹deg⁷ 德】(well) deserved；due

应该【ying¹goi¹ 格哀¹】should；ought to；must

应有【yng¹yeo⁵ 友】due；proper；deserved

应有尽有【ying¹yeo⁵jên⁶yeo⁵ 进⁶ 友】have everything that one expects to find

应允【ying¹wen⁵ 蕴】assent；consent

应诺【ying¹nog⁸ 那恶⁸】agree；promise

应答【ying³dab⁸ 搭】reply；answer

应变【ying³bin³ 边³】meet an emergency；strain

应酬【ying³qeo⁴ 筹】treat with courtesy；dinner party

应付【ying³ fu⁶ 赴】deal with；handle；do sth. perfunctorily；make do

应急【ying³geb⁷ 格合⁷】meet an emergen-cy

应邀【ying³yiu¹ 腰】on invitation

应时【ying³xi⁴ 是⁴】seasonable；at once

应验【ying³ yim⁶ 艳】come true；be con-firmed

应虫声【ying³xing¹qung⁴ 升从】yesman；echo

应用【ying³ yung⁶ 容⁶】apply；use

应战【ying³ jin³ 箭】meet an enemy attack；accept a challenge

应征【ying³ jing¹ 精】be recruited；respond to a call for contributions

应接不暇【ying³ jib⁸ bed⁷ ha⁴ 支叶⁸ 毕霞】have more visitors or business than one can attend to

应运而生【ying³ wen⁶ yi⁴ xeng¹ 混移笙】arise at the historic moment

迎 【ying⁴ 营】go to meet；greet；welcome；receive；move towards

迎接【ying⁴ jib⁸ 支叶⁸】meet；welcome；greet

迎合【ying⁴ heb⁹ 盒】cater to；pander to

迎战【ying⁴ jin³ 箭】meet head-on = 迎击【gig⁷ 激】

迎面【ying⁴ min⁶ 缅⁶】head-on；in one's face

迎风【ying⁴ fung¹ 丰】facing the wind；with the wind

迎刃而解【ying⁴ yen⁶ yi⁴ gai² 孕移介²】（of a bamboo）split all the way down once it's been chopped open—（of a problem）be readily solved

盈 【ying⁴ 仍】be full of；be filled with；have a surplus of

盈利【ying⁴ lēi⁶ 俐】profit；gain

盈余【ying⁴ yū⁴ 如】surplus；profit

盈亏【ying⁴ kuei¹ 规】profit and loss

荧 【ying⁴ 莹】glimmering；dazzled

荧光【ying⁴ guong¹ 胱】fluorescence；fluorescent light

莹 【ying⁴ 荧】jade-like stone；lustrous and transparent；

萤 【ying⁴ 荧】firefly；glow-worn（萤火虫【ying⁴ fo² qung⁴】）

萦 【ying⁴ 仍】entangle；encompass

萦怀【ying⁴ wai⁴ 槐】occupy one's mind

萦绕【ying⁴ yiu⁵ 扰⁵】hover；linger

楹 【ying⁴ 仍】principal columns of a hall

楹联【ying⁴ lūn⁴ 栾】couplet written on scrolls and hung on the pillars of a hall

蝇 【ying⁴ 仍；ying¹ 英】fly

蝇拍【ying⁴ pag⁸ 柏】flyswatter；flyflap = 乌蝇柏【wu¹ ying¹ pag⁸】

嬴 【ying⁴ 仍】a surname

瀛 【ying⁴ 形】sea；ocean

赢 【ying⁴ 仍；yēng⁴ 衣镜⁴】win；beat；gain（profit）

赢得【yēng⁴ deg⁷ 德】win；gain

仍 【ying⁴ 营】remain；＜ad.＞still；yet

仍旧【ying⁴ geo⁶ 柩】remain the same；still；yet

仍然【ying⁴ yin⁴ 言】still；yet

扔 【ying⁴ 仍；wing¹ 咏；fing⁶ 夫英⁶】throw；toss；cast；throw away；cast aside

营 【ying⁴ 形】seek；operate；run；camp；battalion

营业【ying⁴ yib⁹ 叶】do business

营造【ying⁴ jou⁶ 做】construct；build

营救【ying⁴ geo³ 够】succour；rescue

营生【ying⁴ xeng¹ 笙】earn a living；job

营私【ying⁴ xi¹ 司】seek private gain

营养【ying⁴ yêng⁵ 氧】nutrition；nourishment

营垒【ying⁴lêû⁵ 吕】succour；rescue

营房【ying⁴fong⁴ 防】barracks

邢 【ying⁴ 形】a surname

刑 【ying⁴ 形】punishment；torture；corporal punishment

刑罚【ying⁴fed⁹ 佛】penalty；punishment

刑法【ying⁴ fad⁸发】penal code；criminal law；torture

刑律【ying⁴lêd⁹ 栗】criminal law

刑事【ying⁴xi⁶ 士】criminal；penal

形 【ying⁴ 刑】form；shape；body；entity；appear；look

形体【ying⁴tei² 睇】shape；physique；body；form and structure

形态【ying⁴tai³ 太】form；shape；pattern

形象【ying⁴jêng⁶ 丈】image；form；figure

形状【ying⁴jong⁶ 撞】form；appearance；shape

形迹【ying⁴ jig⁷ 织】a person's movements and expression；formality

形容【ying⁴yung⁴ 熔】appearance；describe

形成【ying⁴xing⁴ 诚】take shape；form

形式【ying⁴xig⁷ 色】form；shape

形势【ying⁴xei³ 细】terrain；features；situation

形形色色【ying⁴ ying⁴ xig⁷ xig⁷】of every hue；of all shades；of every forms

形单影只（隻）【ying⁴dan¹ying²jêg⁸ 丹映脊】a solitary form, a single shadow—extremely lonely；solitary

形影不离【ying⁴ying²bed⁷lēi⁴ 映毕漓】inseparable as body and shadow；always together

型 【ying⁴ 刑】mould；model；type；pattern

型号【ying⁴hou⁶ 浩】model；type

认 【ying⁶英⁶】recognize；know；identify；make out；adopt；admit；own；undertake to do sth.；accept as unvoidable

认住【ying⁶jū⁶ 注⁶】think that ∽【普】留意并记住

认真【①ying⁶ jen¹ 珍；②ying² jen¹ 影珍】①earnest；serious；take to heart；②really；true ∽【普】的确；真的

认底威【ying⁶dei¹wei¹ 帝 卫¹】admit that one loses ∽【普】认输；承认比不上对方

认识【ying⁶ xig⁷ 式 】know；understand；knowledge；cognition

认为【ying⁶wei⁴ 维】think；consider；hold；deem

认清【ying⁶qing¹ 青】see clearly；recognize

认得【ying⁶deg⁷】know；recognize

认可【ying⁶ho² 河²】approve

认帐【ying⁶jêng⁶ 涨】acknowledge a debt

认定【ying⁶ding⁶ 锭】firmly believe；hold；set one's mind on

认错【ying⁶qo³ 挫】acknowledge a mistake

认罪【ying⁶jêû⁶ 坠】admit one's guilt

叶 【yib⁹ 业 】leaf；foliage；leaf-like thing；page；part of a historical period；a surname

叶片【yib⁹pin³ 骗】leaf blade；vane

叶子【yib⁹ji² 止】leaf

叶绿素【yib⁹lug⁹xou³ 六扫】chlorophyll

叶落归根【yib⁹log⁹guei¹gen¹ 洛⁹ 龟斤】Falling leaves settle on their roots — a person residing elsewhere finally returns to his ancestral home.

业【yib⁹ 叶】line of business; trade; industry; occupation; profession; employment; job; course of study; cause; enterprise; property; engage in; already

业务【yib⁹mou⁶ 冒】vocational work; business

业绩【yib⁹ jig⁷ 织】outstanding achievement

业主【yib⁹jū² 煮】owner; proprietor

业余【yib⁹yü⁴ 如】sparetime; after-hours

业已【yib⁹yi⁵ 尔】already

页【yib⁹ 叶】page; leaf

页码【yib⁹ma⁵ 马】page number

靥【yib⁹ 叶】dimple

孽【yib⁹ 业; yid⁹ 热】evil; sin

孽障【yib⁹ jêng³ 帐】evil creature; vile spawn

蘖【yib⁹ 业; yid⁹ 热】tiller

谒【yid⁸ 热⁸】call on; pay one's respects to

谒见【yid⁸gin³ 建】call on; have an audience with

热【yid⁹ 谒⁹】heat; hot; heat up; warm; fever; temperature; ardent; craze; fad; eager; popular; thermal

热能【yid⁹neng⁴ 那莺⁴】heat energy

热量【yid⁹lêng⁶ 亮】quantity of heat

热气【yid⁹hēi³ 戏】steam; heat

热浪【yid⁹long⁶ 朗⁶】heat wave; hot wave

热潮【yid⁹qiu⁴ 瞧】great mass fervour; upsurge

热度【yid⁹dou⁶ 道】degree of heat; fever

热天【yid⁹tin¹ 田¹】hot weather; hot days

热血【yid⁹hüd⁹ 黑月⁸】warm blood—righteous ardour

热心【yid⁹xem¹ 深】enthusiastic; ardent; earnest

热情【yid⁹qing⁴ 程】enthusiasm; zeal; warmth

热忱【yid⁹ xem⁴ 岑】zeal; warmheartedness

热诚【yid⁹xing⁴ 成】warm and sincere; cordial

热爱【yid⁹ ngoi³ 哀³】ardently love; have deep love for

热恋【yid⁹liin² 联²】be passionately in love

热烈【yid⁹lid⁹ 列】warm; enthusiastic; ardent

热切【yid⁹qid⁹ 设】fervent; earnest

热闹【yid⁹nao⁶ 那坳⁶】lively; liven up; a thrilling sight; have a jolly time

热门【yid⁹ mun² 们²】in great demand; popular

热带【yid⁹dai³ 戴】the torrid zone

热线【yid⁹xin³ 扇】heat ray; hot line

热痱【yid⁹fei² 肺²】rashes on the skin

热辣辣【yid⁹lad⁹lad⁹ 罗压⁹】burning hot; very hot; burning

热烘烘【yid⁹hung³hung³ 控】very warm

热乎乎【yid⁹fu¹fu¹ 夫】warm

热气腾腾【yid⁹hēi³teng⁴teng⁴ 戏藤】steaming hot; seething with activity

热火朝天【yid⁹fo²qiu⁴tin¹ 伙樵田¹】in full swing

热锅上的蚂蚁【yid⁹guo¹xêng⁶dig⁹ma⁵ngei⁵ 戈尚嫡码魏⁵】ants on a hot pan

益【yig⁷ 乙】benefit; profit; beneficial; increase; all the more; increasingly

益处【yig⁷qü³ 次于³】benefit；profit；good

益友【yig⁷yeo⁵ 有】friend and mentor

益鸟【yig⁷nіu⁵ 那天⁵】beneficial bird

益虫【yig⁷qung⁴ 从】beneficial insect

膉 【yig⁷ 益】the unpleasant smell of oily food after it has turned bad（臭膉【qeo³yig⁷】=【普】花生、黄豆等油类食物发霉变质时的味道）

臆 【yig⁷ 益】chest；subjectively

臆测【yig⁷qog⁷ 策⁷】conjecture；surmise；guess

臆断【yig⁷dün³ 段³】assume；suppose

臆造【yig⁷jou⁶ 做】fabricate；concoct

弋 【yig⁹ 亦】a retrievable arrow with a string attached to it

亿 【yig⁷ 益】a hundred million

亿万【yig⁷man⁶ 慢】hundreds of millions；millions upon millions

忆 【yig⁷ 忆】recall；recollect

忆苦思甜【yig⁷fu²xi¹tim⁴ 府司添⁴】contrast past misery with present happiness

抑 【yig⁷ 益】restrain；repress；curb；or

抑制【yig⁷jei³ 济】restrain；control；check

抑郁【yig⁷yug⁷ 沃】depressed；despondent；gloomy

抑扬【yig⁷yêng⁴ 羊】rise and fall；modulate

抑或【yig⁷wag⁹ 划】< conj. >or

亦 【yig⁹ 译】also；too

亦即【yig⁹jig⁷ 积】that is；namely；viz；i. e.

亦步亦趋【yig⁹bou⁶yig⁹qêü¹ 部吹】ape sb. at every step

亦都【yig⁹dou¹ 刀】also；as well as =【普】也都

译 【yig⁹ 役】translate；interpret

译本【yig⁹bun² 苯】translation

译名【yig⁹ming⁴ 明】translated term or name

译述【yig⁹xêd⁹ 术】translate freely

译文【yig⁹men⁴ 民】translated text

译音【yig⁹yem¹ 阴】transliteration

译者【yig⁹jê² 姐】translator

役 【yig⁹ 亦】labour；use as a servant；servant；battle

役使【yig⁹xei² 洗】work（an animal）；use

驿 【yig⁹ 亦】post；post road（驿道【yig⁷dou⁶】）

绎 【yig⁹ 亦】unravel；sort out（see "演绎"【yin²yig⁹】）

奕 【yig⁹ 亦】< a. > 奕奕【yig⁹yig⁹】radiating power and vitality

弈 【yig⁹ 亦】play chess

疫 【yig⁹ 亦】epidemic disease；pestilence

疫病【yig⁹bêng⁶ 柄⁶】epidemic disease

疫情【yig⁷qing⁴ 程】epidemic situation

翌 【yig⁹ 亦】next

翌日【yig⁹yed⁹ 逸】next day

蜴 【yig⁹ 亦】（see "蜥蜴"【xig⁷yig⁹】）

翼 【yig⁹ 亦】the wing of a bird, aeroplane, etc.；assist（a ruler）；aid

翼翼【yig⁹yig⁹】cautiously

易【yig⁹ 亦；yi⁶ 义】change；exchange；easy；amiable；a surname

易手【yig⁹xeo² 守】change hands

易经【yig⁹ging¹ 京】The Book of Changes

易货协定【yig⁹fo³hib⁸ding⁶ 课胁锭】an agreement on the exchange of commodities

易如手掌【yi⁶ yü⁴ fan² jêng² 余返奖】as easy as turning one's hand over

易过借火【yi⁶guo³jê³fo² 戈³ 蔗伙】very easy；without difficulty ＝【普】很容易；没困难

于【yü¹ 迂】< prep. >∽at；on；in；of；for；to；from

于今【yü¹ gem¹ 金】 up to the present；since；nowadays；today；now

于是【yü¹xi⁶ 示】< conj. > thereupon；hence；consequently；as a result

迂【yü¹ 于】winding；roundabout；pedantic

迂回【yü¹wui⁴ 汇⁴】circuitous；roundabout

迂腐【yü¹fu⁶ 付】pedantry

竽【yü¹ 于】< n. > an ancient wind instrument

淤【yü² 于²】become silted up；silt；stasis

淤积【yü²jig⁷ 织】silt；deposit

淤塞【yü²xeg⁷ 是克⁷】silt up

淤泥【yü²nei⁴ 那矮⁴】silt；sludge；ooze

瘀【yü² 淤】stasis（of blood）

瘀血【yü²hüd⁸ 黑月⁸】extravasated blood

瘀黑【yü² heg⁷ 克 】a part of the body which is swollen and blue-black as blood clogs in that area ＝【普】瘀血的紫黑色

俞【yü⁴ 余】a surname

揄【yü⁴ 余；yü² 淤】draw；raise；deride

揄人【yü²yen⁴ 仁】ridicule other people ＝【普】揶揄别人；嘲弄别人；揭人之短

逾【yü⁴ 俞】exceed；go beyond；even more

逾期【yü⁴kēi⁴ 其】be overdue

逾越【yü⁴yüd⁹ 月】exceed；go beyond

渝【yü⁴ 俞】（of one's attitude or feeling）change

愉【yü⁴ 俞 】pleased；happy；joyful；cheerful

愉快【yü⁴fai³ 块】happy；joyful；cheerful

愉悦【yü⁴ yüd⁹ 月】joyful；cheerful；delighted

瑜【yü⁴ 俞】fine jade；gem；good points；virtues

榆【yü⁴ 俞】elm（榆树【yü⁴xü⁶】）

觎【yü⁴ 俞】（see "觊觎" 【gēi³yü⁴】）

虞【yü⁴ 如】supposition；worry；deceive；cheat；fool；a surname

舆【yü⁴ 如】carriage；sedan chair；area；public；popular

舆论【yü⁴lên⁶ 沦⁶】public opinion

隅【yü⁴ 如】corner；nook；border

愚【yü⁴ 如】foolish；fool；make a fool of；I

愚蠢【yü⁴qên² 春²】foolish；stupid；silly

愚笨【yü⁴ben⁶ 奔⁶】foolish；stupid；clumsy

愚昧【yü⁴mui⁶ 妹⁶】ignorant；benighted

愚弄【yū⁴nung⁶ 龙⁶】stupid but conceited

喁 【yū⁴ 如】< a. > 喁喁【yū⁴yū⁴】whisper

娱 【yū⁴ 如】amuse; joy; pleasure

娱乐【yū⁴log⁹ 落】amusement; entertainment

谀 【yū⁴ 如】flatter

谀辞【yū⁴qi⁴ 迟】flattery

萸 【yū⁴ 如】(see "茱萸"【jü¹yū⁴】)

腴 【yū⁴ 如】fat; plump; fertile

臾 【yū⁴ 如】(see "须臾"【xêū¹yū⁴】)

蝓 【yū⁴ 如】< n. > 蛞蝓【fud⁸yū⁴ 阔】slug = 蜒螺虫【yin⁴lo⁴qung⁴】

盂 【yū⁴ 如;yū² 淤】jar (see "痰盂" 【tam⁴yū²】)

欤 【yū⁴ 如】< int. > show the question and the exclamation

余 【yū⁴ 如】surplus; spare; odd; over; beyond; I; a surname

余地【yū⁴ dēi⁶ 得希⁶】leeway; margin; room

余毒【yū⁴dug⁹ 独】residual poison

余波【yū⁴bo¹ 坡】repercussions

余悸【yū⁴guei³ 季】lingering fear

余孽【yū⁴yib⁹ 叶】leftover evil

余数【yū⁴xou³ 扫】remainder

余味【yū⁴mēi⁶ 未】agreeable aftertaste

余暇【yū⁴ha⁴ 霞】spare time

余兴【yū⁴hing³ 庆】lingering interest

鱼 【yū⁴ 如;yū² 淤】fish; a surname

鱼笥【yū⁴geo² 九】a type of cage used to catch fishes = 虾笥【ha¹geo²】

鱼云【yū⁴wen² 揾】brain of fish = 鱼头云【yū⁴teo⁴wen²】=【普】鱼脑

鱼春【yū⁴gên¹ 椿】(fish) roe =【普】鱼卵

鱼鳃【yū⁴ wog⁷ 乌学⁷】the seminal vesicle of fish =【普】鱼的精囊

鱼鲂【yū⁴ pug⁷ 扑⁷】air bladder (of fish) =【普】鱼鳔

鱼翅【yū⁴qi³ 刺】shark's fin

鱼鳞【yū⁴lên⁴ 伦】fish scale; scale

鱼肉【yū⁴yug⁹ 玉】the flesh of fish; fish and meat; cruelly oppress

鱼饵【yū⁴nēi⁶ 腻】(fish) bait

鱼钩【yū⁴ngeo¹ 欧】fishhook

鱼网【yū⁴mong⁵ 妄】fishnet; fishing net

鱼贯【yū⁴gun³ 灌】in single file

鱼雷【yū⁴lêū⁴ 擂】torpedo

鱼露【yū⁴lou⁶ 路】fish sauce

鱼跃【yū⁴yêg⁴ 约】fish dive

鱼丝袋【yū⁴xi¹doi⁶ 司代】nylon fishing nets

鱼肝油【yū⁴gon¹yeo⁴ 竿由】cod-liver oil

鱼米之乡【yū⁴mei⁵ji¹hêng 迷² 支香】a land of fish and rice — a land of plenty

鱼龙混杂【yū⁴ lung⁴ wen⁶ jab⁹ 隆运习】good and bad people mixed up

鱼目混珠【yū⁴mug⁹wen⁶jü¹ 木运朱】pass off fish eyes as pearls — pass off the sham as the genuine

渔 【yū⁴ 鱼】fishing; take sth. one is not entitled to

渔业【yū⁴yib⁹ 叶】fishery

渔民【yū⁴men⁴ 文】fisherman

渔船【yū⁴xün⁴ 旋】fishing boat

渔港【yū⁴gong² 讲】fishing port

渔具【yū⁴gêū⁶ 巨】fishing tackle

渔歌【yū⁴go¹ 哥】fisherman's song

如【yū⁴ 余】in compliance with; according to; like; as; as if; compare with; be as good as; such as; if; go to

如常【yū⁴xêng⁴ 嫦】as usual

如此【yū⁴qi² 次²】so; such; in this way; like that

如下【yū⁴ha⁶ 夏】as follows = 如次【yū⁴qi³】

如上【yū⁴xêng⁶ 尚】as above

如故【yū⁴ gu³ 固】as before; like old friends

如何【yū⁴ho⁴ 河】how; what

如果【yū⁴ guo² 戈²】if; in case; in the event of

如今【yū⁴gem¹ 金】nowadays; now

如来【yū⁴loi⁴ 莱】Tathagata; Buddha

如期【yū⁴kēi⁴ 其】as scheduled; on schedule

如实【yū⁴ xed⁹ 失⁹】strictly according to the facts; as things really are

如数【yū⁴xou³ 扫】exactly the number or amount

如同【yū⁴tung⁴ 铜】like; as

如意【yū⁴yi³ 薏】as one wishes

如此而已【yū⁴qi²yi⁴yi⁵ 始移耳】That's what it all adds up to.

如法炮制【yū⁴fad⁸pao³jei³ 发泡³济】follow a set pattern = 照版煮碗【jiu³ban²jü²wun²】

如火如荼【yū⁴fo²yū⁴tou⁴ 伙图】like a raging fire

如意算盘【yū⁴yi³xün³pun⁴ 薏蒜盆】wishful thinking

如愿以偿【yū⁴yün⁶yi⁵xêng⁴ 县尔嫦】have one's wish fulfilled

茹【yū⁴ 如】eat

茹苦含辛【yū⁴fu²hem⁴xen¹ 府勘⁴申】(see "含辛茹苦"【hem⁴xen¹yū⁴fu²】)

儒【yū⁴ 如】Confucianism; scholar; learned man

儒家【yū⁴ga¹ 加】the Confucianists; the Confucian school

濡【yū⁴ 如】immerse; linger

濡染【yū⁴yim⁵ 艳⁵】immerse; imbue

孺【yū⁴ 如】child ("孺子"【yū⁴ji² 止】)

蠕【yū⁴ 如】wriggle; squirm

蠕动【yū⁴dung⁶ 洞】wriggle; peristalsis

汝【yū⁵ 乳】you

汝曹【yū⁵qou⁴ 槽】= 汝辈【yū⁵bui³ 背】you people

乳【yū⁵ 与】breast; milk; any milk-like liquid; give birth to; sucking

乳猪【yū⁵ jü¹ 朱】young pigs = 【普】幼猪; 猪娃

乳房【yū⁵fong⁴ 防】breast; mamma; udder

乳头【yū⁵teo⁴ 投】nipple; teat; mammilla; papilla

乳罩【yū⁵jao³ 找³】brassiere; bra

乳汁【yū⁵jeb⁷ 执】milk

乳酪【yū⁵log⁸ 洛】cheese

乳胶【yū⁵gao¹ 交】emulsion

乳剂【yū⁵jei¹ 挤】emulsion

乳酸【yū⁵xün¹ 孙】lactic acid

乳牛【yū⁵ ngeo⁴ 偶⁴】dairy cattle; milch cow

乳名【yū⁵ming⁴ 明】child's pet name

乳制品【yū⁵jei³ben² 济禀】dairy products

乳臭未干【yū⁵qeo³mēi⁶gon¹ 溴味竿】still smell of one's mother's milk —be young and inexperienced

与【yū⁵ 乳】give; offer; grant; get along with; help; support; and; together; take part in; ＜prep.＞ for, to, from, etc.

与其…不如…【yū⁵kēi⁴ … bed⁷yū⁴ …】 ＜conj.＞ show to select the latter

与会【yū⁵wui² 汇²】participate in a conference

与众不同【yū⁵jung³bed⁷tung⁴ 种毕铜】out of the ordinary

与世无争【yū⁵xei³mou⁴jeng¹ 细毛憎】hold oneself aloof from the world

与世长辞【yū⁵xei³qêng⁴qi⁴ 细祥迟】pass away

与日俱增【yū⁵ yed⁹ kêu¹ jeng¹ 逸拘憎】grow with each passing day

予【yū⁵ 与】give; grant; bestow; I

宇【yū⁵ 与】eaves; house; space; universe; world

宇宙【yū⁵jeo⁶ 袖】universe; cosmos

宇航【yū⁵hong⁴ 杭】astronavigation; space navigation

屿【yū⁵ 与；jêû⁶ 聚】small island; islet

妪【yū² 淤】old woman

伛【yū² 淤】＜n.＞ 伛偻【yū²leo⁴ 楼】with one's back bent

羽【yū⁵ 与】feather; plume

羽毛【yū⁵mou⁴ 无】feather; plume

羽翼【yū⁵yig⁹ 亦】wing; assistant

羽化【yū⁵ fa³ 花³】 ascend to heaven and become immortal; (of a Taoist) die; emergence

羽毛球【yū⁵mou⁴keo⁴ 无求】badminton; shuttlecock

羽毛未丰【yū⁵mou⁴mēi⁶fung¹ 无味风】unfledged

雨【yū⁵ 与】rain

雨云【yū⁵wen⁴ 魂】nimbus

雨点【yū⁵dim² 店²】raindrop

雨水【yū⁵xêu² 瑞²】rainwater; rain; Rain Water (2nd solar term)

雨溦【yū⁵mēi¹ 眉¹】light rain that drizzles ＝【普】毛毛雨

雨季【yū⁵guei³ 贵】rainy season

雨具【yū⁵ gêu⁶ 巨】rain gear (i.e. umbrella, raincoat, galoshes, hood, etc.)

雨露【yū⁵lou⁶ 路】rain and dew; favour

雨褛【yū⁵leo¹ 留¹】a raincoat ＝【普】雨衣

雨后春笋【yū⁵heo⁶qên¹xên² 候椿荀²】(spring up like) bamboo shoots after a spring rain

语【yū⁵ 与】language; speak; say; saying; sign; tall

语言【yū⁵yin⁴ 然】language

语音【yū⁵yem¹ 阴】speech sounds; pronunciation

语调【yū⁵diu⁶ 掉】intonation

语句【yū⁵gêu³ 据】sentence

语法【yū⁵fad⁸ 发】grammar

语气【yū⁵hēi³ 戏】tone; mood

语文【yū⁵ men⁴ 民】language and literature; Chinese

语无伦次【yū⁵mou⁴lên⁴qi³ 毛纶刺】speak incoherently

语重心长【yū⁵jung⁶xem¹qêng⁴ 仲深祥】

sincere words and earnest wishes

囹【yū⁵ 语】< n. > 囹圄【ling⁴ yū⁵ 玲语】jail; prison

庾【yū⁵ 语】an enclosure for storing grain

龃【yū⁵ 与】< a. > 龃龉【jêū² yū⁵ 嘴与】discord

禹【yū⁵ 与】the reputed founder of the Xia Dynasty; a surname

驭【yū⁶ 预】drive (a carriage)

吁【yū⁶ 预;hêū¹ 虚】appeal; plead; sigh; oh

峪【yū⁶ 预;yug⁹ 浴】valley; ravine

预【yū⁶ 遇】in advance; beforehand

预报【yū⁶bou³ 布】forecast

预卜【yū⁶ jou² 蚤】foretell; forewarn; in advance =【普】提前；预先

预备【yū⁶bēi⁶ 鼻】prepare; get ready

预测【yū⁶qag⁷ 策⁷】calculate; forecast

预感【yū⁶ gem² 敢】premonition; have a premonition

预告【yū⁶gou³ 诰】herald; advance notice

预见【yū⁶gin³ 建】foresee; foresight

预兆【yū⁶xiu⁶ 肇】omen; presage; sign

预料【yū⁶liu⁶ 辽⁶】expect; predict

预示【yū⁶xi⁶ 是】betoken; indicate

预言【yū⁶yin⁴ 然】prophesy; predict; prediction

预算【yū⁶xūn³ 蒜】budget

预计【yū⁶gei³ 继】calculate in advance; estimate

预谋【yū⁶ meo⁴ 牟】premeditate; plan beforehand

预期【yū⁶kēi⁴ 其】expect; anticipate

预约【yū⁶yêg⁸ 跃】make an appointment

预订【yū⁶dēng⁶ 得镜⁶】subscribe; place an order

预购【yū⁶keo³ 构】purchase in advance

预制【yū⁶jei³ 济】prefabricate

谕【yū⁶ 预】instruct; tell

喻【yū⁶ 预】explain; make clear; inform; know; understand; analogy; a surname

裕【yū⁶ 预】abundant; plentiful; make rich

誉【yū⁶ 预】reputation; fame; praise; eulogize

寓【yū⁶ 预】reside; live; residence; abode; imply; contain

寓所【yū⁶xo² 锁】residence; abode

寓言【yū⁶yin⁴ 然】fable; allegory; parable

寓意【yū⁶yi³ 薏】implied meaning; moral

遇【yū⁶ 预】meet; treat; receive; chance

遇到【yū⁶dou³ 都³】run into; come across

遇见【yū⁶gin³ 建】meet; come across

遇难【yū⁶nan⁶ 那晏⁶】die in an accident; be murdered

遇险【yū⁶him² 欠²】meet with a mishap

遇救【yū⁶geo³ 够】be rescued; be saved

御【yū⁶ 预】drive; of an emperor; imperial; resist; keep out

御侮【yū⁶ mou⁵ 武】resist foreign aggression

御用【yū⁶yung⁶ 容⁶】for the use of an emperor; serve as a tool

愈【yū⁶ 预】heal; recover; become well; better; the better

愈合【yū⁶heb⁹ 盒】heal

愈加【yū⁶ga¹ 家】all the more; even more;

豫【yü⁶ 预】pleased; comfort; another name for Henan Province

酗【yü³ 雨³; hêü³ 去】< v. > 酗酒

【yü³jeo² 走】excessive drinking

鸳【yün¹ 渊】< n. >鸳鸯【yün¹yêng¹ 央】mandarin duck; an affectionate couple

渊【yün¹ 鸳】deep pool; deep

渊源【yün¹yün⁴ 元】origin; source

渊博【yün¹bog⁸ 搏】broad and profound

渊薮【yün¹xeo² 手】den; haunt

渊痛【yün¹tung³ 同³】ache; painful =【普】疼痛;酸痛

冤【yün¹ 渊】wrong; injustice; hatred; enmity; bad luck; loss

冤仇【yün¹xeo⁴ 愁】rancour; enmity

冤屈【yün¹wed³ 乌核⁷】wrong; injustice

冤枉【yün¹wong² 汪²】wrong; not worthwhile

冤家【yün¹ga¹ 加】enemy; foe

冤臭【yün¹ qeo³溴 】= 冤崩烂臭【yün¹beng¹lan⁶qeo³ 蹦兰⁶ 溴】stained; bad smell =【普】恶臭

丸【yün² 院】ball; pill; bolus

蜿【yün²】< a. > 蜿蜒【yün²yin⁴ 言】wriggle; wind

烷【yün² 丸】alkane

纨【yün² 丸; yün⁴ 元】fine silk fabrics

纨裤子弟【yün²fu²ji²dei⁶ 富止第】profligate son of the rich; fop; playboy

皖【yün² 丸】another name for Anhui Province

宛【yün² 丸; yün¹ 渊】winding; tortuous; as if

宛然【yün²yin⁴ 言】as if

宛如【yün²yü⁴ 鱼】just like

婉【yün² 丸】gentle; gracious; beautiful; elegant

婉言【yün²yin⁴ 然】gentle words

婉约【yün²yêg⁸ 跃】graceful and restrained

婉转【yün²jün² 专²】mild and indirect; sweet and agreeable

苑【yün² 阮】enclosed ground for growing trees, keeping animals, etc.; gardens; centre; a surname

院【yün² 阮】courtyard; yard; compound; a designation for certain government offices and public places

院落【yün²log⁸ 洛】courtyard; yard; compound

阮【yün² 院】a surname

怨【yün³ 苑³】resentment; enmity; blame; complain

怨恨【yün³hen⁶ 很⁶】have a grudge against sb.; hate; resentment; grudge; enmity

怨愤【yün³fen⁵ 奋】discontent and indignation

怨府【yün³fu² 苦】object of general indignation

怨气【yün³hêi³ 戏】grievance; complaint

怨言【yün³yin⁴ 然】complaint; grumble

怨声载道【yün³xing¹joi³dou⁶ 升再度】Cries of discontent rise all round.

怨天尤人【yün³ tin¹ yeo⁴ yen⁴ 田¹ 油仁】blame god and man — blame everyone and everything but oneself

完【yūn⁴ 元】intact; whole; run out; use up; finish; complete; be over; be through; pay

完整【yūn⁴jing² 正²】complete; integrated; intact

完备【yūn⁴bēi⁶ 鼻】complete; perfect

完好【yūn⁴hou² 蒿²】intact; whole

完满【yūn⁴ mun⁵ 螨】satisfactory; successful

完美【yūn⁴mēi⁵ 尾】perfect; consummate

完全【yūn⁴qūn⁴ 存】complete; whole; fully; completely; wholly

完善【yūn⁴xin⁶ 膳】perfect; consummate

完毕【yūn⁴bed⁷ 不】finish; complete; end

完成【yūn⁴ xing⁴ 承】accomplish; complete; fulfil

完结【yūn⁴ gid⁸ 洁】come to an end; be over

完蛋【yūn⁴ dan² 旦²】be done for; be finished

完璧归赵【yūn⁴big⁷guei¹jiu⁶ 碧龟照⁶】return sth. to its owner in good condition

元【yūn⁴ 原】first; primary; chief; basic; unit; the Yuan Dynasty (1271～1368); a surname

元旦【yūn⁴dan³ 诞】New Year's Day

元件【yūn⁴gin² 坚²】element; cell

元老【yūn⁴lou⁵ 鲁】senior statesman

元气【yūn⁴hēi³ 戏】vitality; vigour

元首【yūn⁴xeo² 手】head of state

元素【yūn⁴xou³ 扫】element

元凶【yūn⁴hung¹ 空】prime culprit

元勋【yūn⁴fen¹ 分】founding father

芫【yūn⁴ 元】＜n.＞芫茜【yūn⁴xei¹ 西】a type of vegetable; the parsley

园【yūn⁴ 元】an area of land for growing plants; a place for public recreation

园地【yūn⁴dēi⁶ 得希⁶】garden plot; field; scope

园丁【yūn⁴ding¹ 叮】gardener; teacher

园林【yūn⁴ lem⁴ 淋】garden; ground used for growing vegetables, flowers or fruit

园艺【yūn⁴ngei⁶ 毅】horticulture; gardening

爰【yūn⁴ 元；wun⁴ 桓】whence; hence

原【yūn⁴ 元】primary; original; former; raw; excuse; pardon; level, open country; plain; a surname

原本【yūn⁴bun³ 苯】original; former＝【普】原来

原底【yūn⁴dei² 抵】original＝【普】原来

原庄【yūn⁴jong³ 装】be left intact; undamaged＝【普】（货物）原封未动，完好无损

原始【yūn⁴qi² 齿】original; primitive; firsthand

原形【yūn⁴ying⁴ 型】original shape

原料【yūn⁴liu² 撩】raw material

原先【yūn⁴xin¹ 仙】former; original

原理【yūn⁴lēi⁵ 李】principle; tenet

原谅【yūn⁴lēng⁶ 亮】excuse; forgive; pardon

原配【yūn⁴pui³ 沛】first wife

原委【yūn⁴wei² 伟²】the whole story

原野【yūn⁴ yē⁵ 惹】open country; champaign

原意【yūn⁴yi³ 薏】meaning; original intention

原因【yūn⁴yen¹ 恩】cause; reason

原则【yūn⁴jeg⁷ 仄】principle

原子【yūn⁴ji² 止】atom
原状【yūn⁴jong⁶ 撞】original state
原告【yūn⁴gou³ 诰】plaintiff; prosecutor
原籍【yūn⁴jig⁹ 直】ancestral home
原稿【yūn⁴gou² 高²】master copy
原作【yūn⁴jog⁸ 昨】original work = 原著
　　【jü³ 注】
原文【yūn⁴men⁴ 民】original text
原原本本【yūn⁴yūn⁴bun⁹bun² 苯】from be-
　　ginning to end

圆【yūn⁴ 元】round; circular; spherical;
　　tactful; justify; the monetary unit of
　　China (圆＝元)
圆规【yūn⁴kuei¹ 亏】compasses
圆心【yūn⁴xem¹ 深】the centre of a circle
圆周【yūn⁴jeo¹ 邹】circumference
圆形【yūn⁴ying⁴ 型】circular; round
圆桌【yūn⁴jêg⁸ 雀】round table
圆滑【yūn⁴wad⁹ 挖⁹】smooth and evasive
圆润【yūn⁴yên⁶ 闰】mellow and full
圆满【yūn⁴mun⁵ 螨】satisfactory
圆圈【yūn⁴hün¹ 喧】circle; ring

袁【yūn⁴ 元】a surname

猿【yūn⁴ 元】ape
猿猴【yūn⁴heo⁴ 侯】apes and monkeys
猿人【yūn⁴yen⁴ 仁】ape-man

源【yūn⁴ 元】source (of a river); foun-
　　tainhead; cause
源头【yūn⁴teo⁴ 投】fountainhead; source
源泉【yūn⁴qün⁴ 存】source; fountainhead
源流【yūn⁴leo⁴ 留】source and course
源远流长【yūn⁴yün⁵leo⁴qêng⁴ 软留祥】a
　　distant source and a long stream

辕【yūn⁴ 袁】shafts of a cart or carriage;
　　the outer gate of a government office
in ancient times; a government office
in ancient times

缘【yūn⁴ 元】reason; edge; fringe;
　　along; predestined relationship
缘分【yūn⁴fen⁶ 份】lot or luck by which
　　people are brought together
缘故【yūn⁴gu³ 固】cause; reason = 缘
　　由【yeo⁴】
缘木求鱼【yūn⁴mug⁹keo⁴yü⁴ 目球如】
　　climb a tree to catch fish — a
　　fruitless approach
缘起【yūn⁴hēi² 喜】genesis; origin

沿【yūn⁴ 元】along; follow; trim; edge;
　　border; water's edge; bank
沿岸【yūn⁴ngon⁶ 按⁶】along the bank or
　　coast
沿边【yūn⁴bin¹ 鞭】trim
沿海【yūn⁴hoi² 凯】along the coast; coastal
沿路【yūn⁴lou⁶ 露】along the road; on the
　　way
沿线【yūn⁴xin³ 扇】along the line
沿袭【yūn⁴jab⁹ 习】carry on as before; fol-
　　low
沿用【yūn⁴yung⁶ 容⁶】continue to use

铅【yūn⁴ 沿】lead (Pb); black lead; lead
　　(in a pencil)
铅笔【yūn⁴bed⁷ 毕】pencil
铅球【yūn⁴keo⁴ 求】shot
铅印【yūn⁴yen³ 因³】letterpress printing
铅字【yūn⁴ji⁶ 自】type; letter
铅中毒【yūn⁴jung³dug⁹ 种³ 独】lead poi-
　　soning

悬【yūn⁴ 元】hang; suspend; feel
　　anxious; imagine; far apart
悬案【yūn⁴ngon⁶按】unsettled law case;
　　unsettled question
悬挂【yūn⁴gua³ 封】hang; fly; suspension

悬空【yūn⁴hung¹ 凶】hang in the air

悬念【yūn⁴ nim⁶ 粘⁶】be concerned about；audience involvement in a film or play

悬赏【yūn⁴xê̂ng² 想】offer a reward

悬殊【yūn⁴ xū⁴ 薯 】great disparity；wide gap

悬崖【yūn⁴ngai⁴ 捱】precipice

悬崖勒马【yūn⁴ngai⁴leg⁹ma⁵ 捱簕码】rein in at the brink of the precipice — wake up and escape disaster at the last moment

玄【yūn⁴ 元】black；dark；profound；unreliable

玄妙【yūn⁴miu⁶ 庙】mysterious；abstruse

玄虚【yūn⁴ hêû¹ 墟】deceitful trick；mystery

眩【yūn⁴ 玄】dizzy；giddy；dazzled

眩晕【yūn⁴wen⁴ 云】dizziness

炫【yūn⁶ 愿；yūn⁴ 原】dazzle；show off

炫耀【yūn⁴yiu⁶ 要⁶】show off；flaunt

苆【yūn⁵ 远】the young stems of trees；the stem ending of trees =【普】植物茎叶的末梢

远【yūn⁵ 软】far；distant；remote

远程【yūn⁵qing⁴ 情】long-range

远大【yūn⁵dai⁶ 歹⁶】broad；ambitious

远道【yūn⁵dou⁶ 度】a long way

远方【yūn⁵fong¹ 芳】distant place

远见【yūn⁵gin³ 建】foresight；vision

远近【yūn⁵gen⁶ 靳】far and near；distance

远景【yūn⁵ging² 境 】distant view；prospect；long shot

远虑【yūn⁵lêû⁶ 类】foresight；long view

远期【yūn⁶kēi⁴ 其】forward

远亲【yūn⁵qen¹ 陈¹】distant relative

远视【yūn⁵xi⁶ 示】long sight；hyperopia

远行【yūn⁵heng⁴ 衡】go on a long journey

远征【yūn⁵jing¹ 精】expedition

远走高飞【yūn⁵jeo²gou¹fēi¹ 酒糕非】fly far and high；be off to distant parts

远水救不了近火【yūn⁵xêû²geo³bed⁷liu⁵ gen⁶fo² 瑞² 够毕辽⁵ 靳伙】Distant water won't put out a fire close at hand — a slow remedy cannot meet an urgency.

软【yūn⁵ 远】soft；flexible；supple；pliable；mild；gentle；weak；feeble；easily moved or influenced

软熟【yūn⁵xug⁹ 孰】soft =【普】柔软

软揸揸【yūn⁵ dad⁸ dad⁸ 达⁸】weak；not energetic =【普】软弱的；疲软而没生气、没积极性的

软茬茬【yûu⁵yem⁴yem⁴】soft and fine =【普】柔软而又纤细的；很柔软的

软皮蛇【yūn⁵pēi⁴xē⁴ 脾余】one who does not have much of his own ideas but follows what others say ∽【普】（形容某人）做事没劲儿，没积极性、懒洋洋，推而不动

软腭【yūn⁵ngog⁹ 岳】soft palate

软膏【yūn⁵gou¹ 高】ointment；paste

软管【yūn⁵ gun² 莞】flexible pipe or tube；hose

软片【yūn⁵pin³ 骗】（a roll of）film

软件【yūn⁵gin² 建²】software

软化【yūn⁵ fa³ 花³】soften；bating；win over by soft tactics

软和【yūn⁵wo⁴ 禾】soft；gentle；kind

软禁【yūn⁵ gem³ 咁】put sb. under house

arrest

软弱【yūn⁵yê̂g⁶ 药】weak; feeble; flabby

软席【yūn⁵jig⁶ 直】soft seat or berth

软硬兼施【yūn⁵ngang⁶gim¹xi¹ 罨⁶ 检¹ 司】use both hard and soft tactics

愿【yūn⁶ 县】hope; wish; desire; be willing; be ready; vow; honest and cautious

愿望【yūn⁶mong⁶ 亡⁶】desire; wish; aspiration

愿意【yūn⁶yi³ 薏】be willing; be ready; wish; like; want

县【yūn⁶ 愿; yūn² 阮】county

县份【yūn²fen⁶ 分⁶】county

县城【yūn⁶ xing⁴ 成】county seat; county town

县长【yūn⁶jêng⁴ 掌】the head of a county

县志【yūn⁶ji³ 至】county annals

月【yūd⁹ 越】the moon; month; full-moon shaped; round

月光【yūd⁹guong¹ 胱】the moon =【普】月亮;月儿

月大【yūd⁹dai⁶ 歹⁶】a month old =【普】大月(阴历 30 天;阳历 31 天)

月小【yūd⁹ xiu² 少²】the months with 30 days =【普】小月(阴历 29 天;阳历 30 天)

月头【yūd⁹ teo⁴ 投】the beginning of the month =【普】月初

月尾【yūd⁹mēi⁵ 美】the end of the month =【普】月底;月末

月饼【yūd⁹bēng² 柄²】moon cake

月份【yūd⁹fen⁶ 分⁶】month

月份牌【yūd⁹fen⁶pai⁴ 分⁶ 排】monthly calendar =【普】月历

月食【yūd⁹xig⁹ 蚀】lunar eclipse

月宫【yūd⁹ gung¹ 工】the palace of the moon—the moon

月华【yūd⁹wa⁴ 铧】moonlight =月色【yūd⁹xig⁷式】

月台【yūd⁹toi⁴ 抬】railway platform

月季【yūd⁹guei³ 桂】< n .>Chinese rose

月经【yūd⁹ging¹ 京】menses; period

月刊【yūd⁹hon² 罕】monthly magazine

月夜【yūd⁹yê̄⁶ 野⁶】moonlit night

月薪【yūd⁹xen¹ 辛】monthly pay

月息【yūd⁹xig⁷ 式】monthly interest

月下老人【yūd⁹ha⁶lou⁵yen⁴ 夏鲁仁】the old man under the moon—the god who unites persons in marriage; matchmaker

悦【yūd⁹ 月】happy; pleased; delighted; please; delight

悦耳【yūd⁹yi⁵ 尔】pleasing to the ear; sweet-sounding

悦目【yūd⁹mug⁹ 木】pleasing to the eye; good-looking

阅【yūd⁹ 月】read; go over; review; inspect experience; pass through

阅读【yūd⁹dug⁹ 独】read

阅览【yūd⁹lam⁵ 揽⁵】read

阅兵【yūd⁹bing¹ 冰】review troops

阅历【yūd⁹lig⁹ 力】see, hear or do for oneself; experience

越【yūd⁹月】get over; jump over; exceed; overstep; be at a high pitch

越发【yūd⁹fad⁹ 法】getting more and more; all the more; even more =【普】更加;更为

越来越…【yūd⁹loi⁴yūd⁹ 莱】more and more...

越…越…【yūd⁹…yūd⁹…】the more... the more

越冬【yüd9dung1 东】live through the winter

越轨【yüd9 guei2 鬼】exceed the bounds; transgress

越过【yüd9guo3 戈3】cross; surmount

越界【yüd9gai3 介】cross the border

越位【yüd9wei6 卫】offside

越南【yüd9nam4 男】Viet-Nam

越俎代疱【yüd9jo2doi6pao4 阻待刨】exceed one's functions and meddle in others' affairs

粤【yüd9 月】another name for Guangdong Province

粤剧【yüd9kêg9 屐】Guangdong opera

穴【yüd9 月】cave; den; hole; grave; acupuncture point; acupoint

穴居【yüd9gêü1 据1】live in cave

穴位【yüd9 wei6 卫】acupuncture point; acupoint

锥【yêü1 锐1; jêü1 追】awl; anything shaped like a awl; bore; cone; poke a hole

锥仔【yêü1jei2 济2】awl =【普】锥子

锥窿【yêü1lung1 隆1】make a hole with an awl =【普】锥孔;钻孔

锥形【jêü1ying4 型】taper; cone

汭【yêü5 锐5】the sticky liquid that is produced form the bark of trees

蕊【yêü5 汭】stamen or pistil

蚋【yêü6 锐】buffalo gnat; blackfly

锐【yêü6 蚋】sharp; keen; vigour; fighting spirit

锐利【yêü6lēi6 俐】sharp; keen

锐气【yêü6hēi3 戏】dash; drive

锐角【yêü6gog8 各】acute angle

锐不可挡【yêü6bed7ho2dong2 笔贺2 当2】can't be held back; be irresistible

睿【yêü6 锐】farsighted

睿智【yêü6ji3 至】wise and farsighted

央【yêng1 秧】entreat; entreaty; end; finish

央求【yêng1keo4 球】beg; plead; implore

泱【yêng1 央】<*a*.>泱泱【yêng1yêng1】(of waters) vast; magnificent

殃【yêng1 央】calamity; disaster; bring disaster to

秧【yêng1 央】seedling; sprout; vine; young; fry

秧苗【yêng1miu4 描】rice shoot; rice seedling

秧田【yêng1tin4 填】rice seedling bed

鸯【yêng1 央】(see"鸳鸯"【yün1yêng1】)

怏【yêng2 央2】<*a*.>怏怏【yêng2 yêng2】disgruntled; sullen

佯【yêng2 怏; yêng4 羊】pretend; feign; sham

佯攻【yêng2gung1 工】feign attack

佯言【yêng2yin4 然】tell lies; lie

佯死【yêng2 xēi2 四2】feign death; play dead

佯作不知【yêng2jog8bed7ji1 昨毕之】feign ignorance; pretend not to know

羊【yêng4 阳】sheep; a surname

羊毛【yêng4mou4 无】sheep's wool; fleece

羊肉【yêng4yug9 玉】mutton

羊皮【yêng4pēi4 脾】sheepskin

羊羔【yêng4gou1 高】lamb

羊肠小道【yêng4qêng4xiu2dou6 场少2 度】narrow winding trail; meandering footpath

羊毛出在羊身上【yêng⁴ mou⁴ qêd⁷ joi⁶ yêng⁴xen¹xêng⁶ 无次律⁷ 再⁶ 辛尚】After all, the wool still comes from the sheep's back—in the long run, whatever you're given, you pay for.

羊咩【yêng⁴mē¹ 莫夜¹】a goat =【普】山羊

阳【yêng⁴ 羊】(in Chiness philosophy, medicine, etc.) "yang", the masculine or positive principle in nature; the sun; south of a hill or north of a river; in relief; open; overt; belonging to this world; positive; male genitals

阳光【yêng⁴goung¹ 胱】sunlight; sunshine
阳历【yêng⁴lig⁹ 力】solar calendar
阳间【yêng⁴gan¹ 奸】this world
阳极【yêng⁴gig⁹ 击⁹】positive pole; anode
阳电【yêng⁴din⁶ 甸】positive electricity
阳性【yêng⁴ xing³ 姓 】positive; masculine gender
阳痿【yêng⁴wei² 毁】impotence
阳台【yêng⁴toi⁴ 抬】balcony
阳关道【yêng⁴guan¹dou⁶ 惯¹ 度】broad road; thoroughfare
阳春白雪【yêng⁴qên¹bog⁹xüd⁸ 椿伯⁹ 说】the Spring Snow; highbrow art and literature
阳奉阴违【yêng⁴fung⁶yem¹wei⁴ 风音维】overtly agree but covertly oppose

扬【yêng⁴ 阳;yêng² 佯²】raise; throw up and scatter; winnow; spread; make known; make way
扬名【yêng⁴ming⁴明 】make a name for oneself

扬花【yêng⁴ fa¹ 化¹】flowering (of cereal crops)
扬帆【yêng⁴ fan⁴凡 】hoist the sails; set sail
扬程【yêng⁴ging⁴ 情】lift
扬言【yêng⁴yin⁴ 然】threaten (that one is going to take action)
扬弃【yêng⁴hēi³ 戏】develop what is useful or healthy and discard what is not; sublate
扬琴【yêng⁴kem⁴】dulcimer
扬州【yêng⁴jeo¹ 洲】Yangzhou
扬声器【yêng⁴xing¹hēi³ 升戏】loudspeaker
扬长而去【yêng⁴ qêng⁴ yi⁴ hêü³场移虚³】stalk off
扬眉吐气【yêng⁴mēi⁴tou³hēi³ 微兔戏】feel proud and elated
扬扬自得【yêng⁴ yêng⁴ ji⁶ deg⁶治德】be very pleased with oneself; be complacent

杨【yêng⁴ 羊】poplar; a surname
杨柳【yêng⁴ leo⁵ 楼⁵】poplar and willow; willow
杨树【yêng⁴xü⁶ 署⁶】poplar
杨梅【yêng⁴mui⁴ 霉】red bayberry
杨桃【yêng⁴tou² 土】carambola

疡【yêng⁴ 杨】sore (see "溃疡"【kui² yêng⁴】)

抉【yêng² 扬²】make way ∽【普】出示而加以张扬

洋【yêng⁴ 羊】vast; multitudinous; ocean; foreign; modern; silver coin
洋溢【yêng⁴yed⁹ 日】be permeated with; brim with
洋葱【yêng⁴qung¹ 冲】onion
洋行【yêng⁴hong² 项²】foreign firm

洋气【yêng⁴hêi³ 戏】foreign flavour; out-landish ways

洋人【yêng⁴yen⁴ 仁】foreigner

洋相【yêng⁴xêng³ 商】make an exhibition of oneself ＝ 出洋相【qêd⁷ yêng⁴ xêng³】

洋洋【yêng⁴ yêng⁴ 】numerous; copious; triumphantly

洋烛【yêng⁴jug⁷ 竹】candles

洋楼【yeng⁴ leo² 留²】a bangalow; West-ern-style house＝【普】洋房

洋货铺【yêng⁴fo³pou³ 课普³】a shopping centre＝【普】洋货店

洋洋大观【yêng⁴yêng⁴dai⁶gun¹ 歹⁶ 官】spectacular; grandiose

徉【yêng⁴ 羊】(see "徜徉"【xêng⁴yêng⁴】)

仰【yêng⁵养 】face upward; admire; re-spect; look up to; rely on

仰慕【yêng⁵mou⁴ 务】admire; look up to

仰望【yêng⁵mong⁶亡⁶】look up at; look up to

仰卧【yêng⁵ngo⁶ 饿】lie on one's back

仰仗【yêng⁵jêng⁶ 丈】rely on

仰人鼻息【yêng⁵yen⁴bêi⁶xig⁷ 仁备色】be dependent on the pleasure of oth-ers

养【yêng⁵ 卬】support; provide for; raise; keep; give birth to; foster; form; acquire; rest; convalesce; maintain

养育【yêng⁵yug⁹ 玉】bring up; rear

养殖【yêng⁵jig⁹直】breed (aquatics)

养生【yêng⁵xeng¹ 笙】preserve one's health

养神【yêng⁵xen⁴ 臣】repose

养老【yêng⁵lou⁵ 鲁】provide for the aged; live out one's life in retirement

养料【yêng⁵ liu⁶ 辽⁶】nutriment; nourish-ment

养病【yêng⁵bêng⁶ 柄⁶】recuperate

养护【yêng⁵wu⁶ 户】maintain; conserve

养精蓄锐【yêng⁵ jing¹ qug⁷ yêu⁶贞畜睿】conserve strength and store up en-ergy

养尊处优【yêng⁵jun¹qü²yeo¹ 专次于² 丘】enjoy high position and live in ease and comfort; live in clover

养兵千日，用在一时【yêng⁵bing¹qin¹yed⁹, yung⁶joi⁶yed⁷xi⁴ 冰仟逸，庸 再⁶ 壹是⁴】maintain an army for a thousand days to use it for an hour

氧【yêng⁵ 养】oxygen (O)

氧气【yêng⁵hêi³ 戏】oxygen

氧化【yêng⁵fa³ 花³】oxidize; oxidate

痒【yêng⁵ 养】itch; tickle

恙【yêng⁶ 让】ailment; illness

样【yêng⁶ 让；yêng² 扬²】appearance; shape; sample; model; pattern; kind; type

样板【yêng⁶ ban² 版】sample plate; tem-plet; model; example

样本【yêng⁶bun² 苯】sample book; sample

样品【yêng⁶ ben² 禀】sample (product); specimen

样式【yêng⁶xig⁷ 色】pattern; type; form

样子【yêng⁶ ji² 止】appearance; shape; manner; sample; model; tenden-cy; likelihood

漾【yêng⁶ 样】ripple; brim over; over-flow

让【yêng⁶ 漾】give way; give ground; give up; invite; offer; let; allow; make; let sb. have sth. at a fair price

让步【yêng⁶bou⁶ 部】make a concession; give in; give way; yield

让开【yêng⁶hoi¹ 海¹】get out of the way; make way

让路【yêng⁶lou⁶ 露】make way for sb. or sth.; give way

让位【yêng⁶wei⁶ 卫】abdicate; offer one's seat to sb.; yield to; give way to

让座【yêng⁶jo⁶ 助】offer one's seat to sb.; invite guests to be seated

嚷【yêng⁶ 让】shout; yell; make an uproar

攘【yêng⁶ 让】reject; resist; seize; grab; push up one's sleeves

攘外【yêng⁶ ngoi⁶ 碍】resist foreign aggression

壤【yêng⁶ 让】soil; earth; area

酿【yêng⁶ 让】make (wine); brew (beer); make (honey); lead to; wine

酿酒【yêng⁶ jeo²走 】make wine; brew beer

酿造【yêng⁶jou⁶ 做】make (wine, etc.); brew (beer, etc.)

酿成【yêng⁶xing⁴ 承】lead to; bring on; breed

跃【yêg⁸ 约;yêg⁹ 若】leap; jump

跃进【yêg⁸jên³ 俊】make a leap; leap forward

跃然【yêg⁸yin⁴ 言】appear vividly

跃跃欲试【yêg⁸yêg⁸yug⁹xi³ 玉史³】be eager to have a try

约【yêg⁸ 跃】make an appointment; arrange; ask or invite in advance; pact; agreement; restrict; economical; frugal; simple; about; reduction of a fraction; weigh

约定【yêg⁸ ding⁶ 锭】agree on; appoint; arrange

约会【yêg⁸wui⁶ 汇】appointment; engagement; date

约计【yêg⁸gei³ 继】count roughly

约略【yêg⁹lêg⁸ 掠】rough; approximate

约莫【yêg⁶mog⁸ 膜⁸】about; roughly

约数【yêg⁸xou³ 扫】approximate number; divisor

约请【yêg⁸qing² 逞²】invite; ask

约束【yêg⁸ qug⁷促 】keep within bounds; restrain; bind

约法三章【yêg⁸fad⁸xam¹jêng¹ 发叁张】agree on a three-point law — make a few simple rules to be observed by all concerned

钥【yêg⁹ 药】key

钥匙【yêg⁹xi⁴ 时】key

曰【yêg⁹ 药;yūd⁹ 月】say; call; name

药【yêg⁹ 若 】medicine; drug; remedy; certain chemicals; cure with medicine; kill with poison

药材【yêg⁹ qoi⁴才 】medicinal materials; crude drugs

药铺【yêg⁹pou³ 普³】herbal medicine shop

药店【yêg⁹ dim³掂³】drugstores; chemist's shop; pharmacy

药方【yêg⁹fong¹ 芳】prescription

药草【yêg⁹qou² 曹²】medicinal herbs

药费【yêg⁹fei³ 废】expenses for medicine;

yêg. yē   · 581 ·

charges for medicine

药剂【yêg⁹jei¹ 挤】medicament; drug

药膏【yêg⁹gou¹ 高】ointment; salve

药酒【yêg⁹jeo² 走】medicinal liquor

药粉【yêg⁹fen² 分²】(medicinal) powder

药力【yêg⁹lig³ 历】efficacy of a drug

药品【yêg⁹ ben² 禀】medicines and chemical reagents

药片【yêg⁹pin³ 骗】(medicinal) tablet

药水【yêg⁹ xêü² 瑞²】liquid medicine; lotion

药丸【yêg⁹yün² 院】pill

药瓶【yêg⁹ping⁴ 平】medicine bottle

药物【yêg⁹ med⁶ 勿 】medicines; medicaments

药性【yêg⁹ xing³ 姓】property of a medicine

疟 【yêg⁹ 药】malaria

疟疾【yêg⁹jed⁶ 嫉】malaria; ague

虐 【yêg⁹ 药】cruel; tyrannical

虐待【yêg⁹ doi⁶ 代 】maltreat; ill-treat; tyrannize

虐杀【yêg⁹xad⁸ 萨】cause sb.'s death by maltreating him

若 【yêg⁹ 药】like; seem; as if; if; you

若是【yêg⁹xi⁶ 示】if = 若然【yêg⁹yin⁴ 言】 = 若果【guo²】

若非【yêg⁹fēi¹ 飞】if not

若干【yêg⁹ gon¹ 肝】a certain number or amount; how many; how much

若无其事【yêg⁹mou⁴kêi⁴xi⁶ 毛奇士】as if nothing had happened; calmly; casually

若即若离【yêg⁹jig⁷yêg⁹lēi⁴ 积漓】be neither friendly nor aloof

若要人不知, 除非己莫为【yêg⁹yiu³ yen⁴fēi⁷ji¹, qêü⁴fēi¹gēi² mog⁶wei⁴ 仁毕支, 徐飞几膜维】If you don't want others to know about it, don't do it.

弱 【yêg⁹ 若】weak; feeble; young; inferior; lose; a little less than

弱点【yêg⁹ dim⁶店²】weakness; weak point; failing

弱小【yêg⁹xiu² 少²】small and weak

弱不禁风【yêg⁹bed⁷gem³fung¹ 毕咁丰】too weak to stand a gust of wind; fragile

弱肉强食【yêg⁹yug⁹kêng⁴xig⁹ 玉卡香⁴ 蚀】The weak are the prey of the strong—the law of the jungle.

箬 【yêg⁹ 若】< n. > 箬竹【yêg⁹jug⁷ 足】 indocalamus

耶 【yē⁴ 爷】< auxil. > ∽呢(see "呢"【nē¹】)

耶稣【yē⁴xou¹ 苏】< n. > Jesus

耶路撒冷【yē⁴lou⁶xad⁸lang⁵ 露杀罗罂²】 < n. > Jerusalem

椰 【yē⁴ 耶】coconut palm; coconut tree; coco

椰子【yē⁴ji² 止】coconut palm; coconut tree; coco; coconut

椰菜【yē⁴qoi³ 蔡】white lettuce

椰蓉【yē⁴ yung⁴ 容 】shredded coconut stuffing

椰衣【yē⁴yi¹ 依 】the outer fibre of coconuts = 【普】椰子皮

爷 【yē⁴ 耶; yē¹ 耶¹】father; grandfather; uncle; a form of address for an official or rich man; god

爷娘【yē⁴nêng⁴ 那香⁴】father and mother

爷爷【yē⁴yē²】grandfather; grandpa

挪【yē⁴ 耶】< v. >挪揄【yē⁴yū⁴ 如】ridicule; deride

冶【yē⁵ 野】smelt（metal）; seductively dressed or made up

冶金【yē⁵gem¹ 今】metallurgy

冶炼【yē⁵lin⁶ 练】smelt

野【yē⁵ 冶】open country; the open; not in power; out of office; limit; boundary; wild; uncultivated; rude; rough; unrestrained; unruly; thing; object

野外【yē⁵ngoi⁶ 碍】open country; field

野草【yē⁵qou² 曹²】weeds

野仔【yē⁵jei² 济²】a bastard, i. e, an illegitimate child =【普】野种;私生子

野菜【yē⁵qoi³ 蔡】edible wild herbs

野果【yē⁵guo² 裹】wild fruit

野火【yē⁵fo² 伙】prairie fire; bush fire

野餐【yē⁵qan¹ 残¹】picnic

野生【yē⁵xeng¹ 笙】wild; uncultivated; feral

野兽【yē⁵xeo³ 秀】wild beast; wild animal

野味【yē⁵mēi⁴ 未²】game（as food）

野人【yē⁵yen⁴ 仁】savage

野性【yē⁵xing³ 姓】wild nature; unruliness

野心【yē⁵ xem¹ 深】wild ambition; careerism

野蛮【yē⁵ man⁴万⁴】uncivilized; savage; barbarous; cruel; brutal

野鸡【yē⁵ gei¹计¹】（ring-necked）pheasant

野猪【yē⁵jū¹ 朱】wild boar

野营【yē⁵ying⁵ 仍】camp; bivouac

惹【yē⁵ 野】invite or ask for（sth. undesirable）; offend; provoke; tease; attract; cause; infectious; infect; aggravate

惹祸【yē⁵wo⁶ 和⁶】court disaster; stir up trouble

惹气【yē⁵hēi³ 戏】get angry

惹事【yē⁵xi⁶ 士】stir up trouble

惹是生非【yē⁵xi⁶xeng¹fēi¹ 示笙飞】provoke a dispute; stir up trouble

惹屎上身【yē⁵xi²xêng⁵xen¹ 史尚⁵ 辛】stir up trouble; ask for trouble; invite trouble ∽【普】自找麻烦;惹祸

偌【yē⁶ 夜】such; so

偌大【yē⁵dai⁶ 歹⁶】of such a size; so big

夜【yē⁶ 偌】night; evening; late

夜啲【yē⁶did⁷ 得热⁷】decline =【普】晚点儿

夜晚【yē⁶man⁵ 万⁵】= 夜晚黑【yē⁵man⁵ heg⁷万⁵ 克】at night =【普】夜里;晚上

夜班【yē⁶ban¹ 斑】night shift

夜半【yē⁶bun³ 伴³】midnight = 半夜【bun³ yē⁶】

夜叉【yē⁶ qa¹ 查】yaksha（a malevolent spirit）; a hideous, ferocious person

夜车【yē⁶ gē¹ 奢】night train; work deep into the night

夜间【yē⁶gan¹ 奸】at night

夜景【yē⁶ging² 境】night scene

夜色【yē⁶xig² 式】the dim light of night

夜幕【yē⁶mog⁹ 莫】curtain of night

夜曲【yē⁶kug⁷ 卡屋⁷】< n. >nocturne

夜盲【yē⁶ mang⁴ 孟⁴】nyctalopia; night blindness

夜宵【yē⁶xiu¹ 烧】food taken late at night;

midnight snack = 宵夜【xiu¹ yē²】

夜莺【yē⁶ngeng¹ 额亨¹】nightingale

夜总会【yē⁶jung² wui² 种² 汇²】nightclub

夜游神【yē⁶yeo⁴xen⁴ 油臣】the legendary god on patrol at night—a person who is up and about at night; night owl

夜来香【yē⁶loi⁴hēng¹ 莱乡】< n . > cordate telosma

夜明珠【yē⁶ming⁴jū¹ 名朱】a legendary luminous pearl

夜长梦多【yē⁶qêng⁴mung⁶do¹ 场蒙⁶ 朵¹】A long night is fraught with dreams — a long delay means many hitches.

夜郎自大【yē⁶long⁴ji⁶dai⁶ 廊治歹⁶】ludicrous conceit of the king of Yelang — parochial arrogance

夜以继日【yē⁶yi⁵gei³yed⁹ 耳计逸】day and night; round the clock

偌【yēng² 衣镜²】rely on; be dependent on

偌人【yēng² yen⁴ 仁】be dependent on others = 【普】依赖别人

Z

(It is not used in Cantonese.)

音节索引(Syllabic index)

敬告国内读者

本书虽是应外国出版公司之约而编写的，但它沟通英语、汉语粤方言与汉语普通话的联系，国内人士也可能垂爱。故有几句不必译为英语的话要敬告诸位。

孔夫子说："苛政猛于虎。"广州话今天还保留着它的语法结构："苛政猛过老虎。"普通话却部分颠倒其语序了："苛政比老虎还凶猛。"

《战国策·楚策》有云："狗恶之，当门而噬之。"当今的普通话口语已经不用"噬"这个词了，要说"噬"的意思，必须换上"咬"或"吃"才能使人听懂；可是广州话还保留着原有的用法："𠮩（xei⁴）佢（kêü⁵）一啖（dam⁶）"就是古语"噬之"的意思。

"故人西辞黄鹤楼（leo⁴），烟花三月下扬州（jeo¹）。孤帆远影碧空尽，唯见长江天际流（leo⁴）。"用广州话来诵读，它的韵脚和平仄都很合唐诗的格律，显得特别悠扬动听；可是用普通话来念，却起码不很押韵了，"楼"（lóu）、"州"（zhōu）还是同韵的，可是它们与"流"（liú）就不很协和了。诵读大量的唐诗、宋词，您会碰到很多类似上述的情况。

这些情况表明：粤语比普通话更接近我们老祖宗的语言。此无他，南粤是历代战乱的避风港，广东人本质上是南来汉人与土著百越民族的混血儿。南来汉人带来了北方当时先进的文化，由于五岭阻隔，交通不便，这文化变化较少；不像北方文化那样，因受西北少数民族文化影响而变化显著。

可是，近世的封建统治者却忘了本，他们鄙称南粤文化为"蛮方文化"，嘲笑粤语为"蛮方语言"；御用文人学者自然趋附有加，一味标榜"京畿文化"，而对南粤文化不屑一顾。新中国成立以后，五六十年代曾经一度掀起过南粤文化的研究热潮。本书使用的注音方法，就是以广东省教育行政部门 1960 年制定的《广州话拼音方案》为依据的。可是，由于众所周知的原因，这股热潮随后便冷却和衰落了。

南粤文化是有丰富内涵的，其中的语言，表现力就特别强，并有独到的深刻和细腻。它和南粤文化的整体风格是一致的，一言以蔽之曰：吸纳，兼容，心胸无限宽广。甚至连一些西方语汇也融合进来了。这当然无法形成赖以清高的"纯种"，但我以为，"拿来主义"是有益于自己的精神富有的。

尽管有学者认为粤语是古汉语的活化石，但由于上述种种缘故，粤语的研究典籍甚少，特别是记录它的特殊语汇的文字符号，一向缺乏规范，写法往往不一致。这就给本书的编写造成极大的困难。我无意通过本书的编写来给粤语方言词的书写作出规范，但作为实际存在的语言客体，它是必须形之于文字符号的。本书反映粤方言特殊词汇的文字符号，仅据部分民间资料，如粤剧脚本、地方志等，甚至连境外、国外出版物上的一些写法也吸收过来了。这些特殊文字符号，我用下加波浪线（"﹏﹏"）的方法一一标出。敬请读者诸君，切莫把它们当作规范汉字来行文，否则难免北方同胞的误会。至于"生猛海鲜"之类，同胞认同了，那是不在忌讳之列的。

杨明新

1999 年春于广州